The Literature of British Domestic Architecture 1715–1842

The Literature of British Domestic Architecture 1715–1842

John Archer

The MIT Press, Cambridge, Massachusetts, and London, England

© 1985 by The Massachusetts Institute of
Technology

This book was set in Palatino by The MIT
Press Computergraphics Department and
printed and bound by The Murray Printing
Co. in the United States of America.

Library of Congress Cataloging in
Publication Data

Archer, John, 1947–
  The literature of British domestic
architecture, 1715–1842

  Includes index.
  1. Architecture, Domestic—Great
Britain—Bibliography. 2. Architecture,
Modern—17th–18th centuries—Great
Britain—Bibliography. 3. Architecture,
Modern—19th century—Great Britain—
Bibliography. I. Title. Z5944.G7A7 1984
[NA7328]   016.728′0941   84-880
ISBN 0-262-01076-3

The MIT Press wishes to thank the
Publication Program of The J. Paul Getty
Trust for making it possible to maintain
high quality standards in producing this
book.

For My Mother

Contents

List of Illustrations

Photographs (following page 148)
In the limited number of illustrations here I have attempted to offer a taste of the various architectural styles, dwelling sizes, and illustration techniques found in British architectural books of the period. In doing so, I have tried not to reproduce illustrations already available elsewhere in the literature of architectural history, but instead to include some of the less well-known but equally interesting and handsome designs.

All photographs were made by Christopher Faust at the University of Minnesota and—except as noted—from books at the University of Minnesota.

1 Richard Brown, "A Grecian Villa," Pl. XXXI in *Domestic Architecture* (first edition 1841; photograph from [1842] edition, Entry 24.2 [private collection]).

2 Batty and Thomas Langley, "Gothick Pavillion," Pl. LX in *Gothic Architecture* (first edition [1742]; photograph from 1747 edition, Entry 172.2).

3 John Claudius Loudon, "The Beau Idéal of an English Villa," Fig. 1438 in *An Encyclopaedia of Cottage, Farm, and Villa Architecture* (first edition 1833; photograph from 1846 edition, Entry 184.8).

4 Robert Lugar, Design "in the style of an Italian villa," Pl. XXVIII in *Architectural Sketches* (first edition 1805; photograph from 1815 edition, Entry 192.2).

5 Peter Nicholson, "Plan of the Town of Ardrossan," Pl. II (Art. "Town") in *An Architectural and Engineering Dictionary* (first edition 1819; photograph from 1835 edition, Entry 223.2).

6 James Paine, "Front to the Lawn or principal Entrance at Stockeld in Yorkshire," Vol. I, Pl. XLIII in *Plans, Elevations, and Sections* (first edition 1767; photograph from 1783 edition, Entry 243.2).

7 John Buonarotti Papworth, "Cottage Ornée," Pl. 7 in *Rural Residences* (photograph from 1818 edition, Entry 246.2).

8 Charles Parker, "Residence of a Bailiff or Steward," in *Villa Rustica* (Pl. XLVIII in first edition, 1832–1841; photograph from Pl. XLVI as renumbered in 1848 edition, Entry 249.2 [Cornell University]).

9 John Plaw, "Lodge or Cottage," Pl. 13 in *Ferme Ornée* (first edition 1795; photograph from 1803 edition, Entry 259.4).

10 Peter Frederick Robinson, "Binswood Cottage," N.S. Pl. 4 in *A New Series of Designs* (photograph from 1838 edition, Entry 295.1 [University of Kentucky]).

11 Abraham Swan, "A Design for a House," Vol. II, Pl. 12 in *A Collection of Designs* (photograph from 1757 edition, Entry 326.1).

Chart (page 18)
Architectural Publication Activity in the United Kingdom, 1715–1842.

Acknowledgments

At the end of a project that has extended over a dozen years, it is both a relief and a pleasure to remember the scores of people who have given their time, resources, and good will in a great variety of ways.

It is perhaps the greatest pleasure to recall the hospitality afforded me in my travels by family and friends who, I suppose, never quite understood why I was *always* in the library. If Laurence and Sandra in London had not generously taken me in as I struggled with an academic budget, I might never have stayed long enough to get the project under way. Dick and Charlotte cheerfully put me up for weeks on end in Belmont—within striking distance of Cambridge, Boston, and Providence—while kindly assuring me what an "easy guest" I was. In addition I have enjoyed no small measure of hospitality from Joanna in London, Meg and Andrew at Calder House, Helen and Jim in Washington, Anne and Joe in Alexandria, Beth in Arlington, Pete and Trish in Baltimore, Anne in Philadelphia, Dick and Elly in Basking Ridge, Steve in New Hampshire, and David, Hugh, and Leah in New York. Finally, Gloria and Dave always were ready with the comforts of home in Chicago.

At several times I presumed upon the good will of friends and colleagues, either by enlisting their help in tracking down and checking editions of certain books, or by asking their advice on subjects that otherwise would have remained obscure to me. I must especially thank Richard Archer, David Arnheim, Pierre Du Prey, Patricia Erhart, Hilliard Goldfarb, Richard Leppert, Anne Prosseda, Beverly Schreiber Jacoby, Peter Siegel, and Pauline Yu. At various stages, senior colleagues have reviewed portions of my manuscript or offered advice on a variety of subjects; and while deficiencies in this book are entirely my own fault, my work has benefited greatly from the help of James Ackerman, John Coolidge, John Harris, Henry Millon, Damie Stillman, Sir John Summerson, and Dora Wiebenson.

It was, of course, essential to *see* the books that I have described in the following entries. Traveling on a limited schedule often meant that I needed to see dozens of books in a single day. Without the enthusiastic assistance and numerous courtesies extended to me by librarians wherever I went, my task would have approached the impossible. Sometimes their efforts included physical labor: in rare book libraries, for instance, transporting the many large folio volumes that I requested was no mean task; and everywhere, I owe more than a word of thanks to those who reshelved books in my wake. I also bothered countless reference librarians with queries about books that had been lost, mislaid, sold, discarded, or catalogued incorrectly; their patient efforts cleared up many mysteries.

In England, I was well served by the staffs of six libraries: The British Library; Cambridge University Library; The Bodleian Library; the British Architectural Library at the Royal Institute of British Architects; the library of Sir John Soane's Museum (with special thanks to Christine Scull); and The Victoria and Albert Museum Library (especially John P. Fuller).

In America, where I had more time to spend, the list of those who aided me is correspondingly longer; and while I cannot detail all the generous favors offered in so many places, I want at least to recognize the following individuals and institutional staffs whose efforts particularly smoothed my way: the Boston Athenaeum (in particular Jack Jackson, Donald Kelley, and Robert F. Perkins); the Fine Arts Department and Department of Rare Books, Boston Public Library (especially Theresa D. Cederholm and Ellen M. Oldham); the Brown University Library; the John Carter Brown Library, Brown University; The Library of the Carpenters' Company of the City and County of Philadelphia (especially F. Spencer Roach); The Joseph Regenstein Library, The University of Chicago (particularly James Green); the Avery Architectural Library, Columbia University (above all Herbert Mitchell); The Franklin Institute Library (particulary Emerson W. Hilker); The Free Library of Philadelphia; the Arnold Arboretum, Fine Arts Library, Fogg Art Museum, Frances Loeb Library, Houghton Library, Kress Library of Business and Economics, and Widener Library, Harvard University (especially Wolfgang Freitag, Richard Simpson, Marjorie B. Cohn, Angela Giral, Christopher Hail, F. Thomas Noonan, Kenneth E. Carpenter, Ruth Reinstein Rogers, Lucile Hicks, and Stephanie Tournas); The Library Company of Philadelphia; The Library of Congress (in particular Josephus Nelson); Edward J. Sweny at the New England Deposit Library; The New York Public Library; the Fine Arts Library, University of Pennsylvania (particularly Alan E. Morrison and Marjorie Morgan); the Enoch Pratt Free Library (especially Ernest Siegel); the George Peabody Department of the Enoch Pratt Free Library; the Firestone Library and the Marquand Library of Art and Archaeology, Princeton University; the Providence Public Library, Providence, Rhode Island; the St. Paul Seminary, St. Paul, Minnesota (especially Sr. Emilia Francis); the Art and Architecture Library, Sterling Library, Beinecke Rare Book and Manuscript Library, and Yale Center for British Art, Yale University (particularly Judith M. Bloomgarden and Joan M. Friedman).

The library collections of the University of Minnesota have been exceptionally useful to me, since they contain a fair proportion of the books and periodicals that I have included in this study. From time to time I have made heavy demands on many librarians here, and their continual eagerness to help has been gratifying. In particular I want to thank Austin McLean, John Jenson, and Kathy Tezla in Special Collections and Rare Books; John Parker of the James Ford Bell Library; Herbert Scherer and Dennis Skrade in the Art Library; Kristine Johnson at the Architecture Library; Dorothy Peterson and Peggy Johnson in the St. Paul Campus Library; and Ruth Makinen at the Bio-Medical Library. Still, given all the books that are not at the University of Minnesota, my project might well have failed were it not for the help of the Interlibrary Loan Division. Having achieved some notoriety by making more requests per year than any other patron, I am doubly grateful for the occasions on which the staff worked overtime on my requests, put through "rush" orders, and otherwise managed to get me the books I needed when I needed them. Thanks are due to Erika Linke and Joan Fagerlie, respectively present and former Heads of the Division, and to staff members who worked ceaselessly on my requests: Helen Burke, Robert Gunderson, Jennifer Lewis, and Alice Welch.

When time or distance prevented me from consulting specific books, I relied on a host of correspondents throughout the United States and Britain who cheerfully and carefully answered a variety of questions ranging from the exhaustive to the picayune. The following brief mention of their names and institutional affiliations is minimal recompense for their efforts; but I hope they will take some pleasure in at last seeing the volume to which they contributed many months or years ago: Robert Balay, Reference Department, Yale University Library; Fred Batt, University Libraries, University of Oklahoma; Bibliographical Information Service, Department of Printed Books, The British Library; The City Librarian, Birmingham, England; Ruth Breen, Albert R. Mann Library; Jane Brennan, The New York Botanical Garden Library; Mary Alice Carswell, The Academy of the New Church Library, Bryn Athyn, Pennsylvania; Theresa D. Cederholm, Fine Arts Department, Boston Public Library; Marilyn S. Clark, University of Kansas; William T. Dameron, Chalmers Memorial Library, Kenyon College; Duane Davies, Brown University Library; James Davis, Special Collections, University of California Research Library, Los Angeles; Miss M. Deas, National Library of Scotland; Stuart Dick, Special Collections, Morris Library, University of Delaware; Mary C. Dunnigan, Fiske Kimball Fine Arts Library, University of Virginia; Michael J. Durkan, Swarthmore College Library; Linda M. Ellis, Special Collections Department, University of Cincinnati; Rebecca P. Ellis, Massachusetts Horticultural Society; Peter W. Farrell, Reference Department, Alderman Library, University of Virginia; Alexander Fenton, National Museum of Antiquities of Scotland; H. Ferguson, District Library, Stirling, Scotland; Louise Fitton, Rare Book Room, University of Illinois at Urbana-Champaign; Stephanie Frontz, Art Library, Rush Rhees Library, University of Rochester; John P. Fuller, Victoria and Albert Museum Library; Alan Fusonie, National Agricultural Library; Wilma Garrett, Arts & Recreation Department, Mitchell Library, Glasgow; J. A. Gere, Prints and Drawings, The British Museum; Roy E. Goodman, American Philosophical Society; David E. Green, Saint Mark's Library, General Theological Seminary, New York; Henry Grunder, Rare Books, Earl Gregg Swem Library, The College of William and Mary; Peter E. Hanff, Bancroft Library, University of California, Berkeley; Dorothy T. Hanks, History of Medicine Division, National Library of Medicine; Deborah Hardy, George Arents Research Library, Syracuse University; Lyn Hart, George Peabody Department, Enoch Pratt Free Library; Howell J. Heaney, Rare Book Department, The Free Library of Philadelphia; Richard Heinzkill, University of Oregon Library; James Hodgson, Fine Arts Library, Harvard University; Patricia M. Howell, The Beinecke Rare Book and Manuscript Library, Yale University; Sidney Ives, Rare Books and

Manuscripts, The University of Florida; Norma P. H. Jenkins, The Corning Museum of Glass; Carol John, Library, Scottish Office, Edinburgh; Stephen C. Jones, The Beinecke Rare Book and Manuscript Library, Yale University; John B. Ladley, Bowdoin College Library; Jon Lanham, Harvard College Library; Phil Lapsansky, Reference Services, The Library Company of Philadelphia; Diane S. Lauderdale, The Joseph Regenstein Library, University of Chicago; Kenneth A. Lohf, Rare Books and Manuscripts, Columbia University; Lothian Lynas, The New York Botanical Garden Library; Anne McArthur, Marquand Library of Art and Archaeology, Princeton University; R. Russell Maylone, Special Collections Department, Northwestern University Library; Karen Middleton, Special Collections, Aberdeen University Library; Julia E. Miller, The Charles Patterson Van Pelt Library, University of Pennsylvania; Mary M. Mintz, William R. Perkins Library, Duke University; Herbert Mitchell, Avery Architectural Library, Columbia University; John Neu, University of Wisconsin, Madison; Ellen M. Oldham, Department of Rare Books, Boston Public Library; Shirley N. Pelley, University Libraries, University of Oklahoma; Karola Rac, The Franklin Institute Library; Mrs. M. N. Ramsay, The Royal Highland & Agricultural Society of Scotland; M. E. Reinacher, Elijah P. Lovejoy Library, Southern Illinois University at Edwardsville; Peter Reynolds, Inverness Library, Scotland; F. Spencer Roach, The Carpenters' Company of the City and County of Philadelphia; Ethel L. Robinson, Cleveland Public Library; Duane D. H. Roller, History of Science Collections, University of Oklahoma; Nick Savage, The British Architectural Library, The Royal Institute of British Architects; Fran Schell, Tennessee State Library; Antony P. Shearman, Edinburgh City Library; Jayne Schneider, Clifford E. Barbour Library, Pittsburgh Theological Seminary; Andrea Schulman, Harvard College Library; Debra Skaradzinski, Rare Book Collection, University of North Carolina; Katharine M. Smith, Virginia State Library; Richard Goff Smith, Reference Department, University of Illinois Library at Urbana-Champaign; Frank H. Sommer, Winterthur Museum Library; Sally Jo Sorenson, The Library Company of Philadelphia; Lee W. Stanton, The New York State Library; Patricia Sullivan, Fine Arts Library, Cornell University; Jill M. Tatem, Special Collections, Case Western Reserve University; Jerry Thornton, University Library, University of Michigan; Peter VanWingen, Reference and Reader Services Section, Rare Book and Special Collections Division, The Library of Congress; Glenys A. Waldman, The Historical Society of Pennsylvania; David Warrington, The Lilly Library, Indiana University; L. Terry Warth, Special Collections and Archives, University of Kentucky Libraries; Arthur Waugh, Environmental Design Library, University of California, Berkeley; Everett C. Wilkie, Jr., The John Carter Brown Library; Charles Wilt, The Franklin Institute Library; Carol Ann Winchell, University Libraries, The Ohio State University; Mary Lou Wolfe, Pennsylvania Horticultural Society; Priscilla Wrightson, B. Weinreb Architectural Books, London.

I have been especially fortunate over the past several years to have had the assistance of three librarians who in effect put their collections at my disposal by mail. They examined scores of books on my behalf, searched for odd and obscure bits of information, and then alerted me to many things that otherwise I would have overlooked. After sending me countless letters, lists, and photocopies, they cheerfully accepted further requests for even more information. In transcribing and synthesizing what they have sent me, I hope I have done justice to their efforts: Cathy Henderson at the Humanities Research Center, The University of Texas, Austin; Jennifer B. Lee, who was then at The Library Company of Philadelphia; and especially Neville Thompson at the Winterthur Museum Library.

In addition to the personal assistance of all those I have listed above, I also received important material and financial support from several sources. The Graduate School of the University of Minnesota provided funds for research assistance, materials, and travel. I also received travel support from the Kingsbury Fund at Harvard University and from the Putnam Dana McMillan Fund at the University of Minnesota. A research grant from the University of Minnesota Computer Center supported large-scale sorting and storage of information. Finally, I apologize to my colleagues in the Humanities Program for having nearly monopolized our word processor for over six months; using it, however, easily saved six months of working time, and now at last I may be able to devote a little more time to my collegial and collegiate responsibilities.

Christopher Faust handsomely prepared all the photographs at the University of Minnesota Space Science Graphic Arts Center.

I would like to thank the University of Wisconsin Press and the editors of *Eighteenth-Century Studies* for permission to reuse in a different form material that I previously contributed to *Studies in Eighteenth-Century Culture*, Vol. XII, and to *Eighteenth-Century Studies*, Vols. XII and XVI.

I have saved a few special acknowledgments for the end. Over the years Renee Antonow and Mary Finn-Carlson took on various editorial and organizational tasks, and I warmly appreciate their tireless perseverance. Many years ago Marlos Rudie undertook a project far beyond the call of duty, and much larger than she at first suspected, when she agreed to type much of the manuscript for me—not just the final copy, but draft after draft as well. More recently Monika Stumpf also voluntarily took on huge chunks of typing. I am grateful to Marlos and Monika not only for their typing, but also for their daily good humor.

Finally, I owe the greatest debt of all to my wife, Jane H. Hancock. More than generously, she diverted time from her own research and writing to read nearly every word I wrote, making invaluable suggestions and criticisms on nearly every page. She also offered encouragement when I needed it the most, from which I suppose that I have not totally destroyed her interest in Britain, the eighteenth and nineteenth centuries, or architecture.

Minneapolis
Thanksgiving 1983

Postscript

In a book of this size it is inevitable that oversights and errors have gone undetected, despite the greatest care. I regret the inconvenience and confusion these may cause. Undoubtedly some new titles, and hitherto unrecorded editions of many other titles, remain to be discovered in private and public collections throughout the world. I would welcome correspondence from readers who wish to offer corrections and additions.

Introduction

This book approaches British domestic architecture in the eighteenth and early nineteenth centuries through the literary output of architects and others concerned with domestic design. To accomplish this study in as broad a manner as possible, I have first provided an essay that addresses matters of book publication in the eighteenth and nineteenth centuries, and then analyzes several of the important aesthetic and social issues raised in the literature of British domestic architecture during this time. Following the essay are bibliographic descriptions of the individual books and periodicals that make up this body of literature. Finally, each description is accompanied by a commentary containing a detailed discussion of the text and plates. The commentaries focus in particular on the authors' ideas and approaches, with special attention to issues of domestic design.

**1
Scope of
Inquiry**

The importance of domestic design in eighteenth- and nineteenth-century British architectural literature is unquestioned. Dwellings are the most common building type illustrated in Colen Campbell's *Vitruvius Britannicus* (1715), an early and important manifesto of Palladian taste. In the second half of the century both the progress and the excellence of British domestic architecture were proclaimed in several major treatises, including later volumes of *Vitruvius Britannicus* prepared by John Woolfe and James Gandon, James Paine's *Plans, Elevations and Sections, of Noblemen and Gentlemen's Houses*, the *Works in Architecture* of Robert and James Adam, and James Lewis's *Original Designs in Architecture*. Of the most authoritative and popular treatises of the nineteenth century, many were largely or entirely devoted to domestic architecture, particularly John Claudius Loudon's *Encyclopaedia of Cottage, Farm, and Villa Architecture* and Richard Brown's *Domestic Architecture*.

To examine and discuss such a large body of literature first requires careful attention to criteria used for inclusion. A study such as this may be expanded, for example, to include literature on other subjects—such as agriculture or perspective—that are related to the design and practice of domestic architecture.[1] The study also may necessarily be restricted according to medium (books, periodicals, single sheets, etc.), place of publication, chronology, and subject matter. In order to focus the present inquiry as much as possible on British domestic architecture, and to keep it of manageable size, certain limitations were necessary: I have included only books and periodicals published in Great Britain and Ireland, first issued between 1715 and 1842, that contain original designs for habitations. These criteria are discussed in more detail below.

Medium	I have considered only printed books and periodicals.[2] I have excluded single sheets, manuscripts, and drawings.
Place of Publication; Editions of Foreign Books	Because of the difficulties involved in locating Continental editions of British books, and the sheer number of American editions, I have included only books and periodicals with British or Irish imprints.[3]

Place of
Publication;
Editions of
Foreign Books

Because of the difficulties involved in locating Continental editions of British books, and the sheer number of American editions, I have included only books and periodicals with British or Irish imprints.[3]

Of books first published outside Britain or Ireland, I have included only those British or Irish editions that incorporate new or significantly different illustrations. I have specifically excluded translations of major Italian architectural treatises that contain only copies or "corrected" versions of the original plates.

Chronological
Limits

Before the eighteenth century only two Britons, John Shute and Henry Wotton, had published major architectural treatises.[4] The next was Colen Campbell's *Vitruvius Britannicus*, issued in 1715. Campbell was the first British author to devote considerable attention to domestic architecture, and suggested that its advancement was crucial to Britain's future architectural achievement. Thus it is clearly appropriate to begin a study of British domestic architectural literature with Campbell.

The choice of an end date is more problematic. Toward the middle of the nineteenth century, changes in building technology and the burgeoning growth of middle-class housing portended important changes in domestic design as well as practice. A terminus in the 1840s is suggested by the continued publication of volumes titled *Vitruvius Britannicus* until 1847.[5] Yet changes in domestic taste and practice during this decade were not marked by the appearance of any single major treatise.[6] Three events in 1842 do, however, make this year the best choice for a terminus. First, John Claudius Loudon issued the *First Additional Supplement* to his *Encyclopaedia*. Since Loudon died the next year, the *Supplement* marks the final state to which he brought this voluminous and influential treatise.[7] Another major treatise, Richard Brown's *Domestic Architecture*, also was issued in 1842.[8] More so than Loudon's *Encyclopaedia*, Brown's book was a comprehensive and thorough study of domestic architecture, with attention to history, design, and practice. Finally, the first issue of *The Builder* appeared on the last day of 1842. This was a major professional journal, and it was one of the earliest periodicals devoted entirely to architecture.[9] With the contemporary appearance of *The Ecclesiologist* (1841) and *The Building News* (1854) the importance of periodicals steadily increased, and the character of architectural publication changed considerably.[10] Thus in the same year that Loudon's *Supplement* and Brown's *Domestic Architecture* signaled the maturation of comprehensive treatises on domestic architecture, *The Builder* was a harbinger of change. Consequently 1842 is an appropriate, if not necessarily pivotal, date at which to conclude the present study.

Subject Matter   A general examination of all eighteenth- and early nineteenth-century architectural literature reveals at least nine principal subject categories:[11] aesthetic theory; archaeology and historical analysis; original designs for buildings, including ecclesiastical, public,[12] military, and domestic structures; interior decoration and furniture; pricing, measuring, surveying, and perspective; mechanics and engineering; landscape and garden design; town planning; and travel and topography. None of these categories is absolute, of course, and they frequently overlap within individual treatises.

I have limited the present study to books containing original designs for residential structures. This is only a portion of one of the cateogories listed above, but a portion that in fact includes much of the architectural literature of the period. Limiting the study in this manner, however, means the exclusion of certain significant classes of material that deserve brief mention here. The voluminous literature of the Greek Revival and Gothic Revival, containing archaeological reports and historical reconstructions, is of unquestioned importance to domestic design in the eighteenth and nineteenth centuries. Nevertheless it is reasonable to exclude this material here because it is studied most appropriately within the context of British eighteenth- and nineteenth-century historiography.[13] Numerous topographical treatises published during this period provide important views and valuable descriptions of many important dwellings, but they too have been excluded: they contain few original remarks on domestic design, and are best analyzed as a separate class of literature.[14]

I have further limited my study to publications that include at least one design in three dimensions for a whole dwelling: there must be at least one view, or one elevation plus one plan. To incorporate a broad range of designs for domestic structures, I have extended the term "dwelling" here to include enclosed garden buildings such as lodges and hermitages. Nevertheless the restriction to designs for whole dwellings excludes some important classes of architectural literature, principally builder's handbooks, artisan's manuals, and collections of ornaments. These contain designs for the orders, doors, windows, staircases, moldings and other ornaments, instruction in carpentry, and a host of other practical materials. While such books are nearly equal in number to those I have included, and were an important source of motifs for dwellings throughout Britain and North America, they also form a sufficiently large and coherent class of publications to be considered separately. The most prolific authors of such books were John Crunden, William and John Halfpenny, Batty and Thomas Langley, Peter and Michael Angelo Nicholson, William Pain, George Richardson, William Salmon, and Abraham Swan; Appendix A is a checklist of each of these authors' publications, apart from books that appear in the principal bibliographic entries below.

Examples of other types of books that could not be included are the following: those depicting heating installations but showing the building only in partial plan or elevation; those showing shop fronts attached to houses but without a full view or plan of the building; town planning treatises that do not include elevations or views of dwellings; and agricultural treatises containing illustrations of formal gardens laid out in front of mansions that are depicted only in a very flat, two-dimensional manner.[15]

Also excluded are books that contain designs for the interior decoration of entire rooms, but which do not depict complete exteriors. The number of such books is very small, and a checklist appears in Appendix B.

Finally, several important treatises concerning domestic architecture could not be included among the principal entries because they failed to depict an entire dwelling, or consisted entirely of topographical views rather than original designs. These books nevertheless deserve attention, and are considered in Appendix C.

2 Publications Examined

Thorough exploration of domestic architecture in the eighteenth and nineteenth centuries requires examination of publications concerned with architecture as well as many other subjects. Below I have indicated the range and depth of subjects that I have considered.

Architecture

Architectural treatises were the principal body of material that I examined. To gather as many titles and editions as possible I consulted standard bibliographies of the subject,[16] publishers' advertisements bound in eighteenth- and nineteenth-century books, reviews in periodicals, cross-references in other architectural books and articles, and modern library catalogues.[17] I discovered additional material by browsing through library shelves at Harvard, Yale, Columbia, the University of Chicago, and the University of Minnesota.

Agriculture

Many agricultural writers believed that improving the living conditions of rural laborers would lead to increased productivity, and so included exemplary designs for farm houses, cottages, and other structures in their books and essays. I have not examined all the agricultural literature of the period, but I have thoroughly pursued references in architectural and landscape treatises to agricultural publications, and cross-references from one agricultural treatise to another. I examined the entire series of county surveys prepared for the Board of Agriculture between 1793 and 1817; those with views or plans and elevations of dwellings are found under the heading "Great Britain. Board of Agriculture. Reports."

Landscape Design and Gardening

Throughout the eighteenth and early nineteenth centuries theories of pictorial design and "picturesque" composition, developed in treatises on landscape, became increasingly important to architecture as well.[18] Likewise, many landscape treatises included remarks on domestic design, as well as designs for dwellings, reflecting a concern among landscapists that buildings accord with the aesthetic order of the landscape. Working from references in contemporary architectural treatises as well as standard bibliographies of the subject,[19] I have examined landscape and gardening publications from Switzer's *Nobleman, Gentleman, and Gardener's Recreation* (1715) through mid-nineteenth-century periodicals such as *The Horticultural Register* and *Paxton's Magazine of Botany*.

Drawing

Several important aspects of picturesque architectural design were explored at an early date in drawing treatises.[20] Architectural students who used drawing manuals for practice in the late eighteenth and early nineteenth centuries necessarily were exposed to numerous illustrations of picturesque and rustic vernacular dwellings, as well as buildings in other styles, that were used as drawing studies. Although I have not exhaustively examined all the drawing literature of the period, I have included below those treatises and manuals in which I found a dwelling as the principal subject of one or more plates.

Perspective

A knowledge of perspective was requisite for the practicing architect, and dwellings are prominent subjects in many perspective treatises. Unfortunately only limited bibliographies of perspective are available.[21] I have discovered many titles by perusing publishers' advertisements, periodical reviews, and the book stacks of major research libraries.

Encyclopedias and Dictionaries

I have examined all titles issued from 1715 through 1842 that are listed in two specialized bibliographies of encyclopedias and dictionaries, plus additional titles discovered on the shelves of major research libraries.[22] Frequently articles on "Architecture," "Perspective," and other subjects incorporated material borrowed from recent major monographs; less often, they contained original designs for dwellings. In either case these articles provide useful insights into architectural taste and practice at the time.

In the commentary for each encyclopedia or dictionary, I have included a précis of the article titled "Architecture" (if any), plus a précis of each article that includes a view or plan and elevation of a dwelling.

Periodicals

I have not examined the entire corpus of British periodical literature, which is voluminous, but have focused primarily on specialized architectural, agricultural, horticultural, and drawing periodicals.[23] References in these directed me to other periodicals that were addressed to different audiences.[24] I have not examined issues of periodicals that appeared after 1842.[25] Within the individual entries below, I have cited only those articles that contain illustrations of dwellings.

I have not considered daily newspapers, nor weekly journals such as John Claudius Loudon's *Gardeners' Gazette*.

3
Sources
Consulted

In compiling lists of titles and editions for examination, I found the following sources useful, in addition to the printed and public catalogues of major research libraries listed in note 17, and the standard references included in the List of Symbols and Abbreviations at the beginning of the principal entries.[26]

Abbey, John Roland. *Life in England in Aquatint and Lithography 1770–1860*. London: Curwen Press, 1953.

Amery, Colin, ed. *Three Centuries of Architectural Craftsmanship*. London: Architectural Press, 1977.

Architectural Association, London. *Catalogue of the Books in the Library*. London: Langley & Son, 1895.

Averley, G., A. Flowers, F. J. G. Robinson, E. A. Thompson, R. V. and P. J. Wallis. *Eighteenth-Century British Books: A Subject Catalogue Extracted from the British Museum General Catalogue of Books*. Folkestone: Dawson, 1979.

Baggs, A. P., and E. A. Gee. *Copy Books*. York: Institute of Advanced Architectural Studies, University of York, 1964.

Berlin. Staatliche Kunstbibliothek. *Katalog der Ornamentstichsammlung*. Reprint, New York: Burt Franklin, [1958?].

Blutman, Sandra. "Books of Designs for Country Houses, 1780–1815." *Architectural History* 11 (1968), 25–33.

Boston Public Library. *Catalogue of the Books Relating to Architecture, Construction and Decoration*. 2nd ed. Boston: The Trustees, 1914.

The British Library General Catalogue of Printed Books. Five-year Supplement 1971–1975. London: British Museum Publications, 1978–1979.

British Museum General Catalogue of Printed Books. Five-year Supplement 1966–1970. London: The Trustees of the British Museum, 1971–1972.

British Museum General Catalogue of Printed Books. Ten-year Supplement 1956–1965. London: The Trustees of the British Museum, 1968.

Clarke, Ernest. "The Board of Agriculture, 1793–1822." *The Journal of the Royal Agricultural Society of England*, 3rd ser., IX (1898), 1–41.

Collison, Robert Lewis. *Encyclopaedias: Their History throughout the Ages*. New York: Hafner, 1966.

Darley, Gillian. *Villages of Vision*. London: Architectural Press, 1975.

Descargues, Pierre. *Perspective*. New York: Abrams, 1977.

Dobai, Johannes. *Die Kunstliteratur des Klassizismus und der Romantik in England*. Bern: Benteli, 1974–1977.

Donner, Peter F. R. [pseud. for Nikolaus Pevsner]. "The End of the Pattern-Books." *Architectural Review* XCIII:555 (March 1943), 75–79.

Draper, John W. *Eighteenth Century English Aesthetics*. Heidelberg: C. Winter, 1931.

Esdaile, Katherine A. "The Small House and Its Amenities in the Architectural Hand-Books of 1749–1827." *Transactions of the [Royal] Bibliographical Society* XV (October 1917 to March 1919), 115–132.

Fischer, Marianne, ed. *Kunstbibliothek Berlin. Staatliche Museen Preußischer Kulturbesitz. Katalog der Architektur- und Ornamentstichsammlung. Teil 1: Baukunst England*. Berlin: Bruno Hessling, 1977.

Fussell, George Edwin. *More Old English Farming Books: From Tull to the Board of Agriculture 1731 to 1793*. London: Crosby Lockwood & Son, 1950.

Fussell, George Edwin. *The Old English Farming Books from Fitzherbert to Tull 1523 to 1730*. London: Crosby Lockwood & Son, 1947.

Hind, Charles. *English Architectural Pattern Books, 1730–1810: A Bibliography*. Aberystwyth: The author, 1979.

Hitchcock, Henry-Russell. *Early Victorian Architecture in Britain*. New Haven: Yale University Press, 1954.

Hunt, John Dixon, and Peter Willis, eds. *The Genius of the Place: The English Landscape Garden 1620–1820*. New York: Harper & Row, 1975.

Jenkins, Frank. "Nineteenth-Century Architectural Periodicals." In John Summerson, ed., *Concerning Architecture: Essays on Architectural Writers and Writing Presented to Nikolaus Pevsner*. London: Allen Lane The Penguin Press, 1968. Pp. 153–160.

Lyall, Sutherland. "Minor Domestic Architecture in England and Pattern Books 1790–1840." Ph.D. dissertation, University of London, 1974.

McDonald, Donald. *Agricultural Writers, from Sir Walter of Henley to Arthur Young, 1200–1800.* London: Horace Cox, 1908.

McMordie, Michael. "Picturesque Pattern Books and Pre-Victorian Designers." *Architectural History* 18 (1975), 43–59.

Nachmani, Cynthia Wolk. "The Early English Cottage Book." *Marsyas* XIV (1968–1969), 67–76.

Park, Helen. *A List of Architectural Books Available in America before the Revolution.* Los Angeles: Hennessey & Ingalls, 1973.

Perkins, Walter Frank. *British and Irish Writers on Agriculture.* 3rd ed. Lymington: C. T. King, 1939.

Pevsner, Nikolaus. *Some Architectural Writers of the Nineteenth Century.* Oxford: Clarendon Press, 1972.

Pilcher, Donald. *The Regency Style.* London: Batsford, 1947.

Robinson, John Martin. "Model Farm Buildings of the Age of Improvement." *Architectural History* 19 (1976), 17–31.

Rothamsted Experimental Station Library. *Catalogue of the Printed Books on Agriculture Published between 1471 and 1840.* Aberdeen: University Press, [1926?].

Royal Agricultural Society of England. *Catalogue of the Library.* London: Royal Agricultural Society, 1918.

South Kensington Museum, London. *Drawing, Geometry, and Perspective.* London: South Kensington Museum, 1888.

Southampton University Library. *Catalogue of the Walter Frank Perkins Agricultural Library.* Southampton: The University Library, 1961.

Teyssot, Georges. "Cottages et pittoresque[:] Les Origines du logement ouvrier en Angleterre." *Architecture, Mouvement, Continuité* 34 (July 1974), 26–37.

Walsh, S. Padraig. *Anglo-American General Encyclopedias: A Historical Bibliography 1703–1967.* New York: Bowker, 1968.

Wiebenson, Dora, ed. *Architectural Theory and Practice from Alberti to Ledoux.* Chicago: University of Chicago Press, 1982.

Wittkower, Rudolf. *Palladio and Palladianism.* New York: Braziller, 1974.

Wrightson, Priscilla. *The Small English House: A Catalogue of Books.* London: B. Weinreb Architectural Books, 1977.

Notes

1. See Section 2, "Publications Examined."

2. Two examples of printed material bound without a title page are included: John Hassell's cottage designs and Michael Searles's designs and estimates for roofs (Entries 142 and 305). It cannot be determined whether these examples were intended for issue as books.

3. One French edition, a reprint of the Adams' *Works* (Paris, 1900–1902; Entry 1.4), has been included because it contains reproductions of the original title pages (1778–1822).

4. Shute, *The First and Chief Groundes of Architecture* (London: Thomas Marshe, 1563), and Wotton, *The Elements of Architectvre* (London: Iohn Bill, 1624). For more on the place of these two treatises in British architectural history see Rudolf Wittkower, "English Literature

on Architecture," Chapter 7 in *Palladio and Palladianism* (New York: Braziller, 1974), pp. 99–100.

5. From 1827 through 1844 Peter Frederick Robinson issued a series of five parts with this title, each illustrating one major residence (Entry 298). In 1847 a new edition appeared, with additions and deletions.

6. One might argue that A. W. N. Pugin's *True Principles of Pointed or Christian Architecture* (London: J. Weale, 1841) was such a treatise, and that 1841 would be a suitable closing year, since the second edition of Pugin's *Contrasts* and the first issue of *The Ecclesiologist* also appeared then. Nevertheless these publications primarily concern ecclesiastical rather than domestic architecture, and so do not form a fitting terminus for this study.

7. But note that Loudon's wife, Jane, prepared a somewhat expanded Supplement for the 1846 edition of the *Encyclopaedia*, prepared according to directions Loudon had given before his death (Entry 184.8).

8. N.B. The copy in the British Library has a title page dated 1841 (Entry 24.1); nevertheless the Preface is dated May 2, 1842.

9. Loudon's short-lived *Architectural Magazine* appeared from 1834 to 1839, *The Civil Engineer and Architect's Journal* commenced publication in 1837, and *The Surveyor, Engineer and Architect* first appeared in 1840. The introductory "Address" in the "Precursor Number" of *The Builder* deplored "the costly, not to say exorbitant, price of Architectural books." *The Builder*, by contrast, would become "a direct and fitting medium for conveying instruction from the liberal and enlightened of every department—a free exchange of knowledge—which we anticipate may result in mutual good service to all" (I:1 [31 December 1842], 1, 2).

10. For further discussion of architectural periodicals in the nineteenth century see Michael McMordie, "Picturesque Pattern Books and Pre-Victorian Designers," *Architectural History* 18 (1975), 45–46, and especially Frank Jenkins, "Nineteenth-Century Architectural Periodicals," in John Summerson, ed., *Concerning Architecture* (London: Allen Lane The Penguin Press, 1968), pp. 153–160.

11. For comparison, note that in Roman times Vitruvius classified architecture into three divisions: building, making timepieces, and construction of machinery. He subdivided building into two parts: erecting private structures for individuals, and constructing fortified towns and public buildings. He defined three classes of public buildings: defensive, religious, and utilitarian. The latter class included "harbours, markets, colonnades, baths, theatres, promenades, and all other similar arrangements in public places" (*The Ten Books on Architecture*, trans. Morris Hicky Morgan [Cambridge, Mass.: Harvard University Press, 1914], Bk. I, Ch. III, pp. 16–17). In the mid-nineteenth century John Ruskin classified architecture under five "heads": devotional, memorial, civil, military, and domestic (*The Seven Lamps of Architecture* [1849; Sunnyside: George Allen, 1890], p. 16).

12. "Public" structures include office buildings, shops and stores, schools, hotels, clubhouses, bridges, stations, hospitals, prisons, libraries, monuments, palaces, and theaters.

13. For a bibliography of the Greek Revival see James Mordaunt Crook, *The Greek Revival* (London: John Murray, 1972); for the Gothic Revival see Crook, "Introduction" and "Bibliography" in Charles L. Eastlake, *A History of the Gothic Revival* (1872; Leicester: Leicester University Press, 1970). The literature of the Tudor and Elizabethan revivals is surveyed in a note to the commentary on Thomas Frederick Hunt's *Designs for Parsonage Houses* (1827; Entry 154). For British architectural historiography see Nikolaus Pevsner, *Some Architectural Writers of the Nineteenth Century* (Oxford: Clarendon Press, 1972), and especially David Watkin, *The Rise of Architectural History* (London: Architectural Press, 1980).

14. For bibliographies of British topographical literature see William Upcott, *A Bibliographical Account of the Principal Works Relating to English Topography* (London: Richard and Arthur Taylor, 1818); John P. Anderson, *The Book of British Topography* (London: W. Satchell & Co., 1881); and John Harris, *A Country House Index* (London: Pinhorns, 1979). The distinction between a monographic architectural study of a house and a topographical survey of a house is sometimes exceedingly fine. Treatises devoted to Holkham and Houghton (Entries 21 and 288), with detailed plans and elevations, are clearly architectural studies. The literature of Fonthill Abbey, by comparison, consists primarily of popular guide books and sale catalogues (see Appendix C). Other treatises are more complex: John Britton's *Union of Architecture, Sculpture, and Painting*, for example, is a detailed description of Sir John Soane's house and museum. In deciding whether to include this and similar books, I adopted the following arbitrary, but necessary, rule: only monographic studies prepared by an architect of the

house itself should be included among the principal entries. Some of the most important books that have been excluded are discussed in Appendix C.

15. See for example: Thomas Tredgold, *Principles of Warming and Ventilating Public Buildings* (London: Josiah Taylor, 1824); John Young, *A Series of Designs, for Shop Fronts* (London: J. Taylor, 1828); James Craig, *A Plan for Improving the City of Edinburgh* (Edinburgh: The author, 1786); Sydney Smirke, *Suggestions for the Architectural Improvement of the Western Part of London* (London: Priestley, 1834); Richard Bradley, *New Improvements of Planting and Gardening* (1717–1718; 6th ed., London: J. and J. Knapton [etc.], 1731); Charles Evelyn, *The Lady's Recreation* (London: J. Roberts, 1717); John Lawrence [or Laurence], *Gardening Improv'd* (London: W. Taylor, 1718); and Laurence, *The Gentleman's Recreation* (London: Bernard Lintott, 1716).

16. These are found in the list of "Sources Consulted" at the end of this introduction.

17. These include the published catalogues of the American Philosophical Society, the Avery Library at Columbia University, the British Library, the Fowler Architectural Collection of the Johns Hopkins University, the Goldsmiths' Library of Economic Literature at the University of London, the Kress Library of Business and Economics at the Harvard Graduate School of Business Administration, the Metropolitan Museum of Art, the Royal Institute of British Architects, the South Kensington (later Victoria and Albert) Museum, and the Winterthur Museum Libraries, plus the *National Union Catalogue*. I also methodically checked most titles in library catalogues at thirteen major research institutions in England and America: the Bodleian Library, the British Library, the Cambridge University Library, The British Architectural Library at the Royal Institute of British Architects, Sir John Soane's Museum, the National Art Library at the Victoria and Albert Museum, the Avery Library at Columbia University, the Boston Athenaeum, the Boston Public Library, the Harvard College, Design, Fine Arts, and Kress libraries at Harvard, the New York Public Library, the Yale University Library, and the Yale Center for British Art.

18. On the close relationship between pictorial aesthetics, landscape design, and architecture see especially Christopher Hussey, *The Picturesque* (London: Putnam, 1927), Nikolaus Pevsner, *Studies in Art, Architecture and Design* (London: Thames and Hudson, 1968), I, 78–155, and the commentaries below on the following books: Robert Castell, *Villas of the Ancients* (1728); Robert Morris, *Rural Architecture* (1750); Isaac Ware, *A Complete Body of Architecture* (1756); Robert and James Adam, *Works in Architecture* (1778–1779); James Lewis, *Original Designs* (1780–1797); George Richardson, *New Designs in Architecture* (1792); Edmund Bartell, *Hints for Picturesque Improvements* (1804); John Buonarotti Papworth, *Hints on Ornamental Gardening* (1823); and Richard Brown, *Domestic Architecture* (1841).

19. Standard bibliographies are included in the list of "Sources Consulted" at the end of this introduction.

20. See for example John Thomas Smith, *Remarks on Rural Scenery* (1797), and W. Pickett, *Twenty-Four Plates* ([1812]).

21. See for example *Drawing, Geometry, and Perspective* (London: South Kensington Museum, 1888).

22. Robert Lewis Collison, *Encyclopaedias: Their History throughout the Ages* (New York: Hafner, 1966), and S. Padraig Walsh, *Anglo-American General Encyclopedias: A Historical Bibliography 1703–1967* (New York: Bowker, 1968). The collections of British encyclopedias and dictionaries at the University of Minnesota, the University of Chicago, and Yale University are particularly comprehensive.

23. Following is a list of specialized periodicals in which I have found designs for dwellings. They are discussed in the principal entries or in Appendix D below. Architectural: *The Architectural Magazine; Essays of the London Architectural Society.* Agricultural: *Annals of Agriculture; Communications to the Board of Agriculture; Letters . . . of the Bath and West of England Society; Prize-Essays and Transactions of the Highland Society of Scotland.* Horticultural: *The Gardener's Magazine; The Horticultural Register; Paxton's Magazine of Botany.* Drawing: *The Artist's Repository and Drawing Magazine; Hassell's Drawing Magazine.*

24. I have found designs for dwellings in these periodicals: *Facts and Illustrations Demonstrating the Important Benefits Which Have Been, and Still May Be Derived by Labourers from Possessing Small Portions of Land; The Imperial Magazine; Mechanics' Magazine; The Repository of Arts, Literature, Fashions, Manufactures, &c.* These are discussed in the principal entries or in Appendix D below.

25. N.B. I have followed *The Gardener's Magazine* through to its final volume in 1843.

26. Sources useful in the analysis of individual books and periodicals are mentioned in the appropriate commentaries. Sources useful in studying the history of book publication, ideas, style, building types, and other matters are mentioned in the essay on "The Literature of British Domestic Architecture, 1715–1842."

I have not systematically consulted the computer-based *Eighteenth Century Short Title Catalogue* because it is as yet incomplete, and because for purposes of the present study its contents are largely duplicated by other sources I have consulted.

The Literature of British Domestic Architecture 1715–1842

I *Architecture and the Book Trade*

Architectural books, in addition to being examined for their content, also may be studied as artifacts manufactured under particular social and economic circumstances. Just as an architect requires the collaboration of a client with sufficient material resources in order to erect a building, so an author needs the resources of a publisher, a patron, advance subscriptions, or private wealth to publish a book. In the eighteenth and nineteenth centuries the means of engaging such resources were complex; the discussion below will help explain the available choices, and suggest reasons for their great variety. I also will examine the relative importance of various cities and towns as places of publication for architectural books, and survey chronological trends in publication activity. Finally, from the books themselves I will draw some conclusions about the different audiences to which various types of architectural treatises were directed. Altogether, this analysis will help illuminate the geographical, chronological, and sociological contexts in which architectural books appeared, and thus provide a better understanding of these books as products of the society in which they were created.*

1
Publication
Practices

Book publishing underwent fundamental transformations in the eighteenth and early nineteenth centuries. One of the most important trends was the increasing specialization of trades: early in the eighteenth century a single individual carried out the duties of publisher, wholesaler, and retailer; toward the end of the century these became distinct and separate activities. Copyright was virtually nonexistent at the beginning of the eighteenth century. A copyright Act was passed in 1709, yet authors and publishers gained comprehensive protection only through subsequent court decisions and additional legislation in the nineteenth century. Methods of payment and sale in the eighteenth century differed markedly from practices in the nineteenth and twentieth centuries. Authors usually received a single payment for all rights to their work, which then became the sole property of the publisher. At the same time the level of royal

*Throughout this and the following chapters, I have often quoted material from books and articles that appear among the principal entries; I have done so in order to render my arguments here as thorough and accessible as possible. To keep the apparatus of references and notes manageable, no citation is given when the precise reference can be determined by consulting the commentary to the appropriate entry.

and aristocratic patronage was low, so authors and publishers in need of initial capital increasingly resorted to selling books by subscription or in weekly or monthly "numbers." London publishers enjoyed a virtual monopoly over the British book trade for most of the eighteenth century; only toward the end of the century, as the London monopoly began to decline, did provincial publishers begin to issue architectural publications frequently. Concurrently some London publishers began, for the first time, to specialize in books on the arts. Few eighteenth-century publishers had an interest in more than a handful of architectural books,[1] while major nineteenth-century firms such as Ackermann, Bohn, Carpenter, Kelly, Longman, Priestley and Weale, and especially Taylor began to make architecture an important part of their trade.[2]

Publisher, Wholesaler, and Retailer

In the mid-eighteenth century the functions of publisher, wholesaler, and retailer generally were carried out by the same person. The business of such a tradesman, as described in 1747, was fourfold: "to purchase original Copies [i.e., copyrights] from Authors, to employ Printers to print them, and publish and sell them in their Shops; or to purchase Books from such as print them on their own Account, or at Auctions, and sell them at an advanced Price: But their chief Riches and Profit is in the Property of valuable Copies."[3] Fourteen years later another guide to the trades divided bookselling into five classes:

1. The wholesaler dealer, who subsists by his country trade, and by serving some of our plantations. 2. Those who deal only or principally in bibles, common prayers, almanacks, &c. who are also wholesale dealers. 3. The retale dealers, who generally deal in new books. 4. Those who deal chiefly in foreign books. 5. And those who sell old books.[4]

While this classification suggests that booksellers were becoming increasingly specialized, it is clear from other evidence that midcentury tradesmen commonly engaged in both wholesale and retail business,[5] trading in books issued by other publishers while purchasing new manuscripts from authors and also making arrangements with printers.[6]

After publishing a successful book, it was unusual for an eighteenth-century bookseller to maintain a sole interest in the property. He would normally divide the copyright into shares, to be sold at an auction open only to members of the trade.[7] There were two principal reasons for this practice: first, it allowed tradesmen to share the risk that future editions might remain unsold;[8] and more important, it served to restrain competition.[9] The division of individual copyrights into 12, 24, or as many as 128 shares guaranteed that many firms would have a direct interest in the retail sale of each title. If another firm chose to bring out its own edition, whether officially permitted by copyright law or not, the share-owning firms would refuse all trade with that firm. Any tradesman thus cut off from most sources of wholesale supply would soon be unable to fill customers' orders and shortly be forced out of business. This system of dividing publication rights among closed trade associations, or "congers," could exert powerful restraint on the book trade: competition could be eliminated, and prices could be fixed.[10] But while maintaining high prices, such arrangements also meant that individual publishers' interests were spread thinly. For example William Johnson, not a major figure in the London book trade, stated in 1774 that he was a part proprietor of three-fourths of the books currently in trade.[11] Building up a successful business required purchasing an interest in numerous titles, a requirement that clearly discouraged specialization—particularly in architecture and other fields that appealed to a limited audience.

In the last quarter of the eighteenth century the share system declined, in part because the House of Lords invalidated the principle of perpetual copyright in 1774, and in part for economic reasons. With improvements in provincial transportation and banking arrangements, country booksellers no longer depended on private relationships with one or two London firms. Instead of paying with personal letters of credit or through other ad hoc arrangements, a provincial tradesman now could order from any London firm, paying with negotiable bills drawn on a local bank. As wholesalers sent agents into the provinces, trying to expand their shares of the country book trade, they found their efforts were best rewarded when they retained a full interest in the titles they were selling.[12] At least one retailer, James Lackington, found that by requiring cash for each sale he could reduce prices while still building up a highly profitable business. Despite opposition from other firms Lackington flourished, benefiting from the demand for books among London's increasingly literate population.[13] As a result of such changes many wholesalers began to limit their activity to distribution, and publishers began to restructure their capital investments, finding it profitable to build their trade through specializing in the acquisition and sale of books in limited fields.[14] Thus Thomas Rees noted that late in the eighteenth century the trade comprised three distinct classes of booksellers:

The first comprehends publishers only, whose sale of books was confined to their own property. The second might be designated book-merchants, who were chiefly wholesale dealers, and carried on an extensive and important trade with country booksellers; they were also publishers upon a large scale, both of periodicals, under the designation of magazines, and reviews; and likewise works on general literature and science, of the larger and more important and costly descriptions. The third were chiefly retail traders, mostly in old books, but in some instances were publishers of pamphlets, and books of comparatively small expense.[15]

For several decades the trade continued to become increasingly specialized. The *New Picture of London* for 1818 lists ten different types of booksellers, among which are "Wholesale Booksellers and Publishers who supply the town and country trade," "Wholesale Booksellers and Publishers who chiefly confine themselves to their own Publications," "Wholesale Booksellers, who chiefly supply the town and country booksellers," and "Retail Booksellers and Publishers."[16] In 1839, however, brief remarks in *The Author's Printing and Publishing Assistant* suggest a consolidation of interests among London publishers. Of two principal groups, the first comprised "those who reside at the West End of the Town, and who confine their attention to Publishing only"; their stock in trade included "the Literature of the Day—Works of Amusement and light reading, Travels, Memoirs, Novels, Tales, Poems, and other productions of a similar character." The other class of publishers consisted of "those who reside in the City, and who are also engaged in Wholesale

Bookselling." As wholesalers they dealt in "what are called Standard Works—Works on Education, Science, &c., and such as are in regular and constant demand."[17] In the first half of the nineteenth century prominent architectural publishers were found among both groups, in the City and in the West End: both Thomas Kelly and the Longman firm traded in the shadow of St. Paul's Cathedral on Paternoster Row, while Priestley and Weale, Henry Bohn, and Rudolph Ackermann were located in the vicinity of the Strand and Covent Garden, James Carpenter traded in Mayfair, and Taylor's Architectural Library, the most active architectural publishing firm of the period, was located in High Holborn.

Arrangements between Author and Publisher	From 1694 to 1710 no law protected the interests of authors or publishers in literary properties. Britain's first formal copyright statute, enacted in 1709, provided a period of 21 years' protection from 10 April 1710 for books already in print, and 14 to 28 years' protection for books published thereafter. But ambiguities in the Act, as well as subsequent court rulings, left authors and publishers without sufficient protection, particularly against abridgments and foreign reprints.[18] One solution was to apply, often at great expense, for a Royal Licence. This conferred protection against reprinting or abridgment for 14 years, and did so in the name of a more incontestable authority, the king.[19] The situation improved somewhat in 1774, when the House of Lords invalidated the principle of perpetual copyright, under which some publishers had claimed partial immunity from the provisions of the 1709 Act.[20] In 1814 the term of copyright protection was set at 28 years or the life of the author, whichever was longer. In 1842 this was extended to 42 years, or seven years after the author's death, whichever was longer.[21]

At the beginning of the eighteenth century an author would normally sell the full copyright of his work to a publisher. Royalties were unusual. Payment could be as little as £4 or £5, although by midcentury some amounts were much larger: Dr. Johnson received £125 for *Rasselas*, for example, and Fielding received £1,000 for *Amelia*. Yet there remained a significant disparity among payments to authors of lesser and greater repute. In 1793 Joseph Johnson offered James Hurdis £35 for the copyright of his works. Hurdis, who had just become Professor of Poetry at Oxford, was insulted. At the same time Johnson advanced Erasmus Darwin 1,000 guineas for *The Loves of the Plants*, and then gave Darwin £800 for the copyright of all of *The Botanic Garden*.[22] In 1843 a statistical analyst observed that British authors were paid at approximately one-fifth the rate of French writers. "There is no author now living in this country who could obtain 500*l.* per volume for any prose work," he noted, while French writers of fiction and drama regularly commanded 30,000 francs (£1,200) for a single piece.[23]

If an author could not or did not want to sell his work to a publisher, he had the option of publishing it himself, usually by raising money through the advance sale of subscriptions.[24] By the end of the eighteenth century there were two additional possibilities. One provided for the author and publisher to share the risk and the profit according to a formula to be set in advance. Figures available for one example, the second edition of Lemprière's *Bibliotheca Classica* (1792), show that a quarter of the retail price went to the retailer, advertising and distribution costs were approximately 8.5 percent of the retail price, and production costs were 40 percent of the retail price; in this example, the remaining 26.5 percent was divided equally between publisher and author.[25] When a publisher was less confident of a book's success, the firm would offer to publish on commission: the author would pay the costs of publication and retain all receipts, paying a commission to the publisher for distribution and other services.[26]

In 1839 *The Author's Printing and Publishing Assistant* neatly categorized the three "modes of Publishing" then in effect: "that in which a Work is Published entirely for, and at the expense of the Author," a method clearly reserved for "First Productions"; "that in which the Publisher takes all or part of the risk, and divides the profit," employed "where a certain demand can be calculated upon"; and "that in which the Publisher purchases the Copyright, and thus secures to himself the entire proceeds," a method used "where an Author has become so popular as to ensure an extensive circulation."[27]

Edition Size | Evidence is scarce concerning the number of copies printed for editions of architectural books. For books printed in the early and mid-eighteenth century, subscription lists are often the best indication, although they are most profitably used to establish the relative size of an edition rather than the absolute number of copies printed. For the late eighteenth and early nineteenth centuries, records of a few publishing firms and testimony before Parliament give a better idea, although available figures pertain mostly to books in fields other than architecture. Nevertheless, taken all together the evidence shows that architectural books generally were printed in editions of a few hundred copies. Editions of more than 1,000 copies were rare, while editions printed on large paper or with hand-colored illustrations might be issued in as few as 25 or 50 copies. Expensive, extensively illustrated volumes by such prominent eighteenth-century designers as Campbell, Gibbs, and Chambers enjoyed comparatively large runs. Other titles, issued in runs of under 250 copies—considered by many publishers to be the absolute minimum run—apparently also were financially successful. Presumably the utility of such books to members of the building trades, or the appeal of their elegantly executed plates to the gentry and aristocracy, could justify a sufficiently high price that the publisher need sell only a small number of copies.

Since there are few remaining records pertaining to the publication of architectural books in the early and mid-eighteenth century, the most reliable method of estimating the size of an edition is to examine subscription lists. These contain the names of people who were willing to advance money to an author or publisher, and also indicate the number of copies that each subscriber ordered.[28] Early in the eighteenth century Colen Campbell's *Vitruvius Britannicus* (3 vols., 1715–1725; Entries 32–33) was clearly an extraordinary success: 303 people ordered nearly 370 copies of the first volume, 461 people ordered well over 500 copies of the second volume, and 696 people ordered almost 900 copies of the third volume. James Gibbs's equally important *Book of Architecture* (1728; Entry 88) attracted 481 subscribers. By way of comparison only 149 people, mostly tradesmen, subscribed to William Halfpenny's *Art of Sound Building* (1725; Entry 129), a compendium of practical solutions to "problems" in building construction. A note accompanying the first fascicle of Batty and Thomas Langley's *Ancient Architecture* (1741; Entry 172) stated that "To enable the compleating of the last Part, Encouragers are Humbly desired to pay $7^s = 6$ on Receiving this first Part, and $7^s = 6$ more on receiving the last Part." The completed treatise includes a list of 115 "Encouragers To the Restoring of the Saxon Architecture."[29] For Sir William Chambers's thin but very fashionable folio, *Designs of Chinese Buildings* (1757; Entry 38), 165 subscribers ordered 185 copies. Two years later 262 subscribers placed orders for 336 copies of his authoritative *Treatise on Civil Architecture* (Entry 40). In 1766 Thomas Collins Overton's *Original Designs of Temples* (Entry 234), a collection of designs for 28 garden structures and dwellings, attracted orders for 192 copies, including 12 copies for "Mr. Henry Webley, Bookseller."[30] The next year there were orders for 222 copies (including 25 for Webley) for John Crunden's *Convenient and Ornamental Architecture* (Entry 49), containing designs for farm houses and other town and country dwellings.

Records of late eighteenth- and early nineteenth-century publishing firms provide more precise information concerning the number of copies actually printed. For Joseph Johnson and for Cadell and Davies the minimum print run was 250 copies; for books with a modest popular appeal 750 copies was more common.[31] Testimony before a Parliamentary committee on copyrights in 1813 showed that Longman and other publishers also established a normal minimum of 250 copies.[32] The maximum number printed in any run depended on such factors as the author's reputation, the expected demand, and the success of any previous runs. In the 1770s and 1780s the maximum run was approximately 4,000, and the total number of copies in all editions combined did not usually exceed 19,000.[33] Early in the nineteenth century, however, a growing and increasingly literate population with an appetite for novels changed these figures dramatically: the 10,000 copies in the first edition of Sir Walter Scott's *Rob Roy* sold out in three weeks; thereafter, 10,000 copies became a minimum run for a Scott novel.[34]

The market for architectural books was hardly so great. Those printed on large paper, or containing hand-colored plates, served an even smaller audience. Evidence given in Parliamentary hearings on copyright regulation shows that Samuel Lysons's *Reliquae Britannico-Romanae* (1813), an archaeologial treatise similar in format to many large, illustrated architectural books, was issued in only 200 copies, and the plates were printed only on demand.[35] Architectural books were frequently quarto or folio in size, and a typical run for such large books would often be under 250 copies. In the first dozen years of the nineteenth century John White (later White, Cochrane & Co.), who published large books on a variety of subjects, issued quartos and folios in runs averaging 216 copies; the minimum run was 50 copies. When the firm issued both quarto and folio editions of the same title, only 20 copies would be printed in folio size, with 300 printed in quarto. Large-paper and hand-colored copies of quarto or folio titles were occasionally manufactured, in quantities of 25 to 130.[36]

In a seminal study of literary patronage in the eighteenth century, Paul Korshin demonstrated that following the Restoration, direct Crown support of literary activity declined sharply, particularly in comparison with the level of royal support on the Continent.[37] Throughout the eighteenth century the peerage provided equally meager support for authors, and in fact most of the principal eighteenth-century libraries were created by academic and professional men.[38] Korshin showed that in the 1730s a dedicatee might reward an author with a modest gift of £10, and occasionally £20 or £30. By the 1750s dedications were seldom added in expectation of a reward, and instead were included in the hope that the dedicatee's name would help to increase sales.[39] The declining popularity of dedications can be demonstrated in a sample of approximately three-fourths of the books listed in the principal entries. In the period 1715 to 1749, over half contained dedications; from 1750 onward, the number declined to about 28 percent. Yet well into the nineteenth century dedications remained a useful means of encouraging sales. In dedicating *Domestic Architecture* (Entry 91) to Sir John Soane in 1833, Francis Goodwin deprecated the practice of flattering noble patrons through dedications, while indicating that his purpose was to advertise Soane's "sanction" of this book:

the custom of adulatory addresses to such [noble] personages, alike discreditable to patron and author, though so common heretofore, is now nearly grown out of date; for the sanction of such courtly patronage will no longer advance an author one single step in professional reputation, beyond the boundary of just pretension, and well earned desert. . . .

That sanction alone, which a writer, on his own art or science should seek, is the approbation of one amongst the few, who in the same profession have established for themselves, such a reputation as the world will acknowledge as authority. . . .

Your sanction then of this Work, which I have the honour by your kind permission to dedicate to you, cannot fail to procure for me, an advantage such as I could obtain only by your means.

A more profitable method of achieving support in the eighteenth century was to solicit subscriptions. In some cases a wealthy individual would subscribe for several copies of a book, in effect creating a new form of literary patronage.[40] The sale of subscriptions also capitalized on the literary appetite of eighteenth-century Britain's growing and increasingly literate middle class, helping to render previous forms of patronage and largesse unnecessary and obsolete.

The first subscription book, John Minsheu's *Ductor in Linguas*, was issued in 1617 as a matter of expedience, since booksellers had refused to stock it.[41] The subscription trade grew slowly in the seventeenth century, and it became popular only early in the eighteenth.[42] Authors as well as publishers solicited subscriptions by advertising in daily and weekly newspapers, and by means of prospectuses bound into other books or circulated separately. Although terms varied considerably, the subscriber usually had to pay a substantial portion of the price in advance, with the rest due on delivery of individual fascicles or the completed book. To subscribe, however, did not insure speedy delivery, or even delivery at all. Introductions to many books are filled with abject apologies for long delays, sometimes praising the subscribers' forbearance and sometimes expressing indignation at their complaints. In some cases the funds raised were insufficient to begin publication, while incompetence or death kept other authors from completing their work.[43] Still, there were important incentives to subscribe: tradesmen could be listed as "Carpenter," "Plasterer," or the like, thus advertising their services, while members of the peerage might wish their names displayed for reasons of vanity. Because authors and publishers were eager to demonstrate a great demand for their books, they usually withheld subscription lists until the end of the production process, numbering these pages separately or not at all so they could be inserted easily among the already completed parts. In addition, subscription lists could change from volume to volume, edition to edition, or even within a single edition, to incorporate the names of additional subscribers.[44]

A decline in the frequency of subscription publication parallels the decline in the incidence of dedications. In a sample of three-fourths of the books in the principal entries, 32 percent of those published between 1715 and 1749 were offered for sale by subscription. In the next 35 years the proportion dropped to 24 percent, then to 10 percent in 1785–1819. Only 2 percent of the books issued from 1820 through 1842 contain subscription lists. Economic and legal changes during the late eighteenth and early nineteenth centuries suggest reasons for this decline. As publishers increasingly divested themselves of the wholesale trade, they freed additional capital for the purchase of copyrights and for publication expenses. At the same time changes in copyright law, providing for an increased term of protection, enhanced the ability of publishers to recoup their investments.[45] As a result of these changes, the time and energy necessary to raise subscriptions proved comparatively unrewarding.

Subscription lists are often a useful index of a book's popularity as well as the character of its audience.[46] Not surprisingly, large and elegant folio volumes depicting designs for large mansions appealed to royalty and the aristocracy. In addition subscription lists in many such treatises reveal considerable interest among Continental architects and nobility, as well as British booksellers, architects, and artisans in the construction trades. An analysis of several representative subscription lists illustrates these points. James Leoni's folio translation of Alberti (1726), including *Some Designs for Buildings Both Publick and Private* (Entry 177), attracted 260 subscribers. Among these were the Prince and Princess of Wales, the dukes of Modena and Parma, 84 British peers, and 13 baronets. In addition there were six booksellers, who reserved 23 copies, and 53 persons such as painters, engravers, and carpenters, who were engaged in professions and trades related to architecture. No subscribers were identified as "Architect," although prominent architects did in fact subscribe: Vanbrugh, for example, is listed as "Comptroller of his Majesty's Works deceased," Hawksmoor is styled "Esq.," and Wren is listed as "deceased." There are 97 peers and 50 baronets among the 481 subscribers to James Gibbs's *Book of Architecture* (1728; Entry 88). Only two individuals, both Scots (William Adam and Alexander McGill), are listed as "Architects," and the list includes only one "Carpenter," one "Carver," and one "Mason." There are several English architects in the list as well (e.g., Nicholas

Hawksmoor, William Kent, Roger Morris, and Thomas Ripley), but the appellation "Architect" clearly suited none of them.

Sir William Chambers listed three members of the immediate royal family and 36 peers among the 165 subscribers to his elegant and fashionable folio volume, *Designs of Chinese Buildings* (1757; Entry 38). In addition the list includes such prominent painters and architects as James and John Adam, William Kent, James Paine, Sir Joshua Reynolds, Thomas and Paul Sandby, and John Vardy. Two years later 47 members of the peerage and royal family were among the 262 subscribers to his *Treatise on Civil Architecture* (Entry 40). Financial support of Chambers's work through subscription is clear: Viscount Charlemont ordered six copies, Sir Charles Hotham, Bart., ordered six, Sir Thomas Robinson, Bart., ordered 12, and others also ordered multiple copies.[47] Four booksellers ordered a total of 35 copies.[48] At least 50 copies went to individuals listed as architects or as other professionals and artisans in related trades in Britain and France, although the total was certainly greater since major figures such as Kent, Reynolds, and Vardy continued to eschew the use of a professional title.[49] The list of 212 subscribers in the 1783 edition of James Paine's elegant *Plans, Elevations, and Sections, of Noblemen and Gentlemen's Houses* (Entry 243) includes five members of the immediate royal family, 36 peers, and 10 baronets. In addition, a variety of professions and trades related to art and architecture are represented. There are 12 painters, ten architects,[50] ten carpenters, six bricklayers, six joiners, five masons, four sculptors, four plasterers, two carvers, a cabinetmaker, a designer in perspective,[51] an engraver, an inspector of bridges, a land surveyor, a medalist, a member of the Board of Works, a miniature painter, a painter in enamel, a plumber, a seal engraver, a smith, a surveyor, and an upholsterer. A similarly large and elegant work, James Lewis's *Original Designs in Architecture* (1780–1797; Entry 178), contains a list of 217 subscribers; heading the list are three members of the Russian royal family and two members of the English royal family. Below are the names of one Russian prince, 24 peers, 3 baronets, several M.P.'s, and a variety of architects, sculptors, painters, and artisans.

Among subscribers to books containing practical instructions and designs for smaller dwellings, the proportion of peers to architects and artisans is predictably lower. Only 13 peers are listed among the 337 subscribers to John Joshua Kirby's *Dr. Brook Taylor's Method of Perspective* (1754; Entry 167). Of 171 subscribers to Thomas Collins Overton's *Original Designs of Temples* (1766; Entry 234), the peerage is represented only by Lady Pococke and the Countess of Stamford. In addition there are a few subscribers with a professional interest in architecture: three masons, two carpenters, two surveyors, one architect,[52] and one plasterer. John Crunden's *Convenient and Ornamental Architecture* (1767; Entry 49), a modest collection of domestic designs prepared "at the request of a few particular friends" for use by "gentlemen and workmen" alike, contains a list of subscribers that reflects the intended audience: there are just eight peers, no one is described as an "Architect,"[53] and there are 52 individuals connected with the arts of building and decoration. Thomas Rawlins's *Familiar Architecture* (1768; Entry 273), "a Work of general Use" intended for "remote Parts of the Country," includes the names of 11 peers and baronets among the

142 subscribers. In addition there are 13 architects, painters, and sculptors, plus 38 tradesmen including carpenters, bricklayers, masons, plumbers, plasterers, and surveyors. Even William Thomas's *Original Designs in Architecture* (1783; Entry 331), with the author's lofty appeals to "Imagination," "Genius," and "Judgment," attracted only one duke and two earls, plus 12 architects and seven surveyors, among 176 subscribers.

Books containing picturesque designs for modest villas and cottages appealed to a broad spectrum of society, particularly the middle class. This may be seen in the list of 215 subscribers to the 1790 edition of John Plaw's *Rural Architecture* (Entry 260.2). Besides ten peers there are four baronets, seven M.P.'s, six clergymen, and ten military officers. Among those connected with the arts and the building trades are 32 surveyors, 16 architects,[54] 15 bricklayers, eight builders, eight carpenters, seven painters,[55] three members of the Royal Academy, two engravers, two masons, a landscape draughtsman, and a plasterer. The list also includes a bookseller, an alderman, a surgeon, and two comedians. Richard Elsam addressed his *Essay on Rural Architecture* (1803; Entry 69), a similar collection of picturesque designs, to "the nobility and gentry of taste" and "persons of fortune," but there are only two peers listed among the 148 subscribers, while 69 subscribers are described as architects, builders, carpenters, glaziers, plumbers, and other artisans.

Later in the nineteenth century, as the popularity of subscription publication declined sharply, subscribers were generally limited to gentry, professionals, and artisans. The exceptions are found in books with a philanthropic appeal. Arthur Creagh Taylor's *Designs for Agricultural Buildings* (1841; Entry 328), for example, contains plans of model dwellings for the Irish "tenantry." The list of 157 subscribers includes at least 45 peers and baronets.

Another important but less common method of publication was issuance in fascicles, or "numbers." The advantages of this method were twofold. First, as with subscription publication, an author or publisher could test the market with a small portion of a book, hoping to raise the necessary capital to continue publication. Second, purchasers who could not afford the entire book if it were sold as a single unit could more easily afford weekly or monthly installments, resulting in increased sales. The first monthly installment of the first true number book, Joseph Moxon's *Mechanick Exercises*, appeared in January 1678.[56] Comparatively few number books were issued before 1728, however, and it was not a usual method of publication until 1732.[57] By 1842, nevertheless, number publication was considered responsible for widespread dissemination of literature that otherwise would have remained beyond the resources of many readers.[58]

Important examples of number publication include the fourth edition of Ephraim Chambers's *Cyclopaedia*, issued in weekly numbers in 1741, and Samuel Johnson's *Dictionary*, issued in weekly numbers shortly after its first publication in 1755.[59] The first and only edition of Dennis de Coetlogon's *Universal History of Arts and Sciences* (Entry 64) was issued on both a weekly and a monthly basis in 1741–1745.[60] Among early architectural books published in numbers there were both successes and failures. Among the successes, a second impression of the second edition of James Gibbs's influential *Rules for Drawing* (Entry 451.3) was issued in weekly numbers in 1738.[61] Fortnightly issues of Batty Langley's *Young Builder's Rudiments* (Entry 175.2) were advertised in 1733, and weekly installments of his *Ancient Masonry* (Entry 387) were first advertised in the same year.[62] Thomas Rowland's ambitious *General Treatise of Architecture* (Entry 299) was far less successful. When begun in 1732 it was supposed to be completed in 16 monthly numbers; 11 years later Rowland had only begun the third of seven books, and no further books were completed. At the end of the century Robert Morison issued the first part of a series of *Designs in Perspective for Villas* (1794; Entry 211), but no more appeared.

The number trade flourished well into the nineteenth century. John George Jackson's collection of *Designs for Villas* (Entry 157), for example, was completed in six numbers from 1827 through 1829.[63] Yet there were also many cases in which an author's vision found little support in the marketplace. In 1800 Lewis William Wyatt began issuing *A Collection of Architectural Designs* (Entry 359) in bimonthly parts, but publication ceased in 1801 after the third number. John Pike Hedgeland's *First Part of a Series of Designs* (1821; Entry 146) was an important early example of lithographic architectural illustration, but no further parts were issued. John Claudius Loudon proposed to complete his *Illustrations of Landscape-Gardening* (1830–1833; Entry 188) in 20 quarterly parts, but only three eventually appeared.

Individual Publishing Firms

The list of publishers in Appendix F permits identification of several individuals and firms who were particularly active in the field of architecture: these include Ackermann, Bohn, Carpenter, Dodsley, Kelly, Longman, Priestley and Weale, Sayer, and Taylor. Detailed and complete histories of most architectural publishers still await scholarly inquiry. Nevertheless, available studies of some firms offer limited insight into eighteenth- and early nineteenth-century publishing activity,[64] and warrant brief mention here of just four publishers.

Eighteenth-century publishers did not generally specialize in one subject,[65] and architecture was not the major stock in trade of the two most prominent publishers of architectural books during this period. Robert Dodsley published important books by Sir William Chambers and John Wood, but is better known for his connections with such prominent literary figures as Akenside, Gray, Johnson, Pope, Shenstone, Spence, and Walpole. Robert Sayer, who published books by Chambers, Halfpenny, Morris, and several other architects, was chiefly engaged in selling maps, charts, and prints.

The two most prominent architectural publishers in the early nineteenth century, Josiah Taylor (1761–1834) and Rudolph Ackermann (1764–1834), merit somewhat more extensive discussion.[66] The history of the Taylor firm properly begins with Josiah's brother Isaac (1759–1829), an engraver, who traded in Islington and Holborn from 1777 to 1786. Isaac's name appears in the imprint of several architectural books issued from 1768 to 1785. In 1786 he left London for Lavenham, and from 1787 Josiah's name appears in imprints together with that of Isaac.[67] From this time to 1822 the firm was known as "Taylor's Architectural Library" or simply the

"Architectural Library." The partnership dissolved in or about 1796, when Isaac moved to Colchester, becoming a pastor to an independent congregation. Josiah remained the sole proprietor of the firm from 1798 until his death in 1834. Thereafter John Weale took a temporary interest in the firm, trading at "Taylor's Architectural Library" until 1835, when the business passed to Josiah's nephew, M. Taylor.[68]

Ackermann's activities were chronicled by two contemporaries, Thomas Rees and Wyatt Papworth.[69] Born in 1764 in Stolberg, Saxony, Ackermann moved to London sometime between 1783 and 1787, working as a carriage designer until 1795. In that year be began trading in prints at No. 96, Strand; the next year he moved his business to No. 101, Strand, where he previously had conducted a drawing school. About 1806 he closed the school in order to concentrate more on his trade in books, prints, papers, medallions, screens, other fancy articles, and artists' materials. Ackermann was particularly influential in furthering lithographic illustration in Britain: he published the first English treatise on lithography, a translation of Alois Senefelder's *Vollständiges Lehrbuch der Steindruckerey*, to which he added a new set of lithographed plates based on English and other subjects.[70] Ackermann published many important, elegantly illustrated topographical books, as well as *The Repository of Arts, Literature, Commerce, Manufactures, Fashions, and Politics*, a highly successful monthly periodical in which many of John Buonarotti Papworth's designs first appeared.[71] In 1827 Ackermann returned to his former premises at No. 96, Strand, which had recently been remodeled by Papworth. He transferred the business to his sons and his principal assistant in 1829, five years before his death in 1834.

2
Place of Publication

Throughout the eighteenth and nineteenth centuries London was the center of fashion, taste, and innovation in architecture and in publishing. Over 90 percent of the editions listed in the principal entries were published in London. The remaining volumes were issued by publishers throughout England, Scotland, and Ireland,[72] but so few books were issued in any one provincial location that none could be considered a serious rival to London.

Dublin and Edinburgh were the two most important centers of architectural publishing outside of London. The architectural books issued in these cities were of diverse types, including general treatises, practical manuals, and collections of designs, as well as agricultural reports and encyclopedias containing architectural material. Four of the architectural books listed in the principal entries were issued in Dublin, as were editions of other books on related subjects.[73] Among the architectural books a progression is readily apparent from the comprehensive to the narrow and practical. The first was John Aheron's *General Treatise of Architecture* (1754; Entry 3), an ambitious work in conception but lacking the authority of the major Continental treatises. Three years later an anonymous "Gentleman" published a collection of *Twelve Designs of Country-Houses* (Entry 87). The designs, one of which had been executed, are modest in scale and composed in a plain, spare, Neoclassical style. William Stitt's *Practical Architect's Ready Assistant* (Entry 325), issued in 1819, is a collection of tables for measuring and estimating, accompanied by a few designs for dwellings. Arthur Creagh Taylor addressed a very different clientele in *Designs for Agricultural Buildings Suited to Irish Estates* (1841; Entry 328): it is a collection of designs, with estimates, intended to improve the living and working conditions of the Irish "tenantry."

The first architectural book published in Edinburgh was George Jameson's *Thirty Three Designs, with the Orders of Architecture, According to Paladio* (1765; Entry 158). His emphasis on proportionality and on the authority of Palladio demonstrates the northward progress of Palladianism in the mid-eighteenth century, but the retardataire style of several designs reflects the continuing importance of Scottish tradition.[74] Shortly afterward the first two editions of *The Rudiments of Architecture* (1772, 1773; Entry 303) were published in Edinburgh; later editions were published in London, Edinburgh, and Dundee. This builder's manual provides instruction in the orders, in geometry, and in other subjects, along with designs for 23 houses in a competent Palladian manner. William Adam's *Vitruvius Scotius* (Entry 2) was conceived no later than 1726, but published only circa 1812. The book contains illustrations of country houses and other Scottish buildings designed by Adam, his predecessors, and his contemporaries. It implicitly suggests the coming of age of architecture in Scotland, in a manner similar to Colen Campbell's announcement of British preeminence in *Vitruvius Britannicus* (1715; Entry 32). Toward the middle of the nineteenth century James Cunningham completed a far more utilitarian treatise, *Designs for Farm Cottages* ([1842?]; Entry 51), issued in Edinburgh and London. The book contains designs and specifications for cottages and steadings. Other practical designs for laborers' dwellings appear in agricultural surveys of Scottish counties drawn up for the Board of Agriculture.[75]

Outside of London at least a few architectural books were published in every region of England. The earliest was John Wood's *Origin of Building* (Bath, 1741; Entry 351), an examination of the origins of architecture according to scriptural evidence, and an attack on Vitruvian principles. Henry Aldrich's scholarly treatment of Vitruvian civil architecture, far more conventional than Wood's, was published in Oxford in 1789 (Entry 5).

Early nineteenth-century publishers in the Midlands issued architectural books on a variety of subjects. In 1813 two philanthropic works appeared in Oswestry, containing altogether three designs for model cottages: Thomas Netherton Parker's *Plans, Specifications, Estimates, and Remarks on Cottages* (Entry 250) and the *First Report* of the Society for Bettering the Condition of the Poor (Entry 321). The first two editions of James Smith's *Panorama of Science and Art* (1815, 1816; Entry 311), published in Liverpool, contain Thomas Rickman's important essay on the history of English Gothic styles. Only one English encyclopedia was issued outside London: the *Encyclopedia Mancuniensis* was first issued in Manchester in 1815, and then reissued two years later in Nottingham as *The New School of Arts, Science, and Manufactures* (Entry 77). In 1816 William Hawkes Smith issued his *Outline of Architecture* (Entry 314) in Birmingham; the second edition (1820) was the first lithographically illustrated architectural book in England. Finally, in 1835 Rev. William Carus Wilson issued *Helps to the Building of Churches and Parsonage Houses* (Entry 350) in Kirkby

Lonsdale, a treatise devoted to practical designs and useful measures for advancing the mission of the Church.

In the 1820s two modest books were published on or near the south coast. One, J. E. Bartlett's *Essay on Design* (Lymington, 1823; Entry 15), deals with the study and practice of architecture. William Allen published the other, *Colonies at Home* (Lindfield, 1826; Entry 6), as part of a comprehensive program of philanthropic reform.[76] In the southwest T. J. Ricauti issued *Sketches for Rustic Work* (Exeter, 1842; Entry 282), a collection of picturesque designs for the improvement of large country estates.

Many of the books published outside London concern drawing and perspective. John Joshua Kirby issued his important treatise on perspective (Entry 167) in Ipswich in 1754, and Daniel Cresswell published another (Entry 45) not far away in Cambridge in 1811. Early in the nineteenth century, editions of two drawing manuals appeared in the Midlands: *The Artist's Assistant; or School of Science* (Birmingham, 1801; Entry 9), and *The Artist's Assistant in Drawing* (Gainsborough, 1810, 1814; Entry 8). An edition of James Ferguson's treatise on perspective (Entry 80) appeared in Macclesfield in 1807. During the next decade two treatises on projection were printed or published in Newcastle: Thomas Sopwith's in 1836 (Entry 322), and Peter Nicholson's in 1837 (Entry 230). In 1841 John Wood, Jr., published his *Manual of Perspective* (Entry 353) in Worcester.

In Scotland the earliest publication outside Edinburgh was a late edition of *The Rudiments of Architecture* (Dundee, 1799; Entry 303). The *Encyclopaedia Perthensis* (Entry 76) was issued in Perth from 1796 to 1806, and county surveys prepared for the Board of Agriculture were issued in Aberdeen and Glasgow in 1811.[77] The first wholly architectural work issued in Glasgow was George Smith's *Essay on the Construction of Cottages* (1834; Entry 310), an important treatise that called for a functional approach to cottage design in the face of modern social problems.

In sum, the treatises most frequently issued outside London were designs for laborers' dwellings and manuals of drawing and perspective. The former were issued in locations close to perceived need for philanthropic improvement,[78] while the latter perhaps paralleled increasing attention to picturesque landscape in provincial areas.[79] A few extraordinary treatises, such as Wood's *Origin of Building* or Adam's *Vitruvius Scotius*, were the exceptions that proved the rule: few comprehensive, original, or innovative architectural treatises were published outside London. Distribution arrangements were perhaps partly responsible for this situation.[80] Until the early nineteenth century, books published in London were distributed to the provinces through exclusive arrangements between London publishers and provincial booksellers. Such arrangements allowed London publishers to appropriate nearly the entire book trade to themselves, and thus permitted provincial publishers few outlets in London. Consequently it was in the best interest of provincial publishers to take on only those architectural books likely to appeal to the local market.

3	Over the past three decades researchers have approached the history of
Chronological	domestic building activity in Britain through records of the production of
Trends in	building materials, import and trade figures, studies of birth, marriage,
Publication	and death rates, and other means of economic and social analysis.[81] As
Activity	the authors of these studies have noted, such analysis is fraught with

pitfalls: numerical records of brick production, for example, reflect the use of bricks in warehouses and factories as well as in dwellings, while census data on buildings are inaccurate because they do not account for the demolition or conversion of existing structures.[82] Analysis of the frequency of publication of architectural books is an equally imprecise method of measuring building activity, yet it does establish important parallels between publishing and building. In particular such analysis helps to confirm the peaks and troughs in building activity established by previous researchers, and demonstrates that the production of architectural books was in part dependent on economic conditions.

The titles listed in Appendix E represent publications concerning domestic architecture issued in Britain between 1715 and 1842. For purposes of the present analysis, it will be useful to refer to the accompanying chronological chart showing all titles in Appendix E except for general encyclopedias and dictionaries, publications of the Board of Agriculture, and periodicals.[83] In the ten years from 1715 to 1724, too few books were published to support a meaningful analysis. But from 1725 until the end of the decade there was a rise in publication activity that corresponds closely with a cycle of building activity described by Parry Lewis:[84] the peak of the building cycle (1724) immediately precedes a surge in publishing, and the trough in building (1729) coincides with a decline in the number of books issued. Parry Lewis identified another peak of building activity in 1736; architectural publication was not particularly strong at this time, reaching only modest peaks in the mid-1730s and again toward the beginning of the 1740s.

As the growth of population and commerce leveled off in the early 1740s, and as the War of the Austrian Succession demanded an increasing share of public and private resources, building activity declined markedly, particularly in London.[85] Following the 1744 trough in building activity identified by Parry Lewis, no architectural books appeared in 1745 or 1746. The pace of publication resumed quickly, however, and in the early 1750s a flurry of books issued by the Halfpennys and others coincided with a fall in interest rates.[86] Parry Lewis's next peak year for building, 1753, corresponds to a trough in publishing: only the Halfpennys' *Country Gentleman's Pocket Companion* (Entry 131) appeared that year. Thereafter publishing activity rebounded again, remaining strong through most of the Seven Years' War (1756–1763), then declining along with the building depression that arrived at the war's end. Although a strong recovery in building began in the late 1760s and extended until the financial crisis of 1778,[87] the pace of architectural publishing during this period was not so consistently strong. In 1766 through 1768 collections of modest designs by Overton, Crunden, Wrighte, and Rawlins appeared along with major treatises by Paine, Woolfe and Gandon, and Riou (Entries 234, 49, 358, 273, 243, 356, 287). But in 1769 no new architectural books were issued. Five very popular books were first issued in 1774 and 1775: *The Builder's*

1715 ●●
1716
1717 ●○
1718 ○
1719
1720
1721
1722
1723 ●
1724 ●
1725 ●●●●
1726 ●●●○
1727 ●
1728 ●●●●●○
1729 ○○
1730 ●
1731 ●○
1732 ●
1733 ○
1734 ●○
1735 ●●
1736 ●○○
1737 ●
1738 ○
1739 ●●○○
1740
1741 ●●
1742 ●○
1743 ○
1744 ●
1745
1746
1747 ●○
1748 ●○
1749 ●●●
1750 ●●○
1751 ●●●●●●●
1752 ●●●●○○
1753 ●
1754 ●●●
1755 ●●○○○○○
1756 ●●●○
1757 ●●●●●○○○○○○
1758 ●●●○○○
1759 ●●●○○○○○
1760 ○○○
1761 ●●●●●
1762 ●○
1763 ●●○
1764 ○○
1765 ●○○○
1766 ●●●○
1767 ●●●●○○
1768 ●●●○○○○○
1769 ○○○
1770 ●○○
1771 ●●●
1772 ●●○○○
1773 ●○○○
1774 ●●○○○
1775 ●●●○
1776 ●○○○○
1777 ○○○
1778 ●●○○○○○
1779 ●○○

1780 ●●
1781 ●
1782 ●○○
1783 ●●●○
1784
1785 ●●○○
1786 ●○○○○○
1787 ●○○○
1788 ●●○○○○
1789 ●●○○○○○
1790 ○○○○○
1791 ●○○○○○
1792 ●●○
1793 ●●●○○○○○○
1794 ●●●●○○○○○
1795 ●○○○○
1796 ○○
1797 ●●●○○○○○
1798 ●○○
1799 ●○○○○○○
1800 ●●●●●●●●●●○○○○
1801 ●●●○○○
1802 ●●●●●●●○○○○○○
1803 ●●●●○○○○○
1804 ●●●○○○○○
1805 ●●●●●●○○○○○○○○
1806 ●●●●○○○○
1807 ●●●●●●○○○○
1808 ●●●●●
1809 ●●●○○○
1810 ○○○○○○○
1811 ●●●●●○
1812 ●●●○○○○
1813 ●●●●●○○○○
1814 ●○○○○○
1815 ●●●●●●●○○○○○○○
1816 ●●●○○○
1817 ●●●○
1818 ●○○○○○○
1819 ●●●●●●○○○
1820 ●●●●○○○○○
1821 ●●●○○○
1822 ●●●●○○○○
1823 ●●●○○○○○○○○○○○○○○○○
1824 ●●○○○○
1825 ●●●●●●●○○○○○○○○
1826 ●●●●○○○○○
1827 ●●●●●●○○○○○
1828 ●●●●○○○○○○○
1829 ●●●○○○
1830 ●●●●●●●○○○○○
1831 ●●●○
1832 ●○○○○○○
1833 ●●●●●●●○○○○○○
1834 ●●●●○○○○○
1835 ●●●●○○○○○○○○○○○○○○○○○○○
1836 ●●○○○○○○○○
1837 ●●●●○○○○○○○○
1838 ●●○○○○○
1839 ●○○○○○○
1840 ●●●●●●○○○○○
1841 ●●●●●●●●○○○○○○○○○○
1842 ●●●●●●●●○○○○○○○○
n.d. ●●●●●●●●●●●

Architectural Publication Activity in the United Kingdom, 1715–1842

This chart is based on the short-title chronological list of architectural publications in Appendix E. Excluded from this chart are all general encyclopedias and dictionaries, publications of the Board of Agriculture, and periodicals. First editions are represented by "●". Later editions are represented by "○". Multiple editions or parts of editions that were issued in a single year, and which are mentioned individually in Appendix E, also are entered individually here. Multivolume works that appeared over the course of more than one year are entered here according to the years in which they appeared. For more detailed information see the introductory remarks to Appendix E.

Magazine, Pain's *Practical Builder,* Kent's *Hints to Gentlemen of Landed Property,* and perspective treatises by Ferguson and Malton (Entries 26, 240, 165, 80, 200). But in the next two years, perhaps due to the onset of the American Revolutionary War, no new architectural titles appeared.

From the beginning of the war until 1783 most of Britain remained in a building depression.[88] During this period the pace of architectural publication was modest: the Adam brothers completed the first two volumes of their *Works,* Soane issued his *Designs,* Newton published his French commentary on Vitruvius, and Pain issued his *Builder's Golden Rule* and *Supplement* (Entries 1, 317, 221, 237, 242). Some may have considered the Treaty of Versailles a portent of economic recovery: in 1783 Malton finally published the *Appendix* to his treatise on perspective, Paine issued his second volume of *Plans,* and Thomas completed his collection of *Original Designs* (Entries 199, 243, 331). But the ongoing need to finance the large war debt meant that funds for building were scarce, and no new architectural books appeared in 1784. Healthier publication activity in the next several years may reflect the reduction of interest rates beginning in 1785.[89]

In the early 1790s building activity increased, only to collapse following the financial crisis of 1793 and to reach another trough in 1799.[90] In the first half of this decade architectural book publishing lagged slightly behind changes in economic conditions. The pace of publication declined slightly about 1790, increased sharply during and immediately after the financial crisis of 1793, and then fell sharply in 1795 and 1796. Beginning in 1800 there was a strong recovery in the book trade, closely paralleling a resurgence of building construction from 1800 to 1813 fueled by the Napoleonic Wars.[91] But the war eventually took its toll, and in 1814, the year before Waterloo, only one new book appeared—the first volume of Pasley's military *Course of Instruction* (Entry 253). Following the end of the Napoleonic Wars there was a marked recovery in architectural publishing, with at least five new titles and six new editions in 1815 alone. A building depression in 1816 and 1817 then preceded a decline in the number of new books issued through 1818.

Building activity was strong in 1819 and again in 1825, and weak in 1832.[92] In these years architectural publication no longer lagged behind such fluctuations: six new treatises appeared in 1819, eight in 1825, and just one in 1832. Nevertheless a later peak (1836) and trough (1842) in construction[93] correlate poorly with the number of books issued in those years. Indeed publishing activity remained strong from the mid-1830s through the early 1840s, with the exception of a single trough in 1839. This may suggest that the increasing pace and scale of building activity in the nineteenth century could now support a healthy architectural book trade despite temporary declines and recessions. During these years there was extensive building activity in such resort areas as Bath, Brighton, Cheltenham, Leamington, and Tunbridge Wells, and in the newly fashionable suburban outskirts of London,[94] Manchester, Liverpool, and other major urban centers. The appetite of middle-class families for picturesque country and suburban houses in such locations contributed markedly to the health of the architectural book trade during this period: designs for picturesque cottages, villas, and suburban houses were frequently illustrated in some of the most popular architectural treatises of the period, including books by Goodwin, Loudon, Robinson, and many others.[95]

4
Audience

The audience for domestic architectural books in the eighteenth and nineteenth centuries was nearly as diverse as the population: it ranged from the royal family, at whose expense Chambers published his *Plans, Elevations, and Sections* of buildings at Kew (1763; Entry 39), to emigrants and poor laborers, for whom William Wilds wrote *Elementary and Practical Instructions* (1835; Entry 347). Between these extremes, many other treatises clearly were oriented toward specific groups and classes. A modest selection of such treatises for discussion here includes examples of five types: folio collections of elegant designs for aristocratic clients and amateurs, handbooks for artisans and laborers, manuals for those who lived in remote areas or who had little education, picturesque "idea books" for middle-class clients of modest means, and commentaries for members of the architectural profession.

Among the most important and influential eighteenth-century architectural books, large folio volumes with elegant designs for great mansions appealed primarily to aristocratic and gentleman connoisseurs, who owned or contemplated building large houses or who wished to cultivate a sophisticated taste for architecture. The names of such readers are clearly displayed in subscription lists at the front of each volume, along with the names of prominent architects. In many cases the author's introductory remarks were prepared with this same elite clientele in mind. Such books include Campbell's *Vitruvius Britannicus* (1715–1725; Entries 32, 33),[96] Gibbs's *Book of Architecture* (1728; Entry 88),[97] and Chambers's *Treatise on Civil Architecture* (1759; Entry 40), as well as collections of designs published later in the century by James Paine (1767–1783; Entry 243), Robert and James Adam (1778–1779; Entry 1), James Lewis (1780–1797; Entry 178),[98] and Sir John Soane (1788; Entry 319). Most of these books include remarks on important matters of aesthetic theory, and few if any remarks on architectural practice.

Other books are specifically addressed to laborers and artisans. Besides providing instruction in building and design, the authors frequently hoped to alleviate frustrations and problems these readers encountered in their relations with architects. In *The Art of Sound Building* (1725; Entry 129), for example, William Halfpenny censured the architectural profession for keeping their knowledge of the principles of proportion to themselves; it was, he said, "every man's Duty to reveal whatever he thinks may be of Service to the Publick." In 1729 Batty Langley included a special "Advertisement to Workmen" in his *Sure Guide to Builders* (Entry 174.2), and complained that previous authors preferred "to shew the Theory of . . . [their] Works, than to lay down Practical Rules for the Workman." Yet Langley tried to address as broad an audience as possible: in addition to providing material specifically for workmen, he also included matter of interest to "Gentlemen, Surveyors, [and] Master Builders." Edward Hoppus's *Gentleman's and Builder's Repository* (1737; Entry 151) likewise concerned practical aspects of building, and was the first such book directed primarily to an audience of "young Practitioners," or students.[99] A generation later *The Rudiments of Architecture* (1772; Entry 303) was addressed to artisans of "the lowest capacities." Early nineteenth-century drawing manuals and perspective treatises were frequently addressed to amateurs and children,[100] but few architects wrote for such audiences. Rather, during the first half of the century the most elementary architectural books were directed to artisans and laborers outside the building trades, providing advice and instructions for building one's own home.[101]

Some architects particularly appealed to uneducated and geographically remote audiences. In *Familiar Architecture* (1768; Entry 273), for example, Thomas Rawlins addressed those living in "remote Parts of the Country, where little or no Assistance for Designs is to be procured." The text is directed to those interested in theory as well as practitioners, combining ten pages of practical remarks on the construction of arches with commentary on planning, expression, and proportion. William Pain likewise tried to combine practical instruction with aesthetics, in a manual specifically directed at the "workman" and those who were "Ignorant" and "Uninstructed" in architecture. In *The Practical Builder* (1774; Entry 240) he advertised a variety of designs in a new "Taste (so conspicuous in our modern Buildings)," together with "A Table for the Cutting of Timber" and "the most approved and easy methods for drawing and working the whole or separate part of any building."

In the late eighteenth and early nineteenth centuries the growing middle class became a ready market for books of picturesque designs for modest cottages and villas suitable for country "retreats," resorts, and suburbs. Many authors addressed their books directly to potential clients. John Plaw, an author of several such books, openly solicited business: in *Sketches for Country Houses* (1800) he stated his willingness to provide "Designs, and working Drawings, and . . . attend to their usual execution (if required), at the usual commission."[102] Likewise James Malton candidly advertised his services in *A Collection of Designs for Rural Retreats* (1802; Entry 196), offering to furnish designs, drawings, and estimates, and to direct alterations in "any particular style desired." Charles Middleton was more subtle in his salesmanship: he submitted that the picturesque designs in his *Architect and Builder's Miscellany* (1799; Entry 206) would serve "as an Assistant to the Professional Man, and a Guide to the Public in the choice of buildings." Thomas Downes Wilmot Dearn was less felicitous in introducing his first book, *Sketches in Architecture . . . for Public & Private Buildings* (1806; Entry 61): explaining that he was "About to embark" on the profession of architecture and "Ambitious of professional reputation," he spoke baldly of his "pretensions . . . to public favor." The authors of nearly all these books directed their designs toward the gentry and middle classes. Edward Gyfford's *Designs for Elegant Cottages and Small Villas* (1806; Entry 127) were specifically intended for "persons of moderate and of ample fortune." Likewise in *Architectural Sketches* (1805) Robert Lugar offered several types of designs "suitable to persons in genteel life," plus cottages for those who wished "to accommodate their peasantry and dependants with dwellings" in a picturesque manner, as well as larger designs for persons "of a higher class of life, with suitable domestic conveniences in the plan."[103]

Throughout the eighteenth and nineteenth centuries architects also addressed each other concerning their own profession. To the 1791 edition of his *Treatise* Sir William Chambers added approximately eight pages of text concerning the qualifications of an architect. He stipulated that the architect must have a knowledge of technical skills, but far more important were such qualities as character, genius, learning, and above all imagination, in order "to produce sublime or extraordinary compositions." Chambers stressed the artistic nature of an architect's work: he distinguished between designers, who were well versed in aesthetics, and mechanics, whose work the architect must fully comprehend and supervise, but who otherwise would produce designs that are "discordant: without determined stile; marked character; or forcible effect: always without novelty; and having seldom either grandeur or beauty to recommend them."[104] As architects in the 1820s increasingly sought to establish themselves as professionals,[105] John Buonarotti Papworth added to his *Hints on Ornamental Gardening* a short discussion of architects' abilities, sensibilities, and duties. Like Chambers, he presumed the architect would have a knowledge of practical crafts and skills; but Papworth noted that unlike a builder, the architect is far "less dependant on physical than intellectual skill." Indeed the architect must be "full of imagination," "practically an artist," having "the qualifications both of the painter and the sculptor; and the power of combining the theories of art with scientific excellence" (Entry 248.2).

In 1834 architects achieved new professional stature with the founding of the Institute of British Architects, and in the same year John Claudius Loudon issued the first number of his *Architectural Magazine*. His lead article was a discussion of "the Present State of the Professions of Architect and Surveyor, and of the Building Trade, in England,"[106] and included recommendations for establishing professional standards of performance. Seven years later Richard Brown prefaced his authoritative study of *Domestic Architecture* (Entry 24) with remarks on the necessary qualifications of an architect. He recommended a knowledge of geometry, optics, and perspective, but emphasized history and the fine arts as most appropriate to the professional demands placed upon the architect. Brown stated that an architect should have a mind "enriched by study, and stored by travel and observation," in order "to compose or select good combinations of forms and purity of style, or to observe the proper choice and appropriate adoption of the decorations required."

The appearance and content of British architectural books changed considerably during the eighteenth and early nineteenth centuries, in response to important changes in architectural practice, fashion, techniques of book illustration, the professional status of architects, and the clientele for whom designs were prepared. While adequate treatment of all these changes would require a far more lengthy study of British aesthetics, architecture, and society than is possible here, a more narrowly focused study of three distinct publication types and two innovative techniques of illustration will highlight some of the most important changes in format and content.

1
Three Major
Publication
Types

Of the hundreds of books concerning domestic architecture published in Britain during this period, most can be classified into a few distinct types according to subject matter and format. The three principal types to be discussed here, which overlap somewhat and also extend beyond the bounds of domestic architecture, are "general" treatises of architecture, treatises on the orders, and books of picturesque cottage and villa designs.[1] The "general" treatises, large folio volumes that appeared primarily in the first two-thirds of the eighteenth century, emulate such major Classical and Renaissance treatises as the *De architectura* of Vitruvius, Serlio's *Architettura*, and Palladio's *Quattro libri*—works that were the principal sources of early eighteenth-century British architects' knowledge of architecture.[2] The more narrowly focused treatises on the orders were progeny of Renaissance as well as French seventeenth-century publications—Vignola's *Regola* and the first book of Palladio's *Quattro libri*, for example, as well as Fréart de Chambray's *Parallèle* and Perrault's *Ordonnance*. The third type, collections of picturesque cottage and villa designs, originated in late eighteenth-century Britain.[3] These volumes are generally quarto in size, usually embellished with handsome aquatinted or lithographed plates, often hand colored, and served as architects' advertisements or idea books for potential middle-class clients in Britain's growing provincial towns, suburbs, and resort communities. The brief examination below of these publication types will help to reveal their roles in furthering some of the important changes in architectural theory and practice during the eighteenth and nineteenth centuries.[4]

Before 1760 just five authors—Aldrich, Rowland, Aheron, Ware, and Chambers—attempted to publish "general" or "complete" treatises of architecture. To varying degrees all five authors discussed principles of design, the orders, and ornament, and offered a variety of original illustrations as well as designs borrowed from Continental treatises. Yet despite these ambitious undertakings only one author, Ware, completed a thorough exposition of architectural theory and practice. From 1760 to 1842 there were no further serious attempts to undertake treatises of comprehensive scope,[5] in part because archaeological discoveries, designs for picturesque dwellings, and discussion of individual "genius" and creativity seriously challenged the claim of such treatises to general utility.

Early in the eighteenth century Henry Aldrich, Dean of Christ Church, Oxford, undertook a treatise on the general rules of architecture, public and private buildings, ornaments, fortifications, naval architecture, and instruments of war. The book remained incomplete and unpublished at his death in 1710.[6] The portions that he did finish—concerning materials, construction, the orders, proportions of rooms, apertures, staircases, and domestic architecture—were finally published only in 1789 as *The Elements of Civil Architecture* (Entry 5).

Thomas Rowland began his *General Treatise of Architecture* (Entry 299) in 1732, issuing a title page that promised seven books, containing "all that is necessary to be known in building." But 11 years later, after several numbers were issued, the project languished far short of completion. The portions of two books that were finished treat only arithmetic, geometry, mensuration, the orders, and their parts. Shortly after midcentury John Aheron published his *General Treatise of Architecture* (1754; Entry 3) in Dublin. As with Rowland's work, the title promises more than the book contains, but the contents of Aheron's book are clearly more diverse: the text treats mathematical subjects, materials, the orders, stairs, roofs, doors, windows, plus other structural and ornamental elements used in building. The plates illustrate these subjects and also include designs for churches, schools, and dwellings.

Isaac Ware was the first author in the United Kingdom to complete a comprehensive treatise of architecture. His *Complete Body of Architecture* (1756; Entry 339) remained a respected and authoritative reference at least until the end of the century.[7] In the Preface Ware announced a comprehensive approach: he would "collect all that is useful in the works of others," to which he would add information concerning recent improvements: "By this means we propose to make our work serve as a library on this subject to the gentleman and the builder; supplying the place of all other books." While the text and plates are not universally comprehensive, three subjects are presented with particular interest and care: an aesthetic based on the practices of the "Ancients," a general system of architectural proportion based on the proportions of the orders, and the principles and practice of domestic architecture.

Three years later Sir William Chambers completed his *Treatise on Civil Architecture* (1759; Entry 40), limited to aspects of civil design and thus a more narrowly focused work than Ware's. To the *Treatise* Chambers added a proposal for a second volume devoted to matters of "Conveniency, OEconomy, and Strength." This was never completed, however, and the original volume was later retitled to reflect its primarily "decorative," i.e., not practical, subject matter. Chambers explained that his purpose was to impart "precepts" of architecture, and in the text he focused on such topics as the origin of building, the forms and proportions of the orders, and the form and decoration of such structural elements as doors, windows, gates, piers, chimney pieces, and ceilings.

Treatises on the Orders

As fundamental elements of the Classical architectural vocabulary, the orders were of particular importance to European architects of the sixteenth through eighteenth centuries. Correct scale, proportion, and articulation of the orders were central to effective architectural expression. Despite the importance of the subject—or perhaps owing to its importance—eighteenth-century British architects often were content to adopt the principles and proportions established by previous French and Italian writers. During the first two-thirds of the century, English esteem for Neoclassical standards of proportion and uniformity fostered a particular respect for Claude Perrault's *Ordonnance des cinq espèces de colonnes* (1683),[8] in which the author attempted to establish uniform proportions that ostensibly mirrored those of the Ancients. Other architects, wishing to emulate the cool regularity and proportionality of Palladio's villas, adopted the formulation of the orders in his *Quattro libri* (1570).[9] After midcentury the publication of archaeological remains in Greece and elsewhere increasingly called into question the validity of such fixed standards,[10] while at the same time aestheticians encouraged designers to pursue the fruits of their own genius and originality.[11] The proper formulation of the orders increasingly became a matter for archaeological research, while innovative architects neglected the orders in favor of increased attention to picturesque composition, expressive style, utility, and comfort.

At the very beginning of the Palladian movement Colen Campbell made no specific mention of the orders in his major manifesto, *Vitruvius Britannicus* (1715; Entry 32). Nevertheless Campbell obviously recognized the importance of the orders and eventually published his own translation of *Andrea Palladio's Five Orders* (London: S. Harding, 1729). Contemporary handbooks paid close attention to the subject. Sometimes they presented an eclectic discussion of the orders as "laid down and improved from the best masters,"[12] but just as frequently the author relied entirely on "the proportions of the celebrated Palladio."[13] A major purpose of these handbooks was to simplify and codify a system of architectural proportion, based on the orders, for the use of workmen: Halfpenny, for example, offered "useful tables of the proportions of the members of all the orders," while Langley presented the five orders "in a more easy and concise method than any yet published."[14]

The first major eighteenth-century British treatise on the orders was James Gibbs's *Rules for Drawing the Several Parts of Architecture* (1732; Entry 451).[15] Like most of his contemporaries Gibbs enthusiastically adopted Palladio as his principal authority (p. 2), but in addition he proposed to simplify and improve upon Palladio's method of drawing the orders. Gibbs found that Palladio's division of modules into minutes, seconds, thirds, and fourths was "very difficult," particularly for beginners, and he offered instead a "method of dividing the Orders Mechanically into equal parts," by which "Fractions are entirely avoided" (p. 2). Two years later William Salmon published his equally influential *Palladio Londinensis*,[16] in which the second of three parts is devoted entirely to the orders. Salmon's approach, like Gibbs's, was entirely pragmatic: he presented a method of finding modules that "is intirely new; whereby the Module, or Diameter, in proportion to any given Height, is found three ways"—arithmetically, geometrically, and by use of an "Inspectional plain Table."

At midcentury John Wood published his *Dissertation upon the Orders of Columns* (London: James Bettenham, J. Leake, 1750), the first major British attempt to transcend traditional formulations of the orders. In a restrospective assessment of European architectural treatises, he complained of the "Confusion and Disorder" that "modern Architects" had brought to the subject of proportion. He praised Fréart de Chambray, who in his *Parallèle de l'architecture antique et de la moderne* (1650)[17] considered ancient Greece the source of all proper principles, but he also criticized Fréart for numerous errors. Perrault's *Ordonnance* was more to Wood's liking since it had brought its English readers "nearer to the primitive Rules of the Antients . . . than any other Book" so far.[18] Following a history of the orders based on his own *Origin of Building* (1741; Entry 351), Wood concluded that "The Human Body was therefore the Source of the general Proportions given to Columns" (pp. 24–25). He then discussed the three Greek orders—Doric, Ionic, Corinthian—depicting them with heights equaling eight, nine, and ten diameters, respectively.[19] These were, he observed, the proportions of a man considered in three different ways: as "a solid Round Pillar," as "a solid Square Pillar" and as "a Pillar retaining the Thickness of the Human Body when viewed in Profile." Alternatively he proposed that the three orders might be characterized in a manner reminiscent of Vitruvius: as expressions or "lively Symbols" of "the Robust Man," of "the Grave Matron," and of the "Sprightly young Girl" (pp. 26–27).

Other treatises of the 1750s were less imaginative but far more influential. Isaac Ware's formulation of the orders in *A Complete Body of Architecture* (1756; Entry 339) was largely derived from Perrault's *Ordonnance*.[20] In his *Treatise on Civil Architecture* (1759; Entry 40) Sir William Chambers presented a notably eclectic treatment of the orders that was respected well into the nineteenth century.[21] In discussing the orders he frequently referred to the writings and designs of other architects, including Alberti, Barbaro, Blondel, Cataneo, de Chambray, de Cordemoy, de l'Orme, Gibbs, Le Clerc, Palladio, Perrault, Scamozzi, Serlio, Vitruvius, and Wotton. He particularly respected Vignola's formulation of the Tuscan, Doric, and Corinthian.[22] Chambers also referred to his own measurements of "many ancient and modern celebrated buildings, both at Rome and in other parts of Europe," such as the Pantheon, the Basilica of Antoninus, the arches of Titus and Septimius Severus, and the Theater of Marcellus. Clearly he was unwilling to accept the authority of any historical practitioner or of an ideal standard, and instead selected the individual examples that he felt were proven best by time and by common consent. But he recognized the potential for licentiousness in adopting such a method. If, for example, the ancient Roman practice of using a Corinthian order with an Ionic entablature would "contribute towards the perfection of that which all see, and all approve; it cannot justly be censured"; yet such "liberty" must always be "exercised with great caution."

George Jameson's *Thirty Three Designs, with the Orders of Architecture, According to Paladio* (1765; Entry 158) was the first book of domestic designs published in Scotland. It also was a unique attempt to harmonize Palladio's proportions with the authority of "the Divine Architect" and with such biblical precedents as the Tabernacle of Moses and Solomon's Temple. Jameson's approach was reminiscent of Wood in his attention to biblical sources, but he clearly yielded to convention in his deference to Palladian proportion. Stephen Riou appealed to a wholly different standard in *The Grecian Orders of Architectvre* (1768; Entry 287). Praising the recent archaeological activities of James Stuart and Nicholas Revett in Athens, Riou used their findings "to establish documents for the three orders, and to make a modulary division of all their component parts for practical uses." He also provided a parallel examination of the orders as formulated by Palladio, Scamozzi, and Vignola.

One year later Peter de la Roche wrote the first British commentary on the orders that appealed more to personal "taste" and "genius" than to historical authority. In *An Essay on the Orders of Architecture* (London: The author, 1769) he rejected the notion that an architect's taste must be "modelled" by a knowledge of "Antique Remains" in Italy. Rather, the architect should foster the "growth" of architecture, surpassing the work of the Ancients, by looking "for models in his own genius" (p. iii). Indeed the Ancients themselves were guided only by their own "genius, regulating its dictates by those of reason, nature, and propriety." De la Roche lamented that architects examining the ruins of Classical structures did not realize this, since attempts to extract general systems of proportion from such evidence clearly could not succeed (pp. 3–4). Yet this was not a manifesto of diversity: his main purpose was to establish greater uniformity among the orders. He wanted "to unite the *Five Orders*" within "one *General Order,* whose [five] different *Modes* correspond with each other"—according to a modular system of proportion largely based on Perrault (pp. iii, 5–6). His principal concession to originality was a proposal for a new, sixth order, called the "Britannic Order," incorporating many ornamental features closely associated with aspects of British history and tradition. The most prominent of these features was the capital, composed of ostrich feathers like those in the badge of the Prince of Wales.[23]

Twelve years later Henry Emlyn published *A Proposition for a New Order of Architecture,*[24] with components derived from nature as well as from aspects of British history. Noting that the three Greek orders all imitated trees and foliage, Emlyn proposed that the "Twin Tree," a pair of trunks rising from a single base, could likewise be "stripped of its rude form, and embellished with as noble and necessary ornaments as a Grecian or Roman Column" (p. ii). The order consists of twin shafts rising from a single base and supporting a single entablature. Its ornament represents "the particular character of our ancient English chivalry," with capitals, for example, derived from "the Plumage of the Caps of the Knights" (pp. iv–vii).

In the late eighteenth and early nineteenth centuries increasing attention to the remains of Classical civilization tended to diminish the opportunity for outright invention, although refinements and improvements through the application of genius and taste were still encouraged. Two of the largest, most elegant British treatises on the orders appeared during this period. In *A Treatise on the Five Orders* (1787; Entry 434) George Richardson presented "elegant and correct examples, representing the most approved forms, proportions, and decorations, peculiar to the several orders; as exhibited in the remains of the beautiful edifices of antiquity." One of the earliest British architectural books illustrated by the aquatint process,[25] this handsome volume is over 50 centimeters tall, with letterpress in parallel columns of English and French. Perhaps taking his cue from Sir Joshua Reynolds's sixth Discourse,[26] Richardson espoused the Neoclassical doctrine that "study and observation of the beauties . . . of Antiquity" would improve the taste and inspire the genius of the connoisseur or artist. Such examples, he said, were the best models for "forming a correct taste," for discerning "what is graceful and elegant," and for distinguishing "what is destitute of harmony" (p. vii). The best examples of all were those from "the celebrated age of Augustus, at which happy period the universe enjoyed a perfect state of tranquillity" (p. viii). Yet these examples served only as points of departure for artistic refinement and perfection. While touting the experience he gained in travels through Italy, Istria, and southern France, he also explained that he adhered to no system, nor to any "Master, ancient or modern"; rather, he "selected and formed his Designs according to the best of his judgment, and agreeable to the style, forms, and proportions which constitute beauty and harmony" exhibited in general throughout ancient Roman architecture (p. ix). William Bradshaw's *Civil Architecture* ([1800?]; Entry 19) is even larger than Richardson's treatise and contains several elegant, large-scale illustrations of the five orders. Nevertheless it lacks a letterpress text and thus contributed little to the intellectual appreciation of the orders.

After the turn of the century the only nonarchaeological treatises on the orders were handbooks for builders and artisans. These are exemplified by two of Peter Nicholson's books, both of which rely on previous commentaries or archaeological reports rather than the author's own contributions. Many of the illustrations in *The Student's Instructor in Drawing and Working the Five Orders of Architecture* (1795; Entry 421) are based on Athenian examples recorded by Stuart and Revett,[27] while *A Theoretical and Practical Treatise on the Five Orders of Architecture* (1834; Entry 228) is more comparative, presenting "the Opinions of the most eminent Architects" on the proportions of the orders, and contrasting the orders as formulated by "Ancients" with those of the "Moderns."

Books of
Picturesque
Cottage and
Villa Designs

Late in the eighteenth century a new type of architectural book appeared, reflecting important changes in architectural aesthetics: the increasing belief that general principles of design no longer could be applied with equal validity to all circumstances and situations, new confidence in the integrity of the architect's own creative "genius," and a growing interest in the application of picturesque aesthetics to architecture.[28] Sometimes informally described as "villa books,"[29] examples of this type generally contain a brief prefatory essay, short descriptions of the plates, and plans and elevations of designs for modest dwellings, usually shown surrounded by lush plantings and scenery. Such dwellings particularly suited the desires of the growing middle class to live in a rural setting outside of town, in suburbs, resorts, and country "retreats." Often the illustrations were accompanied by evocative descriptions of romantic locations, "retired" activities, and expressively articulated facades.

The earliest of these books was John Plaw's *Rural Architecture* (Entry 260), the first part of which was issued in 1785. A thin quarto containing brief descriptions and aquatinted illustrations of villas, cottages, and other small dwellings, it differs markedly from other contemporary publication types.[30] Plaw's elevations and plans are generally uniform and symmetrical, but his commitment to the picturesque is apparent in the careful coordination of elegant architectural forms with surrounding scenery. Three years later Sir John Soane issued his *Plans Elevations and Sections of Bvildings Executed* (Entry 319). Its folio size, the dedication to the king, and the introductory remarks extolling the importance and greatness of architecture all are reminiscent of earlier, more comprehensive general treatises. But the substance of the book—which includes designs for several modest, picturesque dwellings—also ties it to the "villa book" genre.

More sophisticated examples of the type appeared in the mid-1790s. Soane's *Sketches in Architecture* (1793; Entry 320) contains designs for cottages, villas, and other small dwellings "on a smaller scale" than his previous designs, and "within the reach of moderate fortunes." Many of the designs are embellished in a picturesque manner, with thatch roofs, brick arches, wall surfaces suggestive of rough plaster or stucco, and occasional tree trunks used as columns. All the designs are shown surrounded by what Soane termed "characteristic" landscape scenery. Plaw's next book, titled *Ferme Ornée* (1795; Entry 259), includes a wide variety of highly picturesque designs for lodges, cottages, villas, and other small dwellings. One year earlier Robert Morison issued a far less attractive volume, a small octavo collection of aquatinted and watercolored but crudely drawn and impossibly grandiose proposals, titled *Designs in Perspective for Villas* (Entry 211). James Malton's important and highly influential *Essay on British Cottage Architecture* (1798; Entry 197) was a fundamental dissertation on the picturesque in architecture, stressing the importance of irregular composition and of pictorial harmony with the surrounding environment. His skillfully aquatinted designs for "huts" and larger "retreats" display such features as porches, asymmetrical projections, brick walls, and thatch roofs that shortly became standard elements of the picturesque architectural vocabulary.

The type of book that Plaw introduced in 1785 fully matured only in the first decades of the nineteenth century. The century opened with the appearance of his third book, *Sketches for Country Houses* (1800; Entry 261), containing designs in a variety of picturesque styles for cottages and other small dwellings, executed with careful attention to relations between each house and the surrounding landscape. Within the next three decades several dozen similar collections of designs were issued by other architects, including Aikin, Atkinson, Barber, Bartell, Busby, Dearn, Elsam, Gandy, Gyfford, Hunt, Laing, Lugar, Miller, Papworth, Pocock, and Robinson.[31]

These volumes, generally octavo in size, included elegant, often colored, illustrations of picturesque designs in a variety of styles for cottages, villas, and other modest dwellings. In addition many of these authors included texts that addressed important aesthetic and social concerns, including economy, utility, philanthropy, landscape design, the conflict between picturesque irregularity and ordered symmetry, expression, and style.[32]

The culmination of the type is exemplified by two books issued in 1827, containing fashionable designs for modest dwellings particularly suited to Britain's rapidly growing demand for middle-class housing. Peter Frederick Robinson's *Designs for Ornamental Villas* (Entry 293) contains 16 designs for dwellings and other, smaller, buildings. They are composed in perhaps the most varied collection of styles in British architectural literature to date: Swiss, Greek, Palladian, Old English, Castellated, "Ancient Manor House," Modern Italian, Anglo-Norman, Decorated (Gothic), Elizabethan, "Ancient Timber Building," and Tuscan. Each design is illustrated in plan, elevation, and a "Scenic View," and is accompanied by several pages of descriptive letterpress. In discussing his designs Robinson stressed their individual picturesque characteristics as well as the pictorial integration of each building with the surrounding landscape.

In the same year James Thomson issued *Retreats* (Entry 333), a collection of designs for cottages, villas, and "ornamental buildings," and perhaps the epitome of the "villa book." The text includes important observations on matters of style, landscape setting, function, and expression, and the plates contain designs in Doric, Ionic, Corinthian, and Gothic styles. The prose descriptions indicate Thomson's attention to his clients' vanities and pretensions, as well as their practical, social, and occupational circumstances. There are designs, for example, suited to "an active partner in a mercantile house," a "family residence," and "persons fond of retirement and study." Each design is illustrated in plan and elevation, and the elevations—depicted in aquatint and in many copies hand colored—are well integrated with surrounding lawns, shrubbery, trees, and distant hills.

2
The
Introduction of
Aquatint and
Lithography

Before 1785 British architectural books were illustrated primarily by intaglio techniques, including engraving, etching, and mezzotint. Woodblock prints are found in some early British architectural books,[33] and wood engraving appears as early as 1802,[34] but these techniques were used rarely in architectural books in the eighteenth century. Since exact proportionality and precise detail were characteristic of the Palladian aesthetic that reigned from 1715 through the 1780s, etching and engraving were particularly appropriate techniques for illustrating designs in Palladian style, as well as the intricate detail of midcentury Rococo designs. Executed by the architect himself or by such master engravers as Fourdrinier, Rocque, and Rooker,[35] the plates to many architectural volumes are among the most attractive works of eighteenth-century British art. I will focus here on the subsequent introduction of two new techniques, aquatint and lithography, and the changes in architectural illustration that these techniques facilitated.

The aquatint process was perfected in the late 1760s by the French printmaker Jean-Baptiste Le Prince. Shortly thereafter Paul Sandby added further refinements, and in 1775 he produced the first English book illustrated by this method, *XII Views in Aquatinta from Drawings Taken on the Spot in South Wales*.[36] Significantly, this new technique arrived during a period in which architects increasingly preferred a more informal, picturesque style of dwelling design,[37] a style that involved greater attention to light and shadow, advance and recession, and the textures of architectural materials and natural scenery.[38] The introduction of aquatint significantly aided rendition of all these qualities.

John Plaw was the first British architect to employ aquatint as a means of book illustration, using the technique to depict each design in his *Rural Architecture* (1785; Entry 260). His generally symmetrical facades, embellished with Neoclassical ornament, gain added depth and texture because of the wide range of tones and shades made possible by aquatint. Perhaps not coincidentally, his plates were the first in any British architectural book in which landscape was an important part of the entire composition. Aquatint facilitated portrayal of varied textures and shadings in trees, shrubs, lawns, and stones, which correspond with similar textures and shadings in elements of a building, thus establishing close relationships between a house and its surrounding landscape.

The next book of domestic designs containing aquatinted plates, George Richardson's *New Designs in Architecture* (Entry 284), appeared in 1792.[39] In his introductory remarks Richardson endorsed such qualities as movement, advance, and recession in architecture, and in his elevations he used aquatint to achieve corresponding effects of planar advance and recession, light, and shadow. The plates depict no landscape scenery, however, and Richardson's dead-frontal elevations do not fully achieve the illustrative potential of aquatint.

Later architects exploited that potential, however, particularly in conjunction with picturesque architectural styles. Advance, recession, and irregularity in plan and elevation could be emphasized by gradations of light and shade, and deeply textured materials such as thatch and tree bark could be rendered very effectively in aquatint. Between 1785 and 1819 well over half of all newly issued architectural books included aquatinted plates, with the highest concentration occurring in the years 1800 through 1811. Among these books are highly attractive collections of designs by Atkinson, Barber, Bartell, Busby, Dearn, Elsam, Gandy, Gyfford, Laing, Lugar, Malton, Mitchell, Pocock, and Randall.[40]

Lithography, a process by which drawings may be transferred from a specially treated type of limestone onto paper, was developed in Germany in the 1780s and 1790s, and perfected there by Alois Senefelder in 1796. Early examples of the process, then called "polyautography," appeared in London in 1803. One English book with a lithographed illustration appeared as early as 1807, but British architects remained shy of the process until the end of the next decade. During the same period, however, such German architects as Weinbrenner, von Gärtner, and Schinkel made very effective use of lithography in rendering varied qualities of line and texture in building materials as well as in surrounding landscape scenery.[41]

For British architects, serious attention to lithography had to await translations of Senefelder's *Complete Course of Lithography* (1819) and Antoine Raucourt's *Manual of Lithography* (1820).[42] The first British architectural book to contain a lithographed plate was the second edition of William Hawkes Smith's *Outline of Architecture* (1820; Entry 314.2), which contained, in addition to the six intaglio plates of the first edition, one new lithographed plate, an illustration of the Doric order. Unfortunately the subject was illustrated in a linear manner that hardly made full use of the expressive potential of the medium. In 1821 John Pike Hedgeland issued the *First Part of a Series of Designs for Private Dwellings* (Entry 146), containing ten designs, each illustrated in a lithographed view, and an etched plan. The elevations are typified by severe lines, plain surfaces, and minimal ornamentation, for which lithography was perhaps not the most appropriate technique. Nevertheless Hedgeland did make effective use of lithography in representing the surrounding foliage and landscape scenery, and also in suggesting light, shadow, and three-dimensional space.

Peter Frederick Robinson and Thomas Frederick Hunt were the first British architects to exploit the technique to its fullest potential.[43] In the mid-1820s both men published books in which lithography markedly enhanced the picturesqueness of their designs: they used it to reproduce irregularities of form and texture in rustic sheds, vernacular cottages, and Old English dwellings, to render effects of light and shade, and to establish visual correspondences between buildings and lush surrounding scenery. Following such effective demonstrations of this technique, it quickly became an important and popular method of architectural illustration. Between 1825 and 1831 lithographic illustrations appeared in nearly half of all newly issued architectural books, including treatises by Hall, Jackson, Meason, Soane, Trendall, and Whitwell.[44]

III   *Theory and Design*

In the eighteenth and early nineteenth centuries domestic architecture was the most common and perhaps the most important subject in British architectural literature. Very few major treatises, particularly those containing original designs, failed to include at least one design for a dwelling. More often, descriptions and illustrations of dwellings were a book's principal subject matter. To some degree this emphasis simply paralleled contemporary architectural practice. For most of the eighteenth century, residential building activity remained strong in Britain, while governmental and ecclesiastical building proceeded at a relatively slow pace—especially in comparison with Continental practice.[1]

Whatever the relative prominence of different building genres in Britain, authors of books concerning domestic architecture made a substantial contribution to the study of theory and design. Designs for dwellings frequently were accompanied by discussion of important aesthetic issues, including proportion, creativity, meaning, expression, economy, utility, style, and picturesque composition. These remarks, together with additional observations on progress, "retirement," characteristics of specific dwelling types, and town planning, reveal a broad range of aesthetic and social concerns among architects during this period.

The temptation is strong to emulate the ecumenical and eclectic eighteenth-century "virtuoso" by undertaking here a broad review of British architectural aesthetics. Yet this subject in its diversity and complexity demands examination from such varied perspectives that a comprehensive treatment becomes ungainly if not impossible. Study of the arrangement and use of interior spaces, for example, demands close attention to social history.[2] Discussion of architectural practice should be based on examination of handbooks and manuals[3] and requires familiarity with the history of building technology. Picturesque landscape aesthetics is central to architectural theory in the late eighteenth and early nineteenth centuries; I have discussed this topic briefly below, but further analysis would require closer examination of the history of painting and landscape design.[4] Study of other subjects ranges farther afield, requiring special attention to Gothic and Classical archaeology, ecclesiology, topography, and agriculture.[5]

Therefore in dealing with the diverse literature represented in the entries below, I have tried to limit the scope of my endeavor. My principal concern has been to define issues and ideas that play an important role in the treatises under examination, and to provide a synthetic discussion of the authors' approaches to these topics. Where analysis of this material requires attention to related subjects, I have done so briefly, discussing for example Continental sources and parallels, and concurrent developments in British theory and practice outside the literature of domestic architecture. Ample opportunity still remains to illuminate these cross-cultural and cross-disciplinary connections more fully. In sum, I hope that I have provided a useful discussion of issues and ideas that were central to eighteenth- and early nineteenth-century domestic architecture, and an introductory examination of their origins, contexts, and influences.

<table>
<tr>
<td>

1
The Ancients, Vitruvius, and Progress in Modern Britain

</td>
<td>

In the first two volumes of *Vitruvius Britannicus* (1715–1717; Entry 32) Colen Campbell raised three concerns that remained central to British architectural theory for the next hundred years: the authority of "Ancient" versus "Modern" principles of design, the authority of the Roman author Vitruvius in particular, and the opportunity in modern Britain for achieving progress in architecture. I shall first examine Campbell's treatment of each of these points in *Vitruvius Britannicus,* mentioning a few immediate consequences of his assertions; then I shall turn to the reception and debate of these issues among his successors.

</td>
</tr>
</table>

•

In taking up the controversy between "Ancients" and "Moderns" Campbell alluded to a philosophical quarrel that had engaged members of the Royal Society in London from the date of its foundation in 1660.[6] Although the "quarrel" had little effect on English architecture before Campbell, it was the subject of acrimonious debate among French academic architects: François Blondel and the "Ancients" called for strict adherence to Classical models, while Claude Perrault and the "Moderns" suggested that a degree of moderation and change would be appropriate in the orders and in composition.[7] The French controversy notwithstanding, it may have been the literary aspects of the debate in England that most interested Campbell: without explicitly allying himself with the "Moderns," he echoed their call to surpass Ancient practice by reviving "principles" supposedly embraced by the Ancients.[8] Like the "Moderns," Campbell rejected the authority of Ancient example: comparison of modern British architecture with "the *Antiques*," he said, was "out of the Question." Instead Campbell turned to principles: rather than travel and study in foreign lands, he recommended one "judge truly of the Merit of Things by the Strength of Reason." He claimed that the success of such an approach could be seen in the work of Palladio, "whose ingenious Labours will eclipse many, and rival most of the Ancients." Indeed a return to Ancient principle was still possible: Inigo Jones's work, for example, exhibited all the "Regularity" of Palladio. Campbell called attention to Vitruvian, Palladian, and Jonesian elements in many of the designs he illustrated, but he stressed the importance of principles. He also emphasized the great difference between Ancient principle and modern Continental practice: "The Ancients placed their chief Beauties in the justness of the Intercolumnations, the precise

Proportions of the Orders and the greatness of Parts"; contradictory practices among modern European architects "must be imputed either to an entire Ignorance of Antiquity, or a Vanity to expose their absurd Novelties, so contrary to those excellent Precepts in *Vitruvius*, and so repugnant to those admirable Remains the Ancients have left us."[9]

Campbell's respect for Vitruvius is, of course, apparent in the title of his book. A manuscript copy of Vitruvius's *De architectura* had been discovered early in the fifteenth century, and for the next several centuries it remained the principal source of information on Roman architectural theory and practice. Of particular interest to eighteenth-century architects were his remarks on the origins of architecture, the origins and proportions of the orders, and the design of dwellings. Campbell placed Vitruvian "Precepts" at the center of his architectural aesthetic, and also suggested that the proportions of Ancient "Remains" would agree with those precepts. Nevertheless this presumption proved untenable in the face of ongoing archaeological research: not only Roman remains, but also those in Greece—from which Vitruvius supposedly derived his knowledge of architecture—failed to agree with Vitruvian dictates. As early as 1650 Roland Fréart de Chambray's *Parallèle de l'architecture antique et de la moderne* had provided visual comparisons of the orders as executed by ancient and Renaissance architects. Campbell could disregard such comparisons in his appeal to principle, but by the mid-eighteenth century this was no longer possible. In 1759, for example, Sir William Chambers noted significant variances among orders described by previous writers and in his own examination of ancient remains; his solution was to adopt individual examples that he felt were proven best by time and by common consent (Entry 40). Three years later James Stuart and Nicholas Revett published the first part of their *Antiqvities of Athens*, the first British publication of actual Greek remains.[10] In the Preface to *The Grecian Orders of Architectvre* (1768; Entry 287) Stephen Riou praised the work of Stuart and Revett, noting that their "authentic records and perfect models of the Grecian orders" would promote preparation of correct "documents for the three orders." Riou's accompanying reassessment of contributions by Vitruvius was, by this time, almost gratuitous.

By linking British architecture with the name of Vitruvius, Campbell's title also suggested a new preeminence for Britain. In exhorting architects and patrons to adopt the principles of the "Ancients" that were exemplified in Vitruvian precepts and Palladian designs, Campbell hoped to create a new standard of "Modern" design that would equal and perhaps surpass the work of any other nation. Indeed he claimed that most of the designs he illustrated would "admit of a fair Comparison with the best of the *Moderns*." And with a great proportion of his illustrations devoted to country houses, he implicitly promoted a reordering of the architectural genres. Instead of paying greatest attention to churches, civic buildings, and palaces, he indicated that the modern country house, despite its remote and rustic location, would be the principal vehicle for Britain's return to "Ancient" principles of design. Indeed *Vitruvius Britannicus* was the first British collection of designs devoted primarily to dwellings, and the first anywhere in which domestic designs were tied to a program of architectural reform.[11] At a time when Lockean epistemology and Newtonian physics were laying the foundations for Enlightenment theories of progress, Campbell's program for architectural reform may have seemed to many of his readers to be following a parallel course.[12]

•

Respect for Ancient "principles" remained central to British architectural thought for the next half century. Robert Morris, a disciple of the Earl of Shaftesbury and Britain's first major architectural theorist, agreed that only the Ancients understood the fundamental principles of architecture. The title page of his *Essay in Defense of Ancient Architecture* (1728; Entry 214) compared the "beauty and harmony" of Ancient architecture with the "irregularity" and "abuses" of the Moderns. In the text Morris drew a parallel between the experience of architecture and the appreciation of harmony, and recommended a return to the "Principles" and "Rules" of the Ancients. Six years later in his *Lectures on Architecture* (1734; Entry 215) he explored in some detail a "Principle of the Harmonick Proportions" that had been invented by the Ancients but since lost. Working from a recent translation of a treatise by Lambert ten Kate, Morris identified seven ideal harmonic intervals in Ancient music, and argued that the corresponding numerical ratios established ideal proportions for architectural facades, plans, and room interiors. Classical authority was so important to Batty and Thomas Langley that they titled the first edition of their treatise on Gothic architecture *Ancient Architecture* (1742; Entry 172), and their plates depict Gothic columns and arches regularized into five measured "orders."

Isaac Ware's authoritative Palladian treatise, *A Complete Body of Architecture* (1756; Entry 339), stresses architectural principles based on the practices of the "Ancients." Working to develop a general system of architectural proportion based on the proportions of the orders, Ware criticized the "violent liberties" taken by modern architects, especially the practice of altering established proportions simply to accommodate fanciful ideas. The Ancients, he explained, had loftier goals: they espoused principles of regularity in order to give "that proportion to their works in which subsists the harmony of a building." But Ware's support for Ancient principles extended only to a general concern for proportion and harmony; he was unwilling to be bound by precise rules or measurements. Emulating Claude Perrault's *Ordonnance des cinq espèces de colonnes* (1683), Ware sought to "review" the Classical "remains" of the orders, and then establish a "mean or middle proportion" for each. He noted that in designing orders to suit individual buildings the Ancients did not limit themselves to fixed proportions; rather, "they indulged their genius in its regulated flights," allowing variations of proportion that resulted in a variety of "original" beauties. Thus, Ware contended, "very differently proportioned features can constitute beauty, provided a proper harmony be preserved among them."[13] In *Original Designs in Architecture* (1780; Entry 178) James Lewis concurred. Following a brief account of the historical excellence of Greek architecture, he noted that "the fine Arts were in their full meridian" in Rome. Nevertheless he decried "implicit obedience to the exact proportions dictated by any master" and recommended that "proportions . . . be varied according to different circumstances," and "adapted to their situation in the building." In the same spirit Edmund Aikin counseled readers of *Designs for Villas* (1808; Entry 4) to "think like an Ancient placed in modern times, [while] avoiding equally the servility of frigid copying, and the license of incongruous alteration." More of a modernist than his predecessors, however, Aikin found that contemporary architectural style was not "founded upon what is called the antique," and recommended sparing use of ornament: the beauty of a design should depend on its "general forms and proportions" alone.

Early in the eighteenth century Robert Castell searched for examples of Ancient practice among Roman literary accounts.[14] Many of his contemporaries paid homage indirectly to the Ancients: the rising esteem for Palladio and Jones, spurred in part by Campbell's favorable comparison of their work with that of the Ancients, stimulated several new publications of designs, orders, and ornaments by these masters.[15] But a few British architects questioned or disregarded the authority of Classical example. Among the earliest was John Wood, who in *The Origin of Building* (1741; Entry 351) criticized the Vitruvian thesis that man had progressively evolved architectural forms, styles, and techniques. Instead, according to Wood, knowledge of architecture had been revealed directly to man by God. Principles of order and proportion figure prominently in Wood's account, but unlike his contemporaries he derived these principles from biblical authority, obviating the need to account for inconsistencies and variations among Classical remains. A more fanciful disregard for Ancient example appears in *The Country Gentleman's Pocket Companion* by William and John Halfpenny (1753; Entry 131). The authors included designs for two awkward, rude structures, ostensibly in "Ancient" style, constructed of rough boulders and rubble, and roofed with thatch. They reveal little attention to Classical example or to principles of order and proportion, and instead suggest the origins of architecture in a ruder, more primitive time.

Sir William Chambers attempted to trace more definitely the primitive origins of architecture within the scope of the account given by Vitruvius. Chambers, like Abbé Laugier in France,[16] accepted the Vitruvian notion that architecture had evolved slowly through history, in tandem with the progress of human civilization from a primitive state to Classical perfection. In his *Treatise* (1759; Entry 40) Chambers presented conjectural illustrations of progressive stages in the evolution of primordial dwellings or "primitive huts." The first is a conical hut, followed by a rude rectangular structure made of tree-trunk columns and rough-hewn lintels, and finally a gable-roofed building with primitive Doric columns and entablatures.[17] In the text Chambers stressed that such primitive examples were hardly worthy of imitation. Nature, he said, was the model on which the architect's "taste must be formed," but it was only the foundation from which the architect should proceed toward perfection. Thus just as Greek architecture had evolved from the rude beginnings he illustrated, so Roman architecture "quickly vanquished that of Greece," and subsequent improvements in construction and expression would lead to even greater progress.

Support for Vitruvian tenets remained strong in many other quarters. Dennis de Coetlogon's encyclopedic *Universal History of Arts and Sciences*

(1741; Entry 64) and articles in later encyclopedias[18] relied heavily on the authority of Vitruvius. Early in the century Henry Aldrich undertook an ambitious literary analysis of Vitruvius, "other ancients," and modern authors such as Palladio, hoping to compile a complete treatise of civil and military architecture. The portions that he finished before his death in 1710 were published, finally, in 1789 as *The Elements of Civil Architecture* (Entry 5). About the same time William Newton published the first English translation of Vitruvius (1771–1791; Entry 221), plus a lengthy commentary on Vitruvius in French (1780; Entry 222). In 1812 William Wilkins, a Classical scholar of high repute, published a new translation of Vitruvius's Books III through VI, titled *The Civil Architecture of Vitruvius* (Entry 348), in order to undo "the corruptions with which the early editors have loaded it." Wilkins argued that Vitruvius had derived his knowledge of architecture from direct observation of ancient Greek buildings. Failure to realize this point, Wilkins said, had occasioned misguided attempts to correlate Vitruvius's stated principles with actual buildings in ancient Rome. The implied result had been widespread misunderstanding and distrust of Ancient principles.

Joseph Gwilt, who published a complete translation of Vitruvius in 1826,[19] used his introduction to a new edition of Chambers's *Treatise* (1825; Entry 40.4) to suggest limits to Vitruvius's authority. Asserting that "true architecture was reared" in Greece, he charged that Vitruvius's account of the primitive hut had been disproved by modern archaeology. Gwilt declared that in at least one respect Vitruvius's account was "absurd": ideal proportions originally established in primitive wooden structures would necessarily have been changed when architects began building in stone, due to inherent differences in the two materials. But another author, Peter Legh, maintained an undiluted confidence in the authority of Vitruvian principles. In *The Music of the Eye* (1831; Entry 176) he proposed "to restore architecture to the dignity it had in ancient Greece" by focusing on five "principles of composition" expounded by Vitruvius: utility, proportion, disposition, distribution, and decor or character. Legh's desire to develop "a simple and scientific scheme" of architecture is curiously belied by his plates: there are designs in a wide variety of styles, including Greek, Gothic, Indian, Chinese, and Egyptian. The preponderance of Egyptian designs, however, perhaps reflects a desire to be true to elementary principles by emulating a style then considered to be the most "primitive" form of ancient architecture.[20]

Several architects quarreled not only with the authority of Vitruvius or Ancient example but also with the assumption that Ancient achievements could never be exceeded. In *Vitruvius Britannicus* Campbell suggested that British architecture might soon equal or even surpass that of the Ancients. Two authors expressed their confidence in architectural progress through allegorical illustrations. The frontispiece to William Halfpenny's *Art of Sound Building* (1725; Entry 129) shows a figure of Architecture, a colossal shaft, a Corinthian capital, and an obelisk. Off in the distance a large mansion or palace, three stories high and 15 windows wide, suggests the present and future excellence of domestic architecture in Britain. Isaac Ware referred to the subject of progress more explicitly in the frontispiece to his *Complete Body of Architecture* (1756; Entry 339). Four structures—

an Egyptian pyramid, a Greek temple, the Colosseum, and a portion of a Palladian mansion—are arranged in chronological order from background to foreground, suggesting the historical progress of architecture from Ancient times to the present. One year later Abraham Swan, introducing his *Collection of Designs* (1757; Entry 326), stated his confidence in England's future achievements: he encouraged his countrymen to "strive to excell in their several Professions and Employments," since then it would become evident that *"England* is blest with as happy Geniusses as any Nation under Heaven" (I, vi).

Soon afterward, architects explicitly proclaimed the advanced state of British architecture. In the first volume of *Plans, Elevations and Sections, of Noblemen and Gentlemen's Houses* (1767; Entry 243) James Paine advised other architects not to reproduce the designs of ancient Rome, and especially condemned copying "the most despicable ruins of ancient Greece." Indeed such attention to ancient example was unnecessary: "The rapid progress of architecture in Great-Britain . . . is perhaps without example, in any age or country since the Romans." If architects properly cultivated their own "judgment," instead of copying examples from "ruder" times, England might soon "vie with, if not exceed (at least in the splendour and magnificence of its villas) the most flourishing periods of the ancient Roman empire."[21] John Woolfe and James Gandon, who issued additional volumes of *Vitruvius Britannicus* in 1767 and 1771 (Entry 356), concurred: in modern Britain "architecture was brought to as great a point of perfection in this kingdom in the eighteenth century, as ever it was known to be among the Greeks and Romans." George Richardson conceived his *New Vitruvius Britannicus* (1802–1808; Entry 285) as a record of the "superior taste and elegance" in English architecture, and suggested that studying his illustrations would be rewarding to Englishmen and "ingenious foreigners" alike. Indeed some claims for British preeminence made little or no reference to the Classical past. James Malton emphasized the wholly British nature of the designs shown in his *Essay on British Cottage Architecture* (1798; Entry 197). And in *Domestic Architecture* (1841; Entry 24) Richard Brown praised England's "decided superiority over every other nation in Europe, in the grand display of numerous country-seats." Of his 25 exemplary designs for dwellings, only three were in Classical Greek or Roman styles, while the rest comprised a variety of medieval, Renaissance, picturesque, Palladian, exotic, and other designs.

In sum, the high esteem of early eighteenth-century architects for Ancient "Principles" and for Vitruvius in particular soon was supplemented by the fruits of extensive archaeological research. Some architects chose to correlate the new data with established conventions, making revisions in Vitruvian theory where necessary. Others used the discrepancies between literary and archaeological accounts, as well as confidence in their own original creative abilities, to justify their belief in the present and future potential of British architecture to progress well beyond the standard of Ancient achievements.

2

**Aesthetic
Ideals:
Harmonic
Proportion,
Genius,
Imagination,
and Taste**

During the eighteenth century architectural writers embraced diverse ideals in their desire to invent and justify original designs. Apart from appeals to the authority of past example, discussed above, two ideals were invoked frequently: first, a timeless and universal standard of harmonic proportion, revealing through the design of a building a greater or universal order; and second, the creativity of the individual's own genius and imagination, tempered only by taste (or judgment), placing a premium on the uniqueness of the individual architect's conception. The first ideal figured prominently in early eighteenth-century aesthetics. It was closely related to the Neoplatonism that underlay much Italian Renaissance architecture and the work of many French academic architects, and that also informed important movements in late seventeenth-century English philosophy—particularly the ideas of Anthony Ashley Cooper, Third Earl of Shaftesbury.[22] In *Characteristicks* (1711) Shaftesbury briefly discussed matters of order, proportion, and harmony in architecture, tying them to a universal sense of order within the human soul:

> whatever Things have *Order*, the same have *Unity of Design*, and concur *in one*, are Parts of *one* Whole, or are, in themselves, *intire Systems*. Such is . . . an *Edifice*, with all its exteriour and interiour Ornaments.

> Nothing surely is more strongly imprinted on our Minds, or more closely interwoven with our Souls, than the Idea or Sense of *Order* and *Proportion*. . . . What a difference there is between *Harmony* and *Discord* . . . between the regular and uniform Pile of some noble Architect, and a Heap of Sand or Stones! and between an organiz'd Body, and a Mist or Cloud driven by the Wind!"

But at the same time Shaftesbury also introduced the seeds of fundamental change: he stressed the importance of the artist's individual creativity and the role of the viewer's imagination in appreciating the inner meaning or content of a design. The artist's creative faculty, or genius, he said, imitates that of the Genius of the universe:

> Like that Sovereign Artist or universal Plastick Nature, he forms *a Whole*, coherent and proportion'd in it-self, with due Subjection and Subordinacy of constituent Parts. He notes the Boundarys of the Passions, and knows their exact *Tones* and *Measures*; by which he justly represents them, marks *the Sublime* of Sentiments and Action, and distinguishes *the Beautiful* from *the Deform'd, the Amiable* from *the Odious*.[23]

My discussion of these ideas will focus on their progress in architectural theory and on their application to certain problems of architectural design.

Robert Morris, Britain's first important architectural theorist, was a professed disciple of Shaftesbury and a major proponent of theories of harmonic proportion in architecture. In *An Essay in Defence of Ancient Architecture* (1728; Entry 214) he described the experience of architecture as an intellectual appreciation of harmony. For Morris, a successful design embodied such qualities as "Symmetry," "Concordance," "Proportion," and "Reason," all orchestrated in such a manner that the observer could obtain a highly pleasurable experience of beauty and harmony:

> Architecture, or Order itself, is a beautiful and harmonious Production arising from the Ideas of an unlimited Judgment; and where artfully compos'd and happily executed, nothing can raise the Mind to a more advanc'd Pleasure, than to behold the agreeable Symmetry and Concordance of every particular separate Member, centred and united in the Oeconomy of the whole.

In his *Lectures on Architecture* (1734–1736; Entry 215) Morris elaborated a more detailed and comprehensive theory of "Harmonick Proportions," according to which musical intervals established fundamental ratios for all architectural proportions.[24] Altogether he identified seven ratios for use in determining the geometric volume of an entire dwelling as well as of the individual rooms within: 1:1:1 (a cube), 1:1:1 1/2 (a cube and a half), 1:1:2 (a double cube), 1:2:3, 2:3:4, 3:4:5, and 3:4:6. Morris explained that by applying these proportions to designs such as he depicted in his book, the architect could lead the viewer into "a Profundity of Thought." In this state the order of the entire universe becomes apparent: "we must feel Emanations of the Harmony of Nature diffus'd in us, and must immediately acknowledge the Necessity of Proportion in the Preservation of the whole Oeconomy of the Universe."

Other architects strove to extend principles of order and proportion to provinces where they had not previously been recognized. In *Ancient Architecture* (1742; Entry 172) Batty Langley devised a system of order and proportion for Gothic columns that emulated the proportionality of the five Classical orders. After examining two columns in Westminster Abbey, he calculated that their parts had been "determined and described" with certain proportions and geometric rules that had never been "excelled (if equalled) in any parts of the Grecian or Roman orders." With little further evidence in hand he and his brother Thomas then prepared 16 plates illustrating five Gothic "orders," carefully delineated according to fixed proportions. A decade later William and John Halfpenny issued a series of *New Designs* for buildings in Chinese style (1750–1752; Entry 134). In a brief preface William tried to overcome the reluctance of some readers to accept this style by suggesting that "a graceful Symmetry, and an exact Proportion" were inherent in Chinese design. Indeed the "Chinese" designs the Halfpennys offered, because of their inherent regularity, conspicuously betrayed their European origin.

Proportionality remained important to British architectural theorists through midcentury and beyond, although few authors made it as central to their aesthetics as Morris did. In his voluminous compendium of Palladian theory and practice, *A Complete Body of Architecture* (1756; Entry 339), Isaac Ware paid careful attention to the proportions of facades, doors, windows, chimneypieces, decorations, and almost all other parts of a building, but he also argued that judicious variations in the proportions of the orders were necessary. The Ancients, he said, realized "that beauty in any order was not restrained to an exact proportion of parts." Instead, by paying more attention to the proportions of the entire building, they sought to make each column "a regular part of a regular whole," and so arrived at a result much like that advocated by Morris: they gave "that proportion to their works in which subsists the harmony of building."[25] Likewise James Lewis, in presenting his elegant *Original Designs in Architecture* (1780; Entry 178), recommended that proportions could be varied to suit different circumstances, although the architect should always attend to the harmony of the whole: "The effect of a building . . . [is] produced by a perfect harmony in the constituent parts, so as to exhibit a pleasing appearance in every point of view" (I, 4).

Well into the nineteenth century some architects continued to assert that regular proportions, and especially a cubic form, were ideally suited to domestic design; their reasons, however, were usually economic rather than aesthetic. In 1805 Robert Lugar suggested in *Architectural Sketches* (Entry 192) that houses should be as nearly cubical as possible, for reasons of compactness and convenience. But at the same time he recommended "varied" contours, "broken" lines, asymmetrical lean-tos, and other features that would contribute an overall picturesque irregularity to the design. Likewise in *The Suburban Gardener, and Villa Companion* (1838; Entry 190) John Claudius Loudon recommended a "cubic" house because it would "enclose more space with the same quantity of walling and roof" than any other type, while also facilitating increased comfort, cleanliness, "habitableness," economy in heating, and ease of repair. Unlike Lugar he added little on the subject of style, saying it "may be left to the taste of the occupant," and instead focused on such practical concerns as fitness, location, and construction.

Disaffection with universal standards of proportion and harmony appeared with increasing frequency in the third quarter of the eighteenth century. Ware and Lewis, mentioned above, both argued that proportions might need to be varied to suit individual circumstances. Sir William Chambers agreed. In his *Treatise* (1759; Entry 40) he contended that standards of proportion, far from being absolute, were developed by custom within a local cultural context: pleasure at the sight of particular proportions "must, I am persuaded, be ascribed . . . to convenience, custom, prejudice, or to the habit of connecting other ideas with these figures, than to any particular charm inherent in them, as some are disposed to maintain."[26] Lord Kames offered a medial viewpoint between the positions of Morris and Chambers. In his highly respected treatise on the *Elements of Criticism* he emphatically denied that architectural proportions resemble musical harmonies, but also characterized as "extreme" the assertion that the beauty of certain proportions is "entirely the effect of custom." Instead, he argued that human beings "are framed by nature to relish proportion," and that columns, rooms, and entire houses all can take on a variety of legitimate proportions, all "equally agreeable."[27]

After midcentury the new taste for Rococo ornament often discouraged attention to the proportionality of underlying forms. In *Chinese and Gothic Architecture* (1752; Entry 130), for example, the Halfpennys presented designs covered with wildly proliferating ornament, often without evident support. The authors ostensibly justified this with the lame excuse that "if Gracefulness and true Symmetry are found in the Structure, they will be sufficient Bars to any false or frivolous Aspersions that . . . may be . . . attempted against our Endeavours." But their inattention to "Structure," which is readily apparent in their designs, also is evident in their prefatory announcement that "Invention and Variety of Construction" were their paramount concerns.

From outside the realm of architecture came additional challenges to theories of universal order and harmony. Historical research and geographic exploration were producing substantial evidence of human and natural diversity, and soon geographers, political and economic philosophers, and linguists realized that one system of order could not be applied with uniform success to all people, locations, and ideas.[28] The result—increasing respect for human individuality—encouraged aestheticians to devote special attention to problems of imaginative expansion and the exercise of individual creative genius.

Earlier in the century Lord Shaftesbury had described "genius" as the means by which an observer's imagination—contemplating a thought, a building, or a scene in nature—might expand to entertain an image of the ideal. Such imaginative expansion, while implying a creative capacity within the observer as well as in the artist, necessarily respected traditional rules of proportion and symmetry.[29] But two decades later David Hume discussed the appreciation of architecture instead in quite different terms. He described the experience of a building as a process of expanding the imagination to encompass, by means of "sympathy," an understanding of the building's convenience and of the character of the proprietor:

A man, who shews us any house or building, takes particular care among other things to point out the convenience of the apartments, the advantages of their situation, and the little room lost in the stairs, anti-chambers and passages. . . . The observation of convenience gives pleasure, since convenience is a beauty. . . . [Convenience] must delight us merely by communication, and by our sympathizing with the proprietor of the lodging. We enter into his interest by the force of imagination, and feel the same satisfaction, that the objects naturally occasion in him.[30]

In 1759 Alexander Gerard discussed at some length three distinct processes involved in appreciating architecture—association, sympathy, and imaginative expansion—that went well beyond a respect for harmony and proportion, and involved the active participation of the spectator's own creative ability. Gerard observed that a spectator's first reflection on seeing a building is an appreciation, by association, of its end. Then, within the imagination, a process of sympathy causes the spectator to experience the delights and discomforts of the structure:

When . . . we see a work, it leads us by a natural association to conceive its end; prone to comparison, we examine the propriety of the parts in relation to this end. . . . We dwell in imagination on the inconveniences which must arise from the unfitness of the structure; we form strong ideas of them, which produce [by sympathy] almost the same uneasy sentiments and passions, as if we actually experienced them. . . . But when, on examination, the fitness of all the parts appears, the satisfaction, with which we think on the skill and ingenuity thus displayed, communicates itself to the effect so nearly allied to it, so closely connected with it by causation: and we sympathetically enter into a strong feeling of the delight which must attend the possession or use of what is so well designed and executed.[31]

Necessary to this process of imaginative expansion, in both artist and spectator, is the faculty of genius, which has the power to make connections among ideas:

The first and leading quality of genius is *invention*, which consists in an extensive comprehensiveness of imagination, in a readiness of associating the remotest ideas, that are any way related. In a man of genius the uniting principles are so vigorous and quick, that whenever any idea is present to the mind, they bring into view at once all others, that have the least connection with it.

Yet because genius was potentially a source of random and licentious thoughts, Gerard was careful to portray its activity as regulated by taste.

This faculty serves to "guide and moderate" the efforts of genius, acting as "a check on mere fancy," interjecting "judgment, either approving or condemning." The result is both ordered and regular: "from a confused heap of materials, collected by fancy," he said, "genius, after repeated reviews and transpositions, designs a regular and well proportioned whole. . . . Thus genius is the grand architect, which not only chooses the materials, but disposes them into a regular structure."[32]

Eight years later William Duff argued in his *Essay on Original Genius* that the quality "most essentially requisite to the existence of Genius" was imagination. This he discussed boldly in terms of invention and creativity:

[Imagination is] that faculty whereby the mind not only reflects on its own operations, but which assembles the various ideas conveyed to the understanding by the canal of sensation; . . . and which, by its plastic power of inventing new associations of ideas, and of combining them with infinite variety, is enabled to present a creation of its own, and to exhibit scenes and objects which never existed in nature.[33]

Not surprisingly, Duff complained that "modern Architects" had made "no improvements" in their art. By copying the remains of "ancient Architecture" they had only obstructed "Originality of Genius." Duff proposed that a "truly original" architectural genius would instead create "new and surprising Models in this Art" through the "native force and plastic power of Imagination."[34] Nevertheless Duff was concerned, like Gerard, to forestall possible licentious applications of genius; thus he also discussed the need for "judgment" and "taste" to guide the artist: judgment would guard him "against the faults he may be apt to commit," while taste would serve "as a supplement to the defects of the power of judgment," and bestow "elegance" on the fruits of both imagination and judgment.[35]

Genius was discussed in a major architectural treatise as early as 1756, the year in which Gerard also delivered remarks on the subject in a prize essay.[36] In *A Complete Body of Architecture* (Entry 339) Isaac Ware appealed to genius in order to justify a measure of freedom in proportioning the orders. The Ancients, he said, "indulged their genius," although they took care to restrain that genius with rules. He complained that modern architects, in comparison, simply substituted rules for genius. He proposed that modern architects return to the manner in which the Ancients designed, allowing the genius renewed freedom in which to "form" and "display" itself (pp. 131–132).

Authors of three important architectural treatises published in the last third of the eighteenth century likewise addressed the problem of individual creativity either implicitly or explicitly in terms of genius and imagination, while also appealing to "taste" to insure the legitimacy of the results. In his collection of *Plans, Elevations and Sections* (1767–1783; Entry 243) the late-Palladian architect James Paine found it "unnecessary to give the five orders of architecture" in his book, noting widespread variances in the proportions of Ancient examples and those given by modern authors. He explained that "Mankind think differently, and what one approves, another condemns"; Palladio, Scamozzi, Vignola, and others could not "by demonstration, fix a standard of architecture." Thus all subsequent architects were left to "their own determination," in which they were guided solely "by what is called taste."[37] In 1779 Robert and James Adam completed the first volume of their *Works in Architecture* (Entry 1), in which they complained that attention to rules and proportions frequently was "minute and frivolous." Like Ware they imputed a great respect for individual creativity to Classical architects: the "great masters of antiquity . . . varied the proportions as the general spirit of their composition required," because they recognized that rules "often cramp the genius and circumscribe the ideas of the master." In discussing their own designs the Adams stressed the importance of originality: "The novelty and variety of the following designs will, we flatter ourselves, not only excuse, but justify our conduct, in communicating them to the world.------We have not trod in the path of others, nor derived aid from their labours." The principal constraint they observed was a due respect for taste. By way of demonstration they pointed out that taste had not controlled the excesses of Sir John Vanbrugh's creativity: "unluckily for the reputation of this excellent artist, his taste kept no pace with his genius, and his works are so crouded with barbarisms and absurdities . . . that none but the discerning can separate their merits from their defects." In *Original Designs in Architecture* (1783; Entry 331) William Thomas professed a similar respect for creativity. Stipulating that the orders "are determined by the fixed Rules of Architecture," and that "certain general Rules" are necessary for the "Perfection" of architecture, he also contended that "the Art of Designing is scarcely to be reduced to any fixed Precepts." Unlike the sciences, architecture is "not founded wholly on a System of Problems and Deductions." Rather, it "depends in a great Measure on the Imagination." The design of a building is, finally, a collaboration between the faculties of genius and judgment: "Genius considers it in *Theory*; in practice it can only be the Fruit of Judgment, matured by Habit and constant Application."[38]

Early in the nineteenth century the imagination was accorded greater freedom, but creative liberty soon was challenged from other quarters. In *A Collection of Architectural Designs* (1806; Entry 271) James Randall employed a musical analogy to demonstrate that the architect's imagination, like the musician's, ought to produce nearly limitless original ideas: "Architecture, like music, is susceptible of innumerable combinations, which, if properly united, although very dissimilar, may possess real beauties, and produce pleasing emotions on the mind." Rather than being "confined to the rigid rules of the school," he argued, the architect's "fancy may surely be allowed to play, if kept within proper bounds!" But he suggested that such "bounds," invoked by the faculty of taste, were now defined by a respect for economy rather than proportion: his own designs were intended to accommodate "those . . . who prefer a chastity of taste in buildings constructed for accommodation upon economical principles" (p. iv). The next year William Fuller Pocock expressed the same concerns in *Architectural Designs for Rustic Cottages* (Entry 262). Wanting "to serve the cause of humanity in providing comfortable dwellings for a numerous part of our fellow-creatures," he warned that "giving reins to the imagination, and designing, by the force of fancy only," might well result in designs "impracticable in execution."

A quarter century later John Claudius Loudon, author of the voluminous and immensely popular *Encyclopaedia of Cottage, Farm, and Villa Architecture* (1833; Entry 184), also proclaimed that his "main object" was "to improve the dwellings of the great mass of society." Thus "fitness" was his primary concern in designing houses. Nevertheless he endorsed a renewed respect for some of the aesthetic ideals mentioned above. Of some interest was "taste," which Loudon discussed in terms of the "beauties" of architectural form. He divided these beauties into two types: first, "universal and inherent beauties," such as unity, variety, and symmetry; and second, "historical or accidental beauties of particular styles" that had become "consecrated" through use over a long period of time. In particular he recommended close attention to the first type, especially such "universal principles" as order, proportion, and harmony, which are "altogether independent of any style of Architecture which has hitherto existed." In a manner reminiscent of Lord Kames and Edmund Burke as well, Loudon argued that the "effect" of this type of beauty is due to the influence of certain formal qualities in a building making "organic impressions, and associations of a general nature" on the human mind. Loudon's remarks on the "historical and accidental" beauties of style clearly parallel Claude Perrault's suggestion that the beauties of proportion derive from custom. But Loudon was not sanguine about the "beauties" of style: he placed much greater emphasis on "the general principles of composition, than . . . the details of any particular style," and recommended that the five orders, so important for architects in previous centuries, should be relegated to "the very last part" of any course of instruction.[39]

Thus for some authors, including Loudon as well as Randall and Pocock, eighteenth-century aesthetic ideals—particularly harmony, genius, imagination, and taste—were subordinated to considerations of fitness, utility, and economy. Yet even for these authors such ideals still remained significant, if secondary, components of architectural design, and provided a rationale for aesthetic expression.

3
Expression and Affectivity: Theories of Character and Association

Buildings not only accommodate certain functional requirements, they also serve as means of communication. In my discussion above of imaginative expansion, I focused in particular on the creative roles played by designers and observers of buildings. But a building itself also may be endowed with expressive and affective faculties. Expression is the act or process of making manifest an idea, mood, feeling, quality, or other meaning. Affectivity is the related ability to impress that meaning on a spectator, reader, listener, or other observer. To endow a building with such faculties provides a means of engaging the spectator's mind and emotions, and so of encouraging imaginative expansion.

Theories of expression and affectivity had been the subject of intense concern among French aestheticians throughout the seventeenth and eighteenth centuries. By the mid-eighteenth century French painters applied these theories with the specific intent of eliciting spectator response.[40] Early in the eighteenth century British aestheticians, including Shaftesbury, John Dennis, and Joseph Addison, explored general problems of affective response to objects of human perception. Toward the middle of the century, their successors began to explore in greater detail the role of expression and affectivity in landscape design, music, and literature.[41] In architecture, expression and affectivity concurrently were recognized as central theoretical concerns, having particular relevance to problems of architectural character and associational response.

•

Early in the eighteenth century British architects and poets were aware of the expressive potential of architecture, particularly its ability to reveal the personality or position of the inhabitant. In *Vitruvius Britannicus* (1715; Entry 32), for example, Colen Campbell said of a house designed by John James that "everything contributes to express the refined Taste, and great Politeness of the Master" (I, 6). Conversely, in Alexander Pope's description of Timon's Villa the vapid architecture reflects poorly on the proprietor:

Greatness, with Timon, dwells in such a draught
As brings all Brobdingnag before your thought.
To compass this, his building is a Town,
His pond an Ocean, his parterre a Down:
Who but must laugh, the Master when he sees,
A puny insect, shiv'ring at a Breeze!
. . .
    But hark! the chiming Clocks to dinner call;
A hundred footsteps scrape the marble Hall:
The rich Buffet well-color'd Serpents grace,
And gaping Tritons spew to wash your face.
Is this a dinner? this a Genial room?
No, 'tis a Temple, and a Hecatomb.[42]

As early as 1700 Timothy Nourse, drawing on the country house poem tradition of Jonson, Carew, and Marvell, alluded to the affectivity of both architecture and landscape. He suggested that the siting of a country house should be appropriate to the kind of mood the inhabitant wanted to cultivate, and that the house should express something of the inhabitant's own character:

it looks great in a Man, and carries something of a divine Character stampt upon it, to be able to frame a Building after the Idea he has within himself; that is, to be able to give a durable Existence to something which was not before, and to adorn it with all the Graces of Symmetry and Beauty. And if he be a Man of a Contemplative Genius, the Seat of his House cannot but suggest manlike Thoughts.[43]

John Shebbeare's discussion in 1755 of recent changes in landscape gardening contains some of the earliest explicit remarks on affectivity in landscape design. He found that design had become a matter of selecting objects that could each produce one particular passion, and then combining them to increase their affectivity: "The art lies in selecting the most striking objects, which have affected the mind with any kind of passion or sensation, and then by recalling those ideas, give a combination to these objects which has never yet been seen in nature." The goal, he concluded, was to make "one whole that shall be striking, characteristic, and affecting"— in other words a composition that would impress certain passions or sensations directly on the mind of the spectator.[44] Edmund Burke discussed affectivity at greater length in his *Philosophical Enquiry into the Origin of*

Our Ideas of the Sublime and Beautiful (1757), suggesting that natural objects could produce both beautiful and sublime emotions in the spectator by means of a physiological response to formal characteristics of the objects.[45]

In 1762 Lord Kames, in his influential treatise on critical theory, paid special attention to expression and affectivity in architecture. He argued that "every building ought to have a certain character or expression suitable to its destination; yet this is a refinement which artists have scarce ventured upon." Kames's idea of "character or expression" owes much to the Vitruvian notion of decorum, according to which the form and style of a building should be suited to its use and to the station of its proprietor. Kames elaborated:

The sense of propriety [a synonym for decorum] dictates the following rule, That every building ought to have an expression corresponding to its destination. A palace ought to be sumptuous and grand; a private dwelling, neat and modest; a play-house, gay and splendid; and a monument, gloomy and melancholy. . . . Columns, beside their chief destination of being supports, may contribute to that peculiar expression which the destination of a building requires: columns of different proportions, serve to express loftiness, lightness, &c. as well as strength. Situation also may contribute to expression: conveniency regulates the situation of a private dwelling-house; but, as I had occasion to observe, the situation of a palace ought to be lofty.[46]

Kames also indicated the affectivity of such a design: individual elements as well as the entire design could convey a broad range of ideas and feelings to the spectator. "A great room," for example, "enlarges the mind and gives a certain elevation to the spirits."[47]

Authors of architectural books paid close attention to expression and affectivity only after midcentury—i.e., concurrently with Shebbeare, Burke, and Kames. One of the first was Thomas Wright, who issued the first volume of his *Universal Architecture* (Entry 357) in 1755. In this collection of twelve designs for arbors and grottoes, individual plate descriptions contain hints that the designs were meant to accommodate a variety of psychological dispositions and moods. One arbor or hut suited a need for sheltered solitude, for example, while another, a "Druid's Cell," was meant for "Study or philosophical Retirement." In his authoritative and influential *Treatise on Civil Architecture* (1759; Entry 40) Sir William Chambers, unlike Wright, did not offer designs that simply accommodated a mood. Rather, like Burke two years earlier and Lord Kames three years later, Chambers argued that a building should actively communicate to the observer some attribute of the resident or the site. For example: "with regard to elevations, if the breadth be predominant, we are struck with the ideas of majesty and strength; and, if the height predominates, with those of elegance and delicacy: all which occasion pleasing sensations" (1759 ed., p. 64). Perhaps inspired by contemporary studies of literary and linguistic expression,[48] Chambers also suggested a parallel between architecture and language: "Materials in architecture are like words in Phraseology; which singly have little or no power, and may be so arranged as to excite contempt; yet when combined with Art, and expressed with energy, they actuate the mind with unbounded sway." In *Familiar Architecture* (1768; Entry 273) Thomas Rawlins enthusiastically discussed the degree to which a building could affect the mind, the passions, and the soul:

It must give the highest Satisfaction to a speculative Genius, to consider the utmost Extent of Architecture, and to weigh the different Effects it impresses on the Mind, according to the different Structures presented to the View! How awe-struck must be the Passions, when we behold the antient Buildings of *Greece* and *Rome*! How sooth'd and mollify'd, when we descend to the pleasing rural Cot, where simple Elegance, Proportion, and Convenience unite! The Soul may then be said to be tun'd and exhilarated by the Objects which strike the Attention.[49]

By the late 1760s, then, British authors had clearly recognized the expressive and affective faculties of architecture. Moreover, they soon found that these faculties were fundamentally relevant to two increasingly important considerations in architectural theory: notions that a building should possess a prevailing "character," and that it should be able to affect the observer by stimulating an associational response in the mind.

•

Thomas Whately, a Shakespearean scholar as well as a landscape theorist, completed his *Observations on Modern Gardening* in 1770.[50] In his discussion of landscape theory he synthesized much that had previously been written on expression and affectivity, and provided for the first time in Britain a comprehensive theory of "character" that applied to both landscape and architectural design.[51] Any successful landscape, he said, must be informed by a single theme, a "prevailing idea" or "prevailing character": examples include magnificence, tranquility, cheerfulness, and simplicity. Buildings too, according to Whately, "are intitled to be considered as *characters*" (p. 118). Like a landscape, a building can have a wide variety of expressive characters: it might, for example, be "grave, or gay; magnificent, or simple" (p. 124). Whately also discussed at length the affective faculty of that building's character. The Temple of Concord and Victory at Stowe, for example, "is seen from every part, and impressing its own character of dignity on all around, it spreads an awe over the whole; but no gloom, no melancholy attends it; the sensations it excites are rather placid; but full of respect, admiration, and solemnity" (pp. 224–225).

One year later William Newton, concluding the preface to his translation of Vitruvius (Entry 221), was the first British architect to discuss in print the notion that a building should be informed by a single, expressive, prevailing "character":

I imagine that every building should by its appearance express its destination and purpose, and that some character should prevail therein, which is suitable to, and expressive of, the particular end it is to answer. . . . The characters or effects, which there may be occasion to express, in buildings, may be distinguished into the pleasing and the elevating, or those of beauty and dignity.

Thomas Sandby professed a nearly identical doctrine of character in his series of six lectures on architecture presented to the students at the Royal Academy beginning in 1770. "Every building ought to have a character, or expression, united to its destination," he wrote; "we cannot call the application of trite or frivolous ornaments the expressive signs of purpose and destination." No doubt one of Sandby's students, John Soane, had in mind a quite similar notion of character when he designed cottages and villas with "characteristic scenery" for *Sketches in Architecture* (1793; Entry 320). Unfortunately Soane provided no textual remarks on character in his short introduction or plate descriptions; his sense of the term must be inferred instead from the "characteristic" forms shared by buildings and scenery within individual illustrations.[52]

In the late eighteenth and early nineteenth centuries the most important remarks on character continued to appear in books devoted primarily to landscape design, especially the works of Humphry Repton. In *Sketches and Hints on Landscape Gardening* (1794; Entry 280) Repton stressed the need to identify a prevailing character within any landscape before making improvements: without a character, there could be no common theme or idea around which to organize those improvements. Turning to buildings, Repton identified two fundamental architectural characters, but now in terms of formal rather than expressive qualities: the "perpendicular," corresponding to Gothic styles, and the "horizontal," corresponding to Greek styles. For visual effect, each architectural character would accord best with its landscape opposite: horizontal architecture would complement pointed or conical trees, while vertical, pointed architecture would best suit rounder trees. He explained that the bold vertical projections of Gothic style would lose their effect if surrounded by trees with similar silhouettes; a similar argument justified the use of Greek architecture in conjunction with mountainous or coniferous scenery.

Later, in *Observations on the Theory and Practice of Landscape Gardening* (1803; Entry 279), Repton indicated that character involved something more than formal characteristics. Early in the text he had stressed the importance of "fitness" as a general principle of composition. When he arrived at a definition of "Characteristic Architecture," he identified its two principal qualities as visual coordination with the landscape and fitness to perform a function: "the adaptation of buildings not only to the situation, character, and circumstances of the scenery, but also to the purposes for which they are intended; this I shall call *Characteristic Architecture*." The "purposes" he had in mind were the varied uses of dwelling types such as the mansion, villa, or sporting seat. Depending on their functions, dwellings might display "compactness," "durability," "greatness," and "magnificence"; when allied with scenery of an appropriate visual character, they would become the most successfully "characteristic" architecture possible.

In the years between and immediately following Repton's two treatises, many architectural authors used the term "character" in a manner similar to his. In *Ferme Ornée* (1795; Entry 259), for example, John Plaw offered interchangeable elevations for a shed so that the client could choose "whichever character" (i.e., style) accorded best with adjoining buildings. Perhaps building on Repton's concern for fitness, David Laing suggested in *Hints for Dwellings* (1800; Entry 170) that the character of a dwelling should suit the needs of the inhabitant's social station. In designs for villas, for example, he tried to accommodate the need of potential clients for luxury and display: "I have indulged in more Ornament and Variety of Contour, as allowable to such Buildings, whose Inhabitants may be considered of some Rank in Life, and entitled to more Show as well as Conveniences." In 1805 Robert Lugar included a 16-page essay on the "Style and Character of Buildings" in his *Architectural Sketches* (Entry 192). Like Repton, he argued that the architect must "form a whole appropriate to the locality or situation, to the circumstances and wishes of his employer."

Other architects used the term "character" in an expanded sense, to denote the expression and affectivity of a building in addition to its form and function. Richard Elsam did so in a discussion of various Gothic styles in his *Essay on Rural Architecture* (1803; Entry 69). The Church Gothic style, for example, was a "character . . . well calculated to impress the mind with a just and awful solemnity," while the style of Gothic used in private dwellings should embody "a more cheerful character." The next year Edmund Bartell, in *Hints for Picturesque Improvements in Ornamented Cottages* (Entry 14), noted that cottages and other small dwellings were characterized by "humility and simplicity," and that the object of his book was "to endeavour to preserve this character" and to enhance it with appropriate surrounding scenery.[53]

John Claudius Loudon considered character at length in one of his earliest publications, *Observations on the Formation and Management of Useful and Ornamental Plantations* (Edinburgh: Archibald Constable, et al., 1804). He equated character with expression: just as "objects in a picture should tend to the particular character, or expression, of that picture," so in a landscape all "the parts belonging to a place should have a similar relation to the whole," and all subordinate parts should "agree in expression" (p. 221). His remarks on the placement of buildings in a landscape are brief but they emphasize both affectivity and expression: "Edifices of every kind have a powerful and striking effect upon the eye"; when a building is made part of a landscape, "the most important consideration is to accommodate [it] . . . to the character of the scene to which it belongs, so as it may heighten the effect, and give additional force and expression to this particular character" (p. 275).[54]

Sir John Soane affirmed the importance of character in his eleventh lecture at the Royal Academy, about 1817. He stressed that any composition required a prevailing character: "Too much attention cannot be given to produce a distinct Character in every building, not only in the great features, but in the minor details likewise; even a Moulding, however diminutive, contributes to increase or lessen the Character of the assemblage of which it forms a part."[55] The most comprehensive formulation of a theory of character in the early nineteenth century appeared in an article in Loudon's *Architectural Magazine* (1834, Entry 182), "On Character in Architecture." Perhaps indebted to the writings of Ledoux,[56] the anonymous author argued that character is the supreme affective medium of architectural communication. More than "style" or "expression," character is "the simple, though forcible, language of the features in architecture." On viewing a building, "we recognize its style, we perceive its expressions, but we are impressed with [i.e., affected by] its character. Hence it becomes, as it were, the conducting medium between the intrinsic beauties and qualities of the art, and the pleasures and feelings they excite."[57]

•

In addition to expanding and refining the notion of a building's prevailing character, eighteenth- and nineteenth-century architects also explored in detail the ability of a design to raise in the observer's mind, by means of association, a train of ideas illuminating the building's program. As a philosophical notion, association had been described as early as 1644 by Descartes; the actual term "association" was introduced by Locke in 1700 to describe sources of diversity and therefore error in human reasoning.[58] As the notion achieved greater acceptance among epistemologists and aestheticians early in the eighteenth century,[59] it provided architects a useful means for advancing beyond the Vitruvian notion of decorum and making buildings expressive of their inhabitants and uses.[60]

As early as 1683 Claude Perrault suggested a notion resembling architectural association in his *Ordonnance des cinq espèces de colonnes* (English translation, 1708). In analyzing architectural beauty he divided the subject into two types. The first involves a direct experience of grandeur and richness in a building. The second requires appreciation of beauty by the process of "connexion," similar to association: an object with no intrinsic beauty might be considered beautiful if "connected" with an item that had intrinsic beauty.[61] Nevertheless Perrault's argument concerned only the appreciation of beauty, and not the generation of further ideas in the spectator's imagination.

In 1709 Sir John Vanbrugh called for preservation of the medieval Woodstock Manor because of its historical associations:

There is perhaps no one thing, which the most Polite part of Mankind have more universally agreed in; than the Vallue they have ever set upon the Remains of distant Times[.] Nor amongst the Severall kinds of those Antiquitys, are there any so much regarded, as those of Buildings; Some for their Magnificence, or Curious Workmanship; And others; as they move more lively and pleasing Reflections (than History without their Aid can do) On the Persons who have Inhabited them; On the Remarkable things which have been transacted in them, Or the extraordinary Occasions of Erecting them.[62]

A building, in other words, could initiate trains of thought or "move Reflections" in the minds of spectators. But despite the promise of such an approach, no other British architect published substantial remarks on association until Chambers's *Treatise* appeared in 1759 (Entry 40). During the first half of the century, Palladian respect for order and uniformity dominated architectural aesthetics, and so there was little interest in a manner of expression that seemed to invite irregularity and undisciplined fancy.

Widespread confidence in the use of association for designing and appreciating buildings had to await greater understanding of the process of imaginative expansion, a subject explored in depth by theorists and practitioners alike in the first half of the eighteenth century. Likewise, greater confidence in "taste" as a means of insuring aesthetic uniformity helped allay fears that architectural association would become a source of erroneous or licentious ideas.[63] One of the most important treatises in effecting these changes, Alexander Gerard's *Essay on Taste* (1759), also was particularly influential in demonstrating the role of association in aesthetic pleasures, especially the appreciation of grandeur in architecture.[64] That same year Chambers discussed the beauties of proportion in his *Treatise*. In a manner reminiscent of both Perrault and Gerard he derived the pleasures of such beauties from a connection or association of ideas: "the pleasure or dislike, excited in us [at the sight of certain proportions] . . . must, I believe, be ascribed either to prejudice, or to our habit of connecting other ideas with these figures, rather than to any particular charm inherent in them, as some people are apt to imagine" (p. 64). In the 1791 edition of the *Treatise* he discussed association at greater length. Analyzing the affectivity of visible objects in general and of architectural ornaments in particular, Chambers noted:

Their effect is not alone produced, by the image on the organ of sight; but by a series of reasoning and association of ideas, impressed, and guiding the mind in its decision. Hence it is that the same object pleases one, and is disliked by another; or delights to-day, is seen with indifference, or disgust, tomorrow. For if the object seen, had alone the power of affecting; as is the case with sounds; it must affect all men alike, and at all times in the same manner, which by long and repeated experience, we know is not the case. (p. 108)

Chambers thus accounted for differences of aesthetic perception among individuals and among entire cultures, while still relying on a uniform intellectual process—association—that was fundamental to all tastes.[65]

British architects and landscapists had consciously employed associational techniques in their work since early in the eighteenth century,[66] but architectural authors did not treat the subject in conjunction with original or exemplary designs for buildings until very late in the century. In 1797 John Thomas Smith published *Remarks on Rural Scenery* (Entry 312), in which he discussed the affective associations of humble and picturesque cottage scenes. He remarked that seeing a man or woman

at a cottage-door, benevolently engaged in advising, consoling, or assisting a distressed family, we should instantly perceive a propriety of action, and a probable combination of circumstances; and the expanding heart would be hurried into a train of grateful ideas, before a thought could be bestowed on the mechanism [association] by which it was affected.

The next year James Malton completed his influential *Essay on British Cottage Architecture* (1798; Entry 197). He disagreed with Smith on the visual characteristics of beauty in cottages, yet he too offered designs that were meant to stimulate associationally such concepts as friendship, neighborliness, hospitality, and freedom from care or constraint. In 1815 Francis Stevens also discussed meanings associated with porches in his study of *Domestic Architecture* (Entry 324). A porch, he said, might encourage the viewer to imagine a family group resting there after a hard day's work—presumably suggesting, by extension, ideas of togetherness and deserved relaxation. Cottages done in vernacular style carried a special meaning, derived from historical "associations connected with the times when these venerable edifices were supported with that hospitality which prevailed up to the middle of the last century." Even Peter Frederick Robinson, who repeatedly asserted that pictorial considerations should be foremost in architectural design, could not escape the associational connotations of individual styles. Describing a residential design in Castellated style, illustrated in his *Designs for Ornamental Villas* (1827; Entry

293), Robinson remarked that aspects of the style itself "insensibly lead the mind back to the days of our feudal system, and in wandering among the neighbouring hills we almost expect to see the ancient Baron, surrounded by his followers, ascending the valley."[67]

A few authors challenged the legitimacy of association as a means of architectural expression. In his *Idler* essay (No. 82, 1759) Sir Joshua Reynolds discouraged all attention to custom and association in aesthetics, recommending instead the pursuit of general standards of beauty. Significantly Reynolds changed his mind, and in his thirteenth Discourse (1786) he praised the use of association, while referring specifically to the architecture of Sir John Vanbrugh.[68] In 1812 George Hamilton-Gordon, Fourth Earl of Aberdeen, raised the subject in his introduction to William Wilkins's *Civil Architecture of Vitruvius* (Entry 348). Aberdeen queried whether the perceived beauty of Greek architecture derived from intellectual associations or from properties inherent in Greek style and form. He treated the matter as part of an ongoing conflict between adherents of associational psychology and Edmund Burke's account of the physiological sources of aesthetic pleasure.[69] But having raised this problem, Aberdeen could not arrive at a conclusive answer.

In *The Music of the Eye* (1831; Entry 176) Peter Legh openly discounted any possible role for association in architectural expression. Instead he focused on the visual "characters" of individual forms and styles. "In character," he wrote, "both consistency and harmony are essential requisites." He further argued that union of consistency with harmony was equivalent to the Vitruvian ideal of decorum. A worthy architectural composition, therefore, would achieve the Vitruvian ideal through coordination of all parts to display a single, coherent character. Legh considered architectural expression through form and style to be parallel to human expression through facial physiognomy:[70] in both cases, he said, individual lines are arranged in meaningful combinations that express the inner nature or spirit of the whole.

•

As the nineteenth century progressed, authors increasingly tied architectural expression to the functional or utilitarian nature of a building. In *Rural Residences* (1818; Entry 246) John Buonarotti Papworth stated that a small villa residence must be considered first in terms of its fitness to house a family. Next, and perhaps more important for Papworth, was the matter of expression—providing "external claims to respectability." He especially appreciated the use of historical styles for their associations with particular eras and societal forms. Tudor and Elizabethan styles, for example, recalled a time when "the security of the sovereign and the subject began to depend less on the strength of fortifications and the force of arms, than on the equitable administration of the laws of the country." In addition to style, certain qualities of form could produce affective expression as well, particularly when suited to the function of the dwelling. In laborers' dwellings, for example, "simplicity" could inculcate certain positive moral qualities, while conversely too much ornament would "ill associate with the modest and moderate claims of this respectable and useful class of society."

In 1833 John Claudius Loudon completed his *Encyclopaedia* (Entry 184), one of the most comprehensive and popular architectural books of the entire nineteenth century. Even more than Papworth, he stressed the importance of "fitness" as the first principle of architectural design. The second principle, "expression of the end in view," also was related to the function of a building. Loudon's third principle, "expression of some particular Architectural style," was both "temporary and accidental," and for Loudon far less important than the first two principles. Thus while Loudon paid serious attention to the problem of expression, he considered only expression of function as primary. Other types of expression included "creating in the mind, emotions of sublimity or beauty," through association or other means, but while these were desirable forms of expression they were not necessary for the success of a design. In particular he found little use for expression of character, perhaps because a central, informing character would detract from the expression of a building's purpose and function. On the other hand, for those who did pursue "temporary and accidental" beauties, Loudon readily approved association as a means of expression. The owner of a house might want to use Greek ornament, for example, to express his love of learning, or a Castellated style to stimulate memories of childhood, family, and friends. Loudon even offered one basic design for a dwelling that could be clad with any of six different styles of exterior ornament, facilitating a wide variety of associations that the owner might wish to communicate to the viewer.

The next year John Billington added material to a new edition of his *Architectural Director* (Entry 18.3) that clearly challenged some of Loudon's assertions. Although Billington agreed that use was a building's principal raison d'être, he argued that use should be expressed through a single, coherent "character" that informed the entire design. In an argument reminiscent of Peter Legh's discussion, Billington noted that creatures in nature are distinguished from each other by their physiognomies, and therefore architectural types should be distinguished from each other by their own "characteristic" features. A prison, for example, could "inspire terror," while a concert room could evoke feelings of "pleasure," and a church could express "greatness, power, and majesty." In this manner the architect could express both the simple use of a building, and also certain related intellectual or metaphysical concepts.

George Wightwick offered a unique discussion of the expressive potential of buildings in his *Palace of Architecture* (1840; Entry 346), prefiguring future developments in nineteenth-century theories of expression. He took the reader on a tour of an imaginary palace, which represented "an epitome of the Architectural world." In language like that of the young Ruskin,[71] Wightwick described a variety of means by which architecture could affect the viewer: through the effect of a building's "MONUMENTAL attributes," as "the leading agent in PICTORIAL ROMANCE," as the vehicle of "glowing ASSOCIATION," and as "MATERIAL POETRY." He further suggested that he would bring all these modes of expression together for the first time, as part of an all-embracing, comprehensive Romantic experience.

Thus expression and affectivity remained central to architectural aesthetics from the mid-eighteenth century through the mid-nineteenth. Many architects enthusiastically embraced related theories of architectural character and associational response, particularly in the last half of the eighteenth century. From the beginning of the nineteenth century, however, these theories received a mixed reception: some architects questioned the degree to which these theories discouraged attention to fitness and utility; others, such as Billington and Wightwick, found association and character the perfect means for advancing the course of architectural Romanticism.

**4
The Ideal of
"Retirement"**

The ideal of "retirement"—retreat from the pressures of city life and politics to the country, with its ready opportunities for physical recreation and spiritual regeneration—has been important in Western thought at least since the time of Classical Rome. Horace considered the subject at length in his Odes, Epistles, and Satires: he found much to praise in city life, but he also lamented his inability to achieve full freedom as an individual, or to make best use of his talent as a poet, within urban confines. Thus such rural retreats as Tibur, Tarentum, Baiae, Praeneste, and especially the Sabine Estate became almost sacred places where, alone, he could achieve the closest contact with his Muse.[72] Retreat and regeneration were likewise fundamental activities at suburban villas in Renaissance Italy.[73] In seventeenth-century England the country house was commonly a place of "retirement" from the pressures of politics at Westminster and business in the City, occasioning an entirely different pattern of daily activity, style of dress, and range of intellectual pursuits.[74] In 1700 Timothy Nourse singled out the regenerative aspects of "retired" life in his "Essay of a Country House": "The True design then of such Places of Pleasure and Retreat is to sweeten the Fatigues both of the Body and of the Mind, and to recover us to our former Bent of Duty, which is but in some measure to restore Man to his lost Station." Nourse also stressed the seriousness of this endeavor, warning that his remarks were not meant to justify "those who abandon themselves to a supine and sleepy course of life, retiring to their Country-Houses as to a Seraglio, where they pass their Time in all manner of Sensuality, or Bestiality rather."[75] In the eighteenth century the ideal of "retirement" remained fundamental to the conception of country residences, and by the nineteenth century it was central even to the design of modest suburban dwellings.

Early in the eighteenth century Alexander Pope, who wrote his own imitations of Horatian odes, laid out a large portion of the grounds at his Twickenham estate to facilitate "retirement" and private inspiration. There were gentle variations in ground level, thick plantings, meandering paths, and a deep, rude grotto to which he could retreat for private contemplation.[76] Not far away at Chiswick, in the 1720s, Lord Burlington built his much-acclaimed villa in Palladian style. In choosing this style he may have had in mind many of the characteristics of "villas" that Palladio described in his *Quattro libri* (1570), a translation of which had recently been completed by Leoni (1715). Palladio described the villa as a place where, through "exercise . . . on foot and on horseback, the body will the more easily preserve its strength and health; and, finally, where the mind, fatigued by the agitations of the city, will be greatly restor'd and comforted, and be able quietly to attend the studies of letters, and contemplation."[77] In the 1730s Burlington engaged William Kent to design an irregular, ostensibly "natural" landscape for the estate surrounding his villa, presumably to facilitate recuperative and restorative processes such as Nourse and Palladio described.[78] Meanwhile Burlington had also commissioned Robert Castell to undertake historical research into "the Rules that were observed in the situating and disposing of the Roman Villas." The results, published in Castell's *Villas of the Ancients* (1728; Entry 36), include an appreciation of the "retired" function of a villa. Pliny's villa at Laurentinum, according to Castell, was not furnished with "Conveniencies" for "all Seasons." Instead, Pliny went there only during "those Hours he had at leisure from the Business of the City," and while there he devoted his time chiefly to "exercising his Mind by Study, and his Body by Hunting"— activities emphasized in Castell's detailed descriptions of the villa's country location, its gardens, baths, and libraries.

"Retired" activities were well provided for in most of the country houses, villas, and lodges illustrated in eighteenth-century architectural literature, and literary accounts show clearly that such activities were part of country life throughout the century.[79] In architectural treatises there are frequent general references to "retired" activities such as hunting, entertaining, and contemplation, but few architects addressed the subject of retirement in detail. One who did left no doubt about its importance. In *Lectures on Architecture* (1734–1736; Entry 215) Robert Morris proposed that the remote countryside was the best environment in which to display the harmonically proportioned style of architecture that he advocated. He also pointed out the restorative and contemplative benefits of retirement in such an environment:

Noblemens Seats, besides Grandeur, are erected for a Retirement, or as a Retreat from Publick Cares, perhaps in some silent unfrequented Glade, where Nature seems to be lull'd into a kind of pleasing Repose, and conspires to soften Mankind into solid and awful Contemplations, especially a curious and speculative Genius, who in such distant and remote Recesses, are [sic] free from the Noise and Interruptions of Visitors or Business, or the Tumult of the Populace, which are continually diverting the Ideas into different Channels. (p. 88)

Other architects mentioned the subject only briefly. Isaac Ware commented that one of the designs for a country house in his *Complete Body of Architecture* (1756; Entry 339) was suitable for "a gentleman [who] intends to retire from *London*" (p. 405), but made no further remarks on retirement. Thomas Rawlins likewise broached the subject in his *Familiar Architecture* (1768; Entry 273): he described his design for one small dwelling as "a Retreat for a Merchant, &c. where divested of the cares of Business he may enjoy the Converse of a few select Friends." In 1794 Robert Morison completed his *Designs in Perspective for Villas* (Entry 211), a collection of six large but crudely drawn designs for dwellings accompanied by brief remarks on domestic architecture. He particularly stressed the function of a country house as a place of "retirement": "The genius of the artist, has, in all civilized nations, been exerted towards the embellishment and convenience of those edifices" that facilitate withdrawal "from the busy scenes of life, for the purpose of enjoying domestic tranquillity, at a distance from the formality of courts or the hurry of cities."

Because of changing social and economic circumstances, architectural authors in the early nineteenth century catered increasingly to middle-class, nouveau-riche clients. In their aspirations and pretensions these clients often aped the aristocratic landholders of previous generations, desiring in particular the trappings of a "retired" country existence. These aspirations could be satisfied, at least in part, by designs that were described by their authors in terms of "retired" activities and picturesque land-scapes—designs that were well suited to Britain's newly popular resort areas and suburbs.[80] James Malton's *Collection of Designs for Rural Retreats* (1802; Entry 196), containing designs for modest villas and lodges, includes a 12-page prefatory essay on "the Necessity and Advantage of Temporary Retirement." He argued that retirement was a useful, perhaps even nec-essary, means to achieve happiness: those "who prefer the pure and tranquil retirement of the country, to the foetid joys of the tumultuous city, are they who take the most likely means to enjoy that blessing of life, happiness." Retirement in the country is particularly "favourable to a train of action at once beneficial to humanity, and conducive to individual enjoyment," since a person residing there will have "more leisure for undisturbed reflection, and opportunity for a steady pursuit of well-digested plans of improvement" (p. v). In addition to strengthening the intellect, retirement also nurtures the emotions: it contributes to the genesis of "every truly social feeling, of every tender sentiment; in sober, steady reflection they have their birth, and in solitude they are cherished" (p. ii). Malton extended these ideas in his Introduction, arguing that the design of a country house should help facilitate the goals of retirement. Just as one is less formal in personal dress and "figure" in retirement, he argued, so one's house in the country should be less formal than one in a city. Thus he concluded that informal, picturesque elevations, plans, and styles were particularly suited to country houses.

Richard Elsam discussed the benefits of retirement in a similarly positive manner in his collection of designs for cottages and villas, *An Essay on Rural Architecture* (1803; Entry 69). Significantly his remarks do not apply to the eighteenth-century practice of retreating to the country for several weeks or months at a time, and instead are prescient of the daily commute between affairs of politics and business in the city and the domestic rec-reations of the suburbs:

Beyond doubt, there is considerable satisfaction in a comfortable convenient retreat, near a town, where a gentleman has an opportunity of participating in the sports of the field, in agriculture, or in gardening; and at other intervals, when the mind is so disposed, to intermix in the company, and gay amusements, of his neighbourhood. These are the great pleasures of such a retreat, situated near the city or town, which, if elevated upon a rising ground, near to a public road, well sheltered by trees, and on a pleasant spot, cannot fail to render it both cheerful and retired.

Edmund Bartell also addressed a middle-class audience in *Hints for Pic-turesque Improvements* (1804; Entry 14). He devoted much of his book to designs for the "ornamented cottage," a type of dwelling "appropriate to the residence of a gentleman" and useful as "a retreat from the hurry of a town-life."

The ideal of retirement remained important in architectural literature well into the nineteenth century, particularly in publications of designs for modest suburban and country dwellings. James Thomson, a successful designer of villas both in resorts and in metropolitan suburbs, issued a very handsome example of such a book in 1827. Suggestively titled *Retreats* (Entry 333), the book includes designs for two types of dwellings well suited to retirement: "COTTAGE RESIDENCES," which Thomson described as " 'RETIREMENTS' of a limited description, adapted more particularly to the [suburban] environs of the metropolis"; and larger designs for villas, or " 'RETREATS' of the higher order," intended for locations further from the city, deeper in the countryside, suitable for longer stays, and conducive to a more thoroughly "retired" existence.

5 Picturesque Retreats for Country and Suburb: Designs for Villas and Cottages

The words "villa" and "cottage" were in common usage in early eighteenth-century England, but over the following century they would acquire a far greater range of meanings. Since the thirteenth century the word "cottage" had applied to dwellings for laborers on farms, in villages, or in mining areas. References to villas, denoting the country retreats of ancient Romans and Renaissance Italians, appeared in English literature from the beginning of the seventeenth century.[81] But expanding interest in the ideal of "retirement" and in picturesque aesthetics, and steadily growing demand for middle-class country and suburban retreats caused fundamental transformations in the cottage and villa types, and also in the meaning of their names. By the early nineteenth century there was considerable confusion: in some quarters the words "villa" and "cottage" retained their earlier definitions, while elsewhere they denoted modest, often picturesque dwelling types suited to suburbs and "retired" rural locations. In this discussion I will explore the origins of the second manner of definition, focusing on changes in use and form these dwelling types underwent from the early eighteenth to the mid-nineteenth centuries. By analyzing the use of the words "villa" and "cottage" in context, and by examining designs to which architects applied them, I will demonstrate the quite broad range of meanings these terms acquired, and the variety of dwelling types to which they referred.[82]

•

The villa in ancient Roman civilization was a special place of retirement, regeneration, and inspiration; it served much the same function in Renaissance Rome.[83] Both Classical and Renaissance villas were frequently located at some distance from the city, as for example at Tivoli, where examples from both eras remain. According to Pliny, Varro, and others, many Classical villas were large farming communities consisting of three parts: a *villa urbana* or dwelling set aside for the master's own use; a *villa rustica* consisting of offices for animal husbandry and farming; and a *villa fructuaria* containing storehouses for corn, wine, oil, and other products.[84] Renaissance villas was usually far more compact, and often built much closer to the city, in "suburban" locations, in order to provide more immediate respite and pleasure. Alberti, for example, spoke of a "sort of private houses, in which the dignity of the town-house, and the delights and pleasures of the country-house are both required; . . . And these are the pleasure-houses just without the town," i.e., "Villa's."[85]

A century later Andrea Palladio executed a variety of designs for villas in the Veneto. These designs were studied carefully by many Englishmen on the Grand Tour, including such ardent admirers as Inigo Jones and Lord Burlington. Like their Classical counterparts, many of these Palladian villas comprised entire farming communities, with the principal dwelling serving as the center of a much greater enterprise.[86] In his *Quattro libri* (1570) Palladio was careful to distinguish this type of dwelling from the city house, noting that villa estates suited such pursuits as agriculture, exercise, contemplation, and "private and family affairs." Like the ancient Romans, Palladio considered the country house to be "a little city," and as such it had two parts: "one for the habitation of the master, and of his family; and the other to manage and take care of the produce and animals of the villa." In siting a villa, Palladio not only recommended careful attention to health, convenience, and transportation, but also mentioned the advantages of a picturesque location, or "beautiful prospect."[87]

English usage of the word "villa" in the first half of the eighteenth century, while based on Latin and Italian precedents, soon grew to encompass a much broader range of meanings. Timothy Nourse was one of the first English authors to modify the definition of the villa. In his "Essay of a Country House" (1700) he clearly differentiated the country house from the villa, which by his definition was small, unpretentious, and suited to private pleasures and entertainments:

By a Country-House I do not understand a Farm, nor the ordinary Mansion-House of a Country Gentleman; nor yet a *Villa*, or little House of Pleasure and Retreat, where Gentlemen and Citizens betake themselves in the Summer for their private Diversion, there to pass an Evening or two, or perhaps a Week, in the Conversation of a Friend or two, in some neat little House amidst a Vineyard or Garden, sequestered from the Noise of a City, and the Embarras and Destraction of Business, or perhaps the anxious and servile Attendance of a Court. By a Country-House then, I understand a greater Fabrick, fit to lodge a Nobleman endu'd with ample Fortunes and a vertuous Mind, where he may sweeten the Travels of a Vexatious Life, and pass away his Days amidst the solid and serene Enjoyments of the Country.[88]

In remarks composed about the same time, but not published until 1789 (Entry 5), Henry Aldrich discussed the difference between the Palladian notion of a villa as a farming estate, and the small villa used as a retreat. His use of the term agreed with Nourse's: "The term villa, taken in its full sense, means a country house with a farm annexed: but we shall here understand no more by it than a house built for rural retirement; in the size, situation, and structure of which the plan of a farm house is not to be lost sight of." Nevertheless English usage of the word remained ambiguous and confusing. In Isaac Ware's translation of the *Quattro libri* (1738), for example, Palladio's term "case di villa" is translated both as "country houses" and also as "villas," while Palladio's use of the word "villa" alone, denoting a farming estate, also is translated as "villa."

The earliest original designs for villas illustrated in English books were conceived precisely in the manner that Nourse described. Just two subjects in James Gibbs's *Book of Architecture* (1728; Entry 88) are identified as villas, and while both are two stories tall and over 80 feet wide, they are clearly designed for temporary habitation and entertainment. The central component of the first villa (Plate 40) is a richly decorated, two-story cube room, 30 feet on a side; to each side are separate suites of "Apartments," each having one bedroom on the ground floor and additional "Lodging Rooms" above. The second villa (Plates 59 and 60) likewise has a two-story central "Room," flanked on each side by an "Apartment," or private suite of rooms. Each suite includes an anteroom and bedroom on the ground floor, plus two more bedrooms upstairs, and smaller closets on both stories. In both villas the large central room is the principal component of the entire building and is clearly intended for entertaining. The separate suites to each side, which do not communicate with each other, are primarily sleeping areas. The absence of any other rooms—dining room, drawing room, hall, or saloon, for example—further confirms the special purpose of these villas as temporary places of private entertainment and retreat.

Certainly the most important English precedent for the type of villa that Gibbs designed was Lord Burlington's villa at Chiswick, erected circa 1723–1729. It was similar in scale to Gibbs's designs, and was used principally for entertainment rather than as a residence.[89] But despite the fact that Chiswick House was modeled on Palladio's Villa Rotonda, Burlington and other English neo-Palladians did not readily adopt the term "villa" to describe this type of dwelling. Indeed Burlington appears not to have used the term at all when referring to Chiswick House. When Sir John Clerk of Penicuik visited Chiswick in 1727 he did discuss "the whole situation of the villa," but this is an ambiguous use that could refer to just the house or to the surrounding estate as well.[90] Colen Campbell, who was close to Burlington, used the term only once in *Vitruvius Britannicus*, writing in Volume III (1725; Entry 33) that the tower at Claremont "has a most prodigious fine Prospect of the *Thames* and the adjacent Villas" (p. 11). This too is an ambiguous reference, although it likely denotes farming estates.[91]

Burlington's reluctance to describe Chiswick as a "villa" may be related to his patronage of Robert Castell's study of the Classical Roman villa (1728; Entry 36). Castell's method was literary: he provided translations of and commentary on Latin texts describing Pliny's two villas at Laurentinum and Tuscum, together with remarks on relevant passages from other Roman authors. Castell described a building type that in function resembled the villas that Nourse and Gibbs conceived, but that differed considerably in form. Castell emphasized that the villa facilitated mental and physical recreation: the time Pliny spent at his villa, for example, was "wholly employ'd in exercising his Mind by Study, and his Body by Hunting." The design of a villa also facilitated enjoyment of the surrounding countryside: the composition as a whole should please "the Eye from several Views, like so many beautiful Landskips." Castell also noted the quasi-suburban character of the villa when describing the principal "Conveniencies" at Laurentinum: "*Vicinitatem Urbis, Opportunitatem Viae, Mediocritatem Villae,* [and] *Modum Ruris.*" The first and last of these— proximity to the metropolis and adoption of a rural way of life—were important aspects of the increasingly popular contemporary ideal of rural "retirement."[92] Nevertheless the type of villa Castell described and illustrated was not the diminutive, picturesque structure that Nourse and

Gibbs proposed. Rather, his conjectural reconstructions include long suites of rooms, large pavilions, and office ranges, all forming part of a large agricultural estate whose population would almost equal that of a small town.[93] The lasting import of Castell's work lay not in his reconstructions, but in his extended discussion of the villa type. His remarks clearly associated the term "villa" with a dwelling set in a rural location near a city, in harmony with picturesque natural surroundings, and facilitating an informal, "retired" existence, with opportunities for mental and physical recreation.

Nourse, Aldrich, and Gibbs all associated the word "villa" with a small residence intended for temporary retreat. Chiswick House, although not originally described as a "villa," was equally small and served the same function. But until the 1720s there were few published designs for small dwellings in British architectural literature. Robert Morris, the major theorist of the early eighteenth century, was the first British architect to publish a collection of such designs, his *Essay in Defence of Ancient Architecture* (1728; Entry 214).[94] Most of the dwellings illustrated are just two stories high and three or five openings wide. Like Castell, he professed strict attention to Classical precedents, but instead of reconstructing villas from literary evidence, he applied Classical "Rules" to the design of original dwellings.[95] In his *Lectures on Architecture* (1734–1736; Entry 215) Morris illustrated more designs for small dwellings, which he described specifically as "villas." In discussing them, Morris adopted two characteristics of villas that had been cited earlier by Nourse, Aldrich, and Castell. First, he emphasized the restorative and contemplative benefits of "Retirement" (p. 88). Second, he extolled the advantages of a picturesque country location: "no Building should be design'd to be erected, without first considering the Extent of *Prospect, Hills, Vales, &c.* which expand and encircle it; its *Avenues, Pastures* and *Waters.*"

Morris and his predecessors thus agreed that a villa should characteristically possess a picturesque location and provide opportunities for retirement. Except for Castell, all also agreed that the villa was generally a small dwelling. The consensus over picturesqueness and retirement prevailed for the next hundred years and more, but on the matter of size opinions diverged greatly. In 1750 Morris published another book of designs, titled *Rural Architecture* (Entry 216), in which he indicated he would pay special attention to the "plain little Villa." Surprisingly, one of the three villas presented is the most expensive design in the book (Plates 22 and 23). The plan is 220 feet wide and 105 feet deep, and one of the 15 rooms on the principal floor is a saloon measuring 50 feet by 40 feet. Morris estimated the design would cost £16,400 to erect. The villa shown in Plate 18, estimated to cost £9,400, also is large: the plan is 110 feet by 100 feet. The third villa design (Plate 36) is the smallest, measuring 66 feet by 56 feet, and the only one as small as Gibbs's villas or Chiswick House. The facade in fact closely resembles Gibbs's second design (Plate 59), but in Morris's villa the six rooms on the principal floor are arranged as in a conventional residence.

Villas that actually were erected on the outskirts of London as suburban retreats, by contrast, could be exceedingly diminutive. In 1754 such dwellings earned the satirical censure of one literary wag in *The Connoisseur*:

A little country box you boast,
So neat, 'tis cover'd all with dust;
And nought about it to be seen,
Except a nettle-bed, that's green;
Your Villa! rural but the name in,
So desart, it would breed a famine.
. . .
'Tis not the country, you must own;
'Tis only London out of town.[96]

The writer had two principal complaints: these so-called villas were too small to justify their pretensions to retirement and recreation, and they were packed too closely together to maintain any semblance of a rural environment. He thus confirmed, in effect, the persistence of two essential characteristics of villas that others had established earlier in the century: opportunity for retirement, and a picturesque rural location.

In the following decade designs for villas appeared more frequently in architectural books. There continued to be great variations in size, and now there were important differences in function as well. In Thomas Overton's *Original Designs of Temples* (1766; Entry 234) the six designs for villas are uniformly small: all are five openings wide or less, and except for corner turrets no design is more than two stories high. The principal floor of each design consists of one large room, presumably for dining or dancing. In some cases this room is flanked by small bedrooms. Offices are generally underneath this floor, and bedrooms are in the story above. All these villas were clearly intended only for temporary habitation—an evening's entertainment or a day's retreat in the country.[97] The seven villas in John Crunden's *Convenient and Ornamental Architecture* (1767; Entry 49) are larger, generally two stories high and seven openings wide, plus offices. The greater number of rooms and offices shows that these designs were intended as permanent or semipermanent residences.[98] The two villas in Stephen Riou's *Grecian Orders of Architecture* (1768; Entry 287), finally, are considerably more grandiose: the principal floor of the design in Plate VIII, for example, contains nine principal rooms surrounding an open court 40 feet in diameter, and includes a gallery measuring 60 feet by 20 feet. This design, which is equal in scale to the larger designs for villas in Morris's *Rural Architecture*, clearly exceeds Nourse's notion of a "little House of Pleasure and Retreat" and instead resembles a modest country mansion.

Half a dozen authors who published designs for villas during the 1770s and 1780s shared little more than the notion that a villa was a rural retreat. Their designs for villas vary greatly in size and function, ranging from a one-room hunting lodge to the equivalent of a mansion. The eight designs for villas in *The Builder's Magazine* (1774; Entry 26) include "a Hunting Villa" that consists of just one circular room 43 feet in diameter, "a rusticated small Hunting Villa" that is not much larger, as well as "a villa for a person of quality" 13 openings wide, and another "Villa" 21 openings wide.[99] Robert and James Adam devoted the second number of *Works in Architecture* (1774; Entry 1) to the "Villa at Kenwood," a conspicuously magnificent suburban retreat. The one villa in William Thomas's *Original Designs in Architecture* (1783; Entry 331) is the largest design in the book, with a facade 17 openings wide. The nine designs for villas in James

Lewis's *Original Designs in Architecture* (1780–1797; Entry 178) are modest in comparison, generally two stories high and five or seven openings wide. The "small villas" mentioned on the title page of James Peacock's Οικιδια (1785; Entry 255) are equally modest, with an average of four principal rooms on the ground floor of each. Likewise one villa in John Soane's *Plans Elevations and Sections of Bvildings Execvted* (1788; Entry 319) is two stories high and three openings wide, and the other is of similar size, flanked by one-story wings.

When describing general characteristics of villas in letterpress, some authors were highly ambiguous: in 1787, for example, John Miller used the term to refer, like Ware, to farming estates as well as to gentlemen's country residences.[100] Usage among other authors was equally varied. In *New Designs in Architecture* (1792; Entry 284), for example, George Richardson described villas as "buildings of considerable extent, in which convenience, utility and solidity have been studied in the plans, and in the elevations variety, elegance, and beauty." This description accorded well with his designs, which were as much as 258 feet wide. The next year he was countered by Charles Middleton, who wrote in *Picturesque and Architectural Views* (1793; Entry 207) that all villas were characterized not only by "Elegance," but also by "compactness, and convenience, . . . in contradistinction to the magnificence and extensive range of the country seats of our nobility and opulent gentry." Middleton categorized three specific types of villa according to use, location, and status of the proprietor:

First, as the occasional and temporary retreats of the nobility and persons of fortune from what may be called their town residence, and must, of course, be in the vicinity of the metropolis.—Secondly, as the country houses of wealthy citizens and persons in official stations, which also cannot be far removed from the capital: and thirdly, the smaller kind of provincial edifices, considered either as hunting seats, or the habitations of country gentlemen of moderate fortune.

This diversity of types is reflected in Middleton's designs, which range in size from one that is three windows wide (Plate XI), to another that is 13 windows wide, with a two-story domed drawing room and 12 bedrooms (Plate XIX). In 1794 George Richardson published the first part of a new collection of designs, this time consisting entirely of "country seats or villas" (Entry 283). Now largely concerned with emulating the decorative magnificence of Classical villas—and slighting such traditional considerations as retirement and picturesqueness—he explained that in designing "interior furnishings" he "attempted to retain the spirit and effect of that beautiful and elegant style . . . used in the private apartments, baths, and villas, of the Ancients; namely, at Rome, Adrian's Villa, and the ruins on the Baian shore." With such imitative concerns foremost in his mind, it is not surprising that Richardson failed to consider other characteristics of the villa type, or that his designs vary greatly in size, ranging from one example just three openings wide to another over 110 feet wide and 50 feet deep.

Toward the beginning of the nineteenth century, architects took increasing interest in the application of picturesque aesthetics to all types of domestic architecture.[101] In order to apply picturesque principles most effectively, they needed to analyze and classify the formal qualities of individual dwelling types, including villas. At the same time they also considered the functional and expressive characteristics of villas. James Malton, who had discussed the irregular, picturesque qualities of cottages in his *Essay on British Cottage Architecture* (1798; Entry 197), added brief remarks on villas in his *Collection of Designs for Rural Retreats, as Villas* (1802; Entry 196). Describing the villa as a "country retreat of a nobleman or gentleman," he identified its formal character as one of "elegance." Considering specific styles, however, he rejected "the Grecian and Roman mode of fabrick, for more picturesque forms," which were better suited to the "retired" pursuits of a country retreat. In *An Essay on Rural Architecture* (1803; Entry 69), conceived in part as an attack on Malton's notion of picturesque irregularity, Richard Elsam provided designs for villas that were symmetrical in plan and elevation, and frequently based on regular geometric figures. Of all dwelling types, he identified the "villa of moderate size" as the most "commodious," "healthy," and "pleasant." He suggested that this type would particularly suit a suburban location, where it could combine "the dignity and consequence of the town residence, with the delights and pleasures of the country seat." Two years later Robert Lugar took a middle course between Malton and Elsam: in *Architectural Sketches* (1805; Entry 192) he encouraged picturesque irregularity, but only in cottages; villas, he said, should be entirely uniform, with "exact proportion and regularity of parts."

For many architects the picturesque relation between a villa and the surrounding landscape continued to be a fundamental consideration. Discussing villas in his *Lectures*, Sir John Soane paid close attention to the use of geometric figures and proportions, but he also stressed the importance of harmonizing the villa with surrounding scenery.[102] In *Hints on Ornamental Gardening* (1823; Entry 248.2) John Buonarotti Papworth explored in some detail the formal relation between villas and a particular type of scenery, the "beautiful." He wrote that in architecture and scenery alike, the beautiful "is expressed in gaiety and luxuriance, by an easy gracefulness of forms and parts, and . . . its qualities are lightness, neatness, symmetry, regularity, uniformity and propriety."

Several nineteenth-century architects described the villa as an intermediate dwelling type between the mansion and the cottage, but like their eighteenth-century counterparts they seldom discussed the architectural hierarchy in detail. In *Architectural Designs for Rustic Cottages* (1807; Entry 262) William Fuller Pocock simply found that the "style and decorations" of a villa could be raised "towards those fit for a regular Mansion" or lowered "to a Building scarcely exceeding a Cottage in simplicity of appearance." In 1825 Papworth described a similar hierarchy; unlike Pocock, however, he analyzed the nature of the English villa in greater depth and further explored its picturesque relation with the surrounding environment. Like Pocock he located the villa between the cottage and the mansion: in size as well as "accommodation" the villa was "a mean between the moderate pretensions of the one, and the stately magnificence of the other." He also identified three principal characteristics of a villa: its "insulated form," its "garden-like domain," and its "external offices for stables and domestic economy." He observed that villas were usually designed "according to the principles of Italian architecture," but unlike Palladian villas the principal floor of the English villa was located at grade level. This provided convenient access to the surrounding lawns, whose "verdure and decorations have become almost a continuation of the furniture of the morning and drawing-rooms," encouraging in turn greater enjoyment of the picturesque natural environment.[103]

Shortly afterward Robert Gunter Wetten examined the English villa in a broader historical perspective, comparing it to villas of Greece, Rome, and the Italian Renaissance (*Designs for Villas in the Italian Style* [1830?; Entry 341]). He concluded that the "magificence" of contemporary English villas hardly equaled that of ancient times, and suggested this was due to "modern habits and customs": the modern villa often included little more than "the merely necessary living and sleeping rooms." His own designs for villas reflect an effort to restore lost magnificence: the plan of one measures 100 feet by 123 feet, and the ground floor includes a drawing room, dining room, combined entrance hall and billiard room, breakfast room, library, staircase hall, cabinet, closets, and servants' rooms; upstairs there are nine bedrooms and three dressing rooms.

With historical precedents such as Pliny's villas in mind, John Claudius Loudon chose the villa as the epitome of English residential architecture. In his *Encyclopaedia of Cottage, Farm, and Villa Architecture* (1833; Entry 184) he stated that the English villa embodied all the necessary characteristics of lesser dwelling types, and also provided more of the "comforts and luxuries of life" than were available in villas anywhere else in the world. To analyze this dwelling type he devoted some 23,000 words to a description of "The Beau Idéal of an English Villa," which he also illustrated in a design for a two-story, H-plan villa in Old English style. The ground floor includes seven large principal rooms, plus service areas and servants' quarters. Contrasting this design to Pliny's villas, Loudon noted that the modern villa was not part of a farming estate but instead a country retreat: it was, he said, a "gentleman's residence" located "at an easy distance from the metropolis." Nevertheless Loudon's ideal did resemble Classical and Renaissance villas in some respects: it should be a central feature of a small village, he said, and the villa household should derive food and other materials as much as possible from the surrounding estate.

Like Wetten and Loudon, John Billington also presented the villa as one of the largest dwelling types. In *The Architectural Director* (1834; Entry 18.3) he stated that villas could be "distinguished from [the rest of] country residences, by their greater extent, dignity, and magnificence." Nevertheless villas still retained their character as places of retreat and informal manners: "they do not require either the same extent, dignity, or sumptuousness as palaces, situated in capitals. In the villa, a sovereign resigns, as may be said, the public character that he holds in the midst of his people."

But despite the remarks of Wetten, Loudon, and Billington, in the middle of the nineteenth century the term "villa" was not applied exclusively to large, quasi-palatial residences. In general parlance it had come to denote the quintessential British middle-class dwelling. Indeed most of the designs for villas in Loudon's *Encyclopaedia* were considerably smaller than his "Beau Idéal," and some were less than 50 feet wide. In *Designs for Cottage*

Figure 3

and Villa Architecture (1839; Entry 23) Samuel H. Brooks recognized the recent growth of middle-class suburbs in many parts of the country and summed up the importance and popularity of the more modest type of villa: Britain, he said, had become preeminently a "country of suburban villas." Suburban life had become the goal of each "Englishman, in whose mind the idea of retirement from business and a country life are inseparably united."

•

During the eighteenth century the word "cottage" was newly applied to a variety of dwelling types, and by the end of the century it referred not only to laborers' dwellings that were little more than hovels, but also to picturesque country residences for the gentry, and a host of types in between. To consider the entire range of cottage types would require examination of far more historical material than is under consideration here.[104] In connection with the discussion of villas, however, it is important to consider one type of cottage in some detail: the middle-class "orna-mented" cottage, which in its genesis closely paralleled the villa. The ornamented cottage resembles the villa in several respects, including pic-turesque composition, "retired" function, rural or suburban setting, and upper- or middle-class inhabitants. In many cases the sole difference between an ornamented cottage and a small villa is a matter of size. All of these characteristics were recognized in a discussion of cottage archi-tecture published in 1845:

The term cottage has for some time past been in vogue as a particular designation for small country residences and detached suburban houses, adapted to a moderate scale of living, yet with all due attention to comfort and refinement. While in this sense of it, the name is divested of all associations with poverty, it is convenient, inasmuch as it frees from all pretension and parade and restraint. For this reason those who possess both townhouses and country mansions, have frequently their 'Cottage' also, as an occasional retreat. With the name, something also has been assumed of a mode of building intended to answer to it—one of homely and rustic character—rejecting architectural rules, yet requiring a studious observance of appropriate expression and picturesque physiognomy.[105]

In 1801 a poet noted that the fashion for such small, picturesque cottages, emulating the "retired" characteristics of villas, had begun to displace proper dwellings for the laboring classes:

No village dames and maidens now are seen,
But madams, and the misses of the green!
Farm-house, and farm too, are in deep disgrace,
'Tis now the lodge, the cottage, or the place!
Or if a farm, *ferme ornee* is the phrase!
And if a cottage, of these modern days,
Expect no more to see the straw-built shed,
But a fantastic villa in its stead!
Pride, thinly veil'd in mock humility;
The name of cot, without its poverty![106]

The heritage of the ornamented cottage dates from the mid-eighteenth century, when British architects began to study the precise characteristics of individual building types as a means of differentiating those types within the architectural hierarchy.[107] The first British architect to discuss formal differences among dwelling types was Daniel Garret, who considered the cottage in particular in his *Designs, and Estimates, of Farm Houses* (1747; Entry 86). He stated that "The Palace or Cottage require different Forms"; and while both required regularity and proportion, the cottage ought to be distinguished by "Plainness and Rusticity." Four years later William Halfpenny went further, suggesting in *Six New Designs* (1751; Entry 137) that the cottage might be the epitome of all dwelling types: he found "More real Beauty and Elegance" in the "due Symmetry and Harmony of a well-constructed Cottage" than could ever be found in a palace. By discussing the cottage in terms of such aesthetic ideals, Halfpenny and Garret helped to raise it above its traditional station as simply a rude, functional shelter for laborers.[108]

Another source of increased respect for cottages was the growing infatuation with the presumed innocence and simplicity of a "primitive" life, passed in harmony with nature, and often epitomized by rural shepherds and shepherdesses living in picturesque cottages.[109] Shortly after midcentury, therefore, one could find designs for cottages that facilitated the same type of "retired" rural pleasures and recreations that were associated with contemporary villas. The "cott" in Thomas Collins Overton's *Original Designs of Temples* (1766; Entry 234), for example, can hardly be distinguished from his designs for villas. The principal room on the ground floor is an octagon, 10 feet in diameter, which "commands an extensive prospect" (p. 14); the structure seems intended primarily for temporary enjoyment of the rural landscape. The major characteristic that differentiates it from Overton's villas is its rustic appearance: the roof is made of thatch, and the walls are covered with "rough cast." The sole design for a cottage in *The Builder's Magazine* (1774; Entry 26) is similarly rustic, with a thatch roof and a distyle portico made of "Rough bodies of trees to represent columns."[110] By the end of the century such rustic, ornamental cottages were commonly and clearly differentiated from practical designs for farmers' and laborers' cottages. Robert Beatson's essay "On Cottages" (1797; Entry 16), for example, was devoted to designs for farm cottages and includes practical remarks on ventilation, insulation, conservation of fuel, stairs, and materials; he dismissed "ornamental" cottages as "pleasing objects in different points of view, from the parks or pleasure-grounds of noblemen and gentlemen of fortune."

Near the turn of the century Charles Middleton and James Malton took advantage of the growing interest in ornamental rustic cottages, as well as the steadily increasing attention to picturesque and associational aesthetics in contemporary architecture.[111] They offered timely discussions of the recreational uses, picturesque forms, and bucolic associations of the ornamented cottage. In *Picturesque and Architectural Views* (1793; Entry 207) Middleton recognized that cottages were habitations of "the poorer sort of country people" but also pointed out that cottages served a variety of functional and recreational ends on large estates:

The cottage built at the entrance of a park will form a convenient lodge. At a small distance from the mansion, the dairy, larder, bath, &c., may assume the characteristic form of a Cottage. Cottages in a more distant situation, are frequently fitted up for the reception of parties engaged in rural amusements. . . . The Bailiff, Gardener, Park and Gamekeepers, &c., are commonly lodged in such habitations.

Middleton's designs for cottages incorporate regular geometric figures in plan and elevation, but also picturesque features such as thatch roofs, rustic columns, trelliswork, rough stucco, and brick. In *An Essay on British Cottage Architecture* (1798; Entry 197) James Malton noted his dissatisfaction with the "regular" designs that previous architects had provided for "neat and convenient" cottages, complaining that such designs were not "characteristic" of cottage design. Instead he proposed to revive and "perpetuate" the ornamental characteristics of Britain's indigenous rural architecture. These included picturesqueness, irregularity, pleasant natural surroundings, comfort, and hospitality. His ideal was:

a small house in the country; of odd, irregular form, with various, harmonious colouring, the effect of weather, time, and accident; the whole environed with smiling verdure, having a contented, chearful, inviting aspect, and door on the latch, ready to receive the gossip neighbour, or weary, exhausted traveller.

In addition to describing the irregular forms and rough materials that were essential to achieving "picturesque effect,"[112] Malton also discussed the wealth of feelings and ideas that could be associated with cottages. These included such notions as rural simplicity, lack of artifice and affectation, and a life innocent of care and anxiety. Combining a concern for picturesque form with attention to bucolic, "retired" associations, Malton established the formal and expressive character of the "ornamented" cottage residence for decades to come.[113]

Ornamented cottages were especially popular subjects during the first decade of the nineteenth century. Designs appeared in a variety of sizes and styles, often accompanied by extensive remarks on rural pleasures, regularity and irregularity in cottage design, and the importance of integrating cottages with picturesque landscape scenery.[114] In *Hints for Picturesque Improvements in Ornamented Cottages* (1804; Entry 14) Edmund Bartell noted that an ornamented cottage could serve as "a retreat from the hurry of a town-life" or as a "residence of people of fortune." Thus he proposed to establish rules of design that would suit the growing taste for picturesque aesthetics and pleasures of country life. Discussing principles of picturesque composition, he especially urged that a cottage should be a "pleasing object in the landscape": thatch and pointed windows, he said, were alone insufficient to give "true character to a cottage scene."

Bartell's designs are largely symmetrical, but those in William Atkinson's *Views of Picturesque Cottages* (1805; Entry 10) are not. Atkinson extolled the "effect of chance" in producing "true characteristic simplicity" in picturesque cottages, particularly when irregularities resulted from utilitarian needs.[115] Joseph Michael Gandy also recognized the role of utility and irregularity in producing picturesque beauty. In *Designs for Cottages* (1805; Entry 84) he proposed to "unite *convenience* and *taste*" in designs characterized by simple, spare, yet asymmetrical elevations. He explained that regular, symmetrical designs appeared so only from one point of view; from any other point of view they would appear irregular. Therefore he suggested that every part should be composed to present a variety of picturesque elevations. William Pocock enthusiastically endorsed irregularity in his discussion of the *cabâne ornée* in *Architectural Designs for Rustic Cottages* (1807; Entry 262). The architect, he said, should take care "to form the whole with attention to the picturesque effect of broken lines, unequal heights, and irregular distribution." The result would be a dwelling more "calculated" than any other type for "the true pleasures of domestic life."

Like Atkinson, Gandy, Pocock, and other contemporaries, Richard Elsam provided designs for cottages that would serve as "rural retreats," facilitating recreational activity in sports, agriculture, and gardening. But he was firmly opposed to picturesque irregularity in cottage design. In *An Essay on Rural Architecture* (1803; Entry 69) he argued that symmetry should prevail in architecture as in "the works of Nature"; irregularity in cottages would only suggest "poverty" and the "grotesque." Edward Gyfford, who argued that the style of a dwelling must correspond to the character of the surrounding landscape, also insisted that the design should be absolutely regular. The plans and elevations shown in his *Designs for Elegant Cottages and Small Villas* (1806; Entry 127) are consequently all based on regular geometric figures, including squares, rectangles, semicircles, and circles.

Designs for picturesque ornamented cottages, intended for middle-class clients, continued to appear for the next several decades, although interest in this type declined somewhat after 1810. During the next twenty years John Buonarotti Papworth, one of the most prominent designers of ornamented cottages, continued to advocate picturesque informality and attention to "retirement" in cottage design. In an early article titled "Cottage Ornée" (1813; Entry 247), he noted that this type of dwelling provided "the means of friendly intercourse and rational retirement" by subordinating "splendour and magnificence" to "the calmer enjoyments of domestic felicity." Ten years later, in *Hints on Ornamental Gardening* (Entry 248.2), he argued that the cottage, like any other dwelling type, must be considered together with the surrounding landscape as "a great whole," in which the architect should create "picturesque effects in every point of view." To this end, the cottage should be surrounded by rustic scenery— "a mixture of the wild with unstudied cultivation"—or else set in a rural landscape, "accompanied by marked evidences of civilization and a desire to possess convenience and comforts."[116]

In the 1830s the ornamented cottage received only modest attention in architectural literature. Edward Trendall's *Original Designs for Cottages and Villas* (1831; Entry 334) contains residences suited to "the environs of the metropolis and large towns," but only three of these are cottages. The descriptions do not mention picturesque composition, and the elevations and plans include no scenery. A major portion of John Claudius Loudon's *Encyclopaedia of Cottage, Farm, and Villa Architecture* (1833; Entry 184) is devoted to cottage designs, but most of these were not of the "ornamented" variety; rather, they were intended for the use of laborers, mechanics, gardeners, bailiffs, servants, and small farmers. Indeed Loudon's principal concern was to encourage "fitness" and "expression of fitness" in dwellings, often to the exclusion of ornament; still, he included some remarks on the relation between villas and surrounding landscape scenery (pp. 773–790), and descriptions of several designs incorporate brief remarks on picturesque style and composition. Loudon's few ornamented designs for small dwellings appear in Book III, in which three of the 23 designs for villas are ornamented "Cottage Villas"; also, portions of the Supplement (1842) are devoted to "Ornamental Cottages" and more "Cottage Villas."

But Loudon clearly understood "Cottage Villas" as a subspecies of villas, and his "Ornamental Cottages" were primarily intended for use as servants' lodges. The "ornamented" cottage that had been of such interest and importance to designers three decades earlier—a hybrid type about the size of a large dwelling for a laborer but in many other respects emulating the villa—was no longer a dwelling type of special importance.[117] Thereafter villas remained the most common and respectable type of country and suburban dwelling, and while interest in "ornamented" cottages did not disappear, it soon was equaled by growing attention to practical designs for housing both urban and rural laborers.[118]

6
Row and Terrace Houses

The row house or terrace house—which may be defined as a town house joined to others by party walls—was perhaps the most common dwelling type built in towns and cities during the eighteenth and early nineteenth centuries. Such houses could be grouped in twos and threes behind facades that suggested single houses of grand scale, or they could be ranged in long rows flanking streets and squares. Most row and terrace houses were erected by speculative builders, without the assistance of architects; the form was therefore a product of convention and the constraints of Parliamentary Building Acts.[119] Consequently terrace houses were not accorded the same respect as other dwelling types within the architectural hierarchy, and they received scant attention in architectural literature. In major treatises by Colen Campbell, James Gibbs, and William Chambers (Entries 32–33, 88, 40), for example, there are no original designs for terrace houses, and only one illustration of an extant example: Campbell depicted Lindsey House, in Lincoln's Inn Fields, primarily because it was a fragment of a larger planning scheme that he associated with Inigo Jones.[120]

Several mid-eighteenth-century authors disparaged town houses in general, finding that other types, such as country houses, were far better suited to display wealth and taste. One writer, discussing what he referred to disdainfully as the "street house," explained: "Many a nobleman, whose proud seat in the country is adorned with all the riches of architecture, porticos, and columns, 'cornice and frise with bossy sculpture grav'd,' is here content with a simple dwelling, convenient within, and unornamented without." As an earlier author noted, the need for convenience without extravagance in town houses was a matter of economics: "The Design of Town Houses should be to contrive as many Conveniences as may be on a small Plan, because the Front of Ground in Streets is valuable."[121]

Despite the plainness and mediocrity of the town house as a building type, a number of architects did publish designs for detached town houses and town mansions, ranging in size from the equivalent of a small villa to a small palace.[122] Nevertheless few architects published designs for terrace houses. Hardly any discussed the theory or practice of terrace house design, apart from brief accounts of Building Acts currently in force. But because such buildings comprised a major portion of all housing built in the eighteenth and nineteenth centuries, and since published designs for terrace houses have received comparatively scant scholarly attention, a brief survey of such designs is appropriate here.

Batty Langley, who addressed his *Sure Guide to Builders* (1729; Entry 174.2) to artisans, was the first architect to publish original designs for row houses. Complaining that previous authors had neglected "to lay down Practical Rules for the Workman" (p. 2), Langley provided designs for the orders, windows, doors, ceilings, and other architectonic elements, plus plans and elevations for several buildings, including an elevation of one pair of attached town houses (Plate 9). Each house is three openings wide and three stories high, plus a dormer story. Stringcourses separate the individual floors, and a cornice divides the dormer story from the facade below. One house is fronted by vertical bands of heavy rustication, while on the front of the other house the main framing elements appear to be exposed. The windows are tall, running nearly from floor to ceiling: they are six feet high on the lower two stories, and five feet high on the upper story. Such vertical emphasis in the rustication and in the articulation of windows is, notably, only typical of terrace houses built from 1700 to 1730.[123]

A quarter century later Isaac Ware published a design for a row house in his *Complete Body of Architecture* (1756; Entry 339) that is articulated quite differently (Plate 34). The ground story, set on a plinth, is separated by a pair of stringcourses from the two upper stories. These, in turn, are separated from the dormer story by a cornice and balustraded parapet. The tallest windows are found on the middle floor, or *piano nobile*,[124] with considerably shorter windows above and below. There is no other major ornament on the facade, and the effect is entirely different from the vertical articulation of Langley's town houses: the facade is divided horizontally into three zones—base, *piano nobile* plus chamber story, and attic. Such a horizontal division of the facade was actually a formula that had been in use since the 1730s by builders of town houses in Palladian style, and was likely inspired by Lindsey House, one of the few remaining monuments of English seventeenth-century Palladian terrace housing.[125] In addition to the elevation, Ware provided a plan of the ground floor, 24 feet wide and 60 feet deep, containing just three rooms, each extending the full width of the building: an entrance hall, a staircase hall, and a large room divided into parts by a columnar screen.

Robert Morris contributed two designs for terrace houses to *The Modern Builder's Assistant* (1757; Entry 132).[126] The first (No. 20, Plate 44) is shown in elevation, section, and plan, and consists of three attached houses. The two end houses are 35 feet deep and 18 feet wide; the center house is the same depth and 24 feet wide. The facade is 11 openings wide and three stories high, plus a dormer story. The overall articulation of the facade is similar to Ware's: a stringcourse separates the ground story from the upper two stories, which in turn are separated from the dormer story by a cornice. The ground-floor plan of each house includes a passage leading in from the front door, a front parlor, a back parlor, and a staircase; the center house has one additional parlor. Morris's other design is a single town house, 20 feet wide and 40 feet deep, with a passage, staircase, and two parlors on the ground floor and two bedrooms on the chamber floor. The three-story facade, topped by a gable-ended roof, is shown in two alternate elevations. In both cases the stringcourse that separates the upper two stories from the lower story also divides the facade exactly into upper and lower halves. This proportionality, which is not found in the Lindsey House facade, reflects Morris's fundamental concern with regularity and proportion in architecture.

Similar designs for attached houses appear in John Crunden's *Convenient and Ornamental Architecture* (1767; Entry 49) and in *The Builder's Magazine* (1774; Entry 26). Plate 27 in Crunden's book shows a pair of houses, each three stories high and three openings wide, with one-story stable wings attached to each side. A double stringcourse separates the ground story from the middle story and, unusually, a cornice separates this story from the top story. The ground floor consists of an entrance area, parlor, library, and staircase; the drawing rooms are "on the chamber floor" (p. 12). Crunden's other design (Plate 28/29) consists of three attached houses fronted by a facade 11 openings wide. A double stringcourse separates the ground story from the two upper stories, and the top story is capped by a cornice, a parapet with urns, and—over the central five window openings—a pediment. On the ground floor of each house are an entrance passage, a library, and a parlor; in the center house are also a servants' hall and a clerk's office. In all three houses the drawing rooms are on the *piano nobile*. The two designs in *The Builder's Magazine* (Plates XX, CXVII, CXXI, CXXV, CXXIX, CXXXIII), each three openings wide and three stories high, have facades that are considerably more ornamented, with additional stringcourses between middle and upper stories, balconies in front of windows on the *piano nobile*, and semicircular relieving arches surrounding some of the window openings.

The detailed listing of rooms for each design in the *Builder's Magazine* is a useful source of information concerning the planning of late eighteenth-century town houses. In the first design the kitchen, pantry, housekeeper's room, and servants' room all are in the basement. On the ground floor are a porter's hall, library, and dining parlor. The drawing room and lady's dressing room are on the next floor, and above them are one bed chamber and another room that could serve either as a "common" dressing room or as a children's bedroom. The servants would be housed "in the roof," obtaining light from openings at gutter level that would be invisible from the street below. The second design, somewhat larger, includes a variety of vaults, offices, and service areas in the basement. On the ground floor are an entrance hall, porter's room (including his bed), circular grand staircase, dining and breakfasting parlor, and gentleman's dressing room or study. On the *piano nobile* are a drawing room in the front of the house, a withdrawing room at the rear, and a saloon in between. On the next floor are two suites each comprising a bedroom, a dressing room, and a wardrobe; the "best" suite is at the front of the house, facing the street. In the garret story are four bedrooms and two closets for female servants. To the rear on the ground level are stables and a coach house, above which is a laundry; on a third level are bedrooms for male servants.

Stephen Riou illustrated a much larger design for terrace housing in his *Grecian Orders of Architectvre* (1768; Entry 287). Along a contemplated new street from the Mansion House to Moorgate, he proposed a single four-story facade fronting 13 houses, each three or five windows wide. One-story Doric porticoes front the two end houses, a pediment caps the center three bays, and obelisks surmounted by orbs flank the entrances; otherwise the facade is ornamented with little more than stringcourses and entablatures.[127]

Robert and James Adam completed the second volume of their *Works in Architecture* (Entry 1) in 1779. They included floor plans and interior views of the Earl of Derby's house in Grosvenor Square, plus an elevation, plans, and details of Sir Watkin Williams Wynn's house in St. James's Square. The facade of the latter design, three stories high and three openings wide, is a very elegant elaboration of the Lindsey House theme. The rusticated ground story is pierced by semicircular openings for the entrance and two windows. Fluted Corinthian pilasters tie together the *piano nobile* and top story, above which are a full entablature and a balustraded parapet. The floor-length pedimented windows of the *piano nobile* are fronted by iron balconies and recessed within semicircular relieving arches. The ground floor plan includes a porter's hall and "Eating room" at the front, grand and back staircases, a music room, a library, a dressing room, a powder room, a paved court, and stables. On the *piano nobile* are two withdrawing rooms, an anteroom, a dressing room, a bedroom, a powder room, and service areas.

In 1780 James Lewis published an elevation of three terrace houses he had erected in Great Ormond Street in Book I of his *Original Designs in Architecture* (Entry 178). The houses, apparently identical in plan, are united behind a facade three stories high and nine openings wide. The center three bays of the facade closely resemble Adam's house for Sir Watkin Williams Wynn: Lewis added a pediment at the roofline, omitted pediments and relieving arches for the windows of the *piano nobile*, and made other minor changes. The left and right portions of the facade—also three stories high and three openings wide—are without pilasters and are topped by balustraded parapets. All nine floor-length windows of the *piano nobile* are fronted by iron balconies.

Later in the decade William Pain, a prolific author of handbooks and manuals, included several designs for row houses. The earliest is a design for a "Double town-house" that appeared in *The Builder's Golden Rule* (1781; Entry 237).[128] The facade, which is four stories high and six openings wide, follows the Lindsey House formula. The ground story, set on a plinth, is fronted by relieving arches surrounding window and door openings. Two-story Ionic pilasters tie the *piano nobile* and chamber story together, and also support a cornice above which the windows of the attic story are framed by relieving arches and pilasters. In plan the ground floor of each house includes an entrance passage, a staircase, and two rooms; the front room measures 22 feet by 18 feet, and the back room is 18 feet by 16 feet. *Pain's British Palladio* (1786; Entry 239) includes an elevation, sections, and plans of a three-story house, seven openings wide (Plates I–IV). Although unusually large for a row house, this design lacks openings in the side walls, suggesting they were meant to face walls of other row houses. The facade is modestly ornamented with a pediment at the top, a distyle portico in front of the entrance, and stringcourses between stories. The ground-floor plan includes a vestibule, dining room, withdrawing room, common sitting parlor, and breakfast room. There are five bedrooms on the chamber floor, six bedrooms in the attic, and offices in the basement. Toward the end of the decade Pain included more designs for detached three-story town houses, three or five openings wide, with few or no openings in the side walls, in his *Practical House Carpenter* (1788; Entry 241).[129]

The article on "Architecture" in William Henry Hall's *New Royal Encyclopaedia* ([1788–1791]; Entry 141) was expanded in later editions to include brief—but also rare—remarks on town houses. The discussion begins with the four "rates" of town houses established by the Building Act of 1774. The author urged architects to avoid being "fettered" by the restrictions of the Act, encouraging instead inventiveness in terrace house design. After briefly treating the difficulties of lighting staircases and fitting them into already crowded plans, he described the three "principal" rooms of a town house: the sitting room or library, the dining room, and the drawing room. In second- and third-rate houses, he noted, the dining and drawing rooms were usually on the *piano nobile*. In short remarks on finishings and ornaments, he briefly mentioned sideboards and cornices and in general advocated plainness and restraint. He prescribed proper dimensions for windows and discussed their role in the overall decoration of a room. Concerning the size and proportion of rooms, he recommended creating a spatial progression through the house, beginning with a small portico on the outside, moving to a larger waiting room within, and finally to a "climax" in the "great room." The article concludes with remarks on offices and exterior ornaments such as blind windows and doors, pilasters and columns, and arches and arched recesses.

In *Hints for Dwellings* (1800; Entry 170), David Laing briefly discussed principles of picturesque architectural composition, which he apparently attempted to apply in his accompanying project for six attached "Houses in a Row" (Plates 32–34). In plan the six dwellings consist of alternately advancing pavilions and narrower receding entrance bays. The facade correspondingly alternates in height between three stories and two. The elevation thus makes use of the "Variety of Contour" that Laing had recommended in villas (p. v) but curiously neglected to mention in discussing town houses (p. vii). There were several precedents for such picturesque variations of height in terrace houses: Michael Searles's Paragon at Blackheath (1793) for one, and earlier examples in the vicinity of Bristol.[130] Nevertheless Laing's was the first original design for such a project to be published. Thereafter original designs for similar projects still appeared only rarely. Sir John Sinclair depicted terrace houses being built in the New Town at Thurso in his *Sketch of the Improvements, Now Carrying On . . . in the County of Caithness* (1803; Entry 309). Each house consists of a two-story unit with parlor and bedrooms, plus a one-story kitchen and service wing. Richard Brown's *Principles of Practical Perspective* (1815; Entry 25) includes a design for a semicircular crescent of five three-story buildings connected by one-story colonnaded annexes. By contrast the design for a semicircular crescent in another perspective treatise, Peter Nicholson's *Treatise on Projection* (1837; Entry 230), is entirely uniform, fronted by a continuous three-story facade.

Authors of nineteenth-century builder's manuals often considered brickmaking, surveying, and the construction of party walls; in the process they occasionally offered designs for attached town houses. Thomas Downes Wilmot Dearn's *Bricklayer's Guide* (1809; Entry 58) includes elevations, sections, and plans of terrace houses four stories high and three openings wide. In the same year Richard Jones issued *Every Builder His Own Surveyor* (Entry 162), which includes a plan and elevation of a "Town House in the South of England," of similar proportions to Dearn's design, with a balcony fronting the principal floor windows. Four years later Thomas Humphreys provided a comparable design for a first-rate Irish town house in the frontispiece to his *Irish Builder's Guide* (1813; Entry 488). In 1823 Peter Nicholson gave detailed plans, sections, and elevations for first-, second-, third-, and fourth-rate houses in his *New Practical Builder* (Entry 225). The first-rate house is four stories high and three openings wide, with banded rustication on the ground story, relieving arches supported by pilasters framing the windows of the *piano nobile*, iron balconies in front of these windows, and decorative Greek ornament between the *piano nobile* and the next floor. The fourth-rate house is smaller but not inelegant: it is three stories high and two openings wide, with iron balconies in front of the windows of the *piano nobile* and decorative brickwork in the arches above all windows. Richard Elsam's *Practical Builder's Perpetual Price-Book* (1825; Entry 71), originally issued as part of Nicholson's *New Practical Builder*, includes several designs for terrace houses. One plate shows a terrace of three first-rate houses. Another plate depicts a terrace of four first-rate houses and two second-rate houses, with a facade that is alternately three and four stories high. One more plate depicts two terraces that had been executed in London—one consisting of third-rate houses, and another composed of third- and fourth-rate houses.

Designs for row and terrace houses appeared only rarely in publications of major architects during the 1820s and 1830s. The Adams' grand scheme for the Adelphi, begun in 1768, was included in the posthumous third volume of their *Works in Architecture* (1822; Entry 1.3). Sir John Soane illustrated his own residence in Lincoln's Inn Fields in *Designs for Public Improvements* (1828; Entries 316.2ff), and then described and illustrated it more fully in his *Description of the House and Museum* (1830; Entry 315). In *Designs for Public Improvements* Soane also included an elevation and two plans for Buckingham House, a major town house in Pall Mall, and also a taller, narrower "Town Mansion" in St. James's Square (Plate 40).

The first book devoted primarily to designs for row houses was James Collis's *Builders' Portfolio, of Street Architecture* (1837; Entry 41). The plates include elevations, plans, and sections of row houses in Greek Revival style, generally three stories high and two to four openings wide. Collis, like many of his contemporaries, had abandoned the neo-Palladian formula based on Lindsey House. In his third plate, for example, the ground floor and first floor are framed and tied together by two Ionic columns rising from tall pedestals and supporting a full entablature; above the entablature the top story is framed by short pilasters and capped by a shallow pediment.

In the early 1840s the few treatises containing designs for row and terrace houses largely concerned architectural practice or philanthropy, and often illustrated a variety of first- through fourth-rate designs. For example the first essay in Christopher Davy's *Architectural Precedents* (1840; Entry 56), a manual for architectural students, contains an elevation, plans, and sections of a three-story double town house. The exterior, decorated in Greek Revival style, is four openings wide and three stories high, with an attic story above the center two bays. The ground floor of each house contains a dining parlor and breakfast parlor, the drawing room is on the first floor, the second floor contains two bedrooms and a dressing room, and there are more bedrooms on the attic floor. The kitchen, back kitchen, and cellars are in the basement. A report to Parliament from the Select Committee on Buildings Regulation (1842; Entry 471) concerning proposed changes to the Building Act includes designs for first-, second-, third-, and fourth-rate row houses, plus designs illustrating methods of building terrace houses back to back. The first- through fourth-rate designs are considerably smaller than in previous decades. The first-rate houses, for example, are two stories high and two openings wide; the ground floor contains an entrance passage, a parlor in front, a sitting room in back, plus a kitchen, scullery, yard, privy, and midden to the rear. The fourth-rate houses are two stories high, and each facade has just one window on the upper floor, plus a door and window below. In the smallest fourth-rate designs the ground floor contains a front room, yard, and privy, while in the larger designs there is also a back kitchen.

Designs for model laborers' houses also appeared in two reports to Parliament from the Poor Law Commissioners, one concerning sanitary conditions in general and the other concerning England in particular (1842; Entries 472, 473). Most of the plates depict attached laborers' cottages, but there are also several illustrations of terrace housing for laborers. Both reports contain plans and an elevation of houses in Great Russell Street, Birmingham, which are three stories high and contain two rooms on each floor. Also in both reports there are elevations and a plan of two "courts of houses" in Bradford Street, Birmingham, most of which are three stories high and one room wide. In the report on England (Entry 473) there are more illustrations, depicting similar row houses—some slightly more spacious, some less so—in Tennant Street, Bromsgrove Street, Ann Street, and Pershore Street, Birmingham.

7 Economy, Philanthropy, Fitness, and Model Housing for Laborers

Agricultural and industrial progress in eighteenth- and nineteenth-century Britain often required sweeping relocation and rehousing of the laboring population. This involved removing and rebuilding entire villages, founding new towns, and providing extensive new accommodations in factory towns and cities.[131] Many architects sought to assist in these changes—and profit from them—by contributing improved, more efficient designs for housing laborers. In doing so they necessarily dealt with three fundamental, often inseparable problems that were of growing concern to all architects in this period: the need for economy in the plan and ornamentation of dwellings; the desire of landowners, entrepreneurs, and benevolent societies to provide increasingly humane and healthy accommodations for laborers; and the expectation that dwellings be fit to perform their functions.

●

THEORY AND DESIGN

British architects first paid serious attention to dwellings for farmers, other laborers, and servants toward the middle of the eighteenth century.[132] Those who published designs in the 1740s and 1750s expressed a concern for economy that was firmly rooted in Neoclassical aesthetics. Daniel Garret's *Designs, and Estimates, of Farm Houses* (1747; Entry 86) was the first British book of designs for farm dwellings. He stressed plainness, regularity, and rusticity in his designs, which he intended primarily for the northern counties of England. Over the next five years William Halfpenny issued three similar collections—*Twelve Beautiful Designs, Six New Designs* (together with *Thirteen New Designs*), and *Useful Architecture* (Entries 138, 137, 139)—that contain designs for farm structures specifically adapted to rural and remote areas of Britain. Like Garret, Halfpenny emphasized formal regularity, and stressed Neoclassical principles of "Symmetry and Harmony." Most of his designs are composed of crisp, regular forms, based on simple geometric figures such as squares, rectangles, and triangles. In order to maintain the "moderate expence" of his designs, he restricted exterior ornament to little more than stringcourses, pediments, and occasional piers and columns.

Most other mid- and late eighteenth-century architects, however, seldom mentioned economy or related ideas. Among the few who did was William Pain, a prolific author of builders' manuals. In *The Builder's Pocket-Treasure* (1763; Entry 238) he deplored excessive attention to "Elegance of Style," and instead recommended that artisans observe "Plainness and Perspicuity" in their work. James Peacock made economy an aesthetic virtue. In Οικιδια (1785; Entry 255), directed to "gentlemen of moderate fortunes," he provided plans for small houses that were designed with particular attention to economy and convenience. Throughout the book he stressed economy at the expense of style and show: "Men who are determined to keep their arms a kimbo, and would sooner lose the point of an elbow, than abate half an hair's breadth of their accustomed strut," he said, "should look into folio volumes" for suitable designs. Three years later Sir John Soane completed a folio volume titled *Plans Elevations and Sections of Bvildings Executed* (Entry 319), which shows implicit respect for some of Peacock's ideas.[133] In preparing many of his designs Soane strove "to unite convenience and comfort in the interior distributions, and simplicty and uniformity in the exterior." Exterior ornament is spare in most of his designs, and dwellings with considerable floor area are effectively disguised behind seemingly modest elevations, some as few as three openings wide.

•

The attention that Pain, Peacock, and Soane paid to economy generally reflected the recent progress of Neoclassical aesthetics in Britain. At about the same time agricultural reformers began to consider architectural economy from a different perspective. Instead of concerning themselves with aesthetic issues such as size, proportion, and ornament, they focused on the welfare of laborers who inhabited rural cottages. The reformers suggested that proper housing might improve the material and spiritual condition of rural laborers, and thereby increase their productivity. This in turn would contribute to the prosperity and philanthropic satisfaction of the estate owner.

The agricultural improver Nathaniel Kent was the first writer to address cottage design in detail from this economic and philanthropic perspective. His remarks appear in *Hints to Gentlemen of Landed Property* (1775; Entry 165), which is otherwise largely devoted to agricultural subjects such as husbandry, horticulture, and timber management. Kent's motives were partly humanitarian. He recommended, for example, that gentlemen of power and influence should "consider themselves as guardians of the poor, and attend to their accommodation." But he also recognized the economic importance of good housing for laborers: shabby, drafty, cramped quarters were destructive of "the most beneficial race of people we have." Material improvements in their living conditions, he said, would substantially increase agricultural productivity.

Kent noted that in preparing his designs he paid little attention to formal principles of architecture. Practicing architects could not disregard principles so readily, but several—including George Richardson, John Soane, and John Wood—did profess concern for laborers' welfare and for agricultural reform. In *New Designs in Architecture* (1792; Entry 284) Richardson presented several picturesque designs for ornamental cottages and farm houses. Describing these designs, he appealed implicitly to the humanitarianism of gentlemen who "take pleasure in building convenient dwellings for the families of their domestics or dependents." In *Sketches in Architecture* (1793; Entry 320) Soane published designs for a variety of elegant lodges and villas, and also cottages specifically "for the laborious and industrious part of the community." Of all eighteenth-century architects, Wood explored economic and humanitarian aspects of laborers' housing to the greatest degree. In 1781, the year of his death, he published a series of plates illustrating designs for laborers' cottages; in 1792 these were gathered in "a new edition," titled *A Series of Plans, for Cottages* (1792; Entry 352). Like Kent, Wood hoped to improve the national agricultural output by making laborers more productive. In addition he demonstrated an especially compassionate, human concern for laborers' comfort and welfare. Having visited actual cottages and interviewed their inhabitants, he was deeply disturbed: "the greatest part of the cottages that fell within my observation, I found to be shattered, dirty, inconvenient, miserable hovels, scarcely affording a shelter for the beasts of the forest; much less were they proper habitations for the human species." With such experiences in mind, and with special attention to ideals of economy, utility, and philanthropy, he formulated seven new principles for designing more healthful, practical, and humane cottages.[134] Wood then applied these principles in his own designs for cottages, creating dwellings composed of completely unornamented, regular forms, while emphasizing the relationships between geometric solids in a manner reminiscent of designs by Garret and Halfpenny. To enhance the utility of his designs, Wood included 11 pages of specifications for masons, ironmongers, and other artisans, plus general remarks on cottage construction.

Agricultural reform and human welfare were also paramount issues in publications issued by agricultural societies in the late eighteenth century.

In 1795 Thomas Davis published an important "Address to the Landholders of This Kingdom" in the *Letters and Papers* of the Bath and West of England Society (Entry 55). Appealing to the reader's compassion and concern for human decency, Davis proposed minimum standards for materials and circulation of air in cottages. He also included several exemplary designs for cottages, some of which already had been erected. These ranged from one very small and plain dwelling to others that were described as "Ornamental." The latter presumably were intended to suit landowners who were more concerned with the picturesque landscape than with its agricultural output, yet who still wished to provide decent housing for their tenants.

The society most actively concerned with rural improvement was the Board of Agriculture, founded in 1793 by Sir John Sinclair. Under his direction the Board issued a series of reports on the agricultural state of each county in England, Scotland, and Wales, first in a draft or preliminary edition, and then in revised form. Several reports include observations on local philanthropic improvements and accounts of exemplary houses erected for farmers and the laboring poor. One of the earliest reports, that for Berkshire (1794; Entry 97), includes illustrations of two cottages in Windsor Great Park, presented as examples of "what poor men of this description ought to have." In the report on the North Riding of Yorkshire (1800; Entry 123) John Tuke complained that the current manner of building cottages contributed to poor health. Citing the economic importance of laborers, he recommended increased attention to "convenience" in cottage design, and the location of cottages closer to one another so that residents could help each other in times of need. In the report on North Wales (1810; Entry 113) Walter Davies listed the consequences of poorly designed cottages: "filth, disease, and, frequently, premature death." Davies praised three groups of cottages recently erected in the region, and illustrated a set of designs for model cottages obtained from a local correspondent.[135] The Board also published a series of *Communications* on many aspects of agricultural improvement, which included several important articles on architecture. Five authors—Robert Beatson, A. Crocker and son, Mr. Crutchley, Henry Holland, and Rowland Hunt—contributed articles on farm houses and cottages to the first volume (1797).[136] Beatson in particular recommended economy and convenience in farm buildings: he found ornament "unnecessary" and argued that laborers' dwellings, if properly designed, should be conducive to prosperity and happiness.

Monographs published from the 1790s through the 1810s encouraged philanthropy and agricultural improvement through a variety of measures, including land reform and the rebuilding of laborers' dwellings. William Morton Pitt appealed directly to the compassion and philanthropy of his readers in *An Address to the Landed Interest* (1797; Entry 258): "It is to the gentlemen of landed property, that the whole body of agricultural Poor look for protection, as well as for employment." He proposed that uncultivated tracts of land be offered to laborers on long leases, so they could build cottages and establish large gardens for themselves. This would provide an incentive for laborers to produce more, Pitt said, and thus they could contribute more to their own support. He included five designs for plain, unembellished single and double cottages. In 1802 Sir John

Sinclair published *Hints Regarding Certain Measures Calculated to Improve an Extensive Property* (Entry 308), an account of improvements on his own 100,000-acre estates in Caithness. He described his diverse improvements, which encompassed agriculture, manufacturing, commerce, fishing, mining, roads, bridges, and harbors, as well as individual dwellings, villages, and towns. He suggested that the benefits resulting from all these improvements were closely interrelated, and argued specifically that architectural improvement of towns and villages would be an important catalyst to the economic improvement of an entire region.[137] In 1813 the philanthropist Thomas Netherton Parker produced a pamphlet titled *Plans, Specifications, Estimates, and Remarks on Cottages* (Entry 250). Like Kent and others, he argued that erecting "well arranged" houses for laborers would increase their efficiency, and thus contribute to long-term economic savings for the "proprietor." Parker provided illustrations of two unornamented model cottages designed by a local builder, plus additional information on materials and costs.[138]

In the early nineteenth century a new generation of young architects issued a host of books containing designs for picturesque rural cottages and villas.[139] Several of these books include designs for laborers' dwellings that, in addition to being picturesque, were meant to enhance the welfare and productivity of their inhabitants. William Barber's *Farm Buildings; or, Rural Economy* (1802; Entry 12) illuminated important parallels between ethics, economics, and aesthetics in cottages. The design of a dwelling, he implied, might well influence the morality and intellect of its inhabitants, while a "rude structure, . . . raised in opposition to reason, taste, rule, or arrangement," was "characteristic of dulness and slovenliness in its inhabitants."[140] Barber argued that peasants were not devoid of taste or intellect and therefore should be encouraged to build their own dwellings according to a "regular system of rural building" that he proposed. In *Hints for Picturesque Improvements in Ornamented Cottages* (1804; Entry 14) Edmund Bartell appealed to the landowner's self-esteem: the current manner of constructing laborers' cottages was "injurious to the health and morals of the inhabitants," and this reflected badly on the humanity of the landowner. After several pages devoted to agricultural economics, Bartell also suggested a more fashionable rationale for adopting his proposals: new cottages could improve the picturesqueness of an estate.[141] In *Architectural Designs for Rustic Cottages* (1807; Entry 262) William Fuller Pocock cited philanthropy and landscape embellishment in connection with one particular dwelling type, the rustic cottage. Not only would new cottages "serve the cause of humanity" while also forming "pleasing and characteristic objects in the landscape," he argued, but national prosperity actually depended on the well-being of the peasantry, and therefore on proper housing. Nearly a decade later Richard Elsam also drew a close parallel between philanthropy and aesthetics in cottage design. He observed in *Hints for Improving the Condition of the Peasantry* (1816; Entry 70) that artistic improvements to an estate, including its cottages and farm houses, would have "a tendency to improve the general morals, manners, and condition of the people" living there (p. 14). By providing suitable habitations for laborers, estate owners could help them raise their families according to "principles of morality, virtue, and religion." Such improvements in physical welfare, Elsam noted, were in fact necessary before any moral or intellectual improvement could be expected. Like Bartell, he also appealed to the estate owner's self-esteem: "wretched and dirty cottages," he said, suggest that "the proprietor has been ruined by his improvements, or is possessed of so much blindness, as neither to feel for himself or others."

•

Many of those concerned with designing economical and humane dwellings paid special attention to considerations of utility and fitness. By the middle of the eighteenth century aestheticians already had established the importance of utility and fitness to beauty in architecture. David Hume and Alexander Gerard, for example, found an appreciation of fitness essential to the aesthetic experience of a building.[142] Lord Kames divided all architectural beauty into just two types, "relative" and "intrinsic"; and he declared that the former, which was based on utility, was of "greater importance."[143] Nevertheless utility and fitness were seldom considered at length in British architectural literature before 1800. Indeed some architects were unwilling to sacrifice other aspects of beauty to considerations of fitness. Sir William Chambers, for instance, treated fitness only briefly and unsympathetically in his discussion of pediments: "Beauty and fitness," he wrote, "are qualities that have very little connection with each other: in architecture they are sometimes incompatible." Especially in the case of objects that were "merely ornamental," Chambers found it "unreasonable to sacrifice other qualities more efficacious, to fitness alone."[144]

Humphry Repton was the first British architect to discuss fitness at length and in a highly positive manner. In *Observations on the Theory and Practice of Landscape Gardening* (1803; Entry 279) Repton introduced two general principles of architectural and landscape composition that parallel Kames's "relative" and "intrinsic" beauties: Repton called them "relative fitness or utility" and "comparative proportion or scale." Fitness, he explained, involved comfort, convenience, and adaptation of a design to the needs of the inhabitant. It also was fundamental to his notion of "characteristic architecture," according to which buildings must be suited visually as well as functionally to the purposes for which they were intended.[145]

Three years later John Claudius Loudon, who differed with Repton on many aspects of landscape design, proved his disciple when it came to architectural theory. Loudon's *Treatise on Forming, Improving, and Managing Country Residences* (1806; Entry 191) echoed Repton in stating that "the use of cottages . . . is the chief source of their beauty" (p. 133). Turning to the design of country residences in general, Loudon identified three fundamental considerations: "*utility, convenience, and beauty.*" These differ little, of course, from principles expounded nearly two centuries earlier by Henry Wotton, "Commoditie, Firmenes, and Delight";[146] but Loudon again betrayed a debt to Repton by saying that attention to these principles would result in "unity of character." In a book review in the third volume of his *Gardener's Magazine* (1828; Entry 187) Loudon discussed utility and fitness more emphatically, arguing that they constituted "first beauty" of a building. He complained that contemporary architects too often focused only on "the accidental associations of classical, historical, and imitative beauty" (III, 76). Loudon's most extensive discussion of fitness, however, remains the Introduction to his *Encyclopaedia of Cottage, Farm, and Villa Architecture* (1833; Entry 184). There he discussed three major principles of architecture; the two most important involve fitness. First is "fitness for the end in view," the foremost principle because architecture is above all a "useful art." Second, "expression of the end in view" is the communication of the function that a building is fit to perform. Third, the "expression of some particular Architectural style" and "creating in the mind, emotions of sublimity or beauty" are desirable ends, but ones that Loudon described as only "temporary or accidental" and thus of limited worth. Loudon further emphasized the importance of fitness and expression of purpose later in the book, in discussing individual designs for cottages and villas.[147]

In 1834, one year after Loudon's *Encyclopaedia* appeared, John Billington revised his *Architectural Director* (Entry 18.3) and included a discussion of function that closely parallels Loudon's and Repton's. Use, he said, is a building's principal reason for existence, and thus a primary component of architectural character:

All edifices and buildings are destined for some use; and it is the apparent adaptation to this use, that constitutes their proper or relative character. . . . There is necessarily then, a rule of taste dictated by nature, which prescribes to each kind of edifice, the character that it ought to present, in correspondence to the use for which it is intended.

Even John Buonarotti Papworth, an enthusiastic advocate of picturesqueness in dwellings and in the surrounding landscape, subordinated considerations of style and pictorial composition to fitness. In *Rural Residences* (1818; Entry 246.2) he identified only two primary considerations in designing a house. Significantly, the first was "fitness for the purposes of the family," which included provision for "the requisites of social life" (p. 61); the second was expression—of "external claims to respectability," and of related ideas such as "cheerfulness, comfort, and . . . elegance."

•

Throughout the early nineteenth century other architects were less sanguine on the subjects of economy, philanthropy, and fitness. These considerations threatened ideals of picturesque beauty, which many architects of this period felt to be paramount. In *Architectural Designs for Rustic Cottages* (1807; Entry 262), for example, William Fuller Pocock complained that architects paid too much attention to the utility of dwellings, and too little attention to beauty. But he also eschewed "giving reins to the imagination," which might result in designs that would be difficult to execute; in effect, he advocated a middle road between considerations of utility and beauty.

Peter Frederick Robinson argued more forcibly in favor of the picturesque. In *Rural Architecture* (1823; Entry 296) he lamented that uninspired, unsophisticated, but utilitarian cottages did not accord with the English countryside. He suggested that such cottages in fact disfigured the picturesque environment, and that truly "scenic" dwellings might be built at no additional cost. And he foresaw a further benefit of erecting picturesque designs such as he proposed: because the landlord would find them more attractive, he would become more willing to visit and take an interest in the welfare of his tenants. In *Village Architecture* (1830; Entry 297) Robinson again attempted to enlist philanthropy in the pursuit of picturesque improvement. He proposed that residents be given "some interest" in their dwellings, thus providing an incentive for aesthetic self-improvement that ultimately would result in a more picturesque village. But twelve years later T. J. Ricauti found little to praise in recent philanthropic work. In *Sketches for Rustic Work* (1842; Entry 282) he described a "professional excursion" through England, during which he was distressed by recently erected buildings that were "anything but compatible with the surrounding scenery." He then illustrated several of his own designs for lodges and cottages that, by contrast, are among the most rustic and picturesque published by any architect in the nineteenth century.

Nevertheless dislocations resulting from enclosure and industrial development continued to elicit new designs for plain, practical laborers' dwellings. In 1820 James Loch published a detailed description of efforts to improve economic conditions on the Sutherland estates, which had involved the dislocation of many people. His report (Entry 180), which also served as an apologia for many of his harsh measures, includes dozens of designs for very plain farm buildings that had been erected as parts of various improvement schemes. Alternatively John Hall, Secretary to the Society for Improving the Condition of the Labouring Classes, hoped to further the cause of "true independence" for laborers by publishing designs for utilitarian structures in *Novel Designs for Cottages and Schools* (1825; Entry 140). These, he explained, would be conducive to physical health, cleanliness, "Delicacy," and "Industrious Morality." A similar concern for laborers' economic independence underlay the introduction of a new periodical in 1831, *Facts and Illustrations Demonstrating the Important Benefits Which Have Been . . . Derived by Labourers from Possessing Small Portions of Land* (Entry 79). The first volume includes designs for five model cottages and a plan for a community of ten laboring families. Meanwhile in *Designs for Agricultural Buildings* (1827; Entry 337) Charles Waistell exhorted landowners to give up the pursuit of fashion for a more realistic appreciation of the economic value of farm laborers. Condemning the practice of erecting picturesque buildings "merely as objects to look at," he recommended that landowners instead promote "the health and comfort of those by whom they are benefitted, and by whose labour and industry they enjoy all the necessaries and all the superfluities." Waistell submitted that doing so would "give more true pleasure to the humane heart of the builder or beholder . . . than can be given by the most magnificent structure devoid of use."

As the economic and social pressures of Britain's growing cities continued to exact a toll on the lower classes, utopian socialists and economic reformers began to propose alternative forms of social organization.[148] One of the most important proposals was Robert Owen's *Report to the Committee of the Association for the Relief of the Manufacturing and Labouring Poor*,[149] in which he proposed to establish "Agricultural and Manufacturing Villages of *Unity* and *Mutual Co-operation*." Each of these communitarian villages would accommodate about 1,200 residents in long terraces of "lodging-houses" ranged on four sides of a square, in the center of which were buildings for cooking, eating, infant care, lectures, and worship. Owen proposed to house individual families—a man, his wife, and two infant childrn—in single "lodging-rooms"; children over three years old would be housed in a common children's dormitory. This arrangement, he felt, would provide the inhabitants "more comforts than the dwellings of the poor usually afford."

Reformer and philanthropist William Allen, who had purchased an interest in Owen's mills at New Lanark in 1814, began plans for his own "colony" of agricultural laborers at Lindfield, Sussex, in 1823. Encouraged by his success there, Allen published *Colonies at Home* (1826; Entry 6), through which he hoped to "wean the Poor from a dependence upon the Parish" and to raise in them "a moral and independent feeling" that would make them self-reliant. He suggested the creation of "Benevolent Societies" to oversee an innovative process of land reform: individual families would be given small plots of land, along with instruction in cultivation, as an inducement to become increasingly productive and self-sufficient. The greatest portion of Allen's pamphlet is devoted to remarks on agriculture, but he also included designs for a model cottage and a plan for an entire village of 24 cottages.

Three more communitarian proposals, all issued in 1830, reflect the continuing need for economic relief and social change, and the continuing influence of Owen's program for reform. Thomas Stedman Whitwell's proposal (*Description of an Architectural Model*, Entry 345) includes a design prepared for Robert Owen's recently founded community in New Harmony, Indiana. Continuous three-story terraces form a large quadrangle, 1000 feet on a side. The top floor contains dormitory accommodations for unmarried persons and children, while below there are individual apartments—sitting room, chamber, and water closet—for married couples. Within the quadrangle are separate buildings for cooking, eating, schooling, and other community activities. John Minter Morgan's *Letter to the Bishop of London* included a similar, but unillustrated, proposal for communities of the "labouring classes." Each community would consist of four equal ranges of workers' "apartments" surrounding a large square. Minter Morgan specified that his communities should be erected within two miles of London, to allow the residents to commute daily for employment.[150] Another social reformer, William Thompson, created a design for a continuous three-story building, 1305 feet on a side, that would surround an open square. As described in his *Practical Directions for the Speedy and Economical Establishment of Communities, on the Principles of Mutual Co-operation* (Entry 332), the community would have 2,000 residents. Children would be housed together in the attic story, and adults would be accommodated in a series of single "sleeping rooms" and single or double "sitting rooms." Unlike Minter Morgan, Thompson was concerned that the community be self-sufficient. He proposed an economic system of "Co-operative Industry" that would assure a continuing market for goods produced by workers who joined together in "voluntary union."

Later in the 1830s improvers and philanthropists provided fewer proposals for entire communities, and instead published more designs for model cottages and farm houses that individual laborers could erect on their own. Perhaps Loudon set the keynote in his *Encyclopaedia* (1833; Entry 184), the "main object" of which was "to improve the dwellings of the great mass of society." Loudon deliberately omitted any methodical instruction in the theory and principles of architecture, and organized the book instead as a series of individual designs, each accompanied by commentary and specifications. This, he said, would insure that his book would be "of more immediate practical utility to persons intending to build or furnish." Two years later William Wilds offered *Elementary and Practical Instructions on the Art of Building Cottages and Houses for the Humbler Classes* (Entry 347), a manual prepared primarily for emigrant laborers and also addressed to those who wanted "to extricate themselves" from England but could not do so. It includes detailed information on building construction, horticulture, and husbandry. Shortly afterward two more collections of model designs for cottages and farm houses were published in Ireland: William Deane Butler's *Model Farm-Houses and Cottages for Ireland* (1837; Entry 31) and Arthur Creagh Taylor's *Designs for Agricultural Buildings* (1841; Entry 328).

Throughout the 1830s the Highland and Agricultural Society of Scotland was particularly active in soliciting designs for model cottages and in encouraging their erection. In 1833 the Society held a competition for essays on "the Construction and Disposition of Dwellings for the Labouring Classes." The first-place winner, George Smith, published his *Essay on the Construction of Cottages* (Entry 310) the next year. Like many of his predecessors, he complained that too many architects considered only "picturesque effect" in designing dwellings and ignored fitness and utility. He stated that his designs, in contrast, would embody "economy and domestic convenience," thus contributing to a general improvement in laborers' physical and moral habits In 1839 the Society adopted a more direct method of encouraging rural improvement, described in "Remarks on Cottage Premiums" (Entry 147): a program of cash awards for the best-kept cottages and cottage gardens, currently available only in certain Scottish parishes, would be expanded throughout Scotland. The Society thus hoped to encourage cottagers to improve their dwellings on their own initiative, with only a small capital outlay on the part of the Society. About 1842 James Cunningham delivered an address to the Society, soon published as *Designs for Farm Cottages and Steadings* (Entry 51), in which he condemned the practice of building cottages only for picturesque effect. Instead, he argued, the "strictly useful must take precedence of the ornamental." He also discussed the connection between dilapidated dwellings and immorality: they were, he said, a major source of "grossness" and "indelicacy." Thus before one could expect to see laborers become "chaste, pure, or elevated in morals, we must provide them with houses in which propriety and common decency may be observed."[151] And further, perhaps in an appeal to landowners' distaste for poor relief, Cunningham also suggested a causal relationship between bad housing and pauperism: "The better the class of cottages designed for the labouring population, the higher will be the class of persons who will occupy them, and the less likely to contain among them the seeds of pauperism." Thus following in the steps of Wood, Owen, and many others, Cunningham in effect transformed Garret's earlier attention to plainness and economy into a more general concern for the welfare of rural laborers and the overall moral and economic health of British society.

8
Style

The history of British architecture in the eighteenth and nineteenth centuries can be written, and often is, as a chronicle of changes in style. There were revivals of many historical styles—Palladian, Chinese, Gothic, Greek, Egyptian, Tudor, and others—as well as broader changes in style that resulted from the introduction of Neoclassical and picturesque aesthetics. Some styles were favored because they produced visual harmony or delight; others were adopted to express political programs, personal allegiances, aspects of personal character, and other ideas. Lengthy studies have been devoted to many of the styles that flourished in the eighteenth and nineteenth centuries, and duplication of these efforts would be inappropriate here.[152] Instead I will examine architects' published remarks concerning style, focusing especially on their reasons for adopting a given style or range of styles. Because not all styles are treated equally—or even at all—in the literature under consideration, the remarks below are necessarily an incomplete account of style in British architecture; they do, however, address important applications, innovations, and problems of style in domestic architecture.

After a brief review of factors contributing to the Palladian Revival, I will discuss the eighteenth-century revival of Gothic, Chinese, and Greek styles in connection with the prevailing Neoclassical, Rococo, and picturesque tastes. Next I will consider the opinions of some architects who argued that style should be subordinated to considerations of function. Finally, I will treat four revival styles that were of special interest to nineteenth-century architects, and which have not been chronicled at length elsewhere: Indian, round-arched "Norman" or Romanesque, Italian vernacular, and "Old English" (which includes half-timbered, Tudor, and Elizabethan styles). In applying these styles to dwellings and in discussing their reasons for doing so, British architects clearly revealed important ideas concerning the nature and purpose of style in architecture.

•

In *Vitruvius Britannicus* (1715; Entry 32) Colen Campbell established the principal direction in which British architectural style would develop during the next half century. He proposed to surpass the prevailing Baroque style by adopting a more chaste and rational "British" style, based on precedents established by Vitruvius, Palladio, and Inigo Jones. He also flattered himself and his audience by suggesting that British architecture might soon equal or surpass the work of his Classical and Palladian predecessors. Campbell's hopes and his reliance on Palladian sources were echoed in following decades by the authors of numerous builders' manuals and by major architects such as William Kent, John Vardy, and Sir William Chambers. The specific contributions of these writers have been discussed at length in Section 1 above.

The Gothic Revival was the first major stylistic departure from the orthodox neo-Palladianism of Campbell and his followers, but the earliest proponents of Gothic were hardly eager to challenge the authority of Palladian and Neoclassical theory. Indeed they had to overcome the strictures of theorists such as Robert Morris, who in his *Lectures on Architecture* (1734; Entry 215) severely criticized the lack of symmetry and proportion in Westminster Abbey and other Gothic cathedrals. Whatever proportionality one might find there, he said, was due only to "blind Chance." In his opinion Gothic architecture was no different from the Goths and Vandals themselves, "having in their Aspect and Deportment, a Rusticity and Wildness not to be imitated." He even suggested it had become "a Proverb amongst Men, to term every thing Gothick which was irregular, disproportioned, or deform'd" (I, 48–49).

In 1742 Batty and Thomas Langley issued the first collection of original Gothic designs published in England, ostensibly based on their own research at Westminster Abbey, and titled *Ancient Architecture* (Entry 172). Their unique designs for five Gothic "orders" show traditional Gothic elements arranged according to Palladian canons of order and proportionality. Yet while the regularity of these designs, and even the title of the book, may have suggested to some a deference to the authority of Classical architecture, the Langleys had a different message in mind. With their Gothic designs they recalled a different "Ancient" era, the period before the Conquest when political freedoms were thought to have been among the greatest in English history. Indeed by depicting a style of architecture thus associated with "Saxon" times, a period of "true" British liberty, the Langleys clearly addressed a circle of potential Whig clients who were increasingly concerned about the erosion of British liberties under recent monarchs.[153]

In subsequent decades, designs in Gothic style were less frequently tied to such historical and political circumstances, while retaining an appearance of Palladian order and regularity. In *Rural Architecture in the Gothick Taste* (1752; Entry 136), for example, William and John Halfpenny provided designs for a variety of garden seats and temples, largely based on geometric figures. Nevertheless these fundamentally regular designs also possess a veneer of exuberant ornament, which served to please the growing anti-Palladian, Rococo taste for irregularity and asymmetry.

As the taste for rococo Gothic architecture expanded in the 1750s, architects and designers also strove to accommodate the fashion for florid, ornate, and exotic forms by providing designs in rococo Chinese style.[154] William and John Halfpenny's series of *New Designs* (1750–1752; Entry 134) was the first collection of original Chinese architectural designs published in Britain. Like many of the Halfpennys' Gothic designs, the Chinese subjects exhibit a rigid symmetry in elevation and geometric proportionality in plan. William Halfpenny made the debt to Palladian aesthetics explicit in the preface, where he invoked principles of "graceful Symmetry" and "exact Proportion." In 1752 the Halfpennys also published *Chinese and Gothic Architecture Properly Ornamented* (Entry 130), containing 12 Chinese and eight Gothic designs for dwellings. The primary visual attraction of the designs is their Rococo ornament, applied with little regard for the structural or stylistic integrity of the whole. There are few remarks in the letterpress concerning principles of composition. The authors recommended "Gracefulness and true Symmetry" but also tried to defend the wild proliferation of ornament, often applied without visible structural support, through a vague appeal to "Invention and Variety of Construction." Two years later Edwards and Darly issued their *New Book of Chinese Designs* (Entry 66), containing the most elaborate, least structurally viable Chinese designs in any English treatise. Here the walls and columnar supports ignore Palladian principles of geometry and symmetry, and instead are overwhelmed by robust Rococo ornament. Meanwhile the Palladian theorist Robert Morris noted with contempt the rising fashion for Chinese style—with all its excesses and excrescences—commenting sardonically that Chinese design was "meer Whim and Chimera, without Rules or Order," and needed "no Fertility of Genius to put in Execution."[155]

Several years later Sir William Chambers published *Designs of Chinese Buildings* (1757; Entry 38), based on his recent travels to China. Whether because of his own predisposition toward Neoclassicism or because his designs were based on actual Chinese models, his designs are far less florid than those of his contemporaries. Nevertheless he discussed the principles of Chinese design wholly in European terms. He found a close affinity between Chinese architecture and that of "the antients," and observed that Chinese buildings have "a justness in their proportion, a simplicity, and sometimes even beauty, in their form." He admitted that the exuberance of Chinese ornament would not suit most European building types but, echoing the Halfpennys' defense of Chinese, he argued that the variety and novelty of Chinese design might be allowed to "take the place of beauty" in parks and gardens.

By 1759 the heyday of Chinese had nearly passed. That year Paul Decker completed the last British volume devoted entirely to Chinese designs, his *Chinese Architecture* (1759; Entry 62). His designs were essentially Palladian in form, overspread with a veneer of Chinese ornament. One year later six plates containing Chinese designs were added to a new and posthumous edition of Edward Hoppus's *Gentleman's and Builder's Repository* (1760; Entry 151.4). Thereafter designs for Chinese structures appeared almost exclusively in encyclopedia articles and in eclectic compendia of designs in many different styles.[156]

As the fashion for Chinese architecture waned, interest in Gothic continued to be fueled by archaeological research and an ongoing desire to exploit the heritage associated with styles indigenous to Britain.[157] Novelists and poets began to capitalize on the connections between Gothic architecture and an era firmly associated with such diverse ideas as liberty, chivalry, mystery, and darkness.[158] Practicing architects frequently adopted Gothic forms for a variety of expressive purposes—to evoke a mood of gloom and doom, for example, or to recall the heritage of a particular family.[159] Nevertheless throughout the last half of the eighteenth century, designs for Gothic dwellings appeared infrequently in British architectural books. Paul Decker's *Gothic Architecture* (1759; Entry 63) was one of the few books containing a substantial number of designs in that style. Issued as a pendant to his volume of Chinese designs, the book contains a comparable array of symmetrical, geometric structures overlaid with rococo Gothic ornament. Interestingly, Decker alluded to primitive, even primordial, aspects of Gothic by including several designs for "Rude" or "Rustic" structures, composed of tree trunks, branches, roots, and stones.

Three years later Timothy Lightoler included five designs with Gothic and Castellated ornament in his *Gentleman and Farmer's Architect* (Entry 179). In Thomas Collins Overton's *Original Designs of Temples* (1766; Entry 234) several Gothic designs are covered with a profusion of crockets, finials, ogee arches, cinquefoil arches, and clustered columns. He also included three designs for "villas," important early examples of the Castellated style, with crenellations, finials, turrets, ogee domes, rusticated window openings, and trefoil or round-headed arches.[160] John Crunden illustrated two Gothic designs for dwellings in *Convenient and Ornamental Architecture* (1767; Entry 49), along with a country house and country inn that are crowned by battlements. Among the rustic garden structures in William Wrighte's *Grotesque Architecture* (1767; Entry 358) there is one "Gothic" grotto, but like many of the other buildings it is composed of flints, irregular stones, and small pebbles, expressing a primitive or "rustic" character more than a sophisticated rendition of medieval Gothic. The designs for Gothic garden temples in N. Wallis's *Carpenter's Treasure* (1773; Entry 338) are not much advanced beyond those published by the Halfpennys two decades earlier: rich Rococo ornament overlays a fundamentally symmetrical and regular structure.

In *The Builder's Magazine* (1774; Entry 26) John Carter, a Gothic antiquarian and restorer of Gothic buildings, briefly suggested reasons for the comparative paucity of designs for Gothic dwellings. Gothic, he implied, was too "awful"—in other words, too affective, and thus unsuited to the decorous calm and repose required in a dwelling:

I must confess myself a zealous admirer of Gothic architecture—affirming with confidence, nothing can be more in character, and better adapted to a place of worship, than that awful style of building, and that Grecian and Roman architecture should be confined to mansions and other structures of ease and pleasure.

Sir William Chambers ignored the expressive potential of Gothic and instead focused on its structural characteristics.[161] In the third edition of his *Treatise* (1791; Entry 40.3) he stated that "the antique" was the "model" on which taste should be formed; but throughout history architects had been unable to realize the full potential of architecture, due partly to the lack of suitable construction techniques. "Gothick architects," however, had introduced "considerable improvements in construction," achieving "a lightness in their works, an art and boldness of execution." Accordingly he encouraged modern architects to investigate structural qualities of Gothic as a means of furthering the progress of modern architecture.

Toward the end of the century Chambers's younger contemporaries became interested in medieval styles for another reason—their picturesqueness. In *Sketches and Hints on Landscape Gardening* (1794; Entry 280) Humphry Repton discussed Gothic in terms of its visual character, stressing its predominantly vertical lines and the manner in which they could produce an effective contrast with deciduous trees and gently undulating landscapes. That same year Robert Morison issued *Designs in Perspective for Villas* (Entry 211), in which he discussed the "rude magnificence" of the "castle style," and the bold, mountainous scenery to which it was suited. Greek style, by contrast, was "dedicated to simplicity" and would, according to Morison, be suited to a plainer and flatter landscape. Emphasizing the need for architectural style to suit the landscape in a picturesque manner, he presented each of three villa designs with a choice of Greek and Castellated elevations, and depicted each separately in an appropriate landscape setting.[162]

Concurrently with the early Gothic Revival, architects and archaeologists had begun to document ever more remote remains of Classical antiquity, from Split and Baalbek to Athens itself. In the 1750s and 1760s detailed accounts of these and other sites were issued by Robert Adam, John Berkenhout, Richard Dalton, Thomas Major, James Stuart, Nicholas Revett, Robert Wood, and others. The information that they published concerning the orders, building types, and ornament often conflicted with previous accounts, from Vitruvius's *De architectura* onward.[163] Since the archaeological accounts showed Greek architecture to be unexpectedly primitive, some architects began to reject Greek architecture out of hand as the creation of a culture less sophisticated than that of ancient Rome.[164] Others saw the growing diversity of Antique examples, all equally authoritative, as proof that no single standard prevailed in Classical times—and that none should prevail in modern times as well. Thus Robert and James Adam noted in the first number of their *Works* (1773; Entry 1) that they had "not trod in the path of others, nor derived aid from their labours." By arguing that architecture was subject to no universal standard, they could emphasize proudly the "novelty and variety" of their own designs.[165] Still other architects considered the examples illustrated by Stuart and Revett—the first accurate delineations of Athenian remains ever published—to be free of the corruptions of ancient Rome and therefore more worthy of study and imitation. In *The Grecian Orders of Architecture* (1768; Entry 287) Stephen Riou praised Stuart for "rescuing" knowledge of Greek architecture from "oblivion." On the basis of Stuart's "authentic records and perfect models," Riou then proposed to make an authoritative "modulary division" of the three Greek orders for application to modern "practical uses."

Early in the nineteenth century the authority of Greece so outweighed that of Rome that William Wilkins felt obliged to help restore the reputation of Vitruvius. In *The Civil Architecture of Vitruvius* (1812; Entry 348) he argued that Vitruvius's account had been corrupted by editors and translators who had mistakenly looked for "illustrations of their author amongst the edifices of Rome." According to Wilkins, Vitruvius actually had derived his knowledge of architecture directly from the architectural monuments of Greece. Likewise in 1825 Joseph Gwilt, editor of a posthumous edition of Chambers's *Treatise* (1825; Entry 40.4), declared that "true architecture was reared" in Greece and had received all its "elementary beauties" there. Thus he found it necessary to add a supplementary essay on the "Elements of Beauty in Grecian Architecture" to redress Chambers's bias toward Rome.

But while these architects discussed the primacy and authority of Greek examples, most who published original designs for dwellings simply focused on the visual characteristics of Greek design. As in his formal analysis of Gothic, Humphry Repton again set the keynote. In *Sketches and Hints on Landscape Gardening* (1794; Entry 280) he discussed the essential horizontality of Greek architecture and its "affinity" for surrounding landscape scenery of a vertical character, particularly evergreens. The same year in *Designs in Perspective for Villas* (Entry 211) Robert Morison described the forms of Greek architecture as an historical, evolutionary response to an increasingly picturesque environment:

when cultivation had changed the rude neglected plain into a verdant lawn, . . . the mild beauty of the scene . . . [required] a more refined species of architecture . . . to suit the genius of the place, and the delicacy of the Grecian orders was called in to embellish and complete the picture.

•

Clearly by the 1790s picturesqueness had become a fundamental concern of British architects.[166] Already in 1773 Robert and James Adam, writing in the first number of their *Works in Architecture* (Entry 1), recognized the importance of picturesque advance and recession in designing a dwelling:

Movement is meant to express, the rise and fall, the advance and recess, with other diversity of form, in the different parts of a building, so as to add greatly to the picturesque of the composition. [Movement thus] . . . creates a variety of light and shade, which gives great spirit, beauty and effect to the composition.

Nearly two decades later George Richardson echoed these remarks in his *New Designs in Architecture* (1792; Entry 284). He proposed that the principal parts of a dwelling should "advance and recede," thus creating a "diversified contour" and a "variety of light and shade." Such "movement," he said, would enhance the picturesque appearance of a building.

As I have shown above, Humphry Repton analyzed Gothic and Greek styles principally in terms of picturesque "vertical" and "horizontal" characters, which ideally would complement opposite characters in the surrounding landscape. His greater purpose was to achieve an integration of architecture with its environment through visual means—in other words to extend the Adams' and Richardson's "movement" beyond the dwelling itself and into the surrounding landscape. Richard Payne Knight analyzed the picturesque less in terms of buildings and landscape, and more as a matter of aesthetic perception. In *The Landscape* (1794; Entry 169) he considered not only visual characteristics of picturesque objects, but also the physiological process of apprehending those features through vision. The picturesque, he concluded, involved rough and irregular objects producing a "grateful irritation" of the eye—so mildly irritating that it avoided discomfort, but strong enough to maintain interest and produce "the sensation of what we call . . . *picturesque beauty.*"[167]

At the very end of the century two authors, John Thomas Smith and James Malton, examined the architecture of traditional British cottages in search of further insights into the picturesque. Smith, who addressed his *Remarks on Rural Scenery* (1797; Entry 312) to artists, lamented that of all picturesque objects the cottage had received so little attention. Hoping to encourage greater awareness of the picturesque, he identified a variety of features typically found in cottages that would offer great "allurements to the painter's eye"; he also provided 20 plates showing examples of cottages made of thatch, decaying planks, crumbling plaster, uneven tiles, and other such materials.[168] One year later, in *An Essay on British Cottage Architecture* (Entry 197), Malton analyzed in more detail the characteristic forms and principles of picturesque design in traditional British cottages. He strongly recommended that architects incorporate a variety of picturesque features and techniques in their designs for cottages, including porches, thatch roofs, irregular "breaks" in wall planes, uneven heights, walls made partly of brick and partly of boards, and casement windows. He also urged builders of cottages never to "*aim* at regularity" but instead to let the shape of the building "conform only to the internal conveniency"; this would insure picturesque irregularity.

During the next decade architects debated the aesthetic value of irregular design. Malton himself was among the first to suggest limits to its application. In his *Collection of Designs for Rural Retreats, as Villas* (1802; Entry 196) nearly half the villas—a more formal type of dwelling than cottages—are regular, symmetrical, and composed in Neoclassical style. The next year Richard Elsam devoted much of his *Essay on Rural Architecture* (Entry 69) to a refutation of Malton's earlier arguments in favor of irregularity. Works of nature, Elsam wrote, exhibit symmetry; to depart from that symmetry would disturb the mind of the viewer. Likewise in architecture, he reasoned, asymmetry and irregularity would only suggest ideas of poverty, the "grotesque," or worse. William Atkinson, by contrast, appeared to support irregularity. In *Views of Picturesque Cottages* (1805; entry 10) he stated that functional considerations often were "superior to design" in producing "true characteristic simplicity." He thus suggested that function could dictate irregular forms for cottages, as long as those forms provided convenience. Also in 1805 Robert Lugar included a 16-page discussion of "Style and Character" in his *Architectural Sketches* (Entry 192), extolling the convenience and beauty of cubic forms, but conceding the attractions of a painterly approach to cottage design. "The broken line," he wrote, "must be considered peculiarly in character for a picturesque Cottage," where irregularities of light and shadow produce "those pleasing varieties which constitute the picturesque in building." In *A Series of Designs* (1808; Entry 30) Charles Augustus Busby contradicted not only Malton, Atkinson, and Lugar, but also Repton and Knight: he admitted the beauty of picturesque natural scenery but denied a role for the picturesque in architecture. Rural buildings should not be composed of "irregular masses, and assemblages of light and shade," he said. Instead, a building "forms only a *component* part of the scenery; and . . . all the beautiful effects of light and shade, of colour and outline, are produced by the contrast of the regularity of the building with the picturesque variety of nature."[169]

•

As Gothic, Greek, and picturesque styles became the subject of increasing discussion toward the end of the eighteenth century, some authors questioned the need for style in domestic design, while others argued the merits of one style versus another. James Peacock's stated goal in Οικιδια (1785; Entry 255), for example, was to provide economical and convenient designs for modest dwellings. Thus he concentrated on designing plans, arguing that elevations could "be supplied by the builder in any style of simplicity or decoration he may affect." Style was, by implication, hardly more than a matter of affectation, and of incidental importance.

Humphry Repton, like Peacock, had insisted on the importance of fitness and utility in dwellings. Following his remarks on the visual characteristics of Greek and Gothic styles in *Sketches and Hints on Landscape Gardening* (1794; Entry 280), he discussed several aspects of style at greater length in *Observations on the Theory and Practice of Landscape Gardening* (1803; Entry 279). Well in advance of major attempts to analyze Gothic styles according to historical periods,[170] Repton offered his own tripartite classification of Gothic according to function. "Castle Gothic," he said, with its small windows and large expanses of wall, was appropriate for defense, but because of its gloomy interiors was ill suited to habitation. The "Church Gothic" let in too much light through large windows; furthermore, it could not be used in dwellings because it looked too much like a church. The "House Gothic," however, perfectly suited "the purposes of modern life." Dating from Elizabethan times, this style included "fragments of Grecian architecture" in its ornament, and was "wonderfully picturesque" because of the play of light and shadow across its surfaces. Discussing the associations of the "House Gothic" style, Repton found that it would "imply that the owner is not only the lord of the surrounding country, but of the town also." Greek architecture, by comparison, would imply "the want of landed property" because it could have been erected only quite recently. Five years later in *Designs for the Pavillon at Brighton* (1808; Entry 276) Repton included a 19-page essay on style in domestic architecture. He found all three types of Gothic unsuitable for modern dwellings; even "Queen Elisabeth's Gothic" would be inappropriate, since an historical style would appear incongruous in a modern building. As for Greek style, Repton doubted whether modern household functions could be accommodated within the Greek temple form, or whether any suitable new combination of Greek forms could be devised. Accordingly he recommended "a new style, which is strictly of no character." Buildings in this style would consist of a plain rectilinear shell, designed primarily to be functional.[171] Ornament could be attached to this shell to suit any expressive needs: addition of a "Grecian Cornice" would make it superficially a "Grecian Building" and crenellations would make it "Gothic." As Peacock had suggested earlier and Loudon would argue later, dwellings ought to be conceived primarily in terms of function; style, being of secondary importance, could be added later at the discretion of the architect or client.[172]

In 1806 John Claudius Loudon completed his first book concerning architecture, *A Treatise on Forming, Improving, and Managing Country Residences* (Entry 191). Declaring that "use" was the chief source of beauty in small dwellings such as cottages, he argued that exterior elevations should be composed entirely with an eye to utility (I, 133). Far from advocating Greek, Gothic, or any other established style, Loudon simply recommended whitewash, a small garden, and a "seat" near the front door (I, 134). He extended his animadversions on style in his magnum opus, the *Encyclopaedia of Cottage, Farm, and Villa Architecture* (1833;

Entry 184). Discussing general principles applicable to all dwelling types, he identified "expression of some particular architectural style" as of only "temporary and accidental" interest. The actual differences among Castellated, Greek, and Gothic styles existed "much more in men's minds, and in the historical associations connected with them, than in the abstract forms belonging to them." Thus Loudon conceded that style could, when applied to the facade of a house, make it aesthetically expressive—but he also insisted that style was not of such fundamental importance as many of his contemporaries had argued. Perhaps Loudon's attitude toward style is best shown in a series of improvements he proposed for "A Dwelling for a Man and his Wife, without Children." Beginning with a plain, undecorated one-story dwelling, he proposed a series of possible improvements. The first was functional: he added another story for extra room and comfort. Having thus satisfied utilitarian concerns, he next showed how the cottage would look with five different styles applied to the exterior. The mechanical and offhand manner in which he applied these styles, with hardly a comment on their expressive potential, clearly reflects his indifference to the entire matter of style.

One year later George Smith plainly demonstrated the lack of interest in problems of style among architects concerned with housing Britain's growing population of laborers. In his *Essay on the Construction of Cottages* (1834; Entry 310) he argued that comfort, utility, and fitness should be the architect's principal objectives, and condemned contemporary designs in which "picturesque effect" had been the architect's principal goal. He noted that historical styles had evolved in response to the needs of their own times, and recommended that "science" now be given a greater role in the design of dwellings that would suit the needs of the nineteenth century.

•

In my discussion of imagination, expression, and affectivity (Sections 2 and 3 above), I showed that during the eighteenth century dwellings frequently were conceived as instruments of personal expression. As the Enlightenment cult of individuality encouraged ever broader psychological diversification, architectural style in particular became a convenient and impressive means of self-expression. Thus the role of style in domestic architecture must be examined not only from the perspective of broad changes in theory and taste, but also from the viewpoint of the client, seeking to express his heritage, status, learning, wealth, and other ideas. All of these factors—aesthetic and expressive—must be considered in examining the progress of various "exotic" and historical styles that were revived in the nineteenth century. For the present discussion I have chosen only four styles—Indian, "Norman," Italian vernacular, and "Old English"—that have not been chronicled at length elsewhere, but which were of special interest to nineteenth-century architects.[173] Significantly in discussing specific reasons for using these styles, architects often revealed more general ideas concerning the nature and purpose of style in architecture.

As the taste for rococo Chinese style began to flourish in the 1750s, William and John Halfpenny published several designs in a similar style that they termed "Indian"; these appear in *Rural Architecture in the Gothick Taste* (1752; Entry 136) and in *The Country Gentleman's Pocket Companion* (1753; Entry 131). The designs clearly were inspired more by Chinese examples and a taste for Rococo decoration than by actual knowledge of India. Indeed the variety of other styles that they included—Chinese, Gothic, "Ancient," "Modern," and the like—suggests that the "Indian," like the others, was meant simply as an exotic, imaginative alternative to the order and regularity of orthodox Palladianism.[174]

In 1794 Thomas and William Daniell returned from India, and shortly afterward began to publish a series of views of Indian architecture in *Oriental Scenery* (London, 1795–1808). Only then could English architects begin to create designs in a reasonably authentic Indian style. About 1805 Samuel Pepys Cockerell completed at Sezincote the first English dwelling executed in Indian style,[175] and in the same year Robert Lugar's *Architectural Sketches* (Entry 192) included a design for a villa in the "Eastern" style, closely modeled on the Mausoleum of Sultan Purveiz as illustrated in the Daniells' first volume. Lugar explained that a house in this style, which "partakes of a grand and sublime conception," would bring "the taste, genius, and skill of a distant people" to England.

Probably the most famous—and notorious—example of Indian architecture in England was the remodeling of the Prince Regent's Brighton Pavilion, discussed at length in Repton's *Designs for the Pavillon at Brighton* (1808; Entry 276), and then illustrated in John Nash's *Royal Pavilion at Brighton* (ca. 1825; Entry 218). In proposing the Indian style, Repton stated that Greek and Gothic styles were functionally unsuited to the requirements of a modern "English Palace." Indian architecture, on the other hand, could be recommended on both picturesque and utilitarian grounds: the architect could choose, for example, from "an endless variety of forms and proportions of Pillars." Repton also tried to counter objections to such an unfamiliar style by stressing the originality of his conception: he likened his contribution to the work of those who pioneered the Gothic and Renaissance styles. The greater implication—which wisely remained unstated—was that Indian architecture, well suited to the needs of modern times, might soon replace current styles and become the predominant style of the nineteenth century.

The round-arched "Norman" or Romanesque style was not commonly used in dwellings until the 1820s; Penrhyn Castle, begun in 1827, was the first major residence in this style.[176] Nevertheless designs with round medieval arches appeared in architectural literature as early as the mid-eighteenth century. Two designs in Batty and Thomas Langley's *Ancient Architecture* (1742; Entry 172) may have been the earliest published attempts to revive the round medieval arch. One design for a "Gothick Pavillion" (Plate LX) incorporates tall, narrow round-headed arches on the second story of each of the four corner towers. The rest of the building, however, is a mélange of crenellations, quatrefoils, lancet arches, round trefoil arches, geometrical tracery, and an ogee arch. The "Gothick Pavillion" in Plate LXII includes a semicircular central arch on the upper floor that is more plausibly Norman in origin, since it apparently is sur-

Figure 2

rounded by billet molding. There is Gothic Y-tracery within this arch, however, and apart from crenellations across the top there is nothing else appreciably Norman about the design.

Over two decades later Thomas Collins Overton included a "villa in the style of a castle" in his *Original Designs of Temples* (1766; Entry 234). In the center of the three-story facade is a pair of round-arched windows, set within a larger semicircular arch and supported by Romanesque colonettes. The facade also includes other round-headed openings, a crenellated parapet, and a Union Jack flying above. This combination of medieval and patriotic features apparently was meant to stimulate ideas of Britain's medieval heritage in the mind of the spectator, in a manner similar to the Langleys' use of Gothic (or "Saxon") architecture to recall Britain's "Ancient" liberties.

Early in the nineteenth century, castellated designs with round Norman arches appeared in Richard Elsam's *Essay on Rural Architecture* (1803; Entry 69) and Robert Lugar's *Architectural Sketches* (1805; Entry 192). Elsam used a round "Saxon" arch to frame an enclosed passageway between two small houses "about to be erected at Ipswich" (Plate 14), and also inserted round-headed windows in a castellated drum rising above his design for a villa "in imitation of a *chateau*" (Plate 25). Lugar illustrated a design for a dwelling "in the Castle style" with crenellations, circular turrets, Tudor drip moldings, plus one triple window supported by Romanesque colonettes and topped by round arches with zigzag ornament. Lugar was primarily interested in this combination of medieval motifs for its visual effect: he extolled "the grand effect which may be produced by bold, broken, and massive outlines, unconfined extent, unequal heights, and numerous towers, which afford an infinity of means to augment effects by broad light and shadow, giving to the whole an awful gloominess productive of grand, majestic, and sublime ideas." He also alluded briefly to the affective character of the medieval ornament: "the exterior," he suggested, "invites to the hospitality of some renowned ancestor" (p. 26).

Thomas Frederick Hunt published a design for an "Old English" gamekeeper's hut in *Half a Dozen Hints on Picturesque Domestic Architecture* (1825; Entry 156) that uncharacteristically incorporates Norman motifs. The entrance is framed by a large round arch, ornamented with zigzag and other moldings, and supported by short Romanesque colonettes. Two ground-floor windows are framed by round arches made of large blocks of stone (Plate 4). Hunt explained that he wanted the building to have "the appearance of being raised on the Ruins of a Priory"—thereby suggesting to the potential client that on a large estate even the huts and lodges could raise important associations with Britain's monastic heritage. Two years later Peter Frederick Robinson, architect of one of the earliest Norman Revival churches, Christ Church at Leamington (1825), included a design for a dwelling in "Anglo-Norman" style in his *Designs for Ornamental Villas* (1827; Entry 293). Picturesquely asymmetrical in plan and elevation, the design includes round-arched window and door openings surrounded by zigzag ornament, blank arcading, and other Romanesque features. Noting that few dwellings had been erected in this style since the Middle Ages, Robinson conceded that "the forms of its apertures"— small, narrow windows—might be "inapplicable to our habits" (p. 27).

Indeed when he executed the design that he illustrated, Robinson had been required to substitute "the old English style" for the Norman (p. 28).

No doubt because of its heavy, massive character the Norman style remained unpopular among domestic architects, and appeared only infrequently in books of original designs. Robinson included an "Anglo-Norman" town hall and market house (Plates 29–31) in *Village Architecture* (1830; Entry 297), with round-headed arcades at ground level and round-headed windows above, but little other specifically "Norman" ornament. Among designs in 25 different styles in Richard Brown's *Domestic Architecture* (1841; Entry 24), there is one "Anglo-Norman Castle" (Plate XLIX). In addition to crenellations and arrow slits, there are round window arches supported by Romanesque colonettes and decorated with zigzag ornament. In his brief remarks on this design, Brown noted that modern customs and manners had required extensive changes in the "internal apartments" since "ancient baronial" times (p. 301). He thus implied that while the Norman style might be exploited for its associations with feudal power and splendor, the thick walls and lack of windows in true Norman style made it highly inappropriate for modern needs.

As eighteenth-century English landscape painters increasingly emulated the vernacular architecture of the Italian countryside that appeared in paintings by Claude, Poussin, and other European landscapists,[177] architects too began to find the picturesque irregularity and informal composition of these buildings attractive. Perhaps the first to execute a building in a picturesque Italianate manner was John Nash, whose Cronkhill (1802) includes a tower, arcade, and open balcony that are clearly reminiscent of buildings in paintings by Claude.[178] One year later Edward Edwards was the first to publish original architectural designs in this style, using them as examples of perspective construction in his *Practical Treatise of Perspective* (Entry 67).

In 1805 Richard Payne Knight completed his *Analytical Inquiry into the Principles of Taste* (London: T. Payne and J. White), in which he discussed the formal qualities of "irregular" and "picturesque" houses. The best models for such houses turned out to be buildings in the "mixed style" of architecture that appeared in paintings by Claude, Nicolas Poussin, and Gaspar Poussin.[179] The same year Robert Lugar included one design "in the style of an Italian villa" in his *Architectural Sketches* (1805; Entry 192). He stated that the design—a two-story pavilion attached asymmetrically to a three-story octagonal tower—was "made for a situation which afforded three most desirable views" (p. 24). Clearly Lugar adopted the style because the landscape surrounding the house closely resembled the environment in many Italian landscape paintings. Also in 1805 Joseph Michael Gandy included a double cottage designed "after the Italian manner" in his *Rural Architect* (Entry 85; Plate XXXIII). This and another equally Italianate design (Plate XVI) each consist of a low wing attached asymmetrically to a taller pavilion or tower. Gandy's interest in this style derived largely from its formal irregularity; he explained that in these designs, as in much of his other work, he employed asymmetrical composition "so as to have a picturesque effect."

Over a decade later John Buonarotti Papworth published a proposal for an artist's villa composed of motifs borrowed directly from Italian

Figure 4

landscape painting. Departing from the concerns of his predecessors, who focused primarily on the adaptation of Italianate architecture to an appropriate landscape, or on the production of picturesque effects, Papworth considered the affective possibilities of the Italianate style. He explained in *Rural Residences* (1818; Entry 246) that there was a certain "poetic feeling" in the forms employed by Claude and Poussin that went well beyond "mere" considerations of fitness and convenience (p. 69). Presumably the incorporation of these forms in an artist's dwelling would result in a remarkably intense utilization of the affective capacity of style to inspire the inhabitant.

Few if any additional Italianate designs were published before 1827, when Peter Frederick Robinson and James Thomson each included just one in their collections of designs for picturesque dwellings.[180] Also in 1827 Thomas Frederick Hunt published *Architettura Campestre* (Entry 153), containing designs somewhat reminiscent of paintings by Claude and Poussin; but in the text Hunt disparaged the use of Italianate architecture in a landscape environment so inappropriate as that of Britain. The next year, however, Gilbert Laing Meason issued his treatise *On the Landscape Architecture of the Great Painters of Italy* (1828; Entry 203), a compendium of architectural subjects that had appeared in Italian landscape painting from the late Middle Ages to the seventeenth century. Noting that the buildings he depicted were composed in what Knight had called the "mixed style," Meason observed the "important advantages" that buildings in this style offered—"whether for comfort and convenience, [or] for gratifying taste or fashion." In addition to such considerations as function and fashion, he particularly recommended use of the style for its picturesqueness, which was the result of "contrast and disposition of large broad masses and extended lines."

One year later Sir Charles Barry executed his Italianate design for the Travellers' Club in London. Formal, symmetrical, and based on Renaissance examples, it had very little in common with the picturesque, irregular structures in Meason's illustrations. Thereafter Barry's manner, not Meason's, dictated the course of most Italianate building in Britain,[181] no doubt because of its associations with the political power and prosperity of Renaissance Florence and Rome. Nevertheless in residential design Meason's influence persisted; the principal echo of his work is Charles Parker's collection of original designs, titled *Villa Rustica* (1832 and later; Entry 249). Parker based his designs on cottages and lodges that he had seen in the vicinity of Florence and Rome, but also suggested modifications that would accord with the needs and customs of English clients.

Published designs for Italianate dwellings were uncommon in the 1830s and 1840s, but in 1840 George Wightwick included a design for an "Anglo-Italian Villa" in his *Palace of Architecture* (Entry 346), accompanied by a highly unusual description. Asymmetrical in plan and elevation, this Italianate villa was designed with particular attention to the many picturesque views available from its elevated site, and also with "principles of *fitness*" in mind (p. 201). Speaking in the first person, the villa described itself as a unique adaptation of function to circumstance: "What am I, then, but an English mansion, adapted to my locality, and to the climate and customs of my country? taking my arrangements from my owner, my

THEORY AND DESIGN

leading external features from modern Italy, and my complexion from fair Greece."

In the first half of the nineteenth century four styles of the late Middle Ages and early Renaissance—"half-timbered," "Old English," "Tudor," and "Elizabethan"—were applied with increasing frequency to designs for dwellings. Architects were attracted not only to the picturesque irregular massing and intricate detail of these styles, but also to their nostalgic associations with important eras in British history. This nostalgia is revealed by the term "Old English" itself, used to describe buildings in both Tudor Gothic and Elizabethan styles, a practice that allowed architects to overlook the differences between the two styles.[182] Because of this imprecision, and because of the common picturesque characteristics of these styles, it will be best to consider them all together.

Among the early advocates of these styles, several architects stressed their picturesqueness. Richard Payne Knight set the keynote in a plate that accompanies his poetic manifesto of the picturesque, *The Landscape* (1794; Entry 169). At the center of the illustration is a richly ornamented Elizabethan dwelling, set in a highly picturesque landscape. The house is richly ornamented with elaborate gable ends, chimneys, and parapets silhouetted against the sky. Like the surrounding landscape, it is clearly capable of producing the "grateful irritation" of the eye that Knight considered essential to the appreciation of picturesque beauty. Four years later, in *An Essay on British Cottage Architecture* (Entry 197), James Malton used half-timbered buildings to illustrate the "peculiar" picturesque beauty indigenous to British architecture. He particularly appreciated qualities of intricacy and variety in examples that he discussed. Humphry Repton discussed the picturesqueness of "Queen Elizabeth's Gothic" in more detail in *Observations on the Theory and Practice of Landscape Gardening* (1803; Entry 279), praising in particular "the bold projections, the broad masses, the richness of . . . [the] windows, and the irregular outline of . . . roofs, turrets, and tall chimnies."[183]

Other architects focused on the expressive capacities of these styles. Robert Lugar nearly anthropomorphized a design in Elizabethan style by explaining that it "shews a character becoming an English gentleman; plain and unaffected."[184] John Adey Repton included half-timbered and Elizabethan designs in *Fragments on the Theory and Practice of Landscape Gardening* (1816; Entry 277) for their ability to recall ideas of particular eras. For the Duke of Bedford he prepared one design as "a specimen of the Timber houses which prevailed in England" from 1450 to 1550; and at Cobham Hall he designed a lodge to "appear to be of the same date" as the Elizabethan mansion itself. In *Rural Residences* (1818; Entry 246.2) John Buonarotti Papworth discussed the "mixed" style of Old English architecture in terms of its associations with political stability and freedom. The style, he said, recalls a period "when the security of the sovereign and the subject began to depend less on the strength of fortifications and the force of arms, than on the charitable administration of the laws of the country."

In the 1820s and 1830s Peter Frederick Robinson and Thomas Frederick Hunt were the two principal exponents of the "Old English" style. As early as 1823, in *Rural Architecture* (Entry 296), Robinson extolled an unnamed "style which once adorned the fair landscape scenery" of England—a clear reference to the Old English style and its well-recognized ability to accord with picturesque scenery. He particularly praised such features as high gables, ornamented chimneys, bargeboards, casement windows, and "ivy-mantled" porches. Two years later, in *Half a Dozen Hints on Picturesque Domestic Architecture* (Entry 156), Hunt likewise described the "Old English" style as "better suited to the scenery of this Country" than any other, and praised its "variety of form and outline." In 1827 Hunt published a collection of *Designs for Parsonage Houses* (Entry 154) entirely in the Old English style. In the accompanying letterpress he now criticized architects such as Robinson who had adopted this style only for its picturesque qualities. Hunt found that there was also great value in the broader historical associations of the style, which he illuminated through descriptions of historical events related to the subjects illustrated in his plates.[185] Hunt's last book, *Exemplars of Tudor Architecture* (1830; Entry 155), was the first collection of designs entirely in Tudor style. He included extensive accounts from historical documents showing how specific building parts and furnishings were used in former times. The detail and authenticity of such accounts not only demonstrated the original utility of the style but also showed that it was "still the most applicable for English habitations." In addition Hunt's frequent quotations from Shakespeare and other contemporary writers suggested a wide range of historical and cultural associations that the prospective owner of a Tudor house might wish to display.

Robinson's arguments in favor of the "Old English" style, in contrast, were based almost entirely on pictorial considerations. In *Designs for Ornamental Villas* (1827; Entry 293) his designs in Old English, Elizabethan, and related styles are well integrated with surrounding landscape scenery. He commented that Old English buildings in particular had gables, chimneys, and windows that "harmonize most agreeably in scenic situations, and produce effects of high interest to the painter." Whatever the style, he recommended close attention to the relationship between architecture and the surrounding scenery: "a man should conceive, in his mind's eye, the whole effect of the picture he is about to produce, even before the foundation be laid."

In his efforts to promote picturesque domestic architecture, Robinson produced numerous designs in half-timbered, Elizabethan, and Tudor styles. In *Designs for Lodges* (1833; Entry 292) he presented designs in several styles—including "Timber Fronted" and Elizabethan—that he found especially picturesque. He contrasted his own work in these styles to "the barbarous attempts" at reproducing medieval styles that had "disgraced the last century"; he hinted that greater authenticity was now possible because of recent advances in the study of "Ancient Architecture" in "polite education." Robinson extolled the beauties of "Old English" architecture in the text of his misleadingly titled *Domestic Architecture in the Tudor Style* (1837; Entry 294), which illustrates his work in both Tudor and Elizabethan styles at a house near Swansea. Finally, Robinson also encouraged the revival of Elizabethan architecture by starting a new series of the venerable *Vitruvius Britannicus* (begun 1827; Entry 298). He devoted each number to a single monument of British architecture, and two of the five subjects are major Elizabethan mansions: Hatfield House and Hardwick Hall.

By the 1830s, then, "Old English" styles had become well respected for a variety of reasons, both aesthetic and practical. In 1833 John Claudius Loudon observed that the Elizabethan style had the most "interesting associations connected with it," and was considered "peculiarly appropriate to country residences" (*Encyclopaedia* [Entry 184], p. 1124). Thus he composed his "Beau Idéal of an English Villa" in this style, citing its "picturesque and ornamental" character, as well as its utility: "it admits of great irregularity of form, [and therefore] it affords space for the various offices and conveniences necessary in a country-house." W. H. Leeds also stressed the picturesqueness and utility of the "Old English" style in the introduction to the second volume of Francis Goodwin's *Domestic Architecture* (1833–1834; Entry 91): in addition to providing advantages of "internal propriety and convenience, . . . hardly any style is so well calculated to produce important character and striking effect with comparatively little finish of detail." The introduction to the first volume also emphasized the romantic associations of this style:

Figure 3

Every thing that savors of the rural economy of great household establishments of olden times, is congenial to all persons of enlightened sentiment, or good taste, whatever may be their rank, or whatever their pursuits. A succession of ages has wrapped almost all the concerns of bygone days in those pleasurable sensations, which, associating with the habits of our forefathers, [also] gave birth to that species of mental delight which constitutes the main charm of poetry. . . . For many ages previously to the seventeenth century . . . the customs and habits of the people were in character with these structures; all was social, hospitable, and delightful to the imagination.

George Wightwick concurred in *The Palace of Architecture* (1840; Entry 346), praising Old English for "the *associations* connected with it,—its festive hall, hung round with antlers, spears, and bows; its wood-blazing hearths, and its love-making bay windows" (p. 203).

•

Nineteenth-century eclecticism sometimes has been understood as a failure on the part of architects to define a style appropriate to their times. But as I have shown, specific styles often were used to express particular ideas and feelings. The diversity of styles in many early nineteenth-century publications, therefore, cannot be taken as evidence of indecision or unoriginality. Rather, architects attempted to provide their clients with a broad range of opportunities for expressing themselves through architecture. A brief look at a few of the books that contain designs in several different styles will suggest the variety of opportunities available.

Late in the eighteenth century, compendia of designs in diverse styles were not unusual.[186] Charles Middleton intended his *Architect and Builder's Miscellany* (1799; Entry 206), for example, to serve "as an Assistant to the Professional Man, and a Guide to the Public in the choice of buildings." His designs range in scale from a primitive hut to a large mansion, and are composed in a broad range of styles, including Primitive (wattle and daub), Gothic, Greek, Palladian, Regency, Chinese, and Turkish. John

Plaw's *Sketches for Country Houses* (1800; Entry 261) and Robert Lugar's *Architectural Sketches* (1805; Entry 192) likewise display buildings in various styles—including Rustic, Gothic, Castellated, Monastic, Tudor, Greek, Italian, and Indian—suited to different scenic and economic circumstances. John Buonarotti Papworth discussed Rustic, Gothic, Greek, Old English, Italian, and other styles at length in his *Rural Residences* (1818; Entry 246.2). He stressed the importance of suiting the style to the surrounding scenery as well as to the character of the inhabitant: a farm house, for example, might be in Cottage style in order to "assimilate with home scenery," while a vicarage should be Gothic because the style "leads the spectator very naturally from contemplating the dwelling, to regard the pious character of its inhabitant."

Peter Frederick Robinson's *Designs for Ornamental Villas* (1827; Entry 293) was perhaps the most diverse collection of styles to date, with buildings in Swiss, Greek, Palladian, Old English, Castellated, "Ancient Manor House," Modern Italian, Anglo-Norman, Decorated (Gothic), Elizabethan, "Ancient Timber Building," and Tuscan styles. Robinson discussed the ability of each style to accord visually with certain types of landscape scenery, and associationally with particular historical circumstances. In the same year James Thomson provided Greek, Gothic, Rural, "Regular," "Irregular," "Uniform," and Rustic designs in *Retreats* (Entry 333). He recommended that every design should "possess a character adapted to the local circumstances connected with it"—circumstances that could include scenic, functional, personal, and other considerations. One design in Greek style, for example, incorporated a "neatness and accommodation sufficient to indicate its vicinity to the metropolis," while a Gothic villa was intended for "persons fond of retirement and study."

Architects of the 1830s and 1840s continued to encourage diversity of expression by providing readers—potential clients—with a selection of styles. In *Domestic Architecture* (1833–1834; Entry 91) Francis Goodwin published 42 designs in Greek, Gothic, Italian, Old English, and other styles. His reasons for adopting them varied according to individual circumstances. The Italian style, for example, was utilitarian, while Gothic suggested the hospitality of ancient monasteries, and "Ancient English" architecture was "well calculated to produce important character and striking effect." Samuel H. Brooks included designs for individually expressive suburban dwellings in Gothic, Old English, Tudor, Elizabethan, Italian, Ionic, Greek, and Swiss styles in *Designs for Cottage and Villa Architecture* (1839; Entry 23). Most impressive of all is Richard Brown's *Domestic Architecture* (1841; Entry 24), an encyclopedic collection of "Exemplars" in 25 styles. These are accompanied, where appropriate, by remarks on historical, religious, and geographical circumstances associated with the style, plus appropriate furniture, gardens, and landscape scenery. The book soon became an important early Victorian compendium of information on architectural style and its various applications.

High Victorian Gothic architects and doctrinaire critics soon decried the diversity of styles in the early nineteenth century. But that variety was an expansion and strengthening of the architectural vocabulary, making for an increasingly rich, complex form of communication that well accommodated growing political, social, economic, and artistic diversity.

9
Picturesque
Aesthetics:
Architectural
Form and the
Surrounding
Landscape

In preceding sections I showed that principles of picturesque composition were fundamental to the application and appreciation of certain architectural styles, and to many other concerns of domestic architects during the eighteenth and nineteenth centuries. The picturesque relationship between a dwelling and its natural surroundings also was an important matter for landscape painters, poets, aestheticians, landscape gardeners, and architects throughout the same period.[187] Residential architects generally devoted their attention to three principal picturesque concerns: making views available from the house, arranging buildings and the surrounding scenery to form a picture-like whole, and establishing overt visual relationships between features of a building and elements of the surrounding landscape. I will treat these concerns in the order in which they historically appeared in architectural literature.

•

As early as 1728 Robert Castell, trying to reconstruct the form of an ancient Roman villa, noted that the natural environment visible from the house must be composed like a "beautiful Landskip."[188] He observed that the immediate surroundings might be arranged in three distinct ways, each of which involved a specific aesthetic rationale. According to one method, nature could appear "in her plainest and most simple Dress," because the ground itself was naturally beautiful. In another, the grounds could be arranged according to the formal "Manner of the more regular Gardens," presumably highly symmetrical and geometric. The final method involved irregularity and explicit rurality: natural objects would be "thrown into . . . an agreeable Disorder."

Eleven years later Robert Morris described the surroundings of country houses explicitly in terms of picture-like views. In his *Essay upon Harmony* (London: T. Cooper, 1739) he praised "Places where the *Thames* affords a beautiful Landscape," particularly where it "spreads and divides itself into a Multitude of pleasing Forms, sufficient to afford many fine Picteresque Views, rather in Appearance romantick, than real" (p. 21). At Richmond in particular he found art and nature "beautifully join'd: Words will hardly paint the Images, the Picteresque Scenes, that adorn the Place, are so inimitably blended" (p. 24).

In *Rural Architecture* (1750; Entry 216) Morris expressly discussed the relationship between a house and its offices in terms of painterly composition:

As in History Painting, one principal Figure possesseth the superior Light, the fore Ground and Eminence of the Piece, and the subordinate Figures are placed Part in Sight, Part in Groups and Shade for Contrast, and keeping in the Design; so in Building, all the subservient Offices should terminate by gradual Progression in *Utility* and *Situation*.

Isaac Ware also adopted the painterly analogy in his *Complete Body of Architecture* (1756; Entry 339). He noted that in designing a country estate the farm house and offices should be placed in full view of the principal building, presumably to facilitate proper supervision. For the aesthetic pleasure of the proprietor, however, the farm house and offices should be arranged "as a picture":

The house of the farmer is to be the principal object, and this must be placed on the highest part of the ground: from this, on either side, the out-buildings are to descend spreading in the form of wings, toward the brook at the bottom. . . . Under the direction of a skilful architect, the barns, stables, and cow-houses, will rise like so many pavillions; and the very sheds will assist in the design.

But in spite of the agreement among Morris, Ware, and other midcentury architects concerning the need to group buildings in a picture-like manner, architects in later decades did not endorse this method of composition so readily. William Marshall, for example, recommended only that views connect the house with distant corners of the estate; in his treatise on planting and rural ornament (1785 and later editions; Entry 453), he cited fundamental differences between nature and painting, and urged that scenery not be artificially composed as if in a picture.

●

Architects did not generally recognize the need for an overt visual correspondence between specific features of a building and elements of the surrounding landscape until the middle of the eighteenth century. Indeed despite a long tradition of topographical illustration in which architecture and landscape were represented in great detail,[189] foliage and landscape scenery seldom appeared in architectural books before 1750. The earliest example is Stephen Switzer's treatise on gardening (1715–1742; Entry 327), which includes illustrations of designs for landscape gardens, some of which incorporate plans or elevations of dwellings. The third and fourth volumes of *Vitruvius Britannicus* (1725, 1739; Entries 33, 11) include many views of extant country estates in their landscape settings. Nevertheless landscape scenery was not to be found in collections of original designs for buildings published before midcentury.

In 1752 William and John Halfpenny observed that some of the designs in *Rural Architecture in the Gothick Taste* (Entry 136) had been prepared for particular settings—"Eminences," for example—but these were not illustrated in the plates. Within the next few years foliage and landscape scenery did appear in several collections of original designs, albeit most frequently in illustrations of garden buildings, rather than with designs for permanent residences. The scenery in the Halfpennys' *Country Gentleman's Pocket Companion* (1753; Entry 131), for example, consists simply of trees and shrubs hesitantly added to the left and right of garden structures, apparently to provide a sense of place and scale. A few plates contain something more substantial: one illustration of a summer house, for instance, includes a rockwork bridge and a stream.

Far more complex and elaborate scenery accompanies the designs for arbors and grottoes in Thomas Wright's *Universal Architecture* (1755–1758; Entry 357). In the text Wright made brief suggestions concerning types of landscape scenery—plants, rocks, and ground—that would correspond with the visual character of his designs. In the plates he created a complex visual dialogue between the rustic Rococo forms of his structures and the exuberant natural surroundings. In some cases Wright expected this union of architecture and landscape to impress the viewer or user in a particularly affective manner. A "Druid's Cell," for example, "designed for a Study or philosophical Retirement," is set into the side of a hill and surrounded by dense foliage, conveying a sense of retreat and isolation. Sir William Chambers also considered the pictorial and the emotionally affective aspects of landscape in *Designs of Chinese Buildings* (1757; Entry 38). He observed that gardens in China were "laid out in a variety of scenes"— a manner of composition that seems little different from Castell's "Picteresque Scenes." But Chambers also added that in China those scenes were given "the appellations of pleasing, horrid, and enchanted," thus suggesting a degree of affectivity not unlike what Wright and many contemporary landscapists proposed.[190]

Five years later Lord Kames took up the problem of the proper visual relationship between a house and the surrounding landscape. He asked "Whether the situation . . . ought, in any measure, to regulate the form of the edifice?"[191] In reply he, like Chambers, considered pictorial as well as emotional effects. The basic principle that he sought was "congruity": an "elegant building," he said, should be surrounded by "a polished field" rather than wild, uncultivated country. The result would be a heightened effect for the spectator, who would enjoy "the pleasure of concordance from the similarity of the emotions produced by the two objects."[192]

•

After midcentury, architects returned to the problem of providing suitable views from within a dwelling. The anonymous Irish "Gentleman" who published *Twelve Designs of Country-Houses* (1757; Entry 87) included one design with a large bow window at the rear, designed to "command the desired Prospect" of a "Town, Wood, Lake or River." In *Familiar Architecture* (1768; Entry 273) Thomas Rawlins likewise published designs that were created expressly to accommodate specific views. He provided one retreat with a triangular plan, for example, so that it could "command three Vistos." In describing a summer retreat, he also considered the affective character of its vistas, noting their power to "exhilarate and add fresh Vigour to the Mind of the wealthy and industrious Inhabitant." John Crunden proudly described the impressive view available from one of his villas in *Convenient and Ornamental Architecture* (1767; Entry 49): "The back front, which includes the best apartments, commands, at a little distance, the river Wey, and a very extensive prospect over a rich vale, bounded by a most beautiful chain of hills, which afford great variety of lights and shades, and consequently very pleasing and picturesque." In *The Gentleman and Farmer's Architect* (1762; Entry 179) Timothy Lightoler provided designs for improving or accenting views that were already available. He depicted several "Facades to place before disagreeable objects," plus a battlemented "Sheep Coat" or shepherd's house that when "seen from a Genteel House" would be "an agreeable object" in the distance.

Architects retained this concern for picturesque vistas well into the nineteenth century. In 1806, for example, James Randall wrote in *A Collection of Architectural Designs* (Entry 271) that "the situation of a house should be considered as well for the prospect from it, as for its own picturesque effect." John Buonarotti Papworth published a design in *Rural Residences* (1818; Entry 246.2) that demonstrates especially well the degree to which a dwelling could be tied to its surrounding environment by a series of vistas. The *cottage ornée* in Plate 13 is encompassed on three sides by one- and two-story verandas, which command views in many different directions and emphatically communicate that fact to the observer. In addition, the trellises and latticework around the perimeter of the verandas help facilitate an integration of interior and exterior space, and thus by extension suggest a penetration of natural vistas into the fabric of the house.

●

In the 1780s and 1790s, architects' concerns for picture-like composition and picturesque vistas were overshadowed by attention to more rigorous means of coordinating architectural forms with elements of the surrounding landscape. John Plaw's *Rural Architecture* (1785; Entry 260) was the first British architectural book to include plates executed in aquatint, a technique that greatly expanded the available range of tones and textures for illustrating buildings and scenery. Plaw applied the technique with considerable success to the depiction of light and shadow, three-dimensional advance and recession, and the tactile qualities of trees, shrubbery, lawns, stone, and stucco. In doing so, he achieved a highly attractive, harmonious coordination of dwellings with the surrounding landscape. Indeed these were the first designs published by a British architect in which landscape was an important component of the entire composition.

Shortly afterward, in *Sketches in Architecture* (1793; Entry 320), Sir John Soane introduced the notion of a "characteristic" relation between architecture and scenery.[193] Although Soane provided no detailed remarks explaining this notion, his illustrations reveal a very close correspondence in form and texture between natural and architectural forms. His design for a "Belle-Vue," for example, consists of a solid rectangular base, set firmly on a small hill, above which rises a two-story round turret. An adjacent tree assists visually in anchoring the base of the building to the top of the hill, with possible associations of "rootedness." A sharp drop at the right to the valley below complements the tower's thrust into the open air. On all sides the flora and topography are smooth and rounded, corresponding to the smooth surfaces and simple geometric forms of the building.

In *Sketches and Hints on Landscape Gardening* (1794; Entry 280) Humphry Repton classified all architecture according to two visual characters, the horizontal and the perpendicular. These, he contended, accorded best with their landscape opposites: trees of a "pointed or conic" shape were best suited to horizontal (Greek) architecture, while smoother, more rounded, deciduous trees complemented the vertical (Gothic) character. Nine years later, in *Observations on the Theory and Practice of Landscape Gardening* (1803; Entry 279), he introduced his own notion of "characteristic architecture." He urged that dwellings correspond visually with their surroundings, while also accommodating their intended functions: "the adaptation of buildings not only to the situation, character, and circumstances of the scenery, but also to the purposes for which they are intended; this I shall call *Characteristic Architecture.*"

Richard Payne Knight, author of *The Landscape* (1794; Entry 169), differed with Repton on many subjects but clearly agreed on the need to coordinate architecture with landscape by pictorial means. In one example, Knight proposed a landscape of dense brush and crooked, irregular foliage, designed to surround an Elizabethan house ornamented with elaborate gables, chimneys, and parapets. The architecture and the landscape—each full of rough, irregular elements—would together produce that "grateful irritation" of the eye that Knight considered fundamental to the appreciation of the picturesque.

Other late eighteenth-century architects also displayed serious concern for the visual accord between architecture and landscape. George Richardson did not depict landscape scenery in *New Designs in Architecture* (1792; Entry 284), but he strongly recommended that advance, recession, and "diversified contour" in building "be compared to the effect that hill and dale, foreground and distance have in landscape." James Lewis disregarded scenery altogether in the first volume of *Original Designs in Architecture* (1780; Entry 178); but in the second volume (1797), issued three years after Repton's *Sketches and Hints* and Knight's *Landscape*, he included several designs that clearly reflected the visual character of the surrounding environment. He gave the facade of one villa, for example, "a strong and bold character," with partially rusticated quoins and columns, and a heavily articulated masonry bond across the entire front. Such features permitted the building to "harmonize" with the surrounding "bold and magnificent" landscape scenery.

In the early nineteenth century, authors of many books containing designs for cottages and villas continued to strive for the picturesque coordination of architecture and landscape. Robert Lugar's remarks in *Villa Architecture* (1828; Entry 195) are representative of many.[194] Having observed that the character of the landscape would often suggest one style "as more appropriate than another," he proposed a direct correspondence between particular types of scenery and specific architectural styles. Thus "bold or mountainous country" would require castellations, while a site near a large town or village would accommodate a Neoclassical design, and a *cottage ornée* "may stand in a small lawn, and requires the accompaniments of plantations and shrubberies."

•

During the first half of the nineteenth century many architects again espoused a picture-like conception of the relation between a dwelling and its scenic context.[195] In *Hints on Ornamental Gardening* (1823; Entry 248.2) John Buonarotti Papworth conceived the relation of a house to its immediate environment in terms reminiscent of Ware: "The house is now viewed as a principal attended by a retinue of subordinates"; "the plantations support and contrast with the building, which by the shrubberies is carried forward until it blends naturally and gracefully with the landscape." The same year Peter Frederick Robinson lamented in *Rural Architecture* (1823; Entry 296) that picturesque country landscapes too often were destroyed through inattention to principles of artistic composition. He especially complained of "impotent attempts" by workmen to erect rural dwellings "unaided by the pencil of the Artist."[196] Later, in *Designs for Ornamental Villas* (1827; Entry 293), he recommended that the architect apply principles of painting to domestic design, and in effect become an "*Architetto-pittore.*" In his last book, *A New Series of Designs* (1838; Entry 295), Robinson again urged a painterly approach: picturesque alterations to extant cottages, he said, were like "the last touches given to a picture by the hand of the master."[197]

Gilbert Laing Meason also favored a pictorial manner of architectural composition. In his treatise *On the Landscape Architecture of the Great Painters of Italy* (1828; Entry 203) he reproduced structures found in "the back grounds of the historical works of the great painters," thereby providing "a new source of studies, for the composition of irregular dwellings." Richard Brown was even more explicit: in *Domestic Architecture* (1841; Entry 24), he offered the most thorough discussion to date of pictorial relations between architecture and the surrounding landscape:

In composing a rural residence, the various opening and distant views, with the close adjacent parts of the scenery around the site on which the house is to be erected, are the first in importance, and must be well considered, before the architect determines either on what style of architecture should be adopted, or begins to compose his design; and that design, if extensive, should, like a picture, have some parts prominent as a foreground, others falling back as a middle group, and the third more retired as a background; this will produce shadow and give effect to the lights. Some parts of the house will probably require to project, or be brought forward from a straight line on the plan; while other parts of the house may, on the contrary, recede on that plan, or, in some parts of the elevation be allowed to rise higher than others, by which the contour of the edifice will produce a playful variation, but which outline is to be regulated by the local scenery. (p. 84)

•

A few architects published illustrations of houses designed specifically for artists; in some cases the picturesque scenery or the house itself may have been composed intentionally to express the artistic character of the inhabitant, or—more affectively—to inspire his creativity. Sir John Soane included two plans and an elevation of a "House designed for an Artist" in *Sketches in Architecture* (1793; Entry 320). Across the two-story elevation, three openings wide, four broad, flat pilasters rise from a plinth to support three segmental relieving arches above the entrance and two ground-story windows. Within the arches, the upper story is unarticulated except for three nine-light windows. The surrounding "characteristic scenery" includes a broad expanse of grass in front of the house, with a lawn roller casually abandoned in the left foreground. The vista to the right is closed by tall, feathery trees, while an opening to the left permits a glimpse of a field, a fence, and a distant wood. The smooth lawn and light foliage thus visually complement the relatively flat, plain facade of the house. In contrast John Plaw's "Design made for an Artist," depicted in Plate 18 of *Sketches for Country Houses* (1800; Entry 261), is an ungainly attempt to combine a variety of picturesque elements in a dramatic landscape setting. The three-story facade is fronted by colossal tree-trunk columns, which support a thatch roof. A two-story semicircular bow projects from the center portion of the facade; above, a smaller bow projects from the top story, and the whole center section is topped by a Tuscan pediment. The windows are composed of double or triple lights, with pointed arches, set within rectangular openings. A serpentine walk crosses the smooth lawn in the foreground, while to the rear a steep hill is densely covered with trees. The complexity of the landscape matches the diversity of motifs in the facade, but otherwise the design appears mannered and disorganized.

John Buonarotti Papworth offered a more unusual—and successful—design for "the Residence of an Artist" in *Rural Residences* (1818; Entry 246.2). Set in a thickly forested, hilly landscape, the villa consists of a solid horizontal mass fronted by a vertical tower with a belvedere at the top. All the elements of the elevation and landscape are clearly reminiscent of Italian landscape painting. Commenting on the design, Papworth remarked that "Claude Lorrain, Poussin, and other celebrated landscape-painters" had used such forms in their paintings because they "were well suited to the poetic feeling" that they wished to express. Accordingly, one might well infer that in Papworth's design these same picturesque, highly poetic forms were meant to stimulate a similar degree of artistic creativity in the resident.[198]

•

In conclusion, I must stress that many architects of the picturesque understood building design in broader terms than form, texture, color, style, and pictorial composition. As early as 1798 James Malton, who analyzed the formal characteristics of British cottages in his *Essay on British Cottage Architecture* (Entry 197), suggested that their picturesqueness derived less from the builder's conscious attention to pictorial relationships than from circumstantial needs. Indeed Malton recommended that the shape of a building should "conform only to the internal conveniency." Likewise in *Architectural Sketches* (1805; Entry 192) Robert Lugar—who recommended designing "with a Painter's eye"—also considered geographic and economic circumstances that contributed to the form and style of a dwelling. The architect, he said, must "form a whole appropriate to the locality or situation, to the circumstances of his employer." Gilbert Laing Meason clearly treated architecture in painterly terms in his study of Italian landscape painting (1828; Entry 203): in one group of buildings, for example, he found "that kind of individuality which distinguishes in painting a portrait from an ideal face." But he also included a lengthy history of domestic architecture, in which he focused on the extent to which war, economics, the rise of political states, and other societal factors influenced design. Thomas Frederick Hunt extolled the picturesque qualities of Tudor architecture in his *Exemplars* (1830; Entry 155) but also commented at length on the original functions of features that he had borrowed from historical examples, thus suggesting a special interest in utility as well as picturesque beauty.

By the 1830s a few architects seriously questioned whether picturesque beauty was at all appropriate in dwellings. Samuel H. Brooks recommended in *Designs for Cottage and Villa Architecture* (1839; Entry 23) that architects pay some attention to "irregularity of form," but he put far greater emphasis on methods of construction, fitness, utility, and the influence of climate and social circumstances on architectural design. In *The Suburban Gardener, and Villa Companion* (1838; Entry 190) John Claudius Loudon lamented that "Many persons, who have not had much experience in the choice of a house, are captivated by the exterior; and are more influenced by its picturesque effect, than by any property in the dwelling connected with habitableness." Accordingly he recommended that architects sacrifice the lesser beauties of irregularity in favor of a "cubic" form, which was "preferable in all that regards comfort, habitableness, and economy of heating, keeping clean, and in repair."

10 Town and Village Planning

During the eighteenth and nineteenth centuries British designers introduced major innovations in town and village planning, many of which were of international importance.[199] As new subdivisions and developments transformed the urban and rural landscape, illustrations of many executed plans appeared in popular and topographical literature. Original proposals and executed plans were depicted less frequently in the literature of domestic architecture; nevertheless the examples illustrated and discussed there provide important insights into the ideals and concerns of town planners.

During this period only a few books were devoted entirely to planning; although they are not included in the principal entries below because they contain no designs for dwellings, it will be useful to review these books briefly. Then I will consider the half-dozen eighteenth- and early nineteenth-century English architectural books that contain views or plans of towns or villages—plans that generally are composed in a regular, geometrical manner. Next I will treat the comparatively large number of town plans that appear in treatises devoted to agricultural improvement and economic development in Scotland—plans that sometimes were composed with attention to the picturesque possibilities of the site. Finally I will consider the work of several English planners in the early nineteenth century: the consciously picturesque manner in which some worked, as well as the more utilitarian proposals for utopian reform issued by others.

•

The major eighteenth-century treatise devoted to planning was John Gwynn's *London and Westminster Improved* (London: The author, 1766). Inspired in part by Wren's century-old scheme for rebuilding London after the fire of 1666, Gwynn offered detailed proposals for the redevelopment and expansion of London and Westminster. He proposed replacing existing streets and buildings with orthogonal streets lined by terraces, laying out undeveloped areas in a similar manner, and everywhere inserting landscaped "squares" in the form of circles, octagons, squares, and other regular shapes. He also proposed a new royal palace for the middle of Hyde Park, to be surrounded by a circular walk a mile in circumference, from which tree-lined avenues would radiate in all directions. Gwynn emphasized the extent to which the convenience and order of his proposed improvements would contribute to "publick magnificence." He promised a wealth of cultural and commercial benefits, including a more refined public taste, improved morality, greater industriousness, and increased trade (pp. v–xv, 1). He feared, justifiably, that "the old cry of private property and the infringement on liberty" would be invoked in opposition to his proposals (p. vi). These were the principal reasons that prevented Wren's plan from being executed, and they remained major impediments to any planning improvements in London.

Subsequent published proposals were likewise devoted to specific improvement schemes, rather than discussion of general planning principles. In 1786 James Craig published *A Plan for Improving the City of Edinburgh* (Edinburgh: The author), in which he proposed a large octagonal space to surround the Tron Kirk, new public markets, a 500-foot-wide crescent facing the College and the Royal Infirmary, and other improvements. In part because these proposals would have required the demolition of existing structures, they were never carried out.[200] Early in the nineteenth century John White published *Some Account of the Proposed Improvements of the Western Part of London*,[201] including illustrations of three recent proposals— his father's and two others—for development of the future Regent's Park. The elder White's design shows detached and semidetached villas around the periphery, with a Grand Crescent filling the southern portion of the park and the remainder embellished with curving footpaths and a lake. Thomas Leverton and Thomas Chawner, in contrast, proposed to cover the park with an orthogonal street plan; continuous terraces would front streets in the southern part of the park, with detached and semidetached villas in the remainder. In the third proposal John Nash projected a series of terraces around the periphery, with two concentric circuses in the center; the rest would be covered with picturesque plantings and a long serpentine "ornamental water." After major revisions Nash's design eventually was selected; but his final scheme—for detached villas set in a residential park—owed much to John White's plan that had been illustrated in *Some Account*.[202]

During the next several decades the rationalization and improvement of the existing London street plan—ever more congested due to the expansion of commerce and population—was of growing concern to politicians, social reformers, and architects. One of the most prominent improvement schemes was Sydney Smirke's *Suggestions for the Architectural Improvement of the Western Part of London* (London: Priestley and Weale, 1834). Citing problems of communication, ventilation, disease, poverty, and vice, as well as a desire to beautify the city, Smirke proposed several new avenues, sewers, and other improvements in the area from Bloomsbury to Pimlico. With particular zeal he called for the demolition of slums, viewing them as a cancerous blight on commerce and health: "Let the rotten core therefore be cut out," he urged, and at one location recommended that a market or "military depôt" be built in their place (pp. 58–59).[203]

•

Among eighteenth- and early nineteenth-century books devoted primarily to architecture, a few contain illustrations of town plans. One of the earliest is Thomas Rowland's *Mensuration* (1739; Entry 300), in which a vignette on Table 39 shows a bird's-eye view of an orthogonally planned town. At the center a large church and two smaller buildings are set within a large square. The three main streets of the town converge at a "T" in front of the square. The streets and the square are bordered by two-story houses, many of which closely adjoin each other, in effect forming long terraces. The remainder of the landscape is given over to tree-lined avenues and cultivated fields. Three decades later Stephen Riou devoted a chapter of *The Grecian Orders of Architecture* (1768; Entry 287) to the "Embellishment of Towns and Cities." The three principal topics he discussed were "entrances," streets, and buildings—the three fundamental constituents of the "beauty and magnificence" of cities. He included designs for a new street in the City, flanked by a terrace of 13 four-story houses, and an "open place at Whitehall, with porticos." The Whitehall proposal, originally conceived in 1760, is reminiscent of recent French planning at Nancy, and of Bernini's work in Rome.[204] Riou depicted two long Doric colonnades, with segmental outward bows in the center, leading from the Horse Guards to the Thames. He also proposed to place an Egyptian obelisk in the center, supported by four colossal statues representing the four quarters of the globe. In contrast the towns and buildings depicted in Edward Noble's *Elements of Linear Perspective* (1771; Entry 231) are far less elegant, and were meant primarily as perspective exercises. One plate depicts row houses, warehouses, and other buildings flanking a river or canal. Another plate shows a small coastal village, with a church and two or three houses facing each other across a small inlet.

John Plaw was the first British architect to publish an original, detailed design for an entire village. The proposal, illustrated in *Ferme Ornée* (1795; Entry 259), was prepared for an entrepreneur in Yorkshire and apparently intended to house lead miners. The plan, based on a simple rectangle, was meant to "unite symmetry and utility." Semidetached cottages line the perimeter of the rectangle, with individual plots of land extending outward from each cottage. In the center an oval green surrounds a church or chapel. A decade later Joseph Michael Gandy illustrated a more perfectly geometrical village in *Designs for Cottages* (1805; Entry 84). At the center is a circular chapel or parish church; arranged in a circle around the periphery of the village are eight additional circular buildings, each consisting of eight attached three-room cottages.

Two years later, in *Architectural Designs for Rustic Cottages* (Entry 262), William Fuller Pocock published a design for a "Hunting Establishment" that was meant to "give the idea of a Village." Consisting of a house, a stable, and four other buildings, this mock settlement differs from previous village designs in its picturesque irregularity. The buildings are partly screened by trees, set at varying distances from the viewer, and provided with irregular Gothic or quasi-Tudor elevations. Pocock professed to demonstrate here that in the buildings of a large estate, "picturesque beauty may be joined to utility." By extension, he encouraged greater picturesque irregularity in future village planning.[205]

•

From 1750 well into the nineteenth century, scores of new villages and towns were founded in Scotland, both to stimulate new industry and commerce, and to accommodate farm laborers dispossessed by new, more efficient agricultural techniques. Some of these settlements were laid out by estate owners and entrepreneurs: in the 1760s, for example, the tenth Earl of Renfrew laid out Eaglesham as a cotton-spinning town, and Sir Archibald Grant of Monymusk laid out Archiestown to house the crofters cleared from his estate. Other settlements were corporate ventures, such as Ullapool (1788) and Tobermory (1788), which were founded by the British Fisheries Society. After 1795 the rate of foundation in the Lowlands declined, while the growing number of enclosures and clearances in the Highlands accelerated the rate of foundation there.[206] Between 1800 and 1820 the plans of several Highland settlements and a few late Lowland examples were illustrated in the literature of agricultural improvement, and deserve brief consideration here.

Sir John Sinclair, as the owner of some 100,000 acres in Caithness, first President of the Board of Agriculture, and editor of the massive *Statistical Account of Scotland* (1791–1799), was extensively involved with many aspects of agricultural improvement. Sometime before 1800 he developed a proposal for establishing experimental farms. This was published in the *Annals of Agriculture*, Volume XXXIV (1800; *see* Entry 479) and also published in Paris by the Institut National as *Projet d'un plan pour établir des fermes expérimentales* ([1800?]; *see* Entry 308). The proposal was accompanied by a design for a small village of 20 circular cottages and two school buildings located around the periphery of a circle 540 feet in diameter. In its geometric perfection it clearly prefigured Gandy's proposal of 1805. Sinclair's proposal, however, is more detailed. Individual gardens radiate outward from the cottages, while the interior of the circle is largely devoted to a lawn for children to play on. At the very center is a square area reserved for a workshop and a common kitchen.

Sinclair described recent improvements on his own estates in *Hints Regarding Certain Measures Calculated to Improve an Extensive Property* (1802; Entry 308). He cited problems that were common to many Highland estates, including the poor climate, inefficient farming methods, bad roads and harbors, the lack of markets for agricultural produce, and almost nonexistent commerce and industry. He intended to rectify these problems in part by developing the fishing industry, new manufacturing industries, and other forms of trade in new villages at Berriedale, Sarclet, and Halkirk, and in the New Town at Thurso. In *Hints* he illustrated the new plan for Thurso: an orthogonal pattern of streets running parallel and perpendicular to the Thurso River, and flanked by uniform houses and terraces. Near the center of the New Town is a square with a statue in the center, and at other major street intersections the corners of the buildings are beveled to create small octagonal plazas. Upstream from the residential area the plan shows a church, a proposed academy, and a projected hospital, while downstream—toward the old town of Thurso—are the town quay, brewery, tanning yard, plough factory, and a variety of markets. Directly adjacent to the river bank, below a long range of residential terraces, there is a "Mall or Public Walk." In the caption to the plate, Sinclair remarked that this highly "regular" plan was "not only ornamental but also peculiarly well adapted for preserving the health & promoting the convenience of the Inhabitants." He especially acclaimed the "complete circulation of air" that the street plan afforded, and the "pleasant & healthy" character of the walks along the river.

Sinclair's *Sketch of the Improvements, Now Carrying On . . . in the County of Caithness* (1803; Entry 309), shorter than *Hints*, is again concerned with the problems of "surplus population" created by "an improved system of agriculture and the enlargement of farms." Sinclair proposed to create "a new race" of industrious, prosperous people by building new towns, villages, roads, and harbors, establishing new industries, and other progressive measures. He again illustrated the plan of the New Town at Thurso, and also included plans and elevations of McDonalds Square and the houses in Janet Street. In addition there is a plan for a fishing village at Sarclet, to be renamed Brodiestown. Five detached houses are arranged in a semicircle facing an estuary. To the left and right two streets extend back at oblique angles, parallel to the shore, and a third street runs directly inland. Houses flank both sides of the inland street and the inland side of the other two streets. Although the low density of the plan and the geometric regularity of the semicircle are reminiscent of Sinclair's project for a circular farm village, the design is clearly adapted to the immediate circumstances of the site, and not meant to be an exemplar of ideal town planning.

The plans of Brodiestown and Thurso are illustrated again in John Henderson's *General View of the County of Caithness* (1812; Entry 99). Henderson also depicted the plan of Halkirk, to be laid out along the Thurso River inland from Thurso. The streets are arranged orthogonally, roughly parallel and perpendicular to the river, with a modest concave curve in the center of the street closest to the river bank. In addition to a church and a school at one corner of the settlement, the streets are lined by approximately 54 detached houses, each set in a private rectangular plot.

In the same year in which Sinclair's *Sketch* appeared, Robert Rennie published a 17-page essay devoted entirely to village planning, titled "Plan of an Inland Village" (1803; Entry 275). He advised that the plan be regular, with straight streets and buildings of uniform height and width. The example that he illustrated is a village formed by the intersection of two streets, 60 to 100 feet wide, lined by rows of attached cottages. The streets intersect in a large marketplace, 180 to 300 feet square, with "some public building, as a church, a bridewell, or a prison" in the center. Smaller streets, running parallel to the principal thoroughfares, provide access to garden plots and fields.

Figure 5

William Aiton's report to the Board of Agriculture on the county of Ayr (1811; Entry 93) depicts a variety of civil improvements, including three town planning schemes. The most important is Peter Nicholson's design for Ardrossan, laid out for the Earl of Eglinton beginning in 1806. Located on the Firth of Clyde and the Bay of Ardrossan, the town includes a marketplace at the far northern end, a dock on a spit of land to the west, and several rows of terraces parallel to the shore of the Bay of Ardrossan. Within the range of terraces closest to the Bay, two indented segmental crescents command dramatic views across the water. Even more dramatic is a very large crescent of 43 detached villas facing an inlet of the sea immediately south of the rest of the town. This is perhaps reminiscent of the smaller crescent of detached houses at Brodiestown, but at Ardrossan the villas form an open, airy, attractively sited residential suburb that is clearly detached from the more densely populated commercial center of town. Such an arrangement, almost unique for its time, is an important precedent for suburbs of detached villas soon to be erected throughout Britain.[207] Aiton also illustrated a plan for a country village, containing sixteen pairs of two- and three-story semidetached houses, with individual front and rear garden plots. The houses are arranged in two rows, on opposite sides of a "bleaching ground," through which runs a "rivulet." Two parallel "village roads," one on each side of the bleaching ground, separate it from the two rows of houses. Finally, Aiton included a plan and elevation of a pair of elliptical crescents, facing each other, that were to be erected in Dreghorn.

The next year William Singer completed his *General View of the Agriculture* of Dumfries,[208] including a plan of the village of Bridekirk, begun in 1800. The plan is generally orthogonal, with two principal streets running northwest-southeast, and five running perpendicular. The northeast side of the town, however, is bounded by a large concave semicircle, facing down a gentle slope toward the bridge over the Annan River. The area between this semicircle and a mill race, which runs generally parallel to the river, was to be "laid out for Large Gardens &c." All the streets are shown lined by rows of semidetached cottages, with individual yards and offices behind each cottage. Various stringent regulations concerning building, selling liquor, and "nuisance" industries had been instituted as "security against having vagabonds in such a place"; the intent was to insure that only "industrious people" could "afford to build or rent such houses."

In 1820, finally, James Loch completed his extensive *Account of the Improvements on the Estates of the Marquess of Stafford* (Entry 180), in which he described a host of measures—many of which were strongly criticized— undertaken for the improvement of the Sutherland estates. Among his most unpopular actions, he shifted residents of many Highland glens to coastal areas, where he expected they would flourish by developing new and expanded fishing industries. Loch included illustrations of two new coastal settlements, both with unremarkable orthogonal plans: the fishing port of Helmsdale, designed in 1814 by John Rennie, and the harbor town of Brora, begun in 1811.

•

While most early nineteenth-century Scottish proposals for new settlements were primarily concerned with economic development and accommodation of displaced population, in many cases there was some recognition of the picturesque possibilities of the site—usually in the form of a segmental or semicircular crescent facing a waterfront. English plans published during the same period were about evenly divided between proposals that specifically emphasized picturesque improvements, and utilitarian projects for laborers' communities.

One of the earliest published proposals for picturesque improvements appears in Charles Vancouver's report on the agriculture of Devon (1808; Entry 102). Set among the dramatic cliffs and hills surrounding the harbor at Torquay, the intended improvements consisted of terraces and semi-detached houses following the contour of the land, arranged where possible into convex or concave crescents. Vancouver noted that the "regularity" of extant buildings added "neatness and beauty to the wild and picturesque scenery" of the site, and implied that the new terraces and villas would do likewise. He indicated that these improvements were intended to ac-commodate "company resorting hither for the convenience of sea-bathing," but also projected that Torquay would become a place "of some maritime consequence" in the future (p. 322). This elaborate scheme was never completed, however, and instead isolated detached villas slowly covered the landscape over the next several decades.

The picturesque also appears much later, in Peter Frederick Robinson's *Village Architecture* (1830; Entry 297). Robinson did not propose to design an entire village according to one uniform picturesque program, but he did recommend careful attention to the pictorial characteristics of every building type. The results, when brought together in a single village, would result in a composition quite reminiscent of picturesque painting: the village would contain forms "which our painters have so long delighted to portray, and which have in fact given real value to their pictures." The conjectural example that Robinson illustrated includes a church, a par-sonage, a school, a workhouse, an inn, a combined town hall and market building, and a pump, arranged in a seemingly casual, irregular manner, and surrounded by picturesque scenery.

A view of a similar village appears in the frontispiece to William Cotton's *Short and Simple Letters to English Folk* (1841; Entry 44). An inn, a church, a market hall, houses, shops, and other structures are shown in a variety of Old English and vernacular styles. Cotton's text, including citations from the Bible, describes a "pattern village" in which everything contributes to the moral well-being of its Christian inhabitants.

A far more secular concern for the economic and social welfare of laborers pervades Robert Owen's 1817 proposal for "Agricultural and Manufacturing Villages of *Unity* and *Mutual Co-Operation*." This proposal, for a square communitarian village surrounded by long terraces of "lodging-houses," became the prototype for several other settlements projected by utopian reformers in the next two decades.[209]

In 1826 William Allen, a reformer and philanthropist who had been an associate of Owen, included a plan for a much smaller model village in a pamphlet titled *Colonies at Home* (Entry 6). A single street is lined with 24 cottages on each side, plus a school in the middle of each side—one school for boys, the other for girls. There is also a plan for a small model community in the first volume of a philanthropic periodical begun in 1831, *Facts and Illustrations Demonstrating the Important Benefits Which Have Been . . . Derived by Labourers from Possessing Small Portions of Land* (Entry 79). This geometrically regular "colony of ten families" was designed by Edward Lance, a land surveyor. A barn and two granaries are located within a central octagonal area. Rectangular meadows extend outward from each of two opposite sides of the octagon. Two more rectangular plots, perpendicular to the meadows, contain the residence, school, and private garden of the schoolmaster, and the residence, shop, and garden of the overseer. Extending out from the remaining sides of the central octagon are four double garden plots; straddling the line between each pair is a double stable and a double cottage.

•

Picturesquely sited detached or semidetached villas are frequently found in town and village plans published in Scotland and England during the first half of the nineteenth century; they soon became essential features of middle-class suburbs in the mid- and late nineteenth century. For reasons that I have discussed in several places above, this dwelling type especially suited the social, recreational, intellectual, and emotional predilections of Britain's middle classes.

Early in the eighteenth century Henry Aldrich already had defined the characteristics of the suburban house:

Neatness should be attended to, but retirement more; its principal requisites are ease and repose. Its appearance is neater than the country house, and not so splendid as one in the city. It neither boasts of pastures, or sumptuous dining rooms; content with a study, a garden, and extensive walks. It will be conducive to health if it be placed somewhat on an eminence, and to pleasure if it has a view of the city you have left behind you.[210]

By 1839 Samuel H. Brooks, introducing his *Designs for Cottage and Villa Architecture* (Entry 23), confirmed the progress of the suburban ideal: suburban life, he said, was the goal of each "Englishman, in whose mind the idea of retirement from business and a country life are inseparably united: and thus, *par eminence*, England becomes the country of suburban villas." Early nineteenth-century plans for picturesque groups of such villas, then, were the forerunners of a quintessential British planning type of the mid-and late nineteenth century—the villa suburb in which ideals of retirement, emotional release, and intellectual regeneration were facilitated not only by the architecture, but also by the picturesque, self-consciously rural character of the plan.[211]

Notes

Some standard references are cited in abbreviated form; explanations may be found in the List of Symbols and Abbreviations at the beginning of the principal entries. All other citations are given in full at their first appearance in each section of a chapter; subsequent citations within sections are given in brief form.

**I
Architecture and
the Book Trade**

1. The major eighteenth-century architectural publisher was Robert Sayer, whose interests extended also to maps, charts, and prints. He published architectural books by Chambers, Garret, Halfpenny, Lightoler, Morris, Over, Pain, and others. Robert and James Dodsley published major treatises by Bardwell, Chambers, Kirby, Malton, Newton, Paine, and Wood; but as one of the principal publishing firms of the mid-eighteenth century, their architectural output was greatly overshadowed by other titles. For further details see note 64 below and Appendix F.

2. See Appendix F.

3. R. Campbell, *The London Tradesman. Being a Compendious View of All the Trades, Professions, Arts, Both Liberal and Mechanic, Now Practised in the Cities of London and Westminster* (London: Printed by T. Gardner, 1747), p. 128. See too Terry Belanger, "From Bookseller to Publisher: Changes in the London Book Trade, 1750–1850," in Richard G. Landon, ed., *Book Selling and Book Buying: Aspects of the Nineteenth-Century British and North American Book Trade* (Chicago: American Library Association, 1978), p. 8. Also on booksellers and publishers see Gerald P. Tyson, "Joseph Johnson, an Eighteenth-Century Bookseller," *Studies in Bibliography* XXVIII (1975), 1–16; and Michael Treadwell's sophisticated analysis of "London Trade Publishers 1675–1750," *The Library*, 6th ser., IV:2 (June 1982), 99–134.

4. J. Collier, *The Parents and Guardians Directory* (London, 1761), p. 69; quoted by Belanger, "From Bookseller to Publisher," p. 9.

5. Ibid.

6. R. W. Chapman, "Eighteenth-Century Imprints," *The Library*, 4th ser., XI (1931), 503.

7. Graham Pollard, "The London Share Book System," in *Hodson's Booksellers, Publishers and Stationers Directory 1855* (Oxford: Oxford Bibliographical Society, 1972), p. vi; and Pollard, "The Sandars Lectures, 1959," *Publishing History* IV (1978), 32. Also see Richard Nels Lutes, "Andrew Strahan and the London Sharebook System, 1785–1825: A Study of the Strahan Printing and Publishing Records," Ph.D. diss., Wayne State University, 1979.

8. Belanger, "From Bookseller to Publisher," p. 10.

9. Ibid.; and Pollard, "The London Share Book System," pp. vi–vii.

10. Pollard, "The Sandars Lectures," p. 29.

11. H. G. Aldis, "Book Production and Distribution, 1625–1800," in *The Cambridge History of English Literature* (Cambridge: Cambridge University Press, 1932), XI, 325; and Leslie F. Chard, "Bookseller to Publisher: Joseph Johnson and the English Book Trade, 1760 to 1810," *The Library*, 5th ser., XXXII:2 (June 1977), 149.

12. Belanger, "From Bookseller to Publisher," pp. 11–12, 15–16; and Pollard, "The Sandars Lectures," pp. 29–30.

13. Belanger, "From Bookseller to Publisher," p. 13.

14. Pollard, "The Sandars Lectures," pp. 35–36, 41. Isaac and Josiah Taylor were two of the earliest publishers to specialize in architecture. Their "Architectural Library" at 56 (later 59) High Holborn was clearly the most prominent architectural bookstore of the late eighteenth and early nineteenth centuries.

15. Thomas Rees, *Reminiscences of Literary London from 1779 to 1853* (New York: Francis P. Harper, 1896), pp. 20–21.

16. *Leigh's New Picture of London* (London: Printed for S. Leigh, 1818); cited in Pollard, "The Sandars Lectures," p. 36.

17. *The Author's Printing and Publishing Assistant*, 2nd ed. (London: Saunders and Otley, 1839), pp. 52–53.

18. For an excellent short analysis of the copyright situation in early eighteenth century Britain, on which my remarks here are based, plus references to several other studies of copyright, see R. M. Wiles, *Serial Publication in England before 1750* (Cambridge: Cambridge University Press, 1957), pp. 154–163. Also see Arnold Plant, "The Economic Aspects of Copyright in Books," *Economica*, new ser., I:2 (May 1934), 167–195; Lyman Ray Patterson, *Copyright in Historical Perspective* (Nashville: Vanderbilt University Press, 1968); and Ian Parsons, "Copyright and Society," in Asa Briggs, ed., *Essays in the History of Publishing in Celebration of the 250th Anniversary of the House of Longman* (London: Longman, 1974), pp. 29–60.

19. Royal Licences appear in at least four of the books listed in the principal entries above: Campbell's *Vitruvius Britannicus* (1715; Entry 32); de Coetlogon's *Universal History of Arts and Sciences* (1745, Licence issued 1741; Entry 64); Hall's *New Royal Encyclopaedia* (1788; Entry 141); and the *Encyclopaedia Londinensis* (1795; Entry 74).

20. Belanger, "From Bookseller to Publisher," p. 11. Patterson, *Copyright*, pp. 172–179.

21. *The Author's Printing and Publishing Assistant*, p. 55; Marjorie Plant, *The English Book Trade* (London: Allen & Unwin, 1939), p. 420.

22. Plant, *The English Book Trade*, pp. 76–77; Chard, "Bookseller to Publisher," p. 142.

23. G. P. R. James, "Some Observations on the Book Trade, as Connected with Literature, in England," *Journal of the Statistical Society of London* VI:1 (February 1843), 53.

24. In the eighteenth century many important architectural treatises were published in part or in whole by the author, including the Adams' *Works in Architecture* (1778–1779), Castell's *Villas of the Ancients* (1728), Chambers's *Treatise on Civil Architecture* (1759), Pain's *Practical House Carpenter* (1788), Plaw's *Rural Architecture* (1785), Rawlins's *Familiar Architecture* (1768), and Riou's *Grecian Orders of Architecture* (1768). For further examples see the "Author" entries in Appendix F.

25. Theodore Besterman, *The Publishing Firm of Cadell & Davies* (London: Oxford University Press, 1938), p. xxx. For a similar example see F. D. Tredrey, *The House of Blackwood 1804–1954* (Edinburgh and London: Blackwood, 1954), p. 15. Further on mutual risk arrangements see Chard, "Bookseller to Publisher," p. 142.

26. Besterman, *Cadell & Davies*, pp. xxx–xxxi.

27. *The Author's Printing and Publishing Assistant*, pp. 54–55.

28. Subscription lists of course were often inaccurate, and cannot be used as an absolute index of the number of copies printed or sold. See F. J. G. Robinson and P. J. Wallis, *Book Subscription Lists* (Newcastle upon Tyne: Book Subscriptions List Project, 1975), pp. II–IV.

29. This information is based on examination of a copy in the Avery Library, Columbia University.

30. In the copy at Yale the names of seven more subscribers were entered in longhand.

31. For Cadell and Davies see Besterman, *Cadell & Davies*, p. xxxi. For one book published on commission, only 150 copies were printed; for another book printed on large paper, only 50 copies were made. For Johnson see Chard, "Bookseller to Publisher," p. 144.

32. *Minutes of Evidence Taken before the Committee on Acts of 8 Anne, and 15 & 41 Geo. III* (London: House of Commons, 1813), pp. 3, 5.

33. R. D. Harlan, "Some Additional Figures of Distribution of Eighteenth-Century English Books," *Papers of the Bibliographical Society of America* LIX:2 (1965), 160–170. Chard reports that one tract published by Johnson, Priestley's *Appeal to the Serious* (1770), ran to at least 30,000, and perhaps 60,000, copies: "Bookseller to Publisher," p. 144.

34. Plant, *The English Book Trade*, p. 94.

35. *Minutes of Evidence Taken before the Committee on Acts of 8 Anne, and 15 & 41 Geo. III*, p. 21.

36. I have extracted this information from figures provided by the firm and printed ibid., p. 23.

37. Paul Korshin, "Types of Eighteenth-Century Literary Patronage," *Eighteenth-Century Studies* VII: 4 (Summer 1974), 457.

38. Ibid., p. 459; and Seymour de Ricci, *English Collectors of Books & Manuscripts (1530–1930) and Their Marks of Ownership* (New York: Macmillan, 1930), pp. 44–53.

39. Korshin, "Types of Patronage," pp. 467–468.

40. Ibid., pp. 463–464. Korshin pointed out that this practice "democratized" literary patronage, while also removing the "sense of obligation which pervades and often exacerbates the traditional patron-client relationship."

41. Frank Arthur Mumby and Ian Norrie, *Publishing and Bookselling* (London: Jonathan Cape, 1974), p. 93.

42. Ibid.; Robinson and Wallis, *Book Subscription Lists*, p. II. On seventeenth-century subscription books see S. L. C. Clapp, "The Beginning of Subscription Publication in the Seventeenth Century," *Modern Philology* XXIX: 2 (November 1931), 199–224; and W. E. Risden, "New Ventures in Publishing between 1680 and 1700," B.Litt. thesis, Oxford University, 1966.

43. Plant, *The English Book Trade*, pp. 227–229; and Robinson and Wallis, *Book Subscription Lists*, pp. II–IV.

44. Robinson and Wallis, *Book Subscription Lists*, pp. III–VII. The steadily increasing numbers of subscribers to the three volumes of Campbell's *Vitruvius Britannicus* (1715–1725) demonstrate its growing popularity. The subscription list in a copy of Thomas Collins Overton's *Original Designs of Temples* (1766) at Yale includes the names of seven additional subscribers entered in longhand. Presumably their subscriptions were received after the list was printed, and the author did not care to have the list reset.

45. See the sections above, "Arrangements between Author and Publisher" and "Publisher, Wholesaler, and Retailer."

46. The numerical analysis of subscription lists conducted here might well be supplemented by detailed research into the identity of individual subscribers, focusing in particular on such matters as their wealth, places of residence, and friendships and associations with authors and with other subscribers.

47. On the subject of support through subscription see note 40.

48. Seven for Messrs. Dodsley, 14 for A. Millar, seven for Piers and Webley, and seven for R. Sayer.

49. On the professional status of architects during this period see Colvin (1978), pp. 26–41; J. Mordaunt Crook, "The Pre-Victorian Architect: Professionalism & Patronage," *Architectural History* 12 (1969), 62–68; Frank Jenkins, *Architect and Patron* (London: Oxford University Press, 1961); Barrington Kaye, *The Development of the Architectural Profession in Britain* (London: Allen & Unwin, 1960); Andrew Saint, *The Image of the Architect* (New Haven: Yale University Press, 1983); and John Wilton-Ely, "The Rise of the Professional Architect in England," in Spiro Kostof, ed., *The Architect* (New York: Oxford University Press, 1977), pp. 180–208.

50. N.B. in addition two prominent architects, William Chambers and Henry Holland, are present but not designated as "Architect" in this list.

51. John Joshua Kirby, "Designer in Perspective to His Majesty." See Entries 167 and 168.

52. Francis Hiorne. John Crunden and John Wood are also listed, but without professional titles. The latter subscribed for six copies.

53. Henry Holland's name is included in the list, but without any professional title.

54. Including one "Professor of Architecture" and one "Architect and Surveyor."

55. Including one "Professor of Landscape."

56. Wiles, *Serial Publication in England*, p. 79. My remarks here are based in large part on Wiles's analysis. Also see Plant, *The English Book Trade*, pp. 232–234, 418–419; and Mihai H. Handrea, "Books in Parts and the Number Trade," in Landon, *Book Selling and Book Buying*, pp. 34–52.

57. Wiles, *Serial Publication in England*, pp. 4–5 and passim.

58. Plant, *The English Book Trade*, p. 419. See too Agnes A. C. Blackie, *Blackie & Son 1809–1959* (London: Blackie & Son [1959?]), pp. 5–6.

59. Ibid., pp. 196, 327, 7. For Chambers see Entry 37.5.

60. Wiles, *Serial Publication in England*, p. 327.

61. Ibid., p. 313.

62. Ibid., p. 291.

63. Also note that in several books by Peter Frederick Robinson (Entries 291–293, 295–297) the pages of letterpress for each design are numbered separately, strongly suggesting that the books were issued in fascicles.

64. Following is a select bibliography of available monographs and articles on many publishers and printers listed in Appendix F. Note that authoritative studies of several major architectural publishers—including Carpenter, Kelly, Priestley and Weale, and Sayer—remain to be written. Additional information on individuals and firms listed below, as well as many others engaged in the print trade, may be found in Trevor H. Howard-Hill, *British Bibliography and Textual Criticism: A Bibliography. Volume IV: Index to British Literary Bibliography* (Oxford: Clarendon Press, 1979).

Ackermann: see note 69.

Arch: Geoffrey Keynes, *William Pickering* (London: The Galahad Press, 1969), pp. 9, 10.

Bagster: Samuel Bagster, *Sameul Bagster of London, 1772–1851: An Autobiography* (London: Bagster, 1972).

Black: *Adam & Charles Black 1807–1957* (London: Black, 1957); Alexander Nicolson, ed., *Memoirs of Adam Black* (Edinburgh: Black, 1885).

Blackie: Blackie, *Blackie & Son* (see note 58); Walter Graham Blackie, *Sketch of the Origin and Progress of the Firm of Blackie and Son* (Printed for private circulation, 1897); *150 Years of Publishing* (exhibition catalogue, 1959).

Blackwood: Margaret Oliphant, *Annals of a Publishing House: William Blackwood and His Sons*, 2 vols. (Edinburgh: Blackwood, 1897); Mrs. Gerald Porter, *Annals of a Publishing House: John Blackwood* (Edinburgh: Blackwood, 1898); Tredrey, *The House of Blackwood* (see note 25).

Bohn: Rees, *Reminiscences*, p. 74.

Brindley: George Smith and Frank Benger, *The Oldest London Bookshop* (London: Ellis, 1928).

Bulmer: Peter C. G. Isaac, "William Bulmer, 1757–1830: An Introductory Essay," *The Library*, 5th ser., XIII:1 (March 1958), 37–50; H. V. Marrot, "William Bulmer," *The Fleuron* V (1926), 63–91; Marrot, *William Bulmer; Thomas Bensley; A Study in Transition* (London: The Fleuron, 1930).

Cadell and Davies: Besterman, *Cadell & Davies* (see note 25).

Clements: Norma Hodgson and Cyprian Blagden, *The Notebook of Thomas Bennet and Henry Clements (1686–1719)* (Oxford: Oxford Bibliographical Society, 1956).

Clowes: W. B. Clowes, *Family Business 1803–1953* (London: William Clowes and Sons, [1953]).

Davies: Edward Marston, *Sketches of Some Booksellers of the Time of Dr. Samuel Johnson* (London: Sampson Low, Marston & Co., 1902).

Dickinson: Joan Evans, *The Endless Web: John Dickinson & Co. Ltd. 1804–1954* (London: Jonathan Cape, 1955).

Dodsley: Aldis, "Book Production," pp. 322–324, 334; Marston, *Sketches of Some Booksellers*; Ralph Straus, *Robert Dodsley* (London: John Lane, 1910).

Hansard: J. C. Trewin and E. M. King, *Printer to the House: The Story of Hansard* (London: Methuen & Co., 1952).

Hatchard: Arthur L. Humphreys, *Piccadilly Bookmen: Memorials of the House of Hatchard* (London: Hatchards, 1893); James Laver, *Hatchards of Piccadilly 1797–1947: One Hundred and Fifty Years of Bookselling* (London: Hatchards, 1947).

Johnson: Chard, "Bookseller to Publisher," 138–154; Tyson, "Joseph Johnson"; Paul M. Zall, "The Cool World of Samuel Taylor Coleridge: Joseph Johnson, or the Perils of Publishing," *The Wordsworth Circle* III:1 (Winter 1972), 25–30.

Lackington: Edward Marston, *Sketches of Booksellers of Other Days* (New York: Charles Scribner's Sons, 1901).

Lintot: Marston, *Sketches of Some Booksellers.*

Longman: Asa Briggs, "Introduction: At the Sign of the Ship," in *Essays in the History of Publishing* (see note 18), pp. 1–28; Harold Cox, *The House of Longman* (London: Longmans, Green and Co., 1925); Charles James Longman, *The House of Longman 1724–1800* (London: Longmans, Green and Co., 1936); Philip Wallis, *At the Sign of the Ship; Notes on the House of Longman, 1724–1974* (Harlow: Longman Group, 1974).

Millar: Marston, *Sketches of Some Booksellers.*

Moyes: Iain Bain, "James Moyes and His Temple Printing Office of 1825," *Journal of the Printing Historical Society* IV (1968), 1–10.

Murray: James Grant, *Portraits of Public Characters* (London: Saunders and Otley, 1841), II, 1–46; Samuel Smiles, *A Publisher and His Friends* (London: John Murray, 1891).

Newbery: Sydney Roscoe, *John Newbery and His Successors 1740–1815* (Wormley: Five Owls Press, 1973).

Nichols: Albert H. Smith, "John Nichols, Printer and Publisher," *The Library*, 5th ser., XVIII:3 (September 1963), 169–190.

Osborne: Marston, *Sketches of Some Booksellers.*

Pickering: Keynes, *William Pickering.*

Quaritch: Charlotte Quaritch Wrentmore, "Foreword" in Bernard Quaritch, Ltd., *A Catalogue of Books and Manuscripts Issued to Commemorate the One Hundredth Anniversary of the Firm* (London: Bernard Quaritch, 1947), pp. v–xvii.

Richardson: Marston, *Sketches of Booksellers of Other Days*; William M. Sale, Jr., *Samuel Richardson: Master Printer* (Ithaca: Cornell University Press, 1950).

Rivington: Septimus Rivington, *The Publishing Family of Rivington* (London: Rivingtons, 1919).

Robson: Smith and Benger, *The Oldest London Bookshop.*

Spottiswoode: Richard Arthur Austen-Leigh, *The Story of a Printing House* (London: Spottiswoode, 1912).

Strahan: Austen-Leigh, *Story of a Printing House*; O. M. Brack, Jr., "William Strahan: Scottish Printer and Publisher," *The Arizona Quarterly* XXXI:2 (Summer 1975), 179–191; J. A. Cochrane, *Dr. Johnson's Printer: The Life of William Strahan* (London: Routledge & Kegan Paul, 1964); Robert Dale Harlan, "William Strahan: Eighteenth Century London Printer and Publisher," Ph.D. diss., University of Michigan, 1960; Patricia Hernlund, "William Strahan's Ledgers: Standard Charges for Printing, 1738–1785," *Studies in Bibliography* XX (1967), 89–111; Hernlund, "William Strahan's Ledgers, II: Charges for Papers, 1738–1785," *Studies in Bibliography* XXII (1969), 179–195; Lutes, "Andrew Strahan" (see note 7).

Taylor (Isaac and Josiah): see notes 66 and 68 below.

Taylor (Richard): Nicholas Barker, "Richard Taylor: A Preliminary Note," *Journal of the Printing Historical Society*, no. 2 (1966), 45–48.

Tegg: Grant, *Portraits of Public Characters*, II, 1–46.

Treuttel and Würtz: Giles C. Barber, "Treuttel and Würtz: Some Aspects of the Importation of Books from France, c. 1825," *The Library*, 5th ser., XXIII:2 (June 1968), 118–144.

Warne: Arthur King and A. F. Stuart, *The House of Warne: One Hundred Years of Publishing* (London: Warne, 1965).

Whittingham: Arthur Warren, *The Charles Whittinghams Printers* (New York: The Grolier Club, 1896).

65. See the section "Publisher, Wholesaler, and Retailer."

66. Biographical information concerning these and other contemporary publishers is available in Ian Maxted, *The London Book Trades 1775–1800* (Folkestone: Dawson, 1977). For information on individuals in the printing trades in the early nineteenth century see William B. Todd, *A Directory of Printers and Others in Allied Trades: London and Vicinity 1800–1840* (London: Printing Historical Society, 1972). For nineteenth century publishers see Philip A. H. Brown, *London Publishers and Printers* (London: British Museum, 1961).

67. See Appendix F: Miller, *The Country Gentleman's Architect* (1787).

68. Weale's trading address is "Taylor's Architectural Library" in the imprints of Sopwith's *Treatise on Isometrical Drawing* (1834; Entry 323.1) and Wilds's *Elementary and Practical Instructions* (1835; Entry 347.1). M. Taylor is listed as "nephew and successor to the late Josiah Taylor" in the imprints of Pocock's *Modern Finishings for Rooms* (1835; Entry 263.3) and Thomson's *Retreats* (1835; Entry 333.3). For further information see John Britton's account of Taylor in Rees, *Reminiscences*, pp. 123–125; DNB; and Doris Mary Armitage, *The Taylors of Ongar* (Cambridge: W. Heffer & Sons, 1939).

69. Rees, *Reminiscences*, pp. 137–143; and Wyatt Papworth, "Rudolph Ackermann," *Notes and Queries*, 4th ser., IV:84 (7 August 1869), 109–112, and IV:85 (14 August 1869), 129–131. The ensuing remarks are based on these accounts and on Maxted, *The London Book Trades*, p. 1. Also on Ackermann see William J. Burke, *Rudolph Ackermann: Promoter of the Arts and Sciences* (New York: New York Public Library, 1935); Phyllis M. Handover, "Rudolph Ackermann," *Motif* XIII (1967), 81–89; Sarah T. Prideaux, "Rudolph Ackermann and His Associates," Chapter VI in *Aquatint Engraving: A Chapter in the History of Book Illustration* (London: Duckworth, 1909), pp. 110–152; Prideaux, "Rudolph Ackermann and the Work of His Press. 1764–1834," *The Printing Art* VII:2 (April 1906), 85–93; and A. Samuels, "Rudolph Ackermann," Ph.D. diss., Cambridge University, 1972.

70. The first edition of Senefelder's book appeared in Munich in 1818. Ackermann's translation (London, 1819) is described in Entry 478. He provided new plates because customs duties would have made the importation of Senefelder's plates prohibitively expensive.

71. Ackermann's topographical publications are listed by Wyatt Papworth in "Rudolph Ackermann," pp. 111–112. There were 3,000 subscribers to the *Repository* by the end of its first year; many of the articles that originally appeared there in series were successfully republished as books (ibid., p. 112). On J. B. Papworth, see Entries 246–248. Ackermann also published the famous *Tours* of Dr. Syntax (Papworth, "Rudolph Ackermann," p. 129).

72. There are no Welsh imprints among the principal entries.

73. A fifth architectural book issued in Dublin is Thomas Humphreys's *Irish Builder's Guide* (1813; Entry 488). Among books with Dublin imprints that concern related subjects are several editions of *The Art of Drawing in Perspective* (Entry 7), several editions of Chambers's *Cyclopaedia* (Entry 37), an edition of Hale's *Compleat Body of Husbandry* (Entry 486) published in 1757, a 1778 edition of Ferguson's *Art of Drawing in Perspective* (Entry 80), and a 1790–1797 edition of the *Encyclopaedia Britannica* (Entry 73). Editions of Batty and Thomas Langley's manual *The Builder's Jewel* were issued in Dublin in 1766 and 1768 (Entries 377.7, 377.10).

74. On the northward progress of Palladianism see Summerson (1969), pp. 224–225. The next architectural books published in Edinburgh that I have found are the 1768 edition of Batty and Thomas Langley's *Builder's Jewel* (Entry 377.11), and the 1769 *Supplement to the Builder's Jewel* (Entry 389.1).

75. Not all reports on Scottish counties were published in Scotland; many were issued in England. Nevertheless four were published in Edinburgh (Entries 104, 111, 116–117, 120), one in Aberdeen (Entry 92), and another in Glasgow (Entry 93). Four other books published in Edinburgh are included in the principal entries below, but are not primarily architectural treatises: the *Encyclopaedia Britannica* (1771; Entry 73), the *Encyclopaedia Perthensis* ([1796–1806]; Entry 76), Brewster's *Edinburgh Encyclopaedia* ([1808]–1830; Entry 22), and late editions of Ferguson's treatise on perspective (1802 and 1803; Entries 80.4 and 80.5). Designs for dwellings in all these works were of incidental importance or else derived from previously published English books.

76. See Helena Hall, *William Allen 1770–1843* (Haywards Heath: Charles Clarke, 1953), p. 117 and passim.

77. See note 75.

78. For example Taylor's *Designs* (Entry 328), Wilson's *Helps* (Entry 350), Parker's *Plans* (Entry 250), the Oswestry Society's *First Report* (Entry 321), and Allen's *Colonies at Home* (Entry 6).

79. Note for example the rise of the Norwich School of painters, which flourished from 1803 to 1833.

80. See the section "Publisher, Wholesaler, and Retailer."

81. See especially A. K. Cairncross and B. Weber, "Fluctuations in Building in Great Britain, 1785–1849," *The Economic History Review*, 2nd ser., IX: 2 (December 1956), 283–297; T. S. Ashton, *Economic Fluctuations in England 1700–1800* (Oxford: Clarendon Press, 1959), especially Chapter 4; and J. Parry Lewis, *Building Cycles and Britain's Growth* (London: Macmillan, 1965). More recently C. W. Chalklin published an extensive examination of "the building process" in Britain based on these and many other sources, plus considerable detailed analysis of primary records: see *The Provincial Towns of Georgian England: A Study of the Building Process 1740–1820* (London: Edward Arnold, 1974), especially pp. 256–299. For much of the discussion in this section I have relied on Chalklin's excellent analysis.

82. Cairncross and Weber, "Fluctuations," p. 287; Chalklin, *The Provincial Towns*, p. 285 and passim.

83. In Appendix E encyclopedias and dictionaries are marked by a bullet (•), and publications of the Board of Agriculture are marked by a diamond (♦). All periodicals are listed in notes 23 and 24 of the Introduction.

84. Parry Lewis's correlations between timber imports and building activity are listed in Chalklin, *The Provincial Towns*, Table 6, p. 258.

85. Ibid., pp. 258–259. Chalklin cites several sources including Parry Lewis, *Building Cycles*, and Sir John Summerson, *Georgian London* (Harmondsworth: Penguin, 1969), p. 112.

86. Ashton, *Economic Fluctuations*, pp. 96, 187. Publications by William and John Halfpenny: Entries 130, 133, 134, 136–139.

87. Chalklin, *The Provincial Towns*, pp. 264–271; Ashton, *Economic Fluctuations*, pp. 98–100.

88. For exceptions see Chalklin, *The Provincial Towns*, p. 270.

89. Ashton, *Economic Fluctuations*, pp. 101, 165, 187.

90. Chalklin, *The Provincial Towns*, pp. 274–283; Cairncross and Weber, "Fluctuations," p. 285.

91. Chalklin, *The Provincial Towns*, p. 285. Indeed the parallels are very close: building activity declined slightly in 1807–1809, and in 1810 no new architectural books appeared.

92. Cairncross and Weber, "Fluctuations," p. 285 and passim. In addition to the peak in production of building materials in 1825, Cairncross and Weber also identified a boom in residential construction from 1822 through 1826 (p. 287).

93. Ibid., p. 285. Cairncross and Weber noted a slow increase in housing construction throughout the 1830s, despite a severe housing depression in London in the early and mid-1830s (pp. 287, 291–293).

94. Cairncross and Weber noted a rapid housing expansion in London after 1836 (ibid., p. 293).

95. See Entries 90, 91, 184, 186, 190, 291–297.

96. In addition to the polemical remarks in his Introduction, Campbell suggested humbly that perusing his plates might be a stimulating or instructive pastime for people of leisure: "I hope, therefore, the Reader will be agreeably entertained in viewing what I have collected with so much Labour" (p. 3).

97. In the Introduction Gibbs said that he was encouraged to prepare this book by people of a certain social class: "What is here presented to the Publick was undertaken at the instance of several Persons of Quality and others; and some Plates were added to what was at first intended, by the particular direction of Persons of great Distinction, for whose Commands I have the highest regard. They were of opinion, that such a Work as this would be of use to such Gentlemen as might be concerned in Building, especially in the remote parts of the Country" (p. i).

98. Elements of self-aggrandizement and self-advertisement, present to some degree in all the books mentioned here, are most evident in Lewis's book. Names of the Russian royal family are prominently displayed at the head of the list of subscribers in Volume I, and in

the Preface he noted the "Other Sets of Designs, upon a more extended scale, are reserved for subsequent publications, should this happily meet with the patronage of the Public" (I, 1).

99. Preface. The title page announced that the book would be useful as well for "all gentlemen, artificers, and others, who delight in, or practice, the art of building."

100. Among perspective treatises see for example Charles Hayter's *Introduction to Perspective* (1815; Entry 145), "adapted to the capacities of youth" and arranged in a series of dialogues "between the author's children."

101. See for example William Wilds's *Elementary and Practical Instructions* (1835; Entry 347), directed specifically to emigrants and those "unable to extricate themselves" from adverse conditions at home in Britain. For additional examples see Chapter III, Section 8.

102. Entry 261.1, p. 8. For further discussion of the type of book that Plaw introduced see Chapter II, Section 1.

103. Entry 192.1, p. 1. For additional discussion of the audiences addressed by late eighteenth- and early nineteenth-century authors see Sandra Blutman, "Books of Designs for Country Houses, 1780–1815," *Architectural History* 11 (1978), 25–33 (especially 26, 28).

104. Entry 40.3, pp. 7–15; quotation from p. 11. Near the end of this edition Chambers explained that his principal goals had been to impart "precepts" to "gentlemen," and to instruct "travellers" in means of appreciating buildings and remains in foreign countries (p. 135).

105. On the rise of the architectural profession see note 49.

106. Entry 182.1, I, 12–16. The pseudonymous author of the article noted that the *Mechanics' Magazine* (Entry 477) had recently contributed to increased respect for mechanics, as had the *Lancet* for doctors and the *Legal Observer* for lawyers. He hoped *The Architectural Magazine* would do the same for architects and surveyors, who frequently suffered from low esteem. The author suggested that the problem derived in part from a neglect of professional standards, a situation that could be remedied by establishing rules and norms under the aegis of a professional society. For later remarks by Loudon himself on the subject of architectural professionalism, see "The Regulations of the Institute of British Architects," *Architectural Magazine* II: 20 (October 1835), 470–472.

II
Format and Content

1. Two additional types require brief mention. The first comprises handbooks and manuals. The present study includes only handbooks and manuals that contain designs for dwellings, and excludes numerous books whose contents are limited to ornaments, details of construction, and the like (see "Subject Matter" in Section 1 of the Introduction). Consequently this type is insufficiently represented here to provide an adequate basis for a balanced discussion. Collections of architects' own designs would likewise benefit from separate consideration, perhaps in conjunction with architects' writings on other subjects, monographs on individual buildings, and other types of topographical literature. Additional publication types are discussed in the Introduction in Sections 1 and 2, "Scope of Inquiry" and "Publications Examined."

2. Also see two important French general treatises: François Blondel, *Cours d'architecture* (1675–1683), and Charles Augustin d'Aviler, *Cours d'architecture* (1691). Dora Wiebenson has compiled a useful survey of European general treatises and treatises on the orders: *Architectural Theory and Practice from Alberti to Ledoux* (Chicago: University of Chicago Press, 1982).

3. On the history of this publication type see the references in note 28.

4. For an analysis of changes in domestic architectural practice concurrent with the rise of picturesque cottage and villa design books, see Summerson (1959).

5. The first edition of Joseph Gwilt's mammoth *Encyclopaedia of Architecture* (London: Longman, Brown, Green, and Longman) appeared in 1842. George Richardson issued *The First Part of a Complete System of Architecture* (Entry 283) in 1794, a book that, when finished, was far less comprehensive than its title suggests. It is primarily "a series of original designs for country seats or villas." John Claudius Loudon's *Encyclopaedia of Cottage, Farm, and Villa Architecture* (1833; Entry 184) was limited to domestic and agricultural subjects.

6. A few copies of the first 44 pages of the Latin text were printed before 1710. See Colvin (1978), p. 3.

7. See for example the *Encyclopaedia Britannica* (Entry 73): in every edition from the second (1778–1783) through the sixth (1823) there are three plates containing designs borrowed from Ware.

8. This was translated into English by John James as *A Treatise of the Five Orders of Columns* (London: Printed by B. Motte, sold by J. Sturt, 1708). A second edition appeared in 1722. On Perrault's theory and his influence on English architects see Wolfgang Herrmann, *The Theory of Claude Perrault* (London: Zwemmer, 1973), especially pp. 95–129 and 155–168.

9. The first book, which treats the orders, was translated into English (from the French edition by Le Muet) by Godfrey Richards as *The First Book of Architecture* (London: Printed by J. M. and sold by G. Richards, 1663). For a discussion of this and later English translations of Palladio see Deborah Howard, "Four Centuries of Literature on Palladio," *Journal of the Society of Architectural Historians* XXIX: 3 (October 1980), 224–241.

10. See especially James Stuart and Nicholas Revett, *The Antiqvities of Athens* (London: 1762 and later), and Stephen Riou, *The Grecian Orders of Architectvre*, (1768; Entry 287).

11. See in particular: Alexander Gerard, *An Essay on Taste* (London: Printed for A. Millar, et al., 1759), and *An Essay on Genius* (London: Printed for W. Strahan, et al., 1774); Edward Young, *Conjectures on Original Composition* (London: Printed for A. Millar, et al., 1759); and William Duff, *An Essay on Original Genius* (London: Printed for E. and C. Dilly, 1767).

12. Batty Langley, *Practical Geometry* (1726; Entry 173.1). Langley's *Ancient Masonry* (1736; Entry 387.2) is an even more comprehensive survey of the orders as delineated by architects throughout Europe.

13. Batty Langley, *The Young Builder's Rudiments* (1730; Entry 175.1). Also see William Halfpenny, *Magnum in Parvo* (1722; Entry 369.1), quoted in Summerson (1969), p. 215. By midcentury the authority of Palladio was acknowledged in a wide variety of treatises. In John Robertson's *Treatise of Such Mathematical Instruments As Are Usually Put into a Portable Case*, 2nd ed. (London: T. Heath and J. Nourse, et al., 1757), for example, which contains extensive instruction in delineating the five orders (pp. 45–71), all the proportions given are according to Palladio.

14. William Halfpenny, *The Art of Sound Building*, 2nd ed. (1725; Entry 129.2); and Batty Langley, *The Young Builder's Rudiments* (1734; Entry 175.2). Cf. too James Smith's *Carpenters Companion* (London: J. Millan, 1733), with five plates depicting the orders in an "easy and concise method" and three more plates containing tables of the modular proportions of the orders and their parts.

15. The first British treatise on the orders was John Shute's *First and Chief Groundes of Architecture* (London: Thomas Marshe, 1563).

16. London: Printed for Mess. Ward and Wicksteed, et al., 1734. This book achieved at least eight editions by 1773. Quotations here are from the preface to the second edition (London: A. Ward, et al., 1738).

17. Translated into English by John Evelyn as *A Parallel of the Antient Architecture with the Modern* (London: Printed by T. Roycroft, for J. Place, 1664); later English editions appeared in 1707, 1723, and 1733.

18. Wood, *Dissertation*, pp. 9–10. Still, he found room to criticize Perrault, particularly for his use of mean proportions to deduce the proportions of the orders.

19. In limiting his attention to these three orders Wood followed the example of Fréart de Chambray.

20. See Herrmann, *Theory of Claude Perrault*, pp. 155–168.

21. Editions of Chambers's *Treatise* appeared as late as 1862. Many writers considered Chambers the principal authority on the orders. See for example Isaac Landmann's *Course of the Five Orders of Civil Architecture* (London: Printed for the author, by James Dixwell, 1785), in which "The Five Orders are taken from Mr. Chambers's Elegant Treatise on Civil Architecture."

22. For further attention to Vignola's orders see Robert Sayer's *Vignola Revived* (1761; Entry 304).

23. On contemporary French proposals for a sixth order see Léonce Lex, "De la Recherche d'un sixième ordre d'architecture depuis la renaissance jusqu'à nos jours," *Annales de l'Académie de Mâcon*, 3rd ser., IX (1904), 159–200.

24. London: Printed by J. Dixwell, 1781. Quotations here are from the third edition (London: Printed by J. Smeeton and sold by Messrs. Taylor, 1797).

25. See note 39.

26. Reynolds wrote: "When we have had continually before us the great works of Art to impregnate our minds with kindred ideas, we are then, and not till then, fit to produce something of the same species." He was thus "persuaded, that by imitation only, variety, and even originality of invention, is produced. I will go further; even genius, at least what generally is so called, is the child of imitation." Quotations from Discourse VI, delivered 10 December 1774, reprinted in *Discourses on Art*, ed. Robert R. Wark (San Marino, Calif.: Huntington Library, 1959), pp. 99, 96.

27. These remarks pertain to the seventh edition (1839; Entry 421.8).

28. On the history of the picturesque in British aesthetics see Christopher Hussey, *The Picturesque* (London: Putnam, 1927); on the picturesque in architecture see especially David Watkin, "The Picturesque House: Vanbrugh to Soane," Chapter 5 in *The English Vision* (New York: Harper & Row, 1982).

29. On this subject see Sandra Blutman, "Books of Designs for Country Houses, 1780–1815," *Architectural History* 11 (1968), 25–33; Katherine A. Esdaile, "The Small House and Its Amenities in the Architectural Hand-books of 1749–1827," *Transactions of the Bibliographical Society* XV (October 1917–March 1919), 115–132; Donald Sutherland Lyall, "Minor Domestic Architecture in England and Pattern Books 1790–1840," Ph.D. diss., University of London, 1974; Michael McMordie, "Picturesque Pattern Books and Pre-Victorian Designers," *Architectural History* 18 (1975), 43–59; and Dora Wiebenson, "A Document of Social Change: The Small House Publication," in R. Cohen, ed., *English Art and Aesthetics in the 18th Century* (forthcoming).

30. Cf. for example large general treatises by Ware and Chambers (Entries 339, 40), elegant folio treatises on the orders by Richardson and Bradshaw (Entries 434, 19), collections of designs by major architects such as Adam, Lewis, and Paine (Entries 1, 178, 243), and collections of designs for smaller houses by Garret, Halfpenny, Kent, and Peacock (Entries 86, 138, 165, and 255). The latter were conceived with far more attention to economy, utility, and convenience than to picturesque beauty and expression. For additional remarks on Plaw's contribution see Hussey, *The Picturesque*, pp. 215–216.

31. Entries 4, 10, 12, 14, 30, 59–61, 69, 70, 84, 85, 127, 128, 153–156, 170, 192–195, 208, 246, 248, 262, 263, 291–297.

32. These and other issues are discussed in Chapter III.

33. See for example the text illustrations to Robert Peake's translation (from the Dutch) of Serlio's *First [Second, etc.] Booke of Architecture* (London: Printed for Robert Peake, 1611), and Godfrey Richards's edition of Palladio's *First Book of Architecture* (see note 9).

34. See the text illustration for the article "Country Houses" on p. 85 of Anthony Florian Madinger Willich's *Domestic Encyclopaedia* (1802; Entry 349). Thomas Bewick made wood engraving—not to be confused with woodcut—an important technique of book illustration late in the eighteenth century. From then well into the nineteenth century it was a popular means of book illustration because the blocks, employing a relief process, could be printed on the same sheets and at the same time as the letterpress. On the history of wood engraving, see especially Douglas Percy Bliss, *A History of Wood-Engraving* (London: J. M. Dent, 1928); John Jackson and William A. Chatto, *A Treatise on Wood Engraving* (London: Henry G. Bohn, 1861); and William M. Ivins, Jr., *Prints and Visual Communication* (Cambridge, Mass.: Harvard University Press, 1953), pp. 86–87 et passim.

For detailed discussion of several innovative graphic processes introduced in the nineteenth century, see Elizabeth M. Harris, "Experimental Graphic Processes in England 1806–1859," *Journal of the Printing Historical Society* IV (1968), 33–86; V (1969), 41–80; VI (1970), 53–89.

35. The following are useful contemporary sources of information on British engravers: Horace Walpole, *A Catalogue of Engravers, Who Have Been Born, or Resided in England; Digested . . . from the MSS. of Mr. George Vertue* (Strawberry-Hill, 1763); Joseph Strutt, *A Biographical Dictionary; Containing an Historical Account of All the Engravers, from the Earliest Period of the Art of Engraving to the Present Time*, 2 vols. (London: Printed by J. Davis, for Robert Faulder, 1785–1786); and Samuel Redgrave, *A Dictionary of Artists of the English School: Painters, Sculptors, Architects, Engravers and Ornamentalists*, 2nd ed., rev. and corr. by Frances M. Redgrave (London: Bell, 1878).

36. A useful though dated and incomplete history of aquatint illustration in England is Sarah T. Prideaux, *Aquatint Engraving: A Chapter in the History of Book Illustration* (London: Duckworth, 1909).

37. On the history of the picturesque house type in England see especially David Watkin, "The Picturesque House: Vanbrugh to Soane," Chapter 5 in *The English Vision* (New York: Harper & Row, 1982). Also see Dora Wiebenson, "A Document of Social Change: The Small House Publication," in R. Cohen, ed., *English Art and Aesthetics in the 18th Century* (forthcoming). Note too the contemporary arrival of picturesque domestic architecture in France, particularly Marie Antoinette's Hameau at the Petit Trianon (1783–1786), designed by the painter Hubert Robert and the architect Richard Mique. For additional discussion of the "hamlet" type in France see Dora Wiebenson, *The Picturesque Garden in France* (Princeton: Princeton University Press, 1978), pp. 99–100.

38. On light, shade, advance, and recession, for example, see Robert and James Adam, *Works in Architecture* (1773–1779; Entry 1). On the express relation between architecture and scenery see Thomas Whately, *Observations on Modern Gardening* (London: Printed for T. Payne, 1770); and Humphry Repton, *Sketches and Hints on Landscape Gardening* (1794; Entry 280).

39. In 1787 in his *Treatise on the Five Orders of Architecture* (Entry 434) Richardson employed aquatint to make "the contour and shadows appear clear and distinct," and to produce "a soft and delicate effect, resembling finished Drawings shadowed with Indian Ink" (p. x).

40. See Entries 10, 12, 14, 30, 59–61, 69, 70, 84, 85, 127, 128, 170, 192, 194–197, 210, 262, 271.

41. On the history of lithography see Elizabeth Robins Pennell and Joseph Pennell, *Lithography and Lithographers* (London: T. Fisher Unwin, 1915); Wilhelm Weber, *A History of Lithography* (New York: McGraw-Hill, 1966); and Michael Twyman, *Lithography 1800–1850* (London: Oxford University Press, 1970). Senefelder included an account of his perfection of the process in his *Vollständiges Lehrbuch der Steindruckerey* (Munich, 1818), translated into English in 1819 as *A Complete Course of Lithography* (Entry 478). The English translation contains lithographed plates by Rudolph Ackermann, including a view of a cottage drawn by Samuel Prout. J. T. Smith's *Antiquities of Westminster* appeared in 1807: see Marjorie Plant, *The English Book Trade*, 3rd ed. (London: Allen & Unwin, 1974), pp. 314–316, 489 n. 65; also see Twyman, *Lithography*, pp. 29–30.

42. On Senefelder see the previous note. Raucourt's book originally was published in French in 1819; it was translated by Charles Hullmandel, a prominent English lithographer. *The Art of Drawing on Stone*, written and illustrated by Hullmandel, appeared in 1824 (Entry 475).

43. Robinson's first collection of designs was *Rural Architecture* (1823), and Hunt's was *Half a Dozen Hints on Picturesque Domestic Architecture* (1825). See Entries 291–298 and 153–156.

44. See Entries 140, 157, 203, 315, 334, 345.

III
Theory and
Design

1. There were, of course, several important archaeological treatises that did not focus primarily on domestic architecture. See for example Robert Adam, *Ruins of the Palace of the Emperor Diocletian at Spalatro* (London: The author, 1764); John Berkenhout, *The Ruins of Poestum or Posidonia* (London, 1767); Richard Dalton, *Antiquities and Views in Greece* ([London, 1751–1752]); Thomas Major, *The Ruins of Paestum* (London: T. Major, 1768); Society of Dilettanti, *Ionian Antiqvities* (London: Printed by T. Spilsbury and W. Haskell, 1769 and later); James Stuart and Nicholas Revett, *The Antiqvities of Athens* (London: Printed by James Haberkorn, 1762 and later); Robert Wood, *The Ruins of Balbec* (London, 1757); and Wood, *The Ruins of Palmyra* (London, 1753). The first major British treatise primarily devoted to ecclesiastical architecture was Pugin's *Contrasts* (London: The author, 1836). (For an earlier book containing designs for churches see William Fuller Pocock, *Designs for Churches and Chapels* [London: J. Taylor, 1819, new ed. 1824].) Other significant books that do not contain original designs for dwellings are mentioned in Appendix C.

For some insight into the political, economic, and social reasons that domestic architecture assumed much greater prominence in British architectural practice than elsewhere, see Summerson (1969), pp. 176, 314, et passim; also Frank Jenkins, *Architect and Patron* (London: Oxford University Press, 1961), pp. 67–70.

2. For recent studies of this subject see John Fowler and John Cornforth, *English Decoration in the 18th Century* (Princeton: Pyne Press, 1974); and Mark Girouard, *Life in the English Country House* (New Haven: Yale University Press, 1978).

3. See the section titled "Subject Matter" in the Introduction.

4. For a comprehensive study and an extensive bibliography of this subject, see David Watkin, *The English Vision* (New York: Harper & Row, 1982).

5. Literature concerning these subjects was intentionally excluded from this study. See the Introduction.

6. For discussion of the quarrel between the Ancients and Moderns in England see Richard Foster Jones, *Ancients and Moderns: A Study in the Rise of the Scientific Movement in Seventeenth-Century England* (St. Louis: Washington University Press, 1961); Joseph M. Levine, "Ancients, Moderns and History: The Continuity of English Historical Writing in the Later Seventeenth Century," in *Studies in Change and Revolution*, ed. Paul Korshin (Menston: Scolar Press, 1972), pp. 43–75; and especially Levine, "Ancients and Moderns Reconsidered," *Eighteenth-Century Studies* XV: 1 (Fall 1981), 72–89.

7. On the conflict between Ancients and Moderns in seventeenth-century France see Wolfgang Herrmann, *The Theory of Claude Perrault* (London: Zwemmer, 1973), passim. T. P. Connor, "The Making of 'Vitruvius Britannicus,' " *Architectural History* 20 (1977), 18–19, indicates that Campbell's ideas "appear to follow some lines in the preface to D'Aviler's *Cours d'Architecture*."

8. This point is discussed in more detail in Entry 32.

9. For references and further discussion see Entry 32. Connor, in "The Making of 'Vitruvius Britannicus,' " p. 21, observed that the principles Campbell praised did not always correspond with elements of the designs he illustrated: a design inscribed to James Stanhope (II, Pl. 86), for example, is copied from Palladio's "most mannerist design" for the Palazzo Valmarana.

10. For a detailed discussion of *The Antiqvities of Athens* see Dora Wiebenson, *Sources of Greek Revival Architecture* (London: Zwemmer, 1969).

11. Published collections of designs for dwellings had appeared earlier in France: see especially the *Livres d'architecture* of Jacques Androuet du Cerceau (Paris, 1559–1572); and Antoine Le Pautre's *Desseins de plusieurs palais* (Paris, 1652).

12. On progress see J. B. Bury, *The Idea of Progress* (New York: Macmillan, 1932); and Sidney Pollard, *The Idea of Progress* (Harmondsworth: Penguin, 1971).

13. Entry 339, p. 131. On the relationship between Ware and Perrault see Herrmann, *Theory of Claude Perrault*, pp. 155–168.

14. In *Villas of the Ancients* (1728; Entry 36) Castell analyzed accounts of Pliny's two villas at Laurentinum and Tuscum, along with relevant material from other Roman authors. From this information he tried to reconstruct the actual appearance of a Roman villa. The validity of such an approach was challenged, after midcentury, by extensive archaeological excavation and analysis (see note 1). Of course the appeal of Roman remains—part aesthetic, part nostalgic—remained strong throughout the second half of the century. In 1794 George Richardson issued *The First Part of a Complete System of Architecture* (Entry 283), in which he "attempted to retain the spirit and effect of that beautiful and elegant style . . . used in the private apartments, baths, and villas, of the Ancients."

15. See for example William Kent's *Designs of Inigo Jones* (1727; Entry 166), *Andrea Palladio's Architecture* by Edward Hoppus (1735; Entry 150), and *Some Designs of Mr. Inigo Jones* by John Vardy (1744; Entry 335). Lord Burlington and others, of course, were also instrumental in the revival of Palladio and Jones. See Rudolf Wittkower, *Palladio and Palladianism* (New York: Braziller, 1974), pp. 71–174.

16. See Marc-Antoine Laugier, *Essai sur l'architecture* (Paris: Duchesne, 1753). For a wide-ranging discussion of Vitruvius, Laugier, Chambers, and previous reconstructions of the primitive hut in architectural literature see Jospeh Rykwert, *On Adam's House in Paradise* (New York: Museum of Modern Art, 1972).

17. Of the three designs, the third most closely resembles one illustrated in Laugier's *Essai*. Chambers also depicted the "Origin" of the Corinthian capital, shown rising from a clump of acanthus leaves.

18. For example almost eight decades later Peter Nicholson's *Architectural Dictionary* (1819; Entry 223), later retitled *Encyclopedia of Architecture*, included descriptions of private houses in Classical times based on the writings of Vitruvius and Pliny.

19. *The Architecture of Marcus Vitruvius Pollio* (London: Priestley and Weale, 1826).

20. On early nineteenth-century interest in Egyptian architecture see Richard G. Carrott, *The Egyptian Revival* (Berkeley: University of California Press, 1978). On the greater history of neo-Egyptian taste see James Stevens Curl, *The Egyptian Revival* (London: Allen & Unwin, 1982).

21. Two years later Peter de la Roche approached the subjects of Classical authority and modern progress in a similar manner in *An Essay on the Orders of Architecture*. See the discussion in Chapter II, Section 1.

22. See in particular Anthony Blunt, *Artistic Theory in Italy 1450–1600* (London: Oxford University Press, 1962); Donald Drew Egbert, *The Beaux-Arts Tradition in French Architecture* (Princeton: Princeton University Press, 1980), pp. 99–120: Rensselaer W. Lee, *Ut Pictura Poesis* (New York: W. W. Norton, 1967); Erwin Panofsky, *Idea: A Concept in Art Theory* (New York: Harper & Row, 1968); Rudolf Wittkower, *Architectural Principles in the Age of Humanism* (New York: Random House, 1956), especially Part IV. The importance of Shaftesbury to British architectural thought has never been fully documented. See in particular his essay "The Moralists" in *Characteristicks of Men, Manners, Opinions, Times* ([London], 1711). On Shaftesbury's aesthetics and influence see R. L. Brett, *The Third Earl of Shaftesbury* (New York: Hutchinson's University Library, 1951); Ernst Cassirer, *The Philosophy of the Enlightenment* (Princeton: Princeton University Press, 1951), pp. 312–331, and *The Platonic Renaissance in England* (Edinburgh: Nelson, 1953); and Harold Francis Pfister, "Burlingtonian Architectural Theory in England and America," *Winterthur Portfolio* XI (1976), 123–151 (including further references [p. 137] to studies of Shaftesbury's influence on architecture).

23. The first two passages are from *Characteristicks*, II, 285; the second is reprinted on the title page to Morris's *Essay upon Harmony* (London: T. Cooper, 1739). The third passage is from *Characteristicks*, I, 207.

24. Morris stated that much of his thinking on proportion derived from a treatise by Lambert ten Kate, recently translated into English as *The Beau Ideal* (London: Bettenham, 1732). There are also important parallels between Morris's ideas and those of René Ouvrard: see his *Architecture harmonique, ou application de la doctrine des proportions de la musique à l'architecture* (Paris: R.-J.-B. de La Caille, 1679). For a brief discussion of Ouvrard and further remarks on the subject of harmony see Joseph Rykwert, *The First Moderns* (Cambridge, Mass.: MIT Press, 1980), pp. 13, 33ff, 68, 148–149, 189–193.

25. Entry 339.1, pp. 131, 681. Ware's ideas on proportion were largely indebted to Claude Perrault; see note 13.

26. For the implicit debt to Perrault in these remarks see Entry 40, note 7. In the 1791 edition of the *Treatise*, the last in Chambers's lifetime, he still could not fully explain the appeal of architectural proportion to the observer. Unlike Morris, he denied that architectural proportions resembled musical harmonies in their universal allure; nor did he entirely support the notion that architectural proportions were simply established by common consent. "Whether there be any thing natural, positive, convincing and self amiable, in the proportions of architecture; which, like notes and accord in musick, seize upon the mind, and necessarily excite the same sensations in all; or whether they were first established by consent of the ancient artists, who imitated each other; and were first admired, because accompanied with other real, convincing beauties," were problems that Chambers referred to "Perrault, Blondel, and other writers upon the subject" (Entry 40.3, p. 107).

27. Henry Home, Lord Kames, *Elements of Criticism* (Edinburgh: A. Kincaid & J. Bell, 1762; these references from 6th ed., with corrections and additions, Edinburgh: Printed for John Bell, et al., 1785), pp. 461–465. Kames referred explicitly to Perrault in discussing proportion as "the effect of custom."

28. For a general discussion of this point, plus additional bibliography, see Peter Gay, *The Enlightenment: An Interpretation* (London: Wildwood House, 1970), II, 319–343, 659–662. Among important linguistic studies see Thomas Blackwell, *An Enquiry into the Life and Writings of Homer* (London: Printed in the year 1735); Joseph Priestley, *A Course of Lectures on the Theory of Language, and Universal Grammar* (Warrington: Printed by W. Eyres, 1762); Thomas Percy, *Reliques of Ancient English Poetry* (London: J. Dodsley, 1765); and James Burnet, Lord Monboddo, *Of the Origin and Progress of Language* (Edinburgh: A. Kincaid and W. Creech, et al. [imprint varies in later volumes], 1773–1792). Further on the relation between language and aesthetics see René Wellek, *The Rise of English Literary History* (Chapel Hill: University of North Carolina Press, 1941), pp. 83–94. On efforts to explain cultural

diversity through differences in climate see Christopher J. Berry, " 'Climate' in the Eighteenth Century: James Dunbar and the Scottish Case," *Texas Studies in Language and Literature* XVI: 2 (Summer 1974), 281–292; and Wellek, *Rise of English Literary History*, pp. 31–33, 54–58, 67, 89.

As early as 1728 Robert Castell, author of *The Villas of the Ancients*, was aware that cultural and climatic circumstances might challenge the authority of Classical rules embodied in Pliny's villas at Laurentinum and Tuscum. But Castell argued that the "judicious Architect" would find "few Parts" of either villa that would not be "of Service" at one season or another in England (Entry 36.2, p. 35).

29. In particular he suggested that art should lead the viewer of a landscape to look for that inner, central quality of any element, its "Sole-Animating and Inspiring Power," which when perceived would elevate the imagination to the realm of Beauty and Virtue (*Characteristicks*), II, 366). Also see ibid., I, 136–139. On proportion and harmony see ibid., III, 182–183. For contemporary discussion of imaginative expansion in the landscape and perception of harmony see Stephen Switzer's remarks in *Ichnographia Rustica* (1718; Entry 327.2).

For additional discussion of the role of imagination in British aesthetics see Eric Rothstein, " 'Ideal Presence' and the 'Non Finito' in Eighteenth-Century Aesthetics," *Eighteenth-Century Studies* IX:3 (Spring 1976), 307–332; Alfred Owen Aldridge, "Akenside and Imagination," *Studies in Philology* XLII:4 (October 1945), 769–792; Donald F. Bond, "The Distrust of the Imagination in English Neoclassicism," *Philological Quarterly* XIV (January 1935), 54–69, and "The Neo-Classical Psychology of Imagination," *E.L.H.* IV:4 (December 1937), 245–264; E. J. Furlong, "Imagination in Hume's *Treatise* and *Enquiry Concerning the Human Understanding*," *Philosophy* XXXVI:136 (January 1961), 62–70; Walter John Hipple, Jr., *The Beautiful, the Sublime, and the Picturesque in Eighteenth-Century British Aesthetic Theory* (Carbondale: Southern Illinois University Press, 1957); Alexander Manson Kinghorn, "Literary Aesthetics and the Sympathetic Emotions—A Main Trend in Eighteenth Century Scottish Criticism," *Studies in Scottish Literature* I:1 (July 1963), 35–47; Harold Taylor, "Hume's Theory of Imagination," *University of Toronto Quarterly* XII (1942–1943), 180–190; Clarence DeWitt Thorpe, "Addison and Hutcheson on the Imagination," *E.L.H.* II:3 (November 1935), 215–234, and "Addison's Theory of the Imagination as 'Perceptive Response,' " *Papers of the Michigan Academy of Science, Arts, and Letters* XXI (1935), 509–530; and Ernest Lee Tuveson, *The Imagination as a Means of Grace* (Berkeley: University of California Press, 1960).

30. David Hume, *A Treatise of Human Nature* (London: J. Noon, 1739), II, 154–155. On sympathy in the previous history of ideas see R. S. Crane, "Suggestions toward a Genealogy of the 'Man of Feeling,' " in *The Idea of the Humanities* (Chicago: University of Chicago Press, 1967), I, 188–213; and Walter Jackson Bate, "The Sympathetic Imagination in Eighteenth-Century English Criticism," *E.L.H.*, XII (1945), 144–164.

31. Alexander Gerard, *An Essay on Taste* (London: Printed for A. Millar, et al., 1759), pp. 41–42.

32. Ibid., pp. 173, 174, 176; and Gerard, *An Essay on Taste*, 2nd ed. (Edinburgh: A. Millar, et al., 1764), pp. 171–172. Also on genius see Mark Akenside, *The Pleasures of Imagination* (London: R. Dodsley, 1744), which Gerard cited in his *Essay*. For an early discussion of taste as an "internal sense" see Francis Hutcheson, *An Inquiry into the Original of our Ideas of Beauty and Virtue*, 2nd ed., rev. and corr. (London: Printed for J. Darby, et al., 1726), p. 8. Also concerning taste see: "On Taste," *The Connoisseur* IV:120 (13 May 1756), 270–272; and the final chapter in Kames, *Elements of Criticism*.

33. William Duff, *An Essay on Original Genius* (London: Printed for Edward and Charles Dilly, 1767), pp. 6–7. For further remarks on genius, invention, and imagination see Alexander Gerard, *An Essay on Genius* (London: Printed for W. Strahan, et al., 1774).

34. Duff, *Essay*, pp. 253–256. In 1759 Edward Young had chastised modern writers for imitating the Ancients rather than inventing original compositions: see *Conjectures on Original Composition* (London: Printed for A. Millar, et al., 1759), especially pp. 19, 46. Young did not consider architecture.

35. Duff, *Essay*, pp. 6, 10, 11, 21.

36. Gerard discussed the circumstances of the prize essay in an "Advertisement" to the *Essay on Taste*.

37. Entry 243.2, I, vi–vii. Two years later Peter de la Roche made quite similar remarks in his *Essay on the Orders of Architecture* (London: The author, 1769), rejecting the authority

of "Antique Remains" and recommending that the architect look "for models in his own genius." The Ancients themselves had been guided only by their own "genius, regulating its dictates by those of reason, nature, and propriety" (p. iii).

38. Entry 331, pp. 5, 3, 5. N.B. Thomas did not ignore the subject of proportion. In designing dwellings, for example, he recommended "a proper Respect . . . to the Rule of Proportion, by which the Beauty and Perfections of Architecture, as well as of all other Arts, will ever be best supported" (p. 5).

39. Quotations from Entry 184.5, pp. 1, 4, 1114, 1124. For Lord Kames see note 27 and text discussion above. Burke argued that the experience of the sublime or beautiful was largely a physiological reaction to qualities of the perceived object. See his *Philosophical Enquiry into the Origin of Our Ideas of the Sublime and Beautiful* (London, 1757; 2nd ed., expanded, 1759). For Perrault see note 13.

40. Seventeenth-century writers on aesthetics discussed expression in connection with representation of the passions. In particular see René Descartes, *Les Passions de l'ame* (Paris: Henry LeGras, 1649) and Charles Le Brun, *Conference . . . sur l'expression* (Amsterdam: J. L. De Lorme, 1698). According to them, variations in one's external facial physiognomy directly represented the internal passions and character of the soul. Among French architects, Germain Boffrand offered important remarks on the subject of architectural affectivity just before midcentury. In his *Livre d'architecture* (Paris: Guillaume Cavelier père, 1745) he indicated the necessity that "le spectateur ressente le caractere qu'il [l'édifice] doit imprimer," and that "un homme qui ne connoît pas ces différens caracteres, & qui ne les fait pas sentir dans ses ouvrages, n'est pas Architécte" (pp. 27, 26). By using the verbs "ressente," "imprimer," and "fait sentir" he stressed the affectivity of the design. Over the next quarter century Jacques-François Blondel built on the work of these authors, drawing parallels between pictorial and architectural expression. The architect, he wrote, had the means at his disposal to "exprimer les divers caracteres des différentes productions de l'Architecture, . . . de même que dans un tableau d'histoire ou dans un bas-relief, le Peintre & le Sculpteur, dans les airs de tête de leurs figures, indiquent, par l'expression de chacune d'elles, l'image des passions qui caractérisent les personnages représentés sur la toile, ou par le marbre" (*Cours d'architecture* [Paris: Dessaint, 1771–1777], I, 259–260).

For an important discussion of the theory of expression in painting see Rensselaer W. Lee, *Ut Pictura Poesis* (New York: W. W. Norton, 1967), pp. 23–32. For parallels in literary theory see Jean H. Hagstrum, *The Sister Arts* (Chicago: University of Chicago Press, 1958), pp. 121–123, 177, 230. For an excellent analysis of character in Aristotelian thought and in French academic architecture see "Character," Chapter 6 in Donald Drew Egbert, *The Beaux-Arts Tradition in French Architecture* (Princeton: Princeton University Press, 1980), pp. 121–138. Spectator response was of increasing concern to English landscapists and French painters alike. See especially John Dixon Hunt, "Emblem and Expressionism in the Eighteenth-Century Landscape," *Eighteenth-Century Studies* IV:3 (Spring 1971), 294–317; Ronald Paulson, *Emblem and Expression* (Cambridge, Mass.: Harvard University Press, 1975), pp. 7–34; H. F. Clark, "Eighteenth Century Elysiums: The Rôle of 'Association' in the Landscape Movement," *Journal of the Warburg and Courtauld Institutes* VI (1943), 165–189; Norman Bryson, *Word and Image* (Cambridge: Cambridge University Press, 1981), especially pp. 239–240; and Michael Fried, *Absorption and Theatricality* (Berkeley: University of California Press, 1980), especially pp. 107–160.

41. On the subject of affectivity early in the eighteenth century see especially Wallace Jackson, "Affective Values in Early Eighteenth-Century Aesthetics," *Journal of Aesthetics and Art Criticism* XXVII:1 (Fall 1968), 87–92. Jackson also discussed the philosophical foundations of aesthetic affectivity in "Affective Values in Later Eighteenth-Century Aesthetics," *Journal of Aesthetics and Art Criticism* XXIV:2 (Winter 1965), 309–314. Walter Jackson Bate, in "The Sympathetic Imagination in Eighteenth-Century English Criticism," *E.L.H.* XII:2 (June 1945), 144–164, suggested the extent to which works of art called on the imagination to participate actively in understanding them. Eric Rothstein, in " 'Ideal Presence' and the 'Non Finito' in Eighteenth-Century Aesthetics," *Eighteenth-Century Studies* IX:3 (Spring 1976), 307–332, considered other aspects of this problem. Nevertheless none of these writers focused on the actual affectivity of individual artistic compositions.

42. *An Epistle to the Right Honourable Richard Earl of Burlington* (London: L. Gilliver, 1731), lines 103–108, 151–156.

43. Timothy Nourse, "An Essay of a Country House," in *Campania Foelix* (London: T. Bennet, 1700), pp. 298, 309, 341, and passim. On the country house poem see G. R. Hibbard, "The Country House Poem of the Seventeenth Century," *Journal of the Warburg and Courtauld Institutes* XIX:1–2 (January–June 1956), 159–174.

44. John Shebbeare, *Letters on the English Nation* (London, 1755), pp. 270–272.

45. Four years earlier the musical theorist Charles Avison described succinctly the close connection between expression and affectivity in his *Essay on Musical Expression* (2nd ed. [London: C. Davis, 1753]). Wanting to distinguish between mere "Imitation" and "Expression," he provided examples of both types of composition. The former, he said, might be "the gradual rising or falling of Notes in a long Succession, [which] is often used to denote Ascent or Descent," or "Sounds resembling Laughter, to describe Laughter." In contrast, expression involves an element of affectivity, raising original passions in the spectator: it provides the "Power of exciting all the most agreeable Passions of the Soul" (pp. 57, 3). Also see Alan Lessem, "Imitation and Expression: Opposing French and British Views in the 18th Century," *Journal of the American Musicological Society* XXVII:2 (Summer 1974), 325–330.

46. Henry Home, Lord Kames, *Elements of Criticism* (Edinburgh: A. Kincaid & J. Bell, 1762), III, 299, 338–339. According to Vitruvius, the form and style of a building should be suited to its use and to the station of the proprietor, albeit not actively expressive of them. See Marcus Vitruvius Pollio, *The Ten Books on Architecture*, trans. Morris Hicky Morgan (Cambridge, Mass.: Harvard University Press, 1914), Book I, Chapter 2, §§5–7; Book VI, Chapter 5. In 1624 Sir Henry Wotton was among the first to discuss this notion in English, writing that "Decor is the keeping of a due Respect betweene the Inhabitant, and the Habitation" (*The Elements of Architectvre* [London: Printed by Iohn Bill, 1624], p. 119; see also pp. 7–8, 66, 74, 82–83, 120).

47. Kames, *Elements of Criticism*, III, 470. On the next page Kames discussed "all the emotions that can be raised by architecture," another reference to affectivity.

Kames devoted much of his treatise to literary subjects. In subsequent decades meaning and expression in language itself were the subject of intense examination. In his six-volume study *Of the Origin and Progress of Language* (Edinburgh: A. Kincaid and W. Creech, et al. [imprint varies in later volumes], 1773–1792), Lord Monboddo analyzed such fundamental topics as rhetoric and style, and drew important connections between the origin of the human race, the development of speech, and human evolution. In 1818 Richard Payne Knight, known also for his work on picturesque aesthetics (see Entry 169), completed *An Inquiry into the Symbolical Language of Ancient Art and Mythology* (London: Privately printed), a study of the communication of meaning in ancient art through allegory and symbolism.

48. See the previous note and Entry 40, note 4.

49. This passage is reminiscent of Shaftesbury's remarks half a century earlier in *Characteristicks of Men, Manners, Opinions, Times* ([London], 1711). See Section 2 above, and Jackson, "Affective Values in Early Eighteenth-Century Aesthetics."

50. First ed., Dublin: James Williams, 1770. Second ed., London: T. Payne, 1770. References here are to the fourth edition (London: T. Payne and Son, 1777), which with very minor exceptions reproduces the text of the second and third editions.

51. I have discussed Whately's contribution at greater length in "Character in English Architectural Design," *Eighteenth-Century Studies* XII:3 (Spring 1979), 339–371. For a detailed discussion of French notions of character see Patrick Coleman, "The Idea of Character in the *Encyclopédie*," *Eighteenth-Century Studies* XIII:1 (Fall 1979), 21–47.

52. Sandby's remarks are quoted in Pierre de la Ruffinière du Prey, *John Soane: The Making of an Architect* (Chicago: University of Chicago Press, 1982), p. 65. For analysis of Soane's "characteristic" style see Entry 320. Soane's use of the term "characteristic" here seems little concerned with expression. Rather, it prefigures Repton's use of the term to denote visual coordination with the landscape. Cf. the remark in Soane's *Lectures on Architecture*, ed. Arthur T. Bolton (London: Sir John Soane's Museum, 1929), p. 115: "surrounding scenery" must determine "the Architectural Character of the Villa." See too my remarks on Repton immediately below and in Section 9, "Picturesque Aesthetics." Du Prey has examined Soane's notion of character and "characteristic" aspects of his work (*John Soane*, pp. 65–67, 318–319, and passim).

53. For similar attention to the expressive character of dwellings both small and large see Joseph Woods, Jr., "An Essay on the Situations and Accompaniments of Villas" (1808; Entry 355); and Thomas Downes Wilmot Dearn, *Designs for Lodges and Entrances* (1811; Entry 59).

54. Loudon's debt to Whately is transparent in his description of three special types of character: the "original," the "imitative," and the "emblematical" (p. 260). These are the precise terms that Whately used (*Observations*, Chapters XLVIII–L).

Two years later Loudon's discussion of character in *A Treatise on Forming, Improving, and Managing Country Residences* (1806; Entry 191) was a mélange of notions borrowed from Whately and Repton. Like Whately, Loudon enumerated a variety of "characters" that "are productive of particular expressions and correspondent effects on the mind." (Loudon identified altogether 15 characters, which are listed in Entry 191, note 4. Cf. Whately, *Observations*, p. 154.) Although he criticized Repton's landscape work as "affectedly graceful," Loudon's own proposal for a "characteristic or natural style" of landscape design is clearly derived from Repton. The principal difference was that Loudon wanted "to create or heighten natural character," while he criticized Repton, somewhat unfairly, for doing "directly the reverse" and so producing "a monotony of artificial character."

55. Sir John Soane, *Lectures*, p. 177. On Soane's notion of character see also note 52.

56. Ledoux conceived character as an autonomous quality that activates a structure to inspire and instruct the observer. "La décoration est le caractère expressif. . . . Elle vivifie les surfaces, les immortalise, les empreint de toutes les sensations, de toutes les passions; elle modifie les irrégularités du sort, abaisse la présomptueuse opulence, et relève la timide infortune; elle flétrit l'ignorance, aggrandit le savoir, et dans sa juste répartition, elle donne aux nations le lustre qui les fait briller, et plonge dans la barbarie les peuples ingrats ou insouciants qui négligent ses faveurs" (Claude-Nicolas Ledoux, *L'Architecture considérée sous le rapport de l'art, des moeurs, et de la législation* [Paris: L'auteur, 1804]).

57. On the subject of character later in the nineteenth century see Colin Rowe, "Character and Composition; or Some Vicissitudes of Architectural Vocabulary in the Nineteenth Century," *Oppositions*, no. 2 (January 1974), 41–60.

58. See René Descartes, *Principles of Philosophy*, Part IV, Principle CXCVII, in *Philosophical Works*, trans. Elizabeth S. Haldane and G. R. T. Ross (Cambridge: Cambridge University Press, 1971), I, 294; and John Locke, *An Essay Concerning Humane Understanding*, 4th ed. (London: Printed for Awnsham and John Churchil and Samuel Manship, 1700), Book II, Chapter 30, §7, pp. 222–223.

59. I have discussed the early eighteenth-century background in "The Beginnings of Association in British Architectural Esthetics," *Eighteenth-Century Studies* XVI:3 (Spring 1983), 241–264. For the later eighteenth and nineteenth centuries see George L. Hersey, *High Victorian Gothic* (Baltimore: Johns Hopkins University Press, 1972). Martin Kallich, in *The Association of Ideas and Critical Theory in Eighteenth-Century England* (The Hague: Mouton, 1970), documented the role of association in aesthetic theory but did not consider specifically the role of association in architecture. Also on association see Walter Jackson Bate, *From Classic to Romantic* (New York: Harper & Row, 1961); and Walter John Hipple, Jr., *The Beautiful, the Sublime, and the Picturesque in Eighteenth-Century British Aesthetic Theory* (Carbondale, Ill.: Southern Illinois University Press, 1957).

60. On the Vitruvian notion of decorum see note 46.

61. Claude Perrault, *Ordonnance des cinq especes de colonnes* (Paris: J. B. Coignard, 1683); *A Treatise of the Five Orders of Columns*, trans. John James (London: Printed by B. Motte, sold by J. Sturt, 1708). I have used a later edition (London: J. Senex, [1722]), p. vi.

62. Sir John Vanbrugh, *The Complete Works*, Vol. IV, ed. Geoffrey Webb (London: Nonesuch, 1928), 29.

63. For fuller discussion of these points see Section 2, and Archer, "The Beginnings of Association."

64. "The principal source of grandeur in architecture is association, by which the columns suggest ideas of strength and durability, and the whole structure introduces the sublime ideas of the riches and magnificence of the owner" (p. 23).

65. Perhaps not coincidentally these remarks appeared just one year after Archibald Alison's manifesto of associational aesthetics, *Essays on the Nature and Principles of Taste* (Edinburgh: J. J. G. and G. Robinson, et al., 1790). Alison stated that objects could, by means of association, raise ideas of personal history, national history, and individual occupations (pp. 15–25). Alison's contribution is discussed further by Hersey, *High Victorian Gothic*, pp. 10–12. For an extended discussion of the sources of Chambers's ideas, see Eileen Harris, "Burke and Chambers on the Sublime and Beautiful," in Douglas Fraser, et al., eds., *Essays in the History of Architecture Presented to Rudolf Wittkower* (London: Phaidon, 1967), pp. 207–213.

66. I have discussed this at greater length, and given examples, in "The Beginnings of Association."

67. Observations on the associations of individual styles were, of course, quite common. William Fuller Pocock, for example, noted in *Architectural Designs for Rustic Cottages* (1807; Entry 262) that certain architectural styles could stimulate memories of past eras. The Castellated style, for instance, might suggest an ancient chieftain's residence (p. 14). Writing in *Rural Residences* (1818; Entry 246.2), J. B. Papworth discussed the use of a Classical style for the "association of ideas produced in the mind of the spectator, by its legitimate, though distant, affinity with the ultimate perfection of Grecian architecture."

68. Sir Joshua Reynolds, *Discourses on Art*, ed. Robert R. Wark (San Marino, Calif.: Huntington Library, 1959), pp. 241–242.

69. On this conflict see Kallich, *The Association of Ideas*; Hipple, *The Beautiful*; Hersey, *High Victorian Gothic*; and Edmund Burke, *A Philosophical Enquiry into the Origin of Our Ideas of the Sublime and Beautiful* (London, 1757; 2nd ed., expanded, 1759).

70. For other authors who introduced parallels between facial physiognomy and aesthetic expression see Le Brun, *Conference*; Johann Kaspar Lavater, *Physiognomische Fragmente zur Beförderung der Menschenkenntnis und Menschliebe* (Leipzig and Winterthur: Weidmanns Erben und Reich, and Heinrich Steiner und Compagnie, 1775–1778); Jacques-François Blondei, *Cours*, I, 259–261; and John Billington, *The Architectural Director* (1829; Entry 18).

71. Ruskin's earliest architectural writings had appeared in the previous decade. See Entry 182.

72. For a thorough analysis of Horace's contribution see Rosemary Louise Mullin, "The Use of the Terms 'Rus' and 'Urbs' in the Poetry of Horace," Ph.D. diss., University of Washington, 1967.

73. See David R. Coffin, *The Villa in the Life of Renaissance Rome* (Princeton: Princeton University Press, 1979).

74. The divorce between country and city, and the characteristic pursuits of country life, are discussed in G. R. Hibbard, "The Country House Poem of the Seventeenth Century," *Journal of the Warburg and Courtauld Institutes* XIX:1–2 (January–June 1956), 159–174; Maren-Sofie Røstvig, *The Happy Man: Studies in the Metamorphoses of an Ideal* (Oslo and New York: Norwegian Universities Press, 1962–1971); Don Cameron Allen, *Image and Meaning: Metaphoric Traditions in Renaissance Poetry* (Baltimore: Johns Hopkins University Press, 1968), pp. 187–225; Raymond Williams, *The Country and the City* (New York: Oxford University Press, 1973); Howard Erskine-Hill, "The Country House Ideal," Chapter 9 in *The Social Milieu of Alexander Pope* (New Haven: Yale University Press, 1975); Mark Girouard, "A Place in the Country," *The Times Literary Supplement*, 27 February 1976, 223–225; and Girouard, *Life in the English Country House* (New Haven: Yale University Press, 1978).

75. In *Campania Foelix* (London: T. Bennet, 1700), p. 339.

76. Pope's relation to his Twickenham estate is discussed at length by Maynard Mack in *The Garden and the City* (Toronto: University of Toronto Press, 1969).

77. The term "villa" was applied to Chiswick as early as 1727: see John Fleming, *Robert Adam and His Circle* (London: John Murray, 1962), p. 26. The quotations from Palladio are from p. 46 in the translation by Isaac Ware (London, 1738), which was dedicated to Burlington.

78. Jacques Carré has recently discussed the work of Burlington and Kent in "Architecture et paysage: Le Jardin de Chiswick," in André Parreaux and Michèle Plaisant, eds., *Jardins et paysages: Le Style anglais* (Lille: Université de Lille, 1977), pp. 69–84.

79. See note 74.

80. On the growing popularity of books containing modest designs for suburban dwellings see Chapter II, Section 1. Middle-class pretensions to rural "retirement" were satirized as early as 1754 in a "Letter on the Villas of Our Tradesmen," in *The Connoisseur* I:33 (17 September 1754); my citations are from the 6th ed. (Oxford: J. Rivington, et al., 1774), 255–262. The author ridiculed the proliferation of "dusty retreats" or "Boxes," all lined up in rows, each with a summer house at the end of a small garden, a small fountain containing frogs instead of fish, and an odd assortment of statues. Also see similarly satirical remarks in "The Cit's Country Box," *The Connoisseur* IV:135 (26 August 1756); 6th ed. (Oxford: J. Rivington, et al., 1774), 233–238.

81. *Oxford English Dictionary*, s.v. "Cottage" and "Villa."

82. The standard history of the villa type in eighteenth-century Britain is still Summerson (1959). Using executed examples and book illustrations, Summerson demonstrated the rise

and progress of one particular architectural type, in which the windows of the facade are grouped in a 1–3–1 pattern. He concluded that this type was "the essential innovation of the century" (p. 552). Nevertheless he acknowledged that the actual word "villa" was never used "with any *architectural* precision at all" and that in identifying just one formal type as the villa he was "going a little beyond the warrant of contemporary usage" (p. 570). My approach is different from Summerson's: I am largely concerned with the meaning of the word "villa" in eighteenth- and early nineteenth-century literature, rather than the rise of a particular building type.

83. See Section 4, especially notes 72 and 73.

84. I have borrowed this typology from Robert Castell's account (Entry 36), which obviously was of special interest and importance to eighteenth-century architects. Further on Pliny's villas and on Classical Roman villas in general see Helen H. Tanzer, *The Villas of Pliny the Younger* (New York: Columbia University Press, 1924); and A. G. McKay, *Houses, Villas and Palaces in the Roman World* (Ithaca: Cornell University Press, 1975).

85. Leon Battista Alberti, *The Architecture of Leon Battista Alberti, in Ten Books*, trans. James Leoni (London: T. Edlin, 1726), Book IX, Chapter 2, fol. 79^r. In describing the location of these villas Alberti used the term "suburbani," which Leoni translated as "just without the town."

86. On Palladio's villas see James S. Ackerman, *Palladio* (Harmondsworth: Penguin, 1966). For Inigo Jones's appreciation of Palladio see John Summerson, *Inigo Jones* (Harmondsworth: Penguin, 1966); and John Harris, Stephen Orgel, and Roy Strong, *The King's Arcadia: Inigo Jones and the Stuart Court* (London: Arts Council of Great Britain, 1973). On Lord Burlington see Rudolf Wittkower, *Palladio and Palladianism* (New York: Braziller, 1974), pp. 114–132. Also on Jones and Burlington see Summerson (1969), pp. 61–67, 189–204. Colen Campbell possibly saw Palladian villas as well: see Howard E. Stutchbury, *The Architecture of Colen Campbell* (Cambridge, Mass.: Harvard University Press, 1967), pp. 18–19; but also see Colvin (1978), p. 182.

87. Quotations are from the important eighteenth-century translation by Isaac Ware: Andrea Palladio, *The Four Books of Andrea Palladio's Architecture* (London: Isaac Ware, 1738), pp. 46–47.

88. In *Campania Foelix* (London: T. Bennet, 1700) p. 297.

89. On Chiswick see Wittkower, *Palladio and Palladianism*, pp. 120–127; Summerson (1969), pp. 199–200; and John Charlton, *A History and Description of Chiswick House and Gardens* (London: HMSO, 1958). There are also precedents for this type of villa in mid-seventeenth-century French architecture. See Antoine Le Pautre, *Desseins de plusieurs palais* (Paris: L'auteur, [1652]), reissued as *Les Oeuvres d'architecture* (Paris: Iombert, 1652), especially Plates 11–15. Robert W. Berger has mentioned this design as a possible source for Chiswick House in *Antoine Le Pautre* (New York: New York University Press, 1969), p. 25 n. 12. I am grateful to Dora Wiebenson for introducing me to Le Pautre.

90. See note 77.

91. Summerson (1959), p. 570, stated that Campbell referred to country estates. Shaftesbury used the word in a like manner in *Characteristicks of Men, Manners, Opinions, Times* ([London], 1711): in a lengthy discussion of the accord between exterior beauty and the sense of harmony within the beholder, Shaftesbury cited as an example "the Disposition and Order of these finer sorts of Apartments, Gardens, Villa's!" (p. 184n). Use of the word to denote a country estate continued well past midcentury. The design in Plate 32 of *The Modern Builder's Assistant* by Halfpenny, et al. (1757; Entry 132) was meant "to be situated in a Country Villa" (p. 27), and several designs in Thomas Rawlins's *Familiar Architecture* (1768; Entry 273) were intended for locations "in a City or Villa," "in a Town or Villa," or "in a pleasant airy Villa." Sir William Chambers used the word in the same sense in the third edition of his *Treatise* (1791; Entry 40.3) to describe the location of the Casino "erected at Marino, a villa belonging to the Earl of Charlemont, near Dublin" (p. 136). Chambers had used the word "Seat" instead of "villa" in his first edition (p. 85).

92. See Section 4.

93. Castell noted on p. 14 that Pliny mentioned approximately 46 rooms in his description of Laurentinum, without describing the other half of the house that was inhabited by servants.

94. On Robert Morris, his relative Roger Morris, and their role in the genesis of the small dwelling type, see Emil Kaufmann, *Architecture in the Age of Reason* (Cambridge, Mass.:

Harvard University Press, 1955); Summerson (1959), pp. 572–574; Summerson (1969), p. 212; and Joseph Rykwert, *The First Moderns* (Cambridge, Mass.: MIT Press, 1980), pp. 185–197.

95. See Section 1 of this chapter.

96. "Letter on the Villas of Our Tradesmen," p. 255; see note 80.

97. In form and function these designs differ little from garden buildings that other architects described as "seats," "lodges," or "casinos." Cf. for example Sir William Chambers's "Casino" at Marino, illustrated in his *Treatise* (1759; Entry 40).

98. See also the two villas depicted in the fourth volume of *Vitruvius Britannicus* (1767; Entry 356), which are only slightly smaller.

99. Plate XLII; Plates LXXIII and LXXXVII; Plates III and IV; Plates LXXX, LXXXIII, and LXXXVI.

100. *The Country Gentleman's Architect* (1787; Entry 208). See also note 91.

101. The picturesque is discussed in greater detail in Section 9.

102. See note 52, and *Lectures on Architecture*, ed. Arthur T. Bolton (London: Sir John Soane's Museum, 1929), pp. 114–118. Also see Soane's remarks on Classical villas (*Lectures*, pp. 149–151).

103. "Remarks on English Villas," in J. Britton and A. Pugin, *Illustrations of the Public Buildings of London* (London: J. Taylor, J. Britton, and A. Pugin, 1825), I, 83–88; quotations from pp. 84–85. For later discussion of the pictorial characteristics of villas and the surrounding landscape see John Ruskin's series of articles on "The Poetry of Architecture" in *The Architectural Magazine* (Entry 182); the portion of the series devoted to villas begins in the June 1838 issue.

For examples of the diverse sizes of villas that appeared in the 1820s see the modest Doric, Ionic, and Gothic villas in Peter Nicholson's *New Practical Builder* (1823; Entry 225), and the equally modest villas in John Soane's *Designs for Public Improvements* (1828; Entry 316.2 and later editions); compare the enormous castellated villa depicted in the frontispiece to Richard Elsam's *Practical Builder's Perpetual Price-Book* (1825; Entry 71).

104. On the subject of cottages in general see Harry Batsford and Charles Fry, *The English Cottage* (London: Batsford, 1939); Martin Shaw Briggs, *The English Farmhouse* (London: Batsford, 1953); R. J. Brown, *The English Country Cottage* (London: Robert Hale, 1979); Lyndon F. Cave, *The Smaller English House* (London: Robert Hale, 1981); Olive Cook, *English Cottages and Farmhouses* (London: Thames and Hudson, 1982); Tony Evans and Candida Lycett Green, *English Cottages* (New York: Viking Press, 1982); G. E. Fussell, *The English Rural Labourer* (London: Batchworth, 1949); G. E. Fussell, *Village Life in the Eighteenth Century* (Worcester: Littlebury, 1947); G. E. Fussell and Constance Goodman, "The Housing of the Rural Population in the Eighteenth Century," *Economic History* II:5 (January 1930), 63–90; M. Dorothy George, *England in Transition* (London: Penguin, 1953); George Llewellyn Morris and Esther Wood, *The Country Cottage* (London: John Lane, 1906); Paul Oliver, *English Cottages and Small Farmhouses* (London: Arts Council of Great Britain, 1975); John Woodforde, *The Truth about Cottages* (London: Routledge & Kegan Paul, 1979). On the utilitarian laborer's dwelling see Eileen Spiegel, "The English Farm House: A Study of Architectural Theory and Design," Ph.D. diss., Columbia University, 1960. On matters of economy and fitness in laborers' dwellings see Section 7 of this chapter.

105. *The Supplement to the Penny Cyclopaedia of the Society for the Diffusion of Useful Knowledge* (London: Charles Knight, 1845), I, 426.

106. Samuel Jackson Pratt, "Cottage-Pictures" (1801), in *Sympathy, and Other Poems* (London: Richard Phillips, 1807), p. 213. On the term *ferme ornée* see Entry 259.

107. See Spiegel, "The English Farm House"; the principal conclusions of this study are also presented in Eileen Harris (née Spiegel), "The Farmhouse: Vernacular and After," *Architectural Review* CXXX:778 (December 1961), 377–379.

108. For an earlier attempt to establish order, proportion, and beauty in "cottages" see John Wood, *The Origin of Building* (1741; Entry 351). Cf. too Thomas Rawlins's remarks in *Familiar Architecture* (1768; Entry 273): "How sooth'd and mollify'd [are the passions], when we descend to the pleasing rural Cot, where simple Elegance, Proportion, and Convenience unite!"

109. On primitivism in Britain see Lois Whitney, *Primitivism and the Idea of Progress* (Baltimore: Johns Hopkins University Press, 1934), and Margaret Mary FitzGerald, *First Follow Nature* (New York: King's Crown Press, 1947). The subject is studied in a larger context in Hoxie Neale Fairchild, *The Noble Savage* (New York: Columbia University Press, 1928), and Maren-Sofie Røstvig, *The Happy Man: Studies in the Metamorphoses of an Ideal* (Oslo and New York: Norwegian Universities Press, 1962–1971). Jean-Jacques Rousseau was particularly influential: see *Émile, ou de l'éducation* (Paris: Duchesne, 1762); and *La nouvelle Héloïse* [originally issued as *Lettres de deux amans*] (Paris: Duchesne, 1764). Rousseau visited England from January 1766 to May 1767. The harmony between nature and cottage domesticity is especially apparent in the work of Thomas Gainsborough, e.g., *The Cottage Door* (Huntington Art Gallery, San Marino, Calif.).

110. Plate XXVII. The building was intended either as a public house or as a residence; it is shown with a kitchen, parlor, brewhouse, washhouse, and bar on the ground floor, and five bedrooms upstairs.

111. The picturesque is reviewed in Christopher Hussey, *The Picturesque* (London: Putnam, 1927), and David Watkin, *The English Vision* (New York: Harper & Row, 1982). See also Richard Payne Knight, *The Landscape* (1794; Entry 169), and Humphry Repton, *Sketches and Hints on Landscape Gardening* (1794; Entry 280). On association, see Section 3 of this chapter.

112. One year earlier John Thomas Smith issued his *Remarks on Rural Scenery* (1797; Entry 312), containing views of 20 extant cottages, illustrated in finely etched detail to reveal the picturesque irregularities of both form and texture. He lamented that "of all pictoresque subjects, the *English cottage* seems to have obtained the least share of particular notice," perhaps because the beauty of cottages was not "of the *heroic* or sublime order." Malton took issue with some of Smith's remarks, but his argument in effect demonstrates his indebtedness to Smith's discussion of the picturesque. For later collections of illustrations of picturesque cottages see W. Pickett, *Twenty-Four Plates* (1812; Entry 256), and Francis Stevens, *Domestic Architecture* (1815; Entry 324).

113. For Malton's later modification of his ideas see his *Collection of Designs for Rural Retreats* (1802; Entry 196). For criticism of Malton see Richard Elsam, *An Essay on Rural Architecture* (1803; Entry 69).

114. In addition to the books discussed here, see treatises by Dearn, Elsam, Gandy, Laing, Loudon, Lugar, Malton, Plaw, and Woods (Entries 58–61, 70, 85, 170, 191, 192, 196, 261, 355). Also see three chapters relating to cottage design in William Mitford, *Principles of Design in Architecture* (London: Luke Hansard, 1809), pp. 269–293; this book has been excluded from the principal entries because it contains no illustrations of dwellings.

115. Like Bartell, Atkinson recognized the importance of scenic context in cottage design. He found that judicious use of light, shade, and irregular outline in the building as well as in the surrounding scenery would heighten the "picturesque effect." In the same year Robert Lugar also recommended the use of light and shadow in "the Cottage Orneé, or Gentleman's Cot" (*Architectural Sketches*; Entry 192).

116. See too John Ruskin's extended analysis of the picturesque character of cottages in relation to surrounding scenery in his articles on "The Poetry of Architecture" in Loudon's *Architectural Magazine* (December 1837 through May 1838; Entry 182).

117. The author of the encyclopedia article above (note 105) lamented that this type of cottage was "considered by some as a hybrid branch of the art, or as hardly belonging to it at all" (p. 426). He noted that in Joseph Gwilt's *Encyclopaedia* (1842) cottage architecture was dismissed "summarily" as a "nondescript sort of building" (ibid.).

118. See for example George Smith's *Essay on the Construction of Cottages* (1834; Entry 310); William Wilds's *Elementary and Practical Instructions* (1835; Entry 347); the report of the Cottage Improvement Society for North Northumberland ([1842]; Entry 483); and the reports of the Poor Law Commissioners (1842; Entries 472, 473). Note too the dry character of the designs and the lack of concern for picturesque principles in Samuel H. Brooks's *Designs for Cottage and Villa Architecture* (1839; Entry 23).

119. It is difficult to distinguish precisely between the "row house" and the "terrace house." Clearly, a group of row houses unified into a whole forms a terrace. More informally, however, a range of generally similar row houses also can be considered a terrace. In cases where the architect's original intention was indeterminate, I have sometimes used the term "terrace house" to refer to a row house that might be grouped into a terrace.

Summerson (1969), pp. 227–229, gives an overview of the genesis of the Georgian town house. Summerson gives a more detailed account of terrace housing in *Georgian London* (Harmondsworth: Penguin, 1969), pp. 65–83, 125–132, and passim. For a useful discussion of London squares and terrace housing see Steen Eiler Rasmussen, *London: The Unique City* (Cambridge, Mass.: MIT Press, 1967), pp. 165–270, 292–306. More recently on terrace houses see the impressively detailed study by Dan Cruickshank and Peter Wyld, *London: The Art of Georgian Building* (London: Architectural Press, 1975). Stefan Muthesius puts greatest emphasis on the mid- and late nineteenth century in *The English Terraced House* (New Haven: Yale University Press, 1982). See also Albert Edward Richardson and C. Lovett Gill, *London Houses from 1660 to 1820* (London: Batsford, 1911).

On terrace houses as the province of speculative builders see Summerson, *Georgian London*, pp. 65–83; and Cruickshank and Wyld, *London*, p. 1. The Building Acts of 1667, 1707, 1709, and 1774 particularly influenced the form of London town houses: see Summerson, *Georgian London*, pp. 68, 125–132; Cruickshank and Wyld, *London*, pp. 22–24, 29–31; and Clifford Cyril Knowles and P. H. Pitt, *The History of Building Regulation in London 1189–1972* (London: Architectural Press, 1972).

120. Plates 49 and 50 in Volume I of *Vitruvius Britannicus* (1715; Entry 32). On the design of Lindsey House see Summerson (1969), pp. 94–95.

121. The first passage is from [James Stuart?], *Critical Observations on the Buildings and Improvements of London* (London: J. Dodsley, 1771), pp. 27–28; the second is from William Halfpenny, et al., *The Modern Builder's Assistant* (1757; Entry 132), p. 36.

122. For small designs similar to country villas see the third volume of *Vitruvius Britannicus* (1725; Entry 33): General Wade's house in Great Burlington Street (Plate 10), and Lord Herbert's House in Whitehall (Plate 48). Typical examples of "town mansions," three stories high and seven openings wide, appear in Plates 46 and 67 of John Crunden's *Convenient and Ornamental Architecture* (1767; Entry 49).

123. See Cruickshank and Wyld, *London*, pp. 42–55.

124. The authors of the designs I am considering here used a confusing variety of terms to describe the story immediately above the ground story, including "principal story" (which also could refer to the ground story), "chamber story," and "one pair stairs story." For consistency I have adopted *piano nobile*, a contemporary Italian term that none of them used in describing town houses, but which clearly denotes the story containing important rooms that is one flight above the ground story.

125. On the importance of Lindsey House in establishing a Palladian "schema" for town houses from 1730 to 1830 see Summerson (1969), p. 228.

126. William Halfpenny also contributed a design for "a Town House" (No. 14, Plate 36). The presence of window and door openings only in the front and rear facades suggests that it might have been intended as a row house; nevertheless the plan shows that the two side walls were articulated with pilasters or buttresses, indicating that this house would not have directly adjoined another.

127. In Riou's own copy, at the Winterthur Museum Library, there are sketches—presumably in Riou's hand—showing more elaborate treatments of the facade. I am indebted to Mrs. Eleanor McD. Thompson, Librarian of the Printed Book and Periodical Collection, for bringing this to my attention.

128. The plate is numbered LXXXIII in the 1787 edition. The vicissitudes of Pain's plate numberings are discussed in Entry 237.

129. See for example plates numbered 95, 100, and 103 in the 1794 edition.

130. For references to Searles's work at Blackheath and to related buildings, see the note to Entry 230. Two examples of alternating high-low facades for attached houses are illustrated in Andor Gomme, Michael Jenner, and Bryan Little, *Bristol: An Architectural History* (London: Lund Humphries, 1979), pp. 224–225. The earliest is Ashley Place, Montpelier (by Thomas or William Paty, ca. 1788): each house consists of a ground story six openings wide, plus two additional stories rising above the right half of the ground story. Prince's Buildings (begun in 1790 by William Paty) consisted of three-story units, four openings wide, divided down the center by a party wall, which were linked to each other by one-story wings.

131. On economic and social aspects of the agricultural revolution see Eric L. Jones, *Agriculture and the Industrial Revolution* (New York: John Wiley & Sons, 1974); and G. E. Mingay, "The

Agricultural Revolution in English History: A Reconsideration," in W. E. Minchinton, ed., *Essays in Agrarian History* (Newton Abbot: David & Charles, 1968), II, 11–27. For a broader discussion of the history of philanthropy, see David Edward Owen, *English Philanthropy, 1660–1960* (Cambridge, Mass.: Harvard University Press, 1964). On the housing of agricultural laborers see G. E. Fussell, *The English Rural Labourer* (London: Batchworth, 1949); G. E. Fussell and Constance Goodman, "The Housing of the Rural Population in the Eighteenth Century," *Economic History* II:5 (January 1930), 63–90; and Eileen Spiegel, "The English Farm House: A Study of Architectural Theory and Design," Ph.D. diss., Columbia University, 1960. For a variety of perspectives on transformations in workers' housing that resulted from the industrial revolution see Leonardo Benevolo, *History of Modern Architecture* (Cambridge, Mass.: MIT Press, 1971); Benevolo, *The Origins of Modern Town Planning* (Cambridge, Mass.: MIT Press, 1971); John Burnett, *A Social History of Housing 1815–1970* (Newton Abbot: David & Charles, 1978); Martha Huff Carroll, "Cottage and Slum: The Nineteenth Century British Housing Debate," Ph.D. diss., Columbia University, 1978; Stanley D. Chapman, ed., *The History of Working Class Housing* (Newton Abbot: David & Charles, 1971); Enid Gauldie, *Cruel Habitations: A History of Working-Class Housing 1780–1918* (London: Allen & Unwin, 1974); Henry-Russell Hitchcock, *Early Victorian Architecture in Britain*, 2 vols. (New Haven: Yale University Press, 1954), especially Chapter XIV; Francis D. Klingender, *Art and the Industrial Revolution*, rev. and extended ed. (London: Paladin, 1972); Donald J. Olsen, *The Growth of Victorian London* (New York: Holmes & Meier, 1976); Nikolaus Pevsner, "Early Working Class Housing," in *Studies in Art, Architecture and Design* (London: Thames and Hudson, 1968), II, 18–38; John Nelson Tarn, *Five Per Cent Philanthropy: An Account of Housing in Urban Areas between 1840 and 1914* (London: University of Cambridge Press, 1973); and Tarn, *Working-Class Housing in 19th-century Britain* (London: Lund Humphries, 1971).

132. On farm houses in general and Garret's book in particular see Spiegel, "The English Farm House"; and Eileen Harris (née Spiegel), "The Farmhouse: Vernacular and After," *Architectural Review* CXXX:778 (December 1961), 377–379.

133. Note Soane's close relationship with Peacock, described in Pierre de la Ruffinière du Prey, *John Soane: The Making of an Architect* (Chicago: University of Chicago Press, 1982), pp. 18, 22, 26, 28–29, 66.

134. The principles are described in Entry 352.

135. See too the reports on Lincolnshire (1799; Entry 110) and Oxfordshire (1809; Entry 114), in which Arthur Young presented designs that he found of uncommon merit. Other county reports also include exemplary designs for farm houses and cottages (see Entries 92–123).

136. Entries 16, 17, 46, 47, 50, 148, 149, 152. Also see articles in later volumes by James Gillespie and Arthur Young (Entries 89, 360).

137. Also on the subject of agricultural and economic improvement see Sinclair's proposal for establishing experimental farms (1800; described in Entry 308) and his *Sketch of the Improvements, Now Carrying On . . . in the County of Caithness* (1803; Entry 309).

138. Parker was president of a Midlands benevolent organization, the Society for Bettering the Condition of the Poor in the Hundred of Oswestry and Parishes of Chirk and Llansilin, which in 1813 published its *First Report* (Entry 321), including a design for a model cottage that recently had won second place in a competition.

139. Books of picturesque cottage and villa designs are discussed in Chapter II, Section 1.

140. On previous architects who discussed parallels between the design of a dwelling and the character of the inhabitant see Section 3.

141. The next year two more authors, William Atkinson and Robert Lugar, addressed similar problems of welfare and economics, and likewise offered solutions couched in terms of picturesque improvement. In *Views of Picturesque Cottages* (1805; Entry 10) Atkinson stated that cottage building had become an object "of the first national importance." Building new cottages, he contended, would make estates more picturesque, while at the same time improving laborers' character and productivity. Likewise in *Architectural Sketches* (1805; Entry 192) Lugar provided designs "for those persons whose liberal minds may lead them to accommodate their peasantry and dependants with dwellings," while at the same time improving the picturesqueness of their "domains." Cf. Joseph Michael Gandy, who in *Designs for Cottages* (1805; Entry 84) acknowledged the economic value of cottage improvements but concentrated primarily on the application of artistic principles to cottage design. Two

years later, in *The Country Gentleman's Architect* (Entry 193), Lugar offered more designs for "Gentlemen who from philanthropy may wish to build cottages for their labourers, or farm-houses and farm-yards for their tenants."

142. The ideas of Hume and Gerard are discussed above in Section 2. Note that a concern for fitness is quite distinct from a desire for economy.

143. Henry Home, Lord Kames, *Elements of Criticism* (1762; 6th ed., with corrections and additions, Edinburgh: Printed for John Bell, et al., 1785), II, 456ff. In small dwellings in particular Kames recommended that "utility ought to prevail" over other aesthetic considerations such as regularity (p. 455).

144. Chambers, *Treatise*, 3rd ed. (1791; Entry 40.3), p. 99.

145. Further on "characteristic architecture" see Section 3.

146. Wotton, *Elements of Architecvre* (London: Iohn Bill, 1624), p. 1.

147. Loudon's interest in fitness is echoed in an article on ecclesiastical architecture contributed by Thomas Sopwith to the fourth volume of Loudon's *Architectural Magazine* (1837; Entry 182). Sopwith presented nine "principles of fitness" applicable to the design of a cathedral church. Loudon's ideas also appear in Richard Brown's *Domestic Architecture* (1841; Entry 24), an authoritative treatise on the history, design, and execution of dwellings. Although Brown insisted on the importance of picturesque composition in architecture, he also nearly paraphrased Loudon in his discussion of fitness: "the principles of domestic architecture as an art of design and taste may be reduced to the three following divisions: namely, fitness for the end in view, expression, of the end in view, and appropriateness of architectural style" (p. 306). Fitness, according to Brown, involved suiting "the plan and arrangement of the building" to its intended uses (ibid.).

148. Proposals for utopias and communitarian societies, of course, existed long before the nineteenth century. For an overview see W. H. G. Armytage, *Heavens Below: Utopian Experiments in England 1560–1960* (London: Routledge and Kegan Paul, 1961).

149. "Laid before the Committee of the House of Commons on the Poor Laws," [1817]. The quotations here are from captions to the illustration bound in as a frontispiece. In 1821 Owen published a more detailed proposal, his *Report to the County of Lanark, of a Plan for Relieving Public Distress, and Removing Discontent, by Giving Permanent, Productive Employment, to the Poor and Working Classes* (Glasgow: Wardlaw & Cunninghame, 1821). This includes a prospectus for "Establishing an Institution on Mr. Owen's System in the Middle Ward of the County of Lanark."

150. Minter Morgan's proposal is discussed in more detail in Entry 345.

151. Cunningham's remarks on the connection between housing and morality were not entirely original. In 1804 Ledoux had discussed much the same thing in his *Architecture* (see note 56). Cf. too "Remarks on the Erection of Labourers' Cottages" in the *Horticultural Register* for 1834 (Entry 474), which concerns the effect of a "neat cottage and small garden" on the morals of the laborer. Also see the report of the Cottage Improvement Society for North Northumberland ([1842]; Entry 483), in which the influence of housing on morality is examined further, and in which additional designs by Cunningham appear.

152. Among the most important studies of individual architectural styles in this period are: Richard G. Carrott, *The Egyptian Revival* (Berkeley: University of California Press, 1978); Kenneth Clark, *The Gothic Revival* (London: Constable, 1928); H. M. Colvin, "Gothic Survival and Gothick Revival," *Architectural Review* CIII:615 (March 1948), 91–98; J. Mordaunt Crook, *The Greek Revival* (London: John Murray, 1972); James Stevens Curl, *The Egyptian Revival* (London: Allen & Unwin, 1982); Terence Davis, *The Gothick Taste* (Newton Abbot: David & Charles, 1974); Charles L. Eastlake, *A History of the Gothic Revival* (1872; reprint, ed. J. Mordaunt Crook, Leicester: Leicester University Press, 1970); Paul Frankl, *The Gothic* (Princeton: Princeton University Press, 1960); Georg Germann, *Gothic Revival in Europe and Britain* (London: Lund Humphries, 1972); John Harris, *The Palladians* (New York: Rizzoli, 1982), in which a forthcoming study of "Palladianism and neo-Palladianism" is promised as well; Hugh Honour, *Chinoiserie* (London: John Murray, 1961); Honour, *Neo-Classicism* (Harmondsworth: Penguin, 1968); Honour, *Romanticism* (New York: Harper & Row, 1979); S. Lang, "The Principles of the Gothic Revival in England," *Journal of the Society of Architectural Historians* XXV:4 (December 1966), 240–267; James Macaulay, *The Gothic Revival 1745–1845* (Glasgow: Blackie, 1975); Donald Pilcher, *The Regency Style* (London: Batsford, 1947); Robert Rosenblum, *Transformations in Late Eighteenth Century Art* (Princeton: Princeton University

Press, 1967); David Watkin, *The English Vision* (New York: Harper & Row, 1982); Watkin, *Thomas Hope 1769–1831 and the Neo-Classical Idea* (London: John Murray, 1968); Dora Wiebenson, *The Sources of Greek Revival Architecture* (London: Zwemmer, 1969); and Rudolf Wittkower, *Palladio and Palladianism* (New York: Braziller, 1974).

153. On the political background of the Gothic Revival see Samuel Kliger, *The Goths in England* (Cambridge, Mass.: Harvard University Press, 1952).

154. For accounts of recent voyages to Asia that stimulated British interest in Chinese styles see Jean Baptiste du Halde, *Description géographique . . . de la Chine* (Paris: R. G. Lemercier, 1735), Engl. trans. (London: J. Watts, 1736); and Jean Denis Attiret, *A Particular Account of the Emperor of China's Gardens*, trans. Sir Harry Beaumont (London: R. Dodsley, 1752).

155. See *The Architectural Remembrancer* (1751; Entry 213) where, in addition to these remarks, Morris included two designs in Chinese style. These outlandish designs were meant to illustrate the unfortunate consequences of disregard for architectural principles. Also note his reference to "the Chinese unmeaning stile" in *Select Architecture* (Entry 216).

156. As early as 1751 Robert Morris included designs in Chinese, "Arabian," Persian/Gothic, and "Muscovite" styles in *The Architectural Remembrancer* (Entry 213); he added derogatory remarks concerning the Chinese style. William and John Halfpenny included designs in Chinese, Indian, Gothic, "Ancient," and "Modern" styles in *The Country Gentleman's Pocket Companion* (1753; Entry 131). *The Modern Builder's Assistant*, containing designs by William and John Halfpenny, Robert Morris, and Timothy Lightoler (1757; Entry 132), is another early example of such an eclectic compilation. It contains illustrations of the five orders according to Palladio, numerous designs in a very plain neo-Palladian style, some Rococo designs, others in Gothic and Castellated styles, and some Chinese designs. Also: Timothy Lightoler's *Gentleman and Farmer's Architect* (1762; Entry 179) includes designs for a lodge house and Dutch barn in Chinese style; Sir William Chambers's Chinese Pagoda at Kew is depicted in his *Plans, Elevations, and Sections* (1763; Entry 39); in William Pain's *Builder's Pocket-Treasure* (1763; Entry 238) there is a design for a Chinese temple; in *Original Designs of Temples* (1766; Entry 234) Thomas Overton depicted an octagonal "room" with a Chinese roof; William Wrighte included a Chinese Hermitage in *Grotesque Architecture* (1767; Entry 358); and there are designs for a Chinese bridge and Chinese railings in N. Wallis's *Carpenter's Treasure* (1773; Entry 338).

157. On the historiography of medieval architecture see note 152, and: Joan Evans, *A History of the Society of Antiquaries* (Oxford: Oxford University Press, 1956); Thomas D. Kendrick, *British Antiquity* (London: Methuen, 1950); Nikolaus Pevsner, *Some Architectural Writers of the Nineteenth Century* (Oxford: Clarendon Press, 1972); Henry Beauchamp Walters, *The English Antiquaries of the Sixteenth, Seventeenth and Eighteenth Centuries* (London: E. Walters, 1934); and David Watkin, *The Rise of Architectural History* (London: Architectural Press, 1980), Chapter 3.
Important primary treatises concerning medieval architecture issued by 1800 include: James Bentham, *The History and Antiquities of the . . . Church of Ely* (Cambridge: Cambridge University Press, 1771); James Bentham and Brown[e] Willis, *The History of Gothic & Saxon Architecture, in England* (London: C. Boydel, 1798); Henry Boswell, *Historical Descriptions of . . . the Antiquities of England and Wales* (London: Alex. Hogg, 1786); Samuel and Nathaniel Buck, *Buck's Antiquities* (London: D. Bond, 1774; earlier ed., 1726–1752); John Carter, *The Ancient Architecture of England* (London: J. Carter, 1795 and later); Carter, *Specimens of the Ancient Sculpture and Painting* (London: J. Carter, 1780–1787); Carter, *Views of Ancient Buildings* ([London], 1786–1793); William Dugdale, *The History of St. Paul's Cathedral* (London: Printed by T. Warren, 1658); William Dugdale and Roger Dodsworth, *Monasticon Anglicanum* (London: Richard Hodgkinsonne, 1655–1673); James Essex, "Observations on the Origin and Antiquity of Round Churches," *Archaeologia* VI (1782), 163–178; Essex, "Remarks on the Antiquity and the Different Modes of Brick and Stone Buildings in England," *Archaeologia* IV (1776), 73–109; Richard Gough, *Sepulchral Monuments in Great Britain* (London: Printed for the author, and sold by T. Payne and Son, 1786 and later); Francis Grose, *The Antiquities of England and Wales* (London: S. Hooper, 1773–1787); Grose, *The Antiquities of Ireland* (London: S. Hooper, 1791); Grose, *The Antiquities of Scotland* (London: S. Hooper, 1789–1791); Joseph Halfpenny, *Gothic Ornaments in the Cathedral Church of York* (York: J. Todd & Sons, 1795); James Hall, "On the Origin and Principles of Gothic Architecture," *Transactions of the Royal Society of Edinburgh* IV:2 (1798), 3–27; Thomas Hearne, *Antiquities of Great-Britain* (London: Printed by James Phillips, published by T. Hearne and W. Byrne, 1786); Edward King, *Munimenta Antiqua* (London: Printed by W. Bulmer & Co. for G. Nicol, 1799–1805); King, "Observations on Ancient Castles," *Archaeologia* IV (1776), 364–413; King, "Sequel to the Observations on Ancient Castles," *Archaeologia* VI (1782), 231–375; John Milner, *The*

History of . . . Winchester (Winchester: J. Robbins, 1798–1801); James Cavanagh Murphy, "An Introductory Discourse on the Principles of Gothic Architecture," in Luiz de Sousa, *Plans . . . of Batalha* (London: I. & J. Taylor, 1795); Francis Price, *A Series of Particular and Useful Observations . . . upon . . . Salisbury* (London: Printed by C. and J. Ackers, sold by R. Baldwin, 1753); Society of Antiquaries, *Archaeologia* (London, 1770 and later); Society of Antiquaries, *Cathedrals of Britain* (London: 1795 and later); Society of Antiquaries, *Vetusta Monumenta* (London, 1747 and later); William Stukeley, *Intinerarium Curiosum* (London: The author, 1724); William Warburton, *The Works of Alexander Pope* (London: J. and P. Knapton, 1751), commentary on Epistle IV of the Moral Essays; Thomas Warton, et al., *Essays on Gothic Architecture* (London: Printed by S. Gosnell for J. Taylor, 1800); and Browne Willis, *A Survey of the Cathedrals* (London: R. Gosling, 1727–1730).

158. On the importance of medievalism in eighteenth-century British literature see: Robert Kiely, *The Romantic Novel in England* (Cambridge, Mass.: Harvard University Press, 1972); Warren Hunting Smith, *Architecture in English Fiction* (New Haven: Yale University Press, 1934); Montague Summers, *A Gothic Bibliography* (London: The Fortune Press, 1941); Summers, *The Gothic Quest* (London: The Fortune Press, 1938); Devendra P. Varma, *The Gothic Flame* (London: A. Barker, 1957); and René Wellek, *The Rise of English Literary History* (Chapel Hill: University of North Carolina Press, 1941).

Among primary sources see especially: George Ellis, *Specimens of the Early English Poets* (London: Edwards, 1790); Richard Hurd, *Letters on Chivalry and Romance* (London: A. Millar and J. Woodyer, 1762); Thomas Percy, *Reliques of Ancient English Poetry* (London: J. Dodsley, 1765); Warburton, *Works of Alexander Pope*, commentary on Epistle IV of the Moral Essays; Thomas Warton, *The History of English Poetry* (London: J. Dodsley, et al., 1774–1781); and Warton, *Observations on the Fairy Queen of Spenser*, 2nd ed. (London: R. and J. Dodsley, et al., 1762).

159. These uses are discussed at greater length in John Archer, "The Beginnings of Association in British Architectural Esthetics," *Eighteenth-Century Studies* XVI:3 (Spring 1983), 241–264.

160. On the Castellated style see the important study by A. J. Rowan, "The Castle Style in British Domestic Architecture in the Eighteenth and Early Nineteenth Centuries," Ph.D. diss., Cambridge University, Magdalene College, 1965.

161. French architects had paid much greater attention to the structural aspects of Gothic. For a detailed account of French studies of Gothic see Robin Middleton, "The Abbé de Cordemoy and the Graeco-Gothic Ideal: A Prelude to Romantic Classicism," *Journal of the Warburg and Courtauld Institutes* XXV:3–4 (July–December 1962), 278–320; XXVI (1963), 90–123. Also see Wolfgang Herrmann, *Laugier and Eighteenth Century French Theory* (London: Zwemmer, 1962). For contemporary British attention to structure in the Gothic arch see Michael Young, "The Origin and Theory of the Gothic Arch," *Transactions of the Royal Irish Academy* III (1790), 55–88; and James Anderson, "Thoughts on the Origin, Excellencies, and Defects of the Grecian and Gothic Styles of Architecture," *Recreations in Agriculture, Natural-History, Arts, and Miscellaneous Literature* II (1800), 187–203, 280–293, 418–434; III (1800), 115–132; IV (1801), 273–290; 382–394; 448–465.

162. In *Plans, and Views in Perspective* (1801; Entry 210) Robert Mitchell proposed to elucidate the true principles of Gothic style, and he—like Morison—adopted a Reptonian method of analysis. He argued that Gothic buildings, characterized by vertical lines, could achieve "powerful effects, or irresistible impressions." Classical styles, in contrast, were "cut asunder by the horizontal lines."

During this period it became a common practice to provide designs stylistically suited to particular types of scenery. In 1795, for example, John Plaw completed *Ferme Ornée* (Entry 259), containing designs "calculated for landscape and picturesque effects." Several of these were composed in Gothic or Castellated ("Monastic") styles in order to accord visually with nearby buildings and the surrounding landscape.

163. For archaeological accounts of the 1750s and 1760s see note 1. On the historiography of Classical archaeology see note 152, and: Martin Lowther Clarke, *Greek Studies in England 1700–1830* (Cambridge: Cambridge University Press, 1945); Lionel Cust, *History of the Society of Dilettanti*, 2nd ed. (London: Macmillan, 1914); Terence Spencer, *Fair Greece! Sad Relic* (London: Weidenfeld & Nicolson, 1954); and Bernard Herbert Stern, *The Rise of Romantic Hellenism* (Menasha, Wisc.: George Banta, 1940). On the conflict between archaeological accounts and historical treatises, see Section 1 of this chapter.

164. See for example the remarks in the third edition of Chambers's *Treatise* (1791; Entry 40.3), especially p. 19.

165. Also see remarks by Ware, Lewis, and Aikin, discussed in Section 1.

166. On the picturesque in eighteenth-century British aesthetics see Walter John Hipple, Jr., *The Beautiful, the Sublime, and the Picturesque in Eighteenth-Century British Aesthetic Theory* (Carbondale: Southern Illinois University Press, 1957); Christopher Hussey, *The Picturesque* (London: Putnam, 1927); Elizabeth Wheeler Manwaring, *Italian Landscape in Eighteenth Century England* (New York: Oxford University Press, 1925); and Watkin, *The English Vision*.

167. Sir Uvedale Price contributed equally important remarks on the picturesque: he proposed to establish it as a new aesthetic category, equal to the two currently recognized categories, the sublime and the beautiful. His *Essay on the Picturesque* (London: J. Robson, 1794) has been excluded from the principal entries because it does not contain designs for dwellings.

168. For later collections of picturesque cottages see W. Pickett, *Twenty-Four Plates* (1812; Entry 256), and Francis Stevens, *Domestic Architecture* (1815; Entry 324).

169. An extended consideration of the relationship between a dwelling and the surrounding landscape is found in Section 9 of this chapter.

170. In 1815 Thomas Rickman completed the first authoritative classification of English architecture into historical periods by style; see Entry 311. Rickman's contribution is discussed further in Pevsner, *Some Architectural Writers*, pp. 28–31.

171. Cf. Edmund Aikin's remarks on style, published the same year in *Designs for Villas* (1808; Entry 4). Aikin rejected Gothic because its associations with past times and manners were too delusive and deceptive. The only remaining monuments of Greek architecture were temples, which he found inappropriate models for modern dwellings. Asserting that "modern Architecture is by no means the imitator" of Classical architecture, he recommended that the architect instead "endeavour to think like an Ancient placed in modern times." Aikin's goal was to achieve "an economical style of beauty" based on "general forms and proportions," with little or no ornament.

172. Later, in *Fragments on the Theory and Practice of Landscape Gardening* (1816; Entry 277), Repton continued to recommend the dissociation of style and function in dwellings: in discussing interior design he stated that "whatever the style of the exterior may be, the interior of a house should be adapted to the uses of the inhabitants."

173. The literature of domestic architecture that is represented in the entries below includes few of the important scholarly treatises concerning historical styles and buildings. Such treatises are discussed in many of the references listed in note 152.

The four styles that I have chosen to examine here were clearly viewed by most nineteenth-century architects as subordinate to the principal historical styles—Gothic, Greek, and Roman. Among the principal entries below, some examination of Gothic and Classical styles may be found in the following: Bradshaw, *Civil Architecture* (1800; Entry 19); Woods, "An Essay on the Situations and Accompaniments of Villas" (1808; Entry 355); Wilkins, *The Civil Architecture of Vitruvius* (1812; Entry 348); Smith, *The Panorama of Science and Art* (1815; Entry 311); Smith, *An Outline of Architecture* (1816; Entry 314); Nicholson, *An Architectural Dictionary* (1819; Entry 223); Cottingham, *Working Drawings for Gothic Ornaments* (n.d.; Entry 43); Nicholson, *The New Practical Builder* (1823; Entry 225); Nicholson, *The Builder & Workman's . . . Director* (1824; Entry 224); Gwilt, *Rudiments of Architecture* (1826; Entry 125); Billington, *The Architectural Director* (1829?; Entry 18); Wetten, *Designs for Villas in the Italian Style* (1830?; Entry 341); Legh, *The Music of the Eye* (1831; Entry 176); Nicholson, *A Theoretical and Practical Treatise on the Five Orders* (1834; Entry 228); Jones, *Athenian; or, Grecian Villas* (1835; Entry 161); Collis, *The Builders' Portfolio* (1837; Entry 41); Wightwick, *The Palace of Architecture* (1840; Entry 346); Brown, *Domestic Architecture* (1841; Entry 24); and Francis, *A Series of Original Designs* (1841; Entry 83).

174. The designs in "Indian" style are for garden buildings and piers. Gardens were often understood as special environments in which the imagination was given much greater license than elsewhere. See H. F. Clark, "Eighteenth Century Elysiums: The Rôle of 'Association' in the Landscape Movement," *Journal of the Warburg and Courtauld Institutes* VI (1943), 165–189; and John Dixon Hunt, "Emblem and Expressionism in the Eighteenth-Century Landscape," *Eighteenth-Century Studies* IV:3 (Spring 1971), 294–317.

175. On Sezincote, the Daniells, and other aspects of Indian architecture see Mildred Archer, *Indian Architecture and the British* (London: Country Life, 1968); and Thomas Sutton, *The Daniells: Artists and Travellers* (London: Bodley Head, 1954).

176. For further discussion of Norman Revival see Robin Fedden, "Neo-Norman," *Architectural Review* CXVI:696 (December 1954), 380–385; and Pevsner, *Some Architectural Writers*, pp. 66–69.

177. See Manwaring, *Italian Landscape*, and Hussey, *The Picturesque*.

178. See Summerson (1969), p. 290.

179. Knight's remarks are excerpted in Entry 203.

180. Respectively, *Designs for Ornamental Villas* (Entry 293), and *Retreats* (Entry 333).

181. See for example Robert Gunter Wetten's *Designs for Villas in the Italian Style* (1830?; Entry 341).

182. In *Designs for Parsonage Houses* (1827; Entry 154) Thomas Frederick Hunt described Old English architecture as that of the "Tudor period," from Henry VII through Elizabeth I (p. 17). Thus for Hunt, Tudor and Elizabethan apparently were identical. In *Domestic Architecture in the Tudor Style* (1837, Entry 294) Peter Frederick Robinson cited a passage from James Dallaway's *Discourses* in which Tudor and Old English were equated. John Claudius Loudon, in contrast, strictly equated Old English with Elizabethan architecture in his *Encyclopaedia* (1833; Entry 184, p. 1124). George Wightwick clearly differentiated Tudor from Elizabethan. He stated in *The Palace of Architecture* (1840; Entry 346) that "the common habit of applying the term 'Elizabethan' to the older mansions of the Tudor period, is a heinous offence. The Elizabethan style, properly so called, is 'beneath abhorring,' *i.e.* as a style" (p. 147). He also referred to it as "the mongrel Italianised Gothic of Elizabeth" (p. 148). In *Domestic Architecture* (1841; Entry 24) Richard Brown provided designs in each of three separate "Tudor" styles—Henry the Seventh, Henry the Eighth, and Elizabethan. Further on Elizabethan see Mark Girouard, "Attitudes to Elizabethan Architecture, 1600–1900," in John Summerson, ed., *Concerning Architecture* (London: Allen Lane The Penguin Press, 1968), pp. 13–27.

183. Also note Richard Brown's remarks in *Principles of Practical Perspective* (1835; Entry 25.2): in Tudor times, he said, architects "appear to have been well acquainted with the picturesque in building."

184. *Architectural Sketches* (1805, Entry 192). The design is essentially Tudor Gothic; nevertheless Lugar described its style as "house Gothic," a term that for Repton was equivalent to "Queen Elisabeth's Gothic." Whatever the terminology, perhaps one should trace the origins of twentieth-century "stockbroker Tudor" to Lugar.

185. Several historical studies of Elizabethan architecture were published in the 1830s and 1840s. Many of these follow Hunt's approach, discussing aspects of the social and political context; many also contain romantic views of buildings and rooms with people in Elizabethan costume. For a listing see the commentary to Entry 154.

186. For collections of designs in diverse styles issued earlier than those discussed here see note 156.

187. On this subject see especially Christopher Hussey, *The Picturesque* (London: Putnam, 1927); and David Watkin, *The English Vision* (New York: Harper & Row, 1982).

188. *The Villas of the Ancients* (Entry 36). By "Landskip" Castell may have meant either an easel painting of a scene in nature, or the actual prospect of such a scene; see Hussey, *The Picturesque*, pp. 25–26; and *Oxford English Dictionary*, s.v. "Landscape."

189. Since the mid-sixteenth century, illustrators had rendered views of country dwellings accompanied by park and garden scenery. By the early eighteenth century Leonard Knyff and others had made a specialty of topographical views showing country houses and the surrounding landscape in precise detail. See John Harris, *The Artist and the Country House* (Totowa, N.J.: Sotheby Parke Bernet, 1979).

190. For theoretical remarks by contemporaries of Wright and Chambers concerning the affectivity of garden landscapes, see Section 3.

191. Henry Home, Lord Kames, *Elements of Criticism* (1762; 6th ed., with corrections and additions, Edinburgh: Printed for John Bell, et al., 1785), II, 469. Cf. 1762 ed., III, 339–340.

192. In addition to architects and theorists who considered the pictorial and expressive effects that could be achieved by a house and its surroundings, authors of midcentury perspective treatises also explored the integration of architectural form with surrounding scenery. John Joshua Kirby's treatise on *Dr. Brook Taylor's Method of Perspective* (1754; Entry 167) includes "natural" landscape scenes—at least one of which is by Thomas Gainsborough—containing domestic and ecclesiastical architectural subjects. There are other domestic structures surrounded by landscape scenery in Kirby's *Perspective of Architecture* (1761; Entry 168).

Daniel Fournier's *Treatise of the Theory and Practice of Perspective* (1761; Entry 82) includes illustrations of picturesque cottages and farm buildings set in rustic landscapes.

193. For Soane's notion of "characteristic" architecture see Section 3, especially note 52.

194. A representative sample of other treatises exploring the formal relation between architecture and landscape includes: David Laing, *Hints for Dwellings* (1800; Entry 170); William Atkinson, *Views of Picturesque Cottages* (1805; Entry 10); Robert Lugar, *Architectural Sketches* (1805; Entry 192); Lugar, *Plans and Views* (1811; Entry 194); Thomas Downes Wilmot Dearn, *Sketches in Architecture . . . for Public & Private Buildings* (1806; Entry 61); Edward Gyfford, *Designs for Elegant Cottages* (1806; Entry 127); William Fuller Pocock, *Architectural Designs* (1807; Entry 262); John Buonarotti Papworth, *Rural Residences* (1818; Entry 246.2); Peter Frederick Robinson, *Designs for Ornamental Villas* (1827; Entry 293); James Thomson, *Retreats* (1827; Entry 333); and John George Jackson, *Designs for Villas* (1827–1829; Entry 157).

195. Such an approach was encouraged, in part, by the fact that architects derived their knowledge of at least one very popular dwelling type, the vernacular cottage, primarily from illustrations in drawing manuals. One such manual was John Thomas Smith's *Remarks on Rural Scenery* (1797; Entry 312), which depicts 20 extant cottages set amid irregular trees, decaying logs, underbrush, and other picturesque scenery. Similar cottages and scenery also appear in *William Orme's Rudiments of Landscape Drawing* (1802; Entry 232); John Hassell's *Speculum* (1809; Entry 144) and *Hassell's Drawing Magazine* (n.d.; Entry 143); W. Pickett's *Twenty-Four Plates* (1812; Entry 256); and Francis Stevens's *Domestic Architecture* (1815; Entry 324).

196. Like Robinson, T. J. Ricauti complained of the recent visual damage done by the erection of crude and inelegant buildings in styles "whose outlines are anything but compatible with" the pictorial qualities of the surrounding scenery. In *Sketches for Rustic Work* (1842; Entry 282) he also expressed hope that his own highly picturesque designs might help preseve the rustic and picturesque appearance of England's country estates.

197. Similarly, in brief remarks on architectural composition in *Designs for Farm Buildings* (1830; Entry 291), Robinson noted that even "the rudest Hut may give value to the picture." In *Village Architecture* (1830; Entry 297) he encouraged the preservation and restoration of vernacular buildings in the hope of retaining "the forms . . . which our painters have so long delighted to portray, and which have in fact given real value to their pictures."
Thomas Frederick Hunt, another prolific designer of picturesque dwellings in the 1820s and 1830s, found Robinson's work overly devoted to pictorial effect. In *Designs for Parsonage Houses* (1827; Entry 154) Hunt criticized the "factitious effect obtained by the broken, unequal, or *painter's* line."

198. Cf. Thomas Frederick Hunt's design for a residence in Plate IX of *Architettura Campestre* (1827; Entry 153). Hunt did not describe the design as an artist's residence; but, like Papworth's design, it contains forms derived from Italian landscape painting. The facade consists of a massive semicircular arch sheltering a seat or a bench, and two square towers above; one of these culminates in an open belvedere. Ultimately this design was executed as a lodge on the Alton estate in Staffordshire.

199. Among general studies of British planning that touch on the period 1700–1850 see especially: Colin and Rose Bell, *City Fathers* (Harmondsworth: Penguin, 1972); Leonardo Benevolo, *The Origins of Modern Town Planning* (Cambridge, Mass.: MIT Press, 1971); Françoise Choay, *The Modern City: Planning in the 19th Century* (New York: Braziller, 1969); Gillian Darley, *Villages of Vision* (London: Architectural Press, 1975); John G. Dunbar, *The Historic Architecture of Scotland* (London: Batsford, 1966); Arthur M. Edwards, *The Design of Suburbia* (London: Pembridge Press, 1981); Siegfried Giedion, *Space, Time and Architecture*, 5th ed. (Cambridge, Mass.: Harvard University Press, 1967); W. G. Hoskins, *The Making of the English Landscape* (Harmondsworth: Penguin, 1970); J. M. Houston, "Village Planning in Scotland, 1745–1845," *The Advancement of Science* V:18 (July 1948), 129–132; A. E. J. Morris, *History of Urban Form before the Industrial Revolutions*, 2nd ed. (New York: John Wiley & Sons, 1979); Donald J. Olsen, *The Growth of Victorian London* (New York: Holmes & Meier, 1976); Olsen, *Town Planning in London: The Eighteenth & Nineteenth Centuries* (New Haven: Yale University Press, 1964; new ed., 1982); Steen Eiler Rasmussen, *London: The Unique City* (Cambridge, Mass.; MIT Press, 1967); T. C. Smout, "The Landowner and the Planned Village in Scotland, 1730–1830," in N. T. Phillipson and Rosalind Mitchison, eds., *Scotland in the Age of Improvement* (Edinburgh: Edinburgh University Press, 1970), pp. 73–106; Robert A. M. Stern, ed., "The Anglo-American Suburb," *Architectural Design* 51 (October–November 1981); John Summerson, *Georgian London* (Harmondsworth: Penguin, 1969); Anthony Sutcliffe,

ed., *The Rise of Modern Urban Planning 1800–1914* (New York: St. Martin's Press, 1980); and Paul Zucker, *Town and Square* (Cambridge, Mass.: MIT Press, 1970).

200. These proposals, Craig's earlier and far more important design for the New Town (1767), and his other contributions are thoroughly discussed by A. J. Youngson in *The Making of Classical Edinburgh* (Edinburgh: Edinburgh University Press, 1966).

201. The elder White issued *Explanation of a Plan for the Improvement of Mary-le-Bone Park* (London, 1813). The first edition of *Some Account* (London: W. & P. Reynolds) appeared in 1814; the second edition, with additions, was published in 1815 by Cadell & Davies, et al.

202. White's book also includes a plate showing Nash's proposal for Regent Street, with James Wyatt's suggested improvements superimposed. The history of Regent's Park is discussed at length by Ann Saunders in *Regent's Park* (Newton Abbot: David & Charles, 1969). See also John Summerson, *The Life and Work of John Nash* (Cambridge, Mass.: MIT Press, 1980).

203. In addition to Smirke's proposal, see also: [Lewis Wyatt], *Prospectus of a Design for Various Improvements in the Metropolis* (London: J. Barfield, 1816); Sir William Hillary, *Suggestions for the Improvement and Embellishment of the Metropolis*, 2nd ed. (London, 1825), previous edition in *The Pamphleteer* XXIV (1824), 335–350; *A Letter to the Right Hon. Sir Charles Long, on the Improvements Now Proposed, and Now Carrying On in the Western Part of London* (London, 1825); Charles Long, Lord Farnborough, *Short Remarks, and Suggestions, upon Improvements Now Carrying On or under Consideration* (London: J. Hatchard, 1826); William Bardwell, *Westminster Improvements* (London, 1839); "Metropolitan Improvements," *The Westminster Review* XXXVI (1841), 404–435; and Henry Austin, *Metropolitan Improvements* ([London: Society for the Promotion of Metropolitan Improvements, 1842]).

Among eighteenth century treatises on planning that I have not discussed here see: Thomas Lediard, *Some Observations on the Scheme, Offered by Messrs. Cotton and Lediard, for Opening the Streets and Passages to and from the Intended Bridge at Westminster* (London: Brett and Ruth Charlton, [1738]); Edward Tatham, *Oxonia Explicata & Ornata. Proposals for Disengaging and Beautifying the University and City of Oxford* (London: J. Wilkie, 1773); and William Pickett, *Public Improvement, or a Plan for Making a Convenient and Handsome Communication between the Cities of London and Westminster* (London, 1789).

204. The Place Stanislas (1755) in Nancy was designed by Héré de Corny; for illustrations see Siegfried Giedion, *Space, Time and Architecture*, 5th ed. (Cambridge, Mass.: Harvard University Press, 1967), pp. 145–146. Riou noted (p. 78) that his idea for an obelisk supported by four statues was inspired by the Fountain of the Four Rivers in the Piazza Navona in Rome, completed in 1651 by Bernini.

205. For villages that were executed in a picturesque manner shortly afterward see Darley, *Villages of Vision*, Chapters 4 and 5.

206. Houston, "Village Planning in Scotland," pp. 129–130; Dunbar, *The Historic Architecture of Scotland*, pp. 248–250; Bell, *City Fathers*, p. 228. On the efforts of Sir John Sinclair in Caithness see Rosalind Mitchison, *Agricultural Sir John* (London: Geoffrey Bles, 1962).

207. Compare Nicholson's villas at Ardrossan with the line of villas John White proposed to erect around the periphery of Regent's Park, discussed above. There is a precedent for Nicholson's design in the unexecuted proposal published by Spurrier and Phipps in 1794 for St. John's Wood, showing both a circus and a crescent of semidetached villas. See my "*Rus in Urbe*: Classical Ideals of Country and City in British Town Planning," *Studies in Eighteenth-Century Culture* XII, ed. Harry C. Payne (Madison: University of Wisconsin Press, 1983), p. 169. The plan for Ardrossan is also illustrated and discussed in Peter Nicholson's *Architectural Dictionary* (1819; Entry 223).

208. Edinburgh: Printed by James Ballantyne and Co. for John Ballantyne and Co., Edinburgh; and Longman, Hurst, Rees, Orme, and Brown; and Gale and Curtis; London, 1812. This report to the Board of Agriculture is not included among the principal entries because it does not contain an original design for a dwelling. The plan is described on pp. 595–596.

209. I have discussed Owen's proposal and its progeny—including designs by Stedman Whitwell, John Minter Morgan, and William Thompson—in Section 7.

210. Aldrich's remarks were not published until 1789, in his posthumous *Elements of Civil Architecture* (Entry 5).

211. On early villa suburbs see Archer, "*Rus in Urbe*"; and John Archer, "Country and City in the American Romantic Suburb," *Journal of the Society of Architectural Historians* XLII:2 (May 1983), 139–156.

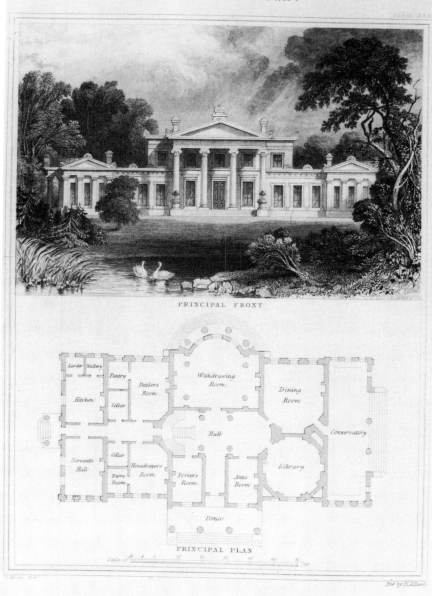

1
Richard Brown, "A Grecian Villa," Pl.
XXXI in *Domestic Architecture* (first
edition 1841; photograph from [1842]
edition, Entry 24.2).

Gothick *Pavillion*

Plate LX

Batty Langley Inv. 1742

T L Sculp.

2
Batty and Thomas Langley, "Gothick
Pavillion," Pl. LX in *Gothic Architecture*
(first edition [1742]; photograph from
1747 edition, Entry 172.2).

3
John Claudius Loudon, "The Beau
Idéal of an English Villa," Fig. 1438 in
*An Encyclopaedia of Cottage, Farm, and
Villa Architecture* (first edition 1833;
photograph from 1846 edition, Entry
184.8).

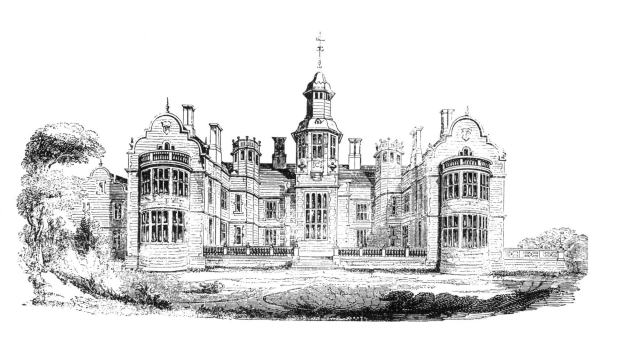

4
Robert Lugar, Design "in the style of
an Italian villa," Pl. XXVIII in
Architectural Sketches (first edition 1805;
photograph from 1815 edition, Entry
192.2).

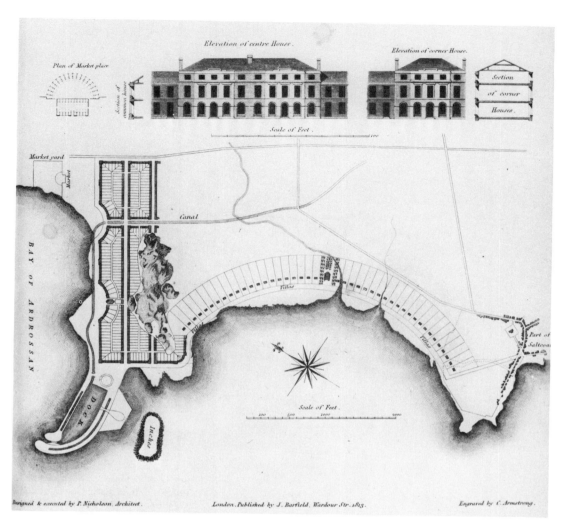

Plan of Market place

Elevation of centre House.

Section of common house

Elevation of corner House.

Section

of corner

Houses.

Scale of Feet.

Market yard

Canal

Villas

Villas

Part of Saltcoats

BAY OF ARDROSSAN

DOCK

Inchee

Scale of Feet.

Designed & executed by P. Nicholson Architect.   London. Published by J. Barfield. Wardour Str. 1813.   Engraved by C. Armstrong.

5
Peter Nicholson, ''Plan of the Town of
Ardrossan,'' Pl. II (Art. ''Town'') in *An
Architectural and Engineering Dictionary*
(first edition 1819; photograph from
1835 edition, Entry 223.2). Also see
Entry 93.

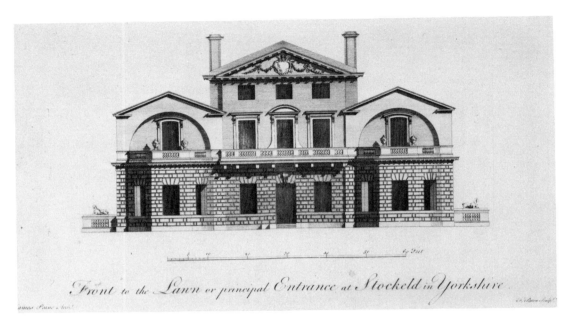

Front to the Lawn or principal Entrance at Stockeld in Yorkshire

6
James Paine, "Front to the Lawn or principal Entrance at Stockeld in Yorkshire," Vol. I, Pl. XLIII in *Plans, Elevations, and Sections* (first edition 1767; photograph from 1783 edition, Entry 243.2).

7
John Buonarotti Papworth, "Cottage Ornée," Pl. 7 in *Rural Residences* (1818; Entry 246.2).

COTTAGE ORNEE.

Pub.d at R.ACKERMANN'S REPOSITORY of ARTS N.o 101, Strand, June, 1818.

8

Charles Parker, "Residence of a Bailiff
or Steward," in *Villa Rustica* (Pl. XLVIII
in first edition, 1832–1841; photograph
from Pl. XLVI as renumbered in 1848
edition, Entry 249.2).

Lodge or Cottage.

9
John Plaw, "Lodge or Cottage," Pl. 13
in *Ferme Ornée* (first edition 1795;
photograph from 1803 edition, Entry
259.4).

Drawn by J.D.Harding.   Designed by P.F.R.   W.Walton lithog.

DESIGN N.º 1.

Printed by Hullmandel

10
Peter Frederick Robinson, "Binswood
Cottage," N.S. Pl. 4 in *A New Series of
Designs* (1838; Entry 295.1).

11
Abraham Swan, "A Design for a
House," Vol. II, Pl. 12 in *A Collection of
Designs* (1757; Entry 326.1).

Principal Entries

Editorial Method

Entries are ordered alphabetically by author, or by title when there is no author. Different works by a single author are arranged alphabetically by title. In cases of joint authorship, entries are arranged only by the first or principal author and then by title; in effect joint authors are ignored for purposes of ordering.

For books first issued from 1715 through 1842, I have included all later editions and reprints through 1950. Reprints and microform editions issued thereafter are located easily through electronic information retrieval systems, which enjoy the advantage of being updated continuously.

Although it was common for periodicals to be reissued in new "editions" years after the original issues, it would be extremely difficult to account for such editions in a thorough manner. Thus I have provided only the date of first publication for any article or volume.

Books and periodicals that became available too late for inclusion in the principal entries are gathered in Appendix D (Entries 468–493). Cross-references to all entries in Appendix D have been inserted among the principal entries.

In determining the appropriate level of detail for the bibliographic descriptions, I have had to balance the advantages of a thorough analysis of every aspect against the exigencies of time and publication expense. The result is the system of description described below.

1
Bibliographic Description: Books (except Encyclopedias)

Each entry consists of several parts—entry number, author, title, imprint, description of pagination and plates, size, and location of the copy consulted—which are explained briefly here. Note that for some books that I could not examine personally, I had to omit portions of the bibliographic description—usually the size, more rarely the imprint or pagination.

Entry Number

Each entry is identified by a two-part number (e.g., 293.6). The portion of the number preceding the point applies to all editions of a single title. The portion of the number following the point is unique for each edition (e.g., 293.1, 293.2, etc.). Note that these numerals are assigned as a convenient means of ordering the material, and so do *not* necessarily correspond to the number of the edition as printed on the title page.

For special symbols following certain entry numbers (e.g., †, ‡, ‖), see the section below, "Location of the Copy Cited."

Author	At the beginning of each entry the author's name is given to the fullest extent known, followed by dates of birth and death when known. When the author's name is not shown on the title page, it is given in square brackets ([ ]). A five-em dash (—————) in place of the author's name indicates that the name is unchanged from the previous entry.[1]
Title	Titles are transcribed in full from each title page. Although many titles are cumbersome and verbose by modern standards, they often provide a valuable account of the contents of the book. For this reason ellipses (. . .) have been used only to indicate omission of biographical information following an author's name. Eighteenth-century orthography frequently was irregular; I have recorded all irregularities as accurately as possible, and therefore I have used "*sic*" only in cases of clear typographical error. I have capitalized only proper nouns, personal titles, and the initial word of each sentence. I have omitted any mention of price that is not part of the title itself. I have not indicated the presence of italics of boldface, nor described the setting of the title on the page. I have also excluded all mottoes, captions, rules, and decorative devices. Description of such features, while of undoubted bibliographic value, would fail to convey effectively the true appearance of the title page, and would distract and confuse the reader trying to understand the content of the title.

In transcriptions of titles a special symbol (=) is used where a hyphen in the original coincides with a line break in this book. All other end-of-line hyphens have been introduced in the typesetting process.

A five-em dash (—————) in place of a title indicates that its wording and punctuation are unchanged from the previous entry. This does not imply that the typeface or setting is unchanged.

Angle brackets (⟨ ⟩) are used to indicate portions of the title that are unchanged from a previous entry. The previous entry to which the reader should refer is always given within the angle brackets. For example, "solids and superfices; ⟨ . . . as 1773 . . . ⟩ copper-plates" indicates that wording and punctuation between the words "solids and superfices;" and "copper-plates" are unchanged from the 1773 edition. This does not mean that typeface or setting is unchanged.

Imprint	The place and date of publication, plus names of printers, publishers, and booksellers, are given as they appear on the title page, adjusted to the following format. The principal place of publication, as shown on the title page, is given first, followed by a colon. Next appear the names of printers, publishers, and booksellers, in the order in which they appear on the title page. I have retained descriptive phrases such as "Printed by" and "Sold by," which identify individuals' roles in the production and sale of a book. For reasons of economy I have deleted biographical information attached to individual names, except for professional titles such as "Bookseller" or "Printer." I have retained names of towns and cities,[2] but deleted all other address information. Within the limitations imposed by this format, I have retained the original punctuation.[3] The date of publication appears last, given in Arabic numerals.

If the place or date of publication is not given on the title page, but can be determined easily from internal or external evidence, it is given within brackets ([ ]). Where no place of publication can be determined, [N. loc.] is given. If no printer, publisher, or seller is mentioned on the title page, [N. pub.] is given. Where no date can be determined, [n.d.] is given.

Pagination and Plates	For each book or volume the letterpress is described first, followed by an indication of frontispieces, portraits, and plates. This method provides an organized account of the contents of the book, but does not always reflect the actual sequence of elements.

In accounting for numbered pages, I have adopted a shorthand convention for numbers that are repeated: for example the pagination "1–55 + 40–122 pp" indicates that page numbers 40–55 are repeated. I have not made special note of any unnumbered pages that are clearly part of a larger numbered sequence. For example "66 pp" could describe a book with a preface on pages 1–4, an introduction on four unnumbered pages, and a text on pages 9–66. Where letterpress appears on unnumbered leaves that are not part of a larger numbered sequence, I have indicated the number of pages in brackets or else specified the number of printed leaves (e.g., "[xxxviii pp]," "[38 pp]," "19 printed leaves"). For brevity I have ignored advertising matter, flyleaves, and blank leaves that are not part of a larger numbered sequence. Likewise I have not accounted individually for half titles at the beginning of a volume, title pages, or lists of errata.[4]

I have accounted for duplicated plate numbers in the same manner as for page numbers: "1–25 + 25–30 pls" indicates that plate number 25 is repeated. For each entry I have tried to determine from plate descriptions and binder's lists the number of plates that should be present. Where there are deficiencies in the copy I examined, I have added brief explanatory remarks—italicized and in brackets—as in the following examples: "52 pls [*2 pls are wanting in this copy*]" means that this copy has 50 plates but should have 52; "25 pls [*Pl. XIII wanting in this copy*]" means that this copy should have 25 plates but has only 24. Some volumes contain duplicate or extra plates; in such cases, and in order to describe aspects of other volumes in more detail, I have added parenthetic comments in roman type. For example, "14 plates (including one duplicate)" describes a copy with a normal complement of 13 plates, plus one duplicate.

Size	Dimensions are given in centimeters, height before width. For a few copies that I was unable to examine personally, only height is given: it is expressed either in centimeters or as sextodecimo (16°), duodecimo (12°), octavo (8°), quarto (4°), or folio (f°).
Location of the Copy Cited	Different copies of a single edition frequently vary in completeness, size, and order of text and plates. The information given in each entry below pertains only to one copy.[5] In each case I have included information concerning its location. For copies that I examined in British libraries, I have adopted abbreviations explained in the List of Symbols and Abbreviations below. For copies in American libraries, I have given the abbreviations used in the *National Union Catalogue*; these are explained at the end of the List of Symbols and Abbreviations.

In some cases I was not able to examine copies personally. Many are cited in standard references: for these I have attached a dagger (†) to the entry number. I have indicated the source of my information by an abbreviation explained in the List of Symbols and Abbreviations. In other cases I was able to examine facsimile reprints or microfilm copies made by libraries possessing the originals: these I have indicated by a double dagger (‡) attached to the entry number, plus a full description of the source of my information. Finally, some copies were examined on my behalf by librarians and other colleagues: for these I have attached a double vertical stroke (‖) to the entry number, and have given the name of the library owning the copy.

"Ghost"
Editions

To make my account of the publication history of each title as complete as possible, I have searched for references to otherwise unknown editions in standard catalogues, bibliographies, and biographical dictionaries.[6] Before including such references among the entries below, I attempted to eliminate editions that in fact never existed—"ghost" editions that for various reasons have made their way into the standard literature on the subject. Unfortunately I discovered too many such editions to list here. Nevertheless some general observations are possible. For each title that I have included in this study, I have traced all the appropriate entries in the *National Union Catalogue* (NUC). Several editions cited there were entered erroneously or inaccurately reported by contributing libraries,[7] and so have been excluded from the entries below. References in NUC to editions that do not appear below may be assumed to be erroneous. Some citations in the *English Catalogue of Books* (ECB) indicate the appearance of a title in October, November, or December of a year preceding the date of an edition that I have confirmed. I have presumed that these citations refer to advance copies or announcements of the confirmed edition, and so I have excluded such citations from the entries below. Likewise I have excluded ECB references to the appearance of a book in January, February, or March of a year following the date of a confirmed edition. The only other ECB citations that I have excluded are those referring to price changes. I have had to take more care in using the *Dictionary* of the Architectural Publication Society (APSD). Titles often are cited imprecisely, and the dates given for some editions are dubious;[8] in a few cases I have included a doubtful APSD citation, but only with cautionary remarks in the accompanying commentary.[9]

2
**Bibliographic
Description:
Encyclopedias**

The format for description of encyclopedias is based on that used for books. Instead of describing pagination and plates for each volume, however, I have described each individual article ("*Art.*") that contains a design for a dwelling. In some multivolume sets the wording of the title or the imprint varies from title page to title page; in these cases I have transcribed one title and imprint in full and, for reasons of economy, simply indicated that others vary. In multivolume sets where title pages are identical except for the volume number, I have transcribed only one title page, replacing the volume number with an ellipsis (. . .). In transcribing imprints, I have used angle brackets (⟨ ⟩) to indicate portions that are unchanged from a previous entry.

Sets of multivolume encyclopedias frequently are incomplete or made up of volumes from more than one edition. In some entries I have combined individual volumes from more than one location to construct a more complete and uniform, albeit artificial, "set."[10] The organizational advantages of such an arrangement need to be weighed against the admitted danger of suggesting a false publication history.

3
Bibliographic
Description:
Periodicals

Depending on the proportion and importance of architectural articles within the run of a periodical, it may be entered below according to its title, its editor or "conductor," or the names of the authors of articles that contain designs for dwellings. In all cases cross references indicate the location of the principal entry.

The format for description of periodicals is based on that used for books. For reasons of economy, there is usually no indication of size. In the case of two periodicals, *The Architectural Magazine* and *Hassell's Drawing Magazine*, the number of volumes is sufficiently small to allow a full account of pagination and plates. For periodicals that extend to many volumes (e.g., *The Gardener's Magazine*) the title, place of publication, publisher, and date are given in full for each volume, but there is no account of pagination or plates. A five-em dash (———) in place of part or all of the imprint indicates that the place of publication, and/or the names of printers, publishers, and booksellers, are unchanged from the previous volume. For periodicals that contain proportionately few articles on architecture (e.g., *Letters . . . of the Bath and West of England Society*) only individual articles concerning domestic architecture are cited; full particulars of the entire volume are not provided.

4
Description
and Analysis
of Text and
Plates

Following the bibliographic description of each book or periodical, there is a commentary with further description and analysis.

Remarks concerning publication history or bibliographic composition are described in the first paragraph(s), and are set off from the rest of the commentary by additional space.

I have provided few biographical remarks concerning authors, since most are discussed at length in Howard Colvin's *Biographical Dictionary of British Architects, 1600–1840* (London: John Murray, 1978).

Each commentary incorporates an explication of the text and description of the plates. In many cases, depending on the originality and importance of the author's remarks, I have provided a critical analysis of his ideas and approach, and tried to set them in historical perspective. Because a full analysis of some texts would be excessively long, I have focused my attention on matters pertaining to domestic architecture. Nevertheless I have briefly indicated the entire range of issues each author discussed. I have kept my analysis close to the texts themselves, preferring to examine an author's ideas in relation to his own designs and to the ideas of other authors, rather than treat each architect's entire oeuvre in monographic detail or analyze his writings in relation to contemporary practice.[11] In discussing the illustrations I have provided a brief account of the entire range of designs in each treatise, and then characterized more fully the designs for dwellings. In many cases I have discussed the largest and smallest dwellings in detail, describing one or more facades, the plan, and the cost when known.

In the commentary for each encyclopedia or dictionary, I have included a précis of the article titled "Architecture" (regardless of whether it has a design for a dwelling), plus a précis of each article that does include a view or plan and elevation of a dwelling.

At the end of a few commentaries I have appended discussions of important collateral material. These remarks are separated from the principal portion of the commentary by a bullet (●).

Notes

1. A five-em dash is not used when the author's name is absent from the title page of one edition, and then appears on the title page of the next. In such cases the author's name appears in brackets in the entry describing the anonymous edition; it appears without brackets for the next edition. Likewise a five-em dash is not used when a periodical edited by a single individual precedes or follows a book written by that individual. For entries describing periodicals, the editor's name is followed by "ed."; for a book by the same person, the author's name is given alone.

2. These include additional places of publication and trade locations of printers and sellers. N.B. for the sake of brevity and wherever possible I have omitted duplicate citations of the principal place of publication. I have not done so when the result would incorrectly associate a name and a location.

3. There is one exception: I have always used a comma to precede the date of publication.

4. All volumes but two have title pages (see note 2 to the Introduction). Most half titles and titles are included in a larger sequence of numbered pages, and therefore no special remarks would be appropriate. Nevertheless sometimes the title page is not part of a sequence of numbered pages. In such cases I have begun my count of pages or leaves *after* the title page; the existence of a title page can be inferred from its transcription as part of the entry. In a few cases the ordering of half title(s) and title page(s) is discussed in individual commentaries.

5. For some multivolume editions I have had to "combine" incomplete sets in two or more libraries to make one entry.

6. The standard sources I consulted are cited in the List of Symbols and Abbreviations below.

7. As confirmed by correspondence with those libraries.

8. For example, for Joseph Michael Gandy's *Designs for Cottages* (1805; Entry 84) the APSD gives "(1803)?" This and similar references are too ambiguous to include among the entries below. For Joseph Gwilt's *Rudiments of Architecture* (1826, 1834, 1835, 1839; Entry 125) the APSD gives "1826, 1835, 1839." I have found no evidence elsewhere of an 1835 edition, and the omission of any reference to the 1834 edition suggests that "1835" may be a typographical error. Nevertheless since this cannot be confirmed, I have included the APSD citation among my principal entries.

9. See for example the commentary on Batty Langley, *A Sure Guide to Builders* (Entry 174).

10. See especially Entry 37, Chambers's *Cyclopaedia*.

11. For such analysis see particularly the forthcoming book by Eileen Harris and Tim Connor, *A Bibliographical Dictionary of British Architectural Books to 1780*.

List of Symbols and Abbreviations

†	Information taken from a standard reference, identified at the end of the bibliographic description.
‡	Information taken from a facsimile reprint or from a microfilm supplied by the institution owning this copy.
‖	Information provided by a librarian or other colleague.
=	In transcriptions of titles this symbol is used where a hyphen in the original coincides with a line break in this book. All other end-of-line hyphens have been introduced in the typesetting process.
⟨ ... ⟩	Words omitted are unchanged from the edition specified.
APSD	Architectural Publication Society. *The Dictionary of Architecture*. London: The Society, [1848]–1892.
Avery (1968)	*Catalog of the Avery Memorial Architectural Library of Columbia University*. 2nd ed. Boston: G. K. Hall, 1968.
BL	The British Library, London. Use of this abbreviation signifies that I personally examined the book at this library.
BLC	*The British Library General Catalogue of Printed Books to 1975*. London: K. G. Saur, 1979–
BM	*British Museum General Catalogue of Printed Books . . . to 1955*. London: The Trustees of the British Museum, 1961–1966.
Bodl.	The Bodleian Library, Oxford. Use of this abbreviation signifies that I personally examined the book at this library.
Colvin (1978)	Colvin, Howard. *A Biographical Dictionary of British Architects, 1600–1840*. London: John Murray, 1978.
DNB	Stephen, Sir Leslie, and Sir Sidney Lee, eds. *The Dictionary of National Biography*. Reprint, Oxford: The University Press, 1967–1968.
ECB	Low, Sampson, comp. *The English Catalogue of Books Published from January, 1835, to January, 1863*. London: Sampson Low, Son, and Marston, 1864.

and:
Peddie, Robert Alexander, and Quintin Waddington, eds. *The English Catalogue of Books ... Issued in the United Kingdom of Great Britain and Ireland 1801–1836.* Reprint, New York: Kraus Reprint, 1963.

ECBB   Robinson, F. J. G., G. Averley, D. R. Esslemont, and P. J. Wallis. *Eighteenth-Century British Books: An Author Union Catalogue.* Folkestone: Dawson, 1981.

NUC   *The National Union Catalogue: Pre-1956 Imprints.* London: Mansell, 1968–1980.

NUC-S   *The National Union Catalogue: Pre-1956 Imprints. Supplement.* London: Mansell, 1980–1981.

RIBA   British Architectural Library, The Royal Institute of British Architects, London. Use of this abbreviation signifies that I personally examined the book at this library.

RIBA   The Royal Institute of British Architects. *Catalogue of the Royal Institute*
(1937–1938) *of British Architects Library.* London: The Institute, 1937–1938.

Soane   Library, Sir John Soane's Museum, London. Use of this notation signifies that I personally examined the book at this library.

Summerson   Summerson, John. "The Classical Country House in 18th-Century Eng-
(1959)   land." *Journal of the Royal Society of Arts* CVII:5036 (July 1959), 539–587.

Summerson   Summerson, John. *Architecture in Britain 1530 to 1830.* Baltimore: Penguin,
(1969)   1969.

Univ. Cat. Committee of Council on Education, South Kensington. *The First Proofs of the Universal Catalogue of Books on Art.* London: Chapman and Hall, 1870.

            and:
            Supplement to the Universal Catalogue of Books on Art. London: Printed for Her Majesty's Stationery Office, by George E. Eyre and William Spottis-woode, 1877.

V&A   National Art Library, The Victoria and Albert Museum, London. Use of this abbreviation signifies that I personally examined the book at this library.

WML   Henry Francis duPont Winterthur Museum. Libraries. *The Winterthur Museum Libraries Collection of Printed Books.* Wilmington, Delaware: Scholarly Resources, 1974.

For additional symbols and abbreviations in Appendixes E and F see the introductory remarks to those appendixes.

Abbreviations of American libraries are explained in *Symbols of American Libraries*, 12th ed. (Washington, D.C.: Library of Congress, 1980). For convenience, a list of the abbreviations used in the present book is given below.

AAP	Auburn University, Auburn, Alabama
C	California State Library, Sacramento, California
CLSU	University of Southern California, Los Angeles, California
CoU	University of Colorado, Boulder, Colorado
CSt	Stanford University, Stanford, California
CtY	Yale University, New Haven, Connecticut
CtY-BA	Yale Center for British Art, Yale University, New Haven, Connecticut
CU	University of California, Berkeley, California
DAU	American University, Washington, D.C.
DeU	University of Delaware, Newark, Delaware
DLC	Library of Congress, Washington, D.C.
DNAL	National Agricultural Library, Beltsville, Maryland
DSI	Smithsonian Institution, Washington, D.C.
FTaSU	Florida State University, Tallahassee, Florida
GAT	Georgia Institute of Technology, Atlanta, Georgia
GU	University of Georgia, Athens, Georgia
ICA	Art Institute of Chicago, Chicago, Illinois
ICJ	John Crerar Library, Chicago, Illinois
ICN	Newberry Library, Chicago, Illinois
ICRL	Center for Research Libraries, Chicago, Illinois
ICU	University of Chicago, Chicago, Illinois
IdU	University of Idaho, Moscow, Idaho
IEN	Northwestern University, Evanston, Illinois
InU	Indiana University, Bloomington, Indiana
IU	University of Illinois, Urbana, Illinois

KyU	University of Kentucky, Lexington, Kentucky
MB	Boston Public Library, Boston, Massachusetts
MBAt	Boston Athenaeum, Boston, Massachusetts
MCM	Massachusetts Institute of Technology, Cambridge, Massachusetts
MdBP	George Peabody Branch, Enoch Pratt Free Library, Baltimore, Maryland
MH	Harvard University, Cambridge, Massachusetts
MH-BA	Graduate School of Business Administration, Harvard University, Boston, Massachusetts
MiU	University of Michigan, Ann Arbor, Michigan
MiU-C	William L. Clements Library, University of Michigan, Ann Arbor, Michigan
MnM	Minneapolis Public Library, Minneapolis, Minnesota
MnSS	Saint Paul Seminary, Saint Paul, Minnesota
MnU	University of Minnesota, Minneapolis, Minnesota
MtU	University of Montana, Missoula, Montana
N	New York State Library, Albany, New York
NBuG	Grosvenor Reference Division, Buffalo and Erie County Public Library, Buffalo, New York
NBuU	State University of New York at Buffalo, Buffalo, New York
NcD	Duke University, Durham, North Carolina
NcRS	North Carolina State University, Raleigh, North Carolina
NcU	University of North Carolina, Chapel Hill, North Carolina
NhD	Dartmouth College, Hanover, New Hampshire
NIC	Cornell University, Ithaca, New York
NjP	Princeton University, Princeton, New Jersey
NjR	Rutgers—The State University, New Brunswick, New Jersey
NN	New York Public Library, New York, New York
NNC	Columbia University, New York, New York
NNU	New York University, New York, New York
NWM	United States Military Academy, West Point, New York

OO	Oberlin College, Oberlin, Ohio
OrU	University of Oregon, Eugene, Oregon
PKsL	Longwood Gardens Library, Kennett Square, Pennsylvania
PP	Free Library of Philadelphia, Philadelphia, Pennsylvania
PPCC	Carpenters' Company, Philadelphia, Pennsylvania
PPF	Franklin Institute, Philadelphia, Pennsylvania
PPL	Library Company of Philadelphia, Philadelphia, Pennsylvania
PU	University of Pennsylvania, Philadelphia, Pennsylvania
PU-FA	School of Fine Arts, University of Pennsylvania, Philadelphia, Pennsylvania
RP	Providence Public Library, Providence, Rhode Island
RPJCB	John Carter Brown Library, Providence, Rhode Island
TxHU	University of Houston, Houston, Texas
TxU	University of Texas, Austin, Texas
Vi	Virginia State Library, Richmond, Virginia
ViU	University of Virginia, Charlottesville, Virginia
ViW	College of William and Mary, Willamsburg, Virginia
WU	University of Wisconsin, Madison, Wisconsin

ACKERMANN, Rudolph (1764–1834), pub.
Architectural recreations *and* Recreaciones arquitectonicas.

See Entry 480.

ACKERMANN, Rudolph (1764–1834), pub.
The repository of arts, literature, commerce, manufactures, fashions, and politics.

See PAPWORTH, **John Buonarotti**, "Architectural hints," *Entry 246.1;* PAP-WORTH, "Cottage ornée," *Entry 247;* PAPWORTH, "Hints on ornamental gardening," *Entry 248.1.*

1.1
ADAM, Robert (1728–1792), and James ADAM (1732–1794)
[*Volume I:*]

The works in architecture of Robert and James Adam, Esquires.
Volume I. Containing the five following numbers, viz.
I. The seat of the Duke of Northumberland, at Sion.
II. The villa of Earl Mansfield, at Kenwood.
III. The seat of the Earl of Bute, at Luton Park.
IV. Public buildings.
V. Designs for the King and Queen, and the Princess Dowager of Wales,
&c. [*The imprint is set at this point on the title page. It is transcribed below.*]
Les ouvrages d'architecture de Robert et Jaques Adam, Ecuyers.
Tome I. Contenant les cinq cahiers suivants, sçavoir,
I. Le chateau du Duc de Northumberland, à Sion.
II. La villa du Comte Mansfield, à Kenwood.
III. Le chateau du Comte de Bute, à Luton.
IV. Édifices publics.
V. Desseins pur le Roi et la Reine, et la Princesse Douairiere de Galles,
&c. [*A French translation of the imprint is set here.*]

London: Printed for the authors; and sold by Peter Elmsly, and by the other booksellers in town and country, 1778.

[*The title page is preceded by a frontispiece and followed by five separate numbers, each with individual title page:*]

[*Volume I, Number I:*]

The works in architecture of Robert and James Adam, Esquires.
Number I. Containing part of the designs of Sion House, a magnificent seat of His Grace the Duke of Northumberland, in the county of Middlesex. [*Imprint in English.*]
Ouvrages d'architecture de Robert et Jacques Adam, Ecuyers. Nombre I. Contenant partie des desseins du Chateau de Sion, magnifique maison de campagne du Duc de Northumberland, dans le contè de Middlesex. [*Imprint in French.*]

London: Printed for the authors; and sold by T. Becket, and the other booksellers in town and country, 1773.

3–12 pp, 8 pls.

[*Volume I, Number II:*]

The works in architecture of Robert and James Adam, Esquires.
Number II. Containing part of the designs of Lord Mansfield's villa at Kenwood, in the county of Middlesex. [*Imprint in English.*]
Les ouvrages d'architecture de Robert et Jâques Adam, Ecuyers. Nombre II. Contenant partie des desseins de la villa de Milord Mansfield à Kenwood, dans le comté de Middlesex. [*Imprint in French.*]

London: Printed for the authors; and sold by T. Becket, and by the other booksellers in town and country, 1774.

3–10 pp, 8 pls.

[*Volume I, Number III:*]

The works in architecture of Robert and James Adam, Esquires.
Number III. Containing part of the designs of Luton House in Bedfordshire, one of the seats of the Earl of Bute. [*Imprint in English.*]
Les ouvrages d'architecture de Robert et Jâques Adam, Ecuyers. Nombre III. Contenant partie des desseins du Chateau du Luton, dans le Comte de Bedford, un des maisons de campagne du Comte de Bute. [*Imprint in French.*]

London: Printed for the authors; and sold by T. Becket, and by the other booksellers in town and country, 1775.

[2] pp, 8 pls.

[*Volume I, Number IV:*]

The works in architecture of Robert and James Adam, Esquires.
Number IV. Containing designs of some public buildings. [*Imprint in English.*]
Les ouvrages d'architecture de Robert et Jâques Adam, Ecuyers. Cayer IV. Contenant des desseins de quelques édifices publics. [*Imprint in French.*]

London: Printed for the authors; and sold by T. Becket, and by the other booksellers in town and country, 1776.

[4] pp, 8 pls.

[*Volume I, Number V:*]

The works in architecture of Robert and James Adam, Esquires.
Number V. Containing designs for the King and Queen, and Her Royal Highness the Late Princess Dowager of Wales, &c. [*Imprint in English.*]
Les ouvrages d'architecture de Robert et Jaques Adam, Ecuyers. Cahier V. Contenant des desseins pour le Roy et la Reine, et pour Feue son Altesse Royale la Princesse Douairiere de Galles, &c. [*Imprint in French.*]

London: Printed for the authors; and sold by Peter Elmsly, and by the other booksellers in town and country, 1778.

[3] pp, 8 pls.

[*Volume II:*]

The works in architecture of Robert and James Adam, Esquires.
Volume II. Containing the five following numbers, viz.
I. The house of the Earl of Derby, in Grosvenor-Square.
II. The house of Sir Watkin Williams Wynn, Baronet, in St. James's-Square.
III. The house of the Earl of Shelburne, in Berkeley-Square.
IV. The seat of the Duke of Northumberland, at Sion, continued.
V. Various designs of public and private buildings. [*The imprint is set at this point on the title page. It is transcribed below.*]
Les ouvrages d'architecture de Robert et Jaques Adam, Ecuyers.
Tome II. Contenant les cinq cahiers suivants, sçavoir,
I. La maison du Comte de Derby, dans la Place de Grosvenor.
II. La maison du Chevalier Watkin Williams Wynn, Baronet, dans la Place de St. Jaques.
III. La Maison du Comte de Shelburne, dans la Place de Berkeley.
IV. La suite des desseins du chateau du Duc de Northumberland, à Sion.
V. Diverses inventions d'edifices publics et particuliers. [*A French translation of the imprint is set here.*]

London: Printed for the authors; and sold by Peter Elmsly, and by the other booksellers in town and country, 1779.

[*The title page is followed by five separate numbers, each with individual title page:*]

[*Volume II, Number I:*]

The works in architecture of Robert and James Adam, Esquires.
Number I. Containing part of the designs of the Earl of Derby's house in Grosvenor-Square. [*Imprint in English.*]
Les ouvrages d'architecture de Robert et Jaques Adam, Ecuyers. Cahier I. Contenant partie des desseins de la maison du Comte de Derby dans la Place de Grosvenor. [*Imprint in French.*]

London: Printed for the authors; and sold by Peter Elmsly, and by the other booksellers in town and country, 1779.

[6] pp, 8 pls (dated 1777).

[*Volume II, Number II:*]

The works in architecture of Robert and James Adam, Esquires.
Number II. Containing part of the designs of the house of Sir Watkin Williams Wynn, Baronet, in St. James's-Square. [*Imprint in English.*]

Les ouvrages en architecture de Robert et Jaques Adam, Ecuyers. Cahier II. Contenant partie des desseins de la maison du Chevalier Watkin Williams Wynn, Baronet, dans la Place de St. Jaques. [*Imprint in French.*]

London: Printed for the authors; and sold by Peter Elmsly, and by the other booksellers in town and country, 1779.

[i] p, 8 pls (dated 1777).

[*Volume II, Number III:*]

The works in architecture of Robert and James Adam, Esquires.
Vol. II. Number III. Containing part of the designs of Shelburne House, in Berkeley-Square. [*Imprint in English.*]
Les ouvrages en architecture de Robert et Jaques Adam, Ecuyers. Tom. II. Cahier III. Contenant partie des desseins de l'Hotel de Shelburne, dans la Place de Berkeley. [*Imprint in French.*]

London: Printed for the authors; and sold by Peter Elmsly, and by the other booksellers in town and country, 1779.

[i] p, 8 pls (dated 1778).

[*Volume II, Number IV:*]

The works in architecture of Robert and James Adam, Esquires.
Vol. II. Number IV. Being a continuation of the designs of Sion House, a magnificent seat of the Duke of Northumberland, in the county of Middlesex. [*Imprint in English.*]
Les ouvrages en architecture de Robert et Jaques Adam, Ecuyers. Tom. II. Cahier IV. Contenant une suite des desseins de la maison de Sion, magnifique château du Duc de Northumberland, dans la comté de Middlesex. [*Imprint in French.*]

London: Printed for the authors; and sold by Peter Elmsly, and by the other booksellers in town and country, 1779.

[i] p, 8 pls (dated 1779).

[*Volume II, Number V:*]

The works in architecture of Robert and James Adam, Esquires.
Vol. II. Number V. Containing various designs of public and private buildings. [*Imprint in English.*]
Les ouvrages en architecture de Robert et Jaques Adam, Ecuyers. Tom. II. Cahier V. Contenant diverses inventions d'edifices publics et particuliers. [*Imprint in French.*]

London: Printed for the authors; and sold by Peter Elmsly, and by the other booksellers in town and country, 1779.

[i] p, 8 pls (dated 1776–1779).

64.5 × 49.5 cm

CtY

1.2

[*Volume I:*]

London: Printed for the authors; and sold by Peter Elmsly, and by the other booksellers in town and country, 1778.

[*The title page is preceded by a frontispiece and followed by five separate numbers, identical to those described in the previous entry.*]

[*Volume II:*]

The works in architecture of Robert and James Adam, Esquires. Volume II. Containing ⟨ . . . as 1779 . . . ⟩ cahiers suivant, sçavoir, ⟨ . . . as 1779 . . . ⟩.

London: Printed for the authors; and sold by Peter Elmsly, and by the other booksellers in town and country, 1786.

[*The title page is followed by five separate numbers, identical to those described in the previous entry, except that the date on the title page of each number now reads 1786.*]

63.8 × 47.6 cm

NNC

1.3

The works in architecture of the late Robert and James Adam, Esqs. Complete in three volumes. Containing plans, elevations, sections, and detail, of the principal buildings, public and private, erected in Great Britain in the reign of George the Third. With designs of every kind, both for interior and exterior decoration. One hundred and twenty-five plates. Engraved by Bartalozzi, Piranesi, Zucchi, Pastorini, Cunego, &c. &c.

London: Priestley and Weale, 1822.

[*The title page is preceded by a frontispiece and followed by three volumes bound as one, with individual title pages:*]

[*Volume I: the title and imprint are identical to those of 1778. The volume consists of five separate numbers, whose titles, imprints, and pagination are identical to those of 1778.*]

[*Volume II: the title, although reset, is otherwise identical to that of 1786. Imprints, in English and French, are of 1822. The volume consists of front matter plus five individual numbers, grouped as three:*]

London: Printed for Priestley and Weale, 1822.

[ii] pp; [2] pp, 8 pls (dated 1777); [2] pp, 8 + 8 pls (dated 1777, 1778); [2] pp, 8 + 8 pls (dated 1778, 1776–1779).

[Volume III:]

The works in architecture of Robert and James Adam, Esquires. Volume III. Containing the remainder of the designs, to complete those in the preceding volumes. [*Imprint in English.*]
Les ouvrages d'architecture de MM. Robert et Jacques Adam. Tome III. Contenant les dessins necessaires pour completer les suites commencèes les tomes précédents. [*Imprint in French.*]

London: Printed for Priestley and Weale, 1822.

2 printed leaves, 25 pls.

65.4 × 48.9 cm

MB

1.4

[Volume I:]

The works in architecture of Robert and James Adam, Esquires.
Volume I. Containing the five following numbers, viz.
I. The seat of the Duke of Northumberland, at Sion.
II. The villa of Earl Mansfield, at Kenwood.
III. The seat of the Earl of Bute, at Luton Park.
IV. Public buildings.
V. Designs for the King and Queen, and the Princess Dowager of Wales, &c. [*Two imprints, dated 1778 and 1900, are set at this point on the title page. The latter is transcribed below.*]
Les ouvrages d'architecture de Robert et Jaques Adam, Ecuyers.
Tome I. Contenant les cinq cahiers suivants, sçavoir,
I. Le chateau du Duc de Northumberland, à Sion.
II. La villa du Comte Mansfield, à Kenwood.
III. Le chateau du Comte de Bute, à Luton.
IV. Edifices publics.
V. Desseins pour le Roi et la Reine, et la Princesse Douairiere de Galles, &c. [*Two imprints in French, dated 1778 and 1900, are set here.*]

Dourdan: Reprinted and published by E. Thézard fils, Publisher, 1900.

10 + 8 + [2] + [4] + [3] pp, 8 + 8 + 8 + 8 + 8 pls.

[Volume II:]

The works in architecture of Robert and James Adam, Esquires.
Volume II. Containing the five following numbers, viz.
I. The house of the Earl of Derby, in Grosvenor-Square.
II. The house of Sir Watkin Williams Wynn, Baronet, in St. James's-Square
III. The house of the Earl of Shelburne, in Berkeley-Square.
IV. The seat of the Duke of Northumberland, at Sion, continued.
V. Various designs of public and private buildings. [*1779 and 1901 imprints in English.*]

Les ouvrages d'architecture de Robert et Jaques Adam, Ecuyers.
Tome II. Contenant les cinq cahiers suivants, sçavoir,
I. La maison du Comte de Derby, dans la Place de Grosvenor.
II. La maison du Chevalier Watkin Williams Wynn, Baronet, dans la Place de St. Jaques.
III. La maison du Comte Shelburne, dans la Place de Berkeley.
IV. La suite des desseins du chateau du Duc de Northumberland, à Sion.
V. Diverses inventions d'edifices publics et particuliers. [*1779 and 1901 imprints in French.*]

Dourdan: Reprinted and published by E. Thézard fils, Publisher, 1901.

[4] + [1] + [1] + [1] + [1] pp, 8 + 8 + 8 + 8 + 8 pls.

[*Volume III:*]

The works in architecture of Robert and James Adam, Esquires.
Volume III. Containing the remainder of the designs, to complete those in the preceding volumes. [*1822 and 1902 imprints in English.*]
Les ouvrages d'architecture de MM. Robert et Jacques Adam.
Tome III. Contenant les desseins necessaires pour completer les suites commencees les tomes precedents. [*1822 and 1902 imprints in French.*]

Dourdan: Reprinted and published by E. Thézard fils, Publisher, 1902.

[iv] pp, 25 pls.

55.2 × 44.5 cm

MH

1.5

The works in architecture of Robert & James Adam[.] Volume I [*or II, or III*]

London: John Tiranti & Co., Architectural Publishers, 1931.

[*Three volumes bound in one:*]

[*Volume I:*] viii pp, frontisp. + 40 pls on 20 leaves.

[*Volume II:*] [i] p, 40 pls on 20 leaves.

[*Volume III:*] [i] + [ii] pp, 25 pls on 13 leaves.

36.7 × 24.8 cm

MnU

The Works in Architecture of Robert and James Adam was published in numbers from 1773 through 1779, and then issued as two volumes of five numbers each, the first volume in 1778 and the second in 1779. A new edition of the second volume appeared in 1786. A posthumous third volume, combined with a new edition of the first and second volumes, appeared in 1822. Reprints of the three volumes were published in France in 1900–1902, and in London (reduced and slightly abridged) in 1931.

Each number in the first volume consists of a preface and plate descriptions, printed in parallel columns of English and French, plus eight plates. In the second volume there is a preface to the first number, printed in English and French; each number also includes descriptions of the plates in English and French, and eight plates. The third volume contains an "Advertisement" in English and French, two pages describing all the plates in the entire volume in English and French, and 25 plates.

The description below is based on examination of the 1822 edition.

This collection of designs illustrating a new and fashionable taste in architecture and interior decoration also contains important remarks on architectural theory in the prefatory essays to the first five numbers. Early in the first essay the authors stressed the importance of originality: "The novelty and variety of the following designs, will, we flatter ourselves, not only excuse, but justify our conduct, in communicating them to the world.------We have not trod in the path of others, nor derived aid from their labours" (I:1, p. 3). In particular the architect should pursue "taste" and "genius" rather than adhere to fixed rules or proportions:[1]

the attention paid to those rules and proportions is frequently minute and frivolous. The great masters of antiquity were not so rigidly scrupulous, [and instead] they varied the proportions as the general spirit of their composition required, clearly perceiving, that however necessary these rules may be to form the taste and to correct the licentiousness of the scholar, they often cramp the genius and circumscribe the ideas of the master. (I:1, pp. 6–7)

Indeed there is no "immediate standard in nature" to which the designer can refer for guidance or inspiration. Rather, the architect must rely on "a correct taste, and diligent study of the beauties exhibited by the great masters in their productions" (I:2, p. 3). Foremost among those masters was Sir John Vanbrugh, whose exuberant Baroque designs were little favored by the Adams' Palladian predecessors: "in point of movement, novelty and ingenuity, his works have not been exceeded by any thing in modern times." Nevertheless, "unluckily for the reputation of this excellent artist, his taste kept no pace with his genius, and his works are so crouded with barbarisms and absurdities . . . that none but the discerning can separate their merits from their defects" (I:1, p. 4).

One of the most important characteristics of Vanbrugh's work was "movement," a quality that in the 1770s, a period dominated by Palladian canons of balance and uniformity, the Adam brothers were eager to champion:

Movement is meant to express, the rise and fall, the advance and recess, with other diversity of form, in the different parts of a building, so as to add greatly to the picturesque of the composition. For the rising and falling, advancing and receding, with the convexity and concavity, and other forms of the great parts, have the same effect in architecture, that hill and dale, fore-ground and distance, swelling and sinking have in landscape: That is, they serve to produce an agreeable and diversified contour, that groups and contrasts like a picture, and creates a variety of light and shade, which gives great spirit, beauty and effect to the composition. (I:1, p. 3)

In their support for this new architectural aesthetic, the Adams not only capitalized on increasing interest in "picturesque" composition in painting,[2] but also built on past discussion of the relation between architectural and pictorial composition.[3] In addition they provided inspiration for future architects to design in a more picturesque and less restrained manner.[4]

The preface to the second number treats the diminution and proportion of columns, plus capitals and moldings. The preface to the third number is primarily a description of Luton, but the fourth and fifth numbers return to more general topics: relations between architecture and painting, and the progress of the arts in Great Britain. Indeed the authors suggested that their work contributed to this progress by helping to "diffuse juster ideas and a better taste in architecture." The current superiority of British architecture could be seen in the arrangement of floor plans, in the design of elevations, and in ornament:

The parade, the convenience, and social pleasures of life, being better understood [in Britain], are more strictly attended to in the arrangement and disposition of apartments. Greater variety of form, greater beauty in design, greater gaiety and elegance of ornament, are introduced into interior decoration; while the outside composition is more simple, more grand, more varied in its contour, and imposes on the mind from the superior magnitude and movement of its parts. (I:5, p. [2])

Works in Architecture was primarily a means for the Adam brothers to display examples of their own work, described on the title pages of individual numbers, and illustrated in plans, elevations, sections, and occasional picturesque views. In introducing these designs the Adams characterized their style as one of lightness and delicacy:

The massive entablature, the ponderous compartment ceiling, the tabernacle frame, almost the only species of ornament formerly known, in this country, are now universally exploded, and in their place, we have adopted a beautiful variety of light mouldings, gracefully formed, delicatedly enriched and arranged with propriety and skill. (I:1, pp. 4–5)

They professed respect for the architecture of Classical antiquity, but were eager to transform it to accord with their own ideals: "we flatter ourselves, we have been able to seize, with some degree of success, the beautiful spirit of antiquity, and to transfuse it, with novelty and variety, through all our numerous works" (I:1, p. 6). Their style in fact employed a combination of Classical and Palladian forms, and drew inspiration from Renaissance Italian and eighteenth-century French modes of composition. The plates were executed with careful attention to advance and recession, fine detail, and shading.

The authors noted that a few copies of each number were colored "with the tints, used in the execution" of their designs, so that "posterity might be enabled to judge with more accuracy concerning the taste of the present age, and that foreign connoisseurs might have it in their power to indulge their curiosity with respect to our national style of ornament," and also so that "the public in general might have an opportunity of cultivating the beautiful art of decoration, hitherto so little understood in most of the countries of Europe" (I:1, p. 7).

1. For contemporary treatises on taste and genius see Alexander Gerard, *An Essay on Taste* (London, 1759); William Duff, *An Essay on Original Genius* (London, 1767); and Alexander Gerard, *An Essay on Genius* (London, 1774).

2. On this subject see Christopher Hussey, *The Picturesque* (London: Putnam, 1927).

3. See for example Robert Castell, *Villas of the Ancients* (1728); Robert Morris, *Rural Architecture* (1750); and Isaac Ware, *A Complete Body of Architecture* (1756), *qq.v.*

4. George Richardson, for example, relied heavily on the Adams' discussion of movement in the introduction to *New Designs in Architecture* (1792; *q.v.*).

2.1

ADAM, William (1689–1748)

Vitruvius Scotius; being a collection of plans, elevations, and sections of public buildings, noblemen's and gentlemen's houses in Scotland: principally from the designs of the late William Adam, Esq. Architect.

Edinburgh: Printed for Adam Black, and J. & J. Robertson, Edinburgh; T. Underwood, and J. Taylor, London, [n.d.].

5 pp, 180 pls (numbered 1–160, plus 19 additional; *one plate wanting in this copy*).

50.7 × 34.5 cm

MB

Following the title page a "List of the Plans, &c." (pp. 3–5) indicates the subjects of the 180 plates. The plates are numbered from 1 through 160, with the following numbers duplicated: 5, 13, 19, 20, 21, 30, 51,[1] 72, 73, 74, 83, 94, 107, 108, 121, 123, 135, 136, 139, and 140.

The publication history of *Vitruvius Scotius* is particularly obscure and complex. A note at the end of the "List of Plans" reads: "The following PLANS, drawn by the late William Adam, Esq. *Architect*, were engraved at his Expence by the most eminent Artists of the time, with a View to Publication. A few complete Sets having come into the Publisher's hands, he now respectfully offers them to the Public" (p. 5). Information amassed by James Simpson[2] reveals that William Adam conceived *Vitruvius Scotius* no later than 1726—one year after publication of the third volume of Colen Campbell's *Vitruvius Britannicus* (q.v.), a collection of illustrations of country houses and other subjects which must have been Adam's model for *Vitruvius Scotius*. There is no evidence that Adam intended his book to promote such a program of architectural reform as Campbell proposed in *Vitruvius Britannicus*;[3] rather, *Vitruvius Scotius* is simply a collection of illustrations of country houses and other Scottish buildings, both executed and proposed, the majority designed by Adam himself.

As Simpson has shown, the first plates were engraved about 1730, and sheets were printed about 1746. On William Adam's death in 1748 the materials for the book passed to his son John, who died in 1792. John's son William (1751–1839) finally sold the prints and copper plates to Constable and Company in 1812. Constable transferred the property to another publisher, Adam Black, who added the title page and list of plates, bound the sheets into books, and together with T. Underwood, J. and J. Robertson, and J. Taylor finally published *Vitruvius Scotius*.

The plates include plans, elevations, and sections of 84 subjects, including 70 houses and palaces, one church, four bridges, five hospitals, two temples, one library, and one kennel. Fifty of the 84 designs are by William Adam; James Gibbs, Sir William Bruce, John Adam, and Roger Morris are among the other architects represented. As Simpson has pointed out, the first plates depict designs by Adam's two chief predecessors, Sir William Bruce (Holyrood Palace) and James Smith (Hamilton House). The next two subjects are Adam's own project for Hamilton House, and his principal executed design, Hopetoun House. Among Adam's other principal designs, those for Yester, Newliston, The Drum, Arniston, Mavisbank, and Floors all appear in the first 49 plates. Other important structures include Robert Morris's Inveraray Castle, and Heriot's Hospital.

1. James Simpson, in "Notes to the Plates" preceding his reprint of *Vitruvius Scotius* (New York: AMS Press, 1980), p. 29, says, "Plate 53 appears to be plate 51 renumbered." Both the Boston Public Library copy and Simpson's reprint have just one plate numbered 51, an elevation of Taymouth Castle. Plate 53 depicts Castle Kenmore.

2. See the "Introduction" to the reprint, op. cit.

3. See the commentary below on *Vitruvius Britannicus*.

3.1
AHERON, John (-1761)
A general treatise of architecture. In five books.

Book I. By way of preparative, contains several rules and examples both in vulgar and decimal arithmetic, together with the art of measuring all kinds of surfaces and solids; likewise, practical geometry, and trigonometry, the one for civil, and the other for military architecture; also an explanation of sines, tangents, and secants, with the use and construction thereof.

Book II. Treats of architecture in general, with useful rules, remarks, and observations; also many useful tables, for the better enabling the reader to make an exact estimate of the charges of erecting any edifice great or small, due regard being had to the conveniency and inconveniency of materials in different situations; the whole illustrated with 140 cuts.

Book III. A parallel of architecture, in a collection of ten principal authors, who have written upon the five orders, viz. Palladio, and Scammozzi; Serlio, and Vignola; Barbaro, and Cataneo; Alberti, and Viola; Perrault, and Le Clerc.

Book IV. Several designs for doors, windows, chimney pieces, piers, gates, entrances, temples, and pavilions.

Book V. A great variety of plans and elevations for parsonage and farm= houses, from 100 *l*. to 500 *l*. expence, also manufactories, charter schools, and country churches; likewise a variety of designs for gentlemen's houses, from 500 *l*. to 100,000 *l*. expence with a calculation of the artificers works, and the quantities of timber, stone, brick, laths, and lime, required for erecting each edifice. By John Aheron, Architect.

Dublin: Printed for the author, by John Butler, 1754.

[*Front matter, five books, dictionary, and contents in one volume:*]

[*Preface and subscribers:*] iii–vi pp.
[*Book I:*] 53 pp, 1 pl.
[*Book II:*] 55–110 pp, 40 pls (on 20 leaves).
[*Book III:*] 8 pp, 7 pls (on 5 leaves).
[*Book IV:*] 1 printed leaf, 16 pls (on 8 leaves).
[*Book V:*] 2 printed leaves, 88 pls (on 49 leaves).
[*Dictionary and contents:*] 8 printed leaves.

41.3 × 26.0 cm

CtY-BA

Aheron was only the third eighteenth-century author in the United Kingdom to attempt a "general treatise" of architecture. The first was Henry Aldrich, whose unfinished *Elements of Civil Architecture* (*q.v.*) was not published until 79 years after his death in 1710. The next attempt, Thomas Rowland's *General Treatise* (1732–[1743]; *q.v.*), is likewise incomplete, and consists only of a short text and few plates.

Aheron's treatise, published in 1754 in five books, contains far more material than Rowland's but is hardly comprehensive. The first and second books, paginated continuously, cover arithmetic, geometry, mensuration, trigonometry, materials, the orders, stairs, roofs, doors, windows, pediments, niches, balusters, balustrades, balconies, and perrons. These subjects are illustrated in the 41 plates that accompany Books I and II. In the brief text and seven plates of the third book Aheron compared ten previous authors' delineations of the orders. The 16 plates that constitute the fourth book illustrate doors, windows, chimneypieces, piers, and designs for eight garden pavilions. On the verso of the half title for Book V is a table for measuring artificers' work, for use in connection with many of the designs illustrated in the following plates.[1] Thirteen plates, numbered 9 through 21, are devoted to designs for schools and churches. All the rest contain plans and elevations for houses. The smallest house is two stories high, with a facade containing five windows and a door; each floor has three principal rooms (Plate 1). The facade of the largest is 29 bays wide. The plan includes two rooms measuring 39 feet by 50 feet and a rotunda 87 feet in diameter (Plate 85).

1. In the copy at the Yale Center for British Art there is a similar, handwritten table—with some different calculations—on a separate leaf following the half title.

4.1

AIKIN, Edmund (1780–1820)

Designs for villas and other rural buildings, by Edmund Aikin, Architect. Engraved on thirty-one plates, with plans and explanations; together with an introductory essay, containing remarks on the prevailing defects of modern architecture and on investigation of the style best adapted for the dwellings of the present times.

London: Printed for J. Taylor, 1808.

1 printed leaf, 23 pp, 31 pls.

30.5 × 24.1 cm

Bodl.

4.2

————

Designs for villas and other rural buildings. By Edmund Aikin, Architect. Engraved on thirty-one plates, with plans and explanations; together with a memoir of the author; and an introductory essay, containing remarks on the defects of modern architecture, and an investigation of the style best adapted for the dwellings of present times.

London: Printed for John Weale (successor to the late Josiah Taylor), 1835.

x + 23 pp, 31 pls.

26.4 × 20.0 cm

NNC

4.3 †

Designs for villas, [. . .] rural buildings . . . .

London: Weale, 1852.

4°

Reference: ECB

The discussion below is based on examination of the second edition (1835), which includes a "Memoir" of the author.

The preliminaries consist of a dedication to Thomas Hope (p. iii) and the Memoir (pp. v–x), which includes an account of Aikin's writings and his professional accomplishments as an architect. In the Introduction (pp. 1–15) Aikin proposed to show that in his designs "I have not been guided by caprice or fashion, but have pursued a system, reasoned if not rational, and consistent if not solid" (p. 1). He began with a discussion of the principal characteristics of Greek, Roman, and Gothic architecture (pp. 1–7). He rejected the assumption that the "style of modern Architecture is . . . founded upon what is called the antique"; rather, "the antique style has never been revived or understood, and . . . modern Architecture is by no means the imitator of the former" (pp. 1, 6). Asking what style of architecture would be most appropriate for modern villas, he first rejected Gothic. Its appeal was largely limited to the associational: "the fancy . . . feels a sensible delight in contemplating the memorials of past times and forgotten manners, and, wrapped in agreeable delusion, enjoys a varied and novel existence" (p. 8). Building in the Gothic style must therefore result in a "delusion" or a "deception," which "is absurd, and productive of disappointment. An English villa can be neither a castle, nor an abbey, nor a temple" (p. 8). Aikin was equally unwilling to design villas imitating monuments of Greek architecture, since "these are public buildings, and principally the edifices of religion," and therefore unsuitable as models for dwellings (p. 10). Yet he believed the principles of Greek design were fundamentally sound, and so recommended that the architect "endeavour to think like an Ancient placed in modern times," adopting "a lighter and more compendious mode; . . . modernizing, without violating, antique simplicity" (p. 10). Aikin identified two particular principles, contrast and variety, as "essential to architectural beauty" (p. 10). The elevation of a villa designed according to these principles "should be either broad and low, or high and narrow, or a combination of both." Through variations in window shapes or the addition of a tower, the architect could achieve a wide range of "expression" in the design (pp. 11–12). Counseling restraint in the use of porticoes, columns, and cornices, Aikin stated that "in almost all the Designs" he "omitted everything which may be called ornament, wishing their beauty, if they possess any, to depend upon their general forms and proportions, and thus endeavouring to attain an economical style of beauty" (p. 13). He concluded the Introduction with brief "observations" on the "Mohammedan" style, which he employed in two of his designs (pp. 14–15).

The remainder of the text (pp. 17–23) is devoted to plate descriptions, with occasional remarks on composition, "effect," and "expression."

The 30 plates depict plans and elevations of 16 designs; the elevations are shown with surrounding scenery, and are elegantly executed in aquatint and color tinting. The designs include a dwelling "adapted for the retirement of a small family," a small country house, eight villas, two sporting lodges, a combination dairy and summer house, a summer house, a bath, and alterations to an existing house. Except for the "Mohammedan" villas all the designs are in a plain Neoclassical style, with large portions of exterior wall surfaces left blank, wide overhanging eaves, and Classical columns supporting porch roofs and porticoes. Only two designs are asymmetrical: his alterations to the existing house at Upper Clapton (Plates 27, 28), and a design for a villa (Plates 14, 15) with a "picturesque character which is produced by a departure from the usual rules of uniformity," and "perhaps better suited to a romantic situation" (p. 20). In the latter design a three-story tower overlooks a small bay in the middle distance, while an adjacent one-story horizontal wing with a bow front complements the verticality of the tower.

One of the smallest residences is the villa in Plates 3 and 4. The ground floor contains a dining room, parlor, kitchen, man's room, and scullery; upstairs there are three chambers, two closets, and a maid's room. The facade is a study in "variety and contrasts in the forms and proportions." The ground-floor windows are located in "receding angles" at the far edges of the elevation, thus leaving "a continuity of wall, which is broken by a projecting porch" in the center. Thus the width of the lower facade, defined by the windows at its edges, "contrasts extremely" with the narrowness of the central porch and the windows above (p. 18). The largest design is the "large Villa or Mansion" (Plates 22–24), which includes a gallery (86 feet by 31 feet), drawing room, dining room, parlor, chamber, dressing room, water closet, servants' hall, housekeeper's room, butler's room, plate room, and store room on the ground floor. The elevation, in "the Mohammedan style," is more richly ornamented than Aikin's Neoclassical designs, although still composed according to principles of variety and contrast (p. 22).

5.1
ALDRICH, Henry (1648–1710)
Elementa architecturae civilis ad Vitruvii veterumque disciplinam, et recentiorum praesertim a Palladii exempla probatiora concinnata. Auctore Henrico Aldrich, S.T.P. Aedis Christi olim Decano.

Oxonii: Prostant apud D. Prince et J. Cooke: T. Payne et Fil. P. Elmsly, J. Robson et W. Clarke; R. Faulder, J. et T. Egerton, Londini, 1789.

[*Additional title page:*]

The elements of civil architecture, according to Vitruvius and other ancients, and the most approved practice of modern authors, especially Palladio. By Henry Aldrich, D.D. formerly Dean of Christ Church. Translated by the Rev. Philip Smyth, LL. B. Fellow of New College.

Oxford: Sold by D. Prince and J. Cooke. And by T. Payne and Son, P. Elmsly, J. Robson and W. Clarke, R. Faulder, J. and T. Egerton, London, 1789.

[viii] + 54 pp, 2 leaves, [ii] + lxvi + 66 pp, frontisp. + 55 pls.

22.9 × 15.2 cm

CtY-BA

5.2

———————

The elements ⟨ . . . as 1789 . . . ⟩ Palladio. By Henry Aldrich. . . .
Translated by the Rev. Philip Smyth. . . . Second edition.

Oxford: Printed by W. Baxter, for J. Parker: Messrs. Payne and Foss; and
Messrs. Law and Whittaker, London, 1818.

viii + 151 pp, frontisp. + 55 pls.

21.0 × 13.3 cm

NN

5.3

———————

———————

Third edition.

Oxford: Printed by W. Baxter, for J. Parker: and Geo. B. Whittaker, London,
1824.

viii + 151 pp, frontisp. + 55 pls.

21.2 × 13.7 cm

CtY

Aldrich originally conceived *The Elements of Civil Architecture* as a treatise
of civil and military architecture, containing six books. These would treat,
respectively, the general rules of architecture, public and private edifices,
ornaments, fortifications, naval architecture, and instruments of war.[1] By
the time of his death Aldrich had finished only the first and second books.
Had the work been completed, its comprehensive scope would have made
it one of the most authoritative early works of English architectural theory
and design, partly filling the gap between earlier works by Shute (1563)
and Wotton (1624) and such later comprehensive treatises as Ware's *Complete Body of Architecture* (1756; *q.v.*) and Chambers's *Treatise* (1759; *q.v.*).

In the event, not even the first two books were published in the author's
lifetime.[2] Only in 1789 did the Rev. Philip Smyth publish Aldrich's Latin
text and 55 plates, plus an original introduction in English and a close
English translation of the text. Although literary analysis of "Vitruvius
and other ancients" might have appeared outmoded in a period of increasing archaeological activity,[3] in fact there was strong demand for
Aldrich's work. The list of subscribers in the 1789 edition includes 213
individuals, and further editions appeared in 1818 and 1824.[4]

Smyth's introduction includes remarks on the origin of architecture, the "present Canons of Architecture" that were developed during the period of Augustan Rome (p. iv),[5] a biographical account of Vitruvius, and accounts of the architectural work of Brunelleschi, Alberti, Bramante, Raphael, Peruzzi, Fra Giocondo, Sanmicheli, Michelangelo, Giulio Romano, Serlio, Pirro Ligorio, Vignola, Palladio, and Scamozzi. There is a brief memoir of Aldrich at the end.

The first book consists of eight chapters, treating materials, construction, the orders, the proportions of rooms, apertures, and staircases. The first chapter of Book II concerns the "private house in a city" (p. 43), which must be located near the proprietor's place of work, and proportioned according to his "office and dignity" (p. 45). In an extension of the Vitruvian notion of "decorum," Aldrich discussed appropriate proportions and ornamentation for various possible proprietors:

Men of ordinary fortune want not houses either large or magnificent. Money lenders and inn holders wish to have them convenient, showy, and well secured from thieves. Lawyers build them with more elegance and space to receive their clients. Merchants require rooms to stow their goods in; well defended, and facing the north. Men in office and noblemen demand houses large, lofty, ornamented, and in short princely. (p. 45)

The second chapter concerns individual rooms and spaces: the vestibulum, oecus, cavaedium, atrium, and peristylium. Chapter III treats "private city houses of other nations." The fourth and final chapter concerns "a villa or country house, and . . . a house built in the suburbs of a town or city."

The remarks on villas are particularly significant, for Aldrich rejected the traditional Latin and Italian definitions of the word "villa" as a "farm" or "farm village," and instead treated it simply as a country house: "The term villa, taken in its full sense, means a country house with a farm annexed: but we shall here understand no more by it than a house built for rural retirement; in the size, situation, and structure of which the plan of a farm house is not to be lost sight of."[6] In thus redefining the term sometime about 1710 Aldrich was well in advance of his contemporaries: Robert Castell, for example, still treated villas as complete farming establishments in his important study, *Villas of the Ancients* (1728; *q.v.*). Indeed in England the term "villa" did not generally denote an isolated, "retired" country residence until Charles Middleton used the word in this sense in *Picturesque and Architectural Views* (1793; *q.v.*).

For related remarks on "suburbs" Aldrich relied in large part on Alberti.[7] Yet Aldrich's description of suburban houses as the median between country and city again seems prescient of late eighteenth-century English architecture:[8]

In the construction of [the suburban house] . . . neatness should be attended to, but retirement more; its principal requisites are ease and repose. Its appearance is neater than the country house, and not so splendid as one in the city. It neither boasts of pastures, or sumptuous dining rooms; content with a study, a garden, and extensive walks. It will be conducive to health if it be placed somewhat on an eminence, and to pleasure if it has a view of the city you have left behind you. (pp. 63–64)

The plates illustrate masonry construction, roof construction, the orders, moldings, proportions of rooms, staircases, and dwellings. The illustrations of dwellings (Plates XXXII–LII), many of which are derived from Perrault or Palladio, include plans and interior views of rooms, atria, and peristylia, plus plans and elevations of houses, villas, and palaces in Greece, Rome, Venice, Vicenza, and other locations in Italy. As examples of the "house built in the suburbs" Aldrich chose two designs by Palladio: the Villa Rotonda at Vicenza, and the Villa Valmarana at Lisiera.

1. English translation, 1789, p. 2.

2. Colvin (1978), p. 63, indicates that a few copies of the first 44 pages of the Latin text were printed before 1710, and that one copy is available in the Bodleian Library. This is cited in ECBB as [Oxford?, 1739?]. There is another copy cited in BLC: *Elementorum architecturae, pars prima* ([1750?]; 44 pp, 12 pls).

3. Several important archaeological accounts of Classical sites had appeared well before 1789. These include Robert Adam, *Ruins of the Palace of the Emperor Diocletian at Spalatro* (London, 1764); Thomas Major, *The Ruins of Paestum* (London, 1768); Society of Dilettanti, *Ionian Antiquities* (London, 1769); James Stuart and Nicholas Revett, *The Antiqvities of Athens* (London, 1762 and later); Robert Wood, *The Ruins of Balbec* (London, 1757); and Wood, *The Ruins of Palmyra* (London, 1753).

4. Note too William Newton's contemporary publication of the first English translation of Vitruvius (1771–1791; *q.v.*), and also his *Commentaires sur Vitruve* (1780; *q.v.*).

5. Page references are to the 1789 edition.

6. P. 59. The Latin text reads, in part, "Nobis stricte sumetur pro domo ipsa vitae rusticae destinata" (p. 49).

7. For a contemporary English translation see Leon Battista Alberti, *The Architecture of Leon Battista Alberti, in Ten Books*, trans. James Leoni (London, 1726). For remarks on suburbs see in particular Bk. IX, Ch. 2.

8. On the merging of country and city in the late eighteenth and early nineteenth centuries see John Archer, "*Rus in Urbe*: Classical Ideals of Country and City in British Town Planning," *Studies in Eighteenth Century Culture* XII (1982), 159–186.

All draughtsmen's assistant.

See Entry 485.

6.1

[ALLEN, William (1770–1843)]

Colonies at home: or, the means for rendering the industrious labourer independent of parish relief; and for providing for the poor population of Ireland, by the cultivation of the soil.

Lindfield, Sussex: Printed by C. Greene; and sold by Longman and Co., London; J. and A. Arch; Harvey and Darton; Hatchards; W. Phillips; and C. Bentham, Dublin, [1826].

ii + 27 pp, 2 pls.

20.6 × 13.0 cm

MH

6.2

———

Second edition.

Lindfield, Sussex: ⟨ . . . as [1826] . . . ⟩ , [1827].

ii + 27 pp, 2 pls.

21.5 × 13.3 cm

NN

6.3
ALLEN, William (1770–1843)
Colonies at home; or, means for rendering the industrious labourer independent of parish relief, and for providing for the poor population of Ireland by the cultivation of the soil. By W. Allen, F.R.S. & L.S.

Lindfield, Sussex: Printed for the Society for Improving the Condition of the Lower Order of Tenantry, and of the Labouring Population of Ireland, by Charles Greene, Printer. Sold by Longman and Co., London; John and Arthur Arch; Hatchard and Co.; and Edmund Fry, 1828.

52 pp.

20.7 × 13.3 cm

MH

6.4

———

A new edition with additions.

Lindfield, Sussex: Charles Greene, Printer. Sold ⟨ . . . as 1828 . . . ⟩ , 1832.

52 + 8 pp, 2 pls.

21.6 × 13.3 cm

MH

In the first two editions the author's name and the date of publication are omitted from the title page, but in each case the Introduction is signed and dated on page ii.

In the 1828 edition Allen revised the text and transferred the illustrations from two plates to text pages 37 and 40. The edition of 1832 is like that of 1828, with the addition of an eight-page appendix describing the "progress" of Allen's settlement at Lindfield. Two new plates accompany the appendix, illustrating a double cottage in plan, section, and elevation.

William Allen was keenly interested in educational improvement and philanthropy. In 1814 he purchased an interest in Robert Owen's mills at New Lanark, and in 1823 he began plans for a school and a "colony" of agricultural laborers at Lindfield, in Sussex. By 1824 the community was well established.[1] Encouraged by his success, Allen prepared this

pamphlet describing similar "colonies" that might be established throughout the country. He wanted "To wean the Poor from a dependence upon
the Parish, and what is falsely called Charity," to enable them "to procure
an education for their children, in moral, religious, and industrious habits,"
and thus raise "a moral and independent feeling in the Poor" that would
keep them self-reliant (1826, p. 1). He suggested forming local "Benevolent
Societies" to oversee this process.[2] Each family would be given a small
parcel of land, along with instruction in cultivation. This, he felt, would
provide an incentive to become both productive and self-sufficient.

Allen devoted much of the pamphlet to remarks on planting, manuring,
crop rotation, and 15 recommended crops (16 in 1828 and 1832). He also
included designs for a cottage and a plan for an entire village. The cottage,
illustrated in plan and elevation on the first plate, is a plain, one-story
structure with a living room in the center, two chambers at one end, and
a work room and dairy at the other. The village consists of one long street
with 24 cottages lining each side, and a school in the middle of each
side—one school for boys, the other for girls. The double cottage illustrated
in the 1832 edition had been erected in 1800 by Joseph Marriage, from
whose *Letters on the Distressed State of the Agricultural Labourers* (Chelms-
ford, 1830) Allen reprinted brief excerpts here. Each cottage includes a
kitchen, pantry, and living room on the ground floor, and three bedrooms
above.

1. On Allen see DNB; *Life of William Allen, with Selections from His Correspondence* (London:
Charles Gilpin, 1846); Helena Hall, *William Allen 1770–1843* (Haywards Heath: Charles
Clarke, 1953), especially pp. 113–124; and W. H. G. Armytage, *Heavens Below: Utopian
Experiments in England 1560–1960* (London: Routledge and Kegan Paul, 1961), pp. 86–89.

2. In the later editions he maintained his support for philanthropic goals, but omitted the
call for "Benevolent Societies."

Annals of agriculture, and other useful arts.

See Entry 479.

The architectural magazine.

See LOUDON, **John Claudius**, ed., *Entry 182.*

Architectural recreations.

See Entry 480.

ARCHITECTURAL **Society, London**
Essays of the London Architectural Society.

See WOODS, **Joseph**, *Entry 355.*

7.1 †

The art of drawing in perspective: wherein the doctrine of perspective is clearly and concisely treated of. . . . To which are annexed, the art of painting upon glass, and drawing in crayons. To which is added a method of casting amber in any form whatever.

London: G. Keith; J. Robinson, 1755.

iv + 92 pp, 1 pl.

12°

Reference: BLC

7.2 ‖

The art of drawing, in perspective: wherein the doctrine of perspective is clearly and concisely treated of, upon geometrical principles; and a mechanical method of perspective and designing invented, for the benefit of such as are strangers to mathematics. Illustrated with variety of copper = plate figures. To which are annexed, the art of painting upon glass, and drawing in crayons; with directions for making them after the French and Italian manner: also the art of etching, and that of Japanning upon wood, or any metal, so as to imitate China; with instructions for making black or gilt Japan-ware, both beautiful and light; and for making the hardest and most transparent varnishes; and, to which is added, a method of casting amber in any form whatever. The second edition.

London: Printed for G. Keith; and J. Robinson, 1757.

iv + 92 pp, frontisp.

15.9 × 8.3 cm

Reference: Collection of the Free Library of Philadelphia.

7.3 ‖

The art of drawing, ⟨ . . . as 1757 . . . ⟩ mathematics. To which are annexed, ⟨ . . . as 1757 . . . ⟩ crayons with ⟨ . . . as 1757 . . . ⟩ Japan ware, ⟨ . . . as 1757 . . . ⟩ whatever. A new edition, corrected, and, besides other improvements, illustrated with copper-plates.

Dublin: Printed by J. Potts, 1763.

iv + 92 pp, 1 pl.

[The above work is bound following, but separately paged from:]

The art of drawing, and painting in water-colours. Wherein the principles of drawing are laid down, after a natural and easy manner; and youth directed in every thing that relates to this useful art, according to the practice of the best masters. To which are annexed, familiar directions, whereby a stranger in the art of drawing, may be readily taught to delineate any view or prospect with the utmost exactness; of colouring any print or drawing in the most elegant manner; and of taking off medals, &c. instantly, after a variety of different ways never before made public; intermixed with curious receipts for the use of painters, statuaries, founders, &c. With instructions for preparing, mixing, and managing all sorts of water-colours used in painting; so as to represent nature in the greatest perfection. A new edition, corrected, and, besides other improvements, illustrated with copper-plates.

Dublin: Printed by J. Potts, 1763.

iv + 92 pp, 3 pls.

16.5 × 9.5 cm

Reference: Information supplied by Fine Arts Library, Fogg Art Museum, Harvard University.

7.4
The art of drawing in perspective: ⟨ . . . as 1757 . . . ⟩ mathematics. To which are annexed, ⟨ . . . as 1757 . . . ⟩ crayons, with ⟨ . . . as 1757 . . . ⟩ Japan ware, ⟨ . . . as 1757 . . . ⟩ varnishes. To which is added, a method of casting amber in any form whatever. A new edition, corrected, and, besides other improvements, illustrated with copper-plates.

Dublin: Printed by J. Potts, 1768.

iv + 92 pp, frontisp. + 2 pls (numbered III and IV).

16.2 × 9.7 cm

BL

7.5
The art of drawing, ⟨ . . . as 1757 . . . ⟩ Japan ware, ⟨ . . . as 1757 . . . ⟩ whatever. The third edition.

London: Printed for G. Keith; and J. Robinson, 1769.

iv + 92 pp, frontisp.

17.3 × 10.3 cm

BL

7.6 ‖
The art of drawing in perspective: ⟨ . . . as 1757 . . . ⟩ mathematics. To which are annexed, ⟨ . . . as 1757 . . . ⟩ crayons, with ⟨ . . . as 1757 . . . ⟩ Japanning upon wood, ⟨ . . . as 1757 . . . ⟩ Japan ware both ⟨ . . . as 1757 . . . ⟩ varnishes. To which is added, a method of casting amber in any form whatever. A new edition, corrected, and, besides other improvements, illustrated with copper-plates.

Dublin: Printed by J. Potts, 1777.

93–188 pp, frontisp.

[The above work is bound following, and paged continuously with:]

The art of drawing and painting in water-colours. ⟨ . . . as 1763 . . . ⟩ manner, and ⟨ . . . as 1763 . . . ⟩ drawing may ⟨ . . . as 1763 . . . ⟩ ways, never before ⟨ . . . as 1763 . . . ⟩ in painting, so ⟨ . . . as 1763 . . . ⟩ copper-plates.

Dublin: Printed by J. Potts, 1778.

2 leaves, 92 pp, 4 pls.

Reference: Information supplied by Winterthur Museum Library.

7.7 †
The art of drawing in perspective. . . .

The fourth edition.

London: G. Keith, 1777.

iv + 92 pp.

12°

Reference: BM

7.8 †
The art of drawing in perspective . . . to which are annexed the art of painting upon glass . . . also the art of etching and that of Japanning. . . . A new edition, corrected. . . .

Dublin: Printed by J. Potts, 1786.

92 pp.

17 cm

Reference: NUC

7.9 †
The art of drawing in perspective. . . . Illustrated with a variety of copper= plate figures. New edition with considerable improvements, designed as a companion to the artist's assistant. . . .

London: R. Sayer, 1786.

31 pp.

Reference: NUC

7.10 ‖

The art of drawing in perspective: 〈 . . . as 1757 . . . 〉 Japan ware, 〈 . . . as 1757 . . . 〉 varnishes. And, 〈 . . . as 1757 . . . 〉 whatever. The fifth edition.

London: Printed for J. Johnson, 1791.

iv + 92 pp, 1 pl.

[*The above work is bound following, but separately paged from:*]

The art of drawing, and painting in water-colours. 〈 . . . as 1763 . . . 〉 down after 〈 . . . as 1763 . . . 〉 drawing may 〈 . . . as 1763 . . . 〉 mixing and managing 〈 . . . as 1763 . . . 〉 perfection. The seventh edition, corrected, and, besides other improvements, illustrated with copper plates.

London: Printed for J. Johnson, [1791?].

96 pp, 1 pl.

Reference: Information supplied by The Library Company of Philadelphia.

7.11 ‖

The art of drawing in perspective: 〈 . . . as 1757 . . . 〉 the arts of painting 〈 . . . as 1757 . . . 〉 directions for making crayons after 〈 . . . as 1757 . . . 〉 Japan ware, 〈 . . . as 1757 . . . 〉 varnishes. And, 〈 . . . as 1757 . . . 〉 whatever. The sixth edition.

London: Printed for J. Johnson, 1797.

iv + 92 pp, 1 pl.

17.5 × 10.0 cm

Reference: Information supplied by Fine Arts Library, Fogg Art Museum, Harvard University.

7.12 ‖

The art of drawing in perspective: wherein the doctrine of perspective is clearly and concisely treated of, upon geometrical principles; and a mechanical method of perspective and designing invented for the benefit of those who are strangers to mathematics. Illustrated with a variety of examples on three copper-plates. The fourth edition, with considerable improvements. Designed as a companion to The artist's assistant—The art of painting in water colours—The art of drawing without a master—The art of painting in miniature—and The art of painting in oil, lately published.

London: Printed for Laurie and Whittle, Map, Chart, and Printsellers, (successors to the late Mr. Robert Sayer), 1798.

32 pp, 3 pls.

Reference: Information supplied by Winterthur Museum Library.

7.13 †

Art of drawing . . . painting . . . glass.

1799.

8°

Reference: ECBB

7.14 †

Art of drawing in perspective.

[London]: Ostell, 1803.

8°

Reference: ECB

7.15 ‖

The art of drawing in perspective: wherein the doctrine of perspective is clearly and concisely treated of upon geometrical principles: and a mechanical method of perspective and designing, invented for the benefit of those who are strangers to mathematics. Illutsrated with a variety of examples on three copper-plates. The eighth edition, with considerable improvements. Designed as a companion to the Artist's assistant—The art of painting in water-colours.—The art of drawing without a master.—The art of painting in miniature.—The art of painting in oil, and the Painter's companion, or treatise on colours, lately published.

London: Printed (by Rider and Weed) for James Whittle and Richard Holmes Laurie, Map, Chart, and Print, Sellers, 1813.

32 pp, 3 pls.

19.5 × 11.5 cm

Reference: Information supplied by Fine Arts Library, Fogg Art Museum, Harvard University.

7.16

The art of drawing in perspective: ⟨ . . . as 1813 . . . ⟩ . The ninth edition, ⟨ . . . as 1813 . . . ⟩ assistant.—The ⟨ . . . as 1813 . . . ⟩ .

London: Printed (by Rider and Weed) ⟨ . . . as 1813 . . . ⟩ , 1817.

32 pp, 3 pls.

19.4 × 12.1 cm

BL

7.17 †

The art of drawing in perspective. . . . The ninth edition, with considerable improvements.

London: J. Whittle & R. H. Laurie, 1818.

32 pp, 3 pls.

8°

Reference: BM

7.18 †

The art of drawing in perspective. . . . Tenth edition, with considerable improvements. . . .

London: R. H. Laurie, 1825.

34 pp, 3 pls.

12°

Reference: BLC

7.19 †

The art of drawing in perspective; wherein the doctrine of perspective is clearly and concisely treated of, upon geometrical principles; illustrated with a variety of examples. Eleventh edition.

London: Printed for R. H. Laurie, 1844.

22 pp, 1 pl.

Nar. 12°

Reference: NUC

Dublin editions of 1763, 1777, and 1791 are bound together with another work, *The Art of Drawing, and Painting in Water-Colours.*

The text remained essentially unchanged from 1755 through 1797, and the 1797 edition will be considered here. The first of two "Parts" concerns perspective. The discussion proceeds from general remarks, definitions, and rules through design, "method," "practice," and a "mechanical Method of Perspective" for those who "are unacquainted with Mathematics" (p. 27). Part II covers the proper materials, colors, and crayons for use in painting on glass, along with remarks on etching, Japanning, varnishing, and casting amber. The editions of 1798 and after are truncated: the first seven chapters (pp. 1–30) repeat Part I of the previous edition; the remainder of the text consists of brief instructions for drawing a street, a double cross, and a "bureau" in perspective (pp. 30–32).

Most editions of *The Art of Drawing, in Perspective* through 1797 have just one plate, usually bound as a frontispiece.[1] Since the plate was redrawn for several editions there are noticeable variations within individual figures. The subjects include geometric diagrams, plus simple objects and a human figure in perspective. The one architectural subject appears in Figure 7, which illustrates the operative principle of a camera obscura.[2] On one side of the figure is a house in late seventeenth-century style, two stories high and three windows wide, flanked by a pair of trees. Opposite is a second house, with one wall cut away so the observer can look into the darkened interior. Light rays from the first house pass through a lens in a wall of the second house onto the opposite interior wall, showing an upside-down image of the first house.

The new edition of 1798 includes three plates. The first reproduces the frontispiece of the earlier editions. The second depicts two scenes in a town, each with buildings facing each other across an open plaza or square, marked off as a geometric grid. In both cases there is a variety of architectural types, including a church, town houses, city walls, and gates.[3] The third plate depicts a bureau, or desk, and a three-dimensional double cross.

1. The exception is the Dublin, 1768 edition. The plates marked "III" and "IV" in the copy at the British Library are identical to Plates III and IV in many editions of the treatise on watercolor painting.

2. The same figure appeared in *A New and Complete Dictionary of Arts and Sciences* (1754–1755; *q.v.*).

3. In describing these scenes the text only mentions "houses." The seventeenth-century style of ornament suggests that the illustrations were borrowed from a Continental perspective treatise.

8.1 ‖

The artists assistant in drawing, perspective, etching, engraving, mezzotinto-scraping, painting on glass, in crayons, and in water-colours. Containing the easiest and most comprehensive rules for the attainment of those truly useful and polite arts. Methodically digested, and adapted to the capacities of young beginners. Illustrated with suitable examples engraved on copper. The second edition, improved.

London: Printed for the author T. Kitchin; Carington Bowles; J. Bowles; J. Smith; and R. Sayer, [n.d.; ca. 1764–1765].

[v] + 48 pp, 4 pls (on 3 leaves).

16.5 × 10.0 cm

Reference: Collection of the Free Library of Philadelphia.

8.2 ‖

The artists assistant in drawing, ⟨ . . . as 2nd edition . . . ⟩ crayons, in water-colours, and on silks and sattins. Containing ⟨ . . . as 2nd edition . . . ⟩ arts, methodically ⟨ . . . as 2nd edition . . . ⟩ copper. The third edition, improved.

London: Printed for Robert Sayer, Map and Print-seller, and John Smith, 1772.

[v] + 48 pp, 2 pls (on 1 leaf).

17.8 × 11.5 cm

Reference: Collection of The Free Library of Philadelphia.

8.3

Bowles's artists assistant in drawing, ⟨ . . . as 2nd edition . . . ⟩ water=
colours, and on silks and sattins. Containing ⟨ . . . as 2nd edition . . . ⟩
arts, methodically ⟨ . . . as 2nd edition . . . ⟩ beginners, illustrated with
suitable examples engraved on four copper-plates.

London: Printed for and sold by the Proprietor, Carington Bowles, [n.d.].

2 printed leaves, 7–55 pp, 4 pls (on 3 leaves).

17.2 × 10.8 cm

BL

8.4

The artists assistant in drawing, perspective, etching, engraving, metzotinto-scraping, painting on glass, in crayons, in water-colours, and on
silks and sattins. Containing ⟨ . . . as 2nd edition . . . ⟩ arts, methodically
⟨ . . . as 2nd edition . . . ⟩ copper. The fourth edition, improved.

London: Printed for R. Sayer and J. Bennet, Map, Chart, Print-sellers, and
Globe-makers, 1786.

[v] + 48 pp, frontisp. + 4 pls (on 3 leaves).

17.6 × 11.3 cm

CtY-BA

8.5 †

Bowles's artists assistant in drawing, perspective, etching. . . . . The seventh
edition. Corrected and greatly improved with additions.

London: Carington Bowles, 1787.

64 pp, 4 pls.

8°

Reference: BM

8.6 ‖

Bowles's artist's assistant in drawing, perspective, etching, engraving,
mezzotinto-scraping, painting on glass, in crayons, and in water-colours,
and on silk or satin. Containing the easiest and most comprehensive rules
for the attainment of those truly useful and polite arts, methodically digested, and adapted to the capacities of young beginners, illustrated with
suitable examples engraved on four copper-plates. By the author of
Bowles's art of painting in water-colours. The seventh edition. Corrected
and greatly improved with additions.

London: Printed for and sold by the proprietor Carington Bowles, [n.d.].

vii + 9–64 pp, 4 pls (on 3 leaves).

17.8 × 11.5 cm

Reference: Collection of The Free Library of Philadelphia.

8.7 ‖

The artists assistant in drawing, ⟨ . . . as 1772 . . . ⟩ copper. The fifth edition, improved.

London: Printed for R. Sayer, Map, Chart, Print Seller, and Globe-maker, 1788.

vii + 48 pp, 4 pls (on 3 leaves).

16.5 × 10.0 cm

Reference: Collection of The Free Library of Philadelphia.

8.8 ‖

The artist's assistant in drawing, ⟨ . . . as 2nd edition . . . ⟩ crayons, in water-colours, and on silks and sattins, containing ⟨ . . . as 2nd edition . . . ⟩ arts, methodically ⟨ . . . as 2nd edition . . . ⟩ copper. The sixth edition, improved.

London: Printed for Laurie and Whittle, Map, Chart, and Printsellers, 1799.

viii + 40 pp, frontisp. + 4 pls.

21 cm

Reference: Information supplied by Winterthur Museum Library.

8.9

The artist's assistant in drawing, perspective, etching, engraving, metzotinto-scraping, painting on glass, in crayons, in water-colours, and on silks and sattins. Containing ⟨ . . . as 2nd edition . . . ⟩ arts, methodically ⟨ . . . as 2nd edition . . . ⟩ copper. The seventh edition improved.

London: Printed for Laurie and Whittle, Map, Chart, and Print-sellers. By J. Wright, 1801.

vii + 40 pp, frontisp. + 4 pls.

19.4 × 12.8 cm

CtY-BA

8.10

The artist's assistant in drawing, ⟨ . . . as 1801 . . . ⟩ copper. The ninth edition, improved.

London: Printed for Laurie and Whittle, Map, Chart, and Print-sellers, 1806.

viii + 36 pp, 4 pls (on 3 leaves).

19.9 × 13.1 cm

CtY-BA

8.11 †

The artists' assistant in drawing perspective. . . . 10th edition.

London: Laurie & Whittle, 1809.

Reference: ECB

8.12 ‖

The artist's assistant in drawing, perspective, etching, engraving, mezzotinto-scraping, painting on glass, in crayons, in water-colours, and on silks and satins. Containing the easiest and most comprehensive rules for the attainment of those truly useful and polite arts, methodically digested and adapted to the capacities of young beginners, illustrated with suitable examples engraved on copper.

Gainsborough: Printed by and for H. Mozley, 1810.

44 + [iii] pp, 3 pls.

16.5 × 9.0 cm

Reference: Collection of The Free Library of Philadelphia.

8.13

The artist's assistant, or, new & improved drawing book; to which are added, the easiest and most comprehensive rules for the attainment of those truly useful and polite arts, etching, engraving, mezzotinto scraping, painting in water-colours, and on silks and sattins; with instructions for mixing the different shades. The whole methodically digested, and adapted to the capacities of young beginners.

London: Printed and published by W. Mason, [1813].

28 pp, frontisp.

19.1 × 11.7 cm

CtY-BA

8.14 †

The artists assistant in drawing, perspective, etching.

Gainsborough: Henry Mozley, 1814.

44 pp.

12°

Reference: BM

8.15 ‖

The artist's assistant in drawing, perspective, etching, engraving, metzotinto scraping, painting on glass, in crayons, in water-colours, and on silks and satins. Containing the easiest and most comprehensive rules for the attainment of those truly useful and polite arts. Methodically digested, and adapted to the capacities of young beginners. Illustrated with suitable examples, engraved on copper. The twelfth edition, improved.

London: Printed for J. Whittle and R. H. Laurie, Map, Chart, and Print, Sellers, 1818.

vi + 7–39 pp, 4 pls (on 3 leaves).

20.3 × 11.5 cm

Reference: Collection of The Free Library of Philadelphia.

8.16
The artist's assistant in drawing, perspective, etching in copper and steel, engraving, ⟨ . . . as 1818 . . . ⟩ copper. The thirteenth edition, improved.

London: Printed for R. H. Laurie, Map, Chart, and Print, Seller, 1825.

vi + 7–48 pp, 3 pls.

17.2 × 10.2 cm

BL

The "Second" edition is the earliest known, and although the title page is undated the date of publication can be fixed circa 1764 or 1765. Among the individuals whose addresses are given in the imprint, Carington Bowles traded no earlier than 1764 in St. Paul's Church Yard, and Thomas Kitchin traded no later than 1765 "at the Star" in Holborn.[1] In some later editions published by Bowles, his name appears at the head of the title, frequently causing the book to be attributed to him. Curiously, Bowles issued a "seventh" edition (1787) in between the "fourth" (1786) and "fifth" (1788) editions issued by Sayer and Bennet. This "seventh" and an undated "seventh" also issued by Bowles differ significantly in pagination from the Sayer and Bennet editions.

All editions ostensibly cover the same subjects, but there are variations in the text and plates. The fifth edition (1788) can be considered representative of most. Chapter I, "Of Drawing" (pp. 1–9), treats copying, enlarging and reducing, "imitation of life," drapery, landscape, light and shade, and historical subjects. Chapter II, "Of Perspective" (pp. 10–20), begins with an explanation of terms and then briefly treats a variety of topics: raising a perpendicular, parallel lines, dividing a line, drawing a circle through three given points, drawing ovals, drawing square "pavements," finding the "proportion" of objects above and below the horizon, drawing direct and oblique views, drawing "a View with accidental Points," and finding "the Center for the Roof of a House." Chapters III through V treat etching, engraving, and mezzotint. Chapters VI through IX describe techniques of painting on glass, in crayon, in watercolor, on silk, and on satin.

Plate I includes examples of facial features and limbs.[2] Plate II includes one entire human figure, three torsos, two busts, and a baby.[3] Plate III, titled "Perspective Plate," contains 16 figures. The first 11 are geometric diagrams and constructions. Figures XII and XIII show rows of columns and human figures in perspective. Figure XIV is an interior view of Sir Christopher Wren's St. Stephen Walbrook. Figure XV shows a two-story house, five windows wide and nearly square in plan, on the bank of a river or canal. Figure XVI is a perspective view of a wide street flanked by rows of three-story houses, with a portion of a two-story church or chapel visible at one side.[4] Plate IV, printed on the verso of Plate III, includes three figures: an outline elevation of the side of a house, a square, and a rectangle. Plate IV is mentioned on page 20, in the context of instructions for finding "the Center for the Roof of a House."

Figures X–XVI from the perspective plate were used in the *Encyclopaedia Britannica* article on perspective (*q.v.*), and Figures I–XVI later appeared on three separate plates in *The Artist's Assistant; or School of Science* (*q.v.*).

1. See Ian Maxted, *The London Book Trades 1775–1800* (Folkestone: Dawson, 1977), pp. 25 and 130.

2. In several editions, including Bowles's "seventh" edition and those published in 1799, 1818, and 1825, this plate also includes examples of hatching.

3. A selection of figures from Plates I and II appears in the frontispiece to the [1813] edition, which includes no other plates.

4. The subjects of Figures XIV–XVI are reversed in several editions, including Bowles's "seventh" and those published in 1799 and 1801. In the Bowles edition the house in Figure XV is three windows wide; in the 1799 edition it is four windows wide.

9.1

The artist's assistant; or school of science; forming a practical introduction to the polite arts: in painting, drawing, designing, perspective, engraving, colouring, &c. With ample directions for Japanning, enamelling, gilding, silvering, lacquering, &c. and a valuable selection of miscellaneous secrets. Illustrated with plates.

Birmingham: Printed for the proprietors, by Swinney & Hawkins; and sold by G. G. & J. Robinson, London; Moore, Dublin; and Creech, Edinburgh, 1801.

xvi + 307 pp, 9 pls.

20.6 × 12.7 cm

MH

9.2 ‖

The artist's assistant, or school ⟨ . . . as 1801 . . . ⟩ plates.

London: Sold by T. Ostell. Printed by M. Swinney, Birmingham, 1803.

xvi + 307 pp, 10 pls.

Reference: Information supplied by Winterthur Museum Library.

9.3 ‖

The artist's assistant; or school of science. Being an introduction to painting in oil, water, and crayons, with biographical accounts of some of the principal artists; the arts of drawing, designing, colouring, and engraving in all its different modes, on copper and wood; of enamelling, gilding on metal, wood, glass, and leather; Japanning, dying, casting, &c. with a great variety of miscellaneous information, relative to arts and manufactories. Illustrated with plates.

London: Printed for Thomas Ostell, by Swinney and Ferrall, Birmingham, and may be had of all other booksellers, 1807.

xvi + 296 pp, 10 pls.

Reference: Information supplied by Winterthur Museum Library.

9.4
The artist's assistant, in the study and practice of mechanical sciences. Calculated for the improvement of genius. Illustrated with copper-plates.

London: Printed for the author: and sold by G. Robinson; and M. Swinney, Birmingham, [n.d.].

v–vi + 7–288 + iv pp, frontisp. + 10 pls.

18.1 × 11.3 cm

CtY-BA

The Preface to the 1801 edition describes this treatise as "a production tending to the increase" of commerce, and to the improvement of Britain's "manufactures" (p. iii). The contents include sections on drawing, perspective, colors, historical "schools" of painting, crayon painting, enamel painting, etching, engraving, mezzotint, aquatint, woodcut, Japanning and staining, casting, bronzing, papier-mâché, gilding, silvering, glass, jewelry, and miscellaneous "secrets."

Bound in the section on drawing are two plates depicting parts of the human face, hands, and feet. Three additional plates following page 10 illustrate the expression of such passions as admiration and contempt, joy and sadness, and love and hatred.[1] The section on perspective (1801, pp. 17–30) consists of brief definitions and several demonstrations and examples. Of the four plates in this section the first three reproduce Figures I–XVI from *The Artists Assistant in Drawing* (q.v.).[2] The subjects include geometric figures, rows of columns and human figures seen in perspective, the interior of St. Stephen Walbrook, a view of a large house—two stories high and six windows wide[3]—on the bank of a river or canal, and a view of a street flanked by three-story row houses. The final plate is a perspective view of a simple gable-roofed house depicted in outline and as a geometric solid.

The undated edition probably was published circa 1806–1813.[4] The contents are similar to previous editions. Three plates between pages 12 and 17 illustrate eyes, noses, lips, hands, feet, and torsos. Three plates between pages 26 and 27 depict the passions. The four plates between pages 42 and 43 contain the same geometric figures and perspective constructions that appeared in previous editions.

1. This description pertains to the 1801 edition. In the 1803 edition the illustrations of human features and the passions are bound together with one additional plate in the section on expression of the passions. In the 1807 edition all these plates, plus the four on perspective, are bound together in the section on "Design."

2. Compared to the illustrations in the "second" edition of *The Artists Assistant in Drawing* (ca. 1764–1765), Figures XIV, XV, and XVI in *The Artist's Assistant; or School of Science* are reversed.

3. In *The Artists Assistant in Drawing* the house was five windows wide.

4. G. Robinson, whose name appears in the imprint, traded alone only in 1772–1785 and 1806–1813. See Ian Maxted, *The London Book Trades 1775–1800* (Folkestone: Dawson, 1977), 191.

The artist's repository and drawing magazine.

See TAYLOR, Charles, *Entries 329.1 and 330.1.*

The artist's repository, or encyclopedia of the fine arts.

See TAYLOR, Charles, *Entries 329.2 and 330.2.*

ATKINSON, James
An account of the state of agriculture & grazing in New South Wales.

See Entry 468.

10.1
ATKINSON, William (1773?–1839)
Views of picturesque cottages with plans selected from a collection of drawings taken in different parts of England, and intended as hints for the improvement of scenery; by William Atkinson Architect.

London: Printed for T. Gardiner, 1805.

viii + 9–29 pp, 20 pls.

29.8 × 23.8 cm

V&A

In an effort to acquire new clients during the lean years of the Napoleonic Wars, Atkinson suggested that landowners could accomplish two worthy goals at once by erecting new cottages on their estates. Doing so, he said, would enhance the picturesque qualities of the landscape while creating better living conditions for resident laborers (pp. v–vi). In addition such improvements would strengthen the proprietor's economic situation. Cleanliness, comfort, and convenience would enhance the "conduct and character" of the laborers, and "tend, in an essential manner, to render them much more useful in their respective stations" (p. v).[1] Atkinson also appealed to the landowner's wartime patriotism, encouraging new cottage building for the economic good of the country: "The building of cottages for the labouring classes of society, and the keeping of them in good repair, are objects of the first national importance; as it is from the active exertions of the industrious labourers, that the other classes derive the greater part of those benefits which they enjoy" (p. v).[2]

Atkinson next turned to the problem of irregularity in cottage design. Unlike his contemporaries Edmund Bartell and Richard Elsam, and like James Malton and Joseph Gandy, Atkinson had no use for strict uniformity and symmetry in cottage design.[3] Rather, "our ideas would be much assisted by observing what has been the effect of chance, as necessity is often superior to design, in producing true characteristic simplicity" (p. vi). In other words simplicity, necessary in such a diminutive structure as a cottage, might be best realized if the cottage were designed explicitly to facilitate specific needs of cottage life. This, presumably, would require an irregular but convenient plan.

Atkinson followed this short Introduction (pp. v–viii) with a short essay on "Cottage Architecture" (pp. 9–24), where he took up the matter of scenic context: "In erecting cottages, the situation and general outline ought to be particularly attended to; in order to produce picturesque effect." This could be achieved by an irregular roof silhouetted against the sky or, "when there is a varied outline, of hills, or trees, to form the background, a straight, or square roof, is not much to be objected to" (p. 9). In either case, picturesque irregularity was a fundamental part of the overall design. Atkinson also recommended close attention to effects of light and shade which he, like the Adam brothers a generation earlier,[4] argued "must be introduced in the building, to produce a picture" (p. 10). But Atkinson had little more to contribute on the subject of aesthetics, and devoted the next 14 pages to materials—stone, brick, mud, pisé, cement, stucco, coloring agents, glass for windows, and brick and iron for stoves.

The plates, described on pages 25–29, include 13 designs for single, double, and attached cottages, both large and small, as well as a farm house, a foot bridge, and details of cottage windows. Some designs are simple half-timbered cottages with thatch roofs, while others make use of Tudor drip moldings, casement windows, crenellations, and bargeboards in a restrained and mature manner to create small but sophisticated designs. Atkinson professed that his designs—unlike those of many other author-designers—were composites of extant examples found in various parts of England (p. vi). But the presence of a Tudor vocabulary does not indicate serious interest in revivalism. Rather, it reflects his study of medieval examples for two characteristics that were applicable to modern needs: irregularity in plan, which presumably facilitated convenience; and irregularity in elevation, which heightened picturesqueness. Atkinson was perhaps the first architect to publish designs based on such observations. The plates also confirm his concern for a marriage of architectural design with scenic context. All designs are shown surrounded by lush, picturesque scenery, which in some cases substantially obscures the design itself (e.g., No. 8).

1. In *An Essay on British Cottage Architecture* (1798; *q.v.*) James Malton had argued that picturesque cottages—the most attractive means of embellishing estate grounds—also were the most effective means of providing comfortable and convenient housing for laborers.

2. For an earlier but less felicitous appeal to landowners to pursue picturesque beauty and rural philanthropy at the same time, see Edmund Bartell, *Hints for Picturesque Improvements* (1804).

3. See Bartell, *Hints for Picturesque Improvements* (1804); Elsam, *An Essay on Rural Architecture* (1803); Malton, *An Essay on British Cottage Architecture* (1798); and Gandy, *Designs for Cottages* (1805).

4. See Robert and James Adam, *The Works in Architecture* (1778–1779).

11.1

BADESLADE, Thomas (ca. 1715–1750), and John ROCQUE (ca. 1704–1762)
Vitruvius Brittanicus, volume the fourth. Being a collection of plans, elevations, and perspective views, of the royal palaces, noblemen, and gentlemens seats, in Great Britain, not exhibited in any collection of this nature hitherto published. Design'd by J. [*sic*] Badeslade and J. Rocque, &c. And engraven by the best hands.

London: Printed for, and sold by John Wilcox, George Foster, and Henry Chappelle, 1739.

3–12 pp, 116 pls (on 54 leaves; plates numbered 1–9, 9–54, 55*, 56*, 55–113).

54.0 × 33.3 cm

Bodl.

Although Badeslade and Rocque adopted Colen Campbell's title and like him produced a volume of views, plans, and elevations of country houses, the purpose of their volume was not to promote any program of architectural reform such as Campbell had proposed.[1] The only letterpress consists of a dedication to the Prince of Wales and brief descriptions of the plates in French and English. The plates are essentially a collection of topographical views. Some were published as early as 1736, and later included in this volume; they emphasize social gatherings in front of the houses rather than the architecture. Other views encompass so much landscape that buildings occupy only a tiny portion of the entire composition. Nevertheless the book serves as an important record of such estate plans as Claremont or Chiswick in the 1730s, at the beginning of the change to a more romantic, natural landscape aesthetic.[2]

The lack of a list of subscribers, and the fact that an important proprietor is named in the legend of each plate, suggest that the book was compiled to encourage patronage or advance the prestige of those whose estates are illustrated. A few of the houses that are illustrated to a large scale, such as Helmingham or Boghengieght, are so retardataire in style and sometimes so ill drawn that they may well have been included primarily as monuments to the proprietors, whose names are displayed in a particularly prominent manner. Other subjects, such as Windsor or Warwick Castle, may have been included more for their royal and historical associations than for any architectural excellence. Finally, the inclusion of Kent's Esher Place (here called "Echa") is of more than incidental interest, for it was an important work of Gothic "restoration" by a prominent Palladian architect, executed during a period when Gothic architecture was nearly in eclipse.[3]

1. See the commentary on Colen Campbell, *Vitruvius Britannicus* (1715).

2. For a brief discussion of the origins of this change, see Nikolaus Pevsner, "The Genesis of the Picturesque," in *Studies in Art, Architecture and Design* (London: Thames and Hudson, 1968), I, 78–101.

3. On Esher see J. W. Lindus Forge, "Kentissime," *Architectural Review*, CVI:633 (September 1949), 187–188. On Gothic architecture in the early eighteenth century see H. M. Colvin, "Gothic Survival and Gothick Revival," *Architectural Review*, CIII:615 (March 1948), 91–98.

12.1
BARBER, William

Farm buildings; or, rural economy. Containing designs for cottages, farm = houses, lodges, farm-yards, &c. &c. With appropriate scenery to each. Dedicated, by permission, to the Farming Society of Ireland. Also a description of the mode of building in pisé, as adopted in several parts of France for many ages; which would be attended with great advantage if practised in this country, particularly in cottages and farm-yards. Designed by William Barber.

London: Printed for the author, by John Tyler, 1802.

1 printed leaf, 13 pp, 6 pls.

30.9 × 24.1 cm

NNC

12.2

Farm buildings; containing designs for cottages, ⟨ . . . as 1802 . . . ⟩.

London: Printed for J. Harding, by B. M'Millan, [1805].

1 printed leaf, 12 pp, 6 pls.

28.9 × 22.9 cm

CtY-BA

The title page and two other leaves of the undated second edition are watermarked 1805.

In the last third of the eighteenth century Nathaniel Kent and John Wood began to address problems of rural poverty and poor agricultural production by publishing designs for healthy, clean, and economical dwellings for laborers.[1] In the 1790s local and national societies concerned with agricultural improvement prepared studies of rural housing and designs for its improvement.[2] William Barber affected a more comprehensive approach to the problem when he published this collection of designs for rural buildings in 1802, for in his appeal to the landowner's sense of philanthropy he invoked ethics and aesthetics as well as economics. In the Preface (pp. 1–2) he suggested that the design of a cottage reflects, and perhaps influences, the moral and intellectual qualities of cottage dwellers:

When we see the rude structure, ill-situated, and worse designed, presenting to the eye a heap of expensive inconveniencies, raised in opposition to reason, taste, rule, or arrangement, we lament the expenditure of time and trouble; and we frequently consider the building as characteristic of dulness and slovenliness in its inhabitant.[3]

Barber recommended showing laborers "the examples of a few compact cottages and farm-houses, arranged with convenience and neatness," and implied they would be eager to emulate these models: "our peasantry are by no means devoid of taste, or a quick intellect." Following this call for a new, "regular system of rural building" (p. 1), there are four pages of plate descriptions (pp. 3–6) in which he stressed "Simplicity, economy, and compactness" in cottage design. The remainder of the text (pp. 6–13) is an essay on working in pisé, a material made of compressed earth and recently described in an article by Henry Holland.[4] Barber hoped his designs would provide tenants with a cheap and efficient manner of building they would be eager to adopt, thus enhancing their own welfare as well as the prosperity of the estate (p. 3). He especially encouraged estate owners to distribute copies of the book among their tenants (p. 3).

Of Barber's six plates, executed in aquatint, the first four include elevations and plans for three plain laborers' cottages, another cottage in Gothic style, a Neoclassical hunting lodge, and a lodge for a small family. The laborer's cottages, all illustrated in Plate I, each include a kitchen and a bedroom, plus a milk room, a closet, or both. Barber estimated the cheapest would cost £34. His professed concern for the plight of peasants is belied by the cost, intended use, and picturesque composition of the designs in Plates II through IV. The cottage in Plate II, he wrote, was intended as "an ornament in a domain, or for a genteel farmer," and would cost £250. The lodge for a small family (Plate IV) includes a hall, a saloon, two parlors, and a study on the ground floor, and would cost £350. Unlike plates in previous treatises devoted to rural improvement, Barber's elevations incorporate picturesque scenery, with spatial advance and recession made more dramatic by the effects of strong light and shadow. These effects are somewhat diminished by the symmetry and regularity of the facades, and by their orientation parallel to the picture plane.

The fifth plate is a plan for an octagonal farm yard. The sixth plate illustrates tools for working in pisé, plus an elevation and plan of a two-room pisé dwelling.

1. See Nathaniel Kent, *Hints to Gentlemen* (1775); and John Wood, *A Series of Plans, for Cottages* (1792; plates executed as early as 1781).

2. See for example the article by Davis published by the Bath and West of England Society (1795); the reports on individual counties commissioned by the Board of Agriculture; and the articles by Beatson, Crocker, Crutchley, Hunt, and Holland published in *Communications to the Board of Agriculture* (1797).

3. P. 1. All page references are to the 1802 edition.

4. See Henry Holland, "Pisé" (1797; *q.v.*), for the first detailed description by a British author of the process of building with this material. N.B. two years earlier John Plaw recommended the use of pisé in very brief remarks in the "Advertisement" to his *Ferme Ornée* (1795; *q.v.*).

13.1 ‡

BARDWELL, Thomas (–1780?)

The practice of painting and perspective made easy: in which is contained, the art of painting in oil, with the method of colouring, under the heads of first painting, or dead-colouring; second painting; third or last painting; painting back-grounds; on copying; drapery-painting; landschape-painting; and a new, short, and familiar account of the art of perspective, illustrated with copper-plates, engraved by Mr. Vivares. By Thomas Bardwell, painter.

London: Printed by S. Richardson; for the author; and sold by him; and by A. Millar; R. and J. Dodsley; and J. and J. Rivington, 1756.

v + 64 pp, 6 pls.

29.0 × 26.5 cm

Reference: Microfilm supplied by Yale University Library.

13.2 ‖
_____

The practice of painting ⟨ . . . as 1756 . . . ⟩ contained the ⟨ . . . as 1756 . . . ⟩ landscape-painting; ⟨ . . . as 1756 . . . ⟩ copper-plates, neatly engraved, ⟨ . . . as 1756 . . . ⟩ Painter. The second edition.

London: Printed for Thomas Miller Bookseller, in Bungay; and sold by B. White, J. Whiston, L. Davis, T. Davies, S. Hooper, T. Cadell. S. Leacroft, C. Parker, Wm. Ottridge, S. Crowder, Robert Sayer, and John Boydell, London, 1773.

v + 64 pp, 6 pls.

27 cm

Reference: Information supplied by Virginia State Library.

13.3
_____

The practice of painting made easy: in which is contained, the art of painting in oil, with the method of colouring, under the heads of first painting, or dead-colouring;—second painting;—third or last painting;—painting back-grounds;—on copying;—drapery, and landscape painting. By T. Bardwell, painter.

London: Printed for, and sold by, the booksellers, 1782.

35 pp.

18.7 × 15.0 cm

V&A

Bardwell's treatise on painting was popular in his lifetime and also was reprinted—perhaps more accurately, pirated—several times after his death. Beginning with the edition of 1795, the section on perspective was omitted, and therefore this and later issues have not been included here.

The organization of the treatise is accurately represented on the title page and is reiterated in the Introduction (1756, p. 3). Bardwell noted that material published here was originally prepared only for his own use (1756, p. 3), and now released "solely for the Benefit of the Art" (1756, p. 4). "Here the Lovers of Painting, who study for their Pleasure and Amusement, may be conducted easily, step by step, to the Secrets of that Art" (1756, p. 4). In assessing the current state of painting in Europe, Bardwell concluded that "Face-painting is no-where so well performed as in England," but remained silent on other aspects of English art (1756, p. 6). He heartily endorsed proposals "to establish an Academy for Painting and Sculpture" in Britain, predicting it would "probably in time improve those Arts to the highest Perfection." It also would "do Honour" to the "Nobility, who will, from frequenting it for their Amusement, learn the Principles of those Arts" (1756, p. 7).

All six plates accompany the section on perspective (1756, pp. 42–64). Each is divided horizontally into two parts. The top portion shows a view of a formal landscape garden, while the bottom is a geometric diagram illustrating the principles on which the scene is composed. The subject of Plate I is the outside wall of a garden and, facing the garden, a two-story house with a small pediment over the door and a larger pediment above the cornice. In the foreground is a line of trees parallel to the front of the house, and there is a steepled church in the distance. The five subsequent plates show scenes with more garden walls, rows of trees, elaborately trimmed hedges, occasional garden buildings, and a glimpse of a larger mansion. Bardwell's architectural and landscape designs were admixtures of late Baroque and early Palladian styles, suitable for the early eighteenth century but definitely retardataire by midcentury.

14.1
BARTELL, Edmund, Jr.

Hints for picturesque improvements in ornamented cottages, and their scenery: including some observations on the labourer and his cottage. In three essays. Illustrated by sketches. By Edmund Bartell, Jun.

London: Printed for J. Taylor, 1804.

xvi + 140 pp, 6 pls.

22.9 × 14.0 cm

MH

Unlike contemporary collections of cottage designs published by Atkinson, Dearn, Gandy, Gyfford, or Lugar,[1] Bartell's book contains a lengthy text and only a small complement of plates. As such it offers a convenient, if not comprehensive, summary of recent ideas on picturesque cottage design. Bartell noted that "Few researches of late years have more occupied the attention of persons of taste, than those which relate to Picturesque Scenery" (p. v). He recognized too the increasing taste for rural or quasi-rural suburban residences: "The love of a country life seems to be innate in the human breast: man seeks the large and populous city from necessity; but when he is fortunately enabled to pursue his own inclinations, he generally dedicates some part of the year to a rural retreat" (p. vi).[2] Disregarding several recent and important studies of picturesque cottages and landscape,[3] Bartell claimed to illuminate a subject as yet only "slightly" explored:

Among the various objects of picturesque beauty, the cottage, whether ornamented or not, has been but slightly noticed; and I do not recollect to have seen any attempt to lay down rules for the management of such buildings upon picturesque principles. . . . [But] as some rule, however imperfect, is more useful than vague and uncertain plans without any fixed principle for their guide, my purpose is, to give a few hints upon the subject. (p. vii)

Despite his professed ignorance of commentary on picturesque cottage design, he quickly introduced such important and topical considerations as external and internal "circumstances," "effect," and "character."[4] For example:

Every building, from the proudest temple to the meanest hovel, possesses a peculiar character; grandeur and magnificence, enriched with every studied ornament, are the pre-eminent features of the former; while humility and simplicity as strongly characterize the latter: to endeavour to preserve this character, is the object of the following Essays. (p. viii)

The first essay concerns only the "ornamented cottage," a dwelling "appropriate to the residence of a gentleman" (p. ix).[5] As "a retreat from the hurry of a town-life," the ornamented cottage should be "rational and elegant" (p. 5). As a "residence of people of fortune," it is "the happy apparent medium between poverty and riches; and, if well executed, throws an air of romance over a rural residence" (p. 5). All these effects depend as much on the surrounding landscape as on the form and ornamentation of the cottage itself:[6]

It is, however, neither a coat of thatch nor Gothic windows that are sufficient to give the true character to a cottage scene; but it is from a combination of pleasing forms and colours, so as to produce an agreeable whole, that we are to expect success: its situation also should be considered; it must, if possible, be so placed, as to make a pleasing object in the landscape, and at the same time to be a comfortable retreat to its inhabitants. (p. 7)

Bartell devoted most of the essay to materials, colors, and styles of cottages. He approved the use of clay, mud, and stone walls, and rejected brick. He debated the merits of thatch, tiles, and slate for roof coverings, and porches made of rustic columns, trellises, and "Chinese work." He also considered painted and stained glass, bow windows, shutters, chimneys, interior decoration, and furniture. He frequently supported his remarks with references to the writings of Kames, Gilpin, and Price.[7]

The second essay concerns grounds and outbuildings connected with an ornamented cottage. He recommended that very few outbuildings accompany any cottage, and that in style all should "correspond as much as may be with the cottage itself" (pp. 68, 67). As for scenery, Bartell counseled restraint: "Where Nature has been lavish of her bounties, be it the artist's business to improve, not to change, the genius of the place; and let his improvements be rather felt than seen" (p. 67). Most of the essay is a discussion of various landscape and garden embellishments: bridges, brooks, willows and alders, pools, seats, inscriptions, huts, sheds, fences, gates and stiles, and cattle.

The third essay calls for improving residences of the laboring poor on gentlemen's estates. Currently cottages were "injurious to the health and morals of the inhabitants," said Bartell, and this reflected badly on the "humanity" of the landowner (p. 89). Bartell devoted several pages to the economics of farm labor,[8] followed by the assurance that new cottages also could improve the picturesque qualities of an estate (pp. 106–107). He argued that cottages had an associational value as well: "Herds, flocks, and human dwellings, fill up vacancies with the most agreeable forms and combinations, and assist in calling forth an association of ideas tending greatly to heighten the beauty of the scene" (pp. 107-108). The rest of the essay, liberally amplified with quotations from Price and Thomson, concerns ventilation, materials, walls, windows, ceilings, plantings, and gardens for laborers' cottages.

The final four pages contain brief descriptions of the plates. These are "six sketches of cottages, such as I think will produce effects pleasing and picturesque" (p. 137). The plates were elegantly executed in aquatint, each showing a thatched "ornamented" cottage, occasionally with rough bark-covered columns supporting a porch or roof overhang. The lattice windows have pointed arches in some cases and round arches in others. Some of the designs are symmetrical, and others exhibit a carefully studied asymmetry. All are surrounded by lush and carefully arranged picturesque scenery.

1. See Atkinson, *Views of Picturesque Cottages* (1805); Dearn, *Sketches . . . for Public & Private Buildings* (1806); Gandy, *Designs for Cottages* (1805) and *The Rural Architect* (1805); Gyfford, *Designs for Elegant Cottages* (1806); and Lugar, *Architectural Sketches* (1805).

2. Later he noted that " 'True and social happiness,' says Zimmerman, 'resides only in the bosom of love, or in the arms of friendship; and can only be really enjoyed by congenial hearts and kindred minds in the domestic bowers of privacy and retirement" (pp. ix–x).

3. See Knight, *The Landscape* (1794); Repton, *Sketches and Hints* (1794); Plaw, *Ferme Ornée* (1795); Smith, *Remarks on Rural Scenery* (1797); Malton, *An Essay on British Cottage Architecture* (1798); Laing, *Hints for Dwellings* (1800); Plaw, *Sketches* (1800); Mitchell, *Plans, and Views* (1801); and Elsam, *An Essay on Rural Architecture* (1803).

4. Humphry Repton treated much the same points in *Sketches and Hints* (1794; *q.v.*). Thomas Whately had also discussed particular "characters" in *Observations on Modern Gardening* (London, 1770). Bartell noted lamely that "Since the final revision of my MSS. Mr. Repton's new work on Landscape Gardening [*Observations* (1803; *q.v.*)] has made its appearance; and it gives me the greatest pleasure to remark, that where his subject in any degree applies to mine, our opinions are nearly the same" (p. xi).

5. A cottage "in its literal sense" is "a house of small dimensions, appropriated to the use of the lower class of people" (p. 4).

6. P. 7. Bartell's argument on p. 6 that the "striking effect" of a cottage can be achieved only when surrounded by appropriate landscape scenery owes much to Repton. See *Sketches and Hints* (1794).

7. Henry Home, Lord Kames, *Elements of Criticism* (Edinburgh, 1762); William Gilpin, *Observations on the Western Parts of England* (London, 1798); Sir Uvedale Price, *An Essay on the Picturesque* (London, 1794–1798).

8. Halfway through he made the hapless statement that "After these remarks were written, Mr. Kent's Agricultural Report of Kent fell into my hands. Never having made rural oeconomics my study, . . . I could not but be highly gratified in finding arguments deduced, with so much good sense, from experience so exactly corresponding with my own" (pp. 98–99). Bartell presumably refers here to the agricultural writer Nathaniel Kent (1737–1810), who wrote *Hints to Gentlemen of Landed Property* (*q.v.*) in 1775, and also prepared a *General View of the Agriculture of the County of Norfolk* (London, 1794 and 1796; Norwich, 1796; and London, 1813) for the Board of Agriculture. But Kent never prepared an agricultural report on the county of Kent. Such a report was indeed prepared for the Board of Agriculture (Brentford, 1794; London, 1796, 1805, and 1813), but the author was John Boys (1794–1824).

15.1 †
BARTLETT, J. E.
An essay on design, as applied generally to edifices both public and private. . . . Intended as a guide to persons engaged in the study of architecture. . . . With plates.

Lymington: The author, 1823.

vi + 128 pp, pls.

8°

Reference: BM

The British Museum *General Catalogue of Printed Books* erroneously includes this book as the work of John Russell Bartlett, an author active in the 1860s who published books relating to Rhode Island history. The British Museum copy of the book was destroyed in World War II, and I have been unable to locate another. Colvin (1978) indicates the book contained designs for castellated mansions (p. 93). See also A. J. Rowan, "The Castle Style in British Domestic Architecture in the Eighteenth and Early Nineteenth Centuries," Ph.D. dissertation, Magdalene College, Cambridge University, 1965, Appendix I.

BATH and West of England Society
Letters and papers on agriculture, planting, &c.

See **DAVIS, Thomas,** *Entry 55.*

16.1
BEATSON, Robert (1742–1818)
"On cottages," *Communications to the Board of Agriculture; on Subjects Relative to the Husbandry, and Internal Improvement of the Country* I:2 (1797), 103–113, and pls. XXXVI–XXXVIII.

MH

The commentary for Entry 16 is combined with that for Entry 17 below.

17.1
BEATSON, Robert (1742–1818)
"On farm buildings in general," *Communications to the Board of Agriculture; on Subjects Relative to the Husbandry, and Internal Improvement of the Country* I:1 (1797), 1–57, and pls. I–XX.

MH

In the 1770s and 1780s individual authors such as Nathaniel Kent and John Wood began to advance the cause of rural improvement through publication of original designs for farm houses and laborers' cottages.[1]

By the 1790s local and national societies concerned with agricultural improvement began to address the problem of rural housing on a more widespread and systematic basis.[2] Foremost among these societies was the Board of Agriculture and Internal Improvement, whose *Communications*, begun in 1797, included several articles on farm house and cottage design.[3]

For the first volume (1797) Robert Beatson prepared two articles, one on farm buildings and one on cottages. He divided the text of the first article into sections treating individual types of farm structures: houses, barns, granaries, stables, "Cow-houses and Feeding-houses," dairies, and "Sheds, Straw and Root-houses, and Hogsties, &c.," plus a final section on the siting and arrangement of farm buildings. He supplemented the text with six plates of houses, seven of barns and mills, one showing a granary, two of stables, three of feeding houses, and one of a dairy and dairy equipment.

In the section on houses (pp. 5–9) Beatson counseled proportion and restraint. The house should have "every conveniency for a family," he said, "but should have a degree of neatness and uniformity," and its size "should be regulated by the size of the farm" (p. 5). In preparing his designs he had "particularly attended to . . . simplicity, uniformity, convenience, and cheapness." Therefore there had been little opportunity for "a display of those architectural ornaments, which, in a higher sphere of buildings, are so pleasing to the eye, and so truly beautiful when disposed by the hand of a skilful architect. Such ornaments are unnecessary in farm buildings" (p. 7). But a farm need not be dismal and dreary, since "neatness and cleanliness" can contribute to a "pleasing" appearance, even suggesting "prosperity and happiness." "A little plot of garden ground or shrubbery" in front "adds greatly to the beauty and neatness" of the farm house, and "large windows add greatly" to its "cheerfulness" (p. 6). Beatson concluded with remarks on the selection of materials and of "tradesmen" to execute the design (pp. 8–9).

The plates show farm houses of the "First," "Second," "Third," and "Fourth" classes, plus two more designs for farm houses with offices. These are accompanied by letterpress explanations on pages 49, 50, and 55 through 57. The "First Class" house is the simplest, and includes a kitchen, parlor, and several smaller offices on the ground floor, plus two bedrooms above. The "Second Class" design "would have a very pretty and uncommon effect, especially if built on an eminence, and having a neat garden in front" (p. 49). The principal facade is composed of a two-story center section with a hipped roof, symmetrically flanked by one-story ells whose roofs, leaning against the central section, echo the lines of the higher roof. The "Third Class" design has a simple rectangular facade, two stories high and three windows wide. The facade of the "Fourth Class" house includes one semicircular window and two square ones on the upper floor, and shallow semicircular relieving arches surrounding the door and two windows on the ground floor. The ground-floor windows are flanked by narrow side lights in a manner reminiscent of Venetian windows. Beatson offered two alternative ground-floor plans, one including a best parlor, common parlor, kitchen, and several smaller offices, and the other substituting a brewhouse for one of the parlors. The farm houses with offices (Plates XIX and XX) are shown in less detail.

The facade of one (Plate XIX) is articulated with narrow pilasters, while the other is a combination of semicircular and round-headed windows with shallow semicircular relieving arches.

The article on cottages has a much shorter text and just three plates, illustrating four designs for cottages. Following general remarks on servants, laborers, relations between landlord and tenant, poor laws, and the benefits of giving cottagers land for a vegetable garden, Beatson turned to specific remarks on cottages. He noted that cottages generally were of one, two, or three rooms; cottages of four rooms "are more in the style of houses of a superior kind" (p. 107). Altogether cottages "could be divided into two classes, the plain, and the ornamental, but it is the former only we mean to treat of here." Ornamental cottages, he said, are chiefly used "as pleasing objects in different points of view, from the parks or pleasure-grounds of noblemen and gentlemen of fortune" (p. 107).[4] Beatson recommended "an apartment 12 feet square" as sufficiently large for a laborer and his family to eat in. A suitably partitioned sleeping room above would then "constitute all the lodging required in a simple cottage" (p. 108). After further remarks on ventilation, insulation, conservation of fuel, stairs, and materials, there are brief explanations of the four cottage designs illustrated. The two designs in Plate XXXVI have just one room on the ground floor and a partitioned bedroom above. Plate XXXVII is an elevation and plan of a double cottage "at Lord Penrhyn's, in Cheshire. This cottage has an exceeding pretty effect from the road, as indeed all his lordship's other cottages have. They are designed by the ingenious Mr. [Benjamin] Wyatt, architect" (p. 113). Each cottage has a small entrance hall and two principal rooms on the ground floor, and although no chamber floor plan is given, there are apparently bedrooms above. All the designs are without ornament, and only Wyatt's design involves a juxtaposition of slightly advancing and receding planes in the facade to create a visual effect.[5]

1. See Nathaniel Kent, *Hints to Gentlemen* (1775); and John Wood, *A Series of Plans, for Cottages* (1792; plates executed as early as 1781).

2. See for example the article by Davis published by the Bath and West of England Society (1795); the reports on individual counties commissioned by the Board of Agriculture (see the entry for "Great Britain. Board of Agriculture. Reports"); and the article by Rennie published by the Highland Society (1803).

3. Also see articles by Crocker, Crutchley, Hunt, and Holland.

4. Beatson remarked: "Of this kind, the completest I have seen are at Lord Penrhyn's, in Cheshire, whose cottages are disposed with great taste" (p. 107).

5. Also on Penrhyn see the following commentaries below: the report to the Board of Agriculture on North Wales (1810; under "Great Britain. Board of Agriculture"); Abraham Rees, *Cyclopaedia* ([1802]–1820); and Lewis William Wyatt, *A Collection of Architectural Designs* (1800–1801).

18.1

BILLINGTON, John

The architectural director: being an approved guide to architects, draughtsmen, students, amateurs, and builders, in the study, employment, and execution of architecture. Containing comprehensive comparative tables of the respective proportions of each member of the orders of antiquity, and those of the modern masters; and detailed tables, presenting the dimensions of every moulding in the orders of Vignola. Together with plates showing the particular form of each distinct part, and the different methods of tracing them; with arcades adapted to the several orders, when employed either with or without pedestals; and also the purest examples of all the other parts which enter into the composition of edifices. The whole reduced to modules and minutes, or parts. To which are added, a history of the art from its origin. A description of, and observations on, the most celebrated antique and modern edifices. A development of the essence of the art, embracing the ideas of order, symmetry, variety, harmony, unity, beauty, invention, &c., and a minute examination of the particular qualities and suitable employment of the constituent parts of edifices. By John Billington, of the Royal Academy of Architecture at Paris. Extensively illustrated by plates and tables.

London: Published by John Richardson, and Josiah Taylor, [1829?].

x + 383 pp, 55 pls, 11 tables.

18.1 × 10.5 cm

Bodl.

18.2

———

The architectural director: ⟨ . . . as 1829 . . . ⟩ invention, &c. and ⟨ . . . as 1829 . . . ⟩ Paris. Illustrated by 55 plates and 14 comprehensive tables.

London: Published by John Richardson, Josiah Taylor, and J. Ainsworth, Manchester, 1833.

xv + 383 pp, 55 pls, 10 tables.

19.7 × 11.7 cm

CtY-BA

18.3

———

The architectural director: being a guide to builders, draughtsmen, students, and workmen, in the study, design, and execution of architecture: containing comprehensive comparative tables of the respective proportions of each member of the orders of antiquity, and those of the modern masters; and detailed tables presenting the dimensions of every moulding in the orders of Vignola, together with plates showing the particular form of each distinct part, and the different methods of tracing them; with arcades adapted to the several orders, when employed either with or without pedestals; and also the purest examples of all the other parts which enter into the composition of edifices; the whole reduced to modules and minutes, or parts; followed by plans, elevations, and sections, of various buildings and edifices: to which are added, a history of the art from its origin: a description of, and observations on, the most celebrated antique and modern edifices: a development of the essence of the art, embracing the ideas of order, symmetry, variety, harmony, unity, beauty, invention, etc.: a minute examination of the particular qualities and suitable employment of the constituent parts of edifices: and a glossary of architecture, including carpentry, joinery, masonry, bricklaying, slating, plumbing, painting, glazing, plastering, etc. By John Billington, Architect. Second edition, greatly enlarged, illustrated by nearly one hundred plates and tables.

London: Printed for John Bennett, 1834.

viii + 344 + 105 + iii pp, frontisp., 77 pls (on 74 leaves), 10 tables.

22.2 × 14.0 cm

MH

18.4

The architectural director: ⟨ . . . as 1834 . . . ⟩ architecture containing ⟨ . . . as 1834 . . . ⟩ without pedestals and ⟨ . . . as 1834 . . . ⟩ sections of ⟨ . . . as 1834 . . . ⟩ development of th [sic] essence ⟨ . . . as 1834 . . . ⟩ tables.

London: Henry G. Bohn, 1848.

viii + iii + 344 + 105 pp, frontisp., 77 pls (on 74 leaves), 10 tables.

21.0 × 13.0 cm

NN

Plates dated 1828 and 1829 provide the principal evidence for dating the first edition. A similar edition was published in 1833, followed by an enlarged "second" edition in 1834. This includes a revised text, a new 105-page glossary, and 22 additional plates. Half of these, numbered 56–66, depict plans and elevations of Renaissance dwellings in Rome. The rest, numbered 67–77, include designs for a theater, a church, and a continuous range of houses and shops, plus illustrations of St. Peter's in Rome and the "Church dell'Annunziata" at Genoa.

The Architectural Director was the first treatise addressed to builders and artisans that, in addition to providing mechanical and technical information, included lengthy discussion of architectural history and principles. Billington wanted to provide "A work on Architecture which would supply the place of a great number of books that treat only on distinct parts of the subject, and also to present a clear and perspicuous detail of the theory and practice of the art" (p. iii).[1] The text is divided into 18 sections, beginning with remarks on the qualifications of an architect, the nature of architecture, its origins, and its history "from the Earliest Period, to the Last Century." There follow sections on "The Antique Orders," "the Five Orders in General," "Rustics," doors, windows, balusters, niches, and entablatures. Two short sections concern "the Form and Proportion of the Interiors of Buildings and Edifices" and "Distribution." Two more technical sections then treat domes and cupolas. The final sections concern decoration and "the Principles and Beauty of Architectural Composition or Design."

The final section on beauty (pp. 280–344), one of the three longest sections in the book,[2] contains few original observations. Nevertheless it brings together several important ideas and attitudes of Billington's time, along with a few idiosyncratic assertions, and so merits brief consideration. Central to his discussion were considerations of use and character:

All edifices and buildings are destined for some use; and it is the apparent adaptation to this use, that constitutes their proper or relative character. . . . There is necessarily then, a rule of taste dictated by nature, which prescribes to each kind of edifice, the character that it ought to present, in correspondence to the use for which it is intended. (pp. 280–281)

Here Billington explored many of the same issues addressed just one year earlier by John Claudius Loudon,[3] but Billington covered them more succinctly and in some cases more thoroughly. Like Loudon, Billington identified use as a building's principal *raison d'être*. The architect could express that use through formulation of a single, coherent "character" that would inform the whole design. Unlike Loudon, Billington likened expression of character to the order of nature which, he said, "has given to all its productions a peculiar physiognomy; which makes them distinguishable from each other, and serves to indicate their several properties" (p. 280). Just as nature distinguishes natural beings from each other by their physiognomies, so do architectural types embody their particular characters.[4]

Billington also noted that architectural character, in addition to facilitating utilitarian ends, also may contribute to the expression of ideas and emotions. The architect, he wrote, should be able to express "intellectual ideas, which are the result of the art metaphysically considered," as well as provide a "true indication of the uses for which edifices are designed" (p. 291). Examples of such expression, and of the affectivity Billington had in mind, include a prison, which "ought to inspire terror," an assembly or concert room, which should inspire "pleasure," and a church, which should express "greatness, power, and majesty" (pp. 297–298).

But the reader expecting to see such affectivity and expression realized in architectural form will be disappointed. Billington gave no specific directions for designing buildings according to these principles.[5] Instead he offered only general rules for applying standard architectural forms to common building types. He proposed, for example, that columns be reserved for public edifices, which then would become relatively more "imposing and significant" (p. 295). Storehouses, warehouses, and custom houses, in contrast, should appear massive and rustic (p. 301); therefore columns and ornament were inappropriate. Since a town hall should represent the wealth and extent of the town, as well as the commerce and opulence of its inhabitants, Billington recommended using the "forms applied to palaces," but made more elaborate, in order to surpass those forms in "greatness, elevation, richness, and decoration" (pp. 301–302).

Billington concluded the section on beauty with a discussion of country residences. "The principal motive in the erection of country seats," he wrote, "is to possess an uninterrupted enjoyment of peaceful pleasure" (p. 331). Following brief remarks on siting and orientation, he discussed five specific types of country residence: villas, seats of nobles, residences of "persons of quality," houses for tradesmen, and cottages. Building on contemporary notions of the villa as a large, substantial residence,[6] Billington argued that villas as a type could be "distinguished from [the rest

of] country residences, by their greater extent, dignity, and magnificence."
But villas also are distinguished by a character of informality: "Although
villas serve as habitations for princes, they do not require either the same
extent, dignity, or sumptuousness as palaces, situated in capitals. In the
villa, a sovereign resigns, as may be said, the public character that he
holds in the midst of his people" (p. 332). The country seats of the nobility
are more formal: "The country is where their interests and influence are
greatest; and therefore their habitations may with propriety be more magnificent than in the capital. Therefore the character of the country seats
of nobles, consists in a mixed though somewhat limited expression of
dignity and magnificence" (p. 332).[7] Country residences of "persons of
quality" are "distinguished by a character of elegance," while houses of
country tradesmen "should be respectable and pleasant; and an expression
of moderation and dignified modesty, [should] be predominant" (p. 332).
Finally, Billington discussed cottages only to deprecate a lack of "unity
of character" in certain examples. In these cases exterior clay walls and
thatch roofs served as a "disguise" for the "interior [which] presents all
the luxuries of life," including "a display of marbles, gilding, paintings,
the most costly furniture, and all the refinements introduced into modern
life" (pp. 332–333).[8] Billington then turned to other aspects of residential
design, including massing, organization of facades, windows, colonnades,
roofs, turrets, decoration, and statues. His final pages describe "pavilions"
that might be distributed throughout an estate for eating, studying, sleeping, hunting, "fowling," bathing, and other purposes.

Plates 1–25 depict the orders and moldings. Plates 26–55 illustrate
pediments, intercolumniations, imposts, archivolts, crowning entablatures,
doors, windows, niches, balusters, rustications, cupolas, and ornaments.
Plates 56–77, described above, include one original design for housing.
As illustrated in Plates 67 through 69, it is a five-story range of houses
and shops, including a shopping arcade. The principal facade is 15 windows
wide and decorated with modest Neoclassical ornament, and the ground
floor consists entirely of shops.

1. This description, and all references, pertain to the 1834 edition.

2. The other two long sections concern architectural history (pp. 49–115) and the orders
(pp. 117–197).

3. See Loudon's *Encyclopaedia of Cottage, Farm, and Villa Architecture* (1833). For earlier
discussion of use and character see Humphry Repton, *Sketches and Hints* (1794) and *Observations* (1803).

4. For similar parallels between physiognomy and architectural character see Peter Legh,
The Music of the Eye (1831).

5. Claude-Nicolas Ledoux, whose notions of character and expression were similar to those
of Billington—and also more sophisticated—presented many examples of characters effectively
realized in architectural form. See Ledoux, *L'Architecture considérée sous le rapport de l'art,
des moeurs, et de la législation* (Paris, 1804).

6. Compare definitions and illustrations of villas given in Robert Gunter Wetten's *Designs
for Villas* (1830) and John Claudius Loudon's *Encyclopaedia* (1833), *qq.v.*

7. The apparent confusion—whether villas or country seats have more dignity and magnificence—is unresolved.

8. Presumably these remarks were an attack on the notion of a "gentleman's cot" or "*cabâne
ornée*," types discussed for example in Robert Lugar's *Architectural Sketches* (1805) and W. F.
Pocock's *Architectural Designs* (1807), *qq.v.*

BIRCHWOLD, Mr.

"Extract of an agricultural and statistick journey."

See Annals of agriculture, *Entry 479.*

BRADLEY, Richard (1688–1732)

A general treatise of agriculture *and* A general treatise of husbandry and gardening.

See Entry 481.

19.1

BRADSHAW, [William?]

Civil architecture by Bradshaw.

[N. loc.: N. pub., 1800?].

34 unnumbered leaves.

71.8 × 51.4 cm

CtY-BA

The book consists of a title page and 34 unnumbered leaves, most of which depict the orders at a very large scale. Five leaves are half titles announcing sections devoted to each of the five orders. Five leaves illustrate the Tuscan order and its parts. One leaf contains a manuscript description of the Doric order. Five leaves illustrate the Doric order and its parts, and another leaf depicts a "Plan & Elevation of a Doric Temple," a circular cella with two distyle porticoes. Illustrations of the Ionic order and its parts appear on eight leaves, the Corinthian order appears on four leaves, and the Composite order appears on three leaves. The two final leaves contain a design for a circular ceiling and illustrations of a "Method of fluting Columns and Pilasters."

20.1

BRANDE, William Thomas (1788–1866), ed.

A dictionary of science, literature, & art: comprising the history, description, and scientific principles of every branch of human knowledge; with the derivation and definition of all the terms in general use. Edited by W. T. Brande. . . . Assisted by Joseph Cauvin. . . . The various departments by eminent literary and scientific gentlemen. Illustrated by numerous engravings on wood.

London: Printed for Longman, Brown, Green, and Longmans, 1842.

viii + 1343 pp.

Art. "Perspective," pp. 914–917.

21.8 × 14.0 cm

BL

20.2

———

———

Second edition, with a supplement.

London: Longman, Brown, Green, and Longmans, 1852.

vii + 1423 pp.

Art. "Perspective," pp. 914–917.

21.7 × 13.8 cm

DLC

20.3

———

———

Third edition, with a supplement.

London: Longman, Brown, Green, and Longmans, 1853.

viii + 1423 pp.

Art. "Perspective," pp. 914–917.

22.0 × 14.0 cm

BL

20.4 ‖

———

A dictionary of science, literature, & art: comprising the definitions and derivations of the scientific terms in general use, together with the history and descriptions of the scientific principles of nearly every branch of human knowledge. Edited by W. T. Brande . . . and the Rev. George W. Cox. . . . In three volumes. Vol. I.

London: Longmans, Green, and Co., 1865.

xi pp, 1 printed leaf, 945 pp.

A dictionary ⟨ . . . as 1865 Vol. I . . . ⟩. In three volumes. Vol. II.

London: Longmans, Green, and Co., 1866.

1 printed leaf, 952 pp.

A dictionary ⟨ . . . as 1865 Vol. 1 . . . ⟩ knowledge. New edition, edited by ⟨ . . . as 1865 Vol. I . . . ⟩. In three volumes. Vol. III.

London: Longmans, Green, and Co., 1867.

2 printed leaves, 1068 pp.

Art. "Perspective," II, 869–873.

23 × 14 cm

Reference: Information supplied by History of Medicine Division, National Library of Medicine.

20.5 ‖

A dictionary of science, literature, & art: comprising the definitions and derivations of the scientific terms in general use, together with the history and descriptions of the scientific principles of nearly every branch of human knowledge. New edition, edited by W. T. Brande . . . and the Rev. George W. Cox. . . . In three volumes. Vol. I [*or* II, *or* III].

[*Volume I:*]

London: Longmans, Green, and Co., 1867.

xi pp, 1 printed leaf, 945 pp.

[*Volume II:*]

London: Longmans, Green, and Co., 1866.

1 printed leaf, 952 pp.

[*Volume III:*]

London: Longmans, Green, and Co., 1867.

2 printed leaves, 1068 pp.

Art. "Perspective," II, 869–873.

22.5 × 12.9 cm

Reference: Information supplied by Rare Book and Special Collections Division, The Library of Congress.

20.6

London: Longmans, Green, and Co., 1867.

[*Volume I:*] xi pp, 1 printed leaf, 945 pp.

[*Volume II:*] 1 printed leaf, 952 pp.

[*Volume III:*] 2 printed leaves, 1068 pp.

Art. "Perspective," II, 869–873.

23.1 × 14.5 cm

ICN

20.7 †

London: Longmans, Green, and Co., 1872.

3 vols.

23 cm

Reference: NUC

20.8

A dictionary of science, literature, & art, [*Vol. III: no comma*] comprising ⟨ . . . as 1866–1867 . . . ⟩ knowledge. Edited by W. T. Brande . . . and the Rev. George W. Cox. . . . New edition, revised. In three volumes. Vol. I [*or* II, *or* III].

London: Longmans, Green, and Co., 1875.

[*Volume I:*] xiii pp, 1 printed leaf, 945 pp.

[*Volume II:*] 952 pp.

[*Volume III:*] 1068 pp.

Art. "Perspective," II, 869–873.

22.5 × 14.3 cm

MnU

Each of the first three editions listed above was published in a single volume. Additional printings in 1845, 1847, 1848, and 1851 are cited by S. Padraig Walsh in *Anglo-American General Encyclopedias: A Historical Bibliography 1703–1967* (New York: Bowker, 1968), p. 40. Beginning with the edition of 1865–1867, the format was expanded to three volumes. In 1866–1867 a "new edition" was issued in three volumes, and reissued in 1867 and 1872. A "new edition, revised" was issued in 1875.

The original purpose of this *Dictionary* was to offer a more "concise" account of "authentic information on the various subjects of science, literature, and art, which a book of reference should furnish . . . to all classes of readers" (Preface). Previous dictionaries and encyclopedias, according to the Preface, were either "too voluminous" or too specialized for "ready reference and general use." The work thus contains thousands of brief definitions and explanations, many of them illustrated, together with major articles of moderate length on such subjects as architecture, chemistry, geology, mineralogy, and music.

The article on "Architecture"[1] was one of the most substantial, having been prepared by Joseph Gwilt (1775–1856), author of numerous architectural treatises.[2] At the very beginning Gwilt defined architecture as "the art of Building, according to certain proportions and rules determined and regulated by nature and taste," but thereafter he devoted little attention to general principles of proportion or taste. Rather, he embarked on a more historical approach, describing the growth of architecture from the primitive "wooden hut" and progressing through the invention of Doric, Ionic, and Corinthian orders. He continued with a brief chronicle of architecture through Roman times, the Middle Ages, the Renaissance, and Baroque England and France. Gwilt then offered a series of subsections treating individual architectural styles: Chinese, Egyptian, Gothic (much expanded in the later editions), Grecian, Indian, Moorish or Saracenic, Mexican, and Roman. A few characteristic illustrations of architectural styles appeared in this article, and others appeared in the following articles: "Arch," "Base," "Cyma," "Curb Roof," "Crossettes," "Corinthian Order," "Composite Order," "Doric Order," "English Architecture," "Fret," "Joists," "Ionic Order," "Inverted Arch," "Guilloche," "Moulding," "Order," "Perspective," "Roof," and "Tuscan Order."[3]

The article on "Perspective"[4] included five illustrations. Three were diagrams of perspective constructions. The other two showed a house first in plan and oblique elevation, and then in an oblique view with surrounding scenery. The house consisted of a central core, square in plan, rising to a third-story lantern; projecting from each side of the square were two-story pedimented facades, each three windows wide and one window deep. Although vaguely reminiscent of projects by Ledoux,[5] the design clearly was chosen for the complexity of forms contained within its biaxial symmetry and thus for its suitability to perspective exercises.

1. Pp. 72–84 in editions through 1853; Vol. I, pp. 147–165, thereafter.

2. Among his approximately 20 publications were treatises on arches, sciography (*q.v.*), and the rudiments of architecture (*q.v.*). He added an introductory essay to the 1825 edition of Chambers's *Treatise* (*q.v.*), published a translation of Vitruvius in 1826, a treatise on criticism in 1837, and *An Encyclopaedia of Architecture* in 1842.

3. This list of articles pertains to the editions of 1842, 1852, and 1853.

4. Pp. 914–917 in editions through 1853; Vol. II, pp. 869–873, thereafter.

5. See, for example, the projects for a *maison de commerce* and a *maison de campagne*, illustrated in Michel Gallet, *Claude-Nicolas Ledoux 1736–1806* (Paris: Picard, 1980), figs. 234 and 411.

21.1
BRETTINGHAM, Matthew (1699–1769)
The plans, elevations and sections, of Holkham in Norfolk, the seat of the late Earl of Leicester. By Matthew Brettingham.

London: Printed by J. Haberkorn, 1761.

2 printed leaves, 27 leaves of plates.

50.8 × 36.8 cm

MH

21.2
_____

The plans, elevations and sections, of Holkham in Norfolk, the seat of the late Earl of Leicester. To which are added, the ceilings and chimney= pieces; and also a descriptive account of the statues, pictures, and drawings; not in the former edition. By Matthew Brettingham, Architect.

London: Printed by T. Spilsbury; and sold by B. White, and S. Leacroft, 1773.

x + 24 pp, 65 leaves of plates.

51.4 × 37.5 cm

MH

In 1735 Isaac Ware published a collection of plates illustrating work executed at Houghton Hall by Colen Campbell, James Gibbs, and Thomas Ripley. This book, titled *The Plans, Elevations, and Sections; Chimney-pieces, and Cielings of Houghton* (*q.v.*), appeared in a new edition in 1760 with

Thomas Ripley cited on the title page as designer of "the whole." The next year Matthew Brettingham, no doubt emulating *The Plans . . . of Houghton*, issued a similar collection of plans, elevations, and sections of house and garden buildings at Holkham, audaciously signing his own name to the plates as architect.[1] Following Brettingham's death *Holkham* appeared in a second edition (1773), with a new text and more than double the number of plates.

In the Preface to the first edition Brettingham noted that the Earl of Leicester (1697–1759), "in whose service and with whom I spent the best and greatest part of my life (thirty years) in the study and execution" of works at Holkham, "before his death, intended publishing the plans and designs of his seat." Some of the plates were finished in the Earl's lifetime, and thereafter "at no small expence and trouble" Brettingham had "continued the engraving of them, that posterity may see the truly fine taste of the noble founder of Holkham." Brettingham also noted the Earl had wanted to publish "the designs of his chimney-pieces, cielings, insides of rooms, statues, bustos, pictures, &c." But while most of these designs had been "prepared for the engravers" for many years, it would have taken too long to engrave them for this occasion, and publication was "deferred till another opportunity." Many of the additional illustrations were published in the second edition.

In the Preface to the second edition (pp. v–x) the architect's son Matthew (1725–1803) carefully acknowledged the sources of architectural motifs in the work of Palladio, Jones, and others, and documented contributions by the Earl of Leicester, the Earl of Burlington, and William Kent toward the conception of the whole; he admitted in effect that the elder Brettingham took too much credit as "Architect." The first 20 pages of text, titled an "Explanation" of Plate I, is a room-by-room tour through the mansion, with detailed description of all the sculptures, paintings, and other furnishings. The final four pages contain a brief description of the house, and a list of the plates, in Italian.

The 27 plates in the first edition are numbered irregularly from 1 to 33,[2] and depict plans, elevations, and interior sections of the house, as well as views and elevations of garden structures, lodges, stables, and a bridge. In the second edition there are 69 plates, numbered from 1 through 69, with two plates numbered 24, three plates numbered 27, two plates numbered 32, and four plates double numbered.[3] The new plates include a plan of the attic floor, another section of the hall, 24 plates of ceilings, two plates of doors, two plates of windows, ten plates of chimneypieces, one plate illustrating the steward's lodge, and a general plan of the stables.

1. The contributions of others were recognized in the second edition. See below.

2. Some are double numbered and others have no number.

3. The numbering scheme is given in the "Spiegazione delle Stampe," pp. 22–23. Several of the plates are not numbered, although they are bound in the correct order. Plates that should bear numbers 59 through 64 are numbered as they were in the first edition: 19, [no number], 29, 31, 33, and 30, respectively.

22.1

BREWSTER, Sir David (1781–1868)

The Edinburgh encyclopaedia; conducted by David Brewster. . . . With the assistance of gentlemen eminent in science and literature. In eighteen volumes. Volume. . . .

Edinburgh: Printed for William Blackwood; and John Waugh, Edinburgh; John Murray; Baldwin & Cradock; J. M. Richardson, London; and the other proprietors, 1830.

[*Eighteen volumes: London, [1808–] 1830. Plus two additional volumes of plates, without title pages.*]

Art. by TELFORD, Thomas (1757–1834), "Civil architecture," VI, 521–663; pls. CXLVIII–CXCII.
Art. by LOUDON, John Claudius (1783–1843), "Landscape gardening," XII, 525–573; pls. CCCXLIII–CCCXLVI.
Art. "Lighthouse," XIII, 1–19; pls. CCCXLVII–CCCXLIX.

26.7 × 19.5 cm

ICU

The title pages of all 18 text volumes of the copy at the University of Chicago are dated 1830.

Originally *The Edinburgh Encyclopaedia* was planned to be 12 volumes; the first issues appeared in 1808 (see Robert Collison, *Encyclopaedias: Their History throughout the Ages* [New York: Hafner, 1966], p. 175). The Library of Congress owns one volume with a title page dated 1813: *The Edinburgh encyclopaedia; or dictionary of arts, sciences, and miscellaneous literature. Conducted by David Brewster, . . . with the assistance of gentlemen eminent in science and literature. Vol. VI.* (Edinburgh: Printed by Andrew Balfour, and sold by John Anderson and Co.; and by Longman, Hurst, Rees, Orme, and Brown, London, 1813). There are no other volumes in the Library of Congress with this imprint, although a copy of Volume VIII, lacking a title page, accompanies the 1813 copy of Volume VI. The 1813 title page likely was meant to be replaced by a new title page, dated 1830, on completion of the set.

Thomas Telford, a prominent bridge and road engineer, prepared the article on "Civil Architecture." Among all encyclopedia articles on architecture, this was the most narrowly historical.[1] Part I, a history of architecture, includes sections on Egyptian, Indian, Persian, Greek, Roman, and Gothic styles. In addition there are remarks on the "Revival" of Roman architecture in the fifteenth century, on architecture in Scotland, and on the design of buildings to facilitate the work of legislative bodies, public exercise and amusement, housing, and commerce. At the beginning of Part II, on "Principles of Architecture," Telford professed strict reliance on Archibald Alison's associationist philosophy: "it is from Mr. Alison's *Essay on the Principles of Taste* [1790] alone, that a satisfactory knowledge of the principles of architecture is to be obtained" (p. 563). Telford summarized Alison's aesthetic (pp. 563–571) and added a few additional observations drawn from William Newton's *Architecture of . . . Vitruvius* (1771–1791; *q.v.*) and Richard Payne Knight's *Analytical Inquiry into the Principles of Taste* (1805). Part III, on architectural practice, includes subsections on Egyptian, Indian, Persian, Chinese, Greek, Roman, Modern, and Gothic architecture. Forty-five plates accompany the article. Illustrations of garden and domestic structures include a pagoda and two temples (Plate CLV) borrowed from Plates IV and V of Sir William Chambers's *Designs of Chinese Buildings* (1757; *q.v.*), a conjectural reconstruction of Greek and Roman villa plans (Plate CLXI), plans and elevations of one house and two villas by Palladio (Plate CLXXVII), and plans and elevations of Longleat, Blenheim, Luton Park, Bowden Park, Montague House, Roseneath, and Ashridge (Plates CLXXVIII–CLXXXI, CXCI–CXCII). The plates thus facilitated a comparison of designs from China, Greece, Rome, Renaissance Italy, Renaissance and Baroque England, and the contemporary Gothic revival.

John Claudius Loudon, the most prominent and prolific writer on horticulture and landscape during the first half of the nineteenth century, prepared the extensive article on "Landscape Gardening." He divided the subject into six chapters: an historical overview, analysis of the "object of this art" and its "principles," discussion of the materials of gardening (ground, wood, water, rocks, and buildings), remarks on the "constituent parts" of a country residence, comments on the formation of "scenes" to give country residences particular "characters," and observations on the "practice" of landscape gardening. In the fifth chapter he specified four particular "characters" of country residences: mansions, villas, ornamented cottages, and "temporary residences" such as "marine villas" or "shooting boxes," each of which required a particular "style" of landscape gardening (p. 568). At the end there is a brief bibliography. The plates for this article include examples of residences laid out in the "geometric" manner and in the "modern" style. Plate CCCXLIII is the plan of a house and grounds in the "geometric" manner, and Figure 1 in Plate CCCXLV is a view of the house and its surrounding landscape. The principal floor plan includes a chapel, library, two dining rooms, and offices. The elevation, in castellated style, is at least 17 windows wide and three stories high. Plate CCCXLIV and Figure 2 in Plate CCCXLV depict a plan and view of a house and grounds laid out in the "modern" style. The house includes a hall, dining room, library, drawing room, music room, chapel, conservatory, and offices. The elevation shows a castellated facade at least 15 windows wide and in some places four stories high. Plate CCCXLVI is a "working plan" for the grounds of this estate.

Most unusual for an encyclopedia, the article on "Lighthouses" includes views or sections of ten operating lighthouses, from Eddystone and Bell Rock in Britain to Corrunna and Genoa in Italy. More detailed plans and an elevation depict the Inchkeith Lighthouse in the Firth of Forth, a design basically Palladian in form but with crenellations along the parapet and atop the portico at the front door. The floor plans simply indicate a kitchen and "apartments" on the ground floor, with "Keepers Rooms" and "Strangers Rooms" upstairs.

1. N.B. during these years Thomas Hope also was preparing his pioneering historical treatise, *An Historical Essay on Architecture*, published posthumously in 1835.

BRIGDEN, Edward

See LOUDON, **John Claudius, ed.,** The architectural magazine, *Entry 182.*

BRITTON, John (1771–1857)
The union of architecture, sculpture, and painting.

See Entry 450.

BRITTON, John (1771–1857)
Vitruvius Britannicus.

See **ROBINSON, Peter Frederick,** Vitruvius Britannicus, *Entry 298.3.*

23.1
BROOKS, Samuel H.
Designs for cottage and villa architecture; containing plans, elevations, sections, perspective views, and details, for the erection of cottages and villas. By S. H. Brooks, Esq., Architect.

London: Thomas Kelly, and sold by all booksellers, [1839].

viii + 148 pp, 111 pls.

27.3 × 21.6 cm

MB

Following treatises by Trendall (1831) and Loudon (1838),[1] Brooks was the next author to address overtly the subject of suburban domestic architecture. From the Introduction (pp. iii–iv) it is clear that he expected England to become an entire nation of suburbs: suburban "retirement" would become the goal of each "Englishman, in whose mind the idea of retirement from business and a country life are inseparably united: and thus, *par eminence*, England becomes the country of suburban villas" (p. iii). As to models for such country retreats, he noted that England was remarkable "in the beauty and neatness of her rural edifices, whether they be considered as specimens of architectural skill, as objects of ornament, or as dwellings adapted for the general purposes of life, on the best and most acknowledged principles of utility, comfort, and economy" (p. iii). Brooks's intended audience included the "experienced" as well as the "amateur" architect, especially the rural builder who could not "be supposed to have had either leisure or opportunity to inspect the different improvements which have gradually or immediately taken place in his own country, or which may be the result of foreign talent" (p. iv). Brooks summarized the scope and application of his book with little modesty:

By a practical application of the principles contained in the following pages, and a strict attention to the details and other minutiae, which are designedly given for the uninitiated in the science of architecture or the art of building, many of the obstacles will be removed which at present stand in the way of the erection of our suburban villas, whilst at the same time, the exterior beauty of the edifice will be improved, with a corresponding increase of interior comfort, convenience, and utility. (p. iv)

In his "Preliminary Remarks" (pp. v–viii) Brooks discussed matters of site, orientation, water, irregular form, picturesque beauty, fitness, expression, style, and imagination in a very cursory manner. But looking forward to the text and illustrations he concluded that "By a simple examination of the designs, details, &c., with a correct estimate of the expense, the individual projecting the erection of a cottage or villa, can render himself at once master of the subject" (p. viii).

The 148 pages of text are devoted to "Specification and Details" of designs for 36 cottages or villas, eight summer houses, three lodges, and several gates. Interspersed throughout the text are additional remarks on a wide variety of subjects: the declining taste for exterior ornament, the influence of climate and social circumstances on architectural design, the adaptability of Greek and Roman forms to public and private buildings, the utility and beauty of architecture, Gothic architecture, Greek architecture, mixed styles, materials, stylistic character, the "national" architecture of Egypt, China, Greece, and Switzerland, methods of construction, arches, Old English style, ventilation, "classic architecture" and the orders, requirements and principles of the architectural profession, preparation of working drawings, siting and drainage, the origin of building, floors, heating and ventilation, general remarks on architectural design, and gardens.

Each design is illustrated in an elevation or perspective view and in plan, and for most designs there are sections, details, and interior views. His range of styles includes Gothic, Old English, Tudor, Elizabethan, Italian, Ionic, Greek, and Swiss. Most of the cottages and villas are two stories high, with facades three or four windows wide. One of the largest is a three-story design in Elizabethan style (Plates 70–72), four windows wide, with a drawing room, dining room, saloon, library, breakfast room, and terrace on the principal floor, and a kitchen, scullery, servants' hall, housekeeper's room, "still room," wine cellar, plate room, and butler's room on the ground floor. Brooks estimated the cost at £2,800. Among the smallest is the two-story double residence in Ionic style shown in Plate 4, with simply a hall, parlor, and drawing room on the ground floor of each side.

The illustrations are executed in a dry, very fine outline, and seldom include shrubbery or other scenery. But while Brooks's designs are neither so elegant nor so picturesque as those of his contemporaries, they were far more practical, and therefore better suited to his audience of suburban builders and inexperienced architects.

1. See Edward Trendall, *Original Designs for Cottages and Villas*, and John Claudius Loudon, *The Suburban Gardener, and Villa Companion*.

24.1

BROWN, Richard

Domestic architecture: containing a history of the science, and the principles of designing public buildings, private dwelling-houses, country mansions, and suburban villas; from the choice of the spot to the completion of the appendages. With observations on rural residences, their situation and scenery; and instructions on the art of laying out and embellishing grounds. By Richard Brown. . . .

London: George Virtue, 1841.

xii + 342 pp, frontisp. + 63 pls.

28.0 × 21.6 cm

BL

24.2

Domestic architecture: containing a history of the science, and the principles of designing public edifices, private dwelling-houses, country mansions, and suburban villas, with practical dissertations on every branch of building, from the choice of the site, to the completion of the appendages. Also, some observations on rural residences, their characteristic situation and scenery; with instructions on the art of laying out and ornamenting grounds; exemplified in sixty-three plates, containing diagrams, and exemplars of the various styles of domestic architecture, with a description, and wood-cuts of the appropriate furniture, garden, and landscape scenery of each. By Richard Brown. . . .

London: George Virtue, [1842].

xii + 342 pp, frontisp. + 63 pls.

28.6 × 22.3 cm

Private Collection

24.3

London: Bernard Quaritch, 1852.

xii + 342 pp, frontisp. [?] + 63 pls [*frontisp. wanting in this copy*].

28.3 × 21.9 cm

MH

The title page of the British Library copy is dated 1841; it is followed by a second, undated title page identical to tht in the [1842] edition, and the Preface, which is dated May 2, 1842. The 1841 title page is the only feature that differentiates the two editions.

A voluminous and authoritative treatise, Brown's book was the first thorough examination of the history and practice of domestic architecture. More than just a pattern book or practical manual, *Domestic Architecture* treated the subject in a comprehensive manner unprecedented in British architectural literature.

In the Preface (pp. v–vii) Brown described his objectives: "the dissemination and advancement of architectural principles, to guide the employer as well as the employed, and to improve or advance our national taste" (p. v). He stressed the need for architects to be widely read, in "history, geometry, the fine arts, optics, and perspective," and also to have a broad fund of experience:

it is quite impossible even for the professional man whose mind has not been enriched by study, and stored by travel and observation, to compose or select good combinations of forms and purity of style, or to observe the proper choice and appropriate adoption of the decorations required, suitable to the destined purposes of a rural residence. (p. v)

Brown praised England's "decided superiority over every other nation in Europe, in the grand display of numerous country-seats, situated in verdant lawns, and spacious parks with ornamental trees. . . ." But he warned of the increasing need to "preserve those noble mansions from tasteless innovations being made by unskilful pretenders" (p. v). Nor would any available architectural treatises help: books written for professional architects contained only "examples and details of classic buildings in Athens and Rome"; handbooks for the country builder provided only "miscellaneous designs for rural dwellings"; and other books contained only "geometrical lines for the operative mechanic."[1] The solution, therefore, could only be a comprehensive treatise on domestic architecture, with particular attention to issues such as those Brown raised in the remainder of his preface: architectural theory, "elementary principles," the history of style, the relationship between style and site, and ornamental landscape gardening. A table of contents (pp. ix–x) and list of illustrations (pp. xi–xii) conclude the preliminary matter.

The text begins with a 66-page "Succinct History" of domestic architecture, first treating Britain, then the ancient world, and leaving only four pages for medieval and postmedieval architecture on the Continent. Next there is a brief discussion of the qualifications of an architect (pp. 67–72), followed by essays on "the Principles of Designing Public Buildings" (pp. 73–80) and "the Principles of Designing Private Dwelling-Houses" (pp. 80–89).

In the latter essay Brown treated several important subjects, including variety, taste, convenience, strength, beauty, ornament, style, climate, the relation between a dwelling and its surrounding landscape, proportion, picturesque beauty, and differences between city and country residences. On the relation between the style of a dwelling and its form, Brown was precise:

in designing a manor-house in the Roman style, grandeur of architecture should be studied; in the Grecian villa, chasteness and sublimity; in the Italian casino, beauty and ornament; and in the Tudor residence, picturesqueness. The rustic cottage, or cottage *ornée*, should also be picturesque in the outline, with dormer windows rising into the roof, and the roof itself hiped [*sic*], or inclined inwards at the ends, and likewise to have rustic awnings to the south front of the house, which give the effect of retirement, and to be partially covered or concealed with ivy, woodbine, and clematis. (p. 83)

Nevertheless, before an architect could choose a style he had to consider the character of "the close adjacent parts" of the site as well as "distant views." Indeed the design,

if extensive, should, like a picture, have some parts prominent as a foreground, others falling back as a middle group, and the third more retired as a background; this will produce shadow and give effect to the lights. Some parts of the house will probably require to project, or be brought forward from a straight line on the plan; while other parts of the house may, on the contrary, recede on that plan, or, in some parts of the elevation be allowed to rise higher than others, by which the contour of the edifice will produce a playful variation, but which outline is to be regulated by the local scenery. Thus, like grouping figures in an historical piece, . . . some parts require to rise in form of triangles, others . . . may require to be horizontal and rise less in height, thus producing an harmonious play of outline along the summit against the sky. . . .[2]

Next follows a brief discussion of the means by which "rocks and caverns frequently suggest an idea for the composition of a building" (pp. 89–91).

The bulk of the text (pp. 91–246) is organized as a series of 47 "Dissertations" on aspects of domestic design. The first eight concern site, air, water, and earth. The next six treat principles of construction, foundations, walls, and chimneys. Another seven treat stairs, floors, partitions, roofs, porches, and porticoes. Dissertation XXII concerns the proper relations between the Classical orders and different types of landscape setting. The next 11 dissertations discuss interior planning and finishing, and include remarks on ground plans, room proportions, halls, vestibules, saloons, galleries, doors, ceilings, and decoration. Two dissertations treat the "Science of Optics" and the art of drawing elevations, followed by five dissertations on external proportions, window and door openings, and external ornament. The final seven dissertations concern sections, color, models, stables and coach houses, lodges, ventilation, and heating.

The next 72 pages (pp. 247–318), accompanied by 55 plates, constitute a separate section of the treatise in which "the elementary diagrams of design, and exemplars of the various styles of domestic architecture [are] displayed and defined; including the appropriate furniture, garden, and landscape scenery of each" (p. 247). Plates I and II depict eight basic elevations and plans for dwellings, ranging from a simple cube to a porticoed rotunda flanked by two wing pavilions. Plate III shows six more complex designs in elevation and plan. Altogether these designs illustrate such basic principles as linearity, horizontality, and verticality, and also the relations between circular and angular forms, and between projecting and receding forms. Plates IV through LII and the accompanying text provide "Exemplars of the Various Styles": plans, elevations, sections, details, and descriptions of designs for dwellings in 25 distinct styles.[3] Some of Brown's attempts were less than successful: for example the "Villa in the Florentine Style" (Plate XVIII), supposedly based on Petrarch's villa at Arqua, more closely exemplifies northern European Mannerism, and "A Pompeii Suburban Villa" (Plate XXII) appears to be a dull attempt at Tuscan Revival more than an accurate rendition of Pompeiian architecture. Other designs are more attractive: the "Cottage Ornée" (Plate IV) is suitably enriched with a thatch roof, ornamental chimneys, pointed windows, half-timbering, and tree-trunk columns supporting the veranda; the facade of the "Tudor Suburban Residence" (Plate XI) is a restrained but picturesque composition of gables ornamented with finials, ornamental chimneys, an oriel window, Tudor drip moldings, crenellations, and heraldic shields. One of the largest designs is the "Grecian Villa" (Plate XXXI). The facade is two stories high in the center, and 15 windows wide. The ground floor includes a hall, withdrawing room, dining room, conservatory, library, anteroom, porter's room, butler's room, housekeeper's room, storeroom, pantry, servants' hall, kitchen, scullery, larder, and cellars. One of the smallest designs, the "Cottage Ornée," is two stories high and three windows wide. The ground-floor plan includes a hall, breakfast room, dining room, withdrawing room, kitchen, pantry, and butler's room. Upstairs there are three bedrooms, two servant's bedrooms, a closet, and a water closet. Plates LIII through LV depict stables, a park entrance, and examples of dwellings in four different styles set in appropriate landscape surroundings.

The final portion of the text (pp. 319–342) is an essay on landscape gardening, accompanied by plates (LVI–LXIII) depicting various elements of landscape scenery, methods of laying out grounds and flower gardens, an "Italian" garden with hothouses, an orangery, and a gardener's residence, a dog kennel, and an ice house.

Figure 1

Brown's contribution lay in providing a comprehensive survey of architectural theory, practice, and style, as well as landscape gardening, plus a visual catalogue of most of the historical and exotic architectural styles of interest to his contemporaries. Nevertheless, as he warned in the Preface, the book was not intended "to make 'every gentleman his own architect' " (p. v); his principal concerns were aesthetic, not practical, and the book was intended primarily "to improve and advance our national taste" (p. v).

1. P. v. It is curious that in this context Brown ignored John Claudius Loudon's *Encyclopaedia* (1833; *q.v.*), a large collection of instructive and informative designs for a wide range of cottages and villas.

2. P. 84. Explicit parallels between pictorial and architectural composition were explored previously by Robert Castell in *Villas of the Ancients* (1728); Robert Morris in *Rural Architecture* (1750); Isaac Ware in *A Complete Body of Architecture* (1756); Robert and James Adam in *Works in Architecture* (1778–1779); James Lewis in *Original Designs* (1780–1797); George Richardson in *New Designs in Architecture* (1792); Edmund Bartell in *Hints for Picturesque Improvements* (1804); and John Buonarotti Papworth in *Hints on Ornamental Gardening* (1823), *qq.v.*

3. Cottage Ornée, Henry the Seventh, Henry the Eighth, Elizabethan, Stuart, Florentine, Flemish, Pompeian, Venetian, Swiss, French, Egyptian, Grecian, Roman, Anglo-Grecian, Anglo-Italian, Persian, Chinese, Burmese, Oriental, Morisco Spanish, Norman, Lancastrian, Plantagenet, and Palladian.

25.1

BROWN, Richard

The principles of practical perspective; or, scenographic projection: containing universal rules for delineating designs on various surfaces, and taking views from nature, by the most simple and expeditious methods. To which are added, rules for shadowing, and the elements of painting. The whole treated in a manner calculated to render the science of perspective and the art of drawing easy of attainment to every capacity. Illustrated with fifty-one plates. By Richard Brown. . . .

London: Printed for Samuel Leigh: sold also by R. Ackermann; J. Harding; and J. Taylor, 1815.

xviii + 96 pp, 51 pls [*pls. 36 and 39 are wanting in this copy*].

29.2 × 22.9 cm

CtY-BA

25.2

———

The principles of practical perspective, or, scenographic projection; containing universal rules for delineating architectural designs ⟨ . . . as 1815 . . . ⟩ capacity. Second edition. In two parts. Illustrated by fifty plates. By Richard Brown. . . .

London: Printed for Leigh and Son. Sold also by J. Weale (late Taylor's Architectural Library), 1835.

2 parts: Part I: xx + 48 pp, frontisp. (= pl. 25) + 24 pls. Part II: xvi + 49–132 pp, frontisp. (= pl. 46) + 26–45 + 47–50 pls.

30.5 × 23.8 cm

DLC

The Principles of Practical Perspective is the most elegantly illustrated perspective treatise of the early nineteenth century, and its text ranges over a wide variety of topics, from elementary perspective constructions to principles of picturesque composition in architecture and painting.[1]

The Preface to Part I begins with remarks on the historical development and importance of perspective. Yet despite much literature on the subject, Brown still found that "an easy, familiar, and practical treatise on the science was still wanting: for the figures and the objects by which most writers on Perspective have illustrated their rules have been uninteresting, and such as seldom occur in practice" (p. vii). His aim, therefore, was "to apply the principles of Perspective to a variety of the most common, pleasing, painter-like, and difficult, but useful objects; and also to show the student how to shadow and colour them" (p. vii). This more practical and useful approach would require "a greater number of plates" than in previous treatises. Nor did Brown want to burden "the mind of the young pupil with too much unnecessary theory. . . . My rules are few and concise, but carefully stated and proved, and then applied to the most common and picturesque objects" (p. vii).

An Introductory Discourse (pp. ix–xvii) describes the principles and applications of perspective in general terms, and is followed by four pages of definitions and two pages of terse remarks on "The Theory of Lines and Planes" (pp. 1–6). Most of Part I is organized as a series of instructive texts accompanying the 25 plates, all demonstrating principles or examples of perspective construction. The first eight plates show drawing apparatus and geometric figures and objects. Plates 9 through 25 illustrate perspective constructions of individual buildings, mostly domestic and ecclesiastical structures, in a variety of styles. Each subject is shown in plan and oblique view, and occasionally in elevation. In order, the subjects are: a rectangular building with a gable roof and projecting eaves and pediments, a martello tower with medieval arrow slits, a park entrance with three arches, a two-story house with semicircular windows on the upper story, a two-story "Country Villa" with wings plus a low attic story over the three central bays, a two-story "Mansion in the Style of a Castle," a three-story Neoclassical "Mansion House," a Neoclassical house with low wings and a semicircular bow at the rear, a "Shot Manufactory" in Doric style, a Gothic "Village Church Tower and Spire," a town square with a rusticated Doric public bath in the center, a vista down a street flanked by houses and with a "Church in the Egyptian Style" at the end, a rustic double cottage "appropriate for a Gamekeeper and Shepherd," a "Culver-House" (i.e., pigeon house or dovecote), a large castellated residence called an "abbey," and finally "the revolving Temple of Concord, which was erected in the Green Park, in commemoration of the return of Peace."[2] The text accompanying each plate focuses almost exclusively on two matters: explaining the mechanical aspects of constructing the perspective view, and discussing the appropriate use of such a view in paintings and drawings. Part I closes with remarks "On the Arts During the Middle Ages" (pp. 45–46) and a conclusion in which Brown explained why he chose so many architectural subjects for his plates: "The reason is, that buildings are more regular than other objects, therefore better adapted for the purpose" of instruction (p. 47).

The second part opens with a Prefatory Address in which Brown claimed his book now had become "a correct treatise on the Elements and Practice of the Fine Arts, embracing Design, Drawing, Shadowing, and Painting" (p. vi). There follows an "Introductory Essay on Picturesque Residences" (pp. ix–xvi) in which he emphasized the need for originality and genius in the designer:

If a man has nothing of that which is called genius to animate him, that, in fact, *which strikes at once*, all the rules that are laid down will never make him a good architect or painter. One who has genius will conceive in his mind the whole of his work, whilst he who is deficient in genius, delights himself only with minor parts, such as the mouldings of cornices, architraves, sash bars, &c., &c. (p. ix)

The rest of the essay primarily concerns the architecture of Tudor times, when architects "appear to have been well acquainted with the picturesque in building, and with that happy mode of producing ornamental effect with little difficulty to the carver, or expense to the employer" (pp. ix–x).[3] Brown discussed a variety of Tudor dwellings, from the "cottage ornée" at Highgate (p. xii) to Hampton Court Palace (p. xi). The plates for Part II, as in the previous part, employ an assortment of building types and styles to demonstrate the techniques of perspective construction. The subjects, generally illustrated in elevation and plan, include: a Greek Revival "Floor-Cloth Manufactory,"[4] crenellated Tudor alms houses,[5] a semicircular crescent of five buildings three stories high connected by one-story colonnaded "annexes,"[6] an "Asylum" or "College," a bridge, the interior of an assembly room, an arcade, a hall or vestibule in a style reminiscent of Sir John Soane, a cylindrical skylight,[7] the Doric interior of a mausoleum, a "cylindro-cylindric Arch,"[8] a lacunary ceiling, "Gothic Arches in the Aisles of a Church," Doric and Ionic orders, two Grecian cenotaphs, houses drawn "in panoramic Perspective," an "Egyptian Cemetery," a "Gallery and Lantern-Light" in a hall, a circular Ionic temple,[9] a view of the Royal Academy in Somerset House, shadows, interior views, and reflections of objects in water. As in Part I, each plate is accompanied by a text explaining the techniques of perspective construction and their application in painting and drawing. Part II closes with several essays specifically on painting: "Definitions of Technical Terms Used by Painters" (pp. 79–83), "The Theory of Light and Shadow" (pp. 84–87), "Practical Remarks on Shadows" (pp. 88–92), brief remarks on drawing, shadowing, landscape, tints, coloring, mounting and varnishing drawings (pp. 93–103), and "The Elements and Practice of Oil Painting" (pp. 104–131).

In the Conclusion (pp. 131–132) Brown reflected on the hybrid treatise he had created, and found it "rather surprising that the authors on perspective (with only one exception) should not have thought of adding an essay on painting to their treatises" (p. 132).[10] Nevertheless the subjects clearly have application to each other, and so "An essay on painting, combined with a treatise on geometry and perspective, cannot therefore but be acceptable; particularly as this work is intended for every class of artists, and to be a complete treatise, alike useful to the student, to the professor, and to the amateur, in every department of the fine arts" (p. 132).

1. The discussion that follows is based entirely on the second edition (1835).

2. Plate 25 is bound as the frontispiece to Part I, and in many copies is colored. Most of the plates are shaded in aquatint.

3. Compare two contemporary treatises on domestic design in Tudor style: Thomas Frederick Hunt, *Designs for Parsonage Houses* (1827), and *Exemplars of Tudor Architecture* (1830), *qq.v.*

4. The building illustrated could be "seen at Whitechapel" (p. 49).

5. These were "erected by the Rev. Rowland Hill," "near Blackfriars-Road" (p. 50).

6. The five principal buildings are three stories high and three or four windows wide, decorated in a restrained Neoclassical manner (Plate 28). They generally resemble contemporary projects for "Polygons" and "Paragons." For further references see the commentary on Peter Nicholson's *Treatise on Projection.*

7. " . . . as seen piercing through a Vault or Groin under the Adelphi Terrace" (p. 57).

8. " . . . as seen in the Gateway at Somerset-House" (p. 60).

9. Plate 45 shows the subject in outline. Plate 46, titled "Temple of Diana" and bound as the frontispiece to Part II, shows the same subject in a different view, with aquatint shading. In many copies this plate is colored. Most of the plates in Part II, as in the previous part, are shaded in aquatint.

10. The exception was Thomas Bardwell, author of *The Practice of Painting and Perspective* (1756; *q.v.*).

26.1

The builder's magazine: or monthly companion for architects, carpenters, masons, bricklayers, &c. as well as for every gentleman who would wish to be a competent judge of the elegant and necessary art of building. Consisting of designs in architecture, in every stile and taste, from the most magnificent and superb structures, down to the most simple and unadorned; together with the plans and sections, serving as an unerring assistant in the construction of any building, from a palace to a cottage. In which will be introduced grand and elegant designs for chimney-pieces, cielings, doors, windows, &c. proper for halls, saloons, vestibules, state rooms, dining rooms, parlours, drawing rooms, anti rooms, dressing rooms, bed rooms, &c. Together with designs for churches, hospitals, and other public buildings. Also, plans, elevations, and sections, in the Greek, Roman, and Gothic taste, calculated to embellish parks, gardens, forests, woods, canals, mounts, vistos, islands, extensive views, &c. The whole forming a complete system of architecture, in all its branches; and so disposed, as to render the surveyor, carpenter, mason, &c. equally capable to erect a cathedral, a mansion, a temple, or a rural cot. By a society of architects. Each having undertaken the department in which he particularly excels.

London: Printed for the authors; and sold by F. Newbery; and all other booksellers in Great Britain and Ireland, 1774.

[ii] + 345 + 100 pp, 185 pls.

26.0 × 21.0 cm

V&A

26.2 ‖

The builder's magazine: ⟨ . . . as 1774 . . . ⟩ Greek, Roman and Gothic ⟨ . . . as 1774 . . . ⟩ excels.

London: Printed for the authors; and sold by F. Newbery; and all other booksellers in Great Britain and Ireland, 1776.

252 + 66 pp, 121 pls [*additional text and plates are wanting in this copy*].

26.6 × 20.5 cm

Reference: Information supplied by The Bancroft Library, University of California, Berkeley.

26.3

The builder's magazine: or, a universal dictionary for architects, carpenters, ⟨ . . . as 1774 . . . ⟩ branches, and so disposed as ⟨ . . . as 1774 . . . ⟩ architects. The second edition.

London: Printed for F. Newbery; and sold by all other booksellers in Great Britain and Ireland, 1779.

[ii] + 345 + 100 pp, 185 pls.

26.4 × 21.0 cm

RIBA

26.4

The builder's magazine: or, a universal dictionary for architects, carpenters, ⟨ . . . as 1774 . . . ⟩ branches, and ⟨ . . . as 1774 . . . ⟩ architects. A new edition.

London: Printed for E. Newbery; and sold by all other booksellers in Great Britain and Ireland, 1788.

[ii] + 345 + 8 + 100 pp, 185 pls.

26.7 × 21.6 cm

MBAt

26.5

The builder's magazine; or, a universal dictionary for architects, carpenters, ⟨ . . . as 1774 . . . ⟩ unadorned. Together ⟨ . . . as 1774 . . . ⟩ architecture in all its branches, and so disposed as ⟨ . . . as 1774 . . . ⟩ architects. A new edition.

London: Printed by T. Maiden, for E. Newbery, Vernor and Hood, and H. D. Symonds, 1800.

[ii] + 345 + 100 + 8 pp, 185 pls [*pl. L is wanting in this copy*].

28.0 × 22.2 cm

MH

26.6

COOK, Andrew George

The new builder's magazine, and complete architectural library, for architects, surveyors, carpenters, masons, bricklayers, &c. as well as for every gentleman who would wish to be a competent judge of the elegant and necessary art of building: consisting of designs in architecture, in every style and taste, from the most magnificent and superb structures, down to the most simple and unadorned: together with the plans, sections, and elevations, serving as an unerring assistant in the construction of any building, from a palace to a cottage. Exclusive of the new and elegant designs, ample instructions are given in the letter-press, concerning all the terms of art, used in every branch of building. Also, under proper heads, the laws for the regulation of buildings—the substance of the Builders' Act, &c.—and a list of the prices allowed by the most eminent surveyors in London to the several artificers employed. The whole forming a complete system of architecture in all its branches; and so disposed, as to render the surveyor, carpenter, bricklayer, mason, &c. equally capable to erect a cathedral, a mansion, a temple, or a rural cot. Embellished with upwards of three hundred elegant quarto and folio engravings. By Andrew George Cook, Architect & Builder.

London: Printed by J. Hartnell, for H. Hogg & Co., [n.d.].

iv + 423 + 106 + lxxx pp, frontisp. + 177 pls.

25.1 × 21.3 cm

V&A

26.7

————

The new builder's magazine, and complete architectural library, for architects, surveyors, carpenters, masons, bricklayers, &c. As well as for every gentleman who would wish to be a competent judge of the elegant and necessary art of building. Consisting of designs in architecture, in every stile and taste, from the most magnificent and superb structures, down to the most simple and unadorned. Together with the plans, sections, and elevations, serving as an unerring assistant in the construction of any building, from a palace to a cottage. Exclusive of the new and elegant designs, ample instructions are given in the letter-press concerning all the terms of art used in every branch of building. Also, under proper heads, the laws for the regulation of buildings—the substance of the Builders Act, &c.—and a list of the prices allowed by the most eminent surveyors in London to the several artificers concerned in building. The whole forming a complete system of architecture in all its branches, and so disposed as to render the surveyor, carpenter, bricklayer, mason, &c. equally capable to erect a cathedral, a mansion, a temple, or a rural cot. Embellished with upwards of three hundred elegant quarto and folio engravings. By Andrew George Cook, Architect and Builder.

London: Printed by M. Allen, for H. Hogg & Co., [n.d].

xcvi + 106 + 423 pp, frontisp. + 177 pls.

25.7 × 20.6 cm

RIBA

26.8

The new builder's magazine, ⟨ . . . as in [n.d.] edition at V&A . . . ⟩ brick-layers, &c. As well ⟨ . . . as in [n.d.] edition at V&A . . . ⟩ terms of art used ⟨ . . . as in [n.d.] edition at V&A . . . ⟩ buildings; the substance of the Builders' Act, &c; and ⟨ . . . as in [n.d.] edition at V&A . . . ⟩ in London, to the ⟨ . . . as in [n.d.] edition at V&A . . . ⟩ architecture, in all ⟨ . . . as in [n.d.] edition at V&A . . . ⟩ engravings. By Andrew George Cook, Architect and Builder.

London: Printed for Thomas Kelly, by Weed and Rider, 1819.

xcvi + 106 + 423 pp, frontisp. + 177 pls.

26.0 × 21.6 cm

BL

26.9

London: Printed for Thomas Kelly, by Weed and Rider, 1820.

xcvi + 106 + 423 pp, frontisp. + 177 pls.

26.7 × 20.3 cm

RIBA

26.10 ‖

London: Printed for Thomas Kelly, by Weed and Rider, 1823.

xcv + [i] + 106 + 423 pp, frontisp. + 177 pls.

27.3 cm

Reference: Information supplied by Fine Arts Library, The Ohio State University.

Although the title page of the first edition is dated 1774, the plates bear publication dates from 1775 through 1778, indicating the work probably was issued serially between 1774 and 1778. The title page indicates the book was prepared by a "society of architects," but most of the plates are signed by John Carter, to whom the entire work has sometimes been attributed.[1] Editions of the work dated 1774 through 1800 were arranged in two parts, one ostensibly "theoretical" and the other "practical." The theoretical part begins with a 306-page dictionary of architectural terms. There follows a section devoted to official government acts regulating building (pp. 307–338), and commentary on Egyptian, Greek, and Roman building (pp. 339–345). The practical section includes 100 pages of plate descriptions and 185 plates. In some editions there is an eight-page list of prices for artificers' work.

When Andrew George Cook took on the duties of "editor" about 1810, he reset the dictionary entries onto 423 pages, and reset the plate descriptions onto 106 pages; he also retained and reset the abstract of the Building Act and the list of prices. The plates, while fewer in number, contain essentially the same designs as those in the earlier editions.

The text of the dictionary is not related to the plates, but was intended to serve as "instructions . . . necessary to form the complete architect" (1800, "Preface," verso). The entries, arranged alphabetically, were supposed to "begin . . . with the most simple instructions, and advance progressively to the sublime parts" (ibid.). Far from sublimities, most entries provide practical information of use to artisans and builders (e.g., "Bricks," "Chimney-Piece," and "Foundation"). Each of the orders is accorded a separate entry, and they are considered together in the article "Order," but altogether there is little more than an account of their proportions. One of the longer articles is "House" (1800, pp. 240–244), which unfortunately elucidates few principles of domestic design. Instead it repeats such commonplace notions as the need to proportion the parts to the whole (1800, p. 243), or the need to dispose the parts in such a manner as to give a harmony to the whole (1800, p. 244). There is little further explanation of these or other points. The author noted the design of a house must suit both the inhabitant and its location (1800, p. 241), but offered no practical advice on how to achieve this end.

Because this book was published during the same years as the first issues of Robert and James Adam's *Works in Architecture* (*q.v.*), many of Carter's designs are in the light and elegant Adam Neoclassical manner. Other designs, less numerous, are in Gothic, rustic, and Palladian styles.[2] These range in size from a rustic one-room hunting villa (Plate XLII), a rustic grotto (Plate CLXXVI), and a Palladian garden seat (Plate XCVI), to a "villa" with a main body nine windows wide and two wings each seven windows wide (Plate LXXX). There is a small Gothic hunting seat (Plate LXVI), a large Gothic church (Plate CX, etc.), and a castellated Gothic mansion (Plates LXII and LXV). Designs for commercial structures include a "Sugar House" (Plate LXXXI) and a market house (Plate LXIV). There are several designs for room interiors, with additional plates devoted to ceilings, vases, moldings, and other ornaments, mostly in Adam style. Some of the designs reveal Carter's talent for manipulation of geometric solids (e.g., Plate LXXXVIII, a farm house composed of octagonal masses), while others reveal his facility for light and elegant decoration in the Adam manner. The plates therefore emphasize no particular style or program. Instead, the variety of designs makes this an important example of increasing late eighteenth-century interest in stylistic diversity.

1. His name also appears at the bottom of the final page of plate descriptions (1800, p. 100).

2. Note Carter's parting comment on the Gothic: "I must confess myself a zealous admirer of Gothic architecture—affirming with confidence, nothing can be more in character, and better adapted to a place of worship, than that awful style of building, and that Grecian and Roman architecture should be confined to mansions and other structures of ease and pleasure" (p. 100). On Carter see also Colvin (1978), pp. 198–200.

27.1 ‡
BURGESS, John Cart (1798–1863)
An easy introduction to perspective, for the use of young persons. By J. C. Burgess. Second edition.

London: Printed for the author, by Tilling and Hughes; and sold by Sherwood and Co.; Orme; Newman; Ackermann; Taylor; Dickinson; Smith and Co., and Hatchard; Murray; Faulkner; and other booksellers, 1819.

vii + 38 pp, 10 pls on 7 leaves.

8°

Reference: Microfilm supplied by The British Library.

27.2

_____

An easy introduction to perspective, for the use of young persons. By J. C. Burgess. Third edition.

London: Printed for the author, by T. Harjette; and sold by Sherwood and Co.; Orme; Newman; Ackermann; Taylor; Dickinson; Smith and Co., Hatchard; Murray; Faulkner; and other booksellers, 1822.

vii + 38 pp, 7 pls on 6 leaves [*additional plates are wanting in this copy*].

21.0 × 13.4 cm

V&A

27.3

_____

An easy introduction to perspective, for the use of young persons. Fourth edition. To which are now added, useful hints on drawing and painting; formerly published in a separate form. By J. C. Burgess.

London: Published by J. Souter; and sold by Dickinson; Hatchard and Son; Ackerman; Fuller; Murray; and by the author, 1828.

vi + 50 pp, 10 pls on 7 leaves.

22.1 × 14.0 cm

BL

27.4 ‡

An easy introduction to perspective, for the use of young persons. Sixth edition, revised, corrected, and improved, with new plates. By J. C. Burgess. . . .

London: Printed for the author, by D. Murray and Co.; sold also, by Simpkin and Marshall; Ackermann and Co.; Dickinson; Fuller's, Temple of Fancy; and Moss, Guernsey, 1835.

xi + 13–39 pp, 6 pls.

8°

Reference: Microfilm supplied by The British Library.

Following the same approach as William Daniel and Charles Hayter (*qq.v.*), John Cart Burgess developed this course of perspective instruction for readers with no technical experience or artistic training. Burgess also slighted works similar to his own by complaining that no such treatise was "sufficiently simple, and concise, for the use of young persons" (1819, p. v). The brief text in the 1819 edition includes sections devoted to lines, points, definitions, explanations of Plates V through X, a description of the camera obscura, and remarks on sketching from nature. Most of the plates show simple geometric and perspective constructions. Plate VII illustrates the interior of a room in outline. Plate IX depicts a pair of two-story houses with gable roofs.[1] Plate X illustrates another small house, with no door and three windows, plus a bridge of two arches spanning a river, with a small village in the distance.

The text and plates of the 1822 and 1828 editions are similar to those of the 1819 edition.

The "sixth" edition, issued in 1835, is entirely different. The "Advertisement" to this edition still complained that other treatises were too "abstract" and "prolix" (p. ix). In addition Burgess claimed that now more than ever "a knowledge of perspective is essentially requisite to all who engage in the study of drawing and painting, sculpture, architecture, and engraving" (p. iii). Citing the importance of perspective construction in paintings by Claude, Poussin, Canaletto, and Turner, he argued that studying perspective would improve the amateur's ability to create art, as well as enjoy all the beauties of both art and nature (pp. iii–iv, vii). The text includes a division of the subject into linear and aerial perspective (p. 15) and running commentaries on the plates. These include a few perspective diagrams, but principally depict furniture, a small country church, a large church with a dome, a bridge of many arches over a river, columns, and one house. The house, Fig. 3 in Plate 6, is rectangular in plan, three stories high, with an ell attached to the rear. The lattice windows suggest a Tudor style.

1. This illustration was a prototype for similar figures used by William Rider and John Wood, Jr. (*qq.v.*).

28.1

[BURKE, John French]

Library of useful knowledge. British husbandry; exhibiting the farming practice in various parts of the United Kingdom. Volume the first. Published under the superintendence of the Society for the Diffusion of Useful Knowledge.

London: Baldwin and Cradock, 1834.

viii + 534 + [2] pp.

20.8 × 12.7 cm

Library of useful knowledge. British husbandry; ⟨ . . . as 1834, Vol. I . . . ⟩ Kingdom. Volume the second. Published ⟨ . . . as 1834, Vol. I . . . ⟩.

London: Baldwin and Cradock, 1837.

ix + 617 pp.

20.9 × 13.2 cm

Library of useful knowledge. Husbandry: volume the third. Comprising reports of select farms; outlines of Flemish husbandry; useful and ornamental planting; road-making; cottage economy. Published under the superintendence of the Society for the Diffusion of Useful Knowledge.

London: Baldwin and Cradock, 1840.

iv + 68 + 65–96 + 35 + 28 pp, 2 printed leaves, 97–156 + 95 + iv + 151 pp, 1 printed leaf, 37 + 68 pp.

20.9 × 13.1 cm

[The following, with separate title page, is included in the final 68-page portion of this volume:]

LOUDON, John Claudius (1783–1843)

Library of useful knowledge. Farmer's series. The cottager's manual of husbandry, architecture, domestic economy, and gardening; originally published in The Gardener's Magazine. By J. C. Loudon. . . . Published under the superintendence of the Society for the Diffusion of Useful Knowledge.

London: Baldwin and Cradock, 1840.

56 pp.

DLC

28.2

Library of useful knowledge. British husbandry; ⟨ . . . as Vol. I in previous entry . . . ⟩.

London: Baldwin and Cradock, 1834.

viii + 534 + [2] pp.

Library of useful knowledge. British husbandry; exhibiting the farming practice in various parts of the United Kingdom. Volume the second. Published under the superintendence of the Society for the Diffusion of Useful Knowledge.

London: Baldwin and Cradock, 1841.

viii + 616 pp.

Library of useful knowledge. Husbandry: ⟨ . . . as Vol. III in previous entry . . . ⟩.

London: Baldwin and Cradock, 1840.

iv + 68 + 65–96 + 35 + 28 + 97–156 + 95 + iv + 151 + 27 + 68 pp.

[*The following, with separate title page, is included in the final 68-page portion of this volume:*]

LOUDON, John Claudius (1783–1843)

Library of useful knowledge. Farmer's series. The cottager's manual ⟨ . . . as in previous entry . . . ⟩.

London: Baldwin and Cradock, 1840.

56 pp.

21.1 × 13.5 cm

MH

28.3
_____

British husbandry; exhibiting the farming practice in various parts of the United Kingdom. Volume the first. Published under the superintendence of the Society for the Diffusion of Useful Knowledge.

London: Robert Baldwin, [1847].

viii + 534 pp, 1 printed leaf.

British husbandry; exhibiting the farming practice in various parts of the United Kingdom. Volume the second. Published under the superintendence of the Society for the Diffusion of Useful Knowledge.

London: Robert Baldwin, [1847].

ix + 616 pp.

Husbandry: volume the third. Comprising reports of select farms; outlines of Flemish husbandry; useful and ornamental planting; cottage economy; structure and improvement of roads. Published under the superintendence of the Society for the Diffusion of Useful Knowledge.

London: Robert Baldwin, [1847].

iv + 68 + 65–156 pp, 2 leaves, 28 + 35 + 95 + iv + 151 + 37 pp, 1 leaf, 68 pp.

[The following, with separate title page, is included in the final 68-page portion of this volume:]

LOUDON, **John Claudius (1783–1843)**

Library of useful knowledge. Farmer's series. The cottager's manual ⟨ . . . as 1840, Vol. III . . . ⟩.

London: Baldwin and Cradock, 1840.

56 pp.

22.1 × 14.1 cm

PU

28.4

British husbandry; exhibiting the farming practice in various parts of the United Kingdom, published under the superintendence of the Society for the Diffusion of Useful Knowledge; with a supplement, comprising modern agricultural improvements, by Cuthbert Wm. Johnson. . . . Volume I.

London: Robert Baldwin, 1847.

viii + 534 + viii + 175 pp.

British husbandry; ⟨ . . . as 1847, Vol. I . . . ⟩ Johnson. . . . Volume II.

London: Robert Baldwin, 1848.

xi + 616 pp.

Husbandry: volume the third. ⟨ . . . as [1847] . . . ⟩.

London: Robert Baldwin, [1847?].

iv + 68 + 65–96 pp, 2 printed leaves, 97–156 + 28 + 35 + 95 + iii–iv + 151 + 37 + [i] + 68 pp.

[The following, with separate title page, is included in the final 68-page portion of this volume:]

LOUDON, **John Claudius (1783–1843)**

Library of useful knowledge. Farmer's series. The cottager's manual ⟨ . . . as in 1840, Vol. III . . . ⟩.

London: Baldwin and Cradock, 1840.

56 pp.

22.1 × 13.6 cm

NIC

There are no major differences among the four editions, except for the addition of a 175-page supplement to the first volume of the final edition.

The principal purpose of this work was to "present a summary of the husbandry of the whole kingdom—embracing Ireland and Scotland as well as England—within a small and unexpensive compass," communicating "the results of real practice, unincumbered by any speculative reasoning" (1834, I, 36). The introduction suggested that a major goal had been to synthesize all the information already gathered in the surveys of individual counties undertaken under the auspices of the Board of Agriculture in the years from 1793 to 1813.[1]

The first volume of *British Husbandry* includes chapters on the history of agriculture, farm size and finances, buildings, human and animal labor, manure and fertilizer, soil, drainage, waste land, grass land and meadows, haymaking, and irrigation. The second volume considers farm machinery, crop rotation, soil, a variety of crops, cattle, sheep, goats, deer, swine, poultry, rabbits, fences, vermin, and cottage gardens. The third volume is a collection of miscellaneous republications, including reports on individual farms in England and Scotland, "Outlines of Flemish Husbandry," an essay on useful and ornamental planting, an essay on roads, and John Claudius Loudon's *Cottager's Manual*. The 1847 supplement contains sections on the history of agriculture, land tenure, agricultural laborers, enclosure, soil, farm machinery, livestock, and miscellaneous topics.

Only two portions of *British Husbandry* relate directly to the subject of architecture. The first is the fifth chapter of Volume I (pp. 85–111), a discussion of "Farm Buildings." The second is John Claudius Loudon's 56-page essay on cottage architecture and gardening in Volume III. Since this is a truncated reissue of his 1830 publication, *A Manual of Cottage Gardening (q.v.)*, it will not be considered here.

The essay on farm buildings covers a wide range of topics: site, materials, costs, water supplies, different types of roofing, and variations in plan found throughout the British Isles. It also offers information on specific building types, including barns, granaries, sheds, dairies, pigsties, poultry houses, and mills. Among the 20 text figures within this chapter, seven show farm houses in plan or elevation. All are shown with attached farm buildings surrounding a farm yard. This reflects "the main object" of farm building design, which "is to have the house and offices so arranged as to save all the time and labour possible, and to enable the farmer to carry on his business with the fewest number of servants" (p. 85). The article offers some advice on siting the house in relation to other farm buildings and in relation to the sun and prevailing winds, but makes little comment on interior plans or external decoration. Of five houses shown in elevation, four are two stories high and three windows wide, with little exterior detail. The fifth house consists of a main story with a door and two windows, and a low attic story. In plan most houses have a kitchen, one or two parlors, a back kitchen, a master's room, and various "offices" on the ground floor; the one upper floor shown in plan includes three bedrooms and one storeroom.

1. See below the entry for "Great Britain. Board of Agriculture. Reports" discussing the history and significance of these county surveys.

29.1

BURROWES, Amyas Deane

The modern encyclopaedia; or general dictionary of arts, sciences and literature, comprehending the latest discoveries in each department of knowledge by Amyas Deane Burrowes of the Honorable Society of Lincolns Inn Esqr. In ten volumes. Vol. . . .

London: Printed and published by Richards & Co., and sold by Simkin & Marshall, Rees, Bristol, and in Dublin by J. Jones, [1820].

[*Ten volumes, issued 1816–1820.*]

Art. "Architecture," I, 666–701; pls. I–XV [*pls. VI, XI wanting in this copy*], and one unnumbered plate.
Art. "Perspective," VIII, 726–741; pls. 1–4, V.

25.9 × 21.0 cm

ICRL

29.2 ‖

The modern encyclopaedia; or, dictionary of arts, sciences, and literature; comprehending a complete history of the various countries, and an accurate geographical description of the principal cities, mountains, seas, and rivers, in the world; with a biography of the most eminent persons of every nation. Illustrated with numerous engravings. By Amyas Deane Burrowes. In ten volumes. Vol. . . .

London: Printed and published by Richards & Co.; and sold by Simpkin & Marshall, 1822.

[*Ten volumes. Plus an additional volume of plates, without title page.*]

Art. "Architecture," I, 677–701; pls. I–XV.
Art. "Perspective," VIII, 726–741; pls. 1–4, V.

Reference: Information supplied by The Library Company of Philadelphia.

The first edition is dated 1816–1820 by Robert Collison in *Encylopaedias: Their History throughout the Ages* (New York: Hafner, 1966), p. 304.

The article on "Architecture" very closely follows that in the fourth edition of the *Encyclopaedia Britannica* (1810; *q.v.*), with only minor omissions and changes. All of the plates were borrowed from the *Britannica*, sometimes with the image reversed. Burrowes did not include any of the plates showing staircases or railings, or the final design for a mansion (*Britannica*, 1810, pls. XLIX–LI, LV).

The articles on "Perspective" and "Perspective-Machine" also closely resemble those in the *Britannica*. Burrowes's plates reproduce some, but not all, of the *Britannica* figures. Among those he did include was Fig. 5, Plate V, using a house to demonstrate the operation of a perspective machine.

30.1

BUSBY, Charles Augustus (1788–1834)

A series of designs for villas and country houses. Adapted with economy to the comforts and to the elegancies of modern life. With plans and explanations to each. By C. A. Busby, Architect.

London: Printed for J. Taylor, 1808.

20 pp, 24 pls.

30.5 × 23.5 cm

V&A

30.2

————————

————————

London: Printed for John Weale (successor to the late Josiah Taylor), 1835.

20 pp, 24 pls.

28.6 × 21.6 cm

Bodl.

The Preface (pp. 5–13) is largely devoted to a history of architecture. Beginning with conical huts made of tree branches, the history proceeds through ancient Egypt to the origin of the orders in Greece. Architecture was "brought to perfection" in Rome (p. 7). Passing quickly through the Italian Renaissance, Busby found that "palaces and villas of Italy exceed in grandeur and magnificence those of our own country." Nevertheless after "the genius of Inigo Jones" revived "the art" of architecture in Britain, such examples as Blenheim, Castle Howard, Holkham, and Wanstead could "rival the proudest examples of Italian splendour" (p. 9). Afterward Robert Adam "produced a remarkable change in the taste of the day": some of his designs "are elegantly conceived, and beautiful in their effect," but in many cases there is "incongruity and confusion" in the decorations as well as "misapplication of members and redundancies of ornament" (p. 10). While Busby praised Sir William Chambers for his "correct and classical taste, derived from the study of the most admired examples of the ancients," he found Adam "a mannerist, and a mere imitator of their defects" (p. 11). Busby found much to praise in the Greek Revival style: the *"boldness* of its parts" and its "elegant ornaments" were "particularly well adapted to small and simple buildings" (p. 11). But the Egyptian Revival was an "absurd" and "sickly fashion" (p. 11).

    Busby concluded the Preface with a few remarks on architectural composition. He disagreed with those "modern theorists"[1] who recommended that rural buildings should have "irregular masses, and assemblages of light and shade," in order to accord with their picturesque natural surroundings. Instead he suggested that a building "forms only a *component* part of the scenery; and that all the beautiful effects of light and shade, of colour and outline, are produced by the contrast of the regularity of the building with the picturesque variety of nature" (pp. 12–13).

The letterpress concludes with a brief announcement that Busby had received the Gold Medal of the Royal Academy (p. 14), and descriptions of the plates (pp. 15–20).

The plates depict plans and elevations of 14 designs; the elevations are shown with surrounding scenery, and are elegantly executed in aquatint and color tinting. The designs include one "small Country House," eight villas, one double house, and four country houses. All are perfectly symmetrical, and embellished with elegant Neoclassical ornament, including segmental and semicircular relieving arches, Doric and Ionic porticoes, gables, and pediments. Several designs include bow fronts or domed rotundas. One of the smallest designs is the "small Country House" suitable for "a small family" (p. 15). Shown in Plate 1, the one-story facade consists of a door framed by a Doric portico and flanked by two windows. The plan includes a hall, a kitchen, a parlor, a drawing room, and two bedrooms. The largest design (Plates 23, 24) measures 104 feet by 43 feet in plan, and includes a dining room, drawing room, library, music room, parlor, and two bedrooms on the ground floor. The chamber floor contains four bedrooms. The facade consists of a two-story tetrastyle Ionic portico flanked by one-story wings, each five windows wide and ornamented with Doric pilasters.

1. See for example James Malton, *An Essay on British Cottage Architecture* (1798; *q.v.*).

31.1 †
BUTLER, William Deane
Model farm-houses and cottages for Ireland, and other improving countries; being a series of designs.

London, 1837.

Reference: Michael McMordie, "Picturesque Pattern Books and Pre-Victorian Designers," *Architectural History* 18 (1975), 56.

I have been unable to locate a copy of this book. The title clearly indicates it contains designs for dwellings.

32.1
CAMPBELL, Colen (1676–1729)
Vitruvius Britannicus, or the British architect, containing the plans, elevations, and sections of the regular buildings, both publick and private, in Great Britain, with variety of new designs; in 200 large folio plates, engraven by the best hands; and drawn either from the buildings themselves, or the original designs of the architects; in II volumes Vol. I [*or* II]. by Colen Campbell Esqr.
Vitruvius Britannicus, ou l'architecte Britannique, contenant les plans, elevations, & sections des bâtimens reguliers, tant particuliers que publics de la Grande Bretagne, compris en 200 grandes planches gravez en taille douce par les meilleurs maitres, et tous ou destinez des bâtimens memes, ou copiez des desseins originaux des architectes: en deux tomes. Tome I [*or* II]. Par le Sieur Campbell.
Cum privilegio regis.

London: Sold by the author, John Nicholson, Andrew Bell, W. Taylor, Henry Clements, and Jos. Smith, 1715 [*or* 1717].

[*Volume I:*] 10 pp, 100 pls.

[*Volume II:*] 8 pp, 100 pls.

42.5 × 27.3 cm

MnU

32.2
_____

_____

London: Sold by the author, John Nicholson, Andrew Bell, W. Taylor, Henry Clements, and Jos. Smith, 1717.

[*Volume I:*] 100 pls.

[*Volume II:*] 8 pp, 100 pls.

47.0 × 29.0 cm

PPL

32.3
_____

Vitruvius Britannicus, ⟨ . . . as 1715–1717 . . . ⟩ deux tomes. Tome. I [*or* II]. ⟨ . . . as 1715–1717 . . . ⟩ .

[N. loc.: N. pub., n.d.].

[*Volume I:*] 12 pp, 100 pls.

[*Volume II:*] 12 pp, 100 pls.

46.7 × 29.8 cm

MH

32.4
_____

[*See Volumes I and II in Entry 33.4.*]

The commentary for Entry 32 is combined with that for Entry 33 below.

33.1
CAMPBELL, Colen (1676–1729)
The third volume of Vitruvius Britannicus: or, the British architect. Containing the geometrical plans of the most considerable gardens and plantations; also the plans, elevations, and sections of the most regular buildings, not published in the first and second volumes. With large views,

in perspective, of the most remarkable edifices in Great Britain. Engraven by the best hands in one hundred large folio plates. By Colen Campbell, Esquire, Architect to His Royal Highness the Prince of Wales.

Vitruvius Britannicus: ou, l'architecte Britannique: contenant les plans des jardins les plus considerables, aussi les plans, elevations, & sections des batimens reguliers, ne sont pas encore publies dans les deux premiers tomes. Avec quelques veues, en perspective, des masons les plus celebres de la Grande Bretagne. Compris en 100 grandes planches gravez en taille douce par les plus habiles maitres. Par le Sieur Campbell, Architecte de Son Altesse Royale le Prince de Galles. Tome III. Cum privilegio regis.

London: Printed; and sold by the author; and by Joseph Smith, 1725.

5–12 pp, 100 pls.

42.5 × 28.3 cm

MnU

33.2 ‡

_____

_____

London: Printed; and sold by the author; and by Joseph Smith, 1725[?].

5–12 pp, 102 pls.

Reference: Reprint (New York: Benjamin Blom, 1967).

33.3

_____

The third volume of Vitruvius Britannicus: or, the British architect. Containing the geometrical plans of the most considerable gardens and plantations; also the plans, elevations, and sections of the most regular buildings, not publish'd in the first and second volumes. With large views, in perspective of the most remarkable edifices in Great Britain. Engraven by the best hands in one hundred large folio plates. By Colen Campbell Esquire, Architect to His Royal Highness the Prince of Wales.

Vitruvius Britannicus: ou, l'architecte Britannique: contenant les plans des jardins les plus considerables, aussi les plans, elevations, & sections des batimens reguliers, qui ne sont pas publiés dans les deux premiers tomes. Avec quelques veues, en perspective, des maisons les plus celebres de la Grande Bretagne. Compris en cent grandes planches gravées en taille douce par les plus habiles maitres. Par le Sieur Campbell, Architecte de Son Altesse Royale le Prince de Galles. Tome III. Cum privilegio regis.

London: Printed in the year 1731.

12 pp, 100 pls.

46.4 × 29.8 cm

MH

Vitruvius Britannicus, ⟨ . . . as 1715–1717 . . . ⟩ architects; in III volumes Vol. I [or II, or III]. by Colen Campbell Esqr. ⟨ . . . as 1715–1717 . . . ⟩ architectes: en trois tomes. Tome. I [or II, or III]. Par le Sieur Campbell. Cum privilegio regis.

[N. loc.: N. pub., n.d.].

[*Volume I:*] 12 pp, 100 pls.

[*Volume II:*] 12 pp, 100 pls.

[*Volume III:*] 12 pp, 100 pls.

52.2 × 37.5 cm

MdBP

Originally conceived as a two-volume work, *Vitruvius Britannicus* was first published in 1715 and 1717. The first volume contains a title page (Plate 1), a dedication to George I (Plate 2), a two-page Introduction, a five-page description of the subjects illustrated in the plates (pp. 3–7), a list of the plates (also on p. 7), a fourteen-year Royal License,[1] a two-page list of subscribers, and plates numbered 3 through 100 (14 double plates and 70 single plates). Volume II consists of a title page (Plate 1), a six-page description of the subjects illustrated in the plates (pp. 1–6), a list of the plates (also on p. 6), a two-page list of subscribers, and plates numbered 2 through 100 (4 quadruple plates, 13 double plates, and 57 single plates).

A new issue of Volume I appeared in 1717. The title page was printed from the same plate as the title page to Volume II: each "II." was altered by erasure to become a "I."

Both volumes were issued again with undated title pages.[2] Volume I contains a title page (Plate 1), a dedication (Plate 2), a two-page introduction, eight pages explaining and listing the plates, and plates numbered 3 through 100. Volume II contains a title page (Plate 1), 12 pages explaining and listing the plates, and plates numbered 2 through 100. The descriptions and lists of plates in both volumes are printed in French as well as in English.

Volume III first appeared in 1725. The edition at the University of Minnesota includes a title page (Plate 1), a dedication to the Prince of Wales (Plate 2), two pages of subscribers, six pages describing and listing the plates, and plates numbered 3 through 100 (24 double plates, 50 single plates).

Another 1725 edition of Volume III, reprinted by Benjamin Blom, Inc., includes an additional double plate with a view, an elevation, and a plan of Umberslade (Plates 101/102). In this edition Umberslade is mentioned briefly in the plate descriptions (p. 12), but is curiously absent from the list of plates.

A new edition of Volume III appeared in 1731. The title page (Plate 1) is followed by a ten-page explanation of the plates in both English and French, a two-page list of the plates in both English and French, and plates numbered 3 through 100. Umberslade is mentioned in the plate descriptions (p. 10). The list of plates provides for a dedication (Plate 2) and an illustration of Umberslade (Plate 101), but neither appears in copies at Harvard University or the Boston Public Library.

All three volumes were issued at least once again, as a set with undated title pages.

The first two volumes of *Vitruvius Britannicus* contain a brief introduction, short letterpress descriptions of each subject illustrated in the plates, other preliminaries, and plans, elevations, and sections of 74 structures, including 61 dwellings. Considered as a collection of plates illustrating architectural subjects, *Vitruvius Britannicus* was impressive but not unique. Indeed the recent collection of views by Leonard Knyff and Johannes Kip, *Britannia Illustrata* (London, 1707), clearly surpassed Campbell's book in the richness and detail of its topographical views. But *Vitruvius Britannicus* was important and unique in two respects: it was the first British book to illustrate a series of the author's own executed designs, and—of special importance—Campbell composed the letterpress and arranged the plates to encourage the redirection and reform of British architectural taste.[3]

Campbell's remarks on architectural taste, which are mostly confined to the Introduction, are too brief, ambiguous, and self-contradictory to constitute a complete and comprehensive theoretical program. Nevertheless his two principal points are clear: that British architecture since Inigo Jones was superior to the work of contemporary Continental architects, and that British architecture should henceforth reject "Modern" practices in favor of "Ancient" principles.

Illuminating his first point, Campbell suggested that British deference to foreign models was the result of traveling abroad at a young and impressionable age, when the young architect or patron would be "more apt to be imposed upon by the Ignorance or Partiality of others, than to judge truly of the Merit of Things by the Strength of Reason" (I, 1). What young tourists saw was the "affected and licentious" work of Italian architects such as Bernini and Fontana, or the "Extravagant" designs of Borromini, "who has endeavoured to debauch Mankind with his odd and chimerical Beauties, where the Parts are without Proportion, Solids without their true Bearing, Heaps of Materials without Strength, excessive Ornaments without Grace, and the Whole without Symmetry" (I, 1). In contrast Campbell praised the architecture of Inigo Jones for its "Regularity," "Beauty," and "Majesty" (I, 2). Wishing perhaps to flatter architects of a senior generation in addition to praising the general excellence of British architecture, he also lauded the work of Bruce, Vanbrugh, Archer, Wren, Wynne, Talman, Hawksmoor, and James (I, 2). Campbell conveniently ignored the contradiction implied by his praise of architects such as Talman and especially Archer, whose work exhibited much of the Continental Baroque style that Campbell had just finished condemning.

The controversy between the "Ancients" and "Moderns" is introduced in the second paragraph of the Introduction. The designs illustrated in *Vitruvius Britannicus*, Campbell said, would "admit of a fair Comparison with the best of the *Moderns*." Unfortunately a comparison of British work with "the *Antiques*" was "out of the Question"; Campbell did not explain this point clearly, but he suggested that Antique practice, like the Latin language, had been corrupted by succeeding generations and therefore could not be known (I, 1). With these brief remarks he recalled the long-standing philosophical quarrel between "Ancients" and "Moderns" that had engaged the Royal Society from its foundation in 1660 in an argument over Classical scholarship and Classical learning, a debate that lasted well into the eighteenth century.[4] Although the "quarrel" had little effect on English architecture before Campbell, it was the subject of acrimonius contention among French architects: François Blondel and the "Ancients" called for strict adherence to Classical models, while Claude Perrault and the "Moderns" suggested that a degree of moderation and change would be appropriate in the orders and in composition.[5] The French debate notwithstanding, it may have been the literary aspects of the debate in England that most interested Campbell. As Joseph Levine has shown, increasingly accurate Classical philology and archaeology among the "Ancients" threatened those "Moderns" who would still rely on imitation of Ancient principles: knowing Homer or Pythagoras too well, for example, would only reveal the broad gulf that differentiated Ancient manners, customs, and society from modern times.[6] The result was that "Ancient" scholars soon became more progressive than the "Moderns," revealing the unique circumstances of Ancient civilization and thus the importance of change and adaptation thereafter. The "Moderns," on the other hand, who agreed that Ancient literature could be equaled or surpassed in modern times, argued that such an achievement could be accomplished only by relying on "principles" supposedly embraced by the Ancients. But in relying on such principles, the "Moderns" still took no cognizance of the particular circumstances of Ancient life that Classical scholars continued to discover.

To some extent Campbell applied the approach of the "Moderns" to architecture. Like them he conveniently dismissed the evidence of ancient example when it suited him: comparison of modern British architecture with "the *Antiques*," he said, was "out of the Question." Instead, Campbell turned to principles: rather than travel and study in foreign lands, he recommended one "judge truly of the Merit of Things by the Strength of Reason" (I, 1). He claimed that the success of such an approach could be seen in the work of Palladio, "whose ingenious Labours will eclipse many, and rival most of the Ancients. And indeed, this excellent *Architect* seems to have arrived to a *Ne plus ultra* of his Art." Unfortunately his successors could not appreciate the principle of "Antique Simplicity," and with Palladio the "great Manner and exquisite Taste of Building" was lost (I, 1). Yet a return to Ancient principle still was possible: Inigo Jones's work exhibited all the "Regularity" of Palladio, and a measure of "Beauty" and "Majesty" as well. Campbell called attention to Vitruvian, Palladian, and Jonesian elements in many of the designs he illustrated, but he stressed the importance of principles. In his own design for a church (II, Plate 27), for example, he found the basic plan agreeable to "*Vitruvius, Palladio,* and the general Consent of the most judicious Architects, both Ancient and Modern." He also used the occasion to emphasize the great difference between Ancient principle and modern Continental practice: "The Ancients placed their chief Beauties in the justness of the Intercolumnations, the precise Proportions of the Orders and the greatness of Parts"; contradictory practices among modern European architects "must be imputed either to an entire Ignorance of Antiquity, or a Vanity to expose their absurd Novelties, so contrary to those excellent Precepts in *Vitruvius,* and so repugnant to those admirable Remains the Ancients have left us."[7]

Over four-fifths of the subjects in the first two volumes are dwellings—a proportion that clearly does not accord with Ancient principle. Indeed

Campbell implicitly suggested a reordering of the architectural genres: instead of paying greatest attention to churches, civic buildings, and palaces, he indicated that the modern country house, despite its remote and rustic location, would be the principal vehicle for Britain's return to "Ancient" principles of design.[8] In addition Campbell reserved a prominent place for his own work: the first plates of Volume I are ecclesiastical subjects, presumably inserted in deference to the traditional hierarchy of architectural types; following these are several domestic designs by Jones and Webb; then come Campbell's own designs, including the seminal design for Wanstead House. Major monuments by his contemporaries, such as Blenheim and Castle Howard, appear only later in Volume I and in Volume II, interspersed among more of his own designs.[9]

The third volume is likewise devoted largely to domestic subjects: following a view of Greenwich Hospital (Plates 3/4), nearly all the plates depict country residences or garden structures. At least five single and 12 double plates in this volume are bird's-eye views or full estate plans, and two more plates incorporate scenery and shrubbery in the vicinity of the house. This return to the topographical manner of Knyff and Kip parallels the weakening of Campbell's polemical vigor—already diminished in the second volume, and wholly absent in the third. Nevertheless these topographical views reveal a new and important interest in the relation between architecture and landscape design.[10]

Some measure of the importance of *Vitruvius Britannicus* may be seen in the list of subscribers for each volume: 303 names for Volume I, with at least a third from the peerage, 461 names for Volume II, and 696 names for Volume III—among the longest such lists in all of British architectural literature. The ratio of peers to artisans is impressively high, perhaps because Campbell's relatives and owners of buildings depicted in the plates account for a substantial portion of each list.[11] The influence of Campbell's work can also be seen in the subsequent course of architectural practice and literature. Summerson has demonstrated the seminal nature of Wanstead House (I, Plates 21, 22),[12] for example, while the role of *Vitruvius Britannicus* in shaping architectural taste is reflected in the number of subsequent volumes published with the same title: one by Badeslade and Rocque in 1739, two by Woolfe and Gandon in 1767 and 1771, two by Richardson in 1802 and 1808, and five by Robinson in 1827–1844 (*qq.v.*). Books published under this title thus extended across five generations and eventually included designs in styles ranging from the most rigorous Palladian to Elizabethan and Gothic.

1. The License was issued to Campbell, John Nicholson, Andrew Bell, William Taylor, Henry Clements, and Joseph Smith.

2. T. P. Connor indicates Vols. I and II were issued again in 1722 and in 1725, but gives no bibliographic particulars. See "The Making of 'Vitruvius Britannicus,'" *Architectural History* 20 (1977), p. 17 and n. 29. It is possible that the undated volumes I have listed as Entry 32.3 may have been issued in 1722 or 1725; but in both volumes there are parallel texts in English and French—a format which resembles the 1731 edition of Vol. III, and thus suggests these volumes were issued in 1731 or later.

3. For some of the observations in this commentary I am indebted to the following important studies: T. P. Connor, op. cit., pp. 14–30; Howard Stutchbury, *The Architecture of Colen Campbell* (Cambridge, Mass.: Harvard University Press, 1967); Summerson (1959); and Summerson (1969).

4. For discussion of the quarrel of the Ancients and Moderns in England see Richard Foster Jones, *Ancients and Moderns: A Study in the Rise of the Scientific Movement in Seventeenth-Century England* (St. Louis: Washington University Press, 1961); Joseph M. Levine, "Ancients, Moderns and History: The Continuity of English Historical Writing in the Later Seventeenth Century," *Studies in Change and Revolution*, ed. Paul Korshin (Menston: Scolar Press, 1972), pp. 43–75; and especially Levine, "Ancients and Moderns Reconsidered," *Eighteenth-Century Studies* XV:1 (Fall 1981), 72–89.

5. On the conflict between Ancients and Moderns in seventeenth-century France see Wolfgang Herrmann, *The Theory of Claude Perrault* (London: Zwemmer, 1973), passim. Connor, op. cit., pp. 18–19, indicates that Campbell's ideas "appear to follow some lines in the preface to D'Aviler's *Cours d'Architecture*."

6. See Levine, "Ancients and Moderns Reconsidered," pp. 82–83, 84, 86.

7. II, 1–2. Note that in this comment, published in 1717, Campbell also acknowledged the authority of Ancient "Remains." However, he did not explore the subject of Classical archaeology any further. Connor, op. cit., p. 21, observed that the strict principles Campbell praised did not always correspond with elements of the designs he illustrated: a design inscribed to James Stanhope (II, Pl. 86), for example, is copied from Palladio's "most mannerist design" for the Palazzo Valmarana.

8. Investigation of the actual form of ancient Roman country villas had to await Robert Castell, whose *Villas of the Ancients* was published in 1728 (*q.v.*).

9. On Wanstead see Summerson (1959) and Summerson (1969). For an analysis of all the designs appearing in *Vitruvius Britannicus* see Paul Breman and Denise Addis, *Guide to Vitruvius Britannicus* (New York: Benjamin Blom, 1972).

10. Campbell provided only brief remarks on individual landscapes in his plate descriptions, but the subject was of great importance to his contemporaries: see for example Stephen Switzer, *The Nobleman, Gentleman, and Gardener's Recreation* (1715; *q.v.*); and Castell, op. cit.

11. Other lengthy subscription lists appear in James Gibbs's *Book of Architecture* (1728; *q.v.*), which has 97 peers among 480 names, and Sir William Chambers's *Treatise* (1759; *q.v.*), which has 261 names but only 52 peers. John Joshua Kirby's *Dr. Brook Taylor's Method of Perspective* (1755 edition; *q.v.*), directed more toward an audience of artisans, has only 13 peers among 337 subscribers.

12. See note 9 above.

34.1
[CARLISLE, Nicholas (1771–1847)]
Hints on rural residences.

London: [Printed by William Nicol], 1825.

[vi] + 107 pp.

24.8 × 19.1 cm

V&A

The sole illustration is a vignette on the title page, a design by John Buckler for a two-story mansion in a Tudor revival style similar to that of Peter Frederick Robinson or Thomas Frederick Hunt.[1] The elevation includes decorative chimneys, finials, bargeboards, crenellations, projecting bays, an oriel, and Tudor moldings.

Following a dedication and a table of contents, Carlisle included a brief prefatory essay in which he stated his purpose in publishing this book: "to communicate the Principles" of this "Art, and to make it's Practice generally intelligible."

The text is divided into 33 short chapters on various aspects of residential architecture, including siting, design, construction, materials, landscaping, and planting. The text is a compendium of excerpts taken from previously published books,[2] and contains no original material.

1. See Robinson, *Rural Architecture* (1823; *q.v.*), and Hunt, *Half a Dozen Hints* (1825; *q.v.*). Carlisle indicated in his conclusion that the design was by Buckler.

2. For the following books, often imprecisely cited by Carlisle, see the separate entries above and below: Richard Elsam, *An Essay on Rural Architecture* (1803); Joseph Michael Gandy, *Designs for Cottages* (1805); David Laing, *Hints for Dwellings* (1800); James Malton, *An Essay on British Cottage Architecture* (1798); John Buonarotti Papworth, *Rural Residences* (1818); Papworth, *Hints on Ornamental Gardening* (1823); James Peacock, Οικιδια (1785); Humphry Repton, *Fragments* (1816); Repton, *Sketches and Hints* (1794); William Robertson, *Designs in Architecture* (1800); Peter Frederick Robinson, *Rural Architecture* (1823); John Thomas Smith, *Remarks on Rural Scenery* (1797); and John Soane, *Sketches in Architecture* (1793). Carlisle also referred to Uvedale Price, *An Essay on the Picturesque* (London, 1794), Thomas Tredgold, *Principles of Warming and Ventilating*, 2nd ed. (London, 1824), and three essays: "Gilbert on the Ventilation of Rooms. Quarterly Journal of Science, *vol.* 13. *p.* 120"; "Journal of Science, Literature and the Arts, *No.* 33. *p.* 70"; and "Loudon's Account of the Paper Roofs used at *Tew Lodge*, in Oxfordshire."

CARR, Ralph
"Hinds' cottages at Hedgeley, Northumberland."

See COTTAGE **Improvement Society for North Northumberland,** *Entry 483.*

35.1
CARWITHAM, Thomas
The description and use of an architectonick sector, and also of the architectonick sliding plates whereby scales of all sizes are most readily and universally obtain'd for fluting pillasters and columns, and drawing the geometrical planes and uprights, in any of the five orders, according to the given diameter of a column. With several other scales, very convenient and ready for the practice of the ingenious designers of buildings. By T. Carwitham of Twickenham.

London: Printed by S. Aris for Thomas Heath, 1723.

vi + 22 pp, 5 pls.

18.2 × 11.2 cm

BL

35.2
___

The description and use of an architectonick sector, ⟨ . . . as 1723 . . . ⟩ plates, whereby ⟨ . . . as 1723 . . . ⟩ geometrical plans and uprights, ⟨ . . . as 1723 . . . ⟩ designers of building. The second edition. To which is added, an appendix, shewing the application and usefulness of the architectonick sector lines in drawing the geometrical plan and upright of a building. By T. Carwitham, Painter.

London: Printed for Thomas Heath, Mathematical Instrument-Maker, 1733.

vi + 42 pp, 10 pls.

18.4 × 11.7 cm

NN

Following a brief preface (pp. iii–vi) the text consists of a description of the sector and instructions for its use (pp. 1–22). In the second edition there is an Appendix (pp. 23–42) describing the use of the sector in "Drawing the Geometrical Plan and Upright of a Building" (pp. 23–28) and its application to other architectural problems.

The five plates in the first edition depict the sector itself and portions of Classical columns to be used for demonstration and practice. The second edition contains five more plates, four of which illustrate the use of the sector in drawing a one-room building. Figures 6 and 9 show a facade with two windows and a door, the latter framed by a pair of pilasters and a Doric entablature. Figures 7 and 8 show the building in plan. Figure 10 illustrates a method of depicting the breadth and height of an elliptical arch.

36.1
CASTELL, Robert (–1729)
The villas of the ancients illustrated. By Robert Castell.

London: Printed for the author, 1728.

[vi] + 128 + [ii] pp, 13 pls.

50.2 × 36.2 cm

CtY-BA

36.2

—————

—————

London: Printed for the author, 1728.

[ii] + 35 + [i] pp, 13 pls.

53.5 × 36.0 cm

CtY

In each edition there is a dedication to Lord Burlington, a preface, a text, an index, and 13 plates. In the larger edition the preliminaries conclude with a two-page list of subscribers; the text includes parallel columns of Latin and English on pages 1–16 and 79–93, giving Pliny's letters to Gallus and Apollinaris in the original tongue as well as in translation. In the smaller edition there is no list of subscribers and the Latin text is omitted.

In the copy of the larger edition at the Yale Center for British Art pages 81 and 82 have been misnumbered 57 and 58, and inserted before page 79. For additional variations among editions, see Laurence Hall Fowler and Elizabeth Baer, *The Fowler Architectural Collection* (Baltimore: Evergreen House Foundation, 1961), pages 67–68.

The commentary below is based on examination of the smaller edition.

On the recto of the first leaf following the title page is the dedication to Castell's patron Lord Burlington; the Preface appears on the verso. Castell suggested in the Preface that his book was only preparatory to a much greater undertaking: "A Desire I have long entertain'd of translating and explaining *Vitruvius*, determin'd me first to set about some inferior Performance in Architecture, as a necessary Preparation." Because Vitruvius had treated the villa only cursorily in his *Ten Books*, Castell chose this as his subject of inquiry: he would determine from other sources "the Rules that were observed in the situating and disposing of the Roman Villas." He noted important accounts of villas in Roman agricultural treatises, and especially descriptions by Pliny the Younger of his villas at Laurentinum and Tuscum. Although Pliny gave no rules for the "disposition" of villas, Castell observed that Pliny did point out the conventions that "were principally regarded in the placing and ordering of them, and how they were at once accommodated by the Architect for enjoying the Benefits, and for avoiding the Inconveniencies of the several Seasons." Thus Castell made Pliny's accounts the central focus of his treatise.

The text is divided into three parts. The first includes a translation, with notes, of Pliny's description of his villa at Laurentinum, "a *Villa Urbana*, or Country House of Retirement near the City" (pp. 1–4).[1] Castell also presented extended remarks on several passages in Pliny's text, including conjectural descriptions of the form and arrangement of the villa (pp. 5–14). Part II contains observations, based on accounts by several Roman authors, on the proper site for a villa, the arrangement of the villa itself, and the treatment of the surrounding grounds (pp. 15–22). Part III includes a translation, with notes, of Pliny's description of his villa at Tuscum (pp. 23–26), followed by lengthier discussions of several passages in Pliny's text (pp. 27–34). A short conclusion on page 35 summarizes Castell's efforts in Parts I through III.

Castell's examination of Roman literature for the principles of "situating and disposing of" villas was in accord with the renewed respect for Antique authority proclaimed in 1715 by Colen Campbell in his remarks on the future of British domestic architecture.[2] Unlike the archaeological researches carried out by later generations,[3] Castell's approach was literary: he analyzed texts describing Pliny's two villas, and brought in relevant material from Varro, Columella, Cato, Vitruvius, and Palladius. His analysis and reconstructions of Roman villas were inaccurate, partly as a result of his literary approach and partly because he sought too eagerly for proportionality, regularity, and symmetry, qualities more important to eighteenth-century architects than to the builders of Roman villas.

Nevertheless Castell's research was highly important for domestic architecture in the eighteenth century because it established certain fundamental characteristics of villa design. Foremost was the villa's function: he stated that it should facilitate the development of the mind and the body. "Besides those Hours which were taken up in the necessary Offices of Life," Pliny's time at his villa was "wholly employ'd in exercising his Mind by Study, and his Body by Hunting" (p. 34). The need for "retirement" from business and public life also was central to the villa: "the *Villa* of *Laurentinum* . . . was not a Mansion House, round which *Pliny* had a large Estate, and all Manner of Conveniencies for Life upon his own Ground; nor was it a Seat which he liv'd in at all Seasons, but where he spent only those Hours he had at leisure from the Business of the City" (p. 5). The notion of the country residence as a place for cultivation of the private individual, familiar from English seventeenth-century literature,[4] was thus confirmed by the authority of the Ancients.

As a prelude to analyzing the villa's proper location and form, Castell provided a gloss on the three parts of a Roman villa: the *villa urbana* was a dwelling set aside for the master's own use; the *villa rustica* consisted of offices for animal husbandry and farming; and the *villa fructuaria* contained storehouses for corn, wine, oil, and other products (pp. 1, 16). Turning specifically to the problem of site, Castell noted that the *villa urbana* at Laurentinum could be described in terms of four "Conveniencies . . . , *Vicinitatem Urbis, Opportunitatem Viae, Mediocritatem Villae, Modum Ruris*" (p. 6). Two of these characteristics—proximity to the metropolis and adoption of a rural way of life—would become fundamental to the location and planning of eighteenth-century English villa estates. Castell further noted that the villa should facilitate enjoyment of the surrounding countryside, "the Whole [of which] must appear like one entire beautiful Landskip," i.e., a painting of a scene in nature. He indicated that such a landscape could be accomplished in three distinct manners. In the first, "Nature appears in her plainest and most simple Dress," because the ground itself is "naturally beautiful." Second, in the formal "Manner of the more regular Gardens," great "Care [is] used in regulating the turning and winding Walks, and cutting the Trees and Hedges into various Forms." Finally, the third manner is highly irregular and explicitly rural: "in the *Imitatio Ruris*, . . . under the Form of a beautiful Country, *Hills, Rocks, Cascades, Rivulets, Woods, Buildings*, &c. were possibly thrown into such an agreeable Disorder, as to have pleased the Eye from several Views, like so many beautiful Landskips" (pp. 28, 32). Such consciously picturesque landscape surroundings became increasingly important accompaniments of villas as the eighteenth century progressed.[5]

The first five plates are lettered A through E. They depict a praetorium and villa rustica in plan, a plan of a villa urbana, villa rustica, and villa fructuaria, a parterre, a small garden structure with a tholus, and a conjectural "Disposition of the Villa . . . with its Environs" (described on pages 21–22). The eight remaining plates depict conjectural reconstructions of the estates at Tuscum and Laurentinum, plus plans of the first and second floors at Tuscum, plans of the first through third floors at Laurentinum, and a plan and elevations of the Cryptoporticus of Laurentinum.

•

For a discussion of Castell's reconstructions of Pliny's villas, along with reconstructions by many others, see Helen H. Tanzer, *The Villas of Pliny the Younger* (New York: Columbia University Press, 1924).

1. The quotation is from the Preface.

2. See Campbell, *Vitruvius Britannicus* (1715; *q.v.*).

3. See for example the following early archaeological accounts of Classical sites: Robert Wood, *The Ruins of Palmyra* (London, 1753); Wood, *The Ruins of Balbec* (London, 1757); James Stuart and Nicholas Revett, *The Antiqvities of Athens* (London, 1762 and later); and Robert Adam, *Ruins of the Palace of the Emperor Diocletian at Spalatro* (London, 1764).

4. See G. R. Hibbard, "The Country House Poem of the Seventeenth Century," *Journal of the Warburg and Courtauld Institutes* XIX:1–2 (January–June 1956), 159–174.

5. For the growing importance of "picturesque" landscape in the eighteenth century, see Christopher Hussey, *The Picturesque* (London: Putnam, 1927). For further discussion of the pictorial relationship between architecture and landscape see Chapter III, Section 9, in "The Literature of British Domestic Architecture, 1715–1842," above.

37.1

CHAMBERS, Ephraim (ca. 1680–1740)

Cyclopaedia: or, an universal dictionary of arts and sciences; containing the definitions of the terms, and accounts of the things signify'd thereby, in the several arts, both liberal and mechanical, and the several sciences, human and divine: the figures, kinds, properties, productions, preparations, and uses, of things natural and artificial; the rise, progress, and state of things ecclesiastical, civil, military, and commercial: with the several systems, sects, opinions, &c. among philosophers, divines, mathematicians, physicians, antiquaries, criticks, &c. The whole intended as a course of antient and modern learning. Compiled from the best authors, dictionaries, journals, memoirs, transactions, ephemerides, &c. in several languages. In two volumes. By E. Chambers Gent.

London: Printed for James and John Knapton, John Darby, Daniel Midwinter, Arthur Bettesworth, John Senex, Robert Gosling, John Pemberton, William and John Innys, John Osborn and Tho. Longman, Charles Rivington, John Hooke, Ranew Robinson, Francis Clay, Aaron Ward, Edward Symon, Daniel Browne, Andrew Johnston, and Thomas Osborn, 1728.

Art. "Levelling," II, 447–449; figs. 9–11 on pl. XVIII.

40.1 × 24.7 cm

MnU

37.2 ‖

Cyclopaedia: or, an universal dictionary of arts and sciences; containing an explication of the terms, and an account of the things signified thereby, in the several arts, both liberal and mechanical; and the several sciences, human and divine: the figures, kinds, properties, productions, preparations, and uses of things natural and artificial: the rise, progress, and state of things ecclesiastical, civil, military, and commercial: with the several systems, sects, opinions, &c. among philosophers, divines, mathematicians, physicians, antiquaries, critics, &c. The whole intended as a course of antient and modern learning. Extracted from the best authors, dictionaries, journals, memoirs, transactions, ephemerides, &c. in several languages. By E. Chambers. . . . The second edition, corrected and amended; with some additions. In two volumes.

London: Printed for D. Midwinter, A. Bettesworth and C. Hitch, J. Senex, R. Gosling, W. Innys and R. Manby, J. and J. Pemberton, R. Robinson, C. Rivington, A. Ward, J. and P. Knapton, E. Symon, D. Brown, T. Longman, H. Lintott, and the executors of J. Darby and F. Clay, 1738.

Art. "Levelling," II, 2 pp; figs. 9–11 on pl. XVIII.

40 × 25 cm

Reference: Information supplied by The Library Company of Philadelphia.

37.3 †

Cyclopaedia.
Third edition.

London: D. Midwinter, 1739.

Reference: Robert Collison, *Encyclopaedias: Their History throughout the Ages* (New York and London: Hafner, 1966), p. 103.

37.4

Cyclopaedia: or, an universal dictionary ⟨ . . . as 1738 . . . ⟩ . By E. Chambers. . . . The third edition corrected and amended; with some additions. In two volumes.

Dublin: Printed for Richard Gunne; Robert Owen; Geo. Risk, Jos. Leathley, Geo. Ewing, Will. Smith, Phil. Crampton, and Abrah. Bradley; John Smith; and Geo. Faulkner, Booksellers, 1740.

[*This copy has only the title page for Vol. II and 29 printed leaves.*]

Art. "Levelling," II, 2 pp [*illustrations wanting in this copy*].

40.2 × 24.5 cm

MH

37.5

Cyclopaedia: or, an universal dictionary ⟨ . . . as 1738 . . . ⟩ . By E. Chambers. . . . The fourth edition, corrected and amended; with some additions. In two volumes.

London: [Prin]ted for D. Midwinter, J. Senex, R. Gosling, W. Innys, C. Rivington, A. Ward. J. and P. [K]napton, E. Symon, S. Birt, D. Brown, T. Longman, R. Hett, C. Hitch, J. Shuckburgh, [—] Pemberton, A. Millar, and the executors of J. Darby, 1741. [*Brackets indicate portions of the page that have been torn away.*]

[*Second volume apparently wanting in this copy. Art.* "Levelling" *therefore wanting.*]

39.6 × 25.0 cm

MH

37.6

Cyclopaedia: or, an universal dictionary ⟨ . . . as 1738 . . . ⟩ of ancient and modern learning, extracted ⟨ . . . as 1738 . . . ⟩ . By E. Chambers. . . . The fifth edition. In two volumes.

[*Volume I:*] London: Printed for D. Midwinter, W. Innys, C. Rivington, A. Ward, J. and P. Knapton, E. Symon, S. Birt, D. Browne, T. Longman, R. Hett, C. Hitch, J. Shuckburgh, A. Millar, J. Pemberton, F. Gosling, M. Senex, and I. Clarke, 1741.

[*Volume II: imprint as for Volume I, but lacking* C. Rivington, E. Symon, *and* I. Clarke; *including in addition* T. Osborn, J. Rivington, and the executors of J. Darby; *dated* 1743.]

Art. "Levelling," II, 2 pp; figs. 9–11 on pl. XVIII.

40.3 × 24.7 cm

MH

37.7 †

Cyclopaedia.
Fifth edition.

Dublin: R. Gunne, 1742.

Reference: Robert Collison, *Encyclopaedias: Their History throughout the Ages* (New York and London: Hafner, 1966), p. 103.

37.8 †

Cyclopaedia.
Fifth edition.

London, 1746.

Reference: Robert Collison, *Encyclopaedias: Their History throughout the Ages* (New York and London: Hafner, 1966), p. 103.

37.9 †

Cyclopaedia; or, an universal dictionary of arts and sciences. . . . The whole intended as a course of antient and modern learning. . . . By E. Chambers. Sixth edition, corrected and amended.

London: Printed for W. Innys, etc., 1750.

42 cm

Reference: NUC

37.10

Cyclopaedia: or, an universal dictionary of arts and sciences containing ⟨ . . . as 1738 . . . ⟩ . By E. Chambers. . . . The seventh edition, corrected and amended. In two volumes. Vol. I.

London: Printed for W. Innys, J. and P. Knapton, S. Birt, R. Ware, D. Browne, T. Osborne, T. and T. Longman, C. Hitch and L. Hawes, J. Hodges, J. Shuckburgh, A. Millar, J. and J. Rivington, J. Ward, M. Senex, and the Executors of J. Darby, 1751.

Cyclopaedia: or, an universal dictionary of arts and sciences; containing ⟨ . . . as 1738 . . . ⟩ . By E. Chambers. . . . The seventh edition, corrected and amended. In two volumes. Vol. II.

London: Printed for W. Innys, J. and P. Knapton, S. Birt, D. Browne, T. Longman, R. Hett, C. Hitch and L. Hawes, J. Hodges, J. Shuckburgh, A. Millar, J. and .J [sic] Rivington, W. Ward, M. Senex, and the Executors of J. Darby, 1752.

Art. "Levelling," II, 2 pp; figs. 9–11 on pl. XVIII.

40.0 × 25.3 cm

ICU

37.11

[Volumes I and II:]

Cyclopaedia: or, an universal dictionary of arts and sciences. Containing an explanation of the terms, and an account of the several subjects, in the liberal and mechanical arts, and the sciences, human and divine. Intended as a course of ancient and modern learning. By E. Chambers. . . . With the supplement, and modern improvements, incorporated in one alphabet. By Abraham Rees. . . . In four volumes. Volume the first [*or* second].

London: Printed for W. Strahan, J. F. and C. Rivington, A. Hamilton, J. Hinton, T. Payne, W. Owen, B. White, B. Collins, T. Caslon, T. Longman, B. Law, T. Durham, T. Becket, C. Rivington, E. and C. Dilly, H. Baldwin, J. Wilkie, W. Nicoll, H. S. Woodfall, J. Robson and Co. J. Knox, W. Domville, T. Cadell, G. Robinson, R. Baldwin, W. Otridge, W. Davis, N. Conant, W. Stuart, J. Murray, J. Bell, W. Fox, S. Hayes, J. Donaldson, E. Johnson, and J. Richardson, 1778 [*or* 1779].

41.1 × 25.9 cm

MB

(*continued*)

† [*Volume III:*]

Cyclopaedia. . . . Volume the third.

London: W. Strahan, 1781.

f°

Reference: NUC [Entry NC 0286749] and NUC-S [Entry NSC 0047853]

† [*Volume IV:*]

Cyclopaedia. . . . Volume the fourth.

London, 1783.

44 cm

Reference: NUC [Entry NC 0286755]

[*Volume V:*]

Cyclopaedia: or, an universal dictionary ⟨ . . . as 1778 Vol. I . . . ⟩ sciences human ⟨ . . . as 1778 Vol. I . . . ⟩ supplement and modern ⟨ . . . as 1778 Vol. I . . . ⟩ Rees. . . . Volume the fifth. Containing the addenda, index, arrangement of the plates, and the plates.

London: Printed for J. F. and C. Rivington, A. Hamilton, T. Payne and Son, W. Owen, B. White and Son, T. Longman, B. Law, C. Rivington, C. Dilly, H. Baldwin, H. S. Woodfall, J. Robson, J. Knox, W. Domville, G. G. J. and J. Robinson, T. Cadell, A. Hamilton, jun. R. Baldwin, W. Ottridge, N. Conant, J. Murray, A. Strahan, W. Fox, S. Hayes, E. Johnson, W. Bent, D. Ogilvy, G. and T. Wilkie, and W. Collins, 1786.

Art. "Perspective machine," illustrated in figs. 52–56 on "Perspective" pl. III.

41.1 × 25.9 cm

MB

37.12

‖ [*Volume I:*]

Cyclopaedia: or, an universal dictionary ⟨ . . . as London, 1778 Vol. I . . . ⟩ .

Dublin: Printed by John Chambers, for W. Whitestone, W. Sleater, B. Corcoran, D. Chamberlaine, J. Potts, J. Williams, W. Colles, W. Wilson, R. Moncrieffe, T. Walker, P. Hoey, L. L. Flin, C. Jenkin, W. Hallhead, J. Beatty, W. Rainsford, and H. M'Kenly, 1778.

Reference: Information supplied by Rare Books and Manuscripts, Butler Library, Columbia University.

[*Volume II:*]

Cyclopaedia: or, an universal dictionary ⟨ . . . as London, 1778 Vol. I . . . ⟩ volumes. Volume the second.

Dublin: Printed ⟨ . . . as Dublin, 1778 Vol. I . . . ⟩ Beatty, and W. Rainsford, 1780.

43.2 × 26.9 cm

MH

[*Volume III:*]

Cyclopaedia: or, an universal dictionary ⟨ . . . as London, 1778 Vol. I . . . ⟩ volumes. Volume the third.

Dublin: Printed ⟨ . . . as Dublin, 1778 Vol. I . . . ⟩ W. Colles, R. Moncrieffe, T. Walker, P. Hoey, C. Jenkin, S. Hallhead, and J. Beatty, 1782.

Art. "Perspective machine," 2 pp.

43.2 × 26.9 cm

MH

[*Volume IV:*]

Cyclopaedia: or, an universal dictionary ⟨ . . . as London, 1778 Vol. I . . . ⟩ volumes. Volume the fourth.

Dublin: Printed by John Chambers, for W. Whitestone, W. Sleater, B. Corcoran, H. Chamberlaine, J. Potts, J. Williams, W. Colles, R. Moncreiffe, T. Walker, P. Hoey, C. Jenkin, J. Beatty, and W. M'Kenzie, 1784.

43.2 × 26.9 cm

MH

[*The fifth, or plate, volume was not issued in Dublin. The London, 1786 volume of plates was used to complete the set. This volume includes illustrations for the article "Perspective machine," figs. 52–56 on "Perspective" pl. III.*]

37.13

[*Volumes I through IV:*]

Cyclopaedia: or, an universal dictionary ⟨ . . . as London, 1778 Vol. I . . . ⟩ volumes. Volume the first [*or second, or third, or fourth*].

London: Printed for J. F. and C. Rivington, A. Hamilton, T. Payne and Son, W. Owen, B. White, T. Longman, B. Law, C. Rivington, C. Dilly, H. Baldwin, H. S. Woodfall, J. Robson, J. Knox, W. Domville, G. G. J. and J. Robinson, T. Cadell, A. Hamilton, jun. R. Baldwin, W. Otridge, N. Conant, J. Murray, A. Strahan, W. Fox, S. Hayes, E. Johnson, J. Bent, D. Ogilvy, G. and T. Wilkie, and W. Collins, 1786.

[*Volume V:*]

Cyclopaedia: or, an universal dictionary ⟨ . . . as London, 1778 Vol. I . . . ⟩ sciences human ⟨ . . . as London, 1778 Vol. I . . . ⟩ supplement and modern ⟨ . . . as London, 1778 Vol. I . . . ⟩ Rees. . . . Volume the fifth. Containing the addenda, index, arrangement of the plates, and the plates.

London: Printed ⟨ . . . as 1786 Vol. I . . . ⟩ , B. White and Son, T. Longman, ⟨ . . . as 1786 Vol. I . . . ⟩ , E. Johnson, W. Bent, D. Ogilvy, G. and T. Wilkie, and W. Collins, 1786.

Art. "Perspective machine," III, 2 pp; figs. 52–56 on "Perspective" pl. III.

41.6 × 26.5 cm

MB

37.14

Cyclopaedia: or, an universal dictionary ⟨ . . . as London, 1778 Vol. I . . . ⟩ .

Dublin: Printed by John Chambers, for W. Sleater, B. Corcoran, H. Chamberlaine, J. Potts, J. Williams, W. Colles, R. Moncrieffe, T. Walker, P. Hoey, C. Jenkin, J. Beatty, and W. M'Kenzie, 1787.

[*This copy of Vol. I is unaccompanied by further volumes.*]

43.2 × 26.9 cm

MH

37.15

‖ [*Volume I:*]

Cyclopaedia: or, an universal dictionary ⟨ . . . as London, 1778 Vol. I . . . ⟩ sciences human ⟨ . . . as London, 1778 Vol. I . . . ⟩ supplement and modern ⟨ . . . as London, 1778 Vol. I . . . ⟩ volumes. Volume the first.

London: Printed ⟨ . . . as London, 1786 Vol. V . . . ⟩ , 1788.

Reference: Information supplied by The British Library.

‖ [*Volume II:*]

Cyclopaedia: or, an universal dictionary ⟨ . . . as London, 1778 Vol. I . . . ⟩ sciences human ⟨ . . . as London, 1778 Vol. I . . . ⟩ supplement and modern ⟨ . . . as London, 1778 Vol. I . . . ⟩ volumes. Volume the second.

London: Printed ⟨ . . . as London, 1786 Vol. V . . . ⟩ , 1788.

Reference: Information supplied by The British Library.

[Volume III:]

Cyclopaedia: or, an universal dictionary ⟨ . . . as London, 1778 Vol. I . . . ⟩ sciences human ⟨ . . . as London, 1778 Vol. I . . . ⟩ supplement and modern ⟨ . . . as London, 1778 Vol. I . . . ⟩ volumes. Volume the third.

London: Printed ⟨ . . . as London, 1786 Vol. V . . . ⟩ , 1788.

Art. "Perspective machine," 2 pp.

42.6 × 26.0 cm

MBAt

‖ *[Volume IV:]*

Cyclopaedia: or, an universal dictionary ⟨ . . . as London, 1778 Vol. I . . . ⟩ sciences human ⟨ . . . as London, 1778 Vol. I . . . ⟩ supplement and modern ⟨ . . . as London, 1778 Vol. I . . . ⟩ volumes. Volume the fourth.

London: Printed ⟨ . . . as London, 1786 Vol. V . . . ⟩ , 1789.

Reference: Information supplied by The British Library.

‖ *[Volume V:]*

Cyclopaedia: or, an universal dictionary ⟨ . . . as London, 1778 Vol. I . . . ⟩ sciences human ⟨ . . . as London, 1778 Vol. I . . . ⟩ supplement and modern ⟨ . . . as London, 1778 Vol. I . . . ⟩ Rees. . . . Volume the fifth. Containing the addenda, index, arrangement of the plates, and the plates.

London: Printed ⟨ . . . as London, 1786 Vol. V . . . ⟩ , 1788.

Reference: Information supplied by The British Library.

37.16 ‖

Cyclopaedia: or, an universal dictionary ⟨ . . . as London, 1778 Vol. I . . . ⟩ .

London: Printed for T. Longman, B. Law, C. Dilly, H. S. Woodfall, W. Domville, G. G. and J. Robinson, T. Cadell, R. Baldwin, W. Otridge, A. Strahan, F. and C. Rivington, W. Goldsmith, T. Payne, S. Hayes, W. Bent, G. and T. Wilkie, B. C. Collins, P. Wynne, C. D. Piguenitt, C. and G. Kearsley, W. March, A. Hamilton, T. Cadell, jun. and W. Davies, W. Owen, H. Murray, A. Galbraith, and E. Johnson, 1795.

[Four volumes, dated 1795, in five.]

Art. "Perspective machine," III, 2 pp; figs. 52–56 on "Perspective" pl. III.

Reference: Information supplied by The New York Botanical Garden Library.

Cyclopaedia; or, an universal dictionary of arts and sciences. Containing an explanation of the terms, and an account of the several subjects, in the liberal and mechanical arts, and the sciences, human and divine. . . . By E. Chambers. . . . With the supplement, and modern improvements, incorporated in one alphabet. By Abraham Rees. . . .

London: Printed for T. Longman, 1795–1797.

5 vols.

45 cm

Reference: NUC-S

In the entries above I have tried as much as possible to arrange individual volumes in discrete and complete sets. In particular, I have attempted to group together volumes having similar or identical imprint dates. Often this has meant combining selected volumes from more than one location to construct a single, hypothetical "set." The organizational advantages of such an arrangement need to be weighed against the admitted danger of suggesting a false publication history.

Six volumes could not be combined conveniently into sets. They are described below in brief:

1781, Volume V: London: Printed for W. Strahan, J. F. and C. Rivington, A. Hamilton, J. Hinton . . . [*and 33 other names*], 1781. Information supplied by the Department of Printed Books, Bodleian Library.

1784, Volume I: London: Printed for W. Strahan, J. F. and C. Rivington, A. Hamilton, T. Payne, W. Owen, B. White, T. Longman, B. Law, C. Rivington, C. Dilly, H. Baldwin, J. Wilkie, H. S. Woodfall, J. Robson, J. Knox, W. Domville, T. Cadell, G. Robinson, A. Hamilton, jun. R. Baldwin, W. Otridge, N. Conant, J. Murray, W. Fox, S. Hayes, J. Bowen, E. Johnson, S. A. Cumberlege, and D. Ogilvy, 1784. Information supplied by The British Library.

1784, Volume II: Imprint as 1784, Volume I. Information supplied by Clifford E. Barbour Library, Pittsburgh Theological Seminary.

1789, Volume V: London: Printed for J. F. and C. Rivington, ⟨ . . . as London, 1786 Vol. V . . . ⟩ W. Collins, 1789. Information supplied by Special Collections, University Library, University of Delaware.

1791, Volume I: London: Printed for J. F. and C. Rivington, A. Hamilton, T. Payne, W. Owen, B. White and Son, T. Longman, B. Law, C. Dilly, H. Baldwin, H. S. Woodfall, J. Robson, W. Domville, G. G. J. and J. Robinson, T. Cadell, A. Hamilton, jun. R. Baldwin, W. Otridge, J. Murray, A. Strahan, W. Goldsmith, W. Fox, S. Hayes, E. Johnson, W. Bent, D. Ogilvy, G. and T. Wilkie, B. C. Collins, and J. Galbraith, 1791. Copy at MBAt.

1791, Volume V: Imprint as 1791, Volume I. Copy at MBAt.

Finally, a few variant issues require brief mention. In addition to the issue of the second edition cited in Entry 37.2, BLC lists another issue, also dated 1738, with a different imprint (London: D. Midwinter, J. Senex . . .). In addition to the issue of the seventh edition cited in Entry 37.10, NUC (Entry NC 0286745) lists another issue, also dated 1751–1752, with a different imprint (London: D. Midwinter). In the 1786 edition described in Entry 37.13 the imprints in Volumes I through IV are identical, while the imprint for Volume V varies slightly; the British Library has copies of Volumes I, II, and IV, also dated 1786, in which the imprints are identical to that in Volume V of Entry 37.13.

The publication history of Chambers's *Cyclopaedia* may be divided into two distinct phases. Between 1728 and 1752 at least ten issues or editions were published, including the first through "seventh" editions published in London, additional "third" and "fifth" editions published in Dublin, and a second issue of the London "fifth" edition. In 1753 a two-volume *Supplement* was added to the final edition. The second phase began in 1778, when Abraham Rees started to combine the original *Cyclopaedia* and the *Supplement* into one continuous text, with additions and changes, and with a new, separate volume for the plates. The exact history of this venture is exceptionally complex; it appears that the first copies of each volume appeared, respectively, in 1778, 1779, 1781, 1783, and 1781. Additional issues of each volume appeared throughout these and subsequent years, published both in London and in Dublin; complete sets were issued in 1786, 1788–1789, and 1795.

Major changes in the architectural subject matter of the *Cyclopaedia* occurred only once, along with the change of editors. In the edition of 1728, the article "Architecture" (I, 129–130; 1 pl.) is essentially an historical account of the subject from biblical Tyre through Greece, Rome, medieval France, and Renaissance France and Italy. The article includes a brief account of architectural publication since Vitruvius.[1] The one plate illustrates details and modular proportions of the five orders. Another article, "Levelling," offers the only illustration of a house. Figure 11 on Plate XVIII, part of this article but bound opposite "Surveying," illustrates the use of a telescope and other instruments to establish the proper elevations of hills, valleys, houses, and watercourses. The house used to illustrate this technique is two stories high and three windows wide; there is a door in the middle of the side elevation. The house lacks any other articulation.

In the first Rees edition (1778–1786) the "Architecture" article again includes an historical account, plus additional brief remarks on solidity, convenience, beauty, order, disposition, proportion, decorum, and economy. There are also short articles on "Architecture, civil," "Architecture, counterfeit," "Architecture, military," "Architecture, naval," and "Architecture in perspective," with cross-references to articles on each of the orders, building,[2] ceilings, doors, foundations, roofs, walls, windows, carpentry and other trades, brick and other materials, and fortification. The sole plate illustrates the five orders, moldings, examples of carving and masonry, and the plan and elevation of a basilica.

The illustrations for "Levelling" were redrawn for the Rees edition, and in the process the figure of the house was omitted. New illustrations for the article on "Perspective" demonstrate the use of a "Perspective machine."[3] The machine is shown from above in Figure 52 and in an oblique view in Figure 53. It is set up to draw the image of a distant house. To use the machine an observer would sight the house through an armature, and then move a pair of wires along the armature so they would intersect directly in front of a given point on the facade of the house. Then, by folding the armature down onto a horizontal surface, and marking the crossing point on paper, a series of points could be established to form the outline of the house. The house shown in this illustration is two stories high and three windows wide, with a door in the center of the ground floor. Curiously, here as in Ferguson's illustration, only the front half of the house is shown. Geometric solids and outlines shaped like buildings appear in Figures 44, 45, and 51.

1. Additional information is included under such headings as "Capital," "Column," "Doric," and so forth.

2. Extending over all or part of three pages, "Building" treats siting, materials, "disposition," foundations, walls, apertures, "compartition," cover, ornament, and rules for judging buildings.

3. These illustrations first appeared in 1775 in James Ferguson's treatise on perspective (q.v.).

38.1
CHAMBERS, Sir William (1723–1796)
Designs of Chinese buildings, furniture, dresses, machines, and utensils. Engraved by the best hands, from the originals drawn in China by Mr. Chambers, Architect, member of the Imperial Academy of Arts at Florence. To which is annexed, a description of their temples, houses, gardens, &c.

London: Published for the author, and sold by him: also by Mess. Dodsley; Mess. Wilson and Durham; Mr. A. Millar, and Mr. R. Willcock, 1757.

4 printed leaves, 19 pp, 21 pls.

53.3 × 36.5 cm

MH

38.2

Desseins des edifices, meubles, habits, machines, et utenciles des Chinois. Gravés sur les originaux dessinés à la Chine par Mr. Chambers, Architecte, membre de l'Académie Impériale des Arts à Florence. Auxquels est ajoutée une description de leurs temples, de leurs maisons, de leurs jardins, &c.

Londres: de l'imprimerie de J. Haberkorn; se vend chez l'auteur; & chez A. Millar & J. Nourse, 1757.

3 printed leaves, 19 pp, 21 pls.

52.1 × 36.2 cm

BL

The English and French editions are virtually identical: the plates are the same, the 19 pages of English text were translated into 19 pages in French, and the English preface and dedication to George, Prince of Wales, also were translated into French. Only the list of subscribers is missing from the French edition.

The fashion for Chinese designs in English architectural literature was nearly limited to the decade of the 1750s.[1] At the pinnacle of this fashion was Chambers's *Designs of Chinese Buildings*, certainly the most authoritative book on the subject, and also the most controversial. His designs were not so fantastic or exuberant as others, ostensibly because they were based on firsthand observations made during a voyage to China (Preface). Although subsequent scholars have seriously challenged this claim,[2] Chambers's work strongly influenced his contemporaries. More than a fourth of the 162 subscribers were peers, including the Prince of Wales and other members of the royal family. Subscribing architects included John and James Adam, James Pain, and John Vardy. Chambers's subsequent commissions for Chinese work at Kew[3] reflect the confidence and interest of the royal family in his work, and further established the Chinese taste in England.

The Preface begins with praise for Chinese "learning" and Chinese accomplishments in politics and the arts.[4] Chambers suggested that there was a "remarkable affinity" between Chinese architecture and that of "the antients," implying both came from a common source. While being careful not to praise Chinese designs too much, and thereby imply a lesser stature for modern European architecture, Chambers noted that Chinese buildings have "a singularity in their manner, a justness in their proportion, a simplicity, and sometimes even beauty, in their form, which recommend them to our notice." These qualities all would have appealed to contemporary Palladian architects in Britain. But the exuberance of actual Chinese ornament seemed at odds with such proportionality and simplicity, a problem Chambers acknowledged by admitting that

Chinese architecture does not suit European purposes; yet in extensive parks and gardens, where a great variety of scenes are required, or in immense palaces, containing a numerous series of apartments, I do not see the impropriety of finishing some of the inferiour ones in the Chinese taste. Variety is always delightful; and novelty, attended with nothing inconsistent or disagreeable, sometimes takes place of beauty.

Thus by invoking variety and novelty—qualities very similar to those which Halfpenny used to justify his Chinese designs in 1752[5]—Chambers argued that a limited number of Chinese forms could be introduced into the European vocabulary. Chambers's argument reflects his concern, as a Palladian, to accommodate the vicissitudes of popular taste without violating the established hierarchies of architectural genre or the canons of appropriate ornament. For his audience, of course, the attractions of taste far outweighed the restrictions of theory, and Chambers needed only this limited apologia before proceeding with a treatise wholly devoted to Chinese design.

Chambers's principal text is a description of Chinese temples, towers, houses, columns, machines, dress, and gardens. He supported his own observations with frequent references to du Halde's *Description géographique* (1735), the most comprehensive description of China published so far. In his account of houses (pp. 7–11; Plates VIII–X) Chambers described the plan of a typical merchant's house in Canton, and discussed the use and furnishings of individual rooms. He also described six examples of Chinese columns (pp. 11–13). Keeping in mind his Palladian audience, who would have been keenly interested in the modular proportions of a "Chinese" order,[6] he carefully specified the proportions of each example.

Chambers's most lasting contribution here was his discussion of Chinese gardens (pp. 14–19). It is doubtful that much of his information was authentic, but his ideas were very relevant to current trends in English landscape aesthetics. In stating that Chinese gardens were "laid out in a variety of scenes" (p. 15), Chambers merely reflected a common English practice, laying out landscape gardens to look like scenes painted on canvas.[7] Of the Chinese he wrote, "Their artists distinguish three different species of scenes, to which they give the appellations of pleasing, horrid, and enchanted" (p. 15). Chambers did not discuss "pleasing" scenes, apparently taking their definition for granted. The "enchanted" scenes are "what we call romantic," and depend on eliciting surprise. Scenes of horror work through the effects of contrast—through sudden transitions, for example, or striking oppositions of forms, colors, and shades.[8] Other aspects of Chinese design that Chambers discussed also reflect current practice in mid-eighteenth-century England: he described designated points from which to admire particular views, individual buildings designed to elicit specific aesthetic or sentimental responses, serpentine rivers, caves, grottoes, cascades, rustic bridges, and so forth.

Chambers's plates include elevations and plans of Chinese temples, a pagoda, a bridge, a house, gates and portals, furniture, pots and vases, teapots, boats, machines, costumes, and samples of Chinese characters. There are no illustrations of gardens. The three plates devoted to the house of a Canton merchant (Plates VIII–X) show plans of the grand and upper stories, one section, and two room interiors. The design of this house appears more substantial and less overburdened with florid ornament than designs by such contemporaries as Halfpenny, Edwards and Darly, and Decker. Nevertheless there is a characteristic European lightness and Rococo ornamentation throughout the design.

1. Serious publication began with the Halfpennys' series of *New Designs* in 1750, Edwards and Darly offered their elaborate collection of Chinese designs in 1754, and Decker published the last book devoted entirely to Chinese subjects in 1759 (*qq.v.*).

2. For an account of this and other matters concerning Chambers's book see Eileen Harris, "Designs of Chinese Buildings," Chapter 10 in John Harris, *Sir William Chambers* (London: Zwemmer, 1970). Also see R. C. Bald, "Sir William Chambers and the Chinese Garden," *Journal of the History of Ideas* XI:3 (June 1950), 287–320.

3. See his *Plans, Elevations, Sections, and Perspective Views of . . . Kew* (1763).

4. The Preface is unpaginated.

5. See below the discussion of Halfpenny's *Chinese and Gothic Architecture*. Such ideas of variety and novelty were quite possibly derived from Sir William Temple's essay on the gardens of Epicurus (1685). See Nikolaus Pevsner, *Studies in Art, Architecture, and Design* (London: Thames and Hudson, 1968), I, 82, 103.

6. Cf. Batty Langley's attempt to design a modular Gothic order in *Ancient Architecture* (1742), and Paul Decker's similar attempt in *Gothic Architecture* (1759), *qq.v.*

7. William Shenstone, for example, wrote: "I think the landskip painter is the gardiner's best designer"; published posthumously in "Unconnected Thoughts on Gardening," in *The Works in Verse and Prose, of William Shenstone* (London, 1764), II, 129. As early as 1728 Robert Castell proposed that the grounds of a villa should be arranged as if part of a picture. In his discussion of Roman villas Castell also mentioned the "Manner of Designing in *China*, [where] . . . Beauty consisted in a close Imitation of Nature; [and] where, tho' the Parts are disposed with the greatest Art, the Irregularity is still preserved" (*Villas of the Ancients*, p. 32; *q.v.*). For a thorough discussion of the relation between landscape painting and garden design see Chapter 5 in Christopher Hussey, *The Picturesque* (London: Putnam, 1927). For a recent discussion of the "Chinese" style of landscape design in eighteenth-century Britain see Patrick Conner, "China and the Landscape Garden: Reports, Engravings, and Misconceptions," *Art History* II:4 (December 1979), 429–440.

8. Chambers's remarks here prefigure those of Edmund Burke in *A Philosophical Enquiry into the Origin of Our Ideas of the Sublime and Beautiful* (London, 1757). Burke later adopted Chambers's discussion as a demonstration of part of his theory. See Eileen Harris, "Burke and Chambers on the Sublime and Beautiful," in *Essays in the History of Architecture Presented to Rudolf Wittkower* (London: Phaidon, 1967), pp. 207–213.

39.1

CHAMBERS, Sir William (1723–1796)

Plans, elevations, sections, and perspective views of the gardens and buildings at Kew in Surry, the seat of Her Royal Highness the Princess Dowager of Wales. By William Chambers. . . .

London: Printed by J. Haberkorn; published for the author, and to be had at his house; likewise of A. Millar, D. Wilson, and T. Becket; of R. and J. Dodsley; R. Sayer, A. Webley, J. Walter, and Dorothy Mercier, 1763.

1 printed leaf, 8 pp, 43 pls.

52.4 × 36.0 cm

MnU

In 1757 Chambers was appointed architect to the Princess Dowager of Wales, and his prime responsibility to her for the next six years was the transformation of Kew Gardens into a showplace of garden architecture. In 1763 Chambers published, at the king's expense, a collection of views, plans, and elevations of his work at Kew. This included general landscaping work as well as the following structures: temples of the Sun, Bellona, Pan, Solitude, Eolus, Victory, Arethusa, and Peace; the Aviary; the House of Confucius; the Alhambra; the Mosque; and especially the Great Pagoda. Chambers illustrated these buildings in plan and elevation, and occasionally in section. He also included plans, elevations, and a view of Kew Palace, and general views of the gardens.

Chambers's descriptions of the plates (pp. 1–8) are factual and dry, containing little comment on principles of landscaping or architectural design. The notable feature of this book is that Chambers included such a wide variety of styles. Only six years before, he had stipulated that a garden should have an essentially Classical disposition, and buildings in more exotic styles should be used only for occasional "variety."[1] At Kew the dominant structure was now Chinese, and the buildings in Roman style had to compete with those in Chinese, "Moresque," Turkish, Gothic, and rustic styles.

1. *Designs of Chinese Buildings* (London, 1757; *q.v.*), Preface.

40.1

CHAMBERS, Sir William (1723–1796)

A treatise on civil architecture, in which the principles of that art are laid down; and illustrated by a great number of plates, accurately designed, and elegantly engraved by the best hands. By William Chambers. . . .

London: Printed for the author, by J. Haberkorn. To be had at the author's house; likewise of A. Millar, J. Nourse, Wilson and Durham, T. Osborne, J. and R. Dodsley, R. Sayer, Piers and Webley, and J. Gretton, 1759.

2 printed leaves, iv + 85 + [i] pp, 50 pls.

52.2 × 37.1 cm

MH

40.2

A treatise on civil architecture, ⟨ . . . as 1759 . . . ⟩. The second edition.

London: Printed by J. Dixwell. To be had at the author's house; likewise of Cadell, Nourse, and Wilson; Durham; R. Dodsley; Sayer; and Webley, 1768.

1 printed leaf, iv + 86 pp, 50 pls.

57.8 × 38.1 cm

Soane

40.3

A treatise on the decorative part of civil architecture. Illustrated by fifty original, and three additional plates, engraved by Old Rooker, Old Foudrinier, Charles Grignion, and other eminent hands. By Sir William Chambers. . . . The third edition, considerably augmented.

London: Printed by Joseph Smeeton. Sold by T. Cadell, Bookseller and Printer to the Royal Academy; I. and J. Taylor; J. Walter; R. Robson; and R. Sayer, 1791.

2 printed leaves, vi + 7–137 pp, 53 pls.

56.8 × 38.1 cm

MH

40.4

A treatise on the decorative part of civil architecture, by Sir William Chambers. . . . With illustrations, notes, and an examination of Grecian architecture, by Joseph Gwilt. . . .

London: Priestley and Weale, 1825.

[*Volume I:*] li + 254 pp, frontisp. + 11 + 15 pls.

[*Volume II:*] 255–514 pp, 16–54 pls.

27.3 × 19.1 cm

MB

40.5

A treatise on the decorative part of civil architecture: illustrated by fifty= three plates, engraved by Rooker, Fourdrinier, Grignion, &c. By Sir William Chambers. . . . The fourth edition, to which are added copious notes, and an essay on the principles of design in architecture, by John B. Papworth. . . . Nine new plates, illustrative of Grecian architecture, are added to this edition.

London: Printed for J. Taylor, 1826.

iv + [iii]–ix + xlv + v–xiii + 159 pp, 9 + 53 pls.

38.7 × 28.7 cm

NNC

40.6

———

A treatise on the decorative part of civil architecture: illustrated by fifty=
three plates. By Sir William Chambers. . . . The fifth edition. To which
are added 〈 . . . as 1826 . . . 〉 Papworth . . . with nine plates illustrative
of Grecian architecture.

London: Printed for M. Taylor (nephew and successor to the late Josiah
Taylor), 1836.

2 printed leaves, 222 pp, 9 + 53 pls.

35.5 × 27.5 cm

PU

40.7 †

———

[A treatise on the decorative part of civil architecture. With illustrations,
notes, and an examination into the principles of Grecian architecture, by
Joseph Gwilt. Revised by W. H. Leeds.]

[London: Issued in installments as a supplement to *The Building News,*
beginning 6 January 1860.]

viii + 319 pp, portr. + 35 pls.

4°

Reference: NUC, BM, and a notice in *The Building News* VI (13 January
1860), p. 21.

40.8

———

A treatise on the decorative part of civil architecture by Sir William Chambers. . . . With illustrations, notes, and an examination of Grecian architecture, by Joseph Gwilt. . . . Revised and edited by W. H. Leeds.

London: Lockwood and Co., 1862.

viii + 336 pp, 11 + 54 pls.

21.6 × 28.6 cm

MnU

The publication history of Chambers's *Treatise* spans more than a hundred years. The first edition, published in 1759, was dedicated to the Earl of Bute and included a two-page list of subscribers. At least a sixth of the 261 subscribers were peers, and another 11 were listed as architects. There followed a four-page preface and 85 pages of text, illustrated by 50 plates. The next edition, in 1768, retained the dedication, omitted the list of subscribers, incorporated minor corrections and modifications in the text, and retained the same 50 plates. The edition of 1791 was the final one of Chambers's lifetime, and included a two-page dedication to the king, a six-page preface, a text expanded to 131 pages, plus the 50 original and three additional plates.

By 1825 continuing demand for the *Treatise* warranted a two-volume edition prepared by Joseph Gwilt. Now quarto rather than folio in size, this edition included a new dedication to the king written by Gwilt, a new list of subscribers, a long preface by Gwilt, a biography of Chambers by Thomas Hardwick, and "An Examination of the Elements of Beauty in Grecian Architecture" with 11 plates, by Gwilt, intended as a complement to Chambers's emphasis on Rome. All of this preceded the full text and plates from Chambers's third edition, to which Gwilt then added notes, four text illustrations, one additional plate of the Corinthian order, a glossary, and an index. In 1826 John Buonarotti Papworth issued another edition, containing a dedication to Sir John Soane written by Papworth, a biography of Chambers, an essay on the principles of architectural design by Papworth with nine plates, a description of these plates, and then all of the material from Chambers's third edition. With some renumbering of pages this also was the format of Papworth's 1836 edition. Another edition, by W. H. Leeds, was issued serially in *The Building News*, Volume VI, beginning with the number for 6 January 1860. Leeds also edited the final edition, published in 1862. Both of the Leeds editions were based on the Gwilt edition of 1825.

Chambers returned to England in 1775 from an extended stay on the Continent, having studied for a year under J. F. Blondel in Paris, with an additional five years in Italy. In 1756 Isaac Ware issued his weighty *Complete Body of Architecture* (q.v.), the first British work to approach the authority and scope of Italian architectural treatises. By comparison the prospectus Chambers issued in 1757 for his own treatise was modest: he proposed "publishing by subscription, designs of villas, temples, gates, doors, and chimney pieces; . . . at least sixty large folio-plates . . . with the necessary descriptions and references."[1] Such a collection of plates and descriptions, if completed as described, might have differed little from typical handbooks by Halfpenny and other contemporary designers.[2] The prospectus revealed no interest in theory, nor any intent to prepare a comprehensive work like Ware's. But as finally issued in 1759, Chambers's *Treatise* displayed an uncommon attention to theoretical matters and incorporated an unusually broad range of material.[3] As announced on the title page, this was an illustrated compendium of the principles of civil architecture, and accordingly Chambers chronicled the origin of building in primitive times, described the orders and their proportions, and considered architectural elements such as doors, windows, gates, piers, chimneypieces, and ceilings. Yet the *Treatise* was patently incomplete: Chambers offered few practical remarks concerning the siting, planning, and massing of buildings, the furnishing and function of rooms, or the work of builders, carpenters, and other artisans. At the end of the 1759 edition he promised that if it were well received, he would complete the treatise with a second volume devoted to "Conveniency, OEconomy and Strength" (1759, p. 84). But by 1791 it was clear that Chambers would never produce an additional volume: he changed the title to reflect his focus on "decorative," i.e., not mechanical, subjects, and remarked that any discussion of "convenience, strength, or economical management of buildings" would be beyond his expertise and therefore presumptuous (1791, p. 135). He noted in retrospect that his goals had been only to impart "precepts" to "gentlemen," and to instruct "travellers"—grand tourists—in means of appreciating the "most valued productions of the countries" they might visit (1791, pp. 135–136).

The preface of the 1759 edition primarily concerns the importance of architecture: "the productions of Architecture are lasting monuments, command universal attention, and record to latest posterity the greatness, wealth, dignity, virtues, and atchievements [sic] of those they commemorate" (1759, p. i). Architecture facilitates commerce, which in turn generates wealth and luxury; likewise, "by furnishing Men with convenient habitations," architecture "procures them that ease of body, and vigour of mind, which are necessary for inventing and improving Arts" (1759, p. ii). Thus architecture is, in effect, fundamentally necessary and responsible for the highest achievements of modern civilization. A short comment on the subject of architectural expression is far more intriguing and original. Perhaps inspired by increasing attention among his contemporaries to the study of linguistics,[4] Chambers attempted to explain the process of architectural expression through an analogy with language: "Materials in Architecture are like words in Phraseology; which singly have little or no power, and may be so arranged as to excite contempt; yet when combined with Art, and expressed with energy, they actuate the mind with unbounded sway" (1759, p. ii).

The first chapter further expands the intellectual scope of the *Treatise.* Unlike contemporary manuals[5] the discussion does not center on such topics as tools, measurement, or drainage. Rather, it concerns the origin of building, from the primitive state described by Vitruvius through the inventions of Greece and Rome. Chambers illustrated a primitive conical hut and a rude post-and-lintel structure as examples of the earliest forms of building, plus a more sophisticated hut, resembling that in Laugier's *Essai* of 1753,[6] to illuminate the metamorphosis from primitive structures to the Doric house or temple.

In the 1791 edition Chambers expanded the first chapter. Considering the progress of architecture in Roman and later times, he addressed a problem that had long concerned French theorists: whether forms and proportions are absolute, and to what extent they may be modified in response to local needs and circumstances.[7] On the one hand he suggested there was a general, paradigmatic model in nature that underlay antique examples: "Nature is the supreme and true model of the imitative arts . . . and the antique is to the architect, what nature is to the painter or sculptor; . . . the model upon which his taste must be formed" (1791, p. 23). But throughout history architects had been unable to achieve this ideal completely, he said, because of poor quality of construction and ineffective expression. Both Greece and Rome had failed in this way. Yet

40.8 CHAMBERS, WILLIAM

others, ignorant of Classical models, had achieved progress: "To those usually called Gothick architects, we are indebted for the first considerable improvements in construction; there is a lightness in their works, an art and boldness of execution" (1791, p. 24). Chambers thus proposed study of Gothic structures as a means to understand better the "taste" and "ingenuity" with which they were built (1791, p. 24). Underlying this proposal was an apparent conviction that architectural beauty is relative to local geographic and climatic circumstances.[8] Chambers emphasized this point in discussing the "distribution" (or plan) of a building and the materials of which it is made:

of distribution, . . . the artist may collect his general idea, from books or observations, made upon buildings erected for various purposes, in different climates and ages; but it is only by practice that he can become expert, in discovering the advantages, or defects of situation; the nature of climates, or expositions; the qualities of air, water, soil, and many other things necessary to be known: and it is only by a thorough acquaintance with the customs, and modes of living of his own times; and with the dispositions, amusements, occupations, and duties, of his cotemporaries; that he can effectually learn, how to supply their wants, or gratify their wishes.

The selection of materials also depends almost entirely on local circumstances:

When therefore an artist has fixed his abode in any particular country, or great city; it will be best, to limit his researches at first, to that place alone: informing himself of the different quarries, woods, kilns, sea ports or other markets from whence it is supplied with materials for building; as also of the different natures and degrees of goodness of these materials, the properest times for providing them, the best means of transporting them to the places of their destination; [and] their value . . . [etc.].[9]

The chapter concludes with a defense of Roman architectural styles. Chambers noted that when "Grecian" architecture was first introduced, it was "extolled into repute"; nevertheless, he claimed, the sight of "Attick designs . . . excited desires for no more," and thus Roman architecture quickly vanquished that of Greece. Unfortunately in recent years the "*Gusto Greco*" had returned, threatening "another invasion," and therefore he had decided to insert remarks defending Roman architecture throughout the third edition (1791, p. 26).[10]

The next seven chapters concern the orders, with attention to their individual parts, their "properties" and characters, their proper use, their "enrichments," their origins, and moldings. In discussing these subjects Chambers frequently referred to the writings and designs of other architects, including Alberti, Barbaro, Blondel, Cataneo, de Chambray, de Cordemoy, de l'Orme, Gibbs, Le Clerc, Palladio, Perrault, Scamozzi, Serlio, Vignola, Vitruvius, and Wotton. Chambers also referred to his own measurements of "many ancient and modern celebrated buildings, both at Rome and in other parts of Europe" (p. 47), such as the Pantheon, the Basilica of Antoninus, the arches of Titus and Septimius Severus, and the Theater of Marcellus. Chambers clearly was unwilling to accept the authority of any historical practitioner or of an ideal standard, and instead selected the individual examples that he felt were proven best by time and by common consent. But in adopting such a method of approach to the orders, he recognized the potential for licentiousness. If, for example, the ancient Roman practice of using a Corinthian order with an Ionic entablature would "contribute towards the perfection of that which all see, and all approve; it cannot justly be censured."

This liberty, however, of deviating from the origin or reason of things, was by the ancients; and must by us, be exercised with great caution: as it opens a wide door to whim and extravagance, and leaves a latitude to the composer, which often betrays, and hurries him into ridiculous absurdities. . . . [For example] Boromini, . . . in attempting to conquer by novelty, and quitting the ancient rules, was submerged in an ocean of extravagance. (pp. 62–63)

Further chapters treat pilasters, Persians, caryatids, pedestals, the "application" of the orders, intercolumniations, arcades, arches, orders above orders, basements, attics, pediments, balustrades, gates, doors, piers, windows, niches, statues, chimneypieces, block cornices and entablatures, proportions of rooms, and ceilings. Examining these subjects in the light of literary argument, archaeological evidence, and modern example, Chambers addressed two theoretical matters that are of special interest. The first is the expressive effect that can be achieved through attention to architectural proportion. For example:

whenever the masses and sub-divisions [of a building] are few in number; firmly marked by quick and opposite transitions; the breadths and widths being predominant; we are impressed with ideas of grandeur, majesty, manly strength, and decorous gravity. And when the composition appears more detailed; the changes gradual and less contrasted; the heights predominant; we are impressed with ideas of elegance, delicacy, lightness, and gaiety.[11]

Questioning the grounds on which certain proportions were traditionally favored, Chambers noted that accepted ratios of height to width in doorways had not been fixed according to any universal standard; instead they had become established through habitual use and custom over a long period of time. Thus he concluded that the beauty of proportions was dependent on circumstance and custom:

We may, I believe, look for the origin of many proportions in the same source. . . . And the pleasure excited in us at their sight, must, I am persuaded, be ascribed, rather to convenience, custom, prejudice, or to the habit of connecting other ideas with these figures, than to any peculiar charm inherent in them, as some are disposed to maintain.[12]

The "habit of connecting" ideas—association—was of growing importance to British aesthetics during the eighteenth century. Chambers did not consider the subject in his first edition, but in the third edition he spoke of association favorably. Continuing his discussion of architectural proportion, he noted that some people believed in an absolute standard of harmonic proportion, while others asserted that beautiful proportions were established by mutual consent and imitation. Chambers adopted the latter rationale, stating that the "effect" of visible objects on the observer

is not alone produced, by the image on the organ of sight; but by a series of reasoning and association of ideas, impressed, and guiding the mind in its decision. Hence it is that the same object pleases one, and is disliked by another; or delights to-day, is seen with indifference, or disgust, to-morrow. For if the object seen, had alone the power of affecting; as is the case with sounds; it must affect all men alike, and at all times in the same manner, which by long and repeated experience, we know is not the case.[13]

The text concludes with brief descriptions of 19 plates containing designs for "Casines [small villas or pavilions], Temples, Gates, Doors, &c.," plus a twentieth plate of "ornamental utensils" that was "partly engraved" but not completed.

The plates, like the text, reflect the goal that Chambers stated in his preface: "to select, from mountains of promiscuous materials, a series of sound precepts, and perfect designs" (1791, p. iv). The first plate depicts the origins of the Doric and Corinthian orders in primitive huts, and the second illustrates moldings and a method for diminishing columns. Ten plates depict the orders and their parts. Twenty-two plates contain examples of pilasters, Persians, caryatids, intercolumniations, arches, arcades, columns upon columns, arches upon arches, pediments, imposts, balusters, doors, gates, piers, windows, chimneypieces, decorative entablatures, and ornaments for ceilings. The next 16 plates include plans and elevations of designs by Chambers for three garden "Casines," five garden temples, a "mausoleum to the memory of Pope, Gay, and Swift," a triumphal arch, and three gates (two of which are based on designs by Palladio and Inigo Jones); one plate depicts a pair of doors designed by Palladio. The final three plates, which do not appear in the 1759 or 1768 editions, illustrate designs for one tripod, two chimneypieces, and "various ornamental utensils."

Only two structures shown in the plates would serve as dwellings, and both were intended only for temporary use. The first is the "casine erected at Marino," consisting of a vestibule, saloon, study, and bedroom on the principal floor and a kitchen, scullery, pantry, butler's pantry, scullery, wine cellar, ale cellar, and servants' hall below. The plan of the principal story is a Greek cross. There are distyle Roman Doric frontispieces on each face, surmounted by pediments on two sides and by attic cornices on the other two.[14] A "Casine" or hunting pavilion designed for Lord Bruce is larger, with two stories raised above a rusticated basement. The principal floor contains a saloon, vestibule, bedroom, and dressing room. The facade is five openings wide; a three-sided bay projecting from the center of the two upper stories is topped by a circular drum with a conical roof and a circular balustrade at the very top.

Responding to changes in taste and advances in archaeology that rendered Chambers's book comparatively limited in scope, later editors added notes in the text to amplify and correct many points; they also included additional essays concerning Greek architecture, to redress Chambers's opposition to this style.

Gwilt declared in the preface to the 1825 edition that he preferred "the Italian school of Architecture," especially the work of Palladio and San-micheli, because it was "more plastic, that is, more capable of being submitted to the wants and habits of this country" (p. xxx). Later, in "An Examination of the Elements of Beauty in Grecian Architecture," Gwilt said that "true architecture was reared" in Greece, and there it "received all the elementary beauties of which she [architecture] was susceptible, as well as those in her general forms with which the habits and character of the nation invested her" (p. 15). Gwilt also declared that Vitruvius's account of the primitive hut had been disproved by modern archaeological evidence. Indeed the account was "absurd" because the proportions supposedly established in the original primitive wooden structures would necessarily have been changed when subsequent buildings were built in stone, because of inherent differences between the two materials.

In Papworth's editions of 1826 and 1836 the "Essay on the Principles of Design in Architecture" helps to redress Chambers's emphasis on Rome, and includes nine plates "illustrative of Grecian architecture."

1. Quoted by Eileen Harris in "The *Treatise on Civil Architecture*," Chapter 9 in John Harris, *Sir William Chambers* (London: Zwemmer, 1970), p. 128. In her chapter on the *Treatise* Harris also provides a thorough discussion of Chambers's ideas of beauty and proportion, his treatment of the orders, and his attitudes toward Greek, Roman, and Gothic styles.

2. See for example Halfpenny, Morris, and Lightoler, *The Modern Builder's Assistant* (1757), or Robert Morris, *Rural Architecture* (1750), *qq.v.*

3. Harris, in "The *Treatise*," op. cit., pp. 128–129, indicates Chambers originally conceived this book as a means to establish his reputation as a designer. The fact that the *Treatise* greatly exceeds the prospectus of 1757 in authority and scope suggests a rapidly growing determination to outdo Ware.

4. Important mid-eighteenth-century studies of Classical and medieval poetry include Thomas Blackwell, *An Enquiry into the Life and Writings of Homer* (London, 1735), and Thomas Percy, *Reliques of Ancient English Poetry* (London, 1765). Eighteenth-century English linguistic studies culminated in the six-volume treatise by James Burnett, Lord Monboddo, *Of the Origin and Progress of Language* (Edinburgh, 1773–1792).

5. For example Edward Hoppus, *The Gentleman and Builder's Repository* (1737), and William Pain, *The Builder's Companion* (1758), *qq.v.*

6. Marc-Antoine Laugier, *Essai sur l'architecture* (Paris, 1753).

7. Chambers's remarks are reminiscent of Claude Perrault, who in 1683 suggested that architectural proportions are not the consequence of natural law, but instead derive from custom: "Thus it is in Architecture, there are Things which Custom only renders so agreeable, that we cannot bear to have them otherwise, tho' they have no Beauty in themselves, that must infallibly please, and necessarily demand Approbation, such as is the Proportion which Capitals generally have with their Columns." See Perrault, *Ordonnance des cinq especes de colonnes selon la méthode des anciens* (Paris, 1683), p. viii; this translation by John James (London, 1708), p. vii. For further discussion see Wolfgang Herrmann, *The Theory of Claude Perrault* (London: Zwemmer, 1973), especially Chs. II, IV, and V.

8. For observations on the eighteenth-century debate concerning the influence of climate on human nature, see Christopher J. Berry, " 'Climate' in the Eighteenth Century: James Dunbar and the Scottish Case," *Texas Studies in Literature and Language* XVI:2 (Summer 1974), 281–292.

9. 1791, p. 25. These remarks are presented in the context of advice to the practicing architect. Chambers also recommended forming "an acquaintance" with local artists and artificers, and making "diligent enquiry into the usual prices" of labor (1791, p. 26).

10. Except as noted, the remaining discussion is based on examination of the 1791 edition, Chambers's last and most complete version.

11. Pp. 106–107. Cf. also the following remarks: "When objects are low, and much extended, we naturally conceive an idea of something mean, abject, and unwieldy: and when they are extremely elevated and narrow, they seem fragile and unstable" (1759, p. 64).

12. P. 106. This is a slightly expanded version of the argument on p. 64 of the 1759 edition. See too note 7 above.

13. P. 108. Cf. the discussion of association found in Alexander Gerard's *Essay on Taste* (London, 1759). On the subject of association in general see John Archer, "The Beginnings of Association in British Architectural Esthetics," *Eighteenth-Century Studies* XVI:3 (Spring 1983), 241–264. For connections between Chambers and Gerard see Harris, "The *Treatise*," op. cit., p. 132.

14. The "casine" and its building history are described by John Harris in *Sir William Chambers*, op. cit., pp. 42–45.

CLARKE, Henry (1743–1818)
Practical perspective.

See Entry 482.

41.1
COLLIS, James (–1886)
The builders' portfolio, of street architecture consisting of a series of original designs for .fronts.of.houses.of.all.classes. With details to a large scale. With an appropriate frontispiece and letter press description by J. Collis. Architect

London: Published by the author in thirty plates. Sold by J. Weale[,] J. Williams. Printed by T. Faulkner, 1837.

9 printed leaves, 30 pls.

36.8 × 26.7 cm

CtY-BA

According to ECB, Collis published a book in 1838 titled *Remarks on Street Architecture*, a title I have been unable to verify; it may be a paraphrase of *The Builders' Portfolio, of Street Architecture*.

This is the first British book devoted principally to designs for terrace and row houses. Nineteen of the 30 plates depict elevations, sections, and plans of facades—mostly of houses but also including a public house, a hotel, and a clubhouse. The remaining 11 plates illustrate entablatures, ornaments, and other details. Most of the designs are three stories high, and range from two to four windows wide. Collis's Neoclassical style is typified by tall, narrow doors, windows running the full room height, and Classical columns, cornices, fretwork, and other moldings.

The text consists of brief descriptions of the plates, with occasional remarks on appropriate materials. In some cases Collis specified the Classical sources of his motifs: in Plate 5, for example, the Temple of Vesta at Tivoli was his source for "a Front suitable for an hotel," and the Pantheon was the source for the Corinthian order in Plate 6.

Communications to the Board of Agriculture.

See BEATSON, **Robert**, *Entries 16 and 17;* CROCKER, **A.**, *Entries 46 and 47;* CRUTCHLEY, **Mr.**, *Entry 50;* GILLESPIE, **James**, *Entry 89;* HOLLAND, **Henry**, *Entries 148 and 149;* HUNT, **Rowland**, *Entry 152;* YOUNG, **Arthur**, *Entry 360.*

42.1 †
The complete farmer: or, a general dictionary of husbandry, in all its branches; containing the various methods of cultivating and improving every species of land, according to the precepts of both the old and new husbandry. . . . By a society of gentlemen, members of the Society for the Encouragement of Arts, Manufactures and Commerce.

London: Printed for the authors; and sold by S. Crowder; J. Coote; and F. Blythe, 1766.

[742] pp, frontisp. + 17 pls.

36.5 cm

Reference: NUC

42.2 †

———————

London: The authors, 1767.

[724] pp, frontisp. + 27 pls.

36.5 cm

Reference: NUC

42.3

The complete farmer: or, a general dictionary of husbandry, in all its branches; containing the various methods of cultivating and improving every species of land, according to the precepts of both the old and new husbandry. Comprising every thing valuable in the best writers on this subject, viz. Linnaeus, Chateauvieux, the Marquis of Turbilly, Platt, Evelyn, Worlidge, Mortimer, Tull, Ellis, Miller, Hale, Lisle, Roque, Mills, &c. Together with a great variety of new discoveries and improvements. Also the whole business of breeding, managing, and fattening cattle of all kinds; and the most approved methods of curing the various diseases to which they are subject. Together with the method of raising bees, and of acquiring large quantities of wax and honey, without destroying those laborious insects. To which is now first added, the gardener's kalendar, calculated for the use of farmers and country gentlemen. Illustrated with a great variety of folio copper-plates, finely engraved; exhibiting all the instruments used in husbandry; particularly those lately invented, and presented to the Society for the Encouragement of Arts, &c. in London; many of which have never yet appeared in a work of this nature. The second edition, corrected and improved. By a society of gentlemen, members of the Society for the Encouragement of Arts, Manufactures, and Commerce.

London: Printed for R. Baldwin, Hawes, Clarke and Collins, S. Crowder, T. Longman, B. Law, T. Lowndes, and Robinson and Roberts, 1769.

343 printed leaves, 111 + [iv] pp, frontisp. + 27 pls.

27.3 × 21.5 cm

MnU

42.4

The complete farmer: ⟨ . . . as 1769 . . . ⟩ Mills, Young, &c. ⟨ . . . as 1769 . . . ⟩ which is added, ⟨ . . . as 1769 . . . ⟩ nature. The third edition, ⟨ . . . as 1769 . . . ⟩.

London: Printed for J. F. and C. Rivington, S. Crowder, T. Longman, B. Law, T. Lowndes, G. Robinson, T. Cadell, and R. Baldwin, 1777.

1 printed leaf, [736] + 111 + [iv] pp, frontisp. + 27 pls.

27.6 × 22.5 cm

ICJ

42.5

The complete farmer: or, a general dictionary of husbandry in all its branches; ⟨ . . . as 1769 . . . ⟩ Mills, Young, Marshall, &c. &c. Together ⟨ . . . as 1769 . . . ⟩ cattle and poultry of all kinds; and the most approved manner of curing the various diseases to which they are subject. Together with the manner of raising bees, ⟨ . . . as 1769 . . . ⟩ insects. Also, the management of vines, and the best method of making all sorts of wines. Illustrated with a great variety of copper-plates, accurately engraved; exhibiting all the instruments used in husbandry; particularly those lately invented, as well as those presented to ⟨ . . . as 1769 . . . ⟩ nature. The fourth edition, considerably improved, and greatly enlarged. By a society ⟨ . . . as 1769 . . . ⟩.
London: Printed for T. Longman, B. Law, G. G. J. and J. Robinson, T. Cadell, R. Baldwin, W. Otridge, and W. Lowndes, [1793].

361 printed leaves, frontisp. + 33 pls.

36.5 × 24.0 cm

MnU

42.6

The complete farmer; or, general dictionary of agriculture and husbandry: comprehending the most improved methods of cultivation; the different modes of raising timber, fruit, and other trees; and the modern management of live-stock: with descriptions of the most approved implements, machinery, and farm-buildings.
The fifth edition, wholly re-written and enlarged. Vol. I [or II].

London: Printed by Rider and Weed, for R. Baldwin; W. J. and J. Richardson; F. C. and J. Rivington; J. Cuthell and Martin; W. Lowndes; W. Otridge and Son; Longman, Hurst, Rees, and Orme; Cadell and Davies; J. Stockdale; Lackington, Allen and Co; B. Crosby and Co; Clarke and Sons; P. and W. Wynne, and J. Booker, 1807.

[*Volume I:*] vii pp, 469 printed leaves, 58 pls.

[*Volume II:*] 581 printed leaves, 50 pls.

26.0 × 20.0 cm

ICJ

More an encyclopedia of agriculture than a dictionary, *The Complete Farmer: or, a General Dictionary of Husbandry* includes a wide variety of articles, ranging from short definitions (e.g., "Cotyledons," "Roughings") to major essays (e.g., "Bee," "Husbandry"). None of the articles in the first four editions concerns domestic architecture, but in the fifth edition (1807) four new articles do: "Cottage," "Farm-House," "Farm-Yard," and "Rammed Earth Buildings."

The article on cottages (I, 6 pp and 2 pls) consists primarily of summaries and paraphrases taken from previously published articles on rural improvement and cottage design.[1] The two plates include elevations and plans for 11 cottages, all reproduced from previous publications.[2]

The article on farm houses (I, 5 pp and 2 pls) was taken from a report on farm buildings by Robert Beatson[3] and from other sources. The two plates contain plans and elevations for four farm houses, all taken from the illustrations to Beatson's report.

The text for the article on farm yards (I, 4 pp and 2 pls) was drawn from the writings of William Marshall[4] and others. The plates include elevations and plans for two farm houses with attached farm yards, also taken from Beatson's article.[5]

The article on "Rammed Earth Buildings" (II, 9 pp and 3 pls) concerns the use of pisé, or rammed clay, to make walls. The first plate illustrates a rude two-room dwelling similar to a design published by Henry Holland, the first to prepare a detailed account of pisé construction in English.[6] The third plate is titled "Pisé cottages," and shows a more sophisticated design: a double cottage in front, rear, and side elevations, plus a section, ground plan, and upper-story plan. Each cottage has three principal rooms on the ground floor, and two on the upper story. There is no ornamentation.

1. See essays in *Communications to the Board of Agriculture* by Beatson, Crocker, Crutchley, and Holland. Also see Davis, "Address to the Landholders" (1795), and Wood, *A Series of Plans* (1792). A portion of the article is based on an essay by Sir John Sinclair that appeared in *The English Encyclopaedia* (1802). The latter in turn was based on an article by Sinclair in the *Annals of Agriculture*, XXXIV (1800; Entry 479) and on a French version titled *Projet d'un plan pour établir des fermes expérimentales* (Paris, [1800?]; *see* Entry 308).

2. In note 1 above see the articles by Beatson, Crocker, Crutchley, Holland, and Sinclair.

3. "On Farm Buildings" (1797; *q.v.*).

4. There are frequent references to Marshall throughout the article.

5. "On Farm Buildings" (1797; *q.v.*).

6. See Holland, "Pisé, or the Art of Building Strong and Durable Walls" (1797).

COOK, Andrew George

See The builder's magazine, *Entries 26.6–26.10.*

COTTAGE Improvement Society for North Northumberland
Report of the Committee . . . for 1842.

See Entry 483.

43.1

COTTINGHAM, Lewis Nockalls (1787–1847)

Working drawings for Gothic ornaments selected and composed from the best examples consisting of capitals, bases, cornices, friezes, finials, pendants, crockets, corbels, spandrils, bosses, roses, battlements, doors, windows, various specimens of mouldings, and a design for a Gothic mansion.

[London]: Pubd. by Priestley and Weale. Printed by C. Hullmandel, [n.d.].

4 pp, 36 pls.

60.0 × 47.0 cm

MBAt

In the copy at the Boston Athenaeum there is no internal evidence of the date of publication except for several plates with various watermarks—1805, 1817, 1818, and 1822. Other libraries have catalogued this book with attributed dates from 1822 through 1830. The publisher traded as "Priestley and Weale"—as printed on the title page—from 1820 through the early 1830s,[1] and C. Hullmandel printed other architectural books in the mid- and late 1820s.[2]

The plates, which measure 60.0 × 47.0 cm, have been folded in half for binding. The four pages of text measure 31.2 × 24.7 cm.

The text includes a brief "Address" and descriptions of the 36 plates. In the Address Cottingham remarked that he chose "such ornaments and mouldings as will produce an elegant effect in execution, without destroying the *character*—an object of the highest consideration in this branch of building" (p. 1).

The subjects of the plates are described adequately in the title. Only the final three plates show more than moldings or ornaments. Plate XXXIV shows a chimneypiece from Strawberry Hill, plus a selection of doors, windows, and niches from other locations. Plates XXXV and XXXVI depict a plan and elevation, respectively, of a mansion designed "for the family of a gentleman of rank and fortune in these times of elegant refinement" (p. 4). Cottingham formulated the design "to imitate the style of architecture of the sixteenth century" (p. 4), and arranged the plan to resemble a monastic cloister, arguing that in the present day no other plan "is so economical and convenient" (p. 4). A grand suite of rooms, he explained, could be arranged with great efficiency along the side of a cloister, together with all the necessary minor rooms, while still facilitating circulation among all. The design for the main entrance hall was adapted from the Chapel of Henry VII. Cottingham said it would "add much to the dignity of the building," particularly in terms of light, shadow, and irregular outline (p. 4).

1. See Ian Maxted, *The London Book Trades 1775–1800* (Folkestone: Dawson, 1977), p. 181. Also see Appendix F.

2. See Appendix F.

44.1

COTTON, William Charles (1813-1879)

Short and simple letters to English folk. No. I. The village. From William Charles Cotton. . . .

London: J. F. and G. Rivington; and W. H. Parker, Oxford, 1841.

5-36 pp, frontisp.

17.9 × 10.8 cm

MnU

This pamphlet was the first in a "Village Series," issued at least through 1842 and including three tracts on "The Village School" and one on "Mary Thompson's Cottage Walls." Cotton projected further tracts on the village parson, the parsonage, the church, the churchyard, the "Village Sunday," forms of prayer, the ordination service, daily prayer, the baptismal service, catechism, and confirmation.[1]

In *The Village* Cotton described a visit to "the pretty village of Brookside," where the narrator "was going to spend a month or so with the Parson, who . . . was now going to help me to fit myself, God helping me, for the holy office of a Pastor" (p. 8). There are lengthy conversations with two residents, John and Mary Thompson, who reveal the wholesome quality of life in this village and the moral well-being of its Christian inhabitants. Cotton concluded with the observation that "many of you who read this may say this is a PATTERN VILLAGE. Yes, so it is. . . . 'Thank God for it!' said Jane Penny, when I told her Brookside was a pattern village; and I hope all will agree with her" (p. 36). Cotton's interest in village life is reminiscent of Peter Frederick Robinson's *Village Architecture* (1830; *q.v.*), which examined both the aesthetic pleasures and the societal advantages of villages. But in making Christian faith such a central part of the residents' well-being Cotton clearly had little in common with Robinson.

The pamphlet has three illustrations: a view of the town from a distance (p. 9), a scene inside the brewhouse (p. 30), and a view of the village center (frontispiece). Within the village are an inn, a church, a market hall, houses, shops, and other structures in a combination of Old English and vernacular styles. The illustration is highly picturesque, but there is no mention in the text of this quality or of features of the individual buildings.

1. Advertised as "In the Press" on the wrapper for *The Village*.

45.1

CRESSWELL, Daniel (1776-1844)

The elements of linear perspective, designed for the use of students in the university.

Cambridge: Printed by Francis Hodson, for J. Deighton; and sold by Longman, Hurst, Rees, Orme, and Brown; and Parker, Oxford, 1811.

xi + 66 pp, 9 pls.

21.9 × 13.5 cm

IU

45.2 †

_____

Elements of linear perspective.

[London]: Longman, 1812.

8°

Reference: ECB

Cresswell explained in the Preface that his treatise "originated" in the "want of a concise treatise on Perspective, adapted to the system of education established in the University of Cambridge" (p. iii). Of books already available, he remarked that the larger ones "contain much more than is wanted for common use," while "the smaller treatises, with the exception of the second edition of that of Dr. Brook Taylor, published in 1719, are, generally speaking, deficient in methodic arrangement and accuracy of demonstration" (p. iv). "Popular works" are even worse, since they "give rules without investigations, and profess to perform what is impossible, to put their readers in possession of the principles of Perspective, without requiring from them the previous knowledge of geometry" (pp. v–vi). Nevertheless Cresswell considered perspective as fundamental a tool for drawing as grammar was for writing:

there is the same absurdity in pretending to delineate, without a knowledge of Perspective, as in attempting to write an epic poem, without being acquainted with the rules of orthography and grammar. To some of the latest and most expensive publications of Travels may be objected the inaccuracy of the drawing in their plates; a censure which a very small portion of information might have prevented. (p. vii)

The main text includes three pages of definitions, followed by four "Sections," treating respectively the delineation of objects on a plane surface, the "Examination of Pictures, supposed to be drawn according to the Principles of Linear Perspective," the representation of pictures seen "from a Point which is not their proper Point of View," and the delineation of shadows. Most of the figures in the nine plates are geometric diagrams, or perspective representations of simple objects such as steps or a ladder. Figure 9, on the fourth plate, shows the interior of a room, with two windows on the left wall, a fireplace at the far end, and a door and a picture on the right wall. The same room appears in Figure 20, on the final plate, now drawn to a larger scale and with shading added. Figure 14, on the sixth plate, shows a geometric outline of a house—just four walls and a gable roof—in oblique view. Also in Figure 14 there is a more detailed view of a larger house, two stories high and five windows wide, with a cornice at the roof line, window frames, a door frame, and a stringcourse between floors. Both houses demonstrate the problems of depicting buildings in pictures "seen from points which are not their proper Points of View" (p. 56).

46.1

CROCKER, A., _Land Surveyor_
"An essay on farm houses, and their various appendant offices, accompanied with plans and elevations, submitted to the consideration of the

Board of Agriculture," *Communications to the Board of Agriculture; on Subjects Relative to the Husbandry, and Internal Improvement of the Country* I:1 (1797), 66–71, and pls. XXVI–XXXII.

MH

The commentary for Entry 46 is combined with that for Entry 47 below.

47.1

CROCKER, A., and Son
"On cottages," *Communications to the Board of Agriculture; on Subjects Relative to the Husbandry, and Internal Improvement of the Country* I:2 (1797), 114–117, and pl. XXXIX.

MH

In the 1770s and 1780s individual authors such as Nathaniel Kent and John Wood had begun to advance the cause of rural improvement through publication of original designs for farm houses and laborers' cottages.[1] By the 1790s local and national societies concerned with agricultural improvement began to address the problem of rural housing on a more widespread and systematic basis.[2] Foremost among these societies was the Board of Agriculture and Internal Improvement, whose *Communications*, begun in 1797, included several articles on farm house and cottage design.[3]

For the first volume (1797) Crocker prepared an article on farm buildings, and with the assistance of his son prepared another on cottages. The first article consists of a brief text followed by illustrations and cost estimates for seven farm houses with farm yards, offices, and "out houses." The principal point of the essay is that "from their sitting room . . . the master or mistress [must] have a direct view into the barn, the stable, the oxstalls," and so forth, thus requiring that all outbuildings "stand at right angles, or nearly so, with lines passing from the windows of the sitting room to those buildings" (p. 67). Thus Crocker's designs all consist of an arc of outbuildings facing the house from across the yard. The one exception (Plate XXXII) is a formal octagon, with the house on one side of the figure. Crocker admitted this "may not be strictly consonant to the general idea . . . of a *direct* and *perpendicular* view . . . into all the out-buildings," but he thought some individuals might be attracted by its "air of snugness" (p. 68). The smallest house (Plate XXVI) consists of a kitchen, parlor, milk house, dairy house, storeroom, and cellar on the ground floor, and a chamber floor above. Crocker estimated it would cost about £263. The rest of the designs are progressively larger and more expensive, the largest (Plate XXXII) costing over £908 and having a best parlor, common parlor, kitchen, china closet, and brewhouse on the ground floor, plus other offices distributed along adjacent sides of the octagon. Some of the larger houses were embellished with modest Georgian cornices, stringcourses, a pediment, and other Neoclassical ornament. In each plate Crocker included an elevation showing the farm house surrounded by trees, fences, and other scenery, making a suitably picturesque composition of each design.

The article on cottages was prompted by "a bill for inclosing the waste land of the kingdom" that was "introduced into the House of Commons, under the auspices of the Board of Agriculture" (p. 114). The Crockers offered elevations and plans for three cottages that would suit the "small estates issuing out of allotments of such wastes" (p. 114). The authors included brief descriptions of their designs and a long annotated excerpt from John Wood's *Series of Plans for Cottages* (*q.v.*), describing seven principles to be observed in the construction of houses for laborers. The first design, with mud walls and a thatch roof, "is the cheapest habitation that we can construct" (p. 114), and has just two rooms—a dwelling room and a working room. The other two designs are made of timber or stone, and have a chamber story over the ground floor. The ground plan of the largest cottage has a parlor, kitchen, back kitchen, and milk room.

1. See Nathaniel Kent, *Hints to Gentlemen* (1775); and John Wood, *A Series of Plans, for Cottages* (1792; plates executed as early as 1781).

2. See for example the article by Davis published by the Bath and West of England Society (1795); the reports on individual counties commissioned by the Board of Agriculture (see the entry for "Great Britain. Board of Agriculture. Reports"); and the article by Rennie published by the Highland Society (1803).

3. Also see articles by Beatson, Crutchley, Hunt, and Holland.

48.1
CROKER, Temple Henry (1730?–1790?) et al.

The complete dictionary of arts and sciences. In which the whole circle of human learning is explained, and the difficulties attending the acquisition of every art, whether liberal or mechanical, are removed, in the most easy and familiar manner. Among the various branches of literature explained in this work are the following, viz. agriculture algebra anatomy architecture arithmetic astronomy botany catoptrics chemistry chronology commerce conics cosmography dialling dioptrics ethics fluxions fortification gardening gauging geography geometry grammar gunnery handicrafts heraldry history horsemanship husbandry hydraulics hydrography hydrostatics law levelling logic maritime and military affairs mathematics mechanics merchandize metaphysics meteorology music navigation optics painting perspective pharmacy philology philosophy physic pneumatics rhetoric sculpture series statics statuary surgery surveying theology, &c. The theological, philological, and critical branches, by The Rev. Temple Henry Croker, A.M. Chaplain to the Right Honourable the Earl of Hillsborough. The medicinal, anatomical, and chemical, by Thomas Williams, M.D. The mathematical by Samuel Clark, author of an easy introduction to the theory and practice of mechanics. And the other parts by several gentlemen particularly conversant in the arts or sciences they have undertaken to explain.

[*Vol. I has no indication of volume; in the second and third volumes, respectively,* Vol. II. *and* Vol. III. *appear directly above the imprint.*]

[*Volume I:*] London: Printed for the authors, and sold by J. Wilson & J. Fell; J. Fletcher & Co.; J. Coote; Mess. Fletcher & Hodson, Cambridge; and W. Smith & Co. Dublin, 1764.

[*Volume II:*] London: ⟨ . . . as 1764 . . . ⟩ , 1765.

[*Volume III:*] London: ⟨ . . . as 1764 . . . ⟩ ; J. Fletcher & Co. J. Coote; ⟨ . . . as 1764 . . . ⟩ , 1766.

Art. "Camera obscura," I, 2 pp; pl. XXXI.

Art. "Levelling," II, 2 pp; pl. LXXIX.

34.8 × 22.0 cm

ICJ

48.2 ‖

─────────

[*Vol. I has no indication of volume; in the second and third volumes, respectively,* Vol. II. *and* Vol. III. *appear directly above the imprint.*]

[*Volume I:*] London: Printed for the authors, and sold by J. Wilson & J. Fell; J. Fletcher & Co.; J. Coote; Mess. Fletcher & Hodson, Cambridge; and W. Smith & Co. Dublin, 1766.

[*Volume II:*] London: ⟨ . . . as Vol. 1 . . . ⟩ , 1765.

[*Volume III:*] London: ⟨ . . . as Vol. 1 . . . ⟩ , 1766.

Reference: Information supplied by University of Illinois Library at Urbana-Champaign.

48.3 †

─────────

The complete dictionary of arts and sciences. In which the whole circle of human learning is explained, and the difficulties attending the acquisition of every art, whether liberal or mechanical, are removed, in the most easy and familiar manner. . . . The theological, philological, and critical branches, by Temple Henry Croker. The medicinal, anatomical, and chemical by Thomas Williams. The mathematical by Samuel Clark. And the other parts by several gentlemen particularly conversant in the arts or sciences they have undertaken to explain.

London: Printed for the authors, and sold by J. Wilson & J. Fell . . . [*Vols. II and III:* London: Printed for Robinson and Roberts], 1766–1769.

38 cm

Reference: NUC-S

48.4

─────────

[*Volumes I and II:*]

The complete dictionary ⟨ . . . as 1764 . . . ⟩ explain. Vol. I [*or* II]. By the King's authority.

London: Printed for Robinson and Roberts, 1768.

Art. "Camera obscura," I, 2 pp; pl. XXXI [*pl. XXXI is wanting in the MnU copy*].

Art. "Levelling," II, 2 pp; pl. LXXIX.

34.2 × 22.4 cm

MnU

‖ [*Volume III:*]

The complete dictionary of arts and sciences. In which the whole circle of human learning is explained, and the difficulties attending the acquisition of every art, whether liberal or mechanical, are removed, in the most easy and familiar manner. . . .

London: Printed for Robinson and Roberts, 1768.

35.3 × 22.2 cm

Reference: Information supplied by Humanities Research Center, University of Texas, Austin.

48.5 ‖
___

[*Volume I:*]

The complete dictionary ⟨ . . . as 1764 . . . ⟩ Croker A. M. ⟨ . . . as 1764 . . . ⟩ explain. Vol. I. By the King's authority.

London: Printed for G. Robinson, 1773.

[*Plus two additional volumes.*]

Art. "Camera obscura," I, 2 pp; pl. XXXI.
Art. "Levelling," II, 2 pp; pl. LXXIX.

Reference: Information supplied by Brown University Library.

In the "Advertisement" to the first volume Croker claimed to have improved on Chambers's *Cyclopaedia* (*q.v.*), the French *Encyclopédie*, and "the other Works of Kind," but his text largely resembled that of Chambers. Croker suggested the work was so complete and definitive that "no *Supplement* will be necessary" (1768, "Advertisement," verso), and also claimed to "augment the Number of Plates" relating to the "Mechanic Arts" (ibid.).

Croker's article on "Architecture" barely fills one page, and chronicles the history of building from biblical times to Rome. There is only brief mention of the Middle Ages, followed by a quick reference to "the last two centuries," when architects "employed themselves wholly in retrieving the primitive simplicity and beauty of ancient architecture" (1768, *Art.* "Architecture"). Croker also discussed the traditional division of architecture into civil, military, and naval branches. Plate XLIII, facing the article "Column," shows the five orders of columns. Brief articles on "Capital" and "Base" are accompanied respectively by Plate XXXIII, showing capitals for the five traditional orders plus "Modern Ionic," and

Plate XI, illustrating bases for the five traditional orders plus "Attic." Plate XCV illustrates the article "Order" with doorways in Rustic, Tuscan, Doric, Ionic, Corinthian, and Composite styles.

A two-story house appears in Plate LXXIX, Fig. 16, to accompany the article on "Levelling." The house, illustrating the use of a telescope to establish the elevation of a distant object, is much like the house used in Chambers's article on the same subject. The only differences are Croker's omission of decorative finials from the roof peak, and his reversal of the entire illustration. In Plate XXXI Croker added an illustration, not in Chambers, demonstrating the operation of a camera obscura. The image of a two-story house and trees is projected, through a lens, onto an interior wall of a second house. The large windows, small window panes, and decorative gable of the first house are reminiscent of seventeenth-century English or Lowland architecture. The illustration closely resembles one published ten years earlier in the *New and Complete Dictionary* (*q.v.*), but Croker's is larger and more detailed.

49.1
CRUNDEN, John (ca. 1745–1835)
Convenient and ornamental architecture, consisting of original designs, for plans, elevations, and sections: beginning with the farm house, and regularly ascending to the most grand and magnificent villa; calculated both for town and country, and to suit all persons in every station of life. With a reference and explanation, in letter-press, of the use of every room in each separate building, and the dimensions accurately figured on the plans, with exact scales for measurement. By John Crunden, Architect. The whole elegantly engraved on seventy copper-plates, by Isaac Taylor.

London: Printed for the author, and Henry Webley, 1767.

viii + iv + 26 pp, 70 pls (on 56 leaves).

26.0 × 18.4 cm

MH

49.2 †
————
Convenient and ornamental architecture.

[London?]: 1768.

4°

Reference: APSD

49.3

Convenient and ornamental architecture, ⟨ . . . as 1767 . . . ⟩.

London: Printed for the author, and A. Webley, 1770.

viii + 26 pp, 70 pls (on 56 leaves).

27.3 × 18.4 cm

MB

49.4

Convenient and ornamental architecture, consisting of original designs, for plans, elevations, and sections: beginning with the farm-house, and regularly ascending to the most grand and magnificent villa; calculated both for town and country, and to suit all persons in every station of life. Engraved on seventy copper-plates, with reference and explanation, in letter-press, of the use of every room in each separate building, and the dimensions accurately figured on the plans, with exact scales for measurement. By John Crunden, Architect. A new edition.

London: Printed for I. Taylor, 1785.

viii + 26 pp, 70 pls (on 57 leaves).

26.0 × 18.1 cm

BL

49.5

Convenient and ornamental architecture, ⟨ . . . as 1785 . . . ⟩ copper-plates. With reference and explanation in letter-press, of the use ⟨ . . . as 1785 . . . ⟩ scales for measurements. By John Crunden, Architect. A new edition.

London: Printed for I. and J. Taylor, 1788.

viii + 26 pp, 70 pls (on 57 leaves).

25.9 × 18.0 cm

PPL

49.6 ‖

Convenient and ornamental architecture, ⟨ . . . as 1785 . . . ⟩ the farm house, ⟨ . . . as 1785 . . . ⟩ copper plates. With reference and explanation in letter press, ⟨ . . . as 1785 . . . ⟩ measurements. By John Crunden, Architect. A new edition.

London: Printed for I. and J. Taylor, 1791.

vi + 26 pp, 70 pls (on 56 leaves).

27.3 × 18.2 cm

Reference: Information supplied by The Library Company of Philadelphia.

49.7

Convenient and ornamental architecture, ⟨ . . . as 1785 . . . ⟩ the farm house, ⟨ . . . as 1785 . . . ⟩ copper plates. With reference and explanation in letter press, ⟨ . . . as 1785 . . . ⟩ edition.

London: Printed for I. and J. Taylor, 1797.

vi + 26 pp, 70 pls (on 57 leaves).

27.3 × 17.8 cm

RIBA

49.8

Convenient and ornamental architecture, ⟨ . . . as 1785 . . . ⟩ the farm house, ⟨ . . . as 1785 . . . ⟩ country, and suitable to persons in every station of life. Engraved on seventy copper plates. With reference and explanation in letter-press, ⟨ . . . as 1785 . . . ⟩ edition.

London: Printed for J. Taylor; by W. Stratford, 1805.

vi + 26 pp, 70 pls (on 56 leaves).

28.6 × 19.1 cm

MH

49.9

Convenient and ornamental architecture, consisting of original designs, for plans, elevations, and sections, beginning with the farm house, and regularly ascending to the most grand and magnificent villa; calculated both for town and country, and suitable to persons in every station of life. Engraved on seventy copper plates. With reference and explanation in letter-press, of the use of every room in each separate building, and the dimensions accurately figured on the plans, with exact scales for measurement. By John Crunden, Architect. A new edition.

London: Printed for J. Taylor; by W. Stratford, 1815.

vi + 26 pp, 70 pls (on 57 leaves).

28.2 × 18.4 cm

RPJCB

Crunden explained in the Preface that "the following designs are the contemplations of my leisure hours for several years past, and, at the request of a few particular friends, . . . [I] have made them public." Reiterating a portion of the title, he pointed out that his designs encompassed nearly the full range of domestic architectural types, "as they begin with the Farm House, and regularly ascend to the magnificent Villa." He achieved this breadth of subject matter in a very compact book by strictly limiting himself to elevations, plans, sections, and descriptions of dwellings, and leaving aside the orders, ornaments, details of carpentry, and all remarks on theory and practice—a highly successful formula that saw the book through nine editions by 1815, well beyond the period when his style of design was fashionable. Crunden sought a broad audience: he stated that he took great care to render his designs "very clear and intelligible to gentlemen and workmen" alike (p. v).[1] Crunden made cursory remarks on the proper heights for rooms, on materials, and also on restraint in the use of ornament: "To be sparing of antique Ornaments, *as they are termed*, on the outside of a building, would shew true taste in an Architect" (p. vii).

The text, an "Explanation" of the plates, consists of descriptions of each design and a key to the plans.

The plates include 42 designs for farm houses, town and country residences, villas, mansions, and inns, plus three designs for room interiors and designs for four doors. The smallest house design (Plate 3), a dwelling "for a single person in some remote country where elegance is not required," is two stories high and three windows wide. The ground-floor plan, 38 feet wide and 16 feet deep, contains an entrance hall, parlor, kitchen, pantry, and storeroom. There are three bedrooms upstairs. Except for modest ornament surrounding the door, the facade is entirely plain. One of the largest designs (Plates 52/53) is a "mansion for a person of distinction, adapted to either town or country" (p. 21). The plan is 209 feet wide and 130 feet deep, containing a marble entrance hall with 12 Corinthian columns, two anterooms, two parlors, two galleries, a dancing room, a saloon (35 feet in diameter), a withdrawing room, libraries for the gentleman and for the lady (each 25 feet in diameter), a principal library (45 feet by 30 feet), a tripartite statue and picture gallery (two octagons, 25 feet in diameter, a either end of a rectangle 45 feet by 30 feet), a grand staircase (39 feet by 35 feet), and a water closet. The facade, "something in the stile of Inigo Jones" (p. 21), is Crunden's most elaborate. It is two stories high and 13 windows wide, with balustrades and statues on the parapet, a rusticated basement, pedimented windows on the principal floor framed by semicircular relieving arches, and engaged Corinthian columns, sometimes paired, between the windows.

Crunden's villas, an intermediate class of country dwelling between the farm house and the mansion, generally include a central pile two stories high and seven windows wide, sometimes connected by arcades to lower office wings (Plates 20, 32/33, 36, 37/38). Some villas are smaller, with central units as little as three windows wide (Plates 24, 65), but still attached to office wings at each side. Two designs for town houses, by contrast, are quite compact. A pair of three-story houses intended for a country town (Plate 27) includes units that are each three windows wide, plus stables attached at the sides. A group of three attached town houses (Plates 28/29), three stories high, contains a unit five windows wide in the center, and units three windows wide at each side.

In plan most of Crunden's designs are regular and orthodox, composed of squares, rectangles, octagons, and occasional three-sided bays. The elevations are symmetrical and generally embellished with restrained Classical ornament, including pediments, porticoes, cornices, stringcourses, rustication, and occasional sculptured garlands, bas-relief panels, balustrades, and urns. A few designs, however, do not follow this description.

Two are composed in "Gothic" style. The elevations (Plates 10, 11) include crenellations, pinnacles, pointed arches decorated with crockets and finials, and Gothic orders framing the front door. The facade of the country house in Plates 62/63 is a pastiche of several styles: in addition to decorative Classical urns and Venetian windows, it incorporates a pediment with Rococo ornament and medieval battlements along the parapet. The country inn in Plates 47/48 likewise is crowned by battlements. A facade in the "Palladion" style (Plates 37/38) has a rusticated basement, curving staircases leading up to the hexastyle portico in front of the entrance, and a balustrade, statues, and urns on the parapet. A design "in the stile of Inigo Jones" has been discussed above. Crunden specified that two designs were in the "modern taste," and they seem to epitomize his goal of restraint in the use of ornament. In one case (Plate 16) the ornament consists merely of quoins at the corners and a small portico in front of the entrance; in the other (Plate 41) there is only a portico at the entrance.

Although none of the plates depicts surrounding foliage or landscape, the descriptions indicate Crunden was keenly aware of scenic considerations. In describing a villa already executed near Weybridge (Plate 36), for example, he made it clear that each facade was composed with a particular setting in mind:

The situation of this building is very desirable: in the fore front is a beautiful lawn, richly adorned with old oak trees, and other fine standards, covered from the north and east, with a plantation of several thousand young firs, of various species, in a flourishing habit, all planted by the worthy proprietor. The back front, which includes the best apartments, commands, at a little distance, the river Wey, and a very extensive prospect over a rich vale, bounded by a most beautiful chain of hills, which afford great variety of lights and shades, and consequently very pleasing and picturesque. (p. 15)

1. This description is based on the 1767 edition. The letterpress includes a dedication (one leaf, verso blank), a Preface (pp. v–viii), a list of subscribers (pp. i–iv), and the text (pp. 1–26).

50.1

CRUTCHLEY, Mr., *of Burleigh*

"Answers to the queries respecting cottagers renting land," *Communications to the Board of Agriculture; on Subjects Relative to the Husbandry, and Internal Improvement of the Country* I:2 (1797), 93–96, and pl. XXXIV.

MH

In the 1770s and 1780s individual authors such as Nathaniel Kent and John Wood had begun to advance the cause of rural improvement through publication of original designs for farm houses and laborers' cottages.[1] By the 1790s local and national societies concerned with agricultural improvement began to address the problem of rural housing on a more widespread and systematic basis.[2] Foremost among these societies was the Board of Agriculture and Internal Improvement, whose *Communications*, begun in 1797, included several articles on farm house and cottage design.[3]

Crutchley's article consists of a list of 27 questions concerning rent and other economic aspects of cottage life, together with his answers.[4] In response to Question 24, "What is the best form of a cottage?," Crutchley supplied an elevation and plan of a house (Plate XXXIV, figs. 3 and 4) which "is thought by most cottagers to be the best," and which he estimated would cost £40 (p. 96). The ground-floor plan includes a living room, a bedroom, a combination washhouse and brewhouse, a combination cellar and pantry, and a dairy. There is a chamber floor above with two "sleeping rooms."

1. See Nathaniel Kent, *Hints to Gentlemen* (1775); and John Wood, *A Series of Plans, for Cottages* (1792; plates executed as early as 1781).

2. See for example the article by Davis published by the Bath and West of England Society (1795); the reports on individual counties commissioned by the Board of Agriculture (see the entry for "Great Britain. Board of Agriculture. Reports"); and the article by Rennie published by the Highland Society (1803).

3. Also see articles by Beatson, Crocker, Hunt, and Holland.

4. On pp. 87–90 Lord Brownlow replied to the same queries. In response to Question 24, "What is the best form of a cottage?," he offered a ground-floor plan and chamber-floor plan of a cottage he had recently erected (Plate XXXIV, figs. 1 and 2). He had taken the design from Nathaniel Kent's *Hints to Gentlemen* (1775), p. 230, "with a little alteration and addition" (p. 89).

51.1
CUNNINGHAM, James
Designs for farm cottages and steadings, with descriptions, specifications, and estimates; general remarks on farm offices; and an appendix of practical information. By James Cunningham, Surveyor, Greenlaw.

Edinburgh and London: William Blackwood & Sons, [n.d.].

[*Part I:*] 26 pp, 2 pls.

[*Part II:*] 43 pp, 5 pls.

26.0 × 15.5 cm

BL

The British Library copy is dated [1842], in agreement with an entry for that date in the ECB. A copy in the Library of Congress, apparently identical to that in the British Library, once was catalogued as [1849]; recently it has been recatalogued as [1842].

Cunningham indicated that the "substance" of his remarks was also "contained in a letter which I had the honour to address to the members of the Highland Society during their late meeting at Berwick-on-Tweed."[1]

The book is divided into two parts, titled "Cottages" and "Steadings." In introductory "General Remarks" on cottages (I, 7–11) Cunningham considered the relation between peasants' living conditions and their "vices":

It is not meant to be alleged that the habits forced upon them by the deficient accommodation of their dwellings, is the only source of such grossness or indelicacy; but this deficiency certainly acts as an effectual barrier to their improvement. Before we can hope to see them chaste, pure, or elevated in morals, we must provide them with houses in which propriety and common decency may be observed. (I, 8–9)

Quoting from a recent study of pauperism in Berwickshire, Cunningham found support for his thesis: "The better the class of cottages designed for the labouring population, the higher will be the class of persons who will occupy them, and the less likely to contain among them the seeds of pauperism" (I, 9).

Offering next a "Description of Present Cottages" in Berwickshire (I, 12–15), Cunningham concluded that "At the best these dwellings are mere sheds, and very far from being fit for the residence of human beings" (I, 13). At the top of the second plate Cunningham depicted "plans of present cottages," showing a pair of attached one-room dwellings, which he criticized in detail in the text.

The remainder of the first part concerns Cunningham's own designs for model cottages. The text includes descriptions, specifications, a discussion of costs, and further remarks on cottage design (I, 15–26). In the first plate there is a plan for a double cottage, each unit having a large kitchen with two bed closets on the ground floor, plus a garret story above. Cunningham provided two elevations: both include a door and a window for each cottage on the ground story, and one includes a dormer window for each garret as well. A longitudinal section illustrates wall and floor construction plus two methods of roof framing. The second plate shows a suggested arrangement of two pairs of cottages with pigsties, ash pits, and coal houses in between. There is also a plan of a double cottage "of less dimensions," and suggestions for rearranging or adding onto existing cottages to make them more habitable. Cunningham indicated that a cottage such as he proposed could be built for £53 or less. In concluding the first part, he observed that for those "who take an interest in Cottage improvement only for the sake of picturesque effect, these proposals can have few recommendations." Nevertheless, he argued, "too high interests are at stake to permit of the question being left *moot* till every village can be made picturesque, and every peasant's dwelling ornamental. The strictly useful must take precedence of the ornamental, and objects of benevolence and humanity have a preferable claim to matters of taste" (I, 25–26).

The second part, on steadings, includes general remarks on barns, stables, byres, cattle sheds, cart sheds, roofing, and masonry, plus specifications for foundations, masonry, carpentry, and slating. There are descriptions of five designs for farmyards and offices that are illustrated in the plates, plus appendixes concerning various aspects of construction and finance. The first two designs for steadings include small "houses" for shepherds and a steward, measuring approximately 20 feet by 15 feet on the ground floor, and including a garret floor upstairs. All five designs include courts, stables, barns, sheds, and other farm offices.

1. I, 7. For earlier communcations to the Highland Society concerning related subjects, see its "Remarks on Cottage Premiums" (1839), and George Smith's "Essay on the Construction of Cottages" ([1833]; published 1835), *qq.v.*

Cunningham's remarks are paraphrased and quoted in the first report of the Cottage Improvement Society for North Northumberland ([1842]; Entry 483). This report also includes additional designs for cottages by Cunningham.

CURWEN, John Christian (1756–1828)
Hints on agricultural subjects *and* Hints on the economy of feeding stock.

See Entry 484.

52.1 †

DANIEL, William

A familiar treatise on perspective, designed for ladies and those who are unacquainted with the principles of optics and geometry; whereby, in a few days sufficient of this useful science may be learned to enable any person, accustomed to the use of the pencil, to draw landscapes and the simpler objects of art with perspective accuracy.

London: Darton and Harvey, 1807.

43 pp, frontisp. + 16 pls.

18 cm

Reference: NUC

52.2 ‡

A familiar treatise on perspective, designed for ladies, and those who are unacquainted with the principles of optics and geometry: whereby, in a few days, sufficient of this useful science may be learned, to enable any person, accustomed to the use of the pencil, to draw landscapes, and the simpler objects of art, with perspective accuracy. By W. Daniel. Second edition, improved.

London: Printed for Darton, Harvey, and Darton, 1810.

46 pp, 16 pls.

17.0 × 10.0 cm

Reference: Microfilm supplied by Yale University Library.

52.3 †

A familiar treatise on perspective, designed for ladies, and those who are unacquainted with the principles of optics and geometry: whereby, in a few days, sufficient of this useful science may be learned, to enable any person, accustomed to the use of the pencil, to draw landscapes and the simpler objects of art, with perspective accuracy, by W. Daniel. Third edition.

London: Printed for Harvey and Darton, 1821.

46 pp, frontisp. + pls.

18.5 cm

Reference: NUC

To help justify writing this new treatise on perspective, Daniel criticized three types of perspective treatise already available (p. 4). One was the "practical or familiar" treatise, which was "not calculated for the instruction of youth." Another was the treatise "written by artists," which Daniel judged to be prohibitively expensive. Finally, there were treatises composed by "scientific men," which had the disadvantage of requiring a knowledge of optics and geometry. Daniel's treatise, as explained in the title, was directed only toward ladies and novices, who had no previous technical knowledge.

The text is arranged as a series of nine letters to "My Dear Madam," containing definitions, demonstrations, and a series of exercises for a young student named "Eliza." Most of the plates are illustrations of mechanical perspective constructions, but three include domestic subjects. Plates 1 and 2 show five different views of a pair of small cottages, connected to each other by a low fence. Each cottage has one door and one window on the facade, and a second floor may be presumed from the presence of a window high up on the side wall. Plate 14 shows three views of the same type of cottage, but now single and with the location of the door and window reversed. All the dwellings are devoid of ornament, and there is no suggestion of the materials used. Plate 8 shows a line of five Tuscan columns in perspective, and Plate 15 shows the unfurnished interior of a room.

53.1 ‡
DAVENPORT, Richard
The amateur's perspective; being an attempt to present the theory in the simplest form; and so to methodize and arrange the subject, as to render the practice familiarly intelligible to the uninitiated in a few hours of study. By Richard Davenport, Esq.

London: Printed for the author: and sold by J. Hatchard; Egerton; and Colnaghi, 1828.

xii + 84 pp, 15 pls (numbered I–XIV, and "Continuation of Plate XIV").

27.2 × 23.5 cm

Reference: Microfilm supplied by The New York Public Library.

The commentary for Entry 53 is combined with that for Entry 54 below.

54.1 ‡
DAVENPORT, Richard
A supplement to "the amateur's perspective." By Richard Davenport, Esq.

London: Printed for the author: and sold by J. Hatchard; Egerton; and Colnaghi, 1829.

viii + 64 pp, 1 leaf, 6 pls (numbered XVI–XXI).

27.2 × 23.5 cm

Reference: Microfilm supplied by The New York Public Library.

To justify writing another treatise in an admittedly crowded field, Davenport strongly criticized the work of his predecessors. Among the problems he cited were ambiguous definitions, excessively intricate arguments, and omission of important steps in the process of instruction (pp. v–vi).[1]

Davenport thus "made an attempt to simplify the theory, and show how the visible lines directed to be drawn within the picture, do represent the imaginary lines defined in the system" (p. vii).

Davenport devoted about a third of his text to the theory of perspective. The rest concerns the practical application of specific rules. Most of his illustrations depict geometric constructions, although dwellings do appear in three plates. Plate VIII shows rude one-room huts in perspective, first in outline and then with solid walls, tile roofs, and shading. Plate IX shows an elevation and two perspective views of a curious "oblong house" without a roof. The opening for the front door is a pointed arch, above which three nearly intersecting arches represent a crude attempt to depict a Gothic window. The final plate, "to face Plate XIV," shows a small, one-story castle-like structure with crenellations across its top edge.

In the *Supplement* Davenport added material on "the theory of the Field of Vision, and Point of Distance; of the height of the Horizon-line; and the position of the prime vertical line in the picture" (p. iii). The six plates depict a variety of subjects, including a small church, a quay, a library wall, an exterior masonry wall and tower, and a landscape scene of a meandering river viewed from above. In Plate XVIII there is a small, approximately cubical masonry structure with three windows and a chimney, which is probably a rude dwelling.

1. In the Preface to the *Supplement*, however, he apologized for referring to Dr. Brook Taylor's work as "somewhat dreaded," and admitted he had never seen it (p. vi). But he continued his attacks on others by referring to Cresswell's *Elements of Linear Perspective* as suited only "for the meridian of Cambridge" (p. vi).

55.1

DAVIS, Thomas

"Address to the landholders of this kingdom; with plans of cottages for the habitation of labourers in the country, calculated to save the expence of the builder as much as is possible, without injuring the health or comfort of the inhabitants thereof," *Letters and Papers on Agriculture, Planting, &c. Selected from the Correspondence of the Bath and West of England Society, for the Encouragement of Agriculture, Arts, Manufactures, and Commerce* VII (1795), 294–310, and 7 pls.

MH

Although Nathaniel Kent and John Wood had been first to advance the welfare of farmers and laborers through publication of original cottage designs,[1] local and national societies concerned with agricultural improvement soon addressed the problem on a more widespread and regular basis. Among the first was the Board of Agriculture and Internal Improvement (*q.v.*), which in its series of reports on individual counties specifically included the subject of cottage design among a variety of other topics relating to horticulture and husbandry. One of the earliest regional societies to consider agricultural improvement was the Bath and West of

England Society, to whom Thomas Davis submitted this short paper in 1795. It consists of a brief introductory essay, followed by designs for three double and four single cottages.[2] Invoking the reader's feelings of compassion and concern for human decency, Davis advocated certain minimum standards for materials and circulation of air as necessary to maintain human well-being (pp. 296–297). He noted the designs could be erected as "ornaments" for parks or plantations (p. 297), perhaps hoping to induce otherwise uninterested landowners to provide decent structures for their laborers.

The plates depict very simple structures with rough stone walls and thatch roofs, ranging in cost from £50 for a single cottage to £100 for a double. The smallest single cottage (No. 6) is 18 feet by 27 feet in plan, with a kitchen, "working room," and "pantry and cellar" on the ground floor, and two chambers above. The "Large Double Cottage, With every necessary Convenience" (No. 5) is 47 feet wide overall, and 17 feet deep. Each cottage has a kitchen and "pantry and cellar" on the ground floor, and a large and small chamber above. The cottages have little ornament. The "Small Double Cottage" (No. 3) and "Useful as well as Ornamental Double Cottage" (No. 4) both have eaves that rise in gentle curves above sets of double or triple arched windows. Designs No. 6 and No. 7, called "Ornamental Cottages," have similarly curved eaves and the windows on the upper floor have mullions that form pointed arches. The facade of each cottage is articulated into vertical bands, and there is a bow in the facade of No. 7.

1. See Nathaniel Kent, *Hints to Gentlemen* (1775); and John Wood, *A Series of Plans, for Cottages* (1792; plates executed as early as 1781).

2. Some of the cottage designs had been executed, but Smith did not specify which: "The plans of cottages on the plates annexed, and hereafter described, have in part been already executed by the Marquis of Bath, part by Joshua Smith, esq; and the rest are new designs" (p. 296).

56.1
[DAVY, Christopher (ca. 1803–1849)]
Architectural precedents; with notes and observations, illustrated with working drawings. Edited by an Architect.

London: John Williams, 1840.

v + 7–76 + 32 + 118 pp, frontisp. + 22 pls.

21.5 × 13.5 cm

NNC

56.2 ‖
DAVY, Christopher (ca. 1803–1849)
Architectural precedents; with notes and observations. By C. Davy, Arch., &c. Illustrated with working drawings.

London: John Williams, 1841.

[i] + v + 7–37 + 32 + 118 + 64 + 67 + 25 + 36 + 48 + 37–179 pp, frontisp. + 45 pls.

21.5 × 13.5 cm

Reference: Information supplied by Humanities Research Center, University of Texas, Austin.

56.3 ‖

————

————

London: John Williams, 1841.

[i] + v + 7–36 + 32 + 118 + 64 + 67 + 25 + 36 + 48 pp, 1 printed leaf, 37–179 pp, frontisp. + 45 pls.

22.0 × 13.5 cm

Reference: Information supplied by Humanities Research Center, University of Texas, Austin.

56.4
WALKER, Thomas Larkins (–1860)
Architectural precedents; consisting of plans, elevations, sections and details, together with specifications, bills of quantities, estimates, and forms of contracts of buildings actually executed. Third edition. Accompanied by Section I. of an essay on architectural practice, (copiously illustrated with working drawings), by T. L. Walker. . . .

London: Library of the Fine Arts, 1841.

v + 7–36 + 32 + 118 + 64 + 67 + 25 + 36 + 48 + 68 + xxxvi pp, frontisp. + 46 pls.

22.5 × 14.1 cm

MBAt

The 1840 edition consists of four separate essays, on second-rate buildings, architectural practice, parochial buildings, and prisons. The second essay begins on page 38, but ends suddenly in midsentence on page 76. The other two essays are paginated separately.

There are at least two 1841 editions by Christopher Davy, and another by Thomas Larkins Walker, all with nine essays. In the first of the Davy editions the first essay ends on page 37—as in the 1840 edition. In the second Davy edition this essay was reset so that it would end on page 36. The essay on architectural practice, beginning in both editions on page 37 and extending through page 179, is bound last in both editions. In between the first and last essays, the letterpress of both editions appears identical; the only variations occur in the order of the plates:[1]

Davy 1841 (56.2)	Davy 1841 (56.3)
Frontispiece	Frontispiece
Title page	Title page
Printed dedicatory leaf	Printed dedicatory leaf
i–v; [vi] blank	i–v; [vi] blank
Essay No. 1, Second-rate Buildings, pp. 7–37, 5 pls. at end	Essay No. 1, Second-rate Buildings, pp. 7–36, 5 pls. at end
Essay No. 2, Parochial Buildings, pp. 1–32, 8 pls. at end	Essay No. 2, Parochial Buildings, pp. 1–32, 8 pls. at end
Essay No. 3, Prisons, pp. 1–118, 9 pls. at end	Essay No. 3, Prisons, pp. 1–118, 9 pls. between pp. 82–83
Essay No. 4, Railway Works, pp. 1–64, 11 pls. at end	Essay No. 4, Railway Works, pp. 1–64, 11 pls. between pp. 32–33
Essay No. 5, Charitable Institutions, pp. 1–67, 11 pls. at end	Essay No. 5, Charitable Institutions, pp. 1–67, 11 pls. between pp. 48–49
Essay No. 6, Repairs and Alterations, pp. 1–25, no pl.	Essay No. 6, Repairs and Alterations, pp. 1–25, no pl.
Essay No. 7, Club-Houses, pp. 1–36, no pl. (but see below)	Essay No. 7, Club-Houses, pp. 1–36, 1 pl. precedes p. 1
Essay No. 8, Churches, pp. 1–48, 1 pl. (of Club House) follows p. 48	Essay No. 8, Churches, pp. 1–48, no pl.
	Half-title to Essay on Architectural Practice
Essay on Architectural Practice, pp. 37–139, no pl.	Essay on Architectural Practice, pp. 37–139, no pl.

Walker made few significant changes in his edition. They include a new title page, a new introduction, and a new frontispiece showing alterations and additions to the Chamberlain Hospital. Walker bound the Davy frontispiece, an elevation of the "New National Scotch Church, London," with Essay No. 8, on churches. Walker also removed Davy's essay on architectural practice and added one of his own, with text illustrations of working drawings for the Church at Friar's Mount, Bethnal Green, prepared under Walker's direction.[2] In remarks on page iv of the introduction Walker implied that he had suddenly taken over as editor from someone else—presumably Davy—and that the nine separate sections of this and previous editions existed prior to his involvement. Yet in the Davy editions Walker's name appears at the head of the section on charitable institutions which, according to the title of the paper, includes "Drawings. . . of and under the Superintendence of Mr. T. L. Walker, Architect, 1840." It remains unclear whether Walker just designed this charitable building, or in addition prepared the text and illustrations for publication.

The common concern of all the essays is the education of architectural students: the "precedents" were meant to provide instructive examples of fully executed buildings, together with specifications and other pertinent information (Walker ed., p. iii). Among a variety of civil and ecclesiastical subjects, only one essay deals with domestic architecture. Its subject is "Second-rate Buildings," and it includes five plates showing an elevation, four floor plans, an attic plan, a roof plan, and two sections of a three-story double town house in Greek Revival style. The ground floor of each house includes a dining parlor and breakfast parlor, the drawing room is on the first floor, the second floor contains two bedrooms and a dressing room, there are more bedrooms on the attic floor, and the kitchen, back kitchen, and cellars are in the basement. The text includes specifications for the excavator, bricklayer, carpenter, joiner, plasterer, plumber, glazier, painter, mason, smith, and paper hanger, plus a "Bill of Quantities."

1. The comparison of editions is based on copies at the Humanities Research Center, University of Texas at Austin. I am grateful to Cathy Henderson of the University of Texas, who painstakingly supplied most of the information given here.

2. This essay also appeared as *An Essay on Architectural Practice. . . . Section I* by Thomas Larkins Walker, issued as a separate volume in 1841. *Section II* of this essay was issued in 1842. The subject of both sections was the Church at Friar's Mount. The pagination of *Section II* is continuous with *Section I*: iv + [69]–136 + xxxvii–xliii pp, with illustrations 28 through 63 in the text.

57.1 ‡
DEACON, Augustus Oakley
Elements of perspective drawing; or the science of delineating real objects. Being a manual of directions for using a set of models composing a variety of picturesque forms, suitable for the practice of beginners. Designed by Augustus Deacon. Illustrated with eight plates.

London: Printed for Taylor and Walton, 1841.

viii + 38 pp, 8 pls.

8°

Reference: Microfilm supplied by The British Library.

57.2 †
_____

Elements of perspective drawing. New edition.

[London]: Dean, 1853.

8°

Reference: ECB

The unique feature of Deacon's instructional method was "the substitution of solid forms in place of sketches or prints for the learner to copy" (p. iii). Deacon felt the student would learn better by viewing three-dimensional forms than by copying illustrations. Therefore he arranged for the manufacture and sale of a set of 57 model blocks, the shapes of which were based on the "simplest" regular solids: cubes, cones, spheres, pyramids, cylinders, and so forth. Students could use the set to construct geometric models of "houses, castles, bridges, steps, crosses, pillars, &c" (p. v).

Deacon devoted a quarter of his text to a lengthy introduction, in which he iterated the need for artisans, mechanics, artists, men of leisure, and men of business to know how to draw (p. 1). In order to delineate any object correctly, he said, one must "understand its form thoroughly" (p. 2). Thus the study of drawing must be divided into two parts: the science of form and the art of delineation. Deacon argued that with a knowledge of drawing one could begin *"intelligent*-seeing" (p. 5): one would become trained in the science of vision, and be able to communicate without the aid of artists or draughtsmen. Further, "clearness and activity of the understanding" actually depend on "the vividness and permanency of the impressions of sight" (p. 9). The rest of the text (pp. 10–38) consists of brief sections devoted to drawing apparatus, definitions of geometric terms, definitions of perspective terms, rules of perspective, and remarks on light and shade.

Most of the plates show geometric constructions and perspective diagrams. In Plates 7 and 8 Deacon illustrated examples of objects that could be built with his blocks—temples, towers, houses, bridges, castles, and the like—but depicted them only as solid three-dimensional stacks of blocks without architectural articulation. He did not discuss these plates except for an incidental reference on page 11.

58.1

DEARN, Thomas Downes Wilmot (1777–1853)

The bricklayer's guide to the mensuration of all sorts of brick-work, according to the London practice, with observations on the causes and cure of smoky chimneys, the formation of drains, and the best construction of ovens, to be heated with coals; also, a variety of practical and useful information on this important branch of the building art, illustrated by various figures, and nine copper plates. By T. D. W. Dearn, Architect.

London: Published by J. Taylor, 1809.

[viii] + 112 pp, 9 pls.

20.7 × 13.2 cm

NNC

In the four-page Preface Dearn indicated that he intended this book for the "mechanic" or artisan as well as the architectural student. Dearn warned that an architect's neglect of this subject often "becomes apparent" too late in his career, when "pride forbids an appeal to those by whose assistance it might be retrieved."

The text begins with a history of brickmaking and remarks on modern methods, followed by a discussion of mortar and cement. There is instruction in arithmetic and in mensuration of a wide variety of subjects. Also there are remarks on smoky chimneys, ovens, drains and sewers, garden and fence walls, coping bricks and buttresses, chimney pots, brick trimmers, centerpieces, centering, stone cornices, and party walls.

Plates 1 and 2 are elevations of walls for town houses, each four stories high and three windows wide. Plates 3 and 4 include an elevation and horizontal sections of a "Flank Wall" and chimneys for a four-story house. Plates 5 through 9 depict more flank walls, brick nogging, arches, ovens, drains, domes, vaults, cornices, and buttresses.

59.1
DEARN, Thomas Downes Wilmot (1777–1853)
Designs for lodges and entrances to parks, paddocks, and pleasure-grounds, in the Gothic, cottage, and fancy styles, with characteristic scenery and descriptive letter-press. On twenty plates. By T. D. W. Dearn, Architect. . . .

London: Published by J. Taylor, 1811.

[iv] + 19 pp, 20 pls.

32.4 × 25.1 cm

Bodl.

59.2
———

Designs for lodges and entrances to parks, paddocks, and pleasure-grounds, in the Gothic, cottage, and fancy styles; with characteristic scenery and descriptive letter-press. On twenty plates. By T. D. W. Dearn, Architect. . . . A new edition.

London: Published by J. Taylor, 1823.

[iv] + 19 pp, 20 pls.

38.1 × 27.9 cm

V&A

Dearn's earlier *Sketches* of 1806 and 1807 (*qq.v.*), published in large part to advertise his abilities as a designer, apparently were successful: in *Designs for Lodges* he indicated that several of the designs illustrated had been executed.[1] Other designs unashamedly repeated formulas first introduced in earlier works.[2] He also included two addresses for readers wanting to write for "more information."[3] Yet although Dearn lived until 1853 his career was undistinguished,[4] and this was the last collection of designs he published.[5]

Having focused on cottages and larger buildings in his two previous collections of designs, Dearn now turned to lodges, "which, although of minor consideration on account of their size, are nevertheless of much consequence."[6] Dearn explained that lodges serve as an introduction to the "character" of an entire estate. Thus an architect's first concern "should be to adapt the Character [of the lodge] to that of the House; as the effect likely to be produced on the mind of a visitor by a first view, should be well considered: for we frequently decide on the Character of places, as well as of persons, by first impressions" (p. iii). Dearn provided designs in "Regular Architecture, in the Gothic, in the Cottage, or in the Modern fancy style," suitable for use on a variety of estates (p. iii). He depicted each design in plan and in an aquatinted view, in which he included "useful hints for Planting."[7]

In the 19 pages of plate descriptions Dearn discussed materials, plan, style, and other aspects of each design. In discussing the plan of the lodge in Plate VI, for example, he counseled only one bedroom in any lodge, since more would suggest to the viewer that children lived there: that would destroy the "neatness and air of comfort, which should mark the approach to a gentleman's residence" (p. 6). In explaining his use of "florid gothic" for the lodge in Plate XI, he found it could "be made suitable to the purposes of domestic life" and would be "very much in character with various situations and ancient mansions in this country" (p. 11).

Most of the lodges contain just three rooms, all on one floor—a living room, bedroom, and "wash house"—with an occasional second bedroom. The only significantly larger design is the entrance lodge for Bayham, in Kent, which incorporates four tenements, each with living room, bedroom, and washhouse, combined in one large "Castle Gothic" structure (Plates 19, 20). Among the more successful compositions in this collection is a "Grecian" lodge spanning a stream with thick foliage on either bank (Plate 14). The facade consists of two windows set within segmental relieving arches, and a pedimented entrance flanked by fluted pilasters and columns *in antis*. One rustic design (Plate 15) is based on four perfect octagons: rough-barked columns of oak hold up the thatch roof of an octagonal porch, behind which three additional octagons form the living room, bedroom, and washhouse.[8] But Dearn did not exploit the potential geometric and compositional complexities of such a tetra-octagonal plan. Rather, he visually emphasized the rusticity of the cottage and its integration with the surrounding scenery through his use of textures, light, and shade. By contrast another design (Plate 12), in "no particular style of architecture" (p. 12), consists of a square plan with a segmental bow on one side and square piers projecting from each of the corners. The elevation shows only slight ornamentation: narrow pilaster bands, a small circular window in the porch, and a large lattice window in the living room.

1. "Advertisement," verso.

2. The "Lodge" in Plate 6, for example, is similar to the "Cottage" in Plate I of *Sketches . . . for Public & Private Buildings.*

3. "Cranbrook, Kent, or at my Publisher's, in London" ("Advertisement," verso).

4. Colvin (1978), pp. 255–256.

5. After 1811 he wrote two more books: *An Historical, Topographical and Descriptive Account of Kent* (Cranbrook, 1814); and *Hints on an Improved Method of Building* (London, 1821).

6. "Advertisement," recto.

7. "Advertisement," verso.

8. In its use of rough-barked columns to hold up a thatch roof for an octagonal porch, the design resembles Plate 22 in Robert Lugar's *Plans and Views of Buildings* (1811), and Plate 4 in Lugar's *Country Gentleman's Architect* (1807), qq.v.

60.1

DEARN, Thomas Downes Wilmot (1777–1853)

Sketches in architecture; consisting of original designs for cottages and rural dwellings, suitable to persons of moderate fortune, and for convenient retirement; with plans and appropriate scenery to each. On twenty plates: with some general observations. By T. D. W. Dearn. . . .

London: Published by J. Taylor, 1807.

vii + 15 pp, 20 pls.

34.6 × 26.7 cm

BL

60.2

_____

_____

A new edition.

London: Published by J. Taylor, 1823.

viii + 15 pp, 20 pls.

34.3 × 26.7 cm

V&A

Sketches in Architecture . . . for Cottages and Rural Dwellings is a sequel to Dearn's *Sketches in Architecture . . . for Public & Private Buildings* (*q.v.*), published one year earlier. In the Preface to the sequel Dearn noted that the earlier book was designed "to secure me some professional reputation with an enlightened public" (p. iv);[1] now he could not refrain from pompously "expressing the pleasure I have experienced, in the commendations bestowed on the former Part" (p. iii). Nevertheless Dearn's subsequent remarks reveal that his designs received a mixed reception at best (pp. iii–iv).

Dearn excused the plainness and simplicity of his present designs as the result of philanthropic concern: he chose "to render the work beneficial to others rather than honourable to myself, by choosing subjects which, though generally interesting, yet preclude the possibility of displaying much architectural knowledge or acquaintance with the sciences." He also invoked two long recognized principles of design: "It has been attempted in these designs for dwellings to unite the two grand essentials, *convenience* and *economy*" (pp. iv–v). He concluded the Preface with reasons for not supplying cost estimates, and then a promise that clients who "call for the exercise of my professional talents" will not "repent the election made in my favour" (p. vii).

The 15 pages of text are romantic, often diffuse descriptions of the designs. The double cottage in Plate I, for example, is introduced through a long account of the enjoyments it might provide the prospective client:

The man of business, whose days have been spent among the busy scenes of life, without the attainment of affluence yet not entirely destitute of success, may here, free from the noise and bustle to which he has hitherto been accustomed, enjoy the fruits of his industry, unalloyed by those anxious cares and solicitudes inseparable from business. (p. 1)

Following another 300 words devoted to the pleasures of rural life, Dearn concluded the description with brief comments on materials and color.

Dearn's 13 designs include four cottages, two double cottages, two small residences, two villas, a double residence, a rural dwelling, and a farm house, each shown in plan and view. Among the smallest is the "small residence" in Plate 5, two stories high and 25 feet wide, with just an eating room, study, and parlor on the ground floor. One of the largest designs is the farm house in Plates 13 and 14, 45 feet wide, with a kitchen, parlor, dairy, breakfast room, washhouse and men's kitchen, and an unidentified room on the ground floor, plus four bedrooms (including one for servants) upstairs.

The designs are generally in one of two styles: a plain, spare, Neoclassical style, often ornamented with trelliswork or rustic columns made of tree trunks, and a Gothic or castellated style, with pointed arches, crenellations, pinnacles, and Tudor drip moldings. In two cases (Plates 9 and 16) the styles are combined: the double residence in Plate 9, for example, combines pointed arches with wide, flat, undecorated masonry surfaces. In another case Dearn provided two elevations, "of totally dissimilar characters," for the same villa (Plates 10–12). He described one, with a castellated parapet, as "sober and dignified." He felt that the other elevation, with trelliswork set in between flat, undecorated masonry piers, "lays claim to an appearance *tout à fait riant*" (p. 9), but in fact this elevation is hardly less sober than the other. Dearn's command of perspective and drawing was as poor here as in *Sketches . . . for Public & Private Buildings*. Consequently each dwelling, shown surrounded by trees, shrubbery, grass, and other landscape scenery, appears poorly integrated with its environment.

1. This description is based on the 1807 edition.

61.1
DEARN, Thomas Downes Wilmot (1777–1853)
Sketches in architecture, consisting of original designs for public & private buildings. By Thomas Downes Wilmot Dearn. . . .

London: Printed and published for the author, by John Cawthorn, [1806].

29 printed leaves, 16 pls [*in this copy pl. 6 wanting; pl. 10 incorrectly numbered as 9; two pls. numbered 12*].

32.7 × 25.4 cm

MBAt

61.2 ‖

Sketches in architecture, consisting of original designs for public and private buildings. By Thomas Downes Wilmot Dearn. . . .

London: Printed for William Baynes, 1814.

xvi pp, 20 printed leaves, 16 pls.

30.0 × 23.3 cm

Reference: Information supplied by Humanities Research Center, University of Texas, Austin.

This is the first of two entirely distinct books by Dearn, each of whose titles begins *Sketches in Architecture*. . . . The title page is undated, but the preface is dated 1806. The second book, dated 1807, is discussed above.

Candidly and perhaps naively Dearn began the Preface by admitting his inexperience: "About to embark" on the profession of architecture, and "Ambitious of professional reputation," he spoke of his "pretensions . . . to public favor" and his desire "equally *to deserve well, as to do well*."[1] Following convoluted remarks on variety and novelty, he presented an unenlightening discussion of pictorial design: the artist should study scenes in nature, he said, but also must "select" the best parts and "supply the defects."[2] He also made a few impetuous critical remarks about the current state of architecture in Britain, specifically condemning the "proposed New Front to the Pavillion at Brighton," which he found "extravagant," "monstrous and absurd."[3] Following a brief discussion of obelisks, he concluded with lengthy observations on the progress of architecture in modern Britain, the education of young architects, and "the importance of the science of perspective."

The 20 text leaves are descriptions of Dearn's 14 designs: a cottage, three entrance gates with lodges, a billiard room, a public bath, a private chapel, a private bath, a cenotaph, a corn exchange and council room, a villa, a chapel and cemetery, a national mausoleum, and a naval museum. In his discussion of Gothic entrance lodges (Plate VII) he indicated the architect's "principal aim should be" to give each lodge "that character which will best harmonize with the surrounding scenery and the objects more immediately connected with it." In all of his illustrations Dearn included lush scenery to complement his buildings, and he suggested appropriately picturesque sites. The design for a "Villa in the Castle Gothic Style" (Plate XI), for example, was suited "for a spot bold and romantic, or one more confined and woody." Dearn's aquatint technique effectively conveys advance, recession, light, and shade, but his perspective rendering of many buildings appears awkward and accords poorly with the surrounding landscape.

There are five dwellings in this collection of designs. The cottage "which the author originally intended for himself" (Plate I) has bare ashlar walls, a projecting cornice and pediment, Gothic windows, and rough-barked tree trunks as columnar supports for the porch. The lodges (Plates II, III, VII) include just one or two rooms each. The "Villa in the Castle Gothic Style" (Plate XI) includes a parlor, eating room, drawing room, library, hall, water closet, kitchen, and servants' hall on the ground floor, plus a chamber floor above.

1. The Preface, some 15 pages long, is unpaginated. These excerpts are from the first page. This description is based on examination of the [1806] edition.

2. From the verso of the first leaf of the Preface.

3. From the recto and verso of the third leaf of the Preface.

62.1

DECKER, Paul

Chinese architecture, civil and ornamental. Being a large collection of the most elegant and useful designs of plans and elevations, &c. from the imperial retreat to the smallest ornamental building in China. Likewise their marine subjects. The whole to adorn gardens, parks, forests, woods, canals, &c. Consisting of great variety, among which are the following, viz. royal garden seats, heads and terminations for canals, alcoves, banqueting houses, temples both open and close, adapted for canals and other ways, bridges, summer-houses, repositories, umbrello'd seats, cool retreats, the summer dwelling of a chief bonza or priest, honorary pagodas, Japaneze and imperial barges of China. Also those for the Emperor's women, and principal officers attending on the Emperor, pleasure boats, &c. To which are added, Chinese flowers, landscapes, figures, ornaments, &c. The whole neatly engraved on twenty-four copper-plates, from real designs drawn in China, adapted to this climate, by P. Decker, Architect.

London: Printed for the author, and sold by Henry Parker and Elirabeth [*sic*] Bakewell; H. Piers and Partner, 1759.

24 pls.

[*Bound with*:]

Chinese architecture. Part the second. Being a large collection of designs of their paling of different kinds, lattice work, &c. for parks, paddocks, terminations for vistos, ha ha's, common fence and garden, paling, both close and open, Chinese stiles, stair-cases, galleries, windows, &c. To which are added, several designs of Chinese vessels, ewers, Ganges cups, tureens, garden pots, &c. The whole neatly engraved on twelve copper= plates, from real Chinese designs, improved by P. Decker, Architect.

London: Printed for the author, and sold by Henry Parker and Elizabeth Bakewell; H. Piers and Partner, 1759.

12 pls.

23.5 × 29.8 cm

MB

The appearance of Chinese designs in British architectural literature was almost entirely limited to the 1750s. The principal publications were the series of *New Designs* begun by the Halfpennys in 1750, *A New Book of Chinese Designs* (1754) by Edwards and Darly, and Sir William Chambers's *Designs of Chinese Buildings* (1757), *qq.v.* Decker's was the last British publication solely devoted to Chinese designs.[1]

The book consists entirely of plates, and is divided into two parts. Each part is fully described on its own title page. Altogether eleven plates show designs for retreats, temples, and seats, five illustrate designs for boats, seven include decorative compositions or landscape scenes, 12 have designs for fences and paling, and one depicts a bridge. Decker's designs for temples, seats, and other structures were the least substantial and most Rococo of his time. Many appear more appropriate for transfer to porcelain jars or tapestry than for use as shelter or accommodation. These designs range in size from the "Imperial Retreat for Angling," 50 feet wide and 41 feet high (Plate I), to garden seats approximately eight feet wide (Plate 7). Nearly all the designs are embellished with scenery, which echoes the exuberance of Decker's Rococo ornament, and disguises the structural inadequacies and impossibilities of his designs.

1. *Chinese Architecture* was published in the same format and in the same year as Decker's *Gothic Architecture* (*q.v.*). Clearly the two were conceived as pendants, intended to exploit concurrent fashions for Chinoiserie and the Gothic Revival.

63.1
DECKER, Paul

Gothic architecture decorated. Consisting of a large collection of temples, banqueting, summer and green houses; gazebo's, alcoves; faced, garden and umbrello'd seats; terminari's, and rustic garden seats; rout houses, and hermitages for summer and winter; obelisks, pyramids, &c. Many of which may be executed with pollards, rude branches and roots of trees.

Being a taste entirely new. Likewise designs of the Gothic orders, with their proper ornaments, and rules for drawing them. The whole engraved on twelve copper plates. Designed by P. Decker, Architect.

London: Printed for the author, and sold by Henry Parker and Elirabeth [*sic*] Bakewell; H. Piers and Partner, 1759.

12 pls.

[*Bound with*:]

Gothic architecture, part the second. In forty three designs of paling of various sorts, for parks and clumps of trees, gates, hatches, &c. Likewise doors and windows, with proper heads to them; sashes of different kinds, &c. To which are added, several designs of frets for joiners and cabinet= makers; with frets and frizes for smith's work, brass and iron fenders, borders for marble tables, &c. The whole neatly engraved on twelve copper= plates. From the designs of P. Decker, Architect.

London: Printed for the author, and sold by Henry Parker and Elizabeth Bakewell; H. Piers and Partner, 1759.

12 pls.

23.5 × 29.8 cm

MB

In 1752 William and John Halfpenny issued their *Chinese and Gothic Architecture*, which illustrated a few designs in rococo Gothic Revival style, although the majority of designs was Chinese. In the same year William Halfpenny issued *Rural Architecture in the Gothick Taste*, his first publication entirely devoted to Gothic Revival.[1] The next major collection of Gothic designs was Paul Decker's *Gothic Architecture* and he, like the Halfpennys, catered to all possible clients: the volume was clearly intended as a pendant to his *Chinese Architecture*, identical in format to *Gothic Architecture* and issued in the same year.

The fashion for Chinese died quickly after these publications, but the taste for Gothic grew steadily, encouraged by increasing interest in archaeology, British history, and structural principles of architecture.[2] Nevertheless Decker's work was designed merely to satisfy a rococo taste, and like Langley and Halfpenny he made little reference to actual Gothic examples. The influence of his work therefore was short lived.

Decker offered no introductory or explanatory text. The limited variety of subjects in his plates—with as many as seven designs per sheet—is indicated on the two title pages. Many of his designs, like the Halfpennys', reflect a Palladian concern for geometry and symmetry, especially in plan. The hermitages in Plate 11, for example, are segmental in plan, while the "Gezebo" in Plate 6 is a semicircle. All elevations, including those made of rustic tree trunks and branches, are bilaterally symmetrical. Like Langley, Decker illustrated a Gothic "Order," its height equal to 12 diameters (Plate 6), but it seems more an afterthought than a fundamental component of Decker's style.[3] Four of the designs in the first part are not Gothic at all, but in "Rude" or "Rustic" style, with rough tree trunks, branches, roots, and stones used to make a garden seat (Plate 9), three hermitages (Plates 10 and 11), and "A Hermatic Retirement" (Plate 12). The illustrations in the first part include ornamental scenery—small trees, bushes, and the like—adjacent to each design, but this achieves little sense of landscape space. Rather, it serves as additional rococo embellishment for the highly fanciful "Gothic" ornamentation of the structures themselves. The first six plates of the second part show gates, railings, paling, and fences. The next three plates show designs for fretwork. The final three plates show designs for window heads, sashes, and doors that, like much rococo Gothic Revival work, bear little resemblance to actual examples of medieval window tracery.

1. The first major British publication concerning Gothic architecture was Batty and Thomas Langley's *Ancient Architecture* (1742; *q.v.*).

2. On the role of these issues in the Gothic Revival see Kenneth Clark, *The Gothic Revival* (London: Constable, 1928); J. Mordaunt Crook, "Introduction" to Charles L. Eastlake, *A History of the Gothic Revival*, reprint (Leicester: Leicester University Press, 1970); Georg Germann, *Gothic Revival in Europe and Britain* (London: Lund Humphries, 1972); and Terence Davis, *The Gothick Taste* (Newton Abbot and London: David & Charles, 1974).

3. The illustration of the "Gothic Order" in the center of Plate 6 overlaps the image to its left, suggesting that the layout of the plate was not carefully planned. This "Order" appears only once in Decker's illustrations, in the "Alcove Seat" in Plate 9.

64.1

DE COETLOGON, Dennis (–1749)

An universal history of arts and sciences: or, a comprehensive illustration, definition, and description of all sciences, divine and human; and of all arts, liberal and mechanical. The origin and progresses of all religions, sects, heresies and schisms: the description of all countries; their government, ecclesiastical, civil and military; their different climates, soils, products, and the manners of the inhabitants: the different systems of philosophers, curious and accurate observations of astronomers, both antient and modern: the history of all orders, religious and military: with curious and entirely new treatises on the duties of embassadors and plenipotentiaries, the education of princes and their subjects, and the manner of travelling into foreign parts. The whole extracted from the best authors in all languages, and enriched with the new systems, hypotheses, maxims, and reflections of the author. By the Chevalier Dennis de Coetlogon. . . . Volume the first [*or second*].

London: Printed and sold by John Hart, 1745.

[*Two volumes: London,* [1741–] *1745.*]

Art. "Building," I, 389–409; 1 pl.

40.1 × 24.5 cm

MnU

The Royal Licence, bound preceding the frontispiece, is dated 13 March 1740/41. The title page of each volume is dated 1745.

Compared to Chambers's *Cyclopaedia* (*q.v.*), de Coetlogon's *Universal History* is far more substantial, containing lengthier articles on many subjects. De Coetlogon began his work in the year after Chambers died, perhaps hoping to capture some of Chambers's market. But the reputation of the *Cyclopaedia* was well established; de Coetlogon could not compete with the several editions of Chambers published between 1741 and 1746, and the *Universal History* never achieved another edition.

The article on "Architecture" (I, 162–178; 1 pl.) observes the traditional division of the subject into Civil, Military, and Naval Architecture, and indicates that Civil Architecture is considered in the article on "Building." There is a brief account of the differences among Ancient, Gothic, and modern architecture. The greatest portion of the article is devoted to the parts and proportions of the five orders. The single plate accompanying this article illustrates the five orders, a variety of moldings, the diminution of columns, and two examples of intercolumniation.

The *Universal History* is one of the few eighteenth-century encyclopedias to have an article on "Building." Its text concerns materials, such as stone, brick, and timber, and such tectonic elements as foundations, walls, gates, doors, windows, chimneys, stairs, and roofs. Aesthetic concerns, such as the size and proportion of rooms, are considered briefly. There are short remarks on the design of churches and bridges. Throughout the article de Coetlogon included frequent references to Vitruvius and especially Palladio. The one plate accompanying the article includes illustrations of doors, windows, chimneypieces, ceilings, stairs, and roof trusses. The principal figure in the plate is a house nine windows wide and two stories high, with a heavily rusticated basement, a projecting center section three windows wide, and above that an attic story of three circular windows. On the skyline there are sculpted figures on pedestals.

DICKSON, R. W.
The farmer's companion *and* Practical agriculture.

See Entry 469.

65.1
[DOMVILE, Lady Helena Sarah]
Eighteen designs for glebe houses and rural cottages, with ground plans.

London: Published by John Mitchell, and John Weale, [n.d.].

37 pls.

21.6 × 28.6 cm

Bodl.

65.2
———
———

London: Published by John Mitchell, and John Weale, [n.d.].

37 pls.

23.0 × 29.0 cm

NNC

The name of the lithographer, Perey Fitzpatrick, and the words "Designed by Lady Domvile" appear in several plates. There is no other indication of author or artist.

There are at least two distinct editions of this book. In the Bodleian Library copy the view of each design is surrounded by a border. In the Avery Library copy the views of Designs 13 and 16 are drawn without any border; the other views retain borders, as in the Bodleian copy.

The discussion below pertains to the Avery copy.

The 37 plates include views and plans of 18 designs for modest cottages and houses. Design No. 6, for example, includes just three rooms, 12 feet wide by 12 or 14 feet long, plus offices. Design No. 9 contains only two rooms, 12 feet square, plus offices. Design No. 18 includes a drawing room, bedroom, dining room, and breakfast room on the ground floor, and bedrooms above. The first nine designs clearly resemble the work of Peter Frederick Robinson (*q.v.*) who, like Lady Domvile, made use of irregular, almost informal plans and elevations, picturesque gables, elaborate bargeboards, oriels, lattice windows, Tudor drip moldings, and ornate chimneys. Both authors depicted their designs in highly picturesque settings, surrounded by mature shrubbery and trees. Domvile's fourth design bears particularly close comparison to the second design in Robinson's *Designs for Lodges* (1830; *q.v.*), which Robinson claimed to have executed in South Wales by 1830. Both designs consist of two small gabled pavilions with elaborate bargeboards and Tudor windows, flanking a recessed portico with two rustic columns *in antis*. Among the differences between the two designs are small porches at each side of Domvile's design that do not appear in Robinson's, variations in the articulation of windows and chimneys, and the fact that Domvile's design is a double cottage while Robinson's is a single gatekeeper's lodge.

The rest of Domvile's designs (Nos. 10–18) are consistently plainer or more crudely rustic than the first nine, with less ornament and a less sophisticated manner of picturesque composition.

DOUGALL, John (1760–1822)
The cabinet of the arts.

See Entry 487.

The draughtsman's [*or* draughtsmen's] assistant.

See Entry 485.

DUNN, Robert
"Sketches of cottages."

See COTTAGE **Improvement Society for North Northumberland,** *Entry 483.*

66.1

EDWARDS, E., and Matthew DARLY

A new book of Chinese designs calculated to improve the present taste, consisting of figures, buildings, & furniture, landskips, birds, beasts, flowrs. and ornaments, &c. By Messrs. Edwards, and Darly.

[London]: Published, & sold by the authors, & by the print & booksellers in town & country, 1754.

[i] p, 121 pls (numbered 1–56, 56–120).

27.9 × 21.6 cm

BL

The fashion for Chinese subjects in English architectural literature was nearly limited to the decade of the 1750s. Serious publication of Chinese designs began with the Halfpennys' series of *New Designs* in 1750 (*q.v.*), and Paul Decker offered the last book devoted entirely to Chinese architecture in 1759 (*q.v.*). During this decade Chinese designs were exceptionally popular: the Palladian theorist Robert Morris implicitly recognized this in his scathing condemnation of Chinese fashion in 1751,[1] while Sir William Chambers issued his important book of designs for Chinese buildings in 1757 (*q.v.*).

Among all these books the collection of designs published by Edwards and Darly in 1754 was the most elaborate. Following a single page of text (an "index" of the plates), there are designs in a highly rocco Chinese style for gates, rails, clothing, idols and other "figures," beds, landscape paintings, conversation pieces, genre scenes, mirrors, cartouches, boats, furniture, birds, and flowers. Architectural subjects include bridges, a pagoda, temples (Plates 1, 15, 53, 54, and 60), porticoes (Plate 8), windows (Plate 11), "Terminaries" (Plates 42, 44, and 59), an "Orchestra" (Plate 49), alcoves, summer houses, and garden seats (Plates 50–52, 57, 103, 112, and 114), and a hermitage (Plate 58). In addition there are "Pannels," doors, and other "Appendages to Buildings."

Most designs are little more than two-dimensional panels or facades; the shallow interiors of most garden temples and alcoves are just large enough for a bench or two. The architectural designs are even less substantial than contemporary Chinese designs by the Halfpennys: walls and columnar supports are not organized according to Palladian principles of geometry and symmetry, but instead are dominated by irregular, robust Rococo ornament, including flaring pagoda roofs, fretwork, urns, and lush plantings.

1. This is found on pp. xv–xvi of Morris's *Architectural Remembrancer* (1751; *q.v.*).

67.1 ‖

EDWARDS, Edward (1738–1806)

A practical treatise of perspective, on the principles of Dr. Brook Taylor. By Edward Edwards. . . .

London: Printed by Luke Hansard, for Leigh, Sotheby and Son, 1803.

xii + 316 + [1] pp, frontisp. + 40 pls.

Reference: Information supplied by Winterthur Museum Library.

Practical treatise of perspective. New edition with 40 plates.

[London]: Leigh, 1806.

4°

Reference: ECB

Following a dedication to the king, the Preface (pp. v–ix) opens with Edwards's division of all previous treatises on perspective into two classes: those which "appear clear and instructive at the first view" but are "deficient in science and theory," and those which "contain the truest principles of the science" but which are so "mathematical" and "abstruse" that there is nothing to interest "the eye of a practical artist" (p. v). Edwards suggested his own treatise would better serve "those artists who have neither time nor resolution sufficient to investigate the science of Perspective, under its present obscurities and difficulties" (pp. vi–vii). The Preface is followed by an illustration of a Tuscan base and capital on page x, and a table of contents (pp. xi–xii).

The first 14 pages of text are devoted to geometry, and are followed by 79 pages of terms, definitions, examples, and illustrations of perspective construction. Subsequent sections treat objects inclined toward the picture plane, objects inclined toward both the picture plane and the horizon, shadows, and additional examples. The text concludes with a "Discourse on the Application of the Science of Perspective, in the Composition of a Picture, and Other Works of Art" (pp. 279–308).

The plates include diverse subjects: geometric figures and diagrams, landscape views including some with geometric objects or human figures, moldings, bases, cornices, and other elements of the Classical orders, room interiors, a country church, and a variety of dwellings. In Plate III there are two buildings described as "houses" (p. 31) whose wide eaves and rooftop belvederes are reminiscent of Italianate buildings in landscape paintings by Claude or Poussin.[1] Garden seats appear in Plates IV and XVII, the former a simple arcaded loggia open on two sides, and the latter resembling an enclosed and pedimented triumphal arch. Edwards's largest project is a mansion, illustrated in Plate V (dated 1795). A three-story pedimented central pile, five windows wide, is connected by low arcades to two wings, each three stories high and three windows wide. Apart from the central pediment there is minimal ornament, consisting of string-courses, a cornice, and a blocking course. A smaller house in Plate XIII is three stories high, five windows wide, and without pediment or wings. Outline figures of small gable-roofed houses appear as part of perspective exercises in Plate XXVII. In Plate XXXI Figure 1 depicts a thatched cottage, with walls constructed of rough wooden planks, located on the side of a hill overlooking a prospect of fields and rolling hills. Figure 2 in the same plate shows a three-story brick or masonry house, five windows wide, on the side of a hill. There is an open vista to the rear, while the foreground is framed by a tree on the right and a barn made of wooden planks on the left. Figures 1 and 2 in Plate XXXIV each show a small "building" (pp. 223, 225), irregular in elevation and plan, set in an open landscape. Figures 1 and 2 in Plate XXXVIII show "two small houses or villas" (p. 264), square in plan, two stories high, with three window openings on the upper-story facade and just a doorway opening below. Figures 3 and 4 in the same plate are views of a bridge crossing a river, with a town house and a campanile on the opposite bank. Figure 1 in Plate XL is a "view of the back part of a village" (p. 271), including a church tower and a barn. Figure 2 in the same plate shows a curving street in a town, flanked on each side by three- and four-story houses and, on the right, a chapel.

1. Compare the Italianate forms in John Nash's design for Cronkhill, erected approximately one year earlier. See Summerson (1969), p. 290 and Pl. 193.

68.1
[ELISON, Thomas]
Decorations for parks and gardens. Designs for gates, garden seats, alcoves, temples, baths, entrance gates, lodges, facades, prospect towers, cattle sheds, ruins, bridges, greenhouses, &c &c. also a hot house & hot wall: with plans & scales on 55 plates

London: Published by J. Taylor, [ca. 1800].

55 pls.

22.9 × 14.6 cm

MB

This anonymous book was traditionally attributed to Charles Middleton (*q.v.*), but Colvin (1978) has argued convincingly that the author was Thomas Elison.[1] Colvin dates the book to ca. 1810, and major libraries have catalogued it with attributed dates from 1800 through 1810. The designs themselves show a formal elegance that might have been stylish for 1800, but was retardataire by 1810, and so I have suggested the earlier date.

The book contains a wide selection of designs for park and garden structures in a variety of styles. Plates 1 through 4 include designs for gates based on a range of motifs from mid-eighteenth-century fretwork to ovals and circles in the style of Sheraton or Hepplewhite. The seats and alcoves in the next four plates are highly architectonic: the structure is well expressed through columns or pilasters, and there is a geometric regularity in plan and elevation. Plates 9 through 24 show garden houses, a seat, temples, pavilions, mausolea, a dairy, and a bath, in a wide range of styles, from Doric to Gothic, primitive, and rustic. Plates 25 through 29 show entrance gates and lodges in Classical styles. Plates 30 and 31 each depict two-story keeper's lodges, one in Tuscan and one in Ionic style. The former has only a kitchen and parlor on the ground floor, and the latter has a kitchen, parlor, store closet, pantry, and entrance hall. Plates 32 and 33 depict Classical porticoes. Plate 34 is a Gothic "Cattle Shed & Ruins," Plates 35 and 36 are Gothic prospect towers, partly in ruins, Plate 37 is a Gothic "Façade," and Plates 38 and 39 are Gothic prospect towers combined with a lodge or cattle shed. Plates 40 through 49 depict bridges in rustic, Gothic, and Classical styles. Plate 50 illustrates an aviary, Plate 52 is a design for a conservatory, and Plates 51 and 53 through 55 are designs for greenhouses, a hothouse, and a hot wall. All designs are shown in elevation and plan.

1. Colvin (p. 287) cites an edition published in Leipzig, *Décorations pour parcs et jardins*, with Elison's name on the title page. This appears to be the same edition as one at Yale, with both French and German title pages, entered in NUC according to its German title: *Verzierungen für Parcks und Gärten, hrsg. von Thms. Elison, Architect des Prinzen von Wallis* (Leipzig: Baumgärtner, [18—]); 55 pls. A catalogue card is maintained at Yale for this title, but the book itself could not be found.

69.1
ELSAM, Richard

An essay on rural architecture, illustrated with original and oeconomical designs; being an attempt, also, to refute, by analogy, the principles of Mr. James Malton's essay on "British cottage architecture," supported by several designs: to which are added, rural retreats and villas, in the Gothic, Castle, Roman, and Grecian styles of architecture; with ideas for park= entrances, a mausoleum, and a design for the naval pillar, to immortalize British naval heroism: the whole comprising thirty plates, in aquatinta; designed by Richard Elsam, Architect.

London: Printed by the Philanthropic Society; and published for the author, by E. Lawrence; and to be had at Taylor's Architectural Library; at Edgerton's Military Library; Hookham and Carpenter's; Evans's; J. Asperne's; Palser's; and of the author, 1803.

1 printed leaf, ii pp, 2 printed leaves, ii + 52 pp, 31 pls (pl. 31 is numbered 33).

32.4 × 25.1 cm

MB

69.2

——————

An essay on rural architecture, illustrated with original and oeconomical designs; to which are added, ⟨ . . . as 1803 . . . ⟩ architecture, with ⟨ . . . as 1803 . . . ⟩ heroism; the whole ⟨ . . . as 1803 . . . ⟩ Architect. Second edition.

London: Printed for Lackington, Allen, and Co., 1805.

[v] + ii + 52 pp, 31 pis (pl. 31 is numbered 33).

33.4 × 26.6 cm

PU

Although Elsam addressed this book to "the nobility and gentry of taste" and "persons of fortune" (pp. 1, 5),[1] there are only two peers identified in the list of 148 subscribers, while 69 subscribers are described as architects, builders, carpenters, glaziers, plumbers, and other artisans. In the introductory "Address" Elsam indicated that the designs included here already had been executed and that in anticipation of further commissions he had given up his public office in order to devote more attention to his clients.[2]

In *An Essay on British Cottage Architecture* (1798; *q.v.*) James Malton strongly advocated rough texture and irregular form as positive qualities in architectural design. In 1802 he reversed himself, offering highly regular, symmetrical compositions in his *Collection of Designs* (*q.v.*). Elsam conceived his *Essay* of 1803 in part as an attack on Malton's earlier ideas, and wholly supported regularity and symmetry in cottage design. But Elsam also had broader objectives, and in the "Essay and Introduction" (pp. 1–21) he identified his principal goal as "improving the taste for Rural Architecture" (p. 1). To do so would involve analysis of three different types of dwelling: not only the "thatched cottage or retreat," but also "Small rural dwellings in the Gothic and castle style," and "Country houses in the modern *elegant* style" (p. 2).

Unlike Malton, Elsam argued that the "beauties" of cottage architecture were not due to "chance" or "inadvertency." Rather, the "beauties" of a cottage derive from quite specific and rational causes, including "the effects of its situation, of its age, . . . our inconstant climate, and . . . the surrounding scenery" (p. 2). Elsam admitted that picturesque irregularity might suit certain buildings and squares in London, but insisted that "uniformity" is necessary in "the retired cottage" (p. 3). He explained that symmetry is "the leading feature in the great outlines" of "the works of Nature," and that any deviation disturbs the mind of the viewer (p. 4). Likewise any irregularity in cottages built as "rural retreats" for "persons of fortune" would only suggest "poverty" and the "grotesque" (p. 5).

Elsam briefly addressed matters of construction, materials, plan, site, and use (pp. 6–8). Clearly he visualized many of his ostensibly "rural" designs in suburban locations, enjoying the benefits of both town and country:

Beyond doubt, there is considerable satisfaction in a comfortable convenient retreat, near a town, where a gentleman has an opportunity of participating in the sports of the field, in agriculture, or in gardening; and at other intervals, when the mind is so disposed, to intermix in the company, and gay amusements, of his neighbourhood. These are the great pleasures of such a retreat, situated near the city or town, which, if elevated upon a rising ground, near to a public road, well sheltered by trees, and on a pleasant spot, cannot fail to render it both cheerful and retired. (p. 8)

In a short discussion of Gothic and Castellated styles (pp. 10ff) Elsam raised important issues of expression and affectivity in architectural style. In churches "there is no character of building so well calculated to impress the mind with a just and awful solemnity, or with a greater religious veneration" as Gothic (p. 11). He also recommended the use of Gothic in "private dwellings" but said it must "be divested of that gloominess conspicuously becoming in solemn structures" (p. 12) and "partake of a more cheerful character than the style usually practised in churches" (p. 16). Elasm also addressed the issue of expression in larger, more formal buildings. The "city mansion" must be grave, sober, and serious, while a country villa should have "cheerful, and even extravagant embellishments" (p. 18).[3] The implication is that architectural style should reflect the nature of one's activities and pursuits: politics, commerce, and formal society in the city, or rest and informal relaxation in the country. In between these extremes the "villa of moderate size" might offer a combination of "the dignity and consequence of the town residence, with the delights and pleasures of the country seat." No other type of dwelling would be "so commodious, so healthy, or so pleasant" (p. 17).

Most of the text (pp. 23–52) is devoted to plate descriptions, with additional remarks on the commissioning and siting of some designs. The

31 plates include aquatinted elevations and plans for one single cottage, one double cottage, a group of four attached cottages, two cottages and a villa each in a choice of styles, a pair of small houses, two individual small houses, five villas, a mausoleum, a monumental pillar, and two park entrances with lodges. The plans all are based on symmetrical geometric figures, and the elevations too are symmetrical and regular. The villa "in the Style of an Abbey" (Plate 13), for example, includes a kitchen, library, bedchamber, and saloon, all of which are circular in plan, plus an eating room and drawing room each measuring 20 feet by 30 feet. Among the smallest designs is a two-story double cottage (Plate 3), with just a kitchen, parlor, closet, and pantry on the ground floor of each side. One of the largest designs is shown in Plate 19, "a Villa intended to be erected in the County of Suffolk." The ground floor is over 80 feet wide and approximately 55 feet deep, and includes an entrance hall, staircase hall, parlor, library, drawing room, eating room, greenhouse, kitchen, housekeeper's room, pantry, and water closet.

Elsam included several designs in "Gothic" and "Castle" or "Chateau" styles. Plate 11, for example, shows a cottage with crenellations, pointed windows, and a porch made of columns in a style reminiscent of Batty Langley Gothic. Plate 14 depicts "two small houses" in "the Gothic Style, with a Saxon Gateway in the Center." Plate 25, an alternative elevation for Mr. Pettyward's villa, is an "imitation of a chateau," with crenellations, machicolations, turrets, and arrow slits. Other designs are in Doric, Ionic, or a very plain Neoclassical style. The elevations include lush surrounding scenery, with an occasional vista past the house to a distant range of hills. Elsam rendered textures and effects of light and shade skillfully, and they contribute to the pictorial depth and elegance of his plates.

1. The description here is based on examination of the 1803 edition.

2. Colvin (1978), p. 292, indicates Elsam was "employed in the Barrack Department of the War Office."

3. Just one year earlier James Malton expressed a similar aversion to the dull regularity of many Palladian country houses in *A Collection of Designs* (q.v.).

70.1

ELSAM, Richard

Hints for improving the condition of the peasantry in all parts of the United Kingdom, by promoting comfort in their habitations: interspersed with plans, elevations, and descriptive views of characteristic designs for cottages, contrived for the use and convenience of the peasant and small farmer, as well as occasional retreats for persons of moderate income. Illustrated on ten plates, handsomely engraved in aquatinta, and embellished with picturesque scenery, elegantly coloured to imitate the drawings. To which are prefixed, introductory observations on the cheapest, best, and most approved manner of building them, under the impression that the materials of every description will be found by the landed proprietor. To which are added, explanations and estimates made accordingly. By Richard Elsam. . . .

London: Printed for and published by R. Ackermann; and may be had of the author, 1816.

viii + 39 pp, 11 pls.

34.3 × 23.5 cm

V&A

In remarks "To the Reader" (pp. vii–viii) Elsam set his work apart from previous treatises on rural improvement by indicating the broad range of issues he would consider:[1]

This work embraces a general view of our peasantry in all parts of the united kingdom, with the causes of their distress in certain districts, as also the ulterior advantages that may be expected by the kingdom at large, and in particular by the landed and agricultural interest uniting to promote the comfort, health, morals, and condition of those useful members of the community; at the same time introducing a more characteristic style of building their habitations than at present prevails. (p. vii)

For those not interested in philanthropic, economic, or picturesque improvement, Elsam also indicated his designs could be "converted at a small expence into occasional retreats for persons with moderate incomes" (p. vii). For those of greater means he also mentioned his previous experience of "near thirty years . . . in designing and estimating public and private buildings, as well as improvements and additions to country seats, in the Grecian, Roman, Gothic, and Castle styles" (p. viii).

The first 20 pages of text address a wide variety of issues relating to rural improvement. The return of peace following the Napoleonic Wars, he said, provided the appropriate "moment when we should turn our eyes towards the condition of the poor" (p. 1). He lamented the "miserable state" of laborers' dwellings, while focusing in particular on opportunities for picturesque improvement: surrounded by "wild and romantic scenery" there were "many thousands . . . destined to live under hovels fit only to shelter the inhabitants of the forest from the inclemencies of the weather." Enlightened improvement could turn all this into "fruitful vallies, rich glens, and mountain scenery . . . clothed with peasants in comely attire, and in the occupation of cottages suited to their humble stations" (pp. 1–2). Elsam also injected moral and philanthropic concerns: he argued that the estate owner had a duty to provide "suitable habitations" for laborers "to bring up their families with comfort in the principles of morality, virtue, and religion"; and having done so, "how happy must he feel in the bosom of those . . . who have been raised by his benevolence from a state of misery to that of comparative independence" (p. 3).

Turning to more practical subjects, Elsam recommended that the owner provide laborers with a "small garden well planted with fruit trees" for their own sustenance as well as additional income, and that laborers should reside as near the farm as possible to minimize the time necessary for travel to and from work (p. 4). He also discussed schemes for generating "a spirit of enthusiasm" among the peasants (p. 5), and noted that improvements in peasants' physical welfare were necessary before any moral or intellectual improvement could be expected (pp. 6–7). In particular, he recommended that cottages include sufficient living space for the large families that peasants generally have (p. 6). He warned that to ignore the peasants' welfare would reflect poorly on a landowner's own character:

"When we therefore see wretched and dirty cottages, miserable and dilapidated farms, upon good but ill-cultivated ground," we naturally conclude "either that the proprietor has been ruined by his improvements, or is possessed of so much blindness, as neither to feel for himself or others" (p. 9). Elsam also proposed economic reforms: "commutation" of tithes owed to the church (pp. 10–11), and the abolition of public poor relief. He specifically contrasted the British tradition of "hospitality" with the loss of "honest pride" among those dependent on poor relief (pp. 12–13).

Elsam also discussed the relation between building materials and picturesque composition. He found brick the best material for cottages, and far superior to pisé, which cost less but was much less durable (p. 15). Yet while he recommended that the "greatest economy should be observed in the construction of peasants cottages," he did not ignore the value of picturesque composition. Indeed where brick and stone were scarce, a wall of mud mixed with lime and straw and "dashed" with a yellow ocher wash would "produce very pleasing and harmonious effects, particularly when contrasted with the neutral tints of shady scenery" (p. 16). Likewise where rough building stones are "mingled" with brick, a "strong wash of lime whiting mixed with umber and sharp grit sand indiscriminately dashed on the walls, is all that is requisite to give them a rich and mellow effect when viewed with the surrounding scenery" (p. 18). Elsam also briefly discussed the construction of brick walls, roofs, and windows (pp. 16–17, 19–20).

The plate descriptions (pp. 20–39) provided additional opportunities for Elsam to comment on cottage design. He particularly emphasized the possibilities for associational expression: "every building should convey to the idea of the spectator the use for which it is intended; and as we understand by the word PEASANT an humble individual, the character of his habitation should mingle with such an association of ideas as are most likely to approximate with the occupier's humble station" (p. 21). Just as important, however, were the effects of picturesque composition: "rural buildings owe many, nay, indeed most of their charms to the scenery; and . . . without the aid of trees, broken foregrounds, herbage, and the surrounding circumstances, the peasant's cottage, as well as the villa, may be justly compared to a fellow-creature cast on the desert island" (p. 22). Earlier in his career Elsam had argued strongly in favor of regularity in architecture,[2] but here he became more equivocal: "regularity in the higher orders of architecture is indispensable; but such is the prevailing taste for irregularity in modern improvements, that it is almost dangerous to propound any thing new in architecture which does not relate to irregular structures or to the picturesque in building" (p. 24). He found that irregularity in Castellated and Gothic structures would "in general please," and that in "the rustic cottage . . . nothing can be more characteristic or consistent than its irregularity" (p. 25).[3]

The first ten plates show plans, elevations, and views of six designs for "a peasant's or farmer's cottage," one of which (Plate X) had been erected in Ireland in 1813. The smallest (Plate IX) includes a kitchen, two bedrooms, and a pantry; the largest (Plates III and VII) contains a kitchen, three bedrooms, plus a pantry and cow shed. All the cottages are designed in the same style, with thatch roofs, hipped gables, and wide windows composed of multiple narrow casements surmounted by a Tudor drip molding. Elsam's elevations and views include lush shrubbery, trees, and lawns, with occasional picturesque laborers or travelers enlivening the foreground. The final plate includes details of a window, a door, a chimney, and a fireplace.

1. Compare earlier books such as Nathaniel Kent's *Hints to Gentlemen* (1775; *q.v.*) or John Wood's *Series of Plans* (1792; *q.v.*), which focus on efficiency, health, and comfort, or Edmund Bartell's *Hints for Picturesque Improvements* (1804; *q.v.*) which concentrates on matters of picturesque composition.

2. See his *Essay on Rural Architecture* (1803).

3. In contrast to his earlier enthusiasm for symmetry and regularity, Elsam now took special interest in chance, which he found "often very superior to design" (p. 25).

71.1
ELSAM, Richard
The practical builder's perpetual price-book: elucidating the principles of ascertaining the correct average value of the different artificer's works usually employed in building; with cursory observations on the customs of measuring in the various parts of the United Kingdom, in reference to the recent act for establishing uniformity in weights and measures. By Richard Elsam, Esq. Architect and Surveyor, assisted by the most eminent professors in the art of building. To which is attached, an appendix, comprehending the substance of every clause in the building act; with information of the utmost importance to the practical builder, not only in the metropolis, but in every part of Great Britain and Ireland.

London: Printed for Thomas Kelly, by J. Rider, and sold by the booksellers in all parts of the British Empire, 1825.

x + 160 + [ii] + 161–180 pp, frontisp. + 7 pls.

23.9 × 14.5 cm

NNC

71.2

————————

————————

London: Printed for Thomas Kelly, by J. Rider, and sold by the booksellers in all parts of the British Empire, 1826.

x + [ii] + 180 pp, frontisp. + 7 pls.

23.5 × 15.0 cm

MH

71.3

_____

_____

London: Printed for Thomas Kelly, by J. Rider, and sold by the booksellers in all parts of the British Empire, 1827.

x + 3–180 + [iv] pp, frontisp. + 7 pls.

23.5 × 15.0 cm

MH

71.4 ‖

_____

_____

London: Printed for Thomas Kelly, by J. Rider, and sold by the booksellers in all parts of the British Empire, 1828.

x pp, 2 printed leaves, 180 pp, frontisp. + 7 pls.

25 cm

Reference: Information supplied by University of Rochester.

71.5 †

_____

The practical builder's perpetual price–book: elucidating the principles of ascertaining the correct average value of the different artificer's works . . . with cursory observations on the customs of measuring. . . . By Richard Elsam. . . . To which is attached, an appendix, comprehending the substance of every clause in the building act. . . .

London: Printed for T. Kelly by J. Rider, 1832.

x + 180 pp, 8 leaves of pls.

23 cm

Reference: NUC-S

71.6

_____

The practical builder's perpetual price-book: for ascertaining the correct average value of the different artificers' works employed in building; with observations on the customs of measuring in the various parts of the United Kingdom, in reference to the act for establishing uniformity in weights and measures. By Richard Elsam, Esq., Architect and Surveyor, assisted by the most eminent architects. With an appendix, comprehending the substance of the building act; with information of the utmost importance to the practical builder, not only in the metropolis, but in every part of Great Britain and Ireland. Revised, corrected, and improved to the present day.

London: Thomas Kelly, 1841.

x + [iii] + 3–180 pp, frontisp. + 7 pls.

23.7 × 15.0 cm

NjP

71.7 †

The practical builder's perpetual price-book. . . . With an appendix comprehending the substance of the building act. . . . Revised, corrected, and improved to the present day.

London: Thomas Kelly, 1842.

x + 180 pp, 8 pls.

8°

Reference: BLC

71.8 ‖

The practical builder's perpetual price-book ⟨ . . . as 1841 . . . ⟩ day.

London: Thomas Kelly, 1844.

x + 180 + [1] pp, frontisp. + 7 pls.

24.4 × 15.0 cm

Reference: Information supplied by Humanities Research Center, University of Texas, Austin.

71.9

London: Thomas Kelly, 1847.

x + 3–168 + 17–40 pp, frontisp. + 6 pls.

24.0 × 15.3 cm

MH

71.10 ‖

[ELSAM, Richard]

Kelly's practical builder's price book, or safe guide to the valuation of all kinds of artificer's work: with the modern practice of measuring and a copious abstract of the new building act, for regulating the construction of buildings. Revised and corrected by new calculations upon the present value of materials and labour, and founded upon the most approved modes of measurement. The whole arranged by an architect of eminence, assisted by several experienced measuring surveyors. Illustrated and exemplified by steel engravings and numerous wood-cuts.

London: Thomas Kelly, 1864.

iv + 5–168 + 31 pp, frontisp. + 5 pls.

25 cm

Reference: Information supplied by Winterthur Museum Library.

This book originally appeared with an undated and anonymous title page as part of Peter Nicholson's *New Practical Builder* (1823–[1825]; *q.v.*). Occasionally this first "edition" has been bound and catalogued separately from *The New Practical Builder*.[1]

The frontispiece to the *Price-Book* shows an elevation and plan of a design by Elsam for a large castellated "Villa." A central cylindrical tower, flanked by turrets and rectangular wings receding at 45-degree angles, fronts a large rectangular kitchen and service pavilion. The main facade is covered with parapets, crenellations, machicolations, Tudor and round-headed windows, and arrow slits. On the ground floor three of the four principal rooms are circular or oval in plan—the staircase hall, the drawing room, and the library. The dining room is a multilateral oblong. Elsam was perhaps too ambitious in attempting such complexity of plan and ornament, but the design is still more successful than other projects by contemporary architects for large castellated residences.[2]

In the Preface (pp. v–vi) Elsam complained that "to persons in search of intellectual knowledge, it is impossible their minds can be gratified by the perusal of books, containing only a series of prices without any preparatory explanation." By contrast the *Price-Book* "conveys the fullest instructions for altering, methodizing, and arranging, all manner of Builder's charges, in accordance to the local and existing circumstances of the places where they are performed" (1826, p. vi). The text includes a lengthy chapter on measuring carpenters' and joiners' work (pp. 3–85), and shorter chapters on sawing, bricklaying and masonry, plastering, slating, plumbing, painting, glazing, and smithing. The final 20 pages include an abstract of the Building Act of 1774 and of other Acts relating to building.[3]

In addition to the frontispiece there are seven plates. One concerns sawing, two more depict "Party and External Walls," and another illustrates the "Backs of Chimnies in Party Walls." The three remaining plates depict houses. One is an elevation of three first-rate houses joined to form a single terrace, four stories high and 11 windows wide. The next depicts a group of four first-rate and two second-rate houses forming a terrace 18 windows wide, and alternately three and four stories high. Another plate includes elevations of two designs: four third-rate houses, "being the front of Cardigan Place, Kennington-Cross," built for Thomas Evans in 1806; and one third-rate and two fourth-rate houses, built in 1806 by Elsam "and known as the Villa-House, or Buildings, near Vauxhall" (p. 160). The three-story facade of the latter design has a bow at each end and a one-story tetrastyle Tuscan portico in the center.

1. I have not determined whether it was issued as a separate title, independently of *The New Practical Builder*.

2. See for example the enormous "Mansion in the Castellated Style" that Nicholson illustrated in Plate XII of *The New Practical Builder*.

3. In the 1847 and 1864 editions pages 169–180 were omitted, and portions of the Metropolitan Buildings Act (1844) were substituted.

72.1
[EMERSON, William (1701–1782)]
The elements of optics. In four books.
Book I. Simple optics, or direct vision.
Book II. Catoptrics, or reflected vision.
Book III. Dioptrics, or refracted vision.
Book IV. The construction of optical instruments.

London: Printed for J. Nourse, 1768.

xii + 244 pp, 13 pls.

[*Bound with:*]

Perspective: or, the art of drawing the representations of all objects upon a plane. In two sections.
Sect. I. Demonstrates the principles whereon this art is founded.
Sect. II. Gives the practical rules for operation; with great variety of examples.

[N. loc.: N. pub., n.d.].

vi + 111 pp, 15 pls.

21.0 × 12.5 cm

ICU

Although the essay on perspective has a separate title page and is paginated separately, all copies I have examined are bound with *The Elements of Optics*. The author's name does not appear on either title page, but the preface to each part is signed "W. Emerson."

Emerson approached the subject of perspective as a branch of optics, referring to it as "a kind of projection" (*Perspective*, p. iii). He noted that perspective would be useful to practitioners of drawing, architecture, fortification, engraving, carving, and other "mechanical arts." He argued that knowledge of perspective was particularly necessary in painting, denying the criticism of some that perspective at best provided a "deceitful illusion."

Two figures in the perspective essay depict dwellings. Figure 68 in Plate XIII shows a village with buildings and formal gardens in the foreground and open countryside in the distance. In the left foreground is the facade of a three-story house, ornamented with a wide cornice and stringcourses between the stories. Other buildings in the scene include two churches on the right, a two-story house in the middle distance, and several farm houses beyond. Figure 71 is a crudely drawn perspective view of a two-story house or cottage. The facade contains three windows on each of two stories, plus one door at the far left end.

73.1 ‡

Encyclopaedia Britannica; or, a dictionary of arts and sciences, compiled upon a new plan. In which the different sciences and arts are digested into distinct treatises or systems; and the various technical terms, &c. are explained as they occur in the order of the alphabet. Illustrated with one hundred and sixty copperplates. By a society of gentlemen in Scotland. In three volumes. Vol. I [or II, or III].

Edinburgh: Printed for A. Bell and C. Macfarquhar; and sold by Colin Macfarquhar, 1771.

Art. "Levelling," II, 971–972; pl. CIV.
Art. "Perspective," III, 469–473; pls. CXLIII, CXLIV.

Reference: Reprint [Chicago: Encyclopedia Britannica, 1967].

73.2

――――――

London: Printed for Edward and Charles Dilly, 1773.

Art. "Levelling," II, 971–972; pl. CIV.
Art. "Perspective," III, 469–473; pls. CXLIII, CXLIV.

25.0 × 19.8 cm

MnU

73.3 ‖

Encyclopaedia Britannica; or, a dictionary of arts, sciences, &c. on a plan entirely new: by which, the different sciences and arts are digested into the form of distinct treatises or systems, comprehending the history, theory, and practice, of each, according to the latest discoveries and improvements; and full explanations given of the various detached parts of knowledge, whether relating to natural and artificial objects, or to matters ecclesiastical, civil, military, commercial, &c. Together with a description of all the countries, cities, principal mountains, seas, rivers, &c. throughout the world; a general history, ancient and modern, of the different empires, kingdoms, and states; and an account of the lives of the most eminent persons in every nation, from the earliest ages down to the present times. The whole compiled from the writings of the best authors, in several languages; the most approved dictionaries, as well of general science as of particular branches; the transactions, journals, and memoirs, of learned societies, both at home and abroad; the MS. lectures of eminent professors on different sciences; and a variety of original materials, furnished by an extensive correspondence. The second edition; greatly improved and enlarged. Illustrated with above two hundred copperplates. Vol. II.

Edinburgh: Printed for J. Balfour and Co. W. Gordon, J. Bell, J. Dickson, C. Elliot, W. Creech, J. McCliesh, A. Bell, J. Hutton, and C. Macfarquhar, 1778.

[*Ten volumes, 1778–1783. The title page for Vol. I is lacking in this copy. The title and imprint for Vol. II are given here. Others vary.*]

Art. "Architecture," I, 597–629; pls. XXV(B), XXVI–XXXIX, 2nd Plate XXXIX, 3rd Plate XXXIX, 4th Plate XXXIX.
Art. "Levelling," VI, 4198–4199; pl. CLXII.
Art. "Perspective," VIII, 5974–5979; pls. CCXXXVI–CCXXXVIII.

Reference: Information supplied by The Library Company of Philadelphia.

73.4 †
Encyclopaedia Britannica; or a dictionary of arts, sciences, and miscellaneous literature. . . .

Dublin: Printed by J. Moore, 1790–1797.

[*Eighteen volumes.*]

4°

Reference: NUC-S

73.5
Moore's Dublin edition. Encyclopaedia Britannica; or, a dictionary of arts, sciences, and miscellaneous literature, on a plan entirely new. By which the different sciences and arts are digested into the form of distinct treatises or systems, comprehending the history, theory, and practice, of each, according to the latest discoveries and improvements; and full explanations given of the various detached parts of knowledge, whether relating to natural and artificial objects, or to matters ecclesiastical, civil, military, commercial, &c. Together with a description of all the countries, cities, principal mountains, seas, rivers, &c. throughout the world. A general history, ancient and modern, of the different empires, kingdoms, and states; and an account of the lives of the most eminent persons in every nation, from the earliest ages down to the present times. Compiled from the writings of the best authors in several languages; the most approved dictionaries, as well of general science as of particular branches; the transactions, journals, and memoirs of learned societies, both at home and abroad; the MSS. lectures of eminent professors on different sciences; and a variety of original materials, furnished by an extensive correspondence. Vol. . . . Dedicated by permission to His Majesty. Illustrated with near four hundred copperplates.

Dublin: Printed by James Moore, 1791.

[Eighteen volumes, 1791–1797. The title and imprint for Vols. I and II are given here. Others vary.]

Art. "Architecture," II, 217–256; pls. XXXIII–LII.
Art. "Perspective," XIV, 194–196; pls. CCCLXXXIII–CCCLXXXVII.

25.7 × 21.2 cm

ICU

73.6
Encyclopaedia Britannica; ⟨ . . . as 1791 . . . ⟩ literature; constructed on a plan, by which the different sciences ⟨ . . . as 1791 . . . ⟩ practice of each,⟨ . . . as 1791 . . . ⟩ commercial, &c. Including elucidations of the most important topics relative to religion, morals, manners, and the oeconomy of life: together with a description of all the countries, ⟨ . . . as 1791 . . . ⟩ world; a general ⟨ . . . as 1791 . . . ⟩. Compiled from the writings of the best authors, in several languages; the most approved dictionaries, as well of general science as of its particular branches; the transactions, journals, and memoirs, of learned societies, both at home and abroad; the MS. lectures of eminent professors on different sciences; and a variety of original materials, furnished by an extensive correspondence. The third edition, in eighteen volumes, greatly improved. Illustrated with five hundred and forty-two copperplates. Vol. II.

Edinburgh: Printed for A. Bell and C. Macfarquhar, 1797.

[Eighteen volumes, 1797. The title and imprint for Vol. II, containing the article "Architecture," are given here. Others vary.]

Art. "Architecture," II, 217–256; pls. XXXIII–LII.
Art. "Perspective," XIV, 181–196; pls. CCCLXXXIII–CCCLXXXVII.

26.5 × 21.0 cm

MH

73.7
Encyclopaedia Britannica; or, a dictionary of arts, sciences, and miscellaneous literature; enlarged and improved. The fourth edition. Illustrated with nearly six hundred engravings. Vol. . . .

Edinburgh: Printed by Andrew Bell, the proprietor, for Archibald Constable and Company; and for Vernor, Hood, and Sharpe, London, 1810.

[Twenty text volumes and two volumes of plates, 1810.]

Art. "Architecture," text vol. II, 553–592; plate vol. XXI, pls. XXXVII–LVI.
Art. "Perspective," text vol. XVI, 170–187; plate vol. XXII, pls. CCCCX–CCCCXV.

26.7 × 19.9 cm

ICU

73.8

Encyclopaedia Britannica: or, a dictionary of arts, sciences, and miscellaneous literature; enlarged and improved. The fifth edition. Illustrated with nearly six hundred engravings. Vol. . . .

Edinburgh: Printed at the Encyclopaedia Press, for Archibald Constable and Company; Gale and Fenner, London; and Thomas Wilson and Sons, York, 1817.

[*Twenty volumes, 1817.*]

Art. "Architecture," II, 553–592; pls. XXXVII–LVI.
Art. "Perspective," XVI, 170–187; pls. CCCCX–CCCCXV.

26.6 × 20.9 cm

ICU

73.9

Encyclopaedia Britannica: or, a dictionary of arts, sciences, and miscellaneous literature; enlarged and improved. The sixth edition. Illustrated with nearly six hundred engravings. Vol. . . .

Edinburgh: Printed for Archibald Constable and Company; and Hurst, Robinson, and Company, London, 1823.

[*Twenty volumes, 1823.*]

Art. "Architecture," II, 553–592; pls. XXXVII–LVI.
Art. "Perspective," XVI, 170–187; pls. CCCCX–CCCCXV.

26.9 × 21.4 cm

MH

Supplements to the *Encylopaedia Britannica* were published in 1801, 1803, and 1815–1824, but contained no extensive remarks relating to domestic architecture, nor any illustrations of dwellings. A full history of the *Encyclopaedia Britannica* is found in Herman Kogan, *The Great E. B.* (Chicago: University of Chicago Press), 1958.

The article on "Architecture" (1771, I, 346–361, pls. XXIV–XXXVII) became a prototype for subsequent encyclopedia articles on the subject.[1] In the first edition the text begins with a discussion "Of Architecture as an Object of Taste," treating such matters as "intrinsic" and "relative" beauty, utility, variety and regularity, proportion, grandeur, and ornament. The second section, on "Architecture as a Mechanical Art," opens with a brief history of the origin of building, followed by detailed descriptions of the five orders and such other elements as pilasters, Persians and caryatids, pedestals, arches, basements, attics, pediments, balustrades, gates, doors, piers, windows, niches, chimneypieces, ceilings, staircases, and roofs. This section closely follows the organization of Sir William Chambers's *Treatise* (1759; *q.v.*), the premier architectural treatise of the time. The plates include illustrations of the orders, doorways, windows, chimneypieces, staircases and railings, and roof trusses.

The only major change in the second edition was the addition of four new plates, numbered XXV(B), 2nd XXXIX, 3rd XXXIX, and 4th XXXIX. Plate XXV(B) directly reproduces four illustrations from Chambers's *Treatise*, depicting the origins of architecture: a conical hut, a rectangular, flat-roofed hut, a gabled-roofed rectangular hut in which a primordial version of the Doric order first appeared, and an illustration of the "Origin of the Corinthian Order."[2] In the "2nd Plate XXXIX" there are elevations and plans of two houses, taken respectively from Plates 36 and 37 of Isaac Ware's *Complete Body of Architecture* (1756; *q.v.*). The first is two stories high, with a parlor, kitchen, brewhouse, dairy, and cellar on the ground floor. The second is also two stories high, but with two parlors, a study, a kitchen, a washhouse, and a stable within the ground-floor plan. The "3rd Plate XXXIX" illustrates more designs from Ware (Plates 106 and 54/55), a bridge and a country seat. The latter consists of a central pavilion three stories high and five windows wide, plus two end pavilions, each two stories high and three windows wide, connected to the center by a curving wall and colonnade. The basement story is heavily rusticated. An even larger design, derived from Ware's Plates 39 and 45, appears in the "4th Plate XXXIX." The facade is three stories high across the entire width of seven windows. A two-story portico frames the central three bays. In plan the saloon is 35 feet square, and of the other seven rooms on the principal floor, even the smallest is 15 feet by 20 feet. All four of these plates were retained through the sixth edition, and the table below chronicles their passage through two renumberings:

2nd edition	Moore's edition and 3rd edition	4th, 5th, and 6th editions
XXV(B)	XXXIV	XXXVII
2nd XXXIX	XLIX	LIII
3rd XXXIX	L	LIV
4th XXXIX	LI	LV

By the third edition the article on architecture had been expanded to include three sections, devoted to history, principles, and practice. The first section chronicles architecture from the primitive hut through Egypt, Greece, Rome, the Middle Ages, and "ancient" and medieval Britain. The section on principles includes the entire text of the first edition article, with very few changes. The final section, devoted to the "practice" of architecture, considers siting, construction, distribution of rooms, bridges, and harbors. In addition to all the plates of the first edition, plus the four plates added to the second edition, there are two new plates. Plate XXXIII (XXXVIII in later editions) illustrates Saxon capitals, Saxon arches, Gothic arches, a Gothic column, and Norman columns. Plate LII (LVI in later editions) shows designs for gates and piers.

In the edition of 1842, all practical designs were omitted. Instead, perhaps signaling a general change in the nature of encyclopedias, the text and illustrations for "Architecture" no longer offer instruction in design, but focus instead on history and archaeology.

The articles on "Levelling" and "Perspective" include the only illustrations of houses in the first edition. The illustrations for "Levelling" are like those used by Chambers, Croker, and other previous encyclopedists (*qq.v.*): a small two-story house, three windows wide and three windows deep, demonstrates the use of a telescope to find the height of distant objects. Several of the figures for "Perspective" are derived from illustrations in *The Artists Assistant in Drawing*.[3] Figure 5, for example, an interior view of Wren's St. Stephen Walbrook, is very close to the same subject in the *Artists Assistant*, although the columns in the *Britannica* version are unrealistically attenuated. Figure 6 depicts a canal or river, with a substantial house, two stories high and five windows wide, on the opposite bank—a reversal of the corresponding *Artists Assistant* plate. Figure 7 shows a street in a town, bordered by continuous three-story facades on each side, and with part of a church or town hall facade at the far right, cut off by the edge of the picture. There is no major difference between this version and that in *The Artists Assistant*.

The same illustrations accompany the "Levelling" and "Perspective" articles in the second edition of the *Britannica* (1778–1783). All these illustrations were omitted in the next edition, in which only Fig. 5 on Plate CCCLXXXVII depicts a house. The figure demonstrates the use of a "perspective machine," and had been used previously in Ferguson's *Art of Drawing in Perspective* (1775; *q.v.*) and Chambers's *Cyclopaedia* (Vol. V, 1786; *q.v.*). The same illustration appears in reverse on plate CCCCXV of the fourth through sixth editions.

1. See for example Burrowes, *The Modern Encyclopaedia* (1816–1820); Hall, *The New Royal Encyclopaedia* (1788–1791); and Johnson and Exley, *The Imperial Encyclopaedia* (1812), *qq.v.*

2. On this plate there is also an illustration of "Nicomedes's Instrument."

3. Figures 10–11 on Plate CXLIII and Figures 3–7 on Plate CXLIV in the *Britannica* closely resemble Figures X–XVI in *The Artists Assistant in Drawing* (1st ed. n.d., 2nd ed. 1772; *q.v.*). Also Figures 2–6 and 9 on Plate CXLIII are taken from Figures 1–5 and 9 in *The Art of Drawing in Perspective* (1755; *q.v.*).

74.1

Encylopaedia Londinensis; or, universal dictionary of arts, sciences, and literature. Comprehending, under one general alphabetical arrangement, all the words and substance of every kind of dictionary extant in the English language. In which the improved departments of the mechanical arts, the liberal sciences, the higher mathematics, and the several branches of polite literature, are selected from the acts, memoirs, and transactions, of the most eminent literary societies, in Europe, Asia, and America. Forming a comprehensive view of the rise, progress, and present state, of human learning in every part of the world. Embellished by a most magnificent set of copper-plate engravings, illustrating, amongst other interesting subjects, the most curious, rare, and elegant, productions of nature, in every part of the universe; and enriched with portraits of eminent and learned personages, in all ages of the world. Together with a comprehensive system of heraldry, finely illuminated, and enriched with the armorial bearings of the royal family; of the English, Scotch, and Irish, nobility; of the Baronets of the United Kingdom; and of numerous distinguished families, patrons of this work. Compiled, digested, and arranged, by John Wilkes, of Milland House, in the County of Sussex, Esquire; assisted by eminent scholars of the English, Scotch, and Irish, universities. Volume II.

London: Printed for the proprietor, by J. Adlard: sold at the Encyclopaedia Office; by J. White; and Champante and Withrow, 1810.

[Twenty-four volumes, 1810 [i.e., 1795]–1829. The title and imprint for Vol. II, containing the article "Architecture," are given here. Those in other volumes vary.]

Art. "Architecture," II, 64–127; pls. I–XXXVIII.
Art. "Optics," XVII, 541–673; pls. I–XX.
Art. "Pise," XX, 519–522, 1 pl.

26.7 × 21.7 cm

MnU

Although the title pages of the 24 volumes bear dates from 1810 through 1829, publication began much earlier. Some plates are dated as early as 1795, and the Royal Licence, appearing in Volume I, was granted by George III in 1795.

The article on "Architecture" is accompanied by plates dated 1795, 1797, 1798, and 1799. The first part of the article concerns "Ancient Architecture," and includes an account of the origin of the orders, brief histories of Chinese, Hindu, and Egyptian styles, descriptions of the five Classical orders, a discussion of Classical temples, and remarks on ancient Greek and Roman houses. The next part concerns Gothic architecture, and includes an historical account as well as particular remarks on Gothic columns, arches, domes, spires, doors, windows, churches, and castles. The final part, "Of Modern or Practical Architecture," includes brief commentaries on intrinsic and relative beauty, proportion, siting, interior arrangement of rooms, ornament, and "the respective merits of the Grecian and Roman architecture." These theoretical remarks are followed by "Rules for Working the Five Orders," directions for drawing and constructing moldings and capitals, and methods for "Diminishing Columns," making flutes and fillets, and drawing the five orders. Further sections treat intercolumniations, "Orders upon Orders," basements, pediments, balustrades, niches, statues, chimneys, chimneypieces, doors, windows, ceilings, staircases, soffits, niches, pediments, groins, skylights, roofs, entrance gates and piers, foundations, superstructures, bridges, quays, and harbors. The 38 plates include illustrations of primitive huts,[1] "Hindu" sculptured columns, Classical orders and moldings, the Parthenon, a conjectural "Plan and Elevation of a Roman Villa,"[2] a "Norman Gothic Column and Entablature" and an "enriched" entablature,[3] Gothic arches, the Church at Batalha, Salisbury Cathedral, the castle at Old Sarum, Somerset House, St. Paul's Cathedral, and four bridges over the Thames in London. In addition there are designs for ceilings, staircases, soffits, niches, pediments, groins, roof trusses, and entrance gates, and designs by James Paine for a mansion house and a chapel.[4] The mansion house is fronted by a hexastyle Corinthian portico, and the plan of the principal floor includes a domed circular drawing room 42 feet in diameter, a hall with 14 freestanding columns supporting a coved ceiling, a saloon, a library, a great dining room, a common dining room, a withdrawing room, and a state bedroom.

The lengthy and frequently technical article on "Optics" includes illustrations of a "perspective machine," Figures 1 and 2 in Plate XX. These illustrations, which originally appeared in James Ferguson's *Art of Drawing in Perspective* (1775; *q.v.*), include a small house, two stories high and five windows wide, representing a distant object to be drawn with the aid of the machine.

The article on "Pise," a building material made of compressed earth, cites earlier accounts of its use published by John Plaw and Henry Holland,[5] and mentions a pisé house and offices built by Robert Salmon at Woburn Park Farm. Most of the article consists of instructions for working with pisé. Figures 1–7 in the accompanying unnumbered plate depict special implements for working with this material, plus the plan and elevation of a two-room pisé cottage.

1. Plate I includes five illustrations of "Primitive Huts." Two are taken from Sir William Chambers's *Treatise* (1759; *q.v.*). Another depicts a monk reading in front of a structure made of massive cylindrical piers, a fourth shows an ascetic sitting in a grove, and a fifth depicts a thatch-roofed hut supported by tree-trunk columns.

2. This appeared previously in William Newton's *Architecture of Marcus Vitruvius Pollio* (1771–1791; *q.v.*), II, Fig. LIX.

3. The column and entablature in Plate XI appeared originally in Batty and Thomas Langley's *Ancient Architecture* ([1742], *q.v.*) as Plate VII, "The Third Order of the Gothick Architecture." The entablature in Plate XII of the *Encyclopaedia* corresponds with Langley's Plate IX, "A Second Gothick Entablature for Order III," but there are significant differences between the two plates.

4. The chapel was built "in the Gardens at Gibside." See James Paine, *Plans, Elevations and Sections* (1767–1783; *q.v.*), I, 21, and Pls. LXVII–LXIX.

5. John Plaw, *Ferme Ornée* (1795; *q.v.*); Henry Holland, "Pisé" (1797; *q.v.*).

75.1

Encyclopaedia metropolitana; or, universal dictionary of knowledge, on an original plan: comprising the twofold advantage of a philosophical and an alphabetical arrangement, with appropriate engravings. Edited by the Rev. Edward Smedley. . . ; the Rev. Hugh James Rose. . . ; and the Rev. Henry John Rose. . . . Volume V. (Mixed Sciences, Vol. 3.)

London: B. Fellowes; F. and J. Rivington; Duncan and Malcolm; Suttaby and Co.; E. Hodgson; J. Dowding; G. Lawford; J. M. Richardson; J. Bohn; T. Allman; J. Bain; S. Hodgson; F. C. Westley; L. A. Lewis; T. Hodges; and H. Washbourne; also J. H. Parker, and T. Laycock, Oxford; and J. and J. J. Deighton, Cambridge, 1845.

[*Twenty-six text volumes and three plate volumes, London, [1817–] 1845. The title and imprint for Vol. V, containing the articles "Architecture," "Engraving," and "Painting," are given here. Other volumes vary.*]

Art. By JAMES, The Right Rev. J. Thomas, D.D., and LINDSAY, Rev. John, "Painting," text vol. V, 466–586, + 6 unnumbered pp; plates vol. I, pls. I–XII.

Art. by LINDSAY, Rev. John, "Engraving," text vol. V, 780–851; plates vol. I, pls. I–IV.

Art. by NARRIEN, John, "Architecture," text vol. V, 237–432; plates vol. I, pls. I–XXIII.

27.1 × 21.5 cm

MnU

75.2

The encyclopaedia of the fine arts: comprising Architecture. By John Narrien. . . . Sculpture. By Richard Westmacott, Jun. . . . Painting. I. History of the Art. By the late Right Rev. J. T. James. . . . II. Theory and practice of the art. By the Rev. John Lindsay. . . . Heraldry. By the Rev. Henry Thompson. . . . Numismatics. By Benjamin R. Green. . . . Poetry. By John Hughes. . . . Music. By Joseph Gwilt. . . . Engraving. By the Rev. John Lindsay. . . . Illustrated by numerous engravings. Forming a portion of the encyclopaedia metropolitana.

London: Published by John Joseph Griffin and Company; and Richard Griffin and Company, Glasgow, 1848.

Art. "Painting," pp. 466–586, + 6 unnumbered pp; pls. I–XII.
Art. "Engraving," pp. 780–851; pls. I–IV.
Art. "Architecture," pp. 237–432; pls. I–XXIII.

27.8 × 22.3 cm

NN

75.3 ‖

Encyclopaedia metropolitana; or, universal dictionary of knowledge: on an original plan, projected by the late Samuel Taylor Coleridge; comprising the twofold advantage of a philosophical and an alphabetical arrangement. Edited by the Rev. Edward Smedley. . . ; the Rev. Hugh James Rose. . . ; and the Rev. Henry John Rose. . . . Volume V. Second Division.—Mixed Sciences, Vol. III. Meteorology. Figure of the earth. Tides and waves. Architecture. Sculpture. Painting. Heraldry. Numismatics. Poetry. Music. Engraving.

London: Published by John Joseph Griffin and Company; and Richard Griffin and Company, Glasgow, 1848.

[*Twenty-six text volumes, one index volume, and three plate volumes, 1848–1849. (Vols. III and V, 1848; all others, 1849). The title and imprint for Vol. V, containing the articles "Architecture," "Engraving," and "Painting," are given here. Other volumes vary.*]

Art. "Painting," text vol. V, 466–586, + 6 unnumbered pp; plates vol. I, pls. I–XII.
Art. "Engraving," text vol. V, 780–851; plates vol. I, pls. I–IV.
Art. "Architecture," text vol. V, 237–432; plates vol. I, pls. I–XXIII.

Reference: Information supplied by Bowdoin College Library.

From its inception the *Encyclopaedia Metropolitana* was the focus of considerable attention, primarily because of the unique topical arrangement of its contents, according to a system devised by Samuel Taylor Coleridge. But although the work received much critical acclaim and encouragement, it was not completed rapidly. Parts were issued as early as 1817, yet the set was not completed until 1845, by which time four different editors had overseen its preparation.

In the first edition cited above, all title pages in the set (26 text volumes, three plate volumes) bear the imprint date 1845. An entry in ECB, dated 1829 to 1836, indicates a set of 25 volumes plus index offered by Baldwin and by Fellowes. An incomplete set at the Humanities Research Center, The University of Texas, Austin, contains title pages dated 1829 (Vols. I and III), 1830 (Vol. IV), 1835 (Vol. V), and 1836 (Vols. VI and VIII). The articles on "Painting," "Engraving," and "Architecture" in the 1835 Volume V are paginated identically to those in the 1845 Volume V.

In 1848 all but the first 236 pages of the fifth volume were reissued separately as *The Encyclopaedia of the Fine Arts*.

The entire encyclopedia was reissued, in 30 volumes, in 1848–1849.

In 1849 a prospectus for a revised edition appeared. Titled *Cabinet Edition of the Encyclopaedia Metropolitana. Prospectus*, it was issued in London by John Joseph Griffin and Company, and in Glasgow by Richard Griffin and Company. The text includes a revised version of the original prospectus for the first edition, plus a description of particulars for the cabinet edition, projected to fill 80 volumes. Accompanying advertisements indicate that 12 weekly parts were scheduled for publication in the next three months, and that six articles—including "Architecture"—were "in active preparation." The *Encyclopaedia Britannica* (11th ed. [Cambridge: Cambridge University Press, 1910–1911], IX, 381) indicates that altogether 42 volumes were issued from 1849 to 1858. The sets of the "Cabinet Edition" that I have examined include no volumes devoted in whole or in part to architecture.

Although many of the articles were prepared by contributors of particular prominence, the article on "Architecture" was not: its author was John Narrien of the Royal Military College at Bagshot. Nearly 200 pages in length, the article begins with a history of architecture in Greece, Egypt, and Persia. Part II is a history of Roman and Saracenic architecture, and Part III treats Gothic and Indian architecture. The final part commences with a history of "Modern Architecture," beginning with the Italian Renaissance and extending through the eighteenth century. Narrien also discussed "Characteristics and Examples" of "Modern" churches, houses, government offices, banks, post offices, theaters, hospitals, prisons, bridges, streets, and villas. Most of the "Characteristics" were commonplaces of architectural theory: in domestic architecture, for example, "the style of construction should be suited to the quality of the occupier of the building" (p. 401), a gloss on the Vitruvian notion of "decorum." Narrien likewise commended the prevailing practice of laying out streets with "great squares" and "curvilinear forms," and praised the practice of combining town houses into large, unified "ranges of buildings" as at the Adelphi or in Regent's Park. He noted further that in Palladian architecture the principal story usually was "elevated on a basement," but due to changes "in the habits and manners of the people of England within the last fifty years," the "principal apartments are now near the level of the ground"

(p. 407). Narrien next treated "General Principles" of architecture, including propriety, proportion, symmetry, and unity. Turning to "Modern Domestic Architecture," he discussed plans, exterior elevations, entrances, vestibules, the necessary rooms for a dwelling of "considerable magnitude," proportions of rooms, galleries, stairs, doorways, windows, niches, fireplaces, interior ornament, and ceilings. His remarks on "Proportions and Distribution of the Ornamental Features of Edifices" largely concern the application of the Classical orders to the exterior. Following observations on materials and on the "Practice of Building," the text concludes with a discussion of "Modern Architecture" in Turkey, Persia, India, and China.

The plates for this article illustrate Classical Greek and Roman moldings and arches, Egyptian columns, and monuments of Egyptian, Greek, Roman, Byzantine, Romanesque, Gothic, Chinese, Palladian, and English Baroque architecture. Illustrations of domestic architecture are limited to elevations and plans of a Chinese house at Canton and to Palladio's designs for the Palazzo Porto and Villa Pojana.

The article on "Engraving" includes remarks on various techniques and biographical accounts of many of the major practitioners. Plate I depicts tools, instruments, and a press. Plate II illustrates examples of five intaglio techniques: soft-ground etching, chalk engraving, mezzotint, aquatint, and two stages of making a line engraving. Three of these illustrations depict picturesque rural cottages, one or two stories high and irregular in plan and elevation. Plates III and IV contain facsimiles of the monograms of 126 engravers.

The article on "Painting" begins with an account of the various historical and national "schools" of painting. The remainder of the article, on "Theory and Rules of the Art," consists of 69 pages on the subject of outline and 19 pages on composition. The plates depict geometric outline figures, skulls, skeletons, heads, clothed and unclothed human figures, perspective constructions of ships, wheels, boxes, and other objects, animal heads and skulls, examples of "Expression" in human faces and hands, and color diagrams. In addition Plate V depicts Gothic arches and side elevations of houses in outline, and Plate XII includes perspective renderings of geometric outlines of gable-roofed houses.

The encyclopaedia of the fine arts.

See Entry 75.2.

76.1 ‖

Encyclopaedia Perthensis; or universal dictionary of knowledge, collected from every source; and intended to supersede the use of all other English books of reference. Illustrated with plates and maps. In twenty three volumes. Volume. . . .

Perth: Printed for C. Mitchel and Co. and sold for them by Mr Thomas Ostell, London. Sold also by Mess. Vernor, Hood, and Sharpe, London; and all respectable booksellers. R. Morison, Printer, [1796–1806].

[*Twenty-three volumes.*]

Art. "Architecture," II, 406–445; pls. X, XVIII–XXI, XXIII.
Art. "Castle," V, 98–100; pl. LX.
Art. "Drawing," VII, 473–482; pls. CXI–CXXIII.
Art. "Perspective," XVII, 235–243; pl. CCLXXIII.

23.3 × 15.1 cm

Reference: Information supplied by University of Illinois Library at Urbana-Champaign.

76.2 ‖

The new encyclopaedia; or, universal dictionary of arts and sciences. In which the different sciences and arts are digested into the form of distinct treatises or systems; including the latest discoveries and improvements; with the natural, civil, military, and commercial history, and biography of eminent men, of all nations; a description of all the countries, cities, seas, rivers, &c. of the known world. Including also the whole of Dr. Johnson's dictionary of the English language. Compiled from every source of domestic and foreign literature; and illustrated with upwards of three hundred and forty plates, and a complete and accurate atlas. In twenty three volumes. Vol. . . .

London: Printed for Vernor, Hood, and Sharpe; and Thomas Ostell. R. Morison, Printer, 1807.

[*Twenty-three volumes. The title and imprint for Vol. I are given here.*]

Art. "Architecture," II, 406–445; pls. X, XVIII–XXI, XXIII.
Art. "Castle," V, 98–100; pl. LX.
Art. "Drawing," VII, 473–482; pls. CXI–CXXIII.
Art. "Perspective," XVII, 235–243; pls. CCLXXIII, "1st. Plate CCLXXIV" (the latter is marked "XIV" in this edition).

8°

Reference: Information supplied by The British Library.

76.3

Encyclopaedia Perthensis; or universal dictionary of the arts, sciences, literature, &c. Intended to supersede the use of other books of reference. Illustrated with three hundred and seventy plates and maps. Second edition, in twenty-three volumes. Volume. . . .

Edinburgh: Printed by John Brown, for the proprietors, and sold by all the booksellers in the United Kingdom, 1816.

[*Twenty-three volumes.*]

Art. "Architecture," II, 406–445; pls. X, XVIII–XXI, XXIII.
Art. "Castle," V, 97–100; pl. LX.
Art. "Drawing," VII, 472–482; pls. CXI–CXXIII.
Art. "Perspective," XVII, 235–243; pls. CCLXXIII, "1st. Plate CCLXXIV."

24.6 × 16.4 cm

MnU

The *Encyclopaedia Perthensis* was issued in weekly parts from 1796 to 1806 (see Robert Collison, *Encyclopaedias: Their History throughout the Ages* [New York: Hafner, 1966], pp. 177–178). An entry in ECB indicates that the 23-volume set was advertised by Vernor in September 1806.

The article on "Architecture" begins with a history of "Ancient" architecture from biblical times through ancient Rome, including an account of the invention of the primitive hut and the origins of the orders. Next follows a history of "Modern" architecture, focusing primarily on the Middle Ages and devoting only one paragraph to Renaissance architecture of the fifteenth century and after. Following these introductory essays, Part I of the article concerns such "General Principles" as composition, harmony, proportion, the "internal division of houses," ornament, and expression. Part II, on the orders, describes their individual parts, their origins, "Diminution of Columns," intercolumniation, arches, pilasters, attics, and "Orders upon Orders." Part III concerns "Other Necessary or Ornamental Parts of Buildings," including Persians, caryatids, termini, pediments, gates, doors, piers, niches, statues, chimneypieces, staircases, handrails, balustrades, roofs, and ceilings. Part IV treats "Principles to be observed in Erecting Buildings," foundations, walls, chimneys, roofs, floors, and "the Distribution of Apartments of Houses." Part V concerns bridges, piers, and harbors.[1] The plates include illustrations of Classical orders and arches, masonry construction, Classical moldings and ornaments, gates and piers, a bridge, roof trusses, primitive huts,[2] "Nicomedes's Instrument for diminishing Columns," and Gothic or "Saxon" arches, capitals, and columns.[3]

The article titled "Castle" includes histories of English and Scottish castles and remarks on their "materials, form, situation, &c." One illustration accompanies the article: Figure 5 in Plate LX shows a five-story keep surrounded by three concentric walls with turrets and crenellations, plus a moat around the whole.[4]

Following a few introductory remarks, the article on "Drawing" is divided into 14 sections, treating materials and instruments, geometric figures, parts of the human face and flora and fauna, human limbs, the face as a whole, the human figure, proportions of the human body, "Attitudes" of the human body, "Effects of the Exertion of the Muscles," "Effects of the Passions in General," "Particular" effects of the passions, light and shade, drapery, and landscapes and buildings. The 13 plates primarily depict human figures and passions. The final plate includes illustrations of rustic country landscapes, castles, and two picturesque, irregular two-story cottages.[5]

The article on "Perspective" includes seven principal sections, which provide a history of the subject, a discussion of principles, definitions, "General Rules," "Mechanical Methods," remarks on "Scenographic Perspective," and conclusions. Additional sections treat aerial perspective, bird's-eye views, "Perspective Glass," and the perspective machine. Figures 4 and 5 in Plate CCLXXIII illustrate the use of this apparatus; in Figure 5 a house two stories high and five windows wide represents a distant object to be drawn with its aid.[6] Another plate, titled "Perspective," does not appear in the first edition. It is one of two plates numbered CCLXXIV in the 1816 edition. Except for Figure 9, which depicts drawing apparatus, all the figures on this plate appeared previously in *The Art of Drawing, in Perspective* (1755, *q.v.*). Most of the figures depict perspective constructions, but one, Figure 10, demonstrates the operation of a camera obscura: an image of one house is projected upside down onto a wall inside another house. This illustration also appeared earlier in the *New and Complete Dictionary* (1754–1755; *q.v.*).

1. The organization of this article is very similar to that of the article on "Architecture" in *The English Encyclopaedia* (*q.v.*).

2. These figures, and others, are borrowed from Sir William Chambers's *Treatise* (1759; *q.v.*). They depict a conical hut, a trabeated hut with flat roof, and a gable-roofed hut supported by primitive Doric columns.

3. The Gothic and "Saxon" figures appeared previously in the third edition of the *Encyclopaedia Britannica* (1797; *q.v.*).

4. This figure also appeared in Plate 61, Volume II, of *The English Encyclopaedia* (*q.v.*).

5. Most of these figures also appeared in Plate 9, Volume III, of *The English Encyclopaedia* (*q.v.*).

6. These figures appeared originally in James Ferguson's *Art of Drawing in Perspective* (1775; *q.v.*).

77.1

Encyclopedia mancuniensis; or the new school of arts, science, and manu-factures; being an elementary circle of the sciences, and general display of useful knowledge; designed as a familiar introduction to natural phi-losophy, chemistry, &c. &c. showing their application and value to every elegant and useful purpose: containing (with the latest discoveries and improvements,) treatises on the following subjects, viz. agriculture anatomy architecture astronomy bleaching botany chemistry commerce divinity drawing dyeing electricity galvanism gardening geography geology gram-mar history husbandry hydraulics hydrostatics law mathematics magnetism mechanics music natural history optics painting perspective philosophy pneumatics printing rhetoric short-hand surgery, &c. Vol. I [*or* II]. Illustrated with twenty-four engravings. Compiled and arranged by F. M. Hodson.

Manchester: Printed and published by J. Gleave, 1815.

[*Two volumes.*]

Art. "Architecture," I, 96–143; 1 pl.

21.2 × 13.0 cm

MnU

77.2

The new school of arts, science, and manufactures; ⟨ . . . as 1815 . . . ⟩ chemistry, &c. &c. shewing their ⟨ . . . as 1815 . . . ⟩ subjects:---viz. ⟨ . . . as 1815 . . . ⟩ with twenty-five engravings.

Nottingham: Printed and sold by R. Dowson, 1817.

[*Two volumes.*]

Art. "Architecture," I, 97–144; 1 pl.

20.2 × 12.4 cm

OrU

The first edition does not appear in NUC; in BLC it is catalogued under the name of the compiler, F. M. Hodson. Neither edition appears in Collison's standard bibliography of encyclopedias.[1] Because the second edition was published in Nottingham rather than Manchester, the reference to Manchester was expunged from the title. The article on "Magnetism" promised on the title page was never included.[2]

The article on "Architecture" opens with the traditional division of the subject into civil, military, and naval architecture (pp. 96–97). There follows a stylistic division of civil architecture into Ancient, Gothic, and Modern, but Gothic and Modern are subsequently ignored while orders and ornaments of ancient architecture are covered in four pages. The major portion of the article concerns the "general principles" of architecture, treating such topics as harmony, beauty, proportion,[3] siting, and planning. The discussion of ornament includes remarks on pilasters, caryatids, pedestals, intercolumniations, arches, pediments, gates, doors, piers, niches, statues, the proportions of rooms, staircases, balustrades, and ceilings (pp. 105–121). Other sections concern roofs, windows, chimneys, and problems of construction. The final 12 pages are devoted to bridges and piers.

The only plate accompanying the article depicts the five orders, two roof trusses, and one elevation of a mansion. The house is 13 windows across, including low wings at either side, a porticoed central pavilion three stories high, and an additional lantern story projecting above the central portion of the roof.

1. Robert Collison, *Encylopaedias: Their History throughout the Ages*, 2nd ed. (New York and London: Hafner, 1966).

2. The first edition thus contains just 35 articles in two volumes of 675 and 702 pages, respectively.

3. The discussion of harmony and proportion was based entirely on Robert Morris's *Lectures* (1734–1736; *q.v.*), published nearly a century earlier. The encyclopedia article wholeheartedly recommended cubic forms, geometric ratios, and seven "harmonic" proportions (pp. 101–104) that were identical to those proposed by Morris.

78.1

The English encyclopaedia: being a collection of treatises, and a dictionary of terms, illustrative of the arts and sciences. Compiled from modern authors of the first eminence in the different branches of science. In ten volumes. The whole illustrated with upwards of four hundred copper= plates. Vol. . . .

London: Printed for G. Kearsley. Sold by Bell and Bradfute, Edinburgh; Brash and Reid, Glasgow; Brown and by Burnett, Aberdeen; Colbert, Dublin; and all other booksellers in the United Kingdom, 1802.

[*Ten volumes.*]

Art. "Architecture," I, 275–301; pls. 17–28.
Art. "Castle," II, 301; pl. 61.
Art. "Drawing," III, 59–65; pls. 5–9 [*7, 8 wanting in this copy*].
Art. "Perspective," VII, 589–601; pls. 34–38.
Art. "Farm," X, 660–663; pl. 28.

25.8 × 19.5 cm

ViU

The article on "Architecture" begins with an introductory essay on the history of architecture (pp. 275–280). Starting with "the origin of architecture" and the invention of the orders, it proceeds quickly through Egypt, Greece, and Rome. Much of the essay is devoted to architecture of the Middle Ages, particularly in Britain, following which there is a single paragraph on Renaissance architecture of the fifteenth and sixteenth centuries. Part I of the article treats "General Principles of Architecture," including composition, harmony, proportion, the "internal division of houses," ornament, and expression. Part II concerns the orders, and includes descriptions of their individual parts, their origins, "Diminution of Columns," intercolumniations, arches, pilasters, attics, Persians, caryatids, termini, pediments, gates, doors, piers, niches, statues, chimneypieces, staircases, handrails, balustrades, orders upon orders, basements, roofs, and ceilings. The third part treats matters of construction and "Principles Necessary to Be Observed in the Erection of Buildings." Part IV concerns "Aquatic Architecture," including piers, bridges, and harbors.[1] The 12 plates depict three primitive huts,[2] a half elevation and plan of a basilica,[3] a variety of Saxon and Gothic capitals, arches, and columns,[4] "Nicomedes's Instrument for diminishing Columns,"[5] Classical orders, moldings, and arches, examples of masonry construction, techniques of dome and staircase construction, a bridge, roof trusses, gates and piers, doors, the Ark of the Covenant, and Noah's Ark.

The article titled "Castle" includes historical remarks on English and Scottish castles. An illustration at the top of Plate 61 shows a five-story keep surrounded by three concentric walls with turrets and crenallations, plus a moat around the whole.[6]

The article on "Drawing" is divided into 12 sections, on materials, parts of the human body, the face, the whole human figure, proportions of the human figure, "Attitudes" of the human figure, "Effects of the Exertion of the Muscles," light and shade, drapery, the "Effects of the Passions," flora and fauna, and landscapes and buildings. The plates primarily depict the human figure and its parts. Only Plate 9 contains different subjects, including animals, castles, rustic country landscapes, and two picturesque, irregular two-story cottages.[7]

The article on "Perspective" consists of a brief history of the subject followed by a series of theorems, corollaries, problems, and solutions. The article concludes with remarks on anamorphosis and a more general discussion of the "art of perspective." Separate subheadings are devoted to aerial perspective, bird's-eye views, and the use of a perspective machine. The plates depict geometric figures and diagrams, plus perspective views of pyramids, steps, and other objects. In addition there are illustrations demonstrating the use of a perspective machine (Figures 4 and 5, Plate 38); these include a two-story house, five windows wide, representing a distant object to be drawn with the aid of the machine.[8]

Among the additional and supplementary articles collected in the final volume of *The English Encyclopaedia*, the article titled "Farm" is partly devoted to the subject of domestic architecture. The article commences with a detailed description of Woburn Farm, an epitome of "what an *ornamental farm* should be."[9] The greater part of the article concerns a proposal by Sir John Sinclair to establish "experimental farms."[10] There is a list of the nobility and others who supported such a plan, a financial analysis of the proposed venture, a list of "Conditions" for joining a society to support such a farm, a summary of Sinclair's arguments in favor of experimental farms, and answers to several objections that critics might raise. The figures in the plate accompanying this article are copied from illustrations in Sinclair's French treatise on the subject.[11] One shows a 400-acre experimental farm divided into 52 separate fields, with indications of the crops to be raised in each field. The remaining figures depict four circular cottages, three of which are two stories high, and one of which is just one story. Each floor contains two or three rooms.[12]

1. This article is organized much like the article on "Architecture" in *Encyclopaedia Perthensis* (1796–1806; *q.v.*).

2. These figures are borrowed from Sir William Chambers's *Treatise* (1759; *q.v.*). They depict a conical hut, a trabeated hut with flat roof, and a gable-roofed hut supported by primitive Doric columns.

3. The full elevation and plan appeared previously in the fifth volume of Abraham Rees's edition of Ephraim Chambers's *Cyclopaedia* (1786; *q.v.*), on the plate titled "Architecture."

4. All these figures appeared previously in the third edition of the *Encyclopaedia Britannica* (1797; *q.v.*).

5. This and several more figures in this article appeared previously in Sir William Chambers's *Treatise* (1759; *q.v.*).

6. This illustration also appeared in Figure 5, Plate LX, of *Encyclopaedia Perthensis* (*q.v.*).

7. This plate closely resembles Plate 67 in *Pantologia* (1813; *q.v.*). Some of the subjects in this plate appear in Plate CXXIII of *Encyclopaedia Perthensis* (*q.v.*).

8. These figures appeared originally in James Ferguson's *Art of Drawing in Perspective* (1775; *q.v.*).

9. P. 660. For a discussion of the "ornamental" or "ornamented" farm, see the commentary on John Plaw's *Ferme Ornée* (1795).

10. Sinclair's proposal originally was published in the *Annals of Agriculture*, XXXIV (1800; Entry 479) and in a French version titled *Projet d'un plan pour établir des fermes expérimentales* ([Paris, 1800?]; see the commentary to Entry 308).

11. *Projet d'un plan*, Pls. 1 and 2.

12. Two of these designs later appeared in *The Complete Farmer* (1807; *q.v.*), and Abraham Rees's *Cyclopaedia* ([1802]–1820; *q.v.*).

Essays of the London Architectural Society.

See WOODS, **Joseph,** *Entry 355.*

79.1

Facts and illustrations demonstrating the important benefits which have been, and still may be derived by labourers from possessing small portions of land: proving [t]he low amount of poor's rates, where such holdings have been granted or continued to the labouring population, and its advantages to the farmer, the land-owner, and the country.

London: Published by the Labourers' Friend Society. Printed for the Society, and sold by Dean and Munday, London, [1831–1832].

[*Volume I:*] 278 pp, pls.

MH

The first volume consists of 278 pages, published in 18 numbers from 1831 to 1832. The second volume begins with No. XIX, on page 279. In October 1834 the title changed to *The Labourer's Friend Magazine*. Judging from the sets at Yale and in the Kress Library at Harvard, architectural designs appear only in the first volume.

In the first volume there are designs for five dwellings, illustrated on four plates and three text pages. Apart from descriptive material that accompanies some of the designs, there is no discussion of any design in the text of the *Magazine*.

The first design appears on a plate facing page 32, and is a "View of the Model Cottages of the Labourers Friend Society," designed by W. Bardwell. The plate depicts a double cottage two stories high and two windows wide, with slight Italianate decoration on the exterior. Floor plans for these cottages appear on the verso of the same plate, facing page 33. The ground floor consists of a kitchen, pantry, and porch, and there are two chambers upstairs. Letterpress text below the plans includes suggestions for construction and remarks on the "warm, cheerful, and comfortable" character of the design.

On the plate facing page 46 a double cottage designed by J. B. Watson is shown in end elevation and in a perspective view, surrounded by trees and shrubbery. No text accompanies this design.

The plate facing page 184 is a view of a "Design for a double cottage" by L. B. Watson—presumably a misprint for J. B. Watson—dated January 1832. Brief remarks in letterpress at the bottom of the plate indicate that the design, two stories high and four windows wide, could be erected for £120 a cottage.

Two plans, a section, and an elevation of "Two Agricultural Cottages" by W. Farlar appear on text pages 238 and 239. The two cottages, forming an attached pair, each include a sitting room, washhouse, and pantry on the ground floor, and three bedrooms above. The legend indicates that each cottage, plus outbuildings, would cost £100. No text accompanies this design.

On page 263 there is an elevation of a rustic single cottage with columns made of rough-barked tree trunks, walls made of rough-hewn vertical boards, and a thatch roof. On the same page is a "Plan of Colony for Ten Families" by Edward Lance, a land surveyor. The plan includes a central octagonal reservation with a barn and two granaries. On two sides of this area rectangular meadows extend outward. Also radiating from the center, and perpendicular to the meadows, are two large plots: one for the residence, school, and private garden of the schoolmaster, and the other for the residence, shop, and garden of the overseer. Extending out from the remaining sides of the central octagon are four double garden plots. Straddling each pair is a double stable and a double cottage.[1] On pages 264–265 Lance described his design, indicating that it was designed for ten families, and included suggestions for growing crops.

1. For a contemporary proposal for an agricultural community see William Allen, *Colonies at Home* (1826).

80.1

FERGUSON, James (1710–1776)

The art of drawing in perspective made easy to those who have no previous knowledge of the mathematics. By James Ferguson, F.R.S. Illustrated with plates.

London: Printed for W. Strahan; and T. Cadell, 1775.

xii + 123 pp, 9 pls.

20.5 × 12.0 cm

ICJ

80.2 †

———————

The art of drawing in perspective, made easy to those who have no previous knowledge of the mathematics. Illustrated with plates.

Dublin: Printed by James Williams, 1778.

xii + 123 pp, 9 pls.

21 cm

Reference: NUC

80.3 †

———————

The art of drawing in perspective, made easy to those who have no previous knowledge of the mathematics. By James Ferguson. Second edition. Illustrated with plates.

London: Printed for W. Strahan [etc.], 1778.

123 pp.

21 cm

Reference: NUC

80.4 †

———————

The art of drawing in perspective, made easy to those who have no previous knowledge of the mathematics. New edition.

Edinburgh: Denham & Dick, etc., 1802.

[1] + 125 pp, 9 pls.

Reference: NUC

80.5
_____

The art of drawing in perspective made easy to those who have no previous knowledge of the mathematics. A new edition. By James Ferguson, F.R.S. Illustrated with plates.

Edinburgh: Printed for Denham & Dick. Sold by Stewart Cheyne, Edinburgh; A. H. Nairn, London; Archer & Ward, and J. Storie, Belfast, 1803.

vii + 9–124 pp, 9 pls.

20.5 × 11.0 cm

MiU

80.6
_____

The art of drawing in perspective, made easy to those who have no previous knowledge of the mathematics. By James Ferguson F.R.S. A new edition, illustrated with plates.

Macclesfield: Printed by J. Wilson, for T. Ostell, London, 1807.

vii + 9–124 pp, 9 pls.

22.4 × 14.3 cm

BL

80.7 †
_____

The art of drawing in perspective made easy to those who have no previous knowledge of the mathematics. New edition.

London: Edinburgh printed, 1810.

vii + 124 pp.

8°

Reference: BM

80.8 †
_____

The art of drawing in perspective, made easy to those who have no previous knowledge of the mathematics. . . . Illustrated with plates. New edition.

London, 1820.

vii + 9–124 pp, 9 pls.

23 cm

Reference: NUC

In the Preface Ferguson explained that late in life he became "amused . . . with studying *Perspective*," and had prepared a set of illustrations to demonstrate "that branch of science" to "others . . . who came to me to learn" (pp. i–ii).[1] Friends who saw these drawings "expressed their desire that I should write a description of the rules by which they were delineated," and as a result he "consented to this publication" (p. ii). Ferguson complained that he saw "bad and distorted figures of machines and engines in printed books," and "many historical paintings . . . put together without any regard to what painters call *keeping*" (p. iii). In particular he cited two errors of perspective in works by Raphael (pp. iii–vi). Ferguson indicated he did not conceive this as "a complete system" of perspective, although anyone who could "fully master" the book "will not find any great difficulty in proceeding to what length he pleases in the attainment of this science" (p. vi).

The text is a series of problems and demonstrations, illustrated by geometric diagrams and perspective renderings of complex three-dimensional objects such as arches, steps, and rows of cubes and pyramids. In Plate IX Ferguson illustrated a "Perspective Machine," described in the Preface as an instrument for drawing objects in perspective "without knowing any rule at all." Ferguson hoped there would be "very few who will have recourse to such an unscientific method" (p. vii), but devoted his final chapter (pp. 115–124) to its use. He explained that some years earlier he was given a sketch of this machine "by the late ingenious Dr Bevis, who then told me he had never seen one of the like construction; and . . . I have great reason to believe that the Doctor was the inventor of it, although he never made it public" (pp. 115–116).[2] The machine consists of a curved armature with two cross wires, perpendicular to a horizontal surface on which a distant object would be drawn in perspective. The distant object in this example is a plain, unornamented two-story house, five windows wide, with a small dormer in the center of the roof.[3] To operate the machine, a user would sight the house through the armature, aligning the two wires to intersect directly in front of a given point on the house facade. Then by folding the armature down onto the drawing surface, and marking the crossing point of the wires, a series of points could be established to form the outline of the house.

1. References here are to the 1803 edition.

2. I have found no earlier depiction of this machine in British literature. Ferguson's illustration appeared over the next half century in a variety of articles on perspective. See for example Burrowes, *The Modern Encyclopaedia* (1816–1820); Chambers, *Cyclopaedia* (1778 and later); *Encyclopaedia Britannica* (3rd and later eds.); *Encyclopaedia Londinensis* (1795–1829); *Encyclopaedia Perthensis* (1796–1806); *The English Encyclopaedia* (1802); Hall, *The New Royal Encyclopaedia* (1788–1791); *The London Encyclopaedia* (1829); and *Pantologia* (1813), *qq.v.*

3. The house is shown in an oblique view from above. It appears that only half the house is shown: it is too shallow for its width, and the roof—which ought to descend in two equal pitches from a central ridge line—has only one pitch, descending from a ridge line at the very rear of the figure.

FIELDING, Theodore Henry Adolphus (1781–1851)
The art of engraving.

See Entry 470.

81.1

FIELDING, Theodore Henry Adolphus (1781–1851)

Synopsis of practical perspective, lineal and aerial. By T. H. Fielding. . . .

London: Printed for the author; sold by Carpenter & Son; Longman & Co.; Parbury, Allen, & Co.; and Smith & Elder, 1829.

1 printed leaf, 7–136 pp, 17 pls [*of which many in this copy have been destroyed*].

21.3 × 12.8 cm

ICU

81.2

Synopsis of practical perspective, lineal and aerial. By T. H. Fielding. . . . Second edition, enlarged.

London: Published for the author; by W. H. Allen & Co., 1836.

2 printed leaves, xi–xii, v–viii, 9–156 pp, 17 + 2 pls.

24.2 × 15.0 cm

CtY

81.3 †

Synopsis of practical perspective, lineal and aerial, with remarks on sketching from nature. . . . Third edition.

London: The author, 1843.

viii + 9–126 pp, 13 pls.

8°

Reference: NUC

The author taught painting and drawing at the Military Seminary of the East India Company, to whose Directors he dedicated this book. The following description is based on examination of the second edition, dated 1836.

Fielding indicated in the Preface (pp. v–viii) that in preparing this "concise System of Perspective" he had excluded "theoretical" remarks, trusting instead that the reader could rely on "the plain demonstration of facts." He wanted "to enable the student to come immediately to the point required, *viz.* the simplest mode of working a question" (pp. v–vi).

The text begins with a history of the subject and remarks on other authors' contributions, followed by several pages of definitions. Pages 38–110 are organized as explanations of the first 16 plates. The subject of Plate I is a cube. Plates II through VII depict plans, elevations, and perspective views of buildings. These include a simple gable-roofed house with one door and no other openings (Plate III), a house with a hipped roof and a central chimney (Plate IV), a "Double House" with an L-shaped plan (Plate V), a room interior with two windows and a door (Plate VI), and a "Street" flanked by three-story houses (Plate VII). All these figures are executed in simple outline, and none includes any architectural ornament. Plates VIII through XVI depict a bridge, an arcade, various geometric figures, a tub, a box, a "Target," a church, columns, turrets, and stairs.

Pages 111–144 include material new to the second edition on "Perspective of Colours" and "Perspective of Shadows" plus remarks on aerial perspective, sketching from nature, ruined buildings, roads, rivers, wild plants, trees, "figures," reflections in water, weeds, moorland scenery, cattle, broken ground and rocks, and clouds. The text concludes with a "List of Lost Books on Painting," remarks on vision, and "Additional Remarks on Sketching or Painting from Nature" (pp. 145–156). Plate XVII and the two new plates in this edition are landscape scenes; the latter two pertain specifically to "Perspective of Colours" and aerial perspective.

FITZGERALD, Francis [pseud. for Charles TAYLOR]

See TAYLOR, Charles, *Entries 329.1 and 330.1.*

82.1
FOURNIER, Daniel (–1766?)
A treatise of the theory and practice of perspective. Wherein the principles of that most useful art, as laid down by Dr. Brook Taylor, are fully and clearly explained, by means of moveable schemes, properly adapted for that purpose. The whole being designed as an easy introduction to the art of drawing in perspective, and illustrated by a great variety of curious and instructing examples. By Daniel Fournier, Drawing-Master, and Teacher of Perspective.

London: Printed for the author: and sold by Mr. Nourse; and by Mr. Lacey, 1761.

viii + 68 pp, 39 pls.

26.0 × 20.3 cm

NNC

82.2
―――――

A treatise ⟨ . . . as 1761 . . . ⟩ curious and instructive examples, engraved by the author. By Daniel Fournier, Drawing-Master, and Teacher of Perspective. The second edition, corrected, and greatly enlarged.

London: Printed for the author, and sold at his house: also by Mr. Nourse, 1764.

viii + 94 pp, [51 pls listed, but wanting, in this copy].

27.0 × 20.7 cm

ICA

In the dedication to the Master of the Military Academy at Noreland (pp. iii–iv) Fournier indicated this treatise was "drawn up for the use of the noblemen and gentlemen, whose military education you superintend. . . ." In the Preface (pp. v–vi) Fournier admitted the limited scope of this book: "As Dr. Brook Taylor's Perspective is undoubtedly the most excellent performance of its kind . . . I chose rather to attempt an explanation of his principles, than to offer any thing of my own." The text is divided into two sections. The first 31 pages, devoted to theory, include definitions, problems, theorems, and demonstrations. The remainder (pp. 32–68) consists of examples of "practical perspective."

The plates include geometric figures and diagrams, illustrations of furniture and other common objects in perspective, room interiors (Plates XVI and XX), parts of the orders (Plates XVII, XVIII, and XXVI), a vault, inclined planes, stairs, and landscape scenes. Plates XXVIII–XXX and XXXII–XXXIII include picturesque cottages and farm buildings set in rustic landscapes. Plate XXXI is a scene in a town with a church, shops, and houses adjacent to an open square. Plate XXXVII is a view of a larger town with three-story buildings fronting an open plaza with a three-story house, three windows wide, in the center.

83.1

FRANCIS, Frederick John

A series of original designs for churches and chapels, in the Anglo-Norman, Early English, Decorative English, and Perpendicular English styles of ecclesiastical architecture: including also designs for rectory houses and schools, in the domestic English and Tudor styles. By Frederick J. Francis. . . .

London: John Weale; Hatchard and Son; R. B. Seeley and W. Burnside; and Williams, 1841.

xi + 14 + [1] pp, 50 pls.

36.6 × 27.0 cm

NNC

Forty of Francis's 50 plates illustrate designs for churches in three different styles: four designs are Anglo-Norman, five are Early English, and five are "Decorative" English. The remaining ten plates show four designs for rectory houses, two in "Domestic English" style and two in "Perpendicular and English" style.

Francis's introduction was a rather belated argument in favor of the revival of Gothic style. He appealed to the reader's sense of history and patriotism in observing that Gothic is "our national architecture,"[1] and that "in no country have the various styles of Gothic architecture attained greater perfection than in England" (p. vi). As for the aesthetic excellence of Gothic, Francis stated that "for a happy union of grandeur with simplicity,—a due admixture of the ornate with the undecorated,—a proper maintenance of relative proportion in the parts, leading and subordinate, so as to conduce to the harmony of the whole,—the most experienced critics have allowed our principal ancient edifices to stand conspicuous, surpassing those on the Continent. . ."(p. vi).

Francis devoted eight pages of text to ecclesiastical subjects, followed by six pages on rectories. He described the two rectory designs in "Domestic English" style as "picturesque," and estimated they would cost £850 and £1020, respectively. Each design was two stories high, with dining room, drawing room, library, kitchen, scullery, pantry, and, in the case of the second design, a larder on the ground floor. In both cases there were three bedrooms on the upper floor. On the exterior both had bargeboarding, finials, casement windows, and other ornamentation reminiscent of the work of Peter Frederick Robinson (q.v.). The other two rectory designs, in a style ostensibly brought to "perfection" under the Tudors, were far more expensive, estimated to cost £2730 and £2950, respectively. Design No. 3 included a drawing room, dining room, library, hall, kitchen, scullery, pantry, and servants' hall on the ground floor, with three bedrooms, two dressing rooms, and three servants' rooms above. The final design had in addition a conservatory and larder on the ground floor, and one more bedroom—but no servants' rooms—on the floor above. The exterior ornamentation consisted of stepped gables and crenellations, along with casement windows and other Tudor details. Francis provided five pages of specifications for use by a variety of artisans, including the excavator, concrete layer, bricklayer, mason, slater, plumber, carpenter, joiner, plasterer, smith, glazier, and painter. He noted that the materials used might vary according to local "circumstances," and "the amount of internal decoration assumed, has been of that intermediate and average character which, while plain and simple in design, yet produces a Gothic Ecclesiastical effect" suitable for a rectory (p. 9).

1. P. vii. Thomas Rickman, whom Francis cited in his text, was not the first to understand Gothic as the English national architecture, but did publish the first comprehensive classification of Gothic architecture into distinct historical periods on the basis of style, *An Attempt to Discriminate the Styles of Architecture in England* (London, 1817). This treatise was first published in 1815 as an essay in James Smith's *Panorama of Science and Art* (q.v.).

84.1
GANDY, Joseph Michael (1771–1843)
Designs for cottages, cottage farms, and other rural buildings; including entrance gates and lodges. By Joseph Gandy, Architect. . . .

London: Printed for John Harding, 1805.

x + 28 pp, 43 pls.

28.3 × 22.9 cm

MBAt

Gandy's ambitions for an architectural career were frustrated from the start by the lack of building activity in England during the Napoleonic Wars. Like many of his contemporaries he resorted to publishing books in which he offered designs for cottages and other small structures and argued that erecting such buildings would contribute to the national welfare.[1]

Gandy noted that a series of articles in the first volume of *Communications to the Board of Agriculture* (1797) had originally given him the idea to publish *Designs for Cottages*. These articles concerned construction and planning of rural cottages and farm buldings, and particularly emphasized matters of cost and efficiency.[2] Gandy acknowledged the economic value of such improvements, but suggested that a further goal—"the advancement of Public Taste"—required more than technical hints on construction (p. iii). To achieve the goal of taste required the abilities of an "Artist," who would prepare designs that "unite *convenience* and *taste* in a greater degree than has hitherto prevailed in this class of Buildings." He therefore offered his designs as "hints for the consideration of Country Gentlemen, and others, who build, and who are sufficiently aware of the use and importance of consulting Architects upon these occasions" (p. iv).

Turning to matters of aesthetic principle, Gandy argued that what might be pleasing in vernacular farm houses and cottages was not the result of design or taste, but rather the accidental consequence of age, color, siuation, variations in form, or surrounding scenery (p. v). An architect, however, would be able to apply principles of design to achieve a far more powerful effect. A well-composed dwelling would encourage its residents in "the early habit of contemplating fine forms," which "produces a correspondence in ideas of beauty, and creates a natural good taste" (p. vi). This in turn would increase the welfare and taste of the laboring classes in general.

Like James Malton and William Atkinson,[3] Gandy believed that variety of form was the most important principle of beauty in building. He criticized those who espoused regularity and symmetry by arguing that "uniform" designs appear so only from one particular point of view (p. vii). From any other point of view, they would appear irregular, and therefore fall into the category of the picturesque (p. viii). Therefore he suggested that each part should be designed with many perspectives in mind, and so present a variety of picturesque elevations. In 43 plates Gandy offered six designs for lodges and 34 designs for cottages, ranging from a simple one-room laborer's cottage to a large farm dwelling, plus one design for a "picturesque" Italianate public house, a design for eight attached cottages that together would form a circle, and a design for a village of circular cottages. These designs demonstrate that elevations such as Gandy recommended—spare and simple yet also picturesque from many points of view—could be attractive and highly sophisticated. The individual forms he used were simple and often severe geometric solids, usually combined in an irregular and asymmetrical manner. The resulting facades were further animated only by thin pilaster strips, shallow semicircular relieving arches, and other spare features related in style to the work of his teacher, Sir John Soane. In many cases Gandy's arrangement of forms generates a tension between long, low, earth-hugging horizontal masses, and vertically aspiring prospect towers or belvederes that rise above the landscape. In one example the vertical tower at one side is balanced by a corresponding vista on the other side (Plate XXVII), thus exercising the viewer's perceptions in all three dimensions. In other designs the tower is complemented by a large tree or hill in the opposite distance (Plates IX, XV). In the village design, Gandy's preference for elemental geometric forms resulted in a curious and not altogether comfortable plan for a circular group of eight detached circular buildings, each consisting of eight wedge-shaped cottages. A circular chapel or parish church occupies the center of the village. This plan, which at least established a bold dialogue between differently scaled circular forms, was reminiscent of similarly elemental compositions recently published by Claude-Nicolas Ledoux.[4]

1. This also was the rationale for such contemporary works as William Barber's *Farm Buildings* (1802), William Atkinson's *Views* (1805), Richard Elsam's *Hints* (1816), and Gandy's *Rural Architect* (1805), *qq.v.* On the need to publish books during this period of slack building activity, and on other aspects of Gandy's career, see John Summerson, "The Vision of J. M. Gandy," Chapter 5 in *Heavenly Mansions* (New York: Norton, 1963).

2. *Designs for Cottages*, p. iii. For the articles in *Communications to the Board of Agriculture*, see entries for Beatson, Crocker, Crutchley, Holland, and Hunt.

3. See entries for Atkinson, *Views of Picturesque Cottages* (1805), and Malton, *Essay on British Cottage Architecture* (1798).

4. *L'Architecture considérée sous le rapport de l'art, des moeurs, et de la législation* (Paris, 1804). For an earlier circular village with circular cottages, see the proposal that Sir John Sinclair published in his *Projet d'un plan pour établir des fermes expérimentales* ([1800?]; described in Entry 308).

85.1
GANDY, Joseph Michael (1771–1843)

The rural architect; consisting of various designs for country buildings, accompanied with ground plans, estimates, and descriptions. By Joseph Gandy. . . .

London: Printed for John Harding, 1805.

1 printed leaf, 27 pp, 42 pls.

29.2 × 24.1 cm

V&A

85.2

————

————

London: Printed for John Harding, 1806.

1 printed leaf, 27 pp, 42 pls.

28.6 × 24.8 cm

MH

In the "Advertisement" dated August 1805, Gandy stated that the success of his first work (*Designs for Cottages; q.v.*) led him to present these designs to the public with "more confidence."

The text consists entirely of plate descriptions, usually just a few lines of prose plus a key to the plan and an estimate of the cost. Despite their brevity the descriptions give an ample sense of the varied uses and locations for which Gandy intended these designs. Some representative examples include a "Cottage for a Labouring Gardener in a Pleasure-Ground" (Plate V), a "Double Cottage for Workmen of the Superior Class, supposed to be situated near a Market-Town" (Plate XI), a "Double Cottage for La-bourers, whose Work is chiefly within-doors" (Plate XV), "Three Cottage-Dwellings, calculated for Summer Residences, and adapted to the vicinity of a Watering or Sea-bathing Place" (Plate XIX), a group of cottages "adapted to the respective necessities of Inhabitants in different circum-stances" (Plates XXII–XXIV), and a "Picturesque Dwelling on the Seacoast, designed for the Retirement of a Naval Officer" (Plate XXXII). The plate descriptions also reveal Gandy's concern for picturesque composition: Plate XXXIII, for example, is a "Double Cottage, containing each three Rooms, after the Italian manner, and distributed so as to have a picturesque effect, rather than any uniformity."

The 42 plates include plans and elevations for three cottages, eight double cottages, eight groups of three or more attached cottages, six lodges, five farm houses, a picturesque dwelling, a small villa, a cottage and dairy, two dairies, a land steward's office, an overseer's residence, a water mill, a public house, an inn, a group of workshops and offices, and a rural institute. In addition the first two plates contain eight elevations, without plans, for very small, simple laborer's cottages. Apart from these the least expensive single design is the "Cottage, of two Rooms" in Plate IV, estimated to cost £90 and containing just a kitchen and a bedroom. The most expensive design is the "small Villa" in Plate XXXIV, estimated at £1000. It includes a kitchen, scullery, storeroom, parlor, small parlor, and library on the ground floor, plus three or four bedrooms upstairs.

Generally more sophisticated than the designs in Gandy's previous book, the plans and elevations illustrated here exhibit a careful integration of squares, circles, octagons, and other geometric figures into regular, symmetrical designs as well as asymmetrical, picturesque compositions. The plan of the cottage in Plate V, for example, is formal and regular, comprising a double square with a semicircular bow projecting from the front. In contrast the "Cottage and Dairy for a Nobleman's Park" (Plate XVI) consists of a two-story octagonal tower attached asymmetrically to one corner of a low, one-story horizontal wing. The double cottage in Plate XXXIII is likewise massed in a picturesque "Italian manner," with a large pavilion at one end balanced by a low wing at the other. Gandy also incorporated a suggestion of picturesque expression in some of his regular, symmetrical facades: the three attached cottages "adapted to the vicinity of a Watering or Sea-bathing Place" (Plate XIX), for example, each incorporate a two-story pavilion topped by a roof with wide overhanging eaves. Directly below the eaves a continuous band of windows 20 feet wide extends nearly the full width of each facade, signaling that extensive landscape or seascape views may be obtained from each cottage.

The gardener's magazine.

See LOUDON, **John Claudius,** *Entry 187.*

86.1
GARRET, Daniel (-1753)
Designs, and estimates, of farm houses, &c. for the county of York, Northumberland, Cumberland, Westmoreland, and Bishoprick of Durham. By Daniel Garret.

London: Printed for J. Brindley, 1747.

[ii] + 2–11 pp, 10 pls.

40.0 × 24.8 cm

V&A

86.2

———

———

London: Printed for J. Brindley, 1758.

[ii] + 2–11 pp, 10 pls.

41.3 × 28.0 cm

PU

86.3

———

———

The second edition.

London: Printed for and sold by Mess. Piers and Webley; and R. Sayer, 1759.

[ii] + 2–11 pp, 10 pls.

37.0 × 27.0 cm

CtY-BA

86.4

———

———

The third edition.

London: Printed for and sold by R. Sayer; and I. Taylor, 1772.

[ii] + 2–11 pp, 10 pls.

37.8 × 24.1 cm

BL

The title page for the 1758 issue appears to be an altered impression of the 1747 title page. Two changes were made in the date: the "X" in "MDCCXLVII" was covered by a small printer's ornament, and a crude "I" was added to the end, resulting in "MDCC LVIII."

Garret's Introduction (pp. i–ii) begins with the assertion that "Architecture is a Science," and thus is "founded on the most plain and simple Principles." Garret could well be expected to emphasize plainness and simplicity since he was clerk of the works to Lord Burlington, a principal advocate of proportionality and regularity in the Palladian Revival.[1] Garret also stressed the importance of convenience in architecture, while calling ornament "rather a Profusion, than a useful Branch" of the subject (p. i). But he distanced himself from most Palladian architects—and also from the long-standing notion of a hierarchy of architectural types—by presenting only designs for farm houses. This was a lesser class of house than other architects would have included in their publications, let alone make the subject of an entire treatise.[2] In addition, while acknowledging a general need for proportionality in architecture, Garret proposed that different classes of house require significantly different designs: "The Palace or Cottage require different Forms; and though Decoration and Magnificence are required in the One, and Plainness and Rusticity in the Other, yet Regularity is necessary in Both: Due Proportion in every Object will always attract the Eye and Attention" (p. i). This is the earliest attempt in British architectural literature to establish formal differences among different classes of domestic design. Garret's work also was original in another respect: it is a collection of designs ostensibly suited to just one region of the country. Garret intended his designs for gentlemen in the northern counties of England, who may have wished to erect regular, cheap, and convenient houses for farmers, but who could not obtain the services of an architect (p. i).

The first page of text is blank, but pages 2 through 11 are detailed estimates of labor and materials costs for the ten designs. These are illustrated in ten plates on eight leaves. The first plate shows a two-story house with kitchen, parlor, back kitchen, milk house, and closet on the ground floor, plus an attached farm yard and farm buildings. The next three designs are similar in plan. Plates 5 through 8 depict smaller houses: that in Plate 5 has just a kitchen, parlor, back kitchen, and milk house on the ground floor. The designs in Plates 9 and 10 are even more compact. That in Plate 9 has a kitchen, parlor, milk house, and closet on the ground floor, together with two of the farm buildings—the pigsty and the byre—attached directly to the house as ells. Some of the designs are Palladian in style (Plates 4, 9, and 10), while others are nearly devoid of ornament (Plates 1, 5–7). In addition, a few are crenellated (Plates 2–4, 7–10), recalling Vanbrugh's castellated walls with bastions at Castle Howard (1706).[3] Garret's crenellated designs perhaps reflect survival of Gothic in vernacular structures in the north of England or, like contemporary designs by Carr of York, they may be early examples of romantic Gothic Revival.[4]

1. On Burlington's Palladianism see Summerson (1969), pp. 197–200; and Rudolf Wittkower, "Lord Burlington and William Kent," "Lord Burlington's Work at York," "Pseudo-Palladian Elements in English Neoclassicism," and especially "English Neo-Palladianism," all reprinted in Wittkower, *Palladio and Palladianism* (New York: Braziller, 1974), pp. 115–132, 135–144, 155–174, 177–190.

2. For an extended discussion of the history of farm houses in architectural literature, and the historical context of Garret's contribution, see Eileen Harris, "The Farmhouse: Vernacular and After," *Architectural Review* CXXX:778 (December 1961), 377–379.

3. Garret was apparently employed at Castle Howard in 1736. See Colvin (1978), p. 333.

4. On Gothic Revival in the north of England see James Macaulay, *The Gothic Revival 1745–1845* (Glasgow: Blackie, 1975). On the early revival of castellated styles see A. J. Rowan, "The Castle Style in British Domestic Architecture in the Eighteenth and Early Nineteenth Centuries," Ph.D. dissertation, Cambridge University, Magdalene College, 1965.

87.1

GENTLEMAN, A

Twelve designs of country-houses, of two, three and four rooms on a floor, proper for glebes and small estates, with some observations on the common errors in building. By a gentleman.

Dublin: Printed for the author, and sold by G. and A. Ewing, 1757.

16 + [viii] pp, 24 pls.

21.6 × 14.0 cm

V&A

By way of apology for "any Defects" in this collection of designs the author noted in the Advertisement (pp. 3–16) that he was "no Architect, but of a quite different Profession," and made these designs "from his own Fancy and for his own Amusement" (p. 3). Yet there was a serious purpose to publishing these designs, and in order to make this book "more truly useful" the author included "a few Rules or Directions whereby some Errors too manifest in modern Practice may be avoided" (pp. 3–4). Pages 4 through 9 contain such "directions" for mortar, chimneys, doors, windows, stairs, roofs, siting, cornices, and pediments. The rest of the Advertisement consists of plate descriptions, generally a few brief remarks on construction techniques, dimensions, ornament, or convenience. Only one design had been executed: that shown in Plate I "Was drawn for the Revd. Adam Lyndon, D.D. late Vicar of Trim," was erected in 1751, "and is now the parsonage House." The letterpress concludes with an eight-page list of subscribers.

The 24 plates illustrate 12 designs, each shown in one elevation and three plans. Designs I–VII, X, and XI consist of a basement or ground story plus two upper stories, and are three or five windows wide. Among the smallest is Design II, with a plan measuring approximately 30 by 40 feet, just three rooms on the "parlour floor," and three rooms plus three closets on the "upper floor." The remaining designs are somewhat larger. Design XII, the largest, has a facade seven windows wide, with rustications on the principal story. Above the "kitchen" floor the principal floor consists of three rooms each 15 feet square, a staircase hall of like size, and a central hall measuring 18 feet by 26 feet. The elevations of all the designs are executed in a plain, spare, Neoclassical style with little ornament. In his remarks on one design (No. VI) the author indicated his awareness of the relation between a house and its scenic context. A large "return" or ell, measuring 20 feet by 26 feet, projects from the rear of the house, and there is a large bow window at the end to "command the desired Prospect" of a "Town, Wood, Lake or River" (pp. 12–13). All of the illustrations are devoid of landscape scenery.

88.1

GIBBS, James (1682–1754)

A book of architecture, containing designs of buildings and ornaments. By James Gibbs.

London: [N. pub.], 1728.

[ii] + xxviii pp, 150 pls.

52.4 × 37.5 cm

MH

88.2

————

————

The second edition.

London: Printed for W. Innys and R. Manby; J. and P. Knapton; and C. Hitch, 1739.

[ii] + xxv pp, 150 pls.

45.1 × 29.8 cm

V&A

Gibbs was the only major architect of his time whose work was not illustrated in Campbell's *Vitruvius Britannicus*; his architecture was too Baroque and too Italianate for the new Palladian aesthetic. Gibbs more than made up for the omission by the publication of his own book. The list of 481 subscribers, including 18 dukes and 38 earls, rivaled that of Campbell.

The letterpress consists of a two-page dedication followed by a brief introduction (pp. i–ii), descriptions of the plates (pp. iv–xxv) giving dimensions as well as the names of those who commissioned designs from Gibbs, and the list of subscribers (pp. xxvi–xxviii). He expected his book to be of use to "Gentlemen" who might be "concerned in Building, especially in the remote parts of the Country." He explained that he provided designs for "useful and convenient Buildings and proper Ornaments; which may be executed by any Workman who understands Lines" (p. i). Nevertheless he warned that "the Forwardness of unskillful Workmen, or the Caprice of ignorant, assuming Pretenders" could ruin his designs in the execution (p. ii). For his own part, Gibbs had "taken the utmost care" to form his designs "in the best Tast[e] I could form upon the Instructions of the greatest Masters in *Italy*, as well as my own Observations upon the antient Buildings there."

This was the first major eighteenth-century British architectural treatise to depict only the author's own designs.[1] The order of the designs in the 150 plates reflects a clear architectural hierarchy. The first 31 plates show ecclesiastical subjects: St. Martin in the Fields, St. Mary le Strand, Marylebone Chapel, and the Church of Allhallows in Derby. The next four plates depict designs for King's College in Cambridge, and Plate 36 is a design for a "Publick Building" in Cambridge. The next 30 plates show designs for 25 dwellings, most of which are described as "Houses," and two of which are called "Villas." Plates 67 through 84 contain designs for garden buildings, including temples, pavilions, "Rooms," summer houses, seats, and a menagerie. Plates 85 through 90 depict landscape ornaments: obelisks, columns, piers, and iron fences. Domestic furnishings such as chimneypieces, door cases, and windows are shown in Plates 91 through 108. Plate 109 contains designs for niches. Two designs for windows at St. Martin in the Fields are shown in Plate 110. Designs for monuments, sarcophagi, and "Compartments for Monumental Inscriptions" appear in Plates 111 through 137. The final 13 plates contain designs for ornamental vases, "cisterns" for buffets and other locations, tables, and pedestals.

It is notable that Gibbs omitted remarks or illustrations concerning proportions, the orders, and the principles and practice of architectural construction,[2] all frequent topics in Continental architectural treatises. This was simply a book of designs, and as such made an important statement about the architect as a designer and stylist, rather than as a theorist, builder, or technician. In the Introduction Gibbs stressed his learning and experience in Italy, but also revealed an affinity between his own ideas and those of his Palladian contemporaries:

For it is not the Bulk of a Fabrick, the Richness and Quantity of the Materials, the Multiplicity of Lines, nor the Gaudiness of the Finishing, that give the Grace or Beauty and Grandeur to a Building; but the Proportion of the Parts to one another and to the Whole, whether entirely plain, or enriched with a few Ornaments properly disposed. (pp. ii–iii)

Nevertheless Gibbs's designs are stylistically more exuberant than those of his Palladian contemporaries, with a livelier disposition of massing and plan, and less stringent reliance on exactness of proportion. Thus his designs have much in common with the work of such Baroque predecessors as Wren and Archer, and may have appeared retardataire in comparison with the spare, rationally proportioned designs of the Palladians. But such a contrast is not surprising given Gibbs's Catholic faith and alliance with the Tory party; his practice succeeded in part because his designs appealed to patrons disturbed by the aesthetic and political changes being wrought by the Whigs.[3] The special importance of the *Book of Architecture*, however, is that it provided a comprehensive selection of designs and details that were frequently copied by provincial architects throughout England and especially the American colonies.[4]

Gibbs's smallest domestic design, "a little House propos'd to my Lord *Ilay*" (Plate 61), is three openings wide, with a basement below grade and two stories above grade. The facade is ornamented with quoins, attic balusters, architraves surrounding all windows, entablatures over the ground-story windows, and a distyle Ionic portico in front of the entrance. The ground floor contains three rooms: the largest is 40 feet by 20 feet, and the other two are 18 1/2 feet by 14 feet. One of the largest designs is that for Ditchley (Plate 39). Overall the design is 346 feet wide, with a central pavilion 138 feet wide and 90 feet deep connected by low quadrants to wing pavilions each 80 feet wide. The central pavilion is three stories high and 11 openings wide, with a hall (35 feet 2 inches by 31 feet 6 inches) and nine other principal rooms on the principal floor. The facade is ornamented with quoins, architraves surrounding the windows, and a pediment over the entrance, plus urns and statues along the parapet. The two "Villas" (Plates 40 and 59–60) are, by comparison, of intermediate size: each is two stories high, one is nine windows wide, and the other is seven windows wide.[5] The larger design (Plate 40) has distyle porticoes *in antis* on both facades. A 30 foot "cube room" between the two porticoes is flanked on both sides by "two Apartments . . . , and over them Lodging Rooms" (p. xi). The other "Villa" has a pedimented distyle portico *in antis* on one facade, between which and the opposite facade is a single room, 30 feet by 40 feet in plan, and 30 feet high. On each side of this room there is a suite of six rooms on two stories; each suite includes three bedrooms and two anterooms or dressing rooms.

1. In 1726 James Leoni issued a collection of his own designs, titled *Some Designs for Buildings Both Publick and Private*, bound at the end of the third volume of his translation of Alberti's treatises on architecture, painting, and sculpture. See Entry 177.

2. The sole exception is a pair of plates simply depicting "The Proportions of Gates and Doors, square or arch'd, according to the five Orders of Architecture" (p. xxii; Pls. 98–99).

3. Summerson (1969), p. 206.

4. For America see especially Chapter IV, "Gibbs and Palladio in the Colonial World," in William H. Pierson, Jr., *American Buildings and Their Architects: The Colonial and Neo-Classical Styles* (Garden City, N.Y.: Anchor Press, 1976), pp. 111–156.

5. For further discussion of the "villa" as a building type see Chapter III, Section 5, in the essay above on "The Literature of British Domestic Architecture, 1715–1842."

GIBBS, James (1682–1754)
Rules for drawing the several parts of architecture.

See Entry 451.

89.1
GILLESPIE, James (1776–1855)
"Cottages," *Communications to the Board of Agriculture; on Subjects Relative to the Husbandry, and Internal Improvement of the Country* VI:2 (1810), 469, and pl. XIX.

MH

This article, which is only two paragraphs long, introduces a design for a one-story double cottage shown in plan, elevation, and section on the accompanying plate. Gillespie indicated that the arched roof, to be constructed "without timber," was inspired by Sir John Sinclair's designs for circular cottages.[1] Both of Gillespie's cottages include a large room ten feet square, plus two beds and one closet set within partitions. Gillespie suggested the pair could be erected for £30.

1. These first appeared in an article by Sinclair in the *Annals of Agriculture*, XXXIV (1800; Entry 479) and in a French version titled *Projet d'un plan pour établir des fermes expérimentales* ([Paris, 1800?]; *see* Entry 308).

90.1

GOODWIN, Francis (1784–1835)

Cottage architecture; being a supplement to the first [*or* second] series of Goodwin's rural architecture, lately published. The supplement contains designs of peasants' cottages, both plain and ornamental, separate and in groups, gate lodges, small dairy farm houses, &c. With specifications and estimates of each design. The whole planned and carefully revised in aid of the improving state of rural economy. By Francis Goodwin, Architect. . . .

London: Printed for the author; and published by John Weale, 1835.

[*Part I:*]

4 + 4 pp, 9 pls.

30.5 × 24.1 cm

MH

[*Part II:*]

4 + 4 pp, 7 pls.

30.5 × 25.4 cm

Bodl.

These two volumes were issued as supplements to the two volumes of Goodwin's *Domestic Architecture* (1833–1834; *q.v.*).

The first volume contains five designs illustrated in views, elevations, and plans on nine plates: a peasant's cottage, a small dairy farm house, an ornamental cottage, a group of eight attached peasants' cottages, and an inn. The text includes brief descriptions and cost estimates for all the designs (pp. 3–4), and detailed specifications for the first design (pp. 1–4). All the designs are in Old English or Tudor style, with picturesque chimneys, bargeboards, half-timbered walls, casement windows, drip moldings, and ornamental buttresses. The cheapest design is the peasant's cottage, which includes a living room and kitchen on the ground floor, and two bedrooms above. The most expensive residence is the farm house, with a living room, scullery, dairy, pantry, and closets on the ground floor, plus four bedrooms and a servant's bedroom upstairs. Of the eight attached cottages, four simply have one room, and the rest have a living room on the ground floor and a bedroom upstairs. This group was "designed to form a little neighbourhood for the social convenience of the labourers employed on a private Gentleman's demesne, or for a great farm; or may form, with detached Cottages to either, [*sic*] a separate hamlet, or additions to one already formed, or to a village, or other community of rustics" (p. 4).

The second volume includes four designs illustrated in views, elevations, and plans on seven plates: two ornamental cottages, a cottage suitable for use by "a Forester," or by "a Peasant," or as "a small Dairy Farm," and a group of seven attached cottages for peasants. There are brief plate descriptions and cost estimates (pp. 3–4), and complete specifications for the first design (pp. 1–4). The style of these designs is similar to that in the first volume, but in all cases the ornamentation is somewhat more elaborate. The first and third cottage designs each have a kitchen and living room on the ground floor, and three bedrooms upstairs. The second cottage design has a living room, dairy, combination bake house and scullery, and two bedrooms on the ground floor, and a cheese room and servants' bedrooms upstairs. Six of the seven attached peasant's cottages have only a living room and a bedroom, both on the ground floor. The seventh cottage, in the center, has a living room and a kitchen on the ground floor, plus two bedrooms above.

91.1
GOODWIN, Francis (1784–1835)
[*Volume I:*]

Domestic architecture, being a series of designs for mansions, villas, rectory houses, parsonage houses, bailiffs' lodge, gardener's lodge, game-keeper's lodge, park gate lodges, etc. in the Grecian, Italian, and Old English styles of architecture. With observations on the appropriate choice of site; the whole designed with strict reference to the practicability of erection, and with due attention to the important consideration of uniting elegance, convenience and domestic comfort with economy; the whole being the result of upwards of thirty years professional experience. With accurate estimates appended to each design. By Francis Goodwin, Architect.

London: Printed for the author; and sold by Messrs. Longman and Co.; Taylor; Priestley and Co.; Ackerman; Treuttel, Würtz and Co.; Waller; Calkin and Budd; Paine; and Williams, 1833.

viii pp, 14 printed leaves, frontisp. + 40 pls (numbered 2–40, 40).

[*Volume II:*]

Domestic architecture, being a second series of designs for cottages, lodges, villas, and other residences, in the Grecian, Italian, and Old English styles of architecture. With an introduction, containing observations on the English domestic style, by W. H. Leeds, Esq. With forty-two plates, and a plan of the public rooms in the town hall at Manchester: also with specifications, etc. as well as estimates to each design. By Francis Goodwin, Architect.

London: Printed for the author; and sold by Messrs. Longman and Co.; Taylor; Weale; Ackermann; Treuttel and Co.; Waller; Calkin and Budd; Paine; and Williams, 1834.

xvi pp, 26 printed leaves, 71–75 pp, frontisp. + 41 pls (numbered 1–4, 6, 6–41).

31.8 × 24.1 cm

MB

91.2

Rural architecture: first [or second] series of designs for rustic, peasants', and ornamental cottages, lodges, and villas, in various styles of architecture; containing fifty [or forty-nine] plates. To which is added, a specification of artificers' works. An estimate is prefixed to each design. The whole planned and carefully revised in aid of the improving state of rural economy. By Francis Goodwin. . . . Second edition, with considerable additions.

London: Printed for the author; and published by John Weale, 1835.

[*Volume I:*] viii pp, 14 printed leaves, frontisp. + 40 pls (numbered 2–40, 40). (Bound with the first part of *Cottage architecture* [1835], described above.)

[*Volume II:*] xvi pp, 26 printed leaves, 71–75 pp, frontisp. + 41 pls (numbered 1–4, 6, 6–41). (Bound with the second part of *Cottage architecture* [1835], described above.)

31.1 × 23.5 cm

BL

91.3

Domestic architecture, being a series of designs for mansions, villas, rectory houses, parsonage houses, bailiff's lodge, gardener's lodge, game-keeper's lodge, park gate lodges, etc. in the Grecian, Italian, and Old English styles of architecture. With observations on the appropriate choice of site; the whole designed with strict reference to the practicability of erection, and with due attention to the important consideration of uniting elegance, convenience and domestic comfort with economy; the whole being the result of upwards of thirty years professional experience. With accurate estimates appended to each design. By Francis Goodwin, Architect. Vol. I [or II]. Second edition.

London: Henry G. Bohn, 1843.

[*Volume I:*] viii pp, 14 printed leaves, frontisp. + 40 pls (numbered 2–38, 38–40). (Bound with the first part of *Cottage architecture* [1835], described above.)

[*Volume II:*] xvi pp, 27 printed leaves, 71–76 pp, frontisp. + 41 pls (numbered 1–4, 6, 6–41). (Bound with the second part of *Cottage architecture* [1835], described above.)

31.6 × 24.9 cm

Private Collection

91.4

Domestic architecture, ⟨ . . . as 1843 . . . ⟩ architecture, with ⟨ . . . as 1843 . . . ⟩ Architect. Vol. I [*or* II]. Third edition.

London: Henry G. Bohn, 1850.

[*Volume I*:] vii–viii pp, 14 printed leaves, 69–72 pp, frontisp. + 40 pls (numbered 2–38, 38–40) + 9 pls.

[*Voume II*:] vii–xvi pp, 24 printed leaves, 61–68 + 73–78 pp, frontisp. + 41 pls (numbered 1–4, 6, 6–41) + 7 pls.

30.4 × 23.2 cm

DLC

The first edition of *Domestic Architecture* was issued in two volumes, in 1833 and 1834 respectively. The Victoria and Albert Museum copy of Volume II, apparently identical to that in the Boston Public Library in all other respects, does not have the words "by W. H. Leeds, Esq." on its title page. The next edition was issued in 1835 under the title *Rural Architecture*, with a new supplement at the end of each volume. Both supplements are titled *Cottage Architecture*, and each has a separate title page dated 1835. The next edition of *Domestic Architecture*, nominally the "second," appeared in 1843 and also includes the 1835 title pages, text, and plates of *Cottage Architecture*. The final, or "third" edition of *Domestic Architecture* was issued in 1850. The text of each volume and of each supplement was entirely reset, and separate title pages for *Cottage Architecture* were omitted.

Volume I is dedicated to Sir John Soane (pp. v–vi), and Volume II is dedicated to Edward J. Littleton (pp. v–vi). The title page to the 1834 edition of Volume II at the Boston Public Library indicates that W. H. Leeds wrote the introduction to this volume (pp. vii–xvi). At least one reviewer believed that Leeds also wrote the letterpress descriptions of individual designs.[1] Leeds also may have written the introduction to Volume I: both introductions argue strongly in favor of "Old English" architecture, and are seemingly at odds with the more balanced distribution of designs among "Grecian, Italian, and Old English Styles" advertised on the title page and illustrated in the plates. In the previous decade Tudor and Elizabethan (or "Old English") styles were of growing interest to British architects, particularly Thomas Frederick Hunt, who had explored the historical associations of the Tudor style as well as its adaptability to the needs of modern society.[2] The introduction to Goodwin's first volume particularly romanticizes Old English architecture:

Every thing that savors of the rural economy of great household establishments of olden times, is congenial to all persons of enlightened sentiment, or good taste, whatever may be their rank, or whatever their pursuits. A succession of ages has wrapped almost all the concerns of bygone days in those pleasurable sensations, which, associating with the habits of our forefathers, [also] give birth to that species of mental delight which constitutes the main charm of poetry. . . . To those imbued with such feelings, . . . the architectural designs in this work are particularly addressed. (1843, I, vii)

This precedes an important analysis of the relation between Old English architecture and its social context:

For many ages previously to the seventeenth century . . . the customs and habits of the people were in character with these structures; all was social, hospitable, and delightful to the imagination. It is evident, that our forefathers felt united in their habits of life, what is now understood, under the general attributes of the picturesque. . . . It was in the indulgence of this taste, that the architect of old, designed the cathedral, the monastery, the college, the town-hall, the market-house, the market-cross, the village church, and even the parsonage house; each being studied and wrought in the character and style admirably suited to its intended purposes, touching the sentiment comprehended in the picturesque.[3]

In the introduction to the second volume Leeds further explored the application of "ancient English" style to modern dwellings, recommending attention to "internal propriety and convenience" (1843, II, ix) while exploring at much greater length the picturesqueness of this style:

Admitting far greater variety of outline both in plan and elevation, and consequently bolder effects of light and shade, and more picturesque masses, it is particularly well calculated for detached buildings, which are beheld from various points of view. . . . For buildings upon a moderate scale, hardly any style is so well calculated to produce important character and striking effect with comparatively little finish of detail. (1843, II, x, xii)

The introduction concludes with a list of 22 "public buildings . . . designed and executed by Mr. Goodwin" (1843, II, xiii), and a discussion of Goodwin's Public Room in the New Town Hall at Manchester (1843, II, xiii–xvi).

Altogether Goodwin illustrated and described 32 designs, in Greek, Italian, "Old English," "Gothic," and "cottage" styles. The latter style (II, Designs 8, 9, and 16) is described as "the Tudor or Elizabethan in their *undress*," permitting "inattention to strict architectural costume" (II, Design 8). Designs in this style incorporate bargeboarding and rustic tree-trunk columns, and at least one is said to resemble "such 'cottages' as young ladies build in their dreams," incorporating "a dash of the fantastic" (II, Design 9).

Altogether the 32 designs include 11 lodges, a parsonage house, a rectory house, a Swiss cottage, a farm house, two park entrances with lodges, 12 villas, two mansions, and a group of laborers' cottages. The smallest design (I, Plates 2–3) is a double lodge for two gamekeepers, each lodge costing £143 and including a living room, a scullery, two bedrooms, a water closet, and a closet. The largest design is the mansion at Lissadell Court, County Sligo, begun in 1830 and "not yet entirely completed" in 1834 (II, Design 15). Goodwin estimated that the cost for a similar design executed in England, "with all the fronts faced with stone," would be £18,000. The ground floor includes a "Gallery and Music room" measuring 64 feet by 23 feet, a dining room, "Anti room," drawing room, library, hall, billiard room, "Studio & Audience room" bedroom, dressing room, and boudoir. Upstairs there are 11 bedrooms, three nursery rooms, and a bath. There are extensive offices and bedrooms for the servants in the basement. Goodwin's final design, for attached laborers' cottages that could be erected in pairs or in groups of four, incorporates "some diversity of form, and pictorial character." Goodwin recognized that "economy is a primary object," but argued that "external effect ought not to be disregarded," since "the objects immediately around [a laborer] exert more or less of moral influence on the feelings." The more cheerful and comfortable the design, the more a laborer and his family will have an "incentive to study neatness," and a "regard for comfort and decency." Each cottage includes a living room, a dairy, two bedrooms, and closets, and the larger cottage of each pair also includes a scullery. A pair of cottages would cost £390, and a row of four would cost £700.

Each design is illustrated in a picturesque view as well as in plan and elevation. The plate descriptions frequently include suggestions for siting the design in a picturesque manner, along with a cost estimate, but no further specifications.[4] Goodwin's choice of style was based on associational as well as pictorial criteria. Gothic, for example, was the obvious choice for a parsonage (I, Design 5), and entirely appropriate for a mansion in a valley or near a river, recalling "the monastic institutions, whether priories, convents, colleges, halls, or ancient manorial houses" that were found in similar locations. Likewise "in mountain regions, amidst or upon bold eminences, the bold castellated style corresponds with the character of the surrounding scenery" (I, Design 10). Goodwin designed one villa in Italian style specifically "to occupy a spot on elevated ground, its general character being suited to a conspicuous site" (I, Design 13). Another Italianate villa was designed to project "stability and strength" as well as "largeness of style, or what, in the painter's art, is expressed in the significant phrase, breadth of effect" (I, Design 11). He composed a "Park-gate Lodge" in Greek style to suit "the extensive, and romantic region of Lissadel" (I, Design 3). But the Old English style was most compatible with "picturesque" scenery for pictorial as well as associational reasons:

A residence in this style of architecture should have its site in the immediate neighbourhood of old timber, as tall stately trees associate with the times which a building in the old English style affects. Hence, low grounds are considered to afford more pictorial features than high lands; the enclosures, where old timber abounds, supplying an endless series of views of a rural character, which are subject to effects of light and shadow, that constitute a delight to the imagination, which no other species of the picturesque can produce. (I, Design 12)

Goodwin considered problems of function and circulation only infrequently. In one case he noted the Italian style "admits abundant internal arrangements, and convenient accommodations on every floor" (I, Design 11), and his remarks on Lissadell Court demonstrate his concern to separate the circulation of family and servants throughout the house (II, Design 15).

1. *Arnold's Magazine of the Fine Arts* IV:8 (June 1834), 180–181.

2. See especially the commentaries on *Designs for Parsonage Houses* (1827) and *Exemplars of Tudor Architecture* (1830).

3. 1843, I, vii–viii. Concern for the relation between a style and its social context dates at least to Richard Hurd's *Moral and Political Dialogues* (London, 1759), in which the medieval architecture of Warwick Castle is understood to suggest the tournaments, feasts, music, and pageants of the time. But the passages quoted above show a deeper concern for the effect of architecture on social mores. These passages prefigure the remarks of A. W. N. Pugin, who in *Contrasts* (London, 1836) suggested a direct correlation between Gothic architecture and the benevolent, tightly knit, Roman Catholic society of the Middle Ages, versus the hunger, crime, and spiritual desolation that accompanied Neoclassical architecture in his own time.

4. Detailed specifications for the first design in Volume II, an entrance lodge or cottage, appear in the "Appendix," pp. 71–75 in editions through 1843, and pp. 61–65 in the 1850 edition.

GREAT BRITAIN. Board of Agriculture
Communications to the Board of Agriculture.

See BEATSON, **Robert,** *Entries 16 and 17;* CROCKER, **A.,** *Entries 46 and 47;* CRUTCHLEY, **Mr.,** *Entry 50;* GILLESPIE, **James,** *Entry 89;* HOLLAND, **Henry,** *Entries 148 and 149;* HUNT, **Rowland,** *Entry 152;* YOUNG, **Arthur,** *Entry 360.*

92.1–123.1
GREAT BRITAIN. Board of Agriculture

Reports

As early as 1769 Arthur Young published a proposal in his *Northern Tour* for an institution to promote agricultural improvement. Seven years later Lord Kames called for an agricultural "Board" in *The Gentleman Farmer* (1776), and in 1790 William Marshall submitted a similar proposal to the Society of Arts.[1] Sir John Sinclair insisted that he independently originated the idea for a board of agriculture about 1792.[2] In 1793 Sinclair won the support of Pitt and others in the House of Commons for his proposal; following its passage and the Royal Assent, a charter was issued for the Board of Agriculture on August 23, 1793.[3] Sinclair was elected first President of the Board.

One of Sinclair's principal goals was to make an agricultural survey of each county in England, Scotland, and Wales. The findings for each county were to be published as draft reports and circulated for comment by interested readers, then revised and published once again. Sinclair hoped that collectively the reports would help identify means by which Parliament, through legislation, could improve Britain's agriculture; in addition the reports would disseminate information to individual landowners and farmers about successful agricultural techniques in local as well as distant areas of the kingdom.[4] He did not wait for approval from the rest of the Board before authorizing individuals to prepare some 80 different reports;[5] nor did he specify limits to the charges and expenses for which the Board might reimburse individual authors. The result was a series of financial embarrassments for the Board, and Sinclair lost the presidency in 1798.

The first of the draft reports appeared in 1793, most were issued in 1794, and the series was essentially complete by 1797. All were published on large paper with wide margins,[6] so that readers could enter emendations and revisions to submit to the Board. Revised editions appeared as early as 1799. During Sinclair's second term as president, from 1806 to 1813, one of his major concerns was to complete the revised series. Most of the revisions were finished by 1813, although a few final volumes appeared over the next four years. When finished in 1817, the series included 143 separate titles.[7] Sinclair hoped to prepare "an abstract of the whole" in two or three volumes, giving a "general view of the agricultural state of the kingdom at large," plus a "General Report" containing an "arranged system of information on agricultural subjects."[8] These volumes never came to fruition.

Sinclair developed a single uniform model for the series of revised and expanded reports: each would consist of 17 chapters treating geography, property, buildings, "modes" of occupying land, implements, enclosure, arable land, grass, gardens and orchards, woods and plantations, commons and wastes, improvements, livestock, "Rural Economy," "Political Economy," obstacles to improvement, and miscellaneous observations. A conclusion at the end would contain suggestions for agricultural improvements, and additional material could be included in appendixes. Authors of individual reports omitted certain topics when appropriate, while in other cases topics were expanded into additional chapters.

In Sinclair's system of organization the third chapter, on buildings, was divided into three parts treating "Houses of Proprietors," farm houses and offices, and cottages. In some cases there were accompanying plates depicting manor houses, farm houses, laborers' cottages, and plans for towns and villages.

The 31 reports (and one separately published *Appendix*) listed below have been selected because they include illustrations of dwellings.[9] The entries are arranged alphabetically according to the counties or regions described in each report. Since all the individual reports were issued in just two series, an abbreviated form of bibliographic entry is appropriate: the size and the names of printers, publishers, and sellers have been omitted.[10] Each commentary below contains a brief account of all plates in the volume, plus more detailed descriptions of plates illustrating architectural subjects. There are brief remarks on passages in the text concerning architecture, construction, and town planning.

1. The efforts of Young, Kames, and Marshall are described by Ernest Clarke in "The Board of Agriculture, 1793–1822," *Journal of the Royal Agricultural Society of England*, 3rd ser., IX (1898), 3–5. See too Rosalind Mitchison, "The Old Board of Agriculture (1793–1822)," *The English Historical Review* LXXIV:290 (January 1959), 41–69.

2. "I knew nothing of such a measure having been recommended by any other individual, previously to its having been proposed by myself." See his "Preliminary Observations on the Origin of the Board of Agriculture, and Its Progress for Three Years after Its Establishment," in *Communications to the Board of Agriculture; on Subjects Relative to the Husbandry, and Internal Improvement of the Country* I:1–2 (1797), iii–lxxxii, especially iii and vii. Also on Sinclair's contributions see his *Account of the Origin of the Board of Agriculture, and Its Progress for Three Years after Its Establishment. By the President* (London: W. Bulmer and Co., 1796); Rev. John Sinclair, *Memoirs of the Life and Works of the Late Right Honourable Sir John Sinclair, Bart.* (Edinburgh: Blackwood and Sons, 1837); and Rosalind Mitchison, *Agricultural Sir John* (London: Geoffrey Bles, 1962).

3. Sinclair, "Preliminary Observations," pp. ix–xi, xxv–xxx.

4. Ibid., p. xxxii.

5. On Sinclair's actions see Clarke, "Board of Agriculture," pp. 12–14. Sinclair listed the original series of 80 reports in "Preliminary Observations," pp. xlix–li.

6. These volumes measure approximately 24 × 20 cm when trimmed.

7. This figure is based on my own bibliographic research, and includes both preliminary and revised reports. N.B. the list of reports given by Clarke in "Board of Agriculture" (p. 16) is quite incomplete. The revised volumes are octavo, measuring approximately 21 × 13 cm when trimmed. Many of the revised surveys were included in a uniform series published in 1813.

8. Sinclair, "Preliminary Observations," p. lxx.

9. In some cases it has been difficult to distinguish plates intended as illustrations of exemplary buildings from those that are simply topographical views. Where the house itself forms a very small part of the illustration, I have considered the plate topographical; if such a plate is the most detailed architectural illustration in the volume, I have not listed the volume below. On the other hand I have assumed that larger and more detailed views of extant dwellings were intended to reveal the state of housing in the county, and so I have included volumes with such illustrations below.

10. For sizes, see notes 6 and 7.

ABERDEENSHIRE

92.1
KEITH, George Skene (1752–1823)

A general view of the agriculture of Aberdeenshire; drawn up under the direction of the Board of Agriculture; and illustrated with plates. By George Skene Keith. . . .

Aberdeen, 1811.

5 + vi–viii + 9–15 + 672 pp, 7 pls (incl. map).

MH

A soil map of Aberdeenshire faces the title page. Two other plates depict a "Plan of the New Orchard belonging to James Ferguson" and a "View of the Summit of Loch-na-gar." The remaining plates illustrate architectural subjects. Three of these are scenic views: the "Abbey of Deer, as it existed in 1770," Haddo House, and Keith Hall. The plate facing page 134 shows an elevation and plan of the "Farmers Offices at Wester Fintray," plus a plan of the farmer's residence there, with a kitchen, a brewhouse, cellars, and a "house" on the ground floor. In the text Keith indicated that the kitchen and brewhouse each measured 30 feet by 20 feet, and the "house" measured 43 feet by 21 feet (p. 135).

AYR

93.1
AITON, William (1760–1848)

General view of the agriculture of the county of Ayr; with observations on the means of its improvement: drawn up for the consideration of the Board of Agriculture, and Internal Improvements. With beautiful engravings. By William Aiton. . . .

Glasgow, 1811.

xxix + 56 + 49–725 pp, 20 pls (incl. maps; *2 pls. are wanting in this copy*).

ICN

The plates include a map of Ayrshire facing the title page, a plan of the harbor and dry docks at Troon, a map of a canal from Glasgow to Ardrossan, a plan of a proposed railway from Kilmarnock to Troon, and illustrations of a bridge, ploughs, and farm animals. Eight more plates contain views of extant houses and castles, including Loudoun Castle, Culzean Castle, Dumfries House, Eglinton Castle, Dalquharran Castle, Coilsfield House, and Kilkerran House.

Figure 5

Three plates depict examples of town planning in Ayrshire. The first, facing page 56, shows Peter Nicholson's design for Ardrossan, laid out beginning in 1806 for the Earl of Eglinton.[1] The plan includes long terraces lining streets parallel to the shore, plus 43 detached villas arranged in a crescent facing an inlet of the sea. This formal arrangement of detached villas is one of the earliest in British planning history, and is a significant precursor of Regent's Park and other planning schemes later in the century.[2] In addition there is a "Market place" at the far northern end of the town, and a dock on a spit of land to the west. The plate also depicts row houses in two elevations and a section, and a plan of the marketplace.

A plate facing page 130 illustrates the plan of a "Country Village," in which a wide "public road" crosses a pair of smaller "village roads." Lying between the two village roads is a "bleaching ground," in the center of which there is a "rivulet." Across each village road from the bleaching ground are eight pairs of two- and three-story semidetached houses, with individual garden plots attached.

A plate facing page 131 depicts a plan and elevation of a pair of elliptical crescents, facing each other, to be erected in the village of Dreghorn.

1. The plan is discussed in further detail in Nicholson's *Architectural Dictionary* (1819; *q.v.*).

2. In 1794 Spurrier and Phipps published a proposal for a crescent of semidetached villas to be erected in St. John's Wood, London, but this was never executed. For further discussion see my "*Rus in Urbe*: Classical Ideals of Country and City in British Town Planning," *Studies in Eighteenth-Century Culture* XII, ed. Harry C. Payne (Madison: University of Wisconsin Press, 1983), pp. 159–186. On John Nash's work at Regent's Park see John Summerson, *The Life and Work of John Nash* (Cambridge, Mass.: MIT Press, 1980), pp. 58–74. For a crescent of detached houses similar to that proposed by Nicholson, but smaller, see Sir John Sinclair, *A Sketch of the Improvements* (1803; *q.v.*).

BANFF

94.1

SOUTER, David

General view of the agriculture of the county of Banff; with observations on the means of its improvement. Drawn up for the consideration of the Board of Agriculture, and Internal Improvement. By David Souter, Farmer.

Edinburgh, 1812.

xiv + 339 + 85 pp, 4 pls.

DLC

A map of the county of Banff faces the title page. One plate, facing page 91, accompanies the section on farm buildings (pp. 89–96). The plate illustrates "a Farm House and Offices in Banffshire" in plan and elevation. Just one story high, the house includes a parlor, dining room, drawing room, bedroom, two bed closets, a "Servants Bed Chamber and Victual House," a kitchen, a milk house, a beer cellar, and an ash house. Souter considered the design "amongst the best of the second class of steadings in this country" (p. 91). On pages 91–96 he gave detailed estimates for the cost of materials and labor necessary to erect it, totaling £868 4s 6d. Illustrations of a turnip drill and a horse hoe face pages 131 and 135 respectively.

95.1

BATCHELOR, Thomas

General view of the agriculture of the county of Bedford. Drawn up by order of the Board of Agriculture and Internal Improvement. By Thomas Batchelor, Farmer.

London, 1808.

xvi + 636 pp, 9 pls (incl. map, portr.).

MH

95.2

————

General view of the agriculture of the county of Bedford. Drawn up for the consideration of the Board of Agriculture and Internal Improvement. By Thomas Batchelor, Farmer.

London, 1813.

xvi + 636 pp, 9 pls (incl. map, portr.).

MH

A portrait of Francis Russell, Fifth Duke of Bedford (1765–1802), faces the title page. A soil map of the county faces page 1. Five plates illustrate farm implements and machinery. Two plates, facing page 20, accompany the section on "Farm-Houses and Offices" (pp. 19–20). Plate I shows an octagonal house erected by the Duke of Bedford at Eaton Socon. "Designed by Mr. R. Salmon" and estimated to cost £671 8s 8d, the house includes a parlor, dining hall, kitchen, dairy, pantry, and combined bake house and washhouse on the ground floor, plus five bedrooms above and "Two large Garrets for Men Servants" under the roof. For comparison Batchelor offered a design for a house "of the usual square form" (p. 20), illustrated in Plate II, with the same number of rooms on the ground and chamber floors, and estimated to cost £733. Neither exterior is ornamented. The section on cottages (pp. 20–24) includes remarks taken from the *Annals of Agriculture*, Vol. XXXIX, on the subject of "Pisé Building." An Appendix (pp. 629–630) also concerns pisé.

For more thorough commentary on the work of the Duke of Bedford and Robert Salmon at Woburn Abbey (including the Park Farm and the Tithe Farm at Eaton Socon) see John Martin Robinson, *Georgian Model Farms: A Study of Decorative and Model Farm Buildings in the Age of Improvement, 1700–1846* (Oxford: Clarendon Press, 1983).

96.1

MAVOR, William (1758–1837)

General view of the agriculture of Berkshire. Drawn up for the consideration of the Board of Agriculture and Internal Improvement. By William Mavor. . . .

London, 1808.

xii + 548 pp, 37 pls.

BL

96.2

———

———

London, 1809.

xii + 548 pp, 37 pls [*of which 5 are wanting in this copy*].

MH

96.3

———

———

London, 1813.

xii + 548 pp, 37 pls.

NN

A soil map of the county faces the title page, and a "Map of the Rivers Thames and Isis" faces page 37. Preceding page 545 is a "Map of the Strata of the Different lines of Inland Navigation between London & Bristol." An elevation and plan of a "fish-house which cannot be robbed" face page 44, and are described on pages 44–45. Two plates facing page 63 depict a "cart-lodge" and farmyard of E. L. Loveden. The farm house, near the center of the farmyard, is shown in plan only: the ground floor includes a parlor, kitchen, brewhouse, dairy, and offices. Elevations and a plan for a cattle shed face page 69. The section on cottages (pp. 70–77) includes a plate, facing page 73, depicting two cottages in Windsor Great Park. This is a reduced copy of the plate accompanying Pearce's 1794 report on Berkshire (*q.v.*). Mavor noted that "To build lodges and cottages round domains, is not less ornamental than it is humane. It is providing an ayslum for servants who have merited protection by diligent labor, and it is at the same time securing their own property from depradations, by multiplying the means of superintendence. The magnificent seat may evince the opulence of the possessor; but it is the state of the cottages and farms on his estate that bespeaks the character of the man!" (p. 73). Eighteen plates illustrate ploughs, other farm implements, and machinery, and the remaining six plates depict farm animals.

97.1
PEARCE, William
General view of the agriculture in Berkshire, with observations on the means of its improvement. By William Pearce. Drawn up for the consideration of the Board of Agriculture and Internal Improvement.

London, 1794.

74 pp, 3 pls.

MH

Pearce praised recent improvements in Windsor Great Park, particularly the "Flemish Farm" created on 300 acres at the extreme north end of the park. Among the notable structures on this farm Pearce cited one new cottage and "an old banqueting house converted into two others, in which His Majesty has put three of the most exemplary farm, or park labourers, and their families" (p. 65). Pearce found these dwellings "so truly what poor men of this description ought to have" (p. 65) that he included plans and elevations of each in Plate I. The two-story elevation of the new cottage includes a semicircular relieving arch that encompasses a semicircular window on the upper floor and four rectangular windows below. The ground-floor plan includes just a kitchen and a washhouse. The old banqueting house, subdivided into two cottages, includes a kitchen and a pantry for each on the ground floor.[1] Plate II shows "Ploughs used in Windsor Great Park" and Plate 3 depicts "The Moveable Barn in Windsor Great Park."

1. A reduced version of this plate appears in later reports on Berkshire by William Mavor (*q.v.*). Also on royal lodges see two books in Appendix C below: John Weale, *Designs of Ornamental Gates, Lodges . . . of the Royal Parks* (1841); and Henry Bryan Ziegler, *The Royal Lodges in Windsor Great Park* (1839).

BERWICK

98.1
KERR, Robert (1755–1813)
General view of the agriculture of the county of Berwick; with observations on the means of its improvement. Drawn up for the consideration of the Board of Agriculture, and Internal Improvement; and brought down to the end of 1808. With several plates. By Robert Kerr. . . .

London, 1809.

xxxii + 504 + 73 pp, map + 3 pls.

ICU

98.2
───────

General view of the agriculture of the county of Berwick; with observations on the means of its improvement. Drawn up for the consideration of the Board of Agriculture and Internal Improvement; and brought down to the end of 1808.

London, 1813.

xxxii + 504 + 73 pp, map + 3 pls.

MH

A map of the county is bound to face the title page. The plate facing page 282 illustrates the "Berwickshire mode of turnip culture," described on pages 281–283. Facing page 97 is a "Plan of a Farm Yard adapted for the turnip husbandry." Kerr noted on page 102 that "There is nothing particular in the cottages of this county. Upon the farms they are for the most part built in rows of one story only, having alternately a thick gable wall, with the fire places of two cottages, and a thin wall as the other division." The plate facing page 102 depicts such a row cottage in plan and elevation. The interior space measures 16 by 21 feet, and includes a "room" with table, dresser, plate rack, and two chests, plus a "back room" with two beds. As illustrated the design could be built for £16 to £21 (p. 103).

99.1

HENDERSON, John (1759?–1828)

General view of the agriculture of the county of Caithness, with observations on the means of its improvement. Drawn up for the consideration of the Board of Agriculture and Internal Improvement. By Capt. John Henderson. With an appendix, including an account of the improvements carried on, by Sir John Sinclair, . . . on his estates in Scotland.

London, 1812.

xii + 371 + 222 pp, 13 pls (incl. map).

MH

99.2

————

————

London, 1815.

xii + 371 + 222 pp, 13 pls (incl. map).

NN

A soil map of the county precedes the title page, and a "Chart of the Town, River, & Bay of Wick" faces page 251. The rest of the plates accompany the Appendixes, in which Henderson described recent improvements by Sir John Sinclair on his Caithness estates. Some of the plates had appeared in earlier publications by Sinclair: the plan of Thurso in "Hints Regarding Certain Measures" (1802; *q.v.*), and the plans of Thurso and Brodiestown in *A Sketch of the Improvements . . . in the County of Caithness* (1803; *q.v.*).

As with the notorious clearances carried out by James Loch for the Duke of Sutherland, the displacement of laborers to coastal areas of Caithness required new towns and harbors for manufacturing, fishing, and commerce.[1] These towns usually had geometric, orthogonal plans laid out with the twin goals of economy and commerce in mind; they were generally unlike the more romantic, picturesque villages and towns soon to be laid out elsewhere in the United Kingdom.[2] Of three town plans illustrated by Henderson, one is not cast in an orthogonal mold, although it retains a geometric order and symmetry. Plate IV, facing page 67, shows a "Sketch of the Fishing Village of Brodiestown, Intended to be erected at Sarcilet." In the center of the plan five houses arranged in a semicircle face the water. To the left and right two streets extend back at oblique angles, parallel to the shore, and a third street runs directly inland. Houses flank both sides of the inland street and the inland side of the other two streets. The plate also depicts an elevation of one of the houses, with a one-story facade consisting of one door and two windows, plus a chimney at each end.

Plate V, facing page 68, shows the "Plan of a Village to be erected at Halkirk," an orthogonal plan of streets parallel and perpendicular to the Thurso River, with just a slight concave curve in the center of the street closest to the river bank. There are approximately 54 houses, a church, and a school, individually sited in rectangular plots.

Plate VI, facing page 69, shows the orthogonal "Plan of the New Town of Thurso," a plan that would contain "about 300 houses" (p. 69) when complete. According to the caption, "the Proprietor resolved to build it according to the most regular plan that could be contrived and in a manner not only ornamental but also particularly well adapted for preserving the health & promoting the convenience of the Inhabitants." Plates VII and VIII, facing page 71, include elevations and plans of a gate, a bank, a factory, Macdonalds Square, and Caithness and Janet Streets. The street facades incorporate some variations in height, depth, and style that provide interest and animation in what otherwise could have been a dull, uniform environment. Plate IX, facing page 73, shows the location of the new town and harbor at Thurso in relation to the old town. Plates X through XIII show proposed designs for the church, infirmary, academy, and wash-house at Thurso. Plate III, facing page 50, is a plan of "Certain Farms on the River Thurso."[3]

1. On James Loch and the Duke of Sutherland see Eric Richards, *The Leviathan of Wealth* (London: Routledge & Kegan Paul, 1973). Loch discussed his work in *An Account of the Improvements . . . on the Estate of Sutherland* (1815; see Entry 180).

2. On planning elsewhere in Scotland see John G. Dunbar, *The Historic Architecture of Scotland* (London: Batsford, 1966), pp. 248–250. New town plans also were illustrated in the Board of Agriculture report on Ayr by William Aiton (1811; *q.v.*). On romantic villages and towns see Gillian Darley, *Villages of Vision* (London: Architectural Press, 1975).

3. For a twentieth-century assessment of Sarclet, Halkirk, and Thurso, see Rosalind Mitchison, *Agricultural Sir John* (London: Geoffrey Bles, 1962), pp. 190–192.

CORNWALL

100.1
WORGAN, G. B.
General view of the agriculture of the county of Cornwall. Drawn up and published by order of the Board of Agriculture and Internal Improvement. By G. B. Worgan.

London, 1811.

xvi + 192 pp, map + 15 pls.

MH

100.2
_____

General view of the agriculture of the county of Cornwall. Drawn up for the consideration of the Board of Agriculture and Internal Improvement. By G. B. Worgan.

London, 1815.

xvi + 192 pp, 15 pls.

MH

Of a total of 15 plates, four show pigs and five others show a bull, "linneys" or sheds for cows, a scheme for draining land, several fences and a wheat rick, and farm implements. Plates I through IV depict plans of "very superior Farm Offices" and farmyards, described on pages 24–26. Plates V and VI contain plans and elevations of cottages "presented by Capt. V. Penrose, of Ethy," and are described in the section on "Cottages" (pp. 26–30). Plate V shows a one-story double cottage, with a kitchen, pantry, and two bedrooms in each cottage. The first design in Plate VI is a circular laborer's cottage 26 feet in diameter, shown in plan only, with a kitchen, pantry, and two bedrooms all on one floor.[1] Mr. Hugh Rowe, a builder in Lostwithiel, had erected such a cottage for £42 (p. 29). The second design in Plate VI, "A small Farm House, or House for a Gentleman's Hind, on One Floor," would cost £89. Shown in plan only, it has straight sides and semicircular ends. It includes a kitchen, a parlor, three bedrooms, and a "wood corner" or pantry.

1. Other designs for circular laborers' cottages appeared in the article "Farm" in *The English Encyclopaedia* (1802; *q.v.*).

DERBYSHIRE

101.1
FAREY, John, Sr. (1766–1826)
[Volume I:]

General view of the agriculture and minerals of Derbyshire; with observations on the means of their improvement. Drawn up for the consideration of the Board of Agriculture and Internal Improvement. Vol. I. Containing a full account of the surface, hills, valleys, rivers, rocks, caverns, strata, soils, minerals, mines, collieries, mining processes, &c. &c. Together with some account of the recent discoveries respecting the stratification of England; and a theory of faults and denuded strata, applicable to mineral surveying and mining. Illustrated by five coloured maps, and sections of strata. By John Farey, Sen.[,] Mineral Surveyor. . . .

London, 1811.

xlvii + 532 pp, 5 pls.

[Volume II:]

General view of the agriculture of Derbyshire; with observations on the means of its improvement. Drawn up for the consideration of the Board of Agriculture and Internal Improvement. Vol. II. Containing a full account of the state of property and its occupancy, the buildings, and implements used in agriculture. The improvement of lands, by inclosing and converting of waste and open tracts, draining, embanking, irrigating, manuring, marling, liming, &c. The culture and cropping of arable lands with the various grains, roots and useful plants, the management and conversion of grass lands; of gardens and orchards, and of woods and plantations. Under which last head, the scarcity of large timber, its profit to the owner, and means of future increase, by pruning, &c. are fully considered. Illustrated by four plates. By John Farey, Sen.[,] Mineral Surveyor. . . .

London, 1813.

xx + 28 + 522 pp, 4 pls.

[Volume III:]

General view of the agriculture of Derbyshire; with observations on the means of its improvement. Drawn up for the consideration of the Board of Agriculture, and Internal Improvement. Vol. III. Containing a full account of the various breeds of live stock, their food, management, uses, and comparative advantages; their houses, stalls, &c.; with accounts of the preparation of cheese, butter, bacon, &c. Rural details regarding modes and prices of labour, cottages, prices of provisions, fuel, &c. Politico= economical details, regarding game, roads, rail-ways, canals, fairs, markets, weights and measures, various manufactures, commerce; parish maintenance of the poor and their own benefit societies, &c.; and regarding the increase of the population, their healthiness, modes of living, &c. The obstacles to improvements, and facilities for their adoption; with a concluding brief recapitulation of the various hints and suggestions, of measures calculated for improvement, scattered through these volumes. Illustrated by a map of roads, canals, &c. and two plates. By John Farey, Sen.[,] Mineral Surveyor. . . .

London, 1817.

xxvii + 725 pp, 3 pls.

MH

101.2

————

[Volume I:]

————

London, 1815.

xlvii + 532 pp, 5 pls.

[Volume II:]

General view of the agriculture of Derbyshire; ⟨ . . . as 1813 . . . ⟩ in agriculture: the improvement ⟨ . . . as 1813 . . . ⟩ and plantations; under which ⟨ . . . as 1813 . . . ⟩.

London, 1815.

xx + 28 + 522 pp, 4 pls.

[Volume III:]

————

London, 1817.

xxvii + 725 pp, 3 pls.

MH

Volumes I and II were issued in 1811 and 1813, respectively, and then reissued in 1815. Volume III was issued once, in 1817.

In Volume I a map of ridges and hills in Derbyshire faces page 1, a map of soil and strata faces page 97, two plates illustrating sections of geological strata face page 113, and a diagram of the strata at Matlock Tor faces page 129. Plate I of Volume II, facing page 10, shows a plan and elevations of farm buildings at Bradby Park. William Martin was the architect and builder. The Bailiff's House, constructed as part of the farm buildings, is two stories high and three windows wide, with a kitchen pantry, storeroom, parlor, dairy parlor, and offices on the ground floor. Plates II, III, and IV show farm machinery and implements. The first two plates in Volume III depict a "Lambing Fold" and a "Sheep-wash." The third plate is a map of turnpike roads, canals, and railways in Derbyshire.

DEVON

102.1
VANCOUVER, Charles (fl. 1785–1813)
General view of the agriculture of the county of Devon; with observations on the means of its improvement. Drawn up for the consideration of the Board of Agriculture, and Internal Improvement. By Charles Vancouver.

London, 1808.

xii + 479 pp, map + 7 tables + 28 pls.

MH

102.2

General view of the agriculture of the county of Devon; ⟨ . . . as 1808 . . . ⟩ Agriculture and Internal Improvement. By Charles Vancouver.

London, 1813.

xii + 479 pp, map + 7 tables + 28 pls.

MH

This *Report* includes 28 plates and a folding map of the county. Eight plates illustrate farm implements, six show farm animals, two show leaves, two show a weir at Black Torrington, one is a diagram of the dry rot process in trees, one is a plan of the Crediton and Exeter Canal, and one shows a bird's-eye view of Dartmoor Prison. Two plates accompany the text section on "Cottages" (pp. 92–98). The first of these illustrates a row of twelve attached ottages with a uniform two-story facade, erected by Reverend Luxmore in the village of Bridestow "for the occupation of the labouring poor" (p. 94). Vancouver reported that the principal room on each floor was 16 feet square, and offered other details of layout and construction. The next plate shows a two-story detached cottage, "built on Oldridge Wood in the Parish of St. Thomas near Exeter by John Prawl for Mr. Sillifant of Coombe." The ground floor is divided into a kitchen, approximately 15 feet square, and a shop 7 feet by 15 feet.

Between pages 322 and 323 are a detailed plan and distant view of Sir Lawrence Palk's proposed improvement scheme for the harbor at Torquay, plus a series of terraces and semidetached houses to be erected among the picturesque hills and cliffs surrounding the harbor. Vancouver noted ongoing efforts to provide "for the accommodation of company resorting hither for the convenience of sea-bathing," and praised the "regularity of buildings lately raised" because they added "neatness and beauty to the wild and picturesque scenery" of the harbor (p. 322). The plan shows a series of concave and convex curving terraces, plus five pairs of semi-detached villas forming a large convex curve, to be erected on the land of Sir Lawrence Palk and Mr. Carey. This elaborate scheme was never completed, and instead isolated detached villas slowly covered the hills surrounding the harbor over the next several decades.[1]

Between pages 472 and 473 three plates show plans and elevations of Sir Lawrence Palk's farmyard at Haldon. A brief explanation of the plates appears on pages 472–474. The complex includes a barn, stable, slaughterhouse, piggery, ox sheds, cattle sheds, and a farm house two stories high and three windows wide. The plan of the ground floor of the house shows four rooms: a kitchen, parlor, cellar, and pantry.

1. For a general history of development at Torquay see James Thomas White, *The History of Torquay* (Torquay: The "Directory" Office, 1878); Arthur Charles Ellis, *An Historical Survey of Torquay* (Torquay: The "Torquay Directory," 1930); and Percy Russell, *A History of Torquay* (Torquay: The Torquay Natural History Society, 1960).

ESSEX.

103.1
[YOUNG, Arthur (1741–1820)]
General view of the agriculture of the county of Essex. Drawn up for the consideration of the Board of Agriculture, and Internal Improvement. By the Secretary of the Board. In two volumes. Vol. I [*or* II].

London, 1807.

[*Volume I:*] xv + 400 pp, map + 43 pls.

[*Volume II:*] vii + 450 pp, 15 pls.

MH

103.2
––––––––––

General view of the agriculture of the county of Essex. ⟨ . . . as 1807 . . . ⟩ of Agriculture and Internal ⟨ . . . as 1807 . . . ⟩.

London, 1813.

[*Volume I:*] xv + 400 pp, map + 43 pls.

[*Volume II:*] vii + 450 pp, 15 pls.

MH

In Volume I a soil map faces the title page. Plate I, facing page 43, is a landscape view of Mistley Hall, the "new church" by Robert Adam at Mistley, and the nearby quay, warehouses, and dockyard. Plates II through IV depict a calf pen, a wheat rick stand, and a Dutch barn. The 39 remaining plates illustrate ploughs, other farm implements, and farm machinery.

In Volume II there are five plates of ploughs, one plate depicting the "Original Hatfield Broad Oak," a view of a chalk quarry, two plates illustrating quarry wagons, an elevation of a wheeled "Passing Bridge for Sheep," illustrations of a pig and a sow, two plates with elevations of a "pig case," and one plate depicting a "Horse Hoe."

FIFE

104.1

THOMSON, John

General view of the agriculture of the county of Fife: with observations on the means of its improvement: drawn up for the consideration of the Board of Agriculture & Internal Improvement. By John Thomson, D.D.

Edinburgh, 1800.

viii + 9–413 pp, map + 3 pls.

MH

In addition to a map of the county this volume includes three plates. One shows a Fife bull. Two others accompany the text section on farm houses and offices (pp. 77–80), and show farm steadings. One shows the "Farm Stead of Kinninmonth in the Parish of Kinglassie," a rectangular court surrounded by a barn, stables, sheds, byres, and a farm house. The ground floor of the house consists of a "Lobby," two bedrooms, and a kitchen, plus ells for hogs, hens, and milk. The upper story includes a bedroom, a bed closet, and a dining room. The next plate is the "Plan of a Farm Steading belonging to Wm. Hunt Esqr. of Loggie," but shows only structures for animals and crops, and excludes the farm house. The accompanying text emphasizes deficiencies in farm structures throughout the county, and does not discuss the two illustrated steadings.

GLOUCESTER

105.1

RUDGE, Thomas (1754–1825)

General view of the agriculture of the county of Gloucester. Drawn up for the consideration of the Board of Agriculture and Internal Improvement, by Thomas Rudge, B.D.

London, 1807.

viii + 408 pp, 5 pls (incl. maps).

MH

105.2

————

General view of the agriculture of the county of Gloucester. ⟨ . . . as 1807 . . . ⟩ Improvement. By Thomas Rudge, B.D.

London, 1813.

viii + 408 pp, 5 pls (incl. maps).

MH

The volume includes a map of the soil of Gloucestershire, a map of the Thames & Severn Canal, and a map of drains in the vicinity of Kempsford. Another plate shows a machine for digging drains. The plate facing page 50 shows four cottages and a schoolroom united in a uniform semicircular range two stories high. This structure was built by E. Chamberlayne of Maugersbury, near Stow, in 1800 (p. 50). On the ground floor each cottage had a "lower room" approximately 12 feet square, and a pantry 5 feet by 12 feet. Upstairs were two bedrooms, each 8 feet by 12 feet, and under the roof there was "a low room . . . capable of containing beds, lighted by a sky-light at the back" (p. 50).

HAMPSHIRE

106.1
VANCOUVER, Charles (fl. 1785–1813)
General view of the agriculture of Hampshire, including the Isle of Wight. Drawn up for the Board of Agriculture and Internal Improvement. By Charles Vancouver.

London, 1810.

xii + 520 pp, map + 13 pls.

MH

106.2
———

General view of the agriculture of Hampshire, including the Isle of Wight. Drawn up for the consideration of the Board ⟨ . . . as 1810 . . . ⟩.

London, 1813.

xii + 520 pp, map + 13 pls.

MH

Facing the title page is a soil map of Hampshire and the Isle of Wight. Eleven of the 13 plates illustrate ploughs, a gate, a roller, a wagon, a cart, a pump, and a harrow. Plate II, facing page 71, shows the plan and elevation of "Mr. Bramstone's Poor House Cottages," an attached pair of houses approximately 90 feet long and 15 feet deep. According to the plate caption they were "built with Mud, or Cob Walls, and floord with Brick." Just one story high, each cottage contains one "Setting Room" 15 feet square, with an oven and a hearth, plus four bedrooms each measuring 15 feet by 7 feet 4 inches and intended for one "pauper" family. The final plate, facing page 286, shows two designs for zigzag garden walls.

HEREFORD

107.1
DUNCUMB, John (1765–1839)
General view of the agriculture of the county of Hereford; drawn up for the consideration of the Board of Agriculture and Internal Improvement. By John Duncumb. . . .

London, 1805. [*Separate editions published by Bulmer for Nicol, and by McMillan for Phillips.*]

viii + 173 pp, 2 maps + 3 pls.

MH

107.2

General view of the agriculture of the county of Hereford. Drawn up for the consideration of the Board of Agriculture and Internal Improvement. By John Duncumb. . . .

London, 1813.

viii + 173 pp, 2 maps + 3 pls.

MH

A soil map of the county faces the title page, and a map of rivers and streams in Herefordshire faces page 11. The first two plates illustrate a section and elevation of Arrendal Farm House and a plan of the house, farmyard, and farm buildings. This house was "recently finished, in the parish of Pipe, on Arrendal farm, belonging to the Governors of Guy's Hospital, and being of the rent of 210*l*. per annum, it is recommended as a model worthy of adoption" (p. 30). The elevation is two stories high and devoid of ornament except for a modest architrave surrounding the door. The ground-floor plan includes a parlor, a best kitchen, a servants' kitchen, a dairy, and a brewhouse. The third plate is an elevation and plan of "Ten Dwellings for the Parish of ___ or for a Gentleman's laborers." Each of the ten attached units contains a single "room" and a shed on the ground floor, and a bedchamber above. Duncumb noted that a row of ten cottages like this was "recently built by the parish of Holmer, for the accommodation of as many poor families" at a cost of £32 10s per unit (p. 30).

KINCARDINE-SHIRE

108.1
ROBERTSON, George (1750?–1832)
A general view of Kincardineshire; or, The Mearns; drawn up and published by order of the Board of Agriculture. By George Robertson. . . .

London, 1810.

1 printed leaf, 12 + 477 + 63 pp, tables, 4 pls (incl. map).

DLC

108.2

A general view of the agriculture of Kincardine-shire or, The Mearns, drawn up under the direction of the Board of Agriculture; and embellished with plates, by George Robertson. . . .

London, [n.d.].

1 printed leaf, 12 + 477 + 63 pp, tables, 4 pls (incl. map).

ICU

108.3

General view of the agriculture of Kincardineshire, or The Mearns. Drawn up for the consideration of the Board of Agriculture and Internal Improvement. By George Robertson. . . .

London, 1813.

12 + 477 + 63 pp, tables, 4 pls (incl. map).

MH

A map of the county faces the title page. The plate facing page 182 is a plan of the farmstead at Stone of Morphy. Facing page 184 is a landscape view of an unidentified farm house, two stories high and three windows wide, together with attached farm buildings. A protrait of Mr. Barclay of Ury faces page 323.

**LEICESTER and
RUTLAND**

109.1

PITT, William (1749–1823), and Richard PARKINSON (1748–1815)

A general view of the agriculture of the county of Leicester; with observations on the means of its improvement, published by order of the Board of Agriculture and Internal Improvement. By William Pitt. . . .
To which is annexed a survey of the county of Rutland, by Richard Parkinson.

London, 1809.

xlviii + 401 + [11] + vii + 187 + [i] pp, map + 19 + 5 pls.

MH

109.2

General view of the agriculture of the county of Leicester; with observations on the means of its improvement. Drawn up for the consideration of the Board of Agriculture and Internal Improvement. By William Pitt. . . .
To which is annexed, a survey of the county of Rutland, by Richard Parkinson.

London, 1813.

viii + 401 + [11] + vii + 187 + [i] pp, map + 19 + 5 pls.

MH

The "annexed" *Survey of the County of Rutland* is paginated separately and bears a separate title page, dated 1808. It is considered separately below.

A map of Leicestershire and Rutlandshire faces the title page. Among the 19 plates in the report on Leicester just two illustrate domestic structures. The plan of the first, "Mr. Johnson's Farmery at Ashby Wolds," shows a stable, barns, and offices surrounding a rectangular fold yard. Along one side is a three-story farm house, with a parlor, kitchen, two pantries, a brewhouse, and a dairy on the ground floor. The asymmetrical, unornamented facade of the house appears in an elevation. The other plate shows a plan and elevation of "a cottage for a labourer, erected by Mr. Smith, attorney of Ashby upon the Wolds." Pitt noted that Smith wanted to give the two-story cottage "a picturesque appearance," and so "finished the back side and ends with sham Gothic arches in the brick-work." Likewise the roof was "covered with thatch, to give a more rural appearance" (pp. 25–26). Smith estimated the cost at £70 without the sham Gothic arches, and at least £100 with them.

The other plates in this report illustrate methods of embanking and draining, rick stoles and staddles, and farm implements.

LINCOLNSHIRE

110.1
[YOUNG, Arthur (1741–1820)]
General view of the agriculture of the county of Lincoln; drawn up for the consideration of the Board of Agriculture and Internal Improvement. By the Secretary to the Board.

London, 1799.

vii + 455 pp, 13 pls.

MH

110.2
_____

General view of the agriculture of Lincolnshire. Drawn up by order of the Board of Agriculture and Internal Improvement. By the Secretary of the Board. Second edition.

London, 1808.

vii + 490 pp, map + 13 pls.

MH

General view of the agriculture of Lincolnshire. Drawn up for the consideration of the Board of Agriculture and Internal Improvement. By the Secretary of the Board. Second edition.

London, 1813.

vii + 490 pp, map + 14 pls (including one duplicate in this copy).

MH

In addition to the 13 plates of the 1799 edition, the 1808 and 1813 editions include a soil map of the county. In the copy of the 1813 edition in the Kress Library there is a duplicate of one plate titled "Woad Apparatus."

The section on "Farm Houses"[1] includes a plate with front and side elevations, two plans, and a section showing stud work of "Mr. Hoyte's House," a design that Young found "convenient" and "remarkably cheap."[2] Young included a detailed estimate of costs totaling £919 18s 11 1/2d. The ground-floor plan includes a drawing room, sitting room, breakfast room, "sellar," kitchen, and scullery; upstairs there are eight chambers. A pair of pilasters flanks the front door, above which there is a modest fanlight and a pediment. In the section on "Cottages"[3] Young described double cottages built by Mr. Linton: one set made of "stud and mud, and thatch" cost £40, and another made of brick and tile cost £60. The plan of this double cottage, shown in a text figure, includes a "room," a dairy, and a washroom or storeroom on the ground floor, plus one "room" upstairs.

The rest of the plates illustrate farm implements, a corn stack, a boat for conveying sheep, the south drainages of Lincolnshire, "the Warping of Morton Carr," and "Woad Apparatus"—large structures for processing and fermenting plant material to produce blue dye.

1. 1799, pp. 28–35; 1808 and 1813, pp. 32–39. The plate faces p. 28 in the 1799 edition, p. 32 in the other editions.

2. 1799, pp. 28–33; 1808 and 1813, pp. 32–37.

3. 1799, pp. 35–36; 1808 and 1813, pp. 39–41.

MIDLOTHIAN

111.1
ROBERTSON, George (1750?–1832)
General view of the agriculture of the county of Mid-Lothian: with observations on the means of its improvement. Drawn up for the consideration of the Board of Agriculture and Internal Improvement, from the communications of George Robertson . . . , with additional remarks of several respectable gentlemen and farmers in the county.

Edinburgh, 1795.

xv + 17–223 + 135 + [4] pp, 12 pls.

MH

An earlier edition by Robertson, published in 1793, contained no plates.

Of twelve plates in the 1795 edition, one is a map of the county, eight show farm equipment and animals, and three are illustrations of farm buildings. Two plates bound between pages 40 and 41 show a view and plan of the "Farmer's Mains at Grogar Bank."[1] The buildings illustrated include a farm house two stories high and three bays wide with a small ell at each side, plus a barn, stables, and cottages. Robertson noted the farm houses of the county generally had five or six rooms (plus kitchen, dairy, larder, etc.), and were made of masonry. Houses usually had blue slate roofs, while other farm buildings had tile roofs (pp. 40–42). Another plate, facing page 166, illustrated a "Mid Lothian Cottage," a one-story semidetached pair of residences shown in a heavily wooded setting. This plate and the view of the Farmer's Mains showed people and animals in the foreground and some surrounding scenery, thereby suggesting the scale of the dwellings and offering some picturesque animation.

1. According to the legend on the plate, a "mains" was "a set of low buildings, in the form of a square."

NORFOLK

112.1
[YOUNG, Arthur (1741–1820)]
General view of the agriculture of the county of Norfolk. Drawn up for the consideration of the Board of Agriculture and Internal Improvement. By the Secretary of the Board.

London, 1804.

xx + 532 pp, map + 7 pls.

MH

112.2
_____

General view of the agriculture of the county of Norfolk. Drawn up for the consideration of the Board of Agriculture and Internal Improvement. By the Secretary of the Board.

London, 1813.

xx + 532 pp, map + 7 pls.

MH

A folding "Map of the Soil of Norfolk" faces the title page. Of seven additional plates three concern architecture. Plate I, facing page 22, illustrates a support post resting on a brick foundation, and a barn roof. The unnumbered plate facing page 25, "A Cottage near Dereham," shows a two-story structure with a tile roof. The ground floor consists of a "Keep Room" 12 feet square and a closet, a chimney, stairs, and two "Leanto" rooms. Plate II, facing page 24, is described as "a double cottage of flint-work," with a tiled roof and pointed Gothic windows. The ground-floor plan shows each cottage with a main room 15 by 11 feet, a closet, and separate areas for wood and for a bed.

113.1

DAVIES, Walter (1761–1849)

General view of the agriculture and domestic economy of North Wales; containing the counties of Anglesey, Caernarvon, Denbigh, Flint, Meirionydd, Montgomery. Drawn up and published by order of the Board of Agriculture and Internal Improvement. By Walter Davies. . . .

London, 1810.

xvi + 510 pp, 2 maps + 2 pls.

MH

113.2

General view of the agriculture and domestic economy of North Wales; ⟨ . . . as 1810 . . . ⟩. Drawn up for the consideration of the Board of Agriculture and Internal Improvement. By Walter Davies. . . .

London, 1813.

xvi + 510 pp, map + 2 pls.

MH

In the edition of 1810 the "Directions to the Binder" (p. 510) specify a map to face the title page, a plate facing page 60, and another facing page 86. In the copy in the Kress Library a map of North Wales, dated 1810, faces the title page. Another, undated, map of North Wales faces page 1. The plate facing page 60 illustrates "Veins of Lead Ore at Llangynog Lead Mine." The plate facing page 86 shows a plan and elevation of a cottage, and six plans for tenement farms of six, nine, and twelve acres.

Davies began his discussion of cottages in North Wales (pp. 82–87) with a condemnation of their wretchedness: "One smoky hearth, for it should not be styled a kitchen; and one damp litter-cell, for it cannot be called a bed-room, are frequently all the space allotted to a labourer, his wife, and four or five children. The consequences are obvious; filth, disease, and, frequently, premature death" (p. 82). In contrast with these dwellings, Davies praised three recent efforts at improvement. In the first case Mr. Wilding of Llanrhaiadr and Mr. Edwards of Cerrigllwydion had recently erected "neat brick-built cottages" in the Vale of Clwyd (p. 83). Second, Arthur Blayney of Gregynog wanted to keep "*industrious* labourers . . . more attached to his neighbourhood, by building for them, not only convenient but elegant houses and offices, and annexing land to each sufficient for the keeping of a cow" (pp. 83–84). Third, Lord Penrhyn had erected 63 dwellings in Caernarvonshire between 1790 and 1800 (p. 84).[1] In Plate II Davies presented a plan and side elevation of a cottage designed by "Mr. Daniel of Varchwell Hall, near Welsh Pool" (p. 86). The elevation shows a simple one-story cottage with a gable roof and a chimney. The plan shows a kitchen, pantry, and bedroom together in one part of the cottage, separated by a wall from the adjacent barn, cow house, and pigsty. The rest of the plate shows six recommended arrangements for "tenements, divided into fields, with the rotation of crops to be pursued."

1. Cottages on Lord Penrhyn's estates in Cheshire were illustrated in Abraham Rees's *Cyclopaedia* ([1802]–1820; *q.v.*) and discussed in the article titled "Cottage." Also see the commentary above on Robert Beatson's article "On Cottages" (1797), and the commentary below on Lewis William Wyatt's *Collection of Architectural Designs* (1800–1801).

114.1
[YOUNG, Arthur (1741–1820)]
View of the agriculture of Oxfordshire. Drawn up for the Board of Agriculture and Internal Improvement. By the Secretary of the Board.

London, 1809.

xii + 362 pp, 28 pls (*pl. I is wanting in this copy*; the rest are numbered II–XXVIII).

MH

114.2

_____

General view of the agriculture of Oxfordshire. Drawn up for the consideration of the Board of Agriculture and Internal Improvement. By the Secretary of the Board.

London, 1813.

xii + 362 pp, 28 pls (numbered I–IV, VII–XIII, XIII, XIV, XIV–XVII, XVII–XX, XXII, XXV–XXVIII, XLVIII–XLIX).

MH

For the 1813 edition ten plates were renumbered, and the order of the plates was changed, but the subject matter of the plates remained the same. A reprint of another 1813 edition (Newton Abbot: David & Charles, 1969) includes plates numbered as in the 1809 edition.

A soil map of the county (Plate I) faces the title page. Three plates accompany the chapter on buildings. The first two (Plates II and III) illustrate plans of the ground and bedchamber floors of Woodeaton House, which Young recommended as a model to anyone who "would build a house and offices at the expense of about 20,000*l*." (p. 18). The ground floor includes a hall, a library, two dining rooms, a breakfast room, and a boudoir. The upper floor includes five bedchambers and three dressing rooms. Plate IV, facing page 24, shows two plans, a side elevation, and a front elevation of "The Bishop of Durham's Cottages." Young found the cottages of "uncommon merit, and almost equally deserving commendation, whether the design or the execution be considered" (p. 24). At a cost of "something above £100 each" (p. 24), the cottages were erected in pairs and included three rooms on each of two floors, the largest room measuring 15 feet by 15 feet 6 inches.

The remaining plates depict ploughs, other farm implements, wagons, ox stalls, and racks.

115.1

PARKINSON, Richard (1748–1815)

General view of the agriculture of the county of Rutland; with observations on the means of its improvement, drawn up for the consideration of the Board of Agriculture and Internal Improvement. By Richard Parkinson.

London, 1808.

vii + 187 + [i] pp, 5 + 19 pls.

NN

The *General View of the Agriculture of the County of Rutland* usually appears bound with the *General View of . . . Leicester* (*q.v.*), but is paginated separately and has a separate title page, dated 1808, as well as a separate list of plates. The copy of *Rutland* in the New York Public Library is bound as a separate volume.

The three copies of *Rutland* I have examined—bound separately, bound with the 1809 edition of *Leicester*, and bound with the 1813 edition of *Leicester*—are nearly identical. All include vii + 187 pages, with directions to the binder and errata on the verso of page 187, and in all cases page 28 is misnumbered 82. The title page does not appear to have been reset. All copies have five plates, although in one copy the binder confused plates from *Rutland* with those of *Leicester* and so they are incorrectly bound. The copy of *Rutland* in the New York Public Library also includes 19 plates from *Leicester*. Also in this copy the legend in the upper right corner of two plates—titled "Plan 1, Cottage House" and "Plan 3, Cottage House"—does not read "P. 28," as in other copies, but instead reads "PL. LXII Page 113."[1] All 24 plates in the New York Public Library copy are bound at the end.

Three of the five plates in *Rutland* illustrate plans and elevations for cottage houses. Parkinson explained on page 28 that the designs were given to him by "Mr. H. Wilson, steward to Earl Winchelsea." All three are two stories high and without exterior ornament. The upper story of each includes two chambers. The smallest design (Plan 3) has just a kitchen and pantry on the ground floor, while the largest (Plan 1) has a kitchen, parlor, and several offices. Parkinson estimated the cost of these designs at £45 to £100. The other two plates illustrate Earl Winchilsea's "Sheep Wash-Dike" and "Cow-House" at Burley.

1. Both these plates appear facing page 113 in R. W. Dickson's *Farmer's Companion,* an abridged edition of his *Practical Agriculture* (*q.v.* in Appendix D).

116.1

SINCLAIR, Sir John (1754–1835)

Appendix to the general report of the agricultural state, and political circumstances, of Scotland. Drawn up for the consideration of the Board of Agriculture and Internal Improvement, under the directions of The Right Hon. Sir John Sinclair. . . .

Edinburgh, 1814.

[*Volume I:*] xv + 510 pp, 2 tables.

[*Volume II:*] xii + 440 + 20 pp, 9 pls.

MBAt

The commentary for Entry 116 is combined with that for Entry 117 below.

117.1
SINCLAIR, Sir John (1754–1835)
General report of the agricultural state, and political circumstances, of Scotland. Drawn up for the consideration of the Board of Agriculture and Internal Improvement, under the directions of The Right Hon. Sir John Sinclair. . . .

Edinburgh, 1814.

[*Volume I:*] xvi + 608 pp, map + 24 pls.

[*Volume II:*] xiii + 676 + 6 pp, 26 pls.

[*Volume III:*] xi + 447 + 44 + ii pp, 1 pl.

MH

Between 1791 and 1799 Sir John Sinclair published *The Statistical Account of Scotland*, a 21-volume survey of agricultural and living conditions in each county of Scotland. His *General Report* and the *Appendix to the General Report*, issued in five volumes in 1814, surveyed the whole of Scotland at once, and was arranged according to the general format of the previous *Reports* to the Board of Agriculture concerning individual counties of England and Scotland.

In Volume I of the *General Report* a map of Scotland faces the title page. In Chapter III, "On Buildings, as Connected with Agriculture" (pp. 125–164), there are 19 plates of houses, farm offices, and other structures; these plates are discussed below. Two plates accompany a chapter on land enclosure, and in the chapter on managing arable land there are two plates of corn stands and one plate illustrating "the Scotch Mode of Cultivating Turnips in Drills." In Volume II four plates illustrate a vinery, a peach house, pine pits, a pine stove, a greenhouse, a hot wall, flues, and furnaces. There are 17 plates illustrating methods of drainage and five plates depicting embankments. The sole plate in Volume III shows "The Pyramid of Statistical Inquiry," celebrating the completion over 24 years of the *Statistical Account* (written 1790–1798), the individual county reports (published 1795–1814), and the *General Report* (written 1811–1814). The *Appendix* contains only nine plates, all in Volume II. One depicts a water wheel and the rest concern irrigation. An illustration of a wooden bridge is mounted on page 349.

The 19 plates that accompany the chapter on buildings are mentioned briefly in the text, but for greater detail the reader is referred to the *Appendix*, where 11 short articles (I, 257–294) concern farm buildings and residences. Plate I depicts two one-story cottages, each with just one room, 15 feet deep and 18 or 19 feet wide.[1] Plate II shows part of a row of cottages, two stories high, with a shared door for each pair. The ground floor of each cottage contains a "Living room" and offices in a lean-to at the rear. Upstairs there are two bed chambers.[2] Plate III is a side elevation and floor plan of a one-story cottage with a living room, a pantry, two beds, and two closets.[3] In Plate IV a two-story double cottage appears in elevation and plan, with a living room, pantry, scullery, and entrance porch on the ground floor, and two bed chambers above.[4] Plate V includes plans and an elevation for "a small farm of from 50 to 100 acres" (p. 137), with a parlor, a kitchen, two pantries, an area for "stores," a "Milk house," and a scullery on the ground floor of the house. Plate VI shows a farmyard and a house with a dining room, parlor, business room, two kitchens, and several offices on the ground floor. Unlike designs in previous plates, the farm house facade is modestly articulated with a semicircular relieving arch projecting into a broken pediment. Plate VII depicts a farmyard and the elevation of a house articulated in a manner similar to the house in Plate VI. In plan the house in Plate VII contains two parlors, a business room, a pantry, a kitchen, and several offices on the ground floor. Plates VIII and XVI–XVIII illustrate farmyards and offices.[5] Plate IX shows a two-story house with a fanlight over the door and quoins at the ends of the facade. On the ground floor there are three principal rooms plus three more rooms in ells, and upstairs there are three chambers and a nursery.[6] Plate X is a plan and view of cattle stalls, and Plates XI and XII illustrate "Apparatus for Steaming Potatoes for Horses." Plate XIII shows a house designed "for a proprietor of moderate fortune; namely, from L.1000 to L. 3000 *per annum*" (p. 159). Sinclair described the house and its construction briefly (pp. 159–163) and estimated that with offices it would cost £3022 10s. The facade is fronted by a one-story tetrastyle Ionic portico. The ground-floor plan includes a hall, a parlor, a dining room, a drawing room, a study, a hothouse, a greenhouse, and offices. Upstairs are four bedrooms, a dressing room, closets, a nursery, and servants' quarters. Plate XIV is a "Section of rubblestone Arched rooffs [*sic*] at Meigle."[7] Plate XV illustrates a block of four one-story attached cottages, each with a kitchen, a "room," and two bed areas.[8] Plate XIX is an elevation, two floor plans, and a roof plan for a two-story house with a Tuscan frontispiece surrounding the door and semicircular relieving arches over the windows. The ground floor includes a lobby, drawing room, dining room, business room, bedroom or family work room, kitchen, barrack room, storeroom, and dairy. Upstairs are four bedrooms, a bed closet, and three closets.[9]

1. Specifications and estimates in *Appendix*, I, 273.

2. Description and estimate in *Appendix*, I, 274–275.

3. Description and estimate in *Appendix*, I, 277.

4. Description and estimate in *Appendix*, I, 277.

5. Specifications and estimates for Plate VIII in *Appendix*, I, 288–290. Description of Plate XVII in *Appendix*, I, 277–279.

6. Specifications and estimates in *Appendix*, I, 286–289.

7. Description in *Appendix*, I, 275.

8. Description and estimate in *Appendix*, I, 279–280.

9. Description in *Appendix*, I, 278–279.

118.1

PITT, William (1749–1823)

General view of the agriculture of the county of Stafford: with observations on the means of its improvement. Drawn up for the consideration of the Board of Agriculture and Internal Improvement, by W. Pitt, of Pendeford, near Wolverhampton; with the additional remarks of several respectable gentlemen and farmers in the county.

London, 1796.

xvi + 241 + [6] pp, map + 14 pls.

ICN

118.2

———

General view of the agriculture of the county of Stafford; with observations on the means of its improvement. By William Pitt . . . with the additional remarks of several respectable gentlemen and farmers in the county. Drawn up by order of the Board of Agriculture. The second edition.

London, 1808.

xii + 327 pp, 16 pls.

MH

118.3

———

General view of the agriculture of the county of Stafford; with observations on the means of its improvement. Drawn up for the consideration of the Board of Agriculture and Internal Improvement. By William Pitt. . . . With the additional remarks of several respectable gentlemen and farmers in the county. The second edition.

London, 1813.

xii + 327 pp, 16 pls.

MH

The first edition, written by Pitt and published in 1794, contained no plates and no discussion of building.

Of sixteen plates in the final edition (1813) eight illustrate farm animals, one is a map of the county, and the rest are plans and elevations of farm structures. These include a "Sheep Cote," a "Cow Shed on an Economical Plan," two original designs for paired cottages, and three original designs for farm houses. The dwellings are mentioned only briefly in the section of text devoted to "Farm-Houses, Offices, and Repairs" (pp. 24–28), where the author described them as "farm-houses upon different scales, adapted either for the proprietor of a farm, or a respectable tenant; with some upon a smaller scale for less occupations, as well as cottages for labourers; in all of them, convenience and economy have been attended to" (pp. 25–26). There follow brief remarks on siting, materials, thatch, repairs, and expense. In all cases, "compactness, regularity, and neatness should certainly be studied and attended to," and "strength and durability should be more particularly attended to than elegance" (pp. 27–28).

The three farm houses, two or three stories high and three windows wide, are shown in elevation and in plan with attached farm yards and offices. Only the two larger designs have any ornamentation, a modest molding surrounding the front door. The plan of the ground floor of the largest house shows a kitchen, common parlor, best parlor, brewhouse, and dairy. The other two houses have a kitchen, parlor, brewhouse, and dairy. The three designs were "adapted" for farms of 200 to 500 acres, 100 to 200 acres, and 50 to 100 acres, respectively. The next two plates each illustrate a pair of attached two-story cottages. The first pair, with hog sties and cow houses attached, would cost £80 to £100. The second, with hog sties only, would cost £60 to £80.

SUTHERLAND

119.1

HENDERSON, John (1759?–1828)

General view of the agriculture of the county of Sutherland, with observations on the means of its improvement. Drawn up for the consideration of the Board of Agriculture and Internal Improvement. To which is annexed, a particular account of the more recent improvements in that county. By Capt. John Henderson.

London, 1812.

xi + 238 pp, 10 pls (incl. map).

MH

119.2

————

General view of the agriculture of the county of Sutherland; with observations on the means of its improvement. Drawn up for ⟨ . . . as 1812 . . . ⟩.

London, 1815.

xi + [i] + 238 pp, 10 pls (incl. map).

NN

Facing the title page is a soil map of the county. Other plates show a plan of the pier being erected in Dunrobin Bay, a section of a coal shaft, an elevation of the proposed mound and bridge to cross the Little Ferry, a view of a machine for dressing barley, a view of the ruined Gothic church at the east end of Dornoch Castle, and views of two ancient ruins, Castle Cole and Dun Dornadil. A view of Dunrobin Castle accompanies the text on "Buildings," which merely offers brief descriptions of this and other major residences in the county. The plate facing page 138 illustrates Earl Gower's farm steading at Skelbo, showing plans and elevations of various buildings for animals and crops.

WEST LOTHIAN

120.1
TROTTER, James
General view of the agriculture of the county of West-Lothian: with observations on the means of its improvement, drawn up for the consideration of the Board of Agriculture and Internal Improvement. With several plates. By James Trotter. . . .

Edinburgh, 1811.

iv + 340 pp, map + 6 pls.

MH

The first edition of this report was published in 1794. Only 38 pages long, it included no architectural illustrations.

A "Map of the Soils in Linlithgowshire" faces the title page. Three plates illustrate threshing machinery and another depicts a "Hay Drag." Appendix No. I, "Prices of Mason and Carpenter Work in building the Farm-house at Stacks, A.D. 1806--1807" (pp. 241–242), includes a plate showing a farmyard and farm house in plan. A plate labeled "Appendix No. II," for which there is no accompanying text, includes a plan and elevation for a double cottage. The caption indicates that one cottage would cost "about £30, & if more than one are built in the same Row, the expense is considerably diminished." Each cottage, just one story high, contains two rooms, one measuring 8 1/2 by 8 feet and the other 9 feet square, plus a small area labeled "Beds" and another labeled "Bed Places."

WORCESTER

121.1
PITT, William (1749–1823)
A general view of the agriculture of the county of Worcester; with observations on the means of its improvement; published by order of the Board of Agriculture and Internal Improvement. By W. Pitt. . . .

London, 1810.

xx + 428 pp, map + 6 pls.

MH

121.2

General view of the agriculture of the county of Worcester; with observations on the means of its improvement. Drawn up for the consideration of the Board of Agriculture and Internal Improvement. By W. Pitt. . . .

London, 1813.

xx + 428 pp, map + 6 pls.

MH

A map of the county faces the title page. Plate I depicts a "Feeding Shed for Cattle." Plate II "is a sketch of three cottages erected on the new inclosure of the Lickey, but built by a person to let" (p. 22). The cottages form a single row, with a brewhouse attached at one end and a shop at the other. Each cottage is two stories high, with a kitchen and pantry on the ground floor. Pitt estimated the cost of the entire group at £210. Plates III through VI depict ploughs, methods of drainage and irrigation, and stalls for feeding cattle.

**YORKSHIRE,
EAST RIDING**

122.1

LEATHAM, Isaac

General view of the agriculture of the East Riding of Yorkshire, and the Ainsty of the City of York, with observations on the means of its improvement. By Isaac Leatham. . . . Drawn up for the consideration of the Board of Agriculture and Internal Improvement.

London, 1794.

68 pp, 3 maps + 7 pls.

MH

Facing the title page is a map of Yorkshire and a map of the East Riding with the "Ainsty Liberty." Another map of the East Riding and the Ainsty of York faces page 7. Plates 1 through 3 depict elevations and plans of "Mr. Parker's Barn Stable." Plate 4 illustrates a plan and elevation of "the Farming Mans House, & part of the Farm Buildings belonging to a Gentleman" in the East Riding. The two-story house includes a kitchen, back kitchen, meal room, pantry, dairy, and other offices on the ground floor. Plate 5 is a "Plan of a Farm House & Buildings, for a middle sized farm," with a parlor, pantry, dairy, back kitchen, and fore kitchen on the ground floor. This particular design, according to Leatham, was "not to be found in the Riding, although many farm offices nearly on the same construction, but not so complete as this, are to be met with" (p. 29). The final two plates illustrate a ewe and a ram.

123.1

TUKE, John (–1841)

General view of the agriculture of the North Riding of Yorkshire. Drawn up for the consideration of the Board of Agriculture and Internal Improvement. By John Tuke. . . .

London, 1800. [*Separate editions printed for G. Nicol and for R. Phillips.*]

xv + 355 pp, map + 14 pls.

MH, CU

An earlier edition, *General View of the Agriculture of the North Riding of Yorkshire, with Observations on the Means of Its Improvement. By Mr. Tuke* (London, 1794), has no plates.

A map of the North Riding faces the title page.

In the section on "Cottages" (pp. 41–46) Tuke reported that laborers' cottages were "generally small and low, consisting only of one room, and, very rarely, of two, both of which are level with the ground, and sometimes a step within it. This situation renders them damp, and frequently very unwholesome, and contributes, with the smallness of the apartments, to injure the health both of parents and children" (p. 41). Considering "the importance of this class of people; that they are the powers by which the business of agriculture is performed," Tuke recommended that laborers should be "accommodated with every convenience . . . for their health" and housed in "cottages adjoining each other, that the families may have better opportunity of rendering mutual assistance" (pp. 41–42).

Five plates which accompany this section are described on pages 44–46 under the heading "COTTAGES," but the designs themselves are clearly labeled farm houses. The design in Plate I, for a farm "of £100 to £150" per annum, is shown in elevation and plan. The two-story house includes a parlor, kitchen, scullery, pantry, and dairy on the ground floor. Plates II and III depict plans and elevations for a two-story house, a farmyard, offices, and a circular barn "for a farm of £200 per Annum." The house includes a parlor, kitchen, study, pantry, dairy, and scullery on the ground floor. Plates IV and V illustrate "A House & Offices for a Farm of £300 per Annum" in plan and elevation. The two-story house has a parlor, a "Common keeping-room," a kitchen, a dairy, a pantry, and wine and ale cellars on the ground floor. All three designs are devoid of ornament except for a pediment over the door of the second house and an entablature over the door of the third.

Plates VI through XIV depict farm implements, fences, hedges, gates, and cattle.

GREAT BRITAIN. Parliament. House of Commons. Select Committee on Buildings Regulation, and Improvement of Boroughs.

See Entry 471.

GREAT BRITAIN. Poor Law Commissioners.

See Entries 472 and 473.

124.1

GREGORY, George (1754–1808)

A dictionary of arts and sciences. By G. Gregory. . . . In two volumes. Vol. I [*or* II].

London: Printed for Richard Phillips: and sold by all booksellers and dealers in books in the United Kingdom, 1806 [*or* 1807].

[*Two text volumes, plus one additional volume of plates.*]

Art. "Perspective," II, 379–383; pl. CIV.

26.6 × 21.1 cm

ICU

124.2 †

A new & complete dictionary of arts & sciences, including the latest improvement & discovery and the present state of every branch of human knowledge. . . . By G. Gregory.

[*Volume I:*] London: W. Lewis, 1815.

[*Volume II:*] London: S. A. Oddy, 1815.

29 cm

Reference: NUC-S

The discussion here is based on examination of the 1806–1807 edition.

The article on "Architecture" (I, 135–142) begins with a short history of the subject, followed by descriptions of the five orders. There are brief remarks on ornaments, moldings, bases, diminution of columns, pedestals, pilasters, attics, caryatids, and termini. There is a longer discussion of "the temples of the antients," followed by observations on Gothic architecture and a paragraph on "domes or cupolas." The article ends with an essay on "modern or practical architecture," which includes remarks on siting, materials, construction, function and arrangement of rooms, fireplaces and chimneys, windows, skylights, and roofs. "References to the Plates" on page 139 indicate there are illustrations of the five orders in Plates I and II.

The single plate accompanying the article on "Perspective" includes several figures borrowed from *The Art of Drawing, in Perspective* (1755; *q.v.*), plus outline drawings of two houses, each two stories high and three windows wide, shown in perspective. One is shown with its facade parallel to the picture plane, the other with its facade oblique to the picture plane. Both these illustrations appeared again in Johnson and Exley, *The Imperial Encyclopaedia* ([1812]; *q.v.*), and Mitchell, *The Portable Encyclopaedia* (1826; *q.v.*); that with the facade parallel to the picture plane appeared in Partington, *The British Cyclopaedia* (1833–1835; *q.v.*).

125.1

GWILT, Joseph (1784–1863)

Rudiments of architecture, practical and theoretical. With plates. By Joseph Gwilt. . . .

London: Priestley and Weale, 1826.

xix + 236 pp, 11 pls.

23.5 × 15.2 cm

NN

125.2

Rudiments of architecture, practical and theoretical. Illustrated with seventeen plates. By Joseph Gwilt. . . . The second edition.

London: Printed for J. Taylor, 1834.

xiv + [ii] + 230 pp, 17 pls (numbered I*–VI*, I–XI).

24.1 × 15.2 cm

NNC

125.3 †

Rudiments of architecture, practical and theoretical.

[London?], 1835.

8°

Reference: APSD

125.4

Rudiments of architecture, practical and theoretical. Comprising sections upon the materials employed in building. The methods of combining the principal materials. The five orders of architecture with their parts, profiles, and proportions. A cursory view of ancient architecture. A dictionary of technical terms used by architects and artificers. A table of foreign measures of length. By Joseph Gwilt. . . . Second edition. Illustrated with seventeen plates.

London: M. Taylor, (nephew and successor to the late J. M. Taylor,) 1839.

xiv + [ii] + 230 pp, 17 pls (numbered I*–VI*, I–XI).

24.8 × 15.9 cm

MH

The preliminary matter includes a dedication, a preface, a table of contents, and lists of the plates.[1] In the Preface (pp. vii–xi) Gwilt noted that if Sir William Chambers had fulfilled "his intention of giving to the public a practical work" then Gwilt would not have "thought it necessary" to prepare this book (p. x). He indicated that his aim was "to divest the entrance to this art as much as possible of its ruggedness and perplexity," and to give the student the means "to make himself intelligible to the artificer when choice or necessity may lead him to indulge his fancy in designing" (p. ix). He suggested the *Rudiments* might well serve as "an useful introduction" to Chambers's *Treatise*.[2]

Following a short introduction (pp. 1–8) the text is divided into five sections, treating materials, "Methods of Combining the Principal Materials," the orders, "Antient Architecture," and "Technical Terms used by Architects and Artificers, and Foreign Measures of Length." The first six plates, marked I* through VI*, illustrate flooring, roof construction, scarfing, domes, vaulting, arches and piers, and a truss for a girder. The next 11 plates, numbered I through XI, illustrate the orders, arcades, piers, and bases for columns. In addition Plate X, titled "Of Designing," depicts a small one-story house in elevation, plan, and section. The plan of the house is square, with hexastyle Ionic porticoes on each of the four facades and a square lantern rising above the square central chamber.

1. This description is based on examination of the 1839 edition.

2. In 1825, one year before the first edition of *Rudiments*, Gwilt published a revised edition of Chambers's *Treatise* (*q.v.*).

126.1 ‖
GWILT, Joseph (1784–1863)
Sciography; or, examples of shadows; and rules for their projection: intended for the use of architectural draughtsmen. By Joseph Gwilt, Architect. Lithographed on eighteen plates.

London: Printed for J. Taylor, 1822.

viii + 9–43 pp, 18 pls.

21.2 cm

Reference: Information supplied by Fiske Kimball Fine Arts Library, University of Virginia.

126.2

Sciography; or, examples of shadows; with rules for their projection: intended for the use of architectural draughtsmen, and other artists. By Joseph Gwilt, Architect. . . . Second edition, with considerable additions and improvements, and six additional plates.

London: Printed for Priestley and Weale, 1824.

viii + 55 pp, 24 pls.

22.1 × 13.3 cm

MBAt

126.3

Sciography; 〈 . . . as 1824 . . . 〉 Architect. . . . Third edition, with considerable additions and improvements, and six additional plates.

London: Printed for Priestley and Weale, 1833.

viii + 55 pp, 24 pls.

22.0 × 14.0 cm

NNC

126.4

Sciography, or examples of shadows: with rules for their projection. Intended for the use of architectural draughtsmen and other artists. With twenty-four plates. By Joseph Gwilt. . . . A new edition, with considerable additions and improvements.

London: M. Taylor, 1842.

viii + 55 pp, 24 pls.

21.0 × 13.0 cm

CtY-BA

126.5

Sciography; 〈 . . . as 1824 . . . 〉 Architect. . . . Fourth edition, with considerable additions and improvements, and six additional plates.

London: Henry G. Bohn, 1866.

iv + 5–32 pp, 24 pls.

22.2 × 13.8 cm

MH

In the Preface (pp. iii–viii)[1] Gwilt noted the "non-existence, in our own language, of an useful and practical Treatise on the projection of Shadows" (p. iii). Thus *Sciography* is "presented to the Architectural Draughtsman and artist with the view of assisting him in a more scrupulous accuracy of the delineation of shadows than is usually attended to" (p. iii). Gwilt offered "no new theory" here, and instead was "contented with smoothing a path already cleared . . . by the French writers." Indeed his "original intention was to have published a mere version of the excellent work of Stanislas L'Eveillé (Etudes d'Ombres)," but it "would have been too complex to have been generally useful." He also acknowledged a debt to La Vallée. Nevertheless the method Gwilt finally adopted "is more simple than that used by either of those writers."

The text is organized as a series of problems and examples. References to the plates often are numbered incorrectly, causing some confusion over the identity and purpose of some figures. The 24 plates depict geometric objects, moldings and parts of the Classical orders, an urn, a niche, an arcade, a handrail, balusters, steps, and room interiors, all with shadows. In addition Plate 20 is an elevation and partial plan of a two-story dwelling, apparently square in plan, with tetrastyle Ionic porticoes on each facade and a small dome over the center.

1. This description is based on examination of the 1824 edition.

127.1
GYFFORD, Edward (1773–1856)
Designs for elegant cottages and small villas, calculated for the comfort and convenience of persons of moderate and of ample fortune; carefully studied and thrown into perspective. To which is annexed, a general estimate of the probable expense attending the execution of each design. By. E. Gyfford, Architect. Engraved on twenty-six plates. Forming part the second of a series of select architecture.

London: Published by J. Taylor; J. Harding; and J. Carpenter, 1806.

viii + 20 pp, 26 pls.

30.8 × 23.5 cm

RIBA

The Introduction (pp. v–viii) clearly reveals Gyfford's sense of self-importance: he was "proud to have the power of annexing to the Library of Arts, a work which can convey any additional information on the progress of this science, in which national pride and character, in ages of civilization, are eminently connected" (p. vi). In his early years Gyfford had shown some promise, receiving the Royal Academy Silver Medal at age 18, and the Gold Medal at 19. But he accomplished little more until he was 33, when he published *Designs for Elegant Cottages*, in which his only known executed design appears. Outside of his other book of *Designs* (1807; *q.v.*), his career was unremarkable.[1]

On the final page of the Introduction Gyfford indicated some of his aesthetic concerns in preparing this collection of designs for dwellings. Elegance, utility, and economy were of special interest, but more important was the character of the whole: "the very end of these studies has been to give the importance of the villa to the cottage, not the cottage character to the villa." The "cottage style," he noted, too easily produces "an idea nearer allied to a barn than to a cottage." Gyfford also explained that his designs were composed to accord with particular aspects of the surrounding landscape: "The different styles adopted, although analogous to the Grecian and Gothic characters, are nevertheless governed by the immediate circumstances of each, consequently form select compositions, deduced discretionally from either" (p. viii).

The text (pp. 1–20) contains descriptions of the ten designs illustrated in the plates, together with occasional remarks on cost, construction, style, furnishings, and the scenic character of the site. He noted that the "Gothic character" of the fifth design, for example, was "particularly well adapted to the romantic scenery in the north and west of England" (p. 9). By contrast the sixth design, "constructed in the modern style of elegance," was "calculated to ornament the polished scenery of the landscape garden" (p. 11).

Each of the ten designs is illustrated in two plans and one or two views. There are four cottages, one "somewhat more commodious residence," a "small villa," a "cottage villa," a "commodious residence," and two villas. The plans are based on regular geometric figures, including squares, rectangles, semicircles, and circles. Seven designs have spare, Neoclassical elevations, aptly described as a "modern style of elegance" in the case of one villa (p. 11). Sometimes embellished with light iron trelliswork, Ionic porticoes, or other Classical ornament, these elevations are symmetrical and carefully proportioned, often including figures of squares and circles raised in low relief on wall surfaces or incorporated in window tracery. Three other designs are in the Gothic or Castle style. Like the Neoclassical designs, they have symmetrical plans and elevations and are composed of regular geometric figures, but they are differentiated by crenellations along the parapets, and windows with pointed arches. Remarks in the text suggest the style was adopted to accommodate more "romantic" scenery (Design No. 5, p. 9), but only in one plate does the scenery appear appreciably bolder (Design No. 8, Plate XXI).

The cheapest design, shown in Plates VII through IX, is a cottage in Gothic style. The ground-floor plan includes a dining room, study, kitchen, and pantry, and the chamber floor contains four bedrooms. Gyfford estimated it would cost £500. The most expensive design, shown in Plates XXV and XXVI, is a villa estimated at £4,300. The ground-floor plan includes a library, dining room, saloon, and drawing room. There are five bedrooms on the chamber floor, and four servants' rooms above that. The bow-fronted facade includes a two-story Ionic portico.

1. Colvin (1978), p. 374. The executed design is shown in Plates XXIII–XXIV, and is described as "a villa, built for C. Cooke, Esq. in Essex, on an eminence commanding an extensive prospect of a rich and most beautiful country" (p. 17).

128.1
GYFFORD, Edward (1773–1856)
Designs for small picturesque cottages and hunting boxes, adapted for ornamental retreats for hunting and shooting; also some designs for park entrances, bridges, &c. carefully studied and thrown into perspective. By E. Gyfford, Architect. Engraved on twenty plates. Forming part the first of a series of select architecture.

London: Published by J. Taylor; J. Harding; and J. Carpenter, 1807.

vii + 9–16 pp, 20 pls.

29.2 × 23.2 cm

Bodl.

Gyfford explained in the Preface (pp. v–vii) that "The Designs contained in this volume form the First Part of a Series of Studies and Designs in *Select Architecture*" (p. vi). The second part had been published the previous year as *Designs for Elegant Cottages and Small Villas* (q.v.). He noted that

"The Plans in this volume are constructed on a small scale of accommodations, yet the elevations present an ornamented and picturesque appearance" (p. v). Although most of the designs were intended "for a temporary retreat from the more elegant amusements of the metropolis, or the more enlarged circle at the villa," some of the plans were "sufficiently large for the permanent residence and required conveniences of a small family" (p. vi). In addition several designs might "form suitable residences for a bailiff, keeper, &c. to be built on picturesque situations, which may be seen at a distance from the mansion" (p. vi). The remainder of the letterpress (pp. 9–16) consists of brief descriptions of each design, touching on such matters as use, materials, cost, and the type of site for which the design was intended.[1]

The 20 plates include plans and views of two "residences," two bridges, a "decorative Temple . . . in the Chinese style," a greenhouse, and 11 "boxes" or residences for hunting, shooting, and "sporting." The cheapest hunting residence (Plate 4), estimated at £160, is 45 feet wide and contains a hall, parlor, kitchen, and eating room on the ground floor, plus three bedrooms above. The most expensive is a "Shooting Box in the castle style" (Plate XII), estimated at £1000. Octagonal in plan and two stories high, the design includes a drawing room, eating room, kitchen, and library on the ground floor, plus four bedrooms upstairs. The facade is ornamented with pointed windows, turrets, a crenellated parapet, and a crenellated lantern rising above the central circular staircase.

Most of the plans are based on regular geometric figures, particularly circles, squares, hexagons, and octagons. In some cases these figures are especially well expressed in the elevation too, as in the case of the "shooting box" in Plate VIII. The view shows two cylindrical towers flanking, and partially set into, a lower one-story rectangular solid. The style is a curious combination of rational Neoclassicism, consisting of geometric solids embellished with thin bands of vertical flutes, and Perpendicular Gothic Revival, with pointed arches used for window mullions and in the entrance. The two-story "Residence" in the first plate, square in plan, is more purely Neoclassical, with a heavily rusticated ground floor, buttress-like pilasters projecting at 45-degree angles from all four corners, and light, segmental iron balconies attached to each face of the upper story. Several other designs with thatch roofs, hipped gables, and tree-trunk columns are executed in a combination of Neoclassical and rustic styles. Two designs in the "Castle" style incorporate crenellations, arrow slits, buttresses, and other medieval features. The Chinese temple incorporates a pagoda roof and a few decorative frets in an otherwise very plain rectangular Neoclassical composition.

1. The residence in Plate I, for example, was "calculated to be erected on an eminence where the prospect is particularly interesting or extensive" (p. 9).

HALE, Thomas
A compleat body of husbandry.

See Entry 486.

129.1

HALFPENNY, William (–1755)

The art of sound building, demonstrated in geometrical problems: shewing geometrical lines for all kinds of arches, niches, groins, and twisted rails, both regular and irregular. With several other draughts of buildings and staircases. All curiously engraven on copper plates. Wherein are laid down (suited to every capacity) easy practical methods for carpenters, joiners, masons, or bricklayers, to work by. By William Halfpenny, Architect and Carpenter.

London: Printed by Sam. Aris for the author; Benjamin Cole Engraver; Tho. Taylor Printseller; Bowen Whitledge Bookseller; Tho. Bowles Printseller; Tho. Wright Mathematical Instrument-Maker; John Senex; Francis Fayram; Tho. Worrall; and John Walthoe, 1725.

4 printed leaves, 56 pp, frontisp. + 20 pls.

30.5 × 19.7 cm

NN

129.2

The art of sound building; demonstrated in geometrical problems, shewing ⟨ . . . as 1st edition . . . ⟩ staircases all ⟨ . . . as 1st edition . . . ⟩ work by. The second edition: to which are added, useful tables of the proportions of the members of all the orders, calculated in feet and inches, for the use of practical builders. By William Halfpenny, Architect and Carpenter.

London: Printed for Sam. Birt; and B. Motte, 1725.

2 printed leaves, 65 pp, frontisp. + 19 + 5 pls.

30.4 × 19.3 cm

RP

The preliminary matter includes a dedication, a preface, and a list of subscribers which is printed on the rectos of two leaves. In the Preface Halfpenny stated he was moved to prepare this book by "the daily Errors that I saw Workmen commit in framing their Works for Buildings, on account of their Want of the Knowledge of the Proportions contain'd in this Book." He did not want to "teach" architects, but instead blamed them for keeping to themselves their knowledge of the principles of proportion.

The allegorical frontispiece—a feature seldom found in architectural handbooks—suggests the extent of Halfpenny's ambition. A figure of Architecture, holding a plan, is surrounded by the instruments of her profession. She sits in front of a wall supporting a colossal column and drapery, and leans on the base of another column. Lying in the foreground are a Corinthian capital and base. In the middle distance is an obelisk, recalling the architecture of Egyptian antiquity. In the distance is a large mansion or palace, three stories high and 15 windows wide, suggestive of the present and future progress of domestic architecture in Britain.[1]

The text is divided into five sections, treating "the Description of Arches by the Intersection of Lines," groins, niches, twisted rails, and the construction of arches and niches in stone and brick. All five sections are composed of individual "Problems," such as "How to form an Elliptical Nich" or how "To find the Angle, or Mitre-Bracket of a Cove." The explications of the problems are illustrated by figures in Plates 1 through 16. These include geometric diagrams and illustrations of niches, railings, arches, columns, "Raking-Collonadoes," a staircase, and a lathe.

Plates 17, 18, and 19 contain one elevation, two sections, and three plans of "a House of my Invention," three stories high and seven windows wide, with a hexastyle Corinthian portico in front and Corinthian pilasters across the facade. The plan is 200 feet square, with an open courtyard, 75 feet square, in the center. This design is not discussed in the text. The final plate in the first edition is a design for Holy Trinity Church in Leeds.

The second edition includes additional text (pp. 57–65), with tables for determining the proportions of the five orders, and instructions for using the tables. Five additional plates depict the orders.

1. Cf. Colen Campbell's remarks on this subject in *Vitruvius Britannicus* (1715; *q.v.*).

130.1
HALFPENNY, William (–1755), and John HALFPENNY (fl. 1750)
Chinese and Gothic architecture properly ornamented. Being twenty new plans and elevations, on twelve copper-plates: containing a great variety of magnificent buildings accurately described; as also, several of a smaller kind elegantly design'd, with all necessary offices, of great strength, easy construction, and graceful appearance. Scales are annexed, and regular estimates are made for each design. The whole carefully calculated by the great square; with instructions to workmen, &c. in several pages of letter-press. Intended as an improvement of what has been published of that sort. Correctly engraved from the designs of William and John Halfpenny, Architects.

London: Printed for, and sold by Robert Sayer, 1752.

16 pp + 12 pls.

[*This copy is bound with six additional plates of designs for gates and palings.*]

27.6 × 26.0 cm

NNC

Apparently conceived as a means of capitalizing on recent innovations in fashion, this is a collection of designs in both Gothic and Chinese styles. Unlike most of the Halfpennys' other works, there is almost no mention here of Palladian ideas of order and proportion. Instead there are just two brief comments in apparent defense against possible criticism from the Palladian camp. First, the authors justified their often whimsical designs by noting that "Invention and Variety of Construction" were paramount in architectural design (Preface). What the authors conveniently ignored in this argument was the equally great need for a balance between that variety and some standard of uniformity. Second, they suggested that "if Gracefulness and true Symmetry are found in the Structure, they will be sufficient Bars to any false or frivolous Aspersions that . . . may be . . . attempted against our Endeavours" (p. 4). Thus the authors tried to excuse and perhaps justify the wild proliferation of ornament added to the facades of their designs, often without structural support.

The letterpress consists of detailed explanations and specifications for the plates. Individual illustrations reveal the symmetry the authors promised, but there is seldom any apparent proportionality. Plates 1 through 8 include 12 designs for two- and three-story houses in Chinese style, some with offices attached, and ranging from 67 to 203 feet wide. The Chinese ornament was attached more with an eye for Rococo design than with a sense of structural or stylistic integrity. The eight Gothic designs in Plates 9 through 12 range from 63 to 230 feet wide, but the ornament is curiously far more restrained. Most of these designs consist of a Palladian facade to which pointed windows and perhaps a few crenellations or finials have been attached. One design has just one identifiably Gothic feature, a cupola (Pl. 12, No. 1).

131.1

HALFPENNY, William (–1755), and John HALFPENNY (fl. 1750)
The country gentleman's pocket companion, and builder's assistant, for rural decorative architecture. Containing, thirty-two new designs, plans and elevations of alcoves, floats, temples, summer-houses, lodges, huts, grotto's, &c. in the Augustine, Gothick and Chinese taste, with proper directions annexed. Also, an exact estimate of their several amounts, which are from twenty-five to one hundred pounds, and most of them portable. Correctly engraved on twenty-five copper plates, from the designs, and under the direction of William and John Halfpenny, Architects.

London: Printed for, and sold by Robert Sayer, 1753.

14 pp, 25 pls.

19.4 × 11.7 cm

Bodl.

131.2

The country gentleman's pocket companion, ⟨ . . . as 1753 . . . ⟩ Gothic and ⟨ . . . as 1753 . . . ⟩ designs and ⟨ . . . as 1753 . . . ⟩, Architects. The second edition.

London: Printed for, and sold by Robert Sayer, 1756.

14 pp, 25 pls.

20.7 × 13.4 cm

MH

The text (pp. 3–14) is devoted to descriptions of designs in Plates 1 through 21, and includes dimensions, remarks on construction and materials, and cost estimates.

Plates 1 through 21 depict 28 designs for garden structures: 12 temples, five summer houses, four lodges, four huts, two grottoes, and one "Termini

Seat." These are composed in Chinese, Indian, Gothic, "Ancient," and "Modern" styles. Plates 22 through 25 illustrate designs for two Chinese "Floats" and two Chinese boats.

Some of the garden structures are little more than flat facades. Those with enclosed spaces are generally square in plan, although there are occasional hexagonal, pentagonal, and circular forms as well. The only design with more than one room is the Gothic lodge in Plate 20, containing a circular "Room" ten feet in diameter, plus a parlor and a kitchen to either side and a "passage" in the rear.

The Chinese and Indian styles closely resemble each other, with wide eaves, extensive treillage, and a profusion of Rococo ornament. The Gothic designs incorporate thatch roofs, pointed windows, buttresses, crenellations, and finials. The "ancient" designs—two huts in Plate 11—are constructed of rough boulders and rubble, topped by thatch roofs. The "modern" designs incorporate ornamental motifs from the late English Baroque as well as scrolls and Venetian windows from the Palladian Revival.

The Country Gentleman's Pocket Companion was the first British architectural treatise to depict original designs flanked by landscape scenery.[1] In most cases the scenery consists of trees and shrubs at either side of the structure, but in some it is more elaborate. The "Modern summer house" (Plate 4), for example, is set atop a rockwork bridge that crosses a small stream.

1. Previously scenery appeared only in topographical views of extant buildings. See for example the third volume of *Vitruvius Britannicus* by Colen Campbell (1725), and the fourth volume by Badeslade and Rocque (1739), *qq.v.*

132.1

HALFPENNY, William (–1755), John HALFPENNY (fl. 1750), Robert MORRIS (ca. 1702–1754), and T. LIGHTOLER

The modern builder's assistant; or, a concise epitome of the whole system of architecture; in which the various branches of that excellent study are establish'd on the most familiar principles, and rendered adequate to every capacity; being useful to the proficient, and easy to the learner. Divided into three parts. Containing

I. A correct view of the five orders, explained in several sheets of letter= press.

II. Consisting of regular plans, elevations, and sections of houses, in the most elegant and convenient manner, either for the reception of noblemen, gentlemen or tradesmen with large or small families, adapted to the taste of town or country. To which part is added, a great variety of other plans for offices or out-houses adjoining to them of different dimensions for domestic uses; such as kitchens, wash-houses, malt-houses, bake-houses, brew-houses, dairies, vaults, stables, coach-houses, dog-kennels, &c. &c. Together with the estimates of each design, and proper instructions to the workmen how to execute the same.

III. Exhibiting (ornamental as well as plain) a variety of chimney-pieces, windows, doors, sections of stair-cases, rooms, halls, saloons, &c. skreens for rooms, also cielings, piers, and gate-roofs, &c. &c.

The whole beautifully engraved on eighty five folio copper plates, from the designs of William and John Halfpenny, Architects and Carpenters, Robert Morris, Surveyor, and T. Lightoler, Carver.

London: Printed for James Rivington and J. Fletcher, and Robert Sayer, MDCCVLII.

ii + 52 pp, 85 pls (pl. I is on p. 3).

31.8 × 20.3 cm

Soane

132.2

The modern builder's assistant; ⟨ . . . as MDCCVLII . . . ⟩ sheets of letter press. ⟨ . . . as MDCCVLII . . . ⟩ Carver.

London: Printed for Robert Sayer, [n.d.].

ii + 52 pp, 85 pls (pl. I is on p. 3).

31.5 × 18.6 cm

NNC

The edition published by "James Rivington and J. Fletcher, and Robert Sayer" is dated "MDCCVLII" on the title page. This improper Roman numeral is the source of some uncertainty, but the date of publication may easily be fixed between 1756 and 1760: Rivington and Fletcher traded together only during those years.[1] Thus "MDCCVLII" appears to be a printer's error for "MDCCLVII" (1757).

The undated edition was "Printed for Robert Sayer," who traded alone from 1751 to 1774.[2] Since William Halfpenny died in 1755 and Robert Morris died in 1754, it would be plausible to date this edition ca. 1751–1754. But the book is described on the title page as a collection of subjects taken "from the designs of" the Halfpennys, Morris, and Lightoler—suggesting that an unnamed compiler, rather than the architects themselves, may have prepared this treatise. For this reason and because undated first editions are highly unusual among British eighteenth-century architectural books, it is perhaps best to suggest that the 1757 edition was the first.[3]

According to the Preface (pp. i–ii), "it has been an established Custom amongst the ablest and most experienc'd Architects, both Antient and Modern, to exhibit the Five Orders belonging to that Science by way of Introduction," and this book was to be no exception: it would begin with the five orders "as laid down by the celebrated Palladio" (p. 1). The Preface also includes brief remarks on convenience, strength, beauty, materials, site, foundations, and wall construction.

Part I of the text (pp. 1–20) is a description of the orders taken from Palladio. Plates I–XXII depict the orders, their parts, and arches.

Part II (pp. 21–50) is devoted to descriptions of the designs illustrated in Plates 23–64; these descriptions include keys to the plans, dimensions, cost estimates, and remarks on interior furnishings, materials, and construction. Among the 29 designs there are 14 country "seats" or residences, six summer houses, five "houses" or residences, two single town houses, one row of three town houses, and one "Seat in a pleasant Situation in the Country, . . . [which] may be adapted to the Town." Fourteen designs are by William Halfpenny, ten are by John Halfpenny, four are by Morris, and one is by Lightoler.[4]

The smallest design is a summer house designed by Halfpenny (Plate 23, No. 1), and estimated to cost £100. Intended for use "in a Garden, or some rural Place," the ground floor consists of a single room 12 feet square, and the bedroom upstairs is the same size. The elevation includes a three-sided bay projecting from the ground floor; the entire facade is framed by pilasters at the sides and a cornice above, with statues flanking the pyramid roof. The largest design is a country seat designed by John Halfpenny (Plates 41, 42), estimated to cost £16,810. The facade is 196 feet wide, and includes a central pile three stories high and seven windows wide, connected by colonnades to two-story wing pavilions. A one-story tetrastyle Corinthian portico frames the entrance, and the windows are ornamented with architraves and entablatures. The colonnades are topped by balustrades and ornamental urns. The ground-floor plan includes a hall, two parlors, a study, saloon, back parlor, butler's pantry, servants' hall, pantry, kitchen, back kitchen, larder, laundry, rooms for the steward and housekeeper, a stable, and harness and saddle rooms.

The only design in Gothic style is a summer house by William Halfpenny (Plate 24). The elevation includes crockets, finials, pointed arches, and ornamental "Gothic" pilasters. Some of the offices for Lightoler's country seat are in the Castellated style (Plates 59, 60), with arrow slits, crenellations, and pointed arches. The Classical ornamentation of the remaining designs often is sober and restrained, and generally consists of little more than stringcourses, pediments, porticoes, and occasional rustication. In some designs individual wings, pavilions, and rooms are crisply isolated from each other, making striking compositions of geometric forms.[5] Other designs are organized in a more typical country house manner, with a central two- or three-story pile flanked by colonnades and wings.[6]

The designs for town houses include one group of three attached houses and one single house that would be suitable for row housing. The three attached houses (Plate 44) each include a basement, three floors, and an attic. The central unit is 24 feet wide, and the end units are 18 feet wide; all are 35 feet deep. The ground floor of each contains front and back parlors, and the central unit has one additional front parlor. The single town house (Plate 46) is 20 feet wide and 40 feet deep. There are three stories plus a basement: the ground floor contains front and back parlors, and the chamber and attic floors each contain two bedrooms.

Part III of the text (pp. 65–85) contains a listing of the subjects in Plates 65 through 85, plus more detailed descriptions of Plates 82 and 83. The plates include designs by Lightoler for chimneypieces, windows, staircases, room interiors, a screen, ceilings, and an alcove, plus designs by William Halfpenny for roof trusses, a dove house, and piers. The designs are composed in a variety of styles, including Palladian, Rococo, Chinese, and Gothic.

1. Septimus Rivington, *The Publishing Family of Rivington* (London: Rivingtons, 1919), pp. 42, 45.

2. Ian Maxted, *The London Book Trades 1775–1800* (Folkestone: Dawson, 1977), p. 199.

3. This hypothesis is given further credence by a notice announcing *The Modern Builder's Assistant* in *The Gentleman's Magazine* XXVII (1757), p. 243. This presumably was the first appearance of the book. If the 1757 edition is indeed the first, the undated edition necessarily appeared sometime between 1757 and 1774.

4. The sole design by Lightoler in Part II is the most extensively illustrated in the whole book: the "Seat in a pleasant Situation in the Country" is shown in Plates 53–56, and Plates 57–64 depict the accompanying offices and coach houses. The house was estimated to cost £10,676, and the offices and coach houses an additional £6,065.

5. Most of these designs are by Halfpenny. See especially Plate 32, a country house which appears progressively fragmented into a hierarchy of ever smaller pyramidal and cubic units. Emil Kaufmann found this "concatenation" and "gradation" of forms particularly important in his history of eighteenth-century European architecture. See his *Architecture in the Age of Reason* (Cambridge, Mass.: Harvard University Press, 1955), p. 29.

6. Many of the designs by John Halfpenny fall under this description.

133.1

HALFPENNY, William (–1755)

A new and compleat system of architecture delineated, in a variety of plans and elevations of designs for convenient and decorated houses. Together with offices and out-buildings proportioned thereto, and appropriated to the several uses and situations required. As also an estimate of each by the great square. Prefix'd to these are ten different sorts of piers, with gates of various compositions suitable to the same; intended for entrances to courts, gardens, &c. As also new architectonic rules for drawing the members, in all kinds and proportions of the orders. And to them are also added a perspective view of the sinking pier of Westminster = Bridge, with the two adjoining arches; and a method proposed by trusses &c. to take off $\frac{3}{4}$ of the weight, or abutment and pressure now on the pier, and discharge it as set forth on the plate. The whole comprised on 47 copper plates, with explanations thereto in common press-work. Neatly engraved, and design'd by William Halfpenny, Architect.

London: Printed for John Brindley, 1749.

[ii] + 25 pp, 47 pls.

25.7 × 34.3 cm

Soane

133.2 †

Système nouveau et complet de desseins d'architecture, en un recueil de plans . . . des maisons commodes et ornées. . . . En 46 planches . . . suivies de leurs explications.

Londres, 1749.

Obl. 4°

Reference: BM

133.3
____

A new and compleat system of architecture, delineated in a variety of plans and elevations; together with offices and out-buildings proportioned thereto, and appropriated to the several uses and situations required; and estimates of each design. Prefixed to these are ten different sorts of piers, with gates of various compositions suitable to the same; intended for entrances to courts, gardens, &c. Also new architectonic rules for drawing the members, in all kinds and proportions of the orders. To which is added, a method of discharging and supporting of arches in bridges, as it often happens that there is a sinking in the piers. The whole comprised on forty-seven copper-plates, with explanations thereto in common press work. Designed by William Halfpenny, Architect and Carpenter.

London: Printed for R. Sayer, Map and Printseller, 1759.

[ii] + 25 pp, 47 pls.

20.0 × 25.1 cm

MB

133.4
____

A complete system of architecture, ⟨ . . . as 1759 . . . ⟩ explanations in letter-press. Designed by William Halfpenny, Architect.

London: Printed for Robert Sayer, [n.d.].

[ii] + 28 pp, 47 pls.

Oblong 4°

RIBA

133.5 †
____

A new and complete system of architecture, delineated in a variety of plans and elevations. . . . Second edition.

London: Printed for R. Sayer, 1772.

28 pp, 47 pls.

24 × 30 cm

Reference: Yale University Library Card Catalogue.

The undated edition contains a list of books for sale (pp. 25–28). Darly's *Ornamental Architect*, containing plates dated 1769 and 1770, was the latest book in the list, suggesting a date ca. 1770 for this edition of Halfpenny's *Complete System*.

In the Preface, printed on two sides of one leaf,[1] Halfpenny explained that when he began this book, "I intended only 15 designs for small edifices, from 200*l*. to 700*l*. value, but by the advices of some friends who approv'd of what I had begun, I have added to them 16 designs more: The value of the largest of which does not exceed 6000£." With these designs completed, Halfpenny also "consider'd the usefulness of some orders, and proportions necessary for piers, and gates, for entrances to courts, gardens, &c. and these I have regulated and proportion'd in a method entirely new, and I have prefix'd them to the work as a preparatory introduction in 12 plates; also one plate shewing the use of architectonick rules, which is more methodically explain'd in the latter part of this book." Finally, having recently viewed the "sunk pier" at Westminster Bridge, he added a plate suggesting a remedy for this "evil." At the end of the Preface he acknowledged the assistance of his friend "Mr. *Robert Morrice*."

The text (pp. 1–25) is organized as a series of plate descriptions. Pages 1 through 4 refer to the cornices, moldings, piers, and gates in Plates 1 through 12. The text offers instruction in how to draw cornices and moldings, and gives dimensions and suggested uses for the piers. Pages 5 through 24 concern the houses shown in plan and elevation in Plates 13 through 45. In addition to dimensions and cost estimates, the text includes keys to the plans and remarks on materials and construction. Pages 24 and 25 refer to Plate 46 and describe "the use of a n[e]w invented architectonick rule, with the method of making them [*sic*] suitable to the proportions of any mouldings." The final plate, not described in the text, is "A Perspective View of the Sunk Pier, and the two Adjoining Arches, at Westminster."

In Plates 13 through 45 there are 31 designs for residences, including five summer lodges or summer houses, one chapel with "apartments" for a chaplain, one farm house, and 24 houses. Apart from two summer houses, the cheapest design is No. 8, estimated to cost £464 10s. The facade is two stories high in the center, plus a dormer story above, and 741/2 feet wide. The ground-floor plan includes a kitchen, common kitchen, parlor (20 feet square), pantry, common pantry, entrance porch, master's closet or counting house, closet or study, stable, and saddle room. The most expensive design (No. 28), estimated to cost £5,685 15s, is 1961/2 feet wide. The central portion of the facade is two stories high and nine windows wide, and fronted by a two-story tetrastyle pedimented portico made of engaged Ionic and Corinthian columns. Above this facade is an attic story, three windows wide. To either side are two-story wing pavilions, two windows wide, attached by one-story walls. The ground-floor plan includes a hall, two parlors, a "Lobby" (511/2 feet by 15 feet), a "Great room" (two stories high, 38 feet by 24 feet), a drawing room, a dining room, five closets, a "Master's boating room, or steward's hall," a stable, coach houses, a housekeeper's room, a kitchen, a cook's larder, a back kitchen, and a scullery.

Halfpenny's plans are composed primarily of rectangles, with occasional circles, squares, hexagons, and octagons added for interest. The elevations are more engaging: instead of composing large monolithic facades, Halfpenny divided his designs into smaller advancing and receding units, emphasized by individual pediments or angled roofs, lending a three-dimensional excitement and tension to the facade.[2] Occasionally simple geometric forms rise directly from the plan through the elevation: in No. 31, for example, the rectangular and circular elements of the plan form prisms and cylinders in the elevation. The designs are modestly ornamented with quoins, Venetian windows, parapets, and stringcourses. Some of the smaller designs have richer ornament: the chapel and summer house (Nos. 14 and 15), for example, include colonnades, an arcade, and domes, and one of the larger houses (No. 29) incorporates Ionic columns across the two principal stories, herms across the attic story, and statues along the parapet.

1. This commentary is based on examination of the 1749 edition.

2. For similar reasons Halfpenny's designs were of special importance in Emil Kaufmann's account of "concatenation" and "gradation" in English eighteenth-century architecture. He reproduced three of Halfpenny's designs (Nos. 27, 29, and 31) among the plates in *Architecture in the Age of Reason* (Cambridge, Mass.: Harvard University Press, 1955).

134.1
HALFPENNY, William (-1755), and John HALFPENNY (fl. 1750)
New designs for Chinese temples triumphal arches, garden seats, palings &c. on fourteen copper plates, by William Halfpenny Architect.

London: Printed for R. Sayer Printseller, and I. Brindley, 1750.

14 pls (pl. 1 is the title page).

New designs for Chinese bridges, temples, triumphal arches, garden seats, palings, obelisks, termini's, &c. on fourteen copper plates. Together with full instructions to workmen annex'd to each particular design; a near estimate of their charge, and hints where with most advantage to be erected. The whole invented and drawn by Will. and John Halfpenny, Architects. Part II.

London: Printed for R. Sayer, Printseller, and J. Brindley, 1751.

8 pp, 15–28 pls.

New designs for Chinese doors, windows, piers, pilasters, garden seats, green houses, summer houses, &c. on sixteen copper plates. Together with instructions to workmen, annex'd to each particular design; the whole invented and drawn by Will. and John Halfpenny, Architects. Part III.

London: Printed for Robert Sayer, Map and Printseller, 1751.

8 pp, 29–44 pls.

New designs for Chinese gates, palisades, stair-cases, chimney-pieces, cielings, garden-seats, chairs, temples, &c. on sixteen copper-plates, with full instructions to workmen. By Wil. and John Halfpenny, Architects. Part IV.

London: Printed for Robert Sayer, Map and Print-seller, 1752.

2 pp, 45–60 pls.

19.5 × 11.3 cm

NNC

134.2

Rural architecture in the Chinese taste, being designs entirely new for the decoration of gardens, parks, forrests, insides of houses, &c. on sixty copper plates with full instructions for workmen also a near estimate of the charge and hints where proper to be erected the whole invented & drawn by Willm. & Jno. Halfpenny Architects. Divided into four parts. The 2d. edition.

London: Printed for & Sold by Robt. Sayer Map & Printseller, 1752.

[*This title page is followed by four separate parts, each with individual title page:*]

[*Part I:*]

New designs for Chinese temples ⟨ . . . as 1st edition, Part [II] . . . ⟩ Architect. Part I.

London: Printed for and sold by Robt. Sayer, 1750.

8 pp, 14 pls (pl. 1 is the title page for Part I).

[*Part II:*]

New designs for Chinese bridges, ⟨ . . . as 1st edition, Part II . . . ⟩.

London: Printed for R. Sayer, Printseller, 1751.

8 pp, 15–28 pls.

[*Part III:*]

New designs for Chinese doors, ⟨ . . . as 1st edition, Part III . . . ⟩.

London: Printed for Robert Sayer, Map and Printseller, 1751.

8 pp, 29–44 pls.

[*Part IV:*]

New designs for Chinese gates, ⟨ . . . as 1st edition, Part IV . . . ⟩.

London: Printed for Robert Sayer, Map and Print-seller, 1752.

2 pp, 45–60 pls.

19.9 × 12.4 cm

CtY

134.3

Rural architecture in the Chinese taste, being designs entirely new for the decoration of gardens, parks, forrests, insides of houses, &c. on sixty copper plates with full instructions for workmen also a near estimate of the charge, and hints where proper to be erected. The whole invented & drawn by Willm. & Jnn. Halfpenny, Architects. The 3d. edition. With the adition of 4 plates in quarto, of roofs for Chinese & Indian temples, the manner of fixing their ornaments, covering and carrying off the water, their cornices with the several members adjusted to regular proportion.

London: Printed for Robt. Sayer, 1755.

[*This title page is followed by four separate parts, each with individual title page:*]

[*Part I:*]

New designs for Chinese temples ⟨ . . . as 1st edition, Part [II] . . . ⟩ Architect. Part I.

London: Printed for and sold by Robt. Sayer, 1750.

8 pp, 14 pls (pl. 1 is the title page for Part I).

[*Part II:*]

New designs for Chinese bridges, ⟨ . . . as 1st edition, Part II . . . ⟩ garden = seats, ⟨ . . . as 1st edition, Part II . . . ⟩ where, with ⟨ . . . as 1st edition, Part II . . . ⟩.

London: Printed for R. Sayer, Printseller, 1751.

8 pp, 15–28 pls.

[*Part III:*]

New designs for Chinese doors, windows, piers, pilasters, garden-seats, green-houses, summer houses, &c. on sixteen copper plates; together with instructions to workmen, annexed to each particular design; the whole invented and drawn by Will. and John Halfpenny, Architects. Part III.

London: Printed for Robert Sayer, Map and Printseller, 1751.

8 pp, 29–44 pls.

[*Part IV:*]

New designs for Chinese gates, ⟨ . . . as 1st edition, Part IV . . . ⟩ Architects, Part IV.

London: Printed for Robert Sayer, Map and Print-seller, 1752.

4 + 3–6 pp, 45–64 pls.

19.1 × 11.4 cm

Bodl.

London: Printed for Robt. Sayer, [n.d.].

[*This title page is followed by four separate parts, each with individual title page:*]

[*Part I:*]

London: Printed for and sold by Robt. Sayer, [n.d.].

8 pp, 14 pls (pl. 1 is the title page for Part I).

[*Part II:*]

New designs for Chinese bridges, temples, triumphal arches, garden=
seats, palings, obelisks, termini, &c. on fourteen copper plates. Together
with full instructions to workmen, annexed to each particular design. A
near estimate of their charge, and hints where, with most advantage, to
be erected. The whole invented and drawn by Will. and John Halfpenny,
Architects. Part II.

London: Printed for Robert Sayer, Map and Print-seller, [n.d.].

8 pp, 15–28 pls.

[*Part III:*]

New designs for Chinese doors, windows, piers, pilasters, garden-seats,
green-houses, summer-houses, &c. on sixteen copper plates. Together
with instructions to workmen, annexed to each particular design. The
whole invented and drawn by Will. and John Halfpenny, Architects. Part
III.

London: Printed for Robert Sayer, Map and Print-seller, [n.d.].

4 pp, 29–44 pls.

[*Part IV:*]

New designs for Chinese gates, palisades, stair-cases, chimney-pieces,
ceilings, garden seats, chairs, temples, &c. on sixteen copper plates. With
full instructions to workmen. by Will. and John Halfpenny, Architects.
Part IV.

London: Printed for Robert Sayer, Map and Print-seller, [n.d.].

viii pp, 45–64 pls.

22.2 × 13.7 cm

MH

By the early 1750s romanticism and the pursuit of fashion had increased
interest in a style of architecture only recently judged to be backward and
barbaric, the Gothic.[1] As early as 1742 Batty and Thomas Langley had
begun to exploit the appeal of Gothic in *Ancient Architecture* (*q.v.*), but
they were at pains to demonstrate that Gothic embodied the same order

and proportion the Palladians had found in Classical architecture. Also about midcentury interest in the romantic possibilities of Chinese architecture had been piqued by accounts of recent voyages to the East and by a growing taste for the exotic in fashion.[2] William Halfpenny's *New Designs for Chinese Temples*, issued in 1750, was the first collection of Chinese architectural designs to be published. His work apparently sold well, for over the next two years he and his son John issued three additional collections of designs, brought together under a new title in 1752 as *Rural Architecture in the Chinese Taste*. Like Langley, Halfpenny sought to overcome the reluctance of clients to accept the Chinese style by establishing its validity from a theoretical standpoint: he suggested in his 1752 preface that "a graceful Symmetry, and an exact Proportion"—two fundamental canons of the current Palladian aesthetic—were as much a part of Chinese architecture as of any other style.

The plates include designs for garden seats, alcoves, temples, and the many other subjects specified on the title pages. These designs all carefully maintain a rigid symmetry in elevation, and geometric proportionality in plan. Many structures, for example, are square in plan (e.g., Plates 8, 12, 13, 14, 18, 19), while two seats are semicircular (Plates 7, 16), two temples are circular (Plates 9, 53), three temples are octagons (Plates 10, 44, 52), and one seat is a combination of four semicircles (Plate 8). Many of the designs were meant to be seen only from the front, although one temple supported over a pond by four diagonal cantilevers (Plate 52) is a successful three-dimensional composition. Most designs are elaborately decorated with Chinese latticework, scrolls, bells, snakes, and other motifs in a manner that ranges from delightful and pleasant to exceedingly ornate and structurally impossible. A few designs are accompanied by scenery, suggesting the parterres, allees, and forests these structures might adorn. Following the Preface, the text consists entirely of plate descriptions, which give dimensions and other information of use to artisans.

1. For an account of the romantic origins of the Gothic Revival see Kenneth Clark, *The Gothic Revival* (London: Constable, 1928); J. Mordaunt Crook, "Introduction" to Charles L. Eastlake, *A History of the Gothic Revival*, reprint (Leicester: Leicester University Press, 1970); Georg Germann, *Gothic Revival in Europe and Britain* (London: Lund Humphries, 1972); and Terence Davis, *The Gothick Taste* (Newton Abbot: David & Charles, 1974).

2. See for example Jean Baptiste du Halde, *Description géographique . . . de la Chine* (Paris, 1735), Engl. trans. (London, 1736); and Jean Denis Attiret, *A Particular Account of the Emperor of China's Gardens*, trans. Sir Harry Beaumont (London, 1752). On the origins of English taste for Chinoiserie see especially Osvald Sirén, *China and Gardens of Europe of the Eighteenth Century* (New York: Ronald Press, 1950); and Hugh Honour, *Chinoiserie* (London: John Murray, 1961).

135.1

HALFPENNY, William (–1755)

Perspective made easy: or, a new method for practical perspective. Shewing the use of a new-invented senographical protractor; so easy, that a person, tho' an intire stranger to perspective, may, by reading a few lines, become master of the instrument, without the help of a master. It's useful in taking the perspective draughts of towns, countrys, houses, and gardens, or any objects whatever; much easier than what has hitherto been practised. With several useful examples in practical perspective. Together with the draughts of several remarkable places, in and about the cities of Bristol and Bath; in twenty-six copper plates. By William Halfpenny.

London: Printed for John Oswald, 1731.

vi + 36 pp, 26 + 2 pls.

18.6 × 11.4 cm

BL

The Preface (pp. iii–iv) primarily concerns the "Senographical Protractor," a "Practical Instrument so useful in Perspective" (p. iii). Halfpenny provided an illustration of the instrument (Plate 1), a description of it (p. iv), and instructions for its use (p. v).

The text consists of a series of problems in perspective and their solutions, all of which are illustrated in Plates 2 through 21. The plates depict geometric figures and diagrams, plus perspective views of geometric solids, pavements, "A Stage for Masters of Defence to decide their Combats in," a floor plan with three rooms, chairs, tables, bed frames and a tester, a cove cornice, a drawbridge, and a crane in a stone quarry. In addition Plate 20 depicts a three-story house, three windows wide, set in a formal garden with trees, hedges, and walls arranged in a regular geometric pattern. Plate 21 depicts a more complex garden plan, with no dwelling. Plates 22 and 23 contain a plan and view of "Mr. Benjamin Holloways House at Bridgewater." Plate 24 is a view of the King's Bath at Bath, and Plates 25 and 26 are a plan and view of "an Exchange" for the City of Bristol. Two unnumbered plates at the end depict the "Hot Well" near Bristol and Queen Square in Bristol. Plates 22 through 26 and the two additional plates are not discussed in the text.

136.1
HALFPENNY, William (–1755), and John HALFPENNY (fl. 1750)
Rural architecture in the Gothick taste. Being twenty new designs, for temples, garden-seats, summer-houses, lodges, terminies, piers, &c. on sixteen copper plates. With instructions to workmen, and hints where with most advantage to be erected. The whole invented and drawn by William and John Halfpenny. Architects.

London: Printed for and sold by Robert Sayer, Map and Printseller, 1752.

8 pp, 16 pls.

22.2 × 13.7 cm

MH

Rural Architecture in the Gothick Taste serves as a pendant to *Rural Architecture in the Chinese Taste*, a collection of designs begun in 1750 under the title *New Designs for Chinese Temples* and completed in four parts in 1752 (*q.v.*).

The text (pp. 3–8) consists of brief plate descriptions, which include dimensions and keys to the plans. In some cases there are brief remarks on appropriate landscape settings. The small temple or summer house in Plate 3, for example, would be "most suitable on an Eminence in a rural Plantation," and the temple in Plate 5 would be "suitable for an Eminence to be seen at a great Distance, or for the Center of a Wood, where its top can be seen above the Trees" (pp. 4, 5). The summer house in Plate 10, by contrast, was designed to be "elevated on a pavement or green Sod" (p. 6). Despite the authors' obvious awareness of landscape considerations, none of the illustrations includes scenery.

The designs include a semicircular "Cove Seat" with a room for musicians above, a "Terminy-Seat," six temples, three summer houses, four lodges, four piers, and one "Gate Way." Most of the plans are composed of one or more squares, sometimes with bows, buttresses, or turrets. The largest design, a "Lodge, or House of Retirement" (Plate 12) includes a three-story circular drum in the center, with a balcony and gazebo above. To either side are wings containing a parlor and a dining room, each 19 feet by 15 feet. The chamber and attic floors above these rooms contain two bedrooms plus garret accommodations for the servants.

The designs in Plates 1 through 13 are embellished with exuberant rococo Gothic ornament, while the lodge and the summer house in Plates 14 and 15 are composed in a more sober, nearly Palladian, "Modern" style. A "Gate Way" in Plate 3 is composed in an eclectic "Composite Taste," and the piers in Plate 16 are based on Chinese, "Indian,"[1] and Gothic motifs.

1. The term "Indian" does not appear in this book but cf. the designs ostensibly in "Indian" style in *The Country Gentleman's Pocket Companion* (1753; q.v.).

137.1

HALFPENNY, William (–1755)

Six new designs for convenient farm-houses, with their proper offices, &c. Wherein are laid down, all the necessary dimensions and estimates of each design, and every separate part, both in brick and stone. Adapted more particularly to the western counties in England, and the whole Principality of Wales. Calculated on a plan more practicable than any published heretofore. The largest estimate not exceeding 480 pounds, and the smallest under 280. By William Halfpenny, Architect and Carpenter. Part I.

London: Printed for Robert Sayer, Map and Printseller, 1751.

[i] + 22 pp, 6 pls [*pl. IV wanting in this copy*].

Six new designs for convenient farm-houses, with their proper offices, &c. Wherein are laid down, all the necessary dimensions and estimates of each design, and every separate part, both in brick and stone. Adapted more particularly to the northern counties in England, and all Scotland. Calculated on a plan more practicable than any published heretofore. The largest estimate not exceeding 494 pounds, and the smallest under 264. By William Halfpenny, Architect and Carpenter. Part II.

London: Printed for Robert Sayer, Map and Printseller, 1751.

[i] + 25–46 pp, 7–12 pls.

Thirteen new designs for small convenient parsonage and farm-houses, with their proper offices, &c. Wherein are laid down all the necessary dimensions and estimates of each design, and every separate part, in brick, stone, and timber. Calculated for every part of Great-Britain and Ireland. The largest estimate not exceeding 287*l.* and the smallest under 97*l.* By William Halfpenny, Architect and Carpenter. Part III.

London: Printed for, and sold by Robert Sayer, Map and Printseller, 1752.

47–49 pp, 13–20 pls.

19.6 × 12.5 cm

NNC

In 1747 Daniel Garret published a series of designs for farm houses suited to the counties of northern England.[1] Two years later William Halfpenny published *Twelve Beautiful Designs for Farm Houses* (*q.v.*), intended for southern counties. *Six New Designs*, issued in two parts, plus a third part issued as *Thirteen New Designs*, are a continuation of that work, including designs for western England and Wales, northern England and Scotland, and "Every Part of Great-Britain and Ireland."

Following Robert Morris, who in 1750 recommended greater attention to cottages and small villas,[2] Halfpenny suggested in the Preface that in small buildings there was greater potential for aesthetic perfection than in large ones. "More real Beauty and Elegance," he wrote, "appears in the due Symmetry and Harmony of a well-constructed Cottage, than can be found in the most exalted Palace." Here, in effect, he inverted the Renaissance hierarchy of architectural genres, suggesting that smaller buildings, rather than cathedrals or palaces, epitomized architectural ideals.

The text consists of keys for the plans, specifications, and cost estimates. Plates 1 through 15 each depict one design for a house and offices. Plates 16–19 each depict two houses, and Plate 20 illustrates one house and a building for "fothering of Cattle." The design in Plate 1 is typical: the ground-floor plan includes a best kitchen, common kitchen, pantry, dairy room, closet, and open shed. Executed in stone, the design would cost £186 12s 5½d, or £227 11s 8½d if executed in brick. With the accompanying barn, stable, and outbuildings the cost would be £301 16s 4d in stone, and £363 1s 7d in brick. The most expensive design, illustrated in Plate 12, includes a common kitchen, pantry, milk room, best kitchen or parlor, and offices on the ground floor. Executed in brick the house would cost £327 7s alone, or £493 13s 10d with barn and stables.

In several plans and elevations there is an attractive clarity to the design, achieved through use of simple geometric forms such as squares, rectangles, and triangles. Occasionally major elements of the plan are disposed at 45-degree angles (e.g., Plates 11, 12, 18), creating diagonal tension and interest. The crisp isolation of masses and forms is further enhanced through frugal use of ornament, generally little more than pediments and stringcourses.

1. Daniel Garret, *Designs, and Estimates, of Farm Houses* (1747; *q.v.*).

2. Robert Morris, *Rural Architecture* (1750; *q.v.*)

HALFPENNY, William (-1755)
Thirteen new designs.

See his Six new designs, *Entry 137.*

138.1 †
HALFPENNY, William (-1755)
Twelve beautiful designs for farm houses.
Second edition [*sic*].

[London?], 1749.

Reference: APSD

138.2

Twelve beautiful designs for farm-houses, with their proper offices and estimates of the whole and every distinct building separate; with the measurement, and value of each particular article, adapted to the customary measurements of most part of England, but more particularly for the following counties, viz. Middlesex, Surry, Essex, Kent, Sussex, Hampshire, Hertfordshire, Cambridgeshire, Berkshire, Buckinghamshire, Oxfordshire, Wiltshire, Gloucestershire, Somersetshire, &c. Useful for gentlemen, builders, &c. By William Halfpenny, Carpenter and Architect.

London: Printed for R. Sayer, Printseller, and sold by J. Brindley; Mr. Heath, Mathematical Instrument-Maker; Mr. Bowles; and Mr.Ware, 1750.

28 pp, 12 pls.

27.3 × 22.9 cm

CtY

138.3

Twelve beautiful designs for farm-houses, with their proper offices, and 〈 . . . as 1750 . . . 〉 Architect. The second edition.

London: Printed for Robert Sayer, Map and Printseller, 1759.

1 printed leaf, 28 pp, 12 pls.

29.8 × 22.2 cm

NN

138.4

Twelve beautiful designs for farm-houses, with their proper offices, and ⟨ . . . as 1750 . . . ⟩ measurement and ⟨ . . . as 1750 . . . ⟩ Architect. The third edition.

London: Printed for Robert Sayer, Map and Print Seller, 1774.

28 pp, 12 pls.

28.3 × 22.9 cm

MH

The 1749 edition listed in the APSD has not been confirmed; the entry, which reads "2nd edit.," may well be an erroneous reference to the 1759 second edition. Nevertheless in the Preface to *Six New Designs* (1751; *q.v.*) Halfpenny referred to a collection of designs for farm houses prepared in 1749.

In the brief Preface (1 leaf, verso blank) Halfpenny stated he was "importun'd to make a Collection of useful Farm-Houses by several Gentlemen and Builders in the different Counties mentioned in the Title Page." Nevertheless he also must have known Daniel Garret's *Designs, and Estimates, of Farm Houses* (1747; *q.v.*), a collection of designs quite similar to Halfpenny's, but prepared for northern, rather than midland and southern, counties of England.

The text includes keys to the plans, detailed cost estimates, and remarks on construction and materials. The plates depict 12 designs for farm houses, some with attached offices. One of the smallest designs (Plate 12), estimated to cost £231 17s 3d, contains an octagonal parlor, closet, kitchen, pantry, and dairy on the ground floor, and a chamber floor above. One of the largest (Plate 10), estimated to cost £498 19s 6d, consists of two floors plus a dormer story, and is five windows wide. The ground floor includes a kitchen, a parlor, a closet, a dairy, sheds, stables, a "Cow-House," "Bog-Houses," and a hog sty.

The designs are minimally ornamented with pediments, stringcourses, and occasional piers and columns. Several elevations are attractively composed of crisply defined pyramids, cubes, and other geometric units.

139.1 †
HALFPENNY, William (–1755)
Useful architecture for erecting parsonage houses, farms, inns, bridges. . . .

London, 1751.

8°

Reference: APSD

139.2

Useful architecture in twenty-one new designs for erecting parsonage=houses, farm-houses, and inns; with their respective offices, &c. of various dimensions at the most moderate expence, the largest not exceeding five hundred pounds, and the smallest under one hundred pounds. As will evidently appear by their several dimensions and estimates particularly set forth with respect both to brick and stone, adapted to the usual measurement of Great Britain and Ireland. Together with a supplement, containing several designs for building with timber only, with estimates annext in like manner. The whole intended as an improvement of what has hitherto been given on that subject, and rendered both practicable and beneficial to all concerned in building. By William Halfpenny, Architect and Carpenter.

London: Printed for and sold by Robert Sayer, Map and Printseller, 1752.

[ii] + 23 + 26–79 pp, 20 pls.

18.4 × 12.1 cm

Bodl.

139.3

The second edition, with four additional designs, of useful architecture; being the last work in this kind of William Halfpenny, Architect and Carpenter, in twenty-five new designs, with full and clear instructions, in every particular, for erecting parsonage-houses, farm-houses, and inns, with their respective offices, &c. of various dimensions, at the most moderate expence, the largest not exceeding five hundred pounds, and the smallest under one hundred pounds. As will evidently appear by their several dimensions and estimates particularly set forth with respect both to brick and stone, adapted to the usual measurement of Great Britain and Ireland. Together with a supplement, containing several designs for building with timber only, with estimates annext in like manner. The four designs added, are for bridges, which in rural situations are generally necessary and always pleasing, being suited to small pieces of water, brooks, &c. and the chief ornament where strength with beauty is needful. The whole intended as an improvement of what has hitherto been given on that subject, and rendered both practicable and beneficial to all concerned in building.

London: Printed for and sold by Robert Sayer, Map and Print-seller, 1755.

[ii] + 82 pp, 21 pls.

20.0 × 12.4 cm

V&A

The third edition, with four additional designs of useful architecture; being the last work ⟨ . . . as 1755 . . . ⟩.

London: Printed for and sold by Robert Sayer, Map and Print-seller, 1760.

[ii] + 78 pp, 21 pls.

20.3 × 12.7 cm

BL

The 1751 edition listed in the APSD has not been confirmed. Dora Wiebenson and Elise M. Quasebarth indicate that the first edition was issued in four parts: the first as *Designs for Farmhouses* in 1750, and the remaining three in 1750, 1751, and 1752. See Wiebenson, *Architectural Theory and Practice from Alberti to Ledoux* (Chicago: University of Chicago Press, 1982), Entry III-D-26. The plates in the 1752 edition are undated.

Apparently encouraged by the success of *Twelve Beautiful Designs* (1749?; *q.v.*) and *Six New Designs* (1751; *q.v.*), Halfpenny also offered this collection of 24 more designs for farm houses and parsonages, plus one building for the "fothering of Cattle."

The Preface is a short pastiche of remarks made in some of Halfpenny's other books. The text includes brief descriptions of the designs, together with keys to the plans, remarks on materials and construction, and detailed estimates for the execution of each design in stone and in brick.

Halfpenny indicated that 11 designs were farm houses, and 13 designs were suitable for parsonages or farm houses. The smallest design is a parsonage or farm house (Plate 18, No. 2) estimated to cost £96 12s 11½d executed in stone, or £117 17s 3½d in brick. The geometric clarity of the individual parts is characteristic of many of the designs in this collection: a two-story central core, containing the kitchen on the ground floor, is flanked by one-story wings to either side containing the cellar and the little parlor. The kitchen is fronted by a one-story milk room, and an entry porch and a pantry project from the angles where the milk room joins the kitchen.

The largest design is a parsonage or farm house, with offices, that would cost £493 13s 10d if erected in brick. It includes a best kitchen, common kitchen, pantry, milk room, and offices on the ground floor. The house has two equal facades, each four windows wide and two stories high, which are joined at a right angle and set at one corner of a farmyard. As shown in Plate 12, both facades are seen at once, with the corner of the house facing the viewer at a 45-degree angle. Other designs also make use of 45-degree angles: some facades have higher and lower portions joined by 45-degree roofs, and some plans include wings and single rooms canted at 45-degree angles to the main body of the house.

In keeping with Halfpenny's goal of "moderate expense," ornament is minimal: it rarely exceeds one or two stringcourses and an occasional pediment.

In the 1755 and 1760 editions the "four designs added," all bridges, appear on one additional plate.

140.1

HALL, John (fl. 1825)

Novel designs for cottages and schools with observations thereon; by John Hall, Secretary to the Society for Improving the Condition of the Labouring Classes.

[London: Published for the author; text printed by C. Baynes; plates by C. Hullmandel], 1825.

11 pp, 15 pls.

42.2 × 31.8 cm

MB

In the introductory essay (pp. 7–11), headed by the single word "TRUTH," Hall announced his goal: to promote "an increase of comfort and happiness to the labouring classes:—an encouragement toward the attainment of a true independence" (p. 7). Cottage design, he believed, should be conducive to the physical health, cleanliness, "Delicacy," and "Industrious Morality" of the resident (p. 7). Hall included brief remarks on cottage gardens, and on suitable materials for constructing cottages, the walls of which he "proposed to be built in Pisé" (pp. 8–9). He concluded with a short discussion of financial support for schools (pp. 10–11).

Twelve of the fifteen plates are lithographed and colored elevations and plans for dwellings, including a pilot's or fisherman's cottage, two pairs of laborer's cottages, two single laborer's cottages, three pairs of small farm houses, a single small farm house, a school and schoolmaster's residence, a woodman's cottage, and a lodge cottage. The final three plates depict designs for schools. Each design is shown surrounded by lush scenery, with mountains, villages, and mansions in the distance and industrious laborers busily working in the foreground. Many of the plans are based on simple geometric figures, including squares, rectangles, and octagons. A typical dwelling includes a living room, a kitchen, and perhaps a pantry on the ground floor, and up to three sleeping rooms either on the ground floor or on an upper story. Nearly all the elevations incorporate some ornament, such as a veranda with Regency trelliswork (No. 9), rustic columns *in antis* (Nos. 2, 6, 8), or a Classical pediment (Nos. 4, 6, 7, 8, 10).

141.1

HALL, William Henry

The new royal encyclopaedia; or, complete modern dictionary of arts and sciences, on an improved plan. Containing a new, universal, accurate, and copious display of the whole theory and practice of the liberal and mechanical arts, and all the respective sciences, human and divine, arranged systematically, and digested into distinct treatises. Also the various detached parts of knowledge, copiously and critically explained, according to the best authorities. Comprizing a regular and general course of ancient and modern literature, from the earliest ages, down to the present times: including all the late discoveries and improvements in the various branches of literature; particularly acoustics aerology aerostation agriculture alchymy algebra altimetry amphibiology analytics anatomy anemography architecture arithmetic astrology astronomy bell-lettres book-keeping botany brachygraphy catoptrics chemistry chronology commerce conchology conics cosmography criticism dialling dioptrics drawing electricity engineering engraving entomology ethics farriery fencing financing fluxions fortification gardening gauging geography geometry grammar gunnery handicrafts heraldry history horsemanship husbandry hydraulics hydrography hydrology hydrostatics ichthyology laws and customs levelling logic longimetry magnetism manegery maritime affairs mathematics mechanics mensuration merchandize mercantile business metallurgy metaphysics meteorology microscopical discoveries military matters mineralogy modelling music mythology navigation natural history nautical matters optics oratory ornithology painting perspective pharmacy philosophy phlebotomy physic physiology phytology planometry pneumatics poetry projectiles pyrotechny recreations religion rhetoric rites and ceremonies sculpture series and statics statuary stereometry surgery surveying synonymies tactics theology trades and arts trigonometry zoology, &c. &c. &c. The whole entirely freed from the errors, obscurities, and superfluities of former writers on the various subjects; and forming a more methodical, intelligent, and complete repository of universal knowledge, than any other work, of a similar nature, ever published in the English language. Illustrated with upwards of 150 large superb copper plates, accurately descriptive of the subjects to which they refer. In three volumes. Vol I. By William Henry Hall, Esq. . . . Assisted by other learned and ingenious gentlemen.

London: Printed for C. Cooke, [n.d.].

[Three volumes, [1788–1791]. The title pages for Vols. II and III differ significantly from that above. The title page for Vol. III is identical to that transcribed below for the edition of [1795?]. The title page for Vol. II is like that of Vol. III, with the following exceptions:

Vol. II.	Vol. III.
arts and sciences,	arts & sciences,
knowledge alphabetically	knowledge. Alphabetically
amphibiology	
chemistry	chymistry
fossilogy	
legerdemain [*following longimetry*]	
manegery	
	mammalia
maritime affairs	
mechanics	mechanies
metallurgy	
meterology	
nautical	naval
phlebotomy	
pyrotechny	
statuary	
tetrapodology	
vermeology, &c.	vermeology zoology, &c.
Vol II.	Vol. III.
and other gentlemen	and by other gentlemen

Certain terms appear on the title page of one volume but not another; the absence of a particular term on a given title page is indicated above by a space. The additional terms for each volume appear in alphabetical order, except as noted.]

Art. "Perspective," III, 10 pp; 4 pls.

38.2 × 23.9 cm

MnU

141.2

_____

The new royal encyclopaedia; or, complete modern universal dictionary of arts & sciences, on a new and improved plan. In which all the respective sciences, are arranged into complete systems, and the arts digested into distinct treatises. Also the detached parts of knowledge. Alphabetically arranged and copiously explained, according to the best authorities. Containing a digest and display of the whole theory and practice of the liberal and mechanical arts. Comprizing a general repository of ancient and modern literature, from the earliest ages, down to the present time: including all the new improvements and latest discoveries made in the arts and sciences, particularly acoustics aerology aerostation agriculture algebra anatomy annuities architecture arithmetic astronomy belles-lettres book= keeping botany brewing catoptrics chymistry chronology commerce comparative-anatomy conchology conics cosmography criticism dialling dioptrics drawing electricity engineering engraving entomology ethics farriery fencing financing fluxions fortification gardening gauging geography geometry grammar gunnery handicrafts heraldry history husbandry hydraulics hydrography hydrology hydrostatics ichthyology laws logic longimetry magnetism mammalia mathematics mechanies medicine mensuration merchandize metaphysics military affairs mineralogy modelling midwifry music mythology navigation natural history naval affairs optics oratory ornithology painting perspective pharmacy philosophy physic physiology phytology pneumatics poetry projectiles religion rhetoric rites sculpture series and statics stenography surgery surveying tactics theology trades and arts trigonometry vermeology zoology, &c. The superfluities which abound in other dictionaries are expunged, for the purpose of incorporating complete systems, and distinct treatises. By means of this addition and deviation from the old plan it comprizes a general circle of science, and forms the most comprehensive library of universal knowledge, that was ever published in the English language. The whole entirely freed from the errors, obscurities, and superfluities of other dictionaries. Illustrated with upwards of 150 large superb copper plates, accurately descriptive of the subjects to which they refer. In three volumes. Vol. III. By William Henry Hall, Esq. . . . And by other gentlemen of scientific knowledge, whose names and addresses appear in the work.

London: Printed for C. Cooke; and sold by the booksellers of Bath, Bristol, Birmingham, Canterbury, Cambridge, Coventry, Chester, Derby, Exeter, Gloucester, Hereford, Hull, Ipswich, Leeds, Liverpool, Leicester, Manchester, Newcastle, Norwich, Nottingham, Northampton, Oxford, Reading, Salisbury, Sherborn, Sheffield, Shrewsbury, Worcester, Winchester, York; and by all other booksellers in England, Scotland, and Ireland, [1795?].

[*Only Vol. III of this set is cited here; Vols. I and II are of the previous edition.*]

Art. "Perspective," III, 10 pp; 4 pls.

37.7 × 23.9 cm

MB

141.3 ‖

The new encyclopaedia; or, modern universal dictionary of arts and sciences. On a new and improved plan. In which all the respective sciences are arranged into complete systems, the arts digested into distinct treatises, and philosophical subjects introduced in separate dissertations. Also, the detached parts of knowledge alphabetically arranged, and copiously explained, according to the best authorities. Including all the material information that is contained in Chambers's Cyclopaedia, the Encyclopaedia Britannica, and the French Encyclopedie. The whole containing a copious digest and display of the complete theory and practice of the liberal and mechanical arts. And comprising an universal repository of ancient and modern literature, freed from the obscurities, errors, and superfluities of other dictionaries. And including all the new improvements and latest discoveries made in the arts and sciences, particularly acoustics aerology aerostation agriculture algebra amphibiology anatomy annuities architecture arithmetic astronomy belles-lettres book-keeping botany brewing catoptrics chemistry chronology commerce comparative anatomy conchology conics cosmography criticism dialling dioptrics distillation drawing dyeing electricity engineering engraving entomology ethics farriery fencing financing fluxions fortification fossils gardening gauging geography geometry grammar gunnery handicrafts heraldry history husbandry hydraulics hydography hydrostatics ichthyology laws logic magnetism mammalia mathematics mechanics medicine mensuration merchandize metallurgy metaphysics military affairs mineralogy midwifery music mythology navigation national affairs natural history naval affairs optics oratory ornithology painting perspective pharmacy philosophy physic physiology pneumatics poetry politics projectiles rhetoric rites sculpture surgery surveying tactics theology trade trigonometry vermeology zoology, &c. By the new and improved plan of incorporating complete systems on the sciences, and distinct treatises on the respective arts, this work comprises, independent of the alphabetical arrangement, a general circle of science; and forms the most comprehensive library of universal knowledge that was ever published in the English language. In three volumes. By William Henry Hall, Esquire. The third edition. Revised, corrected, and enlarged, with considerable additions, improvements, and modern discoveries, by Thomas Augustus Lloyd, assisted by gentlemen of scientific knowledge. Vol. I. Illustrated with upwards of one hundred and fifty large superb copper-plates, accurately descriptive of the different subjects to which they refer.

London: Printed for C. Cooke; and sold ⟨ . . . as [1795?] . . . ⟩, and Ireland, [n.d.].

[*Three volumes. The set at Northwestern University has a title page for Vol. I only. The set at the University of Michigan has a title page for Vol. I identical to that at Northwestern, no title page for Vol. II, and for Vol. III an undated title page for the second edition.*]

Art. "Perspective," III, 10 pp; 4 pls.

Reference: Information supplied by the Special Collections Department, Northwestern University Library, and by the University Library, University of Michigan.

The publication history of *The New Royal Encyclopaedia* is particularly complex. Elements of its chronology appear below, but many questions remain.

A first edition of three volumes apparently was issued in the years 1788–1791. This may be established from publication dates on the plates (1788–1791), from a list of "Advantages" in Volume I dated 1788, and from a Royal Licence granted by George III, also dated 1788, and published in Volume I. I have also found variant issues of Volumes I and III. The title page for Volume I at the University of North Carolina at Chapel Hill does not contain the words "on an improved plan." It includes the Licence from George III, dated 1788. In the Boston Public Library copy, the title page does contain the words "on an improved plan," but the Licence is undated. Copies of Volume II at these two locations and at the University of Minnesota appear identical. In all three copies of Volume III the title pages are identical, but the copy at the Boston Public Library has four additional or revised plates, all bearing dates later than 1791: one at "Ornithology" dated 1795, one at "Pelvis" dated 1794, and two at "Steam engine" dated 1795. This suggests that a revised issue of Volume III was prepared about 1795, but I have found no corresponding revisions in copies of Volumes I or II of the first edition.

At the University of Michigan there is a copy of the third volume, described on the title page as "the second edition." At both the University of Michigan and at Northwestern University there is a copy of Volume I, described on the title page as "the third edition." I have been unable to locate any other volumes of these editions. In both these editions there are plates bearing dates as late as 1795, but no internal evidence why these sets have been catalogued as [1797?]. The University of Michigan volumes each have a flyleaf dated 1799 in manuscript, offering a *terminus ante quem* for the third edition.

The first volume in each edition contains a significant article on architecture by John Plaw.[1] It begins with brief biographies of architects from Greece to the mid-eighteenth century, an account of the origins of architecture, and a description of architectural practice in Greece, Rome, and early Britain. The bulk of the article is devoted to architecture in medieval Britain, an emphasis in marked contrast to contemporary encyclopedias' concentration on Greece and Rome.[2] The next section, patterned after the *Encyclopaedia Britannica*, treats such theoretical matters as "intrinsic" and "relative" beauty, proportion, and ornament. The final portion of the article, admittedly derived from Chambers's *Treatise*, concerns the five orders, pilasters, pedestals, arches, basements, pediments, gates, doors, piers, windows, design, and "structure." Plaw intended to illustrate this article with eight plates. He included six, which depict the five orders and several examples of ornament. The two other plates, in which he proposed "to illustrate the Principles of Executive Designs, Historical Circumstances, and Periods of the different Stages of Architecture in this Country," never appeared.[3]

The same six plates appear in later editions, but the article was revised. The following note appears at the end: "The System of Architecture, in the first edition of this work, was the production of Mr. Plaw, architect, Paddington; but in this new edition it has undergone many alterations and received considerable additions." The entire article was reorganized into three "Parts," on the "Origin and Progress of Architecture," "Principles of Architecture," and the "Practice of Architecture."[4] The first part is a historical survey from primitive huts to modern Britain. The second part covers invention, taste, judgment, beauty, the orders, pilasters, attics, Persian columns, caryatids, termini, pedestals, intercolumniations, arches, orders above orders, and tectonic components from basements to ceilings. The final part discusses foundations, materials, and aspects of town house construction "essential to be noticed by a builder."

The only house depicted in the entire encyclopedia is two stories high and five windows wide, included in Plate 4 of the "Perspective" article to illustrate the use of the "perspective machine." This machine, illustrated in Figures 76 and 77, is nearly identical to that illustrated in Ferguson's *Art of Drawing in Perspective* (1775), Chambers's *Cyclopaedia* (Vol. V, 1786), and the *Encyclopaedia Britannica* (3rd and later editions), *qq.v.*

1. In 1785 Plaw had just issued his *Rural Architecture*, and soon would issue his *Ferme Ornée* (1795) and *Sketches for Country Houses* (1800), *qq.v.* All of these were important and successful collections of cottage and villa designs.

2. See for example *Encyclopaedia Britannica* and *Encyclopaedia Perthensis*.

3. A note at the end of the article, signed by Plaw, indicates that he intended to engrave the additional plates sometime in the future. He died in 1820.

4. Compare the similar organization of the third and later editions of the *Encyclopaedia Britannica* (*q.v.*).

HARDING, James Duffield (1798-1863)
Nine lithographic views of the cottages, composing Blaise Hamlet.

See Entry 452.

HARRISON, Joseph, ed.
The horticultural register.

See Entry 474.

142.1
HASSELL, John (1767-1825)
[Cottage designs].

[London: Plates published by J. Cooper, 1820].

3 printed leaves, 9 pls.

26.0 × 36.5 cm

NNC

No title page accompanies these designs. The format is similar to Hassell's *Aqua Pictura* (London, [1818]): each leaf of text accompanies three or four plates that show a drawing in successive stages of completion, beginning with an outline sketch and ending with a completely aquatinted and colored print. Perhaps these cottage designs, dated 1819 and 1820, were intended to form part of an expanded edition of *Aqua Pictura* or to become a sequel.

The plates depict three designs—a turf cottage, a miller's cottage, and a Swiss cottage—each ornamented with such picturesque features as half-timbering, thatch, columns made of rough-barked tree trunks, and lattice windows. In each scene a strong sidelight or backlight ties much of the architecture and scenery together while also emphasizing space and depth through strong contrasts of light and shadow. The text describes each cottage and its surrounding scenery. Major portions of the text are devoted to the use of tint. These passages are embellished by samples of each tint used in the finished plates.

143.1
HASSELL, John (1767-1825)
Hassell's drawing magazine. Vol. 1 [*or 2, or 3, or 4*].

[N. loc.: N. pub., n.d.].

[*Volume 1:*] 100 pls.

[*Volume 2:*] 100 pls.

[*Volume 3:*] 100 pls.

[*Volume 4:*] 96 pls.

17.7 × 12.2 cm

DLC

Each volume consists of an etched and aquatinted title page, followed by 100 plates (96 in Volume 4) that were executed in etching, aquatint, or both. There is no text.

Most of the subjects are rendered twice—once etched in outline and once with aquatint added. This demonstrates simple line drawing as well as techniques for adding tone and shading. The two renderings usually appear together on the same plate, or facing each other on adjacent plates. Occasionally they are separated by one or more unrelated plates.

Many of the plates are simply titled "Rural Scenery," and others have legends identifying the subject (e.g., "Chepstow Castle," "Vallecrusis Abbey," "Hot Wells," "Keswick Lake," "Otter"). Picturesque subjects predominate, and include abbeys, churches, castles, cottages, farm buildings, farm scenes, boats, hunting scenes, places of natural beauty, rocks, plants, and animals. Nearly all the illustrations emphasize picturesque irregularity of form, texture, and shading in the subject and its surrounding scenery.

144.1 ‖

HASSELL, John (1767–1825)

The speculum: an essay on the art of drawing in water colours; with instructions for sketching from nature, comprising the whole process of a water coloured drawing, familiarly exemplified in drawing, shadowing and tinting a complete landscape; in all its progressive stages; directions for compounding and using colours, indian ink, or bister. By J. Hassell.

London: Printed by W. Flint, for the author; and sold by T. Tegg, and M. Jones. And to be had of all the booksellers in the United Kingdom, 1809.

32 pp, frontisp.

Reference: Information supplied by the Department of Prints and Drawings, The British Museum.

144.2

The speculum; or, art of drawing in water colours: with instructions for sketching from nature; comprising the whole process of a water-coloured drawing, familiarly exemplified in drawing, shadowing, and tinting a complete landscape, in all its progressive stages: with directions for compounding and using colours, sepia, indian ink, bister, &c. By J. Hassell. The third edition, with additional plates.

London: Printed for the author, and sold by Sherwood, Neely, and Jones; and to be had of all the booksellers in the United Kingdom, 1816.

32 pp, 2 pls.

21.1 × 13.3 cm

PPL

The 1809 edition in the Department of Prints and Drawings at the British Museum has one plate, bound as a frontispiece. The subject, "A Sketch from nature," is drawn in outline. Copies of the third edition at Yale and at the Library Company of Philadelphia include this plate plus one additional plate, depicting the same subject in aquatint. S. T. Prideaux indicated that a "3rd edition" published in 1818 contains 3 plates.[1]

In the first section of the treatise, headed "Proportion" (pp. 3–11), Hassell discussed perspective, pictorial composition, and proper subjects for landscape scenes.[2] The "Sketch from nature" serves to demonstrate these points, and depicts a variety of picturesque subjects—a thatched cottage, trees, underbrush, hills, clouds, a stream, and a bridge—organized by several lines converging at a vanishing point. The next section, headed "Simplicity" (pp. 11–14) concerns both simplicity and "emulation" in pictorial composition. The rest of the treatise concerns more practical matters, with sections titled "Directions for Mixing Colours," "Shadowing and Colouring," "Preparation of Tints," "Colouring," "How to Prepare the Paper for Drawing," and "Drawing Materials."

1. S. T. Prideaux, *Aquatint Engraving* (London: Duckworth, 1909), p. 339.

2. This description pertains to the 1816 edition. The text of the 1809 edition differs significantly.

145.1 †
HAYTER, Charles

An introduction to perspective, adapted to the capacities of youth, in a series of pleasing and familiar dialogues, between the author's children accompanied with illustrative plates, appropriate diagrams, and a sufficiency of practical geometry. To which is added, a compendium of genuine instruction in the art of drawing and painting. . . .

London: Printed for the author, 1813.

viii + 168 pp, frontisp. + 14 pls.

Reference: NUC

145.2
———

An introduction to perspective, drawing, and painting, in a series of pleasing and familiar dialogues between the author's children; illustrated by appropriate plates and diagrams, and a sufficiency of practical geometry. And a compendium of genuine instruction, comprising a progressive and complete body of information, carefully adapted for the instruction of females, and suited equally to the simplicity of youth and to mental maturity. By Mr. Hayter, Portrait Painter, in miniature and crayons, and Teacher of the principal elements of the art. The second edition, considerably enlarged and improved.

London: Published by Black, Parry, and Co.; sold also by Egerton; Lindsell; and by the author, 1815.

xi + [xii–xvi] + 197 pp, frontisp. + 17 pls.

20.2 × 13.2 cm

IU

145.3 †

An introduction to perspective, ⟨ . . . as 1815 . . . ⟩ genuine instruction. . . . Third edition, considerably enlarged and improved.

London: Black, Kingsbury, Parbury, and Allen, 1820.

263 pp.

Reference: NUC

145.4

An introduction to perspective, ⟨ . . . as 1815 . . . ⟩ practical geometry, and ⟨ . . . as 1815 . . . ⟩ mental maturity. By Charles Hayter, Professor of Perspective . . . ; Portrait Painter, in miniature and crayons, and Teacher of the principal elements of the arts. The fourth edition, considerably enlarged and improved.

London: Printed for Kingsbury, Parbury, and Allen, [1825].

xix + [i] + xx–xxii + [i] + 300 pp, frontisp. + frontisp. for the "Letters" + 20 pls.

21.0 × 13.5 cm

MnU

145.5 †

An introduction to perspective, practical geometry, drawing and painting. In a series of dialogues, between the author's children, and in epistolary instruction to pupils. Fifth edition.

London: S. Bagster, 1832.

xxvi pp, 1 leaf, 259 pp, 26 pls.

8°

Reference: NUC

145.6 †
___

Treatise on perspective drawing. . . .

[London]: Bagster, 1844.

8°

Reference: ECB

145.7 ‖
___

An introduction to perspective, practical geometry, drawing and painting; a new and perfect explanation of the mixture of colours; with practical directions for miniature, crayon, and oil painting; in a series of familiar dialogues between the author's children, and letters addressed to his pupils. Illustrated with numerous wood engravings, from drawings by John Hayter, Esq. and coloured plates. By Charles Hayter, Esq. The sixth edition.

London: Samuel Bagster and Sons, 1845.

xiv + 276 pp, frontisp. + 7 pls.

21.5 × 14.0 cm

Reference: Collection of the George Peabody Branch, Enoch Pratt Free Library, Baltimore.

There are significant variations in the text and plates among the six editions. This discussion is based on examination of the fourth edition, dated [1825].[1]

In the Preface (pp. v–vii) Hayter observed the need to study "this branch of elementary knowledge," and lamented "the prevailing antipathy to geometrical illustration, especially among those whose professional success" depends on it (p. v). The "Addenda" (pp. viii–xix) include one page of remarks by Hayter, followed by several pages of "encomiums"—excerpts from complimentary letters that Hayter had received—concerning previous editions. A table of contents and a "Note" conclude the preliminary matter.

The text begins with definitions and remarks on the theory and "extensive powers" of perspective. Hayter then treated geometry, bird's-eye views, horizon lines and perspective planes, the point of sight, vanishing points, the section line, reflections, and shadows, and also included several demonstrations and examples. The remainder of the book (pp. 129–300) consists of 21 "Letters," treating materials, line drawing, the human figure, chalk drawing, India ink, light and shade, reflection, color, outline, miniature painting, crayon painting, oil painting, and other subjects.

The frontispiece depicts three figures sitting at a window, and demonstrates a point concerning horizon lines (p. 34). The frontispiece to the "Letters" shows three figures engaged in drawing and painting. The plates depict drawing instruments, geometric figures, objects in perspective, and color charts, and also illustrate points made in the text concerning level planes, horizon lines, point of distance, foreshortening, and reflections. Several plates include architectural subjects. Plate VIII includes outline drawings of three solids shaped like houses; one has a pyramidal roof, and two have gable roofs.[2] Plate X depicts a row of three columns parallel to the picture plane. Plate XII includes a plan and a perspective view of a house, both in outline.[3] Plates XIII and XV contain perspective views of room interiors, and Plate XV also illustrates architectural backgrounds for portraits. Plate XVIII includes a perspective view of a gable roofed cottage to which an ell and two high, thin walls are attached.[4] Plate XIX contains outline elevations of two garden temples and a garden bridge, all curiously in a retardataire mid-eighteenth-century style.[5]

1. The title page is undated, but the dedication (of the "*Fourth* Edition") to Sir Thomas Lawrence is dated June 15, 1825, and all the plates are dated 1825.

2. These also appear in Plate VIII in the 1815 edition.

3. These figures appear in Plate XII in the 1815 edition.

4. This subject does not appear in the 1815 edition. In the 1845 edition it appears as Fig. 133 on p. 120.

5. These appear in Plate XVI in the 1815 edition.

146.1
HEDGELAND, John Pike (1791–   )

First part of a series of designs for private dwellings. By J. Hedgeland.

London: Printed for G. and W. B. Whittaker, 1821.

11 printed leaves, 20 pls.

27.9 × 22.2 cm

V&A

Following this *First Part of a Series of Designs* no further parts were issued.

The *First Part* consists of ten designs for dwellings, each illustrated in a lithographed view and an etched plan, and described on one leaf of letter-press. In a short Preface Hedgeland expressed his particular concern for three criteria in residential design: "comfort and convenience in the internal arrangement; economy in the mode of building; and simplicity of character in the external appearance."

There are designs for a "small dwelling," a "small house," a "country dwelling," a "Gothic residence," five "gentleman's residences," and a group of laborer's cottages. The "small dwelling" (Plates I, II) consists of a dining room, sitting room, and offices on the ground floor, and three bedrooms upstairs. The largest "gentleman's residence" (Plates XIII, XIV) has a vestibule, dining room, drawing room, lobby, breakfast room, and billiard room on the ground floor, plus five bedrooms, two dressing rooms, two servant's rooms, and a water closet upstairs, and offices in the basement.

All the designs are based on simple, regular geometric figures. The design for a group of laborer's cottages (Plates XV, XVI) consists of just four units: a central hexagon, and three squares attached to alternate faces of the hexagon. Eight designs are in Classical styles, and two in Gothic. The "gentleman's residence" shown in Plate XIII is fronted by a two-story Tuscan portico, but there is little other ornament. The facade is five windows wide, and surmounted by a circular lantern rising over the center of the house. The Gothic residences illustrated in Plates XVII and XIX are each two stories high and three windows wide, with Tudor drip moldings over the windows plus a central window with a pointed arch. The design in Plate XIX includes turrets at each side of the elevation.

Hedgeland's *First Part* was, with one minor exception,[1] the first British architectural book to be illustrated with lithographed plates.[2] Unfortunately Hedgeland's designs, typified by severe lines, plain surfaces, and minimal ornamentation, were perhaps better suited to engraving or etching. Nevertheless he made effective use of lithography in representing surrounding foliage and landscape scenery, and also to suggest light, shadow, and three-dimensional space.

1. One lithographed plate was added to the second edition of William Hawkes Smith's *Outline of Architecture* (1820; *q.v.*).

2. The first manual of lithography published in English was Alois Senefelder's *Complete Course of Lithography* (1819; *q.v.* in Appendix D), translated from the German edition of 1818. The English edition was published by Rudolph Ackermann, who added a lithographed view of a cottage drawn by Samuel Prout. Next appeared Antoine Raucourt's *Manual of Lithography* (1820; *q.v.* in Appendix D), translated from the French edition of 1819 by Charles Hullmandel, a prominent early English lithographer. In 1824 Ackermann and Hullmandel together published *The Art of Drawing on Stone*, written and illustrated by Hullmandel.

147.1

HIGHLAND and Agricultural Society of Scotland

"Remarks on cottage premiums, and description and specification of cottages built on the estate of the Earl of Rosebery," *Prize-essays and Transactions of the Highland and Agricultural Society of Scotland* XII (n.s. VI; 1839), 527–534, and pl. 9.

DLC

This article describes a scheme of premiums, at £4 each, to be awarded annually for the best-kept cottages and cottage gardens in four parishes in each of certain Scottish counties. The author noted that in several places cottagers had already begun to compete for these premiums (p. 528). The Society expected that expansion of the premium scheme would encourage cottagers to improve their dwellings and gardens on their own initiative. As one correspondent wrote, the scheme might improve the state of rural housing throughout Scotland, with only a small investment of capital:

If . . . the peasantry can, even under their present unfavourable circumstances, be induced to throw off their slovenly habits, [then] proprietors, in place of forcing upon them conveniences which they do not appreciate, would only have to supply what is absolutely necessary to enable them to carry into effect their own plans of improvement. (p. 531)

As models for cottagers to learn from, the article recommended designs by George Smith that had placed first in a competition held by the Society in 1833. These designs were published subsequently in both serial and pamphlet form (*q.v.*). In addition, one plate of designs was included here: it depicts a double cottage that was "Erected upon the Earl of Rosebery's Estates." Each cottage includes a porch, a pantry, a kitchen, and a "room," with a privy, ash pits, and storage areas for coal and potatoes attached to the exterior. Pages 533–534 contain specifications for erecting these cottages.

HIGHLAND and Agricultural Society of Scotland

See also MITCHELL, **John,** *Entry 491;* SMITH, **George,** *Entry 310.2.*

HIGHLAND Society of Scotland

See RENNIE, **Rev. Robert,** *Entry 275.*

HODSON, F. M.
Encyclopedia mancuniensis.

See Entry 77.1.

HODSON, Thomas
The cabinet of the arts.

See Entry 487.

148.1
HOLLAND, Henry (1745–1806)
"On cottages," *Communications to the Board of Agriculture; on Subjects Relative to the Husbandry, and Internal Improvement of the Country* I:2 (1797), 97–102, and pl. XXXV.

MH

The commentary for Entry 148 is combined with that for Entry 149 below.

149.1
HOLLAND, Henry (1745–1806)
"Pisé, or the art of building strong and durable walls, to the height of several stories, with nothing but earth, or the most common materials. Drawn up and presented to the Board of Agriculture, by Henry Holland, Esq.," *Communications to the Board of Agriculture; on Subjects Relative to the Husbandry, and Internal Improvement of the Country* I:3–4 (1797), 387–403, and pls. XLVIII–LIV.

MH

In the 1770s and 1780s individual authors such as Nathaniel Kent and John Wood had begun to advance the cause of rural improvement through publication of original designs for farm houses and laborers' cottages.[1] By the 1790s local and national societies concerned with agricultural improvement began to address the problem of rural housing on a more widespread and systematic basis.[2] Foremost among these societies was the Board of Agriculture and Internal Improvement, whose *Communications*, begun in 1797, included several articles on farm house and cottage design.[3]

Henry Holland, a prominent builder and architect with a flourishing practice,[4] contributed two articles to the first volume. At the very beginning of the first article, on cottages, he established four "essential considerations" in cottage design: the site, the "distribution" or plan of the building, its "superstructure" and materials, and the supply of water and fuel (p. 97). He elaborated each of these points, and then gave a detailed estimate of labor and materials for a double cottage "of the smallest size," as illustrated in plan and elevation in Plate XXXV. He divided the ground floor of each cottage into two areas, one "for kitchen, and parlour, and all," and the other for "cellar, pantry, dairy, &c." Upstairs were two chambers, one for children and the other for the parents. The elevation shows a thatch roof with an upward bow in the center to accommodate two windows in the middle of the upper story. Holland concluded the article with a useful classification of cottages into five sizes: the smallest size was for a laborer, the second size was for "the labouring man who by his skill, and working task work, earns more than the common labourer," the third size was for a village shopkeeper, shoemaker, tailor, butcher, or baker, the fourth size was for a farmer, maltster, small farmer, alehouse, and "trades requiring room," and the fifth size was for the "large farmer" (p. 102).

The second article concerns pisé, a substance made of compressed clay and used for walls in rural French farm buildings. Holland's article, the first in English thoroughly to discuss building in this material, was closely based on a recent publication by François Cointeraux.[5] Holland began with a brief history and bibliography of the subject, followed by a description of necessary implements, remarks on "working" pisé, instructions for making windows and doors, advice on the selection of proper earth for making pisé, suggestions for exterior and interior finishing of a pisé dwelling, and remarks on other practical matters. Holland's illustrations, reproduced from Cointeraux, depict implements, construction methods, and a rude two-room pisé dwelling. The dwelling is shown in plan, two end elevations, and an oblique view.[6] Over the next 28 years citations and paraphrases of Holland's article appeared in several encyclopedias and one agricultural dictionary;[7] in 1821 it was reprinted verbatim in an American agricultural periodical.[8]

1. See Nathaniel Kent, *Hints to Gentlemen* (1775); and John Wood, *A Series of Plans, for Cottages* (1792; plates executed as early as 1781).

2. See for example the article by Davis published by the Bath and West of England Society (1795); the reports on individual counties commissioned by the Board of Agriculture (see the entry for "Great Britain. Board of Agriculture. Reports"); and the article by Rennie published by the Highland Society (1803).

3. Also see articles by Beatson, Crocker, Crutchley, and Hunt.

4. Colvin (1978), pp. 423–426.

5. *École d'architecture rurale, premier cahier, dans lequel on apprendra soi-même à bâtir solidement les maisons de plusieurs étages avec la terre seule; ouvrage dédié aux Français en 1790, revu et corrigé par l'auteur, l'an 2me de la République Française, une et indivisible, dans le mois de Floréal. Seconde édition.* Paris [1790]. 32 pp, 10 pls. Mr. Roy E. Goodman, Reference Librarian at the American Philosophical Society, kindly supplied me a copy of relevant material from this treatise. N.B. John Plaw was the first British author to discuss the use of pisé, albeit very briefly; see his *Ferme Ornée* (1795; *q.v.*).

6. Plan: Holland, Plate LI; Cointeraux, Plate IV. End elevations: Holland, Plate LII; Cointeraux, Plate V. Side view: Holland, Plate LIII; Cointeraux, Plate VI.

7. See *Pantologia* (1813); Abraham Rees, *The Cyclopaedia* ([1802]–1820); *Encyclopaedia Londinensis*, Vol. XX (1825); and *The Complete Farmer*, 5th ed. (1807). For a broader discussion of the impact of pisé see John Martin Robinson, *Georgian Model Farms: A Study of Decorative and Model Farm Buildings in the Age of Improvement, 1700–1846* (Oxford: Clarendon Press, 1983), pp. 52–56.

8. *The American Farmer* III:1–5 (30 March–27 April 1821), 4, 11–13, 20–21, 28–29, 33–35.

150.1
HOPPUS, Edward (–1739), trans.

Andrea Palladio's architecture, in four books containing a dissertation on the five orders & ye most necessary observations relating to all kinds of building. As also the different constructions of public and private-houses, high-ways, bridges, market-places, xystes, & temples, wth. their plans, sections, & elevations. The whole containing 226 folio copper-plates carefully revis'd and redelineated by Edwd. Hoppus Surveyor . . . and embellish'd wth. a large variety of chimney pieces collected from the works of Inigo Jones & others.

London: Printed for & sold by the proprietor, & engraver, Benj: Cole and by ye booksellers of London & Westminster, 1735.

[*This title page is followed by four separate books, each with individual title page:*]

[*Book I:*]

Andrea Palladio's first book of architecture, with all ye plates exactly copied from ye first Italian edition, printed in Venice anno Dom MDLXX.

London: Engrav'd printed & sold by B. Cole, [n.d.].

[i] + [vi] + 7–70 pp, frontisp. (= title page) + 35 pls.

[*Book II:*]

The second book of Palladio's architecture. In which are contained, the designs of several houses erected by himself either in town or country. With divers other designs of the manner of building formerly practis'd amongst the Greeks and Romans. Translated from the Italian; and the designs carefully copied by B. Cole, Engraver.

London: [N. pub.], 1733.

71–122 pp, 61 pls.

[*Book III:*]

The third book of Palladio's architecture. Treating particularly on high=ways, streets, bridges, squares, basilicas, or courts of judicature, xistes, or places of exercise, &c. Translated from the Italian; and the designs carefully copied by B. Cole, Engraver.

London: [N. pub.], 1733.

123–178 pp, 22 pls (on 20 leaves).

[*Book IV:*]

The fourth book of Palladio's architecture. Treating particularly on the ancient Roman temples, and some churches, which are now seen to be in Italy, and divers other parts of Europe. Translated from the Italian; and the designs carefully copied by B. Cole, Engraver.

London: [N. pub.], 1734.

179–251 + [x] pp, 104 pls (on 93 leaves).

30.8 × 19.6 cm

RIBA

150.2 ‡

Andrea Palladio's architecture, in four books containing a dissertation on the five orders & ye most necessary observations relating to all kinds of building. As also the different constructions of public and private-houses, high-ways, bridges, market-places, xystes, & temples, wth. their plans, sections, & elevations. The whole containing 226 folio copper-plates carefully revis'd and redelineated by Edwd. Hoppus Surveyor to ye Corporation of the London Assurance and embellish'd wth. a large variety of chimney pieces collected from the works of Inigo Jones & others.

London: Printed for Benjn. Cole Engraver, & John Wilcox, 1736.

[*This title page is preceded by a frontispiece and followed by four separate books; three books have individual title pages:*]

[*Book I: No individual title page.*]

1 printed leaf, vi + 7–70 pp, 35 pls (numbered I–XXXV).

[*Book II:*]

The second book of Palladio's architecture. In which are contained, the designs of several houses erected by himself either in town or country. With divers other designs of the manner of building formerly practised amongst the Greeks and Romans. Translated from the Italian; and the designs carefully copied by B. Cole, Engraver.

London: [N. pub.], 1736.

73–121 pp, 61 pls (numbered I–LXI).

[*Book III:*]

The third book of Palladio's architecture. Treating particularly on high=ways, streets, bridges, squares, palaces, basilicas, or courts of judicature. Xistes, or places of exercise, &c. Translated from the Italian, and the designs carefully copied by B. Cole, Engraver.

London: [N. pub.], 1736.

125–177 pp, 22 pls (numbered I–XXII, on 20 leaves).

[*Book IV:*]

The fourth book of Palladio's architecture. Treating particularly on the ancient Roman temples, and some churches which are now to be seen in Italy, and divers other parts of Europe. Translated from the Italian, and the designs carefully copied by B. Cole, Engraver.

London: [N. pub.], 1736.

181–250 + [ix] pp, 104 pls (numbered I–CIV, on 93 leaves).

35.0 × 21.5 cm

Reference: Johns Hopkins University Library, Fowler Architectural Collection (microfilm), published by Research Publications, Inc., Woodbridge, Connecticut. No. 228.

The first fascicle was announced in November 1732: see R. M. Wiles, *Serial Publication in England before 1750* (Cambridge: Cambridge University Press, 1957), pages 284–285.

Although the first edition was successful enough to warrant a second the next year, the contents are hardly an accurate representation of Palladio's work. The translation is a pastiche of excerpts from works by Campbell and Leoni.[1] Hoppus claimed to copy Palladio's illustrations faithfully, but in fact he altered several and also added—sometimes without attribution—other designs by his English contemporaries.[2] On page 19, for example, he illustrated a small domed garden pavilion that is identical to a design in Plate 43 of Isaac Ware's *Designs of Inigo Jones*. There it is attributed to William Kent and described as a garden seat designed for Sir Charles Hotham. Other unattributed designs are also similar to illustrations in Ware's book. Hoppus depicted designs for chimneypieces and additional ornaments that he attributed to Palladio and Jones. Despite its shortcomings, Hoppus's treatise was influential: one unattributed design for a small pavilion (p. 185), for example, eventually became the model for Peter Harrison's Redwood Library in Newport, Rhode Island.

1. For a more thorough commentary on the quality and sources of Hoppus's work, see Rudolf Wittkower, *Palladio and Palladianism* (New York: Braziller, 1974), pp. 88–89.

2. Among Hoppus's additions were headpieces and tailpieces on pp. i, vi, 7, 19, 23, 25, 31, 34, 42, 48, 73, 112, 114, 120, 121, 125, 129, 131, 134, 141, 177, 181, and 185, plus substantial alterations and additions to the plates, including a total of ten chimneypieces illustrated in Pls. XXXII–XXXV. Hoppus added no introduction or explanatory matter of his own to the text.

151.1

HOPPUS, Edward (–1739)

The gentleman's and builder's repository: or, architecture display'd. Containing the most useful and requisite problems in geometry. As also, the most easy, expeditious, and correct methods for attaining the knowledge of the five orders of architecture, by equal parts, and fewer divisions, than any thing hitherto published. Together with all such rules for arches, doors, windows cieling-pieces, chimney-pieces, and their particular embellishments, as can be required. Likewise, a large variety of designs for truss roofs; with the method of finding the hip, either square or bevel. Also, the most certain and approved methods of forming a number of different stair-cases, with their twisted rails, &c. The whole embellished, not only with fourscore plates, in quarto, but such variety of cieling-pieces, shields, compartments, and other curious and uncommon decorations, as must needs render it acceptable to all gentlemen, artificers, and others, who delight in, or practice, the art of building. The designs regulated and drawn by E. Hoppus, and engraved by B. Cole.

London: Printed for James Hodges; and Benjamin Cole, Engraver, 1737.

101 pp, [2] pls on one leaf, 84 pls [*pl. I is wanting in this copy*].

24.4 × 18.4 cm

CtY

151.2

———

The gentleman's and builder's repository: or, architecture display'd. Containing the most useful and requisite problems in geometry. As also the most easy, expeditious, and correct methods for attaining the knowledge of the five orders of architecture, by equal parts, and fewer divisions, than any thing hitherto published. Together with all such rules for arches, doors, windows, ceiling-pieces, chimney-pieces, and their particular embellishments, as can be required. Likewise a large variety of designs for truss roofs; with the method of finding the hip, either square or bevel. Also, the most certain and approved methods of forming a number of different stair-cases, with their twisted rails, &c. The whole embellished, not only with eighty-four plates, in quarto, but such variety of cieling= pieces, shields, compartments, and other curious and uncommon decorations, as must needs render it acceptable to all gentlemen, artificers, and others, who delight in, or practice, the art of building. The designs regulated and drawn by E. Hoppus, Surveyor, and engraved by B. Cole. The second edition, carefully revised and re-examined from the press; with the addition of a new frontispiece, representing the intended front of the new mansion-house for the Lord Mayors of the City of London; and a complete table of contents, alphabetically digested by E. H. aforesaid.

London: Printed for A. Bettesworth, and C. Hitch; J. Hodges; and B. Cole, Engraver, 1738.

[vi] + 99 pp, frontisp., [2] pls on one leaf, 84 pls [*pl. LV is wanting in this copy*].

24.8 × 19.1 cm

NNC

151.3

The gentleman's and builder's repository: ⟨ . . . as 1738 . . . ⟩ bevel. Also the ⟨ . . . as 1738 . . . ⟩ Cole. The third edition, ⟨ . . . as 1738 . . . ⟩ aforesaid.

London: Printed for C. Hitch; J. Hodges; and B. Cole, 1748.

101 pp, frontisp., [2] pls on one leaf, 84 pls.

25.4 × 20.3 cm

CtY-BA

151.4

The gentleman's and builder's repository: ⟨ . . . as 1738 . . . ⟩ bevel. Also the ⟨ . . . as 1738 . . . ⟩, not only with ninety plates, ⟨ . . . as 1738 . . . ⟩ Cole. The fourth edition, carefully revised and re-examined from the press; with the addition of Chinese architecture, being new designs for paling of different kinds, common fences, garden-paling, both close and open, stiles, parks, stair-cases, windows, galleries, &c. and a complete table of contents, alphabetically digested.

London: Printed for C. Hitch and L. Hawes; S. Crowder; and B. Cole, 1760.

iv + 101 pp, frontisp., [2] pls on one leaf, 90 pls.

25.0 × 20.4 cm

NNC

The letterpress of the 1737 edition consists of a preface (pp. 1–2) and the text (pp. 3–101). The 1738 edition contains a preface (one leaf, recto and verso), a table of contents (two leaves, recto and verso), and the text (pp. 1–99). The 1748 edition contains a preface (pp. 1–2) and the text (pp. 3–101). The letterpress of the final edition is like that of 1748, with the addition of a table of contents (pp. i–iv). In all editions there are two unnumbered plates on one leaf between pages 24 and 25, as well as plates numbered I through LXXXIV. In the final edition there are six more plates, numbered LXXXV through XC. The description below is based on examination of the 1737 edition.

In the Preface Hoppus observed that "young Practitioners must, of Necessity, have Recourse to a Variety of Books, and put themselves to a large Expence, before they can be able to form a just Idea of so useful an Art in all its various Branches." He therefore prepared "this *New Magazine*" with the idea of saving his readers both time and expense in their architectural studies.

The first part of the text is "A Dissertation on Practical Geometry" (pp. 3–32, with 2 plates), consisting of rules for drawing polygons, Gothic arches, ovals, "the Angle or Mitre Arch of Groins," other arches, and niches. The rest of the text is "A Dissertation on Architecture" (pp. 33–101, with 84 plates) treating the five orders, their parts, intercolumniations, arches, doors, gates, windows, chimneypieces, moldings, ceilings, obelisks, balusters, roofs, staircases, railings, and ornamental "Shields, or Compartments, . . . for Carvers, Painters, Sculptors, &c."

There are no complete designs for dwellings in the plates accompanying the text, but the frontispiece is an elevation and partial plan of the Mansion House in London. The headpiece to the Preface is an elevation of a one-story building, five openings wide, that would easily serve as a gate lodge. The headpiece to the Dissertation on Practical Geometry is a two-story structure, 11 openings wide, perhaps a stable or an orangery. The headpiece to the Dissertation on Architecture is an elevation of a two-story dwelling, seven windows wide, fronted by a two-story tetrastyle Ionic portico.

The six additional plates in the final edition contain 17 designs for Chinese paling, fences, windows, and staircases.

The horticultural register.

See Entry 474.

HULLMANDEL, Charles Joseph (1789–1850)
The art of drawing on stone.

See Entry 475.

HUMPHREYS, Thomas
The Irish builder's guide.

See Entry 488.

152.1
HUNT, Rowland
"Memoir on the distribution of farms, farm buildings, &c.," *Communications to the Board of Agriculture; on Subjects Relative to the Husbandry, and Internal Improvement of the Country* I:1 (1797), 58–65, and pls. XXI–XXV.

MH

In the 1770s and 1780s individual authors such as Nathaniel Kent and John Wood had begun to advance the cause of rural improvement through publication of original designs for farm houses and laborers' cottages.[1] By the 1790s local and national societies concerned with agricultural improvement began to address the problem of rural housing on a more widespread and systematic basis.[2] Foremost among these societies was the Board of Agriculture and Internal Improvement, whose *Communications*, begun in 1797, included several articles on farm house and cottage design.[3]

In this article on the "Distribution of Farms," Rowland Hunt indulged in tiresome equivocation over several questions: whether to place all farm houses of one estate in one village, "what number of acres in *one* farm is the best quantity for the good of the country,"and "what is the best quantity of acres for *agriculture* as such" (pp. 58–59). In partial answer he suggested the *"principle* of *improvement"*: that "the real and permanent interest of a landlord and tenant are the same, nor can there be a more degrading or ridiculous position, than that of landlord and tenant sitting down to try who most shall impoverish the other" (p. 59). Hunt recommended cooperation between both parties and financial planning that considered the long-term interests of all.

The bulk of the article consists of suggestions for siting farm houses and yards in relation to each other, the rest of the farm, roads, and the "pleasure ground" of a gentleman's estate. The five plates include an elevation and plan of a farm house, a farmyard and offices suited to that house, two floor plans of a smaller farm house, a farmyard and offices for that house, and a plan for "a farm yard belonging to a gentleman's house, at some distance from the mansion itself" (p. 64). The three-story farm house in Plate XXI contains a parlor, small parlor, kitchen, back kitchen, milk house, and smaller offices on the ground floor. The elevation is arranged in an unsophisticated, asymmetrical fashion: the door is off center, the arched window lintels are large and ungainly, and the ground-floor window lintels violate the stringcourse above. The house in Plate XXIII, shown in plan only, includes a parlor, best kitchen, back kitchen, and other offices on the ground floor, plus five bed chambers and a cheese room on the upper story.

1. See Nathaniel Kent, *Hints to Gentlemen* (1775); and John Wood, *A Series of Plans, for Cottages* (1792; plates executed as early as 1781).

2. See for example the article by Davis published by the Bath and West of England Society (1795); the reports on individual counties commissioned by the Board of Agriculture (see the entry for "Great Britain. Board of Agriculture. Reports"); and the article by Rennie published by the Highland Society (1803).

3. Also see articles by Beatson, Crocker, Crutchley, and Holland.

153.1
HUNT, Thomas Frederick (ca. 1791–1831)
Architettura campestre: displayed in lodges, gardeners' houses, and other buildings, composed of simple and economical forms in the modern or Italian style; introducing a picturesque mode of roofing. By T. F. Hunt. . . .

London: Longman, Rees, Orme, Brown, and Green, 1827.

xix + 28 pp, 12 pls.

30.5 × 24.1 cm

MB

153.2

————

————

London: Henry G. Bohn, 1844.

xix + 28 pp, 12 pls.

29.8 × 24.1 cm

MBAt

Thomas Frederick Hunt, Gilbert Laing Meason, and Charles Parker all fostered a revival of interest in Italianate architecture between 1827 and 1832.[1] Hunt was the first, publishing *Architettura Campestre* in 1827, but he was the least enthusiastic. He tried to excuse these designs, atypical of his other work,[2] by explaining that his "patrons" had requested them (p. v). He suggested the reader would easily perceive the "inferiority" of Italian architecture to British medieval styles (p. v). Indeed he intimated the indigenous architecture of the British Isles surpassed that of Greece and Rome since "the beauties of English Architecture were felt by men of genius, taste, and experience, long before one was found bold enough to contend against the deeply rooted prejudices which existed in favour of what is termed Classical Art" (p. v).

The Introduction (pp. ix–xix) conveniently ignores Italian architecture and instead is a history of landscape and garden architecture in England since the time of Inigo Jones. Hunt chronicled the development of the English style in landscaping—the turn toward more serpentine, natural contours—and in particular noted the contributions of Vanbrugh, Pope, Addison, Kent, and Lord Bathurst. He briefly discussed the "rural buildings," or country houses, of several eighteenth-century architects. He concluded with a "hope" that Italian roof tiles might "be brought into general use": they "are light and economical, most beautiful in form, and secure as a covering, affording no harbour either for birds or vermin" (p. xviii).

The 12 lithographed plates, described on pages 2–25, include designs for a summer house and gardener's residence, a garden cottage, a gate lodge, a dairy and gamekeeper's residence, a gardener's cottage or gate lodge, a small residence or "superior" gate lodge, an orangery and garden seat, another gate lodge, a prospect tower and garden seat, a bridge, a small villa, and a casino. One of the largest designs is the casino, "adapted for the residence of a gentleman" (p. 24), with a dining room, drawing room, gentleman's room, boudoir, and arcade on the ground floor. The "small villa" includes a drawing room, eating room, and three bedrooms on the ground floor, plus four bedrooms upstairs.

The design in Plate II for a garden cottage is clearly in an English "cottage" or "rustic" style, with a thatch roof and rough-barked columns, and Hunt admitted the design was "not strictly Italian." Other designs (especially Plates III, IX, XI) incorporate square towers, belvederes, Classical orders, and other clearly Italianate elements. Perhaps most interesting is the design in Plate IX for a prospect tower and residence: the facade consists of a seat or bench set within a massive semicircular arch, above which rise two square towers; one of these culminates in an open belvedere. Hunt no doubt intended these forms to recall the highly geometric examples of vernacular Italian architecture seen in paintings by Claude or Poussin. Ultimately this design was executed as a lodge on the Alton estate in Staffordshire.

1. Also see Meason, *On the Landscape Architecture of the Great Painters of Italy* (1828); and Parker, *Villa Rustica* (1832 and later). Italianate forms appeared in British practice about 1802, in works such as Cronkhill, by John Nash: see Summerson (1969), p. 290.

2. Compare his earlier work in a picturesque Old English manner in *Half a Dozen Hints* (1825) and *Designs for Parsonage Houses* (1827), *qq.v.*

154.1

HUNT, Thomas Frederick (ca. 1791–1831)

Designs for parsonage houses, alms houses, etc. etc. with examples of gables, and other curious remains of old English architecture. By T. F. Hunt, Architect. . . .

London: Longman, Rees, Orme, Brown, and Green, 1827.

viii + 34 pp, 21 pls.

29.8 × 23.5 cm

MB

154.2

————

Designs for parsonage houses, ⟨ . . . as 1827 . . . ⟩ architecture, by T. F. Hunt, Architect. . . .

London: Henry G. Bohn, 1841.

viii + 34 pp, 21 pls.

30.5 × 24.1 cm

MH

Following the Dedication there is a short Preface (pp. v–vi), in which Hunt explained that he conceived this book as a sequel to his *Half a Dozen Hints on Picturesque Domestic Architecture* (1825; q.v.), one of the earliest collections of designs in the Old English style. The first such collection had been Peter Frederick Robinson's *Rural Architecture* (1823; q.v.), but Hunt clearly disparaged Robinson's narrow appreciation of this style, which was limited to its picturesque qualities. In *Designs for Parsonage Houses* there would be "no factitious effect obtained by the broken, unequal, or *painter's* line: the individual forms are represented with the sharpness of recent finishing; and the small portions of vegetation which appear on some of the roofs are only such as a few months would produce" (p. vi). The preliminary matter concludes with a table of contents and a list of the different scales to which the plans are drawn.

The text is interleaved with the plates, and contains brief descriptions of each design as well as observations on materials, colors, chimney shafts, oriel windows, general characteristics of the Old English style, and historical events associated with particular gables and other features that Hunt illustrated.[1]

The plates include illustrations of three "Curious Old Gables" and one "Curious Old Chimney-Piece." In addition there are plans and views of 14 designs for dwellings: four parsonage houses, a rectory, vicarage, a curate's house, a parish clerk's house, a gravedigger's hut, and five alms-houses. One of the largest designs is the rectory (Plates III, IV), in "the style of the latter part of the reign of Henry VII., or the early part of Henry VIII" (p. 5). The elevation is irregular, asymmetrical, and richly embellished with ornamental chimneys, Tudor windows, gables of various heights, and elaborate bargeboards. The ground-floor plan, also asymmetrical, includes a drawing room, a dining room, a library, a butler's pantry, a housekeeper's room, a kitchen, and several closets. Apart from the almshouses and gravedigger's hut the smallest design is the parish clerk's house (Plates X, XI), with an office, parlor, and kitchen on the ground floor, and three bedrooms upstairs. The elevation includes an oriel window, elaborate bargeboards, and ornamental chimneys, crockets, finials, and pendants.

1. Hunt included several excerpts from historical treatises to establish the accuracy of his designs as well as the historical context of the style; he also adopted this procedure in *Exemplars of Tudor Architecture* (1830; *q.v.*). Shortly afterward several authors, perhaps in part inspired by Hunt, published historical accounts of "Old English" and Elizabethan architecture; in many cases they paid close attention to contemporary furniture, costume, and society as well as architecture. See in particular Thomas Hutchings Clarke, *The Domestic Architecture of the Reigns of Queen Elizabeth and James the First* (1833), James Hakewill, *An Attempt to Determine the Exact Character of Elizabethan Architecture* (1835), Matthew Habershon, *Ancient Half-Timbered Houses of England* (1836), Charles John Palmer, *History and Illustrations of a House in the Elizabethan Style of Architecture* (1838), Henry Shaw, *Details of Elizabethan Architecture* (1839), Joseph Nash, *The Mansions of England in the Olden Times* (1839–1849), and three books by Charles James Richardson: *Observations on the Architecture of England during the Reigns of Queen Elizabeth and King James I* (1837), *Architectural Remains of the Reigns of Elizabeth and James I* (1840), and *Studies from Old English Mansions* (1841).

155.1
HUNT, Thomas Frederick (ca. 1791–1831)
Exemplars of Tudor architecture, adapted to modern habitations: with illustrative details, selected from ancient edifices; and observations on the furniture of the Tudor period. By T. F. Hunt, Architect. . . .

London: Longman, Rees, Orme, Brown, and Green, 1830.

viii + 200 pp, 37 pls.

27.9 × 23.5 cm

MH

155.2

————

————

London: Longman, Rees, Orme, Brown, Green, and Longman, 1836.

viii + 200 pp, 37 pls.

29.8 × 24.8 cm

V&A

155.3

————

————

London: Henry G. Bohn, 1841.

viii + 200 pp, 37 pls.

28.6 × 22.9 cm

MH

According to ECB the first edition was advertised in November 1829; Hunt's preface is dated October 22, 1829.

The first thorough and comprehensive stylistic analysis of British medieval architecture was Thomas Rickman's "Attempt to Discriminate the Styles of English Architecture," published as part of a larger work in 1815 and then independently in 1817.[1] John Britton made further remarks on this subject in Volume V of his *Architectural Antiquities* (1826).[2] But neither author considered architecture of the Tudor period. Earlier in the nineteenth century some architects published designs for cottages and other dwellings that included Tudor features, but no one before Hunt attempted such a lengthy account of the Tudor style.[3]

Hunt conceived *Exemplars of Tudor Architecture* with the aim of "shewing that English Architecture is still the most applicable for English habitations" (p. v). To do so, he adopted an unusual format: a series of plates illustrating plans, views, and details of designs for houses, with further illustrations of suitable furnishings, all based on "characteristic examples of the beautiful, though long-neglected Architecture of my own country" (p. v). He added a long descriptive text (pp. 1–193) with quotations and references describing the precedents on which he had based his designs. Hunt frequently commented on the original functions of individual features in Tudor times, and used quotations from Shakespeare and other contemporary authors to add some of the flavor of the period. Such a concern for historical context was rare in British architectural literature, although common since the mid-eighteenth century in the literature of British history and archaeology.[4]

Frequent references to Uvedale Price demonstrate Hunt's awareness of recent theories of picturesque composition, but Hunt preferred to trace an intuitive appreciation for the picturesque to the sixteenth century. The gate house in Plate 26, for example, was "designed rather to produce an agreeable and picturesque effect, than to accord with any fixed rules or customs of art: such, indeed, was the practice towards the latter end of the sixteenth century, when it would appear that—like the fashion of the present day—every man wished to display his taste and learning in architecture" (p. 86).

Hunt's 37 plates include designs for three houses, a dog kennel, a dowry house, gate houses, a wide variety of architectural details, and furniture. The first house (Plates I, II) "is an attempt to combine modern convenience with the splendour of an ancient quadrangular form," and the ground floor includes an entrance hall and cloister, a parlor, a hall or dining room, a library, a "private room," a drawing room, a music room, a housekeeper's room, a butler's room, a plate room, and a passage to the offices. In the second design (Plates XI, XII), slightly smaller than the first, Hunt applied "Henry the Eighth's style of building to the exterior, without reference either to the forms or arrangements of ancient plans" (p. 45). The third design (Plates XXII, XXIII), with just an entrance hall, dining room, library, breakfast room, drawing room, and offices on the ground floor, was designed with a specific function in mind: to "secure . . . every ray of sunlight" possible for rooms which are occupied in the daytime. Hunt's elevations are symmetrical or nearly so, and greatly enriched by judicious use of gables, crenellations, oriels, Tudor arches, finials, and ornamented chimneys.

1. See the commentary below on James Smith's *Panorama of Science and Art* (1815).

2. For further discussion of Rickman and Britton see Nikolaus Pevsner, *Some Architectural Writers of the Nineteenth Century* (Oxford: Clarendon Press, 1972), pp. 25–32.

3. Previously Hunt had discussed certain aspects of the Tudor style in *Half a Dozen Hints* (1825) and in *Designs for Parsonage Houses* (1827), *qq.v.* In particular he praised the picturesque "variety of form and outline" of the "Old English" style, which for him encompassed architecture of the period from Henry VII through Elizabeth I (*Designs for Parsonage Houses*, p. 17).

4. Compare, for example, the attention given to "manners and customs" in Edward King's address to the Society of Antiquaries in 1776: "As an acquaintance with ancient manners and customs is essentially necessary in order to our well understanding the History of past ages, so those Antiquities which tend to illustrate and explain the arts, usages, and modes of living, of our forefathers, both in war and in peace, become daily more interesting objects of our enquiries" (*Archaeologia* IV [1786], 365). By 1821 the relation between architecture and its historical context was clearly a major concern of British historians. A reviewer for *The Quarterly Review* wrote:

The edifices which nations raise are inseparably associated with the deeds which they perform. Architecture performs a perpetual commentary upon the pages of the historian, who can ill dispense with the aid which the imagination thus receives. In vain do we attempt to view the countenances of the actors, or to listen to their voices, unless we can also duly decorate the glowing scene around them.

(Excerpted from "Normandy—Architecture of the Middle Ages," *The Quarterly Review* XXV:49 [April 1821], 117.)

156.1
HUNT, Thomas Frederick (ca. 1791–1831)

Half a dozen hints on picturesque domestic architecture, in a series of designs for gate lodges, gamekeepers' cottages, and other rural residences. By T. F. Hunt.

London: Published by Longman, Hurst, Rees, Orme, Brown, and Green, 1825.

14 printed leaves, 12 pls (numbered 1–9 and A–C).

29.5 × 23.5 cm

BL

156.2
———

Half a dozen hints ⟨ . . . as 1825 . . . ⟩ Hunt, Architect. Second edition.

London: Published by Longman, Rees, Orme, Brown, and Green, 1826.

15 printed leaves, 12 pls (numbered 1–9 and A–C).

30.5 × 24.1 cm

V&A

156.3

Half a dozen hints ⟨ . . . as 1825 . . . ⟩ Hunt, Architect. Third edition, with additions.

London: Published by Longman, Rees, Orme, Brown, Green, and Longman, 1833.

16 printed leaves, 14 pls (numbered 1–9, 13, and A–[D]).

29.5 × 23.9 cm

Private Collection

156.4

London: Henry G. Bohn, 1841.

16 printed leaves, 14 pls (numbered 1–9, 13, and A–[D]).

30.2 × 23.8 cm

Bodl.

In the "Address" Hunt made clear his strong preference for "the Old English Domestic Style": he preferred it "to every other [style], as admitting of greater variety of form and outline, and as being better suited to the scenery of this Country, than the Greek Temple or Italian Villa."[1] Hunt's enthusiastic endorsement of the style followed by two years Peter Frederick Robinson's commentary on many of its picturesque attributes, and Hunt's designs clearly resemble Robinson's in both composition and ornament.[2] Also like Robinson, Hunt directed his designs "to those who have the taste to encourage a style which may be said to be indigenous to this soil, and the liberality to make comfortable provision for their dependents." But unlike Robinson, Hunt illustrated his designs "as they would appear when left by the workmen,—the outline new and unbroken; no attempt having been made to give them that pictorial effect which they could only acquire by time, and the growth of ivy, roses or other embellishing plants."

Following the "Address" there are designs for ten residences, each shown in one lithographed view and described briefly on one leaf of letterpress. The designs include two gate lodges, dwellings for a gamekeeper and under gamekeeper, a house for a bailiff or forester, a double cottage, a hunting box, an entrance lodge, and a gentleman's house. Four additional plates include plans for these dwellings, and an "Appendix" (four leaves) contains cost estimates for the first nine designs.[3]

All the designs are highly picturesque, making effective use of thatch roofs, half-timbering, hipped gables, bargeboarding, projecting bays and porches, Tudor windows and drip moldings, and ornamented chimneys.

The smallest design (Plate II) is a hut for an under gamekeeper, estimated to cost £240. The single story contains just a "lobby" or porch, a living room, a bedroom, and a shed. The elevation includes two slightly projecting window bays flanking the central porch and doorway, and rustic tree-trunk supports for the overhanging thatch roof at each end. One of the largest designs is the hunting box (Plate VIII), estimated to cost £820. The ground-floor plan includes an entrance hall, library, dining room, kitchen, and pantry. The chamber floor includes five bedrooms and a water closet. The elevation includes some exposed timber framing, elaborate barge-boards, decorative chimneys and finials, ornamental columns and bosses, and Tudor windows. Hunt's least successful design, not included until the third edition, also was his largest: "a House very recently erected in Sussex, for a sum not exceeding £4,500."[4] The ground-floor plan includes a library, dining room, drawing room, entrance hall, butler's room, house-keeper's room, and kitchen. Absent here are the innovative juxtapositions of picturesque forms that make his smaller designs so successful. Instead the principal gables are all the same height and nearly the same width, the facade is articulated only by shallow projections and recesses, and there is much less ornamental detail; instead of being picturesque, the facade is uniform, regular, and dull.

1. Quotations are from the 1833 edition, on which all of this commentary is based.

2. Robinson analyzed the picturesque characteristics of a "style which once adorned the fair landscape scenery" of England, while Hunt referred precisely to the Old English style. See Robinson, *Rural Architecture* (1823; *q.v.*).

3. In the first and second editions there are only nine designs. The gentleman's house, shown in a view on Plate 13 and in plan on an unmarked plate, and described on one leaf of letterpress, appeared first in the 1833 edition.

4. Colvin (1978), p. 439, identifies this as Danehurst, near Danehill, Sussex (1828).

HUNT, Thomas Frederick (ca. 1791–1831)
A series of designs for gate lodges.

See his Half a dozen hints, *Entry 156.*

The imperial magazine.

See Entry 476.

157.1
JACKSON, John George (ca. 1798–ca. 1852)
Number [*blank; 1 inserted in pen*] designs for villas, on a moderate scale of expense; adapted to the vicinity of the metropolis, or large towns. By J. G. Jackson. The work will be completed in six numbers, each containing ground and chamber plans, elevations, and perspective views.

London: Printed for James Carpenter and Son, 1828 [i.e., 1827–1829].

[*Numbers I through V:*] 6 printed leaves, 25 pls.

28.3 × 21.0 cm

Bodl.

157.2

Designs for villas. By J. G. Jackson.

London: Printed for James Carpenter and Son, 1829.

7 printed leaves, 30 pls.

27.6 × 21.7 cm

V&A

The Bodleian Library copy is fronted by a title page for the first Number, and contains text and plates for Numbers 1 through 5. The copy at the Victoria and Albert Museum has a lithographed title page dated 1829, an "Address" (one leaf, verso blank), and text and plates for Numbers 1 through 6. The discussion below is based on examination of the 1829 edition.

In the Address Jackson explained that his object was to design "a comfortable Villa on the most moderate scale, and adapted to the vicinity of a City or Metropolis." Accordingly he incorporated only three "principal apartments" in each design, plus "the utmost accommodation in sleeping rooms" and the necessary offices. He adopted the "Grecian and Italian styles" because they were best suited to the "light and cheerful features" of a villa. In contrast the Old English style, with its bay windows, spacious halls, and "sombre dignity," was more appropriate for "mansions." For landscaping, a mansion would need terraces, gardens, groves of trees, oak-lined avenues, or an extensive park with trees and deer, while a villa required only "elegance of appearance, and a compact arrangement"—a well-dressed lawn, a flower garden, and a "Shrubbery Walk," set within an estate of a "few acres."

The six leaves of text contain descriptions of each design, including remarks on the use and decoration of individual rooms, possible modifications to some designs, and visual relationships within individual elevations. The descriptions of two designs mention suitable locations: Number 3, composed of two wings flanking a central tower, was "calculated for a site much exposed to the Sun, and surrounded by a small Pleasure Ground"; Number 5, an irregular Italianate design with a four-story octagonal tower at one corner, was "adapted for a bold and rocky country."

Each design is illustrated in five plates: a basement plan, a ground-floor plan, a chamber-floor plan, an elevation, and a perspective view. The three "principal rooms" on the ground floor of each design are the drawing room, dining or eating room, and library. In addition there is a large "Hall" on the ground floor of Designs 2 through 6. In the largest design (Number 6) the drawing room is 30 feet by 20 feet, and the smallest room on the ground floor is the library (20 feet by 20 feet). Upstairs there are three bedrooms and three dressing rooms. The two facades shown are both symmetrical, three or five windows wide, and two stories high, plus an attic story for servants' rooms. On each facade there is a two-story tetrastyle Corinthian portico. A circular lantern above the roof lights the hall on the ground floor. Pilasters at the corners of the facades support a full entablature above the chamber story, and windows on the ground floor are embellished with architraves and entablatures. In the smallest design (Number 1) the drawing room and dining room each measure 24 feet by 18 feet, and the library is 20 feet by 16 feet. Upstairs there are four bedrooms and two dressing rooms. The elevations are asymmetrical, two stories high and three or six openings wide. The exterior is embellished with a tile roof, an octagonal lantern, pediments, ornamented chimneys, bas-relief sculptures, pilasters, and an iron balcony running along two sides of the ground story.

The remaining designs are likewise articulated with prostyle porticoes, octagonal and square towers, and projecting balconies, all introduced for their picturesque effect. To reinforce this effect each design is shown surrounded by picturesque scenery: winding walks, lawns, shrubs, trees, distant mountains, and even a distant castle.

158.1

JAMESON, George

Thirty three designs, with the orders of architecture, according to Paladio [*sic*]. The mouldings enriched with proper ornaments. Together with observations on each order. By George Jameson, Carver.

Edinburgh: Printed for the author, and sold by him at his house, 1765.

23 pp, 37 pls (incl. frontisp. and dedication).

25.1 × 20.0 cm

V&A

The frontispiece shows "the Author" with a compass, a chisel, a mallet, and other tools of the building trade. Following the title page are an engraved dedication, a letterpress dedication, and a plate showing ornamental moldings and diagrams for constructing flutes, ridges, fillets, and volutes. Facing this plate is a leaf of letterpress titled "Goldman's Volute Described" and giving directions for constructing the volute shown in the adjoining plate. Next follows an address to "Gentleman Operatives, . . . intended to give you some assistance, amidst so many intricacies" (pp. 4–19). Jameson began by discussing the proportions of the orders, contending that "the Antients made use of the module, which is three tens. This law being once established, we shall find, that thirds of a module, threes, squares, and right angled triangles, regulate the whole, observations that have escaped most of our late writers" (p. 4). To support these and other assertions he alluded to the authority of "the Divine Architect" and such historical precedents as the Tabernacle of Moses and Solomon's Temple (pp. 4–5).[1] In a general discussion of the parts of an order he relied on Palladio, who "at present, in his proportions, is generally received, and mostly approven of" (p. 6). The greatest part of the text consists of speculation on the origin of the Doric, Ionic, Corinthian, and "Composed or Roman" orders, and analysis of their individual parts and proportions (pp. 7–17). Jameson also discussed specific instances in which Palladio's account was "defective" (p. 17). Toward the end of the address Jameson explained that he had kept the book small "that it might be in the hands of every mechanick concerned in a building" (p. 18). The letterpress concludes with a list of subscribers (pp. 20–23).

The frontispiece, the engraved dedication, and the plate of moldings and diagrams are marked as Plates 1, 2, and 3. Plates 4 through 8 illustrate the orders. Plates 9 through 37 each depict one design for a house in an elevation and three plans.[2] Most houses have a "lodging storie," a "principal storie," and a "ground storie."[3] The designs are generally three or five windows wide, sometimes with additional one-story ells to either side.[4] Among the smallest is the house in Plate 9, approximately 45 feet wide, with three rooms on the principal floor and three bedrooms above. One of the largest is that in Plate 36, over 100 feet wide, with eight rooms on the principal floor and four bedrooms plus dressing rooms and closets upstairs.

Jameson's book enjoys the distinction of being the first Scottish book of domestic architectural designs to be published.[5] The emphasis on proper proportions for the orders, and on the authority of Palladio, reflect the steady progress of Palladianism north from England in the middle of the eighteenth century.[6] Nevertheless the stylistic diversity of Jameson's designs reveals that acceptance of that style was neither immediate nor absolute. A stepped gable appears in Plate 14, and the house in Plate 35 has crenellations and Gothic windows with fleurs-de-lis growing out of the pointed arches. In Plate 36 a Chinese feeling is suggested by latticework in the parapet and by a pediment with concave sides above the front door. Other designs incorporate a more orthodox Palladian vocabulary, including Venetian windows, quoins, and rusticated window and door frames (e.g., Plates 22, 25, 28, 29, 32). Yet Jameson often handled these forms in a mechanical and awkward manner. For example in Plate 32 giant pilasters rise three stories to frame just a single central bay, and in Plate 33 a Venetian window in the middle of the principal floor is balanced uncomfortably over a triangular pediment framing the entrance on the ground floor.

1. Jameson's remarks are reminiscent of John Wood's *Origin of Building* (1741; *q.v.*).

2. There are two exceptions. Plate 18 includes an additional elevation, plan, and two sections for "Plate 9th," i.e., Plate 17. Plate 26 contains an additional elevation and three sections for "Plate 8th"—probably Plate 20.

3. The "ground storie" could be at grade, partly below grade, or entirely below grade.

4. The one exception is Plate 37, a double house six windows wide.

5. The illustrations for William Adam's *Vitruvius Scotius* (*q.v.*) were engraved and printed much earlier, but were not published until the early nineteenth century.

6. See Summerson (1969), pp. 224–225.

159.1 ‡
[JEWITT, Arthur (1772–1852)]
The hand-book of practical perspective, for the use of artists in general.

London: Robert Tyas, 1840.

xi pp, 1 printed leaf, 78 pp, frontisp. + 22 pls [*frontisp. wanting in this copy*].

12°

Reference: Microfilm supplied by The British Library.

159.2

———

Hand-book of practical perspective, containing the principles and practice of perspective, for the use of beginners and artists in general, giving ample directions for drawing any object in perspective.

London: James Cornish; Liverpool; and Dublin, 1847.

xii + 78 pp, 23 pls.

13.7 × 8.9 cm

BL

159.3

———

———

London: James Cornish & Sons; Liverpool; and Dublin, [n.d.].

xi + 78 pp, 23 pls.

13.7 × 8.7 cm

MH

The preliminaries consist of a one-page table of contents, a Preface (pp. vi–xi), and a one-page list of "Corrections, &c." necessitated by the substitution of a frontispiece other than the one originally planned.[1] In the Preface Jewitt complained that previous treatises were "too high priced for . . . humble aspirants," overly concerned with abstruse theory and "profitless demonstration," and often written more for the sake of showing the *"author's learning"* than for instruction. Even well-written treatises such as those by Ferguson or Priestley[2] were of little use to those who wanted to pursue "pictorial" subjects (p. viii). The remainder of the Preface is devoted to a description of the frontispiece and advice to beginners.

The first 14 pages of text contain definitions and a table of tangents and secants. Instructions for preparing the drawing board are provided on pages 15 through 17. The remainder of the text is a series of problems and explanations: how to locate a point, and how to draw lines, a square, an octagon, a hexagon, a pentagon, circles, a "small square building," houses, an octagonal obelisk, and the arch of a bridge. The plates consist of figures illustrating each problem. The "small square building" that is the subject of problem 11 is two stories high, with a dovecot or poultry house on the upper floor, and an area for storing carts or other items below. Problems 12 through 16 involve houses, all of which are drawn in outline. Those in Problems 12 and 14 are gable roofed, two stories high, and five openings wide. There are two gable-roofed houses without window or door openings in Problem 13, and the house in Problem 15, also without openings, has a hipped roof. The house in Problem 16 is more complex: the central portion has a door and two windows on the ground story, and a dormer with lattice windows above; to either side are one-story ells, each with a door and one with a lattice window.

1. This discussion is based on examination of the 1840 edition.

2. See James Ferguson, *The Art of Drawing in Perspective* (1775; *q.v.*), and Joseph Priestley, *A Familiar Introduction to the Theory and Practice of Perspective* (London, 1770).

160.1

JOHNSON, William Moore, and EXLEY, Thomas

The imperial encyclopaedia; or, dictionary of the sciences and arts; comprehending also the whole circle of miscellaneous literature. In this work all the sciences are digested in a systematic form, and exhibited according to the present highly improved state of knowledge; and every term of art amply explained in alphabetical order. The whole including all the modern discoveries in astronomy, chemistry, electricity, galvanism, geography, domestic and political oeconomy, &c. &c. &c. with a general view of all empires, kingdoms, states, countries, mountains, seas, rivers, lakes, &c. &c. and a concise account of patriarchs, prophets, apostles, philosophers, poets, painters, authors and their works, heroes, lawyers, and statesmen, with every other topic of information essential to a work of this nature. By the Rev. W. M. Johnson, A.M. . . . and Thomas Exley, A.M. . . . In four volumes. Vol. I [*or* II, *or* III, *or* IV].

London: Printed by and for J. and J. Cundee; and sold by Sherwood, Neely, and Jones, [1812].

Art. "Architecture," I, 206–217; pls. 11–14.
Art. "Levelling," III, 263–264; pl. 97.
Art. "Perspective," IV, 264–272; pls. 139–141.

26.5 × 21.3 cm

ICU

The date assigned here is that at the end of the Preface (I, xiv). Robert Collison, in *Encyclopaedias: Their History throughout the Ages* (New York: Hafner, 1966), p. 176, offers the date 1809–1814.

The article on "Architecture" begins with a history of the subject, from the origin of building through Egyptian, Greek, Roman, Gothic, and Renaissance styles. A discussion of "General Principles" includes brief remarks on solidity, convenience, beauty, disposition, proportion, decorum, and economy, plus lengthier commentary on utility, ornament, intrinsic and relative beauty, proportion, and siting. The greatest portion of the article is devoted to the five orders and related topics, including intercolumniations, arches, pilasters, attics, Persians, caryatids, termini, pediments, gates, doors, piers, niches, statues, chimneypieces, staircases, balustrades, roofs, and ceilings. A final page is devoted to the construction of foundations, walls, chimneys, roofs, and floors. Plate 11 includes several illustrations borrowed from Sir William Chambers's *Treatise* (1759; *q.v.*), including designs for two gates and four piers, a depiction of the "Origin of the Corinthian Capital," and three "Antient" or primitive huts—one conical, one with a flat trabeated roof, and one with a gable roof supported by primitive Doric columns. This plate also contains illustrations of "Saxon" or Romanesque columns, "Saxon Capitals," and Gothic arches that appeared previously in the third edition of the *Encyclopaedia Britannica* (1797; *q.v.*). Plates 12 and 14 depict the five orders, and Plate 13 illustrates arches, moldings, a Persian, a caryatid, a term, a diagram of a volute, and "Nicomedes Instrument for diminishing Columns."

The illustrations to the article on "Levelling" appear on Plate 97. These include a small figure of a house, two stories high and three windows wide, ornamented only by a stringcourse across the facade.

Among the illustrations to the article on "Perspective" are two outline drawings of houses, each two stories high and three windows wide, seen in perspective (Plate 140, Figs. 21 and 22). The facade of the first house is parallel to the picture plane, and the facade of the second is oblique to the picture plane. These two figures appeared earlier in George Gregory's *Dictionary* (1806–1807; *q.v.*).

161.1
JONES, Edward
Athenian; or, Grecian villas: being a series of original designs for villas, or country residences: to exemplify in effect its applicability to domestic edifices of this country, and its adaptation in plan to the modern arrangement of their usual apartments. By Edward Jones, Architect.

London: Printed for the author. Sold by J. Weale, Taylor's Architectural Library; J. Williams, Library of the Fine Arts; and R. Akermann & Co. T. R. Drury, Printer, 1835.

viii pp, 3 printed leaves, 6 pls.

54.6 × 39.4 cm

Bodl.

The preliminaries consist of a dedication and a preface. In the latter (pp. v–viii) there is lavish praise for the cities of antiquity, "with their suburbs and villas unfolding to the eye grandeur and perfection in Architecture, and to the reflecting mind the result of wisdom and genius." Jones suggested that of all ancient peoples none achieved the "pre-eminence in purity, and chasteness of style," or equaled "that copiously rich, refined, and elegant taste and feeling" found among the citizens of Athens. He praised the "harmony and perfection" of their buildings, qualities heightened by locations such as a "picturesque eminence," a "fertile valley," or "delightful banks of the meandering river" (p. v). For these reasons Jones adopted the style of the "Architecture of Athens" for his own designs. He admitted that little archaeological evidence of Greek dwellings remained, but felt confident in his understanding of the Athenian style based on evidence in antique bas reliefs, writings of Classical authors, and the remains of Herculaneum and Pompeii. These Roman remains, he explained, did not have the "purity and chasteness" of Greek architecture, but they did have "much of the simplicity and character" of Greek design. At the end of the preface Jones turned to the "beautifully enriched landscape and picturesque scenery of the British Islands," which he found perfectly suited to the "chasteness, simplicity, and grandeur of Grecian Architecture," the style best suited to producing "the most pictorial effect" (p. viii).

The six plates depict three designs for villas. Each is shown in a ground-floor plan, a chamber-floor plan, and a view, and described in one leaf of letterpress. The first design, estimated to cost £800, has an entrance hall, drawing room, dining room, library, butler's room, and water closet on the ground floor; the chamber floor contains five bedrooms and a dressing room. The elevation is two stories high and 40 feet wide, embellished with porticoes fronting the entrance and the window directly above, plus palmettes and other ornamental motifs. The second design has an entrance hall, library, dining room, study, three drawing rooms, an "Anti Drawing Room," a billiard room, a butler's room, and a water closet on the ground floor, plus six bedrooms, a water closet, a bathroom, and two dressing rooms upstairs. Jones estimated the cost at £2,200. The facade is two stories high and 88 feet wide, ornamented with palmettes, and divided by engaged pedimented tetrastyle porticoes into a composition of multiple temple fronts, emphasizing the underlying cubic geometry. The plan of the final design, estimated to cost £2,800, is similar to the second design in number and type of rooms shown. The facade is two stories high and nine openings wide; a prostyle tetrastyle portico fronting the entrance is flanked by two semicircular bows, which are complemented by a semicircular portico on the side of the house and a circular conservatory to the rear. Three engaged porticoes visible on the upper story suggest multiple temple fronts. The perspective views of all three designs incorporate approach drives, entrance gates, and dramatic scenery, including lawns, shrubs, trees, meadows, woods, hills, and mountains.

162.1
JONES, Richard (ca. 1756–1826)
Every builder his own surveyor, or, the builder's vade-mecum: containing, in Part I. the practice of surveying, measuring, & valuing buildings in the north of England, viz. Lancashire, part of Yorkshire, Cheshire, Derbyshire, &c.; the mode of making specifications and estimates for new buildings; the masters' prices for materials and labour and for labour only; sawyers' prices; &c. &c. &c. In Part II. the principles of surveying and valuing buildings in the south of England, viz.—in London, Bath, Bristol, Gloucester, &c. (which are very different from those in the north); including the masters' prices of materials and labour, journeymen's task-work prices, &c. &c. &c. The whole written to enable masters and journeymen, in every branch, to measure and value their own work. By Richard Jones, Builder and Surveyor.

London: Printed for the author; published by James Carpenter; Gale and Curtis; and J. Taylor, 1809.

[vi] + 160 pp, frontisp. + 1 pl.

19.7 × 12.7 cm

CtY-BA

To obviate "frequent disputes between the Builder and his Employer" arising from builders' inability to estimate the cost of their work accurately, Jones offered here "the result of above Thirty Years' experience, in an extensive practice, both as Builder and Surveyor, in the North as well as the South of England." He proposed "to give both to the Northern and Southern builder, not only every information requisite to enable him to estimate Buildings *when finished*, but likewise (which must be highly desirable) to specify the value of *designed Edifices*, by plain and simple rules" (Preface).

Jones also noted in the Preface that the practice of surveying and valuing in the North "differs very essentially" from that in the South. Thus the text is divided into separate sections for North (pp. 3–92) and South (pp. 95–149). The section on northern practice begins with instruction in measuring various types of artisans' work (e.g., carpentry, plumbing), followed by specifications for a house shown in the frontispiece and a table of dimensions based on those specifications. The section concludes with lists of prices for artisans' work and labor as of 1807. The section on southern practice includes instruction in measuring artisans' work and a list of prices for artisans' work and labor as of 1808. There are no specifications or dimensions given for any example.

The subject of the frontispiece is a "Country House in the North of England," three stories high and five windows wide, with four rooms on the principal floor. The facade is modestly ornamented with a cornice, stringcourses, ornamental surrounds for two windows, plus sidelights and a fanlight for the front door. The other plate is bound at the beginning of Part II, and shows a "Ground Plan & Elevation of a Town House in the South of England," four stories high and three windows wide. The facade includes a Regency-style balcony at the level of the principal floor.

163.1
JONES, William (–1757)
The gentlemens or builders companion containing variety of usefull designs for doors, gateways, peers, pavilions, temples, chimney-pieces, and other decorations by Wm. Jones Archt. Part the first illustrated with 31 copper= plates neatly engrav'd.

[London?: N. pub., n.d. (ca. 1735?)].

3 leaves, 31 pls (including frontispiece and one duplicate).

22.9 × 17.8 cm

CtY-BA

163.2

The gentlemens or builders companion containing variety of usefull designs for doors, gateways, peers, pavilions, temples, chimney-pieces, slab tables, pier glasses, or tabernacle frames, ceiling peices, &c. Explained on copper= plates by Wm. Jones Architect.

London: Printed for the author, and sold at his house, 1739.

6 leaves, 60 pls (on 56 leaves: pls. 53/54, 55/56, 57/58, and 59/60 are printed on single leaves).

24.1 × 18.4 cm

NNC

William Jones was a minor Palladian architect whose principal executed work was the Rotunda in Ranelagh Gardens. He contributed 26 "Designs for Frontispieces" to James Smith's *Specimen of Antient Carpentry* (1736), and later included these designs in *The Gentlemens or Builders Companion*.[1]

The 1739 edition is fronted by an engraved title page, with the title flanked by elevations and plans of niches with statues. The next six leaves, also engraved, contain a table of contents. There is no letterpress.

Plates 1–4 and 6–9 depict frontispieces for doors, and Plates 5, 10, and 11 show garden gateways. Plates 12 and 13 illustrate piers. Plates 14 through 20 include designs for garden structures: a "Garden Seat," a "Square Open Temple to be Erected in the Center of four Walks in a Garden," an "Octangular Pavillion," two "Circular Pavillions," an "Open Temple," and a "Square Room Design'd at the end of a middle walk to a Garden." One of the more elaborate designs is the domed "Circular Pavillion" (Plate 17), 20 feet in diameter, with engaged columns and pediments framing each of the four entrances, and niches with busts and statues in the exterior walls. Equally ornamented is the "Square Room" in Plate 20, 16 feet square in plan, with four engaged Ionic columns on the facade and niches flanking the entrance. The other garden structures are much plainer. Plates 21–26 and 33–40 illustrate designs for chimneypieces, Plates 27–32 depict table frames, Plates 41–50 include frames for pier glasses and "tabernacles," and Plates 51–60 show designs for ceilings.

1. Colvin (1978), p. 476; see also p. 758.

164.1
JOPLING, Joseph

The practice of isometrical perspective. By Joseph Jopling, Architect.

London: Published for the author. Sold by M. Salmon; Longman and Co.; Priestly and Weale; William Elliot, Instrument-Maker; and by all other booksellers and instrument-makers, [1833?].

iv + 60 pp, 1 pl.

21.0 × 24.0 cm

CtY

164.2

————

————

Second edition.

London: M Taylor. (Nephew and successor to the late Josiah Taylor), 1839.

96 pp, 3 pls.

22.2 × 14.0 cm

ICJ

164.3

———
———

A new edition, improved.

London: M Taylor. (Nephew and successor to the late Josiah Taylor), 1842.

96 pp, 3 pls.

21.0 × 14.0 cm

CtY

164.4

———
———

A new edition, improved.

London: M. Taylor. (Nephew and successor to the late Josiah Taylor), [n.d.].

96 pp, 3 pls.

21.0 × 12.7 cm

NWM

164.5 †

———

Practice of isometrical perspective, new edition.

London: M. Taylor, 1861.

8°

Reference: ECB

The first edition is dated [1833?] for two reasons: the Preface is dated 1833, and the first part of the text ("To be completed in Four Parts") was reviewed that year in the *Mechanics' Magazine* (XIX:520 [27 July 1833], 289–295). This edition includes 170 numbered figures, of which Fig. 170 is the only one printed on a separate, folding leaf. The second edition includes 177 numbered figures, including three plates numbered I, 2, and 3. Plate 3, described as Fig. 177 in the text, was originally Fig. 170 in the first edition, and still bears the inscription "Fig. 170." There is also a new Fig. 170 on text page 89. Later editions retain the format of the second edition.

Following brief prefaces to the first and second editions (1842, pp. 3–6) the text consists of demonstrations and explanations of the use of isometric perspective in representing three-dimensional geometric objects. The text figures consist primarily of geometric objects shown in isometric perspective, and a few explanatory diagrams. Plate I (Fig. 174) is a cutaway view of a house showing the full ground-floor plan, with rooms divided by "walls and partitions a foot or two" high (1842, p. 94). Plate 2 (Fig. 175) is a view of a fluted column and pedestal. Plate 3 (Fig. 177) is an isometric view of "a farm-house and outbuildings" (1842, p. 95), which previously appeared in Jopling's edition of Waistell's *Designs for Agricultural Buildings* (1826; *q.v.*). The house is two stories high and three windows wide, with lower two-story ells on each side. Shallow relieving arches surround the two ground-floor windows, and a modest architrave and entablature frame the door. The attached farm buildings form a large enclosed quadrangle to the rear.

KENT, I. J.

See LOUDON, **John Claudius, ed.,** The architectural magazine, *Entry 182.*

165.1
KENT, Nathaniel (1737–1810)
Hints to gentlemen of landed property. By Nathaniel Kent, of Fulham.

London: Printed for J. Dodsley, 1775.

vii + 268 pp, 10 pls.

22.2 × 14.0 cm

MH

165.2

————

————

The second edition.

London: Printed for J. Dodsley, 1776.

vii + 283 pp, 10 pls.

21.0 × 12.7 cm

MBAt

165.3

————

Hints to gentlemen of landed property. To which are now first added, supplementary hints. By Nathaniel Kent, of Fulham. A new edition.

London: Printed for J. Dodsley, 1793.

vii + 286 pp, 10 pls.

21.6 × 13.3 cm

Hints to gentlemen of landed property. To which are added supplementary hints. By Nathaniel Kent, of Fulham. A new edition.

London: Printed for G. Nicol, J. Walker, Longman and Rees, and Cadell Jun. and Davies, 1799.

vii + 286 pp, 10 pls.

21.0 × 12.7 cm

MH

Kent cautioned the reader "not to expect anything systematical in . . . the following Remarks," since they were "such as have arisen in the course of a three years residence, and observation in the Austrian Netherlands, and an extensive practice since in the superintendance, and care, of several large estates, in different parts of England" (1775, p. iii). He noted that practical experience was the source of all his observations: "Nothing is borrowed from books, or built upon hearsay-authority." Rather, he offered "chiefly a description of such practical points of Husbandry as may be adopted in many parts of England to great advantage" (1775, pp. iii–iv).

This is principally a treatise on agricultural improvement, and the text covers such matters as soil use, drainage, grass planting, pasture land, husbandry, horticulture, and timber management. But Kent also believed that attention to the welfare of agricultural laboreres would promote agricultural improvement, and so included chapters on modes of land tenure, "the great importance of Cottages," and means for relieving "the Distress of the Poor" (1775 edition).

In 1747 Daniel Garret was the first to publish a collection of designs for farm houses (q.v.). These were small but architecturally correct designs for farm buildings, presumably intended as appendages to larger Palladian estates. Kent devoted 31 pages to the subject of cottages, and was the first to discuss them from an agricultural, not an architectural or picturesque point of view. "The labourer is one of the most valuable members of society," he wrote (1775, p. 228). Arguing on economic grounds, Kent noted that estates are "of no economic value without hands to cultivate them." Therefore "there is certainly no object so highly deserving the country gentleman's attention" as provision for the laborer's welfare (1775, p. 228). Cottages as currently constructed were shabby, drafty, and cramped, entirely destructive of "the most beneficial race of people we have" (1775, pp. 229–230). To improve the cottagers' living conditions and thereby the landowner's agricultural production, Kent offered his own hints and instructions for constructing better cottages. These include remarks on site, materials, construction, and costs. He suggested that in every parish gentlemen of "power and influence" should "consider themselves as guardians of the poor, and attend to their accomodation" for philanthropic as well as economic reasons (1775, pp. 239–240). Kent also offered a scheme whereby a landlord could lease cottages to "industrious labourers" at less than rack rent, but still preserve "the value of all other parts of his estate, by keeping up a proper number of inhabitants" (1775, pp. 241–242).

Two of the ten plates in this book illustrate drainage systems. The remaining eight, showing four designs for double cottages, are accompanied by letterpress cost estimates for labor and materials (pp. 247–258). Two designs are of the "smallest size" and two are of the "largest size." All are shown in elevation, ground-floor plan, and chamber-floor plan. Kent indicated that one design of each size was to be executed in brick, and provided "Studd Work" elevations for the others. The "smallest" designs have a principal room, "celler," and pantry on the ground floor, plus two chambers above. The "largest" designs are arranged in a nearly identical manner, with only slight variations in room size. The principal rooms in the "largest" and "smallest" studwork cottages, for example, are all 13 feet square. Nor is the difference in price substantial: the "largest" pair costs £133, while the "smallest" costs £116. All designs are illustrated in plain outline, with no suggestion of stylistic ornament.

Kent advanced the cause of agricultural improvement by drawing on personal experience instead of study and speculation. Also he was the first to argue that cottage improvement could contribute to the economic development of an estate, and then support his argument with plans and specifications for model cottages. In both these respects his book was an important precedent for the series of county agricultural surveys prepared for the Board of Agriculture between 1793 and 1815 (q.v.). The Board, like Kent, aimed to improve British agriculture by publishing practical solutions, gathered from around the country, to common agricultural problems and needs.[1]

1. For remarks on Kent in the context of agricultural improvement, see John Martin Robinson, *Georgian Model Farms: A Study of Decorative and Model Farm Buildings in the Age of Improvement, 1700–1846* (Oxford: Clarendon Press, 1983) pp. 15, 20, 30–31, 81, 109, 144.

166.1
KENT, William (1684–1748)
The designs of Inigo Jones, consisting of plans and elevations for publick and private buildings. Publish'd by William Kent, with some additional designs. The first [*or* second] volume.

[London: William Kent], 1727.

[*Volume I:*] 6 printed leaves, frontisp. + 73 pls.

[*Volume II:*] 3 printed leaves, 63 pls.

43.2 × 27.9 cm

MH

166.2

The designs of Inigo Jones, consisting of plans and elevations for public and private buildings. Published by William Kent, with some additional designs.

London: Printed for Benjamin White, 1770.

[*Volume I:*] 7 printed leaves (including a title page in French), frontisp. + 1 + 73 pls.

[*Volume II:*] 7 printed leaves (including a title page in French), 65 pls.

55.2 × 37.5 cm

MB

166.3

———————

London: Printed for J. B. Nichols and Son, 1835.

[*Volume I:*] 3 printed leaves, frontisp. + 1 + 73 pls.

[*Volume II:*] 3 printed leaves, 65 pls.

52.5 × 35.5 cm

MBAt

Since the title page refers to William Kent only as the publisher of this posthumous collection of Inigo Jones's work, the book frequently is cataloged under Jones's name. Therefore it is occasionally confused with another collection of Jones's designs, different in format and content, published by John Vardy in 1744 (*q.v.*). Two important bibliographies indicate editions of Kent's *Designs* in 1785 and 1825, but these citations apparently are misprints.[1]

The 1770 edition includes additional material in each volume: a French title page and an explanation of the plates in French. An added plate, numbered 1*, appears in the editions of 1770 and 1835, and shows a design for Whitehall Palace. Plate 64, also added in 1770 and 1835, shows the Palladian design by Henry Flitcroft for Wentworth Woodhouse, in Yorkshire.

In 1726 Giacomo Leoni added several of his own designs to his illustrated English translation of Alberti's *Dieci Libri*.[2] Leoni apparently expected to raise his own reputation by association with this master of the Italian Renaissance. One year later Kent followed the example: he included several of his designs in this collection of work by Inigo Jones, who had become a principal source of inspiration for architects of the Palladian Revival. Compared to Leoni's book, Kent's was far more calculated to impress: it includes a list of subscribers nine times longer, with 18 dukes and 21 earls, and a dedication to the king. The frontispiece shows Britannia holding an architectural plan, and accompanied by a bust of Inigo Jones. This was a determined effort, therefore, to establish the excellence of the English architectural heritage, and Kent placed himself in the center of the enterprise.

Kent noted that his illustrations of Jones's work were based on original drawings by Jones and by John Webb then in the possession of Kent's patron, the Earl of Burlington ("Advertisement," recto). Nearly three-fourths of the plates in the first volume are plans, elevations, sections, and details of Whitehall Palace. Other plates include designs by Jones for windows, doors, and interior furnishings. Plates 70 through 73 illustrate designs for Chiswick House by Burlington. Plate 59 includes two designs for "Rustic-Gates" by Burlington. Plates 63 through 65 show five chimneypieces by Kent, and Plates 67 through 69 show five designs for room interiors and one ceiling design by Kent. The second volume includes 47 plates illustrating 23 domestic designs ascribed to Jones, ranging in size from a two-story country house 55 feet wide, with farmyard and farm buildings attached (Plate 1), to a palace approximately 200 feet wide (Plates 37 through 43). Plates 10 through 12 show two house designs by Burlington. The first is two stories high and nine windows wide, and has a heavily rusticated ground story. The second is three stories high and seven windows wide, with an open loggia on the ground level. Plates 51 through 53 illustrate Burlington's design for the dormitory of the Westminster School. Plates 54 through 56 show the plan and elevation of Jones's portico for Old St. Paul's Cathedral. The final seven plates are devoted to a plan, elevation, and sections of Palladio's church of S. Giorgio in Venice.

1. Helen Park, *A List of Architectural Books Available in America before the Revolution* (Los Angeles: Hennessey & Ingalls, 1973), and Laurence Hall Fowler and Elizabeth Baer, comps., *The Fowler Architectural Collection* (Baltimore: The Evergreen House Foundation, 1961).

2. The first edition of Alberti's work appeared in 1485. See also the entry for Leoni, *Some Designs for Buildings both Publick and Private*.

167.1

KIRBY, John Joshua (1716–1774)

Dr. Brook Taylor's method of perspective made easy, both in theory and practice. In two books. Being an attempt to make the art of perspective easy and familiar; to adapt it intirely to the arts of design; and to make it an entertaining study to any gentleman who shall chuse so polite an amusement. By Joshua Kirby, Painter. Illustrated with fifty copper plates; most of which are engrav'd by the author. Book I.

Ipswich: Printed by W. Craighton, for the author; and sold by him in Ipswich: and in London, by J. Swan; F. Noble; and J. Noble, 1754.

[*Book I:*] [ii] + xvi + iv + [ii] + 78 pp, frontisp. + 22 pls.

[*Book II:*] title page for Book II (which differs from that for Book I), 2 printed leaves, 5–84 + [xi] pp, 27 pls [*pl. XVIII is wanting in this copy*], 2 pls.

25.4 × 20.3 cm

CtY-BA

167.2

Dr. Brook Taylor's method of perspective ⟨ . . . as 1754 . . . ⟩ author. The second edition.

Ipswich: Printed by W. Craighton, for the author. Sold by the author, London; and also by J. and P. Knapton; T. Osborn and Co.; T. and T. Longman; R. and J. Dodsley; W. Meadows; W. Owen; J. Swan; F. Noble; and J. Noble. At Cambridge, by W. Thurlbourn; at Oxford, by J. Green, Engraver; at Norwich, by J. Gleed; and at Ipswich, by W. Craighton, 1755.

[*Book I:*] [ii] + iv + xvi + 78 pp, frontisp. + 22 pls.

[*Book II:*] title page for Book II (which differs from that for Book I), 2 printed leaves, 5–84 + [xi] + [i] pp, 27 + 2 pls.

26.0 × 19.7 cm

CtY-BA

167.3

Dr. Brook Taylor's method of perspective made easy; both in theory and practice: in two books. ⟨ . . . as 1754 . . . ⟩ Kirby, Designer in perspective to their Majesties. Illustrated with many copper-plates, correctly engraved under the author's inspection. The third edition, with several additions and improvements. Book I.

London: Printed for the author, by Mess. Francklin and Bunce: and sold by T. Payne; J. Dodsley; T. Longman; R. Horsefield; T. Davies; and J. Robson, 1765.

[*Book I:*]

xvi + 104 pp, frontisp.

25.9 × 20.7 cm

[*Book II:*]

title page for Book II (which differs from that for Book I), xii + 95 pp.

25.9 × 20.7 cm

[*Plate volume, without title page:*]

14 + 21 pls.

45.7 × 31.8 cm

MH

Dr. Brook Taylor's method of perspective made easy; both in theory and practice: in two books. ⟨ . . . as 1754 . . . ⟩ Kirby, Designer in perspective to their Majesties. . . . Illustrated with many copper-plates, correctly engraved under the author's inspection. The third edition, with several additions and improvements. Book I.

London: Printed for the author: and sold by T. Payne; T. Longman; J. Wilkie; T. Davies; Brotherton and Sewell; and I. Taylor, 1768.

[*Book I:*] viii + ix*–x* + ix–x + 69 pp, 14 pls.

[*Book II:*] title page for Book II (which differs from that for Book I), viii + 66 pp, 21 pls.

56.5 × 39.4 cm

CtY

Linear Perspective (1715) and *New Principles of Linear Perspective* (1719) by Brook Taylor, a respected mathematician and fellow of the Royal Society, were among the most important theoretical works on perspective published in the eighteenth and early nineteenth centuries.[1] In 1754 John Joshua Kirby, a landscapist and architectural draughtsman, prepared this explanation and adaptation of Taylor's method for "the Arts of Design." Kirby dedicated Book I to William Hogarth, who in turn provided an engraved frontispiece captioned "Whoever makes a Design without the Knowledge of Perspective will be liable to such Absurdities as are shewn in this Frontispiece." The subject of the frontispiece is a country landscape with a river, a bridge, a church, boats, sheep, fishermen, houses, and other subjects all in impossible perspective relationships. The second book is dedicated "To the Academy of Painting, Sculpture, Architecture &c. in London." The list of subscribers includes 337 names, with only 13 identified as peers, and 94 listed as architects, painters, engravers, "mathematical instrument makers," carvers, and other artists and artisans.[2]

In the Preface Kirby indicated that his intention was "to steer between the abstruse mathematical Reasoning of some, and the tedious and false Explications of others; and from thence to produce a System of Perspective upon certain and simple Principles, easy to be understood and applied to Practice" (1755, p. i). The "Principles" were those of Dr. Brook Taylor, which Kirby hoped to make "of more universal Use" (1755, p. ii). To this end Kirby divided his treatise into "two Books; the first I have called A compleat System of Perspective, which contains the Theory and its Application to Practice; and the second, The Practice of Perspective, which contains the practical Part only," intended for those lacking "Time or Capacity to go through the theoretical Part" (1755, p. iii). The first book contains seven chapters, concerning drawing instruments and geometry, the eye and light, the theory of perspective, parallel and inclined pictures, shadows, the size of the picture and the position of the eye relative to it, and aerial perspective, chiaroscuro, and keeping. The first chapter of the second book is a general introduction with definitions and axioms. Subsequent chapters treat objects lying on the ground, perpendicular to the ground, and "inclined to the ground," vanishing points and lines, architectural figures, "Horizontal Perspective," shadows, "Scenography," and methods of perspective construction described by Vignola, Marolois, Vredeman de Vriese, "The Jesuit," and Andrea Pozzo. An Appendix ([xi] pp, 2 pls) includes explanations and addenda to matters discussed in the text.

Most of the plates in Parts I and II are geometric figures and diagrams. In accord with his wish to "adapt" perspective "intirely to the Arts of Design," Kirby included a few architectural subjects among his illustrations in Book II. Plates XIII through XV depict bases and capitals. Plate XX shows moldings and Plate XXI depicts domes. Figures 67 and 68 in Plate XVI use a simple, boxy form to demonstrate drawing a house in perspective, and Figure 69 in the same plate shows an unfurnished room interior with a door and two windows on each side wall and a fireplace at the end. Figure 70 in Plate XVII is a landscape scene, with a collection of three-dimensional geometric objects set surrealistically in the foreground, and a modest house with twin gables surrounded by trees and shrubbery in the distance. Figures 71 and 72 in Plate XVIII also are landscape scenes. The first depicts the walled perimeter of Framlingham Castle in Suffolk, and the second, by Thomas Gainsborough, shows a small Gothic church in a rustic setting. These examples are unlike illustrations in contemporary architectural treatises, which seldom depicted buildings in a "natural" scenic context, or even flanked by a few trees or shrubs.[3] Thus Kirby, whose audience included architects, must be understood as one who significantly aided appreciation of the relationship between a building and its picturesque scenic context.[4]

For the edition of 1765 Kirby retained the Hogarth frontispiece, the dedications to Hogarth and the Academy of Painting, and the Preface. In an added "Advertisement" (pp. xiii–xiv) he explained his revisions to the text. In the first book he "found it proper to enlarge the theory of perspective, and to demonstrate this part by a few mathematical notes, and by references to Euclid," and added some "new diagrams." In the second book he "made many additions, and disposed some articles in a different manner." He also "omitted a few figures, and added many others," including "many more practical examples."

All the illustrations for this edition were engraved on new, much larger plates. Among the new illustrations in Book II are several houses, depicted in outline and as geometric solids, in Figures 5 and 6 on Plate VIII, Figures 1–4 on Plate IX, and Figure 5 on Plate XIII. Figures 67–69 of the former edition now appear as Figures 3, 4, and 6 on Plate XIII. A new illustration of a two-story house, two windows wide, appears in Figure 6 on Plate XIV. Plate XVII includes domes and moldings formerly in Plates XX and XXI. The landscape scenes in Plates XVII and XVIII of the 1755 edition have been omitted. Instead, Plates XX and XXI of the 1765 edition contain new landscape scenes, described as "some common examples, intended for the improvement of learners" (II, 95). The subjects include a road through a village, a farm house, a ruined castle, a scene in a village, and Battle Abbey.

1. *Linear Perspective; or a New Method of Representing Justly All Manner of Objects as They Appear to the Eye in All Situations* (London: R. Knaplock, 1715). *New Principles of Linear Perspective; or, the Art of Designing on a Plane the Representations of All Sorts of Objects, in a More General and Simple Method Than Has Been Done Before* (London: R. Knaplock, 1719).

New Principles of Linear Perspective . . . the Third Edition . . . Revised and Corrected by John Colson (London: Printed for John Ward, 1749). *New Principles of Linear Perspective . . . Fourth Edition* (London: J. Taylor, 1811). Authors of early-nineteenth-century perspective treatises repeatedly complained that no truly original treatise had been published since Brook Taylor's; Arthur Parsey, in *The Science of Vision* (1840; *q.v.*), p. vii, suggested Taylor's method had not been challenged or improved upon since its introduction. Taylor, according to DNB, was the first to describe the principle of vanishing points.

2. This count is based on the list in the 1755 edition at Harvard.

3. The only example I have found with a date earlier than Kirby's treatise is William and John Halfpenny's *Country Gentleman's Pocket Companion* (1753; *q.v.*).

4. For developments after Kirby see Christopher Hussey, *The Picturesque* (London: Putnam, 1927), Chapter 6. For architects' remarks on building design as a form of pictorial composition, see Robert Castell, *The Villas of the Ancients* (1728); Robert Morris, *Lectures* (1734–1736) and *Rural Architecture* (1750); and Isaac Ware, *A Complete Body of Architecture* (1756). For theoretical arguments on the relation between landscape and architectural form see John Plaw, *Rural Architecture* (1785); Richard Payne Knight, *The Landscape* (1794); and Humphry Repton, *Sketches and Hints* (1794), *qq.v.*

168.1 ‖
KIRBY, John Joshua (1716–1774)
The perspective of architecture. A work entirely new; deduced from the principles of Dr. Brook Taylor; and performed by two rules only of universal application. Begun by command of His Present Majesty, when Prince of Wales. By Joshua Kirby, Designer in Perspective to His Majesty.

London: Printed for the author, by R. Francklin; and sold by T. Payne; Messrs. Knapton and Horsefield; Messrs. Dodsley; T. Longman; T. Davies; and J. Gretton, 1761.

2 printed leaves, ii + 60 + [ii] pp, frontisp. + engraved dedicatory leaf + 73 pls [*pl. LV is wanting in this copy*].

56.4 × 38.5 cm

Reference: Correspondence and microfilm supplied by the British Architectural Library, Royal Institute of British Architects.

168.2 ‖
——·——
[*Part I:*]

The perspective of architecture. In two parts. A work entirely new; deduced from the principles of Dr. Brook Taylor; and performed by two rules only of universal application. Part the first, contains the description and use of a new instrument called the architectonic sector. Part the second, a new method of drawing the five orders, elegant structures, &c. in perspective. Begun by command of His Present Majesty, when Prince of Wales. By Joshua Kirby, Designer in Perspective to His Majesty.

London: Printed for the author, by R. Francklin; and sold by T. Payne; Messieurs Knapton and Horsefield; Messieurs Dodsley; T. Longman; T. Davies; and J. Gretton, 1761.

2 printed leaves, 82 pp, frontisp. + engraved dedicatory leaf + 25 pls.

[*Part II:*]

The perspective of architecture. A work entirely new; deduced from the principles of Dr. Brook Taylor; and performed by two rules only of universal application. Begun by command of His Present Majesty, when Prince of Wales. By Joshua Kirby, Designer in Perspective to His Majesty. Part the second.

[London]: Printed for the author, [1761].

ii + 60 + [ii] pp, 73 pls.

53.4 × 37.1 cm

Reference: Information supplied by Yale Center for British Art.

The copies at the Royal Institute of British Architects and the Yale Center for British Art differ in two principal respects. First, there are differences in both title and imprint. Second, unlike the RIBA copy, the Yale copy includes a separate title page announcing "two parts," plus letterpress and plates constituting the "first part," which is a treatise on the architectonic sector.[1]

The RIBA copy includes a frontispiece, title page, engraved dedication to the king, Preface (two leaves), Introduction (pp. i–ii), text (pp. 1–60), index (two sides of one leaf), and 73 plates.[2] The Yale copy is bound as two volumes. Volume I contains a frontispiece, title page,[3] engraved dedication to the king, Preface (two leaves), 82 pages of text describing the use of the architectonic sector, and 25 plates illustrating the same subject. Volume II contains a title page, Introduction (pp. i–ii), text (pp. 1–60), index (two sides of one leaf),[4] and 73 plates.

Acknowledging in the Preface that the principles of Dr. Brook Taylor were "universally established," Kirby announced he would proceed in Taylor's "track" while treating the subject "in a manner entirely new" and establishing "new principles for a compleat system of the Perspective of architecture." The text of the first volume consists of an "Introduction to the Use of the Sector" (pp. 1–4), separate chapters detailing its use in drawing each of the five orders (pp. 4–75), and a final chapter describing "other uses" of the sector (pp. 76–82). The plates depict the sector, the five orders, colonnades, arches, archivolts, imposts, block cornices, balusters, doors, entablatures, consoles, and geometric constructions.

The text of the second part is divided into four books. The first (pp. 1–13) contains rules for "preparing the picture" and depicting planes, solid bodies, and moldings. Book II (pp. 14–24) concerns the orders, and Book III (pp. 25–43) treats the perspective of shadows. Book IV (pp. 44–60) concerns the depiction of columns, colonnades, arches, houses, temples, and an amphitheater.

Most of the plates in the second volume depict geometric figures and objects, the Classical orders, and their parts, in perspective (Plates I–XXXV, XLIII–XLV, LXXI). Other plates show more varied and complex architectural subjects. Plates XXXVI and XXXVII depict columns, walls, flat and pedimented roofs, and a rustic stone hut with a hermit standing by its side. Plates XXXVIII and XXXIX show covered passageways. Steps are the subjects of Plates XL and LVIII. Plates XLI, XLII, and XLVI–LIV depict a variety of structures with walls, niches, piers, columns, arches, entablatures, and flat and pedimented roofs. Plates LVI and LVII show a two-story house, L-shaped in plan. In Plates LIX and LX there is a view of "A House from a design of Inigo Jones," three stories high and five windows wide. Plates LXI and LXII show the Banqueting House in Whitehall. Two plates numbered LXIII depict a large house consisting of a central pile two stories high and five windows wide, plus one-story colonnades leading to two-story wings two windows wide and three windows deep. The design for this house was prepared by George III, who as Prince of Wales had studied drawing with Kirby as his master.[5] Plates LXV–LXVIII illustrate doors and pediments. Two plates numbered LXX depict the Temple of Victory at Kew. Plates LXXII and LXXIII depict a large and complex "Scene for an Amphitheatre."

1. This treatise also was issued separately as: *The description and use of a new instrument called, an architectonic sector. By which any part of architecture may be drawn with facility and exactness* (London: printed for Joshua Kirby, Designer in Perspective to His Majesty, by R. Francklin, in Russel-Street, Covent-Garden; and sold by T. Payne at the Mews-Gate; Messrs. Knapton and Horsefield, in Ludgate-Street; Messrs. Dodsley, in Pall-Mall; T. Longman, in Pater-Noster-Row; T. Davies, in Russel-Street, Covent-Garden; and J. Gretton, in Bond-Street, 1761). This information was kindly supplied by Mr. Nick Savage, Early Works Cataloguer, British Architectural Library.

2. The imprint reads in full: "Printed for the Author, by R. Francklin, in Russell-Street, Covent-Garden; And Sold by T. Payne, at the Mews-Gate; Messrs. Knapton and Horsefield, in Ludgate-Street; Messrs. Dodsley, in Pall-Mall; T. Longman, in Pater-Noster-Row; T. Davies, in Russell-Street, Covent-Garden; and J. Gretton, in Bond-Street."

3. The imprint reads in full: "Printed for the Author, in Duke-Street, Grosvenor-Square, by R. Francklin, in Russel-Street, Covent-Garden; and Sold by T. Payne, at the Mews Gate; Messieurs Knapton and Horsefield, in Ludgate Street; Messieurs Dodsley, in Pall-Mall; T. Longman, in Pater-Noster Row; T. Davies, in Russel-Street, Covent-Garden; and J. Gretton, in Bond Street."

4. The indexes of the two copies are not identical. The "Index" in the RIBA copy is a table of contents for Books I through IV (pp. 1–60) plus a list of errata. The "Index" in the Yale copy is a table of contents for both volumes, followed by a list of errata and binding directions.

5. Colvin (1978), p. 496.

169.1
KNIGHT, Richard Payne (1750–1824)
The landscape, a didactic poem. In three books. Addressed to Uvedale Price, Esq. By R. P. Knight.

London: Printed by W. Bulmer and Co.: and sold by G. Nicol, 1794.

77 pp, 3 pls.

25.0 × 19.5 cm

MnU

———

———

The second edition.

London: Printed by W. Bulmer and Co.; and sold by G. Nicol, 1795.

xv + 104 pp, 3 pls.

27.7 × 23.3 cm

MB

In 1794 three authors each published influential treatises on one of the most important aesthetic issues of the time, the picturesque. Humphry Repton offered his *Sketches and Hints on Landscape Gardening* (q.v.), a collection of recommendations based on his work as a landscape architect. In *An Essay on the Picturesque* Sir Uvedale Price proposed—far more methodically—to establish a new aesthetic category, the picturesque, as an equal to the two currently recognized categories, the sublime and the beautiful. Price had conceived his essay as a reply to Knight's didactic poem *The Landscape*, itself originally "addressed" to Price.[1]

Knight's first aim was to establish the existence of a common standard of taste among all humankind. He argued that all observers would necessarily arrive at the same judgment of any given object. "In taste, one may found his principles in a division of the sublime, the picturesque, and the beautiful; and another, in a certain unison of sympathy and harmony of causes and effects; at the same time that both agree in what is, or is not good taste, and approve or disapprove the same objects" (p. vii).[2] In other words the exercise of taste may involve a variety of criteria, but a given object should stimulate like responses in any two observers. The response, therefore, must be independent of interpretation or modification by cultural and personal associations.

This argument entails that objects of beauty be defined in objective, not relative, terms. Thus in a footnote on page 19 Knight described picturesque beauty as "merely that kind of beauty which belongs exclusively to the sense of vision; or to the imagination, guided by that sense. It must always be remembered in inquiries of this kind, that the eye, unassisted, perceives nothing but light variously graduated and modified." Knight thus implicitly rejected the argument that appreciation of the picturesque could be a process of associational psychology. Rather, like Edmund Burke before him, he focused on physical qualities of picturesque objects and on the physiological process of apprehending those qualities through the sense of vision.[3]

In order to define the picturesque more exactly, Knight introduced two extremes of pictorial design: on the one hand he suggested a "harmony, either in colour or surface," that might become so unified that "it sinks into what, in sound, we call monotony"; on the other hand he suggested harshness, contrast, and pointed or irregular surfaces that "produce a stronger or more varied impression than the organ [of sense] is adapted to bear," and in the end become "painful" (p. 21). In between there was the picturesque, so mildly irritating that it avoided discomfort but still maintained interest: "Between these extremes lies that grateful medium of grateful irritation, which produces the sensation of what we call *beauty*; and which in visible objects we call *picturesque beauty*" (p. 22).

Knight made a passionate plea for the inclusion in country landscape of more such picturesque objects, especially those with gently varied colors and irregular surfaces (pp. 1–24). He labeled the excessively smooth landscaping of Repton "deformity," finding it injurious to both nature and taste:

... that strange disease,
Which gives deformity the power to please;
And shews poor Nature, shaven and defaced,
To gratify the jaundiced eye of taste. (lines 17–20)

Knight also criticized serpentine, wavy paths that traversed the landscape in patterns unrelated to need or use. He recommended leaving dense or impassable terrain alone, presumably as an object of picturesque interest, and redirecting paths to suit the more efficient patterns of "common use" (p. 11).

Knight illustrated these points with a pair of plates, bound between pages 14 and 15, which he discussed briefly in the text and notes. Plate 2 shows a three-story house on a country estate that is landscaped "in the modern style" (p. 15). The facade of the house is embellished with a segmental pediment over the door, and a Venetian window above that. In front are smooth, undulating lawns, with a river and a path that intersect each other twice in gently oscillating serpentine lines. Plate 1 shows the same scene done over according to Knight's preference. The house is now clad in Elizabethan style, with elaborate gable ends, chimneys, and parapets silhouetted against the sky, and other ornamentation across the facade of the house. The landscape has changed just as strikingly. The serpentine walk is suppressed and the river almost completely camouflaged by dense and irregular foliage. The foreground and middle ground are covered by dense brush, and a rude rustic bridge now crosses the river. New trees have been added to block off former vistas of open, undulating landscape. Knight felt that all of these features, both architectural and natural, clearly partook of that "grateful irritation" that he tied to perception of picturesque beauty. The rest of the poem considers in greater detail the picturesque elements of such a landscape, including trees, water, lawns, shrubs, walks, "seats," and so forth.

1. On Price's reasons for writing *An Essay on the Picturesque*, see p. iii of his Preface. In addition to stimulating Price's *Essay*, Knight's first edition also sparked acerbic comments from Humphry Repton. Knight responded to these in the 1795 edition through long footnotes, his "Advertisement to the Second Edition" (pp. iii–xiii), and his "Postscript to the Second Edition" (pp. 98–104). For important discussion of the contribution made by all three authors see Walter John Hipple, Jr., *The Beautiful, the Sublime, and the Picturesque in Eighteenth-Century British Aesthetic Theory* (Carbondale: Southern Illinois University Press, 1957); and Nikolaus Pevsner, *Studies in Art, Architecture and Design* (London: Thames and Hudson, 1968), I.

2. The 1795 edition includes certain corrections and additions made in response to Price's *Essay*. Because the 1795 edition is therefore more authoritative, it is the source of all references here.

3. On Burke see *A Philosophical Enquiry into the Origin of Our Ideas of the Sublime and the Beautiful* (London, 1757; expanded edition, London, 1759). Knight later published an extended discussion of association in aesthetics in his *Analytical Inquiry into the Principles of Taste* (London, 1805).

LABOURERS' Friend Society, London

See Facts and illustrations demonstrating the important benefits which have been, and still may be derived by labourers from possessing small portions of land, *Entry 79.*

170.1
LAING, David (1774–1856)
Hints for dwellings: consisting of original designs for cottages, farm-houses, villas, &c. plain and ornamental; with plans to each: in which strict attention is paid to unite convenience and elegance with economy. Including some designs for town houses. By D. Laing, Architect and Surveyor. Elegantly engraved, in aqua-tinta, on thirty-four plates, with appropriate scenery.

London: Printed by S. Gosnell, for J. Taylor, 1800.

vii + 9–15 pp, 34 pls.

31.1 × 24.8 cm

Soane

170.2

————

————

London: Printed by S. Gosnell, for J. Taylor, 1801.

vii + 9–15 pp, 34 pls.

31.1 × 24.8 cm

V&A

170.3

————

————

London: Printed by T. Bensley, for J. Taylor, 1804.

19 pp, 34 pls.

28.9 × 23.5 cm

CtY

170.4

————

————

Hints for dwellings: ⟨ . . . as 1800 . . . ⟩ Laing, Architect. Elegantly engraved, in aqua-tinta, on thirty-four plates, with appropriate scenery. A new edition.

London: Printed by S. Gosnell, for J. Taylor, 1818.

19 pp, 34 pls.

39.9 × 23.2 cm

MdBP

170.5

Hints for dwellings: consisting ⟨ . . . as 1800 . . . ⟩ scenery.

London: Printed for J. Taylor, 1823.

5–19 pp, 34 pls.

28.2 × 22.7 cm

PPCC

170.6

Hints for dwellings: consisting of original designs for cottages, farm-houses, villas, &c. &c. plain and ornamental. With plans to each: in which strict attention is paid to unite convenience and elegance with economy. Including some designs for town-houses. By D. Laing, Architect and Surveyor. Engraved on thirty-four plates, with appropriate scenery. A new edition.

London: M. Taylor, 1841.

16 pp, 34 pls.

31.8 × 24.8 cm

MB

In the Preface (pp. iii–vii) Laing invoked several important aesthetic principles, including variety, symmetry, regularity, convenience, economy, simplicity, and elegance. Nevertheless in so short a space he was unable to organize them all into a wholly coherent aesthetic. "Architecture," he asserted, "is capable of an infinite Variety of Distributions and Combinations, as well internal as external" (p. iii). His own designs are scrupulously symmetrical, and his attention to regularity in plan and elevation is readily apparent. "The nearer the Plan of a Building approaches to a Square," he wrote, "the greater are its Conveniences, and the Cost proportionably less." Citing Uvedale Price, Laing admitted the importance of "painter-like Effects" in architecture,[1] but he also criticized "some Schemes which I have lately seen by an ingenious Artist, in which his Anxiety to produce Variety and *Want of Uniformity* has led him to devise Plans void of Convenience and Economy" (p. vi).[2] Laing claimed that in his own designs he worked "to unite Simplicity of Character with Elegance of Form" (p. iv), but seems to have reserved "Simplicity" primarily for cottages and "Elegance" more for villas:

In the Designs for Dwellings in the Cottage Style, I have attended to a Simplicity suited to the Character of the Structure; rejecting all Superfluity of Ornament, as inconsistent with the Building: in the Plans on a larger Scale, and in the Designs for Villas, I have indulged in more Ornament and Variety of Contour, as allowable to such Buildings, whose Inhabitants may be considered of some Rank in Life, and entitled to more Show as well as Conveniences. (pp. iv–v)

The plate descriptions (pp. 9–15) include remarks on materials, site, and interior decoration. In addition Laing indicated which designs had been built or commissioned. All designs are shown in one elevation and one or two plans. There are six designs for cottages, farm houses, or lodges, plus designs for one "country residence," seven villas, four "houses," three "sporting" residences, one mansion, and a row of six attached houses. Laing's uniformly symmetrical elevations are ornamented in a variety of styles. There are rustic facades with trelliswork, hipped gables, thatch roofs, and tree trunks used as columnar supports. Neoclassical designs incorporate semicircular arches, smooth rustication, Classical porticoes, and one large dome. Gothic designs include windows and niches with pointed arches. In several cases elements of more than one style are combined, no doubt reflecting Laing's professed interest in "Variety." There is some variety in the plans as well, with rooms and wings occasionally disposed at other than right angles, or composed of circles, ovals, and other nonrectilinear shapes.

The largest design, for a "Mansion" (Plates 29, 30), is approximately 90 feet wide and nearly 100 feet deep. The ground-floor plan includes a dining room, anteroom, gallery or withdrawing room, salon, boudoir, library, chamber, vestibule, and various lesser rooms. The facade is topped by a dome and fronted by a pedimented hexastyle Ionic portico. Even the "Cottage" designs are substantial. That in Plate I includes a parlor, kitchen, scullery, and pantry on the ground floor, plus chamber and attic stories above. Perhaps the most unusual design is the project for "Six Houses in a Row," a group of attached dwellings with a continuous facade alternating in height from two to three stories. This was the first original published design for attached town houses that incorporated such picturesque variations in height;[3] it is also reminiscent of the Paragon at Blackheath, a group of attached dwellings with alternating one- and three-story facades erected by Michael Searles in 1793.[4]

1. P. iv. Laing referred to Sir Uvedale Price's *Essay on the Picturesque* (London, 1794).

2. This appears to be a veiled reference to James Malton's *Essay on British Cottage Architecture* (1798; *q.v.*). Malton advocated irregularity in cottage design, based on principles of picturesque painting.

3. On attached town houses see Section 6 of Chapter III in "The Literature of British Domestic Architecture, 1715–1842" above.

4. For further discussion see the commentary on Peter Nicholson's *Treatise on Projection* (1837).

171.1
LAING, David (1774–1856)

Plans, elevations, and sections, of buildings public and private, executed in various parts of England, &c including the new custom-house, London, with plans, details, and descriptions. Engraved on fifty-nine plates. By David Laing. . . .

London: Printed by Bensley and Sons; and published by J. Taylor, 1818.

4 printed leaves, xiv + 44 pp, 57 pls.

56.2 × 38.2 cm

MH

When this book appeared in 1818, Laing was at or near the height of his career. His executed commissions included the Custom Houses at Plymouth and London and several private houses,[1] and his *Hints for Dwellings* (1800; *q.v.*) had achieved four editions. *Plans . . . of Buildings Public and Private* is dedicated to the prince regent and includes a list of over 500 subscribers.

Most of the Introduction (pp. i–xiv) concerns the history of trade and customs collection in London. The first 30 pages of text and 41 or the 57 plates are devoted to Laing's work on the new Custom House. Another eight pages of text and four plates concern his work at the Church of St. Dunstan in the East. Just four text pages and 12 plates are devoted to his work on "Private and Miscellaneous Designs," including six villas and four other residences, all of them either built or commissioned. The final two pages of text are "Cursory Hints on Planting, Aspect, Soil, Dry Rot, &c."

All but one of the domestic designs are Neoclassical in style, and none is elaborately ornamented. In two designs Laing specifically strove for "chaste and plain simplicity" and "a character of simplicity and plainness" (Plates XLVII, XLVIII). The Gothic design (Plates XLIII, XLIV) is "plain" and "undecorated." Its elevation is a formal, symmetrical combination of Tudor and Decorated Gothic motifs with a thatch roof. Laing suggested the style was "in harmony with the general scenery and situation" (p. 32), but he made no further mention of the site and illustrated no scenery in this or any of the other plates. In several plate descriptions (pp. 32–34) Laing mentioned the "prospects" and "views" his designs were meant to accommodate, but he offered few details of any individual location. The houses range in size from a two-story villa (Plate XLII) three windows across to a much larger design, also termed a "Villa" (Plates LII, LIII), a complex combination of angled pavilions, wings, and a central domed rotunda.

1. Colvin (1978), pp. 500–501. Following a partial collapse of the London Custom House in 1825 there were serious charges of incompetence and dishonesty laid against Laing, and his practice was ruined.

LAMB, Edward Buckton (1806–1869)

See LOUDON, **John Claudius, ed.,** The architectural magazine, *Entry 182.*

172.1
LANGLEY, Batty (1696–1751), and Thomas LANGLEY (1702–1751)
Ancient architecture, restored, and improved, by a great variety of grand and usefull designs, entirely new in the Gothick mode for the ornamenting of buildings and gardens exceeding every thing thats extant. Exquisitely engraved on LXIV large quarto copper-plates and printed on superfine royal paper. By Batty and Thomas Langley. . . .

[N. loc.: N. pub., 1742].

[viii] pp + 64 pls (numbered 1–62, A, B).

28.9 × 22.2 cm

Soane

172.2

Gothic architecture, improved by rules and proportions. In many grand designs of columns, doors, windows, chimney-pieces, arcades, colonades, porticos, umbrellos, temples, and pavillions &c. With plans, elevations and profiles; geometrically explained. By B. & T. Langley.

London: Printed for John Millan, 1747.

64 pls (numbered A, B, 1–62).

29.8 × 22.5 cm

MnU

172.3

Gothic architecture, ⟨ . . . as 1747 . . . ⟩ explained. By B. & T. Langley. To which is added an historical dissertation on Gothic architecture.

London: Printed for I. & J. Taylor, [n.d.].

8 pp, 64 pls (numbered A, B, 1–62).

29.2 × 23.2 cm

MB

The three editions of this work all include the same set of plates, but the front matter varies considerably. The first edition, titled *Ancient Architecture*, has no date on the title page. The plates, which were issued in two sets, are dated 1741 and 1742. The first set of plates was accompanied by a title page indicating that 32 plates comprised this "first Part" and another 32 plates and a new title page "will be delivered in June 1742." As completed, the 1742 edition includes two dedicatory leaves, one to the Duke of Richmond and the Duke of Montagu, and another to "the Dean and Chapter of the Collegiate Church of St Peter Westminster." The verso of the second leaf contains a list of subscribers, whom Langley called "Encouragers To the Restoring of the *Saxon* Architecture." There follows a four-page "Dissertation on the Antiquity of the Principal Ancient Buildings," signed by Batty Langley and dated 16 August 1742, plus a brief list of plates. In the penultimate paragraph of the "Dissertation" Langley optimistically projected a second volume, with "many other *useful Designs*, for *Ceilling-Pieces, Insides* of *Rooms, Pavements, Stair Cases, Pagan Temples, Sylvan Towers, Saxon Tents, Niche's, Canopys, Monumental Pyramids*, &c. which I have extracted from the Works of the Ancients, and whose Magnificence and Beauty greatly excee [*sic*] all that have been done by both Greeks and Romans." In the final paragraph he offered "to erect all Sorts of Buildings in the *Saxon Mode* that may be required."

The next edition, titled *Gothic Architecture*, is dated 1747. There is no introductory matter. The final edition is undated, but the imprint "I. & J. Taylor" suggests publication no earlier than 1787.[1] The plates are still dated 1741 and 1742. The introductory essay (pp. 1–7) is titled "An Historical Dissertation on the Antiquity of the Principal Ancient Buildings."

The text varies slightly from that of the 1742 edition, and it is now signed "B. L." and dated 1742. Page 8 contains a brief list of the plates.

A principal aim of this treatise was to demonstrate a system of order and proportion in Gothic architecture that would equal that already established for Classical architecture. The original title, *Ancient Architecture*, implied that Gothic style was as much a part of ancient culture as the Classical styles that were the foundation of contemporary architectural aesthetics. But the British associations of Gothic style also were attractive, and Langley used the introductory essay to locate his material in a historical context that should have appealed to the predominantly Whig—but also Palladian—tastemakers of the time.[2] Concerned with the erosion of liberty under recent monarchs, Whig leaders of the 1740s looked to pre-Conquest, or "Saxon" times, as a period of true British liberty.[3] Perhaps to his advantage, Langley found that during the "Saxon monarchy there was no distinction of Goths from Saxons," that all buildings erected during that period "were in general called Saxon," and "that the Goths first taught the Saxons how to build" (p. 1).[4] Under Canute the Danes razed all Saxon buildings except St. Paul's; that too now being gone, no true example of "Gothic," or Saxon, building remained (p. 3). Nevertheless Langley maintained that many buildings constructed during the reigns of Edward the Confessor through James I were built according to models found in Saxon ruins, and thus could be studied for evidence of underlying rules and principles (pp. 3–6). In particular he examined two columns in Westminster Abbey, illustrated in Plates A and B, for underlying geometric proportions. He found that the "members" of these columns "are determined and described with those beautiful proportions and geometrical rules, which are not excelled (if equalled) in any parts of the Grecian or Roman orders. Nor is that delicacy and deception, which is contained in these columns, to be seen in any Grecian or Roman columns of the same diameters" (p. 7).

Figure 2

Ostensibly from this kind of evidence, the Langleys prepared 16 plates illustrating five Gothic "orders," with measurements and details of each. Other plates illustrate possible uses for these new orders: there are designs for 12 Gothic doorways, an arcade, a colonnade, a portico, 18 windows, eight chimneypieces, eight "umbrello's," four temples, and three "pavillions." Within a few decades careful scrutiny of actual monuments made it clear that the proportionality so vaunted by the Langleys had no basis in fact. Their fanciful creations soon became an object of ridicule as archaeologists began to appreciate Gothic remains in the greater context of medieval culture and not as a basis for pseudo-Palladian canons of regularity and proportionality.[5]

1. See Ian Maxted, *The London Book Trades 1775–1800* (Folkestone: Dawson, 1977), p. 222. The title appears in catalogues issued by the Taylor firm during the 1790s.

2. For an analysis of the political background of the Gothic Revival see Samuel Kliger, *The Goths in England* (Cambridge, Mass.: Harvard University Press, 1952). Eileen Harris has suggested that Langley's interest in Gothic derived from his interest in Freemasonry; see "Batty Langley: A Tutor to Freemasons," *Burlington Magazine* CXIX:890 (May 1977), 327–335.

3. A close parallel to this calculated political appeal can be found in the Gothic Temple at Stowe, begun in 1741—the year of the Langleys' prospectus—and embellished with statues of the seven Saxon deities. The temple, a particularly early example of Gothic Revival,

was at first called the Temple of Liberty, and was built as a symbol of the opposition of Cobham, Chatham, and their Whig circle against the regime of Walpole. See George Clarke, "Grecian Taste and Gothic Virtue," *Apollo* XCVII:136 (June 1973), 566–571; and Clarke, "The History of Stowe—X," *The Stoic*, no. 142 (July 1970), 113–121.

4. References here are to the essay as printed in the undated edition of *Gothic Architecture*.

5. For eighteenth-century reaction to this book and a lengthier discussion of several points, see Alistair Rowan, "Batty Langley's Gothic," *Studies in Memory of David Talbot Rice* (Edinburgh: Edinburgh University Press, 1975), pp. 197–215.

173.1
LANGLEY, Batty (1696–1751)
Practical geometry applied to the useful arts of building, surveying, gardening and mensuration; calculated for the service of gentlemen as well as artisans, and set to view in four parts. Containing,
I. Preliminaries or the foundations of the several arts above-mentioned.
II. The various orders of architecture, laid down and improved from the best masters; with the ways of making draughts of buildings, gardens, groves, fountains, &c. the laying down of maps, cities, lordships, farms, &c.
III. The doctrine and rules of mensuration of all kinds, illustrated by select examples in building, gardening, timber, &c.
IV. Exact tables of mensuration, shewing, by inspection, the superficial and solid contents of all kinds of bodies, without the fatigue of arithmetical computation:
To which is annexed, an account of the clandestine practice now generally obtaining in mensuration, and particularly the damage sustained in selling timber by measure.
The whole exemplifi'd with above 60 folio copper plates, by the best hands. By Batty Langley.

London: Printed for W. and J. Innys, J. Osborn and T. Longman, B. Lintot, J. Woodman and D. Lyons, C. King, E. Symon, and W. Bell, 1726.

viii + [viii] + 136 pp, 40 pls (numbered I–XXIX, XXXI, XXXI–XXXIX, XLI).

34.4 × 22.7 cm

CtY-BA

173.2 †

Practical geometry applied to . . . building, surveying, gardening, and mensuration.

London, 1728.

Reference: DNB

173.3

Practical geometry ⟨ . . . as 1726 . . . ⟩. The whole exemplify'd with a large number of folio copper plates, curiously engraven by the best hands. By Batty Langley. The second edition.

London: Printed for Aaron Ward, 1729.

[ii] + viii + [viii] + 136 pp, 40 pls (numbered I–XXIX, XXXI, XXXI–XXXIX, XLI).

34.9 × 22.2 cm

CtY

The letterpress consists of a dedication (one leaf, recto and verso), a preface (pp. i–viii), a table of contents (four leaves, recto and verso), and the text (pp. 1–136). There are 40 plates. The plate that should be numbered "XL" is labeled "XLI," although on page viii Langley described it as the "fortieth" plate. Since Langley mentioned only 40 plates in the Preface, the reference to "60" plates on the title page is clearly erroneous. The discussion below is based on examination of the 1726 edition.

In the Preface Langley admitted that others had treated the "subjects of the present treatise"—architecture, gardening, mensuration, and land surveying—"but generally in a theoretical, rather than in a practical manner" (p. 1). He proposed to lead the reader methodically from first principles to the most complex aspects. Thus he would begin with geometry, the "basis" of all four disciplines (p. ii). He devoted much of the Preface to a summary description of his text and plates, but in the middle he interjected a lengthy discussion of the proportions of the "principal parts" of columns.

The text is divided into four parts. The first (pp. 1–43) contains geometrical definitions, problems, axioms, and theorems, and treats compound figures, compound lines, and the "Contruncation" of the cube into other solids. Part II (pp. 44–106) concerns architecture. After discussing plans, elevations, and the five orders, he turned to "Architectonical Axioms and Analogies," a series of remarks on doors, windows, gates, halls, galleries, antechambers, chambers, floors, chimneys, joists, rafters, girders, staircases, and materials. He also discussed the use of "an inspectional plain Scale," trigonometry, and the making of drafts, plans, and maps of lands, gardens, farms, and buildings. Part III (pp. 107–127) contains brief remarks on cross multiplication, followed by discussion of mensuration of lines, plane surfaces, solids, carpenters' work, glazing, joinery, painting, plastering, masonry, bricklayers' work, and land. Part IV (pp. 128–136) concerns the "*Inspectional* Tables of *Mensuration*" in Plate XVII.

A few of the plates illustrating geometric and architectural subjects include designs for landscape gardens. In these designs and the accompanying letterpress Langley introduced "a new system of gardening" (p. vii), soon to be expanded in his *New Principles of Gardening* (London, 1728). The "system," explained here only in a fragmented manner, is based on two principles. According to the first, a single geometric pattern need not control the entire design: "The beauty of a garden (in my humble opinion) consists in a regular, irregularity, that the parts may appear as equal, and at the same time be unequal among themselves, and thereby, at every step forward, a new scene, or fresh object appears, and the whole becomes an everlasting entertainment" (p. 34). Thus small portions of a garden could be devoted to spiraling walks, "wildernesses," or isolated seats, clearly separated from the ordered regularity of a central parterre or major cross-walks. The second principle concerns the use of "artinatural walks," irregular and serpentine paths so named because "they are described by art, and represent the product of nature, which in all woods and wildernesses should be imitated as near as possible" (p. 34; Plate III, Fig. V). Langley's garden design in Plate XIII contains "some few artinatural lines," appropriate to a "rural manner" of gardening, and "preferable to the most regular set forms hitherto practised . . . in most parts of *England*" (p. 101). The best manner of landscape gardening combines geometric and "artinatural" lines, as shown in Plate XIV: "an entire garden according to the truth of designing, wherein you may behold art and nature in conjunction with each other, which in gardening is a general axiom to be observed, &c." (p. 102). But while much of Langley's "system" was of fundamental importance to the progress of the picturesque landscape movement,[1] his approach was not entirely original: the serpentine "artinatural" line, for example, was anticipated in Stephen Switzer's *Nobleman, Gentleman, and Gardener's Recreation* (1715, 2nd ed. 1718; *q.v.*).

In addition to the garden designs already mentioned, Langley illustrated a variety of plans for fountains, basins, fish ponds, ornamental borders, and intersections of walks. There are also several circular or rectilinear "places of retirement" designed for "a wilderness, labyrinth, grove, &c.," which are approached by serpentine "artinatural" paths (p. 30; Plate II). Other plates include geometric figures and diagrams, and exercises in drawing architectural plans and elevations. In Plate V there are two elevations and two plans for a house, 37 feet high, 60 feet wide, and 40 feet deep. The elevation consists of three stories and a basement, seven openings wide. Langley devoted several plates to the five Classical orders as laid down by "ancient, antique, and modern" masters; he also depicted "French," "Spanish," Persian, and caryatid orders. In addition there are designs for doors, windows, "neathes," entrances to "shady walks," an "Amphitheatrical mount of ever Green's for ye Termination of a grand Walk," entrances for grottoes, Corinthian and Composite capitals, an elevation of a building "Design'd according to ye Grand manner of Palladio," chimneypieces, a portico, and imposts. In Plate 10 there is an "Inspectional Scale" useful in making flutes and fillets and in finding the position of the sun on any day of the year. Plate 15 depicts the plan of a farm. Plate 17 contains "Inspectional Tables" for measuring surfaces, quantities of timber and stone, and land.

1. For an unfortunately unsympathetic treatment of Langley's role, see Nikolaus Pevsner, "The Genesis of the Picturesque," in *Studies in Art, Architecture and Design* (London: Thames and Hudson, 1968), I, 78–101.

174.1 †
LANGLEY, Batty (1696–1751)
A sure guide to builders, or the principles and practice of architecture made easy for the use of workmen.

[London], 1726.

4°

Reference: APSD

174.2

———

A sure guide to builders: or, the principles and practice of architecture geometrically demonstrated, and made easy, for the use of workmen in general. Wherein such geometrical definitions, theorems, problems, &c. as are the basis of architecture, are render'd easy and intelligible to every capacity. As also their various uses illustrated, in the construction of decimal and diagonal scales, measuring and drawing geometrical plans and uprights of buildings; describing all the moldings used in architecture; diminishing, fluting, cabling, and wreathing the shafts of columns and pillasters; describing the Ionick volute, division and proportion of rusticks; delineating the five orders of columns according to any proportions assign'd, and to determine the pitch of pediments, &c. Together with the general proportions of pedestals, columns, entablatures, imposts, &c. and their various dispositions or intercolumnations in portico's, columnades, arches, doors, windows, &c.
Curiously selected and drawn from the most rare antique, as well of Rome, and other places where architecture has flourish'd, as of Vitruvius, Palladio, Scamozzi, Vignola, Serlio, Perault, Bosse, Angelo, and other celebrated architects, antient and modern.
To which is added, an appendix. Wherein the several acts of Parliament, now in force, relating to builders, building, and materials, are explain'd for the service of surveyors, master-builders, workmen, and proprietors of buildings. The whole illustrated with great variety of grand designs for frontispieces doors, windows, cieling-pieces, pavements, &c. with the Thermes and columns, enrich'd after the antient Grecian and Roman architects, curiously engraven on eighty-two large copper plates. By B. Langley.

London: Printed for J. Wilcox; and T. Heath, Mathematical Instrument-Maker, 1729.

[xvi] + 179 pp, 82 pls (numbered 1–38, 38A, 39–81).

25.4 × 19.4 cm

MB

The APSD indicates that the first edition was issued in 1726, but I have found no corroborating evidence. At least two issues of the 1729 edition are known: one "Printed for J. Wilcox, at the Green Dragon in Little Britain; and T. Heath, Mathematical Instrument-maker, next the Fountain

Tavern in the Strand" (Boston Public Library); and the other "Printed for W. Mears, at the Lamb without Temple-bar; J. Wilcox, at the Green Dragon in Little Britain; Tho. Wright, Mathematical Instrument-maker, (to his Majesty) at the Orrery and Globe in Fleet-street; and by the Author, at Palladio's Head, near Exeter-Change in the Strand" (University of London, Goldsmiths' Library).[1]

Following the dedicatory leaf there is a four-page preface, titled "An Advertisement to Workmen, To be first Read by them before they proceed to the following Work," and dated June 20, 1729. Langley indicated that his "real Design herein is to render the Proportions and Practice of Architecture more accurate, easy, and familiar, than has been yet done by all the Authors hereon extant." In addition, "for the Use of Gentlemen, Surveyors, Master Builders, and Workmen, I have enrich'd the whole with a great Variety of curious and useful Designs of Doors, Windows, Chimney-pieces, Cieling-pieces, Pavements, Arches, Rusticks, &c. according to the grand establish'd Proportions of the most celebrated Architects, as well antique, as antient and modern." The prefatory matter concludes with a four-page table of contents and a six-page index.

In the Introduction (pp. 1–4) Langley again addressed his audience of workmen: "Architecture: Or, The Art of Building, wholly depends on the Principles and Practice of Geometry," he declared. "And therefore those who are desirous to well understand the Reasons of all the beautiful Proportions contain'd in Architecture, must be first acquainted with such Elements of Geometry that are absolutely necessary thereto" (p. 1). He criticized previous authors for their lack of attention to geometry: each wanted "more to shew the Theory of his Works, than to lay down Practical Rules for the Workman" (p. 2). Nor did Langley spare his contemporaries any criticism: he censured William Halfpenny and the authors of *The Builder's Dictionary*, and complained that many "Modern Buildings," except those of Lord Burlington and Lord Herbert,[2] suffered from "the Want of well-digested Rules and Proportions to work after" (pp. 2–3). Even the "excellent Patterns" of the Ancients languished "for want of their Practical Rules being made publick" (p. 3). Toward the end of the Introduction Langley acknowledged that "The first Part of this Work was publish'd about two Years ago, intitled, *The Builders Chest-Book*" (p. 3).[3] He concluded with a list of "Mathematical Instruments" that every workman should have (p. 4).

The text (pp. 5–159) consists of 12 chapters containing the following subjects: geometric definitions, geometric theorems, geometric problems, plans and elevations, the proportions of the five orders, pedestals, columns and their ornaments, entablatures, pilasters, errors in the use of columns and pilasters, pediments, the proportions of rooms and their parts according to Palladio, and finally brief remarks on floors, ceilings, pavements, chimneys, and staircases.

The first six plates depict geometric figures and diagrams. Plate 7, discussed on pages 64–68, shows the "Plan of the Out-Lines" of a building and its flanking offices. Plate 8, described on pages 70–75, illustrates two floor plans of a house: a basement or ground floor with four rooms, and a principal floor with a hall, parlor, and drawing room. On pages 76–77 Langley described the elevation of a garden "Banquetting House," illustrated in Plate 9. A single room enclosed by tall windows is surmounted by a hemispherical dome. On page 77 Langley briefly mentioned the elevations of two attached town houses. These are shown in Plate 9: each is three openings wide and three stories high, and above the cornice line each also has a dormer story. One facade is fronted by heavily rusticated vertical bands; in the other facade the principal framing members are apparently open to view. The window openings are three feet wide and five or six feet high, and placed close to each other, leaving little room for further ornament. Despite their plainness these town house designs are of special interest because this dwelling type appears so infrequently in early and mid-eighteenth-century British architectural literature; indeed these designs appear to be the first published by any British architect. Plates 10–41 illustrate moldings, the proportions of the orders, and parts of the orders. Plate 58 demonstrates the construction of arches. The remaining plates contain designs for windows, doors, ornamented cornices, grotesque columns, pediments, room interiors, pavements, ceilings, terms, "simbolical columns," other columns, and pedestals.

1. The description that follows refers to the issue in the Boston Public Library.

2. Presumably Langley had in mind Chiswick House, which Lord Burlington was building in the mid- and late 1720s, and Marble Hill House (1724–1729), a collaborative effort between Roger Morris and Henry, Lord Herbert, later ninth Earl of Pembroke.

3. *The Builder's Chest Book* was first published in 1727. This casts further doubt on the existence of a 1726 edition of *A Sure Guide*.

175.1
LANGLEY, Batty (1696–1751)
The young builder's rudiments: or the principles of geometry, mechanicks, mensuration and perspective, geometrically demonstrated. Together with the five orders of columns in architecture. Acccording to the proportions of the celebrated Palladio. Calculated for the use of workmen, gentlemen and others, who delight in designing, drawing, painting, engraving, and gardening, &c. Adorn'd with about thirty large copper plates, curiously engrav'd by J. Vandergucht and B. Cole. By B. Langley.

London: Printed for J. Millan at his shop, 1730.

[iv] + 130 + [ii] pp, frontisp. + 28 pls (numbered I–II, II, III, V–XXIII, XXV, XXV–XXVIII).

24.5 × 19.5 cm

NjP

175.2
[LANGLEY, Batty (1696–1751)]
The young builder's rudiments, teaching the meanest capacity in a plain, familiar manner (by questions and answers) the most useful parts of geometry, architecture, mechanicks, mensuration, several ways and perspective, &c.
The second edition, to which are added, the five orders of architecture, in a more easy and concise method than any yet published. Also, great

variety of beautiful doors, windows, and chimneys, &c. according to Inigo Jones, and others. Calculated for the use of gentlemen, architects, sculptors, painters, masons, and all others concerned in the noble art of sound building. Illustrated with above 40 large copper plates, engraved by the late famous Mr. Vandergucht, &c.

London: Printed for J. Millan, and sold at his shop, 1734.

[iv] + 130 + [ii] pp, frontisp. + 41 pls.

24.1 × 19.1 cm

NNC

175.3 †
LANGLEY, Batty (1696–1751)
The young builder's rudiments.

London, 1736.

Reference: DNB

Following the frontispiece and title page are a dedication and a table of contents. The text is divided into two parts: Part I (pp. 1–76) includes geometric terms, geometric problems, the five orders, mechanics, and mensuration; Part II (pp. 77–130) is an essay titled "Perspective made easy." There is a two-page index at the end.

The frontispiece depicts six subjects in perspective: a bridge, houses with Dutch gables flanking a canal, waterfront piers, and three different views of buildings with vaulted interior spaces. Plates I and II show geometric figures and diagrams. Another Plate II depicts the orders. Plate III illustrates pulleys and other mechanical instruments. Plates V through XXVIII show a variety of subjects in perspective. These include rows of arches (Plates XVIII, XIX), multiple arcades and colonnades (Plates XXV through XXVIII), and a house (Plates XXI–XXIII, XXV). The house, a Greek cross in plan, is one story high with an additional story over the center crossing. It is shown in perspective view and in plan from several different angles. Plate XXXI, found only in the second edition, depicts a house "Design'd by Paladio"; it is two stories high and seven windows wide, with colonnades leading from each side to one-story end pavilions.

LEEDS, William Henry (1786–1866)

See LOUDON, **John Claudius, ed.,** The architectural magazine, *Entry 182.*

176.1

LEGH, Peter

The music of the eye; or, essays on the principles of the beauty and perfection of architecture, as founded on and deduced from reason and analogy, and adapted to what may be traced of the ancient theories of taste, in the three first chapters of Vitruvius. Written with a view to restore architecture to the dignity it had in ancient Greece. By Peter Legh. . . .

London: Printed for William Walker; James Carpenter and Son; and Priestley & Weale, 1831.

xxiii + 262 pp, frontisp. + 43 pls.

25.4 × 15.2 cm

MnU

Serious English analysis of Vitruvian texts first appeared in Newton's annotated translation in 1771, and then in Aldrich's *Elements of Civil Architecture* in 1789 (*qq.v.*). A late edition of Aldrich appeared in 1824, and in 1826 Gwilt's more authoritative translation of Vitruvius appeared. But despite such continuing interest in Vitruvius, Legh in 1831 was clearly out of step with most of his contemporaries. He traced the principles of beauty to one source—ancient architecture as recorded by Vitruvius—and used those principles to illuminate a new, presumably purer architectural aesthetic. In this he was fundamentally at odds with the increasingly eclectic tastes of his time. Indeed Legh conceived his treatise in part "with a view to restore architecture to the dignity it had in ancient Greece" (title page). To appreciate that dignity, however, required intellectual sophistication: "It is the object of these essays to show that Architecture is not within the reach of every illiterate mechanic, but that it opens a field to enlarged intellect, and deep research, and that it is full of unlimited novelty and invention" (p. viii). Architecture, Legh said, is "an art, that enlarges the intellect, assists the judgment, directs the taste, and, to adopt the appropriate language of Vitruvius, an art, by whose principles the merits of the works in other arts may be tried, and examined" (p. ix). In a broader context, he suggested that by "throwing at least a glimmering light on the noblest of peaceful arts" he would be doing his part "to promote universal civilization" (p. xi).

The text consists of nine "Essays." The first includes remarks on the "dignity" and "nobility" of architecture, on historical styles, on eighteenth-century criticism, and on siting, materials, and machinery. The second Essay, ostensibly explaining "the object" of the entire work, argues in favor of a "regular, systematic, universal, and scientific arrangement of important theories, well weighed, compared, and modified by each other, that can alone establish the restoration of architecture" (p. 27). These theories would "reduce to a simple and scientific scheme, the hitherto . . . ungovernable wanderings of fancy" (p. 27). Indeed the decline of architecture since Greek times was in great part due to the loss of fundamental governing "principles" (p. 26).

In the third Essay Legh admitted somewhat ironically that "Vitruvius is undoubtedly very obscure" (p. 31), while assuring the reader that Vitruvius clearly expounded five "principles of composition." These principles, respectively the subjects of the next five "Essays," were utility, proportion, disposition, distribution, and decor or character (pp. 36–37).

Legh concluded the third Essay with an attack on "association of ideas." He argued that pleasure can come directly only from pleasing ideas (p. 39). An ordinary idea that by association brings a pleasing idea to mind, he said, is not necessarily a source of pleasure; only the pleasing idea itself is a source of pleasure. Thus Legh claimed to discredit association as a source of pleasure.[1]

Among the five Essays devoted to Vitruvian "principles," Legh's most original contribution was on the subject of character.[2] Most early nineteenth-century architects understood "character" as a central expressive quality within a design, perhaps related to the character of the surrounding landscape, the personality of the inhabitant, or his occupation. Often this quality would be expressed through a combination of forms that, by association, stimulated the intended ideas in the mind of the beholder. Legh adopted a stricter interpretation, however, closer to eighteenth-century writers on character, identifying it with the Vitruvian notion of propriety, or decor. "In character," he wrote, "both consistency and harmony are essential requisites. In all ages Architects seem to have confessed some quality in a design coincident with this principle: Vitruvius . . . gives us the Latin term 'decor,' which . . . literally means nothing more than propriety. . . . [But] we may very properly consider the Latin word decor as technically the same as character" (p. 192). Again he rejected the role of association in communicating ideas to the viewer (p. 196), and instead claimed that character inhered in individual forms and styles, where the observer could perceive it directly. Doric, for example, "gives the ideas of strength, and the Corinthian of lightness" (p. 194). Since possible combinations of different architectural forms were in effect limitless, the potential number of architectural characters likewise would be limitless (p. 195). Nevertheless a successful design must necessarily exhibit a single, coherent character. To achieve that character the design must in fact display uniformity according to all five essential principles of design: uniformity of use, uniformity of proportion (equivalent to Vitruvian "Harmony"), uniformity among forms (or distribution), and uniformity in the arrangement of forms (or disposition)—all to be subsumed under a comprehensive uniformity of character (pp. 198–205).

These arguments differed little from eighteenth-century French and English writings on character. But Legh went further in explaining the means by which observers perceive architectural character, suggesting a novel parallel between architecture and human physiognomy. Perhaps inspired by publications of Le Brun, Lavater, and especially Jacques-François Blondel,[3] he concluded that individual lines, whether in a face or a facade, were the source of all expression (pp. 208–223). Thus just as certain lines can express masculinity and femininity in the human face (p. 220), similar lines have like effects in the Doric and Ionic orders (p. 221). But Legh made little further use of such parallels, and even admitted they were "of remote use in Architecture" (p. 223). He concluded his discussion with an analysis of such traditional architectural "characters" as lightness, heaviness, dignity, neatness, prettiness, handsomeness, strength, solidity, greatness, boldness, grandeur, sublimity, beauty, richness, luxuriance, and magnificence.[4]

The final Essay is a summary of major points in the previous essays, and ends with a rather lame plea that less money be spent on easel painting so that more could be devoted to architecture (pp. 261–262).

Some of the plates illustrate architectural ornament and human physiognomy, but nearly three-fourths show temples, palaces, and garden
structures. Apparently contradicting Legh's earlier enthusiasm for Greece
and the antique, these designs are in a variety of styles, including Greek,
Gothic, Indian, Chinese, and especially Egyptian. The emphasis on designs
in an Egyptian vocabulary perhaps reflects a desire to be true to elementary
principles by emulating a style considered to be the most "primitive"
form of ancient architecture.[5]

1. For further discussion of association see Chapter III, Section 3, in "The Literature of British
Domestic Architecture, 1715–1842" above.

2. For further discussion of character see ibid.

3. See Charles Le Brun, *Conference . . . sur l'expression* (Amsterdam and Paris, 1698); Johann
Kaspar Lavater, *Physiognomische Fragmente zur Beförderung der Menschenkenntnis und Menschliebe* (Leipzig and Winterthur, 1775–1778); and Jacques-François Blondel, *Cours d'architecture* (Paris, 1771), I, 259–261. John Billington, an English contemporary of Legh, offered
another discussion of the relation between physiognomy and architectural character in *The
Architectural Director* (1829; *q.v.*).

4. The seven to which he devoted most attention—greatness, boldness, grandeur, sublimity,
beauty, richness, and luxuriance—differed little from those discussed as early as 1770 by
Thomas Whately in *Observations on Modern Gardening*. But Whately, unlike Legh, derived
the affectivity of his characters from principles of association.

5. On early nineteenth-century interest in Egyptian architecture see Richard G. Carrott, *The
Egyptian Revival* (Berkeley: University of California Press, 1978). On the greater history of
neo-Egyptian taste see James Stevens Curl, *The Egyptian Revival* (London: Allen & Unwin,
1982).

177.1
LEONI, Giacomo (James) (1686–1746)
Some designs for buildings both publick and private by James Leoni,
Architect.

London: Printed for Thomas Edlin, 1726.

[*Additional title page:*]

Alcuni disegni di edificj pubblici e privati, di Giacomo Leoni Architetto.

Londra: Presso Tommaso Edlin, 1726.

[x] pp, 6 numbered folios, 27 pls.

43.2 × 27.9 cm

MB

177.2
_____

Some designs for buildings both public and private, by James Leoni,
Architect.

London: Printed for the proprietor, 1758.

8 pp, 27 pls.

41.6 × 26.0 cm

CtY

In the 1726 edition there are separate title pages in English and Italian; the preface and plate descriptions are set in parallel columns of Italian and English. This edition is bound at the end of the third volume of Leoni's translation of Alberti's treatises on architecture, painting, and sculpture.[1] In the 1758 edition there is no Italian title page nor any Italian letterpress. The following discussion is based on examination of the 1726 edition.

The separate title pages in English and Italian, each dated 1726, are followed by a ten-page Preface plus plate descriptions on the recto and verso of six numbered folios. The 27 plates bear dates from 1723 through 1729.[2]

In the Preface Leoni argued strongly in favor of principles of regularity and proportion, and particularly the authority of "Antique" precedent, while condemning the work of "Modern" architects. He complained of builders who deprived architecture of "simple Gracefulness" and instead "introduced uncouth Members, barbarous Ornaments, and new-fangled Proportions which give pain to the sight of any Man that views them with attention and judgment." Many "modern Fabricks" were little more than "great heaps of Stone piled up one upon the other, . . . put together with much the same regularity as the Chinese Paintings." He criticized a host of faults in modern buildings, including alcoves more appropriate for rats and mice than for human beings, festoons good for nothing except "to harbour dirt and vermin," and windows that too much resembled "lanterns." Because "antique proportions" had been "forgotten or neglected by the Moderns," the "Conveniencies and Beauties" that arose solely from proportion were absent in modern building. At great length Leoni criticized modern architects' ignorance of perspective, the orders, drawing, construction, and the proper arrangement of rooms in a dwelling. He concluded this call for a more rational, ordered, architectural aesthetic with effusive praise for one of the leading patrons of the Palladian Revival, Lord Burlington.[3]

The plates depict several of Leoni's projects and executed designs: a plan and elevation of a project for a triumphal arch in memory of George I intended for the Ring in Hyde Park; a plan of the grounds at Carshalton House; two floor plans, three elevations, and a section depicting Leoni's proposed work at Carshalton; three alternate floor plans for Carshalton; a plan and elevation for a greenhouse at Carshalton; four floor plans and an elevation of a town house erected for the Duke of Queensberry and Dover in Burlington Gardens circa 1721–1723; a plan and an elevation for a country seat in the style of Inigo Jones that, according to Leoni, would have been executed had the client not died; a plan and an elevation for a country seat in the style of Andrea Palladio, including an Egyptian Hall, and inscribed to Burlington; two plans and an elevation for "a little Country-House";[4] a plan and an elevation for each of two town houses; and a plan and an elevation for a stone bridge.

The largest design is the country house in the style of Inigo Jones (Plates 17, 18). The two-story elevation is 25 openings wide. The articulation of the facade is elegant but restrained: the ground story is rusticated, a two-story hexastyle portico in the center has Doric columns on the ground floor and Ionic columns above, statues adorn the parapets and pediment above this portico, and a central lantern crowns the whole. Alternating segmental and triangular pediments top the windows on the upper floor, and engaged pedimented porticoes frame the front ends of the two wings. There are bas reliefs in all three pediments and in recessed panels on the upper story. The principal rooms include a vestibule (60 feet by 30 feet), an oval hall (55 feet by 45 feet), a gallery (125 feet by 30 feet, two stories high), and a chapel.

The smallest design is the "little Country-House" shown in Plates 20–22. The ground floor and upper floor each contain four principal rooms, and the two-story elevation is just five windows wide. The facade is modestly ornamented with stringcourses, a cornice, an engaged one-story portico at the entrance, an architrave and entablature surrounding the center window of the upper story, and cornices above the other four windows on that floor.

1. The title pages to the first and third volumes, both dated 1726, mention that "several designs" by Leoni are included.

2. N.B. the Royal Licence in Vol. I is dated 24 March 1729/1730.

3. On Burlington's role in the Palladian Revival see Rudolf Wittkower, *Palladio and Palladianism* (New York: Braziller, 1974), Chapters 7–9; and Summerson (1969), pp. 197–200. On the rejection of "Modern" practice in favor of "Ancient" principle see the discussion in the commentary on Colen Campbell's *Vitruvius Britannicus* (1715).

4. Argyll House, King's Road, Chelsea (1723). See Colvin (1978), p. 513.

Letters and papers on agriculture, planting, &c. selected from the correspondence of the Bath and West of England Society.

See DAVIS, **Thomas,** *Entry 55.*

178.1
LEWIS, James (ca. 1751–1820)
[*Book I:*]

Original designs in architecture: consisting of plans, elevations, and sections, for villas, mansions, town-houses, &c. and a new design for a theatre. With descriptions, and explanations of the plates, and an introduction to the work. By James Lewis. Book I.
Disegni originali di architettura: consistenti in piante, elevazioni, e spaccati di varie case di campagna, et di città; con un progetto di un teatro. Preceduti da una introduzione, ed accompagnati dalle necessarie spiegazioni. Da Giacomo Lewis. Libro I.

London: Printed for the author, 1780.

ii + 13 pp, 22 pls.

[*Book II:*]

Original designs in architecture; consisting of plans, elevations, and sections of various publick and private buildings: executed, or proposed to be erected, in different parts of England and Ireland. With descriptions and explanations. By James Lewis, Architect. Book II.

London: Printed for the author by Cooper and Graham, 1797.

[ii] + iv + 5–14 pp, 41 pls.

57.8 × 38.1 cm

V&A

178.2

[*Book I:*]

Original designs in architecture; consisting of plans, elevations, and sections for villas, mansions, town-houses, &c. and a new design for a theatre. With descriptions and explanations. By James Lewis, Architect. Book I. The second edition with corrections.

London: Printed for the author by Cooper and Graham, and sold by Messrs. Taylor; and R. Faulder, 1797.

[ii] + vi + 9–18 pp, 22 pls.

[*Book II:*]

Original designs in architecture; ⟨ . . . as previous transcription of 1797 Book II . . . ⟩.

London: Printed for the author by Cooper and Graham, 1797.

[ii] + iv + 5–14 pp, 41 pls.

54.0 × 37.5 cm

CtY

This pair of large folio volumes illustrating the architect's domestic designs and a few other projects clearly followed the example of similar collections by such prominent architects as James Paine (1767) and Robert and James Adam (1773–1779).[1] Lewis's volumes, published in 1780 and 1797, imitated those of his predecessors in size, content, and also format: the text of the Adams' *Works in Architecture* appeared in parallel columns of English and French, and Lewis, who was in Italy from 1770 to 1772, offered parallel columns of English and Italian.[2] But unlike his predecessors Lewis was not an accomplished architect at the time of publication: his only executed work before 1780 was a set of three houses in Great Ormond Street (I, Plate VII).[3] Clearly his designs were published to attract new clients, Europeans as well as Britons, as may be inferred from the Italian text and from the names of several members of the Russian royal family prominently displayed at the head of the list of 217 subscribers.

In the Preface to the first Book Lewis noted his attention to utility as well as beauty: "This Work is chiefly applicable to the erection of Edifices for private use, wherein convenience and cheapness, blended as much as possible with stability and elegance, have been the principal objects of attention" (I, 1). The Introduction (pp. 2–5) consists of general remarks on civil architecture, followed by a short account of the historical excellence of Greek architecture, the elements of which were established "as standards of perfection and elegance to succeeding ages" (I, 2). In the "Augustan age" of Rome "the fine Arts were in their full meridian," followed by a long decline to a period of "chaos, . . . ignorance, superstition, and fantasy" (I, 3). But while Lewis praised the revival of "Grecian Architecture" during the Renaissance (I, 4), he was unwilling to recommend a "servile attachment to any system whatever." Rather, he recommended suiting proportions to prevailing conditions: "Proportions which can most distinctly mark the character of a building, are to be preferred; consequently demand to be varied according to different circumstances" (I, 5). Likewise proportions of the orders of architecture should be "adapted to their situation in the building" (I, 4). Thus in designing buildings there is "ample scope for the judgment and taste of the Artist" who otherwise might be constrained by "too close an adherence to fixt rules" (I, 5).[4]

In the Preface to Book II (1797) Lewis tempered his remarks on proportion. He deplored "a prevalent disposition" among architects "to neglect, . . . [and] to innovate upon, the established orders, proportions, and general principles of Architecture," often committing "a capricious disregard and violation of them" (II, i). In contrast to these "licentious deviations" Lewis offered the "monuments of antient Architecture" as proven standards: "in proportion as these models, and the principles deduced from them, have been deviated from, or relinquished, the Art itself has declined, and its productions . . . have been mean and without effect, or disgusting, extravagant, and ridiculous" (II, i–ii). Lewis argued that such departures "from the rules of our best ancient models" were due in large part to "a vain and presumptuous opinion of the superiority of our own judgment and abilities" (II, ii). Nevertheless he recommended against "an implicit obedience to the exact proportions dictated by any master," and he averred that "the character, the situation, the destination of the work proposed, and a variety of other circumstances relative thereto, will afford ample room for the exercise of the taste and judgement, and even fancy, of the Artist" (II, iii).

In the first book there are designs for eight "villas" or "houses," three attached town houses, and one theater. The smallest villas (Plates I, II, VIII–XI) are two stories high and five windows wide. The principal floor of the villa shown in Plate I includes a library, dining room, drawing room, parlor, and vestibule. The "Attick Floor" has five bedrooms and five dressing rooms. The largest residence (Plates XIV–XVIII) consists of a central two-story pile, five windows wide, connected by low colonnades to end pavilions each two stories high and three windows wide.[5] In the second book there are designs for a market and store houses, three villas, four houses, a casino, two temples, a greenhouse, a theater, a park entrance, a museum, a hospital, and alterations to a house. Despite Lewis's panegyric on Greece in the Introduction, these designs incorporate only a modest assortment of Greek elements within overwhelmingly Roman and Palladian formulas.

Several of Lewis's plate descriptions in Book II demonstrate his concern for integration of architecture with surrounding landscape scenery. But unlike his contemporaries Lewis chose not to include landscape scenery in his plates.[6] Plates XXV and XXVI, for example, depict a villa "to be built at Lodore, in Cumberland." It is a small, compact dwelling with a projecting semicircular bow in the center. The "surrounding objects being bold and magnificent, it has been attempted to give a strong and bold character to the style of Architecture, that the effect of the building might in some measure harmonize with the character of the country" (II, 11). The plate is devoid of scenery, but the villa is well adapted to the surroundings Lewis described: the masonry bond is emphasized across the entire face of the building, and quoins and engaged columns around the central bow are partially rusticated—features that clearly reflect the "bold character" of the surrounding scenery.

1. See Paine, *Plans, Elevations and Sections*; and Adam, *Works in Architecture*.

2. The parallel Italian text appears only in the 1780 edition of Book I. The description here is based on that edition.

3. Colvin (1978), p. 518, lists no other buildings completed before 1780. Colvin also notes that in preparing *Original Designs* "Lewis was apparently assisted by an Italian draughtsman called Vincenzo Berrarese, who told Milizia in a letter that he had been responsible for the drawings although his name did not appear in the book" (p. 517).

4. These remarks are reminiscent of Claude Perrault, who in 1683 suggested that architectural proportions are not the consequence of natural law, but instead derive from custom: "Thus it is in Architecture, there are Things which Custom only renders so agreeable, that we cannot bear to have them otherwise, tho' they have no Beauty in themselves, that must infallibly please, and necessarily demand Approbation, such as is the Proportion which Capitals generally have with their Columns." See Perrault, *Ordonnance des cinq especes de colonnes selon la méthode des anciens* (Paris, 1683), p. viii; this translation by John James (London, 1708), p. vii. For further discussion of Perrault's argument and its implications see Wolfgang Herrmann, *The Theory of Claude Perrault* (London: Zwemmer, 1973), especially Chapters II and IV. Perrault's observations led subsequent theorists to inquire whether proportions simply were relative to local circumstances, or perhaps were dependent on the artist's taste alone. See Herrmann, op. cit., Chapter V. Sir William Chambers considered the problem in his *Treatise* (q.v.), and suggested that local climate, geography, and materials have a necessary effect on the development of architectural form (1791 edition, p. 25). Likewise Chambers argued that forms of a given proportion derive their appeal not from any universal standard but rather from "convenience, custom, prejudice, or . . . the habit of connecting other ideas with these figures" (1791 edition, p. 106). For further discussion of Chambers's ideas of proportion see Eileen Harris, "The *Treatise on Civil Architecture*," Chapter 9 in John Harris, *Sir William Chambers* (London: Zwemmer, 1970), especially pp. 135–137.

5. Although the largest of Lewis's designs, this was modest in comparison with designs published by some of his contemporaries. See for example George Richardson, *A Series of Original Designs* (1795; q.v.).

6. In the following books, all of which appeared less than five years before Lewis's Book II, there was substantial attention to the relation between architecture and landscape: Sir John Soane, *Sketches in Architecture* (1793); Humphry Repton, *Sketches and Hints* (1794); Richard Payne Knight, *The Landscape* (1794); and John Plaw, *Ferme Ornée* (1795).

179.1

LIGHTOLER, Timothy

The gentleman and farmer's architect. A new work. Containing a great variety of useful and genteel designs. Being correct plans and elevations of parsonage and farm houses, lodges for parks, pinery, peach, hot and green houses, with the fire-wall, tan-pit, &c. particularly described. Dutch, and other barns, cow-houses, stables, sheepcots, huts, facades; with all other offices appertaining to a well-regulated farm; their situations rendered convenient, and aspects agreeable. With scales and tables of reference, describing the several parts, with their just dimensions and use. Designed and drawn by T. Lightoler, Architect. And well engraved on twenty-five folio copper-plates.

London: Printed for Robert Sayer, Map and Print-seller, 1762.

25 pls.

29.5 × 22.9 cm

MH

179.2

The gentleman and farmer's architect. ⟨ . . . .as 1762 . . . ⟩ their just demensions and use. ⟨ . . . as 1762 . . . ⟩ copper-plates.

London: Printed for Robert Sayer, Map and Print-seller, 1764.

25 pls.

26.7 × 21.0 cm

NNC

179.3

The gentleman and farmer's architect. ⟨ . . . as 1762 . . . ⟩, stables, sheep= cots, huts, ⟨ . . . as 1762 . . . ⟩, Architect, and well engraved on twenty= five folio copper-plates.

London: Printed for Robert Sayer, Map and Printseller, 1774.

25 pls.

28.3 × 22.9 cm

MH

On Lightoler's Christian name see Colvin (1978), p. 520. For earlier designs by Lightoler see Halfpenny, et al., *The Modern Builder's Assistant* (1757; *q.v.*).

There is no letterpress. The 25 plates include dimensions and keys to the plans.

Among the 33 designs there are three parsonage houses, seven farm houses, one "House," three lodge houses, one group of "Out Offices" that includes a dwelling, one "Kitchen Dairy, &c.," two ox sheds, one group of coach houses and stables, four barns, one hothouse, one firewall, and one peach and vine wall. In addition there is a design for a "Sheep Coat," an enclosed yard with a small two-story residence for a shepherd. Finally there are six designs for "Facades to place before disagreeable objects," three to front farm buildings and three to front a two-story house.

All designs but one are shown in plan plus one or more elevations and occasionally a section; the sole exception is the peach and vine wall, which is not shown in plan.

One of the largest designs is the "House" shown in Plate 5. The elevation is five openings wide; in the center it is two stories high plus an attic story. There is only restrained ornament, consisting of an entablature over the entrance and stringcourses. There is a semicircular window within the pediment fronting the attic story. The ground floor consists of a hall, parlor, kitchen, pantry, laundry, cellar, milk house, brewhouse, back house, and offices. One of the smallest dwellings is the two-story shepherd's house or "Sheep Coat" (Plate 24), containing one room and a closet on the ground floor, and attached to a triangular enclosure for sheep. The composition is one of Lightoler's most picturesque, with the battlemented house and walls shown in two alternate elevations: in one case the structure is intact, and in the other it is a ruin. Lightoler suggested the design should be built on a hill so that when "seen from a Genteel House" it would be "an agreeable object." Six additional picturesque designs appear in Plate 25. Three are elevations in Rustic or Castellated style, all based on the same plan for a barn attached to a stable or cow house. The other three designs are interchangeable elevations for a two-story house, which has a kitchen, parlor, milk house, brewhouse, washhouse, and pigsty on the ground floor. One of the elevations is composed in a very plain Palladian style, another is a combination of Gothic and Castellated styles, and the third is entirely in Castellated style.

Most of Lightoler's designs are composed in a plain and symmetrical Palladian style. He made limited use of such features as quoins, semicircular and Venetian windows, stringcourses, a three-sided two-story bay, and a portico. Designs in Chinese style for a lodge house and a Dutch barn (Plates 17, 22) have pagoda roofs; in addition the lodge house has bells hanging from the corners of the roof, and above the main roof there is an open belvedere with its own pagoda roof. Elements of both Gothic and Castellated styles appear in five designs for dwellings (Plates 5, 8, 11, 16, 18); there are Tudor drip moldings, windows and doorways with pointed arches, quatrefoils, battlements, and arrowslits.

180.1
LOCH, James (1780–1855)

An account of the improvements on the estates of the Marquess of Stafford, in the counties of Stafford and Salop, and on the estate of Sutherland. With remarks. By James Loch, Esquire.

London: Printed for Longman, Hurst, Rees, Orme, and Brown, 1820.

xx + 236 + 118 pp, frontisp. + 38 pls, 1 table.

21.3 × 13.0 cm

MH

Five years earlier Loch anonymously published *An Account of the Improvements on the Estate of Sutherland* (London: Printed by E. Macleish, 1815), an unillustrated 20-page pamphlet, and the predecessor of the book considered here.

By 1813 the Board of Agriculture had virtually completed publishing a series of agricultural surveys of the counties of England, Scotland, and Wales; supplementary and revised volumes appeared as late as 1817.[1] James Loch ostensibly conceived his *Account* in the same spirit of agricultural improvement. In the Preface (pp. xi–xx) he described problems of enclosure and alluded to pressing economic difficulties, and in the address to the Marquess of Stafford (pp. v–ix) he touted his own role in providing timely models for rural improvement throughout the country. In the text (pp. 1–236) he described a host of economic, geographic, agricultural, and architectural improvements he had undertaken in Sutherland, Staffordshire, and Shropshire to ameliorate a variety of problems.

But the book also serves as Loch's own apologia, for as manager of the Sutherland estates under the second Duke (1786–1861), Loch had instituted controversial, almost Draconian measures to improve the economic conditions of the Duke's Highland estates.[2] Loch shifted the residents of many Highland glens to coastal areas, where he expected they would flourish by developing new and expanded fishing industries. Meanwhile Loch turned the depopulated Highland areas over to sheep pasturage, hoping that it would be a more profitable enterprise than collecting rents from subsistence-level farmers. But the fishing industry could not completely support the expanded coastal population, and such wholesale and occasionally inhumane clearances caused much public criticism.

Loch supported his account with nine appendixes (pp. 1–102), summarizing statistical information on rentals, sheep losses, trade, and harbor tonnages for certain locations in Sutherland, and detailing agricultural improvements in Sutherland, at Trentham in Staffordshire, and at Lilleshall in Shropshire.

In addition to a map of "the Late Arrangements Adopted in the County of Sutherland" there are 38 plates, most of which are described on pages 103–118 following the Appendixes. The first 11 plates accompany the text. Plates 1–3, 5, and 6 depict four inns plus a curing yard and red herring house erected in Sutherland between 1809 and 1819. Plate 4 shows John Rennie's orthogonal plan for the town of Helmsdale, begun in 1814, and Plate 7 is the orthogonal plan for Brora, begun in 1811.[3] Plates 8 through 11 show lands in Shropshire improved by enclosure, drainage, and other changes.

Plates 12 through 20 accompany Appendix No. II, "An Account . . . of the Agricultural Improvements on the Estate of Sutherland." Plates 12 and 17 depict elevations and plans of houses and farm buildings. The larger of the two farm houses, in Plate 12, is three stories high and three windows wide, with a parlor, family room, pantry, and kitchen on the ground floor, plus three bedrooms, a bed closet, and a maidservant's room on the chamber floor. Plate 14 includes an elevation and two plans of Morvich Cottage, erected in 1812. The ground floor includes a family room, a dining room, a family bedroom, several closets and offices, a pantry, and a kitchen. Upstairs there are five bedrooms plus a sitting room and a linen room. Plates 13, 15, 16, 19, and 20 show farm buildings. Plate 18 illustrates a distillery.

Plates 21 through 38 are part of Appendix No. IX, a "Sketch of the Improvements Made by Some of the Tenants . . . at Trentham and Lilleshall." Each plate illustrates a farm house and its accompanying farm buildings in elevation and plan. Most of the farm houses are two stories high and three or four windows wide, occasionally with ells to the sides and rear. A typical plan is that in Plate 31, with a family room, parlor, pantries, kitchen, dairy, brewhouse, and scullery on the ground floor, five bedrooms on the chamber floor, and two rooms in the attic. The house in Plate 32 is slightly larger, with a parlor, master's room, family room, storeroom, kitchen, brewhouse, pantry, and milk house on the ground floor, plus seven bedrooms and a cheese room upstairs.

Most of the house designs are symmetrical and regular, with ornamentation generally confined to decorative stringcourses or pilasters framing the front door.

1. See the entries for Great Britain, Board of Agriculture.

2. For a fuller discussion see Eric Richards, *The Leviathan of Wealth* (London: Routledge & Kegan Paul, 1973), on which the account here is based. Also see John Martin Robinson, *Georgian Model Farms: A Study of Decorative and Model Farm Buildings in the Age of Improvement, 1700–1846* (Oxford: Clarendon Press, 1983), pp. 8, 9, 14, 50, 131, 141, 169–170.

3. Other contemporary Scottish town plans are illustrated in the Board of Agriculture reports on Ayr by William Aiton (1811), and on Caithness by John Henderson (1812 and 1815), *qq.v.* Also see Sir John Sinclair, "Hints Regarding Certain Measures" (1802); and *A Sketch of the Improvements . . . in the County of Caithness* (1803).

LONDON Architectural Society
Essays of the London Architectural Society.

See WOODS, **Joseph,** *Entry 355.*

181.1
The London encyclopaedia, or universal dictionary of science, art, literature, and practical mechanics, comprising a popular view of the present state of knowledge. Illustrated by numerous engravings, a general atlas, and appropriate diagrams. By the original editor of the Encyclopaedia metropolitana, assisted by eminent professional and other gentlemen. In twenty= two volumes. Vol. . . .

London: Printed for Thomas Tegg; sold by N. Hailes; E. Wilson; J. Mason; Bowdery & Kerby: Griffin & Co. Glasgow: J. Cumming, Dublin: M. Baudry, Paris: F. Fleischer, Leipsic; and Whipple & Lawrence, Salem, North America, 1829.

[*Twenty-two volumes.*]

Art. "Architecture," II, 583–635, and 10 pls.
Art. "Farm," IX, 59–70.
Art. "Perspective," XVII, 42–52, and 3 pls on one leaf.
Art. "Rural architecture," XIX, 82–90, and 2 pls.

24.0 × 15.0 cm

MnU

181.2 ‖

———

London: Printed for T. Tegg & Son; R. Griffin & Co., Glasgow; T. T. & H. Tegg, Dublin; also J. & S. A. Tegg, Sydney and Hobart Town, 1837.

[*Twenty-two volumes, 1836–1837. The imprint for Vol. I is given above. Others vary.*]

Art. "Architecture," II, 583–635, and 10 pls.
Art. "Farm," IX, 59–70.
Art. "Perspective," XVII, 42–52, and 3 pls on one leaf.
Art. "Rural architecture," XIX, 82–90, and 2 pls.

Reference: Information supplied by The Ohio State University.

181.3 ‖

———

London: Printed for Thomas Tegg; R. Griffin & Co., Glasgow; Tegg and Co., Dublin; also J. & S. A. Tegg, Sydney and Hobart Town, 1839.

[*Twenty-two volumes. The imprint for Vol. I is given above.*]

Art. "Architecture," II, 583–635, and 10 pls.
Art. "Farm," IX, 59–70.
Art. "Perspective," XVII, 42–52, and 3 pls on one leaf.
Art. "Rural architecture," XIX, 82–90, and 2 pls.

Reference: Information supplied by Southern Illinois University.

181.4 ‖

The London encyclopaedia, ⟨ . . . as 1829 . . . ⟩ engravings and appropriate diagrams. ⟨ . . . as 1829 . . . ⟩.

London: Printed for Thomas Tegg; Charles C. Little and James Brown, Boston; Thomas Cowperthwaite and Co., Philadelphia, 1844.

[*Twenty-two volumes. Vol. I, 1844. Vols. II–XXII, 1845. The imprint for Vol. I is given above.*]

Art. "Architecture," II, 583–635, and 10 pls.
Art. "Farm," IX, 59–70.
Art. "Perspective," XVII, 42–52, and 3 pls on one leaf.
Art. "Rural architecture," XIX, 82–90, and 2 pls.

Reference: Information supplied by Brown University Library.

The article on "Architecture" consists of a short "Introduction" and six "Parts." Part I is a "History of the Art" from biblical times through the ancient Near East, Egypt, India, Phoenicia, China, Greece, Rome, medieval Britain, Renaissance Italy and France, and England of the seventeenth to nineteenth centuries. Part II describes the individual orders and their origins, plus intercolumniations, arches, pilasters, attics, and arrangements of orders above one another. In Part III a discussion of "General Principles of the Art" treats composition, harmony, proportion, siting, "Internal Division of Houses," ornament, and expression. Part IV includes brief remarks on Persians, caryatids, termini, pediments, gates, doors, piers, niches, statues, chimneypieces, staircases, handrails, balustrades, roofs, and ceilings. "Principles to be observed in Erecting Buildings" are considered in Part V, with specific remarks on foundations, walls, chimneys, roofs, floors, and "distribution" of rooms within the plan. The final part treats bridges, piers, and harbors.[1] The ten plates accompanying this article include illustrations of Egyptian capitals, a bridge, roof trusses, and a variety of Classical orders, moldings, and ornaments. The conical, flat-roofed, and gable-roofed examples of primitive huts in Plate III were borrowed from Sir William Chambers's *Treatise* (1759; *q.v.*). Plate VIII includes figures of "Saxon Capitals," Gothic and Saxon arches, and Gothic and Norman columns borrowed from the third edition of the *Encyclopaedia Britannica* (1797; *q.v.*).

The article "Farm" includes sections on laying out farm land, farm buildings, and enclosures, and "keeping Farm Accounts." Figures on pages 64–65 illustrate the plan of one farmyard, and the plan and elevation of another, including a two-story residence with a dairy, pantry, and offices on the ground floor and bedrooms above.[2] On pages 65–66 there are two alternate ground-floor plans and one elevation of a farm house, two stories high and three windows wide. The larger of the two plans includes a parlor, kitchen, bedroom, dairy, and offices, while the smaller includes just a parlor, kitchen, and offices. The elevation is without ornament.

The article on "Perspective" begins with a brief history of the subject, followed by definitions and "General Rules." Separate sections are devoted to mechanical methods of perspective construction and to "Scenographic Perspective." There is an extensive bibliography of perspective treatises published from 1508 to 1813. The article concludes with brief discourses on aerial perspective and perspective machines. Three plates, all printed on one leaf, illustrate techniques and examples of perspective construction, a camera obscura, a perspective machine, and special drawing instruments. All of the figures in Plates I and II can be found in *The Art of Drawing, in Perspective* (1755; *q.v.*). Figure 9 in Plate I illustrates the operation of a camera obscura.[3] On the left is a two-story house flanked by two trees; its image is projected through an opening in the front of a second house onto the rear wall. Figures 1 and 2 in Plate III demonstrate the operation of a "perspective machine," and are taken from James Ferguson's *Art of Drawing in Perspective* (1775; *q.v.*).[4]

This is the only encyclopedia that includes an article specifically titled "Rural Architecture." Intended as a companion to the articles on "Agriculture" and "Farm," this article includes excerpts from John Wood's *Series of Plans, for Cottages* (1792; *q.v.*), and descriptions of several designs for houses and farm buildings. Figures 1–3 in Plate I show a design for a two-story farm house, three windows wide, with lattice windows and a fanlight over the front door. The ground-floor plan includes a parlor, kitchen, back kitchen, bedroom, and dairy, and there are three bedrooms upstairs. Figure 4 in Plate I consists of elevations and plans for a farm house and a farm yard. The house includes two parlors, a dining parlor, a kitchen, a dairy, and a pantry on the ground floor, and four bedrooms upstairs. The elevation is two stories high and three windows wide, with no ornament. Plate II includes designs for barns and a corn stand.

1. For earlier articles organized in a similar manner, see "Architecture" in *Encyclopaedia Perthensis* and *The English Encyclopaedia*.

2. The farm yard, house, and offices illustrated on page 65 are reproduced from Plate XIX in Robert Beatson's article "On Farm Buildings" (1797; *q.v.*).

3. This also resembles Figure 7, Plate XXXV, in *A New and Complete Dictionary* (1754–1755; *q.v.*). In *The London Encyclopaedia* the illustration is reversed, and the larger house does not have the ornamental gable or window mullions and transoms that appear in the *New and Complete Dictionary*.

4. The house in Ferguson's illustration is five windows wide. In the *London Encyclopaedia* it is just three windows wide, and shown in much less detail.

182.1
LOUDON, John Claudius (1783–1843), ed.

The architectural magazine, and journal of improvement in architecture, building, and furnishing, and in the various arts and trades connected therewith. Conducted by J. C. Loudon. . . . Vol. I [*or* II, *or* III, *or* IV, *or* V].

[*Volume I:*]

viii + 396 pp.

London: Longman, Rees, Orme, Brown, Green, & Longman, 1834.

[*Volume II:*]

viii + 564 pp.

London: Longman, Rees, Orme, Brown, Green, & Longman; and Weale, 1835.

[*Volume III:*]

xvi + 584 pp.

London: Longman, Rees, Orme, Brown, Green, & Longman; and Weale, 1836.

[*Volume IV:*]

viii + 600 pp.

London: Longman, Orme, Brown, Green, & Longmans; and Weale, 1837.

[*Volume V:*]

x + 728 pp.

London: Longman, Orme, Brown, Green, & Longmans; and Weale, 1838 [–1839].

MH

The Architectural Magazine was the first British periodical devoted entirely to architecture. In the "Introduction" to the first issue (March 1834; pp. 1–12) Loudon announced objectives and a format that closely resembled those of his *Encyclopaedia*, published one year earlier (*q.v.*). He wanted first of all "to diffuse among general readers a taste for architectural beauties and comforts, and to improve the dwellings of the great mass of society in all countries." Like the *Encyclopaedia* the *Magazine* would consist of short articles on architectural subjects; but the *Magazine* also would "embrace a more extensive range of subjects than the Encyclopaedia; since, in addition to the private dwellings of every class of society residing in the country, it will include also dwellings in cities and towns, and public buildings, in a word, the whole of civil architecture, building, and furnishing" (I, 1). The bulk of the Introduction consists of remarks on the advantages of studying architecture, and the resulting potential for improving the taste of the aristocracy, of women, of carpenters and a variety of other artisans, and of the nation as a whole. Loudon concluded with a brief description of the organization of each issue: the first part would consist of "Original Communications," the second would contain reviews, and the third would include "Miscellaneous Intelligence" (I, 10).

The subject matter of the *Magazine* is indeed catholic: the fourth issue, for example, includes an article "On the Gin Temples of the Metropolis," and other articles treat churches, market buildings, town planning, the Houses of Parliament, workhouses, stoves, chimneys, the Classical orders, Gothic architecture, materials (e.g., iron and slate), construction, and principles of design; in addition there are critical remarks on new and proposed buildings. Loudon illustrated several important recent structures, including the Hungerford and Covent Garden market buildings, the new Town Hall in Birmingham, the National Gallery in London, the Customs House in New York City, and Girard College in Philadelphia.

A large proportion of articles in the *Magazine* concerns domestic architecture, treating interior and exterior ornament, furnishings, materials, construction, heating, planning, principles of design, landscaping, and style. Space does not permit a comprehensive review of all these articles, but a chronological synopsis of those accompanied by plans or elevations of dwellings is possible, followed by remarks on several articles concerning important aspects of architectural theory.

• **An Observer,** "On Certain Deceptive Practices Adopted by Some Authors of Architectural Designs for Villas," I:3 (May 1834), 117–120. The author objected to the "deception" created when architects illustrated their designs with landscape scenery, or overly emphasized "the shadows of slight projections," or concealed chimney shafts. He included a plan and elevation of a villa in Greek style taken "from a book of designs recently published," and then provided his own, corrected elevation with proper chimney tops, no ground-story rustication, and other changes.

• **A Self-taught Architect and Landscape-Gardener,** "A Series of Designs, with Descriptive and Historical Particulars, of Characteristic and Ornamental Buildings, and Objects for Gardens and Pleasure-Grounds," I:3 (May 1834), 120–123. The article includes three illustrations of sundials, plus a view of a "round seat, with thatched roof" erected ca. 1812 by the Duke of Marlborough at White Knights. The seat is circular in plan, with a conical roof.

• **W. H. Leeds,** "Specimen of Studies of Plan," I:6 (August 1834), 226–229. Leeds complained that some houses he had seen "would almost convince any one that the chief object, on the part of the architect, was to get through his task with the least possible trouble and expense of thought." He illustrated the plan of a villa with certain defects and suggested remedial improvements, which he depicted in an additional illustration.

• **I. J. Kent,** "On the Domestic Offices of a House," I:8 (October 1834), 302–308; "On the Dwelling-Rooms of a House," II:12 (February 1835), 59–61; "The Dwelling-Rooms of a House," II:15 (May 1835), 228–233; "On the Dwelling-Rooms of a House," II:16 (June 1835), 275–281; "On the Dwelling-Rooms of a House," II:18 (August 1835), 348–358; "On the Dwelling-Rooms of a House," II:19 (September 1835), 404–407. This series of six articles treats the function, construction, decoration, and furnishing of rooms within a house. The first article, unillustrated, primarily concerns the kitchen, but also includes remarks on the coal cellar, scullery, larder, cistern, beer and wine cellars, housekeeper's room, footman's room or butler's pantry, and passages. The second article, also unillustrated, discusses rooms "placed on the principal or entrance floor," including the breakfast parlor and storerooms. The third and fourth articles concern the dining room: there is a detailed plan of a dining room (24 feet by 15 feet) on page 231, and a plan and elevation of an octagonal dining room (20 feet in diameter) on pages 279 and 280. The fifth article, unillustrated, treats the drawing room. The final article, also unillustrated, concerns the library. Cf. the corrected elevation of the octagonal dining room in II:17 (July 1835), 327–328.

• **E. B. Lamb,** "Design for a Villa in the Norman Style of Architecture," I:9 (November 1834), 333–348. The plan and elevation are asymmetrical and irregular, composed of rectangular units of different heights surrounding a round tower. The ground floor contains a porch, hall, drawing room, library, dining room, conservatory, and offices. Lamb's illustrations include a plan and elevation of the house, interior views of the drawing room and of a room furnished with several "articles of furniture in the Norman style," and details of a porch, a doorway, windows, "interlacing arches," chimneys, a tower, a turret, and a fireplace.

• **W. H. Leeds,** "Remarks on Closets, &c., in Sitting-Rooms," I:9 (November 1834), 348–351. Leeds illustrated a plan for part of "a small cottage villa" that has several closets, including "a small light closet between the two sitting rooms." One wall of the light closet is formed by a three-sided bay window.

• **J. Thompson,** "Foreign Notices.—Australia," I:10 (December 1834), 375–377. The article includes a plan for a cottage and surrounding grounds intended to be carried out near Sydney. The one-story house, an "exact square" in plan, has a dining room, a drawing room, three bedrooms, two dressing rooms, a nursery, a storeroom, and a veranda; an office wing is attached.

• **W. H. Leeds,** "Plans for Rooms Adapted to Houses Where a Corner Is Curved Off," II:12 (February 1835), 56–58; "Plans for Rooms, &c.," II:19 (September 1835), 393–400. Considering the recent trend toward "rounding off the angles of corner houses," Leeds noted the possible "injurious" results to room interiors unless "some study and contrivance be employed to produce internal regularity of plan." In the two articles Leeds provided four plans for rooms with rounded or truncated corners. N.B. a corrected engraving of one plan appears in II:20 (October 1835), p. 475.

• **Tyro,** "A Design for a Turnpike Lodge, with Remarks," II:14 (April 1835), 159–161. The article includes side and front elevations, a plan, and two details. The one-story elevation is fronted by a distyle Doric portico. The plan includes a combination waiting room and office, a combination dining room and bedroom for the keeper, a closet, and a water closet.

• **E. B. Lamb,** "Design for a Villa in the Style of Architecture of the Thirteenth Century," II:16 (June 1835), 257–275. Lamb indicated that the design was intended for "a romantic situation, upon a rocky eminence, backed by lofty wood, and a richly cultivated country; with, at the base of the rock, a rapid stream winding through a fertile valley." The illustrations include a ground-floor plan, an elevation, a view of the entrance porch, two interior views, and details of windows, doors, chimneys, and a bell turret. The ground floor contains a hall, saloon, drawing room, breakfast room, business room, dining room, library, and conservatory. Cf. Lamb's additional remarks and illustrations in II:19 (September 1835), 425–428.

• **William J. Short,** "Remarks on Street Architecture," II:19 (September 1835), 389–393. The author recommended that houses be combined "together in such a manner as to form a mass of one style, of sufficient consequence to bear some comparison with public buildings; but not to be carried to such an extent as to produce sameness or mannerism." He wanted architects to "take a lesson from landscape-gardeners, and endeavour to obtain something like the delightful effects and endless variety which they do in laying out walks in pleasure-grounds." Short cited Waterloo Place as "one of the most beautiful gems of street architecture in the metropolis," although not without faults. He included an elevation of "a private residence in Great James Street, Buckingham Gate" as an example of the Elizabethan style used "with good effect."

• **William Ross,** "Street Houses of the City of New York," II:21 (November 1835), 490–493. Ross offered brief remarks on differences in construction and design between houses in London and New York. He provided a basement plan of a New York house with a kitchen, a "large room," and four closets.

• **William Wells,** "Perspective View and Ground Plan of a Cyclopean Cottage," II:22 (December 1835), 533–534. The cottage had been erected on Wells's estate in Kent as a residence for the under gardener. The term "Cyclopean" refers to the walls of the ground story, which are formed of irregularly shaped blocks of sandstone. The upper story is half-timbered. The ground-floor plan has a kitchen, parlor, pantry, "light closet," and shed. Wells provided an elevation and a plan.

• **Edward Brigden,** "Design for a Labourer's Cottage," III:25 (March 1836), 120–128. In this design Brigden attended to "convenience," noting that "all ornament of an elaborate or costly kind is out of order." The illustrations include two plans, a section, two elevations, and several details. The ground-floor plan includes a kitchen and back kitchen, and there are two bedrooms upstairs. The text gives specifications for masonry, carpentry, joinery, plumbing, tiling, plastering, glazing, and painting. Cf. the additional remarks and illustrations offered by "A Young Architect" in III:29 (July 1836), 331–332.

• **E. B. Lamb,** "Design for a Suburban Villa with Two Acres of Ground," III:26 (April 1836), 155–168. The text includes a detailed description of the interior and remarks on landscaping. The Italianate design is shown in four plans, four elevations, a site plan, and a detail of an iron railing. The elevation includes a basement, principal story, chamber story, and attic. The principal floor plan has a porch, hall, drawing room, dining room, and library.

• **Edward Brigden,** "Design for an Entrance Lodge," III:29 (July 1836), 314–315. Bargeboards and Tudor moldings embellish the two-story elevation. The ground-floor plan consists of an octagonal living room with one-story square rooms attached to four of the octagon's eight faces. In addition to the elevation and plan there are details of a gate pier and eave boards.

• **E. B. Lamb,** "Design for a Villa in the Style of the Second Class of Gothic Architecture," III:32 (October 1836), 456–464. The text consists primarily of a description of the interior. The design is shown in two plans and two elevations, and the ground floor contains a dining room, drawing room, study, kitchen, pantry, scullery, and cellar.

• **Richard Varden,** "Design for a Suburban Villa, on Half an Acre of Ground, in an Unfavourable Situation," III:32 (October 1836), 464–475. The design was prepared for a site "of somewhat less than half an acre" in the vicinity of Worcester. The sole illustration is a ground plan of the house combined with a plan for a formal parterre.

• **Edward Brigden,** "Design for a Lodge in the Italian Style," III:33 (November 1836), 512–513. The lodge is shown in elevation and plan, and includes a living room and bedroom on the ground floor, plus an additional room in the tower above.

• **W. H. Leeds,** "An English Version of a French Plan," III:34 (December 1836), 573–581; "An English Version of a French Plan," IV:35 (January 1837), 28–32. The first article concerns a "flat" in a building erected by Poirier in Paris in 1829, in which Leeds discovered numerous examples of the architect's "defective performance." A plan of the flat appears on page 577. In the second article Leeds offered two alternative plans for the flat, incorporating many improvements.

• **M.,** "On the Effect Which Should Result to Architecture, in Regard to Design and Arrangement, from the General Introduction of Iron in the Construction of Buildings," IV:40 (June 1837), 277–287. The illustrations depict two iron roof trusses, a "skeleton exemplification (with some variation)" of the porch of Peterborough Cathedral, the interior of a church constructed of iron, an iron steeple, and the plan and elevation of a house constructed of iron. The facade of the house, five openings wide and two stories high in the center, is covered with elaborate ornamental ironwork. The ground-floor plan includes a saloon, breakfast room, library, dining room, drawing room, and conservatory.

• **Selim,** "On the Necessity of Connecting Buildings in the Country, and Especially Dwelling-houses, with the Surrounding Scenery, by Means of Architectural Embellishments," IV:42 (August 1837), 380–382. The author suggested that just as paintings require frames, so buildings should be framed "with such objects as will show them off to the best advantage." He illustrated an outline plan of a house flanked by office wings and "architectural gardens."

• **J. A. Picton,** "On Cemeteries," IV:43 (September 1837), 426–437. The illustrations include an elevation and plan of the "house for the officiating minister." The ground-floor plan contains a study, dining room, and kitchen. The two-story elevation is composed in Tudor style.

• **G. B. W.,** "A Gate Lodge, or Cottage," IV:44 (October 1837), 490. The irregular elevation is two stories high and four openings wide. The ground-floor plan includes a living room, kitchen, and bedroom; there are two rooms upstairs.

• **Kata Phusin** [pseud. for **John Ruskin**], "The Poetry of Architecture; or the Architecture of the Nations of Europe Considered in Its Association with Natural Scenery and National Character," IV:45 (November 1837), 505–508; IV:46 (December 1837), 555–560; V:47 (January 1838), 7–14; V:48 (February 1838), 56–63; V:49 (March 1838), 97–105; V:50 (April 1838), 145–154; V:51 (May 1838), 193–198; V:52 (June 1838), 241–250; V:53 (July 1838), 289–301; V:54 (August 1838), 337–344; V:55 (September 1838), 385–392; V:56 (October 1838), 433–442; V:57 (November 1838), 481–494; V:58 (December 1838), 533–554. This important series of articles treats function, expression, and composition in vernacular architecture. At the outset Ruskin proposed "to trace in the distinctive characters of the architecture of nations, not only its adaptation to the situation and climate in which it has arisen, but its strong similarity to, and connection with, the prevailing turn of mind by which the nation who first employed it is distinguished" (IV, 505). "We shall consider the architecture of nations as it is influenced by their feelings and manners, as it is connected with the scenery in which it is found, and with the skies under which it was erected" (IV, 508). Ruskin treated lowland cottages in England, France, and Italy, mountain cottages in Switzerland and Westmorland, chimneys, the mountain villa in Italy, the lowland villa in England, and the "British Villa" in "blue" cultivated country, in "green" wooded country, and in "brown" hilly country.

• **W. S.,** "A Design for a Small Cottage Villa," IV:45 (November 1837), 524–529. The design, in "classical" style, is shown in three plans and three elevations. The ground-floor plan has an entrance hall, drawing room, dining room, and library.

• **E. B. Lamb,** "Design for a Suburban Residence to be Erected at Stuttgart, by Direction of His Majesty the King of Würtemberg," V:47 (January 1838), 18–26. The "Anglo-Italian" design is three stories high and five openings wide, and illustrated in two plans and one view. The ground-floor plan contains a hall, dining room, library, breakfast room, butler's room, lobby, and water closet.

• **N.,** "On Selecting the Position of a House on the Side of a Hill," V:47 (January 1838), 29–30. The author recommends that any ground cut away from a slope on one side of a house should be used to build up the slope on the other side. Two diagrams illustrate his argument.

• **Edward Brigden,** "A Design for a Labourer's Cottage or Gate Lodge, in the Grecian Style," V:48 (February 1838), 74–75. The one-story lodge, three openings wide, contains just a living room, bedroom, and washhouse.

• Review of John Britton, *The History and Description, with Graphic Illustrations, of Cassiobury Park, Hertfordshire, the Seat of the Earl of Essex,* V:49 (March 1838), 114–120. A large portion of the review is devoted to cottages and lodges at Cassiobury, and ten of Britton's illustrations are reproduced: a view and a plan of the half-timbered Ridge Lane Cottage, and plans of eight other cottages and lodges.

• **T. K.,** "A House for an Invalid," V:56 (October 1838), 459–464. The house "was designed by an invalid architect (who is so infirm as not to be able to stand or walk), for his own occupation." The illustrations include a combination ground-floor plan and site plan, a first-floor plan, and a detail of the front steps. The ground floor consists of a lobby, closet, water closet, hall, dining room, library, and parlor.

• **W. H. Leeds,** "Design for a Villa Comprising Two Distinct Residences," V:58 (December 1838), 554–564. The design is for "two villas, so disposed as to secure to each nearly all the advantages of a detached and independent residence, at the same time that, from being thus united, they derive importance as an object, which neither of them would possess singly." Leeds provided a site plan, ground plan, and chamber-floor plan. Each unit contains a vestibule, dining room, drawing room, morning room, anteroom, and conservatory on the ground floor, plus seven bedrooms and two other rooms upstairs.

•

The following articles concern selected aspects of architectural theory:

• **W. H.,** "On Character in Architecture," I:9 (November 1834), 324–328. The author carefully distinguished "character" from "style" and "expression." "Style," he said, is "a particular description of order," and "there may be many expressions contributing to the same character." Character, then, is "the simple, though forcible, language of the features in architecture." On viewing a building, "we recognise its style, we perceive its expressions, but we are impressed with its character. Hence it becomes, as it were, the conducting medium between the intrinsic beauties and qualities of the art, and the pleasures and feelings they excite." The author described certain architectural "characters" and then discussed their influence "on the mind," the contributory effects of light and climate in creating them, and the means of creating them with architectural forms.

• **J. Dowson,** "Essay on the Metaphysics of Architecture," III:28 (June 1836), 245–249. Dowson established four "denominations" of architecture: Beautiful, Sublime, Grand, and Magnificent. In addition he mentioned four principles of composition: grace, expression, proportion, and harmony. A large part of the article concerns the ability of Gothic, Greek, and Egyptian styles to produce beauty, sublimity, grandeur, and magnificence.

• **T. Sopwith,** "On the Principles of Design," IV:44 (October 1837), 457–463. The article concerns the design of churches, and concludes with nine "principles of fitness" applicable to the design of a cathedral church.

LOUDON, John Claudius (1783–1843)
"Colleges for working men."

See Mechanics' magazine, *Entry 477.*

LOUDON, John Claudius (1783–1843)
The cottager's manual of husbandry.

See his Manual of cottage gardening, *Entry 189;* and [BURKE, **John French**], British Husbandry, *Entry 28.*

183.1
LOUDON, John Claudius (1783–1843)
Designs for laying out farms and farm-buildings, in the Scotch style; adapted to England: including an account of the buildings and improvements recently executed on Tew Lodge Farm, Oxfordshire, with an opinion on the subject of breaking up grass lands. Illustrated by forty plates. By J. C. Loudon. . . .

London: Published by J. Harding; and Longman, Hurst, Rees, Orme, and Browne. Printed by T. Hood and Co., 1811.

105 pp, 38 pls.

36.5 × 26.7 cm

BL

Observations on laying out farms, in the Scotch style, adapted to England. Comprising an account of the introduction of the Berwickshire husbandry into Middlesex and Oxfordshire. With remarks on the importance of this system to the general improvement of landed property. Illustrated by forty plates, descriptive of farm buildings, rural improvements, &c. &c. recently executed. By J. C. Loudon, F.L.S.

London: Printed for John Harding, 1812.

105 pp, 38 pls.

37.4 × 27.3 cm

MH

In the copy of *Designs for Laying Out Farms* in the British Library the first three plates are watermarked 1817.

In both editions the plates are numbered irregularly. Although the title page announces 40 plates, there are only 38. Loudon explained that "By reason of the distance of the Author from the Press, some confusion has occurred in the numeration of the Plates, which was not discovered before the title-page was printed off" (p. 12). The Table of Contents (pp. 9–12) indicates that the plates should be numbered I–XII (with VII and VIII together forming one plate), XVI–XXXII, XXXIV–XXXIX, XXXIX–XLII. This numbering scheme generally corresponds with the Arabic numbers on the plates[1] but not, unfortunately, with several references in the text.

The first chapter, including nearly half the text and almost a third of the plates, is an account of Loudon's improvements at Tew Lodge Farm, Oxfordshire, between 1808 and 1810. Chapters II and III detail his work at Wood Hall Farm and Kenton Lane Farm, both in Middlesex.[2] Chapter IV concerns formation of farms "from recently-enclosed Commons, and Common-field Lands," and Chapter V is a brief discussion of farm land reclaimed from the sea. Chapter VI presents "Miscellaneous Examples" of farms and farm buildings. The final chapter concerns more elegant farm landscapes: "Park Farms, or Domain Lands, Fermes Ornées, &c."

The plates that accompany the first three chapters depict plans, elevations, and views of buildings on the three estates that Loudon improved, and plans and views of improvements to the grounds. The farm house at Tew Lodge (Plate 4) is two stories high and three windows wide, with a kitchen, parlor, bedroom, pantry, dairy, and counting house shown in the plan. Plates 7 through 12 depict plans, elevations, and views of Tew Lodge itself, designed in a very spare Neoclassical style. The ground-floor plan includes a dining room, drawing room, library, kitchen, pantry, and offices, and there are five rooms on the chamber floor. Loudon designed the plan with efficiency in mind:

From the bedroom, and from almost any part of the library, the whole of the farm buildings, and nearly one half of the farm, may be viewed without any change of position. By this means the farmer, when he sees any thing amiss, or which requires his notice, has only (uninterrupted by weather) to walk out under the porch, and with a French horn first direct the attention of the party, and then give orders through a speaking-trumpet. (p. 49)

Plates 18 and 19 show the farm house at Woodhall Farm, formerly a "comfortless, ill-arranged dwelling," now "altered and repaired so as to be a neat and commodious residence" (p. 65). The plan of the farm house at Kenton Farm is shown in Plate 23, and an alternative design "which may be erected at less expence" (p. 10), with a two-story cylindrical tower in the center of the rear elevation, appears in Plates 19 and 24.

Among the plates in Chapters IV through VI are three designs for houses and residential improvements. Plates 28 and 35 (misnumbered 30 and 19, respectively) include the plan and elevation of a house for "the estate of W. Colhoun" at Wrentham. The plan is a Greek cross, with triangular porches filling the angles between the arms of the cross. Plate 32 includes an elevation and plan for improvements in a castellated style to the house at Mimbury Fort. Plates 34 and 35 include the plan of a house and the plan and elevation of farm buildings for the Birchden and Hamsel estate near Tunbridge Wells.

In the discussion of park farms in Chapter VII (pp. 100–105), Loudon argued that a designer's attention to fitness and utility in roads, fences, and buildings, as well as in "culture and management," would give the owner pleasure and also serve as "an example to tenantry" (p. 100).[3] In addition the designer would want to "dignify and ennoble the farming of an independent gentleman or noble agriculturalist" (p. 100). Dignity, Loudon said, could be displayed in "the buildings, fences, and roads of a farm, by a superiority of design, by exhibiting a plan sufficiently extensive to attain, with ease, what in common cases is rather attempted than attained" (p. 101). And *"wealth* or *distinction"* can be expressed through "a superiority of execution; by employing durable, in place of temporary, materials; by selecting them from principles of taste rather than of economy; and by displaying in their use, *abundance* rather than *scarcity* or penuriousness" (p. 101). He cited Holkham and Woburn as "instances of park farms, in which these ideas have been carried into effect in the grandest manner"; in particular Holkham was a "proper *ferme ornée* . . . where elegance takes place of magnificence, and beauty of extent" (pp. 101–102). Plates 36 through 38 illustrate a project for "a park and farms" at Scone Park, Perthshire, that Loudon prepared in 1804. He proposed moving the town of Scone "to a distant part of the estate" (p. 103), dividing up the estate into farm land and pasture land, building a new set of farm buildings, and installing "the necessary accommodations of a farmery" in the "old castle of Ardgillan," which would be "heightened in effect as a ruin" (p. 104). The principal farm buildings, shown in Plate 38, are arranged in two concentric curves facing a rectangular barn at the center point. The entrance to the farmyard passes directly through the center of the two-story "Stewards House," which also includes two parlors, a kitchen, and a dairy on the ground floor.

The two plates numbered 39 show a "Mansion, Farmery & Stables, Calculated to form One Pile of Architecture," designed in 1809 for Colonel Richard Mytton, of Garth in Montgomeryshire.[4] The house, farm buildings, and circular stables all form a single range of buildings fronted by a continuous Gothic veranda, with Perpendicular Gothic windows in the house facade and crenellations and finials at the top. The ground-floor plan of the house includes an entrance hall, library, drawing room, dining room, business room, laundry, housekeeper's room, brewhouse, kitchen, and many smaller offices. Plate 40 is a distant view of "the ancient palace of Scone, with additions in the cathedral or palace style, in order to render it a fit residence for a modern nobleman" (p. 12).

1. Exceptions include Plate 28, which is misnumbered 30, and Plate 35, which is misnumbered 19.

2. For fuller discussion of Loudon's farm improvements see Melanie Louise Simo, "Loudon and the Landscape: A Study of Rural and Metropolitan Improvements 1803–1843," Ph.D. dissertation, Yale University, 1976.

3. On the importance of fitness and utility for Loudon's aesthetic, see commentaries below on his *Gardener's Magazine* (1826 and later) and *Encyclopaedia of Cottage, Farm, and Villa Architecture* (1833).

4. Loudon described the design as "now executing" (pp. 104–105). Elevations and a plan for the stables also appear in Loudon's *Encyclopaedia* (1833; *q.v.*), pp. 965–966. Colvin (1978), p. 525, calls the house Loudon's "principal architectural work," and "crudely detailed."

LOUDON, John Claudius (1783–1843)
An encyclopaedia of agriculture.

See Entry 489.

184.1
LOUDON, John Claudius (1783–1843)
An encyclopaedia of cottage, farm, and villa architecture and furniture; containing numerous designs for dwellings, from the cottage to the villa, including farm houses, farmeries, and other agricultural buildings; several designs for country inns, public houses, and parochial schools; with the requisite fittings-up, fixtures, and furniture; and appropriate offices, gardens, and garden scenery; each design accompanied by analytical and critical remarks, illustrative of the principles of architectural science and taste on which it is composed. By J. C. Loudon. . . . Illustrated by nearly one hundred lithographs, and above two thousand engravings on wood. The designs by upwards of fifty different architects, surveyors, builders, upholsterers, cabinet-makers, and others, of whom a list is given.

London: Longman, Rees, Orme, Brown, Green, & Longman; Treuttel, Würtz, and Richter, London; Treuttel and Würtz, Paris and Strasburg; Black, Edinburgh; Carvill, New York; Gray and Bowen, Boston; Carey and Lea, Philadelphia; Howe, Sydney; and Melville, Hobart Town, 1833.

xx + 1138 pp.

21.6 × 14.0 cm

MB

184.2

———————

London: Longman, Rees, Orme, Brown, Green, & Longman. Treuttel, ⟨ . . . as 1833 . . . ⟩ Melville, Hobart Town, 1834.

xx + 1138 pp.

21.7 × 13.0 cm

MH

184.3

———————

An encyclopaedia ⟨ . . . as 1833 . . . ⟩ Loudon. . . . Illustrated by more than two thousand engravings: the designs by upwards of fifty different architects, surveyors, builders, upholsterers, cabinet-makers, landscape-gardeners, and others, of whom a list is given. A new edition, with numerous corrections, and with many of the plates re-engraved.

London: Longman, Rees, Orme, Brown, Green, & Longman; and sold by John Weale, 1835.

xx + 1138 pp.

21.6 × 13.7 cm

CtY

184.4

———————

An encyclopaedia ⟨ . . . as 1833 . . . ⟩ Loudon. . . . Illustrated by more than two thousand engravings: the designs by upwards of fifty different architects, surveyors, builders, upholsterers, cabinet makers landscape-gardeners, and others, of whom a list is given. A new edition, with numerous corrections, and with many of the plates re-engraved.

London: Longman, Rees, Orme, Brown, Green, & Longman; and sold by John Weale, 1836.

xx + 1138 pp.

21.3 × 13.3 cm

MBAt

184.5

An encyclopaedia ⟨ . . . as 1833 . . . ⟩ Loudon. . . . Illustrated by more than two thousand engravings: the designs by upwards of fifty different architects, surveyors, builders, upholsterers, cabinet-makers landscape-gardeners, and others, of whom a list is given. A new edition, with numerous corrections, and with many of the plates re-engraved.

London: Longman, Orme, Brown, Green, & Longmans, and sold by John Weale, 1839.

xx + 1138 pp.

21.6 × 13.3 cm

MH

184.6 ‖

London: Longman, Brown, Green, and Longmans; and sold by John Weale, 1841.

xx + 1138 pp.

Reference: Information supplied by Ricker Library of Architecture and Art, University of Illinois at Urbana-Champaign.

184.7

An encyclopaedia of cottage, farm, and villa architecture and furniture: containing ⟨ . . . as 1833 . . . ⟩ parochial schools, with the requisite fittings = up, fixtures, and furniture, and ⟨ . . . as 1833 . . . ⟩ Loudon. . . . Illustrated by more than two thousand engravings: the designs by upwards of fifty different architects, surveyors, builders, upholsterers, cabinet-makers landscape-gardeners, and others, of whom a list is given. A new edition: with a supplement containing above one hundred and sixty pages of letter-press, and nearly three hundred engravings, bringing down the work to 1842.

[*In an otherwise identical copy at MdBE, a comma follows the word* cabinet-makers.]

London: Longman, Brown, Green, and Longmans; and sold by John Weale, 1842.

xx + 1306 pp.

21.6 × 14.0 cm

BL

184.8

An encyclopaedia of cottage, farm, and villa architecture and furniture; containing numerous designs for dwellings, from the villa to the cottage and the farm, including farm houses, farmeries, and other agricultural buildings; country inns, public houses, and parochial schools: with the requisite fittings-up, fixtures, and furniture; and appropriate offices, gardens, and garden scenery: each design accompanied by analytical and critical remarks. By the late J. C. Loudon. . . . Illustrated by more than two thousand engravings. A new edition, edited by Mrs. Loudon.

London: Longman, Brown, Green, and Longmans, 1846.

xxiv + 1317 pp.

21.9 × 13.7 cm

MB

184.9

London: Longman, Brown, Green, and Longmans, 1853.

xxiv + 1317 pp.

21.6 × 13.7 cm

MH

184.10

London: Longman, Brown, Green, Longmans, & Roberts, 1857.

xxiv + 1317 pp.

21.6 × 13.5 cm

MdBP

184.11

London: Longman, Green, Longman, Roberts, & Green, 1863.

xxiv + 1317 pp.

22.2 × 14.0 cm

CtY

184.12

London: Longmans, Green, and Co., 1867.

xxiv + 1317 pp.

22.2 × 14.2 cm

MH

184.13

London: Frederick Warne and Co. New York: Scribner, Welford, and Co., 1869.

xxiv + 1317 pp.

21.3 × 13.6 cm

PP

184.14 ‖

An encyclopaedia ⟨ . . . as 1846 . . . ⟩ schools; with ⟨ . . . as 1846 . . . ⟩ scenery; each ⟨ . . . as 1846 . . . ⟩ Mrs. Loudon.

London: Frederick Warne & Co., [n.d.].

xxiv + 1137 pp.

Reference: Information supplied by Environmental Design Library, University of California, Berkeley.

Loudon's *Encyclopaedia* was unquestionably the most voluminous and most frequently reissued architectural treatise of the mid-nineteenth century. It achieved at least 14 editions or impressions over approximately 40 years, passing through two major editorial revisions and several minor ones.

The first edition, issued by Loudon in 1833, contained xx + 1138 pages. He made minor corrections and changes in the text for the edition of 1835. In 1842 he offered an extensive body of additions as a "Supplement," issued both as a separate title and as part of the edition of 1842. In that edition the Supplement added 164 pages to the length of the book, and the Index was expanded by four pages. Following Loudon's death in 1843 his wife Jane undertook the final changes, which first appeared in the edition of 1846. She expanded the Supplement to 172 pages, in most cases according to directions Loudon had given before his death; she also revised the "Glossarial Index," increasing its length by three pages, and she expanded the introductory matter by four pages. Through all these revisions Loudon's original 1124 pages of text remained largely unchanged.

At the very beginning Loudon announced the two principal goals of his work. His "main object" was "to improve the dwellings of the great mass of society." Later it becomes clear that by "great mass" he meant not only working-class people but also the middle classes, who in the 1830s were clearly the ascendant element of British society. Second, Loudon wanted "to create and diffuse among mankind, generally, a taste for architectural comforts and beauties" (p. 1).[1] Thus his work would have a dual social benefit: it would contribute to physical improvements in housing while furthering a greater understanding of architectural aesthetics. But while these goals were complementary, he recognized they were not necessarily linked. The first, he said, was by now an imperative need, given the state of existing housing, while the second goal was merely desirable.

Loudon felt the format of his book would help in pursuing both goals: he presented individual designs for scores of dwellings, discussed and analyzed each in a brief text, and illustrated each in one or more diagrams, plans, or views. He believed this would be more palatable for the "general reader" than a long treatise proceeding methodically through all the principles and practices of architectural design, and so would be "of more immediate practical utility to persons intending to build or furnish." To this compendium of practical instructions he then added occasional criticism and commentary "initiating the general reader in the principles of architectural taste" (p. 1).

But instruction in the fundamental principles of taste was not left entirely to the reader's ability to synthesize from examples. In the Introduction Loudon specified what he believed to be the three "leading" principles of architecture. The first was "fitness for the end in view," because architecture above all was a "useful art."[2] The second was "expression of the end in view," i.e., communication of the building's function through its design.[3] Loudon considered both these principles to be necessary and permanent features of architectural design. The third principle was only "temporary and accidental," and defined simply as "expression of some particular Architectural style" (p. 4), or "creating in the mind, emotions of sublimity or beauty" (p. 6). Later he indicated that this could involve stimulating the imagination through association and other means (pp. 1114–1124). In the Introduction, however, Loudon offered only the somewhat unorthodox notion that "expression of style," while desirable, was not necessary for the success of any architectural design. Loudon's three principles thus were a significant—if not complete—departure from the traditional architectural principles formulated by Vitruvius (structure, function, and aesthetic pleasure) and Wotton (firmness, commodity, and delight).

Loudon devoted the bulk of his treatise to short individual analyses of designs for dwellings and other structures. In the first of four "Books" he presented dwellings for laborers, mechanics, gardeners, bailiffs, "upper servants," and small farmers. The second book included designs for farm houses, farmeries, country inns, and parochial schools. He devoted the third book entirely to villas, and featured a design for the "Beau Idéal of an English Villa." The final book—only 19 pages—explored theoretical issues and in particular "principles of criticism." The shortness of this portion reflects Loudon's preference for instruction by example.

Within the first three books there are designs for at least 81 cottages and 23 villas—plus 35 more cottages and 17 more villas in the Supplement. Loudon accompanied each design with a discussion of specific points, including the situation of the building in the landscape, the fitness of the design for its purpose, technical information necessary for its erection, instructions for artisans, and possible expression of taste or style. Not all designs were presented as paradigmatic. Design XVI in Book I, for example, had two major defects: a thatch roof which Loudon criticized as giving the dwelling a mean, crouching appearance; and truncated gable ends which appeared to be an imperfection of form and therefore suggested restricted resources and meanness of character. Presenting negative as well as positive examples was clearly part of Loudon's method of teaching by example.

Among the instructive examples making up this treatise, Loudon presented one in great detail, as an epitome of residential architecture. This was "the English villa," chosen because it embodied all the necessary characteristics of lesser types while exhibiting a standard of excellence unparalleled elsewhere. Even "the humblest cottage," he explained, "ought to contain all the essential comforts of a villa dwelling" (p. 763), while the English villa also combined "more of the comforts and luxuries of life than the villa of a man of wealth and taste in any other country in the world" (p. 6). Thus a cottage was essentially a villa reduced in size and cost. The only qualitative difference between the two was one of aesthetic expression: the villa alone could express the wealth, position, or taste of its inhabitant.

Certainly behind Loudon's thinking there was the Utilitarian sentiment that those who were industrious and educated to taste also would be able to amass the wealth necessary to erect a dwelling of the villa class. Others, who were less fortunate financially as well as aesthetically, should not need the opportunity for expression that a villa provided. But there was also a more defensible Neoclassical rationale for Loudon's apotheosis of the villa: the essential principles incorporated in the most ideal dwelling ought to underlie the design of all other dwellings, no matter what their size or function. Loudon applied this reasoning to invert the arguments of several eighteenth-century theorists. In the 1750s Marc-Antoine Laugier and Sir William Chambers had canonized the "primitive hut" or cottage, not the villa, as the principal model of domestic design.[4] They considered villas and mansions to be elaborations and improvements on this basic form. Loudon essentially adopted the same parallel but now chose the villa—the most fully realized of all domestic types—instead of a primordial cottage as his paradigm.

As a preliminary to detailed analysis of the English villa, Loudon offered the following definition:

a country residence, with land attached, a portion of which, surrounding the house, is laid out as a pleasure-ground. . . . In this view of a villa, the dwelling is to be considered as only an amplification of the cottage [i.e., a more perfect version of a cottage]; and the lands, [are to be considered] as those of a farm, in which ornament and effect have been studied in the vicinity of the house. . . . [The] only essential requisites are, that the possessor should be a man of some wealth, and either possess taste himself, or have sense enough to call to his assistance the taste and judgment of others, who profess to practise this branch of the art of design. (p. 763)

Figure 3

Loudon augmented this definition with a 23,000-word description of the epitome of such a dwelling, "The Beau Idéal of an English Villa." Like many of his predecessors[5] he looked to Pliny's description of two ancient

Roman villas for insight into the general nature of the villa. But Loudon quickly determined that more could be learned from a putative "modern Pliny" (p. 790). No longer was the villa necessarily a farm house, for example; instead, it was better described as a "gentleman's residence in the country . . . [but also] at an easy distance from the metropolis" (pp. 790–791). Loudon did retain a few characteristics of the Roman villa in his description of the "Beau Idéal," notably the notion that a villa should be a central feature of a small village (p. 791). Likewise he recommended that the villa household should derive food and other materials as much as possible from the surrounding estate. But he also specified that the villa should be executed in the "old English style" of architecture. He justified this choice entirely in terms of nineteenth-century principles of picturesque beauty and utility: the Old English style "is more picturesque and ornamental; it accords best with rural scenery; and, as it admits of great irregularity of form, it affords space for the various offices and conveniences necessary in a country-house" (p. 792).

Loudon provided a plan of the landscaped garden surrounding this ideal estate, plus three elevations and two plans of the villa itself. The building, forming an H in plan, is two stories high, with nine windows across the facade. The ground-floor plan includes seven principal rooms, plus numerous service areas and servants' quarters. The text discusses almost every room in great detail, as well as the exterior landscaping, the architectural style, the farm, lodges on the farm, the dairy, the village, and the village church. Unfortunately the design as illustrated appears awkward and unsophisticated. Loudon's perspective is too forced, his forms are too rigid, and his ornamentation is too coarse.

Loudon made occasional remarks on architectural theory in his commentaries on individual designs, with more extensive discussion reserved for Book IV. There he treated seven major issues: fitness, expression, character, association, architectural style, scenic context, visual composition, and historical context. A brief look at Loudon's treatment of each will suggest the catholicity of his text.

Fitness was Loudon's primary theoretical concern. He made it his fundamental criterion in the analysis of individual designs, and also devoted a third of Book IV to the subject. He established the historical primacy of fitness by tracing a regard for it back to Vitruvius. But Loudon eschewed an elaborately reasoned theoretical analysis, instead simply defining fitness as efficiency of plan, economy of construction both in design and materials, and moderation in cost. Accordingly he then addressed such practical matters as the durability of building materials, the proper way to lay stones, precautions against fire, and ventilation.

Closely related to fitness was the "first and most essential beauty" of architecture: "expression of the purpose" for which a building was erected (p. 5). In his discussion of expression, however, Loudon seems to have confused two things: expression of *the purpose* of a structure, and expression of its *component functions*. Although the reader might have expected instructions for a grand synthetic expression of "purpose," Loudon presented only an elementary vocabulary of lesser architectural functions. For example he suggested that multiple chimney tops would indicate numerous fireplaces in a house that was well suited to a cold climate, that large areas of glass, by contrast, would express fitness for a southern exposure or for warmer climates in general, and that the largest window of a dwelling would indicate the room suited to most frequent use, the living room.

Several contemporary architects who were concerned with the problem of expression had advocated the choice of a single, unified expressive quality, or "character," to inform the design of each individual building.[6] Loudon too had said much about character in his earlier treatises,[7] but there was little mention of character in the *Encyclopaedia*. He used the word most frequently as a synonym for "signification" or "style." For example, in discussing interior furnishings, Loudon noted that "Every apartment, therefore, on being entered, ought to display a marked character of use; as well as a particular character of style, with reference to its finishing and furnishing" (p. 259). In the sole paragraph entirely devoted to character, Loudon offered another possible meaning for the term. He suggested that distinctive architectural features might be added to a design solely for the purpose of giving that design a marked "character," i.e., a visually distinctive—but not necessarily meaningful—appearance. "*Character*, in Architecture," he explained, "as in physiognomy, is produced by the prevalence of certain distinctive features, by which a countenance, or a building, is at once distinguished from every other of the same kind" (p. 1120). Perhaps hindered by his insistence on fitness and use as primary considerations in architectural design, Loudon was unable to retain his youthful enthusiasm for the notion of character as the central, informing quality of an architectural design.

In contrast, Loudon still supported association as a means for conveying architectural meaning to the spectator. Throughout his remarks on individual designs, he emphasized that association was a principal consideration in selecting a site and in choosing or appreciating architectural styles. One might want to adjust a site, for example, to recall the place where one was born, or the property of one's ancestors; this would establish the location as a "home." Discussing the relative merits of Castellated, Greek, and Gothic styles, Loudon concluded that "The difference between the styles unquestionably lies much more in men's minds, and in the historical associations connected with them, than in the abstract forms belonging to them" (p. 774). Loudon also identified specific notions normally associated with these styles. The primary associations of Greek style were a love of learning and a well-developed taste. In the Castellated style, "Towers, battlements, buttresses, pointed windows, mullions, and porches . . . recall a thousand images connected with the place of our birth, the scenes of our youth, the home of our parents, and the abodes of our friends," partly because parish churches in this style presumably held a prominent place in one's memories of childhood, family, and friends (p. 773). Alternatively, Castellated architecture in a landscape of hills and cliffs might suggest more romantic ideas of a fortified castle in medieval times. Loudon was less precise about the associations of Gothic, exclaiming only, "How various the associations which rise up in our minds, when viewing a successful imitation of a baronial castle, or of an old English manor-house!" (p. 774). But perhaps he made his point most clearly when he offered a single basic design for "A Dwelling for a Man and his Wife, without Children," illustrated with a choice of six different styles applied to the exterior. Beginning with a plain, undecorated one-story dwelling, one room deep with one window and a door on the facade, Loudon first added another story for extra room and comfort; he then experimented by sequentially applying five different styles to the exterior, looking like so much cladding. The example made clear Loudon's contention that style was secondary to function and fitness, but that whatever associations the proprietor wished to communicate to the viewer were deemed suitable and were in fact an asset to a successful design.[8]

Given the possible associations that different kinds of scenery might stimulate in a viewer's mind, Loudon recognized the importance of adjusting an architectural design to suit its scenic context. Unlike P. F. Robinson and other contemporaries[9] he did not insist that a building be united by pictorial means with its surrounding scenery; but in a discussion reminiscent of Humphry Repton[10] he noted that certain types of scenery were suited only to particular architectural styles. "Rude, rocky, hilly, and very irregular surfaces are said to require the Castle Gothic; fertile valleys, the Abbey Gothic, or monastic style; and rich extensive plains the Grecian or Roman manner" (p. 773). Loudon also referred extensively to Meason's study of connections between rural Italian villas and the Italian landscape,[11] and in fact reproduced nine designs from Meason's book to illustrate his points.

But Loudon skirted a related problem: whether pictorial composition was a necessary component of architectural design. An affirmative answer would have put him more closely in agreement with such contemporaries as P. F. Robinson and T. F. Hunt,[12] but it also would have seriously challenged his opening premise that fitness and its expression were the primary considerations in architectural design. Thus comparatively few passages in Loudon's text suggest concern for visual principles. On page 763 the reference is at best oblique: he noted that a "principal defect" of designs for English villas might be the want of "sufficient union" between house and grounds.

Finally, Loudon's concern for historical context resulted in a special approach to the understanding of architectural meaning. Loudon proposed that a building could be appreciated only in terms of its own physical and historical context. Just as social and historical events could not be evaluated out of context, he reasoned, so a building could not be understood apart from the circumstances of its own time and place.

In judging of a building of any particular age or country, the circumstances of that age or country at the time, require to be taken into consideration. In judging of the modern buildings of Italy, for instance, it must not be forgotten that almost all the modern Italian Architects were painters as well as Architects; and that almost the whole of their public buildings are addressed more to the eye than to the reason. In judging of the buildings of the reign of Louis XIV., it must be considered that the great object of the Architects was to follow the taste of the court, which was that of extravagant decoration. In judging of the taste of churches, and of sumptuous public buildings in all countries, it must not be forgotten that the great object was to excite the admiration and the astonishment of the spectator. . . . Thus, a critic must always have two standards of comparison to judge by: the one, that (as well as he can conceive it) of the time when the building was erected; and the other the *beau idéal* of perfection in his own mind. (pp. 1121–1122)

Such a relativistic mode of assessing past and present designs was unusual among Loudon's contemporaries, and particularly at odds with the ideas of architects such as Robinson, who viewed architectural design as a matter of visual composition alone.[13] Loudon's approach entailed two important consequences, significant for the further course of architectural theory in the nineteenth century. First, he demonstrated that by means of association any design could suggest a geographic, historical, or biographical context to a spectator. Second, this approach, highly attractive to John Ruskin and others,[14] suggested a revised standard of architectural judgment, and required the critic to assess any design, past or present, as a component of an entire scenic, social, cultural, and aesthetic context. Here may be found, among other consequences, the roots of modern architectural history with its attention to matters of geographic, social, and intellectual context in addition to the history of style and technology.

1. All citations refer to the 1839 edition.

2. P. 4. Both Loudon and his predecessor Humphry Repton (*q.v.*) owed much of their concern for fitness to eighteenth-century French theory, and also set important precedents for the widespread attention given to fitness and function by architects later in the nineteenth century. On the origin of concern for the expression of fitness through structural rationalism, see Robin Middleton, "The Abbé de Cordemoy and the Graeco-Gothic Ideal," *Journal of the Warburg and Courtauld Institutes* XXV:3–4 (July–December 1962), 278–320, and 26 (1963), 90–123.

3. P. 4. Loudon here extended eighteenth-century English and French notions that the scale, facade, and massing of a building should reveal the character of its inhabitant or reflect its use (e.g., as a palace, mansion, cottage, etc.). Loudon suggested that the function of individual rooms, circulation patterns, and the occupation of the inhabitant might also be expressed in the design.

4. On the primitive hut see Joseph Rykwert, *On Adam's House in Paradise* (New York: Museum of Modern Art, 1972). Also see Marc-Antoine Laugier, *Essai sur l'architecture* (Paris, 1753), and Sir William Chambers, *A Treatise on Civil Architecture* (1759; *q.v.*).

5. See for example Stephen Switzer, *Ichnographia Rustica* (1715) and Robert Castell, *Villas of the Ancients* (1728), *qq.v.*

6. See Chapter III, Section 3, in "The Literature of British Domestic Architecture, 1715–1842" above.

7. See especially his *Treatise on . . . Country Residences* (1806; *q.v.*).

8. See Humphry Repton, *Designs for the Pavillon at Brighton* (1808) for a possible precedent for Loudon's notion of interchangeable styles.

9. See Robinson, *Designs for Ornamental Villas* (1827) and *A New Series of Designs* (1838). Also see James Thomson, *Retreats* (1827), and T. F. Hunt, *Architettura Campestre* (1827) and *Designs for Parsonage Houses* (1827).

10. See Repton, *Sketches and Hints* (1794) and *Observations* (1803), *qq.v.*

11. Gilbert Laing Meason, *Observations on the Landscape Architecture of the Great Painters of Italy* (1828; *q.v.*).

12. See note 9.

13. See especially Robinson's *Designs for Ornamental Villas* (1827).

14. See the early series of articles written by Ruskin under the pseudonym Kata Phusin and published in Loudon's *Architectural Magazine*: "The Poetry of Architecture," *The Architectural Magazine* IV (1837), 505–508, 555–560; V (1838), 7–14, 56–63, 97–105, 145–154, 193–198, 241–250, 289–301, 337–344, 385–392, 433–442, 481–494, 533–554.

LOUDON, John Claudius (1783–1843)
An encyclopaedia of gardening.

See Entry 490.

185.1

LOUDON, John Claudius (1783–1843)

Engravings, with descriptions, illustrative of the difference between the modern style of rural architecture and the improvement of scenery, and that displayed in a treatise on country residences, and practised by Mr. Loudon.

Loudon: Printed by C. Whittingham; for Longman, Hurst, Rees, and Orme, 1807.

16 pp, 8 pls.

27.9 × 21.3 cm

V&A

On page 5 Loudon noted that "some gentlemen" had recently asked him for "sketches of gentlemen's seats" that he was currently improving. He selected eight plates, numbered XIII, XIV, 16, XXI, XXII, XXIII, XXV, and XXVI, from his *Treatise on Forming, Improving, and Managing Country Residences* (1806; *q.v.*). These include views of the house and grounds at Barnbarrow both before and after Loudon's intended improvements, landscape improvements proposed for Harewood, architectural improvements intended for the house at Barnbarrow, landscape improvements proposed for Farnley Hall, landscape and architectural improvements completed at Kingswood Lodge, and a series of plans showing a landscape as it might have been laid out "a century ago" as well as in the style of Capability Brown and in Loudon's own manner.

In the text Loudon briefly discussed each of his improvements, and then compared aspects of his landscaping style with the approaches of Brown and Humphry Repton. Loudon noted differences in cost as well as in the use of trees, buildings, water, ground, parks, pleasure grounds, and kitchen gardens. Clearly indebted to notions of "character" recently developed by Thomas Whately and Repton,[1] Loudon termed his approach "the characteristic style of forming residences," in which his goal would be to "harmonize" the building with the surrounding "country," in contrast with the "affectedly graceful system of Brown and Repton" (p. 14).

1. See Thomas Whately, *Observations on Modern Gardening* (London, 1770), and Humphry Repton, *Sketches and Hints* (1794; *q.v.*).

186.1

LOUDON, John Claudius (1783–1843)

First additional supplement to Loudon's encyclopaedia of cottage, farm, and villa architecture and furniture.

[London], 1842.

1133–1306 pp.

22.3 × 14.0 cm

CtY

The first edition of Loudon's *Encyclopaedia* (*q.v.*) appeared in 1833. He made minor corrections and changes in the text for the edition of 1835. The only major additions that he completed before his death were brought together in 1842 in a Supplement that he attached to the end of the *Encyclopaedia*. The Supplement is paginated continuously with the *Encyclopaedia*, but has its own table of contents, introduction, text, and index.[1]

The *First Additional Supplement* begins with a table of contents, an "Additional List of Books Quoted," and a "List of Contributors" (pp. 1133–1135). In a brief Introduction (p. 1135) Loudon indicated that ever since 1833 he had been collecting additional material "with a view to a new edition, or a Supplement." The material came from a variety of sources, including Loudon's own *Architectural Magazine* (*q.v.*), the report of the Poor Law Commissioners (*q.v.* in Appendix D), information Loudon garnered on his travels throughout England and Scotland, and designs submitted by correspondents in Great Britain, North America, and Australia.

The text (pp. 1135–1296) is divided into seven chapters, treating subjects similar to those in the *Encyclopaedia*: cottages, cottage villas, villas, farm buildings, schools, inns, workhouses, almshouses, details of construction, fittings, furnishings, furniture, and "Hints to Proprietors Desirous of Improving the Labourers' Cottages on Their Estates." The format likewise resembles that of the *Encyclopaedia*: short articles treating particular problems or describing individual designs. These include 35 designs for cottages and 17 for villas. The letterpress concludes with a "General Index" (pp. 1297–1306).

1. I have therefore presumed that some copies of the *First Additional Supplement* would have been issued separately, for the convenience of owners of previous editions. The copy of the supplement at Yale is separate from any copy of the *Encyclopaedia*; and bound at the end of the supplement there is a title page for the 1842 edition of the *Encyclopaedia*.

187.1
LOUDON, John Claudius (1783–1843), ed.
The gardener's magazine, and register of rural & domestic improvement. Conducted by J. C. Loudon. . . .

[*Volume I:*] London: Printed for Longman, Rees, Orme, Brown, and Green, 1826.
[*Volume II:*] ————— , 1827.
[*Volume III:*] ————— , 1828.
[*Volume IV:*] ————— , 1828.
[*Volume V:*] ————— , 1829.
[*Volume VI:*] ————— , 1830.
[*Volume VII:*] ————— , 1831.
[*Volume VIII:*] London: Printed for Longman, Rees, Orme, Brown, Green, and Longman, 1832.
[*Volume IX:*] ————— , 1833.
[*Volume X:*] ————— , 1834.
[*Volume XI:*] ————— , 1835.
[*Volume XII:*] ————— , 1836.

[*Volume XIII:*] London: Printed for Longman, Orme, Brown, Green, and Longmans, 1837.
[*Volume XIV:*] ———— , 1838.
[*Volume XV:*] London: Printed for the conductor; and sold by Longman, Orme, Brown, Green, and Longmans; and A. and C. Black, Edinburgh, 1839.
[*Volume XVI:*] ———— , 1840.
[*Volume XVII:*] London: Printed for the conductor; and sold by Longman, Brown, Green, and Longmans; and A. and C. Black, Edinburgh, 1841.
[*Volume XVIII:*] ———— , 1842.
[*Volume XIX:*] ———— , 1843.

MH

The Gardener's Magazine was the first of Loudon's serial publications. Most of the articles concern practical aspects of horticulture, "arboriculture," "floriculture," new tools, new machines, and new instruments. There are also significant articles on landscape design, garden structures such as conservatories and hothouses, and dwellings.[1]

Throughout the 18 years of the *Magazine*'s publication, Loudon reprinted many domestic designs from recently published books by contemporary architects, including T. F. Hunt, P. F. Robinson, and R. G. Wetten.[2] In addition he reviewed other recent architectural publications, often unsympathetically.[3] He published original designs for dwellings by such architects as Robert Abraham, E. B. Lamb, B. Mathews, J. Robertson, and Richard Varden, as well as some of his own designs.[4] Frequently he offered views of extant houses. These include recently built examples, others in fashionable, recently rediscovered vernacular styles, and many whose landscape surroundings he found of particular interest. The original designs that he illustrated encompass a wide range of types and styles, including a Scottish roadside thatched cottage (XIX, 254–255), small symmetrical villas in simplified Classical style (X, 24–25), small houses in elaborate Tudor style (V, 318–322), others with more restrained Tudor ornament (VI, 660–663), and his own designs embellished only with simplified Classical or rustic ornament (VI, 153–167).

In the Preface to Volume I Loudon described the two "objects" of his magazine: "to disseminate new and important information on all topics connected with horticulture, and to raise the intellect and the character of those engaged in this art." In the Introduction he expressed his wish to "put all Gardeners in distant parts of the country *on* a footing with those about the metropolis" (I, 2). He also intended to "extend the sources of enjoyment to be procured from a garden," especially to "gentlemen in the country, who have not paid any attention to gardening themselves, and whose worthy and industrious gardener has, perhaps, gone on in the same track for twenty or thirty years" (I, 3). He remarked proudly that "landscape gardening has created in Britain parks and pleasure-grounds unequalled in any other part of the world," but lamented that "in laying out new, or improving old residences, there seems to be a great want, either of industry or ability to profit from" those excellent examples (I, 5). Citing prominent authors on the subject of landscape design, Loudon noted that "the modern art of laying out grounds" is "an art of imagination," and subject to artistic principles, just as is painting. But since landscaping, like architecture, contributes to the "convenience and comfort of man," it also must be subject to principles of "fitness and utility."[5]

1. Of 100 engravings in Volume I, for example, three show residences (Grange Park, Hampshire, and Waltham House, Massachusetts). In Volume IX there are 84 major articles (excluding reviews and "notices"), of which just one illustrates a design for a residence, two discuss the construction of garden fountains, one describes a "Garden Chair," two concern designs for hothouses and greenhouses, and one is a collection of plans and diagrams for garden walls and sheds. The rest of the articles are descriptions and plans of gardens, and remarks pertaining directly to "arboriculture," "floriculture," and horticulture.

2. Hunt, *Architettura Campestre* (*q.v.*), reproduction of Plates I, II, VI, IX, in Volume IV, 43–46. Robinson, *Designs for Ornamental Villas, Rural Architecture*, and *Designs for Farm Buildings* (*qq.v.*), nine plates reproduced in Volume V, 318–322. Wetten, *Designs for Villas* (*q.v.*), two illustrations reproduced in Volume V, 541–542.

3. Ideas of central importance to Loudon's architectural theory, later to be elaborated in his *Encyclopaedia* (*q.v.*), were introduced in an 1828 review of two books by T. F. Hunt (III, 76–78; the books under review were *Half a Dozen Hints* and *Designs for Parsonage Houses*). Loudon complained that many architects could not "separate the accidental associations of classical, historical, and imitative beauty, from the more permanent associations of fitness, grandeur, uniformity, and variety" (III, 76). In other words architects too often used style to achieve an expressive end, while ignoring more fundamental principles of beauty. Foremost among these principles was utility, or fitness (III, 76; for an earlier discussion of this principle see Humphry Repton, *Observations on the Theory and Practice of Landscape Gardening*). The other "grand principle of beauty is that every building should, by its appearance, communicate the idea or expression of what it is" (III, 76). Needless to say Loudon disparaged the rich ornament and picturesque massing of Hunt's designs for lodges, cottages, and parsonage houses (III, 77).

4. Abraham: VI, 34–35. Lamb: XIX, 254–255. Mathews: III, 135–138. Robertson: X, 24–25, 261–263, 375; XI, 64–66, 173–174. Varden: VI, 660–663. Loudon: VI, 153–167, 551–554, 659–660. Some of Loudon's designs were part of a larger article on "Cottage Husbandry" (VI, 139–167) which also was expanded and issued as a separate title, *A Manual of Cottage Gardening* (1830; *q.v.*).

5. See the discussion of these principles in note 3. For an extended discussion of *The Gardener's Magazine* as a horticultural journal see Ray Desmond, "Loudon and Nineteenth-Century Horticultural Journalism," in Elisabeth B. MacDougall, ed., *John Claudius Loudon and the Early Nineteenth Century in Britain* (Washington, D.C.: Dumbarton Oaks, 1980), pp. 77–97.

188.1 ‡
LOUDON, John Claudius (1783–1843)

Illustrations of landscape-gardening and garden architecture; or, a collection of designs, original and executed, for laying out country residences of every degree of extent, from the cottage and farm, to the national palace and public park or garden; kitchen-gardens, flower-gardens, arboretums, shrubberies, botanic gardens, scientific gardens, cemeteries, &c. In different styles, by different artists, of different periods and countries. Accompanied by letter-press descriptions in English, French, and German. Edited by J. C. Loudon, F.L.S. H.S. G.S. & Z.S. . . . In twenty parts, to appear quarterly. Part I [*or* II]. . . .

Illustrations de jardinage paysagiste et de l'architecture de jardin; démontrés [*or* démontres] dans une collection de desseins, originaux, et en exécution, pour la disposition des maisons de plaisance de toute espece, depuis la chaumière et la ferme, jusqu'au palais national et au jardin public; des jardins potagers, des jardins a fleurs, des arboretums, des bosquets, des jardins botaniques, des jardins scientifiques, des cimetiéres, &c. En différens genres, par des artistes de différentes périodes et de pays différens. Accompagnés de descriptions en anglais, en français, et en allemand. Ouvrage rédige par J. C. Loudon, F.L.S. H.S. G.S. & Z.S. . . . En vingt livraisons, dont une paraîtra tous les trois mois. Premiere [*or* Seconde] livraison. . . . Erläuterungen über Landschaft Gartenkunst und Garten Bau Kunst; oder, eine Sammlung von originellen und ausgeführten Plänen zur Anlegung von Landsitzen jeder Art und Grösze, von der Bauerhütte und dem Bauergute bis zum national Pallast, und öffentlichen Park oder Garten; von Gemüse und Blumengärten, Baumpflanzungen und Lustgebüschen, von botanischen und wissenschaftlichen Gärten, Begräbnisz Plätzen, u.s.w. In verschiedenen Stylen, von verschiedenen Künstelern, von verschiedenen Zeiten und Landern. Begleitet von gedruckten Beschreibungen in englischer, französischer und deutscher Sprache. Herausgegeben von J. C. Loudon, F.L.S. H.S. G.S. u. Z.S. . . . In zwanzig, vierteljährig erscheinenden, Theilen. 1ster [*or* 2ter] Theil. . . .

London: Published by Longman & Co. Booksellers; and by G. Charlwood, Seedsman; and also by Treuttel & Wurtz, London, Paris, and Strasburg, 1830 [*or* 1831]. [*The imprint also appears in French and German translations.*]

[*Part I. / Premiere livraison. / 1ster Theil:*] 4 + [1] pp, 4 pls.
[*Part II. / Seconde livraison. / 2ter Theil:*] 5–8 + [2] pp, 4 pls.

f°

Reference: Microfilm supplied by The British Library.

The title page for Part II promised the publication of Part III on 1 April 1831. According to Loudon's wife, Jane, it finally appeared in 1833.[1] The ECB also indicates that Part III appeared, but gives 1831 as the date. I have been unable to locate a copy of Part III.

In Parts I and II the text appears in parallel columns of English, French, and German.

Loudon's introductory text (I, 1) indicates the essentially ad hoc nature of his approach. He proposed to publish a series of exemplary designs rather than any carefully argued synthesis of principles or theories:

It is the object of the present work to increase the knowledge, and improve the taste, of the amateur and practical gardener in all that relates to design in Gardening. For this purpose, it is intended to select and publish plans and descriptions of a number of the principal Country Residences, Parks, Pleasure-Grounds, and other garden departments, which have been executed in different parts of the world, in different styles, in different times, and by different artists. (I, 1)

To these "executed" designs, Loudon intended to add an equal number of "original" designs, i.e., similar but unexecuted proposals by himself and others. Altogether these designs would suit a variety of locations, including farms owned and cultivated by small proprietors, larger "splendid residences" used as gentlemen's country retreats, public parks, and even "the most extensive domain." Loudon would include all styles of landscaping as well, from those used in ancient Rome to the latest fashion, although most designs would be in "the modern English or natural style." He claimed this style was best suited to the climate and "state of civilization" of Europe, America, and their colonies as well (I, 1).

Loudon conceived this series of *Illustrations* as a parallel to the articles in his *Gardener's Magazine* (1826–1843), and also in part as preparatory to undertaking publication of an *Encyclopaedia of Landscape-Gardening* (I, 1). The early termination of the *Illustrations* may well have resulted from Loudon's increasing involvement with his mammoth *Encyclopaedia of Cottage, Farm, and Villa Architecture* that appeared in 1833.

In both Parts each plate is accompanied by one or two sheets of explanatory letterpress. The first plate in Part I includes 154 separate illustrations, or "lessons," in landscape drawing. Most show land forms and arrangements of trees, although there are several sketchy illustrations of houses. Numbers 127 through 130 show a small house, two stories high and three windows wide, in plan, elevation, and section. Number 132 shows this house in oblique view. Number 131 shows a street bordered on each side by two-story row houses. Numbers 133 and 134 show an isometric projection of a farm house and offices, taken (without credit) from Plate VII of Waistell's *Designs for Agricultural Buildings* (1826) and later included in Jopling's *Practice of Isometrical Perspective* (1833) (*qq.v.*). Numbers 135 and 136 show a bird's-eye view and roof plan of a two-story house with three windows across both the front and side facades.

Plate 2 in Part I is a diagram for the layout of arboretums, showing in 64 strips a path some 18,800 feet long, designed to display all the trees and shrubs known to survive in open air in Britain. Plates 3 and 4 are working plans for landscaping a country residence and estate designed by Joshua Major.

Plate 5, in Part II, is a design by P. Masey, Jr., for laying out the estate at Brandon Hill, Bristol, as a public garden. Plate 6 consists of plans by Loudon for the organization of an arboretum according to the Jussieuean system, with trees in circular groups and masses. Plate 7 shows a design for arranging herbaceous plants according to the same system. Plate 8 is a design by Loudon for laying out a ten-acre estate as a "villa residence."

1. Jane Loudon, "A Short Account of the Life and Writings of John Claudius Loudon," reprinted in John Gloag, *Mr. Loudon's England* (Newcastle upon Tyne: Oriel Press, 1970), p. 205.

189.1
LOUDON, John Claudius (1783–1843)
A manual of cottage gardening, husbandry, and architecture; including plans, elevations, and sections of three designs for model cottages; descriptions of a mode by which every cottager may grow his own fuel; a new mode of heating cottages; a scheme for labourers and others to build their own cottages, on the cooperative system; calendarial tables of the culture and produce of cottage gardens throughout the year; directions for brewing, baking, &c. and the process for making sugar from mangold wurzel. By J. C. Loudon. . . . Assisted by Mr. Ellis, Mr. Gorrie, Mr. Taylor, and seven other experienced gardeners, farmers, and cottagers. Extracted from the Gardener's magazine.

London: Printed for the author; by A. & R. Spottiswoode; and sold, without profit, by Mr. Charlwood, Seedsman, 1830.

72 pp.

21.0 × 12.7 cm

BL

In 1830 Loudon published an article "On Cottage Husbandry and Architecture, Chiefly with Reference to Certain Prize Essays Received on Cottage Gardening, and to Projected Encyclopaedias on These Subjects," in his *Gardener's Magazine* (VI, 139–167; *q.v.*). In the article he discussed "attaching" land to cottages so the inhabitants could grow their own produce. He also included brief essays on malt, "pot-barley," hops, sugar, cider, perry, wines, spirits, hedges, tobacco, and medicinal plants. Approximately half the article (pp. 153–167) is devoted to detailed plans, elevations, and specifications for "A Model Cottage for a Country Labourer." Loudon actually offered three different designs suiting the same general criteria. The first design (Figs. 30–34) has a cellar story and a principal floor with a "kitchen or living-room," parlor, three bedrooms, and water closets, plus areas at the rear for pigs, ducks, fuel, a cistern, and the like. Apart from a small pediment over the front door, the elevation shows no ornament. The plan of the second design is similar to the first, but Loudon added a veranda around the exterior, "supported by trunks of larch or spruce fir trees, with the bark on" (p. 162). In the third design Loudon omitted the cellar story, added a floor with four bedrooms, and made the principal rooms on the ground floor a kitchen, parlor, back kitchen, and "dairy and pantry" (p. 162).

In 1830 Loudon also issued *A Manual of Cottage Gardening*, containing this article (pp. 3–31) and three others from *The Gardener's Magazine*. There are few differences between the pamphlet and periodical versions; most changes simply involve page and figure numbers.

The third volume of Burke's *British Husbandry* (1840; *q.v.*) includes a collection of four articles by Loudon titled "The Cottager's Manual." These concern "Cottage Husbandry," "Cottage Architecture," "Cottage Economy," and "The Garden." The article on architecture (pp. 16–30) contains the same designs and specifications as in *The Gardener's Magazine* and *A Manual of Cottage Gardening*. The text has been reset.

Loudon also incorporated the same cottage designs into the first chapter of his *Encyclopaedia* (1833; *q.v.*).

LOUDON, John Claudius (1783–1843)
A manual of cottage gardening.

For later editions see [BURKE, John French], British husbandry, *Entry 28.*

LOUDON, John Claudius (1783–1843)
Observations on laying out farms.

See his Designs for laying out farms, *Entry 183.*

190.1
LOUDON, John Claudius (1783–1843)
The suburban gardener, and villa companion: comprising the choice of a suburban or villa residence, or of a situation on which to form one; the arrangement and furnishing of the house; and the laying out, planting,

and general management of the garden and grounds; the whole adapted for grounds from one perch to fifty acres and upwards in extent; and intended for the instruction of those who know little of gardening and rural affairs, and more particularly for the use of ladies. By J. C. Loudon. . . . Illustrated by numerous engravings.

London: Printed for the author; and sold by Longman, Orme, Brown, Green, and Longmans; and W. Black, Edinburgh, 1838.

xvi + 752 pp.

22.9 × 14.0 cm

MH

190.2

The villa gardener: comprising the choice of a suburban villa residence; the laying out, planting, and culture of the garden and grounds; and the management of the villa farm, including the dairy and poultry-yard. Adapted, in extent, for grounds from one perch to fifty acres and upwards. And intended for the instruction of those who know little of gardening and rural affairs, and more particularly for the use of ladies. Illustrated by numerous engravings. By J. C. Loudon. . . . Second edition. Edited by Mrs. Loudon.

London: Published for the editor, by Wm. S. Orr & Co., 1850.

xii + 516 pp.

21.6 × 13.3 cm

MH

In 1831 Edward Trendall published the first book of house designs intended specifically for the suburban environs of large cities (*q.v.*). Loudon was the next, and the first to use the word "surburban" in his title. Loudon also was the first to discuss suburban design per se, focusing on matters of architecture and building as well as on the aspirations and ideals involved in suburban living. Suburban residences, according to him, embodied the integration of two things: the refinement and cultural advantages of urban society, together with the opportunity for relaxation and regeneration found in the country. This goal was not new. Attempts at integration of *"rus"* (country) and *"urbs"* (city) data from the time of Horace, and a desire to combine these ideals had been a central problem in British poetry, aesthetics, architecture, and landscape gardening throughout the eighteenth century.[1] But Loudon was the first to discuss at length the unification of these two ideals in one type of dwelling, the suburban villa. On the one hand, the suburban villa offered advantages of country life: "The master of a suburban residence, however small may be his demesne, may thus procure health and enjoyment at the same time" (p. 9).[2] On the other hand,

such residences may be considered at the ultimatum, in point of comfort and enjoyment, of the great mass of society. . . . One immense advantage of a suburban residence over one isolated in the country consists in its proximity to neighbours, and the facilities it affords of participating in those sources of instruction and enjoyment which can only be obtained in towns: for example, public libraries and museums, theatrical representations, musical concerts, public and private assemblies, exhibitions of works of art, &c. (p. 10)

Presumably aware of contemporary suburban growth around Regent's Park, in St. John's Wood, and close to his own home in Bayswater,[3] Loudon recognized that certain qualities were essential for a successful suburban residence and community. These were discussed in his first chapter, "On the Choice of a Situation for a Suburban or Country House and Grounds," pp. 12–34. One requisite was the social homogeneity of the residents: the best choice of neighborhood for a prospective buyer would be one in which "the houses and inhabitants are all, or chiefly, of the same description and class as the house we intend to inhabit, and as ourselves" (p. 32). Another requisite was opportunity for meaningful social intercourse: one must look for neighbors with comparable "education and morals" (p. 32). Finally, the residence itself should offer the inhabitant several opportunities "of a personal nature." First among these was the opportunity to erect a dwelling suitable to one's economic situation. Second, the suburb's quasi-rural location could provide a variety of opportunities for health, recreation, retirement, and seclusion, including raising horses and dogs or pursuing such interests as astronomy, botany, gardening, or entomology. Third, one might want to establish or advance business connections among one's neighbors. Finally, health concerns might cause some families to choose specific suburbs for such characteristics as warmth, "bracing" air, or high humidity (pp. 32–34). All these features together would contribute to a flourishing suburban community.

Following these remarks on the location and advantages of a suburban residence, Loudon turned to the specific aspects of "Construction," "External Appearance," and "Interior Arrangements" necessary to build a suburban house (Chapter II, pp. 34–131). Most of the text consists of practical information, but there are a few general observations on utility and aesthetics. Loudon lamented that "Many persons, who have not had much experience in the choice of a house, are captivated by the exterior; and are more influenced by its picturesque effect, then by any property in the dwelling connected with habitableness" (p. 114). He recommended greater attention to fitness, already a major theme in his *Encyclopaedia* (1833; *q.v.*). Among the principal considerations of fitness were good drainage and a dry site, a compact shape for the house, diagonal orientation between the cardinal points so that all sides received sunlight, good illumination and ventilation, and a secure roof (p. 116). These were clearly the most important considerations: after discussing them, Loudon quickly dismissed "architectural style," saying it "may be left to the taste of the occupant" (p. 117).[4] He further implied that picturesque composition was not appropriate for architecture:

It will be said, by some architects, that a square house affords less architectural beauty than any other form, from the sameness of the general shape; but . . . our opinion is that variety, however prominent a beauty it may be in landscape, is only a subordinate one in architecture; and that the grand characteristic beauties of that art are magnitude and symmetry. (p. 118)

Therefore the best form for a house was "cubic," which is "known to enclose more space with the same quantity of walling and roof than any other," and "preferable in all that regards comfort, habitableness, and economy of heating, keeping clean, and in repair" (p. 117). Gothic and Elizabethan houses, he noted, originally were built in square or quadrangular form for just these reasons (p. 119). But Roman and Greek styles were preferable to Gothic, because they were comparatively more compact, less ornamented, and less expensive to furnish (pp. 119–120).

The third chapter, on "Laying out and Planting the Gardens and Grounds of Suburban and Other Country Residences," constitutes nearly three-fourths of the entire book. At the very beginning Loudon again discussed the notion of architectural fitness. He listed a few brief "Rules" pertaining to the design of walls and window openings, and also asserted that "Fitness of a Building for the End in View ought not only to be real, but apparent" (p. 135). He devoted most of the chapter to plans and estimates for suburban gardens. In addition to illustrating designs for grounds and plantings, Loudon often included plans and views of exemplary dwellings.[5] These include his own house in Porchester Terrace, a three-story pair of dwellings designed to look like one compact cubic villa (pp. 325–350). Elsewhere he illustrated designs by Glendinning, Lamb, Rutger, and Varden.

The final chapter includes "Supplementary Details" pertaining to houses, "Domestic Offices," and "The Scenery of a Suburban Residence." In the section on scenery he included 15 designs for lodges and gate houses, composed in considerably more picturesque and varied styles than he had advocated for suburban residences. There are designs by Brigden, Hunt, Lamb, Robinson, and Wells, in such styles as Italian, Rustic, Old English, and Grecian. Clearly Loudon admitted irregularity, stylistic expression, and pictorial effect as proper characteristics for entrance lodges and gate houses, perhaps because these structures merited consideration only as parts of landscape scenery. On the other hand residences of a higher class—suburban cottages and villas in particular—necessarily had to be designed according to principles of use, function, and efficiency, all central to his most fundamental principle of architecture, fitness.

1. For a fuller discussion see John Archer, "*Rus in Urbe*: Classical Ideals of Country and City in British Town Planning," *Studies in Eighteenth-Century Culture*, XII, ed. Harry C. Payne (Madison: University of Wisconsin Press, 1983), 159–186.

2. All page references are to the 1838 edition. The 1850 edition was substantially reorganized by Loudon's wife Jane after his death in 1843. She noted he had intended to omit "a portion of the Suburban Gardens" and include "more descriptions of villas." These he had published already in *The Gardener's Magazine*. She also added "numerous Designs for Plant-houses," an index, names of new plants, and "details respecting New Improvements in Gardening" (1850, Preface, p. [v]).

3. On Regent's Park see Thomas H. Shepherd and James Elmes, *Metropolitan Improvements; or London in the Nineteenth Century* (London: Jones, 1827), passim; Ann Saunders, *Regent's Park* (Newton Abbot: David & Charles, 1969); John Summerson, *The Life and Work of John Nash* (Cambridge, Mass.: MIT Press, 1980); and the published *Reports* of the Commissioners of His Majesty's Woods, Forests, and Land Revenues in the British Parliamentary Papers for 1812, 1816, 1819, 1823, and 1826. There is no thorough study of the early growth of St. John's Wood, but see Hugh C. Prince, "North-west London 1814–1863," in J. T. Coppock and Hugh C. Prince, eds., *Greater London* (London: Faber and Faber, 1964), p. 104; *Laurie and Whittle's New Map of London* (London: Laurie and Whittle, 1817); and John Smith, *A Topographical Account of the Parish of St. Mary-le-Bone* (London: John Smith, 1833), map. On suburban developments in Notting Hill, just west of Bayswater, see *Survey of London XXXVII: Northern Kensington* (London: Greater London Council, 1973). On Loudon's own house see the description in *The Suburban Gardener*, pp. 325–350. Also see John Gloag, *Mr. Loudon's England* (Newcastle: Oriel Press, 1970), pp. 73–80.

4. Elsewhere Loudon found architectural styles almost superfluous, and of such minimal importance as to be interchangeable. See his *Encyclopaedia* (1833).

5. Altogether there are 343 engravings in the 1838 edition and 378 in the 1850 edition, all printed on text leaves. No illustrations appear separately on plates.

191.1
LOUDON, John Claudius (1783–1843)

A treatise on forming, improving, and managing country residences; and on the choice of situations appropriate to every class of purchasers. In all which the object in view is to unite in a better manner than has hitherto been done, a taste founded in nature with economy and utility, in constructing or improving mansions, and other rural buildings, so as to combine architectural fitness with picturesque effect; and in forming gardens, orchards, farms, parks, pleasure-grounds, shrubberies, all kinds of useful or decorative plantations, and every object of convenience or beauty peculiar to country seats; according to the extent, character, or style of situations, and the rank, fortune, and expenditure of proprietors; from the cottage to the palace. With an appendix, containing an enquiry into the utility and merits of Mr. Repton's mode of shewing effects by slides and sketches, and strictures on his opinions and practice in landscape gardening. Illustrated by descriptions of scenery and buildings, by references to country seats, and passages of country in most parts of Great Britain, and by thirty-two engravings. By John Loudon. . . . In two volumes.—Vol. I [*or* II].

London: Printed for Longman, Hurst, Rees, and Orme, by C. Whittingham, 1806.

[*Volume I:*] xii + [xli] + 353 pp, 14 pls.

[*Volume II:*] 355–723 + [vii] pp, 15–32 pls.

25.1 × 21.0 cm

MB

191.2

A treatise on forming, improving, and managing, country residences: including the construction and arrangement of rural buildings, and the formation of gardens, orchards, farms, parks, pleasure grounds, shrubberies, plantations, &c. &c. Illustrated by descriptions of scenery and buildings, by references to country seats, and passages of country in most parts of Great Britain, and by thirty-two engravings. By J. C. Loudon, F.L.S. In two volumes.

London: Printed for John Harding, 1812.

[*Volume I:*] xii + [xli] + 354 pp, 11 pls.

[*Volume II:*] 355–701 + [viii] pp, 12–32 pls.

26.0 × 21.0 cm

Soane

In the Preface (I, vii–xii)[1] Loudon discussed his method of approach to rural architecture and landscape gardening. He indicated that he had developed a "theory" that was "sufficient to establish an art (which has hitherto been guided chiefly by fashion or caprice) upon principles inherent in the nature of man" (I, vii). Despite the length of his text, Loudon warned that he had not treated all aspects of the subject. Rather, he described the book as "but a short transcript of the leading ideas and general principles which are prominent in the author's mind on the subject of his profession." He stressed that his information was acquired through practical experience (I, viii), in contrast to the "dogmatical manner" of the adherents of Capability Brown, who "give their plans and opinions, without being able to reconcile what they propose with *common sense*." He also condemned "geometrical architects," who "do every thing by geometrical elevations," and never consider picturesque effect (I, ix–x). The preliminaries also include a lengthy and detailed table of contents, and a seven-page "List of Country Residences Referred to in the Following Work."

The Introduction (I, 3–16) begins with observations on the delights of "rural scenery," to which the owner of a country residence could add "the pleasures resulting from agriculture and gardening" (I, 3–4). In contrast commerce and urban society were "unnatural," and the only reason for engaging in commerce was to be able one day to "retire to the country" and enjoy "the *ease*, *liberty*, and *independence* of a country residence" (I, 4–5). Loudon offered a conjectural account of the historical genesis of country residences from "primitive" times to the eighteenth century (I, 6–10), when William Kent produced "a new style of Ornamental or Landscape Gardening" (I, 11). Loudon criticized the "defects and absurdities" of Capability Brown's landscape work later in the eighteenth century, and praised Uvedale Price and Richard Payne Knight for their efforts in encouraging landscape architects to "think for themselves" in creating picturesque compositions (I, 11–12).[2] Turning to architecture, Loudon complained that designers of country mansions paid too little attention to the relation between a building and its surrounding landscape, and praised recent efforts to introduce "irregularity" and "characteristic beauty" in country houses. He also established three fundamental "qualities" to be sought in a country residence: "*utility, convenience,* and *beauty*" (I, 14).[3]

The text begins with an analysis of "*Taste,* or intellectual feeling" (I, 17) to provide a foundation for understanding rural architecture and landscape gardening. Loudon identified 11 fundamental components of beauty, ranging from utility and fitness to harmony (I, 34–35), and then enumerated 15 "characters" that "are productive of particular expressions and correspondent effects on the mind" (I, 35–43).[4] After examining the principles of landscape painting, Loudon discussed architectural theory, focusing on principles of beauty and "characters" similar to those he cited in his discussion of taste. There is a lengthy discussion of Greek and Gothic architecture (I, 79–119), including an analysis of seven Gothic styles: Pointed Gothic, Saxon Gothic, and several varieties of the Irregular or Mixed Gothic—Cathedral Style, Castle Style, Quadrangular Style, Tower Style, and Turret Style. Loudon concluded that Greek architecture was unsuited to Britain for reasons of climate as well as its inability to accommodate certain utilitarian needs. Gothic architecture, by contrast, was "capable of supplying every internal convenience" and in addition "may produce expression by a great variety of ways" (I, 105). He next discussed the "application" of design principles to individual architectural types: he treated churches and bridges quickly, and then turned to "private" architecture, including cottages, villages, towns, cities, factories, farm buildings, and especially "the habitations of the wealthy and noble," placing great emphasis on the relation between mansions and the surrounding landscape (I, 119–186). The remainder of the first volume is devoted to agriculture (I, 187–252), "useful or culinary gardening" (I, 253–313), and "ornamental gardening" (I, 314–353).

The second volume opens with a lengthy discussion of "picturesque improvement" (II, 355–440), which is based on two fundamental principles: "unity of design and character" within the whole, and a "grouping, or connexion" of individual parts (II, 358). Loudon discussed individual elements of picturesque landscapes, such as earth, water, rocks, flora, and buildings, as well as the means of unifying them to form picturesque compositions, and the particular requirements of parks and pleasure grounds. The next major subject is the "picturesque plantation"; Loudon attended to aesthetic as well as horticultural considerations (II, 441–587). He also remarked briefly on such "conveniences" of country residences as approaches, drives, lodges, gates, offices, ponds, aviaries, kennels, tennis courts, and bowling greens (II, 589–598).

Having dealt only with "principles" of architecture and landscape so far, Loudon next turned to the "practice" of forming and improving country residences, and managing country estates (II, 599–653). He discussed the different styles in which estates could be laid out, including the "formal or ancient style" of London, Wise, and Switzer, the "affectedly graceful or modern style" of Brown, White, Repton, and Eames, and his own "characteristic or natural style." He explained that he adopted the term "characteristic" because the "leading principle" of his style was "to create or heighten natural character. The other styles effect directly the reverse—they produce a monotony of artificial character" (II, 644). The final major division of the text concerns the choice of a site for a country residence and the advantages of improving country estates (II, 655–699).

In the Conclusion Loudon summed up his ideas: the art of rural improvement "is founded in *beauty, use,* and *adaptation* to the proprietor; which, applied to a residence as a whole, may be comprehended in one epithet, UNITY OF CHARACTER" (II, 700). The letterpress concludes with an Appendix concerning Repton's "mode of using slides and sketches" and his "manner of operating with the principal materials of landscape" (II, 703–723), an index, binding directions, and errata.

Loudon clearly had his differences with Repton, who in trying to establish fixed principles of landscape gardening "displayed only confusion and incongruity" (II, 700). Nevertheless Loudon was dependent on Repton and others for fundamental elements of his theory: Repton, Archibald Alison, and Thomas Whately all had discussed landscape "character" well before Loudon developed the notion of "characteristic" landscape gardening.[5] Loudon's text is seldom original and frequently repetitive, but its strength is its methodical and comprehensive approach to the subject. In his attention to diverse aspects of theory and practice he clearly surpassed the principal landscape treatise of the previous decade, Repton's admittedly ad hoc and fragmentary *Sketches and Hints on Landscape Gardening*.[6]

The plates include several examples of Loudon's own designs for architectural and landscape improvements, but do not illustrate the numerous aspects of his theory in a comprehensive manner. The first four plates depict elevations of houses in the Cathedral, Castle, Tower, and Turret styles. Plates 5 and 6 illustrate examples of English and Scottish cottages "naked" in the landscape and also surrounded with decorative scenery. Also in Plate 6 there are diagrams of "an approved mode of constructing Cottage Fire Places." Plates VII and 8 illustrate examples of Greek and Gothic buildings "harmonized" with surrounding scenery. Plates 9 and 10 concern drainage and embankment, Plate 11 illustrates hothouses, and Plate 12 depicts the plan of a "House with a large Conservatory and Vinery attached to it." Plates XIII and XIV are views of the house and grounds at Barnbarrow before and after Loudon's suggested improvements, and Plate XV contains before-and-after views of landscape improvements at Llanarth. Plate 16 shows proposed landscape improvements at Harewood. Plate XVII concerns cascades and other forms of water, and Plate XVIII shows fences and other barriers. Plates 19 and XX depict methods of bending and grouping trees. Plate XXI shows architectural improvements intended for the house at Barnbarrow, and Plates XXII and XXIII illustrate landscape improvements proposed for Farnley Hall. Plates 24 and 25 show landscape and architectural improvements completed at Kingswood Lodge. Plate 26 contains four plans of a rural landscape, the first showing the original arrangement of fields and meadows, and the others illustrating conjectural improvements "in the style prevalent about a century ago," in the style of Capability Brown, and in Loudon's own manner. Plates XXVII through XXXI depict proposed improvements at Barnbarrow, Hopton Court, and Maybo. The final plate depicts the deceptive "mode of using Slides as practised by Mr. Repton," a criticism of Repton's use of plates with folding flaps to depict landscapes before and after proposed improvements.

1. This commentary is based on examination of the 1806 edition.

2. See Uvedale Price, *An Essay on the Picturesque* (London, 1794), and the commentary above on Richard Payne Knight, *The Landscape* (1794).

3. These qualities differ little from those described nearly two centuries earlier by Henry Wotton: "Commoditie, Firmenes, and Delight." See his *Elements of Architectvre* (London, 1624), p. 1.

4. These are sublimity, beauty, deformity, picturesque beauty, sculpturesque beauty, antique beauty, romantic beauty, wildness, tranquility, melancholy, age and ruin, elegance, gaiety, novelty, and ridicule.

5. See Humphry Repton, *Sketches and Hints* (1794; *q.v.*). In his discussion of architectural character (I, 78) Loudon cited Archibald Alison's *Essays on the Nature and Principles of Taste* (Edinburgh, 1790). Alison in turn based much of his discussion of character (e.g., pp. 277–279) on Thomas Whately's *Observations on Modern Gardening* (London, 1770). For further discussion of "character" see John Archer, "Character in English Architectural Design," *Eighteenth-Century Studies* XII:3 (Spring 1979), 339–371.

6. In the "Advertisement" to *Sketches and Hints* (1794; *q.v.*) Repton stated that he wanted to create a "complete system of Landscape Gardening," but the expense of preparing a sufficient number of plates forced him instead to present a collection of "detached fragments."

LOUDON, John Claudius (1783–1843)
The villa gardener.

See his Suburban gardener, *Entry 190.*

192.1
LUGAR, Robert (ca. 1773–1855)
Architectural sketches for cottages, rural dwellings, and villas, in the Grecian, Gothic, and fancy styles, with plans; suitable to persons of genteel life and moderate fortune. Preceded by some observations on scenery and character proper for picturesque buildings. By R. Lugar, Architect and Land Surveyor. Elegantly engraved on thirty-eight plates.

London: Printed by T. Bensley, for J. Taylor, 1805.

1 printed leaf, 27 pp, 38 pls.

29.2 × 22.9 cm

Bodl.

192.2
——————

Architectural sketches, for cottages, ⟨ . . . as 1805 . . . ⟩ buildings. By R. Lugar, Architect. Elegantly engraved on thirty-eight plates.

London: Printed by W. Stratford, for J. Taylor, 1815.

1 printed leaf, 27 pp, 38 pls.

31.1 × 34.1 cm

MB

192.3
——————

Architectural sketches for cottages, ⟨ . . . as 1805 . . . ⟩ buildings. By R. Lugar, Architect. Elegantly engraved on thirty-eight plates. A new edition.

London: Printed for J. Taylor, 1823.

31 pp, 38 pls.

30.2 × 23.5 cm

MB

Perhaps encouraged by a small rise in building activity in Britain following the depression of 1799, three architects in their mid-thirties published modest books of architectural designs in 1805. William Atkinson, Joseph Michael Gandy, and Robert Lugar all offered a modest range of cottage and villa designs, perhaps catering to two groups of potential clients: middle-class merchants and others who had reaped wartime profits, and landowners who for agricultural or philanthropic reasons might want to improve conditions for laborers on their estates. Lugar addressed this book to both groups. Many of the cottages illustrated, Lugar announced, were "for those persons whose liberal minds may lead them to accommodate their peasantry and dependants with dwellings, and at the same time to embellish their domains with a variety of picturesque buildings, which shall be both ornamental and useful" (p. 1).[1] To these, Lugar added many more designs that would be full of "beauty, elegance, and convenience," and suitable as dwellings for people of "a higher class of life" (p. 1).

Lugar also included a 16-page discussion of the "Style and Character of Buildings." In his opening remarks he suggested that local circumstances or needs could justify variety and irregularity in architecture: the architect must "form a whole appropriate to the locality or situation, to the circumstances and wishes of his employer" (p. 3). Thus many of Lugar's designs exhibit "dissimilarity and variety" because they "have been made for particular situations, and for particular persons" (p. 4). Nevertheless the architect should aim for regularity: "a house which partakes in form much of the cube will be more compact in the plan and elevation, afford more conveniencies with less cost, than any other form" (p. 4). As for cottage design in particular, Lugar argued in favor of a painterly approach:[2] "the Architect, not less than the Painter, should feel the true value of varied lines in the contour of buildings, and he frequently should compose with a Painter's eye. The broken line must be considered peculiarly in character for a picturesque Cottage, whether it be the habitation of a gentleman or a peasant. It is thus . . . [that] the pleasant effects of light and shadow are made to produce those pleasing varieties which constitute the picturesque in buildings" (p. 5). These effects could be achieved by making such functional additions to a cottage as a "lean-to closet, a bow-window, a pent-house, chimneys carried high and in masses, or gable-ends" (p. 5).

Following several pages of remarks on color, materials, and utility, Lugar considered three specific types of dwelling: the lodge, the *cottage ornée*, and the villa. Essentially a residence for a laborer or a retainer on a large estate, the lodge "should be in due character with the house," to avoid an otherwise "gross violation and incongruity of design" (pp. 9–10). The "Cottage Ornée, or Gentleman's Cot" is a simple rural retreat for a gentleman, and "should possess particular neatness, without studied uniformity" (p. 10). Here Lugar especially encouraged picturesque irregularity, with "deep recesses and bold projections" producing a "play of light and shadow" (p. 10). In the third type of residence, the villa, "the style should at once declare it to be the residence of the Gentleman" (p. 15). Quite opposite from the cottage, the villa should be entirely uniform in design, with "exact proportion and regularity of parts" (p. 15). Nevertheless there must always be a quality of "lightness" to the villa, where "great architectural enrichments, such as colonnades and porticos," are entirely inappropriate (p. 15).

Figure 4

The plate descriptions (pp. 19–27) include remarks on siting, materials, and the intended uses of individual rooms. Lugar's designs are far more ambitious than those of Atkinson and Gandy.[3] Even the smallest thatched lodges and cottages are two stories high, with rough-barked tree-trunk columns and a multitude of picturesque angles and projections.[4] The "ornamented cottage with ruins" in Plate VIII is a modest two-story dwelling set next to a much larger artificial ruin. "A house in the style of true house Gothic" (Plate X) is a regular, symmetrical design in an ornamented late Tudor or Elizabethan style. The style no doubt was chosen for its associations: "the elevation shews a character becoming an English gentleman; plain and unaffected" (p. 21). A design in Castle Gothic, by comparison, was intended for "a family of the first rank," using "bold, broken, and massive outlines, unconfined extent, unequal heights, and numerous towers . . . giving to the whole an awful gloominess productive of grand, majestic, and sublime ideas" (Plates XXXIII–XXXIV; p. 26).[5] An "Italian Villa" (Plate XXVIII) consists of a principal mass two stories high and three windows wide, plus a three-story tower in the rear, reminiscent of similar towers in Italian landscapes by Claude. More fantastic was a villa in the "Eastern" style, including a central dome and corner turrets, and closely modeled on an Indian example.[6]

All designs are shown in plan and elevation. The elevations, executed in aquatint, show lush foliage in the foreground and surrounding the house, together with such picturesque accompaniments as winding roads and picket fences. Among the designs of average size, the ground-floor plan of the Ornamented Cottage (Plate XI) is typical: it includes a living room, kitchen, dining room, bake house, china closet, and library. The farm house (Plate XIII) is similar, with a living room, kitchen, dining room, bake house, breakfast room, closet, pantry, and dairy.

1. All references here are to the 1805 edition.

2. Lugar likely was indebted to James Malton for these ideas. See Malton, *An Essay on British Cottage Architecture* (1798).

3. Most of the cottage and villa designs are at least two stories high and three windows wide. Altogether Lugar's designs include two Peasant's Cottages, three Lodges, three Ornamented Cottages, three Villas, six designs labeled "Dwelling," "Residence," or "House," one Mansion, two Farm Houses, two Pavilions, and one plate of designs for Gothic windows.

4. The ground-floor plan of the Lodge in Plate III includes only a best room, a living room, a washhouse, and a porch. No kitchen is shown.

5. In brief remarks on the Gothic style (pp. 12–15) Lugar adopted Repton's classification: Castle Gothic, Church Gothic, and House Gothic. See Humphry Repton, *Observations on the Theory and Practice of Landscape Gardening* (1803). Lugar recommended "consistency of character" in Gothic designs, a quality often lacking when "the village carpenter" ignorantly mixes all three styles for the sake of novelty (p. 13).

6. Lugar's design closely resembles the "Mausoleum of Sultan Purveiz, near Allahabad" in Thomas Daniell, *Oriental Scenery* (London, 1796), I, 22. My thanks to Catherine Asher for her help with identifying Lugar's source.

193.1

LUGAR, Robert (ca. 1773–1855)

The country gentleman's architect; containing a variety of designs for farm houses and farm yards of different magnitudes, arranged on the most approved principles for arable, grazing, feeding, and dairy farms;

with plans and sections shewing at large the construction of cottages, barns, stables, feeding-houses, dairies, brew-houses, maltings, &c. with plans for stables and dog-kennels; to which are added, designs for labourers' cottages and small villas. The whole adapted to the use of country gentlemen about to build or to alter. By R. Lugar. . . . Engraved on twenty=two plates, with general observations and full explanations to each.

London: Published by J. Taylor, 1807.

v + 26 pp, 22 pls.

31.1 × 24.1 cm

MB

193.2

The country gentleman's architect; ⟨ . . . as 1807 . . . ⟩ feeding houses, ⟨ . . . as 1807 . . . ⟩ labourers cottages ⟨ . . . as 1807 . . . ⟩ each.

London: Published by J. Taylor. Printed by J. Moyes, 1815.

v + 26 pp, 22 pls.

30.9 × 24.0 cm

MnU

193.3

The country gentleman's architect; ⟨ . . . as 1807 . . . ⟩ sections, showing at ⟨ . . . as 1807 . . . ⟩ dog-kennels: to which are added designs ⟨ . . . as 1807 . . . ⟩ each. The second edition.

London: Published by J. Taylor, 1823.

32 pp, 22 pls.

28.6 × 22.9 cm

MBAt

193.4

The country gentleman's architect: containing a variety of designs for farm-houses and farm-yards of different magnitudes, arranged on the most approved principles for arable, grazing, feeding, and dairy farms; with plans and sections, showing at large the construction of cottages, barns, stables, feeding-houses, dairies, brewhouses, maltings, &c. with plans for stables and dog-kennels: to which are added, designs for labourers' cottages and small villas. The whole adapted to the use of country gentlemen about to build or to alter. By R. Lugar, Architect. A new edition.

London: M. Taylor, (nephew and successor to the late J. Taylor), 1838.

32 pp, 22 pls.

30.5 × 24.1 cm

V&A

Daniel Garret issued the first book devoted to designs for agricultural buildings in 1747. In the 1790s a growing interest in agricultural improvement stimulated publication of many articles in *Communications to the Board of Agriculture*, the inception of a series of reports on the agricultural state of every county in Britain, and several monographs on agricultural improvement.[1] In addition to advice on matters of husbandry and horticulture, these publications provided detailed plans, elevations, and specifications for farm houses and laborers' cottages.

By 1807 Robert Lugar had already published one book of designs,[2] but as yet had received no important commissions.[3] Perhaps as an attempt to broaden his potential clientele he made agricultural improvement the ostensible subject of *The Country Gentleman's Architect*. The preface opens with pompous praise of agriculture as "the most ancient and most useful of those arts which have engaged the attention of man" (p. iii). He noted with pride the role of British "patronage and example" in stimulating agricultural progress. Nevertheless he recognized a growing need for attention to the design and arrangement of farm buildings—matters that "have not, I believe, been duly attended to in any publication by a regular architect" (p. iii). Therefore he provided "various examples of rural buildings suitable to the different intentions of Gentlemen who from philanthropy may wish to build cottages for their labourers, or farm-houses and farm-yards for their tenants" (p. iv). In addition, perhaps to interest a less philanthropically minded clientele, he included "a selection of houses possessing superior internal accommodations, and suited in their external appearance to the rank and style of a Gentleman farmer" (p. iv). Lugar noted he had "occasionally indulged [in] a few practical observations on certain parts of husbandry, which some may think belong rather to the agriculturalist than to the architect." But if "I have transgressed the boundaries of my province, my sole motive has been an anxious wish to render this work useful; and I flatter myself that the real principles of the book will be found of general utility" (p. v).

The principal text (pp. 1–26) does in fact include general remarks on utility, interspersed with descriptive comments on the plates. The first four plates illustrate designs for three cottages, which Lugar accompanied with individual descriptions and remarks on siting, construction, and materials (pp. 1–3). Plates 5 through 12 illustrate four farmyards, four farm houses, and a villa. To accompany these plates Lugar added remarks on siting, soil, and drainage for farmyards, plus extensive comments on husbandry quoted from Arthur Young (pp. 6–11). The remaining plates include more plans for farmyards together with elevations and plans for a dairy, an entrance gate in Doric style, a "Boiling Room," a piggery, a "Feeding

House for Oxen," a barn, a brewhouse combined with a washhouse and bake house, and a malting. Lugar included additional remarks on materials and construction to accompany these plates.

Lugar did not comment on the variety of styles in which his designs for dwellings appeared. Plate 4, for example, shows a rustic thatched cottage with tree-trunk columns supporting the veranda roof. The "Farm House & Offices" in Plate 5 include a pointed arch and lattice windows reminiscent of Tudor style, while the asymmetrically placed three-story tower attached to the farm house in Plate 6 is clearly Italianate. Regency trelliswork and scalloped awnings decorate the "Farm House or Small Villa" in Plate 7, while an elegant Doric portico fronts the "Villa" in Plate 8. Indeed the latter design, with a picturesque vista visible in the distance, seems more suited to suburban building estates in Cheltenham or Tunbridge Wells than to a working farm.[4] In plan Lugar's designs range from the simple "Labourer's Cottage" in Plate 1 with just a living room, closet, and washhouse on the ground floor, to a farm house with two parlors, a kitchen, and other rooms on the ground floor plus eight chambers on the upper floor (Plates 6 and 14).

1. See articles by Beatson, Crocker, Crutchley, Gillespie, Holland, Hunt, and Young; individual county surveys entered under "Great Britain. Board of Agriculture"; and John Wood's *Series of Plans for Cottages* (1792), Thomas Davis's "Address to the Landholders" (1795), and William Morton Pitt's *Address to the Landed Interest* (1797).

2. *Architectural Sketches* (1805; *q.v.*).

3. Colvin (1978), pp. 526–528. Only one subject in *Architectural Sketches* had been prepared for a specific client—a cottage with a ruin (plates 7 and 8). The text of *The Country Gentleman's Architect* does not indicate that any of the designs had been commissioned or executed.

4. Lugar explained that "The accommodations shown in this plan are suitable for a gentleman of rank, or of large estate, who lives in a style of elegance becoming a landholder of extensive possessions, residing on his own domain. The apartments," including a breakfast room, library, drawing room, and dining room on the ground floor, "are numerous and spacious, the elevation neat and important" (p. 5). Villas quite similar to this were erected beginning in the 1830s on The Park Estate at Cheltenham. One called "Arundel Lodge" indeed very closely resembles Lugar's design.

194.1

LUGAR, Robert (ca. 1773–1855)

Plans and views of buildings, executed in England and Scotland, in the castellated and other styles. By. R. Lugar, Architect. Elegantly engraved on thirty-two plates.

London: Printed for J. Taylor, 1811.

28 pp, 32 pls.

30.5 × 23.5 cm

RIBA

194.2

A new edition.

London: Printed for J. Taylor, 1823.

28 pp, 32 pls.

30.8 × 24.1 cm

V&A

194.3

Plans and views of ornamental domestic buildings, executed in the castellated and other styles. By R. Lugar, Architect. Second edition.

London: Published by M. Taylor (nephew and successor to the late Josiah Taylor), 1836.

x + 11–32 pp, 32 pls.

36.8 × 27.0 cm

NNC

In the Preface (pp. 5–12) Lugar treated several aspects of architectural design, including site, comfort, economy, and choice of style.[1] His most important remarks are those on style, even though his discussion of the relation between landscape and the Castellated style is clearly reminiscent of Repton:[2] "In a well-wooded country, abounding with grand and romonantic [sic] scenery, a house in the castle style is peculiarly suitable, as well as in character with an extensive domain" (p. 10). Lugar also noted that the Castellated style could accommodate "a number of rooms, which are essential to modern habits," and its "pleasing irregularity, and . . . play of light and shadow" were "highly conducive to the picturesque" (pp. 10–11). By contrast, "houses of the regular, or Grecian cast" should have "a chaste and simple character, . . . effected more by forms than ornaments" (p.11). Lugar was less precise about "buildings of the cottage class," stating only that "considerable indulgence should be allowed; and the fastidious should be disarmed of the severity of criticism, when the picturesque and the useful are conveniently and pleasingly united" (p. 11).

The remainder of the letterpress is devoted to plate descriptions (pp. 13–28), which offer detailed accounts of the landscape surrounding each design, and also characterize the views available from within.

Unlike Lugar's two previous books (q.v.), which depict few if any executed designs, 12 of the 13 designs in *Plans and Views* had been carried out.[3] Several designs are in "mixed" styles, and all but one incorporate Castellated, Gothic, or Old English features.[4] Such a preponderance of executed designs in non-Classical styles was unprecedented in British architectural literature.

Most of the designs are large country residences, although Lugar also included a lodge and cottage at Tillicheun, a pheasantry and cottage at Cullean, and a double cottage for a laborer and gardener at The Rookery.

Of all the designs shown, the most important is certainly Tillicheun (Plates 1-4), on the west side of Loch Lomond, romantically sited to command "an assemblage of wood, water, lawn, and distant country," and "backed by hills covered with plantations, which plantations extend high up the moors" (p. 13). The elevations depict a romantic assemblage of turrets, towers, crenellations, machicolations, arrowslits, and pointed windows. On the inside, the "hall, the dining-room, the staircase, and the state bedroom, are finished in Gothic. The remainder of the house is of fancy decoration, unshackled by any particular style" (p. 15). In addition to the hall, dining room, and staircase, the ground-floor plan includes a breakfast room, drawing room, billiard room, two dressing rooms, a retiring room, "Mr. Stirling's own Room," a kitchen, a housekeeper's room, a butler's pantry, a servants' hall, and several closets. Upstairs there are six bedrooms, the state bedroom, several dressing rooms, and servants' rooms. By way of contrast one of Lugar's smaller designs, Rose Hill Cottage (Plates 21, 22), includes just a living room, hall, dining room, kitchen, greenhouse, larder, and scullery on the ground floor. The elevation is particularly picturesque, with a thatch roof, Gothic windows and doorways, and a bow front surrounded on three sides by a veranda made of rustic tree-trunk supports and a sloping thatch roof.

1. This discussion is based on examination of the 1811 edition. There is a dedication to the Marquis of Buckingham on p. 3.

2. See Humphry Repton, *Sketches and Hints* (1794; *q.v.*).

3. The exception was the design for The Abbey at Balloch, Dumbartonshire (Pls. 17-20): "Mr. Buchanan . . . ultimately preferred making the additions to his old house" rather than executing this design (p. 21).

4. The Ryes Lodge at Little Henny, Essex (Pls. 7–9), is entirely Neoclassical.

195.1
LUGAR, Robert (ca. 1773–1855)
Villa architecture: a collection of views, with plans, of buildings executed in England, Scotland, &c. On forty-two plates. By Robert Lugar, Architect.

London: Published by J. Taylor, 1828.

x + 34 pp, 42 pls.

41.9 × 29.2 cm

BL

195.2
————

Villa architecture: a collection of views, with plans, of buildings executed in England, Scotland, &c. On forty-two plates. By Robert Lugar, Architect. Second edition.

London: Published by M. Taylor, 1855.

v–x + 34 pp, 42 pls.

41.6 × 27.5 cm

PPL

Much earlier in his career Lugar published *Architectural Sketches* (1805), *The Country Gentleman's Architect* (1807), and *Plans and Views* (1811). These helped to establish him as a residential architect, and his success is demonstrated in *Villa Architecture*, a "selection of Designs from the Author's portfolio" (p. v), nearly all of which had been executed. At the beginning of the Preface (pp. v–x) Lugar expressed the hope that his designs would "do justice to his own professional pretensions" by providing ideas for "any gentleman who contemplates improvement of this kind on his estate" (p. v).

Lugar argued that the design of a house must accommodate the pictorial characteristics of the surrounding landscape as well as the needs of the resident. He described his elevations as "appropriate and ornamental to the scenery in which they are placed," while noting "the still more important consideration of the interior arrangements, upon the fitness and convenience of which . . . the credit of the Architect, as well as the comfort of the occupier, must ultimately depend" (p. vi). In designing the plan the architect must "arrange the distribution of the living rooms that they may not be overlooked in approaching the door, and that the indispensable privacy of a country residence not be invaded; and then carefully . . . adjust the subordinate offices, the kitchen-garden, the stables, the approaches, and plantations, so that each may obtain the contiguity and facility of access which its utility requires" (p. vii).

The architect's choice of style, he said, should be determined by two factors: the general form of the landscape, and the scenery immediately surrounding the site. "It is obvious, that the aspect of the country, as well as the immediate scenery, will often suggest one [architectural style] as more appropriate than another" (p. vii). Lugar mentioned specific locations for which he found certain styles appropriate: "bold or mountainous country" required a castellated style (p. viii), while a location in the "neighbourhood of a large town or village, . . . accompanied by a paddock or a small lawn" would accommodate a parsonage in Neoclassical style, and a cottage ornée "may stand in a small lawn, and requires the accompaniments of plantations and shrubberies" (p. ix).

Lugar continued to emphasize the integration of architecture and landscape in the plate descriptions (pp. 1–34). Cyfarthfa Castle in South Wales, for example, "stands on a bold slope, in the midst of the park, backed by woods and extensive plantations. The south-east front commands an enlarged and very pleasing view down the Vale of Taff, bounded on either side by a fine outline of mountain scenery." The view at night of the ironworks below resembles "the fabled Pandemonium" (p. 33). To complement the mountainous and wooded scenery the design (Plates XLI, XLII) has a castellated elevation, full of turrets, arrowslits, and pointed arches. Nevertheless the elevation is relatively low, and complements rather than dominates the low peaks in the background.

Altogether there are designs for two castles, four mansions, two "houses," one "residence," five lodges, four cottages, two farm houses, a parsonage, a greenhouse, a school house, and a banqueting room. The choice of styles is eclectic but also limited to those that are especially picturesque: most of the designs are in Italianate, Elizabethan, Gothic, and Rustic styles. Among the smallest designs is Puckaster Cottage, Isle of Wight (Plates XI, XII), with a dining room, a drawing room, a hall, two "Rooms" for Mr. Vine, a butler's room, a storeroom, and offices on the ground floor. Upstairs are six bedrooms and two dressing rooms. The elevation is particularly rustic, with a thatch roof and rustic bark columns, plus irregularly disposed gables, oriels, projections, and recessions across the facade. The largest design is Cyfarthfa Castle, and the ground-floor plan includes a hall, a library, two drawing rooms, an anteroom, a dining room, a billiard room, a children's playroom, a schoolroom, a day room, a children's garden, a room for Mr. Crawshay, offices, and stables.

The plates, executed in aquatint and hand colored, are among the most handsome in all cottage and villa design books. Each subject, depicted in view and in plan, is skillfully integrated with surrounding foliage and distant landscape forms. This is accomplished through effects of light and shadow, conscientiously balanced relationships between natural and built objects, and in some cases a misty haze that creates an effect of atmospheric depth. Some of the designs are large, but few appear imposing because the facades are composed with a studied irregularity, large wings and pavilions are concealed behind foliage, and major pavilions and masses are disposed such that all portions of the dwelling cannot be seen at one time.

MACPACKE, Jose

See PEACOCK, **James,** *Entry 255.*

MAIN, James, ed.
The horticultural register.

See Entry 474.

MALLET, R.
"Garden architecture."

See The horticultural register, *Entry 474;* Paxton's magazine of botany, *Entry 254.*

196.1
MALTON, James (–1803)
A collection of designs for rural retreats, as villas. Principally in the Gothic and castle styles of architecture, with their ichnography, or plans, laid down to scale; and other appendages. By James Malton. . . .

London: Published by J. and T. Carpenter, Booksellers; to be had at Taylor's Architectural Library; of all the principal booksellers; and of the author, [1802].

1 printed leaf, xii + 43 pp, 34 pls.

35.2 × 28.6 cm

V&A

Malton's previous books include a seminal treatise on the architecture of cottages (1798) and a treatise on perspective (1800), discussed below. *A Collection of Designs* opens with a candid advertisement of Malton's services as an architect. He offered to furnish new designs, working drawings, and cost estimates, to direct alterations on "any sound old building, to any particular style desired," and even to make arrangements by mail.

The 12-page prefatory essay is titled "Reflections on the Necessity and Advantage of Temporary Retirement." The notion of retirement, or withdrawal from society in order to pursue personal enrichment, had been central to the design of country houses for a century and a half.[1] Malton commenced with an inquiry into the pursuit of happiness, and found that retirement was a useful, perhaps necessary, means to that end: "The wise, the virtuously independent, who prefer the pure and tranquil retirement of the country, to the foetid joys of the tumultuous city, are they who take the most likely means to enjoy that blessing of life, happiness" (p. ii). The rest of the essay further extols the benefits of retirement: it is "the parent of every truly social feeling" (p. ii); in retirement "the mind clearly sees what should be done" (p. iii); and retirement is "relished by persons who find delight in the continual and steady pursuit of information" (p. vi). Thus "the villa," a country retreat, "requires to be supplied with more food for the mind than the mansion in town" (p. vi).

Malton echoed these sentiments in the Introduction (pp. 1–14), where he suggested that a house should express and contribute to one's retirement: just as one is less formal in personal dress and "figure" in retirement, so should one's house in the country be less formal than one in a city (p. 8). Malton found large, regular mansions such as Wentworth, Kedleston, Wanstead, and Worksop entirely inappropriate to the country, and suited instead to the formal regularity of a London square (p. 7). Malton recommended the use of more informal elevations, plans, and styles in country residences while also linking the design of a dwelling to the character and personality of its inhabitant: "nothing can more distinctly mark the character and taste of a man, than the kind of dwelling he shall chuse to erect for the place of his particular residence. In that will indisputably be seen, whether his taste, his judgment, or his wealth, was predominant; or how far all together were called into action" (p. 5).

The 34 plates include 26 designs for villas and lodges in a variety of Gothic and Neoclassical styles. In addition there are three separate designs for a library or museum (Plates 25, 26, 28, 29; the design in Plate 29 also could serve as a bath), a dairy, a bath, Gothic chairs and windows, and illustrations for an essay on lighting rooms. In describing his designs (pp. 15–36) Malton recommended picturesque styles and informal plans. "A villa," he said, is "the country retreat of a nobleman or gentleman. Its character is elegance, and its situation should be retired." Thus Malton "reject[ed] the Grecian and Roman mode of fabrick, for more picturesque forms" (p. 15). Yet his designs are not entirely in medieval or exotic styles. Indeed nearly half the designs are Neoclassical in style and generally characterized by regular, symmetrical plans and elevations. Regularity is especially apparent in one design for a museum (Plate 28): four square pavilions are disposed symmetrically about a circular "saloon" with a dome overhead, each pavilion designated to display a certain type of object or artifact. The plan for Design 18, a Neoclassical villa, is far more exciting and original. Starting with an equilateral triangle, Malton rounded all the corners and then turned one side into a large concave curve, fronted by a portico bowing outward. Inside, the principal rooms include a circular hall, a circular "Ladies Work room," a rectangular dining room, and a rectangular breakfast parlor, plus a library and a drawing room each shaped as a rectangle with a semicircular bow at one end. Malton designed a similar plan, based on a right triangle, for a Gothic hunting lodge (Plates 14 and 16). This includes an oval drawing room measuring 18 feet by 27 feet, a rectangular sitting room and breakfast parlor, and a rectangular dining room. The exterior is heavily ornamented with machicolations, crenellations, pointed windows, arrowslits, and statues in niches. A few designs appear with alternative elevations for the same plan: Designs 1 through 4, for example, are two Neoclassical and two Gothic elevations based on a single plan for a villa (Plate 4) that includes a hall, dining room, study, kitchen, scullery, and water closet on the ground floor.

Malton composed several designs with a particular type of setting in mind, such as the bank of a river or the top of a hill. Clearly aware of Humphry Repton's recent discussion of architectural and landscape "characters,"[2] Malton paid special attention to the picturesque integration of architecture and scenery. He described one "florid" Gothic villa, for example, whose "character is the inland villa, and requires a quiet and enclosed situation on a small lawn, having a gentle rise to the front, with light timber immediately about" (pp. 22–23).

The final portion of the text (pp. 37–43) is an essay "On Lighting Apartments," in which he noted "the cheerfulness of rooms depends chiefly, if not entirely, on the mode of *conveying in* the light; not the *quantity of* it." The accompanying illustrations (Plate 34) depict six different methods of arranging windows in a wall.

1. On matters relating to "retirement" in seventeenth-century country house design see G. R. Hibbard, "The Country House Poem of the Seventeenth Century," *Journal of the Warburg and Courtauld Institutes* XIX:1–2 (January–June 1956), 187–225; and Mark Girouard, "A Place in the Country," *Times Literary Supplement*, 27 February 1976, pp. 223–225.

2. See Repton, *Sketches and Hints* (1794).

197.1
MALTON, James (–1803)

An essay on British cottage architecture: begin an attempt to perpetuate on principle, that peculiar mode of building, which was originally the effect of chance. Supported by fourteen designs, with their ichnography, or plans, laid down to scale; comprising dwellings for the peasant and farmer, and retreats for the gentleman; with various observations thereon: the whole extending to twenty-one plates, designed and executed in aqua = tinta. By James Malton.

London: Published by Hookham and Carpenter, Booksellers; and to be had at Taylor's Architectural Library; at Egerton's Military Library; of Mr. Wilkinson, Map and Print-seller; and of the author, 1798.

27 pp, 21 pls.

33.0 × 27.9 cm

MH

An essay on British cottage architecture. Being an attempt to perpetuate on principle that peculiar mode of building which was originally the effect of chance. Exemplified by fourteen designs, with their ichnography, or plans, laid down to scale; comprising dwellings for the peasant and farmer, and retreats for the gentleman; with various observations thereon: the whole extending to twenty-three plates, designed and executed in aqua= tinta, by James Malton. The second edition, with two additional plates.

London: Published by Thomas Malton; and to be had at Taylor's Architectural Library; at Egerton's Military Library; and at Carpenter's, Bookseller, 1804.

27 pp, 23 pls.

33.7 × 27.3 cm

MB

Unlike contemporary architects who advocated order, regularity, and symmetry in domestic design,[1] Malton wanted to "perpetuate . . . the peculiar beauty of the British, picturesque, rustic habitations" which were "the most pleasing, the most suitable ornaments of art that can be introduced to embellish rural nature."[2] He complained in the Introduction (pp. 1–12) that previous architects designed "regular" dwellings that were "very neat and convenient" but were not "characteristic of that species of building distinguished by the name of COTTAGE" (p. 3). Nor was he satisfied with the definition of "cottage" given in Dr. Johnson's *Dictionary* (1755): "*a mean habitation*" (p. 4). Malton's predecessors had published designs for plain, practical cottages, where the emphasis was on philanthropic and economic improvement rather than pictorial composition.[3] Malton had in mind a more substantial, comfortable, and picturesque cottage:

a small house in the country; of odd, irregular form, with various, harmonious colouring, the effect of weather, time, and accident; the whole environed with smiling verdure, having a contented, chearful, inviting aspect, and door on the latch, ready to receive the gossip neighbour, or weary, exhausted traveller. (p. 5)

He identified certain picturesque and irregular features that would contribute to the "distinguishing character" of this cottage:

A porch at entrance; irregular breaks in the direction of the walls; one part higher than another; various roofing of different materials, thatch particularly, boldly projecting; fronts partly built of walls of brick, partly weather boarded, and partly brick-noggin dashed; casement window lights, are all conducive, and constitute its features. (p. 5)

In addition to this analysis of the physical components of the picturesque rural cottage, Malton also explored the emotions and feelings that traditionally were associated with cottages, and which could be heightened by careful attention to design. "A peculiar regard for this description of building, prevails in all ranks of people," Malton stated. "The greatly affluent . . . involuntarily sigh as as they behold the modest care-excluding mansions of the lowly contented. . . . Often has the aching brow of royalty resigned its crown, to be decked with the soothing chaplet of the shepherd swain" (p. 6). The cottage, in other words, suggests a life innocent of care and anxiety; in addition it connotes simplicity and inartificiality: "The matured eye . . . turns disgusted from the gorgeous structure, fair sloping lawn, well turned canal, regular fence, and formal rows of trees; and regards, with unspeakable delight, the simple cottage, the rugged common, rude pond, wild hedge-rows, and irregular plantations" (p. 7). Altogether, then, the cottage possesses associations of friendship, neighborliness, hospitality, and freedom from care and constraint—a new and complex notion of "cottage," semantically far richer than the "mean habitation" or hovel understood by Johnson and others.[4]

Malton also argued that the state of contemporary British architecture justified greater attention to the picturesque cottage style: "There is no discrimination in the present stile of Architecture. . . . Churches in town are scarcely distinguishable from warehouses; or from stables. . . . Country houses on the common, are reared like town houses in the streets of London. The peculiars of every nation form a mongrel species in England"; Indian, Greek, and Italian buildings all were poorly suited to British customs and the northern climate (pp. 9–10). In contrast the British cottage and "old country Church" were "peculiar, beautiful, and picturesque" structures, indigenous to rural England, "durable," and "gratifying" to the mind and the eye (p. 11).

The "Essay on Cottage Architecture" (pp. 13–27) explores the differences that can occur between drawings and executed designs (pp. 14–16), and the various forms of picturesque cottage windows (pp. 16–19), illustrated in Plates 1 and 2. In brief comments on the subject of irregularity, Malton took issue with John Thomas Smith's assertion that "irregularity of parts" is "a constituent of beauty";[5] Malton found only that "well chosen irregularity" was pleasing, and that to "combine irregularity into picturesque" was "the excellence of Cottage construction" that he aimed to achieve in his own designs (p. 19). Later on he seemed to suggest a natural, organic rationale for picturesque design: the builder, he said, must never "*aim* at regularity," but instead should let the "outward figure" of the building "conform only to the internal conveniency" (p. 27). The remainder of the text consists of brief descriptions of 14 individual designs, with occasional remarks on use, site, and means of achieving "picturesque effect."

Malton presented this series of 14 designs "to those Noblemen and Gentlemen of taste" who wanted to build "retreats" for themselves or dwellings for their tenants, and to farmers for use in making their own dwellings "agree and correspond with the surrounding scenery" (p. 2). The designs are arranged "in regular gradation, from a peasant's simple hut, to a habitation worthy of a gentleman of fortune" (p. 3): the first five designs are "peasant's huts," the next six are "for the farmer, or retired gentleman of small fortune," and the last three are such that "a splendid equipage might be drawn up, and not appear an inappropriate appendage" (p. 3).

The 14 designs are illustrated in Plates 3 through 21; Designs 1 through 4 are each shown in an elevation and an oblique view, and all are based on a single plan. Design 5 is depicted in one elevation and one plan. Designs 6 through 12 are each shown in one elevation and two plans. Design 13 is depicted in one elevation, two plans, and two sections, and Design 14 is illustrated in one elevation and three plans. The elevations are skillfully executed in aquatint, and illustrate Malton's picturesque porches, projections, brick walls, and thatch roofs to best advantage. The smallest designs, Nos. 1 through 4, are 19 1/2 feet wide and 18 feet deep, with a living room (11 feet by 15 feet), children's room or sickroom, and piggery on the ground floor, and a bedroom upstairs. The four different elevations include thatch roofs, hipped gables, half-timbering, lattice windows, and walls made of planking and plaster. Design 14, the largest, has a dining room, library, breakfast parlor, withdrawing room, waiting room, ladies' working room, water closet, and paper closet on the ground floor. The chamber floor contains four bedrooms, a water closet, and bedrooms for the butler and housekeeper. The facade is two stories high and 90 feet wide, with a thatch roof, hipped gables at each end of the facade, and a pedimented "colonnade" supported by four rustic columns in front of the entrance. Malton indicated that in this design, intended as "the residence of a large and opulent family," he "strove to unite elegance of form, to cottage construction and simplicity" (p. 25).

1. See for example Charles Middleton, *Picturesque and Architectural Views* (1793); and John Miller, *The Country Gentleman's Architect* (1797), *qq.v.*

2. P. 1. He explained that "rural nature" could be exemplified by the "savage, sublime, and picturesque" paintings of Salvator Rosa and Loutherbourg, the "grand and beautiful" paintings of Claude and Poussin, and the "beautiful and picturesque" paintings of Ruysdael.

3. See for example Charles Middleton, *Picturesque and Architectural Views* (1793); Nathaniel Kent, *Hints to Gentlemen* (1775); John Wood, *A Series of Plans* (1792); Thomas Davis, "Address to the Landholders" (1795); and Robert Beatson, "On Cottages" (1797), *qq.v.* Only John Thomas Smith, who published *Remarks on Rural Scenery* (1797; *q.v.*) one year before Malton's book, considered cottages as "pictoresque subjects" worthy of the artist's attention.

4. Malton noted that "Dr. Watts" defined the cottage as "*a mean house in the country*" (p. 4). Malton's eagerness to suggest such a variety of associations may have been stimulated by the recent publication of Archibald Alison's fundamental associationist treatise, *Essays on the Nature and Principles of Taste* (Edinburgh, 1790).

5. See John Thomas Smith, *Remarks on Rural Scenery* (1797; *q.v.*).

198.1

MALTON, James (–1803)

The young painter's maulstick; being a practical treatise on perspective; containing rules and principles for delineation on planes, treated so as to render the art of drawing correctly, easy of attainment even to common capacities; and entertaining at the same time, from its truth and facility. Founded on the clear mechanical process of Vignola and Sirigatti; united with the theoretic principles of the celebrated Dr. Brook Taylor. Addressed to students in drawing. By James Malton, Architect and Draftsman.

London: Printed by V. Griffiths; and published for the author, by Carpenter and Co., 1800.

[i] + ii + xiv + 71 pp, 23 pls.

29.8 × 23.5 cm

CtY

In a two-page "Apology" following the Dedication Malton discussed the need for "a practical treatise, which would exemplify the doctrine of delineation, in an easy, familiar, and engaging manner; and wherein its rules might be applied to pleasing and painter-like subjects" (p. i). As a solution he proposed a "method of practice that is followed throughout this work," namely "a mixture of the scientific principles of Brook Taylor, with the clear mechanical mode of Vignola and Sirigatti" (p. i). The Preface (pp. i–xiv) is a lengthy discussion of the need for artists to study perspective, architecture, and drawing. Malton argued that perspective was as fundamental to painting as anatomy, and suggested that artists should not feel constrained by close attention to the rules of either.

The Introduction (pp. 1–17) includes remarks on the principles of perspective vision and a series of definitions. Next follows a discussion of "Practical Geometry" (pp. 18–27), organized as a series of problems. The text concludes with a series of illustrated examples of "Practical Perspective" (pp. 28–71).

The plates include a variety of geometric figures and objects depicted in perspective (Plates 1, 3–4, 6, 7, 9, X, XII, 18). Plate 2 shows two elevations and an oblique view of a small house, two stories high and three windows wide, with semicircular relieving arches in the ground-story front and side elevations. Plate 11 includes an elevation, two plans, and one cutaway view of a "building" approximately 24 feet wide with one principal room inside and a Tuscan portico *in antis* on the facade. Plates V, 8, XII, and XV use outline drawings of gable roofed houses as objects of perspective constructions. Plate 23 demonstrates "angle of vision" with reference to the plan of a mansion, an outbuilding, and surrounding trees. The remaining plates illustrate cubes, cylinders, cones, and other geometric forms in perspective, and demonstrate their application in drawing such picturesque architectural subjects as a castle, a gateway, churches, a barn, a bridge, a lighthouse, and a tower.

199.1

MALTON, Thomas (1726–1801)

An appendix, or second part, to the compleat treatise on perspective. Containing a brief history of perspective, from the earliest and most authentic accounts of it, down to the eighteenth century, when it first began to flourish in England. In which, the methods of practice, used by the ancients, are exemplified, and compared with those now in use. Military perspective, bird's-eye views, &c. The appearances of ascending and descending, on an upright picture; such deceptions in vision accounted for, and illustrated by striking representations; with useful and critical remarks on round objects, in general. The application of perspective to scenery, also to a ship, and in landscape. Projection on curved surfaces, with other distortions, or anamorphoses. Inverse perspective; also, the doctrine of reflection, on plane mirrors. And lastly, it contains a parallel and criticism on all the English authors, who have wrote treatises on perspective; and the principles of Dr. Brook Taylor's perspective compared with Guidus Ubaldus, and, 'sGravesande. The whole delivered in nine sections, and illustrated by ten, large, neat, and curious, folio plates. By Thomas Malton.

London: Printed for the author; and sold by Messrs. Robson; Becket; Taylor; Dilly; and by the author, 1783.

[ii] + 160 pp, 10 pls.

38.1 × 24.1 cm

CtY

199.2

An appendix, or, second part to the complete treatise on perspective; containing a brief history of perspective, from the earliest and most authentic accounts of it, down to the eighteenth century, when it first began to flourish in England; in which the methods of practice, used by the ancients, are exemplified and compared with those now in use. Military perspective; bird's eye views; &c. The appearances of ascending and descending on an upright plane; such deceptions in vision accounted for, and illustrated by stricking representations: with useful and critical remarks on round subjects in general. The application of perspective to scenery; also to a ship; and in landscape; projection on curved surfaces; with other distortions, or anamorphoses; inverse perspective. Also the doctrine of reflection on plane mirrors. And, lastly, it contains a parallel and criticism on all the English authors who have wrote treatises on perspective; and the principles of Dr. Brook Taylor's perspective compared with Guidus Ubaldus, and s'sGravesande. The whole delivered in nine sections, and illustrated by ten plates. Second edition, with additions and improvements. Thomas Malton, Sen.

London: Printed and sold, for the author, by V. Griffiths; sold also by Messrs. Carpenter and Co.; Taylor, and by J. Malton, 1800.

[ii] + 160 pp, frontisp. + 10 pls.

34.2 × 21.8 cm

DLC

Malton's *Compleat Treatise* (1775) achieved four editions by 1779. Four years later he issued this *Appendix* which, according to the Preface, he had intended to publish along with the later editions of the *Compleat Treatise*.

The text (pp. 4–160) is divided into nine sections. Section I includes selective remarks on Continental perspective treatises, and an account of a mechanical apparatus "for taking general Views . . . without understanding Perspective." Section II concerns military perspective, bird's-eye views, and "horizontal Pictures." Section III describes optical "Effects" and "Deceptions" connected with perspective. Sections IV, V, and VI concern the use of perspective in making theatrical scenery, drawings of ships, and landscape pictures. In Section VII Malton discussed distorted representations, anamorphoses, and a method for "delineating on curved Surfaces."

Section VIII treats "Inverse Perspective," reflections in mirrors, and methods of depicting a globe in perspective. The final section includes extensive commentary on other English perspective treatises, as well as a few "Remarks on the Reviewers" of Malton's own treatise.

The ten plates include geometric objects and diagrams, illustrations of drawing apparatus and anamorphoses, and perspective views of bases, pediments, other architectural elements, household objects, furniture, and ships. In addition Figures 6 through 8 in Plate I depict a three-story house, seven windows wide, in a plan and two elevations. Figures 17 through 19 in Plate III illustrate "a Building, having two Courts or large Areas" (p. 29). Figures 21 and 22 in Plate IV are views looking uphill and downhill, respectively, at row houses that flank a sloping street and rise or fall in a stepwise manner.[1] There are two landscape scenes in Plate VII. One depicts a picturesque cottage, stream, bridge, and distant village. The other is a view of Burton Constable (p. 59).

1. For an earlier treatment of a similar subject see Edward Noble's *Elements of Linear Perspective* (1771).

200.1

MALTON, Thomas (1726–1801)

A complete treatise on perspective, in theory and practice; on the principles of Dr. Brook Taylor. Made clear, by various moveable schemes, and diagrams, in the most intelligent manner. In four books. Embellished with an elegant frontispiece and forty-eight plates. Containing diagrams, views, and original designs, in architecture, &c. by the author; elegantly engraved.
Book I. Treats on optics and vision, a necessary introduction to the theory of perspective; and contains some objections to the received opinions of light and colour; reflection, &c.
Book II. Contains the whole useful theory of perspective, both rectilinear and curvilinear; with remarks, and familiar examples, to illustrate and evince the universality of its principles; with a full refutation of the absurd opinions which several persons entertain of perspective.
Book III. Is a copious treatise on practical perspective. In which, is first displayed the true elements of the whole, as deduced from the foregoing theory; their extensive application is pointed out, and exemplified throughout the whole book; and, by the most simple means possible, is shewn how to project, perspectively, all kinds of regular objects, from the simplest to the most complex; also, how far it is applicable to irregular objects. Comprized in twelve sections, on various subjects, and adapted to various professions.
Book IV. Treats on shadows in general, in theory and practice, projected by the sun, also by a torch or candle; of reflected light on objects, and the reflected images of objects, on the surface of water, and polished, plane surfaces, of aireal perspective, or the effect of distance, &c. In six sections, containing nine plates, which illustrate the whole. By Thomas Malton.

London: Printed for the author; and sold by Messrs. Robson; Dodsley; Becket; Taylor; Richardson and Urquhart; and by the author, 1775.

[ii] + viii + 284 pp, frontisp. + 46 pls. [*pls. XL, XLII–XLVI, all mentioned in the text, are wanting in this copy*].

36.5 × 24.2 cm

MH

200.2

A compleat treatise on perspective, in theory and practice; on the true principles of Dr. Brook Taylor. Made clear, in theory, by various moveable schemes, and diagrams; and reduced to practice, in the most familiar and intelligent manner. Shewing, how to delineate all kinds of regular objects, by rule. The theory and projection of shadows, by sun-shine, and by candle-light. The effects of reflected light, on objects; their reflected images, on the surface of water, and on polished, plane surfaces, in all positions. Keeping, aireal perspective, &c. The whole explicitly treated; and illustrated, in a great variety of familiar examples; in four books. Embellished with an elegant frontispiece, and forty-six plates. Containing diagrams, views, and original designs, in architecture, &c. neatly engraved. All originals; invented, delineated, and, great part, engraved by the author, Thomas Malton.

London: Printed for the author; and sold by Messrs. Robson; Dodsley; Becket; Taylor; Richardson and Urquhart; and by the author, 1776.

[ii] + viii + [viii] + 284 pp, frontisp. + 46 pls.

37.5 × 25.0 cm

MH

200.3

A compleat treatise on perspective, ⟨ . . . as 1776 . . . ⟩ manner; shewing how ⟨ . . . as 1776 . . . ⟩ positions. The whole explicitly ⟨ . . . as 1776 . . . ⟩ frontispiece, and forty-eight plates. ⟨ . . . as 1776 . . . ⟩ Malton. The second edition, corrected and improved; with large additions.

London: Printed for the author; and sold by Messrs. Robson; Becket; Taylor; Dilly; and by the author, 1778.

[x] + 296 pp, frontisp. + 48 pls [*pl. XXXI wanting in this copy*].

35.6 × 22.9 cm

CtY-BA

London: Printed for the author; and sold by Messrs. Robson; Becket; Taylor; Dilly; and by the author, 1779.

[xviii] + 296 + 8 + 4 pp, frontisp. + 48 pls.

34.9 × 21.6 cm

NN

The preliminary matter of the final edition (1779) includes a dedication to the "President and Members, of the Royal Academy," where Malton had studied and exhibited since 1773,[1] plus an eight-page preface, a seven-page table of contents, and one page of errata. The text consists of four books, the contents of which are clearly described in the title of the first edition. At the end of the final edition is an eight-page list of subscribers and a four-page list of subscribers "In Dublin."[2]

The frontispiece depicts a domed pavilion with an inscription to the memory of Dr. Brook Taylor in a panel over the central arch. The 48 plates, many of which have folding flaps, depict a variety of geometric figures, diagrams, and objects in perspective. Among these objects are pedestals, entablatures, pediments, arches, arcades, colonnades, capitals, vases, parts of the orders, staircases, doors, domed ceilings, furniture, coaches, and machinery. Malton also included a few major architectural monuments, such as St. Paul Covent Garden, the adjacent "piazza," and the Royal Hospital at Chelsea. Several plates depict church and room interiors. Simple geometric solids shaped like houses are depicted in Plates III, V, and XLIII, and a partial view of a house wall and gambrel roof is shown in PLate VI. A domed building with an Ionic portico appears in Plate XXV. Figures 106 through 109 in Plate XXIII show a two-story house with an octagonal bow at one end rotated through several positions as part of a perspective exercise. Figure 27 in Plate XLIV depicts a small two-story building with an ell attached to one side. Figure 28 in the same plate shows a large two-story house, U-shaped in plan, seven windows wide and five windows deep. Plate XLVIII includes a landscape scene with a bridge over a river, a wharf, and next to the wharf a three-story house, five windows wide.

1. In 1782 Malton received the Gold Medal, but his bid in 1795 to become an Associate failed. See Colvin (1978), pp. 535–536.

2. In the list of Irish subscribers the first page is blank, the second is unnumbered, the third is numbered 3, and the fourth is numbered 4.

MARSHALL, William (1745–1818)
Planting and ornamental gardening *and* Planting and rural ornament.

See Entry 453.

201.1 ‡
MARTIN, Benjamin (1704–1782)

The principles of perspective explained in a genuine theory; and applied in an extensive practice. With the construction and uses of all such instruments as are subservient to the purposes of this science. By Benj. Martin.

London: Printed for, and sold by the author, [1770?].

[ii] + 51 pp, 1 pl.

27.8 × 20.6 cm

Reference: Microfilm supplied by The Library of Congress.

The British Museum assigned the date [1770?] in the nineteenth century.[1] Other libraries occasionally have assigned different dates, but several copies examined appear to be identical.

In the Preface Martin indicated that his interest lay in theoretical aspects of perspective: "No Mathematical Science requires a Theory more than Perspective," he wrote, and "The Manner in which some Authors have treated the Theoretical Part has not been satisfactory to me." Therefore he now presented "a Theory of Perspective which appears to me the most genuine, natural, and perspicuous that possibly can be" (Preface). From "First Principles" he turned to scenography, landscape, mechanical construction, double parallel rules, optics, and spherical perspective. Only one plate accompanies this treatise, and most of the figures in it are geometric constructions. The sole architectural subject appears as part of Figure 8, which illustrates a device for sketching landscape scenes in perspective. The subject here is a half-timbered cottage with thatch roof, set underneath a group of trees, projected on an "imaginary transparent plane" (p. 26) above the perspective device. Lower down, the landscape is shown redrawn in outline with the aid of the machine.

1. The author's address, given in the imprint, is "Fleet-Street, No. 171."

202.1
MATTHEWS, James Tilly (–ca. 1814)
Useful architecture. By James Tilly Matthews, Architect. No. I.

[N. loc.: J. Bass, printer, 1812].

2 pp, 4 pls.

28.6 × 23.5 cm

Soane

The copy of the first number in the Soane Museum is accompanied by a prospectus, dated 31 October 1812, proposing several further numbers. Apparently these never were issued.

All the plates are dated 1812; there is no other evidence of date.

The brief text (pp. 1–2) describes designs for a "small cottage" (Plate 1) and three versions of an "Economical Villa" (Plates 2–4). Matthews indicated the latter might serve "either as a Country Box for those who, having a considerable establishment, want but a temporary dwelling for a few months yearly; or for the permanent Residence of a moderate Family" (p. 1).

The first plate contains two plans and a view of a two-story cottage. The ground-floor plan includes a family room, a washhouse, a cellar, a dairy, and a pantry; the chamber floor includes one bedroom and one large "Family" bedroom. The elevation includes a door and a window on the ground floor, and one window upstairs.

The other three plates include plans and views of three different villas, all with similar elevations: the central three bays are two stories high, and are flanked by one-story bays, one window wide, on either side.

203.1
MEASON, Gilbert Laing

On the landscape architecture of the great painters of Italy. By G. L. M Esqr.

[London]: Printed at C. Hullmandel's Lithographic Establishment, 1828.

3 printed leaves, 147 pp, 55 pls.

27.9 × 22.5 cm

MB

Vernacular architecture of the Italian countryside had been an object of continuing interest in England for more than a century before Meason's book appeared in 1828. The taste for Italianate forms appeared early in the eighteenth century, when English painters looked to the works of Claude and Poussin as prototypes for a new, "picturesque" approach to landscape composition.[1] Englishmen collected, studied, and copied the works of Claude, Poussin, and dozens more Renaissance and Baroque painters, paying close attention to "picturesque" architectural subjects as well as to the Old Masters' methods of composition. Nevertheless British architects, looking instead to ancient Greece and Rome for inspiration and example, were slow to appreciate the irregular and frequently informally composed buildings in the work of French and Italian landscape painters. Perhaps the first to execute a building in a picturesque Italianate manner was John Nash, whose Cronkhill (1802) includes a tower, arcade, and open balcony that are reminiscent of buildings in works by Claude.[2] One year later Edward Edwards was the first to publish original designs in this style, although they were intended as examples of perspective construction, and not projects for actual dwellings.[3]

In 1805 Richard Payne Knight considered architecture at length in his *Analytical Inquiry into the Principles of Taste*. In a discussion of the "irregular" house, he specifically cited the work of Claude, Nicolas Poussin, and Gaspar Poussin:

The best style of architecture for irregular and picturesque houses, which can now be adopted, is that mixed style, which characterizes the buildings of Claude and the Poussins. . . . [In the design of these buildings,] it may be discreet always to pay some attention to authority; especially when we have such authorities as those of the great landscape painters above mentioned; the study of those works may at once enrich and restrain invention.[4]

Also in 1805 Robert Lugar published his collection of *Architectural Sketches* (q.v.). Among designs in Gothic, French, Castle, and Indian styles there was one, illustrated in Plates XXVII and XXVIII, "in the style of an Italian villa." Suggesting a scenic context similar to that in some Italian landscape paintings, Lugar indicated the design "was made for a situation which afforded three most desirable views, and the plan is so constructed as to embrace each separately" (p. 24). The dwelling itself consists of two parts: an entirely symmetrical two-story pile, three windows wide, attached at its left rear corner to a three-story octagonal tower.[5] Individually neither part was remarkable, but their disposition in this asymmetrical, picturesque manner clearly recalls examples in the paintings of Claude and Poussin. In the same year Joseph Michael Gandy included a double cottage designed "after the Italian manner" in his *Rural Architect* (1805; q.v.). The asymmetrical elevation (Plate XXXIII), consisting of a tile-roofed rectangular pavilion attached to a low, horizontal wing, was "distributed so as to have a picturesque effect, rather than any uniformity." Another design in this collection is equally Italianate: a two-story octagonal tower is attached to one corner of a low, one-story horizontal wing (Plate XVI).

In 1818 John Buonarotti Papworth published a proposal for a "Villa, Designed as the Residence of an Artist," composed of forms clearly and openly borrowed from Italian landscape painting. Papworth explained:

Claude Lorrain, Poussin, and other celebrated landscape-painters of the seventeenth century, introduced forms of buildings in their compositions that were well suited to the poetic feeling obvious in the works of those great masters; the [poetic] feature is common to the countries in which they painted, but it was by them brought to a higher degree of elegant and judicious conformity with the chief subjects of their pencils, than could be expected to exist in buildings generally erected without other considerations than such as merely related to fitness and conveniency.[6]

Presumably such Italianate forms, so well suited to "poetic feeling," would serve as an inspiration to the artist residing in this villa.

In the next decade few, if any, Italianate designs were published before 1827. In that year Peter Frederick Robinson published *Designs for Ornamental Villas* (q.v.) and James Thomson published *Retreats* (q.v.), each of which contained one design in that style. In the same year Thomas Frederick Hunt completed *Architettura Campestre* (q.v.), a collection of designs somewhat reminiscent of paintings by Claude and Poussin, but Hunt was openly unsympathetic to the use of Italianate architecture on

British soil. The very next year, however, Gilbert Laing Meason published his voluminous compendium of Italianate architectural designs, titled *On the Landscape Architecture of the Great Painters of Italy.*

There is no mistaking Meason's enthusiasm for Italianate architecture. He repeatedly noted the value of this style for residential design because of its picturesque irregularity,[7] and the plates reproduce architectural subjects found in Italian landscape painting from the late Middle Ages to the seventeenth century.

The text includes a remarkably long discussion of architectural history, and domestic architecture in particular. The first chapter explores the "Rise of Domestic Architecture" in Greece and Rome, and the next focuses on the defensive nature of early country residences. The third chapter concerns Roman villas, and is based in part on accounts of Pompeii and descriptions by Pliny and others of ancient villas. The fourth chapter concerns "The Masonry of Roman Architecture." The next chapter, devoted to the architecture of the Middle Ages, reveals Meason's uncommon interest in the societal context of architecture, including such matters as war, economics, and the rise of political states. Also he compared the expressive potential of architecture to that of painting: one group of buildings, he said, had "the appearance of that kind of individuality which distinguishes in painting a portrait from an ideal face" (p. 55). In the sixth chapter, which concerns the history of domestic architecture in England, Meason lamented that "Italian Villa architecture" of the sixteenth century "was not copied in England" (p. 66).

The seventh chapter, Meason's longest, propounds his principal thesis: that the "Landscape Architecture of the Italian Painters" is suitable for modern dwellings. Acknowledging his debt to Richard Payne Knight's observations on the "mixed style . . . of Claude and the Poussins" (p. 71),[8] Meason observed that "the back grounds of the historical works of the great painters" include numerous examples of that "mixed style," now reproduced here as "a new source of studies, for the composition of irregular dwellings" (pp. 72–73). He noted that this style offered "important advantages" in designing new country residences or adding on to old ones, "whether for comfort and convenience, [or] for gratifying taste or fashion" (p. 73). In choosing his examples Meason excluded buildings "in the foreground or in street architecture, as well as those . . . which had so much Grecian or Roman ruins attached to them as gave them the air of composition architecture of the artist." Instead, the examples selected could not be considered "either Grecian, or Roman, or Gothic." Rather, they were products of "different periods, fortuitously formed by additions made either to a tower, or to ranges of substructions of an ancient date, as suited the convenience or habits of the owners. Its picturesque effect is produced by contrast and disposition of large broad masses and extended lines, which inevitably lead to grandeur" (p. 75). The chapter includes further remarks on the use of light and shade and other techniques in designing picturesque architecture, landscaping grounds around country residences, and interior decoration. The final two chapters concern historical and picturesque aspects of Tuscan and Gothic architecture. In the Appendix (pp. 113–147) Meason presented brief observations on each of his plates.

The 55 plates depict buildings selected from four centuries of Italian landscape painting. Meason included the work of Annibale Carracci, Claude Lorrain, Domenichino, Giorgione, Giotto, Poussin, Palma Vecchio, Raphael, Salvator Rosa, and Titian. The plates, all lithographed, are hardly adequate renderings of the artists' individual styles, but effectively indicate the picturesque relations between architectural form and landscape scenery through subtle shadings of texture, light, and shade.

Meason addressed matters of interest and importance to British architects of the 1820s: he presented a wide selection of picturesquely sited, irregular structures that could be adapted and modified to suit the needs of the designer. Yet his influence remained modest. Many mid-nineteenth-century suburbs and provincial resorts could boast "tower houses" and Italianate villas, but these designs were inspired less by Meason than by such prominent executed examples as the Tower House in Park Village West, London, or Osborne, Queen Victoria's retreat on the Isle of Wight.[9] One year after publication of Meason's book Sir Charles Barry carried out his Italianate design for the Travellers' Club in London (1829). Formal, symmetrical, and based on Renaissance prototypes, it had very little in common with the picturesque, occasionally casual, asymmetry and variety in Meason's illustrations. The principal echo of Meason's work is the collection of original designs based on Italian vernacular prototypes published in 1832 by Charles Parker, titled *Villa Rustica* (q.v.).

1. For a fuller discussion see Christopher Hussey, *The Picturesque* (London: Putnam, 1927). Also see Elizabeth Wheeler Manwaring, *Italian Landscape in Eighteenth Century England* (New York: Oxford University Press, 1925).

2. Summerson (1969), p. 290.

3. Edward Edwards, *A Practical Treatise of Perspective* (1803; q.v.).

4. Richard Payne Knight, *An Analytical Inquiry into the Principles of Taste*, 4th ed. (London: T. Payne and J. White, 1808), p. 225. The passage cited also appeared in the 1805 edition.

5. Nearly the same design without an attached tower appeared in Plate 8 of Lugar's *Country Gentleman's Architect* (1807; q.v.), where he described it merely as a "Villa." Octagonal towers alone were not remarkable; they appeared frequently in British architecture following publication of Stuart and Revett's *Antiqvities of Athens*, I (London, 1762). See Dora Wiebenson, *Sources of Greek Revival Architecture* (London: Zwemmer, 1969), Chapter V.

6. J. B. Papworth, *Rural Residences* (1818; q.v.), p. 69.

7. See especially pp. 71–73. Also, following the half title there is a printed leaf bearing a passage from Reynolds's *Discourses* declaring that a picturesque departure from regularity in architecture enhances buildings by giving them "something of scenery."

8. Also on the subject see S. Lang, "Richard Payne Knight and the Idea of Modernity," in *Concerning Architecture: Essays on Architectural Writers and Writing Presented to Nikolaus Pevsner* (London: Allen Lane, 1968), pp. 85–97.

9. Tower House was built ca. 1824–1828 in Park Village West as part of the general development of Regent's Park carried out under the supervision of John Nash. Cronkhill, also by Nash, may well have been the prototype for Tower House. See John Summerson, *The Life and Work of John Nash, Architect* (Cambridge, Mass.: MIT Press, 1980), p. 128. Osborne was erected in 1845–1849 by Thomas Cubitt, and designed in part by Prince Albert. See Henry-Russell Hitchcock, *Architecture: Nineteenth and Twentieth Centuries* (New York: Penguin, 1978), p. 119.

Mechanics' magazine.

See Entry 477.

204.1 ‡

MERIGOT, James

The amateur's portfolio: being a selection of lessons calculated to make the art of drawing easy, and founded upon the principles of geometry and practical perspective. Dedicated, by permission, to the Marchioness of Stafford. By James Merigot. . . . Vol. I [*or* II].

London: Printed for S. Robinson, 1821.

[*Volume I:*] [i] + iii + 5–50 + 32 + 16 + [ii] pp, frontisp. + 60 pls.

[*Volume II:*] iv + 22 + 17–43 + 29 + 16 + 23–24 + [ii] pp, frontisp. + 61 pls.

25.2 × 19.8 cm

Reference: Microfilm supplied by Yale University Library.

As with Merigot's *Treatise on Practical Perspective*, the chronology of *The Amateur's Portfolio* is problematic. The title pages of Volumes I and II are dated 1821, but the dedication is dated 1816 and the plates were published in 1814, 1815, and 1816. On page 3 of the undated introduction, Merigot promised the work would be completed "in Twenty-four Monthly Numbers," each of which would contain five plates, and which altogether would form two quarto volumes. Since the plates were issued as part of individual "Numbers," they were not numbered serially. This has made it difficult to correlate the plates with the text and to bind them in correct order.

In the Introduction Merigot indicated that the treatise was intended for "young students" in families, academies, schools, and seminaries (I, iii). Because this audience would include people with different abilities and experience, he decided to include lessons with varying levels of difficulty in each number (I, iii).

Merigot projected the first volume to include "the study of rural scenery, cottages, country views, and flowers" (I, ii), while the second would concentrate on the human figure, animals, and landscape embellishment; both volumes would treat the use of color. As completed, each volume includes three separately paginated sections. The first section in each volume treats aspects of drawing technique: in Volume I, the text and plates concern drawing instruments, geometry, outlines, tints, colors, watercolor, and reflections in water; in Volume II, the subjects include design, composition, landscape drawing, the human figure, historical subjects, taste, grace, draperies, miniature painting, and intaglio. The second section of each volume is a series of "progressive lessons," short texts each accompanied by several plates, illustrating such problems as drawing houses, barns, or steeples, outlining, shading, painting on velvet, mounting drawings, using color, and engraving. The third section in each volume treats perspective, and includes illustrations of geometric forms, towers, crosses, churches, bridges, bodies of water, and landscapes.

The plates include a wide range of subject matter, from drawing instruments to landscapes, flowers, and the human figure. Other subjects include geometric figures, bridges, trees, historical scenes, furniture, and staircases. At least 32 plates, most of them accompanying the "progressive lessons" in Volume I, contain domestic subjects. Many of these are picturesque cottages, used in a variety of ways: as convenient examples for demonstrating drawing technique, as subjects in picturesque landscape scenes, as examples of objects reflected in water, and as examples of shading and coloring technique. Other domestic subjects include castles, an ale house, a "villager's" house, summer houses for gardens, and one or two larger dwellings, such as Organ Hall in Hertfordshire.

205.1
MERIGOT, James

A treatise on practical perspective; written for the use and study of young learners and amateurs in the art of drawing and painting. With easy rules, by which also builders, cabinet makers, upholsterers, and other proficients in mechanical invention, may represent on paper their plans and designs previous to execution. With an additional essay on architecture, from the amateur's portfolio. Dedicated by permission to the Marchioness of Stafford. By J. Merigot. . . .

London: Printed for S. Robinson, 1819.

[*Part I:*]
"Treatise on Practical Perspective. Geometry. Sec. I. Definitions."
8 pp, 1 pl.

[*Part II:*]
"Treatise on Perspective."
16 pp, 5 pls.

[*Part III:*]
"Perspective. (Continued from page 16, Vol. 1.)"
20 pp, 6 pls.

[*Part IV:*]
"Additional Essay on Architecture."
41–43 pp, 1 pl.

28.6 × 21.6 cm

CtY-BA

The title page is dated 1819, but the book clearly was begun several years earlier. The dedication is dated 1816, the plates of the "treatise on perspective" are dated 1814, the plates of the "second volume" are dated 1815, and portions of the text are printed on sheets watermarked 1813 or 1814.

The first part consists of the dedication, a brief "Address," definitions, and one plate with geometric figures. The 16-page text of the second part includes sections titled "Definitions" and "Practical Perspective." The five plates show geometric figures, crosses, and other objects in perspective, landscape scenes, and "a house with two wings." The house is U-shaped in plan, two stories high, and five windows wide. The 20-page text of the third part describes illustrations in the six plates. These include hexagonal and octagonal "summer-houses," a round tower, furniture, flowers, staircases, geometric objects, a church, reflections in water, landscape scenes, human faces, and drawing instruments. The "Additional Essay" (pp. 41–43) also appeared in Merigot's *Amateur's Portfolio* (1821; *q.v.*). The text and one plate both concern the five orders.

206.1
MIDDLETON, Charles (1756–1818?)
The architect and builder's miscellany, or pocket library; containing original picturesque designs in architecture, of plans and elevations for cottages, farm, country and town houses, public buildings, temples, greenhouses, bridges, lodges and gates for the entrances to parks and pleasure grounds, stables, monumental tombs, garden seats, &c. Dedicated to His Royal Highness the Prince of Wales. By Charles Middleton. . . .

London: Printed for the author; and sold by J. Debrett; Faulder; J. Taylor; Messrs. White; and E. Jeffrey, 1799.

2 printed leaves, 60 pls [*pl. XXXV wanting in this copy*].

18.1 × 11.4 cm

MBAt

206.2

————

————

London: Printed for the author; and sold by J. Taylor, 1812.

2 printed leaves, 60 pls.

18.7 × 11.1 cm

BL

206.3

————

The architect and builder's miscellany, or pocket library; containing original picturesque designs in architecture, for cottages, farm, country, and town houses, public buildings, temples, green houses, bridges, lodges, and gates for entrances to parks and pleasure grounds, stables, monumental tombs, garden seats, &c. By Charles Middleton, Architect. On sixty plates, coloured.

London: Printed for J. Taylor, [n.d.].

60 pls.

17.9 × 11.0 cm

PPCC

206.4

The architect and builder's miscellany, or pocket library; containing original picturesque designs in architecture, for cottages, farm, country, and town houses, public buildings, temples, greenhouses, bridges, lodges, and gates for entrances to parks and pleasure grounds, stables, monumental tombs, garden seats, &c. By Charles Middleton, Architect. Sixty plates.

London: Printed for J. B. Nichols and Son; and J. Weale, [1843?].

60 pls [*pls. 15–19, and 27, wanting in this copy*].

19.0 × 11.5 cm

BL

The copy of the undated edition in the Library of the Carpenters' Company in Philadelphia has no watermark or other internal evidence of date. Another undated copy is printed on paper watermarked 1827.[1] The undated copy in the British Library, according to the printed *General Catalogue*, was published circa 1850, but the only internal evidence of date is one plate watermarked 1842 and several others watermarked 1843.

Middleton was a pupil of James Paine, but their publications differ markedly in format as well as content. Paine published a large folio collection of designs for substantial mansions.[2] Middleton, by contrast, described his book in the Dedication as a "Pocket Companion, for Amateurs of the Science." The format is in fact so small that his elevations and plans give only a general idea of each building's appearance. Nevertheless the scope of Middleton's book was ambitious: in the "Address to the Public" he proposed to illustrate the complete scale of domestic architectural types, "from the primitive Hut, to the superb Mansion." The book thus could serve "as an Assistant to the Professional Man, and a Guide to the Public in the choice of buildings."

The first 32 plates illustrate designs for dwellings, each shown in elevation and plan, beginning with the smallest and most primitive. Plate I, for example, depicts a primitive wattle-and-daub one-room conical hut. A circular Gothic cottage (Plate VIII) contains a parlor, a best room, and a kitchen. A two-story Regency villa with a thatch roof (Plate XI) has a hall, breakfast room, eating room, study, bedroom, dressing room, kitchen, pantry, and scullery on the ground floor. The design for a Neoclassical mansion in Plate XXIX includes a hall, eating room, music room, conservatory, drawing room, tea room, breakfast room, "anti room," steward's room, housekeeper's room, kitchen, scullery, storeroom, and pantry on the ground floor.

The rest of the plates depict designs for mausolea, Chinese and Turkish tea rooms, Greek, Gothic, and Palladian chapels, a banqueting room, tombs, sundials, stables, gates and lodges, greenhouses, seats, bridges, monumental columns, an aviary, a public bath, a theater, an observatory, a courthouse, and a triumphal arch. Despite his eclecticism in scale and style, however, Middleton adopted a manner of illustration that was peculiarly his own. The designs are etched in a nervous line that obscures smaller details but delineates significant features of the building design and surrounding scenery, and also contributes an uncommon liveliness and animation to the illustration as a whole. The plates are further distinguished by bright, sometimes garish coloring in ocher, salmon, pale green, bright green, and bright blue tints.

1. See No. 184a in Priscilla Wrightson, *The Small English House: A Catalogue of Books* (London: B. Weinreb Architectural Books, 1977).

2. See James Paine, *Plans, Elevations and Sections, of Noblemen and Gentlemen's Houses* (1767–1783).

MIDDLETON, Charles (1756–1818?)
Decorations for parks and gardens.

See ELISON, **Thomas,** *Entry 68.*

207.1
MIDDLETON, Charles (1756–1818?)
Picturesque and architectural views for cottages, farm houses, and country villas. Engraved and designed by Charles Middleton, Architect.

London: Printed for Edward Jeffery; sold by R. Faulder; and T. and J. Egerton, 1793.

16 pp, 21 pls.

45.7 × 29.8 cm

MBAt

207.2

————
————

London: Printed for the proprietor; and sold by H. D. Symonds, 1795.

16 pp, 21 pls.

46.3 × 29.8 cm

V&A

The relatively large size of this volume is reminiscent of major treatises by Gibbs, Ware, Paine, and Adam,[1] but the subject matter is not. Middleton provided only plans and elevations for dwellings, yet within that limitation he developed an important illustrated typology of popular British dwelling types in the late eighteenth century.

The text (pp. 1–16) is divided into three sections, on "Cottages" (pp. 1–4), "Farm-Houses" (pp. 5–8), and "Villas" (pp. 9–16). In each case there are general remarks followed by descriptions of original designs illustrated in the plates. Middleton's comments on each type are sufficiently informative on aspects of use, plan, materials, style, and ornamentation that they warrant detailed examination here.

Middleton characterized cottages as habitations of "the poorer sort of country people," generally "persons in the service of the family on whose estate they are erected." Yet he pointed out that cottages may serve a variety of functions:

The cottage built at the entrance of a park will form a convenient lodge. At a small distance from the mansion, the dairy, larder, bath, &c., may assume the characteristic form of a Cottage. Cottages in a more distant situation, are frequently fitted up for the reception of parties engaged in rural amusements. . . . The Bailiff, Gardener, Park and Gamekeepers, &c., are commonly lodged in such habitations.

The design of a cottage is often "the work of necessity, for which no rules can be given." Cottages may be built of "stone, brick, or timber, stuccoed or rough cast, and covered with thatch." He specified that "a parlour, kitchen, pantry, and scullery, are the rooms required to compose such buildings, on the ground plan, with lodging rooms over them . . . proportionably arranged to accommodate the kind of family intended to inhabit them." Perhaps because of the lack of rules and variety of materials available, Middleton hoped to provide a selection of examples that "serve the twofold purposes of use and ornament" (p. 1).

In shorter remarks on farm houses (p. 5) Middleton stated that outbuildings might vary "according to the nature of the farm to which they belong," but one "general plan" is "applicable" to all farm dwellings. The ground floor should include "a best and common parlour, kitchen, pantry, scullery, and store room," with "the necessary lodging rooms" upstairs. All "should be furnished in a plain and simple manner." Other rooms, including the dairy, scalding room, brewhouse, bake house, and washhouse, are generally "considered as offices."

Turning to villas (p. 9) Middleton identified three principal types serving distinct functions:

First, as the occasional and temporary retreats of the nobility and persons of fortune from what may be called their town residence, and must, of course, be in the vicinity of the metropolis.—Secondly, as the country houses of wealthy citizens and persons in official stations, which also cannot be far removed from the capital: and thirdly, the smaller kind of provincial edifices, considered either as hunting seats, or the habitations of country gentlemen of moderate fortune.

Yet all three types share certain formal qualities: "Elegance, compactness, and convenience, are the characteristics of such buildings, either separate or combined, in contradistinction to the magnificence and extensive range of the country seats of our nobility and opulent gentry." The elements of the plan should form a "general suite of apartments on the ground floor, and be so connected with each other as to allow access to each room without interfering with any branch of the offices." The principal apartments "will, of course, be enriched according to the purposes for which they are intended." The offices "should be nearly on a level with the mansion house," but with the most disagreeable functions placed furthest from the house.

The plate descriptions include dimensions, suggestions for materials and for interior and exterior ornament, and comments on the functions of individual rooms. Occasionally there are remarks concerning an appropriate site. Design Number X in Plate III, for example, "is a circular building, proposed to be erected on an eminence, the upper part of which may form an observatory, as the gallery, encircling the roof, affords an opportunity of gaining an extensive view of the surrounding country" (p. 4).

The plates include designs for 12 cottages (Plates I–III), three farm houses (Plates IV–IX), two "small thatched dwellings" (Plate X), eight villas (Plates XI–XX), and one orangery (Plate XXI), each illustrated in one elevation, one or more plans, and occasionally a section. Middleton's cottage designs incorporate such picturesque features as thatch roofs, rustic columns, and trelliswork, but also a variety of Neoclassical characteristics such as symmetrical plans and elevations featuring circles, squares, and other regular geometric figures, plus quoins, pediments, and semicircular windows. The smallest design (Plate I, No. 2) consists of just three rooms— a kitchen, bedroom, and "hovel" or shed—under a circular thatch roof supported by eight rustic columns. The largest (Plate III, No. 11) includes a domed circular dining room, 17 feet in diameter, plus a parlor and kitchen on the ground floor, with three bedrooms upstairs.

The farm house designs are much plainer than the cottages, and all are roughly the same size. The facade of the design in Plate V is three stories high and five windows wide, and its most striking ornamental features are the wide segmental arches over the ground-floor windows. The ground-floor plan includes a best parlor, a common parlor, a kitchen, a common kitchen, and offices. The two upper stories contain a total of 12 bedrooms.

In Plate X Middleton included designs for two "small thatched dwellings," not discussed in the text as a separate type, but mentioned briefly on pages 7–8. The elevations are two stories high and two windows wide, with one-story ells or porches to each side.

There is a great variety of size and ornament among the villas. The facade of the smallest (Plate XI) is just two stories high and three windows wide, with one-story ells to the left and right. The ground-floor plan consists of an eating room, parlor, drawing room, library, and closet. Shallow relieving arches ornament the ground story of the central portion, while urns and paired pilasters embellish the two ells. Other designs make greater use of Neoclassical ornamentation, including domes, urns, rustication, parapets with decorative bas reliefs, pediments, porticoes, and semicircular relieving arches. The largest design (Plate XIX) is two stories high and 13 windows wide, with a large domed rotunda—a two-story drawing room—in the center. In addition to the drawing room the ground-floor plan includes a music room, library, "Anti Room," eating room, and two long office wings to the rear. The upper floor includes 12 bedrooms, plus servants' quarters. The facade includes a hexastyle colonnade fronting the rotunda. At either end two-story wing pavilions have distyle porticoes *in antis* on the ground floor, and are crowned with pediments supported by paired caryatids.

1. See James Gibbs, *A Book of Architecture* (1728); Isaac Ware, *A Complete Body of Architecture* (1756); James Paine, *Plans, Elevations and Sections* (1767–1783); and Robert and James Adam, *The Works in Architecture* (1778 and later).

208.1

MILLER, John

The country gentleman's architect, in a great variety of new designs; for cottages, farm-houses, country-houses, villas, lodges for park or garden entrances, and ornamental wooden gates; with plans of the offices belonging to each design, distributed with a strict attention to convenience, elegance, and economy. Engraved on thirty-two plates; from designs drawn by J. Miller, Architect.

London: Printed for I. and J. Taylor, 1787.

13 printed leaves, 32 pls.

26.7 × 20.6 cm

BL

208.2

⸻

The country gentleman's architect, ⟨ . . . as 1787 . . . ⟩ , elegance and economy. Engraved on thirty-two plates, from designs drawn by J. Miller, Architect.

London: Printed for I. and J. Taylor, 1789.

13 printed leaves, 32 pls.

24.8 × 20.4 cm

PU

208.3

⸻

The country gentleman's architect, in a great variety of new designs, for cottages, farm houses, ⟨ . . . as 1787 . . . ⟩ plates, from ⟨ . . . as 1787 . . . ⟩ .

London: Printed for I. and J. Taylor, 1791.

13 printed leaves, 32 pls.

25.1 × 19.7 cm

V&A

208.4

⸻

The country gentleman's architect, ⟨ . . . as 1787 . . . ⟩ , elegance and economy. Engraved on thirty-two plates, from ⟨ . . . as 1787 . . . ⟩ .

London: Printed for I. and J. Taylor, 1793.

13 printed leaves, 32 pls.

26.0 × 20.6 cm

NNC

208.5

London: Printed for J. Taylor, 1802.

13 printed leaves, 32 pls [*pls. 1, 2, 25–32 are wanting in this copy*].

26.7 × 21.0 cm

MBAt

208.6

The country gentleman's architect, in a great variety of new designs, for cottages, ⟨ . . . as 1787 . . . ⟩ plates, from ⟨ . . . as 1787 . . . ⟩ .

London: Printed for J. Taylor, 1805.

13 printed leaves, 32 pls.

25.4 × 21.0 cm

MBAt

208.7

The country gentleman's architect, in a great variety of new designs for cottages, ⟨ . . . as 1787 . . . ⟩ plates, from ⟨ . . . as 1787 . . . ⟩ .

London: Printed for J. Taylor, 1810.

13 printed leaves, 32 pls.

26.7 × 21.0 cm

NN

The 13 printed leaves each contain a key, identifying by letter the rooms and buildings illustrated in plan on Plates 3 through 15.

Altogether there are elevations and plans for five cottages, 12 farm houses, six villas, two country houses, and six lodges; there are also six alternative elevations for houses, and 12 patterns for gates. Perhaps reflecting the concern for "economy" stated on the title page, most of the designs appear diminutive and frugally ornamented. With the exception of one country house (Plate 18) and one villa (Plate 21) the principal floor of each design is set at or very near ground level, in accord with contemporary attempts to achieve a greater integration of interior and exterior environments.[1] But Miller's composition was unfortunately retardataire in other respects, recalling the geometric rigidity of William and John Halfpenny or Timothy Lightoler[2] with symmetrical facades composed of rectangles, squares, triangles, and semicircles. Apart from occasional projecting three-sided bays there is only modest advance and recession in Miller's facades, and ornament is generally restricted to plain stringcourses, cornices, pediments, attic balusters, and an occasional portico.

The smallest design, for a cottage (Plate 1), includes just a kitchen, closet, and bedroom. The farm houses generally have two parlors, a kitchen, a back kitchen, and perhaps a dairy or pantry on the ground floor, with one or two chambers above. One of the villas has a farmyard attached, and is similar in plan to Miller's farm house designs. The other villas, without farmyards, have a parlor, library, dining room, dairy, kitchen, and back kitchen, or a similar arrangement, on the ground floor.[3] One country house (Plate 18) includes just a best parlor, common parlor, hall, and storeroom on the ground floor, while the other (Plate 20) has two parlors, a hall, a dressing room, a servants' room, and a dairy.

1. For a later discussion of this point see J. B. Papworth, *Hints on Ornamental Gardening* (1823).

2. See Halfpenny et al., *The Modern Builder's Assistant* ([1757]), and Lightoler, *The Gentleman and Farmer's Architect* (1762).

3. Miller used the term "villa" to refer both to farming estates and to gentlemen's country residences. In this he was not unlike Thomas Rawlins, who used the word in a similar dual manner in *Familiar Architecture* (1768; *q.v.*).

209.1 ‖
MITCHELL, James (1786?–1844)
The portable encyclopaedia: or, a dictionary of the arts and sciences, on the basis of Dr. Gregory's. Comprehending the latest improvements in every branch of useful knowledge. Illustrated by numerous engravings. By James Mitchell. . . .

London: Printed for Thomas Tegg; sold by R. Griffin & Co. Glasgow; R. M. Tims, Dublin; M. Baudry, Paris, and Cary & Lea, Philadelphia, 1826.

Art. "Perspective," pp. 599–602; pl. XLIII.

Reference: Information supplied by The University of Oklahoma.

209.2 †
─────────

The portable encyclopaedia: or, a dictionary of the arts and sciences on the basis of Dr. Gregory's. Comprehending the latest improvements in every branch of useful knowledge.

London: Printed for T. Tegg; sold by R. Griffin, Glasgow; R. M. Tims, Dublin; M. Baudry, Paris; and Cary & Lea, Philadelphia, 1828.

Reference: NUC

209.3
─────────

The portable encyclopaedia: ⟨ . . . as 1826 . . . ⟩.

London: Printed for Thomas Tegg; sold by R. Griffin & Co. Glasgow; R. M. Tims, Dublin; M. Baudry, Paris, and Cary & Lea, Philadelphia, 1831.

Art. "Perspective," pp. 599–602; pl. XLIII.

21.0 × 13.0 cm

ICU

209.4

The portable encyclopaedia: or a dictionary of the arts and sciences on the basis of Dr. Gregory's. Comprehending the latest improvements in every branch of useful knowledge. Illustrated by numerous engravings. By James Mitchell. . . .

London: Printed for T. Tegg and Son; R. Griffin and Co., Glasgow; T. T. and H. Tegg, Dublin; also J. and S. A. Tegg, Sydney and Hobart Town, 1837.

Art. "Perspective," pp. 599–602; pl. XLIII.

13.5 × 21.5 cm

NcD

209.5 ‖

The portable encyclopaedia: ⟨ . . . as 1826 . . . ⟩.

London: Printed for Thomas Tegg; R. Griffin and Co., Glasgow; Tegg and Co., Dublin: also, J. and S. A. Tegg, Sydney and Hobart Town, 1839.

Art. "Perspective," pp. 599–602; pl. XLIII.

Reference: Information supplied by The University of Oklahoma.

In many respects this encyclopedia resembles an earlier one, *The Portable Cyclopaedia; or, Succinct General Dictionary of the Present State of the Arts and Sciences: Serving as a Companion to Johnson's Octavo Dictionary of the English Language. By T. C. Watkins. A New Edition, Corrected, Improved, and Enlarged, by James Mitchell, LL.D. F.A.S.* (London: Printed for Geo. B. Whittaker, 1825).[1] The latter work, however, contains no illustrations of dwellings.

The article on "Architecture" (pp. 65–69, Plates IV–V) begins with brief remarks on the origins of building, followed by descriptions of the five orders. Separate sections are devoted to the parts of an order, the diminution of columns, and "Pedestals, Pilasters, &c." The history of Gothic architecture is divided into Saxon, Norman, Saracenic, and Florid Gothic styles. Concluding remarks on "Modern Architecture" note two characteristics that distinguish eighteenth-century architecture from that of previous times: first, eighteenth-century public buildings are less grand and massive, but "are superior . . . in simplicity, convenience, neatness, and elegance"; second, during the eighteenth century private dwellings became "more spacious, convenient, and agreeable to a correct taste" (p. 69). Plate IV depicts the parts of an order, and Plate V depicts the five Classical orders.

The article on "Perspective" includes just one plate. Five of the ten figures are borrowed from *The Art of Drawing, in Perspective* (1755; *q.v.*). Four of these plus three other figures, including two illustrations of houses, appeared previously in George Gregory's *Dictionary* (1806–1807; *q.v.*).

The houses are both two stories high and five windows wide. The facade of the house in Figure 5 is parallel to the picture plane, while the facade in Figure 10 is oblique to the picture plane.

1. The 1825 edition cited here, and earlier editions dated 1810, 1814, and 1819, are entered in BM, NUC, and UC under C. T. Watkins and/or T. C. Watkins.

MITCHELL, John
"On the dairy husbandry in Holland."

See Entry 491.

210.1
MITCHELL, Robert
Plans, and views in perspective, with descriptions, of buildings erected in England and Scotland: and also an essay, to elucidate the Grecian, Roman and Gothic architecture, accompanied with designs. By Robert Mitchell, Architect.
Plans, descriptions, et vues en perspective, des edifices eriges en angleterre et en ecosse: suivis d'un essai sur l'architecture grecque, romaine et gothique, avec des desseins illustratifs. Par Robert Mitchell, Architecte.

London: Printed, at the Oriental Press, by Wilson & Co. for the author: and sold by J. Taylor; R. Faulder; J. and T. Carpenter; T. Evans; and J. White, 1801.

[ii] + 32 pp, 18 pls.

52.0 × 35.4 cm

CtY

The Introduction is printed in both English and French on a preliminary leaf. Mitchell explained in the Introduction that some of the plates depicted "buildings the author has been employed in constructing," while others (Plates 15–18) had been prepared to illustrate the accompanying "Essay to Elucidate the Grecian, Roman, and Gothic Architecture." He felt the essay would establish the true principles of Gothic architecture and so reveal a "pure" Gothic style, of which few historical examples remained. Indeed the Gothic examples that did remain were so "overcharged with decorations" that they had lost the simplicity appropriate to the "pure" style (Introduction).

The text consists of eight pages of plate descriptions (pp. 1–8) and the essay on Greek, Roman, and Gothic architecture (pp. 9–15), followed by a French translation of the descriptions and the essay (pp. 17–32). The plate descriptions concern Mitchell's work at Selwood Park, Heath Lane Lodge, Cottisbrooke, Moore Place, Preston Hall, and the Rotunda in Leicester Square, and reveal particular attention to the character of the surrounding environment. Mitchell described the setting of Selwood Park, for example, as a *"Ferme Ornée . . .* excelled by none in the kingdom. The beautiful diversity of forms in the pleasure-grounds, which are richly adorned with groups of stately trees, and a noble piece of water, produce the most varied picturesque scenery . . . " (p. 1). Plates I and II correspondingly depict elegant lawns, trees, shrubbery, and drives. In Plate III, a view of the "Front towards the Pleasure-Grounds," a pedimented two-story Composite portico and bows at the two ends of the mansion create an undulation and animation appropriate to the "diversity in the pleasure-grounds" visible from this front (p. 2).

Plates I through 14, executed in aquatint and elegantly colored, depict Mitchell's work at the locations mentioned above. Despite the emphasis on Gothic in the Introduction, all these designs are in Classical styles. He suggested in the "Essay" that the form of a temple especially suited "mansions, or residences of persons of distinction, for which, it is conceived, they are particularly appropriate, as the form of the Temple admits of the highest magnificence" (pp. 9–10). Nevertheless among the designs illustrated here only the tetrastyle porticoes at Selwood clearly suggest ancient temple forms. The plan of the house is clearly commensurate with the "magnificence" such forms might connote: the ground floor includes a hall, library, billiard room, dressing room, powder closet, cold bath, hot bath, drawing room, breakfast room, and eating room, plus offices and servants' rooms.

To accompany the "Essay" Mitchell prepared original designs for residences in Greek, Roman, and Gothic style, all based on the same plan. The ground floor of this plan includes a vestibule, combination dressing room and "powdering-closet," breakfast room, drawing room, eating room, and combination library and picture gallery (Plate 15). The first design (Plate 16), "intended to elucidate the style of the Grecian Architecture," is fronted by a portico in Doric style—the "earliest invented" of the orders and that which exhibits greatest "simplicity" of composition (p. 10).[1] In connection with the second design (Plate 17), he noted that Romans "erected more sumptuous buildings," but however "these excelled in magnificence and richness of decoration, they fell short in the elegance of composition and purity of design" (p. 11). Gothic, on the other hand, was "truly original." Citing a host of differences between Classical and Gothic columns, capitals, and other elements, Mitchell concluded that in Gothic architecture "the parts are constructed for the eye to embrace the whole." Thus "In viewing a Gothic building, all the parts are found united, whilst, in the Grecian or Roman Architecture, they are cut asunder by the horizontal lines." Gothic architecture therefore could produce "powerful effects, or irresistible impressions," while "the Ancients" were limited by their concern for "giving correct proportions to their columns" (pp. 11–13).

In two respects Mitchell was clearly indebted to his contemporary Humphry Repton: first, in emphasizing the picturesque relationship between a house and its surrounding scenery; and second, in basing his entire discussion of architectural style on an observed difference between the horizontality of Classical styles and the verticality of Gothic. Repton had specifically discussed both matters in *Sketches and Hints* (1794; *q.v.*).

1. This design closely resembles Grange Park, erected by William Wilkins in 1809.

211.1

MORISON, Robert (–1825)

Designs in perspective for villas in the ancient castle and Grecian styles, by Robert Morison. Part the first. Printed for the author, where the geometrical plans, &c. of the villas may be seen.

[N. loc.: Printed for the author], 1794.

3 printed leaves, 6 pls.

22.2 × 32.4 cm

CtY-BA

The preliminary leaves include a dedication, an Introduction, and one leaf of plate descriptions. In the Introduction Morison stressed the function of a country house as a place of "retirement": "The genius of the artist, has, in all civilized nations, been exerted towards the embellishment and convenience of those edifices" that facilitate withdrawal "from the busy scenes of life, for the purpose of enjoying domestic tranquillity, at a distance from the formality of courts or the hurry of cities."[1] He also noted that hospitality was an important characteristic of domestic design. In England in particular the "rural mansion seems destined not only for . . . retirement, but likewise for a temple of hospitality, where the proprietor wishes to exercise his munificence, and display his taste." This remark was hardly original: hospitality and display had been important characteristics of domestic design since Vitruvius.[2]

Morison's comments on style were more timely. He wrote that "all the distinction of form which gives character to the modern structure, may be traced to grand sources, viz. the antient Grecian, and the antient castle style." The castle style, developed originally for defense and therefore suited to some "rocky eminence," necessarily displayed a "rude magnificence." Thus in both visual and associational terms the castle style corresponded best with "bold" and "mountainous" scenery. Greek architecture evolved in response to changing circumstances: "when cultivation had changed the rude neglected plain into a verdant lawn, . . . the mild beauty of the scene . . . [required] a more refined species of architecture . . . to suit the genius of the place, and the delicacy of the Grecian orders was called in to embellish and complete the picture."[3] Thus it became "the chief study of this publication, to preserve distinct the most striking features which characterise each manner." To facilitate comparison, Morison provided one elevation in each style for each of three different plans.

Morison's illustrations, executed in colored aquatint and watercolor, are nevertheless crudely drawn. Surrounding each design is scenery supposedly appropriate to the style of the elevation: castellated designs are indeed surrounded by hills, but the landscapes surrounding the Greek elevations are hardly plain or level. The cheapest design (Plate 3), a castellated elevation, was estimated to cost £6,670 to £8,360, depending on materials used. The most expensive design (Plate 6), a Greek elevation, would cost £25,000. Measuring 172 feet by 115 feet in plan, it includes a hall 30 feet in diameter, a tribune 30 feet by 22 feet, two anterooms, two dining rooms, three drawing rooms, a library, two dressing rooms, one bed chamber, a boudoir, a powder room, and water closets.

1. Concerning the role of "retirement" in seventeenth-century country house design see G. R. Hibbard, "The Country House Poem of the Seventeenth Century," *Journal of the Warburg and Courtauld Institutes* XIX:1–2 (January–June 1956), 187–225; and Mark Girouard, "A Place in the Country," *The Times Literary Supplement,* 27 February 1976, pp. 223–225.

2. See Marcus Vitruvius Pollio, *Ten Books on Architecture,* Book VI, Chapter V.

3. Humphry Repton discussed differences between architectural styles in much the same terms in *Sketches and Hints on Landscape Gardening (q.v.),* also published in 1794.

212.1
MORRIS, Richard

Essays on landscape gardening, and on uniting picturesque effect with rural scenery: containing directions for laying out and improving the grounds connected with a country residence. Illustrated by six plates. By Richard Morris. . . .

London: Printed for J. Taylor, 1825.

viii pp, 1 printed leaf, 91 pp, 7 pls.

30.8 × 24.2 cm

DLC

The Library of Congress owns two copies. In Copy 1 none of the plates is colored, while in Copy 2 the first three plates are colored. Both copies contain seven plates, but there is no reference on the title page or in the text to the final plate, a pair of views labeled "Temple N° 4" and "Vista N° 6."

Morris's essay is an important exposition of principles of design common to landscaping and to country house architecture in the first quarter of the nineteenth century. He divided the text into eight essays, on situation and style, external decorations, laying out grounds, planting, water, rural ornaments, distant scenery, and general appearances. But while Morris's work was valuable because of its scope, it was hardly original. The essays on grounds, planting, water, and rural ornaments drew on earlier treatises by Whately and Marshall.[1] The first essay, on "The Situation and Style of Building for Villas," contained Morris's principal theoretical observations. His reference here to the "propriety and advantage of consulting jointly the Architect and Landscape Gardener" (p. 11) reflected a long-standing notion that the two disciplines shared a common regard for principles of picturesque composition. At the very beginning Morris asserted that "the principal considerations" in designing country residences should be "the situation and the character of building" (p. 9), and subsequently he devoted a major portion of his text to these topics. But Humphry Repton already had elucidated these points some three decades earlier, and by 1825 they were generally accepted by most landscape theorists and practitioners.[2] Turning to individual cases, Morris observed that a villa set "on the brow or near the summit of a wooded hill," for example, "excites in the beholders the most pleasing ideas of health and comfort, and of all those various enjoyments which render life delightful" (p. 12). In addition the style of such a dwelling would contribute to the character of the composition: the "castle Gothic," for example, "is an imposing style; its character is strength, and as it carries the mind to circumstances of romance and chivalry, it is suited to wild and romantic scenery" (p. 16). In this manner Morris assigned specific "characters" to a variety of Gothic and Classical styles—again emulating Repton, who had already done this decades earlier.[3]

In his first plate Morris adopted a representational scheme employed earlier by Repton,[4] using one landscape view to show three different houses each located in an appropriate setting. The houses, all in Classical styles, were articulated to suit their respective locations—the top of a hill, the side of a hill, and a wooded vale beside a river. The second plate was a plan for "pleasure grounds," including walks and drives, woods, meadows, a hill, a valley, and a river, surrounding a country villa. The next plate was a plan for a flower garden and rosary. The fourth plate, titled "Decorated Scenery," showed an ornamental circular temple set on a knoll overlooking a distant landscape, and a large country mansion visible in the distance. Plate V showed a waterfall. Plate VI, titled "View Improved," showed a landscape scene with a few trees in the near foreground, through which vistas to the left, the right, and straight ahead revealed open fields, a river, a bridge, and other ornamental features.

1. Thomas Whately, *Observations on Modern Gardening* (London, 1770), especially Chapters II–XI, XXVI–XXXIV; and William Marshall, *Planting and Rural Ornament* (London, 1796). On Marshall see Appendix C.

2. The first chapter of Humphry Repton's *Sketches and Hints on Landscaping Gardening* (London, 1794; *q.v.*) was titled "Concerning Different Characters and Situations." Situation and character were principal subjects of Chapters 11 through 13 in Repton's *Observations on the Theory and Practice of Landscape Gardening* (London, 1803; *q.v.*). In *Fragments on the Theory and Practice of Landscape Gardening* (London, 1816; *q.v.*) Repton devoted considerable attention to the compatibility of "situation" and "character" in country house remodeling.

3. See for example *Observations on the Theory and Practice of Landscape Gardening* (London, 1803), pp. 189–192, and *Designs for the Pavillon at Brighton* (London, 1808), pp. 17–21.

4. The plate facing p. 2 in *Fragments on the Theory and Practice of Landscape Gardening* (London, 1816) illustrated several different "Characters of Houses" set in appropriate landscape contexts.

213.1

MORRIS, Robert (ca. 1702–1754)

The architectural remembrancer: being a collection of new and useful designs, of ornamental buildings, and decorations. For parks, gardens, woods, &c. To which are added, a variety of chimney-pieces, after the manner of Inigo Jones, and Mr. Kent. The whole neatly engraven on fifty copper-plates, in octavo. Designed by Robert Morris, Surveyor. . . .

London: Printed for, and sold by the author; and also by W. Owen, 1751.

xvi pp, 50 pls.

22.2 × 13.7 cm

V&A

213.2

Architecture improved, in a collection of modern, elegant and useful designs; from slight and graceful recesses, lodges and other decorations in parks, gardens, woods or forests, to the portico, bath, observatory, and interior ornaments of superb buildings. With great variety of rich embellishments for chimneys in the taste of Inigo Jones, Mr. Kent, &c. All curiously engraved on fifty copper-plates, octavo. Designed by Robert Morris, Surveyor. . . .

London: Sold by Robert Sayer, 1755.

xvi pp, 50 pls.

21.3 × 13.0 cm

Soane

213.3

London: Sold by Robert Sayer, 1757.

xvi pp, 50 pls.

20.3 × 12.7 cm

RIBA

In the Preface (pp. iii–viii) Morris explained the rationale for this "Remembrancer." He claimed that so much had been written on the subject of architecture that "all indeed that is left necessary to be done, is to improve the Ideas, by well chosen *Examples*," based on "Rules and Proportions" that were established in "preceding Ages" by "the most refined Judgments" (p. iii). Summarizing those rules, he stated that *"Proportion is the first Principle,"* and then "proper Appropriation of the Parts constitute[s] true *Symmetry* and *Hamony*." But just knowing the established rules and proportions was not enough to make someone an excellent architect: the ability to design well "must rise from a Genius formed by *Nature*, as well as cultivated by *Art*" (p. iii). The best way of accomplishing this, according to Morris, was to learn by example. This collection of "hints" was therefore intended for "better Geniuses" to learn from (p. iv), and also to serve as a portable *"Pocket Companion* or a Remembrancer" for gentlemen to use when they wished to express their ideas and needs to architects (p. v). Morris noted that in some examples he might appear to have "deviated from the *Greek* and *Roman* Orders, yet where no established Rules can instruct, I have observed *Proportion*." Thus in his examples the "Beauties of the *Roman Orders*" in fact strike the mind "more forcibly" (p. iv). He concluded the Preface with a brief summary of important considerations in designing and constructing a building: site, use, materials, foundations, variety, proportion, and ornament.

The plate descriptions (pp. ix–xiv) consist of brief comments on each design, with dimensions and occasional remarks concerning appropriate siting and orientation.

The preliminaries conclude with a highly facetious announcement (pp. xv–xvi) for a new book, "A Treatise on Country Five Barr'd Gates, Stiles and Wickets, Elegant Pig-Styes, beautiful Henhouses, and delightful Cowcribs, superb cart-houses, magnificent Barn Doors, variegated Barn Racks and admirable Sheep-Folds." In effect this prospectus served as an attack on contemporary purveyors of designs in exotic, unorthodox styles, an attack made perfectly clear in Morris's prefatory condemnation of the Chinese style: he complained that it was "meer Whim and Chimera, without Rules or Order, [and that] it requires no Fertility of Genius to put in Execution" (p. xv).

The first 34 plates contain designs for 33 structures, each illustrated in plan and elevation. Altogether there are three porticoes, eight summer houses or summer rooms, three temples, five seats, seven pavilions or banqueting rooms, two bridges, a water house, a pair of keeper's lodges, two mausolea, and one "Eye-Trap."[1]

In plan most of the designs are based on regular geometric figures, particularly circles and squares. Two plans (Plates 4, 9) incorporate the curve of the abacus of an Ionic or Corinthian capital. The horizontal dimensions of the rooms, pavilions, and temples are generally ten to 30 feet in each direction. One of the largest designs is a "Pavilion" (Plate 5) that consists of an octagon 30 feet in diameter at the center, attached by 31-foot arcades at either side to end pavilions 20 feet square in plan. The total width, including the thickness of several walls, is 142 feet. Most of the elevations are composed in a restrained, symmetrical Palladian manner, and frequently incorporate regular geometric figures.

Morris presented several designs to illustrate the consequences of disregard for architectural principles. One seat (Plate 25) is covered with fretwork and ornamental patterns of diamonds, circles, and octagons. Morris said that it illustrated "how Order and Uniformity may be disguised by gaudy Tinsel, introduced without Consistency, or Rules." He described a design in Chinese style (Plate 26) as "another chimerical Seat" inserted here "to keep in Countenance all true Lovers of the *Oriental Taste*, and to shew how Trifles may be esteemed, when it is the Fashion to be ridiculous." Morris offered three more designs for summer rooms (Plates 14–16) without disparaging remarks, but their styles are hardly orthodox: the design in "Arabian" taste incorporates windows and doors with diamond and circular latticework, the design in Persian and Gothic styles has a pagoda roof and pointed arches, and the design in the "*Muscovite* Manner" also incorporates unusual ornament.

The remaining 16 plates, as indicated on the title page, contain designs for chimney pieces in the "manner" of Inigo Jones and William Kent.

1. The "Eye-Trap" (Plate 30), to be used for screening a "disagreeable" object, is shown in elevation only.

[MORRIS, Robert (ca. 1702–1754)]
The art of architecture, a poem.

See Entry 454.

214.1

MORRIS, Robert (ca. 1702-1754)

An essay in defence of ancient architecture; or, a parallel of the ancient buildings with the modern: shewing the beauty and harmony of the former, and the irregularity of the latter. With impartial reflections on the reasons of the abuses introduced by our present builders. To which is annexed, an inspectional table, universally useful. Illustrated with sixteen copper= plates. By Robert Morris, of Twickenham.

London: Printed for D. Browne; W. Bickerton; J. Pote; and J. Walthoe, 1728.

xxviii + 114 pp, frontisp. + 14 pls, table.

27.3 × 21.6 cm

MnU

The Dedication (pp. iii–xiv), inscribed "To All Encouragers and Practitioners of Ancient Architecture," traces the progress of architecture from Greek times to the early eighteenth century, with greatest emphasis on Rome. The Preface (pp. xv–xxviii) is a defense of Morris's desire to return to "Ancient" principles. Following a general introduction the body of the book is divided into a discussion of the flourishing state of architecture among the Ancients, a chronicle of its decay in the Middle Ages and resurrection in the Renaissance, a description of the orders in general and the Doric, Ionic, and Corinthian orders in particular, remarks on proportion, and commentary on individual exemplary illustrations. The illustrations include two doorways, a recently erected "irregular" and "disproportionate" house, and designs by Morris for four house facades, two with plans. The book concludes with a chpater discussing the use of an "Inspectional Table" for determining proportional dimensions for the orders.

Morris was the first English author to write at length on architectural theory. In the preface to this, his first book, he stressed that theoretical principles are a necessary foundation for the study and practice of architecture (pp. xv–xxviii). He suggested that one must first comprehend the laws of beauty as they apply to architecture before embarking on any specific design (pp. xvi–xvii).[1] He described the experience of architecture as an intellectual appreciation of harmony (p. 14), and discussed architectural judgment as seeking a balance between intentions and truth: to be "a true Critick" is "to examine thoroughly the Intention, Design, and End of the Things propos'd or taught: To consider the Rules and Methods, if just and pure, to take the Result of the whole Piece, to see if conformable to Truth or Reason, if genuine and free from Theft" (p. xx).

Two major points in the *Essay* center on Morris's desire to return to "Ancient" standards. His first point was that only "Ancient" architecture embodied principles of beauty and harmony, principles that had been lost with the advent of the "Moderns."[2] Here Morris clearly allied himself with other major Palladian authors of the early eighteenth century—Colen Campbell, whose third volume of *Vitruvius Britannicus* (q.v.) had appeared just three years before, and Robert Castell, whose *Villas of the Ancients* (q.v.) appeared in the same year as Morris's *Essay*.[3] Morris developed this argument in the Preface, noting that Ancient architecture exhibited "those unerring Rules, those perfect Standards of the Law of Reason and Nature, founded upon Beauty and Necessity" (p. xviii). These were the same rules that he would like to see in modern design. He suggested they still could be achieved by adopting the same "Principles and Virtues" as the Ancients had, and which a perceptive observer could recognize in remaining examples of Ancient architecture (pp. xviii–xx).

In his second major point, Morris described architectural design as a visible representation of harmony (p. 14).[4] Citing again the rules followed by Ancient architects, he proposed an almost transcendental model of the spectator's experience of a building: the successful design consists of such a perfect orchestration of "Symmetry," "Concordance," "Proportion," and "Reason," reflected in every aspect of the structure from the plan and massing to the materials and workmanship, that the observer is led to a highly pleasurable experience of architectural order. This order in turn embodies both beauty and harmony:

Architecture, or Order itself, is a beautiful and harmonious Production arising from the Ideas of an unlimited Judgment; and where artfully compos'd and happily executed, nothing can raise the Mind to a more advanc'd Pleasure, than to behold the agreeable Symmetry and Concordance of every particular separate Member, centred and united in the Oeconomy of the whole; with the consentaneous Agreement of apt Materials, regulated and adapted in a due Proportion to the distinct Order propos'd, in such a variety of Beauties, whose Dispositions are likewise concurring with the Rules prescrib'd by its ancient Practitioners, which were ever founded upon Reason. (p. 14)

The book includes 14 plates, of which six illustrate designs for houses. The rest show the orders, techniques for proportioning architectural elements, and several designs for doorways. The plate facing page 88 is a late Baroque facade for a house, used to demonstrate the unfortunate consequences of not following Morris's principles. Another design, shown in plates facing pages 84 and 85, closely resembles Marble Hill House, a carefully proportioned villa built in 1724–1729 by the author's relative Roger Morris. Three other houses, illustrated in plates facing pages 90, 93, and 96, are likewise diminutive—five or even three windows wide, and just a principal floor and chamber floor set atop a basement story.[5] Robert and Roger Morris were instrumental in establishing this small, compact, and geometrically perfectible type of house as a new model of taste.[6] Indeed this *Essay* is the first publication to illustrate only this one type of house, to the exclusion of any larger examples such as palaces, mansions, or "great houses."[7]

1. His definition of beauty was commonplace: "Order in Disposition, and Variety in Matter" (p. xvi).

2. This point is announced in the title. For further discussion of "Ancients" and "Moderns" see the commentary above on Colen Campbell's *Vitruvius Britannicus*.

3. Campbell, Castell, and their patron the Earl of Burlington all strongly advocated "Ancient" principles of design. See Rudolf Wittkower, "English Literature on Architecture," in *Palladio and Palladianism* (New York: Braziller, 1974), pp. 95–112. In the *Essay* and his subsequent *Lectures* (1734–1736; *q.v.*) Morris expanded and developed his ideas to become the principal theorist of the Palladian movement.

4. This suggests close affinity with notions of creative and perceptive genius proposed by the Earl of Shaftesbury in "The Moralists," part of *Characteristicks of Men, Manners, Opinions, Times* ([London], 1711). Note too that on the title page of Morris's *Essay upon Harmony* (London, 1739) there is an excerpt from *Characteristicks* on the subject of harmony.

5. The design in the plate facing page 93 also includes colonnades and wings with farm offices attached to each side of the house.

6. See Summerson (1959), pp. 570ff.

7. Compare, for example, Robert Castell's *Villas of the Ancients* (*q.v.*), also published in 1728, which exhibited a very different approach to the design of country dwellings, ostensibly based on historic Roman precedents rather than intellectual models.

215.1
MORRIS, Robert (ca. 1702–1754)

Lectures on architecture. Consisting of rules founded upon harmonick and arithmetical proportions in building. Design'd as an agreeable entertainment for gentlemen: and more particularly useful to all who make architecture, or the polite arts, their study. Read to a society establish'd for the improvement of arts and sciences, and explain'd by examples on copper plates; with the proportions apply'd to practice. By Robert Morris.

London: Printed for J. Brindley, 1734.

[xviii] + 134 pp, 4 pls.

Lectures on architecture. Consisting of rules founded upon harmonick and arithmetical proportions in building, applicable to various situations. Design'd as an agreeable entertainment for gentlemen: but more particularly useful, to all who make architecture, or the polite arts their study. Part the second. Read to a society established for the improvement of arts and sciences, and explain'd by examples on 13 copper-plates; with the proportions apply'd to practice[.] By Robert Morris.

London: Printed for the author, and sold by J. Brindley; J. Wilcox; and J. Millan, 1736.

viii + 135–226 pp, 12 pls.

19.7 × 11.9 cm

NNC

215.2

Lectures on architecture. ⟨ . . . as 1734 . . . ⟩ building, design'd ⟨ . . . as 1734 . . . ⟩ explain'd, by ⟨ . . . as 1734 . . . ⟩ Morris. The second edition.

London: Printed for R. Sayer, 1759.

[xiv] + 132 pp, 4 pls.

Lectures on architecture. ⟨ . . . as 1736 . . . ⟩ practice. By Robert Morris.

London: Printed for the author, and sold by J. Brindley; J. Wilcox; and J. Millan, 1736.

viii + 135–226 pp, 12 pls.

20.3 × 12.8 cm

CtY

The preliminaries in the 1734 edition of Part I include a four-page dedication, a 13-page Preface, and one page of errata. The 1759 edition lacks the dedication but retains the Preface. The text of the first edition of Part I (pp. 1–134) consists of eight "Lectures"; the second edition contains the same eight lectures reset on 132 pages.

Part II (one edition only, dated 1736) includes a dedication to the author's "kinsman," architect Roger Morris (pp. iii–iv), and a Preface (pp. v–viii). The final six lectures are printed on pages 135–226.

The following commentary is based on examination of the first edition (1734–1736).

In 1730 Morris established a "Society for the Improvement of Knowledge in Arts and Sciences,"[1] to which he delivered a series of fourteen lectures on architecture over the next five years. He then published the lectures in two parts, in 1734 and 1736. In the Preface to the first part he noted that the lectures would treat the origins of society, the advantages of learning, the history of architecture, the nature and use of the orders, siting, and proportions. Morris also indicated that the *"Principle* of the *Harmonick* Proportions" was fundamental to the entire course of lectures. He interjected a lengthy criticism of James Ralph's *Critical Review of the Publick Buildings, Statues and Ornaments in, and about London and Westminster* (London, 1734), following which he returned to the subject of harmonic proportion. He explained that he first learned of it from a treatise by Lambert ten Kate, recently translated into English as *The Beau Ideal*.[2] Morris lavished praise on author as well as translator for their contributions to the "universal Good of Mankind" in bringing these principles of proportion to light.

The first five lectures, perhaps conceived before Morris learned of ten Kate's treatise, cover a broad range of historical and theoretical matters, including the origins of society, the advantages of learning, epistemology, the necessary qualifications of an architect, the history of architecture, decorum, and considerations in the siting of buildings. On the subject of decorum Morris was particularly concerned with the expressive capacity of the several orders: the Doric order was suited to "grave and solemn Uses," the Ionic was suited to "Riant Uses," and the Corinthian was appropriate for use "in Palaces, &c." (p. 43). Later on, he described the appropriate correspondence between architecture and certain types of landscape scenery: art, he said, pleases most when it resembles nature, thus establishing "a kind of Sympathy and Attraction, when both are blended or mingled together." Thus the Doric order is most appropriate to a "Champaign open Country," while a "chearful Vale" requires the Ionic order for "more Decoration and Dress," and the Corinthian order suits "silent *Streams*, the gay, [and] the wanton *Scene*" (pp. 66–69).

Late in the fifth lecture Morris turned to harmony and proportion. Before him no English architect had treated these subjects in such a thorough manner, despite encouraging precedents in recent philosophy.[3] Morris began his discussion by drawing analogies among nature, music, and architecture: as "Nature has taught Mankind in *Musick* certain Rules for Proportion of Sounds, so *Architecture* has its Rules dependant on those Proportions." He conceived a hierarchy of disciplines, all based on proportion, with architecture at the top: "The Square in *Geometry*, the Union or Circle in *Musick*, and the Cube in *Building*, have all an inseparable

Proportion" (p. 74). Extending the musical analogy further, Morris established seven fundamental architectural proportions based on musical intervals, and he illustrated geometric solids based on those proportions in a plate facing page 75.[4] The ratios of height, depth, and width in these solids are as follows: 1:1:1 (a cube), 1:1:1 1/2 (a cube and a half), 1:1:2 (a double cube), 1:2:3, 2:3:4, 3:4:5, and 3:4:6.[5] In the sixth and seventh lectures Morris suggested that these architectural proportions would create a kind of beauty that would lead to perception of the greater harmony of all Nature:

Beauty, in all Objects, spring[s] from the same unerring Law in Nature, which, in *Architecture*, I would call Proportion. The joint Union and Concordance of the Parts, in an exact Symmetry, forms the whole a compleat Harmony, which admits of no Medium. . . . When I consider Proportions, I am led into a Profundity of Thought. . . . If we immerse our Ideas into the infinite Tract of unbounded Space, and with the Imagination paint out the numberless Multitudes of Planets, or little Worlds, regularly revolving round their destin'd Orbs . . . we must feel Emanations of the Harmony of Nature diffus'd in us; and must immediately acknowledge the Necessity of Proportion in the Preservation of the whole Oeconomy of the Universe. (pp. 81, 101–102)

In the remainder of Part I Morris discussed the arrangement of house plans, proportions for rooms, and interior and exterior ornament.

There are three plates in addition to the illustration of geometric solids. One, facing page 107, depicts room interiors composed according to four different proportions. The remaining two plates contain a plan and three elevations for a house composed according to the proportion 3:4:5. The plan measures 50 feet by 40 feet, and the house is 30 feet high. Morris provided a choice of three elevations: one with an engaged two-story Ionic tetrastyle portico plus a pediment, ornamental bas-reliefs, and swags; one with more modest ornament; and one with little more than an entablature over the door.

In the Preface to the second part Morris stated that his remaining lectures were composed of "Demonstrations" of the principles elucidated in the first part. On page 137 he explained that he would create one design according to each of his seven harmonic proportions, and that each design would be articulated and embellished with proper ornament in a manner suited to a particular site. The twelve plates in Part II contain plans and elevations for seven houses. Six are composed according to the proportions 1:1:1, 1:1:1 1/2, 1:1:2, 1:2:3, 2:3:4, and 3:4:6.[6] The remaining design, the largest, is a facade 39 openings (540 feet) wide, four stories high in the center, and surmounted by a cupola. This ungainly facade serves to illustrate "a Building compos'd of different Proportions" (p. 201): the elevation is divided into seven "Parts," all of which are five openings wide except for the center, which is nine openings wide; each part is proportioned according to one of the ratios 1:1, 1:1 1/2, or 1:2. The second, middle, and sixth parts are fronted by engaged pedimented Corinthian porticoes; the center portico is hexastyle and the others are tetrastyle. By contrast the smallest design, a "Cube & $\frac{1}{2}$," is just 51 feet across, 34 feet high, and 34 feet deep. The principal floor includes two rooms in the proportion 1:1:1 1/2, and two rooms in the proportion 3:4:5. The facade includes a portico that is square in elevation, with four Ionic columns supporting an ornamented pediment. In all cases Morris demonstrated the fundamental proportionality of his designs by inscribing circles—their diameters related according to one of the seven ratios—within the outlines of his elevations and plans. The text accompanying these designs carefully attends to interior and exterior proportions, and also describes suitable offices, ornament, and appropriate landscape scenery, with special attention to such scenic elements as forests, meadows, water, walks, avenues, and vistas. Nevertheless none of Morris's plates includes landscape scenery.

Indeed siting was of particular concern to Morris: he stated in the Preface to the second part that "no Building should be design'd to be erected, without first considering the Extent of *Prospect, Hills, Vales, &c.* which expand and encircle it; its *Avenues, Pastures* and *Waters*" (p. vi). Earlier, in Part I, he insisted that only in country houses could his ideas be brought to fruition: "There is this great Disadvantage [that] arises in Buildings which are, or are to be erected in Cities or Towns, that neither Proportion [n]or Convenience can be had" (p. 82). In the country, however, site, function, and design all could be free of extrinsic constraints, and therefore could be composed in greatest harmony with Nature.[7] Thus in describing a design for a villa site Morris stressed the relation between landscape and Nature:

I would in some Places, at certain Distances, erect some Statue, or little Building, to retire to in the Summer's Heat, or in the Coolness of an Evening's pleasing Shade, when all Nature is calm, and undisturb'd, and the Mind unbent from Cares or Fatigue. Such Retreats would give unspeakable Raptures to a Soul capable to pursue a Tract of Thought in Infinity of Space, or contemplating upon the immense Wonders of the Universe. (p. 144)

Likewise only in nature could one's thoughts freely pursue the perfection and harmony embodied in an architectural design. "Reflections of this kind, are the Growth of Retirement to a contemplative *Genius*; and the *Design* before us, decorated with those Embellishments, requires a Situation capable of raising such elevated Ideas" (p. 173). The site, he said, should be provided with appropriate rivulets, walks, vistas, trees, bushes, birds, meadows, distant hills, a grotto, a bath, a theater, and other landscape elements. He then concluded that on such a site "Every Sprig of *Grass* may afford a multitude of fine Thoughts, to employ the Imagination; and by a Genius turn'd to *microscopical* Speculations, a Way is open'd to entertain the Fancy with unbounded Reflections" (p. 175).

1. The founding of the society is described on the first page of the Preface to Part I.

2. *The Beau Ideal, by the Late Ingenious and Learned Hollander, Lambert Hermanson ten Kate. Translated from the Original French by James Christopher Le Blon* (London, 1732).

3. Morris was an admitted disciple of Anthony Ashley Cooper, Third Earl of Shaftesbury, who in *Characteristicks* ([London], 1711) advocated system, order, and proportion in architecture: "whatever Things have *Order,* the same have *Unity of Design,* and concur *in one,* are Parts of *one* Whole, or are, in themselves, *intire Systems.* Such is . . . an *Edifice,* with all its exteriour and interiour Ornaments" (II, 285). Morris's devotion to Shaftesbury's ideas is made explicit on the title page to Morris's *Essay upon Harmony* (London, 1739), which includes an excerpt from *Characteristicks* on the subject of harmony.

4. In adopting the musical analogy Morris was following Renaissance precedent: both Alberti and Palladio discussed correspondences between musical intervals and architectural proportions. See Rudolf Wittkower, *Architectural Principles in the Age of Humanism* (New York: Random House, 1965), Part IV. Morris had the advantage of a demonstration by ten Kate and Le Blon that such correspondences were valid, but ten Kate and Le Blon themselves offered no specific architectural proportions. Morris's ratios, which differ from those adopted by Alberti and Palladio, are thus his own.

5. Morris discussed these in detail on pp. 75–77. On pp. 78–79 he provided a table of dimensions for rooms and for chimneys, proportioned according to all seven ratios.

6. The design according to the ratio 3:4:5 is illustrated in Part I.

7. In his preference for a "natural" environment Morris was in large part indebted to Shaftesbury, who praised "Things of a *natural* kind; where neither *Art*, nor the *Conceit* or *Caprice* of Man has spoil'd their *genuine Order*, by breaking in upon that *primitive State*" (*Characteristicks*, II, 393–394).

216.1
MORRIS, Robert (ca. 1702–1754)

Rural architecture: consisting of regular designs of plans and elevations for buildings in the country. In which the purity and simplicity of the art of designing are variously exemplified. With such remarks and explanations as are conducive to render the subject agreeable. Illustrated with fifty quarto copper-plates. By Robert Morris, Surveyor.

London: Printed for the author, and to be had of him at his house, 1750.

iv + [v–xiv] + 8 pp, 50 pls.

29.5 × 21.4 cm

NNC

216.2
_____

Select architecture: being regular designs of plans and elevations well suited to both town and country; in which the magnificence and beauty, the purity and simplicity of designing for every species of that noble art, is accurately treated, and with great variety exemplified, from the plain town-house to the stately hotel, and in the country from the genteel and convenient farm-house to the parochial church. With suitable embellishments. Also bridges, baths, summer-houses, &c. to all which such remarks, explanations and scales are annexed, that the comprehension is rendered easy, and subject most agreeable. Illustrated with fifty copper plates, quarto. By Robert Morris, Surveyor.

London: Sold by Robert Sayer, 1755.

[ii] + 8 + [viii] pp, 50 pls.

27.3 × 20.6 cm

NNC

216.3

London: Sold by Robert Sayer, [n.d.].

[ii] + 8 pp, 50 pls [*pls. 9 and 14 wanting in this copy*].

28.0 × 22.2 cm

Soane

216.4

Select architecture: ⟨ . . . as 1755 . . . ⟩ designing, for ⟨ . . . as 1755 . . . ⟩ hotel; and ⟨ . . . as 1755 . . . ⟩ summer-houses, &c. with estimates to each design by the great square, and such remarks, ⟨ . . . as 1755 . . . ⟩ Morris, Surveyor. The second edition.

London: Sold by Robert Sayer, 1757.

[viii] + 8 pp, 50 pls.

28.3 × 22.9 cm

MH

Only the first edition, published under the title *Rural Architecture*, contains a four-page list of subscribers. The 171 names include barely half a dozen peers. Later editions, published under the title *Select Architecture*, all were issued after Morris's death in 1754. The following discussion is based on examination of the 1757 edition, except as noted.

The title page includes an elevation of a house taken from a plate in Morris's *Lectures* (1734–1736; *q.v.*). The design is two stories high and five openings wide, with a tetrastyle Corinthian portico. Superimposed over this facade is a pattern of four circles demonstrating the underlying proportional harmony of the design.

In the two-page preface[1] Morris explained that he once intended to write a book half on the subject of country houses and half on town houses. He decided to devote this book entirely to country houses for three reasons: many designs for town houses already had been published, there were few people in the country who were "capable of Designing," and others who had written on country houses had "raised nothing but Palaces, glaring in Decoration and Dress; while the Cottage, or plain little Villa, are passed by unregarded." The suggestion that villas were of a scale similar to cottages is noteworthy, since among Morris's contemporaries the term "villa" often denoted a large country estate.[2] Nevertheless Morris's villas are among the very largest designs in this book. Turning to the subject of style, Morris's firm belief in an orthodox Palladian aesthetic fueled his condemnation of recent changes in taste: he complained that "Grecian and Roman Purity and Simplicity" were being neglected while "Gaiety, Magnificence, the rude Gothic, or the Chinese unmeaning stile, are the Study of our modern Architects."[3]

The eight-page introduction is an account of the origins and practice of architecture, with special attention to considerations of use, site, materials, convenience, proportion, regularity, purity, simplicity, and expense. In the course of his remarks Morris discussed two types of proportion. The first, which he called "*natural Proportion*," involved adjusting the plan of a house to suit the needs of the inhabitants: "The Parts should be so disposed, that, from the highest Station, in those little Communities [within the household], all the subservient Apartments should be joined by an easy Gradation, that every Link in the Concatenation should be justly regulated."[4] Furthermore, this "Gradation" and "Concatenation" should be evident in the exterior elevation, composed in a manner that Morris likened to history painting:

As in History Painting, one principal Figure possesseth the superior Light, the fore Ground and Eminence of the Piece, and the subordinate Figures are placed Part in Sight, Part in Groups and Shade for Contrast, and keeping in the Design; so in Building, all the subservient Offices should terminate by gradual Progression in *Utility* and *Situation*.[5]

The second type of proportion could be defined in a more orthodox manner, in terms of "*Geometric* and *Harmonic* Magnitude." Morris noted that he had treated this subject at much greater length in his *Lectures* (q.v.).

The explanations of the plates (pp. 1–8) contain brief descriptions of each design, dimensions, cost estimates, and occasional remarks on use, site, proportion, plan, construction, and landscape setting. Despite Morris's concern for composing buildings in a manner similar to history painting, there is little attention to this subject in the descriptions of individual designs. Perhaps his most extensive remarks pertain to the "Pleasure-Room" in Plate 50, which he designed for a terrace near Windsor. He hoped that in the mind of the spectator this building would link the beauty of the natural landscape to the harmony of nature:

A Building of this Kind would be an Object seen at a Distance, and render it as well an Amusement to entertain the Fancy of others, as to those on the Spot, for a Variety of beautiful Hills, Vales, Landskips, &c. for the Pleasure of the Inhabitants, create a new Succession of pleasing Images, and call forth the Beauty, Order, and Harmony of Nature, to decorate and enliven the Scene.[6]

The only plate showing any surrounding scenery is a design for a private sanctum, or "Adytum," dedicated to Daniel Garret (Plate 8). Morris explained in the plate description that Garret had chastised him for publishing a book titled *Rural Architecture* without depicting any trees. This design, therefore, was enclosed on three sides with shrubs and evergreens. It would serve as "a Retirement in a calm Summer Evening, where divested of Care, and the agonizing Pains of the Gout, and of all other real and *imaginary Maladies*, with a few selected Friends, may he [Garret] enjoy all the Happiness and Tranquility, that they or himself can wish to possess" (p. 2).

The plates contain plans and elevations for 18 dwellings, 14 small "Seats" and other garden structures, two town halls or market buildings, three churches or chapels, two bridges, and one altarpiece. There is also one design (Plate 47) that Morris originally intended as a "cold Bath" but which he also believed would serve as a synagogue, mosque, chapel, surgeon's "Dissecting-Room," auction room, or library (p. 8). The least expensive dwelling is the "Building" in Plate 1, estimated to cost £324.

Three stories high and three openings wide, it is a cube 30 feet high, wide, and deep. On the ground floor there are three rooms plus a staircase and entrance hall. The modest ornament is limited to stringcourses, a weather vane, and an entablature and architrave surrounding the entrance. The largest design, a residential "Seat" shown in Plate 20, is three stories high in the center and 256 feet wide, including offices; the house itself is 70 feet wide. The most expensive design is the "Villa" illustrated in Plates 22 and 23, estimated at £16,400. The north and south elevations, each 17 openings wide, consist of a basement story and two upper stories, with an Ionic portico in the center. The plan is 220 feet wide and 105 feet deep; the 15 rooms on the principal floor include a large hall (40 feet by 20 feet) and saloon (50 feet by 40 feet). The facades are articulated and ornamented in a restrained manner. Both have Venetian windows at each end, with pediments above. In the center of one facade there is an engaged octastyle portico with a balustrade above, and the other facade has a smaller, pedimented prostyle portico. Cornices and stringcourses extend the full length of each facade, and some windows are embellished with entablatures and pediments. One of the other two "Villas" that Morris illustrated (Plate 18) also is large: the plan measures 110 feet by 100 feet, and the estimated cost is £9,400. The third "Villa" (Plate 36) is much smaller—66 feet by 56 feet—but is still a substantial residence. The elevation, seven openings wide, contains a basement story and two upper stories.

Most of Morris's elevations are composed in a modest, often "plain" manner like that in the designs described above. Some garden structures are heavily rusticated, but the dwellings are usually embellished with little more than ornamental swags, porticoes, pediments, and semicircular relieving arches. Morris's plans are generally based on squares and rectangles, with occasional octagons and circles. Many designs exhibit the strict arithmetic or geometric proportionality he advocated in his *Lectures* (*q.v.*).

1. The preface does not appear in the 1757 edition. These remarks are based on examination of the 1755 edition.

2. On the meaning of the word "villa" see the commentary on Robert Castell's *Villas of the Ancients* (1728), Summerson (1959), and Chapter III, Section 5, in "The Literature of British Domestic Architecture, 1715–1842" above.

3. He continued this attack in the introduction, finding the "purity" of the Greek style clearly superior to the "Devastations of *Gothic* Wildness." He argued that "Undecorated Plainness" was far preferable to "Redundancy of Members, Ornament, and Dress."

4. "Gradation" and "concatenation" were central to Emil Kaufmann's analysis of eighteenth-century English architecture in *Architecture in the Age of Reason* (Cambridge, Mass.: Harvard University Press), pp. 3–31, especially p. 24.

5. Parallels between pictorial and architectural composition were explored previously by Castell, op. cit. For subsequent discussion see Issac Ware, *A Complete Body of Architecture* (1756); Robert and James Adam, *Works in Architecture* (1778–1779); James Lewis, *Original Designs* (1780–1797); George Richardson, *New Designs in Architecture* (1792); Edmund Bartell, *Hints for Picturesque Improvements* (1804); John Buonarotti Papworth, *Hints on Ornamental Gardening* (1823); Richard Brown, *Domestic Architecture* (1841), qq.v.

6. P. 8. For further discussion of Morris's ideas of harmony see the commentary on his *Lectures*, especially note 3.

217.1

MULLER, John (1699–1784)

Elements of mathematics. Containing geometry. Conic-sections. Trigonometry. Surveying. Levelling. Mensuration. Laws of motion. Mechanics. Projectiles. Hydrostatics. Hydraulics. Pneumatics. A theory of pumps. To which are prefix'd, the first principles of algebra, by way of introduction. For the use of the Royal Academy of Artillery at Woolwich. Vol. I. By John Muller, Professor of Artillery and Fortification.

London: Printed for the author, and J. Millan, 1748.

liv + 188 pp, 11 pls.

Elements of mathematics. Containing, geometry. ⟨ . . . as Vol. I . . . ⟩ algebra. By way of introduction. For the use of the Royal Academy of Artillery at Woolwich. Vol. II. By John Muller, Professor of Artillery and Fortification.

London: Printed for the author, and J. Millan, 1748.

189–442 pp, 13 pls (numbered XII–XXIV).

20.0 × 12.7 cm

MH

217.2 †

Elements of mathematics. . . . Second edition.

London, 1757.

8°

Reference: NUC

217.3

Elements of mathematics. Containing geometry. Conic-sections. Trigonometry. Surveying. Levelling. Mensuration. Laws of motion. Mechanics. Projectiles. Gunnery, &c. Hydrostatics. Hydraulics. Pneumatics. A theory of pumps. To which is prefixed, the first principles of algebra, by way of introduction. For the use of the Royal Academy of Artillery at Woolwich. Vol I. and II. The third edition improved. With an addition of a new treatise on perspective. By John Muller. . . .

London: Printed for J. Millan, 1765.

xxxvi + 312 pp, 21 + 7 pls.

20.1 × 12.5 cm

ICJ

In the Preface to the 1748 edition Muller noted that there were few authors "who have endeavoured to render this sublime Science useful, by a proper Application of its Principles, to the Practice and Perfection of mechanical

Operations." He intended this treatise "for the Instruction of young Gentlemen, in whatever may be useful and conducive to the Improvement of Military Science" at the Royal Academy of Artillery at Woolwich, and also for use by "others who are desirous of being informed of these useful Branches of the Mathematics" (p. v).

A long Introduction (1748, pp. xix–liv) explains "the first principles of algebra" (p. xix). The text is divided into four books. The first two, in Volume I, treat geometry and conic sections. In Volume II, Book III concerns trigonometry, surveying, leveling, and mensuration, and Book IV treats motion, mechanics, projectiles, hydrostatics, hydraulics, pneumatics, and pumps.

In the 1765 edition the Preface is omitted, and the Introduction and text have been revised, reset, and incorporated in a single volume. Following the last section of Book IV, on pumps, there is a new, final section on perspective (pp. 304–312) with seven new plates. This section includes a short list of definitions, a series of axioms, theorems, corollaries, and problems, plate descriptions, discussion of light and shadow, and remarks on "choice of distances."

The 24 plates in the 1748 edition are principally geometric figures and diagrams, plus several illustrations of fortifications, pulleys, machinery, and hydraulic equipment. Architectural subjects appear in Plate XII, where a house and two buildings with towers are used to demonstrate methods of finding the height of "inaccessible" objects (pp. 202–205). In Plate XV Muller demonstrated techniques of mensuration with a plan of a powder magazine, sections of round and pointed arches, and a diagram of a groin vault. These two plates also appear, with minor changes, in the 1765 edition.

Of the seven new plates on perspective in the 1765 edition, the first four show geometric figures and diagrams. Plate V demonstrates the perspective construction of a plain, unornamented house, two stories high and five windows wide. A parterre in front of the house is flanked on each side by three rows of five trees. Plate VI depicts the interior of a room, with windows in the left and right walls, a door at the end, and an array of geometric solids sitting on the floor. Plate VII "represents the perspective of a house with two wings" (p. 310), three stories high, ornamented only with stringcourses between stories and an awkward pediment over the central bay.

218.1 ‡
NASH, John (1752–1835)
The royal pavilion at Brighton. Published by the command of & dedicated by permission to the King, by His Majesty's dutiful subject and servant, John Nash.

[London, 1825 or after].

1 printed leaf, 54 pls.

f°

Reference: Microfilm supplied by The British Library.

218.2 †

Illustrations of Her Majesty's palace at Brighton; formerly the pavilion: executed by the command of King George the Fourth, under the superintendence of John Nash. . . . To which is prefixed, a history of the palace, By Edward Wedlake Brayley.

London: J. B. Nichols & Son, 1838.

17 pp.

f°

Reference: BM

By 1815 the Prince Regent, the future George IV, was unhappy with the mixture of styles and the awkward room arrangements at his Brighton residence. This was the result of extensive alterations by a host of previous architects—among them Henry Holland, Peter Frederick Robinson, and William Porden.[1] John Nash was therefore authorized to make sweeping changes as the regent's personal architect. Nash altered the function and plan of several rooms, completely unified the exterior facades in the "Indian" style, and redecorated the interior in a variety of "exotic" styles.

Nash's improvements were recorded in a series of plates by Augustus Charles Pugin, issued individually between 1820 and 1825. These illustrations in outline were supplemented with hand-colored copies of the same plates, and published collectively as Nash's *Royal Pavilion*. The engraved table of contents lists the 34 subjects represented in the plates. On each of 26 plates, one or two of these subjects is illustrated in outline. Twenty-three of these subjects plus five others appear in colored versions as well. Altogether the subjects include the exterior, both before and after Nash's alterations, the music room, the music gallery, the salon, the banqueting gallery, the banqueting room, the king's bedroom, the king's library, the kitchen, the stables, and a section through the entire pavilion.

1. For an extensive discussion of the architectural history of the Pavilion, see Clifford Musgrave, *Royal Pavilion: An Episode in the Romantic* (London: Leonard Hill, 1959). Also see Henry D. Roberts, *A History of the Royal Pavilion, Brighton* (London: Country Life, 1939), and John Dinkel, *The Royal Pavilion, Brighton* (New York: Vendome Press, 1981). The most recent addition to the literature is by John Morley: *The Making of the Royal Pavilion* (London: Sotheby Publications, 1984).

219.1 ‖

A new and complete dictionary of arts and sciences; comprehending all the branches of useful knowledge, with accurate descriptions as well of the various machines, instruments, tools, figures, and schemes necessary for illustrating them, as of the classes, kinds, preparations, and uses of natural productions, whether animals, vegetables, minerals, fossils, or fluids; together with the kingdoms, provinces, cities, towns, and other remarkable places throughout the world. Illustrated with above three hundred copper-plates, curiously engraved by Mr. Jefferys, Geographer and Engraver to His Royal Highness the Prince of Wales. The whole extracted from the best authors in all languages. By a society of gentlemen. Vol. I.

London: Printed for W. Owen, 1754.

[*Four volumes in eight parts: London, 1754–1755. The title and imprint for Vol. I are given above.*]

Art. "Camera obscura," I, 436; pl. XXXV.
Art. "Levelling," III, 1894–1896; pl. CLVII.

Reference: Information supplied by The Library Company of Philadelphia.

219.2

A new and complete dictionary of arts and sciences; comprehending all the branches of useful knowledge, with accurate descriptions as well of the various machines, instruments, tools, figures, and schemes necessary for illustrating them, as of the classes, kinds, preparations, and uses of natural productions, whether animals, vegetables, minerals, fossils, or fluids; together with the kingdoms, provinces, cities, towns, and other remarkable places throughout the world. Illustrated with above three hundred copper-plates, engraved by Mr. Jefferys, Geographer to His Majesty. The whole extracted from the best authors in all languages. By a society of gentlemen. The second edition, with many additions, and other improvements. Vol. I.

London: Printed for W. Owen, 1763.

[*Four volumes: London, 1763–1764. The title and imprint for Vol. I are given above.*]

Art. "Camera obscura," I, 444–446; pl. XXXV.
Art. "Levelling," III, 1917–1919; pl. CLVII.

21.6 × 13.2 cm

ICU

A copy of the second edition at the Detroit Public Library consists of four volumes. Each volume is divided into two parts, and each part is bound separately. The title pages for Volume I, Part I, and for Volume II, Part I, are dated 1763. Title pages for the remaining six parts are dated 1764.

The article on "Architecture" (pp. 183–184) observes the traditional division of the subject into civil, naval, and military architecture. Most of the article is a recitation of principles that must be observed in civil architecture (e.g., solidity, convenience, beauty) and a synopsis of architectural history from Greece to "the moderns." There is also a list of ten "antient" or "celebrated" writers on architecture. Other articles, one or two pages long and sometimes accompanied by plates, discuss "Order," "Base," "Capital," and the individual orders. Additional architectural illustrations accompany articles such as "Door" and "Green-House."

The illustration in Plate XXXV, Figure 7, accompanying the article on the camera obscura, appeared here for the first time in British literature.[1]

On one side of the illustration there is a house, two stories high and three windows wide, flanked by a pair of trees. On the other side is a second house, seen in cutaway view. Light rays from the first house are projected through a lens in the wall of the second house onto its rear wall, producing an inverted image of the first house and its flanking trees. The large windows, small window panes, and ornamental gable of the first house all suggest a seventeenth-century English or Lowland architectural style.[2]

The article on "Levelling" includes one illustration (Fig. 1, No. 4), which shows a two-story house, three windows wide. The illustration demonstrates the use of the telescope to determine the height of distant objects, and closely resembles the illustration of the same subject in Chambers's *Cyclopaedia* (*q.v.*).

1. The illustration appeared later in Croker's *Complete Dictionary*, in *The New Complete Dictionary*, and in *A New Royal and Universal Dictionary*, *qq.v.*

2. This suggests that a Continental treatise on perspective may have been the source of this illustration.

The new complete dictionary of the arts and sciences.

See Entry 492.

The new encyclopaedia.

See Entry 76.2.

220.1 ‖

A new royal and universal dictionary of arts and sciences: or, complete system of human knowledge. Containing, not only all the various improvements that have been made by the learned and ingenious in every part of Europe to the present times; but also a very great variety of useful discoveries, which have been communicated to the authors of this work, by gentlemen of distinguished abilities; whereby every difficulty attending the study of the arts and sciences is distinctly cleared, and the whole explained in the most easy and intelligent manner. Among the various branches treated of in this work, are the following, viz. agriculture, algebra, anatomy, architecture, arithmetic, astronomy, book-keeping, botany, chemistry, chronology, commerce, conics, cosmography, criticism, dialing, dioptrics, ethics, farriery, fluxions, fortification, gardening, gauging, geography, geometry, grammar, gunnery, handicrafts, heraldry, horsemanship, husbandry, hydraulics, hydrostatics, law, levelling, logic, maritime, and military affairs mathematics, mechanics, merchandize, metaphysics, meteorology, music, navigation, optics, painting, perspective, pharmacy, philosophy, physic, pneumatics, poetry, rhetoric, sculpture, series and statics, statuary, surgery, surveying, theology, trigonometry, &c embellished with upwards of one hundred copper-plates, drawn from real objects, by the most eminent artists, and engraved by the best hands; containing full and exact representations of the various instruments, machines, tools, plans, figures, &c. necessary to illustrate the work. The anatomical, chemical, and medicinal parts by M. Hinde, M.D. The mathematical parts by

W. Squire, author of The modern book-keeper. Gardening and botany by T. Marshall, Gardener to the Right Hon. the Earl of Shelburne. Criticism, grammar, poetry, theology, &c. by The Rev. Thomas Cooke, A.B. And the other parts by gentlemen of eminence in the several departments they have undertaken to elucidate.

London: Printed for J. Cooke, 1770.

[*Two volumes: London, 1770–1771. The title and imprint for Vol. I are given above.*]

Art. "Camera obscura," I, 1 p; pl. XX.
Art. "Levelling," II, 2 pp; pl. LVI.

Reference: Information supplied by The University of Florida, Gainesville.

220.2
A new royal and universal dictionary ⟨ . . . as 1770 . . . ⟩ , are the following: agriculture, algebra, anatomy, architecture arithmetic, ⟨ . . . as 1770 . . . ⟩, fortification gardening, ⟨ . . . as 1770 . . . ⟩ military affairs, mathematics, ⟨ . . . as 1770 . . . ⟩ copper-plates, (among which are twelve large plates of the zodiac, from original drawings, executed by eminent astronomers) drawn from real objects, ⟨ . . . as 1770 . . . ⟩ illustrate this work. ⟨ . . . as 1770 . . . ⟩ book-keeper; gardening and botany by J. Marshall, Gardener, at Knightsbridge; criticism, grammar, poetry, theology, &c. by The Rev. Thomas Cooke, A.B. Author of The universal letter-writer; or, new art of polite correspondence. And the other parts by gentlemen of eminence in the several departments they have undertaken to elucidate.

London: Printed for J. Cooke, 1772.

[*Two volumes: London, 1772–1771. The title and imprint for Vol. I are given above.*]

Art. "Camera obscura," I, 1 p; pl. XX.
Art. "Levelling," II, 2 pp; pl. LVI.

35.6 × 22.6 cm

ICU

Issues of Volume I appeared in 1770 and 1772; Volume II appeared only in 1771. The title page for Volume II differs from those for Volume I, but has not been transcribed above.

The article on "Architecture" (I, 3 pp) begins with a history of the subject from biblical times through Egypt, Persia, Greece, Rome, and the Middle Ages, up to "the last two centuries, [when] the architects of Italy, England, and France, employed themselves wholly in retrieving the primitive simplicity and beauty of ancient architecture." For a discussion of the five orders, the reader is referred to the article "Order." Figures 1–5 in Plate LXX illustrate the orders, and Figure 8 depicts a modillion.[1] The rest of the article on architecture is arranged under five subheadings: civil, military, naval, and counterfeit architecture, and architecture in perspective. The one paragraph devoted to civil architecture briefly mentions eight "rules to be observed": solidity, convenience, beauty, order, disposition, proportion, decorum, and economy. For military architecture, the reader is referred to the article "Fortification." By far the lengthiest remarks are devoted to naval architecture, or shipbuilding, following which the reader is also referred to a separate article titled "Ship Building." The commentaries on counterfeit architecture, or painted "scene-work," and on architecture in perspective consist of little more than definitions.

The only illustrations of domestic architecture occur in figures accompanying the articles "Camera obscura" and "Levelling." The illustration for "Camera obscura" (Plate XX, Fig. 1) shows the image of a two-story house and trees projected through a lens onto an interior wall of a second house. The illustration is almost an exact copy, reversed, of one in *A New and Complete Dictionary* (1754–1755; *q.v.*).

The illustrations for "Levelling" (Plate LVI, Figs. 3–4) are unlike illustrations of this subject in most other encyclopedias and dictionaries.[2] In Figure 4 a porticoed and pedimented dwelling set on a raised embankment or podium has replaced the usual plain, unornamented house used as part of the demonstration of leveling. The two-story portico includes four columns flanking the center opening on each level, a design perhaps inspired by Palladio's Villa Cornaro or Plate 61 in Book II of his *Quattro Libri*. In Figure 3 a church steeple and three or four cottages form part of a small rural village visible in the distance.

1. Fig. 6 depicts an orrery. There is no Fig. 7.

2. Similar illustrations appeared in *The New Complete Dictionary* (1778; *q.v.*).

221.1
NEWTON, William (1735–1790)
The architecture of M • Vitruvius • Pollio: translated from the original Latin, by W. Newton, Architect.

London: Printed by William Griffin, and John Clark, and published by J. Dodsley, 1771.

viii + vii–x + [ii] + 122 pp, 22 pls.

50.5 × 32.4 cm

CtY-BA

221.2

† [*Volume I:*]

The architecture of M. Vitruvius Pollio: translated from the original Latin, by W. Newton, Architect.

London: Printed for I. and J. Taylor, R. Faulder; P. Elmsly, and T. Sewell, 1791.

2 leaves, [iii]–xix + [2] + 122 pp.

48.5 cm

Reference: NUC

[Volume II:]

The architecture of M • Vitruvius • Pollio: translated from the original Latin, by W. Newton, Architect. Volume the second.

London: Printed for James Newton; and sold by I. and J. Taylor; R. Faulder; P. Elmsly; and T. Sewell, 1791.

1 printed leaf, xix + [iv] + 123–280 + [iii] pp, 46 pls (pls. 1–26 are for the first volume).

47.6 × 31.4 cm

MnU

In a century dominated by the revival of Roman and Renaissance architectural forms, it is curious that publication of the first English translation of Vitruvius's *Ten Books*, a major literary account of Classical architecture, began only in 1771 and was not completed until 1791. Already in 1762 James Stuart and Nicholas Revett had completed the first volume of their *Antiqvities of Athens*, a pioneering and important archaeological account of Greek architecture.[1] But the new fashion for Greek styles did not immediately displace the authority of Vitruvius or the taste for Roman styles among prominent architects, including Sir William Chambers. Indeed as late as 1791, the year Newton's work was completed, Chambers published the third, and most authoritative, edition of his *Treatise on the Decorative Part of Civil Architecture* (q.v.), in which he maintained his support for Roman styles.

The first volume of Newton's translation (1771) includes preliminary matter, the first five books of Vitruvius, and 22 illustrative plates. Newton published nothing further until 1780, when he issued his commentary in French (q.v.) on selected passages drawn from the entire ten books of Vitruvius. Between 1782 and his death in 1790 Newton was occupied with work on the Royal Chapel at Greenwich.[2] The 1791 edition of Vitruvius, including all ten books in translation, was published posthumously by Newton's brother James. The illustrations for the first volume, many of them redrawn, filled 26 instead of 22 leaves, to which 20 new leaves of plates were added for the second volume.

In the Preface to the first volume (1771, iii–viii) Newton lamented the lack of an English translation of Vitruvius, and speculated that "our neglect of the arts hitherto, and the little figure we have made therein, may probably be owing to our intestine [*sic*] commotions, and the unsettled state of the nation for many years past" (p. iii). Following brief remarks on translations of Vitruvius into other languages, he discussed the order of his illustrations, the division of his translation into chapters, and other aspects of his own work. Newton concluded with some tantalizing remarks on architectural "character," remarks he unfortunately cut short because he felt they were not germane to the subject of this treatise. Mindful of the Vitruvian ideal of decorum, requiring consistency and coordination of parts in every design, Newton recommended that every building incorporate a single, prevailing "character":

I imagine that every building should by its appearance express its destination and purpose, and that some character should prevail therein, which is suitable to, and expressive of, the particular end it is to answer. . . .

The characters or effects, which there may be occasion to express, in buildings, may be distinguished into the pleasing and the elevating, or those of beauty and dignity. . . . (1771, vii–viii)[3]

The rest of the preliminary matter includes observations on the life of Vitruvius (pp. vii–x), a table of contents, and a list of errata. The text (pp. 1–122) consists of a translation, with copious notes, of the first five books of Vitruvius. The plates are reconstructive drawings of subjects mentioned by Vitruvius, including a city plan, fortifications, masonry, rectangular and circular temples, the orders, roofs, doorways, basilicas, theaters, harmonic proportions, and baths.

The second volume (1791) includes a dedication to the king, followed by an address "To the Public" by James Newton, assuring the reader that a great portion of the letterpress and plates had been finished before his brother William's death, and that the rest was taken faithfully from William's own manuscripts and drawings. The Preface (pp. iii–viii) is nearly identical to that in the first volume. Extended "Observations Concerning the Life of Vitruvius" (pp. ix–xix) precede a brief "Advertisement" and the table of contents. The text (pp. 123–280) is a translation, again with copius notes, of the last five books of Vitruvius. A three-page "Appendix" includes addenda and emendations. The plates depict cavaedia, reconstructed Roman and Greek town houses and villas, techniques of construction and leveling, geometry, sundials, construction machinery, hydraulic machinery, a water organ, a cyclometer, and military weaponry and attack machinery.

1. For more detailed discussion of Stuart and Revett see Dora Wiebenson, *Sources of Greek Revival Architecture* (London: Zwemmer, 1969). On the Greek Revival see J. Mordaunt Crook, *The Greek Revival* (London: John Murray, 1972).

2. See the "Advertisement" to the 1791 edition, Vol. II.

3. Newton's idea of a central, prevailing character may be traced, at least in part, to a popular treatise on landscape that appeared one year earlier, Thomas Whately's *Observations on Modern Gardening* (London: 1770). For a discussion of Whately's contribution see John Archer, "Character in English Architectural Design," *Eighteenth-Century Studies* XII:3 (Spring 1979), 339–371.

222.1 ‡
NEWTON, William (1735–1790)

Commentaires sur Vitruve, eclaircis par des figures, & propres à être joints aux différentes traductions de cet auteur. Avec une description des machines militaires des anciens. Par W. Newton, Architecte.

A Londres: chez P. Elmsley, 1780.

iv + vi + 78 pp, 25 pls.

f°

Reference: Microfilm supplied by The British Library.

In 1771 Newton published his translation of the first five books of Vitruvius (*q.v.*). From 1782 to 1790 he was occupied with work on the Royal Chapel at Greenwich, and so Books VI through X did not appear until 1791. In between, in 1780, he published this commentary in French on selected passages drawn from the entire ten books of Vitruvius. The first 74 pages of text are the commentary proper, and pages 75–78 are observations on the life of Vitruvius. The illustrations included with this commentary were selected from the figures used (or to be used) in the English translation; in many cases they were redrawn. The following figures are presented on 25 unnumbered plates: I–XIII, XVIII, XXII–XXVII, XXIX–XXXV, XXXV no. 2, XXXVI, XXXVII, XLVIII–LVI, LXII–LXX, LXX no. 2, LXXXVIII, XCI–CVIII, CVIII no. 2, CXIII–CXVII.

The illustrations span the entire range of subjects in Vitruvius, from the orders and a basilica to a water organ and catapults. Dwellings and structures that could be adapted for domestic or garden use appear in at least eight figures. These include Figure XXXII, a rectangular temple, Figure XXXIII, Piranesi's reconstruction of a Roman temple from a fragment, Figure XXXIV, the Temple of the Sibyl at Tivoli, and Figure XXXV, a two-story structure with a colonnaded courtyard. Figures LIII–LVI are plans and sections of cavaedia.

223.1

NICHOLSON, Peter (1765–1844)

An architectural dictionary, containing a correct nomenclature and derivation of the terms employed by architects, builders, and workmen. Exhibiting, in a perspicuous point of view, the theory and practice of the various branches of architecture, in carpentry, joinery, masonry, bricklaying, and their dependence on each other; the sciences necessary to be understood; and the lives of the principal architects. The whole forming a complete guide to the science of architecture and the art of building. In two volumes. Vol. I [*or* II]. By Peter Nicholson, Architect.

London: Printed by J. Barfield, 1819.

[*Volume I:*] xlvi + 475 + 260 pp, 122 pls (including two different plates labeled "Hand Railing. Plate II."; *wanting "Hand Railing. Plate VI." and "Hand Railing. Plate VII."*)

[*Volume II:*] 261–913 + [i] pp, 158 pls.

26.4 × 21.0 cm

NNC

223.2

———

An architectural and engineering dictionary, containing ⟨ . . . as 1819 . . . ⟩ branches of architecture and engineering, in carpentry, ⟨ . . . as 1819 . . . ⟩. In two volumes. 281 plates. Vol. I. By Peter Nicholson, Architect.

London: Published, by assignment, by John Weale, (successor to the late Josiah Taylor); and to be had of Messrs. Appleton and Co., New York, 1835.

[*Two volumes: London, 1835. The title and imprint for Vol. I are given above.*]

[*Volume I:*] xlvi + 475 + 260 pp, 123 pls.

[*Volume II:*] 261–913 pp, 158 pls.

26.7 × 21.3 cm

MH

223.3

_____

Encyclopedia of architecture; being a new and improved edition of Nicholson's dictionary of the science and practice of architecture, building, etc. Edited by Edward Lomax, Esq., C.E., and Thomas Gunyon, Esq., Arch. & C.E. Vol. I [*or* II].

London: Peter Jackson, Late Fisher, Son, & Co. The Caxton Press, [1852].

[*Volume I:*] [vi] + 516 pp, "Vignette" + frontisp. + 109 pls [*one plate is wanting in this copy*].

[*Volume II:*] [i] + 604 pp, frontisp. + 121 pls.

27.1 × 21.3 cm

ICU

223.4 †

_____

Architectural Dictionary [ed. Lomax].

[N. loc.]: Tallis, 1854.

4°

Reference: ECB

223.5 †

_____

[Nicholson's dictionary of the science and practice of architecture.]

[London?], 1855.

Reference: DNB

223.6 †

_____

Nicholson's dictionary of the science and practice of architecture, building, carpentry. . . . New edition. Edited by E. Lomax and T. Gunyon.

London, [1857–1862].

4°

Reference: BM

223.7

_____

Nicholson's dictionary of the science and practice of architecture, building, carpentry, etc., etc., etc. From the earliest ages to the present time. New edition. Edited by Edward Lomax, Esq., C.E., and Thomas Gunyon, Esq., Arch. & C.E. Illustrated by upwards of 1,600 working drawings. Vol. I [*or* II].
[*The period following* time *does not appear on the title page to Vol. I.*]

London and New York: The London Printing and Publishing Company, Limited, [ca. 1861–1864].

[*Volume I:*] iv pp, 2 printed leaves, 516 pp, frontisp. + "Vignette" + 99 pls.

[*Volume II:*] iv + 604 pp, frontisp. + 115 pls.

27.5 × 21.0 cm

MB

223.8

_____

_____

London and New York: The London Printing and Publishing Company, Limited, [n.d.].

[*Volume I:*] iv pp, 2 printed leaves, 516 pp, frontisp. + "Vignette" + 99 pls [plate "Embankment" *is wanting in this copy*].

[*Volume II:*] iv + 604 pp, frontisp. + 115 pls.

26.3 × 20.7 cm

IdU

The *Architectural Dictionary* of 1819 contains plates dated as early as 1811. The *Architectural and Engineering Dictionary* of 1835 is, except for a few changes, nearly a reissue of the 1819 edition. The first edition of the *Encyclopedia* may be dated [1852] according to the date of the Preface, signed by editors Lomax and Gunyon. The ECB indicates an edition published by Tallis in 1854, and according to the DNB another edition appeared in 1855, but I have not located copies of either. The British Museum *General Catalogue* shows an edition published in London and New York in 1857–1862, but that copy was destroyed by bombing and so is unavailable for examination. In the penultimate undated edition (Entry 223.7) there are 17 fewer plates than in the [1852] edition and there are minor alterations in the text.[1] The publisher's address given on the title page dates this edition to 1861–1864.[2] There is no address given for the publisher in the final undated edition (Entry 223.8).

The articles and illustrations address a great variety of subjects relating to architecture, engineering, mechanical drawing, and perspective. These include roofs, doors, windows, moldings, the orders, domes, geometry, "joinery," "plumbery," projection, stereotomy, and more. The discussion below is limited to articles with illustrations that depict entire dwellings.[3] Except for discussion of the article "House," the commentary below refers only to the 1835 edition.

In the editions of 1819 and 1835 the article "House" (I, 92–105, plus 17 plates numbered irregularly, I through XIX)[4] is comparatively long, but hardly original. Nicholson included lengthy quotations from Vitruvius and Pliny of the subject of Greek and Roman dwellings, brief descriptions of houses he had designed himself, and remarks on such historically significant houses as Blenheim, Holland House, Holyrood House, and the Mansion House. He referred the reader to the article "Building" for principles of construction. The plates accompanying the "House" article all illustrate Nicholson's own designs. The smallest are illustrated first: a two-story brick house for a baker in Buckinghamshire; and a double cottage with a thatch roof, a single door flanked by rustic tree-trunk columns, and a total of four rooms inside (Plates I–II). There are three modest designs in late Georgian style, three to seven windows wide and two stories high (Plates III–IV, VI–VII). Another design, Corby Castle, "delightfully situated upon the romantic banks of the river Eden" (p. 103; Plate VIII), is an uncomfortable combination of late Georgian door and window elements with Greek Doric porticoes and Tuscan arcades. A house designed for a location "near Glasgow" (Plates X, XII–XIII) is more successful: it includes a small Doric portico at the central entrance and two flanking pairs of broad, flat pilaster bands rising the full two-story height of the facade. Far more elaborate, and apparently not executed, is the design for a house at Clifden, Buckinghamshire (Plates XIV–XV). A combination of medieval castellation and Decorated Gothic windows, the design consists of a main building 16 windows across. It is surrounded by and perhaps raised above a one-story outer wall with crenellated towers at the corners. The final five plates illustrate a design for a small coffee house at Paisley, richly decorated in Neoclassical style. An additional plate, marked "House. Plate XX," is described in the article on "Windows" in the Appendix (II, 913), and illustrates an elaborate Gothic design for "the tea-room, at the Spring, near Cliffden, Buckinghamshire, . . . which was designed by the Author, and executed by him in 1813." Later editions, compiled by Lomax and Gunyon, do not include Nicholson's domestic designs. The text of the "House" article (I, 503–514) retains long passages from Vitruvius and Pliny, and includes additional remarks on Roman villas in ancient Britain, and a brief history of British domestic architecture through Tudor times. One plate for this article shows the interior remains of "a private house, Pompeii, Italy." This plate was omitted after 1852.

Two other plates in the Lomax and Gunyon editions, discussed in the article "Italian Architecture," show the plan and elevation of Bridgewater House, by Sir Charles Barry.

Several illustrations for the article "Panorama" (II, 421–428, 2 pls) are simple unarticulated house forms—walls and a simple gable roof—shown in a variety of perspective constructions.

The article on "Perspective" (II, 446–509, 40 pls) begins with a modest history and bibliography of the subject. The bulk of the article is a series of "Problems" and "Demonstrations," profusely illustrated in the plates. Several "Problems" require construction of geometric figures, arches, towers, churches, and houses in perspective. A plate demonstrating the use of the centrolinead, for example, shows a two-story house with gable roof, chimneys, windows, and a door, depicted in elevation, plan, and oblique view.[5] Plate VIII shows a similar house, now with a hipped roof, a cornice, window sills, doorsteps, and a front door. In Plates IX and X there is a slightly larger house—four windows wide instead of three—with a more elaborate cornice and a pedimented gable roof. Figures 1 and 2 in Plate XIII show an outline rendering of a two-story house, three windows wide, in oblique view.

The article "Pisé" (II, 526–534, 1 pl) begins with a description of necessary implements and instructions for their use in working with pisé, a substance made of dried, compressed earth. Most of the article consists of detailed instructions for making a pisé house. Nicholson noted that "different kinds of buildings of these earthy materials may be seen in England, at Woburn Abbey, . . . and in other places" (II, 534). The illustrations, which do not correspond exactly with the figure numbers given in the text,[6] depict tools and molds used for working with pisé, and the plan and view of a two-room house built of pisé.[7]

Figure 12 in the plate accompanying "Proportional Compasses" (II, 599–609, 1 pl) is a perspective view of a two-story house with windows and a door but no roof, used as the subject of a drawing exercise.

Figure 5

The article "Town" (II, 774–777, 2 pls) concerns Nicholson's work for "the Earl of Eglinton, in designing and laying out the new town of Ardrossan, in Airshire" (II, 774). Nicholson reprinted 18 regulations that the Earl of Eglinton had established in 1806 for laying out the town, building houses, and maintaining them. Located on the Firth of Clyde and the Bay of Ardrossan, the town plan includes several crescents whose centers are not on land. To lay out those crescents Nicholson devised a special method of forming curves without a center, and described his method on the final page of the article. The first plate is a pair of diagrams illustrating this method, and the second plate is a plan of the town. There is a "Market place" at the far northern end, plus several terraces facing the Bay of Ardrossan, a dock on a spit of land to the west, and to the south a very large crescent of 43 detached villas facing an inlet of the sea. The plate also includes elevations of two three-story terraces.[8] An addendum to the article appears in the Appendix (II, 912), describing an additional plate ("Town. Plate III.") with an elevation and plan of "Carlton-place, Glasgow, executed in the year 1804, from a design of the Author's."

1. For example in the description of the Crystal Palace (II, 385) a comment on the main rib supports has been eliminated, and the following appears instead: "The materials of the building in Hyde-park, were afterwards used in constructing the Crystal Palace at Sydenham." The Sydenham project was completed in 1854. See George F. Chadwick, *The Works of Sir Joseph Paxton 1803–1865* (London: Architectural Press, 1961), pp. 144–149; and Samuel Phillips, *The Palace and Park* (London: Crystal Palace Library, 1854).

2. The address is given as "97, 98, 99, & 100, St. John Street, London," According to London commercial directories the publisher, The London Printing and Publishing Company, traded at that address only in the years 1861–1864. Previously they occupied only 97 and 100 St. John Street, and in 1865 they moved to 26 Paternoster Row. I am grateful to the Keeper of Enquiry Services at the Guildhall Library for this information.

3. Limiting discussion in this manner accords with the general criteria for including any publication in this bibliography; see the Introduction for further explanation. One article that includes no illustrations of houses, but which deserves brief mention, is "Chinese Architecture" (I, 238–245, 3 pls). Apart from a brief introduction Nicholson based the entire text on Sir William Chambers's *Designs of Chinese Buildings* (1757; *q.v.*). The illustrations, taken from Chambers's Plates I, III–V, VII, and XI, depict temples, a pagoda, a triumphal arch, a bridge, and a tower.

4. Plates numbered V, IX, and XI are mentioned in the text but do not appear in the "Directions to the Binder." Only one plate numbered XVII is mentioned in the text, but two appear in the binder's list.

5. The plate is marked "Centrolinead. Plate II." The binder's list indicates that it was meant to accompany the article on perspective.

6. The text mentions figures numbered 1 through 17. In the sole plate accompanying this article there are only 15 figures.

7. Nicholson's illustrations are similar to figures borrowed from a treatise by François Cointeraux and published by Henry Holland in *Communications to the Board of Agriculture* (1797; *q.v.*). Nicholson's illustrations correspond closely with designs for a pisé dwelling published by William Barber in *Farm Buildings* (1802; *q.v.*).

8. Nicholson's plan for Ardrossan was published earlier in *General View of the Agriculture of the County of Ayr* (1811). See the entry above under "Great Britain. Board of Agriculture." Much of Nicholson's design was executed, and remains today.

224.1
[NICHOLSON, Peter (1765–1844)]

The builder & workman's new director; comprehending definitions and descriptions of the component parts of buildings, the principles of construction and the geometrical development of the principal difficulties that usually occur in the different branches of mechanical professions, employed in the formation of edifices.

London: Printed by James Compton. Published by John Day, Mark King, James Pringle, Henry Goll, Edward Sanders, Robert Johnson, William Foster, John Wright & Thomas Prosser, 1824.

iv + viii + 176 + xl + 16 + 16 + [iv] pp, frontisp. + 141 pls.

26.3 × 20.6 cm

NNC

224.2

NICHOLSON, Peter (1765–1844)

The builder and workman's new director; comprehending definitions and descriptions of the component parts of buildings, the principles of construction, and the geometrical developement of the principal difficulties that usually occur in the different branches of mechanical professions, employed in the erection of edifices. By Peter Nicholson, Esq.
Illustrated with 150 copper plates and 480 wood cuts.

London: Printed for Knight and Lacey, Publishers of books connected with the useful arts, 1825.

iv + viii + 176 + xl + 16 + 16 + iv pp, frontisp. + 141 pls.

27.0 × 21.6 cm

CtY

224.3 †

———————

The builder and workman's new director.

[N. loc.], 1827.

Reference: Obituary in *The Civil Engineer and Architect's Journal, Scientific and Railway Gazette*, 7 (November 1844), 427; also DNB.

224.4 †

———————

The builder's and workman's new director, comprising explanations of the general principles of architecture, the practice of building, and of the several mechanical arts connected therewith. . . . A new edition, revised and much enlarged, from the original work, by Peter Nicholson. . . . Illustrated with 141 copper plates. . . .

London: J. Taylor, 1834.

4 prelim. leaves, 2 + lxx + lxx*–lxx*** + lxxi–lxxxiii + 3–338 pp, frontisp. + 140 pls.

28.5 cm

Reference: NUC

224.5 ‖

———————

The builder's and workman's new director, comprising explanations of the general principles of architecture, the practice of building, and of the several mechanical arts connected therewith, consisting of an essay on design and construction, with observations on the qualities and application of different kinds of materials; a descriptive account of the orders of architecture, with many examples of their details and proportions on numerous engraved plates; a compendious treatise on perspective, with a variety of illustrative examples; a development of the geometrical principles of architecture and the building arts, particularly as applied to masonry, bricklaying, carpentry, &c. &c. A new edition, revised, and much enlarged, from the original work, by Peter Nicholson, Esq. Architect. Illustrated with 141 copper plates and numerous wood cuts.

London: Published by assignment of the executors of the late Mr. Josiah Taylor, by Lewis A. Lewis, 1836.

4 printed leaves, 2 + lxx + lxx*–lxx*** + lxxi–lxxxiii + 3–338 pp, frontisp. + 140 pls.

28.5 cm

Reference: Information supplied by Winterthur Museum Library.

224.6 †

The builder and workman's new director.

Edinburgh, 1843.

Reference: DNB

224.7

The builder's and workman's new director: comprising explanations of the general principles of architecture, of the practice of building, and of the several mechanical arts connected therewith; also the elements and practice of geometry in its application to the building art. A new edition, revised and much enlarged, from the original work by Peter Nicholson, Architect. With upwards of one hundred and fifty copperplates and numerous diagrams.

London and Edinburgh: A. Fullarton and Co., 1845.

xi + 471 pp, frontisp. + 156 pls on 155 leaves [*pl. 156, on the 155th leaf, is wanting in this copy*].

27.4 × 21.9 cm

ICU

224.8 ‖

London and Edinburgh: A. Fullarton and Co., 1848.

ix + [1] + 471 pp, 155 pls [*pl. 156 is wanting in this copy*].

Reference: Information supplied by Environmental Design Library, University of California, Berkeley.

224.9

_____
_____

London and Edinburgh: A. Fullarton and Co., 1853.

ix pp, 2 printed leaves, 3–471 pp, 1 + 156 pls (pls. LXXII and LXXIII are on one leaf; in this copy there is a duplicate of pl. XVII).

28.5 × 22.4 cm

MH

224.10

_____

The builder's and workman's new director: ⟨ . . . as 1845 . . . ⟩ of architecture. Of the practice ⟨ . . . as 1845 . . . ⟩ connected therewith also the elements ⟨ . . . as 1845 . . . ⟩ diagrams.

London and Edinburgh: A. Fullarton and Co., 1856.

ix pp, 2 printed leaves, 5–472 pp, 158 pls on 157 leaves.

26.7 × 20.8 cm

NN

224.11 ‖

_____
_____

London and Edinburgh: A. Fullarton and Co., 1865.

ix pp, 3 printed leaves, 5–472 pp, 158 pls on 157 leaves.

27.2 × 21.1 cm

Reference: Information supplied by Humanities Research Center, University of Texas, Austin.

The editions of 1824 and 1825 include a frontispiece, 141 plates, and a 176-page text. The preliminaries and subsidiaries consist of a preface, a table of contents, a memoir of the author, a 40-page appendix on masonry, bricklaying, carpentry, joinery, perspective, the five orders, and the "Cyclograph," a 16-page appendix on geometry, another 16-page appendix on curved lines, and directions for the binder. The text is divided into sections on plane geometry, solid geometry, stereotomy, orthoprojection, "Development of the Surfaces of Solids," "General Principles," and plane trigonometry. The plates are arranged in 25 groups, eight of which accompany the text: these concern plane geometry, curved lines, orthographical projection and orthoprojection, "Development of Surfaces," "General Principles," and architectural solids. The remaining plates illustrate the topics covered in the appendixes. Two plates, both in the appendixes, illustrate dwellings. The first, marked "Perspective, House. Plate I," depicts a two-story dwelling, three windows wide, with a one-room ell at each side of the house. Pilasters flank the front door and support a small pediment. The second plate, marked "Building, Design.

Plate VI," shows "a Country House, designed for a gentleman of moderate fortune" (p. xl). The central portion of the dwelling is two stories high and five windows wide, with a tetrastyle Ionic portico in front of the entrance; one-story wings at either side of the house each include Ionic porticoes *in antis*.

In the 1834 and 1836 editions the letterpress was expanded to 338 pages of text, plus an introduction, a preliminary essay, a long discussion of the orders, a glossary, and an essay on perspective. The text is divided into three parts: "Geometrical Principles of Architecture and the Building Arts" (pp. 3–71), "Practical Architecture" (pp. 73–162), and "Geometry" (pp. 163–338). In addition to the frontispiece there are 140 plates illustrating the orders, perspective, drawing instruments, architectural solids, orthographic projection, "Development of Surfaces," "General Principles," masonry and stonecutting, bricklaying and groin vaults, carpentry, joinery, and practical geometry. The plate marked "Building, Design. Plate VI" is not included. The plate formerly marked "Perspective, House. Plate I" is now marked "Perspective, Plate Y."

In 1845 the book was revised and expanded, with a wider audience in mind: "not only . . . the numerous class of individuals for whose instruction it was originally composed, and also . . . those young workmen whose efforts are directed to qualify themselves to act as 'Clerks of the works' under Architects . . . , but likewise . . . young men about to engage in the practice of Architecture as a profession." The editor therefore aimed "to combine as much useful information as possible on the Theory and Practice of Architecture,—the science of Geometry as connected therewith,—and on the several branches of Artificers' works of primary importance in Building; and at the same time to condense the Work within the smallest limits compatible with these objects."[1] The text, now 471 pages, is divided into eight parts: preliminary remarks, "the application of geometry to the building arts," the orders, "elements and practice of geometry," "geometrical principles of architecture and the building arts," perspective, architectural history, and an appendix. In the editions of 1845, 1848, and 1853 there are 156 plates in addition to the frontispiece, illustrating masonry, carpentry, joinery, "Grecian Orders," geometry, "Geometrical Principles of Architecture," perspective, and the history of architecture.[2] The plate formerly marked "Perspective, House. Plate I" is now marked "Perspective, Plate 147." Other plates demonstrating perspective construction also include houses: Plate 144 shows oblique views of two geometric solids shaped like houses, and Plate 145 includes a view of six attached three-story houses.

1. Quotations from the "Advertisement" to the 1853 edition.

2. The frontispiece, marked "Civil Architecture," depicts examples of Romanesque columns, arches, and ornament from ecclesiastical buildings in Kent. Plates 155 and 156, also marked "Civil Architecture," depict Blenheim Palace and the Pantheon in Rome.

225.1
NICHOLSON, Peter (1765–1844)
The new practical builder, and workman's companion: containing a full display and elucidation of the most recent and skilful methods, pursued by architects and artificers, in the various departments of carpentry, joinery,

bricklaying, masonry, slating, plumbing, painting, glazing, plastering, &c. &c. Including, also, new treatises on geometry, theoretical and practical, trigonometry, conic sections, perspective, shadows, and elevations; a summary of the art of building; copious accounts of building materials, strength of timber, cements, &c.; a description of the tools used by the different workmen; an extensive glossary of the technical terms peculiar to each department; and the theory and practice of the five orders, as employed in decorative architecture. By Peter Nicholson, Architect. The whole illustrated and embellished with numerous plates, from original drawings and designs, made expressly for this work, by the author, and correctly engraved, under his immediate inspection, by Mr. W. Symns, and other eminent artists.

London: Printed for Thomas Kelly, 1823 [–1825?].

10 + [ii] + 596 pp, portr. + frontisp. + additional engraved title page + 183 pls (plus an undated issue of Elsam, *The practical builder's perpetual price-book*: 160 + [ii] + 161–180 pp, frontisp. + 4 pls).

26.0 × 21.0 cm

MH

225.2

The new and improved practical builder, and workman's companion: exhibiting a full display and elucidation of the most recent and skilful methods pursued by architects and artificers, in all the various departments of building. In three volumes. Vol. I. contains geometry, carpentry, joinery, and cabinet-making. Vol. II. contains masonry, bricklaying, plastering, slating, painting, glazing, & plumbing. Vol. III. contains theory and practice of the five orders, Gothic architecture, perspective, projection, fractions, decimal arithmetic, &c. Comprehending a summary of the art of building; extensive accounts of building materials, strength of timber, cements, &c. and a glossary of the technical terms peculiar to each department. Illustrated by numerous diagrams and steel plates, accurately engraved by Mr. Turrell and other eminent architectural artists, from original drawings and designs, and works executed by the most distinguished architects of this country, viz.: Messrs. Brunel, Burton, Clarke, Elsam, Hardwick, Inwood, Johnstone, Laing, Nash, Nicholson, Perronet, Rennie, Shaw, Smirke, Soane, Telford, Tredgold, Wilkins, Wyatville, &c. &c.

London: Thomas Kelly, 1835 [i.e., 1837?].

[*This title page precedes three volumes with individual title pages, each dated 1837.*]

[*Volume I:*] xxxvi + viii + 140 + 36 pp, 84 + 6 pls.

[*Volume II:*] viii + 232 pp, 45 pls.

[*Volume III:*] [ii] + 167 + [i] pp, 108 pls.

27.0 × 21.6 cm

RIBA

225.3

_____

_____

London: Thomas Kelly, 1838 [–1839].

[*This title page precedes three volumes. Vols. I and III have no individual title pages. Vol. II has an individual title page dated 1839.*]

[*Volume I:*] xxxvi + 132 + 36 pp, 75 pls.

[*Volume II:*] viii + 232 pp, 54 pls.

[*Volume III:*] 76 + 133–140 pp, 51 pls.

27.6 × 21.0 cm

RIBA

225.4 †

_____

[The new and improved] practical builder.

London: Kelly, 1847.

3 vols.

4°

Reference: ECB

225.5

_____

The new and improved practical builder, and workman's companion: exhibiting a full display and elucidation of the most recent and skilful methods pursued by architects and artificers, in all the various departments of building. By Peter Nicholson. In three volumes.
Vol. I. contains geometry, carpentry, joinery, and cabinet-making.
Vol. II. contains masonry, bricklaying, plastering, slating, painting, glazing, & plumbing.
Vol. III. contains theory and practice of the five orders, Gothic architecture, perspective, projection, fractions, decimal arithmetic, &c.
Comprehending a summary of the art of building; extensive accounts of building materials, strength of timber, cements, &c. and a glossary of the technical terms peculiar to each department. The whole revised and arranged by Thomas Tredgold; and illustrated by numerous diagrams and steel plates, accurately engraved by eminent architectural artists, from original drawings and designs, and works executed by the most distinguished architects of this country, namely: Messrs. Brunel, Burton, Clarke, Elsam, Hardwick, Inwood, Johnstone, Laing, Nash, Nicholson, Perronet, Rennie, Shaw, Smirke, Soane, Telford, Tredgold, Wilkins, Wyatville, &c. &c.

London: Thomas Kelly, [1848].

[*The title page, preceded by a portrait of the author, an additional engraved title page, and one plate, is followed by a "Preface" (pp. iii–vi) and essays on geometry and trigonometry (pp. vii–xxxvi). Next follows the title page for Vol. I and the rest of Vol. I. Vols. II and III each are preceded by individual title pages.*]

The new and improved practical builder. Carpentry, joinery, and cabinet = making; being a new and complete system of lines for the use of workmen; founded on accurate geometrical and mechanical principles, with their application in carpentry,—to roofs, domes, centring, &c.; in joinery,—to stairs, hand-rails, soffits, niches, &c.; and in cabinet making,—to furniture, both plain and ornamental; fully and clearly explained, illustrated by numerous engravings by artists of the first talent. Vol. I.

London: Thomas Kelly, [1848].

viii + 140 + 36 pp, 84 + 6 pls [*pl. XXXVII is wanting in this copy*].

The new and improved practical builder. Masonry, bricklaying, and plastering, both plain and ornamental: containing a new and complete system of lines for stone cutting, for the use of workmen; with an ample detail of the theory and practice of constructing arches, domes, groins, niches, stairs, columns, &c. bond, foundations, walls, bridges, tunnels, light = houses, &c. the formation of mortars and cements; including, also, practical treatises on slating, plumbing, painting, and glazing; and a full description of the various materials employed in all these arts, illustrated by numerous engravings by artists of the first talent. Vol. II.

London: Thomas Kelly, [1848].

viii + 232 pp, 60 pls.

The new and improved practical builder. The five orders of architecture; containing the most plain and simple rules for drawing and executing them in the purest style; for the use of workmen; exhibiting the most approved modes of applying each in practice, suitably to the climate of Great Britain. Including an historical description of Gothic architecture, illustrated with specimens selected from the most celebrated structures now existing, and numerous plans, elevations, sections, and details of various buildings, executed by architects of great eminence. To which are added, treatises on projection, perspective, fractions, decimal arithmetic, &c. in order to assist the student in drawing architectural objects, concluding with an index and glossary of the terms of art, &c. Illustrated by numerous engravings by artists of the first talent. Vol. III.

London: Thomas Kelly, [1848].

[ii] + 168 pp [*pp. 161–164 wanting is this copy*], 112 pls.

28.5 × 22.0 cm

NNC

225.6

———

———

London: Thomas Kelly, [1850].

[This title page, together with a frontispiece and an additional engraved title page, precede xxxvi pages of preliminary matter. Next follows the title page for Vol. I and the rest of Vol. I. Vols. II and III each are preceded by individual title pages.]

———

London: Thomas Kelly, [1850].

viii + 140 + 36 + 40 pp, 108 pls.

———

London: Thomas Kelly, [1850].

viii + 232 pp, frontisp. + 90 pls.

———

London: Thomas Kelly, [1850].

[ii] + 168 pp, 112 pls.

27.1 × 21.0 cm

MB

225.7 †

———

The new and improved practical builder and workman's companion.

London, 1853.

Reference: DNB

225.8 †

———

The new and improved practical builder. Revised and arranged by T. Tredgold.

London: [1861].

4°

Reference: BM

The title page of the first edition is dated 1823, but publication apparently was not completed until 1825, the date of the portrait, engraved frontispiece, and several plates.[1] The text is divided into 17 chapters, on geometry, carpentry, joinery, terms and tools used in carpentry and joinery, timber, masonry, terms and tools used in masonry, bricklaying, plastering, terms and tools used in bricklaying and plastering, slating, plumbing, house painting, glazing, "Building in General,"[2] the five orders, and perspective. An appendix treats several mathematical subjects.

The plates are divided into four "Series." The first, or "Miscellaneous," series illustrates a wide variety of subjects, including geometry, roofs, moldings, windows, doors, railings, tools, timber, bridges, masonry, and bricklaying. The second series depicts the orders, and the third concerns perspective. Plate IX in the third series shows a plan and view of a two-story house, three windows wide, with a pediment and a "cantaliver [sic] cornice" (p. 538). The fourth series, titled "Plans and Elevations," is accompanied by brief descriptions (pp. 563–578). The first five of these plates are plans, elevations, and sections of first-, second-, third-, and fourth-rate town houses, designed in a typical late Georgian manner with shallow relieving arches, Corinthian pilasters, and decorative iron balconies. The next four plates show country villas: two have Doric or Ionic porticoes, and two have Gothic ornamentation superimposed on a symmetrical, otherwise Georgian elevation and plan. Plate X depicts a pair of Gothic lodges flanking an entrance gate to "a Mansion." Plates XI and XII are designs for a huge mansion "in the Castellated style." At least five stories high, the elevation includes turrets, crenellations, and machicolations running riot over the top, Tudor drip moldings above all the windows on the upper stories, and large Decorated Gothic windows on the ground floor. Plates XIII and XIV are designs for a "Gothic" dwelling, "the Seat of Henry Monteith Esqr.," a more sober exercise in Castellated and Tudor styles. Plate XV is a three-story "Mansion," seven windows wide, with a Doric colonnade across the full width of the facade. Plates XVI through XXXVI, plus ten more numbered irregularly, depict designs for "a Church in the Grecian style," a chapel, two mausolea, a "Grecian monument," roofs and trusses, doors, shop fronts, windows, a chimney piece, "a Country Court House and Prisons," and a small prison. Another dwelling appears in the frontispiece, a Greek Revival house designed by Nicholson for Fulton Alexander, and previously illustrated in Plate X of Nicholson's Architectural Dictionary (q.v.).

The principal title page of the next edition is dated 1835, but the title pages for individual volumes are dated 1837. The subjects treated in each volume are outlined on the principal title page. The contents of the third volume closely parallel Nicholson's Theoretical and Practical Treatise on the Five Orders (1834; q.v.). Most illustrations of dwellings in the first edition of the New Practical Builder, now renumbered, retitled, and redated, are included in the third volume of the 1835–1837 edition.

The letterpress title page of the [1848] edition is undated, but the engraved title page and many of the plates are dated 1848.[3] Few major changes were made for this edition. The illustrations of domestic architecture are generally the same as in earlier editions, although some of the plates underwent minor changes. In Volume III Plates XXIX through XXXII show first- through fourth-rate houses.[4] Greek and Gothic Revival country villas appear in Plates XXXIII through XXXVI. Plate XXXVII shows lodges and an "Entrance to a Mansion." Plates XXXVIII and XXXIX depict a plan and elevation for a mansion in the Castellated style. Plates XL and XLI illustrate the Gothic residence of Henry Monteith, and Plate XLII depicts the three-story mansion with a Doric colonnade across the front. Plate LXXIV is a perspective view of a two-story house, three windows wide, four windows deep, ornamented with a simple stringcourse between stories, widely projecting eaves, and a projecting raking cornice framing the gable end of the roof. Plate LXXXIX depicts Holford House in Regent's Park, and Plate CI illustrates Stafford House. Numerous other architectural subjects also appear in this volume.[5]

The next edition, also with an undated title page, includes a 40-page "Copious Abstract of the Metropolitan Building Act" in Volume I. Eighteen additional plates appear in Volume I, and 30 more appear in Volume II; many of these are dated 1849 or 1850. Volume III remained essentially unchanged.

1. The Preface to Volume I (pp. 5–8) is dated 1822. The copy at Harvard is bound in two volumes, with the single letterpress title page (1823) in Volume II.

2. This chapter (pp. 425–450) includes remarks on terms used in building, proportions of door and window openings, proportions of rooms, stairs, moldings, "the Beauty of Buildings," and "Situations of Country Residences." No plates accompany this chapter. In the [1850] edition this material appears as Book II in Volume III, pp. 52–72.

3. The "Directions to the Binder" in Volume I list 90 plates, numbered I–LXXXIV and 1–6. (The latter group of six plates all concern "Cabinet Making," and include designs for furniture.) Plate XXXVII, mentioned in the binder's list, is wanting in the Avery copy. An additional plate, not mentioned in the binder's list, precedes the title page for the set. Its subject is the "Roof of Chapel in the Bethnal Green Road," and it is dated 1850.

4. Floor plans of these houses appear in Volume I, Plate XIV.

5. Plates XLIII–XLVIII, a "Grecian Church"; XLIX–LIV, a chapel; LV–LXI, mausolea; LXII–LXIII, a country courthouse and prisons; LXIV–LXV, a small county prison; LXVI–LXVII, Middlesex County Lunatic Asylum; LXVIII, St. Peter's in Rome and St. Paul's in London; LXXXIV, Waltham Abbey; LXXXV–LXXXVI, Waltham Cross; LXXXVII, the Royal Palace at Pimlico; LXXXVIII, the National Gallery; XC, Goldsmiths' Hall; XCI, Westminster Hall; XCI.2, Chapel of Henry VII, Westminster Abbey; XCII–XCIV, Lincoln Cathedral; XCIII.2, Freiburg Cathedral; XCV, Palazzo Grimani, Venice; XCVI, thirteenth-century architectural sculpture; XCVII, the Hall, Christ's Hospital; XCVIII, New Church, Chelsea (now St. Luke's); XCVIII.2, Notre Dame, Paris; XCIX, Lady Chapel, St. Saviour, Southwark; C, Church of Batalha; C.2, Basilica of St. Francis, Assisi; CII, Westminster Hospital; CIII, General Post Office, London; CIV, Custom House, London; CV, Norwich Cathedral; CVI, Fishmongers' Hall; CVII, Somerset House; CVIII, a method of constructing wharf walls. For a description of the other plates in this volume, see the commentary on Nicholson's *Theoretical and Practical Treatise on the Five Orders.*

NICHOLSON, Peter (1765–1844)
The practical builder's perpetual price-book.

See ELSAM, Richard, *Entry 71;* NICHOLSON, Peter, The new practical builder, *Entry 225.1.*

226.1

NICHOLSON, Peter (1765–1844), and Michael Angelo NICHOLSON (–1842)

The practical cabinet-maker, upholsterer, and complete decorator. By Peter & Michael Angelo Nicholson. With numerous illustrative engravings.

London: H. Fisher, Son, & Co., [1826–1827].

x + 11–152 + 12 pp, additional engraved title page + 104 pls on 103 leaves [*8 plates are wanting in this copy*].

27.3 × 21.4 cm

CtY

226.2

————

————

London: H. Fisher, Son, & Co., [1826–1827].

x + 11–152 + 12 pp, additional engraved title page + 121 pls on 120 leaves.

26.5 × 20.5 cm

CtY-BA

226.3 †

————

The practical cabinet maker, upholsterer and complete decorator.

London: Fisher, 1828.

4°

Reference: ECB

226.4 †

————

The practical cabinet-maker, upholsterer, and complete decorator: with numerous illustrative engravings. . . . By Peter & Michael Angelo Nicholson.

London: H. Fisher, Son, & Co., [1834?].

152 + 12 pp, additional engraved title page + 104 leaves of plates (dated 1826–1834).

27 cm

Reference: NUC-S

226.5

The practical cabinet-maker, ⟨ . . . as [1826–1827] . . . ⟩.

London: H. Fisher, Son, & Co., [1836–1838].

x + 11–152 + 12 pp, additional engraved title page + 104 pls on 103 leaves [*one plate of drawing room chairs is wanting in this copy*].

27.0 × 21.1 cm

MB

226.6 ‡

The practical cabinet maker, upholsterer, and complete decorator. By Peter & M. A. Nicholson.

London: Published by H. Fisher, Son & P Jackson, Caxton, 1843.

Reference: Reprint, ed. Christopher Gilbert (East Ardsley, England: E P Publishing Limited, 1973).

226.7

The practical cabinet-maker, upholsterer, and complete decorator. By Peter & Michael Angelo Nicholson. With numerous illustrative engravings.

London: Fisher, Son, & Co. The Caxton Press, London; Liverpool; Manchester, [1846].

x + 11–152 pp, additional engraved title page + 104 pls on 103 leaves.

28.8 × 22.0 cm

ICA

The letterpress title pages of the copies in the Art and Architecture Library at Yale and in the Yale Center for British Art are undated. Both copies have etched title pages dated 1826, and both contain plates dated 1827.[1] The copy at the Yale Center for British Art has 17 additional plates, none of which is mentioned in the list of plates.[2] A copy in the Boston Public Library has an engraved title page dated 1836, and plates dated as late as 1838. Another edition has an engraved title page dated 1843, and plates dated 1826, 1827, and 1838. Apparently the final edition was that of [1846], with plates dated 1832 to 1846.

The Introduction (pp. v–x) is dated 1826. The authors recognized a need for "a complete treatise, by the aid of which all the various articles of Cabinet Furniture may be readily executed by the Mechanic with precision and tasteful elegance, and the designs made clearly intelligible to the Gentleman and the Amateur" (p. v). They proposed to furnish "such a variety of designs as shall illustrate the principles upon which these articles are constructed, and afford every requisite information on this important and interesting subject" (p. v). There follows a brief literary exposition of the aesthetic principles underlying these designs: the "first and chief consideration is utility"; but once basic needs are satisfied, "we naturally seek further gratification" (p. v). Frequently such gratification is provided by "novelty," but as time passes its charm is "gradually dissolved." The only solution is constantly to "seek out fresh sources of intellectual gratification; and thus the powerful and inventive genius of man is called forth" (p. vi). The authors recommend that this genius "at all times be governed by certain principles." The artist must make a "judicious selection, then, of the beautiful forms and varieties of nature, and [keep] a strict adherence to curved lines produced by organical description" (p. vi). Since the Greeks understood these principles well, the artist should closely study the works of "the ancients" (pp. vi–vii).

The text (pp. 11–152) treats geometry, projection, and perspective, subjects which are illustrated in the first 23 plates. These depict geometric figures and diagrams, plus perspective views of furniture and other objects. Plate 12 includes a perspective sketch of a one-story house, three windows wide, with an enclosed yard and offices. Two plates numbered 15 show room interiors. The final 12 pages of letterpress include a "Glossary of Technical Terms used in Cabinet-Making." The last 81 plates, many of them colored, contain designs in the Nicholsons' elegant Regency style for household furniture and furnishings, including beds, chairs, tables, curtains, and wardrobes; there are also several plates illustrating Classical ornaments and the orders. Just four designs are Gothic: a bed, a "Drawing Room Gothic Commode," an "Upright Gothic Piano Forte," and a "Gothic Side Board."

1. A copy cited in the printed catalogue of the Rare Book Collection of the Winterthur Museum Libraries has plates dated 1826 to 1834. A similar copy at Indiana University is included here as Entry 226.4.

2. The additional plates all are dated 1826, and all but the first are signed "M. A. Nicholson del." The subjects of these plates are: [I], French bed; [II], cradles; [III], draperies for windows; IV, settee and easy chair; V, window draperies; VI, jardiniere; VII, French bed; VIII, washstands and tables; IX, French bed; X, window curtains; XI, French bed and commode; XII, French bed; XIII, cradle, tea table, and fire screen; XIV, French curtains; XV, Chinese bed and washstand; XVI, easy chair and couch; XVII, French bed.

227.1
NICHOLSON, Peter (1765–1844)

The rudiments of practical perspective, in which the representation of objects is described by two easy methods, one depending on the plan of the object, the other on its dimensions and position, each method being entirely free from the usual complication of lines, and from the difficulties arising from remote vanishing points. By Peter Nicholson. . . . Illustrated by 38 plates, elegantly engraved by Lowry.

London: Printed for J. Taylor, 1822.

xviii + 122 pp, 38 pls.

23.8 × 15.6 cm

MnU

227.2

The rudiments of practical perspective, in which the representation of objects is described by two easy methods, one depending on the plan of the object, the other on its dimensions and position, each method being entirely free from the usual complication of lines, and from the difficulties arising from remote vanishing points. By Peter Nicholson. . . . Second edition, illustrated by 38 plates, elegantly engraved by Lowry.

London: Edward Lumley, 1835.

xviii + 122 pp, 38 pls.

22.2 × 13.7 cm

PU

227.3 †

Rudiments of practical perspective.

[London]: Lumley, 1838.

8°

Reference: ECB

A practicing architect as well as author of several practical manuals on architecture and perspective, Nicholson criticized previous perspective treatises for "a want of familiar examples" (p. iii). These books were "not well calculated to engage the attention of many who are desirous of obtaining a practical as well as a theoretical knowledge of the subject" (pp. iii–iv). Further, Nicholson introduced "the principles of the Science . . . in the form of lectures, instead of the more usual way of propositions" because this method was "better adapted to engage the attention of the student" (p. iv).[1]

The text begins with "Preliminary Considerations," including definitions and elementary propositions. The next three chapters treat perspective "according to three separate methods" (pp. xi–xii). The first is "the representation of objects by means of their vanishing and intersecting points only, and by their geometrical description." The second also employs vanishing points, with a "directing point" used to "terminate" the "definite lengths" of those lines. The third "is by vanishing points, having the representation of the point and the linear dimensions of the objects given." The remaining chapters concern solid objects such as buildings, "the base of the solid being given in the original plane," drawing lines "to an inaccessible converging point," the use of a centrolinead, "representation of solids from their dimensions and position," "representation of objects at different distances," and shadows.

Of 38 plates, 24 are devoted to geometric diagrams, perspective constructions, and simple objects rendered in perspective. Fourteen plates illustrate houses. Two plates accompanying the chapter on objects with bases "in the original plane" illustrate plans, elevations, and perspective views of a two-story house three windows wide. Plate XVIII shows the house in outline, and Plate XIX shows it shaded and with a chimney added. The principal exercise in the chapter on the centrolinead is the representation of a "complete building" (p. xvii). Shown in Plates XXII through XXX, the building is a three-story house, the top floor located under dormers in the roof. The facade is three windows wide, there are chimneys at each end, and the side elevation contains the only door. Each plate shows the progressive addition of one type of tectonic element (e.g., windows, roof, dormers, etc.). Houses also appear as part of other exercises. In Plate XXXV there is an oblique view of a two-story house with a hip roof, and in Plate XXXVI there is a continuous row of 15 attached houses, each two stories high and three windows wide. Plates XXXVI and XXXVIII illustrate geometric solids that resemble houses.

1. Nicholson also noted: "The Practical Part of this work, is the result of many years' experience in teaching the Science of Perspective" (p. v).

228.1
[NICHOLSON, Peter (1765–1844)]

A theoretical and practical treatise on the five orders of architecture; containing the most plain and simple rules for drawing and executing them in the purest style; with the opinions of Sir William Chambers, and other eminent architects, both ancient and modern, exhibiting the most approved modes of applying each in practice, with directions for the design and execution of various kinds of buildings, both useful and ornamental, and suitable to the climate of Great Britain. Including an historical description of Gothic architecture, shewing its origin, and also a comparison of the Gothic architecture of England, Germany, France, Spain, and Italy; together with details of the first, second, and third periods of the pointed arch, or Gothic style; illustrated with specimens selected from the most celebrated structures now existing, and numerous plans, elevations, sections, and details of various buildings, executed by architects of great eminence. To which are added, in order to assist the student in drawing architectural objects with ease and accuracy, treatises on projection, perspective, fractions, decimal arithmetic, &c. Concluding with an index and glossary of the terms of art, &c.

London: Printed for Thomas Kelly, 1834.

[ii] + 163 pp, 100 pls (numbered I–LXXXVI, XCI, XCI.2, XCII, XCIII, XCIII.2, XCIV–XCVIII, XCVIII.2, XCIX, C, C.2).

27.4 × 21.2 cm

NNC

228.2

London: Printed for Thomas Kelly, 1839.

[ii] + 163 pp, 100 pls (numbered I–LXXXVI, XCI, XCI.2, XCII, XCIII, XCIII.2, XCIV–XCVIII, XCVIII.2, XCIX, C, C.2).

27.4 × 21.3 cm

NN

228.3 †

A theoretical and practical treatise ⟨ . . . as 1834 . . . ⟩ ancient and modern. . . . Concluding with an index and glossary of the terms of art &c.

London: T. Kelly, [184–].

2 leaves, 163 + [1] pp, pls.

28 cm

Reference: NUC-S

228.4 †

London: T. Kelly, 1850.

2 leaves, 163 + [1] pp, pls.

28 cm

Reference: NUC-S

The text and illustrations correspond closely with the third volume of Nicholson's *New and Improved Practical Builder* (1837 and later; *q.v.*).

The first 51 pages of text treat the orders. Pages 52–72 concern "Building in General," with special attention to proportions of doors, windows, apartments, and moldings, and "situations for country residences." An essay on Gothic architecture (pp. 73–116) is followed by a discussion of perspective, projection, shadows, and decimal arithmetic (pp. 117–144). There are brief plate descriptions on pages 145–161. The text concludes with a "Glossary of Technical Terms" (pp. 162–163).

Plates I through XXVIII depict the orders, moldings, and ornaments. Plates LXIX through LXXXIII illustrate Nicholson's discussion of geometry, perspective, projection, and the use of the centrolinead. The remaining plates are described above in the commentary on the 1848 edition of the *New and Improved Practical Builder*.

229.1 ‡
NICHOLSON, Peter (1765–1844)
A treatise on practical perspective, without the use of vanishing points; being an application of the centrolinead to perspective, &c. with a general description of the instrument. By Peter Nicholson. . . .

London: Printed and sold by J. Barfield, for the author; sold also by J. Taylor; Longman and Co.; Gardiner and Son; Davis and Dickson; T. Underwood; and W. and S. Jones, Mathematical Instrument Makers, 1815.

vi + iv + 5–35 pp, 13 pls.

8°

Reference: Microfilm supplied by The British Library.

Nicholson's principal aim here was to illustrate the use of a centrolinead, and so this book is considerably shorter and more limited than his later *Rudiments of Practical Perspective* (1822; *q.v.*).[1]

Of 13 plates three illustrate use of the apparatus, and the other ten show exercises that involve plans, elevations, and views of houses. The first two plates show a three-story house, three windows wide, in front elevation, two end elevations, and roof plan.[2] The next eight plates illustrate progressive stages in constructing an oblique perspective view of the same house.

1. He noted in the Preface that "No definitions are here given; the reader is supposed to understand the elements of perspective" (p. v).

2. The same design was also the subject of extensive illustration in Nicholson's *Rudiments of Practical Perspective* (1822; *q.v.*).

230.1 †
NICHOLSON, Peter (1765–1844)
A treatise on projection.

Newcastle: T. and J. Hodgson, 1837.

136 pp, 62 pls.

8°

Reference: Obituary in *The Civil Engineer and Architect's Journal, Scientific and Railway Gazette*, 7 (November 1844), 427; also DNB, APSD.

230.2 ‡
————————

A treatise on projection, containing first principles of plans and elevations, and the modes of delineating solids, and every form of mechanical construction, so as to present the most striking image of the object to be carried into execution; on entirely new principles. Together with a complete system of isometrical drawing, the whole practically applied to architecture, building, carpentry, machinery, shipbuilding, astronomy, and dialling. With numerous plates. By Peter Nicholson. . . .

London: Richard Groombridge; and Charles Turnham, Carlisle, 1840.

xvi + 136 pp, additional engraved title page + frontisp. + 64 pls (numbered 1–62, A, B).

20.9 × 11.9 cm

Reference: Microfilm supplied by Cornell University Libraries.

This was Nicholson's last publication, except for revisions of previously published titles.

Nicholson conceived this book as "a practical work," promising to discuss the subject in terms of "fixed and scientific principles" (p. ix). The work is directed to "the Engineer, the Architect, the Mechanic, and to all employed in the erection of buildings, or the construction of machinery" (p. ix). The text begins with a brief section on elementary principles of projection, and another on the "objects" of projection—geometric solids, regular solids, and circles. The two major portions of the treatise are devoted, respectively, to projection "on the lower plane" and projection "on the oblique plane."

Among Nicholson's didactic examples are several designs for dwellings, as well as geometric solids, machinery, domes, staircases, a cornice, a roof, and subjects in astronomy. Among the domestic examples Plate 14 shows the end elevation, front elevation, plan, and oblique view of two similar one-story houses. Each has a facade with a central door flanked by two windows; one has a simple pitched roof with two gable ends, and the other has a hipped roof.

Plate 15 illustrates two subjects that are unusually complex for a treatise on projection. One is a semicircular crescent of three-story houses joined in one continuous facade. The other is an arrangement of 12 identical detached houses, each three stories high and six windows wide, around the perimeter of a dodecahedron. All the houses face outward and are connected to each other by one-story screen walls that serve to enclose the inner garden area. Nicholson's design was closely related to the so-called Polygon erected earlier in the century in Somers Town, London, and for a while a fashionable Neoclassical rival to John Nash's far more romantic Park Villages to the west.[1]

Plate 43 shows "projections" of a two-story house, five windows across and with a hipped roof, as seen from above, the front, and the side. Plate 44 shows much the same subject, with the addition of a front porch or portico and a simple pitched roof with gable ends. Plates 45 and 46 show projections of geometric forms that were derived from the outlines of the house in Plate 43. Plate 53 shows projections of geometric forms similar to those in Plate 14. Plate 54 shows an oblique projection, as if viewed from above, of an L-shaped dwelling two stories high but with one wing lower than the other. Plate 55 shows three-dimensional geometric outlines of five differently shaped buildings: two in the form of a Greek cross, one with a tall central portion and two lower wings, one with a U-shaped plan, and one in the shape of an L.

1. The Polygon in Somers Town was erected by Jacob Leroux in 1793. See *Survey of London XXIV* (London: London County Council, 1952), 120–121. About 1768 Leroux had designed a similar twelve-sided Polygon in Southampton that was never completed. See *The Southampton Guide: or, an Account of the Ancient and Present State of That Town* (Southampton, 1781), pp. 57–58; *The Southampton Guide: or, an Account of the Antient & Present State of That Town,* 4th ed. (Southampton, [1787]), pp. 79–80; and A. Temple Patterson, *A History of Southampton* (Southampton: At the University Press, 1966), I, 52–55, 57. Other many-sided arrangements of uniform dwellings include Michael Searles's Paragon in the New Kent Road, Southwark (1789–1790, now demolished), and his Paragon at Blackheath (ca. 1793). See James Edwards, *A Companion from London to Brighthelmston* (London, 1801), p. 7; Stanley C. Ramsey, *Small Houses of the Late Georgian Period 1750–1820* (New York: Architectural Book Publishing Company, 1919), I, pls. 71–72, and II, pls. 65–66; *Survey of London XXV* (London: London County Council, 1955), 118–119, 123, pl. 86. Also see Plate 28 in Richard Brown, *The Principles of Practical Perspective* (*q.v.*). Attached houses with alternating high-low facades were erected in the vicinity of Bristol as early as 1788: see Andor Gomme, Michael Jenner, and Bryan Little, *Bristol: An Architectural History* (London: Lund Humphries, 1979), pp. 224–225.

231.1

NOBLE, Edward

The elements of linear perspective demonstrated by geometrical principles, and applied to the most general and concise modes of practice. With an introduction, containing so much of the elements of geometry as will render the whole rationale of perspective intelligible, without any other previous mathematical knowledge. By Edward Noble.

London: Printed for T. Davies, 1771.

2 printed leaves, iii–cxvi [*a misprint for cxv*] + 298 pp, 4 + 48 pls.

20.5 × 13.1 cm

RPJCB

Two preliminary leaves include a dedication to Sir Joshua Reynolds and a table of contents. In the Preface (pp. iii–xi) Noble divided previous writers on perspective into two categories. The first includes those "who have treated this subject in a liberal and masterly manner . . . but as they require some previous geometrical knowledge" on the part of the reader, "they are unintelligible where they are most wanted." Second are "those who endeavour to demonstrate the principles of perspective without having recourse to mathematical speculations. These gentlemen may be compared to an architect who would support a building whilst the foundation is removed" (p. iv). Noble warned that this is not a book for "those who are content with learning by rote the mechanical rules which compose the practice of an art" (p. iii). To bring the reader up to a sufficient level of mathematical sophistication, Noble provided an Introduction "Containing Such Geometrical Propositions, (Extracted from Euclid's Elements) as are Necessary to Demonstrate the Principles of Perspective" (pp. xiii–xvi), followed by a 99-page discussion of "Euclid's Elements" in detail (pp. xvii–cxv).

The text (pp. 1–298) is a series of theorems, problems, examples, and demonstrations. Most of the plates contain geometric figures and objects, but several include architectural subjects. Plates 11, 13, 22, and 23 show perspective constructions of different houses, each two stories high and three windows wide. Plates 25 and 27 illustrate garden temples. Plate 30 depicts a row of columnar bases in perspective. Plates 33 and 41 show stepwise ascending and descending houses. Plates 34, 42, 44, and 45 show room interiors. There are partial views of building facades in Plates 39 and 40. Plate 46 shows the buildings in a small town, and Plate 47 shows several houses and a church near a small inlet.

NORTON, Charles
Proposals, with the plan & specification, for building the crescent, in Birmingham.

See Entry 455.

232.1
ORME, William
William Orme's rudiments of landscape drawing, and perspective. Dedicated to the Society for the encouragement of arts &c. &c.

London: Sold and publishd [by William Orme?] at No 59 New Bond St., [1802].

3 printed leaves, 22 pls [*of which two are wanting in this copy*].

26.8 × 44.1 cm

PPF

The title page and letterpress are undated. The plates were published in 1801 and 1802.

The book consists of six numbers, all described on the first page of letterpress. Each number contains three or four plates. In addition the sixth number, "a small Treatise on Perspective," includes two leaves of letterpress.

Numbers 1 through 5 constitute a short series of lessons in drawing. The four plates in the first number depict lines, then lines "put together into Forms," and studies "from Nature" demonstrating "Character," "Precision," "Outline," and "Touch." The second number includes four plates "intended to shew the Process of describing with the Pencil, Trees, Cottages, &c. more complicate in Form and more finished." All four plates in the third number "are Examples of Trees in the first Process, and continued to a finished State." In the fourth number three plates demonstrate "a simple broad Style of Drawing with Indian Ink," and "the same Subject, in Colours . . . [in] the finished State." The three plates in the fifth number "are finished Lessons for the Learner's Imitation and Practice." The final number contains a series of brief definitions and eight short "Lessons" in perspective drawing.

Many of the plates include rustic cottages, some with thatch roofs, surrounded by picturesque scenery. Lessons VI and VIII in the sixth number are exercises in drawing a house; the example shown in Figures 9 and 11 is two stories high and three windows wide.

233.1

OVER, Charles

Ornamental architecture in the Gothic, Chinese and modern taste, being above fifty intire new designs of plans, sections, elevations, &c. (many of which may be executed with roots of trees) for gardens, parks, forests, woods, canals, &c. Containing paling of several sorts, gates, garden seats, both close and open, umbrello's, alcoves, grotto's and grotesque seats, hermitages, triumphal arches, temples, banqueting houses and rooms, rotundo's, observatories, ice-houses, bridges, boats, and cascades, also, an obelisk or monument, with directions where proper to be erected, and the method how to execute them. The whole neatly engrav'd on fifty four copper-plates. From the designs of Charles Over, Architect.

London: Printed for Robert Sayer, 1758.

8 pp, 54 pls.

19.7 × 12.1 cm

MB

233.2

————

Ornamental architecture ⟨ . . . as 1758 . . . ⟩, and cascades. Also, an obelisk ⟨ . . . as 1758 . . . ⟩ Charles Over, Architect.

London: Printed for Robert Sayer, Map and Printseller, [n.d.].

8 pp, 54 pls.

20.3 × 12.7 cm

V&A

The text (pp. 3–8) consists of brief descriptions of each design and occasional remarks on siting and construction.

The 54 plates include elevations and plans of 44 designs for paling, railing, gates, seats, a retreat, a grotto, a hermitage, a hermit's cell, an arch, a banqueting room, a banqueting house, a "rotundo," an observatory, an ice house, bridges, boats, cascades, and an obelisk. The most common structures are temples, approximately ten feet in diameter and one or two stories high; most are not enclosed. Those that are enclosed (Plates 20, 29) consist of a single room with one door and several windows.

Over's plans and elevations are generally symmetrical and regular, based on squares, double squares, hexagons, octagons, decagons, and circles. The elevations are composed in a wide variety of styles. Many are Gothic, characterized by a profusion of crockets, finials, ogee arches, quatrefoils, and clustered Gothic columns. An "Umbrello'd" seat in "Indian" style (Plate 8) has a concave scalloped umbrella set on a central support. The "Chinese" structures (Plates 5–6, 18, 21, 23, 24, 37, 47) incorporate pagoda roofs with bells hanging from the corners and railings with "Chinese" fretwork. In addition there are designs for Chinese boats in Plates 50 and 51. The grotto, rustic seat, hermitage, hermit's cell, banqueting room, ice house, foot bridge, and two cascades (Plates 14–17, 27, 44, 49, 52–53) all are designed in a rustic style with bold rockwork, rough-hewn masonry, roots, and branches. Apart from an "Italian" iron railing (Plate 2) and a "Modern" iron gate (Plate 3), only three designs are in ostensibly Classical styles: an Ionic temple (Plate 39), a "Bridge in the Paladion Style" (Plate 46), and a rusticated obelisk (Plate 54).

234.1
OVERTON, Thomas Collins
Original designs of temples, and other ornamental buildings for parks and gardens, in the Greek, Roman, and Gothic taste. By Tho. Collins Overton.

London: Printed for the author, and sold by Henry Webley, Bookseller, 1766.

19 pp, 50 pls.

26.0 × 18.4 cm

MH

234.2

———

The temple builder's most useful companion, being fifty entire new original designs for pleasure and recreation; consisting of plans, elevations, and sections, in the Greek, Roman, and Gothic taste: calculated for the ornamenting of parks, forests, woods, gardens, canals, eminences, extensive views, mounts, vistos, islands, &c. Together with a full explanation, in letter press, to each design, and exact scales for measurement. By Thomas Collins Overton.

London: Printed for Henry Webley, 1766.

7–19 pp, frontisp. + 50 pls.

23.2 × 14.5 cm

NNC

234.3

———

———

London: Printed for I. Taylor, 1774.

15 pp, frontisp. + 50 pls.

25.4 × 16.5 cm

MB

In 1766 this book was issued under two different titles, as shown above. Both editions include a list of subscribers (pp. 3–5), text (pp. 7–19), and 50 plates.[1] The list of subscribers was omitted in the 1774 edition of *The Temple Builder's Companion*, and the text leaves were renumbered accordingly.

Although Overton issued this collection of designs at a time when the authority of Palladio and Inigo Jones was beginning to decline,[2] and several designs are in Gothic, Castellated, or Chinese styles, he still displayed his deference to the Palladians in the frontispiece. Two gentlemen in the foreground gesture toward statues of Jones and Palladio set on pedestals in front of a circular Ionic garden temple. An obelisk and a rectangular temple sit on hills in the distance. The inscription is a couplet from Pope:

Jones and Palladio to themselves restore,
And be whate'er Vitruvius was before.

The text consists of brief descriptions of each design, including dimensions and occasional information on materials, construction, and the client for whom the design was prepared. The plates include designs for 20 enclosed garden structures, including temples, summer houses, "rooms," "rotundos," "buildings," and a pavilion, seven open structures including alcoves, a "rotundo," a temple, and a pavilion, plus eight larger structures suitable for use as dwellings: a "cott," six villas, and one "building." The fully enclosed garden structures, in both Classical and Gothic styles, are simple one- and two-story buildings with circular, square, hexagonal, or octagonal plans, and usually just one room to a story. The "cott" (Plate 34) is not much larger: the ground floor includes two rooms, 7 1/2 feet square and ten feet by 12 feet, plus a projecting bay ten feet in diameter. Each of the villas is two stories high, with one principal room to a floor, the smallest being a hexagon 15 feet in diameter (Plates 41, 42) and the largest being a rectangle 18 feet 8 inches by 23 feet 4 inches (Plates 35, 36).[3]

The majority of Overton's designs are composed in a competent Neoclassical style. Most incorporate highly regular, symmetrical elevations and plans based on elementary geometric figures. In many cases Overton superimposed dotted lines to illustrate these figures, which include circles, semicircles, squares, double squares, octagons, and hexagons. One of the most elegant designs is the villa in Plate 45, two stories high and 20 feet square in plan. The elevation includes a rusticated basement and an upper story composed of a Venetian window set in the center of a wall framed by Ionic columns and a pediment. By superimposing geometric figures on the elevation Overton illustrated the proportionality of his design: the top and corners of the pediment are circumscribed within a circle that touches the bottom of the elevation; and another, smaller circle touches the top of the pediment, the outer edges of the Ionic columns on the upper story, and the dividing line between upper and lower stories.

Overton's designs in Gothic style are characterized by a profusion of crockets, finials, ogee arches, cinquefoil arches, clustered columns, and occasional crenellations. Three designs for villas are important early examples of the Castellated style, with crenellations, finials, ogee domes, rusticated window openings, and trefoil or round-headed arches; two of the three Castellated villas have three-story turrets projecting from all four corners.[4] One structure, an octagonal "room" (Plate 3) has a roof described by Overton as "Chinese." He did not specify the style of the "cott" in Plate 34, but the rubble masonry, thatch roof, and pointed windows are clearly in rustic style.

1. The copy of the 1766 *Temple Builder's Companion* in the Avery Library is wanting the list of subscribers, but the copy of the same edition in the Bodleian Library does include this list.

2. Cf. the veneration of Jones and Palladio in the first two-thirds of the century in Colen Campbell's *Vitruvius Britannicus* (1715 and later; *q.v.*); William Kent's *Designs of Inigo Jones* (1727; *q.v.*); John Vardy's *Some Designs of Mr. Inigo Jones* (1744; *q.v.*); and Isaac Ware's *Designs of Inigo Jones* (n.d.; *q.v.*). English translations of Palladio's *Quattro Libri* appeared in 1663 (trans. Godfrey Richards), 1716–1720 (trans. Giacomo Leoni), 1729 (trans. Colen Campbell), and 1738 (trans. Isaac Ware).

3. There is one exception: the villa in Plates 46 and 47 is one story high, and consists of a central room 15 feet square, flanked by two rooms each ten feet by 12 feet, one for "retirement" and the other for a servant.

4. Further on the origins of the Castellated style see A. J. Rowan, "The Castle Style in British Domestic Architecture in the Eighteenth and Early Nineteenth Centuries," Ph.D. diss., Cambridge University, Magdalene College, 1965.

235.1

The Oxford encyclopaedia; or, dictionary of arts, sciences, and general literature. Illustrated with nearly two hundred elegant engravings. By the Rev. W. Harris; J. A. Stewart, A.M.; C. Butler, Esq.; and the Rev. J. H. Hinton, A.M. Assisted by other literary gentlemen. Vol. I.

Oxford: Printed by Bartlett and Hinton, for Thomas Kelly, London, 1828.

[*Six volumes: Oxford, 1828. The title and imprint for Vol. I are given above.*]

Art. "Civil architecture," II, 529–544; 8 pls (numbered 13*, 16, 17, 14, 15, 17*, 18, 18*).
Art. "Perspective," V, 322–332; 5 pls (numbered 121–125).

26.8 × 21.6 cm

DLC

The article titled "Civil Architecture" is divided into four parts. The first treats the history of architecture, beginning with the origins of building in the primitive hut, progressing through the architecture of Egypt, Assyria, and Persia, and describing the origins of the orders in Greece and Rome. There are additional remarks on other aspects of Greek and Roman architecture, followed by a discussion of Saxon, Norman, and Gothic architecture, and very brief comments on the Italian Renaissance. The first part concludes with a history of English architecture from Wren through Wyatt. The second part is a discussion of materials in architecture. The third part concerns styles, including Egyptian, "Hindoo," Chaldean, Median, Persian, Greek, Roman, Saxon, Norman, Gothic, and "modern." The third part concludes with a discussion of the five orders, Persians, caryatids, termini, pilasters, attics, pedestals, basements, pediments, niches, colonnades, and arcades. The fourth part, which concerns construction, treats foundations, walls, chimneys, roofs, domes, groins, floors, ceilings, stairs, balusters, doors, gates, and windows. This part concludes with a discussion of floor plans and other aspects of domestic architecture, much of which is taken from Robert Lugar's *Architectural Sketches* (1805; *q.v.*). At the end of the article there is a list of a few recommended treatises published within the previous 70 years.

Eight plates accompany this article. The first (Plate 13*) depicts three primitive huts and a primordial Corinthian capital, copied from Sir William Chambers's *Treatise* (1759; *q.v.*), plus a "Collection" of 12 "Fragments" of Egyptian architecture. The orders appear in Plates 14, 15, and 17. In Plate 16 there are examples of a "Saxon" arch and Gothic tracery. Plate 17 depicts six "Saxon Capitals" that appeared previously in the third edition of the *Encyclopaedia Britannica* (1797; *q.v.*). Plate 17* contains designs for roof trusses. Plates 18 and 18* contain plans and elevations for villas that previously appeared in Plates XXIX through XXXII of Lugar's *Architectural Sketches*. The first design is a two-story villa, five windows wide, with a hall, dining room, drawing room, and library arranged around the four sides of a central core containing a "Strong Closet" and a staircase. The upper story contains five chambers and two dressing rooms. The ground-floor elevation incorporates floor-length windows with semicircular tops. The second design, a "Villa in the Eastern Style," has a large dome in the center, minarets above the four corners, and profuse Indian ornament. The ground floor contains a dining room, drawing room, ante-room, library, and dressing room; upstairs there are six bedrooms. The design is based on a view of the "Mausoleum of Sultan Purveiz, Near Allahabad," Plate 22 in Volume I of Thomas Daniell's *Oriental Scenery* (London, 1796).

The article on perspective begins with introductory remarks and a history of perspective. The "Principles and Practice" of perspective are explained in a series of problems and demonstrations on pages 324–329. Remarks on the centrolinead are followed by an exercise in drawing a house, taken from Peter Nicholson's *Rudiments of Practical Perspective* (1822; *q.v.*). The article concludes with a discussion of anamorphosis and a reference to Charles Hayter's *Introduction to Perspective* (1813; *q.v.*). The plates contain geometric figures and diagrams, plus illustrations of pyramids, tables, chairs, stairs, and other objects in perspective. Plates 124 and 125 contain several figures borrowed from Nicholson's *Rudiments*, depicting plans, elevations, and perspective views of a house. It is two stories high, plus a dormer story, and three windows wide. The entrance is in the center of the side elevation, which is one window wide.

236.1

PAIN, William (1730?–1790?)

The builder's companion, and workman's general assistant: demonstrating, after the most easy and practical method, all the principal rules of architecture, from the plan to the ornamental finish; illustrated with a greater number of useful and familiar examples than any work of that kind hitherto published; with clear and ample instructions, annexed to each subject or number, on the same plate; being not only useful but necessary to all masons, bricklayers, plasterers, carpenters, joiners, and others concerned in the several branches of building, &c. Also, the figure, description, and use of a new-invented joint-rule; so calculated as to render easy the drawing of any figure, architrave, frize, cornice, or moulding, that can be required to any given scale. The whole correctly engraven on seventy-seven folio copper-plates, from the designs of William Pain. The subjects herein chiefly consist of,

I. Of foundations, walls, and their diminutions, fitness of chimneys, and proportion of light to rooms, with the due scantlings of timber to be cut for building, &c.

II. Great variety of geometrical, elliptic, and polygon figures, with rules for their formation. Centering of all sorts, for groinds, brick and stone arches, &c. both circular and splay'd, also with circular sofits in a circular wall: many examples for glewing and vaneering, niches, &c. with rules for tracing the cover of curve-line roofs, piers, vases, pedestals for sun= dials, busts, &c. and their most suitable proportions.

III. General directions for framing floors and partitions, truss-roofs, &c. and methods to find the length and backing of hips, strait or curve lines to any pitch, square or bevel.

IV. Of stair-cases, variously constructed; the methods of working ramp and twist-rails—profils of stairs to shew the manner of setting carriages for the steps, also the framing of string-boards and rails, and likewise of fixing them.

V. The five orders of architecture from Palladio, with the rule for gauging flutes and fillets on a diminish'd column, by a method extremely easy, and intirely new.

VI. Doors, windows, frontispieces, chimney-pieces, cornices, mouldings, &c. truly proportion'd, in a plain and genteel taste.

VII. Sacred ornaments, viz. altar-pieces, pulpits, monuments. &c.

VIII. Gothic architecture, being a various collection of columns, entablatures, arches, doors, windows, chimney-pieces, and other decorations in that prevailing taste—and it may be noted of these, as of all the foregoing examples, that they are immediately adapted to workmen, and may be executed by the meanest capacity.

London: Printed for the author, and Robert Sayer, 1758.

[iii] + 4 pp, 5–81 pls (= "pages").

35.2 × 21.6 cm

V&A

236.2

The builder's companion, and workman's general assistant: demonstrating, after the most easy and practical method, all the principal rules of architecture, from the plan to the ornamental finish; illustrated with a greater number of useful and familiar examples than any work of that kind hitherto published; with clear and ample instructions annexed to each subject or number, on the same plate; being not only useful but necessary to all masons, bricklayers, plasterers, carpenters, joiners, and others concerned in the several branches of building, &c. The whole correctly engraven on 102 folio copper-plates, containing upwards of seven hundred designs on the following subjects, &c.

I. Of foundations, walls, and their diminutions, fitness of chimneys, and proportion of light to rooms, with due scantlings of timber to be cut for building, &c.

II. Great variety of geometrical, elliptic, and polygon figures, with rules for their formation. Centering of all sorts for groinds, brick and stone arches, &c. both circular and splay'd, also with circular sofits in a circular wall: many examples for glewing and vaneering, niches, &c. with rules for tracing the cover of curve-line roofs, piers, vases, pedestals for sun= dials, busts, &c. and their most suitable proportions.

III. General directions for framing floors and partitions, truss-roofs, &c. and methods to find the length and backing of hips, strait or curve lines to any pitch, square or bevel.

IV. Of stair-cases, variously constructed; the methods of working ramp and twist-rails—profils of stairs to shew the manner of setting carriages for the steps, also the framing of string-boards and rails, and likewise of fixing them.

V. The five orders of architecture from Palladio, with the rule for gauging flutes and fillets on a diminish'd column, by a method extremely easy, and intirely new.

VI. Doors, windows, frontispieces, chimney-pieces, cornices, mouldings, &c. truly proportion'd, in a plain and genteel taste.

VII. Sacred ornaments, viz. altar-pieces, pulpits, monuments, &c.

VIII. Gothic architecture, being a various collection of columns, entabla-tures, arches, doors windows, chimney-pieces, and other decorations in that prevailing taste—and it may be noted of these, as of all the foregoing examples, that they are immediately adapted to workmen, and may be executed by the meanest capacity. By William Pain, Architect and Joiner.

London: Printed for the author, and Robert Sayer, 1762.

[iii] + 4 pp, 5–81 pls (= "pages"), 25 additional pls (plus, in this copy, an extra copy of "page" 11).

36.2 × 23.5 cm

MBAt

236.3

The builder's companion, and workman's general assistant; demonstrating, after the most easy and practical method, all the principal rules of ar-chitecture, from the plan to the ornamental finish; illustrated with a greater number of useful and familiar examples than any work of that kind hitherto published; with clear and ample instructions annexed to each subject or number, on the same plate, with estimates of materials and workmanship; being not only useful to all masons, bricklayers, plasterers, carpenters, joiners, and others concerned in the several branches of building, &c. but also necessary for gentlemen, who will be hereby enabled to know the exact expence of any building, alteration, or repair. The whole correctly engraved on 92 folio copper-plates, containing upwards of seven hundred designs on the following subjects, &c.

I. Of foundations, walls, and their diminutions, fitness of chimneys, and proportion of light to rooms, with the due scantlings of timber to be cut for building, &c.

II. Great variety of geometrical, elliptic, and polygon figures, with rules for their formation, centering of all sorts of groins, brick and stone arches, &c. both circular and splayed, also with circular soffits in a circular wall: many examples for glewing and vaneering, niches, &c. with rules for tracing the cover of curve-line roofs, piers, vases, pedestals for sun-dials, busts, &c. and their most suitable proportions.

III. General directions for framing floors and partitions, truss-roofs, &c. and methods to find the length and backing of hips, straight or curve lines to any pitch, square, or bevel.

IV. Of stair-cases, variously constructed; the methods of working ramp and twist-rails; profils of stairs to shew the manner of setting carriages for the steps, also the framing of string-boards and rails, and likewise of fixing them.

V. The five orders of architecture from Palladio, with the rule for guaging flutes and fillets on a diminished column, by a method extremely easy, and entirely new.

VI. Doors, windows, frontispieces, chimney-pieces, cornices, mouldings, &c. truly proportioned, in a plain and genteel taste.

VII. Sacred ornaments, viz. altar-pieces, pulpits, &c.

VIII. Gothic architecture, being a various collection of columns, entablatures, arches, doors, windows, chimney-pieces, and other decorations in that prevailing taste—and it may be noted of these, as of all the foregoing examples, that they are immediately adapted to workmen, and may be executed by the meanest capacity.

IX. Plans and elevations of elegant buildings, green-houses, hot-houses, temples, seats for gardens, parks, &c.

By William Pain, Architect and Joiner. The second edition, with many improvements and additions by the author.

London: Printed for Robert Sayer, Map and Printseller, 1765.

[ii] + 4 + 10 pp, 5–92 pls (= "pages").

36.2 × 23.5 cm

CtY

236.4

The builder's companion, and workman's general assistant; demonstrating, after the most easy and practical method, all the principal rules of architecture, from the plan to the ornamental finish; illustrated with a greater number of useful and familiar examples than any work of that kind hitherto published; with clear and ample instructions annexed to each subject or number, on the same plate, with estimates of materials and workmanship; being not only useful to all masons, bricklayers, plasterers, carpenters, joiners, and others concerned in the several branches of building, &c. but also necessary for gentlemen, who will be hereby enabled to know the exact expence of any building, alteration, or repair. The whole correctly engraved on 92 folio copper-plates, containing upwards of seven hundred designs on the following subjects, &c.

I. Of foundations, walls, and their diminutions, fitness of chimneys, and proportion of light to rooms, with due scantlings of timber to be cut for buildings, &c.

II. Great variety of geometrical, elliptic, and polygon figures, with rules for their formation, centering of all sorts for groins, brick and stone arches, &c. both circular and splayed, also with circular soffits in a circular wall; many examples for gluing and vaneering niches, &c. with rules for tracing the cover of curve-line roofs, piers, vases, pedestals for sun-dials, busts, &c. and their most suitable proportions.

III. General directions for framing floors and partitions, truss-roofs, &c. and methods to find the length and backing of hips, straight or curve lines to any pitch, square, or bevel.

IV. Of stair-cases, variously constructed; the methods of working ramp and twist rails; profils of stairs to shew the manner of setting carriages for the steps; also the framing of string-boards and rails, and likewise of fixing them.

V. The five orders of architecture from Palladio, with the rule for gauging flutes and fillets on a diminished column, by a method extremely easy, and entirely new.

VI. Doors, windows, frontispieces, chimney-pieces, cornices, mouldings, &c. truly proportioned, in a plain and genteel taste.

VII. Sacred ornaments, viz. altar-pieces, pulpits, &c.

VIII. Gothic architecture, being a various collection of columns, entablatures, arches, doors, windows, chimney-pieces, and other decorations in that prevailing taste—and it may be noted of these, as of all the foregoing examples, that they are immediately adapted to workmen, and may be executed by the meanest capacity.

IX. Plans and elevations of elegant buildings, green-houses, hot-houses, temples, seats for gardens, parks, &c.

By William Pain, Architect and Joiner. The third edition, with many improvements and additions by the author.

London: Printed for Robert Sayer, Map and Printseller, 1769.

[*In this copy, the original title page has been replaced by a photocopy.*]

1 printed leaf, 4 + *1–*10 pp, 5–92 pls (= "pages"; *"page" 69 wanting in this copy*).

38.1 × 24.1 cm

MH

236.5 †

The builder's companion.

[London]: Laurie, ca. 1810.

f°

Reference: ECB

The first two editions, dated 1758 and 1762, include a preface (one leaf, recto only), a table of contents (one leaf, advertisements on verso), and four pages of text (pp. 1–4) containing essays on foundations and "the Proportion of the Openings of Chimneys." The 77 plates, printed individually on separate leaves, are labeled as "pages" 5 through 81. Many of the plates include lengthy inscriptions describing or explaining the subjects represented. The 1762 edition at the Boston Athenaeum contains 25 additional plates, interleaved with the rest, depicting vases, rails, pedestals, moldings, architraves, and Gothic moldings and entablatures. The next two editions (1765 and 1769) contain a table of contents (one leaf, advertisements on verso), the four-page text found in previous editions, an additional ten pages of text concerning rates and prices, and 88 plates, labeled as "pages" 5 through 92. The new plates include designs for Gothic ornaments, two "Gentlemens Houses," several garden seats and temples in Classical as well as Gothic styles, two bridges, a greenhouse, and a hothouse. According to the ECB, a final edition appeared in 1810. The discussion below is based on examination of the 1758 edition, except as noted.

In the brief preface Pain stated that "in all Things Order is to be observed," and therefore in architecture "every Part and Member [must] have its right Order and due Proportion." Since Palladio was among those who had brought architecture to a state of "Perfection," Pain presented the five orders according to Palladio, now "laid down . . . by an intire NEW SCALE."

All the subjects illustrated in the plates are clearly described on the title page except centers for moldings (Plate 30) and intercolumniations for colonnades, arcades, and porticoes (Plate 31). Among the more fully elaborated designs there are five piers, 11 vases, six pedestals, seven frontispieces, eight half pediments, five windows, seven doors, 14 chimneypieces, one altarpiece, two pulpits, two monuments, and three shields. Plates 67 through 81 depict subjects in Gothic style, including five "orders,"[1] several detailed designs for columns, bases, capitals, and entablatures, 13 arches, plus moldings, cornices, frontispieces,[2] doors, windows, and chimneypieces.

The only two designs for dwellings appear in Plate 86 in the 1765 and 1769 editions. Each of these houses is three stories high; one is five openings wide and the other is seven.

1. These are closely related to Batty Langley's designs. See Alistair Rowan, "Batty Langley's Gothic," *Studies in Memory of David Talbot Rice*, ed. Giles Robertson and George Henderson (Edinburgh: Edinburgh University Press, 1975) p. 208.

2. These too are derived from Langley. See Rowan, loc. cit.

237.1
PAIN, William (1730?–1790?)
The builder's golden rule, or the youth's sure guide: containing the greatest variety of ornamental and useful designs in architecture and carpentry, with the most ready practical methods of executing the same, from the

plan to the ornamental finish, in the most prevailing modern taste. The whole correctly engraved, on 104 copper-plates, with a full explanation in letter-press. To which is added, an estimate of prices for materials and labour, and labour only, with references to the respective designs. By William Pain. . . .

London: Printed for the author, by H. D. Steel, 1781.

iii pp, 1 printed leaf, 18 pp, 1 printed leaf, 58 pp, 104 pls.

21.0 × 12.7 cm

NN

237.2

The builder's golden rule, ⟨ . . . as 1781 . . . ⟩ engraved, on 106 copper= plates, ⟨ . . . as 1781 . . . ⟩ designs. By William Pain. . . . The second edition.

London: Printed for the author, by H. D. Steel, 1782.

1 printed leaf, iv + 18 pp, 1 printed leaf, 58 pp, 106 pls.

20.3 × 12.7 cm

CtY

237.3

The builder's golden rule, ⟨ . . . as 1781 . . . ⟩ engraved, on 100 copper= plates, ⟨ . . . as 1781 . . . ⟩ added, a list of prices ⟨ . . . as 1781 . . . ⟩ designs. By William Pain. . . . The third edition, with additions by the author.

London: Printed for and sold by the author, by H. D. Steel, 1787.

1 printed leaf, iv + 18 pp, 1 printed leaf, 54 pp, 100 pls.

20.7 × 12.7 cm

MnU

Over the course of three editions Pain freely adjusted the numbering and order of his plates. The first edition has 98 consecutively numbered plates, plus six more numbered to face Plates 9, 19, 20, 63, 67, and 70. In the 1782 edition plates were added to face Plates 8, 15, and 55, and the plate facing Plate 9 was omitted. In the final edition plates numbered 95 through 98 were omitted, as were those facing Plates 19, 20, 67, and 70; two new plates were added to face Plates 7 and 36, resulting in a net loss of six plates from 1782 to 1787. The subject matter of like numbered plates in the first two editions is generally the same, but in the final edition most subjects were renumbered.[1]

The first part of the text is a series of plate descriptions, giving dimensions and instructions for builders and artisans. Some plates are not described at all. At the end of the volume is a list of prices for materials and labor with occasional references to designs illustrated in the plates.

The plates depict geometric constructions, timber framing, arches, trusses, domes, the orders, moldings, frontispieces for doors, chimney-pieces, staircases, a greenhouse, a hothouse, chimney flues, a church, a pulpit, an altarpiece, ceilings, shutters, and a coach house. Pain included three designs for dwellings. The smallest is a farm house two stories high and three windows wide, with a yard and offices (1787, Plate XCI). The ground floor includes a parlor, kitchen, dairy, "scaulding room," and, in ells, a laundry and brewhouse. Stringcourses, a pediment, and a modest "frontispiece" around the entrance are the sole ornaments. The facade of the four-story "Double town-house" (1787, Plate LXXXIII) includes shallow recessed arches on the top and ground floors, with colossal Ionic pilasters separating the windows of the two middle floors. The "Gentleman's Country House" (1787, Plates LXXXI–LXXXII) is two stories high and nine windows wide, with a two-story Corinthian portico framing the three central bays.

1. Plates numbered 79 through 94 in the 1787 edition correspond to plates numbered 77 through 92 in the 1782 edition. Some subjects retained the same plate number in all three editions. This title, like others by Pain, awaits a detailed collation of editions.

238.1
PAIN, William (1730?–1790?)
The builder's pocket-treasure; or, Palladio delineated and explained, in such a manner as to render that most excellent author plain and intelligible to the meanest capacity, in which not only the theory, but the practical part of architecture has been carefully attended to. Illustrated with new and useful designs of frontispieces, chimney-pieces, &c. with their bases, capitals and entablatures, at large for practice; architrave frontispieces, cornices and mouldings for the inside of rooms, &c. the construction of stairs, with their ramp and twist rails; framing of floors, roofs, and partitions; with the method of finding the lengths and backing of hips streight or curvi-linear; the tracing of groins, angle-brackets, splay'd or circular soffits; with plans and elevations of a dwelling-house, hot-house, garden temple, seat and bridge; and a table of scantlings for cutting timber for building. The whole neatly and correctly engraved on forty-four copper plates, with printed explanations to face each plate. By William Pain. Engraved by Isaac Taylor.

London: Printed for W. Owen, 1763.

iv + 69 pp (incl. 44 pls).

18.7 × 11.4 cm

CtY

238.2

The builder's pocket-treasure; ⟨ . . . as 1763 . . . ⟩ bases, capitals, and entablatures, ⟨ . . . as 1763 . . . ⟩ frontispieces, cornices, and ⟨ . . . as 1763 . . . ⟩ the length and backing of hips, streight ⟨ . . . as 1763 . . . ⟩ Taylor. Second edition, with an appendix of eleven copper plates, with explanations.

London: Printed for W. Owen, 1766.

iv + 92 pp (incl. 55 pls).

19.3 × 11.4 cm

RPJCB

238.3

The builder's pocket-treasure; ⟨ . . . as 1763 . . . ⟩, chimney-pieces, &c. their bases, capitals, and entablatures, ⟨ . . . as 1763 . . . ⟩ cornices, and mouldings ⟨ . . . as 1763 . . . ⟩ the length and backing of hips, streight ⟨ . . . as 1763 . . . ⟩ soffits; besides plans ⟨ . . . as 1763 . . . ⟩ plates. With printed explanations to face each plate. By William Pain. Engraved by Isaac Taylor. A new edition, with an appendix of eleven copper plates, and explanations.

London: Printed for W. Owen, 1785.

iv + 92 pp (incl. 55 pls).

19.4 × 11.4 cm

MH

238.4

The builder's pocket-treasure. In which not only the theory, but the practical parts of architecture are carefully explained. Illustrated with useful designs of frontispieces, chimney-pieces, &c. bases, capitals, and entablatures at large architrave frontispieces, cornices and mouldings for the inside of rooms, &c. the construction of stairs, with their ramp and twist rails; framing of floors, roofs, and partitions; with the method of finding the length and backing of hips, straight or curvi-linear; the tracing of groins, angle-brackets, splay'd or circular soffits; with some plans and elevations, and a table of scantlings for building timbers, &c. &c. Correctly engraved on fifty-five plates. With printed explanations to each. By William Pain. . . . A new edition.

London: Printed for I. and J. Taylor, 1793.

iv + 92 pp (incl. 55 pls).

19.4 × 12.1 cm

CtY

In editions published in 1766 and afterward, Pain included an "Appendix" with 12 additional pages of letterpress and 11 new plates. The discussion below is based on examination of the 1785 edition.

In the Preface (pp. iii–iv) Pain noted that men of "Learning and Abilities" far superior to his own had written architectural treatises, but he complained that unless the reader had "a Capacity almost equal to that of the Writer," he would learn little (p. iii). Pain esteemed Palladio as a great "Master" of architecture and therefore conceived his own book as an attempt to make Palladio's "Performance" useful to builders and workmen. He intentionally made *The Builder's Pocket Treasure* small enough that a workman could "have his whole Trade in his Pocket" (pp. iii–iv). In terms of style, Pain promised "Plainness and Perspicuity. Elegance of Style would be of no Advantage to the Subject," and indeed would detract from his goal, which was "to obviate and remove the many Difficulties which common Mechanics usually meet with in perusing Books of Architecture" (pp. iii–iv).

The pagination of the text (92 pages) includes 37 pages of letterpress and 55 plates numbered as text pages. The half title for the "Appendix" is not included in this pagination. Most text pages were intended to face specific plates, and contain instructions for drawing or constructing objects shown in those plates.[1]

The subjects of most plates are adequately represented on the title page. In addition the Tuscan, Doric, Ionic, and Corinthian orders are illustrated in detail on Plates IV through XI. Plates XXXIX through XLIV contain plans and elevations for nine structures: a house, offices for the house, a hothouse, a greenhouse, a bridge, a garden seat, an alcove, a garden temple, and a Chinese temple.

The house (Plate XXXIX) is three stories high and seven windows wide, with a projecting three-sided bay in the center of the facade rising the full height of the elevation. Ornament is limited to a modest "frontispiece" surrounding the entrance, a cornice, and stringcourses between stories. Of the six principal rooms on the ground floor, the largest is 24 feet by 18 feet. The offices (Plate XXXIX), housed in a separate structure, include stables, a brewhouse, a coach house, a laundry, and a saddle room. The one-story greenhouse (Plate XLI) is seven openings wide. All the windows are Gothic, with pointed arches and complex latticework. Nevertheless there is a Classical pediment with raking cornice above the central three windows. The garden "Seat" (Plate XLII) is simply a bench, while the "Alcove" (Plate XLII) is half an octagon in plan, 15 1/2 feet wide. The front opening of the "Alcove" is framed by three trefoil arches, and the whole is topped by a bell shaped roof. The "Compound Temple to stand on a Mount in a Garden or Pleasure Ground" (Plate XLIII) is a single enclosed room, 12 feet square in plan, plus semicircles eight feet in diameter added to each side of the square. The Chinese temple (Plate XLIV) is shown in elevation only. Two stories high in the center and five windows wide on the ground story, the design is covered with latticework and topped by a pagoda roof with bells hanging from the corners.

1. On pages 3, 6, and 35 there are general remarks on the Tuscan, Doric, Ionic, and Corinthian orders and on the proportions of chimneypieces. Page 63 contains a table of scantlings for cutting timber.

239.1

PAIN, William (1730?–1790?), and James PAIN

Pain's British Palladio: or, the builder's general assistant. Demonstrating, in the most easy and practical method, all the principal rules of architecture, from the ground plan to the ornamental finish. Illustrated with several new and useful designs of houses, with their plans, elevations, and sections. Also, clear and ample instructions, annexed to each subject, in letter= press; with a list of prices for materials and labour, and labour only.

This work will be universally useful to all carpenters, bricklayers, masons, joiners, plaisterers, and others, concerned in the several branches of building, &c. comprehending the following subjects, viz.

Plans, elevations, and sections, of gentlemen's houses.

Designs for doors, chimneys, and ceilings, with their proper embellishments, in the most modern taste.

A great variety of mouldings, for base and surbase architraves, imposts, friezes, and cornices, with their proper ornaments, for practice, drawn to half-size: to which are added, scales for enlarging or lessening at pleasure, if required.

Also, great variety of stair-cases; shewing the practical method of executing them, in any case required, viz. groins, angle-brackets, circular circular flewing and winding soffits, domes, sky-lights, &c. all made plain and easy to the meanest capacity.

The proportion of windows for the light to rooms.

Preparing foundations; the proportion of chimneys to rooms, and sections of flews.

The principal timbers properly laid out on each plan, viz. the manner of framing the roofs, and finding the length and backing of hips, either square or bevel. Scantlings of the timbers, figured in proportion to their bearing. The method for trussing girders, scarfing plates, &c.

And many other articles, particularly useful to all persons in the building profession.

The whole correctly engraved on forty-two folio copper-plates, from the original designs of William and James Pain.

London: Printed by H. D. Steel; for the authors, 1786.

[i] + 14 pp, 42 pls.

43.2 × 27.6 cm

MH

239.2

———

Pain's British Palladio: or, the builder's general assistant. Demonstrating in ⟨ . . . as 1786 . . . ⟩ at pleasure. Also, great variety ⟨ . . . as 1786 . . . ⟩ laid out, on each plan, ⟨ . . . as 1786 . . . ⟩ William and James Pain.

London: Printed for I. and J. Taylor, 1788.

4 + 14 pp, 42 pls.

41.6 × 27.3 cm

NNC

239.3

Pain's British Palladio: ⟨ . . . as 1786 . . . ⟩ friezes and cornices, ⟨ . . . as 1786 . . . ⟩ at pleasure. Also, great variety ⟨ . . . as 1786 . . . ⟩ laid out, on each plan, ⟨ . . . as 1786 . . . ⟩ William and James Pain.

London: Printed for I. and J. Taylor, 1790.

4 + 16 pp, 42 pls.

42.4 × 26.0 cm

MH

239.4

Pain's British Palladio: ⟨ . . . as 1786 . . . ⟩ instructions annexed ⟨ . . . as 1786 . . . ⟩ others concerned ⟨ . . . as 1786 . . . ⟩ sections of gentlemen's ⟨ . . . as 1786 . . . ⟩ friezes and cornices, ⟨ . . . as 1786 . . . ⟩ at pleasure. Also, great variety ⟨ . . . as 1786 . . . ⟩ laid out, on each plan, ⟨ . . . as 1786 . . . ⟩ William and James Pain.

London: Printed for I. and J. Taylor, 1793.

4 + 16 pp, 42 pls.

42.2 × 26.0 cm

MBAt

239.5

Pain's British Palladio: or, the builder's general assistant. Demonstrating, in the most easy and practical method, all the principal rules of architecture, from the ground plan to the ornamental finish. Illustrated with several new and useful designs of houses, with their plans, elevations, and sections. Also, clear and ample instructions annexed to each subject, in letter-press; with a list of prices for materials and labour, and labour only. This work will be universally useful to all carpenters, bricklayers, masons, joiners, plaisterers, and others concerned in the several branches of building, &c. comprehending the following subjects, viz.
Plans, elevations, and sections of gentlemen's houses.
Designs for doors, chimneys, and ceilings, with their proper embellishments, in the most modern taste.
A great variety of base and surbase mouldings, architraves, imposts, friezes and cornices, with their proper ornaments, for practice, drawn to half= size: to which are added, scales for enlarging or diminishing at pleasure.
Also, great variety of stair-cases; shewing the practical methods of executing them, in any case required: also, groins, angle-brackets, circular circular flewing and winding soffits, domes, sky-lights, &c. all made plain and easy to the meanest capacity.
The proportion of windows for the light to rooms.
Preparing foundations; the proportion of chimneys to rooms, and sections of flews.

The principal timbers properly laid out, on each plan, viz. the manner of framing the roofs, and finding the length and backing of hips, either square or bevel. Scantlings of the timbers, figured in proportion to their bearing. The method of trussing girders, scarfing plates, &c.
And many other articles, particularly useful to all persons in the building profession.
The whole correctly engraved on forty-two folio copper-plates, from the original designs of William and James Pain.
A new edition, corrected.

London: Printed for I. and J. Taylor, 1797.

4 + 16 pp, 42 pls.

41.9 × 26.0 cm

MnU

239.6

Pain's British Palladio: ⟨ . . . as 1797 . . . ⟩, circular-circular flewing ⟨ . . . as 1797 . . . ⟩ corrected.

London: Printed by W. Stratford; for J. Taylor, 1804.

4 + 16 pp, 42 pls.

42.2 × 26.7 cm

CtY

Although the pagination varies among editions, the text of all editions includes four parts: a list of the contents, a table of prices for labor and materials, descriptions of the plates, and estimates of prices for materials and labor "adapted to" the designs illustrated in the plates.

The lengthy title accurately reflects the variety of subjects illustrated in the plates, from a large country mansion to details of moldings and staircase railings. The unusually large scale of the designs, especially for a builder's manual, reflects the authors' pretensions to have compiled a comprehensive treatise on British domestic architecture. But the lack of a substantial text and the inclusion of just five houses, all very large in scale, hardly establish this work as a British equivalent of any treatise by Palladio.

The plate descriptions serve as legends, giving the dimensions, proportions, and names of individual rooms or structural members that are illustrated. In some cases there are directions for artisans: e.g., the description to Plate XXXVIII includes directions for laying out groin vaults, and within the description of Plate XXXIX there is a separate section titled "Directions for preparing Foundations" (p. 6).[1]

The first 27 plates include elevations, plans, sections, and some interior details for five large dwellings, all in Palladian style. The first design, for "a gentleman's house" (Plates I–IV), is three stories high and seven windows wide. The second design (Plates V–XI) is similar, but with a two-story portico of engaged Ionic columns on the principal facade. This design is illustrated in one elevation, two sections, five plans, seven diagrams of chimney flues, and two designs for chimneypieces. The principal floor includes a hall, a dining room, a withdrawing room, a common sitting room, a "dressing room for the master," a smoking room, a music room, a water closet, and staircases. The third design is a "town-house" with a rusticated ground story and Ionic pilasters above.[2] The principal floor includes a dining room, withdrawing room, hall, common sitting parlor, breakfast room, saloon, water closet, and stairs. The illustrations of this design in Plates XII through XV include a facade, two sections, and four plans. Seven plates of chimneypieces follow. The fourth design, "a gentleman's country-house" (Plate XXIII) is three stories high and nine windows wide, but uncomfortably proportioned—too wide and too low—and awkwardly ornamented with a Venetian window on the principal story surmounted by an attenuated shell-like motif with a segmental window in its center. The final design, also for a gentleman's country house, is over 370 feet wide. The central pavilion, 11 windows wide and three stories high, is connected by low wings to end pavilions two stories high and five windows wide. The principal floor includes a hall, a drawing room, a withdrawing room, a common sitting room, a great dining room, a little dining room, a hunting room, a "state-room for the reception of company," a library, and "a tribune, which has a gallery." Plates XXIV through XXVII illustrate this design in one elevation, two sections, three plans, and four interior elevations of the drawing room.

The subsequent plates include staircases, ceilings, doorways, moldings, capitals, and arches, with details illustrating techniques of construction as well as decorative schemes.

1. This and subsequent quotations are from the 1786 edition.

2. This design was reproduced, minus some ornament, in Pain's *Practical House Carpenter* (1788; *q.v.*).

240.1
PAIN, William (1730?–1790?)
The practical builder, or workman's general assistant: shewing the most approved and easy methods for drawing and working the whole or separate part of any bulding, as the use of the tramel for groins, angle-brackets, niches, &c. semi-circular arches on flewing jambs, the preparing and making their soffits. Rules of carpentry; to find the length and backing of hips, strait or curved; trusses for roofs, domes, &c.—trussing of girders, sections of floors, &c. The proportion of the five orders, in their general and particular parts, gluing of columns, stair-cases with their ramp and twist rails, fixing the carriages, newels, &c. Frontispieces, chimney-pieces, ceilings, cornices, architraves, &c. in the newest taste. With plans and elevations of gentlemens and farm-houses, yards, barns, &c. By William Pain, Architect and Joiner. Engraved on eighty-three plates.

London: Printed for I. Taylor, 1774.

6 printed leaves, 83 pls.

25.3 × 21.0 cm

MH

240.2

The practical builder, ⟨ . . . as 1774 . . . ⟩ building; as ⟨ . . . as 1774 . . . ⟩ parts; gluing of of [*sic*] columns, ⟨ . . . as 1774 . . . ⟩, cielings, ⟨ . . . as 1774 . . . ⟩ taste; with ⟨ . . . as 1774 . . . ⟩ plates.

London: Printed for I. Taylor, 1776.

5 printed leaves, 83 pls [*pl. XXVIII is wanting in this copy*].

24.8 × 21.0 cm

CtY

240.3

The practical builder, or workman's general assistant; shewing the most approved and easy methods for drawing and working the whole or separate part of any building; as the use of the tramel for groins, angle-brackets, niches, &c. semi-circular arches on flewing jambs, the preparing and making their soffits. Rules of carpentry; to find the length and backing of hips, straight or curved.—Trusses for roofs, domes, &c.—Trussing of girders, sections of floors, &c. The proportion of the five orders, in their general and particular parts.—Glewing of columns, stair-cases with their ramp and twist rails; fixing the carriages, newels, &c. Frontispieces, chimney-pieces, cielings, cornices, architraves, &c. in the newest taste.—With plans and elevations of gentlemens' and farm-houses, yards, barns, &c. A new edition, revised and corrected by the author William Pain, Architect and Joiner. Engraved on eighty-three plates.

London: Printed for I. Taylor, 1778.

8 printed leaves, 83 pls.

26.4 × 21.3 cm

BL

240.4 ‖

The practical builder; or workman's general assistant; shewing the most approved and easy methods for drawing and working the whole or separate part of any building; as the use of the tramel for groins, angle brackets, niches, &c. semi-circular arches on flewing jambs, the preparing and making their soffits; rules of carpentry, to find the length and backing of hips strait or curved; trusses for roofs, domes, &c. Trussing of girders, sections of floors, &c. The proportion of the five orders in their general and particular parts: gluing of columns; stair-cases with their ramp and twist rails, fixing the carriages, newels, &c. Frontispieces, chimney-pieces, ceilings, cornices, architraves, &c. in the newest taste; with plans and elevations of gentle-men's and farm-houses, barns, &c. The fourth edition; revised and corrected by the author, William Pain, Architect and Joiner. Engraved on eighty= three plates.

London: Printed for I. and J. Taylor, 1787.

10 printed leaves, 83 pls.

4°

Reference: Information supplied by B. Weinreb Architectural Books Ltd., London.

240.5
___

The practical builder; ⟨ . . . as 1787 . . . ⟩ building; as, the ⟨ . . . as 1787 . . . ⟩ plates.

London: Printed for I. and J. Taylor, 1789.

9 printed leaves, 83 pls.

26.4 × 21.3 cm

BL

240.6
___

The practical builder; ⟨ . . . as 1787 . . . ⟩ building; as, the ⟨ . . . as 1787 . . . ⟩ barns, &c. The fifth edition; revised and corrected by the author, William Pain, Architect and Joiner. Engraved on eighty-three plates.

London: Printed for I. and J. Taylor, 1793.

9 printed leaves, 83 pls.

26.0 × 21.0 cm

NNC

240.7
___

The practical builder; or, workman's general assistant: shewing the most approved and easy methods for drawing and working the whole or separate part of any building; as, the use of the tramel for groins, angle brackets, niches, &c. semi-circular arches on flewing jambs, the preparing and mak-ing their soffits; rules of carpentry, to find the length and backing of hips strait or curved; trusses for roofs, domes, &c. Trussing of girders, sections of floors, &c. The proportion of the five orders in their general and particular parts; gluing of columns; stair-cases with their ramp and twist rails, fixing the carriages, newels, &c. Frontispieces, chimney-pieces, ceilings, cornices, architraves, &c. in the newest taste. With plans and elevations of gentle-men's and farm houses, barns, &c. The sixth edition; revised and corrected by the author, William Pain, Architect and Joiner. Engraved on eighty= three plates.

London: Printed for J. Taylor, 1799.

9 printed leaves, 83 pls.

26.0 × 21.0 cm

V&A

240.8

The practical builder; ⟨ . . . as 1799 . . . ⟩ barns, &c. The seventh edition; revised and corrected by the author, William Pain, Architect and Joiner. Engraved on eighty-three plates.

London: Printed by W. Stratford, for J. Taylor, 1804.

9 printed leaves, 83 pls.

25.4 × 21.0 cm

RIBA

Following the title page the first leaf of letterpress includes a Preface on the recto and a table of contents on the verso.[1] In the Preface Pain indicated that this collection of designs was "not meant to instruct the professed Artist, but to furnish the Ignorant, [and] the Uninstructed, with . . . a com-prehensive System of Practice." Noting a "very great Revolution (as I may say) which of late has so generally prevailed in the Stile of Archi-tecture, especially in the decorative and ornamental Department," Pain promised that this new "Taste (so conspicuous in our modern Buildings) which is vainly sought in any other practical Treatise, the Workman will here find illustrated in a great Variety of useful and elegant Examples." The next printed leaf contains "A Table for the Cutting of Timber for Building" on the recto, and an explanation of Plate I on the verso. Four additional printed leaves contain explanations of material in Plates IV, VI, IX, and LXIX.

The contents of the 83 plates are well represented in the title and need not be repeated here. Plates LXXV through LXXVIII include plans and elevations for three "Gentleman's" houses and one "House for a large Family." The smallest (Plate LXXV) is three stories high and five windows wide, with a principal floor containing three rooms each measuring 18 feet by 22 feet and another room measuring 20 feet by 16 feet. The central three bays of the facade project forward slightly, and are crowned by a pediment. A small portico frames the front door. The largest design, in-tended for a "large Family" (Plate LXXVIII), includes a two-story central pile 190 feet square in plan, with 17 rooms on the principal floor sur-rounding an open rectangular courtyard. From each side of the central pile one-story colonnades lead to two-story wing pavilions, four windows wide, each with three rooms on the principal floor. The central facade is ornamented in a heavy Palladian manner, with pairs of colossal pilasters and a colossal hexastyle pedimented portico *in antis*. Plates LXXIX and LXXX include designs for a greenhouse, a small dwelling (two stories high and five windows wide), and two hothouses. Plate LXXXI depicts a coach house and stables. Plates LXXXII and LXXXIII each include designs for a farm house, barn, and stable. The smaller of the two houses (Plate LXXXIII), just two stories high and three windows wide, is ornamented modestly with an attic parapet, a cornice, and a frontispiece above the front door. The ground floor includes a parlor and a kitchen, each 14 feet square, plus a pantry, dairy, and combined brewhouse and washhouse.

1. This description pertains to the first edition (1774).

241.1
PAIN, William (1730?–1790?)
The practical house carpenter; or, the youth's instructor: containing a great variety of mouldings at large for practice, with their proper embellishments, two designs for gentlemen's houses, with their plans, elevations, and sections; likewise, a great variety of stair-case work, laid down to a very large scale for practice. To which is added, a treatise on Gothic architecture, with columns, entablatures, frontispieces, chimney pieces, shop fronts, cielings, &c. A plan and elevation of a Gothic temple, and a plan and elevation of a gentleman's house in the Gothic taste. All laid down in a plain and practical manner for practice. Engraved on thirty-four folio copper plates. By William Pain. . . . The second edition, with additions.

London: Printed for, and sold by the author, 1788.

8 pp, 42 pls (numbered A–F, 1–33; and 3 additional).

23.2 × 17.8 cm

RIBA

241.2
————

The practical house carpenter, or the youth's instructor: containing a great variety of useful designs in carpentry and architecture; the five orders laid down by an entire new scale; with frontispieces, chimney pieces, stair cases, and mouldings at large; with their proper embellishments for practice. Plans, elevations, and sections, for town and country houses. Printed on fifty-four quarto copper plates, with explanations to face each plate. By William Pain. . . . The second edition, with large additions, and a list of prices.

London: Printed for the author, 1789.

17 printed leaves, 67 pls (numbered 1–52, A–C; and 12 additional).

21.6 × 17.1 cm

NNC

241.3

The practical house carpenter, ⟨ . . . as 1789 . . . ⟩ houses. Printed on seventy-five quarto copper plates, with explanations to face each plate. By William Pain. . . . The third edition, with large additions, and a list of prices.

London: Printed for the author, 1790.

17 printed leaves, 45 pls (numbered 1–32; and 13 additional).

[Bound and uniform with:]

The practical house carpenter. Part the second. Containing a great variety of plans, elevations, and sections for town and country houses; two designs for ceilings, with several designs for frize and cornices in the first part; a section of a finished room, and a section of a library; mouldings at large, with their proper embellishments; stair-cases in the most plain and practical manner, adapted to the designs in the second part. A design for a church, plan, elevation, and section, two ways, with designs for altar piece and pulpit to ditto. Several designs for chimney pieces, fronts for shops, hot houses, green house, &c. also for a farm house and yard, with brewhouse and landry, adapted to a nobleman's or gentleman's country seat; and a design for coach houses and stables. Printed on sixty-four quarto copper plates. To which is added, a list of prices for materials and labour and labour only, in part first. By William Pain. . . .

London: Printed for the author, [1790].

1 printed leaf, 60 pls (numbered 1–43, A–H; and 9 additional).

21.6 × 17.7 cm

MdBP

241.4

The practical house carpenter; or, youth's instructor: containing a great variety of useful designs in carpentry and architecture; as centering for groins, niches, &c. Examples for roofs, sky-lights, &c. The five orders laid down by a new scale. Mouldings, &c. at large, with their enrichments. Plans, elevations and sections of houses for town and country, lodges, hot-houses, green-houses, stables, &c. Design for a church, with plan, elevation, and two sections; an altar-piece, and pulpit. Designs for chimney = pieces, shop-fronts, door-cases. Section of a dining-room and library. Variety of stair-cases, with many other important articles, and useful embellishments. To which is added, a list of prices for materials and labour, labour only, and day prices. The whole illustrated, and made perfectly easy, by 148 copper plates, with explanations to each, by William Pain. . . . The fourth edition, with large additions.

London: Printed for I. and J. Taylor, 1792.

v pp, 15 printed leaves, 148 pls (numbered 1–2, back plate 3, 3–55, face plate 56, 56–146).

21.8 × 17.4 cm

PP

241.5

_____

The practical house carpenter; ⟨ . . . as 1792 . . . ⟩ Pain. . . . The fifth edition, with additions[.]

London: Printed for I. and J. Taylor, 1794.

v pp, 15 printed leaves, 22 pp, 146 pls (numbered 1–2, back plate 3, 3–31, 32–35 [renum.], 36–37, 38–41 [renum.], 43–45, 46–47 [renum.], 48–50, 51 [renum.], 52, 53–56 [renum.], 57–62, 63 [renum.], 64, 65 [renum.], 66–67, 68 [renum.], 69–76, 77 [renum.], 78, 79–81 [renum.], 81–83, 84 [renum.], 85–89, 90 [renum.], 91, 92 [renum.], 95 [renum.], 94–96, 97 [renum.], 98–99, 100–101 [renum.], 102, 103–104 [renum.], 105, 106–109 [renum.], 110, 111–115 [renum.], 116–120, 121 [renum.], 122–125, 126 [renum.], 127–128, 129–131 [renum.], 132, 133–135 [renum.], 136, 137–145 [renum.], 146.) N.B. [renum.] indicates that the number printed on the plate has been changed to read as indicated here.

21.3 × 17.1 cm

MdBP

241.6

_____

The practical house carpenter; ⟨ . . . as 1792 . . . ⟩ as centring for ⟨ . . . as 1792 . . . ⟩, elevations, and sections ⟨ . . . as 1792 . . . ⟩ stair-cases: with many other important articles and ⟨ . . . as 1792 . . . ⟩ 148 copper-plates, with explanations to each. By William Pain. . . . The sixth edition, corrected.

London: Printed for J. Taylor, 1799.

v pp, 15 printed leaves, 22 pp, 148 pls (numbered 1–2, back plate 3, 3–64, face plate 65, 65–146).

21.0 × 17.1 cm

BL

241.7

_____

The practical house carpenter; ⟨ . . . as 1792 . . . ⟩ elevations, and sections ⟨ . . . as 1792 . . . ⟩ embellishments. The whole illustrated, and made perfectly easy, by one hundred and forty-eight copper-plates, with explanations to each. By William Pain. . . . The sixth edition, with additions.

[*The portion of the title page containing the imprint has been cut off.*]

v pp, 15 printed leaves, 149 pls (numbered 1–2, face plate 3, 3–64, face plate 65, 65–146, including a duplicate of pl. 38).

23.8 × 19.1 cm

MB

241.8 ∥

The practical house carpenter; ⟨ . . . as 1792 . . . ⟩ architecture: as centring for ⟨ . . . as 1792 . . . ⟩, elevations, and sections ⟨ . . . as 1792 . . . ⟩; an altar piece, ⟨ . . . as 1792 . . . ⟩ stair-cases; with many other important articles and ⟨ . . . as 1792 . . . ⟩ each. By William Pain. . . . The seventh edition, corrected.

London: Printed for J. Taylor; by W. Stratford, 1805.

17 printed leaves, 30 pp, 148 pls (numbered 1–2, back plate 3, 3–64, face plate 65, 65–146).

22 cm

Reference: Information supplied by Humanities Research Center, University of Texas, Austin.

241.9

The practical house carpenter; ⟨ . . . as 1792 . . . ⟩ architecture: as centring for ⟨ . . . as 1792 . . . ⟩ at large with their enrichments. Plans, elevations, and section of ⟨ . . . as 1792 . . . ⟩; an altar piece, ⟨ . . . as 1792 . . . ⟩ stair= cases; with many other important articles and useful embellishments. The whole illustrated, and made perfectly easy by one hundred and forty= eight copper-plates, with explanations to each. By William Pain. . . . The eighth edition.

London: Printed for J. Taylor; by W. Stratford, 1815.

17 printed leaves, 148 pls (numbered 1–2, back plate 3, 3–64, face plate 65, 65–146).

21.3 × 17.8 cm

CtY

241.10

The practical house carpenter; ⟨ . . . as 1792 . . . ⟩ architecture: as, centring for ⟨ . . . as 1792 . . . ⟩, elevations, and sections ⟨ . . . as 1792 . . . ⟩ stair= cases: with many other important articles and useful embellishments. The whole illustrated, and made perfectly easy by one hundred and forty= eight copper-plates, with explanations to each. By William Pain. . . . The ninth edition.

London: Printed for J. Taylor, 1823.

17 printed leaves, 148 pls (numbered 1–2, back plate 3, 3–64, face plate 65, 65–146).

21.6 × 17.8 cm

BL

Carpentry and building. The practical house carpenter, more particularly for country practice, with specifications, quantities, and contracts: also containing—

I. Designs for the centering of groins. . . .

II. Designs for roofs and staircases. . . .

The whole amply described, for the use of the operative carpenter and builder. Firstly written and published by William Pain. . . . Secondly re-modernized and improved by S. H. Brooks.

London: John Weale, 1860–1861.

viii + 27 pp, 101 pls.

26 cm

Reference: NUC and BM

Between 1788 and 1861 *The Practical House Carpenter* achieved at least 11 editions, becoming one of the most frequently issued architectural books of the eighteenth and nineteenth centuries.[1]

Brief letterpress remarks on drawing and construction accompany some of the plates, and several editions include a "Table of Scantlings" and price lists for materials and labor.[2] From 1788 until the fourth edition (1792) the number of plates steadily increased, although some plates were changed and others were deleted after one or two editions. After 1792 many of the plates were renumbered, but they were not augmented. The title page includes a partial list of subjects depicted in the plates. In addition there are illustrations of arches, trammels, polygons, domes, soffits, hips, floors, trusses, frontispieces for doors, ornaments, ceilings, farm buildings, gateways, a bridge, vases, and pedestals.

In the 1788 edition designs for houses appear in Plates 13, 15, and 28. Plate 13 depicts a house three stories high and five windows wide, with a Tuscan portico in front. Of the 12 windows in the elevation, ten are Venetian.[3] The facade of the house in Plate 15 is three stories high and three windows wide, including two thermal windows, four Venetian windows, and a rusticated doorway.[4] Plate 28 depicts a three-story castellated house for a gentleman, seven windows wide and three stories high, with crenellations, quatrefoils, and Venetian windows with pointed arches. This was the only non-Classical design in the book, and was eliminated from later editions.

New designs in the 1789 edition include a two-story house, nine windows wide, with an elegant two-story Corinthian portico (Plate 50),[5] and another house consisting of an awkward assemblage of one- and two-story pavilions, 18 windows wide, with a pedimented Ionic portico in front (Plate 52).[6]

Six additional designs for houses appear in later editions.[7] Plates 100, 103, and 107 all depict facades three stories high and five windows wide, with stringcourses between the stories and ornamented doorways. The facade in Plate 116 is similar in size, but the basement story is rusticated and the top two stories are fronted by an Ionic order. The principal floor plan of the design in Plate 107 includes a saloon, a drawing room, great and little dining rooms, a tea room, a library, and a dressing room. The designs in Plates 109 and 112 are larger: the latter is three stories high and nine windows wide, and its principal floor includes an entrance hall, a drawing room, large and little dining rooms, a library, a tea room, and a breakfast room.

1. Few architectural books attained this number of editions. Nicholson's *Builder & Workman's New Director* (*q.v.*) achieved 11 editions between 1824 and 1865. Loudon's *Encyclopaedia* (*q.v.*) achieved 14 editions between 1833 and ca. 1869.

2. In the 1799 edition, for example, p. v is "A Table of Scantlings for Cutting Timber for Buildings," and pp. 1–22 are "A List of Prices, for Materials and Labour, and Labour Only, . . . Corrected to 1799."

3. Plate 47 in the 1789 edition; eliminated from the 1794 and later editions.

4. Plate 49 in the 1789 edition. See Plate 95 in later editions.

5. Plate 97 in the 1794 and later editions.

6. Plate 99 in the 1794 and later editions.

7. The account here is based on the 1799 edition.

242.1
PAIN, William (1730?–1790?)
A supplement to the builder's golden rule: engraved on thirty-four folio copper-plates. By William Pain. . . .

London: Printed for and sold by the author, 1782.

7 pp, 34 pls.

22.9 × 18.4 cm

CtY

One year after the first edition of *The Builder's Golden Rule* (1781; *q.v.*) Pain issued a second edition and also this *Supplement*.

The text of the *Supplement* begins with a half page of "Introductory Remarks" on Doric, Ionic, and Corinthian intercolumniations (p. 3). The remaining four and a half pages consist of plate descriptions.

The plates include illustrations of an "equilateral scale" for proportioning cornices and moldings, and a variety of subjects in Classical and Gothic styles: architraves, cornices, bases, surbases, imposts, columns, pediments, entablatures, arches, frontispieces, chimneypieces, a ceiling, ornamental "trusses," garden seats, a temple, shop fronts, and one house. It is curious that while none of the designs in *The Builder's Golden Rule* is in Gothic style, nearly two-thirds of the subjects in the *Supplement* are.[1] Pain's Gothic orders are reminiscent of those published earlier by Batty and Thomas Langley,[2] particularly in the regularity and proportion of their ornament. Pain's Gothic furniture designs are likewise based on regular geometric figures, with quatrefoils and ogee arches set within squares and rectangles.

Plate 31, a "Plan and elevation of a gentleman's house, in the Gothic taste," is three stories high and seven windows wide, with an awkward assortment of crenellations, finials, quatrefoils, and squat windows with pointed arches, plus a triple window framed by Gothic columns and entablatures. The plan includes a staircase hall and seven rooms on the principal floor. The Gothic temple in Plate 32 is two stories high, with quatrefoil and ogee-arched windows, plus crenellations and machicolations along the parapet. The "umbrella-seats" in Plate 34 are shallow three-sided recesses, fronted by elaborate ogee arches and covered with busy ornament.

1. Of 34 plates, 22 contain Gothic subjects.

2. *Ancient Architecture* ([1742]; *q.v.*).

243.1
PAINE, James (1717–1789)
Plans, elevations and sections, of noblemen and gentlemen's houses, and also of stabling, bridges, public and private, temples, and other garden buildings; executed in the counties of Derby, Durham, Middlesex, Northumberland, Nottingham, and York. By James Paine, Architect. . . . Part the first. Illustrated by seventy-four large folio plates.

London: Printed for the author, and sold by Mr. Davies; Mr. Dodsley; Mr. Brotherton; Mr. Webley; and at the author's house, 1767.

2 printed leaves, iv pp, 1 printed leaf, [1] + ii + 3–11 + [11–20] pp, frontisp. + 74 pls.

Plans, elevations, and sections, of noblemen and gentlemen's houses, and also of bridges, public and private, temples, and other garden buildings; executed in the counties of Nottingham, Essex, Wilts, Derby, Hertford, Suffolk, Salop, Middlesex, and Surrey. By James Paine, Architect. Part the second. Illustrated by one hundred and one large folio plates.

London: Printed for the author; and sold by Mess. Sayer and Bennett; Mr. Beckett; Mr. Robson, at Mr. Boydell's; and at the author's house, 1783.

vi + 32 pp, 101 pls (numbered I–XIV, XIII–XIV, XVII–CI).

54.6 × 36.2 cm

MH

243.2
———
Plans, elevations, and sections, ⟨ . . . as 1767 . . . ⟩ plates. The second edition.

London: Printed for the author, and sold by Mr. White; Mr. Becket; Mr. Robson; Mr. Davies; Mr. Isaac Taylor; Mr. Boydell; and at the author's house, 1783.

viii pp, 2 printed leaves, 22 pp, 75 pls.

Plans, ⟨ . . . as 1783, Part the Second . . . ⟩ plates.

London: Printed ⟨ . . . as 1783, Part the Second . . . ⟩, 1783.

vi + 32 pp, 101 pls (numbered I–XIV, XIII–XIV, XVII–CI).

61.0 × 44.4 cm

MBAt

In the 1750s and 1760s James Paine and Robert Taylor were the two major practicing architects in England: Sir William Chambers's private commissions were generally smaller and fewer in number, and Robert Adam was not as widely recognized until the 1770s.[1] Paine prepared this collection of his executed designs for publication in 1767—supplemented by a second volume in 1783—partly as a means of vaunting his success, and partly to interest additional clients. No doubt mindful of his own prominence, he contended that Britain had developed a new and advanced form of domestic architecture. "The rapid progress of architecture in Great-Britain, within these last thirty years, is perhaps without example, in any age or country since the Romans," he wrote in the Preface. "It may rationally be predicted, that England will vie with, if not exceed (at least in the splendour and magnificence of its villas) the most flourishing periods of the ancient Roman empire" (p. i).

Britain's progress, he felt, was stimulated by such "revivers and patrons" of architecture as the Earl of Burlington, the dukes of Cumberland, Norfolk, Devonshire, and Northumberland, the earls of Scarbrough, Bute, Strafford, Bessborough, Pembroke, and Leicester, and Lord Petre (p. i).[2] Progress itself came from research "into the remains of antiquity, in distant countries" at such sites as "Palmyra, Spolatra, and Balbec" (pp. i–ii). But progress also required advances beyond ancient prototypes. He deplored copying "the most despicable ruins of ancient Greece," and felt that Wood, Stuart, Revett, Le Roy, and others were wasting their time measuring ancient ruins (p. ii). Greek architecture was patently inferior to that of Rome, and the architect who traveled to see either would suffer by imbibing "wrong principles in his art, and a blind veneration for inconsistent antiquated modes" (p. ii). Even the architecture of Rome, a vast improvement over that of Greece, should not be copied indiscriminately, nor were the houses of Palladio suited for copying. In both cases copying would preclude any beneficial adaptation to English customs or climate (p. ii). Paine also remarked on the qualifications of an architect. Detailed analysis of the five orders was "unnecessary": the architect must be "guided by what is called taste," and if he has insufficient "judgment" to properly determine his own forms, then he must be reduced to copying the models of Palladio and others, none of whom had been able "to fix a standard of architecture" (p. iii).

Following the Preface, list of subscribers, and list of plates, the first and most prominent subject in the first volume is Paine's series of improvements at Chatsworth. The volume also includes designs for work at 13 other houses, a chapel, and a few garden structures. Paine's most impressive work, the designs for Worksop, Wardour, and Kedleston, all appear in Volume II. Also in this volume there are designs for five other country houses, some town houses, and a few bridges, ceilings, and chimneypieces.

Much of Paine's aversion to copying ancient examples may be attributed to contemporary ideas of genius and creativity, especially as formulated by Gerard and Young.[3] Paine suggested that the artist's private sensibility, once released from constraint, would continue to improve Britain's domestic architecture. Yet his basic vocabulary remained Roman. The combination of Pantheon and basilica at Kedleston (II, pls. 48–52) is a major case in point.[4] Other elements of Paine's style derive from Inigo Jones and William Kent. Nevertheless the resulting compositions often are highly unusual. In pavilions attached to each side of the house at Stockeld (I, pl. 43), for example, a window topped by a segmental architrave and cornice fits tightly within a recessed semicircular relieving arch that itself presses upward into the broken pediment at the top of the pavilion. These and other elements of this compact house advance and recede slightly in three dimensions to reinforce the sense of a taut but lively surface—quite different from the more rigid, static facades erected earlier in the century. Paine's facility with masses and volumes was impressive, especially in the arrangement of the central mass and four end pavilions at Kedleston—a more dynamic version of Holkham Hall—or in the complex integration of horizontal and vertical spaces seen in the two-story hall at Wardour (II, pls. 40–41).

Figure 6

1. Summerson (1969), pp. 217–221.

2. The list, of course, includes several of Paine's patrons. See Colvin (1978), pp. 607–613.

3. See Alexander Gerard, *An Essay on Taste* (London, 1759), and *An Essay on Genius* (London, 1774); and Edward Young, *Conjectures on Original Composition* (London, 1759).

4. This example is discussed in Summerson (1969), pp. 219–221.

244.1
PAINE, James (1717–1789)
Plans, elevations, sections, and other ornaments of the mansion-house, belonging to the Corporation of Doncaster. By James Paine.

London: Printed for the author, 1751.

[iii] + 3 pp, 21 pls.

44.4 × 29.0 cm

PU

The book is dedicated to the Mayor and Corporation of Doncaster, and also to Godfrey Copley, William Dixon, and John Stead. The Preface describes the history of the Mansion House from its conception in 1744 to its completion in 1748. The text (pp. 1–3) consists of descriptions of the 21 plates. These include exterior elevations, plans, sections, and views of the interior.

245.1

Pantologia. A new cyclopaedia, comprehending a complete series of essays, treatises, and systems, alphabetically arranged; with a general dictionary of arts, sciences, and words: the whole presenting a distinct survey of human genius, learning, and industry. Illustrated with elegant engravings; those on natural history being from original drawings by Edwards and others, and beautifully coloured after nature. By John Mason Good . . . ; Olinthus Gregory . . . ; and Mr. Newton Bosworth . . . ; assisted by other gentlemen of eminence, in different departments of literature. Vol. . . .

London: Printed for G. Kearsley; J. Walker; J. Stockdale; R. Lea; E. Jeffery; Crosby and Co.; Sherwood, Neely, and Jones; Suttaby, Evance, and Co.; J. Blacklock; W. Lowe; J. Booth; J. Rodwell; Bell and Bradfute, Edinburgh; Brash and Reid, Glasgow; and M. Keene, Dublin, 1813.

[*Twelve volumes, 1813.*]

Art. "Architecture," I, 20 pp; pls. 3, 4, 14–18.
Art. "Building," II, 5 pp; pl. 32.
Art. "Drawing," IV, 8 pp; pls. 64–67.
Art. "Perspective," IX, 11 pp; pls. 134–137.

23.9 × 14.2 cm

ICU

245.2

Pantologia. A new cabinet cyclopaedia, ⟨ . . . as 1813 . . . ⟩ literature. Vol. . . .

London: Printed for J. Walker; Sherwood, Neely, and Jones; Baldwin, Cradock, and Joy; Suttaby, Evance, and Fox; E. Jeffery; W. Lowe; J. Booth; J. Blacklock; Rodwell and Martin; Bell and Bradfute, Edinburgh; Brash and Reid, Glasgow; and M. Keene, Dublin, 1819.

[*Twelve volumes, 1819.*]

Art. "Architecture," I, 20 pp; pls. 3, 4, 14–18.
Art. "Building," II, 5 pp; pl. 32.
Art. "Drawing," IV, 8 pp; pls. 64–67 [*pl. 67 is wanting in this copy*].
Art. "Perspective," IX, 11 pp; pls. 134–137.

23.8 × 14.5 cm

MnU

The article "Architecture" begins with a brief history of the subject, starting with the invention of the primitive hut and including Persian, Greek, Egyptian, "Arabian," Gothic, and Renaissance styles. The next portion, devoted to "General Principles," treats composition, harmony, proportion, "internal Division of Houses," ornament, and expression. A discussion of the five orders includes remarks on their individual parts and characteristics, their origins, "Diminution of Columns," intercolumniation, arches, pilasters, attics, pediments, gates, doors, piers, niches, statues, chimneypieces, staircases, balustrades, "Orders upon Orders," basements, roofs, and ceilings. The final portion of the article concerns "the Principles necessary in erecting a Building," and foundations. Plates 3 and 4 illustrate the five orders. Plate 14 illustrates techniques of arch construction and "Nicomedes's Instrument for diminishing Columns." Plates 15 and 16 include Gothic arches and columns, "Saxon Capitals," elevations of the tower of York Minster and the north entrance of Peterborough Cathedral, as well as a few Classical ornaments. Plates 17 and 18 depict Classical arches and imposts.

The article on "Building" includes brief comments on the history of Parliamentary Acts relating to the subject and remarks on the principles of composition. These are followed by a lengthy discourse on "Building *in Pisé*," based on a treatise by François Cointeraux.[1] The sole plate for this article, titled "Building *in Pisè*," depicts tools for working with pisé plus a plan and elevation of a two-room dwelling that could be made of pisé.[2]

The article on "Drawing" is divided into 12 sections, on materials, limbs and other parts of the human body, the human face, the human figure, proportions of the human body, "Attitudes" of the human figure, "Effects of the Exertion of the Muscles," "Distribution of Light and Shade," drapery, "Effects of the Passions," flora and fauna, and landscapes and buildings. Plates 64 and 65 show eyes, ears, limbs, heads, and complete human figures. Plate 66 consists of outline reproductions of two paintings by Raphael. Plate 67 includes figures of animals, rustic country landscapes, castles, villages, and a picturesque, irregular two-story cottage, all of which appeared previously in Plate 9, Volume III, of *The English Encyclopaedia* (*q.v.*).

The article on "Perspective" begins with a history of the subject, followed by two theorems and a series of problems and constructions. The article concludes with remarks on the "practical" application of perspective to drawing and painting, aerial perspective, and perspective machines. The four plates depict geometric constructions, objects in perspective, steps and arches, drawing instruments, and a perspective machine. The two illustrations depicting the use of this machine include a small house, two stories high and three windows wide, representing a distant object to be drawn with the aid of the machine. These two illustrations were borrowed from James Ferguson's *Art of Drawing in Perspective* (1775; *q.v.*).

1. François Cointeraux, *Ecole d'architecture rurale* (Paris, [1791]). For English treatises on pisé, see the commentary above on Henry Holland's article "Pisé" (1797).

2. The illustrations in this plate closely resemble those in Plate 6 of William Barber's *Farm Buildings* (1802; *q.v.*), and differ distinctly from the illustrations in the treatises by Cointeraux and Holland.

246.1
PAPWORTH, John Buonarotti (1775–1847)
"Architectural hints," *The Repository of Arts, Literature, Fashions, Manufactures, &c.*, Second Series:

1:1 (January 1816), 1–5, pl. 1.
1:2 (February 1816), 63–66, pl. 8.
1:3 (March 1816), 125–128, pl. 13.
1:4 (April 1816), 187–190, pl. 19.
1:5 (May 1816), 249–251, pl. 25.
1:6 (June 1816), 311–313, pl. 31.

2:7 (July 1816), 1–3, pl. 1.
2:8 (August 1816), 63–64, pl. 7.
2:9 (September 1816), 125–126, pl. 13.
2:10 (October 1816), 187–190, pl. 19.
2:11 (November 1816), 249–252, pl. 25.
2:12 (December 1816), 311–314, pl. 31.
3:13 (January 1817), 1, pl. 1.
3:14 (February 1817), 63–64, pl. 7.
3:15 (March 1817), 125–126, pl. 13.
3:16 (April 1817), 187–188, pl. 19.
3:17 (May 1817), 249–250, pl. 26.
3:18 (June 1817), 311–312, pl. 32.
4:19 (July 1817), 1, pl. 1.
4:20 (August 1817), 63–64, pl. 6.
4:21 (September 1817), 125–126, pl. 12.
4:22 (October 1817), 187, pl. 18.
4:23 (November 1817), 249, pl. 24.
4:24 (December 1817), 367, pl. 31.

MnU

246.2

___

Rural residences, consisting of a series of designs for cottages, decorated cottages, small villas, and other ornamental buildings, accompanied by hints on situation, construction, arrangement and decoration, in the theory & practice of rural architecture; interspersed with some observations on landscape gardening: by John B. Papworth, Architect. . . .

London: Printed for R. Ackermann, by J. Diggens, 1818.

viii + 9–106 + [iii] pp, 27 pls.

25.4 × 17.8 cm

MH

246.3

___

Rural residences, consisting of a series of designs for cottages, decorated cottages, small villas, and other ornamental buildings; accompanied by hints on situation, construction, arrangement, and decoration, in the theory and practice of rural architecture: interspersed with some observations on landscape gardening. By J. B. Papworth. . . . Second edition.

London: Printed for R. Ackermann, by Sedding and Turtle, 1832.

viii + 9–106 + [iii] pp, 27 pls.

26.7 × 18.4 cm

MH

An earlier series of articles titled "Architectural Hints" appeared in Ackermann's *Repository* from February to July 1813, and contained designs for a "Hall," a staircase and vestibule, a conservatory, a bed chamber and state bed, and two libraries, all in Gothic style.[1] These designs did not appear in *Rural Residences*.

In the Introduction to *Rural Residences* (pp. v–viii) Papworth indicated that the designs shown in the plates had already appeared in the *Repository* during 1816 and 1817, and "further observations have been added to supply, in part, the many deficiencies which necessarily occurred from so desultory a manner of publication." He also complained that "architecture in this country has failed to receive its proportion of public patronage, because the public has not distinguished it as a fine art" (p. v). Indeed in London "the speculative builder has generally superseded the labours of the artist," and the result is "an obvious perversion of true architecture" (p. vi). Thus "the following designs and observations were made, as an introduction to the threshold of art" (p. vii).[2]

The text and plates in *Rural Residences* are those of the original 24 articles published in the *Repository* in 1816 and 1817, with some additions and changes. The original 24 plates are reproduced, in a different order,[3] and three additional plates have been added: Plate 1, a bath; Plate 18, a *cottage ornée*;[4] and Plate 26, a veranda. The text is organized as a series of commentaries on each of the plates, and includes material from the original articles, often abridged, plus substantial additions concerning materials, siting, color, picturesque composition, style, and function. The letterpress concludes with an index (one leaf, recto and verso) and an "Index to the Plates" (one leaf, recto only).

The colored plates, depicting plans and elevations with appropriate landscape scenery, are arranged in a sequence beginning with cottages, progressing through *cottages ornées* and villas, and ending with ancillary structures for large estates such as lodges and seats. There is less rigor and order in the organization of the text, which treats subjects such as siting, style, and function in a loose, sometimes casual manner. Nevertheless Papworth's discussion is important and frequently enlightening on the subject of domestic design.

Figure 7

In discussing the site for a *cottage ornée* (Plate 7), Papworth observed that after attending to soil, water, drainage, and the orientation of the structure, the architect must also consider communication, proximity to supplies and medical facilities, and landscape scenery. Only then would it "be proper to determine on the character and form of the house itself" (p. 29). The size of the house should be determined by the size of the family living in it and the use they would make of it. The style, on the other hand, must be determined by the character of the surrounding landscape. At a low and secluded site, for example, well covered with "large and embowering" trees and divided by shrubs into small areas, "the thatched cottage will be in harmony with its compact and rural situation." For a plain with tall "aspiring" trees, and "lofty" hills or spires of towns and cities in the distance, Greek would be most appropriate. Gothic, on the other hand, would suit hilly ground with round trees.[5]

In describing other designs Papworth provided more detailed remarks on style. In connection with a steward's cottage (Plate 4), for example, he noted that just four styles "have been introduced in small dwellings."

The first was based on "frugality," and was characterized by "a rigid adherence" to "perfect simplicity." The second allowed greater ornament, "but of a very rustic character," no more than "might have been the genuine effort of a tasteful husbandman." In the third style the "forms from Grecian or Gothic architecture have been adopted with a pleasing effect." Finally in the fourth style "a more extended license has been taken, and the [historical] model entirely neglected for further efforts of the fancy to obtain the sentiment of rural or picturesque beauty"—a description that characterizes much of Papworth's own work.[6] A small residence also should be closely related to the particular character of the surrounding landscape: "The cottage orné, the casino, or the villa, should be designed with a studied reference to the spot on which either is to be erected; for circumstances of combination will make some features to be desired, and others to be avoided, that wholly depend on localities and surrounding scenery" (pp. 26–27). In some cases, however, a style might be chosen for its associations. A Classical style could produce an "association of ideas . . . in the mind of the spectator, by its legitimate, though distant, affinity with the ultimate perfection of Grecian architecture" (p. 18). The "mixed" style of Old English architecture, on the other hand, recalls a period "when the security of the sovereign and the subject began to depend less on the strength of fortifications and the force of arms, than on the equitable administration of the laws of the country" (p. 33).[7]

But Papworth's most important remarks are found in his discussions of individual architectural types, specifying forms and styles appropriate to specific classes of inhabitants, ranging from laborers to men of leisure. In remarks on a group of cottages for "the labouring poor" (Plate 2), for example, he stated that the design "cannot be too simple." Too much ornament would "ill associate with the modest and moderate claims of this respectable and useful class of society" (p. 9). Nevertheless within the limits of "simplicity" the designer could easily express and inculcate certain positive moral qualities:

The porch in which [the laborer] . . . rests after the fatigues of the day, ornamented by some flowering creeper, at once affords him shade and repose; neatness and cleanliness connected with these and other means of external cheerfulness, bespeak that elasticity of mind, and spring of action, which produce industry and cheerfulness, and demonstrate that peace and content at least dwell with its inhabitants. (p. 10)

The four attached cottages, which are arranged symmetrically about two axes, are covered by a picturesque thatch roof which includes large semi-circular gables. Underneath are Tudor windows and distyle porches *in antis* for each cottage, made of rustic tree-trunk columns. This picturesque but rustic ornament reflects the accommodations inside: the ground floor of each cottage contains just a kitchen and a parlor, with a common "area" for all four cottages in the center of the structure. Two other cottages for laborers or retainers (Plates 3, 4) are composed in a similar rustic style.

A *cottage ornée* should be composed in an entirely different manner because it serves a different function:

The cottage orné is a new species of building in the economy of domestic architecture, and subject to its own laws of fitness and propriety. It is not the habitation of the laborious, but of the affluent, of the man of study, of science, or of leisure; it is often the rallying point of domestic comfort, and in this age of elegant refinement, a mere cottage would be incongruous with the nature of its occupancy. (p. 25)

The *cottage ornée* described here (Plate 6), designed in Gothic style to accord with "garden scenery," includes a dining room, parlor, hall, kitchen, scullery, and larder on the ground floor, plus four bedrooms upstairs. Another *cottage ornée* (Plate 12) was designed to accord with scenery in "the neighbourhood of the lakes." Since its "situation combines the romantic with the rural" (p. 49) the elevation includes a thatch roof, diagonally latticed windows, a scalloped bargeboard in the semicircular gable surrounding the window in the upper story, and simple wooden shafts with square capitals, suggestive of primordial Doric columns,[8] supporting porch roofs and flanking ground-story windows. The ground-floor plan includes a drawing room, parlor, music room, "Book Room," kitchen, and larder, and there are five bedrooms upstairs. Another *cottage ornée*, designed for an "Exposed and Elevated Situation" (Plate 13), establishes its relation with the landscape even more dramatically. One- and two-story verandas surround the house on three sides, indicating not only the large number of views available from the house, but also the interpenetration of interior and exterior space. On the ground floor a dining room, drawing room, and entrance hall open out onto the verandas, while even the kitchen and scullery windows afford picturesque views of distant vistas.

Papworth suggested that the most appropriate style for a vicarage house would be Gothic: because the style is associated with churches, it readily "leads the spectator very naturally from contemplating the dwelling, to regard the pious character of its inhabitant" (p. 45). The house itself includes a dining room, double drawing room, study, kitchen, closet, larder, and scullery on the ground floor.

The single design for a farm house, by contrast, is in "cottage style" in order to "assimilate with home scenery" (Plate 10). The thatch roof is broken by several pointed, semicircular, and hipped gables, and topped by ornamental chimneys. Below there are Tudor windows and a porch supported by four simple cylindrical wooden shafts with square bases and capitals. But unlike a cottage the design is not diminutive: the elevation is two stories high and three windows wide, and the ground floor includes a drawing room, parlor, library, kitchen, scullery, storeroom, and greenhouse.

Papworth's designs for villas are more formal. He identified one as "a residence for a small family" (Plate 15), and then described its principal characteristics in more detail. "A Residence," he said, "may be considered under two points of view." The first is its fitness to house people. The second is expression—providing "external claims to respectability, including whatever tends to produce those impressions which are recommendatory to the tasteful and judicious."[9] Thus "cheerfulness, comfort, and a due proportion of elegance, are the prevailing features desirable to the exterior" (p. 61). The two-story elevation, three openings wide, is fronted by a two-story semicircular bow with engaged fluted Doric columns. To either side Classically ornamented windows are recessed under semicircular relieving arches, and the parapet above also is decorated with modest Classical ornament. The ground-floor plan includes a dining room which extends into the bow, two drawing rooms, a library, a hall, a staircase hall, and a conservatory. More dramatic is the villa designed "as the Residence of an Artist" (Plate 17). Set in a thickly forested, hilly landscape, the villa consists of a massive horizontal block fronted by a tower with a belvedere at the top. The tower and other Italianate elements of the elevation and landscape are clearly reminiscent of paintings by Claude and Poussin. Papworth observed that "Claude Lorrain, Poussin, and other celebrated landscape-painters of the seventeenth century, introduced forms of buildings in their compositions that were well suited to the poetic feeling obvious in the works of those great masters" (p. 69). Papworth directly transferred those forms to a residence intended for an artist, and thus expressed by association a "poetic feeling" well suited to the creative activity of the resident.[10]

1. 1st ser., IX:50–55 (February–July 1813).

2. These observations are far more pessimistic than the original statement of purpose in January 1816. Papworth observed then that "architectural and rural improvement . . . so intimately connected with the elegancies of social life, are now generally cultivated by the affluent: indeed these arts have acquired a patronage and encouragement unknown in earlier times." He hoped his series of articles would provide much "useful matter" for "the amateur" (*Repository*, 2nd ser., I:1 [January 1816], 1–2).

3. The subjects of the plates are given here in the order of their appearance in *Rural Residences*; following each in parentheses is the issue number of the *Repository* in which the plate originally appeared. A bath [not in *Repository*]; four attached cottages for laborers (21); a cottage (8); a steward's cottage (16); a bailiff's cottage (23); a Gothic cottage (2); a *cottage ornée* (1); a *cottage ornée* (4); a Gothic cottage (22); a *cottage ornée* (20); a vicarage house (10); a *cottage ornée* (14); a *cottage ornée* (11); a hunting lodge (5); a villa (19); a villa (15); a villa (17); a villa or *cottage ornée* [appeared in *Repository* in 1813]; a park lodge and entrance (3); a park entrance (12); a Gothic conservatory (7); a dairy (6); a fishing lodge (13); an ice house (18); two garden seats (9); a veranda [not in *Repository*]; a domestic chapel (24).

4. This design and the accompanying letterpress (pp. 73–76) originally appeared in a separate article by Papworth, "Cottage Ornée" (1813; *q.v.*).

5. Papworth's correspondence between architectural and landscape types is reminiscent of that established by Humphry Repton in *Sketches and Hints* (1794; *q.v.*).

6. The quotations are from p. 18.

7. The plate for which this description was written depicts a *cottage ornée* with lattice casement windows in an oriel. Although not a remarkable example of the "Old English" style, this was one of the first such designs to appear in British architectural literature.

8. Cf. the illustrations of "Primitive Buildings" in Sir William Chambers's *Treatise* (1759; *q.v.*).

9. For earlier remarks on fitness and expression see Humphry Repton, *Observations* (1803); John Claudius Loudon, *A Treatise on . . . Country Residences* (1806); and Loudon, *Designs for Laying Out Farms* (1811), *qq.v.*

10. For further discussion of the revival of Italianate forms in British domestic architecture, see the commentary on Gilbert Laing Meason, *On the Landscape Architecture of the Great Painters of Italy* (1828).

247.1

PAPWORTH, John Buonarotti (1775–1847)

"Cottage ornée," *The Repository of Arts, Literature, Commerce, Manufactures, Fashions, and Politics*, [First Series] 9:49 (January 1813), 53–55, pl. 4.

MnU

In addition to the two major series of articles that Papworth prepared for *The Repository of Arts*, his first contribution was a design for a *cottage ornée*, illustrated in one plate and accompanied by three pages of text, signed "Φ."

The elevation is two stories high and three windows wide; the window and door openings are separated by a horizontal stringcourse and by two-story pilasters. The ground-floor plan includes a dining room, drawing room, and breakfast room, all opening directly onto the lawn in front of the house, plus a vestibule, hall, gallery, kitchen, scullery, other offices, and a courtyard. In introducing the design Papworth noted the "superiority" of English dwellings for accommodating the "elegancies of life." The Englishman, he said, desires above all "the means of friendly intercourse and rational retirement," and so "splendour and magnificence are made subordinate to the calmer enjoyments of domestic felicity" (p. 53). To describe dwellings with such characteristics, Papworth would have preferred a more appropriate name than *"cottage ornée,"* a term borrowed from French yet generally accepted among English architects:[1]

This design is called a *Cottage ornée*; indeed we have no term suited to this character of building, which is certainly superior to the highest class of cottage, and as certainly below the importance of the villa: perhaps a term more suitable might be borrowed from the Italians, whose *Cassines* were those buildings in the Campagna which were prepared for retirement from the scenes of splendour, state, and ceremony. (p. 53)

The plate and an abridged version of the text appear in Papworth's *Rural Residences* (1818; *q.v.*), Plate 18 and pp. 73–76.

1. See the discussion of the related term *"ferme ornée"* in the commentary on John Plaw's *Ferme Ornée* (1795). Also see W. F. Pocock's use of *"cabâne ornée"* in *Architectural Designs* (1807; *q.v.*); Robert Lugar's introduction of the term *"cottage ornée"* in *Architectural Sketches* (1805; *q.v.*); and Edmund Bartell's discussion of the "ornamented cottage" in *Hints for Picturesque Improvements* (1804; *q.v.*).

248.1

PAPWORTH, John Buonarotti (1775–1847)

"Hints on ornamental gardening," *The Repository of Arts, Literature, Fashions, Manufactures, &c.*, Second Series:

7:37 (January 1819), 1–2, pl. 1.
7:38 (February 1819), 63–64, pl. 7.
7:40 (April 1819), 202–203, pl. 20.
7:41 (May 1819), 249, pl. 26.
7:42 (June 1819), 311, pl. 32.
8:43 (July 1819), 1, pl. 1.
8:45 (September 1819), 125, pl. 13.
8:46 (October 1819), 187–188, pl. 20.
8:47 (November 1819), 249, pl. 26.
8:48 (December 1819), 311, pl. 33.
9:49 (January 1820), 1, pl. 1.
9:50 (February 1820), 63, pl. 7.
9:51 (March 1820), 132, pl. 13.
9:52 (April 1820), 187, pl. 19.
9:53 (May 1820), 249–250, pl. 25.
9:54 (June 1820), 311, pl. 31.

10:55 (July 1820), 1, pl. 1.
10:56 (August 1820), 63, pl. 7.
10:57 (September 1820), 125, pl. 13.
10:58 (October 1820), 187, pl. 19.
10:59 (November 1820), 249, pl. 25.
10:60 (December 1820), 311–312, pl. 31.
11:61 (January 1821), 1–2, pl. 1.
11:62 (February 1821), 67, pl. 7.
11:63 (March 1821), 129–130 [*the title varies:* "Hints on landscape gardening"], pl. 13.
11:64 (April 1821), 191, pl. 19.
11:65 (May 1821), 253, pl. 25.
11:66 (June 1821), 315, pl. 31.
12:67 (July 1821), 1, pl. 1.
12:68 (August 1821), 63, pl. 7.
12:69 (September 1821), 125, pl. 13.
12:70 (October 1821), 187, pl. 19.
12:71 (November 1821), 249–250, pl. 25.
12:72 (December 1821), 311, pl. 31.

MnU

248.2

Hints on ornamental gardening: consisting of a series of designs for garden buildings, useful and decorative gates, fences, railings, &c. Accompanied by observations on the principles and theory of rural improvement, interspersed with occasional remarks on rural architecture. By John Buonarotti Papworth. . . .

London: Printed for R. Ackermann, by J. Diggens, 1823.

110 + [ii] pp, 28 pls.

26.7 × 17.8 cm

MH

Papworth's series of 34 articles on landscape architecture and gardening originally appeared between 1819 and 1821 in Ackermann's *Repository*. Most of the articles are little more than brief descriptions of the accompanying plates.[1] In 1823 Papworth published *Hints on Ornamental Gardening*, which contains an important new introductory essay, 28 of the original 34 plates, plus revised and expanded plate descriptions.[2] The discussion below is based on *Hints on Ornamental Gardening*.

The text begins with an essay on the relation between architecture and landscape gardening (pp. 9–32), the first part of which is a brief history of man's attempts "to controul the operations of nature when near the vicinity of his dwelling." Papworth criticized the "ancients," particularly the Romans, for treating nature as subservient to art and creating landscapes that were overly subject to geometric order (p. 9). He noted that William Kent, Capability Brown, and Humphry Repton progressively transformed landscape design into the simultaneous harmonization of art, architecture, and nature. Repton in particular "perceived the necessity of connecting the works of art with nature, by gentle and almost insensible degrees, thus harmonizing the landscape with the buildings" (p. 13). Papworth endorsed this approach, stating that the architect must consider "the house, the offices and the plantations as a great whole, which he combines with a view to create picturesque effects in every point of view, whether near or distant" (p. 16). Indeed the house and landscape could be arranged almost as if in a painting: "The house is now viewed as a principal attended by a retinue of subordinates" (p. 26); and "the plantations support and contrast with the building, which by the shrubberies is carried forward until it blends naturally and gracefully with the landscape" (p. 16).[3]

Papworth discussed specific techniques for achieving this integration of architecture and landscape (pp. 18–23). Perhaps the most effective means was to eliminate the raised basement story of a dwelling: "The chief apartments are now therefore placed on the level of the ground, and have free access to the lawn or terrace by casements that descend to the very floor" (p. 20). Consequently the walks, shrubbery, verandas, colonnades, and interior rooms all could be more closely integrated with each other. Because people would be able to walk into and out of the house more freely, they also would become more inclined to perceive indoors and outdoors as one.[4]

Papworth recognized that individual dwelling types would harmonize better with some kinds of landscape scenery than with others:[5]

It would be a fruitless attempt to harmonize the landscape with the building, if their characters were incongruous with each other—they must be associated therefore with reference to the characteristics of each: that is to say, the cottage with rustic or rural scenery—the villa with the beautiful—the palace with the grand, and the castle with rocks, rugged or alpine scenery, with the forest and the bolder products of nature.[6]

Papworth then suggested an innovative categorical correspondence between these four dwelling types and the affective qualities of appropriate landscape scenery:

[Rustic scenery/cottage architecture:] It has been properly observed of the rustic as it relates to character—that it is simple and inartificial; a mixture of the wild with unstudied cultivation, although not enough of the latter to have produced the pastoral enjoyments of life.
[Rural scenery/cottage architecture:] Of the rural—that it is accompanied by marked evidences of civilization and a desire to possess convenience and comforts, with such embellishments as are not expensive or allied to luxury.
[Beautiful scenery/villa architecture:] Of the beautiful—that it is expressed in gaiety and luxuriance, by an easy gracefulness of forms and parts, and that its qualities are lightness, neatness, symmetry, regularity, uniformity and propriety.
[Grand and sublime scenery/palace and castle architecture:] And of the grand and sublime—that actual magnitude, solemnity and simplicity are its essential qualities. (pp. 14–15)

The introductory essay concludes with remarks on the qualifications and duties of an architect. According to Papworth the architect must possess artistic as well as technical abilities. He must have "the qualifications both of the painter and the sculptor; and the power of combining the theories of art with scientific excellence." This requires both perception and understanding: the architect must be "endowed with a capacious grasp of mind—full of imagination—extensively versed in the mathematics—in the principles of art and science, and practically an artist" (pp. 30, 31). But an architect need not be a master of practical crafts and skills. Unlike a builder, the architect is far "less dependant on physical than intellectual skill" (p. 31).[7]

The remainder of the text consists of revised and expanded descriptions of the 28 plates.[8] These treat important landscape components of residential estates, including the site as a whole, its boundaries, land forms, water forms, lawns, plants, trees, approaches, walks and paths, flower gardens, and fountains.

The plates are aquatinted and elegantly colored, typical of the high degree of finish usually found in publisher Rudolph Ackermann's work. Each design is shown accompanied by handsome landscape scenery. Most designs incorporate a sophisticated combination of rustic and Classical styles. The "Plantation Seat," for example, is composed of spare, thin elements reminiscent of Adam Neoclassicism, but with richer ornament: the bases of the columns are derived from vegetal forms, elaborate gilded brackets support the roof, a rich dentilled cornice surrounds the roof, and the whole is crowned by an ornamental Greek palmette. There is a hint of Egyptian in addition to the Classical and rustic in the "Ice House," which has a pyramidal thatch roof, a low doorway with dramatically battered sides, a large rusticated semicircular arch, and a porch made of rough-barked columns and tree-branch railings.

1. The first two articles are exceptions: they include remarks on the history of English landscape gardening, and on the work of William Kent and Capability Brown. These remarks were reprinted, with some additions, on pp. 10–13 of *Hints*.

2. Following are the subjects of the original 34 plates, listed in the order in which they originally appeared. Plates that also appear in *Hints* are indicated by an asterisk (*), followed by the plate number from *Hints*. A dagger (†) indicates that the subject was excluded from *Hints*. No new plates were added when *Hints* was published in 1823. A Woodland Seat, *XIV. An Aviary, *VI. A Bridge & Boat House, *VII. A Polish Hut, *XII. An Aviary, *XXI. A Bridge Adapted to Park Scenery, *X. A Swiss Cottage, †. A Fountain, *XXII. Park Entrances (four examples), *II. Coppice Wood Fences, Gates, and Hurdles (ten examples), *III. A Garden Seat, *XIX. An Alcove, *XX. A Cenotaph, *XXVIII. A Venetian Tent, *XVIII. An Apiary, *XXVI. A Garden Seat, *V. A Garden Fountain, †. An Ice Well, *XIII. A Bath, *XXV. A Rustic Bridge, *VIII. A Conservatory, *XVIII. A Garden Fountain, *XXIV. A Picturesque Diary, *XI. A Gamekeeper's Lodge, *IV. View of a Lodge, †. A Poultry House, *XVI. Gardener's Cottage, †. A Fountain, *XXIII (frontispiece). Garden Railing (four examples), *XXVII (includes two examples from the original plate and two new examples). Gothic Diary, †. A Bridge & Temple, *IX. Plan of a Garden (showing in plan the house, offices, stables, kitchen garden, conservatory, kitchen yard, stable yard, melon ground, flower garden, "rosiary," entrance gate, and surrounding landscape), *I. A Laundry, *XV. A Small Garden (a formal design consisting of a circular walk and two cross-axial walks), †.

3. The notion that a building could be composed like a picture was explored earlier by Robert Castell in *Villas of the Ancients* (1728), Robert Morris in *Rural Architecture* (1750), and Isaac Ware in *A Complete Body of Architecture* (1756), qq.v. Papworth's remarks concerning a "retinue of subordinates" particularly recall Ware's argument that each element of a structure—central pile, wings, end pavilions, and so forth—necessarily existed in a pictorial relationship with the others. Also see Robert and James Adam, *Works in Architecture* (1778–1779); James Lewis, *Original Designs* (1780–1797); George Richardson, *New Designs in Architecture* (1792); and Edmund Bartell, *Hints for Picturesque Improvements* (1804), qq.v.

4. In 1813 Papworth published a design for a residence in which the principal rooms open directly onto the lawn in front of the house. See the commentary above on his article "Cottage Ornée."

5. In 1794 Humphry Repton analyzed the correspondence between landscape scenery and architectural style (see the commentary on his *Sketches and Hints*). Papworth's analysis was similar, but he focused on architectural *types* instead of *styles*.

6. P. 14. Papworth's "rustic," "rural," "beautiful," "grand," and "sublime" types of landscape may be traced to *Observations on Modern Gardening* (1770) by Thomas Whately, who identified several different landscape "characters" on the basis of visual and associational qualities.

7. Papworth's remarks reflect ongoing changes in the nature of the architectural profession in Britain. On the professional status of architects during this period see Colvin (1978), pp. 26–41; J. Mordaunt Crook, "The Pre-Victorian Architect: Professionalism & Patronage," *Architectural History* 12 (1969), 62–68; Frank Jenkins, *Architect and Patron* (London and New York: Oxford University Press, 1961); Barrington Kaye, *The Development of the Architectural Profession in Britain* (London: Allen & Unwin, 1960); Andrew Saint, *The Image of the Architect* (New Haven: Yale University Press, 1983); and John Wilton-Ely, "The Rise of the Professional Architect in England," in Spiro Kostof, ed., *The Architect* (New York: Oxford University Press, 1977), pp. 180–208.

8. See note 2 above.

249.1
PARKER, Charles (1799–1881)
Villa rustica. Selected from buildings and scenes in the vicinity of Rome and Florence; and arranged for lodges and domestic dwellings. With plans and details. By Charles Parker, Architect.

London: Printed for James Carpenter and Son, 1832.

iv pp, 15 printed leaves, 32 pls.

Villa rustica. Selected ⟨ . . . as 1831 . . . ⟩ details. By Charles Parker, Architect. Second Book.

London: Printed for the author; by J. M'Gowan, 1833.

15 printed leaves, 33–64 pls.

Villa rustica. Selected ⟨ . . . as 1831 . . . ⟩ details. By Charles Parker, F.A.S. Third Book.

London: Printed for the author, by E. Colyer, 1841.

12 printed leaves, 65–93 pls.

30.5 × 24.0 cm

ICU

249.2

Villa rustica: selected from buildings and scenes in the vicinity of Rome and Florence; and arranged for rural and domestic dwellings. With plans and details. By Charles Parker. . . . Second edition, with corrections and additions.

London: John Weale, 1848 [i.e., 1848–1849].

iv pp, 28 printed leaves, 72 pls [*pl. III is wanting in this copy*].

28.0 × 22.2 cm

MB

Issued in parts between 1832 and 1841, Parker's book was the third British treatise devoted to architecture in the rural Italian vernacular style. Thomas Frederick Hunt's *Architettura Campestre* (1827; *q.v.*) was first, but Hunt openly preferred Old English architecture to that of Italy. Gilbert Laing Meason published a compendium of architectural subjects illustrated in Italian landscape painting (1828; *q.v.*), but he provided no suggestions for transforming them into actual dwellings. Parker professed a high regard for the "Domestic Architecture of Italy," and indicated in his Preface that his object was twofold: "to delineate the exterior of these buildings with their surrounding scenery," and to suggest interior modifications to suit "the wants and manners of this country" (1832, iii). Also in the preface Parker explained his choice of Italian villas as models for British dwellings and schools: "many of the habits and customs of the antient Romans are still discernible in the modern structure." Nevertheless he left unexplained his choice of the Villa Rustica as his particular model. He noted that in ancient Roman times there were three types of villas—"Urbana," "Rustica," and "Fructuaria"—but the Villa Rustica contained only "the stables and accommodations for the domestics."[1]

Book I (1832) includes 32 plates illustrating 11 designs, all described individually on unnumbered leaves of letterpress. Among the models on which Parker based his designs were cottages and lodges in the vicinity of Florence and Rome, including two dwellings in the Borghese Gardens. Parker specified new uses for only four designs: a gardener's dwelling (Plates I–III), a residence for a small family (Plates XVII—XIX), a gamekeeper's dwelling (Plates XX–XXII), and a fishing or hunting box (Plates XXIX–XXXI). In a few cases he discussed the particular advantages of Italianate forms. The upper part of the campanile, for example, originally served as "a supping room, where the guests, while reclining at table might enjoy at the same time a pleasant prospect. The modern Campanile is still often resorted to for the same purposes" (Plates IX–XI).

The second Book (1833) includes eight more designs, illustrated on 32 plates and described on separate sheets of letterpress. Parker was less precise about the models for these designs, specifying the "banks of the Tiber" or the Apennine region in three cases, and the Borghese Villa in another. Nevertheless he indicated quite clearly the uses he intended for these designs: a gate lodge, an entrance lodge, a water mill, a bailiff's or steward's residence, a summer fishing residence, a hunting or shooting box, and two more gate lodges.

The final Book (1841) contains designs for ten schools, illustrated in 29 plates, plus descriptive letterpress. Parker noted that he had "again visited the continent to observe the structures there erected" (1841, "Preface"). Two of the designs include a master's residence (Plates LXXI–LXXIII and LXXIV–LXXVII). The capacity of the schools illustrated ranges from 100 children (Plates LXV–LXVII) to 1,000 (Plates LXXVIII–LXXX and LXXXI–LXXXII).

Parker's lithographed renderings of dwellings set amidst bold Italian scenery are among the most expertly executed illustrations in British architectual literature. Perspective, depth, light and shadow, shading, and texture are masterfully handled to produce a dramatic rendering of each dwelling. The design for a gate lodge in Plates XXXIII–XXXVI is typical, with "large projecting roofs . . . covered with tiles, and the external timbers made of oak. The Gables are finished with plain mouldings, and the ends of the plates and purlins are projected from the walls and ornamented with a simple pattern." In the elevation vertical lines predominate, particularly in the tall and sometimes narrow windows, the ornamental chimneys, and the three-story tower. The plan includes a sitting room, scullery, and pantry on the ground floor and two bedrooms on the chamber floor. Likewise in Plates XLVI–XLIX, "the residence of a Bailiff or Steward," the elevation is dominated by vertical lines in ground-floor arcades, an upper-floor balcony, and a three-story tower. These lines are echoed by softer verticals in foreground and background trees, while vistas to distant hills and valleys establish complementary horizontals and a sense of great pictorial depth. Parker admitted that the building was perhaps more than a bailiff or steward required, but explained that it was "intended as a picturesque feature in the general landscape, when viewed from the [main] house."

Figure 8

1. 1832, pp. iii–iv. For a much earlier discussion of Roman villas, see Robert Castell, *The Villas of the Ancients* (1728; *q.v.*). It is possible that Parker chose only the Villa Rustica because he deemed it more picturesque and informal than the Villa Urbana, which in Roman times "contained apartments for the family" (1832, p. iv).

250.1
PARKER, Thomas Netherton
Plans, specifications, estimates, and remarks on cottages, with plates: drawn up at the request of the Oswestry Society, for Bettering the Condition and Increasing the Comforts of the Poor. By T. N. Parker, Esq. And published by their direction.

Oswestry: Printed and sold by T. Edwards; sold also, by Eddowes, Shrewsbury; Hatchard, and Lackington, Allen, and Co. London, 1813.

4 + 23 + [i] pp, 4 pls.

22.3 × 14.0 cm

MH

The "Errata," printed on the verso of page 23, are dated Jan. 22, 1816.

The author, President of the Society for Bettering the Condition of the Poor, in the Hundred of Oswestry, and Parishes of Chirk and Llansilin, proposed that erecting "well arranged" houses for the laboring poor would increase their efficiency and thus produce long-term economic savings for the "proprietor" (p. 2). The text consists of estimates and comments on the use of locally available materials in building cottages, and specifications for erecting the two cottages illustrated in the four plates. The two designs, each depicted in a view, a section, and two plans, were prepared by "Mr. Thomas Jones, junior, builder, of Oswestry" (p. 1). The facade of each is two stories high, with two windows on the upper story, plus two windows and a door below. The ground-floor plan of the first cottage includes a kitchen, a bake house and washhouse, a pantry and milk house, a cow house, and a calf kitchen. Upstairs there are three chambers, one of which could be used as a "store room," plus a hayloft. In the second cottage there are just two bedrooms upstairs, and only a kitchen, pantry, and bake house below. Neither design includes any architectural ornament, although each is depicted partially obscured by picturesque foliage. Jones estimated the first would cost £130 10s 4¼d, and the second would cost £105 8s.

251.1
PARSEY, Arthur
Perspective rectified; or, the principles and application demonstrated. In this treatise the present systems of delineation are compared with a new method for producing correct perspective drawings without the use of vanishing points. By Arthur Parsey. . . . Illustrated with sixteen plates.

London: Published by Longman, Rees, Orme, Brown, Green, and Longman, and sold by all booksellers, 1836.

xiii + 84 pp, 16 pls.

27.4 × 21.6 cm

BL

251.2

_____

The science of vision; or, natural perspective! Containing the true language of the eye, necessary in common observation, education, art and science; constituting the basis of the art of design, with practical methods for foreshortening and converging in every branch of art, the new elliptical or conic sections, laws of shadows, universal vanishing points, and the new optical laws of the camera obscura, or Daguerrèotype, also, the physiology of the human eye, explaining the seat of vision to be the iris and not the retina. Second edition of the original work, entitled "Perspective rectified," with corrections and many additions. With twenty-four plates. By Arthur Parsey. . . .

London: Longman & Co., 1840.

xxxii + 142 pp, 1 printed leaf, 22 pls.

25.3 × 16.0 cm

ICJ

In the first edition the plates demonstrated perspective construction through simple geometric figures and linear diagrams as well as more sophisticated subjects such as pointed arches, ships, chairs, sofas, and a circular staircase. In the Introduction to this edition Parsey suggested he would establish for the first time "a theory which coincides with the true evidence of the senses" (p. xii), but he explained his approach better in the Introduction to the second edition. Discussing his change of title to *The Science of Vision*, Parsey argued that pictorial vision, as opposed to optics, had never been the subject of proper scientific investigation. The system of perspective as currently practiced, therefore, was only an inaccurate substitute for the representation of human vision. He proposed to develop a new system of optics and perspective based on the "natural language of the eye."[1]

Painting and drawing were more important than had ever been realized: pictures were more than mere "luxuries or ornaments." Rather, pictures were influential instruments "in forming our notions or ideas of external nature, from the first picture-book put into our infant hands till we become men of taste and connoisseurs in art and science" (1840, p. vi). But pictures organized according to conventional rules of perspective, particularly the rules formulated over a country earlier by Dr. Brook Taylor, followed only "artificial" systems (1840, p. vii). These pictures offered a false view of the world, since lines that in real life would appear to converge—e.g., the vertical edges of a tall church tower—were instead uniformly represented as parallel. Parsey claimed to have exhibited "the first picture ever drawn with optical accuracy" at the Royal Academy in 1837 (1840, p. vii), presumably with vertical lines converging. He concluded his introduction with an account of the reception of his ideas among various institutions and societies.

In the second edition Parsey included additional subjects in the plates to illustrate his theory more thoroughly. These included a house—Fig. 58 in Plate 10—drawn in "natural perspective." The dwelling is shown in outline in an oblique view, without roof, but with six windows in the facade and a door in the side wall. The "vertical" lines of the walls and windows clearly converge, the walls seeming to tilt away from the viewer.

1. "The popular theory of perspective being only an artificial system, no production has hitherto taught the natural language of the eye. The optical principles of the projection of light and ocular appearances being resolvable to the same common laws, the linear science of vision will constitute the practical manual of optics" (1840, p. v).

252.1
PARTINGTON, Charles Frederick
The British cyclopaedia, of arts and sciences, manufactures, commerce, literature, history, geography, politics, biography, natural history, Biblical criticism and theology, on the basis of the German conversations–lexicon, with such additions as will adapt it to the present state of science. By Charles F. Partington. . . . Arts and sciences.—Vol. I.

London: Published by Orr & Smith; W. and R. Chambers, Edinburgh; W. Curry, Jun. and Co., Dublin; Bancks and Co., Manchester; Wrightson and Webb, Birmingham; Willmer and Smith, Liverpool; Wright and Bagnall, Bristol; and Thomas Wardle, Philadelphia, 1833.

The British cyclopaedia of the arts and sciences; including treatises on the various branches of natural and experimental philosophy, the useful and fine arts, mathematics, commerce, &c. By Charles F. Partington. . . . Complete in two volumes. Second volume.

London: Published by Orr & Smith, 1835.

Art. "Perspective," II, 165–170.

24.5 × 16.5 cm

DLC

252.2 †

The British cyclopaedia of arts and sciences, manufactures, commerce, literature, history, geography, politics, biography, natural history, Biblical criticism and theology. . . . By Charles F. Partington.

London: Orr & Smith, 1834–1836.

3 vols.

25 cm

Reference: NUC-S

252.3

The British cyclopaedia ⟨ . . . as 1833–1835 Vol. II . . . ⟩ volumes. First [*or* Second] volume.

London: Published by Orr & Smith, 1835.

Art. "Perspective," II, 165–170.

24.9 × 17.0 cm

WU

252.4 ‖

The British cyclopaedia of the arts, sciences, history, geography, literature, natural history, and biography; copiously illustrated by engravings on wood and steel by eminent artists. Edited by Charles F. Partington. . . . Complete in ten volumes. Volume I [*or* II]. Arts and Sciences.

London: Wm. S. Orr and Co., 1838.

Art. "Perspective," II, 165–170.

24.5 × 15.5 cm

Reference: Information supplied by Winterthur Museum Library.

The article on "Architecture" (I, 90–102, and 3 pls) begins with a history of architecture in Babylon, Egypt, India, Greece, Rome, medieval Europe, Renaissance Italy, and England from Inigo Jones through the Gothic Revival. Four pages are devoted to the five orders, followed by remarks on Persians and caryatids, funeral monuments, and the Monument of Lysicrates. The remainder of the article (pp. 97–102) is a history and analysis of Gothic architecture. The three plates include examples of Egyptian, Classical, and Gothic architecture. Text figures depict the orders and other subjects.

The article on "Perspective" includes a text illustration on page 168 showing an outline drawing of a house, two stories high and three windows wide, seen in perspective view. This illustration appeared earlier, reversed, in George Gregory's *Dictionary* (1806–1807; *q.v.*).

253.1

PASLEY, Sir Charles William (1780–1861)

[*Volume I:*]

Course of instruction, originally composed for the use of the Royal Engineer Department. By C. W. Pasley. . . . Volume I. Containing practical geometry and the principles of plan drawing.

London: Printed for John Murray, 1814.

xvi + 269 pp.

[*Volume II:*]

Course of military instruction, ⟨ . . . as Vol. I . . . ⟩ Pasley. . . . Volume II. Containing elementary fortification.

London: Printed for John Murray, 1817.

6 + iii–xl + 335 pp, 5 pls [*all pls wanting in this copy*].

[*Volume III:*]

Course of military instruction, ⟨ . . . as Vol. I . . . ⟩ Pasley. . . . Volume III. Containing elementary fortification.

London: Printed for John Murray, 1817.

xxix + 335–702 pp.

20.8 × 12.6 cm

MnU

253.2

_____

A complete course of practical geometry, including conic sections, and plan drawing; treated on a principle of peculiar perspicuity. Originally published as the first volume of a course of military instruction, by C. W. Pasley. . . . Second edition, much enlarged.

London: Published by T. Egerton, 1822.

xlvii + 608 pp.

21.1 × 13.3 cm

DLC

253.3 †

_____

Complete course of practical geometry and plan drawing; &c.

London, 1838.

8°

Reference: RIBA (1937–1938)

253.4 †

——————

Course of practical geometry and plan drawing.

[London]: Parker & Son, 1851.

8°

Reference: ECB

Pasley first issued his treatise on geometry and plan drawing in 1814, as "Volume I" in what by 1817 became a three-volume manual of military instruction. The second and third volumes, concerning fortification, were reissued separately in 1822. The treatise on geometry and plan drawing was reissued separately in an enlarged edition of 1822, and also in 1838 and 1851.

In 1811 Pasley, attached to the Plymouth company of Royal Military Artificers, set out to devise a system of instruction that could enable "the non-commissioned officers and soldiers . . . to understand the nature of a rough sketch, plan or section," but would not require "calling in the assistance of scientific masters of any kind" (1814, pp. v–vi). Pasley had found all existing geometry texts unsuitable for this purpose, and so developed his own text based on methods of instruction "lately introduced into this country for the education of the poor, by Dr. Bell and Mr. Lancaster" (1814, pp. v–vi). Pasley conjectured that his text might also be of use to the general population, enabling "a more general diffusion of some knowledge of Practical Geometry amongst the lower classes," especially masons and carpenters. He further suggested that the work would supplement the learning of "young gentlemen who have received a good classical education" (1814, p. vii).

The treatise on geometry occupied the first 224 pages of the first edition and the first 562 pages of the second. The rest of each edition was devoted to "The Principles of Plan Drawing," a topic that, according to Pasley, had not previously been treated in print (1822, p. vi). In a succession of 76 diagrams[1] accompanied by detailed instructions Pasley demonstrated the formation of a plan, section, elevation, and oblique elevation of a rudimentary dwelling, a simple box with one door, one window, and a gable roof.

1. The diagrams appear to be identical in the editions of 1814 and 1822. The texts are similar, but not identical.

PAXTON, Sir Joseph (1803–1865), ed.
The horticultural register.

See Entry 474.

254.1
Paxton's magazine of botany, and register of flowering plants.

[*Volume I:*] London: Orr and Smith, 1834.
[*Volume II:*] ———— ,1836.
[*Volume III:*] London: Published by W. S. Orr & Co., 1837.
[*Volume IV:*] ———— , 1838.
[*Volume V:*] ———— , 1838.
[*Volume VI:*] ———— , 1839.
[*Volume VII:*] ———— , 1840.
[*Volume VIII:*] London: Published by Wm. S. Orr & Co., 1841.
[*Volume IX:*] ———— , 1842.

[*For volumes published after 1842, see the entry in the* Union List of Serials, *3rd ed., IV, 3281.*]

MnU

Primarily a horticultural journal, *Paxton's Magazine of Botany* includes three articles that contain designs for dwellings and ornamental garden structures:[1]

• "Plan and Description of a Gate Lodge to a Country Residence," I (1834), 178–179. This design and the accompanying description were previously published in Paxton's *Horticultural Register* for September 1833 (*q.v.*). The author of this design, "A Bricklayer's Labourer," contributed several other designs to *The Horticultural Register*, and these are mentioned below.

• "Designs for the Erection of Ornamental Cottages, on Gentlemen's Es-states," I (1834), 251–257. The article contains designs for three double cottages and one quadruple cottage. Each appeared previously in separate articles in Paxton's *Horticultural Register* for August 1831, October 1831, February 1832, and August 1834. There the designs were attributed, respectively, to "Artus," "A Bricklayer's Labourer," idem, and "The Brick-layer's Labourer."

• **R. Mallet, Esq. of Dublin,** "Garden Architecture. On the Various Forms and Characters of Arbours as Objects of Use or Ornament, Either in Garden or Wild Scenery," IV (1838), 82–86. Following references to Milton, the Bible, Horace, and Virgil, Mallet classified arbors into three types: purely natural, partly natural and partly artificial, and wholly artificial. Five text figures provide examples of all three types, including lone trees (Figs. 1 and 2), a tree ornamented with climbing plants (Fig. 3), a ring of trees planted to enclose a circular space (Fig. 4), and a large pedimented arch with wings, largely constructed of treillage (Fig. 5). This article also appeared in Paxton's *Horticultural Register* IV (1835).

1. The editor, Sir Joseph Paxton, was a prolific architect, gardener, and designer of parks. See George F. Chadwick, *The Works of Sir Joseph Paxton 1803–1865* (London: Architectural Press, 1961).

255.1
PEACOCK, James (1738?–1814)

Οικιδια, or, nutshells: being ichnographic distributions for small villas; chiefly upon oeconomical principles. In seven classes. With occasional remarks. By Jose Mac Packe, a bricklayer's labourer. Part the first, containing twelve designs.

London: Printed for the author, and sold by C. Dilly, 1785.

1 printed leaf, 89 pp, 2 + 25 pls.

20.6 × 13.0 cm

MBAt

255.2 †
_____

Οικιδια.

London, 1786.

8°

Reference: APSD

Following the lead set by Daniel Garret, William Halfpenny, and Nathaniel Kent in preceding decades,[1] Peacock set out to provide designs for economical and convenient small houses. But unlike his predecessors, Peacock did not present designs for farm houses. Rather, his plans were "chiefly intended for the more immediate use of gentlemen of moderate fortunes"—in other words, for their own personal residences. Since his clients would not likely be able to afford an architect, Peacock included more specific and practical information than if these had been "hints to the designer" (p. 1).

There are no elevations or views among Peacock's illustrations. He provided only plans, explaining that his "main intention" was "to give the first or elementary principles of designs for small dwellings, leaving the parts less fixed and determinate, to be supplied by the builder in any style of simplicity or decoration he may affect" (p. 2). Peacock implied, therefore, that exterior articulation and style were entirely secondary considerations.[2]

Throughout the book there is a recurring emphasis on economy. Peacock stressed efficient distribution of space, and not style or show: "Men who are determined to keep their arms a kimbo, and would sooner lose the point of an elbow, than abate half an hair's breadth of their accustomed strut, should look into folio volumes" (p. 4). He also deplored the decoration of houses for decoration's sake: "the building should not be made for the ornament, but the ornament for the building. Hence appers the ill oeconomy of those who design their elevation for effect, and make the plan a secondary consideration" (p. 68).

Following the Introduction (pp. 1–4) there is a series of 11 tables with letterpress explanations (pp. 5–24 and plates A and D), giving proper proportions for rooms, passages, staircases, windows, doors, and fireplace openings in each of seven "classes" of building. Pages 25 through 49 give detailed dimensions for the plans illustrated in Plates I–XXV. These include ground- and chamber-floor plans for 12 dwellings, plus a ground-floor plan for "four distinct Dwellings, united to form a single regular pile" (Plate XXV). Most of the plans contain four principal rooms to a floor, plus a staircase hall or landing. Peacock did not designate the use of these rooms, calling them simply a "Room," "A second room," and so forth.

Many floor plans and individual rooms are based on elementary geometric figures, including squares, circles, ovals, and hexagons. Two designs are unusual combinations of such figures: Plates III and IV show ground- and chamber-floor plans consisting of a pair of circles attached to a pair of bow-fronted pavilions; Plates IX and X are plans of a hexagonal house with three hexagonal rooms on each floor.

The last major portion of the book is a long "Appendix" (pp. 51–84), including advice to "the gentleman" on designing and building his own house, dealing with workmen, and understanding the principles of beauty. The book concludes with several pages of endnotes keyed to references in the text.

1. See Garret, *Designs, and Estimates, of Farm Houses* (1747); Halfpenny, *Six New Designs* (1751), *Twelve Beautiful Designs* (1749), and *Useful Architecture* (1751); and Kent, *Hints to Gentlemen* (1775).

2. In this respect Peacock clearly foreshadowed John Claudius Loudon's remarks on the ancillary nature of architectural style. See Loudon's *Encyclopaedia of Cottage, Farm, and Villa Architecture* (1833).

PHUSIN, Kata [pseud. for John RUSKIN]
"The poetry of architecture."

See LOUDON, **John Claudius, ed.** The architectural magazine, *Entry 182.*

256.1 ‡
PICKETT, W.
Twenty-four plates divided into ninety-six specimens of

cottages,—	bridges,—	castles,—	churches,
wind-mills,—	abbeys,—	water-mills,—	lighthouses,
turnpikes,—	ruins,—	barns,—	rocks,
priories,—	kilns,—	waterfalls,—	gateways,
crosses,—	cliffs,—	forts,—	wharfs,
towers,—	alehouses,—	caves,—	wells.

Intended to facilitate the improvement of the student, and to aid the practitioner, in landscape composition: by W. Pickett.

[London]: Published by T. Clay. Printed by J. Hayes, [1812].

24 pls.

30 × 48 cm

Reference: Microfilm supplied by The British Library.

The title page accurately identifies the subject matter of all 24 plates. Each plate contains four individual illustrations, executed in aquatint.

As cottages, bridges, and other picturesque subjects appeared with increasing frequency in the paintings of Gainsborough and Constable, they also became a necessary part of an art student's vocabulary. Pickett's *Twenty-Four Plates* is one of the earliest published collections of rural architectural subjects meant to assist in this aspect of art education.[1] Architects too were concerned with picturesque coordination of buildings with landscape,[2] and this book no doubt interested many architectural students and practitioners.

Pickett's concern for picturesque integration of structures with scenery is revealed in the lush foliage surrounding and sometimes partially obscuring his subjects.[3] Many illustrations include a river in the foreground, creating additional interest through reflections and textural contrasts. Fences, ells, barns, and other picturesque elements make each illustration a balanced and animated composition. Most of Pickett's cottages, turnpike houses, and other residences are composed in an irregular, apparently casual manner, very much like that advocated by James Malton in his *Essay on British Cottage Architecture* (1798; *q.v.*).

1. John Thomas Smith illustrated cottages 15 years earlier in his *Remarks on Rural Scenery* (1797), and cottages were a principal subject in *William Orme's Rudiments* (1802). A cottage also appears in the frontispiece of John Hassell's *Speculum* (1809). Pickett's work was a foretaste of the larger collection of cottage subjects published by Stevens et al. as *Domestic Architecture* in 1815. For all four of these works see the individual commentaries above and below.

2. For discussion of this point see Chapter III, Section 9, in "The Literature of British Domestic Architecture, 1715–1842" above.

3. In this respect Pickett's illustrations are very much like those of William Atkinson in *Views of Picturesque Cottages* (1805; *q.v.*).

PICTON, J. A.
"On cemeteries."

See LOUDON, **John Claudius, ed.,** The architectural magazine, *Entry 182.*

Picturesque sketches of rustic scenery including cottages & farm houses.

See STEVENS, **Francis,** *Entry 324.*

257.1 †
PINNOCK, William (1782–1843)
A catechism of perspective. . . . By a friend to youth.

London: Pinnock & Maunder, [1820?].

34 pp, pls.

12°

Reference: BM

Pinnock's catechisms. A catechism of perspective; intended as a companion to the catechisms of drawing and architecture; containing a variety of useful examples. Fourth edition.

London: Printed for Geo. B. Whittaker, [1823].

34 pp, additional engraved title page, 4 pls.

12°

Reference: Microfilm supplied by The British Library.

The "fourth edition" has been dated [1823] because that date appears on the added engraved title page. The letterpress title page, like that of the other edition, is not dated.

Twelve figures appear on the four plates of the "fourth edition." Some are geometric constructions, while others show human figures, trees, arches, and slopes. Figures 2 and 8 are outline drawings of a one-story house, with one window and one door, shown in an oblique view. Figure 12 shows objects inside a room. The text is a series of brief questions and answers that give definitions and elementary demonstrations.

PITT, William
"Buildings of a farm."

See Annals of agriculture, *Entry 479.*

258.1
PITT, William Morton (1754 or 1755–1836)
An address to the landed interest, on the deficiency of habitations and fuel, for the use of the poor. By Wm. Morton Pitt. . . .

London: Printed for Elmsly and Bremner, 1797.

iii + [4] + 51 pp, 5 pls.

22.9 × 14.0 cm

MH

Agricultural improvement was an object of growing attention in the last decade of the eighteenth century, as the Board of Agriculture began to publish its surveys of individual counties (*q.v.*) and the first volumes of its *Communications.*[1] In 1797 William Morton Pitt published this *Address* concerning the welfare of agricultural laborers. In the Introduction (pp. i–iii) he flattered his audience and appealed to its philanthropic concerns: "It is to the gentlemen of landed property, that the whole body of agricultural Poor look for protection, as well as for employment" (p. i). In the text (pp. 1–31) he recommended that currently uncultivated tracts of land be offered to laborers so they could erect cottages and establish large gardens for themselves. This would increase their self-sufficiency and pride, provide an incentive for laborers to produce more for their own support, and thus reduce the wages the landowner would have to pay (p. 9). Pitt also included remarks on financing and designing laborers' cottages (pp. 17–22), on workhouses and "schools of industry" (pp. 23–28), and on fuel (pp. 29–31). The Appendix (pp. 32–51) concerns "the Institution of Working-Schools for poor Girls, and of Sunday-Schools for poor Boys and Girls, in Chester."

The five plates depict plans, elevations, and sections of one single cottage and four double cottages, uniformly plain and unembellished, described briefly in the text as "simple and economical, and of the smallest size possible, to include all the [necessary] requisites and conveniences" (p. 22). The single cottage in the first plate includes a kitchen, pantry, and three bedrooms all on one floor. The one-story double cottages in the second plate each have a kitchen, a pantry, and three bedrooms. The cottages in Plates 3 and 4 each have a kitchen, a pantry, and four or three bedrooms, respectively, on two floors. The two-story design in Plate 5 includes a kitchen, a pantry, three bedrooms, a "Pigs house," a cow stall, and a "fuel house."

1. See articles in the first volume of *Communications* (1797) by Beatson, Crocker, Crutchley, Holland, and Hunt.

259.1
PLAW, John (1745?–1820)
Ferme ornée; or rural improvements. A series of domestic and ornamental designs, suited to parks, plantations, rides, walks, rivers, farms, &c. Consisting of fences, paddock houses, a bath, a dog-kennel, pavilions, farm = yards, fishing-houses, sporting-boxes, shooting-lodges, single and double cottages, &c. Calculated for landscape and picturesque effects. Engraved on thirty eight plates. With appropriate scenery, plans, and explanations. By John Plaw, Architect.

London: Published by I. and J. Taylor, 1795.

[i] + 13 pp, 38 pls (plus, in this copy, following pl. 1, a duplicate of pl. 11).

29.2 × 20.6 cm

Bodl.

259.2

———

Ferme ornée; ⟨ . . . as 1795 . . . ⟩ effects. Engraved on thirty-eight plates. With appropriate scenery, plans, and explanations. By John Plaw, Architect.

London: Published by I. and J. Taylor, 1796.

[i] + 13 pp, 38 pls [*pl. 4 is wanting in this copy*].

29.2 × 23.5 cm

MH

259.3

————

Ferme ornée; or, rural improvements. ⟨ . . . as 1795 . . . ⟩ effects. Engraved in aqua-tinta on thirty-eight plates. With appropriate scenery, plans, and explanations. By John Plaw. . . . A new edition.

London: Printed by W. Stratford; for J. Taylor, 1800.

[i] + 13 pp, 38 pls.

28.6 × 22.2 cm

V&A

259.4

————

————

London: Printed by W. Stratford; for J. Taylor, 1803.

[i] + 13 pp, 38 pls.

31.8 × 24.4 cm

RIBA

259.5

————

————

London: Printed for J. Taylor, 1813.

[i] + 13 pp, 38 pls.

30.2 × 23.8 cm

NN

259.6

————

Ferme ornée; or, rural improvements. A series of domestic and ornamental designs, suited to parks, plantations, rides, walks, rivers, farms, &c. Consisting of fences, paddock-houses, a bath, a dog-kennel, pavilions, farm= yards, fishing houses, sporting boxes, shooting lodges, single and double cottages, &c. Calculated for landscape and picturesque effects. Engraved in aqua-tinta on thirty-eight plates. With appropriate scenery, plans, and explanations. By John Plaw. . . . A new edition.

London: Printed for J. Taylor, 1823.

[i] + 14 pp, 38 pls.

31.8 × 25.4 cm

MH

The title of Plaw's book recalls the long-standing ideal of the English country estate as a place of rural retirement, a notion current since the seventeenth century, when it appeared in practice as well as in the poetry of Jonson, Marvell, and others.[1] Following publications by Switzer and Castell (*qq.v.*) in the early eighteenth century, there emerged a conscious effort to emulate Roman farm towns, or "villas," in the design of country estates. By 1731 the author of "Dawley Farm" made a point of describing a country estate as both a villa and a farm:

See! Emblem of himself, his Villa stand!
Politely finish'd, regularly Grand!
Frugal of Ornament; but that the best,
And all with curious Negligence express'd.
No gaudy Colours stain the Rural Hall,
Blank Light and Shade discriminate the Wall:
Where thro' the Whole we see his lov'd Design,
To please with Mildness, without Glaring shine;
Himself neglects what must all others charm,
And what he built a Palace calls a Farm.[2]

By the early 1740s the term *ferme ornée*, invoking an artificially elegant pastoralism, had been imported from the Continent and began to augment the Roman villa ideal. Perhaps the earliest mention of the *ferme ornée* in an English treatise was in the "Appendix" to the third volume of the final edition of Stephen Switzer's *Ichnographia Rustica* (1742). Although most of the appendix concerned sunlight, trees, and mushrooms, Switzer also illustrated the plan of one estate that apparently combined both the Latin and the ornamented models: it was "a regulated Epitomy of a much larger Design portraited and lay'd out, by the Right Honourable the Lord *Bathurst* at *Riskins* near *Colnbrooke*, upon the Plan of the *Ferme Ornée*, and the Villa's of the Ancients."[3]

As early as 1734 Philip Southcote had begun to embellish the landscape at his estate, Woburn Farm.[4] The date of completion is uncertain, but his improvements likely constituted the first *ferme ornée* actually completed in England. Indeed no one challenged Joseph Spence's remark that "Mr. Southcote [was] the first that brought in the garden farm, or *ferme ornée*." Spence believed that Southcote took "his idea of a Ferme Ornée" from Italian models, in "Fields, going from Rome to Venice."[5]

The letters of William Shenstone reveal that he too was developing such a farm in 1748. But he apparently took his inspiration from France: "The French have what they call a *parque ornée*; I suppose, approaching about as near to a garden as the park at Hagley. I give my place the title of a *ferme ornée*."[6]

In 1770 Thomas Whately published *Observations on Modern Gardening*, a popular treatise that canonized the *ferme ornée* as one of nine specific types of landscape. Whately devoted 11 pages to the *ferme ornée*, and in a lengthy description of The Leasowes cited Shenstone's improvements as exemplary of the type.[7]

John Plaw was the first to extend the term *"ferme ornée"* to mean more than just a style of landscape or a kind of country estate. He did so in part by associating the term with specific architectural types and groupings of buildings that he depicted in his plates. There, in addition to several designs for fences and ha-has, he illustrated a wide variety of rustic and picturesque structures: a wood pile house (i.e., an outhouse), a garden seat, cattle sheds, paddock sheds, an aviary, a poultry house, dog kennels, a fishing bridge, a combination fishing lodge and keeper's dwelling, a hunting box, shepherd's huts, a bath, cottages, a cottager's lodge, a hunting lodge, a keeper's lodge, a villa in the cottage style, farm houses, farmyards and offices, a fold yard, a cattle yard, stables, a barn, a cow or ox house, a village, and village buildings. Certainly no *ferme ornée* could include all such structures, but each was well suited to the retired, rustic, and picturesque characteristics of a *ferme ornée*.

As illustrated, every building was carefully designed in a picturesque manner, or else well integrated with the surrounding scenery. Several designs were prepared with particular scenic locations in mind, including one for a bath, "designed for John Morant, Esq. Brockenhurst-House, New Forest" (Plates 14, 15; p. 7). The bath itself is a Palladian rotunda with a square, gable-roofed dressing room attached to the front, clearly reminiscent of the Pantheon. The design is surrounded, however, by lush coniferous forest, making for a pleasing contrast between the formal geometry of the bath and the pointed, angular shapes of the trees—precisely the sort of picturesque contrast advocated by Humphry Repton only one year earlier in his *Sketches and Hints on Landscape Gardening* (1794; *q.v.*). Other designs have an intrinsically picturesque rusticity, well suited to a rural environment. The shepherd's hut illustrated in Plate 12, for example, is designed to resemble a haystack. The keeper's lodge in Plate 22 has gnarled tree trunks with the bark still attached supporting the thatch roof, plus walls made of rockwork, and window frames made of branches.

Several designs are a marriage of the rustic and the geometric. The lodge in Plate 13, for example, is a two-story cylinder with a conical thatch roof. Three concave segmental alcoves in the ground story of the cylinder, with Tuscan columns *in antis*, accommodate an entrance and windows. The stylistic character of the design is further confused by the windows, which are Gothic.[8] Nevertheless Plaw considered stylistic harmony an important criterion. In Plate 5, for example, he presented a cattle shed with three different elevations—Classical, Monastic, or Rustic—so that the client could choose "whichever character may best accord with the adjoining buildings." Altogether Plaw presented designs in numerous styles, including rustic, Gothic, Castellated ("Monastic"), Palladian, and a cross between late Adam and early Regency.

Among Plaw's unique offerings were his illustrations of "American cottages," erected by Colonel Montresor in Kent (Plate 17). They had steeply pitched roofs, presumably to shed snow more easily, and had full-width open porches across the front.[9] Another design shows an entire farm estate, square in plan, surrounded by a wall and then by rows of trees, and above which stands the tall central tower of the house itself. All was done in "Monastic" style, to give the whole by association "an air of antiquity, consequence, and grandeur" (p. 10).

Plaw was the first practicing British architect to publish a detailed design for an entire village (Plate 33). Prepared for an entrepreneur in Yorkshire, apparently to house lead miners, the design was rectangular in plan, and therefore "intended to unite symmetry and utility" (p. 12). The houses would be built "in couples," i.e., semidetached, and in the central area there would be a church or chapel and pumps for water. Two following

Figure 9

plates show designs for "cottages" and "village buildings" that were "applicable" to the design for a village (p. 12). Each cottage in one semidetached pair (Plate 34) includes a living room, pantry, and "bed" on the ground floor, and a chamber floor above partitioned into two rooms. The "Village Buildings" in Plate 35 are a semidetached pair just one story high, with dormers in the roof. Each unit contains four rooms: a living room, a kitchen, a bedroom, and either a second bedroom or a "Pantry and Cellar."

The plates were executed in aquatint, thus facilitating a wide range of textures and shadings for depicting building materials and foliage. Plaw achieved a sense of depth in his illustrations by shading the landscape in increasingly light tones as it receded. The text (pp. 1–13) consists entirely of plate descriptions indicating which designs were commissioned and executed, and giving advice on materials and on siting in relation to nearby scenery and the estate as a whole.

Plaw's goal in publishing the book was to attract new clients. He noted in the "Advertisement" that many of his designs already had been executed, and "of most of them I have small models which completely shew their effect in execution; these I shall be happy to explain to any Gentleman who may wish to inspect them." But Plaw's influence was more widespread than his practice.[10] He was, for example, the first British author to recommend the use of pisé, or rammed earth, in building cottages.[11] More important, through *Ferme Ornée* and his other books, he encouraged a romantic, picturesque view of the cottage and other small dwellings. In his emphasis on rusticity, the associational use of style to convey ideas of history or rurality, and the coordination of architectural character with that of surrounding scenery, Plaw helped establish several important Romantic alternatives to the prevailing Palladian canons of architectural design.

1. See Mark Girouard, "A Place in the Country," *The Times Literary Supplement*, 27 February 1976, pp. 223–225; and G. R. Hibbard, "The Country House Poem of the Seventeenth Century," *Journal of the Warburg and Courtauld Institutes* XIX:1–2 (January–June 1956), 159–174.

2. "Dawley FARM," *Fog's Weekly Journal*, Saturday, 26 June 1731, p. [2].

3. Stephen Switzer, "An Appendix to Ichnographia Rustica," *Ichnographia Rustica* (London, 1742), III, p. 9. For more on Switzer see the commentary on *The Nobleman, Gentleman, and Gardener's Recreation* (1715; Entry 327). On the *ferme ornée* in France see Dora Wiebenson, *The Picturesque Garden in France* (Princeton: Princeton University Press, 1978), pp. 98–100. Finally, one article arrived too late for me to profit from it: William A. Brogden, "The *Ferme Ornée* and Changing Attitudes to Agricultural Improvement," *Eighteenth Century Life*, n.s. VIII:2 (January 1983), 39–43.

4. See Joseph Spence, *Observations, Anecdotes, and Characters of Books and Men*, ed. James M. Osborn (Oxford: Clarendon Press, 1966), I, 424, §1126.

5. Ibid., I, 424, §1125; I, 250, §603.

6. William Shenstone, *The Works*, 3rd ed. (London, 1773), III, 142.

7. Thomas Whately, *Observations on Modern Gardening*, 4th ed. (London, 1777), pp. 161–171.

8. Plaw also remarked that "This cottage, if properly built on wheels, might also be moved at pleasure" (p. 6).

9. These were typical of eighteenth-century dwellings in the Mississippi valley. See Hugh Morrison, *Early American Architecture* (New York: Oxford University Press, 1952), pp. 257–260.

10. The list of works actually executed by Plaw is short. See Colvin (1978), pp. 642–643.

11. In the "Advertisement" to the 1795 edition he mentioned "the new method of building Walls for Cottages, &c. as practised in France," described by François Cointeraux "in a little work lately published at Paris, under the title of *Maison de Pisé*" (1792). Plaw recommended the method as "practicable on a small scale" and cheap. Two years later Henry Holland provided the first detailed description in English of the process of building with pisé: see his article titled "Pisé" (1797; *q.v.*).

260.1

PLAW, John (1745?–1820)

Rural architecture: consisting of designs, from the simple cottage, to the more decorated villa; including some which have been built under the author's direction. By John Plaw. . . . London: etch'd and shaded in aqua = tinta by the author; and published by subscription, at his house. . . . Part the first; containing thirty copper-plates.

[London: The author], 1785.

7 pp, 30 pls (numbered I–XXIX, XXXI).

25.4 × 18.4 cm

Soane

260.2

Rural architecture; or designs from the simple cottage, to the decorated villa; including some which have been executed by the author, John Plaw. . . .

London: Etch'd and shaded in aqua-tinta, on sixty-one copper-plates, and published by the author; at Mr. Cust's, Stationer; and J. and J. Taylors, 1790.

8 + viii pp, frontisp. + 60 pls (numbered I–XL, XL, XLII–LX).

24.8 × 17.8 cm

CtY-BA

260.3

Rural architecture; or designs, from the simple cottage to the decorated villa; including some which have been executed. By John Plaw, Architect and Surveyor. Etched and shaded in aqua-tinta, on sixty-two plates.

London: Published by J. and J. Taylors, 1794.

8 + viii pp, frontisp. + 61 pls (numbered I, I*, II–LX).

28.0 × 20.3 cm

BL

260.4

———

———

London: Published by I. and J. Taylor, 1796.

8 pp, frontisp. + 61 pls (numbered I, I*, II–LX).

29.8 × 22.2 cm

MH

260.5 †

———

Rural architecture.

London, 1800.

Reference: APSD

260.6

———

Rural architecture; ⟨ . . . as 1794 . . . ⟩.

London: Published by J. Taylor, 1802.

8 pp, frontisp. + 61 pls (numbered I, I*, II–LX).

20.6 × 28.6 cm

MB

This collection of designs for modest, picturesque country residences is the first example of a genre of British architectural literature often described informally as the "villa book."[1] Such books generally include a brief prefatory essay, short descriptions of the plates, and plans and elevations of designs in a variety of styles, usually surrounded by lush foliage.[2]

The innovative nature of *Rural Architecture* is apparent in its size, its content, its format, and the audience to which it is addressed. Plaw's book is a thin quarto, the text consists of one or two lines describing each plate, and the designs are uniformly modest in size, elegantly ornamented, and surrounded by picturesque scenery. Such a book was not to be found among the established genres of architectural literature in 1785. Comprehensive treatises by Chambers, Gibbs, and Ware[3] were very large folios that treated such subjects as the orders, the principles of composition, and the details of construction, and illustrated designs for dwellings among a variety of other subjects in the plates. Collections of original designs by contemporary architects, such as Adam, Lewis, and Paine,[4] also were large folios, and unlike *Rural Architecture* included elaborately detailed plates and sometimes lengthy descriptions. Collections of smaller designs for farm houses, cottages, and lodges, such as those by Garret, Halfpenny, Kent, and Peacock,[5] were prepared with more attention to economy and convenience than to picturesque beauty.

Rural Architecture was the first British architectural book to include aquatinted plates. The process allowed Plaw an entirely new range of textures and tones to depict light and shadow, three-dimensional advance and recession, and the different tactile qualities of trees, shrubbery, lawns, stone, and stucco. He took advantage of this technique to unify architecture and landscape in picturesque compositions. Indeed Plaw was the first to publish designs in which landscape was an important component of the entire composition. In Plate XXVIII, for example, the large dome of the rotunda at Belle Isle is echoed in the rounded form of a tree to the right, by clouds and hills in the distance, by the gentle rise of ground on which it sits, and by the serpentine path in the foreground.

Plaw's frontispiece is an allegory, something unusual in British architectural literature, but the message is an appropriate comment on his commitment to picturesque architecture and landscape. Two figures stand in the foreground, and one gestures toward a Pantheon-like structure in the middle distance, on an island in a lake. The gesturing figure is dressed fashionably, while the other wears a plain, simple garment:

The Subject is Taste, accompanying Rural Simplicity, and pointing to one of the most beautiful Scenes this County can boast of, viz. The Lake of Winandermere; on the largest Island in which, is built a circular Villa after a Design of the Author's; the Plans, Elevations, &c. are in this Work.[6]

The letterpress includes a list of subscribers (pp. i–viii) and a table of "Contents" (pp. 1–8) composed of brief descriptions of each plate. The 61 plates depict 30 designs, including 13 villas, five cottages, "the Circular House, on the great Island, in the Lake of Winandermere," residences designed for Robert Colt, an Irish client named Scott, the Duke of Gordon, and Humberstone Mackenzie, alterations to Selson House and Wootton Court, plus a hermitage, a "small house," a shooting farm, a "Casine," and a "Mansion House." In plan Plaw's designs are symmetrical or nearly so, with only an occasional office wing or projecting bay attached to one side. The elevations are uniform and symmetrical, and embellished with Neoclassical ornament. This includes semicircular and segmental relieving arches, Doric and Ionic porticoes, decorative urns mounted on parapets, decorative bas-relief panels, and occasional rusticated masonry.

Apart from the one-room hermitage (Plate I*), Plaw's smallest design is a two-story thatched cottage designed for the Duke of Gordon (Plate I), with only a living room, washhouse, and milk house on the ground floor. One of the largest designs, also prepared for the Duke of Gordon, is the residence shown in Plates LII and LIII. The principal facade is two stories high and 11 windows wide; it is framed in the center and at both ends by two-story porticoes. The ground-floor plan includes a withdrawing room, eating room, dressing room, wardrobe, water closet, morning room, bedroom, audit room, steward's room, kitchen, housekeeper's and butler's rooms, and service wings. Certainly Plaw's most impressive design was the circular rotunda at Lake Windermere (Plates XXV–XXX). Set on a rusticated basement, the house is three stories high, 50 feet in diameter, and fronted by a tetrastyle Ionic portico. The principal floor plan includes a library, withdrawing room, eating parlor, vestibule, and closet. Both the chamber floor and the "Attic" floor contain five bedrooms, two servant's bedrooms, and several closets.

1. On this subject see Sandra Blutman, "Books of Designs for Country Houses, 1780–1815," *Architectural History* 11 (1968), 25–33; Katherine A. Esdaile, "The Small House and Its Amenities in the Architectural Hand-books of 1749–1827," *Transactions of the Bibliographical Society* XV (October 1917–March 1919), 115–132; Donald Sutherland Lyall, "Minor Domestic Architecture in England and Pattern Books 1790–1840," Ph.D. diss., University of London, 1974; Michael McMordie, "Picturesque Pattern Books and Pre-Victorian Designers," *Architectural History* 18 (1975), 43–59; and Dora Wiebenson, "A Document of Social Change: The Small House Publication," in R. Cohen, ed., *English Art and Aesthetics in the 18th Century* (forthcoming). Also see Chapter II, Section 1, in "The Literature of British Domestic Architecture, 1715–1842" above.

2. A list of such books would necessarily include dozens of titles. For a representative sample, see books by Aikin, Atkinson, Busby, Dearn, Gandy, Gyfford, Lugar, and Pocock, in addition to Plaw's later books.

3. Sir William Chambers, *Treatise* (1759); James Gibbs, *A Book of Architecture* (1728); and Isaac Ware, *A Complete Body of Architecture* (1756), qq.v.

4. Robert and James Adam, *Works* (1778–1779); James Lewis, *Original Designs* (1780–1797); and James Paine, *Plans, Elevations and Sections* (1767–1783), qq.v.

5. Daniel Garret, *Designs, and Estimates, of Farm Houses* (1747); William Halfpenny, *Twelve Beautiful Designs for Farm Houses* (1749); Nathaniel Kent, *Hints to Gentlemen* (1775); and James Peacock, Οικιδια (1785), qq.v.

6. P. 1. The house was designed by Plaw in 1774–1775, and is now known as Belle Isle. See E. W. Hodge, "Belle Isle, Westmorland," *Country Life* LXXXVIII (3 and 10 August 1940), 98–101, 120–124.

261.1
PLAW, John (1745?–1820)
Sketches for country houses, villas, and rural dwellings; calculated for persons of moderate income, and for comfortable retirement. Also some designs for cottages, which may be constructed of the simplest materials; with plans and general estimates. By John Plaw. . . .

London: Printed by S. Gosnell, for J. Taylor, 1800.

18 pp, 1 + 41 pls.

29.2 × 24.1 cm

MH

261.2 †
___

Sketches for country houses, villas and rural dwellings. . . .

London: J. Taylor, 1802.

20 pp, 41 pls.

30.5 × 24.1 cm

Reference: NUC

261.3

Sketches ⟨ . . . as 1800 . . . ⟩ estimates. By John Plaw. . . .

London: Printed by W. Stratford; for J. Taylor, 1803.

18 pp, 1 + 41 pls.

31.8 × 24.4 cm

RIBA

261.4 †

Sketches for country houses, villas, and rural dwellings. . . .

London: J. Taylor, 1812.

18 pp, 41 + 1 pls.

4°

Reference: Cited in Priscilla Wrightson, *The Small English House: A Catalogue of Books* (London: B. Weinreb Architectural Books Ltd., 1977), no. 206.

261.5

Sketches for country houses, villas, and rural dwellings; calculated for persons of moderate income, and for comfortable retirement. Also, some designs for cottages, which may be constructed of the simplest materials; with plans and general estimates. By John Plaw, Architect. A new edition.

London: Printed for J. Taylor, 1823.

20 pp, 1 + 41 pls.

29.8 × 23.5 cm

MB

In the Preface (pp. 3–8) Plaw strongly recommended qualities of symmetry and simplicity in cottage design. He disagreed with those designers who preferred asymmetrical, irregular designs, and who recommended picturesque vernacular cottages as models to learn from.[1] Instead Plaw relied on established principles:

I beg leave to observe, the following Designs are constructed on the principles of symmetry and correspondence of parts; because I am aware some persons think Dwellings on an humble scale, and Cottages, ought rather to be irregular in their forms, and broken in their parts, taking certain structures for examples, which, in my opinion, should rather serve as beacons of danger, warnings of bad taste.[2]

He also advocated "the most simple forms and finishings, whether in the Greek or Gothic style": cottages should be "snug, low, compact, and dressed in artless and unaffected attire" (p. 3).

Plaw recommended careful attention to the relation between a house and its surrounding landscape. He noted that his own designs were "made for, and adapted to particular situations" (p. 4), and he also included lengthy excerpts concerning "proper Situations for an House" from Humphry Repton's *Sketches and Hints* (1794; *q.v.*).[3] To illustrate his point Plaw included a plate demonstrating the relations between landscape forms and houses of different sizes and shapes.[4] Plaw concluded the Preface with remarks on the prices of materials and an advertisement of his willingness to provide "Designs, and working Drawings, . . . at the usual commission" (p. 8). The rest of the text (pp. 9–18) contains brief descriptions of each plate, and cost estimates for most designs.

The plates depict plans and elevations of 28 designs, including 11 cottages, three double cottages, improvements to two cottages, two houses for clergymen, a summer retreat, a shooting seat, a "Cassino," a "small House," and six houses designed for particular clients. Plaw indicated that many of these designs had been executed. The plans are generally symmetrical and rectilinear, although a few include semicircular bows and porticoes. Two designs are circular in plan: a cottage for a fisherman or a herdsman (Plate 4), "calculated to give the least resistance to the wind" (p. 10); and a two-story cottage with a kitchen, a parlor, and four bedrooms (Plate 12) that "would be a pretty object in a Gentleman's Park" (p. 12). Plaw also included a "Cassino" with a triangular plan (Plate 32), and a house with a symmetrical but irregular octagonal plan (Plate 33) that "admits of elegant apartments conveniently distributed" (p. 17).

Each design is illustrated in one or more views, elegantly executed in aquatint, and clearly indicating the character of the surrounding landscape. Most of the elevations are composed in rustic, Gothic, and Castellated (or "Monastic") styles, with thatch roofs, rusticated masonry, tree-trunk columns, lattice windows, pointed arches, and crenellated parapets. Some of the larger designs are more Neoclassical with semicircular relieving arches, Doric and Ionic porticoes, and recessed panels of decorative bas-relief sculpture.

The smallest design is a two-story cottage (Plate 3), estimated to cost £150, with a kitchen, parlor, and pantry on the ground floor. The walls are made of rubble masonry, with trelliswork surrounding the central door and the windows to either side; the roof is made of thatch, and hipped gables frame the windows on the chamber floor. One of the largest designs (Plates 40, 41), "intended for an elevated spot on Highgate Hill" (p. 18), was estimated to cost £3,400. The ground-floor plan includes a morning parlor, withdrawing room, dining room, butler's room, and gentleman's room; the chamber floor has four bedrooms plus several closets and dressing rooms. The elevation is two stories high and five windows wide, with a crenellated parapet, quatrefoil openings piercing the parapet, Gothic windows, and a small portico topped by Gothic pinnacles.

1. See in particular James Malton, *An Essay on British Cottage Architecture* (1798; *q.v.*).

2. P. 3. References are to the 1800 edition.

3. The excerpts extend from p. 4 through p. 7.

4. The plate faces p. 6, and is based on Plate X in Repton's treatise.

262.1

POCOCK, William Fuller (1779–1849)

Architectural designs for rustic cottages, picturesque dwellings, villas, &c. with appropriate scenery, plans, and descriptions. To which are prefixed, some critical observations on their style and character; and also of castles, abbies, and ancient English houses, concluding with practical remarks on building, and the causes of the dry rot. By W. F. Pocock, Architect. Elegantly engraved on thirty-three plates.

London: Printed for J. Taylor, 1807.

vii + 36 pp, 33 pls.

28.6 × 22.9 cm

MB

262.2 †

———

Architectural designs for rustic cottages.

London, 1819.

4°

Reference: APSD

262.3

———

Architectural designs ⟨ . . . as 1807 . . . ⟩ English houses: concluding ⟨ . . . as 1807 . . . ⟩ plates. Second edition.

London: Printed for J. Taylor, 1823.

vii + 36 pp, 33 pls.

30.5 × 24.1 cm

V&A

According to the Dedication this book was conceived in part to promote "the comforts and happiness of those rustic dependants necessary to an extensive Estate." The Preface (pp. v–vii) concerns the conflict between utility and aesthetics in domestic design.[1] "One error, I trust, I have avoided," is "giving reins to the imagination, and designing, by the force of fancy only, compositions, which . . . might, perhaps, be impracticable in execution." But to this "Charybdis" Pocock opposed the "Scylla" of being "deficient in novelty, variety, and effect" (p. v). In the "Introductory Observations" (pp. 1–25) he complained that recent architects had paid too "little regard to external appearance," and instead "it has become the fashion to regard the usefulness rather than the beauty of what relates to personal accommodation" (p. 1).

The bulk of the "Observations" is devoted to seven brief essays, of which the first four provide a brief but important analysis of specific residential types.[2] The first essay (pp. 5–8) concerns "Rustic Cottages, or

Habitations of the Labourer," buildings of interest to those "wishing to serve the cause of humanity in providing comfortable dwellings for a numerous part of our fellow-creatures" as well as to "a great landed proprietor" pursuing "ideas of improvement." Indeed "the strength, and consequent importance of every country depends upon its possessing a bold, and numerous peasantry," and so this "class of Building" is necessarily of great importance (p. 5). But in addition to their philanthropic, economic, and political value laborers' cottages also could "form pleasing and characteristic objects in the landscape" (p. 6), and Pocock concluded his discussion with remarks on appropriate materials, colors, and sites (pp. 6–8). The next dwelling type, the *cabâne ornée* (pp. 8–10), "though humble in its appearance affords the necessary conveniences for persons of refined manners and habits, and is, perhaps, more calculated than any other description of building for the enjoyment of the true pleasures of domestic life, unincumbered with the forms of state and troublesome appendages" (p. 8). As a type thus suited to relaxation and enjoyment its appearance should "not in any case [be] sacrificed to regularity" (p. 8), and the architect should take care "to form the whole with attention to the picturesque effect of broken lines, unequal heights, and irregular distribution" (p. 9).[3] Turning to "Grecian, or Roman Villas" (pp. 11–12) Pocock said that every part must be "uniform and perfectly symmetrical" but that there was room for "liberties" with established proportions. He found the villa an especially versatile type: its "style and decorations" could be raised "towards those fit for a regular Mansion" or lowered "to a Building scarcely exceeding a Cottage in simplicity of appearance," and distinguished from a cottage only by its size (p. 11). In his discussion of "Buildings of the antient English Character, usually denominated Gothic" (pp. 13–18) Pocock lamented the lack of any "Precepts" or systematic method of classifying Gothic styles. Nevertheless he had no difficulty recommending the use of specific Gothic styles in a manner appropriate to their historical associations and to the site:

The structure in itself [is] to be either simple, magnigicent, or bold, according to the situation for which it is designed, and [according to] the property, influence, and rank of the proprietor, and [whether it is] intended to represent either a proud baronial Castle, built some centuries ago, to display all the 'Pride, pomp, and circumstance of glorious war,' the stately remains of a magnificent abbey, or the simple and unadorned appearance of an old English Mansion. (p. 14)

The next essay, "Of Scenery and Situation" (pp. 18–19), establishes appropriate landscape settings for specific architectural types:[4]

an unadorned regular House is suited for a plain open country, a magnificent Mansion for a country abounding with vegetation, and richly clothed with majestic woods, a modest and retired Cottage is well disposed in a luxuriant valley, while in bold and romantic situations the greatest license may be given to the imagination whether, in designing a Dwelling in the rural manner of a *Cabâne Ornée*, or in the picturesque style of a magnificent Abbey. (pp. 18–19)

The essay on "Execution of Buildings in general" (pp. 20–22) concerns the use of materials appropriate to the character of the design. The final essay explores "the Causes of the Dry Rot" (pp. 22–25).

The plate descriptions (pp. 26–36) indicate the type of resident for whom the design was intended,[5] and include remarks on appropriate sites, suggestions for suitable materials, descriptions of individual rooms, and hints for making the design appear more picturesque. The 33 plates include designs for an ornamental dairy, four cottages, six double cottages, one "picturesque residence," two *cabânes ornées*, one "ornamented Farm House," four villas, two mansions, and one entire "Hunting Establishment." Pocock's cottages and *cabânes ornées* incorporate such rustic and picturesque features as thatch roofs, tree-trunk columns, lattice casement windows, pointed arches, and Tudor drip moldings, with a mixture of regular and irregular elevations. Three of the four villas are Neoclassical, with symmetrical elevations, Classical porticoes, and semicircular relieving arches. The fourth villa and both mansions are in the "ancient English" or "Castle" style, with crenellations, pointed arches, finials, turrets, and other medieval features. The smallest design is the "Labourer's Cottage" in Plate 2, consisting of just a living room and washhouse on the ground floor, and a bedroom upstairs. The largest design is the mansion in Plate XXX, "a fit Residence for a nobleman of the first distinction" (p. 35), measuring approximately 90 feet by 120 feet in plan and with a tower rising several stories. The ground floor includes a large "Gothic Hall and Stair Case," anteroom, drawing room, library, billiard room, dining room, dressing room, servants' hall, housekeeper's room, and butler's pantry.

The final two plates are a plan and elevation of a house, stable, and four other buildings that would form a gentleman's "Hunting Establishment," arranged with special attention to the picturesque relations between the buildings. Indeed Pocock "arranged the whole so as to give the idea of a Village, which, in many situations, will become an object both pleasing and picturesque" (p. 36).

1. A far more thorough discussion of the relation between utility and aesthetics appeared just four years earlier in Humphry Repton's *Observations* (1803; *q.v.*).

2. Few late eighteenth- and early nineteenth-century authors constructed typologies of residential architecture; most assumed that the reader understood the difference between such terms as "cottage," "*cabâne ornée*," and "villa," or intentionally left the distinctions blurred. For a contemporary analysis of "cottages," "farm houses," and "villas," see Charles Middleton, *Picturesque and Architectural Views* (1793; *q.v.*).

3. Compare James Malton's discussion of the importance of irregularity in his *Essay on British Cottage Architecture* (1798; *q.v.*).

4. Compare Repton's more general discussion of the relation between architecture and scenery in *Sketches and Hints* (1794; *q.v.*).

5. In the Preface Pocock mentioned that some designs had been executed, others were prepared for execution, and some had been created just for this book (p. vi).

263.1
POCOCK, William Fuller (1779–1849)
Modern finishings for rooms: a series of designs for vestibules, halls, stair cases, dressing rooms, boudoirs, libraries, and drawing rooms; with their doors, windows, chimney-pieces, and other finishings, to a larger scale; and the several mouldings and cornices at full size: showing their construction and relative proportions. To which are added some designs for

villas and porticos, with the rules for drawing the columns, &c. at large. The whole adapted for the use and direction of every person engaged in the practical parts of building. Engraved on eight-six plates, from designs by W. F. Pocock, Architect.

London: Printed for J. Taylor, 1811.

vi + 7–23 pp, 86 pls.

26.0 × 21.3 cm

MBAt

263.2

Modern finishings for rooms; a series of designs for vestibules, halls, stair cases, dressing rooms, boudoirs, libraries, and drawing rooms; with their doors, windows, chimney pieces, and other finishings, to a large scale: and the several mouldings and cornices at full size: shewing their construction and relative proportions; to which are added, some designs for villas and porticos, with the rules for drawing the columns, &c. at large. The whole adapted for the use and direction of every person engaged in the practical parts of building. Engraved on eighty-six plates, from designs by W. F. Pocock, Architect.

London: Printed for J. Taylor, 1823.

vi + 7–23 pp, 86 pls [*pls. 34 and 59 wanting in this copy*].

26.0 × 20.3 cm

MB

263.3

Modern finishings for rooms: a series of designs for vestibules, halls, staircases, dressing-rooms, boudoirs, libraries, and drawing rooms; with their doors, windows, chimney-pieces, and other finishings, to a large scale: and the several mouldings and cornices at full size; shewing their construction and relative proportions: to which are added, some designs for villas and porticos, with the rules for drawing the columns, &c. at large. The whole adapted for the use and direction of every person engaged in the practical parts of building. Second edition. Engraved on eighty-six plates, from designs by W. F. Pocock, Architect.

London: Printed for M. Taylor, nephew and successor to the late Josiah Taylor, 1835.

vi + 7–23 pp, 86 pls.

25.3 × 20.3 cm

DLC

263.4

Modern finishings for rooms: a series of designs for vestibules, halls, staircases, dressing-rooms, boudoirs, libraries, and drawing-rooms; with their doors, windows, chimney-pieces, and other finishings, to a large scale: and the several mouldings and cornices at full size; shewing their construction and relative proportions: to which are added, some designs for villas and porticoes, with the rules for drawing the columns, &c. at large. The whole adapted for the use and direction of every person engaged in the practical parts of building. Third edition. Engraved on eighty-six plates, from designs by W. F. Pocock, Architect.

London: Printed for M. Taylor, nephew and successor to the late Josiah Taylor, 1837.

vi + 7–23 pp, 86 pls.

28.6 × 22.3 cm

PU

The ECB indicates an edition published by J. Taylor in October 1810. This is likely the edition dated 1811 on the title page, and so is not listed here as a separate entry.

In the Preface (pp. iii–vi) Pocock noted that the "defects of former publications appear to be, that the several parts [of a design] which require to be connected, are scattered through the book, and are not combined in a regular and united series," so that when moldings and "enrichments" are selected "harmony of proportion and fitness of character" often are wanting (p. iii). To alleviate this problem Pocock assembled 16 groups of plates to illustrate comprehensively "Plans and Sections for all the principal rooms of a modern house, with suitable ornaments, enrichments, and mouldings, drawn to a proper scale and proportion" (pp. iii–iv). These groups, labeled A through I and K through Q,[1] and accompanied by brief letterpress descriptions, depict plans, elevations, and details of an entrance vestibule, an entrance hall, two staircases, a dressing room, two dining rooms, a boudoir, two libraries, two drawing rooms, and porticoes in the Tuscan, "Antique Doric," Doric, and "Antique Ionic" orders. Pocock indicated that "many" of these designs had been executed (p. iv).

The final five groups of plates, labeled R, S, T, V, and W,[2] depict plans and exterior elevations for one "small House, or Villa," three "Villas," and one "respectable Farm House." The smallest (Plates R.1, R.2) has a parlor, drawing room, and conservatory on the ground floor, four bedrooms and a closet above, and a kitchen, washhouse, and offices in the basement. The largest (Plates V.1, V.2) was "nearly similar to a house I built some years ago in Essex, for one of the most respectable of that class of society called Gentlemen Farmers" (p. 22). Three stories high, it includes a hall, drawing room, dining room, business room, kitchen, and offices on the ground floor, and five bedrooms on the chamber floor. The facades of these house designs, like Pocock's interior furnishings, are in a spare

Neoclassical style, with little ornament other than cornices, stringcourses, semicircular relieving arches, and small porticoes. The most unusual facade is that of the farm house in Plate W.2, in which a Greek portico is flanked by ground-floor windows with mullions forming Gothic pointed arches.

1. Also numbered 1 through 76.

2. Also numbered 77 through 86.

Prize-essays and transactions of the Highland and Agricultural Society of Scotland.

See HIGHLAND and Agricultural Society of Scotland, *Entry 147;* MITCHELL, **John,** *Entry 491;* SMITH, **George,** *Entry 310.2.*

Prize essays and transactions of the Highland Society of Scotland.

See RENNIE, **Rev. Robert,** *Entry 275.*

264.1
PROUT, Samuel (1783–1852)
Bits for beginners by Samuel Prout: 21 plates, with 100 studies of rustic scenery, picturesque old houses, cottages, ruins, castles, churches, porches, archways, bridges, waterfalls, etc.

[London]: Ackerman's Repository, 1817.

24 pls.

36.6 × 28.0 cm

CtY

264.2

Progressive fragments, drawn and etched in a broad and simple manner; with a comprehensive explanation of the principles of perspective; for the use of young students in landscaping-drawing. By Samuel Prout.

London: Printed for R. Ackermann, by L. Harrison, Printer, 1817.

2 pp, frontisp. + 23 pls.

26.1 × 36.7 cm

MH

264.3

———

London: Printed for R. Ackerman, [n.d.].

2 pp, frontisp. + 23 pls.

26.4 × 36.5 cm

CtY

The title page of *Bits for Beginners* mentions 21 plates, but the copy at Yale contains 24 plates, all dated 1817. *Progressive Fragments* contains the same 24 plates, with the final plate now bound as a frontispiece. *Progressive Fragments* also contains one leaf of letterpress, printed on both sides.

The text of *Progressive Fragments* concerns perspective. Following brief definitions there are several examples of perspective construction, illustrated in Figures 1–11 on the first plate. The other plates depict stones, fences, bridges, barns, Gothic ruins, cottages, and other picturesque structures. Small rural farm houses, rows of attached cottages, and details of larger Tudor dwellings appear in Plates 8, 10, 11, 13, 16, and 19. In depicting these buildings Prout emphasized their picturesque qualities: dormers, windows, porches, steps, benches, ladders, and other weathered and irregular features all contribute to texturally varied, engaging compositions.

265.1
PROUT, Samuel (1783–1852)
Elementary drawing book of landscapes and buildings. By Samuel Prout. . . .

London: Charles Tilt, [1840].

24 pls.

18.9 × 28.9 cm

CtY-BA

265.2

———

Elementary drawing-book of landscapes and buildings. By Samuel Prout. . . .

London and Glasgow: Richard Griffin and Company, [1858?].

24 pls.

18.1 × 26.9 cm

MtU

The British Museum dated the first edition [1840], and this is confirmed by internal evidence. A letterpress sheet of advertisements mentions *Harding's Drawing Book* for 1837 and 1838, and lists *Prout's Microcosm* (1841) as "nearly ready." After 1840 the publisher, Charles Tilt, traded as Tilt and Bogue.[1] The next edition, published by Richard Griffin, corresponds with the "new edition" of 1858 listed in ECB.

Altogether the 24 lithographed plates contain 126 landscape or architectural subjects, some of which are little more than vignettes, while others are more sophisticated compositions. Although none of the figures is identified, several scenes obviously are Continental. The architectural subjects include medieval churches, ruins, bridges, cottages, and villages. Prout's technique emphasized the form and texture of half-timbering, thatch, and crumbling stone walls. Other subjects include fences, cliffs, a mountain lake, and seacoast scenes.

1. Philip A. H. Brown, *London Publishers and Printers* (London: British Museum, 1961), p. 95.

PROUT, Samuel (1783–1852)
Progressive fragments.

See Bits for beginners, *Entry 264.*

PROUT, Samuel (1783–1852)
Rudiments of landscape.

See Entry 493.

266.1
PROUT, Samuel (1783–1852)
A series of easy lessons in landscape-drawing, contained in forty plates; arranged progressively from the first principles in the chalk manner, to the finished landscape in colours. By Samuel Prout.

London: Published by R. Ackermann; and may be had of all the Book and Print-sellers in the United Kingdom. Printed by L. Harrison, 1820.

4 pp, 40 pls.

20.6 × 27.5 cm

ICU

The brief text (pp. 3–4) offers encouragement to beginners and describes the arrangement of the "lessons." The student is first taught to copy a variety of subjects, with special attention to "proportion." The next topic is laying in "flat shade," and the final topic is "coloring."

In accord with this plan of instruction, Plates 1–24 are executed in soft-ground etching, Plates 25–32 in etching and aquatint, and Plates 33–40 in etching and aquatint with hand coloring. Unfortunately Prout did not demonstrate the progressive application of several techniques to a single given subject; the contents of the plates illustrating each technique are different. Among the subjects illustrated in the plates are coastal scenes, a castle, bridges, a ruined abbey, churches, fences, a waterfall, and picturesque cottages. Cottages appear in Plates 10, 11, 13, 18, 20, 26, and 28–30, and a cottage or farm house appears in Plate 39.

267.1
PROUT, Samuel (1783–1852)
A series of views of rural cottages in the north of England, drawn and etched in imitation of chalk. By Samuel Prout. Twelve plates.

[London: R. Ackermann, 1821].

12 pls.

26.8 × 36.7 cm

CtY

The commentary for Entry 267 is combined with that for Entry 268 below.

268.1
PROUT, Samuel (1783–1852)
A series of views of rural cottages in the west of England, drawn and etched in imitation of chalk. By Samuel Prout, twelve plates.

[London: R. Ackermann, 1819].

12 pls.

36.7 × 27.6 cm

CtY

Views . . . in the North of England and *Views . . . in the West of England* each consist of twelve plates, without a title page or any other printed leaves. The titles are taken from original labels on the wrapper of each volume.

The subjects depicted in *Views . . . in the North of England* include cottages and bridges (Plates 1–4, 12), a scene at Helmsley (Plate 5), a windmill (Plate 6), Kirkham Abbey (Plate 7), and several views in York (Plates 8–11). All the *Views . . . in the West of England* depict cottages. As in his other books Prout emphasized the irregular forms and variety of textures in buildings made of such diverse materials as thatch, plaster, tile, half-timbering, stone, brick, and earth. All the subjects are complemented by picturesque scenery, with occasional human figures alone or in groups adding animation and interest.

These vernacular examples, irregular in form and often dilapidated, provided alternatives to the carefully proportioned and stylistically more orthodox designs for "cottages" available in contemporary architectural treatises.[1]

1. Compare, for example, the far more studied, carefully composed designs for cottages in John Buonarotti Papworth's *Rural Residences* (1818).

269.1

PROUT, Samuel (1783-1852)

Studies of cottages & rural scenery. Drawn and etched in imitation of chalk. Samuel Prout. Sixteen plates.

[London: R. Ackermann, 1816].

16 pls.

26.9 × 36.4 cm

NN

The sixteen plates are unaccompanied by a title page or any other printed leaves. The title is taken from an original label on the wrapper.

The plates depict cottages, castles, bridges, picturesque ruins, and scenes of rural life. Prout used the soft-ground etching technique effectively to depict the textures of thatch, wood, brick, and earth, and also to visually integrate his subjects with the surrounding picturesque scenery.

270.1

PYNE, William Henry (1769-1843)

Nattes's practical geometry, or introduction to perspective. Translated from the French of Le Clerc; with additions and alterations. The explanations rendered so simple, that very young people, by attention, may soon be enabled to go through the different problems with perfect ease. A work not only useful to those who cultivate the elegant art of drawing, but also recommended to the student in various branches of the arts and sciences. To which is added, an easy method of making an oval of any given proportions: also the rule for forming a geometrical plan and elevation; being the last problem previous to the commencement of the study of perspective. With forty vignettes, etched from designs analogous to the different geometrical figures, by W. H. Pyne. The problems engraved by T. King.

London: Published by W. Miller; and may be had of Mr. Nattes, 1805.

x + 98 pp (of which 45 are plates, numbered additionally as pls. 1-23, 23-44), additional engraved title page.

23.7 × 15.1 cm

BL

270.2

———

Nattes's practical geometry, ⟨ . . . as 1805 . . . ⟩ perspective. With forty= four vignettes, etched from designs analogous to the different geometrical figures, by W. H. Pyne. Second edition. The problems engraved by T. King.

London: Published by P. Wright; sold by Messrs. Longman & Co. Ogles, Duncan, & Co. Baldwin & Co. Sherwood & Co.; Simpkin & Marshall; and all Booksellers, 1819.

x + 98 pp (of which 45 are plates, numbered additionally as pls. 1–23, 23–44), frontisp.

24.2 × 14.6 cm

MB

The text, based on *Pratiqve de la geometrie* (Paris, 1669) by Sébastien Le Clerc (1637–1714), begins with brief general remarks on geometry (pp. 1–2) and definitions (pp. 3–15). The remainder consists of five "Books" devoted to lines, constructing plane figures, inscribing figures within other figures, circumscribing figures about other figures, and "Proportional Lines."

Many of the geometric figures in the plates are based on illustrations in Le Clerc's treatise, which include ornamental borders and vignettes. Pyne prepared new, colored vignettes for this treatise. Essentially unrelated to the text, they depict picturesque subjects such as farm animals, mills, a county fair, wheelwrights, stonemasons, shipwrights, sawyers, plasterers, and other artisans at work. One of the two plates numbered 23 (page 58) depicts a gate house constructed of rough stonework, two stories high. A pointed archway forms a passage through the ground-floor level. Irregular additions around the sides and back of the house give it a highly picturesque outline. A farmer and child, standing in the foreground near a drying platform, add animation and interest to the scene.

271.1
RANDALL, James (ca. 1778–1820)
A collection of architectural designs for mansions, casinos, villas, lodges, and cottages, from original drawings. By James Randall, Architect. Elegantly engraved in aqua-tinta, on thirty-four plates, with explanations.

London: Printed for J. Taylor, 1806.

vi pp, 13 leaves, 34 pls.

52.1 × 35.6 cm

V&A

The Preface (pp. iii–vi) includes remarks on creativity and picturesque effect. Randall argued that established architectural styles and forms could constrain the architect's creativity, and so recommended giving rein to the imagination:

It is not necessary that chastity of taste be confined to the rigid rules of the school: fancy may surely be allowed to play, if kept within proper bounds! New ideas, and new combinations, if composed with judgment, may add interest to the architectural beauties of the landscape, and increase the comforts of domestic life, and procure the approbation of the judicious critic.[1]

Drawing a parallel between architecture and music, Randall suggested that the imagination could produce nearly limitless combinations of form:

"Architecture, like music, is susceptible of innumerable combinations, which, if properly united, although very dissimilar, may possess real beauties, and produce pleasing emotions on the mind."[2]

On the subject of picturesque composition Randall showed himself to be a disciple of Humphry Repton.[3] Randall recommended careful attention to the relation between a house and its scenic context: "The situation of a house should be considered as well for the prospect from it, as for its own picturesque effect; and this consideration of the *look towards a house*" requires understanding the "peculiar beauties" of both Greek and Gothic styles. Gothic "affords a pleasing variety of outline, and produces an abundant play of light and shadow, while the more classic Grecian style, possesses compactness, and symmetrical proportions that are preferred, in many situations, by highly cultivated minds" (pp. v–vi).

The 34 plates, accompanied by 13 leaves of descriptive letterpress, include elevations, perspective views, and plans for 20 designs. The first 29 plates illustrate designs numbered I through XIII, including five villas, four casinos, two mansions, one "Belle-vue," and one "Gentleman's cottage." Unnumbered and included at the rear, perhaps as an afterthought, are three designs for gate lodges (Plates 30–32) and four designs for "Cottages for Labourers" (Plates 33–34). "It has been my endeavour to exhibit a variety in the Plans and Elevations," he noted (p. iv), and there is also a variety in style: there are designs in Greek, Gothic, and Castellated styles, as well as one of the earliest published designs for a residence in Egyptian style (Design IX).

This "Mansion in the Egyptian Style" is also one of Randall's largest designs. The ground-floor plan includes a "Coridor" measuring 38 feet by 20 feet, a saloon, a drawing room, a dining room, a "Meuseum [*sic*] and Gallery" measuring 43 feet by 20 1/2 feet, a morning room, a vestibule, and a "Gentlemans Parlour or Study." Upstairs there are seven bedrooms. The dramatic two-story elevation is five windows wide, with battered walls, hieroglyphic inscriptions, and Egyptian columns *in antis*. One of the smallest designs is the "Gentleman's Cottage" (Design XIII), with a principal floor including two bedrooms, a kitchen, a parlor, and one other room.

There are three designs for quadruple cottages and one for a quintuple cottage. Randall explained that "Cottages built in clusters . . . are cheaper and warmer than those built singly or detached. Their appearance also is more pleasing and picturesque, a circumstance not unworthy of attention in such buildings as on a gentleman's estate." The ground-floor plan of the Tudor quadruple cottage (Plate 34) shows just one room to a cottage, 12 feet square; each unit also has additional space upstairs. The Neoclassical design for a quintuple cottage, also in Plate 34, consists of five attached units in a row: at either end are octagonal cottages, each 17 1/2 feet wide; the rectangular cottage in the center measures 11 feet by 8 feet; and the two connecting cottages are each 7 1/2 feet by 6 1/2 feet.

Randall's perspective views all include lush and dramatic scenery. He used aquatint to render depth, texture, and tone in a highly effective manner. The designs in Greek and Egyptian style have scrupulously symmetrical elevations. In describing his Gothic designs Randall extolled "variety and play of outline" (p. vi and letterpress for Plate 32), but most appear to be regular, symmetrical compositions onto which a tower or an ell has been grafted to contrive an effect of asymmetry.

1. P. iii. Perhaps this freedom of creativity explains the excessively projecting roof "in the Italian manner" (Design VIII) and the overly florid Gothic ornament of the mansion in Design V.

2. Ibid. Compare Randall's ideas to those of Robert Morris, who in his *Lectures* (1734–1736; *q.v.*) proposed an analogy between architectural and musical proportions. Unlike Randall, Morris used the musical analogy to demonstrate the need for disciplined order, not as a justification for imaginative fancy. Randall's ideas parallel contemporary French musical theory. See for example André Ernest Grétry, *Mémoires, ou essai sur la musique* (Paris, 1797), I, 168–169: "Si vous ne pouvez être vrai qu'en créant une combinaison inusitée, ne craignez point d'enrichir la théorie d'une règle de plus. . . . Ce n'est cependant qu'à l'homme familiarisé avec la règle, qu'il est quelquefois permis de la violer, parce que lui seul peut sentir qu'en pareil cas la règle n'a pu suffire."

3. See especially Repton's analysis of the visual relationships between landscape scenery and Greek and Gothic architecture in *Sketches and Hints* (1794; *q.v.*).

272.1
RAWLINS, T. J.
Elementary perspective, divested of technicalities; as taught at the Training College, Stanley Grove. By T. J. Rawlins, Professor of drawing and perspective.

London: Tilt and Bogue, [n.d.].

6 pls.

24.3 × 30.5 cm

V&A

The date of publication must be within the years 1841 to 1843, since the publishing firm Tilt and Bogue is listed in local directories for those years only.[1]

The work consists of a title page and six plates. Each plate contains three or four "Problems," consisting of individual instructive texts accompanied by illustrations. Of a total of 20 "Problems," 12 relate to the subject of architecture. Problem II shows how to illustrate a room in perspective, while Problems III, IV, VI, VII, and VIII show how to represent different types of arches from various viewpoints. Problems XIV and XV show pediments and gables. Problem XIII demonstrates how to render a house in perspective, using an example two stories high, five windows wide, and three windows deep. A similar demonstration in Problem XVI uses a house just three windows wide, and the house in Problem XVII comprises just one large room on the inside, with a small exterior portico on one side and a bow projecting at the end. Problem XVIII illustrates a plain three-story house facing a two-story crescent.

1. Philip A. H. Brown, *London Publishers and Printers* (London: British Museum, 1961), p. 95.

273.1

RAWLINS, Thomas

Familiar architecture; consisting of original designs of houses for gentlemen and tradesmen, parsonages and summer-retreats; with back-fronts, sections, &c. Together with banqueting-rooms, churches, and chimney-pieces. To which is added, the masonry of the semicircular and elliptical arches, with practical remarks. By Thomas Rawlins, Architect.

[N. loc.]: Printed for the author, 1768.

viii + 9–30 pp, 2 printed leaves, 60 pls.

32.7 × 26.7 cm

MB

273.2

————

Familiar architecture; or, original designs of houses for gentlemen and tradesmen; parsonages; summer retreats; banqueting-rooms; and churches: with plans, sections, &c. To which is added, the masonry of semicircular and elliptical arches; with practical remarks. By Thomas Rawlins, Architect. On fifty-one copper plates.

London: Printed for I. and J. Taylor, 1789.

viii + 9–30 pp, 51 pls (numbered I–XLVIII, LVIII–LX).

33.0 × 26.0 cm

Bodl.

273.3

————

Familiar architecture; or, original designs of houses, for gentlemen and tradesmen, parsonages, summer retreats, banqueting-rooms, and churches; with plans, sections, &c. To which is added, the masonry of semicircular and elliptical arches; with practical remarks. By Thomas Rawlins, Architect. On fifty-one copper-plates. A new edition.

London: Printed for I. and J. Taylor, 1795.

26 pp, 51 pls.

31.1 × 24.1 cm

MH

This description is based on the copy of the 1768 edition in the Boston Public Library. There is a variant issue of this edition in the Library of Congress.[1]

In his introductory remarks "To the Public" (pp. i–viii) Rawlins complained that "many excellent Geniuses, who have largely expatiated" on the subject of architecture, "have form'd Plans too extensive for the plain Villa, the Parochial Church, and elegant Mansion: Their lofty Views, and unlimited strength of Imagination, have so far hurried them away, that they have neglected to render their Designs useful and instructive to Country Builders" (p. i). The "Plans and Designs already published," he charged, "no way answer the Uses required in the Country" (p. 1).[2] One of his principal concerns was the location of offices: too often other designers located them underground, when in fact country locations allow "sufficient Space" above ground (p. i). Indeed Rawlins ascribed unusual importance to the design of offices: "Unmix'd Elegance, and explanative Usefulness in the Offices, I apprehend to be one of the most essential Parts of Design" (p. ii). He devoted two pages to the planning of offices, wings, and other parts of a house. He also included brief remarks on the dimensions of his designs, his reasons for not including cost estimates, and a short discussion of pediments.

Rawlins, who called himself "A Stone Mason" (p. ii), described this book as "a Foundation for a Work of general Use, and especially in the remote Parts of the Country, where little or no Assistance for Designs is to be procured" (p. vii). Yet he also included a few provocative remarks on the nature of architectural expression:

It must give the highest Satisfaction to a speculative Genius, to consider the utmost Extent of Architecture, and to weigh the different Effects it impresses on the Mind, according to the different Structures presented to the View! How awe-struck must be the Passions, when we behold the antient Buildings of *Greece* and *Rome*! How sooth'd and mollify'd, when we descend to the pleasing rural Cot, where simple Elegance, Proportion, and Convenience unite! The Soul may then be said to be tun'd and exhilarated by the Objects which strike the Attention. (p. ii)

In particular, "Arithmetical Proportions being particularly regarded, the internal Parts [of a building] may be made to suit the Temper, Genius, and Convenience of the Inhabitant, by enlarging, or reducing the Scale" (p. iv). These remarks are reminiscent of Robert Morris, who discussed the effects of proportion on the mind in his *Essay in Defence of Ancient Architecture* (1728; *q.v.*). Rawlins's comments also recall a more important and recent treatise, the *Elements of Criticism* (1762) by Lord Kames, who contended

That every building ought to have an expression corresponding to its destination. A palace ought to be sumptuous and grand; a private dwelling, neat and modest; a play-house, gay and splendid; and a monument, gloomy and melancholy. . . . Columns, beside their chief destination of being supports, may contribute to that peculiar expression which the destination of a building requires: columns of different proportions, serve to express loftiness, lightness, &c. as well as strength.[3]

The text consists of "Practical Remarks on Arches, &c." (pp. 9–18), drawing on Rawlins's occupational expertise, and plate descriptions (pp. 19–30) which give the intended purpose and location of individual designs, their dimensions, and a key to each plan. Altogether there are designs for 32 dwellings, two banqueting rooms, and three churches, plus additional plates illustrating chimneypieces and techniques of arch construction.[4] With the exception of a few parsonages, most of the dwellings are "Retreats," intended for the use of such persons as a "Gentleman with a middling Family," a "Gentleman of opulent Fortune," or a "Merchant." Several retreats were designed for locations "in a City or Villa" or "in a Town or Villa"—an unusual use of the term "Villa" to refer to a small town or farming community.[5] Rawlins clearly intended several designs solely for rural retirement and regeneration. Plate XXIV, for example, shows "a small Building to be situate in a pleasant airy Villa, as a Retreat for a Merchant, &c. where divested of the cares of Business he may enjoy the Converse of a few select Friends." A few retreats were specifically designed to accord with picturesque scenery: Plate XXVIII, for example, depicts a "Summer Retreat, to be situated on an Eminence commanding some extensive Prospects which may exhilarate and add fresh Vigour to the Mind of the wealthy and industrious Inhabitant," and Plates XXXVIII and XXXIX show a retreat with an equilateral triangular plan "designed to command three Vistos."

All of Rawlins's designs are composed in a sober Palladian manner, ornamented with Venetian windows, pediments, balusters, stringcourses, rusticated masonry, semicircular relieving arches, and occasional projecting bows. Despite Rawlins's concern for picturesque vistas, none of the elevations includes any scenery. The smallest design is that in Plate I, two stories high and 30 feet wide, with a parlor, large parlor, closet, pantry, and kitchen on the ground floor, and three chambers upstairs. Among the largest designs is the residence "for a Gentleman in the Country" (Plate XXXIII). The facade, 160 feet wide, consists of a central portion three stories high and 72 feet wide, connected by one-story arcades to bow-fronted two-story wing pavilions at either side. The ground-floor plan includes a hall, two parlors, a dining room, a withdrawing room, a library or study, a dressing room, a kitchen, a scullery, a servants' hall, a pantry, a storeroom, a stable, coach houses, and closets.

Facing the final plate is a single leaf of letterpress containing references to "Apparatus in the plate" designed for testing the strength of arches.

1. The variant issue is described in Laurence Hall Fowler and Elizabeth Baer, *The Fowler Architectural Collection* (Baltimore: Evergreen House Foundation, 1961), p. 223. Except for slight variations in the binding order, the Fowler copy matches that in the Boston Public Library.

2. But compare Daniel Garret's *Designs, and Estimates, of Farm Houses* (1747), and William Halfpenny's *Six New Designs* (1751), *Thirteen New Designs* (1752), and *Twelve Beautiful Designs* (1749), all compiled for use in specific counties and regions.

3. Henry Home, Lord Kames, *Elements of Criticism* (Edinburgh, 1762), III, 338–339.

4. Plates XLIX to LVII, illustrating chimneypieces, do not appear in the Bodleian copy of the 1789 edition. Plates LVIII to LX concern arch construction.

5. "Villa" was used in this sense in Renaissance architectural literature, but by the mid-eighteenth century had come to denote an isolated country residence. Rawlins also used the term in the latter sense: see the quotation above from page i of his introduction. The meaning of the word "Villa" is discussed at greater length in Chapter II, Section 5, in "The Literature of British Domestic Architecture, 1715–1842" above.

Recreaciones arquitectonicas.

See Entry 480.

274.1

REES, Abraham (1743–1825), comp. and ed.

The cyclopaedia; or, universal dictionary of arts, sciences, and literature. By Abraham Rees . . . with the assistance of eminent professional gentlemen. Illustrated with numerous engravings, by the most distinguished artists. In thirty-nine volumes. Vol. . . .

London: Printed for Longman, Hurst, Rees, Orme, & Brown, F. C. and J. Rivington, A. Strahan, Payne and Foss, Scatcherd and Letterman, J. Cuthell, Clarke and Sons, Lackington Hughes Harding Mavor and Jones, J. and A. Arch, Cadell and Davies, S. Bagster, J. Mawman, James Black and Son, Black Kingsbury Parbury and Allen, R. Scholey, J. Booth, J. Booker, Suttaby Evance and Fox, Baldwin Cradock and Joy, Sherwood Neely and Jones, R. Saunders, Hurst Robinson and Co., J. Dickinson, J. Paterson, E. Whiteside, Wilson and Sons, and Brodie and Dowding, 1819.

[Thirty-nine text volumes, [1802–]1819, and six plate volumes, [1802–]1820. In the title for the plate volumes, the words In thirty-nine volumes. Vol. . . . *are replaced by* Plates. Vol. . . . *In the imprint for the plate volumes,* James Black and Son *is omitted, and* Ogle Duncan and Co. *is added, following* Sherwood Neely and Jones.]

Art. "Agriculture," text vol. I, 6 pp; plates vol. I, 43 pls.
Art. "Cottage," text vol. X, 18 pp; plates vol. I, "Agriculture" pls. VI, VII, and IX.
Art. "Farm buildings," text vol. XIV, 5 pp; plates vol. I, "Agriculture" pls. XIII, XIV.
Art. "Farm house," text vol. XIV, 3 pp; plates vol. I, "Agriculture" pl. XV.
Art. "Perspective," text vol. XXVI, 31 pp; plates vol. IV, 13 pls.
Art. "Pisé," text vol. XXVII, 8 pp; plates vol. I, 1 pl (bound with "Agriculture" plates).

26.9 × 20.0 cm

ICRL

Between 1778 and 1786 Abraham Rees combined Ephraim Chambers's *Cyclopaedia* (*q.v.*) and its *Supplement* (1753) into a new, uniform, and corrected set. Between 1802 and 1820 Rees issued a new encyclopedia in 39 text volumes and six plate volumes, likewise titled *Cyclopaedia*.[1]

The article on "Architecture" (II, 2 pp) consists of general observations on the purpose and importance of architecture: it is, for example, an art that tends "to secure, accommodate, delight, and give consequence to the human species." This and most of Rees's other remarks are clearly paraphrases of Sir William Chambers's *Treatise* (3rd ed., 1791; *q.v.*). Sixty-nine plates, numbered irregularly, accompany this article. Thirty are signed by Peter Nicholson. The subjects include Roman basilicas, amphitheaters, arches, and baths, the Temple of Pandrosus and the Parthenon, a "Hindoo" temple at Deo, elements of Egyptian architecture, plans of the former and present St. Peter's in Rome, a view of the west door of the cathedral at Carrara, the orders, moldings, joinery, carpentry, roofs, chimneys, groins, domes, arches, doors, and bridges. Cross-references at the end of the text direct the reader to additional articles on civil, military, and naval architecture.

"Civil Architecture" (VIII, 8 pp) opens with a division of the subject into architecture as a "useful" art, to be treated in the article titled "Building," and architecture "as a fine art," to be treated here. The discussion is entirely historical. Six pages are devoted to the progress of architecture in Greece and Rome, including conjectural accounts of the origins of the orders. A final two pages concern the "revival" of "Grecian architecture" in "modern times," and treat Italian architecture from Brunelleschi to Bernini, French architecture from Lescot to Soufflot, and Inigo Jones and Christopher Wren in England. Cross-references direct the reader to separate articles on Norman, Saxon, and Gothic architecture.

Adam Dickson (1721–1776) prepared the article on "Agriculture," which is an historical account of the subject from the time of the "Ancients" through recent improvements and innovations by Anderson, Bakewell, Elkington, Fordyce, Marshall, Sinclair, and Young. Among the 43 plates accompanying the article, six—VI, VII, IX, XIII, XIV, and XV—include illustrations of domestic architecture. Plate VI depicts plans and elevations for two circular cottages, one rectangular cottage, and one rectangular double cottage, plus elevations of four more cottages.[2] Plate VII illustrates three designs for "Ornamental Cottages": two of the elevations incorporate cornice moldings and windows with pointed arches, while the third lacks significant ornament. The ground floor of each has a kitchen and offices, and the two larger designs have back kitchens; upstairs each cottage has two bedrooms. Figures 1–5 in Plate IX show details of a cottage fireplace, staircase, and bedroom. Plates XIII and XIV depict two-story houses and offices for "Corn and Mixed" farms and for "Grass and Dairy" farms.[3] Plate XV shows two two-story farm houses in elevation, ground-floor plan, and chamber-floor plan.[4] These plates are not described in the article on "Agriculture," but rather in separate articles titled "Cottage," "Farm Buildings," and "Farm House," which are discussed individually below. Another plate, titled "Pisè," is bound with the plates on agriculture but described in the article on "Pisé," also discussed below. The remaining agricultural plates depict barns and other farm structures, carts, farm implements and machinery, embankments, yards, fences and gates, harrows, plows, methods of catching moles, grasses, kilns, quarries, pits, and mines.

The article titled "Cottage" includes excerpts from previous treatises by Beatson, Crocker, Crutchley, Davis, Dickson, Holland, Kent, Loudon, Sinclair, and Wood,[5] plus reports to the Board of Agriculture on the state of agriculture in Cheshire, Devonshire, Gloucestershire, and Shropshire. Most of the excerpts address specific methods of housing rural laborers; in addition there are brief remarks on cottage housing at Winnington and other estates owned by Lord Penrhyn.[6]

The article on "Farm Buildings" treats the proper "distribution" of farm buildings according to the type and size of farm. There are brief remarks on Plates XIII and XIV.[7]

The article titled "Farm House" is almost entirely a paraphrase of Robert Beatson's article "On Farm Buildings" (1797; q.v.), and the illustrations are likewise borrowed from Beatson.[8]

The discussion of "Perspective" commences with a brief history of the subject and remarks on individual perspective treatises. The bulk of the article is a series of propositions, corollaries, and theorems, followed by descriptions of the diagrams in the plates and a series of problems and solutions. All but two of the plates are signed by Peter Nicholson. They depict geometric figures and diagrams, capitals and sets of steps in perspective, and a few houses. In Plate VI there is a house with wings and another with a bow front, each represented in a perspective view as a geometric solid. In Plate IX the facade of a house two stories high and three windows wide is shown in an elevation and in an oblique view. In Plate X the same house is shown with a gable roof in plan, in elevation, and in oblique views.[9]

The article on "Pisé" includes a reference to Henry Holland's article on the subject (1797; q.v.), a lengthy paraphrase of "the account of the Rev. Mr. Jancour, as transmitted to the Board of Agriculture," and a reference to *The Complete Farmer* (1807 ed.; q.v.). The one plate, bound with the plates on agriculture, reproduces figures first published by Holland. These include illustrations of implements for working with pisé plus a plan and two elevations of a two-room pisé cottage. The text of this article was excerpted at length as late as 1947 in Clough Williams-Ellis et al., *Building in Cob, Pisé, and Stabilized Earth* (London: Country Life). This practical manual presented alternative building techniques for use during the postwar period when regular building materials such as bricks and timber were in short supply.

1. See Robert Collison, *Encyclopaedias: Their History throughout the Ages* (New York: Hafner, 1966), pp. 109–110.

2. Figs. 1 and 2 in Plate VI appeared previously as Fig. 3, Plate XXXIX, in A. Crocker and Son, "On Cottages" (1797; q.v.). Figs. 3–8, designs by Sir John Sinclair, appeared previously in Plate 28, Vol. X of *The English Encyclopaedia* (1802; q.v.). Figs. 9–10 and 12–14 appeared previously in Plates XXXVI–XXXVIII of Robert Beatson's article "On Cottages" (1797; q.v.). Fig. 11 appeared in Plate XXXIV accompanying "Answers to the Queries Respecting Cottagers Renting Land. By Mr. Crutchley" (1797; q.v.).

3. The designs in Plates XIII and XIV appeared previously in an article by A. Crocker, "An Essay on Farm Houses" (1797; q.v.).

4. These designs appeared previously in Plates I and III in Robert Beatson's article "On Farm Buildings" (1797; q.v.).

5. See individual commentaries on all the following books and articles: Beatson, "On Cottages" (1797); Crocker, "On Cottages" (1797); Crutchley, "Answers to the Queries" (1797); Davis, "Address to the Landholders" (1795); Dickson, *Practical Agriculture* (1805); Holland, "On Cottages" (1797); Kent, *Hints to Gentlemen* (1775); Loudon, *A Treatise on . . . Country Residences* (1806); Sinclair, designs for circular cottages in *The English Encyclopaedia*, Vol. X (1802); and Wood, *A Series of Plans* (1792). The cottage designs illustrating this article appeared in "Agriculture" Plates VI, VII, and IX. See note 2 above.

6. The cottages in Figure 14, Plate VI, had been designed by "Mr. Wyatt" for the estate at Winnington. See also Beatson, "On Cottages," p. 113, pl. 38. The three designs in Plate VII were described as of the same "sort" as other cottages on Lord Penrhyn's estate. Lord Penrhyn's improvements also were discussed in the report to the Board of Agriculture on North Wales; see the commentary above under "Great Britain. Board of Agriculture." See too Abraham Rees's *Cyclopaedia* ([1802]–1820) and Lewis William Wyatt's *Collection of Architectural Designs* (1800–1801), qq.v.

7. See note 3 above.

8. See note 4 above.

9. The illustrations closely resemble figures in Nicholson's *Rudiments of Practical Perspective* (1822; q.v.).

275.1

RENNIE, Rev. Robert

"Plan of an inland village," *Prize Essays and Transactions of the Highland Society of Scotland* II (1803), 250–266, and 1 pl.

CtY

Robert Rennie was not the first British designer to publish a plan for a new town or village. As early as 1795 John Plaw included such a plan in his treatise on picturesque dwellings, *Ferme Ornée* (*q.v.*). In 1800 a design for a circular village by Sir John Sinclair was published in France.[1] Plans for new towns and villages in Scotland are illustrated in Sinclair's "Hints Regarding Certain Measures" (1802; *q.v.*) and in his *Sketch of the Improvements . . . in the County of Caithness* (1803; *q.v.*).[2]

In 1803 Rennie published this 17-page essay entirely devoted to aspects of village planning. His goal was "to point out and explain what seems most necessary for the establishment of inland villages; as the most eligible and expedient conditions of feus and leases, directions for building the houses in a substantial manner, for regulating the settlers, and establishing industry among them" (p. 250).

The first four pages are devoted to such practical matters as siting, foundations, fresh air, soil, water, fuel supply, access to transportation, and building materials. Then he discussed the proper form for a village: above all it should be "regular," with straight streets and buildings of uniform height and width. In addition, it should be "capable of being extended and enlarged at pleasure" (p. 254). The form he chose was a cross; indeed, he remarked, "the common sense of mankind, has almost universally fixed upon this" form (p. 255). The plan shown in the plate includes two major streets, 60 to 100 feet wide, intersecting each other at right angles in a large marketplace, 180 to 300 feet square, with "some public building, as a church, a bridewell, or a prison" in the center (pp. 255–257). A grid of smaller streets, at least 12 feet wide, connects cottages along the principal thoroughfares with garden plots and fields to the rear. Rennie suggested dimensions and building materials for cottages, and recommended that one or more model plans be established for feuers to build from (pp. 257–260). The plate includes an illustration of six attached cottages, each two stories high, with a door and three windows on the ground story and two dormer windows above. Rennie concluded the essay with suggestions for feu and lease arrangements that would ensure the economic vitality of the town (pp. 260–266).

1. This is discussed in the commentary on Sinclair's "Hints Regarding Certain Measures."

2. Other examples of Scottish town planning are illustrated in reports to the Board of Agriculture on the counties of Ayr (1811) and Caithness (1812). These are discussed in the entry for "Great Britain. Board of Agriculture." Also see the commentary on James Loch, *An Account* (1820).

The repository of arts, literature, commerce, manufactures, fashions, and politics.

See **PAPWORTH, John Buonarotti,** "Cottage ornée," *Entry 247.*

The repository of arts, literature, fashions, manufactures, &c.

See PAPWORTH, **John Buonarotti**, "Architectural hints," *Entry 246.1*; PAP-WORTH, "Hints on ornamental gardening," *Entry 248.1.*

276.1
REPTON, Humphry (1752–1818)
Designs for the pavillon at Brighton. Humbly inscribed to His Royal Highness the Prince of Wales. By H. Repton, Esq. with the assistance of his sons, John Adey Repton, F.S.A. and G. S. Repton, Architects.

London: Printed for J. C. Stadler; and sold by Boydell and Co.; Longman, Hurst, Rees, and Orme; White; Cadell and Davies; Payne and Mackinlay; Payne; Miller; and Taylor. The letter press by T. Bensley, 1808.

1 printed leaf, x + 41 pp, 10 pls.

54.4 × 37.2 cm

MH

276.2
———
Designs ⟨ . . . as 1808 . . . ⟩ F.S.A. & G. S. Repton, Architects.

London: ⟨ . . . as 1808 . . . ⟩ Taylor. Printed by Howlett and Brimmer, [n.d.].

1 printed leaf, x + 41 pp, frontisp. + 8 pls.

52.9 × 36.8 cm

MH

The title page of the first edition is dated 1808. Many text leaves and plates are watermarked 1807, and the plates are dated 1808. Other issues bear undated title pages. Often these issues have been dated [1806] because the dedication bears that date, but for two reasons this cannot be correct. In the "Prefatory Observations" Repton included a reference to "a small Work published in 1806," i.e., his *Enquiry;* his use of the past tense suggests that *Designs* was issued later. Second, most of the plates are dated 1808, and many of the watermarks are even later. An undated copy at Harvard has seven plates dated 1808, of which several are watermarked 1825, plus text leaves watermarked 1821 and 1822, and a frontispiece watermarked 1825.

The book begins with "Prefatory Observations" (pp. i–x) on "the united Arts of Landscape Gardening and Architecture" (p. i).[1] Repton complained of the "false principle of mistaking greatness of dimensions, for greatness of character," and lamented its recent application to sculpture, painting, jewelry, and especially architecture (p. ii). Thus Repton "rejoiced" when asked by the Prince of Wales to undertake renovations of "a place which was deemed by every body too small to admit of any improvements," the Pavilion at Brighton (p. iii). Repton recommended a series of landscape improvements that would be appropriate to such a limited site (p. iv). He also presented a lengthy defense of his recommendation to redo the exterior of the Pavilion in Indian style (pp. v–x).

The first part of the text (pp. 1–11) consists of remarks on the site and plan of the Pavilion, and on Repton's intended improvements. At the end of the text (pp. 33–41) there are sections titled "Interior," "Dining Room," "Of Ornaments, &c.," and "Corridor," discussing Repton's specific proposals in more detail. These portions of the text are illustrated by aquatinted plates and text figures, many of them colored, and several with movable "slides" showing the subject both before and after Repton's proposed changes.

The rest of the text (pp. 13–31) is an essay on architectural style, titled "An Inquiry into the Changes in Architecture, as It Relates to Palaces and Houses in England. Including the Castle and Abbey Gothic, the Mixed Style of Gothic, the Grecian and Modern Styles; with Some Remarks on the Introduction of Indian Architecture."[2] Adding slightly to arguments presented five years earlier in his *Observations* (*q.v.*), Repton discussed the characteristics of architectural styles. Castle Gothic, he said, consists of massive walls with small windows. Abbey Gothic has "lofty and large apertures" suited only to use in chapels, churches, halls, and libraries. He recommended the "mixed style," or "Queen Elisabeth's Gothic," for "modern Palaces" if they had to be in Gothic style; but, he added, the mind would not be reconciled easily to the incongruity of a modern palace in an older style (p. 17). Greek style, he said, might be made "applicable to the purposes of modern habitation," if a suitable "combination of forms" could be devised (p. 19). He deplored too strict an adherence to ancient Greek models, especially temples: "houses built from such models would become inconvenient in proportion," and "even a moderate sized residence, cannot be entirely surrounded by a peristyle," because the windows would be blocked or obscured (pp. 19–20).

Repton found that the "Modern" style of building was the consequence of "numerous difficulties in reconciling the internal convenience of a house to the external application of Grecian Columns of any order." The result was the complete banishment of columns and the introduction of "a new style, which is strictly of no character" (p. 21). Buildings in this style consist of a plain rectilinear shell with simple rows of square windows and superficial ornament: with "a Grecian Cornice, it is called a Grecian Building"; with "notches" (crenellations) cut in the top of the wall, "it is called a Gothic Building" (p. 21). In this manner "the rage for simplicity, the dread of mixing dates, and the difficulty of adding ornament to utility, alike corrupted and exploded both the Grecian and the Gothic Style in our modern buildings" (p. 21). Through this analysis Repton criticized the excessive attention that British architects paid to style, and their disregard for more fundamental problems of utility. Some years later John Claudius Loudon discussed problems of function and style at much greater length,[3] but Repton made a fundamental point: he established the difference between the need for functional design in a dwelling, and the decorative or expressive effect that a particular architectural style could add to its exterior.

Pages 23–28 concern principles of construction in Greek, Gothic, and Indian architecture. Pages 29–31 are an essay on the "Application of Indian Architecture." "Having shewn already the difficulty of adapting either the Grecian or Gothic styles to the character of an English Palace,"

Repton recommended Indian architecture, in part because it "presents an endless variety of forms and proportions of Pillars" (p. 29). To counter the possible objections of critics, he noted that an "Artist" finds it "difficult . . . to divest himself of forms he has long studied: this will account for the confusion of Grecian and Gothic in the Works of John of Padua, Inigo Jones, and others," and the same confusion "may be observed in the first introduction of Gothic mixed with the Saxon and Norman which preceded it" (p. 30). Yet despite such appeals for open-mindedness Repton clearly was uncertain of himself, and he also devoted six pages of the Prefatory Observations (pp. v–x) to an extended defense of the Indian style.

No plates accompany the "Inquiry into the Changes in Architecture." Aquatint vignettes on pages 23–25, 28, and 31 illustrate columns, lintels, arches, and other elements of the styles Repton discussed. On page 13 there is an elaborate headpiece depicting a landscape, with a river or inlet in the foreground and in the distance a medieval castle, a Gothic abbey, and large residences in Elizabethan, Palladian, and Indian styles.

1. Comments here are based on the 1808 edition at Harvard.

2. He prepared the essay "In obedience to the Royal Commands, 'That I should deliver my opinion concerning that Style of Architecture would be most suitable for the Pavillon' " (p. 15).

3. The notion that style was a subordinate aspect of exterior design, and the corollary notion that different styles could be applied almost interchangeably to any facade, were prefigured in James Peacock's book Οικιδια (1785; q.v.). Loudon recommended that fitness be the architect's principal concern, and considered style an optional matter of "expression." See his Encyclopaedia (1833; q.v.).

277.1

REPTON, Humphry (1752–1818), and John Adey REPTON (1775–1860)

Fragments on the theory and practice of landscape gardening. Including some remarks on Grecian and Gothic architecture, collected from various manuscripts, in the possession of the different noblemen and gentlemen, for whose use they were originally written; the whole tending to establish fixed principles in the respective arts. By H. Repton, Esq. assisted by his son, J. Adey Repton, F.A.S.

London: Printed by T. Bensley and Son; for J. Taylor, 1816.

xii + 238 + [i] pp, 43 pls.

33.4 × 27.3 cm

MnU

In *Fragments* Repton offered few ideas that had not been explored already in his *Observations on the Theory and Practice of Landscape Gardening* (1803), or *Designs for the Pavillon at Brighton* (1808), qq.v. He included illustrations of many architectural "improvements" he had executed at country houses all over England. As in earlier treatises, he described these improvements and the rationale behind them by reprinting excerpts from his "Red Books," descriptive proposals prepared for the improvement of over 200 estates.

The contents of this book are arranged as a series of 36 "fragments," or essays. Fifteen describe Repton's proposals for improvements at individual country estates,[1] while the rest discuss styles, materials, and principles of landscape gardening. He considered such principles as symmetry, unity of character, outline, color, combination and contrast, "aspects" and "prospects," and variety. Other essays concern water, fences, windows, interiors, rural architecture in general, castles, villas, lodges, cottages, and the "luxuries of a garden."

In the first essay Repton offered an important discussion of the different visual properties of architectural styles. He illustrated his points in the plate facing page 2, labeled "Characters of Houses." Of six houses, all three stories high and 60 feet wide, the first is embellished only with a flat cornice at roof level and with an ornamented doorway. The next illustration shows the addition of a balcony across the full width of the middle floor, while the third illustration depicts vertical articulation of the facade into bays. "The eye seems at once to class the former with the Grecian, and the latter with the Gothic character; and this is the consequence merely of the contrasted horizontal and perpendicular lines" (p. 2). The next three designs show the house completely finished in "Grecian" style (actually Palladian, with a rusticated ground story and an engaged tetrastyle Ionic portico), and two "Gothic" styles, one with pointed arches and one castellated. He added another plate, facing page 4, showing enlarged versions of the "Grecian" and castellated designs set in appropriate landscapes. The former, he said, was suited to "quiet, calm and beautiful scenery of a tame country," and the Gothic accorded with "wild and romantic situations," with "rocks and dashing mountain-streams, or deep umbrageous cells" (pp. 3–4).

In the essay on "Interiors" Repton stated that "whatever the style of the exterior may be, the interior of a house should be adapted to the uses of the inhabitants" (p. 52).[2] Some architects adopted a similar line of reasoning to justify the use of a Classical or exotic style on the exterior of a house, for associational expression or other reasons, while arranging the interior plan in a manner unsympathetic to that style but well suited to modern functional needs.[3]

Throughout the book he reiterated his concern for principles of utility and convenience.[4] In his remarks on Stanage Park, for example, he indicated that "the three following principles, however they may be at variance with each other, have all been considered in the plan here suggested, viz. 1st. Economy, 2d. Convenience, and 3d. a certain degree of Magnificence" (p. 36). In his analysis of aesthetic composition and expression he relied on criteria introduced in his previous books:[5] "style and character" or "situation and character" were central to his discussion of almost every house and its relation to the landscape.[6]

Dwellings in half-timbered and Elizabethan styles appeared only infrequently in British architectural books during the first decades of the nineteenth century.[7] John Adey Repton contributed designs in each style to *Fragments*, and his reasons for doing so are of some interest. He explained that his half-timbered design for a "Timber Cottage" facing page 14 was drawn up at the request of the Duke of Bedford, and "serves as a specimen of the Timber houses which prevailed in England from about the year 1450 to 1550" (p. 14). The younger Repton also included detailed information on the sources and precedents for motifs and materials used in the cottage. In designing a Tudor "Park Keeper's Lodge" at Cobham Hall (p. 184), he intentionally avoided "the modern Gothic Style, with sharp-pointed windows, and a flat slate roof just rising over the battlements," and instead adopted the style "which is distinguished by massive square-headed windows, with pinnacles, mouldings, gables, escutcheons, and the lofty enriched chimneys of former days." He chose this quasi-Elizabethan style so the design would appear to be of the same date as Cobham Hall itself, "built in the reign of Queen Elizabeth" (p. 185).

The plates, like those in *Observations*, consist of aquatinted illustrations, many hand colored, reproduced from Repton's "Red Books." Many of the plates have movable "slides," or flaps, allowing the viewer to see the landscape before and after Repton's suggested improvements. Additional aquatinted and engraved illustrations also appear on text leaves.

1. These include Cobham Hall, Blenden Hall, Beaudesert, Wingerworth, a garden in Portugal, Uppark, Frome House, Longleat, an unidentified villa near London, Ashridge, Woburn Abbey, Sherringham Bower, Endsleigh, and Harestreet. There is also a design for a "House of Industry."

2. His description of the rooms a house "will require . . . for the present habits of life" illuminates aspects of Regency interior planning. A house should include "a dining-room, and two others, one of which may be called a drawing-room, and the other the book-room, if small, or the library, if large: to these is sometimes added a breakfast-room, but of late, especially since the central hall, or vestibule, has been in some degree given up, these rooms have been opened into each other, *en suite*, by large folding doors; and the effect of this enfilade, or visto, through a modern house, is occasionally increased by a conservatory at one end, and repeated by a large mirror at the opposite end" (p. 52).

3. Repton's sometime friend and rival, Richard Payne Knight, explored this idea in designs for his own residence, Downton Castle (1774–1778). See S. Lang, "Richard Payne Knight and the Idea of Modernity," in John Summerson, ed., *Concerning Architecture: Essays on Architectural Writers and Writing Presented to Nikolaus Pevsner* (London: Allen Lane The Penguin Press, 1968), pp. 85–97.

4. He already had discussed these principles in *Observations* and in *Designs for . . . Brighton, qq.v.*

5. See *Observations* and *Designs for . . . Brighton*.

6. See example Stanage Park, pp. 33–35; Beaudesert, pp. 40–42; Wingerworth, pp. 59–60; Uppark, pp. 91–92; Frome House, pp. 101–102; Longleat, pp. 115–118; a villa near London, pp. 129–130; Woburn Abbey, pp. 150–151; Endsleigh, pp. 213–217.

7. See Chapter III, Section 8, in "The Literature of British Domestic Architecture, 1715–1842" above. Humphry Repton had discussed "Queen Elizabeth's Gothic" briefly in his *Observations* (1803; *q.v.*).

278.1

REPTON, Humphry (1752–1818)

The landscape gardening and landscape architecture of the late Humphry Repton, Esq. Being his entire works on these subjects. A new edition: with an historical and scientific introduction, a systematic analysis, a biographical notice, notes, and a copious alphabetical index. By J. C. Loudon, F.L.S., &c. Originally published in one folio and three quarto volumes, and now comprised in one volume octavo. Illustrated by upwards of two hundred and fifty engravings.

London: Printed for the editor, and sold by Longman & Co. and A. & C. Black, Edinburgh, 1840.

xxxi + 619 pp, portr.

21.5 × 14.0 cm

MnU

A portrait of Repton faces the title page. In the Introduction (pp. v–xii) John Claudius Loudon explained that he conceived this collected edition of five of Repton's major books as the first in a series of four or five volumes that would reprint all the "best works" on landscape gardening (p. v). But Loudon did not specify any of the other books he intended to include, and no further volumes in the series appeared.

Also in the Introduction Loudon gave a brief history of landscape gardening, dividing it into two principal styles: the Architectural Style (including Ancient, Roman, Geometric, and Regular Styles), and the Landscape Style (incorporating Modern, English, Irregular, and Natural Styles). He traced the origin of the Landscape Style to William Kent, whose manner was superseded late in the eighteenth century by "Repton's School," a manner that incorporated "all that was excellent in the former schools" (pp. v–viii). In recent years increasing interest in botany and horticulture had "given rise to a school which we call the Gardenesque," a name Loudon gave to his own style of landscape work. The "characteristic feature" of this approach was "the display of the beauty of trees, and other plants, individually" (p. ix).

The preliminaries also contain lists of contents and engravings "classed according to the subjects," as well as a list of contents in the order in which they were printed in the text (pp. xiii–xxxi).

The text begins with a biographical notice of Repton (pp. 1–22), which according to Loudon was "furnished" by a member of Repton's family (p. xii). The remainder of the text consists of Repton's five major treatises on landscape gardening: *Sketches and Hints on Landscape Gardening* (pp. 23–116), *Observations on the Theory and Practice of Landscape Gardening* (pp. 117–320), *An Inquiry into the Changes of Taste in Landscape Gardening* (pp. 321–357), *Designs for the Pavillon at Brighton* (pp. 359–406), and *Fragments on the Theory and Practice of Landscape Gardening* (pp. 407–606). Occasionally Loudon added his own remarks in footnotes. He reproduced Repton's sometimes lavish illustrations as small engravings on text leaves, and the results were often unsatisfactory.[1] Many of Repton's illustrations originally had "slides," or flaps that folded up and down to show scenes before and after his "improvements." Loudon, who had always disliked this method of illustration, included one example of a figure with a movable slide on page 31, but in all other cases showed the subject twice: once reproducing the effect with the slide open, and then showing the effect with the slide closed.[2] The book concludes with an index (pp. 607–619).

1. Loudon indicated that the illustrations in some copies of *Landscape Gardening* were colored (p. xii). Nevertheless engravings of such small size could not do justice to the range of textures and tones in Repton's folio plates.

2. Loudon discussed Repton's method of using slides at length in the Appendix to his *Treatise* (1806; *q.v.*). He made further remarks in a lengthy footnote on pp. 31–38 of *Landscape Gardening*.

279.1

REPTON, Humphry (1752–1818)

Observations on the theory and practice of landscape gardening. Including some remarks on Grecian and Gothic architecture, collected from various manuscripts, in the possession of the different noblemen and gentlemen, for whose use they were originally written; the whole tending to establish fixed principles in the respective arts. By H. Repton, Esq.

London: Printed by T. Bensley, for J. Taylor, 1803.

16 + 222 + [2] pp, portr. + 27 pls.

33.3 × 27.9 cm

MnU

279.2

————

————

London: Printed by T. Bensley, for J. Taylor, 1805.

16 + 222 + [2] pp, portr. + 27 pls.

34.1 × 27.6 cm

MH

This was the second of Repton's books on landscape design, and it was perhaps his most significant and influential publication overall. It addressed several important issues in contemporary architectural and landscape design, among them fitness and the pictorial and associational qualities of architectural style.

The format of *Observations* was like that of his previous book, *Sketches and Hints* (*q.v.*). Repton regretted the difficulty of applying "rules of Art to the works of Nature" ("Advertisement," p. 5), and offered instead a series of "observations" that in sum would tend to "establish fixed Principles" (ibid.). As in the previous book, he borrowed most of his examples from his "Red Books," descriptive proposals prepared for the improvement of over 200 estates ("Advertisement," pp. 6–7).

At the start of the text (p. 2) Repton introduced two "general principles" of architectural and landscape composition, "*relative fitness* or UTILITY, and *comparative proportion* or SCALE." He found the two principles "inseparable," but clearly distinguished utility or fitness as a principle of "the mind," and scale as a principle of "the eye" (p. 2). The principle of fitness involved comfort, convenience, and adaptation of a design to "the uses of each individual proprietor" (p. 2).[1] Scale was a "principle which depends on sight," and "forms the basis of all improvement depending on perspective" (pp. 2, 5). Repton noted that in its "attention to perspective" the "Art of Landscape Gardening is in no instance more intimately connected with that of painting" (p. 6), thus suggesting a close relation between landscape gardening and pictorial composition. Consequently the second chapter concerns optics and vision, and four subsequent chapters treat such landscape forms as water, plantings, woods, and fences as elements of visual composition.

In the next two chapters Repton analyzed specific types of landscape improvement according to visual principles. He dismissed the *ferme ornée* as "inconsistent": "The chief beauty of a *park* consists in uniform verdure," while a "*farm*, on the contrary, is for ever changing the colour of its surface in motley and discordant hues" (pp. 92–93). On the other hand a "Pleasure Ground," a lawn ornamented with flowers and shrubs, clearly encompasses the mansion with a "scene of 'embellished neatness'" and thus separates the residential area from pastures, woods, and so forth (p. 99).

Repton also attempted to define the difference between landscape gardening and painting, reviving his nine-year-old dispute with Richard Payne Knight and Uvedale Price.[2] "The art I profess," he wrote, "is of a higher nature than that of painting." Indeed "nature may be rendered more pleasing than the finest picture; since the perfection of painting seldom aims at exact or individual representations of nature" (p. 110). He alluded to differences between painting and gardening in "general composition," coloring, and scale (pp. 109, 117) but offered no further substantive analysis.

The next two chapters contain remarks on the history of gardening and "Miscellaneous" observations on variety, first impressions, roads, entrances, architectural ornaments, decorations, colors, and metals. Among these observations he included a few remarks on "character," suggesting that this notion encompassed both visual and emotional aspects of a design. On the one hand, the character of a design was a visual characteristic, drawing together both landscape and architecture into a single unified composition:

One of the first objects of improvement should be to adapt the character of the grounds to that of the house; and both should bear some proportion to the extent of property by which they are surrounded. (p. 137)

But the character of a design also was a theme, feeling, or idea that governed the whole. In the case of landscape design, Repton advocated "adding character" to make the design coherent:

The painter copies in their respective places, the eyes, the nose, and mouth, of the individual, but without adding character his picture will not be interesting. The landscape gardener finds ground, wood, and water, but with little more power than the painter, of changing their relative position; he adds character by the point of view in which he displays them, or by the ornaments of art with which they are embellished. (p. 135)

The design of a dwelling should reflect its surroundings and express its function, thereby becoming truly "characteristic architecture":

the adaptation of buildings not only to the situation, character, and circumstances of the scenery, but also to the purposes for which they are intended; this I shall call *Characteristic Architecture*. (p. 206)

The "purposes" Repton had in mind, and which he discussed near the end of the treatise, were the uses associated with different types of dwelling, such as the mansion, villa, or sporting seat (p. 204). A small villa might display "compactness," while a mansion would exhibit "greatness," "durability," and "magnificence" (p. 204). A dwelling expressing one of these characters, when allied with scenery of a similar or other appropriate character, would then become the most successfully "characteristic" architecture possible.

Repton devoted three substantial chapters (pp. 167–212) to the subject of architecture and its relation to landscape gardening. He argued that these two subjects were "inseparable" (p. 167), since "it is impossible to fix or describe the situation applicable to a house, without at the same time describing the sort of house applicable to the situation" (p. 170). To demonstrate his point he analyzed seven different house types, from "prior to the reign of Elizabeth" to "modern" times, according to the shape of the plan, the architectural style employed, and the setting in the landscape.

He also offered a detailed analysis of architectural style, reprinted from his Red Book describing alterations at Corsham. He first discussed the relative merits of Greek and Gothic style in terms of historical associations:

A house of Grecian architecture, built in a town, and separated from it only by a court-yard, always implies the want of landed property; because being evidently of recent erection, the taste of the present day would have placed the house in the midst of a lawn or park, if there had been sufficient land adjoining; while the mansions built in the Gothic character of Henry VIII, Elizabeth, and James, being generally annexed to towns or villages, far from impressing the mind with the want of territory, their size and grandeur, compared with other houses in the town, imply that the owner is not only the lord of the surrounding country, but of the town also. (p. 189)

Repton then contrasted the styles in visual terms:

and although Grecian architecture may be more regular, there is a stateliness and grandeur in the lofty towers, the rich and splendid assemblage of turrets, battlements, and pinnacles, the bold depth of shadow produced by projecting buttresses, and the irregularity of outline in a large Gothic building, unknown to the most perfect Grecian edifice.[3]

He also described three different "species," or types of Gothic style, a classification that was fundamental to much subsequent commentary on the Gothic style:[4]

Gothic structures may be classed under three heads, viz. The *Castle* Gothic, the *Church* Gothic, or the *House* Gothic: let us consider which is the best adapted to the purposes of a dwelling.

The *Castle Gothic*, with few small apertures and large masses of wall, might be well calculated for defence, but the apartments are rendered so gloomy, that it can only be made habitable by enlarging and increasing these apertures, and, in some degree, sacrificing the original character to modern comfort.

The more elegant *Church Gothic* consists in very large apertures with small masses or piers: here the too great quantity of light requires to be subdued by painted glass; and however beautiful this may be in churches, or the chapels and halls of colleges, it is seldom applicable to a house, without such violence and mutilation, as to destroy its general character: therefore a Gothic house of this style would have too much the appearance of a church; for, I believe, there are no large *houses* extant of earlier date than Henry VIII, or Elizabeth, all others being either the remains of baronial castles or conventual edifices.

At the dissolution of the monasteries by Henry VIII, a new species of architecture was adopted, and most of the old mansions now remaining in England were either built or repaired, about the end of that reign, or in the reign of Queen Elizabeth: hence it has acquired in our days the name of *Elizabeth's Gothic*; and although in the latter part of that reign, and in the unsettled times which followed, bad taste had corrupted the original purity of its character, by introducing fragments of Grecian architecture in its ornaments, yet the general character and effect of those houses is perfectly Gothic; and the bold projections, the broad masses, the richness of their windows, and the irregular outline of their roofs, turrets, and tall chimnies, produce a play of light and shadow wonderfully picturesque, and in a painter's eye, amply compensating for those occasional inaccuracies urged against them as specimens of regular architecture. (pp. 190–191)

[I do not hesitate, on the whole, to pronounce that, of all the various dates and styles of architecture proper for a mansion, there is none more dignified, more picturesque, or even better adapted to the purposes of modern life, than might be derived from the best style of Queen Elizabeth's Gothic.][5]

The rest of Repton's discussion of architecture describes his work at Port Eliot, Magdalen College, Ashton Court, and Bayham.

The concluding chapter includes a long essay on "Theory of Colours and Shadows, By the Rev. Dr. Milner," and Repton's final observation that theories of color, while "satisfactory with respect to works of Art," cannot always be reconciled with truth in nature (p. 221).

Certainly the most attractive feature of the book is the plates. Executed in aquatint and hand colored, they are "fac similes of my sketches in the original *Red Books*" (p. 7). Many of the plates, and several additional illustrations printed on text leaves, include "slides," or flaps that can be removed so the viewer can compare both "before" and "after" views. These plates depict Repton's work at Ashton Court, Bayham, Blaise Castle, Brentry Hill, Bulstrode, Burley, Corsham, Garnons, Harewood, Langley Park, Michel Grove, Plas Newydd, Port Eliot, Purley, the Royal Fort at Bristol, Shardeloes, Stoke Park, Wentworth, and West Wycombe. Additional plates illuminate points made in the text (e.g., the difference between a farm and a park), and illustrations in the text accompany his discussions of optics, trees, and water.

1. For later authors who discussed the issue of fitness see John Billington, John Claudius Loudon, and Richard Brown.

2. See the commentary above for Knight, *The Landscape.*

3. P. 189. The alterations he proposed for Corsham were Gothic, explaining the strong argument in favor of Gothic here.

4. This analysis, taken from the Corsham Red Book, had already been printed two years earlier in John Britton's *Beauties of Wiltshire* (London, 1801), II, 271–282. Therefore it is not surprising to find the same scheme of classification already in Elsam's *Essay on Rural Architecture* (London, 1803), published in the same year as Repton's *Observations*. Repton's scheme, based on visual principles, was superseded by Thomas Rickman's somewhat archaeological analysis, first published in James Smith's *Panorama of Science and Art* (1815; *q.v.*).

5. The final paragraph, presumably in Repton's Red Book but not included in *Observations*, is taken from Britton, *Beauties*, II, 279.

280.1

REPTON, Humphry (1752–1818)

Sketches and hints on landscape gardening. Collected from designs and observations now in the possession of the different noblemen and gentlemen, for whose use they were originally made. The whole tending to establish fixed principles in the art of laying out ground. By H. Repton, Esq.

London: Printed by W. Bulmer and Co., and sold by J. and J. Boydell; and by G. Nicol, [1794].

xvi + 83 + [ii] pp, 16 pls.

27.5 × 37.9 cm

MH

In the Advertisement (pp. ix–x) Repton explained that for a long time he had wanted to create a "complete system of Landscape Gardening, classed under *general rules*" (p. ix). But he found "so much variety in their application" that it would be too expensive to bring together a sufficient number of plates to illustrate his points, and therefore he chose instead to present this collection of "detached fragments."[1] In the dedication to the king (pp. v–vi) Repton defended the lack of system in his approach on the grounds of experience and past success: "true taste in every art, consists more in adapting tried expedients to peculiar circumstances, than in that inordinate thirst after novelty."

The Introduction (pp. xiii–xvi) consists of "General Remarks on Landscape Gardening," an "Art which originated in England" and "can only be advanced and perfected by the united powers of the *landscape painter* and the *practical gardener*" (p. xiii). Repton indicated that his present goal was:

not merely to produce a *book of pictures*, but to furnish some hints for establishing the fact, that *true* taste in *Landscape Gardening*, as well as in all the other Polite Arts, is not an accidental effect, operating on the outward senses, but an appeal to the understanding, which is able to compare, to separate, and to combine, the various sources of pleasure derived from external objects, and to trace them to some pre-existing causes in the structure of the human mind. (pp. xv–xvi)

In the first chapter Repton introduced the twin subjects "character" and "situation," the two fundamental features of a landscape that every designer must consider in the process of "improvement":

All rational improvement of grounds is, necessarily, founded on a due attention to the Character and Situation of the place to be improved: the former teaches what is *advisable*, the latter what is *possible*, to be done. . . . In deciding on the *character* of any place, some attention must be given to its situation with respect to other places; to the natural shape of the ground on which the house is, or may be, built; to the size and style of the house, and even to the rank of its possessor; together with the use which he intends to make of it, whether as a mansion or a constant residence, a sporting seat, or a villa. . . . (p. 1)

The rest of the chapter (pp. 2–12) consists of extracts from Repton's "Red Books," which were descriptive proposals prepared for the improvement of individual estates. The extracts here concern aspects of character and situation at specific sites, and identify particular characters such as "gloomy and sequestered" or "picturesque and cheerful" (p. 4).[2] Repton recognized that the character of an estate depended in large part on qualities of the landscape, but also contended that character was a function of architectural style and of the manner in which buildings were sited in the landscape. At Tatton Park, for example, "It is not from the *situation* only that the *character* of Tatton derives its greatness. The command of adjoining property, the style and magnitude of the mansion, and all its appendages, contribute to confer that degree of importance which ought here to be the leading object in every plan of improvement" (p. 9).

In the second chapter, "Concerning Buildings" (pp. 13–19), Repton classified all architecture according to two characters, the horizontal and the perpendicular (p. 14).[3] Greek and Gothic architecture, he said, are far better "distinguished" by attention to the horizontality or perpendicularity of their form than by attention to minute details of style (p. 16). These two architectural characters befit two complementary types of landscape: "trees of a pointed or conic shape have a beautiful effect" with Greek architecture, "chiefly from the circumstance of contrast." But "trees of a conic shape mixed with Gothic buildings displease, from their affinity with the prevalent lines of the architecture"; Gothic therefore is "peculiarly adapted to those situations, where the shape of the ground occasionally hides the lower part of the building, while its roof is relieved by trees, whose forms contrast with those of the Gothic outline" (p. 17). Repton illustrated this point in Plate VII, in which movable "slides" allow the viewer to contrast the appearance of Gothic and Classical structures surrounded either by pointed coniferous trees or by lower, more rounded, deciduous trees.

The third chapter concerns "Proper Situations for an House," and further explores the correspondence between landscape scenery and architectural character and style. Chapters 4 through 7 consider specific landscape forms, such as water, "Park Scenery," and approaches, and also address such aesthetic problems as "Symmetry and Uniformity" and the "Affinity betwixt Painting and Gardening."[4]

In the Appendix (pp. 67–83) Repton reprinted his recent *Letter to Uvedale Price* (1794), occasioned by Price's *Essay on the Picturesque* (1794), and added further remarks on the subject of picturesque landscape.[5] He argued that picturesque effect was an important component of landscape appreciation, but not the only one—and therefore Price and Richard Payne Knight, who focused primarily on the picturesque,[6] had not inquired "deeply enough" into the problem (p. 77). On pages 78–81 Repton added a list of 16 "Sources of Pleasure in Landscape Gardening": congruity,[7] utility, order, symmetry, picturesque effect, intricacy, simplicity, variety, novelty, contrast, continuity, association,[8] grandeur, appropriation, animation, and the seasons.

Five of the 16 plates illustrate architectural subjects. Plates II, III, and IV show Repton's designs for renovations in Gothic style of house facades at Rivenhall, Wembly, and Welbeck. Plate V depicts changes in visual effect caused by the application of Gothic or Greek styles to the facade of a mansion. Plate VII, discussed above, demonstrates the correspondence between architectural and landscape styles. Plates I, VI, VIII, IX, and XI–XVI depict landscape and other improvements, either proposed or executed, at specific estates. Plate X illustrates different visual relationships that exist between a house and convex, concave, or level land forms.

1. Repton indicated that his "Red Book," or bound set of proposals for improvements at Welbeck, was the "ground work of the present volume," and listed 56 other "Red Books" from which he made additional "Extracts" (pp. x–xii).

2. Thomas Whately provided the first comprehensive analysis of landscape character in *Observations on Modern Gardening* (London, 1770). For more on the subject see John Archer, "Character in English Architectural Design," *Eighteenth-Century Studies* XII:3 (Spring 1979), 339–371.

3. He admitted there might be a third character, exemplified by Chinese style, but disparaged it as a "confused mixture" of the two other characters (p. 15).

4. In discussing the extremes of expression achieved in all of the arts, he noted that "*Gardening* must include the two opposite characters of native wildness, and artificial comfort, each adapted to the genius and character of the place" (p. 64).

5. Humphry Repton, *A Letter to Uvedale Price* (London: G. Nicol, 1794). Price replied in *A Letter to H. Repton, Esq., on the Application of the Practice as Well as the Principles of Landscape-Painting to Landscape-Gardening* (London: J. Robson, 1795).

6. See the commentary on Richard Payne Knight, *The Landscape, a Didactic Poem* (1794). On the various debates among Repton, Price, and Knight see Walter John Hipple, Jr., *The Beautiful, the Sublime, and the Picturesque in Eighteenth-Century British Aesthetic Theory* (Carbondale: Southern Illinois University Press, 1957); and Nikolaus Pevsner, *Studies in Art, Architecture and Design* (London: Thames and Hudson, 1968), I.

7. Defined as "a proper adaptation of the several parts to the whole; and that whole to the character, situation, and circumstances of the place and its possessor" (p. 78).

8. "This is one of the most impressive sources of delight; whether excited by local accident, as the spot on which some public character performed his part; by the remains of antiquity, as the ruin of a cloister or a castle; but more particularly by that personal attachment to long known objects, perhaps indifferent in themselves, as the favourite seat, the tree, the walk, or the spot endeared by the remembrance of past events" (p. 80).

281.1
RICAUTI, T. J.
Rustic architecture. The picturesque and pleasing appearance of rough wood, thatch, etc. when applied as the only decorations of rural buildings, illustrated by XLII zincographic drawings; consisting of plans, elevations, sections and perspective views; the doors, windows, chimney shafts, etc. drawn geometrically to a large scale, with a description and the estimated cost of each design.

London: Printed for and published by the author. And to be procured through any bookseller, 1840.

8 printed leaves, 42 pls [*pl. XXXI is wanting in this copy*].

24.1 × 31.8 cm

Bodl.

281.2

Rustic architecture. Picturesque decorations of rural buildings in the use of rough wood, thatch, etc. Illustrated by forty-two drawings, consisting of plans, elevations, sections, and perspective views; the doors, windows, chimney shafts, etc. drawn geometrically to a large scale, with descriptions and estimated costs. By T. J. Ricauti, Architect.

London: James Carpenter, 1842.

8 printed leaves, 42 pls.

[*Title page:*] 31.8 × 25.4 cm

[*Text and plates:*] 25.4 × 31.8 cm

MB

In the Introduction, printed on a single leaf following the title page, Ricauti described this book as an "appeal to Society (particularly American) in favor of those humble, though by no means unimportant features in the Pastoral Landscape," namely, "Rural Cottages." In making these designs he tried "to form an agreeable picture" in the exterior elevation, while also attending to "internal accommodation." Perhaps overly romanticizing the rustic aspects of his designs, he claimed that they "exhibit no ornament (excepting the Chimney Shafts) but such as can easily be procured by a judicious use of the woodman's axe."

Ricauti presented six designs, each described on one leaf of letterpress and illustrated in seven "zincographic" plates. The first four designs—cottages for a peasant, a forester, a gamekeeper, and a gardener—also could be used as residences for a "small family." The fifth design befitted a "small genteel family" or could be used as a bailiff's cottage on a gentleman's estate. The sixth design was a "residence of a small genteel family: or a steward's cottage on a nobleman's estate." In the letterpress descriptions Ricauti provided dimensions, specifications, and cost estimates for each design. The illustrations include plans, elevations, sections, details of chimneys and windows, and designs for rustic bargeboards and furniture. Each house also is depicted in a picturesque view, surrounded by trees, shrubbery, lawns, and distant fields and hills.

Ricauti's architecture is highly picturesque, making extensive use of hipped gables, thatch roofs, lattice windows, half-timbering, rough-barked columns, and other rustic features. In Design No. IV, for example, a large gable with elaborate bargeboards encloses half-timbered walls and an oriel with lattice windows; the small veranda below, running along three sides of the house, is constructed of rustic columnar supports and a thatch roof. Picturesque Tudor ornament tops the chimneys, the many angles and planes of the roof are adorned with ornamental patterns woven into the thatch, and the veranda is furnished with rustic rough-hewn benches. The smallest design (No. I), estimated to cost between £120 and £140, includes a basement with a kitchen, back kitchen, and baking area, plus a living room and two bedrooms on the ground floor. The largest design (No. VI) would cost £600, and includes a hall, waiting room, breakfast room, dining room, kitchen, and other service areas on the ground floor, plus four bedrooms, two dressing rooms, and two servant's bedrooms upstairs.

282.1

RICAUTI, T. J.

Sketches for rustic work; including bridges, park and garden buildings, seats and furniture. The scenic views in the tinted style of zincography, from eighteen plates, printed at the author's offices; with descriptions and estimates of the buildings. By T. J. Ricauti, Architect. . . .

Exeter: Published by P. A. Hannaford. London: Longman, Brown, Green, and Longmans, 1842.

8 printed leaves, 18 pls (numbered 1–7, 17).

30.8 × 23.5 cm

MB

282.2 †

Sketches for rustic work.

[London]: H. Bohn, 1845.

4°

Reference: ECB

282.3

Sketches for rustic work; including bridges, park and garden buildings, seats and furniture. With descriptions and estimates of the buildings. By T. J. Ricauti, Architect. . . .

London: Henry G. Bohn, 1848.

7 printed leaves, 18 pls (numbered 1–17, 17).

31.1 × 25.0 cm

MB

The title page is followed by a dedicatory leaf and an Introduction, in which Ricauti noted that "in the course of a professional excursion through some of the most picturesque counties of England . . . my attention was first directed to this subject." He was distressed by the recent erection of crude, inelegant garden buildings and seats "whose outlines are anything but compatible with the surrounding scenery." Ricauti offered this collection of original designs to encourage preservation of the rustic and picturesque appearance of England's country estates.

The plates include designs for three bridges, a gate lodge, a winter house for plants, a gardener's cottage, a pigeon house, a garden gate, rustic seats and other furniture, and a fishing cottage. Each design is illustrated "zincographically" in one or more plans, elevations, or views. Six leaves of descriptive letterpress accompany these designs, and include brief remarks on materials, construction, picturesque composition, and cost.[1]

Even more intricate and picturesque than Ricauti's previously published designs,[2] the gate lodge, gardener's cottage, and fishing cottage include more elaborate half-timbering and bargeboards, plus overhanging upper stories, thatch roofs, ornamental chimneys, and intricately carved finials, pendants, and supporting brackets. The gate lodge (Plates IV–VI), estimated to cost £110, includes a tool room and lodgekeeper's room on the ground floor, plus a bedroom and seed room upstairs. The gardener's cottage (Plates IX–XI), estimated to cost £160, contains a gardener's room and two fruit rooms on the ground floor, plus a bedroom and "room for summer fruit" upstairs. The design for a rustic fishing cottage is shown only in a view (Plate XVII).[3] Ricauti stated that "this design is so simple that any person possessing a knowledge of architecture and building could prepare the plans, elevations, &c. and by attending to the directions given in the description of the Gate-lodge, might be enabled to execute it."

1. On the final leaf Ricauti also provided a list of his "terms for making designs of buildings, and for superintending the erection."

2. See *Rustic Architecture* (1840).

3. This plate and one other are both numbered "XVII." According to the text, the view of the fishing cottage should be numbered "XVIII."

283.1
RICHARDSON, George (1736?–1817)
The first part of a complete system of architecture; or, a series of original designs for country seats or villas: containing plans and elevations, with sections of the principal apartments, ceilings, chimney-pieces, friezes, capitals of columns, and pilasters, enriched cornices, and other interior decorations. Designed and engraved, in aquatinta, on XXVII plates, with descriptions; by George Richardson, Architect.

London: Printed for the author; and sold by Mr. George Nicol, 1794.

6 pp, 27 pls.

51.4 × 35.6 cm

RIBA

283.2
___

A series of original designs for country seats or villas; containing plans and elevations, sections of the principal apartments, ceilings, chimney= pieces, capitals of columns, ornaments for friezes, and other interior decorations, in the antique style. Comprized in LVII. plates, with descriptions. Designed and engraved, in aquatinta, by George Richardson, Architect.

London: Printed for the author; and sold by the principal booksellers of London, Edinburgh, and Dublin, 1795.

[*Part I:*] 6 pp, 27 pls.

[*Part II:*] ii + 7–12 pp, 28–57 pls.

50.2 × 33.7 cm

V&A

The format and content of this folio collection of plans, elevations, and sections of the architect's own designs clearly recall earlier treatises by James Paine, Sir John Soane, and Charles Middleton.[1] Unlike his predecessors Richardson presented designs for just one class of buildings, "Country Seats or Villas." Within this one class there is a wide range of sizes, from a small two-story villa, three windows wide (Plate I), to one design three stories high in the center and 11 windows wide (Plates LIII–LV).

Richardson included brief remarks on architectural theory in the Introduction (1795, II, i–ii). He indicated that utility and convenience were important considerations in designing a house (II, i), but these did not fulfill a building's potential for aesthetic expression:

there still remains unlimited scope for improvement and invention, not only in the distribution and connection of the several apartments, and the interior finishing of private houses, but also on the exterior parts of buildings, where there is ample latitude for exercising the powers of invention and novelty, consistent with the purest principles of the art. (II, i)

In accord with such principles he advocated restraint in the use of ornament: "on the exterior parts of private buildings a profusion of ornaments should not be recommended; and when any are admitted, they should be designed with regularity, and introduced with judgment and taste." Indeed in his own elevations he placed special emphasis on "proportion, simplicity, and uniformity," so that his designs would "produce an agreeable effect from every point of view" (II, i). For "interior furnishings" he was inspired by ancient Roman examples: he had "attempted to retain the spirit and effect of that beautiful and elegant style . . . used in the private apartments, baths, and villas, of the Ancients; namely, at Rome, Adrain's Villa, and the ruins on the Baian shore" (II, ii).

The 57 plates are accompanied by 12 pages of descriptions, dimensions, and keys (I, 1–6; II, 7–12). Richardson, who had served as draughtsman to the Adam brothers for 18 years,[2] took special care in designing ornamental friezes, chimneypieces, and ceilings. Indeed the most successful designs in the book are probably the rich interior elevations and the details of individual ornaments, all in an Adamesque manner. Richardson's exterior style, in contrast, is often thin and spare, relying on shallow relieving arches and thin pilaster strips to animate the facade. In a few cases the articulation is bolder, with heavy rustication, projecting bows, and ornamented porticoes. Some of the larger designs are broken up into smaller units to allow advance, recession, light, and shadow to enliven the facade in a manner reminiscent of Adamesque "movement."[3]

The ground-floor plan of Richardson's smallest design includes just a lobby, parlor, dining room, kitchen, and servants' room (Plate I). One of the largest designs is over 110 feet wide and 55 feet deep, with a lobby, parlor, dining room, drawing room, lady's dressing room, two "powdering closets," two water closets, a breakfast room, a library, and a gentleman's dressing room on the ground floor. Upstairs there are seven bed chambers and additional rooms (Plates LIII–LV).

1. See Paine, *Plans, Elevations and Sections* (1767–1783); Soane, *Plans Elevations and Sections* (1788), and *Sketches in Architecture* (1793); and Middleton, *Picturesque and Architectural Views* (1793).

2. Colvin (1978), p. 687.

3. See the commentary on Robert and James Adam, *The Works in Architecture* (1778–1779).

284.1

RICHARDSON, George (1736?–1817)

New designs in architecture, consisting of plans, elevations, and sections for various buildings, comprised in XLIV folio plates; designed and engraved by George Richardson, Architect.

Nouveaux desseins d'architecture, ou, plans, elevations, et coupes de divers bâtimens; compris en XLIV planches in folio, dessinées et gravées par George Richardson Architecte.

London: Printed for the author, 1792.

1 printed leaf, ii + 40 pp, 44 pls.

51.4 × 33.3 cm

MH

Richardson's *New Designs* was the second British architectural book to include plates executed in aquatint, following John Plaw's *Rural Architecture* (1785; *q.v.*). But these volumes have little else in common. Plaw's book was small, included only designs for small and modest houses—most of which already were commissioned or executed—and included landscape scenery in the illustrations. Richardson's book was the opposite. In the tradition of Campbell, Gibbs, Chambers, and Adam,[1] Richardson presented his designs in a large folio volume, over 50 cm high. The heavy Neoclassical border around the title page, with titles in both French and English, and a text consisting of parallel columns of French and English, reflect Richardson's aesthetic and professional ambitions. Indeed he proposed to present a progression of building types, from dwellings of "simple form and construction" to "the most complicated and adorned edifices" (p. i). There is no evidence that any of his designs had been executed.

The Introduction (pp. i–ii) includes few original insights into architectural aesthetics. Even the discussion of movement, while important, was indebted to Robert Adam.[2] Richardson strove in his designs

to make the different great parts advance and recede, on purpose that they might not only produce an agreeable and diversified contour in the plans, but also a variety of light and shade in the elevations, which gave beauty, spirit, and effect to the whole compositions. This movement of design adds much to the picturesque appearance of a building, and in some degree may be compared to the effect that hill and dale, foreground and distance have in landscape. (p. ii)

Yet despite such emphasis on the picturesque, Richardson included no scenery in his illustrations.[3]

The plate descriptions (pp. 1–40) include detailed remarks on each design, including descriptions of individual rooms, dimensions, cost estimates, and suggestions for decoration. There are general remarks on some building types, including cottages, country houses, farm houses, and gate lodges.

Altogether there are designs are four cottages, seven country houses, four villas, four farm houses, eight entrances with gates and lodges, five garden temples and pavilions, a town residence, a town mansion, four stables, two greenhouses, two orangeries, six interior elevations, and 19 entablatures, capitals, and other ornaments. The four thatched cottages, illustrated in Plates I and II, were "intended to be erected in the fields or villages belonging to the estates of such gentlemen who take pleasure in building convenient dwellings for the families of their domestics or dependants" (p. i).[4] Like his cottages, Richardson's farm houses (Plates VIII–XIV) were intended for "gentlemen of fortune and taste, who delight in improving their landed property" (p. i). His country houses (Plates III–VII) were designed "for persons in better circumstances in life than the inhabitants" of cottages, and perhaps "for such persons who may be able and inclined, at little expence, to build a convenient residence on pleasant situations in the country" (pp. 3, i). His largest designs (Plates XXXIII–XXXV), up to 258 feet wide, were "villas": "buildings of considerable extent, in which convenience, utility and solidity have been studied in the plans, and in the elevations variety, elegance, and beauty" (p. ii).[5] Finally, his designs for a town mansion and town residence (Plates XXXVIII, XXXIX) include "apartments of parade on the principal floors . . . sufficiently large and numerous for the greatest fortunes and first families in the kingdom" (p. ii).

All of Richardson's designs are Neoclassical. Many features are reminiscent of designs by James Paine and Robert and James Adam,[6] but are executed in a heavier manner, with more rustication, thicker detailing, and less ornament. Nevertheless Richardson's efforts to introduce "movement" were effective: light and shadow enliven the planar advance and recession of the facades.

1. See Colen Campbell, *Vitruvius Britannicus* (1715 and later); James Gibbs, *A Book of Architecture* (1728); William Chambers, *A Treatise on Civil Architecture* (1759); and Robert and James Adam, *The Works in Architecture* (1778 and later).

2. See the commentary on *The Works in Architecture*.

3. Richardson suggested that a building should be composed like a landscape painting. This notion was explored previously by Robert Castell in *Villas of the Ancients* (1728), Robert Morris in *Rural Architecture* (1750), Isaac Ware in *A Complete Body of Architecture* (1756), Robert and James Adam in *The Works in Architecture* (1778 and later), and James Lewis in *Original Designs* (1780–1797), qq.v.

4. In the previous two decades one agricultural writer and one architect had begun to advance the cause of rural improvement through publication of original designs for farm houses and laborers' cottages. See Nathaniel Kent, *Hints to Gentlemen* (1775); and John Wood, *A Series of Plans, for Cottages* (1792; plates executed as early as 1781). Clearly Richardson's designs were intended primarily as landscape ornaments, and only incidentally for their philanthropic or economic value.

5. Compare the "Villas" illustrated by Plaw in *Rural Architecture*: most are under 60 feet wide, two or three stories high, and just three or five windows across. Richardson's definition recalls ancient Roman and Renaissance notions of an extensive and elegant country residence, a notion supported by descriptions in Robert Castell's *Villas of the Ancients* (1728; q.v.).

6. James Paine, *Plans, Elevations and Sections, of Noblemen and Gentlemen's Houses* (1767–1783); and Robert and James Adam, *The Works in Architecture* (1778 and later), qq.v.

285.1

RICHARDSON, George (1736?–1817)

The new Vitruvius Britannicus; consisting of plans and elevations of modern buildings, public and private, erected in Great Britain by the most celebrated architects. Engraved on LXXII plates, from original drawings. By George Richardson, Architect.

Le nouveau Vitruve Britannique; qui comprend les plans et élévations de bâtimens modernes, tant publics que particuliers, érigés dans la Grande Bretagne par les plus célèbres architectes. Contenant LXXII planches, gravées d'après des dessins origineaux.

London: Printed by W. Bulmer and Co., for the author; and sold by J. Taylor, 1802.

iv + 20 pp, 72 pls [*pls. IX, X, XI, XLVII, XLVIII wanting in this copy*].

The new Vitruvius Britannicus; consisting of plans and elevations of modern buildings, public and private, erected in Great Britain by the most celebrated architects. Engraved on LXX plates, from original drawings. Volume II. By George Richardson, Architect.
Le nouveau Vitruve Britannique; qui comprend les plans et élévations de bâtimens modernes, tant publics que particuliers, érigés dans la Grande Bretagne par les plus célèbres architectes. Contenant LXX planches, gravées d'après des dessins origineaux. Tome second.

London: Printed by T. Bensley, for the author; and sold by J. Taylor, 1808.

[ii] + 10 pp, 70 pls [*pls. 11, 12, 19, 20, 63 wanting in this copy*].

56.5 × 38.7 cm

MH

285.2

The new Vitruvius Britannicus; consisting of plans and elevations of modern buildings, public and private, erected in Great Britain by the most celebrated architects. Engraved on LXXII. plates, from original drawings. By George Richardson, Architect.
Le nouveau Vitruve Britannique; qui comprend les plans et élévations de bâtimens modernes, tant publics que particuliers, érigés dans la Grande Bretagne. Par les plus célèbres architectes. Contenant LXXII. planches, gravées d'après des dessins origineaux.

London: Printed by T. Bensley, for the author; sold by J. Taylor, 1810.

iv + 20 pp, 72 pls.

The new Vitruvius Britannicus ⟨ . . . as 1808 Vol. II . . . ⟩ .

London: Printed by T. Bensley, for the author; and sold by J. Taylor, 1808.

[ii] + 10 pp, 70 pls.

54.0 × 40.0 cm

PU

Colen Campbell issued the first book titled *Vitruvius Britannicus* in 1715. Subsequent volumes by Campbell appeared in 1717 and 1725. Badeslade and Rocque issued a fourth volume in 1739, and Woolfe and Gandon completed additional volumes in 1767 and 1771. Campbell's aim was to encourage a British style of architecture, based on "Ancient" examples, that would eclipse the achievements of other modern nations. Badeslade, Rocque, Woolfe, and Gandon implicitly adopted the same goal by borrowing Campbell's title, but their illustrations, increasingly dominated by views of prominent estates, suggest less a commitment to principle than a desire for profit. Richardson's work, published in 1802–1808, includes elevations and plans of several structures by contemporary architects. He offered the illustrations ostensibly "in order to display the taste and science of the English nation in its style of Architecture, at the close of the eighteenth century, and that these might be suitably recorded, and made public, as well for our own use, as for the advantage of ingenious foreigners, who are anxious to know the superior taste and elegance of an English nation" (I, iii). Richardson thus suggested that his contemporaries had finally achieved a standard of architectural excellence worthy of study and imitation.[1]

The first volume illustrates 26 subjects, including 24 residences, the public assembly rooms in Glasgow, and the Middlesex County Session House. In parallel columns of English and French the plate descriptions (pp. 1–20) discuss the building history, site, approaches, dimensions, interiors, and other aspects of the individual designs. All the designs are in Palladian, Adam, Greek Revival, and like classicizing styles. Of 18 designs in the second volume, 12 are residential and six are for civic and commercial structures. The plate descriptions (pp. 1–10) are similar in format and content to those in the first volume. Two of the domestic designs are not in Classical style: William Wilkins's Gothic elevation for Donington Park, and Archibald Elliott's castellated design for Loudoun Castle. Other prominent architects whose work is represented in these two volumes include Robert Adam, Joseph Bonomi, John Carr, S. P. Cockerell, Thomas Leverton, Robert Mylne, John Nash, William Porden, Sir John Soane, George Steuart, James Wyatt, and Samuel Wyatt.

The plates, many of them based on the architects' original drawings, were executed in aquatint. Only plans and elevations are shown; there are no sections or interior details. Although the text descriptions discuss aspects of the surrounding landscape, Robinson included no foliage or scenery in his illustrations.

1. James Paine had made a similar assertion 35 years earlier in *Plans, Elevations and Sections* (1767; *q.v.*).

286.1 ‡
RIDER, William
The principles of perspective, and their application to drawing from nature, familiarly explained and illustrated. By William Rider.

London: Simpkin, Marshall, and Co., 1836.

xii + 63 pp, 14 pls.

8°

Reference: Microfilm supplied by The British Library.

286.2 †
_____

Principles of perspective.

[N. loc.]: Atchley, 1849.

8°

Reference: ECB

Rider noted in the Preface that he prepared this treatise principally as a reference manual for his own students (p. v). He also introduced, without resolving, a problem discussed by Arthur Parsey in *Perspective Rectified* (1836; *q.v.*). Both noted that rules of perspective construction required horizontally receding parallel lines to converge. But vertical parallels, which also in reality recede from the observer, were not permitted to converge. Both authors agreed that this created a distorted image of reality. Parsey's solution was to develop a system for representing vertical convergence as well. Rider simply accepted current practice and defined it as a convention of perspective rendering (p. vii).

Rider divided his text into sections on theory (pp. 1–16), practice (pp. 17–44), and "The Truth of the Foregoing Rules Demonstrated by a Reference to Optical Principles" (pp. 45–55). The section on practice includes subdivisions concerning oblique perspective, and "Observations on Sketching from Nature."

The 28 figures in the plates show drawing apparatus, boxes in perspective, bridges, and other simple objects of perspective construction. Several illustrations accompanying the text portions on oblique and parallel perspective illustrate houses. Figure 11, facing page 23, shows two elevations and an oblique view of a house three windows wide and two stories high. Figure 12, facing page 26, illustrates a pair of attached cottages with pitched roofs.[1] Figure 15, facing page 32, shows a two-story cottage of irregular plan, with bargeboards, drip moldings, and apparently a thatch roof. Figure 16, below Figure 15, depicts the interior of a room, with a door, fireplace, floor-length windows, and paintings on the walls. Figure 17, also on the same plate, represents a street flanked on both sides by three-story terraces and ending in front of a small Gothic church. The plate facing page 36 shows three outdoor scenes. Figure 18 is "a level road," flanked on the left by a terrace of two-story dwellings. Figure 19 is a view looking uphill on a country road. Figure 20 shows a cottage with a thatch roof set into a hillside overlooking a bay.

1. These are similar to a pair rendered in more detail in John Cart Burgess, *An Easy Introduction to Perspective* (1819; *q.v.*), Pl. IX.

287.1
[RIOU, Stephen (1720–1780)]
The Grecian • orders • of architectvre. Delineated • and • explained • from • the • antiqvities • of • Athens • Also. the • parallels • of • the • orders • of • Palladio • Scamozzi • and • Vignola • to • which • are • added • remarks • concerning. pvblick • and • private • edifices • with • designs.

London: Printed by J. Dixwell, for the avthor, 1768.

8 printed leaves, 78 pp, 18 + 10 pls.

44.7 × 29.4 cm

RPJCB

In 1762 James Stuart and Nicholas Revett completed the first volume of their *Antiqvities of Athens*, the first book of Greek archaeology to be published in Britain.[1] Six years later Stephen Riou "inscribed" *The Grecian Orders* to Stuart, and in the Inscription (one leaf, recto) praised Stuart for "rescuing" the "genuine forms of Grecian architecture" from "oblivion."

The Preface (two leaves) is dated at Canterbury, 30 November 1767. In it Riou placed the goals of his own book within the context of Stuart's and Revett's achievements: the *Antiqvities of Athens*, he said, "will transmit to posterity the authentic records and perfect models of the Grecian orders. From those antiquities, it is attempted in this treatise to establish documents for the three orders, and to make a modulary division of all their component parts for practical uses." In addition, Riou would provide "cursory practical considerations concerning publick and private edifices, and . . . give a description of ten plans with their elevations." The preliminaries conclude with an explanation of illustrations in the text (two leaves), a list of 276 subscribers (two leaves), and a table of contents (one leaf).

The first part of the text (pp. 1–50) consists of nine chapters. The first is an introductory survey of architectural history from "the origin of Art" through the seventeenth century, with additional remarks on proportion, eurythmy, and symmetry. Chapters II through VI concern the orders, their proportions, moldings, a "Scroll Medallion," balusters, pediments, acroteria, statues, cornices, and vases. Chapter VII treats doors and windows. Chapter VIII compares descriptions of the orders by Vignola, Palladio, and Scamozzi. The final chapter concerns orders on orders, cornices, and ceilings. Eighteen plates accompany this part of the text, and illustrate the orders, moldings, arcades, a colonnade, "portals," a triumphal arch, and windows.

The second part, "Remarks Concerning Publick and Private Edifices, with Designs" (pp. 51–78), is divided into three chapters. The first concerns the state of architecture in "modern" Europe, and includes remarks on Sir Henry Wotton, Inigo Jones, Ralph Bathurst, Sir Christopher Wren, Sir James Thornhill, Sir John Vanbrugh, William Talman, Sir William Wilson, James Gibbs, the Earl of Burlington, and William Kent. In the second chapter, concerning the architectural "Embellishment of Towns and Cities," Riou stated that the "beauty and magnificence of a city depend principally upon" its "entrances," streets, and buildings (p. 58), each of which he discussed individually. The final chapter treats "Practical Considerations" in building, and also contains descriptions of the ten accompanying plates. These include designs for a temple, a church, a cenotaph, an "open place at Whitehall, with porticos," a new street in the City, a town house with stables and offices, a villa similar to "the castle of Caprarola," another villa, and a hunting pavilion.

The design for a "street in the City" (Plate VI) is simply a terrace of 13 houses, each four stories high and three or five windows wide. The design for a town house, illustrated in two elevations and one plan (Plate VII), is three stories high and seven windows wide. The ground floor includes four principal rooms, a courtyard, offices, and stables. The plan of the villa in Plate VIII incorporates nine principal rooms surrounding an open court 40 feet in diameter, and includes a gallery measuring 60 feet by 20 feet. The principal floor of the villa in Plate IX has a vestibule, two anterooms, a gallery (54 feet by 20 feet), an eating room, a library, a drawing room, a state dressing room, a bed chamber, a chapel, and a chaplain's chamber. The hunting pavilion in Plate X is octagonal in plan, containing a kitchen, storeroom, servants' hall, and drawing room in three octants, and stables in the other five octants.

1. For a thorough discussion of *The Antiqvities of Athens* see Dora Wiebenson, *Sources of Greek Revival Architecture* (London: Zwemmer, 1969).

288.1
[RIPLEY, Thomas (ca. 1683–1758)?]
The plans, elevations, and sections; chimney-pieces, and cielings of Houghton in Norfolk; the seat of the Rt. Honourable Sr. Robert Walpole; First Lord Commissioner of the Treasury, Chancellor of the Exchequer, and Knt. of the Most Noble Order of the Garter.

[N. loc.]: Published by I: Ware, 1735.

1 printed leaf, 35 pls.

53.3 × 35.6 cm

V&A

288.2
RIPLEY, Thomas (ca. 1683–1758)
The plans, elevations, and sections; chimney-pieces, and cielings of Houghton in Norfolk; built by the Rt. Honourable Sr. Robert Walpole; First Lord Commissioner of the Treasury, Chancellor of the Exchequer, and Knt. of the Most Noble Order of the Garter. Who was for his great merit created Earl of Orford &c. The whole designed by Thomas Ripley Esqr. Delineated by Isaac Ware and William Kent Esqrs. And most elegantly engrav'd by the ingenious Mr. Fourdrinier. With a description of the house and of the elegant collection of pictures.

London: Sold by C. Fourdrinier Mr. Lewis, Messrs. Piers & Webley, 1760.

1 printed leaf, 10 pp, 35 + 1 pls.

52.7 × 37.5 cm

MBAt

In 1721 Sir Robert Walpole commissioned Colen Campbell to prepare a design for Houghton Hall, a design that was later published in *Vitruvius Britannicus* (*q.v.*). Over the next decade and a half Walpole entrusted much of the execution and many alterations to his own protégé, Thomas Ripley, and had William Kent complete many of the interiors.

This collection of plans, elevations, sections, details, and one view was first published in 1735. It is traditionally attributed to Thomas Ripley because the title page to the second edition indicates that he designed "the whole." But Campbell was partially responsible for much of the work that is illustrated, and only 14 plates are inscribed "T. Ripley Arch."; another 13 are inscribed "W. Kent Inv." The book is sometimes attributed to its publisher, Isaac Ware, whose name also appears on each plate as delineator.

In the first edition the title page is followed by a prefatory address to the reader in Latin. The 27 plates (19 single, eight double) include a view of the west front; plans of the ground floor and principal floor; elevations of the east, west, and "End" fronts; sections of the east front, west front, hall, "Salone," and staircase; a plan and two elevations of the stables; and illustrations of eight ceilings and ten chimneypieces.

Ten additional pages of letterpress in the second edition contain a description of the interior furnishings and the picture collection. Also in this edition there is one new plate, unnumbered and unsigned, depicting a "Geometrical Plan of the Garden, Park, and Plantation, of Houghton."

289.1
ROBERTSON, John
Supplement to Loudon's manual of cottage gardening, husbandry, and architecture; containing thirty designs for dwellings in the cottage style, varying in accommodation from three to ten rooms each, besides offices. By J. Robertson. . . .

London: Longman, Rees, Orme, Brown, Green, & Longman. Treuttel, Würtz, and Richter, London; Treuttel and Würtz, Paris and Strasburg; Black, Edinburgh; Carvill, New York; Gray and Bowen, Boston; Carey and Lea, Philadelphia; Howe, Sydney; and Melville, Hobart Town, 1833.

48 pp (of which 24 are lithographed plates).

21.0 × 12.7 cm

BL

John Claudius Loudon's *Manual of Cottage Gardening* (q.v.) first appeared in 1830. Three years later Robertson issued this *Supplement*.

The letterpress consists of a one-page table of contents and 18 pages containing brief descriptions of the designs illustrated in the plates. Each description is divided into three parts: the first, titled "Accommodation," serves as a key to the floor plans; the second, titled "Construction," concerns materials; and the third is a "General Estimate" of the cost of the design calculated according to three different rates. The 24 lithographed plates, interleaved and numbered continuously with the text pages, contain 30 designs for dwellings. The first 12 plates depict Designs I through XVIII in one view and one plan each, and the remaining plates illustrate Designs XIX through XXX in one view and two plans each.

The designs include 16 cottages or "Cottage Dwellings," eight "Dwellings," three "Cottage Villas," one "Roman Building," one "Roman Cottage Villa," and one farm house. The smallest is Design VII, "A Cottage of Three Rooms, and Other Conveniences," calculated at 3d per cubic foot to cost £155 1s. The floor plan shows an entrance lobby, kitchen, pantry, cow house, water closet, wood and coal house, milk house, and two bedrooms. The one-story elevation is asymmetrical: an ell to the left contains the offices, the kitchen and entrance lobby are in the center, and on the right a three-sided bay with windows projects from the front bedroom. There are three designs with "Ten Rooms" (XII, XVIII, XXIII), but the largest is "A Dwelling of Nine Rooms" (VI), estimated at 3d per foot to cost £447 6s 9d. On the ground floor there are a porch, kitchen, pantry, scullery, parlor, store closet, and three bedrooms. The chamber floor has three bedrooms, a sitting room, and a closet. The symmetrical elevation is two stories high and three openings wide in the center, with a pair of two-story ells at the sides. The floors of the ells, which contain bedrooms, are lower than the floors in the central portion. The articulation of the facade is restrained: two-story pilasters frame the central unit, a stringcourse separates its two stories, and a prostyle pedimented portico frames the entrance.

Robertson's generally Italianate style is characterized by wide eaves, low pitched roofs, bracketed cornices, and occasional pilasters, semicircular relieving arches, and projecting three-sided bays. These characteristics are particularly prominent in the "Roman Building" (XXVII) and in one "Cottage" (XXIX). In addition there are "Rustic" and "Rural" cottages (XVII, XXIV) with thatch roofs, and a "Grecian" cottage (XXV) with Doric columns *in antis* and banded rustication.

290.1

ROBERTSON, William

Designs in architecture, for garden chairs, small gates for villas, park entrances, aviarys, temples, boat houses, mausoleums, and bridges; with their plans, elevations, and sections, accompanied with scenery, &c. by W. Robertson.

London: Printed by W. Bulmer and Co. And published at R. Ackermann's Repository of Arts; and at J. B. Beygang's, Leipzig, 1800.

14 printed leaves, 24 pls.

34.2 × 24.1 cm

CtY

290.2

———

Desseins d'architecture, représentans des siéges de jardins, des portes de maisons de campagne, des entrées de parcs, des volières, des temples, des hangars pour des bateaux, des mausolées et des ponts, avec leurs plans, leurs élévations, leurs sections et des ornemens, par W. Robertson. Traduit de l'anglais.

Londres: De l'imprimerie d'A. Dulau et Co. et de L. Nardini: et se vend chez R. Ackermann; et chez J. G. Beygand, Leipzig, 1800.

14 printed leaves, 24 pls.

27.3 × 36.2 cm

MB

The title page of the English edition is dated 1800, and several plates bear the following inscription: "London Pub. 1 Jan. 1800. at R. Ackermann's Repository of the Arts, 101 Strand. & I. G. Beygang's, Museum, Leipzig." In the majority of the plates, however, "1820" appears instead of "1800." Whether this indicates completion of the book over 20 years or a late reissue for which the dates were changed cannot be determined. The printer whose name appears on the title page apparently ceased trading as "W. Bulmer" in 1819,[1] and unfortunately nothing else is known of Robertson's work as an architect.[2]

Following a dedicatory leaf and a table of contents there are 24 aquatinted and colored plates illustrating designs for four garden chairs, four garden gates, two garden doors, an aviary, an aviary with music room, two park lodges with gates, two garden seats, two temples, two garden seats with bath, two conservatories, a boat house, a mausoleum, and three bridges. Interleaved with these designs are brief letterpress descriptions of each plate.

All the designs exhibit careful attention to symmetry, regularity, and balance. Without violating these canons of Neoclassical design Robinson also added elegant and highly sophisticated ornament, including heavy rustication, elaborately detailed orders, fanlights, relieving arches, coffered ceilings, urns, garlands, paterae, and medallions. Geometric order is maintained through repeated use of squares, circles, and other regular figures in plans, sections, elevations, and individual details. In several designs (e.g., the temple in Plate 10) projecting porticoes, staircases, and domes enhance the composition through effects of spatial advance and recession.

Each design is shown in elevation and, except for the garden seats and gates, in plan as well. The formality of the elevations—all perfectly parallel to the picture plane—is softened by surrounding trees, shrubs, and lawns, all carefully orchestrated to emphasize the principal lines of the structure as well as to create a very elegant, picturesque illustration. The design in Plate 18, for example, a "Temple of Neptune, intended for a Boat House" is a shallow cella fronted by a tetrastyle Doric portico, raised up above the water's edge on a heavily rusticated elliptical arch. The temple is flanked on each side by two flights of steps ornamented with balustrades and statues of tritons, and the entire composition is reflected in the water below. To each side and the rear, masses of leafy foliage complement the principal elements of the composition by forming a backdrop for the temple itself and strong framing elements at the edges of the illustration. Robertson iterated his concern for compositional harmony in remarks accompanying Plate II: "That nothing adds more to the beauty of a dwelling, than that all its appendages should be in unison with it, is the opinion of the best architects, who, even when those appendages are removed at a distance, still preserve the connection, by their style, &c. which produces harmony."

1. Ian Maxted, *The London Book Trades 1775–1800* (Folkestone: Dawson, 1977), p. 34; and Philip A. H. Brown, *London Publishers and Printers* (London: British Museum, 1961), p. 18.

2. Colvin (1978), p. 698.

291.1

ROBINSON, Peter Frederick (1776–1858)

Designs for farm buildings. By P. F. Robinson. . . .

London: Printed for James Carpenter and Son, 1830.

vii pp, 20 printed leaves, 56 pls.

31.1 × 23.5 cm

MB

291.2

————

Designs for farm buildings, in fifty-six plates. By P. F. Robinson. . . . Second edition, improved.

London: Henry G. Bohn, 1837.

vii pp, 20 printed leaves, 56 pls.

30.5 × 24.8 cm

NNC

291.3

————

Designs for farm buildings, with a view to prove that the simplest forms may be rendered pleasing and ornamental by a proper disposition of the rudest materials. In fifty-six plates. By P. F. Robinson. . . . Third edition.

London: Henry G. Bohn, 1837.

vii pp, 22 printed leaves, 56 pls.

29.8 × 24.1 cm

CtY

In the prefatory "Address" (pp. iii–iv)[1] Robinson discussed the pictorial aspects of architectural design: "the rudest Hut may give value to the picture," he said, "if erected with some regard to its outline" (p. iii). Even "the mere Shed may create a certain degree of interest, by a proper arrangement of the materials" (p. iii). In offering this collection of farm buildings designed according to principles of picturesque composition, Robinson hoped to "improve the unseemly features which the village Carpenter, unassisted, must constantly produce" (p. iii). Robinson also professed "a strict regard to economy," using "plans, the usefulness of which has already been acknowledged" (pp. iii–iv).[2]

Altogether there are 25 designs, in four different styles that he felt were particularly "useful": Old English, Italian, Swiss, and Rustic. The designs include four laborer's cottages, three barns, two cow houses, a granary, a cattle shed, a farmyard, a farm house, fences, seats, mills, smithies, a gate house, a "horse track," a tower for a reservoir, a weighing house, and a dairy. Each design is illustrated in one or more of the lithographed plates, which contain plans, elevations, and views. The unnumbered text leaves include letterpress descriptions of each design. Of the four designs for laborer's cottages (Nos. I–IV) two are in Old English style and the others are Italian and Swiss. All include just a bedroom, kitchen, and washhouse, and the first three have only modest exterior ornament. The fourth is decorated far more elaborately in Swiss style, which Robinson claimed was "peculiarly fitted for agricultural buildings." The ground-floor plan of the farm house (No. XIV) includes a parlor, kitchen, counting house, and brewhouse. Plates 34 and 35 show front and rear elevations in Old English style, while Plates 36, 37, and 38 show alternative elevations in Swiss, Old English, and Italian styles. In some cases Robinson's pursuit of the picturesque fully overcame his concern for utility. In the design for an Italianate barn (No. VII), for example, a low, compact barn is fronted by a tall and exceedingly thin campanile, which according to Robinson was useful only as a dovecote. Other designs, such as the rustic seats in Plate 40, could be used for little more than picturesque embellishment of a landscape.

1. References are to the 1830 edition. The preliminary matter concludes with a list of plates (pp. v–vii).

2. Robinson did not indicate who "acknowledged" the usefulness of his plans.

292.1
ROBINSON, Peter Frederick (1776–1858)
Designs for lodges and park entrances. By P. F. Robinson. . . .

London: Printed for Priestley and Weale; and J. Williams, 1833.

7 pp, 12 printed leaves, 48 pls.

31.4 × 24.1 cm

BL

292.2
_____

Designs for gate cottages, lodges, and park entrances, in various styles, from the humblest to the castellated. By P. F. Robinson. . . . The landscapes drawn on stone by J. D. Harding and T. Allom. Third edition, greatly improved.

London: Henry G. Bohn, 1837.

iv pp, 12 printed leaves, 48 pls.

29.8 × 23.5 cm

MB

In the "Address" (pp. i–ii)[1] Robinson remarked that a gate lodge could be "a feature of considerable importance, inasmuch as it should indicate the character of the structure to which it affords an approach" (p. ii). That character is communicated to the viewer by the style of the lodge: a castellated lodge, for example, is "indicative of great territorial extent, and a residence of the highest class" (p. ii). Altogether Robinson offered designs in three styles: "Timber Fronted," "Elizabethan," and "Castellated." In contrast to "the barbarous attempts" at reproducing medieval styles "which disgraced the last century," Robinson hinted at the authenticity of his own designs by observing that the "study of Ancient Architecture has now fortunately become a part of polite education" (p. i).

The book includes plans, elevations, and lithographed views of 12 designs for lodges. Each is illustrated in four plates, and accompanied by one leaf of letterpress description. The lodges range in size from the "humblest" (p. ii), with just a parlor, kitchen, and cellar (Plates 1–4), to a "timber-fronted" design with a parlor, kitchen, and outhouse on the ground floor and two chambers above (Plates 9–12). Three designs already had been executed: No. 1, a gate lodge, at locations in Scotland, South Wales, and Sussex; No. 2, another gate lodge, in South Wales; and No. 4, a "Cottage Lodge of One Story," also in South Wales.

In the Address Robinson suggested that his designs were meant as "ideas which may be reduced, or enlarged upon," but recommended that actual work be supervised by "the architect" (p. i). Unfortunately for Robinson at least one design was attractive enough to be copied without his supervision. Design No. 2, the gate lodge he had erected in South Wales, appears with only minor changes and no acknowledgment to Robinson in Lady Domvile's *Eighteen Designs* (ca. 1840; *q.v.*).[2] The same design also was executed near Brosely, in Shropshire[3]—a copy possibly supervised by Robinson, but one that easily could have been made directly from the design in his book.

1. All references are to the 1837 edition. The introductory matter concludes with a list of plates (pp. iii–iv).

2. Nor was Robinson's design, dated 1832, entirely original. The same combination of forms—two small gabled pavilions flanking a portico with rustic columns *in antis*—had appeared in Plate 11 of John Plaw's *Ferme Ornée* (1795; *q.v.*).

3. This cottage remained extant in 1976.

293.1
ROBINSON, Peter Frederick (1776–1858)
Designs for ornamental villas. By P. F. Robinson. . . .

London: Printed for James Carpenter and Son, 1827.

24 printed leaves, 96 pls.

29.8 × 23.5 cm

Bodl.

293.2 †
_____

Designs for ornamental villas.

[London]: Carpenter, 1829.

4°

Reference: ECB

293.3

Designs. For ornamental villas. 3rd. edition. By P. F. Robinson. . . .

London: Printed for James Carpenter and Son, 1830.

24 printed leaves (plus one title page dated 1827 and another dated 1830), 96 pls.

30.5 × 23.5 cm

CtY-BA

293.4

Designs for ornamental villas. In ninety-six plates. By P. F. Robinson. . . . The scenic views chiefly by J. D. Harding. Third edition, greatly improved.

London: Henry G. Bohn, 1836.

x + 43 pp, additional lithographed title page, 96 pls.

30.5 × 24.1 cm

MH

293.5 †

Designs for ornamental villas.

[London]: H. Bohn, 1837.

Royal 4°

Reference: ECB

293.6

Designs for ornamental villas. In ninety-six plates. By P. F. Robinson. . . . The scenic views chiefly by J. D. Harding. Fourth edition, greatly improved.

London: Henry G. Bohn, 1853.

x + 43 pp, 96 pls.

29.2 × 22.9 cm

V&A

Peter Frederick Robinson and Thomas Frederick Hunt, the two most prolific authors of domestic design books in the 1820s, each published two books in 1827. Hunt distinguished himself from Robinson by disparaging the work of architects who tried to achieve compositional effects through use of the *"painter's"* line."[1] Robinson, by contrast, tried to adapt different regional and historical styles to his own particularly painterly conception of architectural design, based on the picturesque theories of Sir Uvedale Price.[2] In *Designs for Ornamental Villas* Robinson offered 16 designs, most of which had already been "carried into effect" (1836, p. iii). The range of styles represented perhaps was the most eclectic in British architectural literature to date: Swiss, Greek, Palladian, Old English, Castellated, "Ancient Manor House," Modern Italian, Anglo-Norman, Decorated (Gothic), Elizabethan, "Ancient Timber Building," and Tuscan. The designs include twelve "residences," two lodges, a garden house, and stables. Each is illustrated in plan, elevation, and a "Scenic View," and is accompanied by several pages of descriptive letterpress.

In the "Address" (1836, pp. iii–iv) Robinson lamented that "something is still wanting to reform that absence of taste and good feeling which is so manifest in most of our modern buildings, where the aid of the architect has not been sought in creating them" (1836, p. iii). Considering "the wonderful increase of buildings, not only in the metropolis, but in almost every provincial town, the extensive plans which are now in contemplation, and the rapidity with which our watering places especially have been enlarged,"[3] Robinson described this book as a "reference in aid of those who are about to build, or as hints from which some assistance may be obtained" (1836, pp. iii–iv).

Much of his discussion of individual designs concerns the pictorial integration of form and style with the surrounding landscape. In discussing the first design, for example, he noted that Swiss style was "applicable in southern aspects, particularly under hills, or cliffs, as the large projecting roofs answer all the purpose of awnings, or verandahs" (1836, p. 1). In the fifth design he found the Old English style "peculiarly picturesque," with gables, chimneys, and windows that "harmonize most agreeably in scenic situations, and produce effects of high interest to the painter" (1836, p. ii). Each design is depicted in a lush, mature, and well-composed landscape setting, exemplifying Robinson's conviction that landscape and architectural design are one:

a man should conceive, in his mind's eye, the whole effect of the picture he is about to produce, even before the foundation be laid, and . . . the house, the form of the ground closely connected with it, and every article of furniture, as far as regards its situation, should be well and sufficiently considered, prior to the commencement of the work, without which success cannot be contemplated. It is evident all this must be the operation of one mind; and . . . the great outline of the [entire] undertaking should be the work of the Architect. (1836, p. 29)

Occasionally Robinson's argument in favor of a particular style relies as much on associationism as on picturesque aesthetics. For his sixth design, a house to be built in Yorkshire among "large tracts of moorland and mountain, rarely visited by the foot of the stranger, and still in their primitive state of wild magnificence," he chose a "Castellated character" because it would "lead the mind back to the days of our feudal system, and in wandering among the neighbouring hills we almost expect to see the ancient Baron, surrounded by his followers, ascending the valley" (1836, p. 15).

All the designs Robinson illustrated are of ample size. Even the smallest two, an entrance lodge and a garden house, have several rooms on each of two stories. The larger residences suffer from a rigidity of outline and in most cases a compositional symmetry not entirely appropriate to the style adopted. For example both the Castellated residence in the sixth design and the "Decorated"—actually Tudor—residence in the tenth design are proportioned more like a Palladian mansion than any true examples of medieval work.

1. See Hunt, *Designs for Parsonage Houses* (1827), p. vi.

2. "Uvedale Price, in his excellent Essay on the Picturesque, argues with much truth and feeling, that union of character cannot be expected to prevail, until the principles of painting are applied to whatever in any way concerns the embellishment of our houses; and that the Architect should combine a general knowledge of his own profession with that of the landscape gardener, and become the '*Architetto-pittore*,' in order to render his work perfect as a whole" (1836, p. 29).

3. Robinson himself had recently excuted a residence, a church, and a hotel in Leamington, one of the most important inland resorts of the 1820s. See Colvin (1978), p. 701.

294.1
ROBINSON, Peter Frederick (1776–1858)
Domestic architecture in the Tudor style, selected from buildings erected after the designs and under the superintendence of P. F. Robinson. . . .

London: J. Williams, 1837.

ii + 4 pp, 17 pls.

29.8 × 22.9 cm

MB

In the "Address" (pp. i–ii) Robinson explained that he intended to publish a series of books illustrating buildings "designed and erected under my own superintendence" (p. i). He chose to commence the "series with some account of a house I have recently completed for John Henry Vivian, Esq., M.P. for Swansea" (p. ii).[1]

The text (pp. 1–4) describes Robinson's "improvements" to the house and surrounding landscape, begun in 1823. Within the description he interspersed brief remarks on picturesque composition. Robinson took special pleasure, for example, in the Old English style because it possessed "what Price calls *picturesqueness*, produced by different levels of floors and windows" (p. 2).

The plates include an elevation of the house before Robinson began his improvements (Plate 7), as well as a view of the completed mansion surrounded by formal garden walls and set in a majestic landscape of forests, lawns, grazing cattle, and figures riding horseback through the foreground (Plate 1). Another view shows the mansion with its picturesque gables, chimneys, and pinnacles complemented by distant mountains and by animals grazing peacefully in the foreground (Plate 8). The remaining plates include a ground-floor plan, four exterior elevations, and six interior views, plus detailed elevations of the lamp in the entrance court, the sundial on the terrace, and a stone seat on the terrace.

1. Although Robinson lived another 21 years, no further books appeared in this "series."

295.1

ROBINSON, Peter Frederick (1776–1858)

A new series of designs for ornamental cottages and villas, with estimates of the probable cost of erecting them; forming a sequel to the works entitled rural architecture and designs for ornamental villas. By P. F. Robinson. . . . Fifty-six plates. The landscapes drawn on stone by J. D. Harding and T. Allom.

London: Henry G. Bohn, 1838.

17 printed leaves, 32 + 24 pls.

30.0 × 23.7 cm

KyU

295.2 †
_____

[A new series of] designs for [ornamental] cottages and villas.

[London]: H. Bohn, 1839.

Royal 4°

Reference: ECB

295.3
_____

A new series of designs ⟨ . . . as 1838 . . . ⟩.

London: Henry G. Bohn, 1853.

17 printed leaves, 32 + 24 pls.

29.8 × 22.9 cm

NNC

A New Series of Designs was Robinson's last book, appearing when he was 62 years old. He lived another 20 years, but published nothing further. The title indicates that he conceived the book as a sequel to two earlier books, and like them it includes a selection of his own designs that were "already executed, or now in progress."[1]

In the "Address" (recto and verso of one leaf following the title page) Robinson predictably discussed architectural design as a matter of painterly composition: he indicated that "a judicious improvement" to a cottage, particularly "as regards doors, windows, and chimnies," resembles "the last touches given to a picture by the hand of the master." No doubt with his own contributions in mind, he praised the "improvement which has taken place, during the last ten years, in our Rural Architecture." He noted with some pride that the countryside had been "embellished" while "improving the condition of the peasantry" at the same time.

On separate leaves following the "Address" are two lists of plates, corresponding to the two "divisions" of the book. The eight designs in the first "division" include a smithy, a schoolhouse, a gate cottage, a cottage, a farm house, a mill, and two laborer's cottages. The second division contains designs for one cottage, four villas, and a manor house. Each design is described on one leaf of letterpress and illustrated in four plates. These include plans, elevations, and lithographed views.

All the designs are composed in Robinson's characteristic manner, with irregular plans, overhanging upper stories, elaborate bargeboards, projecting porches and bays, and Tudor windows. The views of these designs include large, mature trees, distant hills, lush shrubbery, lawns, winding paths, and occasional children, animals, passersby, and other figures to provide animation and interest. In several plate descriptions Robinson made brief remarks on picturesque characteristics of individual sites and designs. For example the smithy (First Division, Design No. I) was erected on a "peculiarly beautiful" spot, and a "small dwelling" was attached, so that "the whole groupes well." On the other hand Binswood Cottage in Leamington (Second Division, No. I) "has now lost much of its attractiveness in consequence of the increased number of new buildings surrounding it."

Figure 10

The smallest residence illustrated is the laborer's cottage (First Division, No. VIII). Including only a kitchen, bedroom, and outhouse, the design "has been studied so as to produce the smallest building in which a human being could be placed." Robinson estimated it could be erected for £100 or less. By contrast one of the largest designs, a villa at Little Sampford (Second Division, No. IV), cost approximately £3,500. The ground-floor plan includes a two-story entrance hall, drawing room, library, dining room, gentleman's room, water closet, kitchen, pantry, larder, dairy, housekeeper's room, servant's hall, laundry, and closet. The chamber floor includes five bedrooms and a servant's room.

1. Robinson stated this in the "Address." This commentary is based on examination of the 1838 edition.

296.1
ROBINSON, Peter Frederick (1776–1858)
Rural architecture, or series of designs for ornamental cottages, by P. F. Robinson. . . .

London: Printed for Rodwell and Martin, 1823.

28 printed leaves, 96 pls.

28.6 × 22.2 cm

MB

296.2 ‖

─────────

2nd. edition. Rvral architectvre being a series of designs for ornamental cottages by P. F. Robinson. . . .

London: Printed for James Carpenter and Son, 1826.

3 pp, 25 printed leaves, lithographed title page + 96 pls.

28 cm

Reference: Information supplied by Winterthur Museum Library.

296.3

─────────

3rd. edition[.] Rural architecture being a series of designs for ornamental cottages by P. F. Robinson. . . .

London: Printed for James Carpenter and Son, 1828.

26 printed leaves, 96 pls.

27.9 × 22.2 cm

MB

296.4

─────────

Rural architecture; or, a series of designs for ornamental cottages. In ninety= six plates. By P. F. Robinson. . . . The landscapes drawn on stone by J. D. Harding. Fourth edition, greatly improved.

London: Henry G. Bohn, 1836.

[*In this copy, and in nine other copies examined, there is an additional lithographed title page dated 1837.*]

30 printed leaves, additional lithographed title page + 96 pls.

29.8 × 23.5 cm

BL

296.5

─────────

Rural architecture; or, a series of designs for ornamental cottages. In ninety= six plates. By P. F. Robinson. . . . The landscapes drawn on stone by J. D. Harding. Fifth edition, greatly improved.

London: Henry G. Bohn, 1850.

29 printed leaves, 96 pls.

29.8 × 23.5 cm

CtY

Rural Architecture is the first published collection of designs by Peter Frederick Robinson, one of the most prolific authors of architectural books in the first half of the nineteenth century. In the "Preface to the First Edition" Robinson complained of the destruction of picturesque rural landscapes by uninspired and unsophisticated designs for cottages: "In the most beautiful parts of this Country, the scenery is disfigured by the impotent attempts of the Workman, unaided by the pencil of the Artist; and . . . the square spruce brick house, and tiled roof, obtrudes itself at every turn, and carries back the ideas of the wanderer to the Metropolis and its environs."[1]

In the "Preface to the Second Edition" Robinson noted the "rapid sale" of the first edition, and advanced his argument in more detail. He called for the preservation of an architectural "style which once adorned the fair landscape scenery" of England, "but which has been of late years altogether neglected." Its characteristics include "The high pointed gable, and enriched chimney stack; the ornamental barge board, and mullioned window; the ivy-mantled porch, and lean-to-roof." Robinson argued that where this style is used in a cottage, "it becomes an object of interest in the picture." A landlord building such a cottage on his estate consequently would become more inclined to take an interest in the welfare of tenants living in the cottage, and the "attention of the landlord is met by the assiduity of the tenant, and neatness and even elegance is the result." Even the "rosy-cheeked smiling children, proudly showing the little presents occasionally made to them for good behaviour, exhibit a marked contrast to the neighbouring poor, whose unhealthy countenances betray the neglected state of their habitations." Robinson also promised that "a scenic dwelling may be erected . . . at the same cost [as] with the less attractive structure."

Prefaces to the third and fourth editions both indicate that many of the lithographed illustrations had "been redrawn upon the stone." Following the prefaces there is a three-page "List of the Plates."

The 20 designs include two lodges, five cottages, one double cottage, one group of four attached cottages, four farm houses, two "residences," one parsonage, two alms houses, a dairy, and a "boat house and fishing cottage." Each is illustrated in plan, elevation, and view on four or more plates, and described in one or more pages of letterpress. In several cases Robinson included remarks on aspects of picturesque composition—the proper form and size of window mullions, for example—in the plate descriptions. Except for two designs in the "Swiss" style, all are composed in Robinson's characteristic manner, employing ornamental chimneys, roofs made of stone or thatch, elaborate bargeboards, occasional brick or half-timbered walls, Tudor windows, and ashlar masonry. He made particularly effective use of lithography in depicting the picturesque shapes and textures of these elements. Robinson also indicated in the descriptions that several of the designs had been executed.

One of the smallest designs (No. VII) is a gate cottage, "erected for the late Sir James Macdonald, Bart., near Liphook." The ground floor contains just two rooms, a kitchen measuring 11 feet by ten feet, and a parlor measuring 15 feet by 12 feet. There is one bedroom upstairs. The elevation is asymmetrical and highly picturesque, including tall chimneys, gables with elaborate bargeboards, thatch roofs, a projecting dormer and window bays, and Tudor windows. One of the largest designs (No. XX) is a "residence" that "was erected for Lieut. Gen. Bayly Wallis, near Leatherhead, in Surrey." Although designed in "the Cottage style," the building is not diminutive: the ground floor includes a vaulted entrance hall, a drawing room measuring 37 feet by 17 feet, an eating room, a billiard room, a library, a conservatory, and offices. Upstairs there are five bedrooms plus dressing rooms. The view (Plate 95) is a busy jumble of chimneys, gables, bargeboards, porches, and window bays. Indeed because this design was unusually large for Robinson, his assiduous attention to picturesque detail resulted in an elevation that was unfortunately, and uncharacteristically, complex and disorganized.

1. This discussion is based on examination of the 1836 edition, which includes prefaces from the the first four editions.

297.1
ROBINSON, Peter Frederick (1776–1858)
Village architecture. Being a series of designs for the inn, the schoolhouse, almshouses, markethouse, shambles, workhouse, parsonage, town hall, and church; illustrative of the observations contained in the essay on the picturesque, by Sir Uvedale Price: and as a supplement to a work on rural architecture, by P. F. Robinson. . . .

London: Printed for James Carpenter and Son, 1830.

viii pp, 12 printed leaves, 40 pls.

28.6 × 22.9 cm

V&A

297.2
――――――
Village architecture, being a series of picturesque designs for the inn, the schoolhouse, almshouses, markethouse, shambles, workhouse, parsonage, townhall, and church: forming a sequel to a work on rural architecture. By P. F. Robinson. . . . The landscapes drawn on stone by Scarlett Davis and T. Allom. Fourth edition, greatly improved: with an additional view of the village street.

London: Henry G. Bohn, 1837.

viii pp, 12 printed leaves, frontisp. + 40 pls.

29.2 × 23.5 cm

MB

Robinson may have planned *Village Architecture* as an accompaniment to his *Designs for Farm Buildings*, also first published in 1830. The subjects of the two books do not seem closely related,[1] but their bibliographic form suggests that they were conceived together. *Designs for Farm Buildings* consists of 25 designs, illustrated on 56 plates. The 1830 edition of *Village Architecture* includes 12 designs on 40 plates. The numbering of these 40 plates begins at 57 and ends with 96. The designs, however, bear numbers XXIV through XXXV, making for an imperfect match with the 25 designs in *Designs for Farm Buildings*.

The second and third editions of *Designs for Farm Buildings* (both issued in 1837) retain the format of the first edition. Apparently there was no second or third edition of *Village Architecture*, although a "fourth edition" appeared in 1837. But the designs in *Village Architecture* now were re-numbered I through XIII, and the plates numbered 1 through 40, with an additional frontispiece, clearly establishing *Village Architecture* as a separate work.

As in his other works, Robinson proposed to illustrate the application of aesthetic principles proposed by the prominent landscapist Sir Uvedale Price (1837, p. iii). Robinson noted that in previous books he had considered cottages and humble dwellings individually in their relation to the landscape; in the present work he wanted to develop a picturesque design for an entire village. As a first step, he would examine the picturesque possibilities of every village building type, closely following the lead of Price in "considering how the Inn, the School-house, the Town Hall, Parsonage, and Church, may be rendered attractive [i.e., picturesque], without unnecessarily increasing the expense in erecting them" (1837, pp. iv–v). Robinson's solution was neither to design a whole village according to one uniform picturesque program, nor to design buildings individually according to picturesque principles. Rather, he advocated restoring and preserving extant examples of vernacular architecture. He maintained that this would contribute to the visual improvement of the entire village, while also benefiting the inhabitants socially. Here Robinson, inspired by Price, was the first practicing architect to call for preservation and restoration of *vernacular* structures for their picturesque value.[2] Further, he argued that if the resident could be given "some interest" in his residence he would have a greater incentive to improve his own situation (1837, p. iv).[3] If many cottages were preserved and restored, their diversity would increase the picturesqueness of the entire village. Robinson's notion of the picturesque also incorporated a particularly painterly vision of architecture: "instead of destroying the ancient gabled Cottage, the forms may be preserved which our painters have so long delighted to portray, and which have in fact given real value to their pictures" (1837, p. iii).

As examples of such picturesque possibilities Robinson illustrated an inn, an almshouse, a market house, a village pump, a butcher's shop, a workhouse, a parsonage, a town hall, an entrance to a churchyard, and a church. He primarily employed the "Old English" style (encompassing both Tudor Gothic and half-timbering), and also provided designs in Swiss, Anglo-Norman, and "old timber" styles. He described each subject briefly in one or two pages of text, and illustrated each in one or more plates. These include plans, exterior and interior elevations, and exterior and interior views.

Two subjects clearly were not vernacular survivals, but new designs: a schoolhouse erected by Robinson in 1827, and the "Swiss Room" which he erected the same year in Regent's Park. Other subjects include true vernacular survivals (e.g., Design No. I, The Inn at Patterdale) as well as designs with suspiciously Robinsonian bargeboarding and other picturesque ornament (e.g., Design No. VIII, The Parsonage). The final plate, titled "The Village Street," plus the frontispiece to the "fourth" edition illustrate a hypothetical village composed of several of these buildings. The plate of "The Village Street" shows the church, the school, the workhouse, and the inn; the other plate shows the workhouse, the pump, a combined town hall and market building, the church, the parsonage, and the inn. In describing this scene Robinson lamented that "villages are daily suffering from the . . . mistaken attempt to improve them" (1837, Design No. XIII, p. 2). No doubt he meant that careful restoration and attention to traditional scenic character would result in far more picturesque and successful village scenes than had recent attempts at "uniform" and "modern" improvements.[4] The originality and importance of Robinson's proposals lay in his call to preserve, restore, and imitate styles and structures of the past in an ad hoc manner—not to create a unified plan of uniform style, but to achieve a picturesque design through restoration of extant dwellings in traditional styles.

1. The text of *Village Architecture* does include several references to *Rural Architecture* (1823), a work whose contents do seem closely related.

2. Well over a century earlier, Sir John Vanbrugh had recommended preserving a more formal structure, Woodstock Manor, because of its historic, associational, and pictorial value (*The Complete Works*, ed. Bonamy Dobrée and Geoffrey Webb [London, 1928], IV, 29–30). The pictorial value of picturesque temples and ruins was well recognized by the middle of the eighteenth century. See Christopher Hussey, *The Picturesque* (London: Putnam, 1927). But for an architect to suggest restoring and preserving vernacular dwellings in villages was still highly unusual in 1830.

3. To further support this point, Robinson offered the following passage from Price: " 'There is no way in which wealth can produce such natural, unaffected variety, as by adorning a real village, and promoting the comforts and enjoyments of its inhabitants' " (letterpress description of Design No. III).

4. Robinson was not the first architect to propose schemes for entire villages. Nash had long since built Blaise Hamlet (1810) and the two Park Villages (1823 and later), all highly picturesque examples. Sir William Chambers, John Carr, and others built planned villages in the eighteenth century, occasionally in the form of a picturesque meandering curve, as at Milton Abbas (1773), but more often using only straight lines and right angles. For an extended discussion, see Gillian Darley, *Villages of Vision* (London: Architectural Press, 1975). Other architects had published proposals for stylistically unified villages and for regular, formal town plans long before Robinson. John Plaw included a design for a village in *Ferme Ornée* (1795; *q.v.*); Joseph Michael Gandy included another in *Designs for Cottages* (1805; *q.v.*). Several plans for new towns or for improvements appeared in the series of county agricultural surveys prepared for the Board of Agriculture: significant designs may be found in reports by Aiton on Ayrshire (1811; *q.v.*) and by Henderson on Caithness (1812; *q.v.*).

298.1
ROBINSON, Peter Frederick (1776–1858)
‖ [*Part I:*]

Vitruvius Britannicus. History of Woburn Abbey: illustrated by plans, elevations, and internal views of the apartments, from actual measurement. By P. F. Robinson. . . .

London: Published by James Carpenter and Son, 1827.

[iv] + 20 pp, 8 pls.

59.0 × 40.0 cm

Reference: Information supplied by Winterthur Museum Library.

[*Part II:*]

Vitruvius Britannicus. History of Hatfield House: illustrated by plans, elevations, and internal views of the apartments, from actual measurement. By P. F. Robinson. . . .

London: Printed for the author, and published by J. and A. Arch; Longman and Co.; Molteno and Co.; Priestley and Weale; Pickering; Rodwell; and Williams, 1833.

[4] + 28 pp, engraved dedicatory leaf + 9 pls.

57.8 × 41.9 cm

BL

[*Part III:*]

Vitruvius Britannicus. History of Hardwicke Hall: illustrated by plans, elevations, and internal views of the apartments, from actual measurement. By P. F. Robinson. . . .

London: ⟨ . . . as 1833 . . . ⟩, 1835.

30 pp, engraved dedicatory leaf + 9 pls.

57.8 × 41.9 cm

BL

[*Part IV:*]

Vitruvius Britannicus. History of Castle Ashby: illustrated by plans, elevations, and internal views, from actual measurement. Edited by P. F. Robinson, Architect. . . .

London: Printed by J. B. Nichols and Son; and published by the proprietor and John Weale; B. Hall, Birmingham; H. T. Cooke, Warwick; and Hewett, Leamington, 1841.

24 pp, engraved dedicatory leaf + 10 pls.

57.8 × 41.9 cm

BL

[*Part V:*]

Vitruvius Britannicus. History of Warwick Castle: illustrated by plans, elevations, and internal views, from actual measurement. By Charles William Spicer, Esq.

London: Printed by J. B. Nichols and Son; and published for the proprietor by John Weale; B. Hall, Birmingham; H. T. Cooke, Warwick; Hewett, Leamington; and Robert Best Ede, Dorking, 1844.

ii + 36 pp, additional engraved title page + 9 pls.

57.8 × 41.9 cm

BL

298.2

Vitruvius Britannicus. History of Woburn Abbey: illustrated by plans, elevations, and internal views of the apartments, from actual measurement. By P. F. Robinson. . . .

London: Printed for the author, and published by J. and A. Arch; Longman and Co.; Molteno and Co.; Priestley and Weale; Pickering; Rodwell; and Williams, 1833.

20 pp, engraved dedicatory leaf + 8 pls.

47.8 × 34.3 cm

ICN

298.3

ROBINSON, Peter Frederick (1776–1858), and John BRITTON (1771–1857)
Vitruvius Britannicus. History of Woburn Abbey, Hatfield House, Hardwicke Hall, and Cassiobury Park. Illustrated by plans, elevations, and internal views of the apartments. By P. F. Robinson . . . and John Britton. . . .

London: Henry G. Bohn, 1847.

[*Part I:*] 3 printed leaves, 9 pls.

[*Part II:*] 2 printed leaves, 10 pls.

[*Part III:*] 1 printed leaf, 10 pls.

[*Part IV:*] 1 printed leaf, 11 pls. (numbered 1–3, 3–10).

55.2 × 36.8 cm

MH

In 1715 Colen Campbell published the first book titled *Vitruvius Britannicus* (*q.v.*). By 1808 he and five other authors had completed altogether eight volumes with that title.[1] Peter Frederick Robinson's *Vitruvius Britannicus* appeared in five parts between 1827 and 1844, each part illustrating just one major architectural monument. A second edition, with additions and deletions, appeared in one volume in 1847. Unlike his predecessors Robinson wanted to depict the historical excellence rather than the current progress of British architecture, and so his subjects include Woburn, Hatfield, Hardwick, Castle Ashby, Warwick Castle, and Cassiobury. In his previous books Robinson had emulated the Tudor and "Old English" styles, and his choice of subjects here is clearly in accord; it also indicates a firm rejection of the overwhelmingly Palladian and Neoclassical content of previous volumes of *Vitruvius Britannicus*.[2]

At the beginning of each of the original five parts there is a dedicatory leaf, followed by a brief letterpress history and description of the structure, and eight to ten plates illustrating the structure in plan, elevation, and exterior and interior views.

In the 1847 edition the final plate in the part devoted to Cassiobury includes views of five cottages and one lodge on the estate grounds. Britton found the designs "distinguished at once for their exterior picturesque features, and for the domestic comfort they afford to their humble occupants." "Most" of the cottages consist of "a porch, a sitting room, one or two bedrooms, and a wash-house, with an oven and a copper." Britton described the largest of the cottages, with five rooms on the ground floor and "others" upstairs, as "*Cottage-ornée*" and inappropriate for "the working peasant." He described others as "simple in form and economical in construction, being made of brick nogging and timber, with thatched roofs." All are depicted in picturesque settings, with tall trees in the background and rustic laborers or picturesque family groups in the foreground.[3]

1. See volumes by Badeslade and Rocque, by Woolfe and Gandon, and by George Richardson.

2. Colen Campbell published the original volume (1715) in part to promote a "modern" British style of architecture that would equal or surpass all previous styles. Robinson, in contrast, looked to a period prior to the Palladian revival as the source of an indigenous— and to his mind superior—British architecture. For contemporary historical studies of Elizabethan architecture see the note to the commentary on Thomas Frederick Hunt's *Designs for Parsonage Houses* (Entry 154).

3. John Britton had previously published *The History and Description, with Graphic Illustrations, of Cassiobury Park* (London: The author, 1837; 32 pp, 22 pls). A review of this book in John Claudius Loudon's *Architectural Magazine* (March 1838; *q.v.*) includes the following illustrations borrowed from Britton: a view of Ridge Lane Cottage, which also appears in Plate 10 in *Vitruvius Britannicus*; and nine plans, which do not appear in *Vitruvius Britannicus*, for cottages and lodges.

ROSS, William
"Street houses of the city of New York."

See LOUDON, **John Claudius, ed.,** The architectural magazine, *Entry 182.*

299.1
ROWLAND, Thomas
A general treatise of architecture. In seven books. Containing all that is necessary to be known in building, with several new designs of houses, &c. and also the plans of their different situations. In a manner entirely new and pleasant. Being an easy introduction to the knowledge of architecture and building, and for the better understanding the rules of Vitruvius, Palladio, Scamozzi, and others both antient and modern. By Thomas Rowland, of New-Windsor, Gent. To which is added, a work of infinite labour and expence, consisting of tables for the mensuration of all sorts of works us'd in building, of great use and service to all architects, artificers, and measurers whatsoever.

London: Printed by Henry Parker, for the author, and sold by J. Cole, 1732 [-1743].

ii + 48 pp, 23–30 pls; plus viii pp, 44 pls from the same author's *Mensuration*.

40.0 × 25.0 cm

PPL

Although the title page is dated 1732, a notice on the original wrapper for the second Number at the Yale Center for British Art reads: "The first Number to be deliver'd the 5th of *September*, 1743; and to be continued every Month. . . . " The same month the first Number also was advertised in *The Gentleman's Magazine* (p. 504). Wrappers of later numbers at Yale also bear the date 1743.

According to the wrapper of one Number at Yale, Rowland originally intended the *Treatise* to include "Sixteen Numbers; but in no Case to exceed Eighteen." On the title page and at the end of the Preface he indicated that the text would be divided into "seven Books or Sections." From available copies, it appears the *Treatise* remains incomplete: on page 48, the final page in most copies, Rowland indicated he was just bringing the second Book to a close. One other copy, no longer available, included part of a third Book.[1]

Plates 1 through 22 are printed on text leaves, and Plates 23 through 30 are printed on separate leaves. On pages 41 and 46 there are references to plates numbered 31–35 and 38–41. Plate 34 appears on page 45, and an unnumbered plate appears on page 47; otherwise none of the plates numbered above 30 appears in any copy I have examined.

Rowland's title page promises a major treatise, encompassing diverse aspects of architectural theory and practice. The Preface is less precise: "My Design . . . is not to give you an elegant and curious History of Architecture, that being already done by several . . . Authors; but to give you a plain, easy and familiar Method, adapted to the Understandings of those who are not at all skill'd in Building, and to explain all the difficult Parts (which cannot be so well comprehended in Words) by Drawings graved on Copper Plates with proper Explanations." He complained that other architectural books simply provided "Directions in general, without shewing any Method"; Rowland indicated he would prepare "useful Hints" to remedy these deficiencies.

Also in the Preface Rowland suggested that spending money on architecture could contribute to the economic and social health of the country: he encouraged "our Nobility and Gentry to amuse themselves with delightful Speculations in this fine Science, which may be a Means to induce them to lay out their Money in a good and frugal Way, to employ the poor and industrious Tradesmen, and others, who, for want of Employment, are very often reduced to the utmost Necessity." Perhaps Rowland himself, recently dismissed from the post of Clerk of the Works at Windsor Castle,[2] was among the "others" in need of "Employment."

The first 48 pages of text are divided into two Books. The first is divided into three parts, on arithmetic, geometry, and mensuration. The second, on "Architecture," treats the orders and their parts, with special attention to entablatures.

The first plate, a headpiece on page 1, depicts an equestrian angel blowing a trumpet. The second plate, a headpiece on page 16, depicts a Palladian mansion: the central portion, five windows wide, consists of two stories on top of a raised basement; in addition there is a pair of large office wings. A formal parterre and garden lie to the rear. A slightly different view of the same mansion appears on wrappers of individual Numbers. The next 19 plates, all of which appear on text leaves, depict geometric figures and diagrams. Plate 22, which appears on page 29, depicts the plan of a house with four principal rooms on the main floor. One facade, three windows wide, is fronted by four sets of paired columns;

the other facade incorporates a projecting bow. Plates 23–30 include no illustrations of dwellings, but do depict the orders, plans of two round temples, and the plan and elevation of a round, domed church.

1. The British Museum *General Catalogue of Printed Books* indicates that the text of a third Book extended at least to page 56. Unfortunately this copy was destroyed during the Second World War. The other copy in the British Library, like those at Yale and at the Library Company of Philadelphia, has only 48 pages of text.

2. Colvin (1978), p. 708.

300.1
ROWLAND, Thomas

Mensuration of superficies and solids, by tables of feet, inches, and parts; chiefly applied to the several artificers works in building, but may be used on other occasions; such as gauging, &c. by Thomas Rowland of New= Windsor.

London: Printed by A. Parker, and sold by the author at Windsor; J. Cole, Engraver; and by most of the Booksellers of London and Westminster, and other parts of Great-Britain, [1739].

[ii] + viii pp, printed folding leaf, frontisp. + 52 pls.

38.7 × 22.2 cm

ICJ

On the title page of *A General Treatise of Architecture* (1732; *q.v.*) Rowland indicated that he would include "Tables for the Mensuration of All Sorts of Works Us'd in Building." These tables, which appear in some copies of the *General Treatise*, also were issued as a separate volume. In the preface to this volume, dated 1739, Rowland explained that the tables were "designed to be added to a general Treatise of Architecture now Publishing," but were of such utility that he decided to publish them separately "before the Book above mentioned."

The copy in the John Crerar Library includes a frontispiece, the preface, eight pages of instructions in "The Use of the Tables," a folding leaf on which both the contents and an index are printed, and the engraved tables themselves, numbered 1 through 52, and printed on recto and verso of 26 leaves.

The frontispiece is labeled "Plate 23." In the upper portion a cone, pyramid, sphere, and base of a column are shown in perspective. In the lower portion there is a screen made of Doric and Ionic columns. Several tables are ornamented with vignettes, and four incorporate architectural subjects.[1] The vignette in Table 21 is a landscape that includes a large mansion, a group of cottages, and a small village. Table 39 contains a view of an orthogonally planned town with a large church and two smaller buildings set within a central square. Tables 46 and 47 each contain landscape scenes with country mansions: two stories high and seven windows wide, the mansions closely resemble each other except for one-story wings added to the mansion in Table 47.

1. Vignettes appear in Tables 11, 16, 21, 26, 35, 37, 39, 41, and 43–48.

301.1 ‖

RUDGE, Edward

An introduction to the study of painting, arranged under three heads, viz. geometry, perspective, and light and shadow, elucidated by question and answer. By E. Rudge. . . .

London: Published by Hurst, Chance, and Co, and Ward, Stratford-upon-Avon, 1828.

vi + 85 pp, frontisp. + 15 pls.

25.5 cm

Reference: Information supplied by Winterthur Museum Library.

Following the title page there is a dedication to Rudge's pupils (one leaf, verso blank). In the Preface (pp. i–ii) Rudge set out his reasons for writing this book: previous treatises were too "trifling," "abstruse," "voluminous," or "expensive" for instructing the "youthful mind"; in addition, he complained that painting was often taught without any attention to rules, "as though the eye in Painting, or the ear in Music or Poetry were of themselves the sole guides to lead to excellence in any one of those professions." The preliminaries conclude with a description of the "Arrangement" of the book (p. iii) and a table of contents (p. v).

The text is arranged as a series of questions and answers. Pages 1–2 contain a brief introduction to painting and its "fundamental principles": geometry, perspective, and light and shadow. Geometry is explained in a series of definitions, examples, and problems on pages 3–30. The rest of the text is divided into four chapters treating perspective. The first includes a discussion of the nature of vision, plus definitions, instructions for preparing a drawing board or canvas, and other "remarks." The second chapter concerns objects parallel and perpendicular to the picture plane; the third treats objects "inclined" to the picture plane. The final chapter concerns objects inclined both to the picture plane and to the horizon, light and shadow, and the "proportionate" height of figures in illustrations. There is a glossary at the end.

The 15 plates illustrate subjects treated in the text: the eye and human vision, preparation of a drawing board, objects parallel, perpendicular, and inclined to the picture plane, light and shadow, and objects in artificial light. Among these illustrations are perspective views of several "houses" and "buildings." These include two cubical houses and a pair of two-story houses shown in outline (Plates 3, 4), a pair of two-story buildings with lattice windows on each story (Plate 9), three gable-roofed buildings shown in outline (Plates 10, 11), another two-story building with a three-light window on the upper floor (Plate 13), and a two-story building with one door, two windows, and an attached ell (Plate 14). Other subjects illustrated include trees, steps, a table, spheres, cubes, and a row of pointed arches.

302.1 ‖

The rudiments of ancient architecture, in two parts. Containing an historical account of the five orders, with their proportions and examples of each from the antiques; also Vitruvius on the temples and intercolumniations,

&c. of the Ancients. Calculated for the use of those who wish to attain a summary knowledge of the science of architecture. With a dictionary of terms. Illustrated with ten plates.

London: Printed for I. & J. Taylor, 1789.

vii + 84 pp, frontisp. + 9 pls (numbered 2–10).

Reference: Information supplied by Winterthur Museum Library.

302.2

Rudiments of ancient architecture, containing an historical account of the five orders, with their proportions, and examples of each from antiques; also extracts from Vitruvius, Pliny, &c. relative to the buildings of the ancients. Calculated for the use of those who wish to attain a summary knowledge of the science of architecture. With a dictionary of terms. Illustrated with eleven plates. The second edition, much enlarged.

London: Printed for I. and J. Taylor, 1794.

xvi + 117 pp, frontisp. + 10 pls (numbered 2–4, 4, 5–10).

23.8 × 14.2 cm

MH

302.3 ‖

Rudiments of ancient architecture, ⟨ . . . as 1794 . . . ⟩ plates. The third edition, enlarged.

London: Printed for J. Taylor, 1804.

xvi + 135 pp, frontisp. + 10 pls.

Reference: Information supplied by Humanities Research Center, University of Texas, Austin.

302.4

Rudiments of ancient architecture, ⟨ . . . as 1794 . . . ⟩ antiques also, extracts ⟨ . . . as 1794 . . . ⟩ plates. The fourth edition, enlarged.

London: Printed for J. Taylor, 1810.

xvi + 134 + [i] pp, frontisp. + 10 pls (numbered 2–4, 4*, 5–10).

25.0 × 15.5 cm

Edinburgh University

302.5

Rudiments of ancient architecture, ⟨ ... as 1794 ... ⟩ antiques: also extracts ⟨ ... as 1794 ... ⟩ plates. The fifth edition.

London: Printed for J. Taylor, 1821.

xv + 134 + [i] pp, frontisp. + 10 pls (numbered 2–4, 4*, 5–10).

23.5 × 14.6 cm

MH

According to the Preface to the first edition[1] this book "may be considered as notes or minutes, of what is necessary to be known by one, whose desire, as mine was, is rather general information, than of the minutiae of the science." The author indicated that these "notes or minutes" were based on examination of Sir William Chambers's *Treatise* (*q.v.*) and unspecified "other books" (p. xi). "The guide I followed in selecting and illustrating, was, a recollection of the wants I formerly felt, when desirous of a general knowledge of Architecture" (p. x).

The first part of the text (pp. 1–47) concerns the origins of the orders as well as their proportions in ancient and modern times. A vignette on page 17 depicts "a primitive Hut, which shows the Origin of Columns, and some other parts peculiar to early Examples of original Architecture and antique remains."[2] The hut is a conflation of two figures in the first plate of Chambers's *Treatise*: a flat-roofed structure supported by rustic columns, and "The Third sort of Huts which gave birth to the Doric ORDER," a structure with a pitched roof supported by round shafts with square plinths serving as capitals and bases. The building in the *Rudiments* vignette has a pitched roof supported by rustic columns.

"Part the Second" of the text (pp. 49–70) concerns the "Temples or Sacred Buildings of the Ancients." The next part is a discussion "Of the Houses of the Ancients; Their Situation and Distribution" (pp. 71–89) based on accounts in Vitruvius and Pliny. The final portion of the text is "A Dictionary of Terms Used in Architecture" (pp. 91–134).

The frontispiece shows the five orders together. Plates 2–4, 4*, 5, and 6 show the Tuscan, Doric, Ionic, Modern Ionic, Corinthian, and Composite orders individually. Plates 7 and 8 show bases and moldings. Plates 9 and 10 show parts of the Corinthian and Doric orders. In addition to the vignette on page 17, other vignettes depict "The Fascade of the Temple of Clitumnus," "the construction of an ancient Roman wall," a Roman Doric capital, and a Greek Doric capital.

1. This account is based on the final edition (1821). The Preface to the first edition is printed on pp. ix–xv. It is preceded by the "Preface to the Second Edition" (pp. v–viii).

2. The description is taken from a list of the vignettes which follows p. 134. This vignette does not appear in the 1789 and 1794 editions.

303.1 ‖

The rudiments of architecture; or, the young workman's instructor. Part first, containing the five orders of columns entire, with frontispieces, doors, windows, porticoes, intercolumniations, and arcades, suited to each; rustick doors and windows; block and cantaliver cornices; rustick quoins; the manner of constructing brick and stone-arches; centering for groins and vaulting; stairs, twisted rails, roofs, and domes; inspectional scales, tables, &c. Directions for drawing plans and elevations with Indian ink: likewise, the French and Spanish orders. Part second; containing geometry; the mensuration of solids and superficies; plain trigonometry, and surveying of land. To which is added, the builder's dictionary. Intended for those whose time will not allow them to attend teachers. Illustrated with upwards of 350 examples, accurately engraved upon thirty-seven large copper= plates.

Edinburgh: Printed by Robert Mundell, 1772.

127 + [16] pp, 37 pls.

Reference: Information supplied by Special Collections, University Library, University of Delaware.

303.2

The rudiments of architecture; or, the young workman's instructor. In two parts.
Part first, containing, the five orders of columns entire, with frontispieces, doors, windows, porticoes, intercolumniations, and arcades, suited to each; block and cantaliver cornices; rustic quoins; the manner of constructing brick and stone-arches; centuring for groins and vaulting; stairs, twisted rails, roofs and domes; inspectional scales, tables, &c. Directions for drawing plans and elevations with Indian ink: likewise, the French and Spanish orders.
Part second, containing geometry; the mensuration of solids and super-ficies; plain trigonometry, and surveying of land. With twenty-three elegant designs of buildings, the most of which have been actually executed in North Britain. To which is added, the builder's dictionary. Intended for those whose time will not allow them to attend teachers.
Illustrated with upwards of 373 examples, accurately engraven upon forty= nine large copper-plates.

Edinburgh: Printed by William Auld, 1773.

vii + 127 + [i] + 6 + [16] pp, 49 pls (numbered I–XXXIII, I–III, D, and 12 additional).

26.0 × 20.3 cm

CtY-BA

303.3

The rudiments of architecture; ⟨ . . . as 1773 . . . ⟩, porticoes intercolum-niations, ⟨ . . . as 1773 . . . ⟩; rustic quoins; ⟨ . . . as 1773⟩, containing, ge-ometry: the mensuration of solids and superfices; ⟨ . . . as 1773 . . . ⟩ copper-plates.

London: Printed for John Donaldson, 1775.

vii + 127 + [i] + 6 + [16] pp, 49 pls (numbered I–XXXIII, I–III, D, and 12 additional).

26.0 × 20.3 cm

CtY-BA

303.4

The rudiments of architecture: or, ⟨ . . . as 1773 . . . ⟩. Part first, containing the ⟨ . . . as 1773 . . . ⟩; rustic doors ⟨ . . . as 1773 . . . ⟩; rustic quoins; ⟨ . . . as 1773 . . . ⟩ dictionary: intended ⟨ . . . as 1773 . . . ⟩ teachers. The second edition, corrected. Illustrated with upwards of three hundred and seventy-three examples, accurately engraven upon forty-nine large copper-plates.

Edinburgh: Printed for James Dickson and Charles Elliot, 1778.

vii + 127 + [i] + 6 + [16] pp, 49 pls (numbered I–XXXIII, I–III, D, and 12 additional).

28.6 × 21.0 cm

NNC

303.5

The rudiments of architecture: or, the young workman's instructor. In two parts.
Part first, containing the five orders of columns entire, with frontispieces, doors, windows, porticoes, intercolumniations, and arcades, suited to each; rustic doors and windows; block and cantaliver cornices; rustic; quoins; the manner of constructing brick and stone-arches; centuring for groins and vaulting; stairs, twisted rails, roofs and domes; inspectional scales, tables, &c. Directions for drawing plans and elevations with Indian ink: likewise, the French and Spanish orders.
Part second, containing geometry; the mensuration of solids and superficies; plain trigonometry, and surveying of land. With twenty-four elegant designs of buildings, the most of which have been actually executed in North Britain. To which is added, the builder's dictionary: intended for those whose time will not allow them to attend teachers. The third edition, corrected.
Illustrated with upwards of three hundred and seventy-three examples, accurately engraven upon fifty large copper-plates.

Dundee: Printed for G. Milln, Bookseller; Vernor and Hood, London; J. Dickson, J. Fairbairn, P. Hill, and Mundel & Son, Edinburgh; J. Duncan & Son, Brash & Reid, and J. Murdoch, Glasgow; W. Coke and W. Reid, Leith; A. Brown and J. Burnet, Aberdeen; and I. Forsyth, Elgin, 1799.

vii + 127 + [i] + 6 + [16] pp, 50 pls (numbered I–XXXIII, I-III, D, and 13 additional).

26.0 × 20.3 cm

CtY-BA

According to the Prefatory Introduction (1773, pp. [iii–iv]), the "Compilers" wanted "To remove every impediment which has the least tendency to obstruct the knowledge of Architecture, as well in *theory* as *practice*, from becoming general, and to make it level with the lowest capacities, by application only, without the assistance of a master." Thus they had "very carefully selected whatever is really useful in the most approved books on this subject," including "every thing truly valuable that has been published on this Science for the use of Workmen" (p. [iii]).

The first part of the text (pp. 1–66) is well summarized on the title page. The thirty-three plates that accompany this part include tables and scales, plus illustrations of the orders, colonnades, doors, windows, porticoes, roof trusses, staircases, railings, pediments, and arches. In addition Plate XXV contains an elevation, two plans, and a section of a two-story house. The second part (pp. 67–127) concerns geometry, mensuration, trigonometry, and surveying. The four plates, marked I–III and D, depict geometric figures and diagrams and illustrate surveying techniques. The letterpress concludes with a 16-page dictionary.

The editions of 1773 through 1799 include six pages of letterpress and 12 plates that do not appear in the first edition. The letterpress consists of keys to the figures on the plates, which include elevations and plans for 23 houses, all in a midcentury Palladian manner.[1] The largest house (No. II) is three stories high and seven windows wide, plus wings. The principal floor plan includes a lobby, a dining room, two servants' rooms, a housekeeper's room, a larder, a kitchen, a bake house, a scullery, a coach house, and a stable. Most designs are just two stories high and three or five windows wide, more appropriate for the builders and artisans purchasing this manual. Design XIII, among the smallest, contains a parlor, dining room, three bedrooms, and two closets on the principal floor.

When compared to George Jameson's *Thirty Three Designs* (1765; *q.v.*), the only previous Scottish architectural publication, this book demonstrates the belated but increasing acceptance of Palladian architecture in Scotland.

1. There is one more plate in the 1799 edition, bringing to 24 the number of additional house designs.

RUSKIN, John (1819–1900)
"The poetry of architecture."

See LOUDON, **John Claudius, ed.,** The architectural magazine, *Entry 182.*

SAUL, M.
"Design of a toll-gate cottage."

See Mechanics' magazine, *Entry 477.*

304.1
[SAYER, Robert?]
Vignola revived; wherein is shewn the true and most elegant proportions of the five orders, as laid down by that great master: illustrated by two hundred and twenty-seven designs of palaces and other magnificent buildings, executed by himself in Italy and elsewhere; neatly engraved on fifty-six folio copper-plates, adapted not only to the general use of architecture, but herein particular subjects are treated with the greatest accuracy, viz. the five orders; columns, symbolical, &c. &c. doors, windows, niches, &c. cornishes, French and Italian; ballustrades, mosaic work, mouldings, &c. sections of rooms, with designs for furniture; ornamental iron-work for various purposes; temples, grotto's, and summer retreats,

for parks, gardens, &c. Plan, elevations, and sections of the Castle of St. Angelo at Rome; also of a church, pallaces, &c. With many other particulars relative to the art of building.

London: Printed for Robert Sayer, Map and Print-seller, 1761.

4 pp, 56 pls.

36.2 × 24.1 cm

CtY-BA

Many of the subjects illustrated in the plates were not designed by Vignola, and so this book is traditionally attributed to its publisher and presumed compiler, Robert Sayer.

In deciding to publish this book, Sayer likely recognized the growing respect among architects for Vignola as an authority on the orders,[1] and saw an opportunity to capitalize on the paucity of English publications of Vignola's work.[2] The brevity of the text suggests it was intended as a manual, especially for builders and provincial architects. The houses illustrated in the plates, up to 25 windows wide, clearly were not suited to the enterprise of most small builders, but would have served as impressive examples to show prospective clients, or as quarries from which to borrow individual motifs and details.

The text (pp. iii–iv) includes remarks on the five orders, their proportions, and intercolumniations.

The contents of the plates are accurately summarized on the title page. Plates 33 and 35 include plans and sections of temples for gardens and parks. Plates 38 through 52 depict six dwellings. The first is a "palazzo" 25 windows wide, shown in plans, sections, and elevations (Plates 38–42). The next design is smaller, only 11 windows wide, and shown in three plans and a section (Plates 43–46). Plans for a country house, a nobleman's seat, and a palace, and an elevation of the country house, appear in Plates 47 through 51. The final dwelling, designed "in the Italian taste," is two stories high and nine windows wide (Plate 52).

1. In the first edition of *A Treatise on Civil Architecture* (1759; *q.v.*) Sir William Chambers strongly praised Vignola's rendering of the orders. For the Tuscan order Chambers "chiefly imitated Vignola's" (p. 15). Vignola's Doric was "composed in a greater style, and in a manner more characteristic of the Order" (p. 17) than others. Although "Vignola's Composite has nothing remarkable in it" (p. 26), Chambers found Vignola's Corinthian "extremely beautiful, and beyond dispute superiour to that of any other Master. He hath artfully collected all the perfections of his Originals, and formed a whole preferable to either of them" (p. 29).

2. The only significant earlier publications were Joseph Moxon's translation, *Vignola: or the Compleat Architect* (London, 1655, and later editions), and John Leeke's translation, *The Regular Architect* (London, 1669, and later editions).

305.1

SEARLES, M[ichael]

[Designs and estimates for roofs.]

[N. loc.: N. pub., n.d.].

7 leaves.

22.9 × 31.1 cm

CtY-BA

No title page accompanies these designs. Altogether there are seven leaves, printed on one side only, containing designs and estimates for roofs, some of which are shown supported by simple walls. Searles suggested that these designs had been published before: at the top of the first leaf he indicated that the price of linseed oil had risen "Since the first Publication of these Estimates." Nevertheless the designs do not appear in any of Searles's other known publications, including *The Land Steward's and Farmer's Assistant* (London, 1779), *The Land-surveyor's Vade-mecum* (London, [1780?]), and *The Measurer's Companion* (London, 1781).

The first leaf contains designs and estimates for two roofs, each 50½ by 41¼ feet. The second and fourth leaves each include designs for two roofs, 16½ feet square, supported by simple one-story walls with two window openings. The third and fifth leaves contain estimates for these four roof designs. The sixth leaf has two designs for roofs, and cost estimates for each. The final leaf includes two designs and estimates for roofs, shown supported by simple one-story walls with three window openings.

The estimated prices range from £10 18s 9½d for one of the designs on the second leaf, covered in "artificial slate," to £192 7s 4d for one of the designs on the first leaf, "which was intended for the House late Lord Harrowby's, at Streatham," and estimated "before the Artificial Slate was known of."

SENEFELDER, Alois (1771–1834)

A complete course of lithography.

See Entry 478.

306.1

SHERATON, Thomas (1751–1806)

The cabinet-maker and upholsterer's drawing-book. In three parts. By Thomas Sheraton, Cabinet-maker.

London: Printed for the author, by T. Bensley; and sold by J. Mathews; G. Terry; J. S. Jordan, L. Wayland; and by the author, 1793.

xxxii + [viii] pp, frontisp.

[*The above material is followed by Parts I, II, and III, an Appendix, and an Accompaniment, each titled separately but all in one binding:*]

The cabinet-maker and upholsterer's drawing-book, in three parts.
Part I. Containing such geometrical lines and instructions as are highly useful to persons of both branches; including the methods of finding lines for hip and elliptic domes for state beds, of mitring mouldings of different projections together, and of finding curved lines to answer the various sections of irregular figures.—To which are added, the five orders, proportioned by aliquot parts, and exhibited in one large plate.
Part II. On practical perspective, applied to the art of representing all kinds of furniture in different situations; together with a little of the theory for such as would know some of the reasons on which this useful art is founded. N.B. The examples in perspective are intended to exhibit the newest taste of various pieces of furniture, and likewise to shew the necessary lines for designing them.
Part III. Is a repository of various ornaments, consisting of designs for pediments, with cornices, &c. drawn at large, their springs shewn, and the proper gaging marked off to work the several mouldings by.—To which are added, two methods of representing a drawing-room, with the proper distribution of the furniture. By T. Sheraton, Cabinet-maker.

London: Printed for the author, by T. Bensley; and sold by J. Mathews; G. Terry; J. S. Jordan; L. Wayland; and by the author, 1791.

5–176 pp, 13 pls.

[Part II:]

The cabinet-maker and upholsterer's drawing-book. In three parts. Vol. II. By Thomas Sheraton, Cabinet-maker.

London: Printed for the author, by T. Bensley; and sold by J. Mathews; G. Terry; and J. S. Jordan, 1794.

177–350 pp, 14 pls (numbered 14–25, 25–26).

[Part III:]

The cabinet-maker and upholsterer's drawing-book. Part III. Containing a description of the several pieces of furniture.
1. Of the use and style of finishing each piece.
2. General remarks on the manufacturing part of such pieces as may require it.
3. An explanation of the perspective lines where they are introduced. To which is added, a correct and quick method of contracting and enlarging cornices or other mouldings of any given pattern.

[N. loc.: N. pub., n.d.].

351–446 pp, 41 pls on 43 leaves (pls numbered 27–30, 27–47, 49–54, 54–60, and three without number).

[Appendix:]

Appendix to the cabinet-maker and upholsterer's drawing-book. Containing a variety of original designs for household furniture, in the newest and most elegant style; also, a number of plain and useful pieces, suitable either for town or country; together with a description and explanation to each piece. By Thomas Sheraton, Cabinet-maker.

London: Printed for the author, by T. Bensley; and sold by J. Mathews; G. Terry; J. S. Jordan; and by the author, 1793.

54 pp, 1 printed leaf, 30 pls (numbered 1, 3–15, 17–26, 29–32, 56 [*a mislabeling of pl. 2*], and one with no number; pls. 27 and 28 are bound in Part III).

[*Accompaniment:*]

An accompaniment to the cabinet-maker and upholsterer's drawing-book. Containing a variety of ornaments useful for learners to copy from, but particularly adapted to the cabinet and chair branches: exhibiting original and new designs of chair legs, bed pillars, window cornices, chair splads, and other ornaments, calculated to assist in the decorations of the above branches; together with instructions in letter-press. By Thomas Sheraton, Cabinet-maker.

London: Printed by T. Bensley, for the author, [1794].

27 pp, 1 printed leaf, 14 pls.

25.6 × 20.0 cm

ICA

306.2 †
_____

The cabinet-maker and upholsterer's drawing-book. In four parts. The second edition, with additional plates. By Thomas Sheraton. . . .

London: Printed for the author by T. Bensley, and sold by J. Mathews . . . , 1794–1796.

2 volumes.

27 cm

Reference: NUC

306.3 †
_____

The cabinet maker and upholsterer's drawing book. Second edition. With 120 plates.

[London]: Baynes, 1801.

4°

Reference: ECB

306.4 ‡

The cabinet-maker and upholsterer's drawing-book. In four parts. By Thomas Sheraton, cabinet-maker: recommended by many workmen of the first abilities in London, who have themselves inspected the work. The third edition, revised, and the whole embellished with 122 elegant copper-plates.

London: Printed by T. Bensley, for W. Baynes, (successor to G. Terry): sold also by J. Archer, Dublin; and all other booksellers, 1802.

viii + viii + 5–121 + 172–446 + 60 + 24 + [viii] pp, frontisp. + 121 pls (numbered 1–26, 25–29, 29–56, 56–61, A, 1–30, 30–32, 31, 39, 64, 49, 52, 66, 75, 41, 1–14).

Reference: Reprint, ed. Charles F. Montgomery and Wilfred P. Cole (New York: Praeger, 1970).

306.5

The cabinet-maker and upholsterer's drawing-book by Thomas Sheraton complete with "Appendix" and "Accompaniment" and all the plates revised and prepared for press by J. Munro Bell.

London: Gibbings and Company, 1895.

xvi + 17–440 pp, frontisp. + 121 pls (numbered 1–6, A, 7–26, 25–29, 29–56, 56–61, 1–32, 30A, 31, 39, 49, 52, 66, 75, 41, 64, 1–14).

28.1 × 22.2 cm

MnM

The title page to the first part, issued in 1791, announces three parts in all. Title pages and texts for the second and third parts appeared in 1793, together with a new title page for the whole.[1] The Appendix also was issued in 1793. The Accompaniment has an undated title page, but the plates are dated 1794.

The discussion below is based on examination of the third edition (1802).

A voluminous and authoritative treatise on furniture and interior design, Sheraton's *Cabinet-Maker* originally was conceived, according to the 1791 title page, as a treatise on geometry, the orders, perspective, and ornament. Sheraton observed in his prefatory address (1802, pp. 5–10) that "Books of various designs in cabinet work, ornamented according to the taste of the times in which they were published, have already appeared." But "none of these . . . profess to give any instructions relative to the art of making perspective drawings, or to treat of such geometrical lines as ought to be known by persons of both professions" (p. 5). Nor had previous books provided "accurate patterns at large for ornaments to enrich and embellish the various pieces of work which frequently occur in the cabinet branch" (p. 6). Sheraton hoped to remedy these problems in the present book. He also included remarks on previous books of furniture designs and changes introduced in his own book since the first edition. The preliminary matter concludes with remarks "To the Reader" on Thomas Malton's *New Royal Road to Geometry* (pp. 11–14) and an "Introduction" to the subject of geometry (pp. 15–17).

The text of Part I begins with definitions of geometrical terms, and then turns to lines, two-dimensional figures, three-dimensional solids, practical problems in architecture and furniture design, and the five orders. Part II, on perspective, starts with "principles" and then treats "optical laws," a series of "problems in perspective," the "representation of objects," the application of perspective techniques to representing architecture and furniture, and shadows. Part III concerns the depiction and construction of designs for furniture and ornaments illustrated in the plates. The text of the Appendix includes descriptions of more designs for furniture that appear in additional plates. The Accompaniment contains instructions for drawing ornaments, and descriptions of examples shown in the plates.

The plates include geometric figures and diagrams, illustrations of the orders and moldings, perspective diagrams, perspective representations of geometric solids, furniture, and other subjects, and a wide variety of furniture designs including tables, stands, bookcases, secretaries, desks, cabinets, sofas, chairs, fire screens, knife cases, a traveling box, beds, commodes, sideboards, wardrobes, and steps. In addition there are designs for ornaments and room interiors.

In Part II there are two plates that depict houses in perspective. In Plate 24 a three-story house, three windows wide, with a simple pitched roof and no ornament on the facade, is shown with the facade parallel to the picture plane; in addition a similar house, with no window or door openings, is shown with its side wall parallel to the picture plane. Among several figures in Plate 26, two include houses. One shows perspective views of two identical unornamented houses, each two stories high and three windows wide. The other figure shows three houses next to a canal that recedes into the distance. The largest house is three stories high and three windows wide; all have simple pitched roofs and are without ornament.

1. I have been unable to consult a copy of a first edition that has a 1793 title page to Part II. Nevertheless such a copy is recorded in Charles F. Montgomery's "Bibliographical Note" to a reprint of the third edition of *The Cabinet-Maker and Upholsterer's Drawing-Book* (New York: Praeger, 1970), p. XX. Montgomery indicates that other copies are located at the Winterthur Museum, Yale University, the British Library, the Bibliothèque Nationale, and the Metropolitan Museum of Art. But the Winterthur copy in fact has a 1794 title page to Part II. The copy at the Art Institute of Chicago appears identical to the edition described by Montgomery, except for a 1794 title page to Part II.

SHORT, William J.
"Remarks on street architecture."

See LOUDON, **John Claudius, ed.,** The architectural magazine, *Entry 182.*

307.1

SHORTESS, J.

Harmonic architecture. Exemplified in a plan, elevations and sections, &c. of a building, with four different fronts, upon an harmonic form or cube, now made octangular; being designed for a museum, in a retired situation of a park or garden: to which is added, a table of parts with two scales, one of parts and the other of feet and inches, for measuring and proportioning the members to the aforesaid building. By J. Shortess, Gent.

London: Printed for the Society of Booksellers for Promoting Learning. And sold by Messrs. Osborn and Smith in Gray's-Inn, 1741.

[ii] pp, 8 pls.

27.9 × 21.6 cm

NNC

The "Preface by the Publisher" describes this as "an ESSAY towards ascertaining a Method, in an Harmonic Way, to proportion the Members with the Body of a Building," and asserts that knowledge of this method is "necessary" for architects. The reference to harmonic proportions clearly recalls Robert Morris's lengthy discussion of the subject in his *Lectures* (1734–1736; *q.v.*), and suggests that Morris's work was an important inspiration for Shortess.

The first seven plates include a floor plan, four elevations, a section, and a ceiling plan of a cubical structure, ornamented with Corinthian pilasters, and described on the title page as a "museum" for a park or a garden.[1] The final plate includes a table and two scales for computing proportions.

1. Cf. the following definition of "museum," from the *Oxford English Dictionary*: "A building or apartment dedicated to the pursuit of learning or the arts; a 'home of the Muses.'"

308.1

[SINCLAIR, Sir John (1754–1835)]

Hints regarding certain measures calculated to improve an extensive property, more especially applicable to an estate in the northern parts of Scotland.

[London]: Printed by W. Bulmer and Co., [1802].

[iv] + 47 pp, 2 pls [*both wanting in this copy*].

25.0 × 21.2 cm

CtY

308.2

SINCLAIR, Sir John (1754–1835)

"Hints regarding certain measures calculated to improve an extensive property, more especially applicable to an estate in the northern parts of Scotland," Essay VIII in *Essays on Miscellaneous Subjects. By Sir John Sinclair, Bart.* (London: Printed by A. Strahan, for T. Cadell, Jun. and W. Davies, 1802), 207–271, and 2 pls.

21.0 × 13.0 cm

MnU

308.3 ‖

———————

"Hints regarding certain measures calculated to improve an extensive property," Essay VIII in *Essays on agriculture, farming, breeding and fattening cattle, and on longevity, with the modern improvements in utensils, management of land, &c. Illustrated with descriptive plates; and particularly adapted to North Britain, the United States, and the British Colonies in America. By Sir John Sinclair. . . . Second edition* (London: Printed by A. Strahan, for T. Cadell, Jun. and W. Davies; and G. and J. Offor, 1818), 207–271, and 2 pls.

Reference: Information supplied by Brown University Library.

Sinclair was, next to Arthur Young, the most voluminous writer on agricultural improvement during the late eighteenth and early nineteenth centuries. He was instrumental in the foundation of the Board of Agriculture, editor of a 21-volume *Statistical Account of Scotland* (1791–1799), author of a lengthy report to the Board of Agriculture on the state of agriculture in Scotland,[1] and responsible for numerous other books, essays, and addresses on rural and agricultural subjects.

This essay concerns Sinclair's improvements on his own estates in Caithness, altogether encompassing some 100,000 acres. Unfortunately improvement was difficult in northern Scotland, for "many ancient prejudices still exist," and the region "is in general occupied by small farmers, whose lots or portions are so intermixed together, as to prove an effectual bar to judicious cultivation." In addition the climate was poor, there was little market for agricultural produce, "the commerce and manufactures of the county are at a low ebb," and poor roads and harbors made the area "almost inaccessible."[2]

Turning first to "Agricultural Improvements" (pp. 214–235), Sinclair discussed specific improvements appropriate to arable lands, grasslands, wastelands, cattle farms, sheep farms, farm buildings, leasing arrangements, and plantations. He devoted just one paragraph to the subject of farm buildings, and included one plate illustrating "a house and offices, built for a small farm I am now in possession of, which . . . having the appearance of an ancient Gothic building, has become a distinguished ornament to all the neighbourhood" (p. 230). The house is two stories high and three windows wide, with a kitchen and a "room" on the ground floor. The facade is exceedingly plain except for the pointed arches of the door and five windows. The walls of the farmyard and offices are pierced by narrow openings with pointed arches, and projecting bows at either end of these walls are topped with crenellations.

Next Sinclair considered nonagricultural, or "Miscellaneous" improvements (pp. 235–252) in commerce, manufacturing, fishing, mining, roads and bridges, harbors, new villages, and new towns. Pointing out the advantages of villages as centers of manufacturing and trade, he mentioned briefly his intention to establish new villages at Berriedale, Sarclet, and Halkirk.[3] He also noted that "no district could reach any great degree of prosperity without having a considerable town erected in it" (p. 247), and so with some pride discussed his plan for a new town at Thurso. In the old town, "which contained about 1,600 inhabitants, . . . the houses were very irregularly built, and in many places crowded on each other" (p. 248). Sinclair's new plan, a regular pattern of orthogonal streets flanked by uniform houses and terraces, included a public square, a public mall along the bank of the Thurso River, and a separate market area at the northern end of the town. Sinclair boasted that the plan, illustrated in an accompanying plate, would greatly increase the "comfortable accomodation of the inhabitants," and he predicted great commercial and civic success for the town.[4]

Two appendixes follow the text. The first concerns aspects of the fishing industry (pp. 253–260), and the second is an "Account of the Encouragement Given by Frederick the Great, King of Prussia, for Promoting the Internal Improvement of his Dominions" (pp. 260–271).

•

By 1800 Sinclair prepared another important treatise on the subject of rural improvement, for delivery to "la classe des sciences physiques et mathématiques" in Paris. It was printed, presumably shortly thereafter, by "Baudouin, Imprimeur de l'Institut National" and titled *Projet d'un plan pour établir des fermes expérimentales, et pour fixer les principes des progrès de l'agriculture, par sir John Sinclair, baronnet, membre du parlement et fondateur du bureau d'agriculture britannique* (32 pp, 3 pls).[5] In the first 15 pages Sinclair discussed the advantages of establishing experimental farms. In the light of Thomas Malthus's recent essay on population, at least one of Sinclair's arguments was both timely and persuasive: if the growing populations of London and other major cities were to continue to eat, farm production would have to increase, and that could only occur through agricultural research and experiment. He urged those who had amassed large fortunes in industry, commerce, or the professions, and then retired to country estates, to consider supporting experimental farms or at least adopt on their own estates the improved farming techniques discovered elsewhere.

The final 16 pages contain a synopsis and discussion of Sinclair's proposal. At the end there are three plates, provided by Sinclair. The first depicts a 400-acre farm divided into 52 separate fields, with indications of appropriate crops for each field. The second plate shows designs for four circular cottages; three are two stories high, and one is just one story. Each floor contains two or three rooms. Sinclair indicated that the cottages were to be constructed of stone or brick, and thus would be warm, commodious, and durable. These designs were reproduced later in several English articles on cottage design.[6] In the third plate Sinclair presented one of the earliest published British designs for a small village. It consists of a square plot of land, encompassing 5 to 20 acres. In the center of this plot is a circular area 540 feet in diameter, with 20 circular cottages and two school buildings around the perimeter. Private garden plots radiate outward from the cottages, while the center of the circle is largely devoted to a lawn for children to play on. At the very center is a square area containing workshops and a common kitchen.

1. This report is discussed above in Entry 117.

2. Pp. 211–212. Page references are to the 1802 or 1818 editions of collected essays. For an account of contemporary improvements in the neighboring county of Sutherland, see James Loch, *An Account* (1820; *q.v.*). Also see Rosalind Mitchell's account of Sinclair's life and contribution, *Agricultural Sir John* (London: Geoffrey Bles, 1962).

3. For the plan of Sarclet see the commentary below on Sinclair's *Sketch* (1803). For Halkirk see John Henderson's report to the Board of Agriculture on the county of Caithness (Entry 99).

4. Pp. 248–249. Sinclair "hoped that about one-fifth part of the new town will be completed" by the end of 1802 (p. 250). For further remarks on Thurso see Henderson's report, cited in note 3.

5. Because of its French imprint this treatise has not been included as a separate entry; but its important discussion and illustrations of cottage design require brief discussion here. An English version of this proposal appeared in the *Annals of Agriculture*, XXXIV (1800), and is discussed in Appendix D, Entry 479.

6. See *The English Encyclopaedia* (1802); *The Complete Farmer* (1807); and Abraham Rees, *Cyclopaedia* ([1802]–1820), *qq.v.*

SINCLAIR, Sir John (1754–1835)
"Proposals for establishing . . . a joint stock farming society."

See Annals of agriculture, *Entry 479.*

309.1
SINCLAIR, Sir John (1754–1835)
A sketch of the improvements, now carrying on by Sir John Sinclair, Bart. M.P. in the county of Caithness, North Britain.

London: Printed by W. Bulmer and Co., 1803.

16 pp, 6 pls.

26.3 × 21.2 cm

CtY

One year before publication of this *Sketch*, Sinclair published "Hints Regarding Certain Measures Calculated to Improve an Extensive Property" in two versions: as a 47-page pamphlet, and as part of his collected essays (*qq.v.*). The *Sketch* includes a text entirely different from that in "Hints," but includes two plates that originally appeared in "Hints" and four additional plates.

In the *Sketch* as well as in "Hints," Sinclair's principal concern was agricultural improvement in northern Scotland, particularly on his own estates in Caithness, and the consequent need "to provide employment for the surplus population which an improved system of agriculture and the enlargement of farms necessarily occasion."[1] He proposed as the outcome nothing less than formation of "a new race of people . . . who, from a state of torpor, ignorance, idleness, and its concomitant poverty, are animated, to exertion and inquiry, and impelled to obtain by their industry, the acquisition of wealth." He proposed to accomplish this "by the application of a great capital, and of great attention," to building new towns, villages, roads, and harbors, establishing new "manufactures," and introducing "new breeds of animals, new instruments of husbandry, and . . . new modes of cultivation" (p. 1).

In this account Sinclair limited himself to reporting "a few of the most important particulars" of the "improvements now carrying on in the remotest district of the kingdom" (p. 1). These include improvements on a 23,000-acre sheep farm, a 2,134-acre common, and a farm at Thurso East, establishment of new towns at Halkirk, Brodiestown, and Thurso, and a few "miscellaneous" improvements. Appendix A is a list of conditions under which feus were given for building in Halkirk (pp. 12–15), and Appendix B is a letter from David Brodie concerning his plan for the new village at Sarclet (pp. 15–16).

Two of the six plates, "Plan of a Farm House and Offices," and "Plan of the New Town of Thurso," appeared first in "Hints".[2] Of the four new plates one is a colored version of the Thurso plan.[3] Another plate depicts a plan and elevation of the houses in Janet Street, which faces the Thurso River, a plan of McDonalds Square further inland, and a plan and elevation of a gate for the center of McDonalds Square. In the text Sinclair indicated that the houses in Janet Street "will make a considerable progress this year, and in the course of another season will probably be completed" (p. 10). As shown in the plate they form a continuous range of alternating one- and two-story elevations, with each dwelling consisting of a two-story unit with parlor and bedrooms, plus a one-story kitchen and service wing. The facades are ornamented with stringcourses, modest rustication, and Tuscan colonnades forming screens in front of the service areas. Another plate is a "Plan of Certain Farms on the River Thurso" adjacent to the Loch of Leurary and the Loch of Cathel. Finally there is a "Sketch of the Fishing Village of Brodiestown, Intended to be erected at Sarilet [sic] near Wick." The plan includes a semicircular group of five detached houses facing an estuary, and three streets radiating from that semicircle, lined with houses at intervals of 100 or 150 feet. In the text Sinclair indicated that the location had formerly been known as Sarclet, but in honor of improvements being undertaken by his tenant David Brodie, it was being renamed Brodiestown (p. 9).[4]

1. P. 1. Cf. major "improvements," some of them notoriously ruthless, undertaken by James Loch on behalf of the Duke of Sutherland in the neighboring county of Sutherland, and described in Loch's *Account* (1820; q.v.). For a detailed account of Sinclair's life and work, see Rosalind Mitchison, *Agricultural Sir John* (London: Geoffrey Bles, 1962).

2. These two plates are described above in the commentary on Sinclair's "Hints."

3. There are minor differences between the two verions of the Thurso plan. In one the buildings are hatched, while in the other they are colored. In the colored version "Washington's Monument" on Green Island is identified by an inscription; it is not identified in the other version.

4. The elevations and plans of Thurso and Brodiestown later appeared in John Henderson's report to the Board of Agriculture on the county of Caithness (1812; Entry 99).

310.1

SMITH, George (1793–1877)

Essay on the construction of cottages suited for the dwellings of the labouring classes, for which the premium was voted by the Highland Society of Scotland. Illustrated by working plans of single and combined cottages, on different scales of accommodation and cost. Also with specifications, details and estimates, by George Smith, Architect, Edinburgh.

Glasgow: Blackie & Son, Glasgow, Edinburgh and London, [1834].

38 pp, 11 pls.

22.2 × 14.0 cm

MH

310.2

———

"Essay on the construction of cottages, suited for the dwellings of the labouring classes, and adapted to the climate of Scotland. By Mr George Smith, Architect, Edinburgh," *Prize-Essays and Transactions of the Highland and Agricultural Society of Scotland* X (n.s. 4; 1835), 205–216, and pls. 6 and 7.

DLC

310.3 †

———

Essay on the construction of labourers' cottages.

[Glasgow]: Blackie, 1850.

8°

Reference: ECB

The first architectural treatise to be published in Glasgow, Smith's *Essay* includes an Introduction (pp. 7–9) dated at Edinburgh in June 1834. An earlier version won first place in an 1833 competition for essays on "the Construction and Disposition of Dwellings for the Labouring Classes" (1835, p. 205); the "substance" of this version was reprinted in 1835 by the Highland and Agricultural Society of Scotland in its *Prize-Essays and Transactions*.

The text of the 1833/1835 essay includes lengthy descriptions of four cottage designs, together with commentary on materials and specifications for construction. Near the end Smith explained the need for such cottages in remarks that address the growing social problems of Britain's urban areas:[1]

It would be of immense advantage to the health and morals of the town labourers, if they could be induced to live in the suburbs, in rows of detached cottages, in place of huddling together in the crowded parts of the towns. . . . When crowds of paupers and profligates are allowed to harbour in old decayed tenements, in the central parts of our great towns, the grade of the inhabitants gradually changes. It is much to be lamented, that sober and industrious tradesmen and labourers . . . are apt, in time, to sink into a state of degradation and worthlessness. . . . This great evil might, in some measure, be avoided, by erecting comfortable cottages for the industrious labourers, in the neighbourhood of large towns. (1835, pp. 211–212)

The first plate includes designs for three double cottages. The first two are just one story high, with a kitchen, "room," pantry, scullery, and other "offices" on the ground floor. The third design has bedrooms "over the center part," and a kitchen, "room," and offices on the ground floor. The third design, unlike the first two, has modest exterior ornament: there are Tudor drip moldings over the windows, plus a finial at the peak of the gable, and chimneys with Tudor moldings at base and top. The second plate shows a "combined cottage for four families," a one-story structure with a kitchen, "room," and offices for each family, plus shared courtyards and cisterns, and a common cow house. The modest Tudor ornament is similar to that in the third design on the first plate.

The letterpress of the 1834 edition is almost entirely different.[2] In the Introduction (pp. 7–9) Smith remarked on the growing need for designs "of a far humbler class, than those which generally appear in works on Domestic architecture":

Most of the books on cottage architecture hitherto published, exhibit only designs for dwellings in which picturesque effect is the object principally attended to, while the accomodation of the interior arrangements, to the circumstances of the intended inhabitants is seldom kept sufficiently in view by the architect. (1834, p. 7)

Unlike such contemporaries as Lugar or Robinson,[3] Smith deprecated the notion of laborers' cottages as pictorial compositions, and instead advocated use and fitness as fundamental principles of cottage design.[4] "What are called picturesque cottages," he charged, "are often badly contrived in the interior and are, in general, placed in situations, more with a view of giving effect to a particular scene, than with reference to the comfort of the cottager" (1834, p. 26).

In the text (1834, pp. 11–32), Smith pointed out the economic benefits of erecting new, functional cottages: "the labourers of this country will be gradually elevated in their habits, both physical and moral; towards which desirable end, nothing can conduce more than lodging them in such a way as to place comfort within their reach, by industrious exertion and the adoption of more cleanly habits." Cleanliness, comfort, and decency can be achieved best in dwellings that embody "economy and domestic convenience" in their "arrangement," and which are constructed of strong and durable materials (1834, p. 12). Further benefits can be realized through provision of a suitable site, gardens, good water, plenty of light and air, and gas for cooking and lighting (1834, pp. 12–16). Following a short essay on "Roofing for Cottages" (1834, pp. 17–20) Smith concluded the text with descriptions of nine designs for cottages (1834, pp. 20–32). The Appendix (1834, pp. 33–38) includes specifications and estimates for constructing cottages, and a sketch and description of a gas stove and room heater.

In introducing his cottage designs Smith rejected the use of historical styles and instead recommended a modern, "scientific" approach to design:

310.1 SMITH, GEORGE–310.3 SMITH, GEORGE

There are three distinct styles of ancient Architecture existing in Scotland; namely, the Castellated, the Ecclesiastical or Gothic, and the old Scotch Manor house. Each of these styles, in succession, was composed and adapted to the spirit of the age, by the Architects of the different periods; but the aid of science had never been called to design the more humble erections of farm buildings until about the commencement of the present century. (1834, p. 20)

Four of the nine designs (V through VIII) correspond to the four designs published in the 1835 article. All were redrawn at a much larger scale, on individual plates. Design I consists of two attached one-room cottages. Design II is a single cottage with a kitchen, a "room," and offices. Design III has a kitchen, a "room," a porch, a bed closet, a scullery, and offices. Design IV has a similar complement of rooms, but unlike the other designs is asymmetrical in plan. Design IX is a range of six attached cottages with varying plans. Designs III, IV, and VII–IX all have modest Tudor ornament. Two additional plates show a variety of Tudoresque chimney tops, cope moldings, and base moldings, plus a pinnacle, two cornices, a window mullion and window molding, a section of Design VII, and an elevation and plan of a window for Design VII.

1. These were among the earliest remarks on Britain's growing urban problems to be published by a practicing architect. Smith's comments appeared a year before Pugin's *Contrasts* (1836), an important and influential treatise suggesting architectural solutions to modern social and moral ills. In 1830 Stedman Whitwell and William Thompson published less influential proposals (*qq.v.*) for ideal communities in which laborers could join in a cooperative enterprise to achieve self-sufficiency and thus avoid the evils of modern society.

2. The only portion that remains essentially unchanged is that titled "General Heads of a Specification for the Construction of Cottages," pp. 213–216 in the 1835 edition and pp. 33–35 in the 1834 edition.

3. See for example Robert Lugar, *Villa Architecture* (1828); and Peter Frederick Robinson, *Village Architecture* (1830).

4. Cf. the remarks on utility and fitness in John Claudius Loudon's *Encylopaedia*, published the same year as Smith's original essay (1833). It is clear from a remark on p. 13 of Smith's 1834 edition that he had read Loudon's *Encyclopaedia*.

311.1 ‖
SMITH, James

The panorama of science and art; embracing the sciences of aerostation, agriculture and gardening, architecture, astronomy, chemistry, electricity, galvanism, hydrostatics and hydraulics, magnetism, mechanics, optics, and pneumatics: the arts of building, brewing, bleaching, clockwork, distillation, dyeing, drawing, engraving, gilding and silvering, ink-making, Japanning, lacquering, millwork, moulding and casting in plaster, painting, staining glass, staining wood, and varnishing: the methods of working in wood and metal, applicable in annealing, boring and drilling, filing, grinding, tempering steel, making screws, soldering, common and elliptic turning, &c. And a miscellaneous selection of interesting and useful processes and experiments. By James Smith. With forty-nine illustrative engravings, by eminent artists. In two volumes.—Vol. I [or II].

Liverpool: Printed for Nuttall, Fisher, and Co., 1815.

2 vols.

8°

Reference: Information supplied by Bibliographical Information Service, The British Library.

311.2

The panorama of science and art; embracing the sciences of aerostation, agriculture and gardening, architecture, astronomy, chemistry, electricity, galvanism, hydrostatics and hydraulics, magnetism, mechanics, optics, and pneumatics: the arts of building, brewing, bleaching, clockwork, distillation, dyeing, drawing, engraving, gilding and silvering, ink-making, Japanning, lacquering, millwork, moulding and casting in plaster, painting, staining glass, staining wood, and varnishing: the methods of working in wood and metal, applicable in annealing, boring and drilling, filing, grinding, tempering steel, making screws, soldering, common and elliptic turning, &c. And a miscellaneous selection of interesting and useful processes and experiments. By James Smith. With forty-nine illustrative engravings, by eminent artists. In two volumes.—Vol. I [or II].

Liverpool: Printed at the Caxton Press, by Nuttall, Fisher, and Dixon, [1816].

[*Volume I:*] x + 626 pp, frontisp. + 29 pls.

[*Volume II:*] xii pp, 1 printed leaf, 862 pp, frontisp. + 20 pls.

20.5 × 12.7 cm

DLC

311.3 ‖

The panorama of science and art; ⟨ . . . as [1816] . . . ⟩, making crews [*sic; Vol II:* screws], soldering, ⟨ . . . as [1816] . . . ⟩ two volumes.—Vol. I [or II].

London: Printed at the Caxton Press, by Henry Fisher. Sold by all the booksellers in the United Kingdom, [n.d.; ca. 1816–1822].

[*Volume I:*] x + 626 pp, frontisp. + 28 pls.

[*Volume II:*] xii + 886 pp, frontisp. + 20 pls.

Reference: Information supplied by University of Cincinnati Library.

311.4

_____

_____

London: Printed at the Caxton Press, by Henry Fisher. Sold by all the booksellers in the United Kingdom, [n.d.; ca. 1823].

x + 626 pp, frontisp. + 29 pls. [*The second volume of the set has been lost.*]

21.0 × 12.0 cm

CoU

311.5 ‖

_____

The panorama of science and art; ⟨ . . . as [1816] . . . ⟩, making crews [*sic; Vol. II:* screws], soldering, ⟨ . . . as [1816] . . . ⟩ two volumes.—Vol. I [*or* II]. Ninth edition.

London: Printed at the Caxton Press, by Henry Fisher. Sold by all the booksellers in the United Kingdom, 1823 [–1824].

[*Volume I:*] x pp, 1 leaf, 626 pp, frontisp. + 29 pls.

[*Volume II:*] xii + 886 pp, frontisp. + 20 pls.

21.3 × 13.0 cm

Reference: Information supplied by History of Science Library, The University of Oklahoma at Norman.

311.6 †

_____

The panorama of science and arts, embracing the science of aerostation, agriculture, gardening, architecture, electricity, galvanism, hydrostatics and hydraulics; the arts of building, brewing, inkmaking, casting in plaster, varnishing, etc. The method of working in wood and metal, by James Smith.

[N. loc.: N. pub.], 1824.

2 vols.

Reference: NUC

311.7

The panorama of science and art; ⟨ . . . as [1816] . . . ⟩ architecture, astronomy chemistry, ⟨ . . . as [1816] . . . ⟩ steel making crews [*sic*], soldering, ⟨ . . . as [1816] . . . ⟩ two volumes.—Vol. I. Eleventh edition.

London: Printed at the Caxton Press, by Henry Fisher. Sold by all the booksellers in the United Kingdom, 1825.

x + 626 pp, frontisp. [*The plates to Vol. I are wanting; there is no second volume to the set.*]

21.4 × 13.1 cm

MH

311.8 ‖

The panorama of science and art; embracing the principal sciences and arts; the methods of working in wood and metal; and a miscellaneous selection of useful and interesting processes and experiments. By James Smith. In two volumes, with illustrative engravings. Vol. I [*or* II]. Thirteenth edition.

London: Printed at the Caxton Press, by H. Fisher, Son, & Co. Published at 38, Newgate Street; and sold by all booksellers, [1840?].

[*Volume I:*] x pp, 1 leaf, 626 pp, frontisp. + 29 pls.

[*Volume II:*] xii + 886 pp, frontisp. + 20 pls [*the plate to face p. 816 is wanting in this copy*].

22.2 × 13.2 cm

Reference: Information supplied by The Free Library of Philadelphia.

In the Preface Smith explained that the first essay would introduce techniques of working manually with iron, timber, and mechanical equipment because the progress of science and art was too easily impeded by theorists' lack of "mechanical dexterity."[1] Subsequent essays treated architecture, building, mechanics, optics, astronomy, pneumatics, hydrostatics and hydraulics, aerostation, magnetism, electricity, galvanism, chemistry, dyeing, bleaching, distillation, agriculture, gardening, drawing, painting, engraving, and miscellaneous subjects. This was, Smith noted, a carefully considered order in which the topics "may be conveniently studied."[2]

The position of architecture at the beginning indicates that Smith considered it an elementary subject, but it was also one of some importance. Smith noted in the Preface that he had solicited the article from Thomas Rickman; in the event, Rickman offered here the first authoritative classification of English Gothic architecture into historical periods by style.[3] The 57-page article progressed chronologically through Norman, Early English, Decorated, and Perpendicular styles, treating each separately in terms of doors, windows, arches, piers, buttresses, tablets, niches, ornaments, and steeples. Rickman devoted his final 11 pages to "Grecian" architecture, where he simply considered the five Classical orders. In a brief prefatory statement Rickman sought to establish the importance of studying architecture, and in particular tried to distinguish "between mere building and architectural design" (p. 126). The former, he said, "looks for convenience," while in the latter "the columns are essential parts, and to them and their proportions all must be made subservient." Rickman suggested that the modern architect should search among historical remains for models. Indeed this activity was central to architectural creativity: "in selecting and adopting these [models], the taste and abilities of the architect has [sic] ample space" to flourish (ibid.). Rickman included five plates, the first showing elements of Gothic architecture, the second showing a Gothic arch or door, and the last three showing the Classical orders.

The next article, on "Building," included substantial portions concerning bricklaying and masonry, and "miscellaneous remarks" on siting and planning houses, on constructing rooms, on chimneys, doors, windows, stairs, roofs, and floors, and on proportioning timbers for small and large buildings. The article closed with several pages devoted to the Building Act. Two plates illustrated different kinds of brickwork.

The 33-page article on "Drawing" included 13 pages on perspective. Figures 1 and 2 in Plate III illustrated a machine used for drawing distant objects in perspective.[4] First illustrated in James Ferguson's *Art of Drawing in Perspective* (1775; *q.v.*), the device consisted of a vertical armature, perpendicular to a flat horizontal base, with an eyepiece at one end. The user would sight a distant object through the eyepiece and then manipulate two wires crossing the armature to intersect at a point directly in the line of vision between eyepiece and object. The armature would then be folded down to the horizontal, and the intersection point plotted on a piece of paper. The process would then be repeated for many different points on the distant object, resulting in an image of that object being plotted on the paper. In this illustration, as in Ferguson's original, a house was used as the distant object. It was two stories high and five windows wide, and lacked any ornamentation.

1. [1840] edition, I, iii.

2. Ibid., p. iv.

3. Smith offered no information on the authorship of any other portion of *The Panorama*. Rickman's essay was published separately two years later as *An Attempt to Discriminate the Styles of Architecture in England* (London, 1817), and went through seven editions by 1881.

4. A total of four plates, numbered I through IV, accompanied the essay on "Drawing."

312.1
SMITH, John Thomas (1766–1833)
Remarks on rural scenery; with twenty etchings of cottages, from nature; and some observations and precepts relative to the pictoresque. By John Thomas Smith. . . .

London: Printed for and sold by Nathaniel Smith, ancient Print-seller, and I. T. Smith, 1797.

27 + [ii] pp, 20 pls.

30.5 × 24.8 cm

MH

Smith's *Remarks on Rural Scenery* was the first drawing treatise to pay special attention to picturesque cottages: they are discussed at length in the text and illustrated in each of the plates. The first portion of the text, an essay on "Various Features and Specific Beauties in Cottage Scenery" (pp. 5–10), is a manifesto of the picturesque.[1] Smith lamented that "of all pictoresque subjects, the *English cottage* seems to have obtained the least share of particular notice" (p. 5), with palaces, castles, churches, and monastic ruins receiving far more attention. He surmised that the beauty of cottages had been ignored because it was not "of the *heroic* or sublime order"; yet beauty in general, "equally pervading *every* department of Nature, is found not less perfect in the most *humble* than in the most *stately* structures, or scenery" (p. 6). He noted that such poets as Thomson, Shenstone, and Cooper had long appreciated the "character" of cottage architecture, and also cited Richard Payne Knight's more recent appreciation of the cottage in *The Landscape*. Among painters, Smith praised Gainsborough for making "more profound and accurate observations of Nature," and giving "distinct characteristics and original varieties to his cottagery, and to the furniture and circumstances with which his best works are so eminently enriched" (p. 7). The rest of the text (pp. 11–27) consists of brief essays on "Study," "Freedoms to be Taken with Nature," light and shade, coloring, perspective, "Original Etchers of Rural Scenery," and "Connecting Objects, and Selecting Those Only Which Shall be Suitable to Their Stations."

Smith's most original contribution was his analysis of the expressive value of cottage design. A year before Malton's fundamental treatise on British cottage architecture,[2] Smith, like Malton, suggested the possibilities of associational meaning in scenes involving humble and picturesque cottages. Seeing a well-dressed woman "at a cottage-door, benevolently engaged in advising, consoling, or assisting a distressed family, we should instantly perceive a propriety of action, and a probable combination of circumstances; and the expanding heart would be hurried into a train of grateful ideas [i.e., associations], before a thought could be bestowed on the mechanism by which it was affected" (p. 23). He also identified specific cottage features that would raise certain ideas in the mind of the viewer:

nothing will more easily, or more universally excite the attentions of benevolence, than the appearance of neatness and cleanliness: The regular, whitewashed or new brick wall—the glaring red chimney-pot—the even-thatch'd roof— . . . —the oven, exhibiting a smooth unvarying surface of dead plaster, or decked only with a vine pruned into deformity—the bright yellow foot-path, straight as a line—all tend to impress an idea of frugal propretè, and will be sure to call forth the praises of the good *housewife* and the thrifty *oeconomist*. (pp. 8–9)

But Smith found all such features worth "noting to the artist," and provided an equally long catalogue of irregular, picturesque elements that "offer far greater allurements to the painter's eye" (p. 9).

All the 20 plates are views of real cottages, drawn and etched in detail to show the picturesque irregularities of thatch, decaying planks, crumbling plaster, and uneven tiles, plus trees, bushes, and underbrush slowly overtaking each dwelling. In the foreground of many views there are tools, baskets, fences, and occasional human figures to add further interest and animation to the scene.

1. Three highly important treatises on the picturesque had just appeared: Richard Payne Knight, *The Landscape* (1794; *q.v.*); Uvedale Price, *An Essay on the Picturesque* (London, 1794); and Humphry Repton, *Sketches and Hints* (1794; *q.v.*). Also see Christopher Hussey, *The Picturesque* (London: Putnam, 1927).

2. James Malton, *An Essay on British Cottage Architecture* (1798; *q.v.*).

313.1
SMITH, Thomas
The art of drawing in its various branches, exemplified in a course of twenty-eight progressive lessons, calculated to afford those who are un-acquainted with the art the means of acquiring a competent knowledge without the aid of a master; being the only work of the kind in which the principles of effect are explained in a clear, methodical, and at the same time familiar style. By Thomas Smith. Illustrated with coloured designs and numerous wood engravings.

London: Printed for Sherwood, Jones, and Co., 1825.

xvi + 121 pp, 1 printed leaf, 16 pls.

20. 8 × 12.9 cm

BL

313.2 ‖
_____

The art of drawing ⟨ . . . as 1825 . . . ⟩ the art, the means ⟨ . . . as 1825 . . . ⟩ engravings.

London: Printed for Sherwood, Gilbert, and Piper, 1827.

xvi + 121 pp, frontisp.

Reference: Information supplied by Winterthur Museum Library.

313.3 ‖
_____

The young artist's assistant in the art of drawing in water colours, ex-emplified in a course of twenty-nine progressive lessons, on animals, fruit, flowers, still life, portrait, miniature, landscape, perspective, architecture, and sculpture, calculated to afford those who are unacquainted with the art, the means of acquiring a competent knowledge without the aid of a master; being the only work of the kind in which the principles of effect are explained in a clear, methodical, and, at the same time, familiar style. By Thomas Smith. Illustrated with coloured designs and numerous wood engravings.

London: Printed for Sherwood, Gilbert, and Piper, [1830?].

xiii + v–xvi + 134 + 4 + 8 + [2] pp, frontisp. + 20 pls.

Reference: Information supplied by Winterthur Museum Library.

The final edition, titled *The Young Artist's Assistant*, may be dated [1830] on the strength of an entry for that year in ECB.

The text of the first two editions consists of 28 "Lessons" and a brief conclusion. The first eight lessons concern perspective: one introductory lesson is followed by seven practical lessons on how to draw trees, a house, a circle, a bridge, a barrel, a road, and another house. The two houses, illustrated on pages 6 and 13, are both two stories high; the first is three windows wide and the second is two windows wide. Subsequent lessons concern drawing, landscape, the use of pencil, ink, and color, "Marine" drawing, still life, "Historical or Figure" drawing, portrait and miniature painting, animals, "Effect," contrast, and harmony. Illustrations of architectural subjects accompany some of these lessons and include a rustic barn in the plate titled "Indian Ink," rustic cottages in "Cottage Plate 1st" and "Cottage Plate 2nd," a bridge and pyramids on page 102, distant rows of houses on pages 103 and 114, and a ruined abbey on page 108.

The final edition includes all this material plus a "Preliminary Lesson on Figure and Landscape Drawing" (pp. vii–xvi) and an additional lesson at the end on "The Relative Connection of Drawing, Architecture, and Sculpture" (pp. 120–133). This includes brief remarks on the formal characteristics and expressive capacities of different architectural styles, including Egyptian ("dark and ponderous, . . . immense and gloomy"), Greek, Turkish, Saracenic, Saxon, Norman, Gothic ("vastness, gloominess, and solemnity"), Doric, Ionic, Corinthian, Tuscan, and Composite. Three plates accompany this lesson, and depict the Parthenon, the Classical orders and moldings, and examples of Norman, Early English, Decorated, and Perpendicular styles.

314.1
SMITH, William Hawkes
An outline of architecture, Grecian, Roman, and Gothic. By W. Hawkes Smith.

Birmingham: Printed by W. Hawkes Smith, 1816.

iv + 34 pp, 6 pls.

26.5 × 21.3 cm

CtY-BA

314.2
————

An outline of architecture, Grecian, Roman, and Gothic. By William Hawkes Smith[.] The second eidtion [*sic*].

Birmingham: Printed by W. Hawkes Smith, and sold by Longman, Hurst, and Co.; and Baldwin, Cradock, and Joy, London, 1820.

iv + 33 pp, 7 pls (numbered 1–3, 3*, 4–6).

26.5 × 21.4 cm

NNC

In the Preface (pp. i–iii)[1] Smith explained that in an effort to "cultivate" a knowledge of "taste" he would, curiously, treat the subject in "Outline" because architecture approaches "nearest to the nature of a demonstrative Science" (p. i).

The first 26 pages of text comprise seven chapters, on the origin of architecture, the components of the orders, the five orders, "Various Architectural Decorations," a "Vocabulary of Architectural Terms," a short discussion of Gothic, and a description of Gothic arches illustrated in Plate 6. The text concludes with a set of "Questions for Examination" (pp. 27–31) and a brief address to the reader (pp. 32–33) with references for further reading and study.

The first plate depicts three primitive huts or dwellings—cone shaped, flat roofed, and gabled, borrowed from the first plate in Sir William Chambers's *Treatise* (1759; *q.v.*)—along with illustrations of Ionic and Corinthian capitals. Plate 2 illustrates the "component parts" of the Doric order. Plate 3 depicts entablatures, bases, and pediments. Plate 4 is devoted to the Ionic, Corinthian, and Composite orders. Plate 5 depicts arches, a Persian, and a caryatid. Attached to Plate 6 are several layers of cutout paper figures illustrating different forms of Gothic arches.

In the second edition (1820) an additional plate, marked 3*, illustrates the Doric order. Unlike the other plates it is a lithograph, and thus makes Smith's *Outline* the first lithographically illustrated architectural book published in England.[2]

1. This account is based on the 1820 edition. In the 1816 edition the pages are numbered 1–19 and 21–34, omitting 20.

2. The next lithographically illustrated architectural book was John Pike Hedgeland's *First Part of a Series of Designs* (1821; *q.v.*), in which views of all ten designs are lithographs.

315.1
SOANE, Sir John (1753–1837)
Description of the house and museum on the north side of Lincoln's-Inn= Fields, the residence of John Soane. . . .

London: Printed by James Moyes, 1830.

[ii] + 56 pp, 17 pls.

30.1 × 23.7 cm

CtY-BA

315.2 ‖

———————

———————

London: Printed by James Moyes, 1832.

xix + 27 pp, frontisp. + 18 pls (numbered I–XIII, XIV*, XIV, XV, XV*, XVI).

31 cm

Reference: Information supplied by Humanities Research Center, University of Texas, Austin.

315.3

Description of the house and museum on the north side of Lincoln's Inn Fields, the residence of Sir John Soane. . . .
With graphic illustrations and incidental details.

London: Printed by Levey, Robson, and Franklyn. Not published. Only one hundred and fifty copies printed, [1835].

xiv + 109 pp, frontisp. + 38 pls.

36.4 × 27.0 cm

MH

315.4

Description de la maison et du musée situés au nord de la place de Lincoln's Inn Fields, à Londres, demeure du Chevalier Soane. . . . Avec illustrations graphiques et details accessoires.

Londres: De l'imprimerie de Levey, Robson, et Franklyn, [1835].

xiv, 103 pp.

36.0 × 27.0 cm

PPL

Generally the English title page and letterpress are accompanied by a set of plates, while the French title page and letterpress are bound alone, without plates. In some cases the English title page, English letterpress, French title page, French letterpress, and a set of plates all are bound together.[1]

In 1840, after Soane's death, and abridgment of the *Description* was published principally for use as a guide to the Museum. This and ten more editions published by 1930 have been omitted here.

No British architect before Soane had devoted an entire book to the description and illustration of his own house: his *Plans . . . of Pitzhanger* (1802; *q.v.*) was the first, and *Description of the House and Museum* was the second. Architects of two important country houses, Houghton and Holkham, had prepared monographs of their own work,[2] but these books clearly did not depict the architects' own residences. Like Houghton and Holkham, Soane's house was an important and original monument, and characteristic features of Soane's style are well displayed in his book. The exterior elevation, for example, incorporates thin, fluted pilasters with no capitals and a minimal entablature (Plate I), and the ceiling of the breakfast room is an elegant, shallow vault flanked by narrow skylights, with an octagonal lantern in the center (Plates XXIX–XXXI).

In the "Exordium" (1835, pp. vii–viii) Soane explained the didactic goals of this book: "One of the objects I had in view was to shew, partly by graphic illustrations, the union and close connexion between Painting, Sculpture, and Architecture,—Music and Poetry" (1835, p. vii).[3] He also noted that the *Description* "was chiefly written for the advantage of the Architect, who will, I trust, become sensible, from the examination to which it leads him, that every work of Art which awakens his ideas, stimulates his industry, purifies his taste, or gives solidity to his judgment, is to him a valuable instructor" (1835, p. viii).

Accordingly the text of the 1835 edition—the largest and last before Soane's death—is principally a descriptive guide to objects in his collection, including paintings, sculptures, and architectural drawings. The final nine pages are devoted to the Act of 20 April 1833 "for settling and preserving Sir John Soane's Museum, Library, and Works of Art . . . for the Benefit of the Public, and for establishing a sufficient Endowment for the due Maintenance of the same."

Plate I is a view of the exterior, and the second plate is a plan of the ground floor. Plans of the basement story and the "Drawing Room Floor" appear in Plates XVI and XXXIII, respectively. Plate XXV is a section and plan of the "Museum & Crypt," and Plate XXXVII shows plans of the chamber and attic floors. Plates III–V are views of the interior, as are Plates VI–X, XV, XVII–XX, XXIV, XXVI–XXIX, XXXI, XXXII, XXXIV–XXXVI, and XXXVIII. The rest of the plates depict objects in Soane's collection and sections of individual rooms.

1. I have not located any copy containing just the French title page, French letterpress, and plates. This suggests that Soane may never have intended a complete French edition, and rather had the French material prepared simply to accompany that in English.

2. See [Thomas Ripley], *The Plans, Elevations, and Sections . . . of Houghton* (1735); and Mattew Brettingham, *The Plans, Elevations and Sections, of Holkham* (1761).

3. Also see John Britton, *The Union of Architecture, Sculpture, and Painting* (1827) in Appendix C below.

316.1
SOANE, Sir John (1753–1837)
Designs for public improvements in London and Westminster. By John Soane. . . .

London: Printed by James Moyes, 1827.

[iv] + 21 pp, 34 pls (numbered 1–7, 7.F., 8–33).

49.0 × 30.0 cm

CtY-BA

316.2
_____
Designs for public improvements in London and Westminster. The second impression; with further improvements and explanatory illustrations. By John Soane. . . .

London: Printed by James Moyes, 1828.

vi + 36 + [ii] pp, 55 pls (numbered 1–31, *31, 32–54).

48.9 × 30.0 cm

NNC

316.3

Designs for public and private buildings, by John Soane. . . .

London: Published by Priestley and Weale, Rodwell, Colnaghi & Co, and Ridgeway, 1828.

vi + 36 + [ii] pp, 55 pls (numbered 1–21, 21*, 22–54; *pl. 31 is misnumbered 21*).

48.9 × 29.8 cm

MH

316.4

Designs for public and private buildings, by Sir John Soane. . . .

[London: N. pub., 1832].

xiv + [4] + 67 pp, frontisp. + 77 pls (numbered I, II, 3, IV, 5, 6, VII, 8, 9, IX*, 9**, 10, [no number], X.A, X.B, X.C, X.D, 11, 12, XIII, 14–19, 19*, 20, XXI, 22–31, 31*, XXXII, 33, XXXIV, XXXIV*, XXXIV**, XXXIV***, XXXV, 36–39, XXXIX*, XXXIX**, XL, XLI, 42, XLIII, XLIV, XLIV*, XLIV**, XLV–XLVIII, XLVIII*, XLVIII**, XLVIII***, XLVIII****, XLVIII*****, 49–51, LII, LIII, LIV, LV, LVI).

46.7 × 28.6 cm

Soane

Essentially a vehicle for publishing illustrations of Soane's own work,[1] *Designs for Public Improvements* appeared in four distinct editions, with a host of variations among individual copies.[2]

According to Soane, only 25 copies of the 1827 edition of *Designs for Public Improvements* were "distributed."[3] This edition consists of a list of plates, a dedication to the king, 21 pages of plate descriptions, and 34 plates illustrating designs for an entrance to Hyde Park, two other entrances, two royal palaces, the Board of Trade and Privy Council Office, the Law Courts, a scheme to unify the Houses of Parliament and Law Courts in one architectural style, a Senate House, an entrance to the House of Lords, the Bank of England, a chapel at Tyringham, two churches, and Chelsea Hospital.

The next year a "second impression" was published "with such Alterations and Illustrations as a revision of the Subject suggested" (p. v). Following a dedication to the king (pp. iii–iv) and a brief introduction (pp. v–vi), an expanded text (pp. 1–36) includes descriptions of plates numbered through 51. Twenty-one new plates make the total 55, numbered 1–31, *31, and 32–54. New designs in this edition include a monument to the memory of the Duke of York, two villas, two town mansions, two prisons, additions to Norwich Castle, Dulwich College, the Bank of England, and Soane's own house at 13, Lincoln's Inn Fields.

Also in 1828 Soane issued the first edition of *Designs for Public and Private Buildings*. The contents differ only slightly from *Designs for Public Improvements*.[4]

The copy of the final edition (1832) in the Soane Museum has additional preliminary material, including lists of sovereigns and others mentioned in the plate descriptions, plus expanded plate descriptions, a set of the previous 55 plates, and 22 more plates, most of which are additional illustrations of subjects included in earlier editions. This edition, not published, was made up in approximately 16 copies for presentation to Soane's friends and to the sovereigns of Europe.[5]

In the introduction Soane contended that architecture was an art that subsumed all others—"an Art which, in Imperial Works, combines and displays the mighty powers of Painting and Sculpture—Music and Poetry" (1828, p. v). Extending his argument for the "proud pre-eminence" of architecture even further, Soane proposed awkward parallels between the arts, language, and the order of the universe: speaking of the arts, "we say, Painting, Sculpture, and ARCHITECTURE:—in Grammar, the three degrees of comparison are distinguished by the positive, comparative, and SUPERLATIVE; and in like manner we say, our King, our Country, and our GOD!"[6]

In some plate descriptions Soane suggested embarrassment at the exuberance and pretension of his early work: he described his 1779 design for a Senate House as "a Study made in Rome in 1779, without regard to expense or limits of space, in the gay morning of youthful fancy, amid all the wild imagination of an enthusiastic mind, animated by the contemplation of the majestic Ruins of the sublime Works of Imperial Rome" (1828, p. 23). In contrast the 1794 design for the Houses of Parliament had required "economy and utility . . . to be more consulted than magnificence" (ibid.). In other cases Soane presented his work as an attempt to achieve an ideal synthesis of architectural form and utility. The design for a royal palace (1779), for example, was based on "exemplars of magnificence, intricacy, variety, and movement, uniting all the intellectual delights of classical Architecture. . . . There is no subject more interesting to the young Architect, and better calculated for the exercise of his skill, taste, and imagination, than a Palace for the Sovereign:—To unite the grand and the useful is a most difficult task" (1827, p. 14).

Apart from palaces and his own house, Soane included only four designs for residences. The two town mansions (Plate 40) would have fit in well among existing Neoclassical designs in St. James's Square, for example, but otherwise were unremarkable. The facade of Swinnerton Villa (Plate 39) is more idiosyncratically Soanean. It is organized by a complex rectilinear grid made of columns, pilasters, and cornices, overlying and contrasting with three shallow semicircular relieving arches, two of which are one story high and one of which rises two stories. The facade is partially rusticated, except for areas under and immediately above the arches, thus reinforcing, through a contrast of textures, the tension within the complex pattern of curves and orthogonals.[7] The other design in Plate 39, the "Villa at Tringham," is less exciting. Columns and pilasters run the full height of the two-story facade, which is rusticated on the ground floor and left quite plain above.

1. He described the book as "this abrégé of a long professional life" (1828, p. 29).

2. The variations are complex, especially since some of the plates appear in different states. For remarks on two copies of the 1828 edition of *Designs for Public and Private Buildings* see Laurence Hall Fowler and Elizabeth Baer, comps., *The Fowler Architectural Collection of the Johns Hopkins University* (Baltimore: Evergreen House Foundation, 1961), p. 270.

3. See *Designs for Public Improvements* (1828), p. v.

4. In the Harvard and Fowler copies, there is no dedication to the king. The Harvard copy has 55 plates. The Fowler copy has 61 plates, which include three duplicates and additional designs for the Law Courts.

5. This information accompanies a copy in the Victoria and Albert Museum, shelfmark 93.E.18, which Soane had given to his pupil Charles James Richardson.

6. 1828, p. vi. For further remarks by Soane on the integration of the arts see his *Description of the House and Museum* (1830; *q.v.*) and John Britton's *Union of Architecture, Sculpture, and Painting* (1827; *q.v.* in Appendix C).

7. A similarly organized facade appears in Plate XXII of Soane's *Designs in Architecture* (1778; *q.v.*).

317.1

SOANE, Sir John (1753–1837)
Designs in architecture; consisting of plans, elevations, and sections, for temples, baths, cassines, pavilions, garden-seats, obelisks, and other buildings; for decorating pleasure-ground, parks, forests, &c. &c. Engraved on 38 copper-plates. By John Soan.

London: Printed for I. Taylor, 1778.

38 pls on 37 leaves.

27.3 × 18.4 cm

MB

317.2

Designs in architecture, consisting of plans, elevations, and sections, for temples, baths, cassines, pavilions, garden-seats, obelisks, and other buildings; for decorating pleasure grounds, parks, forests, &c. &c. Engraved on 38 copper-plates. By John Soane, Architect. . . .

London: Printed for I. & J. Taylor, 1789.

38 pls on 37 leaves.

26.3 × 18.4 cm

PU

317.3

_____

_____

London: Printed for I. & J. Taylor, 1790.

38 pls on 37 leaves.

26.0 × 18.1 cm

MBAt

317.4

_____

_____

London: Printed for I. & J. Taylor, 1797.

38 pls on 19 leaves.

53.3 × 36.8 cm

Soane

This collection of 30 designs without text was Soane's first publication. In a 1777 prospectus he promised "designs to please the different tastes in Architecture and to render the work generally useful and immediately calculated for execution."[1] As completed, the book contains designs for six garden seats, a "facade" to terminate a view, two obelisks, a bath, a summer house, a summer room, a tea room, two rotundas, seven temples, a banqueting room, two pavilions, a "Hunting Casine," a "Garden Building," a dairy, and two mausolea. While there is a sufficient variety of styles to please many "different tastes," most of the designs are Neoclassical, and some are quite similar to contemporary work by Sir William Chambers, John Yenn, John Carter, and others.[2] Designs in other styles include the Gothic summer house (Plate XI), decorated in a manner reminiscent of Batty Langley, and the "Dairy House in the Moresque Style" (Plates XXXIII and XXXIV), which is in fact a Neoclassical composition of semicircular arched windows across the facade, a low dome over the center, and tall obelisks at both ends. In several designs there are interesting experiments with geometric forms, particularly in plan. The plan of the Temple of Peace (Plate XXXII), for example, consists of two intersecting ovals circumscribed by a third. The plans of the tea room (Plate XII) and the triangular temple (Plate XIX) are both curved triangles, each side consisting of a concave circular segment.

Two designs are large enough to suggest they might be used as temporary residences. The "Hunting Casine" (Plate XXIX) consists of a dining room, eating parlor, hall, and dressing room or library. The "Dairy House in the Moresque Style" (Plates XXXIII and XXXIV) includes a dairy, dairy kitchen, tea room, dressing room, and cold bath.

1. Arthur T. Bolton, ed., *The Portrait of Sir John Soane* (London: Sir John Soane's Museum, 1927), p. 14. The genesis of the book is described by Pierre de la Ruffinière du Prey in *John Soane: The Making of an Architect* (Chicago: The University of Chicago Press, 1982), p. 88.

2. Du Prey discussed Soane's borrowings ibid, pp. 90–92. Du Prey also noted astutely that Soane's book is an attempt to combine the "high style" of the major midcentury treatises with the small size of designs illustrated in contemporary builders' handbooks (p. 92).

318.1 ‡

[SOANE, Sir John (1753–1837)]

Plans, elevations, and perspective views, of Pitzhanger Manor-House, and of the ruins of an edifice of Roman architecture, situated on the border of Ealing Green, with a description of the ancient and present state of the Manor-House, in a letter to a friend.

London: J. Moyes, 1802.

8 pp, 11 pls (numbered II–XII), supplementary watercolor drawings.

4°

Reference: Microfilm supplied by The British Library.

The copy of the book in the British Library is extra-illustrated with numerous watercolor drawings, most of which were preparatory for the plates.

Soane prepared this book to document the changes and improvements he carried out at Pitzhanger Manor House, Ealing, from 1800 to 1802. His intention was to demolish the old house, with the exception of a two-story wing that he had helped George Dance complete circa 1768–1770. Then he would "erect . . . a small Villa connected with these rooms, as a more suitable and convenient residence for my family" (p. 5). Indeed he wanted this to be the future residence of his son, "whose classical education, and the facilities and advantages he possessed, would enable him to distinguish himself above his fellows in the practice of a profession calculated to increase domestic comforts and the refinements of a civilised society" (p. 4).

The short text is a chronicle of Soane's improvements, and the plates illustrate some of the more prominent results. Plates II through VIII are plans and elevations plus exterior and interior views. Designs for the breakfast room and library (Plate VII) were closely related to Soane's earlier work in the breakfast room (1792) at No. 12, Lincoln's Inn Fields. Plates IX through XII are fantasy illustrations of ancient ruins supposedly discovered on the estate grounds, which Soane imagined excavating and restoring.[1]

1. For discussion and illustrations of Pitzhanger Manor see: Architectural Monographs, *John Soane* (London: Academy Editions, 1983); Arthur Thomas Bolton, *Pitzhanger Manor House Ealing Green* (London: Sir John Soane's Museum, [1918]); Pierre de la Ruffinière Du Prey, *John Soane: The Making of an Architect* (Chicago: University of Chicago Press, 1982), pp. 21–22, 333; Isabella M. (Mrs. Basil) Holmes, *The Home of the Ealing Free Library* (Ealing: Middlesex County Times Printing and Publishing Co., 1902); George Richardson, *The New Vitruvius Britannicus* (1808, *q.v.*), II, 9, and pls. LVII–LIX; Dorothy Stroud, *George Dance Architect 1741–1825* (London: Faber and Faber, 1971), pp. 87–89; and Stroud, "Sir John Soane and the Rebuilding of Pitzhanger Manor," in Helen Searing, ed., *In Search of Modern Architecture: A Tribute to Henry-Russell Hitchcock* (Cambridge, Mass.: MIT Press, 1982), pp. 38–51.

319.1

SOANE, Sir John (1753–1837)

• Plans • elevations • and • sections • • of • bvildings • • executed • in • the • covnties • of • • Norfolk • • Svffolk • • Yorkshire • • Staffordshire • • Warwickshire • • Hertfordshire • • et • caetera • • By • Iohn • Soane • Architect • • Member • of • the • Royal • Academies • • of • Parma • and • Florence •

London: • Pvblished • by • Messrs. • Taylor • at • the • architectvral • library • • Holborn •, 1788.

[vi] + 11 pp, 16 printed leaves, 47 pls.

57.1 × 38.3 cm

MnU

This collection of houses, interiors, outbuildings, lodges, a bridge, a dairy, and a museum documents Soane's increasing success as a domestic architect as he reached his thirty-fifth birthday.[1] Following the dedication to the king, a list of subscribers, and a table of contents, Soane began his Introduction with general remarks on the importance and greatness of architecture, supported by lengthy quotations from Alberti, Vitruvius, Martial, Horace, and Pliny. For his own part Soane suggested the architect "not . . . blindly and servilely copy the ancient buildings," but "cautiously examine them, and if possible catch the spirit of them" (p. 3). Therefore he recommended not only "contemplating the venerable remains of ancient grandeur" but also studying "the works of Raphael, Michael Angelo, Julio Romano, Palladio, Scamozzi, Vignola, and the other great restorers of architecture, and studiously observe, how they cautiously used the inestimable remains of antiquity" (p. 4). He decried the present taste for "fashion" in architecture, "which renders learning and application needless" (p. 5). True architecture, he said, "is a coy mistress that can only be won by unwearied assiduities, and constant attention; but when the mind is wedded to it, the imagination is always filled with wonder and delight" (p. 5). Considering the use of ornament, he counseled restraint: "such ornaments only should be used, as tend to shew the destination of the edifice, [and] as assist in determining its character" (p. 8). Four paragraphs later he revealed great respect for the power of Gothic architecture to stimulate imaginative expansion: Gothic buildings "are so well calculated to excite solemn, serious and contemplative ideas, that it is almost impossible to enter such edifices without feeling the deepest awe and reverence" (p. 9). He concluded the Introduction by noting that every design must be adapted to its own "situation," and that in every case the architect must take into account "the difference in manner of living, and the different ideas of convenience, comfort, and elegance" that every client will have (pp. 10–11).

Soane's designs reflect a growing taste in the late eighteenth century for diminutive, informal residences.[2] The design in Plate I, for example, includes eight principal rooms on the ground floor, but effectively disguises them behind a facade just three openings wide. Other designs for dwellings, such as those at Letton, Tendring, and Hockeril, exhibit a similarly diminutive scale, accented by spare ornamentation. In the Introduction Soane had noted his desire "to unite convenience and comfort in the interior distributions, and simplicity and uniformity in the exterior" (p. 11).

Soane's designs for interior renovations and room additions exhibit more elaborate ornamentation than do his exterior facades. Yet even his elegant frieze sculptures, ceiling coffers, and other ornaments remain subject to a clear geometric order.

A special case is his design for the facade of a dairy at Hammels, in Hertfordshire (Plate 44). A thatch roof suggests rusticity, as do four rough tree trunks serving as columns for the portico. In contrast, the pediment is executed in a precisely delineated and correct Doric style, while a more informal relief sculpture of a cow fills its center. This combination of the formal and the rustic, plus a droll advertisement of the building's function, clearly diverges from the Neoclassical orthodoxy exemplified in Soane's other designs. Yet the divergence, in this case, is excused and even justified by the building's necessarily rural location and romantically primitive function as a retreat for an aristocratic lady.[3]

1. The Introduction is dated 10 September, his birthday.

2. See Summerson (1959).

3. For a recent detailed discussion of this dairy see Pierre de la Ruffinière Du Prey, *John Soane: The Making of an Architect* (Chicago: University of Chicago Press, 1982), pp. 245–252. For a more general discussion of Soane's "primitivism" see John Summerson, "Soane: the Man and the Style," in Architectural Monographs, *John Soane* (London: Academy Editions, 1983), pp. 16–19.

320.1
SOANE, Sir John (1753–1837)
Sketches in architecture; containing plans and elevations of cottages, villas, and other useful buildings, with characteristic scenery. By John Soane. . . . To which are added six designs for improving and embellishing of grounds, with sections and explanations. By an amateur. The whole engraved on fifty-four plates.

London: Printed for I. and J. Taylor, 1793.

[*Part I:*] [i] + iv pp, 43 pls.

[*Part II:*] iv + 20 pp, 11 pls.

43.8 × 29.8 cm

MH

320.2
———
Sketches in architecture; ⟨ . . . as 1793 . . . ⟩ are added, six ⟨ . . . as 1793 . . . ⟩ plates.

London: Printed for J. Taylor, 1798.

[*Part I:*] [i] + iv pp, 43 pls.

[*Part II:*] iv + 20 pp, 11 pls.

42.9 × 27.9 cm

NNC

In the title Soane indicated that he provided his designs "with characteristic scenery," a phrase that prefigured the special attention Humphry Repton gave to the relation between architectural and landscape "characters" in *Sketches and Hints* (q.v.), published one year later.[1] But while Repton analyzed both architectural and landscape forms in an effort to establish principles of compatibility, Soane made no further mention of the "characteristic" relation between landscape and scenery. Fortunately the plates, discussed below, offer some insight into Soane's understanding of this term.

In the single-page Introduction Soane referred briefly to the buildings, "chiefly on a large scale," that he had published five years earlier in *Plans Elevations and Sections* (1788; q.v.), indicating that the present designs were "on a smaller scale" and "within the reach of moderate fortunes." The principal contents of the book are "cottages for the laborious and industrious part of the community, and . . . other buildings generally calculated for the real uses and comforts of life."[2] Following a few short comments on siting and materials for cottages, Soane noted that all these designs, for cottages and "villas," had been "made for particular persons and situations."

The brief plate explanations (pp. i–iv) contain remarks on siting, materials, dimensions, and floor plans, with occasional mention of the client and location for which individual designs were intended. The plates depict each design in one view and one or more plans. Altogether there are 25 designs, including one lodge, seven double cottages, six "Houses," four villas, alterations and additions to one villa, two proposals for a "Hunting Casine," a National Mausoleum, a "Belle-Vue," a "Castello d'acqua," and an "Ice House." The double cottages are generally alike in size and in plan, ranging from 30 to 50 feet wide, with each unit containing a sitting room, washhouse, and pantry on the ground floor, and one to three chambers upstairs. One of the smallest "Houses" is that "designed for an Artist" (Plates XIII, XIV). The ground-floor plan is 66 feet wide and contains a drawing room, breakfast parlor, eating room, library, and kitchen. There are five chambers upstairs. The two-story elevation is unremarkable, with one-story pilasters supporting segmental relieving arches over the ground-floor windows, and little other ornament. The surrounding scenery includes trees, grass, and a lawn roller casually abandoned in the left foreground. Most of the "Houses" and "Villas" are somewhat larger. The "Villa" in Plates XXIV and XXV is typical: the ground-floor plan is 82 feet wide, and includes a vestibule, tribune, dressing room, eating room, breakfast room, drawing room, and library. Upstairs there are four chambers plus dressing rooms and closets.

All of Soane's elevations are scrupulously symmetrical. Many of the cottages are embellished in a picturesque manner, with thatch roofs, brick arches over the windows, a surface treatment suggestive of rough plaster or stucco, and even columns made of tree trunks in Plates VIII and IX. The surrounding scenery includes fences, lawns, water, trees, winding paths, and distant hills. In contrast the houses and villas are ornamented in a Neoclassical manner—sometimes quite plain, and in other cases embellished with fluted pilasters, Classical porticoes, decorative garlands, and similar features. The landscape surroundings include distant hills, streams, trees, fences, curving drives, and clouds. In all these designs the "characteristic" relation between scenery and architecture seems to be founded on the premise that both picturesque and Neoclassical designs accord well with smooth, rounded landscape forms. The symmetry and prismatic clarity of the elevations are complemented by the soft, rounded forms of the lush scenery, forming well balanced and harmonious compositions. Indeed only one design suggests a more dynamic relation between the structure and its environment. In the project for a "Belle-Vue" (Plate XL) a solid rectangular base, set on a small hill, has a scalloped parapet, carved away to complement the two-story round turret rising above and encompassing the view on all sides. An adjacent tree visually anchors the base of the "Belle-Vue" to the top of the hill, with possible associations of "rootedness." A sharp drop-off at the right to the valley below balances the thrust that the tower makes into the open air. Yet even here the "characteristic" scenery is smooth, rounded, and carefully composed to complement the form of the building.

1. In the same year (1794) two more authors considered the matter of picturesque relations between architecture and scenery: see Richard Payne Knight, *The Landscape* (*q.v.*); and Sir Uvedale Price, *An Essay on the Picturesque*.

2. On the subject of cottages compare two contemporary publications: John Wood's *Series of Plans, for Cottages* (1792; *q.v.*) is devoted entirely to plain, unornamented designs, while Charles Middleton's *Picturesque and Architectural Views* (1793; *q.v.*) includes symmetrical, geometric, but picturesquely ornamented designs for cottages.

321.1

SOCIETY **for Bettering the Condition of the Poor, in the Hundred of Oswestry, and Parishes of Chirk and Llansilin**
First report of the Society for Bettering the Condition of the Poor, in the Hundred of Oswestry, and Parishes of Chirk and Llansilin.

Oswestry: Printed and sold by T. Edwards, for the Society, 1813.

16 pp, 2 pls, 1 folding table.

22.3 × 14.0 cm

MH

In 1813 the president of the society, Thomas Netherton Parker, prepared a separate pamphlet illustrating plans for two model cottages for laborers, which he published as *Plans, Specifications, Estimates, and Remarks on Cottages* (*q.v.*). In the same year the society issued this, its *First Report*, including a brief statement of purpose, the society's rules, the prizes it proposed to offer, subscribers' names, and an account of "Friendly Societies, Schools, Population, and Poors Rate [*sic*] in the District." The report also includes two plates illustrating a model cottage in elevation, section, and two plans. The design, prepared by Richard Griffiths, is two stories high with a bedroom, kitchen, pantry, bake house, and other offices on the ground floor, and two bedrooms above.

322.1 ‡
SOPWITH, Thomas (1803–1879)
Practical observations on the easy and rapid delineation of plans and drawings, in isometrical and other modes of projection; intended to accompany and explain the projecting and parallel rulers, and isometrical drawing paper. By T. Sopwith. . . .

[Newcastle]: Printed for the author, 1836.

iv + 40 pp, 1 pl.

17.8 × 10.7 cm

Reference: Microfilm supplied by Yale University Library.

"The immediate object" of this treatise, according to Sopwith, "is to explain certain methods of constructing drawings, by which accuracy and expedition are combined with facility of execution" (p. iii). He intended it in part as "a brief letter-press description" of the use of "Parallel and Projecting Rulers" (p. iv). He prepared the work "in conformity with the rules of a society, established in Newcastle, which has for its object the improvement of its members in various departments of the fine and useful arts" (p. iii).

The text proceeds from definitions to demonstrations, with references to other writings on the subject and lengthy instruction in the use of "isometrical drawing paper." The sole plate, bound as a frontispiece, includes 13 figures. Figures 1–4 and 11–13 are geometric diagrams. Figures 5–10 are perspective views of a two-story house, three windows wide. Two views are isometric, one showing the entire house and the other looking in on the ground floor, with the upper floor removed. The other views show the same subjects rendered according to different methods, described elsewhere by Sopwith as "verti-horizontal" and "verti-lateral" drawing.[1]

1. All six figures depicting the house appear in Sopwith's *Treatise on Isometrical Drawing* (1834; *q.v.*).

323.1
SOPWITH, Thomas (1803–1879)
A treatise on isometrical drawing, as applicable to geological and mining plans, picturesque delineations of ornamental grounds, perspective views and working plans of buildings and machinery, and to general purposes of civil engineering; with details of improved methods of perserving plans and records of subterranean operations in mining districts. With thirty= four copperplate engravings. By T. Sopwith. . . .

London: John Weale, Taylor's Architectural Library, 1834.

xxvi + 239 pp, frontisp. + additional engraved title page + 32 pls.

21.0 × 13.5 cm

DLC

A treatise on isometrical drawing, ⟨ . . . as 1834 . . . ⟩ mining districts. Second edition. Thirty-five engravings. By T. Sopwith. . . .

London: John Weale, 1838.

xxv + 224 pp, frontisp. + additional engraved title page + 33 pls [*frontisp. wanting in this copy*].

21.1 × 13.3 cm

MnM

The frontispiece is a perspective view of Capheaton Hall, Northumberland (1668), and its surrounding grounds; Sopwith wanted to demonstrate that "isometrical drawing is well adapted" to illustrating "the old English style of gardening" (p. 190).[1] A vignette on the engraved title page depicts Chesterholme, Northumberland; the illustration is "an example of the manner in which isometrical drawing may be applied to ornamental as well as useful pusposes" (p. 194).

In the Preface (pp. v–viii) Sopwith indicated that his "object" was "to elucidate the principles of Isometrical Projection, and to explain its application to a variety of useful purposes," including "the construction of Geological Maps, and of Plans and Sections of Mines" (p. v), as well as making "Plans and Elevations of Buildings, and for working details of Machinery," or "representing Gardens and Pleasure grounds," harbors, bridges, and "other engineering Plans" (p. vi). He wanted to provide "a book which may be practically useful and intelligible to every class of readers," including "mathematical students" as well as "Amateur Artists, and especially . . . Ladies, who are thus enabled to combine the beauties of Landscape, Architectural, and Flower Painting, with useful and correct delineations of pleasure-grounds, houses, gardens, or other objects" (pp. vii, vi). A detailed table of contents (pp. ix–xviii), an "Explanation" of the plates (pp. xviii–xxiii), and an index of technical terms (pp. xxiv–xxv) conclude the preliminary matter.

The text is divided into six chapters, on mining plans and surveys, principles of isometric projection, techniques of isometric drawing, the application of isometric drawing to geology and mining, its application to "ornamental and landscape gardening," and its application to "plans of buildings and machinery, and to general purposes of civil engineering."

The plates include maps and plans, geometric figures, landscape views, sections of geological strata, and illustrations of protractors, machinery, and a mine shaft. Several plates include architectural subjects. Plate IX includes a plan, two elevations, and a view of a church, an adjacent house, and the underlying geological strata. Plate XIV shows a perspective view in outline of a house with a hipped roof and a chimney.[2] Plate XVII includes six perspective views of a two-story house, three windows wide. Two views are isometric, one showing the entire house and the other looking in on the ground floor, with the upper floor removed. The remaining four views depict the same house according to two alternative methods of oblique perspective. Dubbed "verti-horizontal" or "verti-lateral" drawings (p. 142), they are by comparison clearly inferior: one pair shows too much roof and not enough side wall, while the other pair suffers from the opposite distortion.[3] Plates XXIII and XXIV show plans and views of landscape gardens. Plates XXV and XXVI include a plan, elevations, and a view of a design for a county prison. Plate XXVII contains a plan, elevation, section, and view of Tanfield Arch, near Newcastle. Figures 1 and 2 in Plate XXX show perspective views of a church tower and the monument to Dugald Stewart on Calton Hill in Edinburgh.

1. This discussion is based on the 1838 edition.

2. This plate and two others are signed by Peter Nicholson, whose assistance Sopwith acknowledged in the Preface (p. vii).

3. These six views also appeared as Figures 5–10 in Sopwith's *Practical Observations* (1836; *q.v.*).

324.1
STEVENS, Francis (1781–1823)
Domestic architecture. A series of views of cottages and farm houses, in England and Wales, built chiefly during the dynasty of the house of Stuart. From drawings by S. Prout; R.C. Burney; A. Pugin; C. Varley; J.J. Chalon; W. de La Motte; R. Hills; W.H. Pyne; and others. The plates etched by Francis Stevens.

[London]: M. A. Nattali, [1815].

iv + 36 pp, frontisp. + 53 pls.

36.2 × 28.3 cm

CtY-BA

324.2

———————

Views of cottages and farm-houses in England and Wales: etched by Francis Stevens, from the designs of the most celebrated artists.

London: Published by R. Ackermann. L. Harrison and J. C. Leigh, Printers, 1815.

iv + 36 pp, frontisp. + 53 pls.

36.2 × 29.2 cm

V&A

324.3
[STEVENS, Francis (1781–1823)]
Picturesque sketches of rustic scenery including cottages & farm houses by Prout, Varley, Wilson, Hill, Munn, Pyne, Samuel, Stevens etc. 54, plates, 1815.

[London: R. Ackermann], 1815.

1 printed leaf, frontisp. (= title page) + 53 pls.

35.2 × 27.3 cm

MBAt

324.4

Picturesque sketches ⟨ . . . as 1815 . . . ⟩ etc. 54, plates, 1860.

[N. loc.: N. pub.], 1860.

Frontisp. (= title page) + 53 pls.

37.1 × 28.3 cm

MB

In the first three editions all the plates are dated 1815. In the final edition, the title page bears the date 1860, and the plates are undated.

The Introduction indicates that the plates were "executed by Francis Stevens, from the paintings, drawings, and sketches of amateurs and professional artists" (p. iv). These included Burney, Chalon, Munn, Prout, Pyne, and others.

In the late eighteenth and early nineteenth centuries architects and artists showed increasing interest in picturesque cottage architecture, and Stevens provided the first comprehensive collection of extant examples from around the country, all illustrated in a manner to emphasize their picturesque characteristics.[1] Each subject is surrounded by abundant foliage, and there is special attention to the textures of thatch, brick, wood, broken plaster, tree bark, and leaves. In some cases figures of people and animals enliven the composition.

In the Introduction (pp. iii–iv) Stevens indicated that his purpose was to "yield instruction to the amateur of painting, and amusement to those who delight in contemplating the rural beauties of our isle" (p. iv). Most of the text concerns pictorial composition and painterly technique. There are general remarks on picturesque landscape as well as descriptions of scenery characteristic of particular geographic areas. Additional remarks concern individual painters' techniques, rendering dark and light masses, and depicting light breaking over rough walls.

Like James Malton,[2] Stevens recognized the role of picturesque subjects in stimulating the imagination. Echoing Malton's comment that a door on the latch might signal a warm reception for a neighbor or weary traveler,[3] Stevens remarked that a porch could suggest pleasing family groups relaxing there, enjoying a rest in the summer evening after a long day's work (p. 22). Stevens also noted the hospitality associated with cottages done in an older vernacular style, and lamented their gradual disappearance:

The associations connected with the times when these venerable edifices were supported with that hospitality which prevailed up to the middle of last century, are interesting to all persons of feeling. . . . But a few years more and not a vestige of these mansions, the seats of ancient British hospitality, will remain. (p. 4)

1. For an important architectural study, see James Malton, *An Essay on British Cottage Architecture* (1798; *q.v.*). W. Pickett's *Twenty-four Plates Divided into Ninety-six Specimens of Cottages* ([1812]; *q.v.*) appeared three years earlier than Stevens's book, but did not necessarily depict extant examples.

2. *An Essay on British Cottage Architecture* (1798; *q.v.*).

3. Ibid., p. 5.

325.1
STITT, William

The practical architect's ready assistant; or, builder's complete companion: exhibiting in a comprehensive form the standard prices, and the various trades connected with it, according to the rise and fall of materials at all periods. Also, the timber merchant's assistant: shewing at a view, the manner of measuring timber in its various scantlings, &c. &c. &c. By William Stitt, Architect and Measurer. Dedicated by permission to Francis Johnston. . . . Embellished with fine engravings.

Dublin: Printed for the author, by James Charles, 1819.

iv + viii + 9–358 pp, frontisp. + 3 pls, 5 folding tables.

20.7 × 12.7 cm

RPJCB

In the Preface (pp. iii–iv, dated 1818) Stitt complained that most architectural treatises published in England were "short of being really useful" (p. iii) for the practitioner. Therefore he brought together this set of tables that he had found helpful in his own work. Following a list of 311 subscribers (pp. i–iv) and an index (pp. v–viii), the 350 pages of text consist principally of Stitt's tables and instructions for their use in measuring and estimating.

The frontispiece shows a plan and elevation of "the Lord Primate's House at Rokeby Hall," two stories high and seven windows wide, with Corinthian pilasters and a pediment framing the central three bays. A "Design for a Country Villa in the Most Modern Style" faces page 97. It is a small, plain dwelling two stories high, three windows wide on the upper story and extending further, to five windows, on the ground floor. Facing page 229 is a "Design for a Villa in the Gothic Style," two stories high and five windows wide. A "Design for a Cottage" faces page 337, a more interesting design because of its irregular elevation. The entrance, framed by a small Ionic portico, is perfectly centered and flanked by single windows to the left and right. The roofline, however, is arbitrarily lowered over most of the left portion of the facade, creating an unpleasant imbalance—perhaps meant to suggest picturesque vernacular cottages, and perhaps useful in demonstrating a more difficult problem in measuring.

326.1
SWAN, Abraham

A collection of designs in architecture, containing new plans and elevations of houses, for general use. With a great variety of sections of rooms; from a common room, to the most grand and magnificent. Their decorations, viz. bases, surbases, architraves, freezes, and cornices, properly inriched with foliages, frets and flowers, in a new and grand taste. With margins and mouldings for the panelling. All large enough for practice. To which are added, curious designs of stone and timber bridges, extending from twenty feet to two hundred and twenty, in one arch. Likewise some screens and pavilions. In two volumes. Each containing sixty plates, curiously engraved on copper. By Abraham Swan, Architect. Vol. I.

London: Printed for and sold by the author; by Mr. Meadows; Messrs. Hitch and Hawes; H. Piers and Partner, 1757.

vi + 8 pp, 60 pls.

A collection of designs in architecture, containing new plans and elevations of houses, for general use. With a great variety of sections of rooms; from a common room to the most grand and magnificent. Their decorations, viz. bases, surbases, architraves, freezes, and cornices, properly inriched with foliages, frets and flowers, in a new and grand taste. With margents and mouldings for the penelling; with some rich sections to a larger scale for proportioning the architraves, freezes and cornices to the heighth of the rooms. To which are added, curious designs of stone and timber bridges, extending from twenty feet to two hundred and twenty, in one arch. Likewise some screens and pavilions. In two volumes. Each containing sixty plates, curiously engraved on copper. By Abraham Swan, Architect. Vol. II.

London: Printed for and sold by the author; by Mr. Meadows; Messrs. Hitch and Hawes; H. Piers and Partner, 1757 [–1758].

iv + 12 pp, 65 pls.

40.1 × 25.4 cm

MnU

326.2

_____

A collection of designs in architecture, containing new plans and elevations of houses, for general use. With a great variety of sections of rooms, from a common room to the most grand and magnificent. Their decorations, viz. bases, surbases, architraves, freezes, and cornices, properly inriched with foliages, frets and flowers, in a new and grand taste. With margents and mouldings for the panelling: all large enough for practice. To which are added, curious designs of stone and timber bridges, extending from twenty feet to two hundred and twenty, in one arch. Likewise some screens and pavilions. In two volumes. Each containing sixty plates, curiously engraved on copper. By Abraham Swan, Architect. Vol. I.

London: Printed for and sold by the author; by J. Buckland; and H. Webley, [n.d.; ca. 1770–1775?].

vi + 12 pp, 60 pls [*the plates are those of Vol. II, and the plate descriptions, pp. 1–12, are those for Vol. II*].

A collection of designs in architecture, containing new plans and elevations of houses, for general use. With a variety of sections of rooms, from a common room to the most grand and magnificent. Their decorations, viz. bases, surbases, architraves, freezes, and cornices, properly inriched with foliages, frets and flowers, in a new and grand taste. With margents and mouldings for the penelling; with some rich sections to a larger scale for proportioning the architraves, freezes and cronices to the heighth of the rooms. To which are added, curious designs of stone and timber bridges, extending from twenty feet to two hundred and twenty, in one arch. Likewise some screens and pavilions. In two volumes. Each containing sixty plates, curiously engraved on copper. By Abraham Swan, Architect. Vol. II.

London: Printed for the author: and sold by Henry Webley; and James Buckland, [n.d.; ca. 1770–1775?].

iv + 8 pp, 65 pls [*pls. 1–60 are those of Vol. I, and the plate descriptions, pp. 1–8, are those for Vol. I*].

38.5 × 24.3 cm

DLC

326.3

A collection of designs ⟨ . . . as previous entry . . . ⟩ copper. Besides a description of the buildings, and directions for executing most of the designs in letter press. By Abraham Swan, Architect. Vol. I.

London: Printed for and sold by Robert Sayer, Map and Printseller, [n.d.].

vi + 8 pp, 60 pls.

A collection of designs ⟨ . . . as previous entry . . . ⟩ mouldings for the panelling; with ⟨ . . . as previous entry . . . ⟩ pavilions. With the addition of five new plates of ornaments. In two volumes. Each containing sixty plates, curiously engraved on copper. Besides a description of the buildings, and directions for executing most the designs in letter press. By Abraham Swan, Architect. Vol. II.

London: Printed for and sold by Robert Sayer, Map and Printseller, [n.d.].

iv + 12 pp, 65 pls.

41.9 × 26.7 cm

MH

The exact publication history of this work remains obscure. Of three apparently different editions only one is dated on the title page (1757). Further confusion arises from the title page of the second volume, which in two editions advertises only 60 plates; all copies that I have consulted contain 65 plates. Nor are the five additional plates mentioned in the text. These are all dated January 1758, while the rest of the plates in both volumes are dated from January through November 1757.[1]

The edition in the Rosenwald Collection in the Library of Congress, which according to the imprint was sold by H. (or Henry) Webley, may be dated to 1770–1775, since the Webley firm operated under that name only during those years.[2] In this copy the text and plates for each volume apparently have been bound with the title page and preface for the other volume.

In the undated edition at Harvard, the wording of the title pages has changed significantly, and the plates are no longer dated.

Swan conceived this book for the use of lesser gentry and builders of small country houses. The size of the book is unusually large for such an audience, but it does not reflect grand pretensions so much as a desire to serve the user by illustrating the orders, moldings, and ornaments at a very large scale. Swan offered a few house designs "to accommodate the Great and Noble" (I, iii), but most were directed to "Gentlemen of moderate Fortunes" (I, iii). In making these designs, Swan noted, he consciously avoided the "grand" and "pompous." Instead he believed that true grandeur would result from careful attention to the fundamental "Rules" of the Doric, Ionic, and Corinthian orders (I, iii–iv). He thus inferred that grandeur derives from adherence to the rules of Classical architecture, and not from the massing or articulation of facades and plans. In view of the burgeoning interest in Gothic and Chinese styles during the 1750s, Swan appears conservative and perhaps defensive in his insistence on Classical orthodoxy, which he supported by invoking his "more than Thirty Years Application to, and Experience in, the Theory and Practice of Architecture" (I, iii).[3]

Apart from the short Preface in each volume, the only text consists of very brief plate descriptions in Volume I and somewhat lengthier descriptions in Volume II. Forty-three plates depict elevations and plans for houses. Fifty-two plates illustrate moldings, the orders, and other ornaments. Twenty-two plates depict designs for rooms, walls, screens, and staircases, and there are eight plates of bridges. Most of the house designs are modest in size, ranging from two or three stories high and three windows wide (e.g., II, Plates 1 and 4), to three stories high and seven windows wide (I, Plates 8 and 14). Plates 16 through 20 in Volume II show designs on a much larger scale: one, for example, is 13 windows wide and another has a large dome over the center. Several of the smaller designs have a geometric proportionality, scale, and elegance that are reminiscent of work by Robert Morris (*q.v.*). Altogether the designs exhibit a variety of taste in ornament, ranging from a single design that is so plain as to be dull (I, Plate 15), to others that have heavily rusticated facades (II, Plates 10 and 11), elegant semicircular relieving arches around the windows (II, Plate 4), asymmetrical rococo ornaments in the pediments (II, Plates 11–13, 17, 19), and rusticated Venetian windows (II, Plate 12). In all cases Swan illustrated the plan of the principal floor on the same plate as the elevation. In some plans there appears to be a concern for geometric proportion (e.g., rooms dimensioned according to ratios of 1:1 and 3:4 in II, Plate 8), but most seem to be the result of fitting a given number of rooms into a floor plan of set dimensions. Swan did not indicate that any of his house designs had been executed.

Figure 11

326.2 SWAN–326.3 SWAN

1. Plate 61 in Volume II also bears the inscription "These five Plates are an addition of 1. shillg."

2. James Buckland, the other seller, traded from 1736 to 1789. See Ian Maxted, *The London Book Trades 1775–1800* (Folkestone: Dawson, 1977), pp. 241, 33.

3. Even Sir William Chambers, who thoroughly praised the architecture of Rome in his *Treatise* (1759; *q.v.*), had earlier extolled the aesthetic potential of Chinese architecture in *Designs of Chinese Buildings* (1757). Chambers also supported associational theories of aesthetic response; see the commentary on his *Treatise*.

327.1 ‖
SWITZER, Stephen (1682–1745)

The nobelman, gentleman, and gardener's recreation: or, an introduction to gardening, planting, agriculture, and the other business and pleasures of a country life. By Stephen Switzer.

London: Printed for B. Barker, and C. King, 1715.

2 printed leaves, xxxiv + 266 + [16] pp.

19.8 × 12.1 cm

Reference: Information supplied by Rare Book and Special Collections Division, The Library of Congress.

327.2

Ichnographia rustica: or, the nobleman, gentleman, and gardener's recreation. Containing [*Vol. II:* Being] directions for the general distribution of a country seat, into rural and extensive gardens, parks, paddocks, &c. And a general system of agriculture, illustrated with great variety of copper = plates, done by the best hands, from the author's drawings. Vol. I [*or* II, *or* III]. By Stephen Switzer, Gardener, several years servant to Mr. London and Mr. Wise.

London: Printed for D. Browne, B. Barker and C. King, W. Mears, and R. Gosling, 1718.

[*Volume I:*] xlv + [iii] + 352 + [xvi] pp, frontisp. + 1 pl.

[*Volume II:*] 2 printed leaves, ii + 271 + [vii] pp, 48 leaves of plates (numbered as Plates II–XXIII; Figures 1–14 on 14 leaves; Figures 1–11 on 5 leaves; Plate XXV; unnumbered plate; Plates XXVIII–XXX, XXXII, XXXIV).

[*Volume III:*] 7 printed leaves, xvi + 255 pp, 2 pls.

19.3 × 11.8 cm

DLC

327.3

Ichnographia rustica: or, the nobleman, gentleman, and gardener's recreation. Containing directions for the surveying and distributing of a country-seat into rural and extensive gardens, by the ornamenting and decoration of distant prospects, farms, parks, paddocks, &c. Originally calculated (instead of inclosed plantations) for the embellishment of countries in general; as also for an introduction to a general system of agriculture and planting. Illustrated with above fifty copper plates, done by the best hands, which, though first published above twenty years ago, has given rise to every thing of the kind, which has been done since. The second edition, with large additions. Vol. I [*or* II, *or* III]. By Stephen Switzer, seedsman and gardener at the seedshop in Westminster-Hall.

London: Printed for J. and J. Fox, B. and B. Barker; D. Browne; and F. Gosling, 1742.

[*Volume I:*] 16 + xlv + [iii] + 352 + [xvi] pp, frontisp. + plate tipped in on title page + 1 pl.

[*Volume II: as 1718 edition*].

[*Volume III:*] 6 printed leaves, xvi + 255 pp, 2 pls; 1 pl, one printed leaf, 96 pp.

19.2 × 12.3 cm

DLC

The Nobleman, Gentleman, and Gardener's Recreation (1715) was reissued as the first volume of *Ichnographia Rustica* (1718 and also 1742). The frontispiece and plate(s) in the first volume of *Ichnographia Rustica*, however, are not present in the Library of Congress copy of the 1715 edition. The major difference between the editions of 1718 and 1742 is the addition of a 96-page "Appendix" to the end of Volume III in the 1742 edition.

The order and nature of the contents vary sightly from edition to edition; this précis reflects the arrangement of the final (1742) edition. The work opens with an extensive and authoritative history of gardening (97 pages) from biblical times to the present, including references to the major Classical and Renaissance writers on horticulture and landscape. Subsequent chapters treat earth, precipitation, sun, air, trees, springs, statues, grass, and gravel. The second volume begins with instruction in geometry, mathematics, and surveying, followed by chapters devoted to various types of landscape forms: courtyards, terrace walks, parterres, woods, groves, wildernesses, parks, espalier trees and hedges, fruit gardens and fruit trees, and orchards and vineyards. In the third volume Switzer addressed more general aesthetic issues, with chapters on design and siting, discussion of individual examples, and a "Description of a beautiful Rural Garden." The greater part of this volume, however, is devoted to "the Management and Improvement of Arable Land," and includes discussion of tools, dung, manure, enclosures, ploughing, sowing, draining, and other miscellaneous topics. The 1742 "Appendix" offers further observations on sun, earth, air, and water, a discussion of the motion of sap in trees, observations on "spontaneous Production of Plants," and a "Dissertation on Mushrooms."

Switzer's principal contributions to the art of landscape gardening were to challenge the prevailing French manner of symmetrical composition on a large scale,[1] and to promote imaginative expansion in the viewer's mind in a manner similar to that proposed by Addison.[2] He proposed that the viewer should no longer by hemmed in by geometry, but rather be free to experience the full beauty and extent of unrestrained nature: "where-ever Liberty will allow, [I] would throw my Garden open to all View, to the unbounded Felicities of distant Prospect, and the expansive Volumes of Nature herself." At the same time he would accommodate another side of the psyche by offering "some private Walks and Cabinets of Retirement, some select Places of Recess for Reading and Contemplation."[3]

Switzer also recognized the potential for human expression in the design of a country residence. Of all the works of Creation, he said, "a Country Seat distributed with Judgment, may well be accounted one of the greatest; in this every Person makes to himself a Kind of new Creation, and when a Seat or Villa, is decently and frugally distributed, what a Harmony does it create in a virtuous Mind."[4] A similar expressiveness could be achieved in smaller structures: he recommended

the Erection of all Lodges, Granges, and other Buildings that Gentlemen are obliged to build, for Conveniency, in the Form of some Antiquated Place, which will be more beautiful than the most curious Architecture: There seems to be a much more inexpressible Entertainment to a Virtuous and Thoughtful Mind, in Desolate Prospects, Cool murmuring Streams, and Grots, and in several other Cheap and Natural Embellishments, than in what many of our modern Designers have recommended.[5]

Switzer offered little comment on the specifics of architectural design, but included views and plans of dwellings in several plates. The frontispiece to Volume I shows a formal parterre, at the far end of which is a two-story mansion, 15 windows wide, in late seventeenth-century style. In Volume II, Plate VI shows a vast parterre with fountains, walks, and beds of plantings, flanked on at least two sides by wings of what appears to be a large palace. At the bottom of Plate VIII there is a vignette showing houses flanking a canal, apparently in a Belgian or Dutch town because of the stepped gables on several of the dwellings. Plate XI shows a portion of a parterre flanked on one side by a dense wall of trees, while on the opposite side there is a three-story structure—perhaps a wing of a mansion or palace—eight windows wide and at least three windows deep. Picturesque towers and farm buildings are included in the vignettes at the bottom of Plates XVII and XX. Figure 1 in Plate XXIII shows "The Genll. Sketch of a Building" in plan, a main pile approximately 200 feet wide and 100 feet deep, flanked by two wings each 200 feet wide and 60 feet deep. Adjacent to the building are gardens extending some 1,200 feet away. Plate XXV shows a more detailed plan of a mansion—including ten principal rooms on the ground floor—and a landscaped parterre beyond. A brief passage titled "A description of Plate the 26th"[6] apparently refers to this plate, and offers some insight into Switzer's ideas of domestic design. Switzer recommended that "a private Gentleman," in order not to exceed the bounds of propriety, should not "begin his House much larger than what is in this Design; he ought to be very moderate and plain in the Furniture of his Building, and of the Magnificence of his adjacent Gardens and Court-Yards" (II, 146). The building would be 80 feet wide and 35 feet deep, encompassing a drawing room and dining room on the central axis, flanked by a pair of drawing rooms ("or Bed-chambers") on each side, with four "Closets" at the four corners of the structure. Switzer offered on remarks on style, and little on the subject of ornament except to suggest that restraint would save money that could be used "for the Embellishment of the adjacent Fields" (II, 146).

1. 1742, I, 10.

2. Quoting from Addison, Switzer remarked that "Our Imagination loves to be filled with an Object" (1742, III, 3). Thus the designer should become 'thoroughly conversant in the various Scenes of a Country Seat" (III, 6) in order to provide the material objects necessary to imaginative expansion. Indeed "the Designer as well as the Poet should take as much Pains in forming his Imagination, as a Philosopher in cultivating his Understanding" (III, 6), since "the chief Satisfaction and Pleasure of the Mind (next to it's own Serenity, Innocence and Tranquillity, and the Noblest Instinct of human Nature, it's Sacred, Inexpressible and Divine Efferviscence) arises from, and it's Flame is maintain'd by exterior Objects" (III, i).

On Addison and imaginative expansion, see *The Spectator*, Nos. 411–421 (21 June through 3 July 1712); Clarence DeWitt Thorpe, "Addison and Hutcheson on the Imagination," *E.L.H.*, II:3 (November 1935), 215–234; Thorpe, "Addison's Theory of the Imagination as 'Perceptive Response,'" *Papers of the Michigan Academy of Science, Arts, and Letters*, XXI (1935), 509–530; and Ernest Lee Tuveson, *The Imagination as a Means of Grace* (Berkeley: University of California Press, 1960).

3. 1742, I, xxxv–xxxvi.

4. 1742, III, iii.

5. 1742, I, 317.

6. 1718 and 1742, II, 145–149.

328.1

TAYLOR, Arthur Creagh

Designs for agricultural buildings suited to Irish estates, including labourers' cottages, lodges for out-door servants, farm houses with their offices, etc. The whole designed with due attention to convenience, comfort, and economy, and having an accurate estimate appended to each design. Engraved on twenty copper plates. By Arthur Creagh Taylor, Architect. To which is added, some remarks on the improvement of the condition of cottagers in this country, by J. Naper, Esq. . . .

Dublin: Grant and Bolton, 1841.

1 printed leaf, iv + 5–13 + [i] pp, 17 printed leaves, 20 pls.

27.3 × 21.6 cm

CtY-BA

Following a list of 157 subscribers (pp. i–iv), Taylor explained in the Introduction (pp. 5–6) that he prepared this collection of 16 designs for dwellings in part because of increasing concern in Ireland for the living conditions of the "tenantry" (p. 5). Four years earlier William Deane Butler had published a similar book,[1] and treatises concerned with the welfare of Scottish laborers and peasants also appeared in the mid- and late 1830s.[2] Taylor wanted to encourage the Irish tenantry to build their own houses, but recognized there could be little progress without "model plans" to work from. Therefore Taylor offered this collection of designs, some of which already had been "adopted" on large estates (p. 5). Taylor also included a letter from Mr. J. Naper of Loughcrew, with remarks on financing such projects (pp. 7–9), general specifications for earthwork, masonry, carpentry, slating, and plastering (pp. 10–12), and "rules for estimating the cost" of the designs (p. 13).

The 16 designs are illustrated in plan and elevation on 20 plates, without scenery or other embellishment. They are described in letterpress on the verso of page 13 and on additional, unnumbered printed leaves. The designs include seven single and double cottages for farmers, laborers, and servants, four single and double farm houses with offices, two lodges, a "farm residence" with offices, and a set of four attached houses suitable for a village or a small town. The smallest design, for a laborer's cottage (Plate I), includes a kitchen, two bedrooms, a scullery, and a dairy. Taylor estimated the cost at £25. The largest design, for a farm residence (Plate XIX), includes a dining room, parlor, kitchen, hall, and two bedrooms, which Taylor estimated would cost £230. He noted that in most designs "nearly all ornament has been dispensed with." The only exceptions were the Tudor forester's lodge (Plate XVIII) and the Neoclassical farm residence (Plate XIX), "which differ in their character and purpose from the others" (p. 6).

1. Butler, *Model Farm-houses and Cottages for Ireland* (1837; *q.v.*).

2. See George Smith, *Essay on the Construction of Cottages* (1834); and Highland and Agricultural Society of Scotland, "Remarks on Cottage Premiums" (1839).

329.1
[TAYLOR, Charles (1756–1823)]
"Of architecture" [by Francis Fitzgerald, pseud. for Charles Taylor], *The Artist's Repository and Drawing Magazine, Exhibiting the Principles of the Polite Arts in Their Various Branches* III (London: Printed for C. Taylor, 1788), 141–196, and 34 pls.

MnU

329.2
———

"Principles of architecture," *The Artist's Repository, or Encyclopedia of the Fine Arts Vol: 2. Perspective, Architecture* (London: Published by C. Taylor, 1808), 1–96, frontisp., and 50 pls.

MnU

The commentary for Entry 329 is combined with that for Entry 330 below.

330.1
[TAYLOR, Charles (1756–1823)]
"Of perspective" [by Francis Fitzgerald, pseud. for Charles Taylor], *The Artist's Repository and Drawing Magazine, Exhibiting the Principles of the Polite Arts in Their Various Branches* III (London: Printed for C. Taylor, 1788), i–iv + 5–140, and 20 pls (numbered 1–16, and 4 unnumbered).

MnU

"On perspective," *The Artist's Repository, or Encyclopedia of the Fine Arts Vol: 2. Perspective, Architecture* (London: Published by C. Taylor, 1808), 5–143, and 51 pls.

MnU

330.3
TAYLOR, Charles (1756–1823)

A familiar treatise on perspective; in four essays:
Essay I. On the theory of vision, and the principles of perspective as therewith connected.
Essay II. Elements of the practice of perspective, definitions and explanation of terms.
Essay III. The perspective of shadows.
Essay IV. On keeping, or aërial perspective.
By Charles Taylor.
The principles developed in this treatise are illustrated by fifty one engravings; accompanied by correct descriptions and familiar explanations.

London: Printed by R. & R. Gilbert, for C. Taylor, 1816.

143 + [i] pp, 51 pls [*pls. VII, VIII are wanting in this copy*].

23.0 × 14.5 cm

ICN

The Artist's Repository and Drawing Magazine was issued in six parts between 1785 and 1794.[1] A revised edition appeared in four volumes in 1808. This contains just seven articles: in Volume I, "The Human Figure"; in Volume II, "Perspective" and "Architecture" (both of which had been in Volume III [1788] of the previous edition); in Volume III, "Landscape" and "A Compendium of Colors"; and in Volume IV, "A Dictionary of Principles and Terms of Art" and "A Concise History of the Arts of Design." The article on perspective was reset and reprinted as a separate volume in 1816, under the title *A Familiar Treatise on Perspective*.

The individual articles were not signed. Taylor's name appears only as publisher in *The Artist's Repository and Drawing Magazine*. Nevertheless the title page of *A Familiar Treatise on Perspective* establishes his authorship of at least the perspective article. The pseudonym Francis Fitzgerald appears on the title pages for the "First Sett" and "Second Set" of lectures (first edition, Vols. I and III), which treat drawing, perspective, architecture, and landscape.

The article on architecture consists of two "Lectures."[2] The first opens with Pope's epithet "the proper study of mankind is man," and a suggestion that "a very proper part of that study, is, to trace the efforts of human ingenuity," particularly in architecture (1808, p. 1). There follow brief remarks on "the original dwelling of man" (1808, p. 1), the progress of civilization and the arts, and architecture in biblical, "Druidical," and

Classical times (1808, pp. 1–11). There is mixed praise for Gothic architecture: it "was peculiar and barbarous; dissimilar in its parts, multifarious, and injudicious, in its ornaments; confused, and perplexed, in its distribution. But . . . it was correspondent to the hood, the cowl, the beads, the superstition of the times, and, even now, has great effect in producing solemnity and reverence, and striking with awe the man of observation" (1808, p. 12). This seeming equivocation over the romantic possibilities of Gothic is soon resolved into a clear denunciation: "Gothic architecture is a striking instance of the necessity of order; for, if the architects of the times . . . had studied uniformity and symmetry . . . they might have discarded . . . those labyrinthine ornaments, with which they endeavoured to conceal disproportion." By adopting "principles of regularity . . . they might have shewn, that their manner was susceptible of effects . . . not always disgusting, or even despicable" (1808, pp. 12–13). This Lecture concludes with remarks on the adaptation of design to climate and praise for the architecture of modern Britain. Accompanying the first Lecture are ten plates, described in ten pages of letterpress (1808, pp. 17–27). They illustrate "primitive" dwellings, biblical, Egyptian, Greek, and Roman temples, and Christian churches (e.g., St. Mark's in Venice and St. Peter's in Rome). The "primitive" dwelling[3] is little more than a square cella with a recessed doorway. Some of the designs for temples are conjectural (e.g., prostyle, peripteral, dipteral, and hypaethral temples),[4] while other plates show Classical monuments that were frequently adapted for use as garden structures (e.g., the Temple of the Winds, the Monument of Lysicrates, and one of the temples at Baalbek).[5]

The second Lecture concerns "principles" of architecture, and briefly mentions uniformity, symmetry, variety, decoration, and ornament (1808, pp. 29–38). Most of the Lecture (1808, pp. 38–50) is devoted to the orders, and it closes with a short, impressionistic description of a house in both Doric and Ionic style where "health and serenity" and "peace and tranquillity shall fix their residence"; where the inhabitants can exercise their "important prerogatives as rational, and immortal, beings, whose views extend beyond the narrow compass of this limited globe" (1808, p. 54). The 40 plates that accompany this Lecture are explained in brief descriptive comments (1808, pp. 55–88). Two plates illustrate the progress of dwellings from rude "Hottentot" huts to conjectural reconstructions of early Doric huts.[6] Other plates show Egyptian temples, columns, and obelisks. Most of the plates are devoted to the Tuscan, Doric, Attic, Ionic, Corinthian, and Composite orders. A few final plates illustrate the Temple of Fortuna Virilis, the Pantheon, the Banqueting House in Whitehall, St. Paul's, and St. Peter's. The article closes with eight pages on "practical building," including remarks on siting, materials, form, foundations, walls, apertures, distribution, roofs, and ornament.

The article on perspective consists of four "Lectures" each followed by plates and plate descriptions.[7] The first Lecture includes remarks on the eye as an organ of sight, perception, lines, and planes. Subsequent lectures consider principles of perspective, shadows, keeping, and foreshortening. Most of the plates depict geometric diagrams or simple objects in perspective. A few show more complex subjects such as room interiors and dwellings. There are two landscape scenes with churches and two-story houses five windows wide,[8] plus three landscapes with one- and two-story cottages and farm houses.[9] Two plates show perspective views of simple box forms with gable roofs.[10]

1. The *Union List of Serials* (3rd ed., I, 500) indicates that the set includes five volumes. Instructions to the binder on the final page of the final part read: "This Work may be bound in Two Volumes or in Four." The four volumes would be constituted as follows: I, the "First Sett of Lectures," on drawing; II, "A Compendium of Colors" and the first series of "Miscellanies"; III, the "Second Set of Lectures," on perspective, architecture, and landscape; IV, the "Dictionary" and Part II of the "Miscellanies." Individual title pages also indicate that the "Compendium of Colors" should be in Vol. II, and the "Dictionary" in Vol. IV.

Somewhat differently dated editions of *The Artist's Repository and Drawing Magazine* are listed in ECBB (II, 492; and IV, 403) and in the *British Union-Catalogue of Periodicals* (New York: Academic Press, 1955), I, 225.

2. This description applies primarily to the 1808 edition.

3. In 1788 and 1808, Pl. I, Nos. 1 and 2.

4. In 1788 and 1808, Pl. III.

5. In 1788 and 1808, Pls. VIII–X.

6. In 1788, Pls. XX–XXI. The Hottentot huts do not appear in the 1788 edition. In 1808, Pls. XI–XII. The Doric structures are copied directly and without attribution from those in the first plate of Chambers's *Treatise* (1759; *q.v.*), where they are identified as "The Second Sort of Huts" and "The Third sort of Huts which gave birth to the Doric Order."

7. This description applies primarily to the 1808 edition.

8. Not in the 1788 edition, but see the view of a town center in one of the unnumbered plates; Pls. XIII and XIV in 1808 and 1816.

9. Pls. XXXI, XLIII, and XLV in the 1808 and 1816 editions. See Pls. X, XV, XVI, and three of the unnumbered plates in the 1788 edition.

10. Pls. XXXVI and XXXVII in 1808 edition; not in the 1788 edition.

331.1
THOMAS, William (–1800)
Original designs in architecture, by William Thomas, M.S.A. Architect and Surveyor: consisting of twenty-seven copper-plates, in folio; which contain plans, elevations, sections, cielings, and chimney pieces, for villas and town houses; dewigns for temples, grottos, sepulchres, bridges, &c. in the most approved taste. To which are prefixed, a suitable introduction, and a description, explaining the several designs.

London: Printed for the author, 1783.

12 pp, 27 pls.

53.3 × 37.5 cm

MH

In the Introduction (pp. 4–5) Thomas noted that "Perfection" in architecture comes from making "*Convenience* go hand in hand with *Elegance*, by reducing, to *certain general Rules*, an Institution which owed its Birth, like most others, to Necessity, the common Parent of Invention" (p. 4). Tracing the history of that "Institution," namely architecture, Thomas concluded that in Rome, together with "Music, Poetry, Painting, and every liberal Science, Architecture was found in its Perfection" (p. 4). But Thomas did not contend that the practice of architecture should be entirely circumscribed by rules. He noted in the Preface (p. 3) that architecture "is not founded wholly on a System of Problems and Deductions, but requires a peculiar Turn of Mind; and . . . it thus depends in a great Measure on the Imagination." The architect must have both "Genius" and "Judgment, matured by Habit and constant Application" (p. 5).

Thomas's designs, described on pages 7–10, include a nobleman's villa, a mausoleum, a banqueting house, a "Casino" or country retreat, a Gothic garden temple, a bridge, a gate with lodges, the offices at Stackpole Court, Surrey Chapel, a house for Mr. Mirehouse, a hunting seat, a grotto, and several projects for interior furnishings. Thomas's style is Neoclassical, symmetrical, and often dry. The elevations and plans make obvious use of squares, double squares, and circles. Even the Gothic temple appears Classically inspired, with a square plan and elevation, a regular tripartite division of the facade, and Classical urns set in niches in the front. The decorative detail of Thomas's ceiling and furniture designs is reminiscent of contemporary work by Robert Adam.

THOMPSON, J.
"Foreign notices.—Australia."

See LOUDON, **John Claudius, ed.,** The architectural magazine, Entry 182.

332.1
THOMPSON, William
Practical directions for the speedy and economical establishment of communities, on the principles of mutual co-operation, united possessions and equality of exertions and of the means of enjoyments. By William Thompson. . . .

London: Strange, and E. Wilson. Sold at the office of the British Association for Promoting Co-operative Knowledge, [1830].

1 printed leaf, iv + 265 + xiii pp, 1 pl, 1 table.

21.0 × 12.7 cm

IEN

At a time when laborers' dwellings and even entire communities for laborers commanded increasing attention from architects,[1] Thompson published this design for a community as part of a proposal for an economic system of "Co-operative Industry" that would assure a continuing market for goods produced by workers who joined together in "voluntary union" (p. i). Thompson considered a wide variety of issues involved in founding a community with economic self-sufficiency as its goal: methods of obtaining initial funds and land, the optimal number of inhabitants (2,000) and how to select them, agricultural and manufacturing enterprises, sources of power, health, education, recreation, and administrative organization.

In an early section of the treatise (pp. 52–93) Thompson discussed his design for a large single structure in which the community would live and work. As illustrated in the frontispiece, the structure would consist of a continuous three-story range completely surrounding a "great domestic Square" of 36 acres. The principal elevation, 1305 feet long, was articulated into seven attached units, each slightly advancing or receding, a total of 130 windows across. Altogether there would be dwelling space for 2,000 "persons of all ages." Domestic "rooms," flanking corridors running the full length of each range, would be of three types: approximately 1,440 "sleeping rooms" for one person, approximately 1,380 "sitting rooms" for one person, and 36 "sitting rooms" for two people. Children would be housed in an attic story above. Other rooms at various intervals along the corridors would accommodate washing, drying, bathing, health care, education, public lectures, printing, bookkeeping, storage, cooking, a library, and a museum. Adjoining the exterior of one side of the great square Thompson indicated another quadrangle, approximately 730 feet on a side, intended to accommodate linen, woolen, and cotton manufacturing, dressmaking and other crafts, a flour mill, cow houses, a dairy, and a threshing machine.

In his text description Thompson was concerned less with matters of style and expression than with such practical matters as access to power, light, heat, ventilation, and water. He suggested that any choice of ornament should reflect the taste of the community as a whole, and that his designs for "internal arrangements" were compatible with "Gothic, Grecian, Egyptian or Barbarian" styles (p. 54). He did not expect that a community would erect such a large structure all at once, but rather recommended that work progress in stages, with a section 100 feet long to be added each year. He firmly believed in the importance of contiguous, communal dwellings, arguing somewhat ironically that detached dwellings result in "loss of *personal independence*" (p. 58). In other words just as economic independence was predicated on a system of "Co-operative Industry," so personal independence relied on the communal support available only in a large, functionally integrated residence such as Thompson proposed.

1. See, for example, the following treatises: Allen, *Colonies at Home* (1826); *Facts and Illustrations Demonstrating the . . . Benefits . . . Derived by Labourers from Possessing Small Portions of Land* (1831 and later); Whitwell, *Description of an Architectural Model . . . for a Community* (1830); Smith, *Essay on the Construction of Cottages Suited for . . . the Labouring Classes* (1834); Butler, *Model Farm-Houses* (1837), *qq.v.* On Thompson, who was an associate of Robert Owen, Jeremy Bentham, and John Stuart Mill, see Richard Keir Pethick Pankhurst, *William Thompson (1775–1833): Britain's Pioneer Socialist, Feminist, and Co-operator* (London: Watts & Co., 1954).

333.1
THOMSON, James (1800–1883)
Retreats: a series of designs, consisting of plans and elevations for cottages, villas, and ornamental buildings. By J. Thomson, Architect.

London: Printed for J. Taylor, 1827.

viii + 32 pp, 41 pls.

27.9 × 22.5 cm

MH

333.2

———

———

London: Printed for J. Taylor, 1833.

viii + 32 pp, 41 pls.

32.1 × 24.8 cm

NNC

333.3

———

———

London: Printed for M. Taylor, nephew and successor to the late Josiah Taylor, 1835.

viii + 32 pp, 41 pls.

29.5 × 23.2 cm

MH

333.4 ‖

———

———

Second edition.

London: M. Taylor, (nephew and successor to the late Josiah Taylor), 1840.

vi + 7–36 pp, 41 pls.

31.2 × 24.5 cm

Reference: Information supplied by Humanities Research Center, University of Texas, Austin.

333.5

———

———

Second edition.

London: M. Taylor, (nephew and successor to the late Josiah Taylor), 1854.

vi + 7–36 pp, 41 pls.

30.5 × 23.5 cm

NN

The discussion below is based on examination of the 1835 edition.

In the Preface (pp. v–vi) Thomson noted that each of his designs "has been made with reference to some particular case which either has arisen or is likely to occur" (p. v)—reflecting his concern that each design should suit its scenic context as well as the particular needs of its inhabitants. He further explained that he "divided" his designs into three classes:

the first class consisting of COTTAGE RESIDENCES, or "RETIREMENTS" of a limited description, adapted more particularly to the environs of the metropolis; the second class containing VILLAS, or "RETREATS" of the higher order; and the third class comprising ORNAMENTAL BUILDINGS, some of which may be considered as appendages to the preceding designs, and others that may be erected independent of them.[1]

The preliminary matter concludes with a table of contents (pp. vii–viii).

The text is organized as a series of commentaries on individual designs, giving dimensions, remarks on materials and construction, and observations on appropriate siting and landscape scenery. The designs are grouped in three "Sections." The first, titled "Cottages," contains designs for seven cottages, a lodge, two "residences," and a pair of "coupled houses." These are composed in Greek, Gothic, Rural, "Regular," "Irregular," "Uniform," and Rustic styles. The second section, titled "Villas," includes designs for a parsonage house, a "family residence," two houses, and five villas, in Gothic, Doric, Ionic, Corinthian, and other styles. The final section, titled "Ornamental Buildings," contains designs for a conservatory, a bridge, a park entrance, a stable, a chapel, a fishing lodge, a bath, an "aquatic temple," a "water gate," and a rustic lodge. The designs in all three sections are shown in elevation and plan, and the elevations—in many copies hand colored—are well integrated with lawns, shrubbery, trees, and other landscape elements.

Although Thomson provided no comprehensive discussion of architectural theory or practice, nevertheless he offered important insight into matters of style, landscape setting, function, and expression. In describing one of his smallest designs, for example, he addressed all of these matters:

As all superior erections, whether public or private, should be suitably designed to their situation, as well as to the particular objects for which they are built; so a Cottage should possess a character adapted to the local circumstances connected with it. To construct a Hermitage, as has sometimes been done, on the road-side of an approach to a populous town or city, would necessarily be out of true character; it is in a wild uncultivated country, amidst the picturesque scenery of the crag and precipice, that such objects strike with effect.

The present design [in Greek style] is for the residence of an active partner in a mercantile house. Its features are calculated for a retirement suited to relieve the mind from the fatigues of the day; and it possesses neatness and accommodation sufficient to indicate its vicinity to the metropolis. (p. 1)

The design itself is two stories high and three openings wide, with a dining room, "private room," drawing room, and two closets on the ground floor, plus three bedrooms and two dressing rooms upstairs. The facade incorporates wide two-story pilasters framing the openings, plus a narrow horizontal band of Greek fretwork between stories and modest Greek ornament surrounding the entrance. The foreground is filled with dense shrubbery, blocking views of the surrounding—presumably suburban—neighborhood.

Thomson also indicated that associations of particular styles rendered them suitable for certain specific applications. In the case of the Ionic order, for example, its feminine associations made it appropriate for the residence of a prosperous family: "where opulence exists independent of rank and title, the matronly Ionic may be considered as the most legitimate style for a family residence" (p. 18). As shown in Plates 22 and 23, the Ionic Villa is fronted by a two-story engaged hexastyle Ionic portico; at each end there is a semicircular hexastyle Ionic portico surmounted by a dome, and an attic story, three windows wide, rises above the center of the elevation. The ground-floor plan includes a drawing room, dining room, library, study, boudoir, hall, and anteroom; there are five bedrooms, four dressing rooms, and a maid's room upstairs. The design is complemented by a smooth lawn in the foreground and gently rolling hills in the distance.

Doric was the earliest of the orders, and therefore offered associations of permanence and longevity, associations implicit in Thomson's description of the Doric Villa:

Surely, to persons of extensive landed property, there is not a more laudable or advantageous exercise of its revenue than the erection of a stately mansion commensurate with it. It enables the possessor to live with becoming dignity; and he has the gratification which none but the wealthy can fully enjoy, of giving aid to national industry and talent, in the various branches that engage the artist and the artisan; while to his posterity he leaves a useful and honourable bequest, to remain for ages—a monument of parental regard and patriotic munificence. (p. 19)

As shown in Plates 25 and 26, the design is two stories high and nine windows wide, fronted by a tetrastyle Doric portico in the center and engaged Doric pilasters to either side. The setting is regular and formal, with a sheet of water leading up to the front of the house, large round trees flanking the house to left and right, a level landscape in the foreground and middle distance, and gently rolling hills in the background. The ground-floor plan includes a large entrance hall, library, dining room, drawing room, morning room, boudoir, gentleman's room, and attendant's room.

By contrast the Corinthian order is associated with elegance and refinement, qualities appropriate to the "residence of a nobleman," a dwelling that "should possess an elevation of character corresponding with the rank of its inhabitant" (p. 21). Thus the Corinthian Villa (Plates 27, 28) is of a more modest scale than the Doric or Ionic villas, but more richly ornamented. The facade is two stories high and five openings wide, and fronted by two-story Corinthian columns plus a pediment over the three central openings. Decorative swags, statues along the parapet, and other ornamental features enrich the facade, while the surrounding landscape is shut off by closely planted trees at either side of the house, thus focusing the viewer's attention on the house alone. The plan includes an entrance hall, morning room, boudoir, drawing room, library, dining room, and gentleman's room, plus a large service wing screened from the observer's view by trees.

In contrast to the ostentation and display found in the Ionic, Doric, and Corinthian designs, the Gothic Villa (Plates 20, 21) was suited to "persons fond of retirement and study. . . . It contains all the requisites for domestic comfort, and conveniences for literary or scientific pursuits" (p. 17). The facade is symmetrical, with a gable in the center framing a projecting window bay on the ground floor, plus smaller window bays at either end of the facade. In between, to the left and right of the central bay, are ranges of window openings with pointed arches providing light to rooms intended for growing flowers. In addition to these rooms the plan includes an entrance hall, library, drawing room, dining room, butler's pantry, closets, and an office wing. The Gothic elevation is complemented by a smooth lawn in the foreground and tall, narrow trees, some coniferous, in the background.

1. Pp. v–vi. N.B. there are similarities in organization and in other respects between Thomson's *Retreats* and *Rural Residences* (1818; *q.v.*), by Thomson's teacher John Buonarotti Papworth.

334.1
TRENDALL, Edward W.
Original designs for cottages and villas, in the Grecian, Gothic, and Italian styles of architecture, in which strict attention is paid to unite convenience and elegance with economy, adapted to the environs of the metroplis [*sic*] and large towns. Consisting of plans, elevations, and estimate to each design, with appropriate details, including roofs, doors, windows, shutters, exterior and interior cornices, &c. In thirty plates, designed and drawn on stone by E. W. Trendall, Architect to the Epsom Grand Stand, &c. &c. &c.

London: Published by the author, to be had of James Carpenter and Son, and Messrs. Priestley and Weale, [1831].

10 pp, 30 pls.

28.6 × 22.9 cm

MB

During the middle and late 1820s several suburban areas on the outskirts of London underwent rapid development. These included Regent's Park and Park Villages East and West, planned by John Nash, and more informally developed areas in St. John's Wood, Paddington, and Bayswater.[1] Similar projects were proposed or well under way in Nottingham[2] and in resort towns such as Cheltenham, Tunbridge Wells, and St. Leonards.[3] Designs for dwellings specifically suited to such suburban areas—"environs of the metropolis and large towns," as Trendall put it—had appeared only infrequently in previous architectural books. James Thomson and Peter Frederick Robinson had included a few designs intended for the outskirts of a town,[4] but no one before Trendall devoted an entire treatise to such designs. In the "Address" Trendall also noted the need for a book on "Cottage and Villa Architecture . . . of a more detailed and simple nature" than those already available (p. 3).

In 30 plates he provided designs for nine dwellings "adapted to the environs of the metropolis and large towns" (p. 3), and illustrated them with plans, elevations, and details of roofs, doors, windows, and moldings. Brief letterpress descriptions (pp. 7–10) list the parts of each design and give cost estimates. The first three designs (Plates 1–5), all in a very spare Neoclassical style, are described as "cottages." The largest consists of a raised basement and two upper stories, with a hall, drawing room, dining room, and parlor on the principal floor, and three bedrooms above. Trendall estimated the cost at £750. The next three designs (Plates 6–12) are described as "Gothic Villas" and range in cost from £1,582 to £2,370. The last three designs, for a "Double Cottage in the Italian Style" (Plates 13,14) and two "Italian Villas" (Plates 15–19), cost from £2,085 to £3,000. The largest (Plates 17–19) includes a staircase hall, parlor, drawing room, dining room, conservatory, library, housekeeper's room, kitchen, store closet, larder, and scullery on the ground floor, three bed chambers and two dressing rooms on the chamber floor, and a servant's bedroom under the roof. The remaining plates (20 through 30) illustrate roof trusses, doors, windows, moldings, and cornices.

1. On Regent's Park and the Park Villages see Ann Saunders, *Regent's Park* (Newton Abbot: David & Charles, 1969); and John Summerson, *The Life and Work of John Nash* (Cambridge, Mass.: MIT Press, 1980). On St. John's Wood see Hugh C. Prince, "North-west London 1814–1863," in J. T. Coppock and Hugh C. Prince, eds., *Greater London* (London: Faber and Faber, 1964), pp. 80–119; John Smith, *A Topographical Account of the Parish of St. Mary-le-Bone* (London: John Smith, 1833); and Alfred Cox, *The Landlord and Tenant's Guide* (London: The Author, 1853), pp. 231–232. Much of this expansion was facilitated by recent extension of short-stage commuter coach service from the City. See T. C. Barker and Michael Robbins, *A History of London Transport* (London: Allen & Unwin, 1963), I, 1–19, 391–392.

2. On Nottingham see Stephen Glover, *The History and Directory of . . . Nottingham* (Nottingham: Glover, 1844), pp. 116–167; Thomas Chambers Hine, *Nottingham: Its Castle* (London: Hamilton, Adams, & Co., 1876), p. 48; and K. C. Edwards, "The Geographical Development of Nottingham," in *Nottingham and Its Region* (Nottingham: British Association for the Advancement of Science, 1966), pp. 389–390. Two studies by Kenneth Brand, focusing specifically on the development of The Park Estate in Nottingham, are forthcoming.

3. On Cheltenham see S. Y. Griffith, *Griffith's New Historical Description of Cheltenham* (London, 1826 and later editions); Gwen Hart, *A History of Cheltenham* (Leicester: Leicester University Press, 1965); and Simonia Pakenham, *Cheltenham, A Biography* (London: Macmillan, 1971). On Tunbridge Wells see John Britton, *Descriptive Sketches of Tunbridge Wells* (London, 1832); and Alan Savidge, *Royal Tunbridge Wells* (Tunbridge Wells: Midas, 1975). On St. Leonards see John Manwaring Baines, *Burton's St. Leonards* (Hastings: Hastings Museum, 1956).

4. See James Thomson, *Retreats* (1827), Peter Frederick Robinson, *Designs for Ornamental Villas* (1827 and later editions), and Robinson, *A New Series of Designs* (1838), *qq.v.*

Twelve designs of country-houses.

See GENTLEMAN, A, *Entry 87.*

VARDEN, Richard (1812–1873)
"Design for a suburban villa, on half an acre of ground, in an unfavourable situation."

See LOUDON, John Claudius, ed., The architectural magazine, *Entry 182.*

335.1
VARDY, John (–1765)
Some designs of Mr. Inigo Jones and Mr. Wm. Kent.

[N. loc.]: Published by John Vardy, 1744.

2 leaves with engraved text, 50 pls.

39.1 × 25.7 cm

V&A

Following the engraved title page there are two engraved leaves containing a "Table of the Several Plates." According to this list Plates 1–17 are the work of Inigo Jones, and Plates 18–50 were designed by William Kent.

The designs by Jones include gates, the screen at Winchester Cathedral, an alcove for a bed, chimney pieces, and a ceiling. Kent's designs include candlesticks, chandeliers, dish covers, vases, a tureen and cover, a "Surtoute," gold cups, mugs, a silver standish, chimney pieces, tables, a settee, chairs, an organ case, a gateway, the screen for the Courts of King's Bench and Chancery, the screen in Gloucester Cathedral, a stable, and four garden structures: Merlin's Cave in the Royal Gardens at Richmond, the Hermitage at Richmond, a seat for Kensington Gardens, and a temple at Rousham.

Three additional plates, numbered 51 through 53, are not mentioned in the list of plates but are present in many copies. They depict more designs by Kent: the pulpit in York Minster, the stern of the Prince of Wales's barge, and a window in the same barge.

Published without a dedication or a list of subscribers, the book is a manifesto of Palladian taste apparently put together by Vardy as a commercial venture, perhaps in imitation of a similar collection of designs recently published by Isaac Ware.[1] Nevertheless several of Kent's Gothic designs are included: the silver standish (Plate 31), Merlin's Cave (Plate 32), the screens at Westminster and Gloucester (Plates 48, 49), and the pulpit at York (Plate 51). Fundamentally regular and Classically proportioned, these designs are made Gothic only through a veneer of pointed arches, crockets, finials, and other Gothic ornament.

1. *Designs of Inigo Jones* (*q.v.*). An edition of this book appeared in 1743, one year before Vardy's book.

336.1
VARLEY, John (1778–1842)
A practical treatise on perspective, published and sold by the author, John Varley. . . .

[London: John Varley, 1815].

2 printed leaves, 1 pl.

34.3 × 48.3 cm

CtY-BA

336.2
————

A practical treatise on the art of drawing in perspective; adapted for the study of those who draw from nature; by which the usual errors may be avoided. By John Varley.

London: Printed for Sherwood, Gilbert, and Piper; and R. Ackerman, [1820].

4 printed leaves, 2 pls.

33.0 × 23.5 cm

NN

A copy of the [1815] edition at Princeton is identical to that at the Yale Center for British Art. Both have two printed leaves and one plate.

The composition of the [1820] edition is sroblematic. The Library of Congress printed catalogue card indicates 11 leaves and four plates, but the book itself cannot be located. The New York Public Library copy of the book contains a title page, four leaves of text, and two plates. All four text leaves are folded, and so could be considered eight leaves; nevertheless the leaves are clearly marked "No. 1," "No. 2," "Page 3," and "Page 4." The text of the first two leaves refers only to the first plate, and the text of the second two leaves refers only to Plate II.

The text treats principles of perspective drawing, and describes examples illustrated in the plates. The first plate, dated 1815, includes geometric figures and illustrations of a church, boats, a bridge, a row of four attached cottages, a two-story house drawn in outline, and two rustic cottages depicting "common errors to be avoided." The second plate, dated 1820, contains 11 figures labeled A through I, K, and L. The architectural subjects depicted include a castellated tower, a "cottage porch" in Old English style, room interiors, and a bridge.

337.1
WAISTELL, Charles
Designs for agricultural buildings, including labourer's cottages, farm= houses and out-offices, conveniently arranged around fold-yards, and adapted to farms of various sizes and descriptions: to which are prefixed, an essay on the improvement of the condition of cottagers, necessary preliminary information (illustrated by wood cuts) for constructing agricultural buildings, and explanations and observations on the several designs; together with an improved field gate, and stand for a corn rick. To which are added, plans and remarks on Caterham farm yard, as it formerly was; and also as it has been improved. By the late Charles Waistell, Esq. . . . Twelve very superiorly engraved copper plates of plans, elevations, isometrical perspective views of homesteads, &c. &c. Joseph Jopling, Architect, editor. . . .

London: Published by Longman, Rees, Orme, Brown, and Green; and by the editor, 1827.

xi + 115 pp, 12 pls.

30.5 × 23.5 cm

MBAt

337.2
————

Designs for agricultural buildings, including labourers' cottages, farm= houses and out-offices, conveniently arranged around fold-yards, and adapted to farms of various sizes and descriptions: to which are prefixed, an essay on the improvement of the condition of cottagers, necessary preliminary information (illustrated by wood-cuts) for constructing agricultural buildings, and explanations and observations on the several designs; together with an improved field gate, and stand for a corn rick. To which are added, plans and remarks on Caterham farm yard, as it formerly was; and also as it has been improved. By the late Charles Waistell. . . . Edited by Joseph Jopling. . . . Twelve copper plates of plans, elevations, isometrical perspective views of homesteads, &c. &c.

London: Published by M. Taylor, (nephew and successor to the late Josiah Taylor), [after 1834].

xi + 115 pp, 12 pls.

30.9 × 23.7 cm

MnU

A notice in *The Edinburgh Review* for December 1826[1] indicates that Waistell's book was issued late in that year, a date confirmed by the Preface, which is dated "7th November, 1826." Nevertheless only two editions are known: one dated 1827 in the imprint, and one which cannot have been published before 1835.[2]

Waistell's treatise is part of the literature of rural and agricultural improvement that began with Nathaniel Kent's *Hints* (1775) and the series of county agricultural surveys prepared for the Board of Agriculture (1793 and later).[3] Waistell's principal aim was to ameliorate the poor living conditions of rural laborers while at the same time increasing agricultural production: "The great object, therefore . . . is to make the cottagers more comfortable, and by that means render them healthy, stout, and active, and capable of that hard and continued labour which their pursuits require. If we effect these, we gain an advantage in the produce of their labour, much beyond any rent that the most penurious can wish to extract from them" (p. 1). Lamenting the dearth of information available to farmers on efficient design and organization of farm structures, he now offered a treatise "pointing out what circumstances ought to be considered, what conveniences are requisite, various reasons for particular arrangement, and a series of practical examples with a view to economy and improvement" (p. 3). He presented "a gradation of plans for labourers' cottages, and also for farm-houses and out-buildings, suited to both arable and grazing farms of different magnitudes." Individual buildings were designed to "be either contracted or enlarged in any of their parts . . . so as to accommodate them to different families, or to farms of different sizes, qualities, districts, and climates" (p. 3).

Chapter I concerns the welfare of cottagers, and Waistell recommended exercise, a healthy diet, and individual plots of land to cultivate. He chastised those who would erect cottages simply as picturesque ornaments:

It has been fashionable with gentlemen to erect buildings in their grounds often merely as objects to look at; it would be happy for themselves, as well as for their poor half-starved labourers, if, in ornamenting their grounds, gentlemen were to direct their attention to the promoting of the health and comfort of those by whom they are benefitted, and by whose labour and industry they enjoy all the necessaries and all the superfluities of life. (p. 9)

He appealed to the consciences of wealthy landowners by asking them to exchange fashion for the satsifactions of philanthropy: "In the plans that have been selected for this work, economy more than elegance has been considered; but even such plain buildings as these, forming comfortable lodgings to honest industrious families, must give more true pleasure to the humane heart of the builder or beholder, in contemplating them, than can be given by the most magnificent structure devoid of use, whether obelisk, pagoda, or other heathen temple" (p. 9).

Chapter II includes brief remarks on siting, water, light, ventilation, the arrangement of buildings around a farmyard, and the form and proportion of buildings. Chapter III concerns individual rooms that must be designed for specific uses, such as the "bake-house," "brew-house," "cider-house," "potatoe-place," and "wood-house." Chapter IV is a discussion of "Out-Offices" such as barns, granaries, hog sties, and tool houses. Chapter V is devoted to building materials and construction, and treats mortar and cement, timber, walls, floors, roofs, and roof coverings. The final section of the text (pp. 80–107) describes individual designs for farm buildings. Also illustrated in the plates, these designs include three pairs of semi-detached cottages and six farm houses with outbuildings, plus a gate, a "Corn-Rick Stand," and plans of Caterham Farm Yard. The cottages for laborers consist of a kitchen and wash house on the ground floor and sleeping rooms above. The farm houses are substantial. The first three designs include a parlor, kitchen, back kitchen, and dairy on the ground floor. The three larger designs have a parlor, living room, kitchen, dairy, pantry, and—in one case—a business room on the ground floor. One farm house is three stories high, and the rest are two. In most cases the facades are plain and unarticulated, but two farm houses have shallow pilasters at the corners, shallow relieving arches surrounding the windows, and pilasters or other ornamentation at the front entrance.

According to a statement by Joseph Jopling in his *Practice of Isometrical Perspective* (London, 1833), p. 60, he provided the design for the farm house and yard illustrated in Plates VIII and IX.

1. Vol. 44, No. 89 (Dec. 1826), 254.

2. The imprint is "M. Taylor, 6 Barnard's Inn, Holborn, (Nephew and Successor to the Late Josiah Taylor)." The latest imprint for Josiah (or J.) Taylor in Appendix F is dated 1834, indicating he was alive until then. The earliest imprint date for M. Taylor is 1835, and Josiah Taylor is likewise described in imprints from 1835 onward as deceased.

3. For remarks on Waistell in the context of agricultural improvement, see John Martin Robinson, *Georgian Model Farms: A Study of Decorative and Model Farm Buildings in the Age of Improvement, 1700–1846* (Oxford: Clarendon Press, 1983), pp. 21, 26–27, 40, 84, 121.

WALKER, Thomas Larkins (–1860)

See DAVY, **Christopher**, *Entry 56.4.*

338.1

WALLIS, N.

The carpenter's treasure; a collection of designs for temples, with their plans, gates, doors, rails, and bridges, in the Gothic taste; with the centres at large, for striking Gothic curves and mouldings; and some specimens of rails, in the Chinese taste: forming a complete system for rural decorations. A new edition. Neatly engraved on sixteen plates, from the original drawings of N. Wallis, Architect.

London: Printed for I. Taylor, [1773].

16 pls.

24.8 × 15.2 cm

BL

Copies in the British Library, the Avery Library at Columbia, the Beinecke Library at Yale, and the Yale Center for British Art all are described on the title page as "A new edition." The plates are dated 1773.

The 16 plates, unaccompanied by text, include designs for moldings, arches, doors, gates, rails, bridges, a "Termination for a Vista," and 13 garden temples. The first 14 plates contain designs in Gothic style, Plate XV has designs for a Gothic bridge and a Chinese bridge, and Plate XVI depicts Chinese railings. Palladian symmetry and proportion are apparent in the designs for Gothic garden temples (Plates IV–VII), but as in earlier designs by Halfpenny and Decker (*qq.v.*) there is also an abundance of Rococo ornament.

339.1

WARE, Isaac (–1766)

A complete body of architecture. Adorned with plans and elevations, from original designs. By Isaac Ware. . . . In which are interspersed some designs of Inigo Jones, never before published.

London: Printed for T. Osborne and J. Shipton; J. Hodges; L. Davis; J. Ward; and R. Baldwin, 1756.

8 printed leaves, 748 + [iv] pp, 3 printed leaves, frontisp. + 115 pls.

41.3 × 25.4 cm

MB

339.2

————

————

London: Printed for J. Rivington, L. Davis and C. Reymers, R. Baldwin, W. Owen, H. Woodfall, W. Strahan, and B. Collins, 1767.

8 printed leaves, 748 + [iv] pp, 3 printed leaves, frontisp. + 114 pls.

41.6 × 26.7 cm

BL

London: Printed for J. Rivington, L. Davis and C. Reymers, R. Baldwin, W. Owen, H. Woodfall, W. Strahan, and B. Collins, 1768.

8 printed leaves, 748 + [iv] pp, 3 printed leaves, 108 pls.

39.4 × 24.8 cm

MH

The letterpress consists of a preface, a list of plates, and a table of contents, all on eight unnumbered leaves, plus 748 pages of text, explanations of plates IX through XVI on three additional unnumbered leaves,[1] and a four-page index at the end. In addition to the frontispiece there are as many as 115 plates in some copies.[2] The description below is based on examination of the 1756 edition in the Avery Library.

The frontispiece reveals Ware's own conception of his contribution to the study of architecture. In the foreground a young man, perhaps a student, holds a drafting square. He walks past five other figures who represent fundamentals of architecture: mensuration, masonry, geometry, perspective, and the orders. In the far distance there is an Egyptian pyramid, and progressively closer to the foreground are a Greek temple, the Colosseum, and a portion of a Palladian mansion, representing the historical progress of architecture from Egypt to the modern Palladian revival. The frontispiece thus suggests the practical as well as the historical breadth of Ware's vision.

The Preface likewise announces a comprehensive approach, and one that is meant to satisfy a diverse audience. Describing "the present state of architecture" Ware lamented that important rules and "discoveries" could be found only in "scattered" treatises, which often failed to include the most recent information.[3] Thus he proposed to "collect all that is useful in the works of others," to which he would add information concerning recent improvements: "By this means we propose to make our work serve as a library on this subject to the gentleman and the builder; supplying the place of all other books." Ware was particularly concerned with architectural practice. Previous writers, he said, paid too much attention to "magnificence" and "pomp," and ignored utility. Thus he promised that "nothing will be omitted that is elegant or great; but the principal regard will be shewn to what is necessary and useful." Most of the Preface is simply an explanation of the sequence in which Ware arranged the text.[4] In brief remarks at the end of the Preface he also revealed the diverse audience to which he hoped his book would appeal:

By these means we hope to lay down in one body the whole science of architecture, from its first rudiments to its utmost perfection; and that in a manner which shall render every part of it intelligible to every reader;

to acquaint the gentleman with what, on every possible occasion, he should design in his edifice; and to instruct the practical builder in not only what he ought to do, but how he should execute it, to his own credit, and to the advantage of the owner.

The contents in fact do not encompass "the whole science of architecture." Instead they accommodate three important and fundamental objectives: Ware's desire to elucidate architectural principles based on the practices of the "Ancients," thus avoiding the "violent liberties" taken by modern architects; his wish to present a thorough discussion of the orders, and to develop a general system of architectural proportion based on the proportions of the orders; and his interest in the principles and practice of domestic architecture, almost to the exclusion of all other building types.[5] Ware thus implicitly supported two principal components of Colen Campbell's program of architectural reform set out over 40 years earlier in *Vitruvius Britannicus* (*q.v.*): restoration of "Ancient" authority, and confidence that Britain's future architectural progress lay in domestic building.

The text is methodically divided into ten Books. The first Book includes definitions and a discussion of building materials, including stone, brick, tile, timber, lead, and iron. Book II treats siting, drainage, foundations, walls, roofs, floors, and chimneys. Most of this Book—144 pages, or approximately one-fifth of the entire treatise—concerns the orders, their "decoration," and their proportions. In describing the orders Ware paid particular attention to Palladio, but his account is even more closely modeled on Perrault's *Ordonnance*.[6] The third Book, nominally devoted to the "general practice of architecture," actually is limited to domestic architecture. The first part of the Book concerns the proportions of houses, their elevations, "exterior ornaments," doors, and plans. The second part treats dwellings in which the orders "are not employed,"[7] while the third and largest part concerns dwellings in which the orders "are used." Ware clearly paid close attention to the proper uses and proportions of each order, but even in designing houses without orders he emphasized the importance of architectural principles. In the design of a "country house with a farm," for example, decorum required that "the principal building" be "proportioned to the dignity of the proprietor, and the number of his retinue." Since the farm house, in turn, would be placed "in full view of the principal building," the farm house and its surrounding offices must be arranged according to principles of pictorial composition. Ware's discussion of this point is an early and important elucidation of principles of picturesque composition in architecture:[8]

[The proprietor] is to consider all this as a picture, and as he knows where the eye is to be placed, he may very happily and agreeably throw the whole into perspective.

The house of the farmer is to be the principal object, and this must be placed on the highest part of the ground: from this, on either side, the out-buildings are to descend spreading in form of wings, toward the brook at the bottom; which terminates the farm territory. These will serve to enclose the proper quantity of ground for the yard, and the very racks and stalls may be so placed in that, with a view to the eye at the proprietor's house, that they shall form a picture.

Under the direction of a skilful architect, the barns, stables, and cowhouses, will rise like so many pavillions; and the very sheds will assist in the design. (p. 353)

Books IV through VI treat doors and windows, interior decorations and ceilings, and chimney pieces. Book VII treats "exterior decorations" such as piers and garden buildings. The eighth Book concerns bridges. Book IX returns to theoretical matters pertaining to domestic architecture. Nominally concerned with constructing elevations "upon true principles of Architecture," this Book bitterly criticizes the "very rash and wild liberty" taken by "modern" architects in their use of the orders. Unlike the Ancients, who would vary the proportions of the orders "by small measures, which are not perceived by the common eye," modern builders had taken to "accommodating an order to the place," in other words "altering its proportions to make it suit the service" (p. 681). The Ancients, according to Ware, sought something more: they made each column "a regular part of a regular whole," in order to "surprize and charm the more correct and knowing artist." Ultimately "they gave that proportion to their works in which subsists the harmony of building" (p. 681).[9] The contents of the final Book are anticlimactic and also unsuitably located at the end, for they concern basic "sciences and arts" that are prerequisite to the practice of architecture: arithmetic, geometry, perspective, and mensuration.

The first 31 plates illustrate the parts of a building facade, the five standard orders and their parts, Persian and caryatid orders, termini, moldings, kilns, chain bars, iron cramps, iron railings, foundations, brick and stone walls, plates, beams, trusses, sewers, drains, a design for a loggia, and part of the lower story of Palladio's Palazzo Chiericati in Vicenza. The next 27 plates depict plans and elevations for 15 houses, one mansion house, one town hall, one garden pavilion, and "an AEgyptian banqueting room." Another 33 plates contain designs for doors, windows, dining rooms, ceilings, and chimney pieces. In the next ten plates there are designs for piers, six garden seats, a cold bath, and three bridges. Three more plates depict temporary bridges and a design for Westminster Bridge. The next four plates illustrate three designs for Corinthian house facades and a composite elevation after Palladio. The final six plates include geometric figures, examples of perspective constructions, and a depiction of piers at Holland House.

Ware's 15 designs for houses in Plates 32 through 61 include proposals as well as executed designs. Several exhibit a strict proportionality: the width of the house in Plate 32 is half again as great as its depth; in Plate 33 the plan is twice as wide as it is deep; and in Plate 35 the plan is "near to a square." Plate 34 contains a plan and elevation for a row house or "town house," three stories high plus an attic, and three windows wide. The modest ornament includes balusters fronting the attic story and stringcourses between the ground and principal floors. The design for a "small farm-house" in Plate 36 consists of a central pavilion two stories high and 36 feet 10 inches wide, flanked by two ells each 10 1/2 feet wide. On the ground floor there is a kitchen, a parlor, a cellar, a dairy, and a brewhouse. One of the larger designs is that for Chesterfield House

(Plates 60, 61), with a central pavilion three stories high and five openings wide, connected by Corinthian colonnades to wing pavilions each three stories high and three openings wide. The ornament of the central pavilion includes architraves surrounding all windows, alternating segmental and triangular pediments over the windows of the principal floor, balustrades in front of these windows, entablatures over windows on the ground floor, and a scrolled pediment over the entrance. The colonnades are topped by balustrades and urns. The wing pavilions, by contrast, are articulated in a very plain manner, with little more than cornices and stringcourses. The principal floor of the central pavilion has a hall and staircase, dining parlor, anteroom, drawing room, library, lobby, waiting room, and dressing room. The wing pavilions contain offices and stables. One of Ware's most interesting designs is Wrotham Park (Plates 52, 53). The central pavilion, five openings wide, consists of a basement plus two stories, fronted by a tetrastyle pedimented Ionic portico and topped by an octagonal drum. To either side are one-story wings with pyramidal roofs connected to octagonal end pavilions with roofs that are semicircular in profile. The whole is a carefully proportioned composition of circles, semicircles, squares, octagons, and triangles.

Four plates accompany the ninth Book, which concerns "the construction of elevations upon true principles of Architecture." The plates depict three designs for Corinthian facades, plus a design for another facade after Palladio (Plates 113–116). The largest facade (Plate 113) is eleven windows wide, with a basement, two upper stories, and an attic story just three windows wide. The other two original designs are nine windows wide and consist of a basement, principal floor, and attic. In all three of Ware's designs a rusticated basement supports engaged Corinthian columns across the entire width of the facade, with colonettes or other ornament surrounding many of the windows, plus additional ornament elsewhere.

Plates 120 and 121, concerning perspective, each contain a view of a three-story house; one house is five openings wide and the other is seven.

In addition to house designs there are also illustrations of garden structures. The "garden pavilion" in Plate 39 is two stories high, with three rooms on the ground floor. The one "cold bath" and six garden seats in Plates 101–105 are all one story high; two are ornamented with heavy rustication, another has a tetrastyle pedimented portico, and others have distyle porticoes *in antis*.

1. Each leaf is printed on both sides. In the Avery Library copy the first is inserted between pp. 96 and 97, and concerns Plates IX and X. The second, between pp. 116 and 117, concerns Plates XII and XIII. The third is between pp. 120 and 121 and concerns Plates XIV–XVI.

2. There are 115 plates in the Boston Public Library copy of the first edition, and 114 in the Avery Library copy. The plates exist in two distinct states, described by Laurence Hall Fowler and Elizabeth Baer in *The Fowler Architectural Collection* (Baltimore: Evergreen House Foundation, 1961), p. 340.

3. Indeed two recent efforts to create a "General Treatise" of architecture were sadly inadequate. Thomas Rowland's book (1732–1743; *q.v.*) hardly treated more than arithmetic, geometry, mensuration, and the orders. John Aheron's treatise (1754; *q.v.*) contained more plates than Ware's, and included illustrations of the orders, windows, doors, and complete houses, but nearly all of his text concerned arithmetic.

4. The arrangement in ten Books no doubt was intended to recall the similar format of treatises by Vitruvius and Alberti; nevertheless Ware's treatise differs markedly both in content and in the audience to which he appealed.

5. On the Ancients and "violent liberties" see especially pp. 681–682. On the orders note his lengthy treatment of the subject on pp. 129–272. His devotion to domestic architecture is apparent in the plates, discussed below.

6. On Ware's debt to Perrault see Wolfgang Herrmann, *The Theory of Claude Perrault* (London: Zwemmer, 1973), pp. 161–168.

7. These include "common houses" in London and in the country, farm houses, and a "country house with a farm."

8. Parallels between pictorial and architectural composition were explored previously by Robert Castell in *Villas of the Ancients* (1728) and by Robert Morris in *Rural Architecture* (1750), *qq.v.* For subsequent discussion see Robert and James Adam, *Works in Architecture* (1778–1779); James Lewis, *Original Designs* (1780–1797); George Richardson, *New Designs in Architecture* (1792); Edmund Bartell, *Hints for Picturesque Improvements* (1804); John Buonarotti Papworth, *Hints on Ornamental Gardening* (1823); and Richard Brown, *Domestic Architecture* (1841), *qq.v.*

9. Cf. Robert Morris's extensive remarks on architectural harmony in his *Lectures on Architecture* (1734–1736; *q.v.*).

340.1
WARE, Isaac (–1766)
Designs of Inigo Jones and others published by I: Ware.

[N. loc.: I. Ware, n.d.].

3 engraved leaves, 53 pls.

24.4 × 17.1 cm

MB

340.2

_____

_____

[London:] Printed for J. Millan, 1743.

1 leaf, 53 pls.

21.9 × 14.0 cm

MBAt

It is not certain when the undated edition appeared. Colvin (1978), p. 865, states that it was issued "not later than 1733." Rudolf Wittkower suggested 1735, while noting that some of the designs in Ware's book had already been copied by Edward Hoppus in *Andrea Palladio's Architecture* (1733–1735; *q.v.*).[1]

On the verso of the title page of the undated edition there is a cartouche inscribed: "Most of these Designs are already Executed, & the rest, are at Burlington House." An engraved "Table of the Several Plates" extends over recto and verso of two leaves plus the recto of a third leaf. In addition to 43 single plates there are five double plates, numbered 10/11, 17/18, 19/20, 28/29, and 46/47.

Ware attributed many, but not all, of the designs shown in the plates to Inigo Jones: six chimney pieces, one staircase, one theater, seven ceilings, piers at Windsor Castle, an altarpiece and screen in Somerset House Chapel, a stable, and a simple rectangular garden "Seat" with Doric columns *in antis*. William Kent is represented by more designs than Jones: 11 chimney pieces, the dining room at Houghton, another room designed for the Duke of Grafton, an obelisk for Shotover, and a variety of garden seats and pavilions: a "Room" at Shotover, two "Rooms" at Claremont, "Seats" for Sir Charles Hotham and Lord Cobham, and a domed "Temple." Kent's garden "Rooms" are simple in plan, and based on octagonal, square, or circular figures. The building at Shotover is domed, and the entrance of one "Room" at Claremont is framed by battered architraves. The largest garden structure is the two-story domed "Seat" depicted in Plates 43 and 44, five windows wide on the ground story, fronted by a hexastyle pedimented Doric portico, with three rooms inside on the ground floor. There is one design by Lord Burlington, for the piers at the entrance to Chiswick House (Plate 25). The design for an "Alcove" (Plate 23) is unattributed.

1. Rudolf Wittkower, *Palladio and Palladianism* (New York: Braziller, 1974), p. 88. For designs copied by Hoppus see for example Pl. 43 in *Designs of Inigo Jones*, a design for a garden seat by William Kent for Sir Charles Hotham. This appeared as a tailpiece to Chapter VII, Book I, of Hoppus's book.

WARE, Isaac (–1766)
The plans, elevations, and sections; chimney-pieces, and ceilings of Houghton in Norfolk.

See RIPLEY, **Thomas,** *Entry 288.*

WEALE, John (1791–1862)
Designs of ornamental gates, lodges, palisading, and iron work of the royal parks.

See Entry 456.

WELLS, William
"Perspective view and ground plan of a cyclopean cottage."

See LOUDON, **John Claudius, ed.,** The architectural magazine, *Entry 182.*

341.1

WETTEN, Robert Gunter (–1868)

Designs • for • villas in • the Italian • style • of • architectvre by Robert • Wetten • Archt.

[London]: Pvblished • by • James • Carpenter • and • Son • Old • Bond • Street, [n.d.].

8 printed leaves, 24 pls.

29.2 × 23.2 cm

Bodl.

341.2

————

————

————

[London]: Pvblished • by • James • Carpenter • and • Son • Old • Bond • Street, [1830?].

viii pp, 7 printed leaves, 24 pls.

32.0 × 25.0 cm

MnSS

Both editions include seven leaves of plate descriptions and 24 plates. The edition in the Bodleian Library begins with an Introduction printed on one leaf. This is lacking in the edition at the St. Paul Seminary, which instead has an eight-page Preface dated at Rome in June 1830.[1] Except for remarks specifically pertaining to the Introduction, this commentary is based on examination of the copy at the St. Paul Seminary.

The letterpress for Designs 3 and 4 is dated 1829; the rest of the letterpress is undated. The plates for all designs are dated 1829 or 1830.

Wetten stated in the Introduction (Bodleian Library copy) that "several amateurs" who were partial to the "beauties" of the Italian style had encouraged him to prepare this book.[2]

In the Preface Wetten discussed the general characteristics of villas in ancient and modern times. He lamented that many of the "noblest domestic productions" of architecture had "been swept away forever" (p. 1). From the little that he knew of Greek villas, derived solely from one chapter in Vitruvius, Wetten concluded that "great magnificence did not prevail, even in the abodes of the most wealthy or renowned citizens" (p. i). In some ways Greek villas were superior to those of Rome: in Greece one could find "the ease and refinement of an accomplished and elegant people, addicted to the lighter pursuits of literature, and the more seducing pleasures of a dreamy and speculative philosophy, rather than that pompous grandeur in which the Romans sought to gratify those ambitious passions which in their private as in their public life nothing could satiate but the certainty of complete possession" (p. ii). Roman villas "surprise us by their extent and splendour; and might, according to the present acceptance of the words, be more justly denominated Palaces" (p. ii). Wetten briefly mentioned several examples of Roman villas, including the Golden House of Nero and Pliny's villa at Tuscum (p. iii), and added general remarks on siting, lighting, "distribution" of rooms, and baths in

Roman villas. He concluded that Roman villas were in some respects the epitome of the type:

In fine, to the construction of a Roman Villa, every science appears to have brought its choicest offerings, and every clime its loveliest fruits; no soft persuasive to ease and pleasure seems to have been wanting within its extended circuit, no gentle combination of all circumstances concurrent to enjoyment, to have been from its magic chambers absent.

Indeed the Roman villa embodied a "complete dominion of nature and art" (p. v).

Wetten treated Palladio's villas quickly and somewhat indifferently: "The plans are very interesting, and the apartments well distributed" (p. vi). Modern British villas had less "magnificence" and fewer "seducing pleasures" than Classical villas, but suited the social conditions of their times: they generally contained only "the merely necessary living and sleeping rooms." Wetten explained that in his own designs, therefore, "a certain scale introduced by modern habits and customs has not been greatly exceeded, that expense has been considered, and the general arrangements of the English habitations [have been] adhered to, without attempting to display that magnificence which might be introduced so happily in a Villa" (p. vii).

Each of Wetten's six designs for villas is described in one or two pages of letterpress and illustrated in four plates. The letterpress includes dimensions, brief descriptions of individual rooms, and occasional remarks on offices, surrounding scenery (Design 4), and the clients for whom certain designs were prepared (Designs 1 and 3). Each set of four plates includes a ground-floor plan, a chamber-floor plan, an elevation, and a perspective view with surrounding scenery.[3] All the designs are composed in an Italianate style characterized by smooth banded rustication, Classical porticoes, cornices, moldings, and decorative urns; some designs have tile roofs. Among the distinctive features in individual designs are the tetrastyle caryatid porch in Design 3 and the octagonal "Tribune" on the ground floor of Design 5.

The largest design contains "under one Roof all the accommodations usually considered requisite to the completeness of a Modern Villa" (Design 6). The plan is approximately 123 feet deep, and the principal facade is nearly 100 feet wide. The ground floor includes a combined entrance hall and billiard room (30 feet by 29 feet), drawing room (34 feet by 21 feet), dining room (34 feet by 21 feet), breakfast room, library, staircase hall, cabinet, china and plate closet, water closet, housekeeper's room, housekeeper's bedroom, combined butler's room and bedroom, stables, coach houses, combined coachman's room and bedroom, manservants' bedroom, servants' hall, kitchen, and scullery. The chamber floor contains nine bedrooms and three dressing rooms. The ground-story facade, nine openings wide, is fronted by a tetrastyle pedimented Corinthian portico, and composed of smooth banded rusticated masonry and tall round-arched window and door openings. This facade is crowned by a parapet decorated with urns, behind which appears the recessed facade of the upper story.

The smallest design (No. 4), approximately 59 feet wide and 63 feet deep, contains "the Apartments necessary in a Modern Villa," arranged "in the most advantageous manner (within a limited space)." The ground floor includes a drawing room (27$\frac{1}{2}$ feet by 17 feet), dining room, breakfast room, study, hall, staircase and corridor, porch, housekeeper's room, water closet, and one bedroom, plus offices in a separate wing. The chamber floor contains two "Bed Rooms," three "Bed Chambers," and three dressing rooms. The smooth ashlar facade is two stories high and three windows wide, with a one-story entrance porch to the right. A terrace in front of the house is enclosed by a low balustrade. The smoothness and regularity of the facade are complemented by the thick foliage in the foreground and the high, gently rolling forested hills in the distance.

1. This copy is apparently identical to copies at Princeton University and the Victoria and Albert Museum.

2. For remarks on Italianate architecture in previous British architectural literature see the commentary above on Gilbert Laing Meason, *On the Landscape Architecture of the Great Painters of Italy* (1828; *q.v.*).

3. The four plates for Design 5 are a principal-floor plan, a ground-floor plan, an elevation, and a view.

342.1
WHITTOCK, Nathaniel
The British drawing-book: or, the art of drawing with pen and ink; containing a series of progressive lessons on drawing landscape scenery, marine views, architecture, animals, the human figure, &c. Also, a complete system of practical perspective. By N. Whittock. . . .
Illustrated by numerous engravings.

London: John Limbird, [n.d.].

101 pp, 72 pls [*pl. 9 is wanting in this copy*].

15.9 × 25.2 cm

DLC

On the title page Whittock is introduced as author of *The Decorative Painters' . . . Guide* (1827) and *Illustrations of York* (1828),[1] thus establishing 1828 as the earliest possible date of publication.

The text consists of 72 "Lessons," each illustrated by one plate. Subjects of instruction include towers and chimneys, bridges, boats and coastal scenes, flowers and leaves, trees, animals, and the human figure. Lessons XVI, XX, XXII, XXVI, and XXXII concern perspective, and include instruction in "how the ground plan of a church or hall may be put in perspective" (p. 39). Over a third of the lessons are devoted to architectural subjects, including a three-story house that is "not picturesque" (Plate 2, p. 13), a rustic cottage (Plate 4), towers, rural churches, Gothic ruins, a two-story house fronted by a large parterre (Plate 26), the West Gate at Canterbury (Plate 36), houses dating from before the Fire of 1666 (Plates 9, 44), parts of the orders, the Temple of Neptune at Paestum (Plate 64), a house in Elizabethan style (Plate 66), and Woburn Abbey (Plate 72).

1. The author and correct title are: Thomas Allen, *A new and complete history of the County of York. . . . Illustrated by a series of views, engraved . . . by Nathaniel Whittock* (London, 1828–1831). The preface is dated 1832.

343.1 †
WHITTOCK, Nathaniel
Oxford drawing book. 100 lithograph drawings.

[N. loc.]: Holdsworth, 1827.

Oblong 4°

Reference: ECB

343.2

———

The Oxford drawing book, or the art of drawing, and the theory and practice of perspective, in a series of letters containing progressive information on sketching, drawing, and colouring landscape scenery, animals, and the human figure with a new method of practical perspective: detailed in a novel, easy, and perspicuous style, for the use of teachers, or for self= instruction. By Nathaniel Whittock, teacher of drawing and perspective, and lithographist to the University of Oxford. Embellished with upwards of one hundred lithographic drawings, from real views, taken expressly for this work.

London: Published by Isaac Taylor Hinton, 1829.

vi + 159 + [2] pp, 107 pls (numbered I–XXIV, XXIV*, XXV–LVII, LVII*, LVIII–CV).

20.9 × 27.0 cm

CtY-BA

343.3

———

The Oxford drawing book, or the art of drawing, and the theory and practice of perspective, in a series of letters containing progressive information on sketching, drawing, and colouring landscape scenery, animals, and the human figure with a new method of practical perspective: detailed in a novel, easy, and perspicuous style, for the use of teachers, or for self= instruction. By Nathaniel Whittock, teacher of drawing and perspective, and lithographist to the University of Oxford. Embellished with upwards of one hundred lithographic drawings, from real views, taken expressly for this work. A new and improved edition.

London: Published by Edward Lacey, [n.d.].

vi + 159 + [2] pp, frontisp. + 107 pls (numbered 1–24, 24–57, 57*, 58–105) on 27 leaves.

20.9 × 27.0 cm

CtY

The 1829 edition and the undated edition include a Preface dated 1825. The publisher of the undated edition, Edward Lacey, traded at the address given on the title page only from 1829 to 1847.[1]

In the Introduction (pp. iii–vi) Whittock proposed to teach the art of drawing "in a style hitherto unattempted," whereby he "condescended to lead the learner step by step, in a plain familiar manner" (p. iii). Among the many subjects to be covered in the text, he promised some attention to architectural style: "In treating of the various styles of Grecian and Gothic Architecture, their distinguishing features are pointed out, to enable the student to determine the era of their invention, and the uses to which they may be properly applied in drawing plans for the erection of modern buildings" (p. vi).[2]

The text, arranged as a series of letters to "My Dear George and Eliza," treats drawing, perspective, architecture, landscape, animal subjects, the human figure, India ink, sepia, and coloring. In addition there are historical anecdotes pertaining to subjects depicted in the illustrations.

The plates include perspective diagrams as well as illustrations of landscapes, trees, animals, human figures, and architectural monuments.[3] Plates VIII and XI also include outline drawings and perspective views of a two-story house and two cottages. Plates XIII and XXI contain, respectively, a view of a picturesque village in Cumberland and a view of a cottage near Woodeaton. In Plates LXXVI, LXXVIII, and LXXXIX there are picturesque views of Clifton, a chapel in Switzerland, and Edinburgh.

1. The address is 76, St. Paul's Church Yard. See Philip A. H. Brown, *London Publishers and Printers* (London: British Museum, 1961), p. 58.

2. Whittock discussed Gothic on pp. 50–58 and the Greek orders on pp. 118–120.

3. E.g., the ruins of Beaumont Palace, the tower of Oxford Castle, Denbigh Castle, and the Bloody Gate of the Tower of London.

344.1

WHITTOCK, Nathaniel

The youth's new London self-instructing drawing book; containing a series of progressive lessons, with instructions for drawing rural scenery, architecture, the human figure, animals, &c. Illustrated by upwards of one hundred engravings, by N. Whittock. . . .

London: Published by G. Virtue, 1833.

iv + 108 pp, 104 pls.

12.9 × 21.4 cm

CtY-BA

344.2

———

———

London: Published by G. Virtue, 1834.

iv + 108 pp, 104 pls.

13.4 × 21.7 cm

CtY-BA

344.3

———

———

London: Published by G. Virtue, 1836.

iv + 108 pp, 104 pls.

13.2 × 21.8 cm

CtY-BA

This book should not be confused with another by Whittock that has a similar title: *The Youth's New London Self-Instructing Drawing-Book in Colours* (n.d.).[1]

Following a table of contents (pp. iii–iv), the text begins with a discussion of "requisite drawing materials" and instruction in outlining and shading. Pages 9–18 concern picturesque architecture. Next there are remarks on trees, landscape, "marine" and coastal scenery, still life, animals, and the human figure (pp. 19–75). Then Whittock turned again to architecture, treating perspective, Indian, Egyptian, Greek, and Roman styles, the five orders, and "Anglo-Norman," Early English, Decorated, and Perpendicular Gothic styles (pp. 75–103). The text concludes with remarks on "marine" drawing, light and shade, and landscapes with figures.

The content of the plates parallels the subject matter of the text. Plates 1–8 include examples of arches, fences, cottages, gables, and other picturesque subjects. The illustrations of landscape and figural subjects (Plates 9–76) contain a few castles, abbeys, and cottages (Plates 13–16, 28–32). Plates 77–96, illustrating architecture and perspective, include several houses shown in perspective (Plates 77, 85, and 87), a room interior (Plate 84), a "Hindoo Temple" (Plate 86), an "entrance court to a Turkish residence" (Plate 88), and examples of Greek, Roman, and medieval architecture (Plates 89–96). Three of the final plates depict architectural subjects: Doune Castle in Scotland, Blarney Castle in Ireland, and an Alpine village (Plates 101–103).

1. Pagination: v + 74 pp, 78 pls. The contents of the two books differ markedly.

345.1

WHITWELL, Thomas Stedman (–1840)

Description of an architectural model from a design by Stedman Whitwell, Esq. for a community upon a principle of united interests, as advocated by Robert Owen, Esq.

London: Hurst Chance & Co., and Effingham Wilson, 1830.

28 pp, 1 pl.

21.0 × 13.0 cm

MH

Along with Robert Owen, John Minter Morgan, and William Thompson, Stedman Whitwell was a prominent advocate of ideal community planning in the late 1820s and early 1830s.[1] From January to August 1826 Whitwell was in New Harmony, Indiana, where Owen was working to carry out his vision of a utopian community. In 1830 Whitwell published this *Description* of a large quadrangle, 1000 feet on a side, designed for Owen's New Harmony community.

Whitwell's design is illustrated in a lithographed view bound following the title page, and pages 5–18 of the text are a description of its site, plan, heating, ventilation, lighting, water supply, drainage, public areas, private apartments, basement, towers, cloister, gymnasiums, baths, gardens, conservatory, and esplanade. Altogether the buildings, promenades, and gardens would cover 33 acres, and the three-story main quadrangle would surround an open courtyard of 22 acres (p. 5). The quadrangle would contain dormitory accommodation for unmarried persons and children on the top floor, while the lower two floors would consist of individual apartments—sitting room, chamber, and water closet—for married couples. Separate structures projecting into the courtyard would accommodate cooking, eating, bathing, washing, schooling, lectures, musical and theatrical performances, and other community activities.

The last ten pages are an "Extract from Mr. J. M. Morgan's Letter to the Bishop of London,"[2] a description of "four distinct and separate plans, by which each class of society may derive great advantages, without the surrender of their present habits and opinions" (p. 20). The first plan, "for the higher and middle classes of society," would be a "Club" or "College, of the size of one of the largest squares" of London (p. 20). The second, and that which most closely parallels Whitwell's project, proposes communities "for the labouring classes," in the form of "Squares to be erected within two miles of London." Each square, consisting of four equal ranges of workers' "apartments," would be "for the residence of those employed during the day in the cities of London and Westminster" (pp. 24–27).[3] Minter Morgan suggested that up to eight "proprietors" might agree to build one square, each erecting as little as half of one side, and becoming "Landlord" of just the portion he built (p. 24). Minter Morgan's third proposal was to provide "separate allotments of land" to "those who are willing and able to work, but can procure no employment" (p. 27). His final recommendation was to open the churches of London on weekdays "for the purpose of instruction, and in the evening for lectures on the sciences, under the direction of the clergy."[4]

1. For further discussion of Owen, New Harmony, Minter Morgan, Thompson, and Whitwell, see W. H. G. Armytage, *Heavens Below: Utopian Experiments in England 1560–1960* (London: Routledge and Kegan Paul, 1961), especially pp. 130–133. Thompson was author of *Practical Directions for the . . . Establishment of Communities* (1830; *q.v.*).

2. At least two editions of Minter Morgan's pamphlet appeared in 1830. I have consulted *Letter to the Bishop of London. By Mr. J. M. Morgan. Second Edition.* (London: Hurst, Chance & Co.; and Effingham Wilson, 1830).

3. Compare George Smith's similar wish to see laborers housed away from the central city, discussed in his *Essay on the Construction of Cottages* (1834; *q.v.*). Smith, unlike Whitwell or Morgan, wanted to see laborers housed in suburban cottages.

4. The quotation is from Minter Morgan, *Letter*, p. 30. At this point Whitwell truncated his extract from Minter Morgan's book, and provided only a brief summary of the fourth proposal.

346.1
WIGHTWICK, George (1802–1872)
The palace of architecture: a romance of art and history. By George Wightwick, Architect.

London: James Fraser, 1840.

xx + 219 pp, 36 pls (including frontisp., map, and of the plates numbered 1–69 those that are not printed on text leaves).

27.9 × 19.1 cm

MnU

George Wightwick, an architect with a flourishing practice in southwestern England,[1] introduced a highly romantic and imaginative approach to architectural design and criticism in this unusual architectural treatise that he called a "romance of art and history." His purpose, he explained in the dedication, was "to promote a just appreciation of Architecture, in the minds of all who are susceptible of the Beautiful, the Poetical, and the Romantic." To this end he adopted the format of a narrative fantasy, deliberately if not accurately modeled after contemporary novels of Sir Walter Scott. The novels had been extraordinarily successful in stimulating popular appreciation of history, he noted (p. vii), implying that his "Romance" would do the same for architecture.

The narration takes the form of a dream sequence, in which "the uncontrolled imagination of a dreamer" (p. 1) was taken into a walled domain of 50 extraordinary temples. Among these awesome structures the viewer soon perceived the Master Mason, and then the Prince Architect himself, "personifying the ART he loved" (p. 3). The Prince Architect, majestically welcoming the visitor, described his palace and what the visitor could expect to see throughout the visit:

You will see, within this domain, an epitome of the Architectural world. Mine is, as it were, a palace of congress, wherein you will be successively addressed by humble (but, it is hoped, characteristic) representatives of the great families of Design in ancient and Mahomedan India, China, Egypt, Greece, ancient and modern Italy, Turkey, Moorish Spain, and Christian Europe. (p. 3)

The Prince exhorted his audience to understand the feelings and ideas behind each of the styles they would encounter. He said he would strive

to arouse your senses to the importance of ARCHITECTURE, in regard to its MONUMENTAL attributes—to arrest your admiration, by its impressiveness as the leading agent in PICTORIAL ROMANCE—to fascinate your sympathies, by exhibiting its venerable forms as the vehicles of glowing ASSOCIATION—and to stimulate your imaginations, by advocating its claims as a MATERIAL POETRY. (p. 4)

Here the Prince identified four different conceptual approaches to architecture—as monument, as pictorial romance, as stimulus to imaginative associations, and as poetry—and implied he would bring them together for the first time as part of an all-embracing, comprehensive Romantic experience.[2]

The first stop on the journey was to view an "Avenue" running past examples of many different architectural styles, an occasion that Wightwick used to discuss principles of architectural meaning. For Wightwick architecture was replete with semantic content, whether it simply recorded information and events for posterity, or also acted as a partner in a visual, intellectual, and associational dialogue with the viewer. "Architecture," on the most basic level, "affords information where history is silent, or confirms the facts which history asserts" (p. 9). But a spectator, contemplating a work of architecture, "becomes *his own poet*; unites himself with it in the bond of a perfect reciprocity . . .[and becomes] stimulated by the abstract associations connecting it with the distinguished character of the age of which it remains to speak" (p. 14). Sometimes Wightwick rivaled and even exceeded Ruskin in his efforts to animate and spiritualize architecture. He observed at one point that "a piece of genuine Architecture is a *creature*," with extraordinary powers of communication, "breathing, as it were, the sentiment of its original and peculiar purpose, and promulgating, in the symbolic eloquence of its particular form and style, the IDEA of its designer" (p. 15). The designer's ideas, in turn, could be affected by his personal situation as well as by society at large, making the building a complex expression of personal predilections as well as broader historical and cultural characteristics.

With these notions fresh in the reader's mind, Wightwick devoted most of the text to a journey around the Prince Architect's "Palace," encountering buildings in 13 prominent styles: Ancient Indian, Chinese, Egyptian, Greek, Roman, Constantinal, Norman-Gothic, Christian Pointed, Mohammedan Pointed, Italian Pointed, Greco-Roman, Anglo-Greek, and Anglo-Italian. Nearly all the structures were ecclesiastical, although he included a few examples of English domestic work, including two views of an "Old English Manor-House." Of particular interest for the modern architect were views of a "Soanean Interior" and "Soanean Exterior," presented as examples of Greco-Roman style. The "Anglo-Italian Villa," ostensibly designed according to laws of fitness,[3] was two stories high, with a campanile projecting above, and nine principal rooms including a chapel on the ground floor. Wightwick's description was anthropomorphic, with the villa speaking in the first person. The soliloquy concluded: "What am I, then, but an English mansion, adapted to my locality, and to the climate and customs of my country? taking my arrangements from my owner, my leading external features from modern Italy, and my complexion from fair Greece" (p. 202). Two vignettes near the end of the text (p. 203) illustrate appropriate landscape settings for Old English mansions and Italian villas. The former is shown in a cultivated valley and the latter is set up on a hillside with a prospect of mountains in the distance.

Following a page and a half of tender and tearful farewells (pp. 208–209), Wightwick concluded the work with a glossary of architectural terms.

1. Colvin (1978), pp. 888–890.

2. None of these approaches was new. Architecture was conceived as monument at least as early as the Egyptian pyramids. Pictorial composition was fundamental to the architectural theories of Robert Adam, Gilbert Laing Meason, and P. F. Robinson (*qq.v.*), to name just a few. For a discussion of association in architecture, see Chapter III, Section 3, in "The Literature of British Domestic Architecture, 1715–1842" above. Ruskin published a series of articles on "The Poetry of Architecture" under the pseudonym Kata Phusin in *The Architectural Magazine* (ed. John Claudius Loudon, *q.v.*).

3. Pp. 201–205. Note John Claudius Loudon's emphasis on fitness in his influential *Encyclopaedia* (*q.v.*), first published in 1833 and in its fifth edition by the time Wightwick published *The Palace of Architecture*. Loudon considered the English villa to be the paradigm of domestic architecture.

347.1
WILDS, William

Elementary and practical instructions on the art of building cottages and houses for the humbler classes; an easy method of constructing earthen walls, adapted to the erection of dwelling houses, agricultural, and other buildings, surpassing those built of timber in comfort and stability, and equalling those built of brick; and at a considerable saving. To which are added, practical treatises on the manufacture of bricks and lime; on the arts of digging wells and draining; rearing and managing a vegetable garden; management of stock, etc.: for the use of emigrants, to the better lodging of the peasantry of Ireland, and to the improvement of those districts to which the benevolence of landed proprietors is now directed. By William Wilds. . . .

London: John Weale, (Taylor's Architectural Library), 1835.

xxiv + 143 pp, 6 pls.

21.9 × 13.3 cm

MB

Unlike predecessors who exhorted philanthropists and benevolent societies to rehabilitate and improve laborers' housing,[1] Wilds directly addressed those "who, through choice, or the force of circumstances, are led from their native country, and thrown into the solitary forest, or the howling desert, in search of that reward for their industry and exertions which their own country no longer affords them" (p. v). In his concern for the welfare of emigrants as well as those "unable to extricate themselves" (p. 5) he claimed "exemption from all motives of a pecuniary nature" and hoped for the "greatest possible circulation" of his book (p. vi).

In the Introduction (pp. vii–xxiv) Wilds commented briefly on the history of building with compressed earth, or pisé,[2] and then discussed at length its superiority over both wood and brick. Chapter I (pp. 1–36) includes practical advice on emigration, instruction in selecting earth and designing molds for making pisé, and remarks on surveying and constructing foundations. Wilds illustrated a plan for a two-room pisé house on page 12, and an elevation of the house on page 18. The chapter concludes with detailed comments on material and techniques of house construction. Chapters II (pp. 36–44) and III (pp. 44–57) concern the use and manufacture of bricks, and Chapter IV (pp. 58–72) concerns lime. Chapter V (pp. 72–141) consists of "short instructions in the arts of well digging, draining, rearing, and managing a vegetable garden, piggery, poultry, sheep, cows, &c., making of bacon, &c., for winter stock, and similar subjects connected with the welfare and enjoyment of the cottager" (p. 72).[3]

Wilds included six plates, described on pages 142–143, showing elevations and plans for four single cottages, a double cottage, and "Four Cottages, Represented as Two." The smallest designs (Nos. I, II) each contain just one room, intended as "a sleeping apartment only," for "an under-keeper or guard to a gentleman's garden or grounds, or person to attend a gate at night" (p. 142). Larger designs, for couples with and without children, include at least a sitting room, bedroom, washhouse, and privy (Nos. III–V). The final design, "for operative mechanics or manufacturers" (p. 143), is the only design with two stories, and consists of four attached units each with a sitting room, washhouse, and bedroom. The facades of all six designs are ornamented in a very spare manner, with simplified pilasters, stringcourses, and window moldings.

1. See for example Thomas Netherton Parker, *Plans, Specifications, Estimates, and Remarks on Cottages* (1813); William Morton Pitt, *An Address to the Landed Interest* (1797); George Smith, *Essay on the Construction of Cottages* (1834); and the *First Report of the Society for Bettering the Condition of the Poor* (1813).

2. John Plaw was the first author to discuss the use of this material: see his *Ferme Ornée* (1795; *q.v.*). Henry Holland published a detailed description of the process of building with pisé two years later in *Communications to the Board of Agriculture* (1797; *q.v.*). Also see William Barber, *Farm Buildings* (1802; *q.v.*).

3. Much of the information in this chapter was obtained from John Claudius Loudon's *Manual of Cottage Gardening* (1830; *q.v.*). Wilds noted that he had obtained Loudon's permission to do this (p. 73).

348.1
WILKINS, William (1778–1839), trans.
The civil architecture of Vitruvius. Comprising those books of the author which relate to the public and private edifices of the ancients. Translated by William Wilkins. . . . Illustrated by numerous engravings. With an introduction, containing an historical view of the rise and progress of architecture amongst the Greeks.

London: Printed by Thomas Davison. For Longman, Hurst, Rees, Orme, and Brown, 1812 [–1817].

[vi] + lxxvi + 282 pp, 14 + 13 + 9 + 5 pls.

36.7 × 27.3 cm

CtY

Although the title page is dated 1812, the ECB indicates that the first part was issued only in 1813. The plates are dated 1813, 1814, and 1817.

William Wilkins, whose *Antiquities of Magna Graecia* (1807) had already established his scholarly reputation, undertook this translation of Books III through VI of Vitruvius's treatise in order to undo "the corruptions with which the early editors have loaded it."[1] Wilkins complained that "Former translators, in following the text of the printed editions, have propagated these errors, which, in many instances, are wholly subversive of the principles of architecture our author intended to inculcate." This occurred in part because the first editors had "searched for illustrations of their author amongst the edifices of Rome; expecting, with some appearance of probability, that the principles he promulgates would be found to prevail in the buildings of the country which gave him birth." But Wilkins argued that Vitruvius's "work" was based "upon the architectural monuments of Greece," an assertion founded on Wilkins's own "acquaintance with the remains of ancient art in Greece and in Ionia, obtained by studying upon the spot the principles of their construction."

The Introduction (pp. i–lxxvi) was the anonymous work of George Hamilton-Gordon, fourth Earl of Aberdeen.[2] It commences with a discussion of an important problem in early nineteenth-century aesthetics: whether the perceived beauty of Greek architecture derives from intellectual associations or from properties inherent in Greek style and form. Aberdeen treated the problem as the consequence of an ongoing conflict between associational psychology and Edmund Burke's account of the physiological sources of aesthetic pleasure (pp. i–viii).[3] The bulk of the Introduction is a history of Classical architecture, beginning with the origins of human habitation in caves and proceeding through Egyptian, Syrian, and Mycenaean architecture to that of ancient Greece (pp. xvii–xxxiv). Aberdeen included a short discussion of residential architecture in Homer's poetry (pp. xxxiv–xxxix), and then turned to the evolution of the orders, porticoes, and temples (pp. xxxix–lxix). Following a brief discussion of arches and domes (pp. lxx–lxxvi) Aberdeen concluded that in Roman times architecture became "barbarous," with the Roman arch contributing to "a more truly vitiated taste, than would probably have been witnessed had it never existed" (p. lxxvi).

Wilkins's translation of Vitruvius's four books is accompanied by detailed notes and four sets of plates. The first 14 plates, described on pages 33–52, depict different types of Greek temples, columns, and porticoes. The next 13 plates are described on pages 97–120 and illustrate the orders, temple fronts, roofs, doors, and round temples. Nine plates, described on pages 175–196, depict such examples of civil architecture as a basilica, theaters, a bath, and the Palaestra at Ephesus. The final five plates are described on pages 239–260 and include conjectural reconstructions of ancient dwellings: a Roman cavaedium, a Roman house, an Egyptian oecus, a Greek house, and the Palace of the Odyssey. The letterpress concludes with a glossary (pages 263–282).

1. All quotations in this paragraph are from the "Advertisement," printed on two leaves following the dedication. Wilkins indicated he chose Books III–VI, Vitruvius's account of civil architecture, because he believed this was the most seriously corrupt portion of Vitruvius's *Ten Books*.

2. For a thorough discussion of Aberdeen's contributions to this book, see R. W. Liscombe, *William Wilkins 1778–1839* (Cambridge: Cambridge University Press, 1980), Chapter V.

3. On associational psychology and aesthetics see Martin Kallich, *The Association of Ideas and Critical Theory in Eighteenth-Century England* (The Hague: Mouton, 1970); and Walter John Hipple, Jr., *The Beautiful, the Sublime, and the Picturesque in Eighteenth-Century British Aesthetic Theory* (Carbondale: Southern Illinois University Press, 1957). On association in architecture see John Archer, "The Beginnings of Association in British Architectural Esthetics," *Eighteenth-Century Studies* XVI: 3 (Spring 1983), 241–264; and George L. Hersey, *High Victorian Gothic* (Baltimore: Johns Hopkins University Press, 1972). On Burke see Hipple, op. cit., and Edmund Burke, *A Philosophical Enquiry into the Origin of Our Ideas of the Sublime and the Beautiful* (London, 1757; expanded edition, 1759).

349.1
WILLICH, Anthony Florian Madinger
The domestic encyclopaedia; or, a dictionary of facts, and useful knowledge: comprehending a concise view of the latest discoveries, inventions, and improvements, chiefly applicable to rural and domestic economy; together with descriptions of the most interesting objects of nature and art; the history of men and animals, in a state of health or disease; and practical hints respecting the arts and manufactures, both familiar and commercial. Illustrated with numerous engravings and cuts. In four volumes. Volume. . . . By A. F. M. Willich. . . .

London: Printed for Murray and Highley; Vernor and Hood; G. Kearsley; H. D. Symonds, and Thomas Hurst; and the author, 1802.

[*Four volumes, 1802.*]

Art. "Country-houses," II, 83–87.

21.1 × 12.6 cm

MnU

The article on "Architecture" (I, 97–100) includes a brief account of the origin of building, a short paragraph on the five orders, and a summary history of Roman, medieval, and Renaissance styles. It concludes with remarks on several recent architectural books, and a few theoretical maxims.

The article on "Country Houses" is the only such article to appear in an encyclopedia before midcentury. The text and illustrations are disappointingly provincial and retardataire. After some initial observations on the susceptibility of houses to fire, Willich described a country house designed according to "certain principles, adopted by Mr. BORDLEY, the ingenious American farmer" (p. 84). As shown on page 85, the plan forms an H, similar to English and American farm houses of the seventeenth and early eighteenth centuries,[1] and has six principal rooms on the main floor. The elevation is three stories high, with tall windows reminiscent of English mansions built before 1730. The remainder of the text concerns dimensions, materials, and methods of construction.

1. See S[tephen] P[rimatt], *The City & Country Purchaser & Builder* (London, [1667]); and Fiske Kimball, *Domestic Architecture of the American Colonies* (New York: Scribner, 1922), pp. 44, 54, 70–71.

350.1

WILSON, William Carus (1791–1859)

Helps to the building of churches and parsonage houses: containing plans, elevations, specifications, etc. By the Rev. William Carus Wilson. . . .

Kirkby Lonsdale: Printed and sold by Arthur Foster: sold also by L. and J. Seeley; J. G. and F. Rivington; J. Hatchard and Sons, London, 1835.

1 printed leaf, 24 pp, frontisp. + 1 + 8 pls.

27.3 × 21.6 cm

V&A

350.2

Helps to the building of churches, parsonage houses, and schools: containing plans, elevations, specifications, &c. By the Rev. W. Carus Wilson. . . . Second edition.

Kirkby Lonsdale: A. Foster: L. and G. Seeley, London, 1842.

viii + 38 pp, frontisp. + 1 + 16 pls.

21.6 × 13.7 cm

Bodl.

In 1824 the Rev. William Carus Wilson founded the Clergy Daughters' School in the village of Cowan Bridge. In 1833 the school was moved to Casterton, where he prepared plans for an adjacent chapel, consecrated in October 1833. The school and chapel figure prominently in the text and illustrations of *Helps to the Building of Churches*.[1] The remarks below are based on examination of the 1842 edition.

Four preliminary pages are devoted to quotations from the Bible and from Wordsworth. The text opens with a statement of purpose—"to help forward the good work of building Churches, Parsonage Houses, and Schools" (p. 1). There are brief remarks on the growing need for such institutions (pp. 3–6), followed by a discussion of the Church Building Act (pp. 6–12). Carus Wilson warned that a "Church destitute of architectural propriety is in no case recommended," but suggested that too costly a design might leave the endowment dangerously small, or even discourage erection of the church in the first place (p. 12). He then put forward his own chapel at Casterton as an exemplary model of "what has recently been done very successfully, and at a very moderate expense" (p. 13). He described the building in detail and added remarks on its construction and financing (pp. 13–22).

In the second edition Carus Wilson also included descriptions of Holme Church and Parsonage (because it "was not easy to convince many persons that Casterton Chapel was really finished for the sum mentioned"), Casterton Parsonage, Casterton Village School and Rooms for the Aged Poor, and an Infant School and Room for Public Meetings and Lectures. He described these designs on pages 24–28, and provided specifications on pages 29–32 for erecting a church. The text concludes with "Suggestions Published by the Incorporated Society for Building Churches" pertaining to the construction of churches (pp. 33–38).

The plates include views, elevations, sections, and plans of Casterton Chapel, Holme Chapel and Parsonage House, Casterton Parsonage, Grimsarch Parsonage, the Village School at Casterton, a "School and Dwelling House," an "Infant School, and Room for Public Meetings," and a pulpit. All of Wilson's designs are in a style that he described as "old English" (p. 20), with casement windows, Tudor drip moldings, occasional bargeboarding, and some decorative finials and ornamental chimneys. Of the three designs for parsonages illustrated, that at Casterton is slightly larger than the other two. The ground floor includes a drawing room, dining room, sitting room, kitchen, scullery, pantry, and storeroom. There are six rooms on the chamber floor, plus "Water, and other Closets," and four more rooms on the top floor. The village school at Casterton includes a "School Room," two "Dwelling Rooms," and one bedroom on the ground floor, plus five bedrooms and three larger rooms on the chamber floor. Carus Wilson indicated that the "rooms above and behind will accommodate twelve aged poor" (p. 26). The one-story design for a "School and Dwelling House" includes two schoolrooms and a four-room "Teachers House." At one end of the "Infant School, and Room for Public Meetings" there is a "House" (a room 14 feet by 11 feet) and two bedrooms.

1. For further details of Carus Wilson's life see Jane M. Ewbank, *The Life and Works of William Carus Wilson 1791–1859* (Kendal, England: Titus Wilson & Son, 1960).

351.1
WOOD, John (1704–1754)
The origin of building: or, the plagiarism of the heathens detected. In five books. By John Wood, Architect.

Bath: Printed by S. and F. Farley, and sold by J. Leake: M. Lewis, in Bristol: W. Innys; C. Hitch; R. Dodsley; J. Pine; and J. Brindley, London, 1741.

[iv] + 235 pp, 36 pls.

42.5 × 25.7 cm

MnU

Wood sharply criticized the Vitruvian thesis that mankind naturally and progressively evolved techniques, styles, and forms of architecture over the course of centuries.[1] Instead he argued that, according to Scripture, architecture was suddenly and divinely revealed to mankind, and that all subsequent architecture, including that of ancient Greece and Rome, derived from this divine revelation.[2] Whatever the pagan Classical civilizations claimed as their own invention was merely plagiarism of the divine:

the *Knowledge* our Ancestors first had in Arts and Sciences, *was given them immediately by* GOD; we purpose, in the following Sheets, not only to weigh and consider, the Origin, Progress, and Perfection of Building, so as to make an Account thereof consistent with Sacred History, with the Confession of the Antients, with the Course of great Events in all Parts of the World, and with itself; but, from Time to Time, to point out the *Plagiarism of the Heathens.* (p. 11)

The first four of Wood's five "Books" therefore chronicle the history of architecture as it appears in Scripture, from the city of Enoch, built by Cain (Genesis 4:17), until the Roman era. In Book V Wood then discussed "the Orders of Columns, . . . the Forms and Proportions of Temples, Basilica's, and other celebrated Edifices of Antiquity; and . . . the Standard Measures of the Antients" (p. 181)—all presented as the Classical remains of what originally had been divinely inspired architectural forms.

Standard Neoclassical tenets such as order, proportion, and beauty figure prominently in Wood's historical chronicle; mankind learned of them too through divine revelation. Nor does Wood's account of the invention of the orders differ seriously from the Vitruvian account except for the intervention of God. Both accounts, for example, extol the imitation of nature, and of trees in particular:

GOD was graciously pleased, in these *Pillars*, to direct how we should supply our Necessities in Building, with the Materials of the Earth, and even reconcile Art with Nature in our future Imitations; to which Purpose, as the *Pillars* imitated *Trees*, so they were made with a Base at the Bottom, to answer the Root, and with a Capital at Top to represent the Head of a *Tree*: GOD showing us, in the very same structure, how we ought to apply the Imitation of natural Things, in natural Places. (p. 70)

Wood chronicled in detail the transmission of these divine revelations from Mosaic times to ancient Greece, whence all subsequent civilizations derived their knowledge of the orders. He focused in particular on cities and structures that are described in the Bible, although his descriptions were based on literary reconstructions by others as well as on biblical accounts.[3] To illustrate and support his discussion Wood included plates depicting the altar at the foot of Mount Sinai, Moses's Tabernacle, the Camp of the Israelites, Moses's plans for a new city, the Temple of Solomon and Solomon's Palace, and Ezekiel's vision of a new city. Plates 6 and 31–36 show the Classical orders and moldings. He also included several plates illustrating stages in the progress of domestic architecture. Plates 4 and 5 depict houses by Zuccari and Palladio. Plates 7–11, in comparison, show plans and elevations for two-story "cottages," Wood's own reconstructions in a Classical vocabulary of dwellings "common" in the time of Moses (p. 93). They are square in plan, with four pilasters on each face. Wood considered each corner pair of pilasters as a single unit, thus making a total of 12 pilasters for each cottage, and enabling Wood to trace his design directly to the original 12 pillars erected by Moses at the foot of Mount Sinai (p. 93). Wood thus suggested that his designs were examples of a divinely revealed and scripturally justified architecture.

1. Wood offered the following synopsis of Vitruvius:

VITRUVIUS tells us, That Men at first were born in Woods and Caverns, like the Beasts, and lived therein on the Fruits of the Earth.

VITRUVIUS says, That an impetuous Wind happened to arise, it pushed the Trees in a certain Wood with such Violence against one another, that by their Friction they took Fire; which drove Mankind out from amongst them: This caused Men to assemble together, to live in the same Place, and to make Huts to dwell in; some with Leaves, others with Branches of Trees and Pieces of Clay; while some dug Lodges in the Mountains. . . .

VITRUVIUS goes on with telling us, that Dorus having built a Temple in the antient City of Argos, that Temple was found by Chance to be of the Order which was afterwards call'd

Dorick; after which several other Temples were erected of the same Order in the neighbouring Cities, but at that Time there were no Rules observed for the Proportions of Architecture. . . . [Later] the Pillars were then adjusted after Proportions taken from the Human Body. (pp. 9–10)

To this Wood opposed a description of the expulsion from Eden, and Moses's account of building the Tabernacle in the Wilderness "by the Direction of God" (p. 10).

2. This argument was a sincere but largely ignored challenge to theses advanced in the 1750s by Abbé Laugier and Sir William Chambers. They argued that architecture evolved in a primitive state of society, according to natural principles and natural instinct, into a "primitive" hut that embodied the fundamental characteristics of the Classical orders. See Marc-Antoine Laugier, *Essai sur l'architecture* (Paris, 1753), and Sir William Chambers, *A Treatise on Civil Architecture* (London, 1759; *q.v.*). For a wide-ranging discussion of these issues see Joseph Rykwert, *On Adam's House in Paradise* (New York: Museum of Modern Art, 1972), Chapters 3 and 5.

3. E.g., Ioannes Baptista Villalpandus, *In Ezechielem explanationes et apparatus Urbis ac Templi Hierosolymitani* (Rome, 1596–1604).

352.1
WOOD, John (1728–1781)

A series of plans, for cottages or habitations of the labourer, either in husbandry, or the mechanic arts, adapted as well to towns, as to the country. Engraved on thirty plates. To which is added, an introduction, containing many useful observations on this class of building; tending to the comfort of the poor and advantage of the builder: with calculations of expences. By the late Mr. J. Wood, of Bath, Architect. A new edition.

London: Printed for I. and J. Taylor, 1792.

38 pp, 28 + 2 pls.

41.9 × 33.0 cm

V&A

352.2 ‖

A series of plans for cottages or habitations of the labourer, either in husbandry, or the mechanic arts, adapted as well to towns as to the country. Engraved on thirty plates. To which is added an introduction, containing many useful observations on this class of building; tending to the comfort of the poor and advantage of the builder: with calculations of expences. By the late Mr. J. Wood, of Bath, Architect. A new edition, corrected to the present time.

London: Printed for J. Taylor, 1806.

31 + [1] pp, 28 + 2 pls.

35 × 28 cm

Reference: Information supplied by Fine Arts Library, Cornell University.

352.3 †

[A series of] plans of cottages. New edition.

[London]: Taylor, ca. 1814.

Royal 4°

Reference: ECB

352.4 †

[A series of] plans for labourers' cottages.

[N. loc.: n. pub.], 1837.

f°

Reference: *The Edinburgh Review* 65:131, April 1837, 267.

For several reasons the first edition is generally assumed to have been published in 1781: the plates are dated that year, the author died that year, and the next edition (1792) is described on the title page as "a new edition." Nevertheless I have been unable to verify that any copy of a 1781 edition exists.

The remarks below are based on examination of the 1806 edition, which closely resembles the 1792 edition but lacks six pages of remarks on the construction of cottages.

The first British book wholly devoted to farm house designs was published in 1747 by Daniel Garret.[1] In an effort to promote agricultural improvement Nathaniel Kent published designs for healthful and economical laborers' dwellings in 1775.[2] Wood's objectives in *A Series of Plans* likewise included an increase in the national output, but he also expressed a compassionate, humane concern for the comfort and prosperity of laborers and farmers in both town and country.

On the first page of the Introduction (pp. 3–19) Wood argued that "no architect can form a decent plan, unless he ideally places himself in the situation of the person for whom he designs: I say it was necessary for me to feel as the cottager himself; and for that end to visit him; to enquire after the conveniencies he wanted, and into the inconveniencies he laboured under" (p. 3). And as he explored various living conditions, there was much to disturb him: "the greatest part of the cottages that fell within my observation, I found to be shattered, dirty, inconvenient, miserable hovels, scarcely affording a shelter for the beasts of the forest; much less were they proper habitations for the human species" (p. 3–4). Wood therefore was indignant "that no architect had, as yet, thought it worth his while to offer to the public any well constructed plans for cottages" (p. 3).

Wood's philanthropic concern and his interest in the practical conditions of life among cottagers were unique among major architects of his generation,[3] but his approach to cottage design was more orthodox. At the very beginning of his essay he recalled the notion of a hierarchy of architectural genres, stating that there is a "regular gradation between the plan of the most simple hut and that of the most superb palace; that a palace is nothing more than a cottage IMPROVED; and that the plan of the latter is the basis as it were of plans for the former" (p. 3).[4] Having thus established the legitimacy of cottages as a type, Wood turned to practical matters of cottage design and construction. He set forth seven fundamental "principles, on which all cottages should be built," and offered practical suggestions for implementing them in cottage design (pp. 4–7). All cottages, he said, should be (1) dry and healthy, (2) warm, cheerful, and comfortable, (3) convenient, (4) greater than 12 feet wide, (5) built in pairs so that residents could render mutual assistance, (6) economically built, strong, and made of the best materials, and (7) provided with garden plots for the cottagers' own use. Noting that his designs were prepared specifically for the region east of Bath (p. 7), Wood also discussed methods of construction and prices of labor and materials for masons, bricklayers, iron-mongers, carpenters, plasterers, tilers, thatchers, and paviors (pp. 9–19).

The plate descriptions (pp. 20–31) serve as a key to the plans and also include remarks on the use, site, and construction of individual cottage designs. The two "Miscellaneous" plates illustrate studwork, trusses, joints, and other aspects of carpentry. The remaining 28 plates include cottage designs in four "Classes." Those in the "First Class" (Plates I–IV) contain just one room, "Second Class" cottages have two rooms (Plates V–XI), "Third Class" cottages have three rooms (Plates XII–XXI), and those in the "Fourth Class" (Plates XXII–XXVIII) have four rooms.[5] With one exception each design is shown in at least one elevation and one plan.[6] Altogether there are designs for 27 single cottages, 16 double cottages, two quadruple cottages, a multiple cottage for six residents, and another for 16 residents. All the designs are clearly in the Garret and Halfpenny tradition of plain, crisp forms, composed with an eye for the relationships between geometric solids.[7] The elevations, completely devoid of ornament, are composed of projecting and recessed flat surfaces, reflecting midcentury Palladian concerns for planarity, geometry, and proportion.

1. Daniel Garret, *Designs, and Estimates, of Farm Houses* (1747; *q.v.*).

2. Nathaniel Kent, *Hints to Gentlemen of Landed Property* (1775; *q.v.*).

3. Wood also executed a number of important works in Bath and elsewhere, the most significant being the Royal Crescent in Bath (1767–1775).

4. Unlike Garret (*q.v.*) Wood did not attempt to define the differences among different architectural genres. Nor did Wood follow William Halfpenny's suggestion in *Six New Designs* (1751; *q.v.*) that cottages, not palaces, epitomized architectural ideals.

5. Wood took some liberties with this classification. Several designs include additional bedrooms, bringing the total number of rooms above that permitted for a given "Class."

6. Plate IV depicts a poorhouse erected for the Borough of St. Ives, with 16 rooms plus an apartment for the overseer. Wood included two plans but no elevation.

7. For Garret, see note 1 above. For Halfpenny, see *Six New Designs* (1751; *q.v.*) and other titles.

353.1 ‡
WOOD, John, Jr.

A manual of perspective, being a familiar explanation of the science, including the rules necessary for the correct representation of objects, the principles of shadows, reflections in water, &c. Adapted more particularly for the use of amateurs. By J. Wood, Junr. With numerous examples.

Worcester: Published by Wood & Son, 1841.

iv + 5–28 pp, 7 pls.

8°

Reference: Microfilm supplied by The British Library.

353.2

A manual of perspective, ⟨ . . . as 1841 . . . ⟩ amateurs. By J. Wood, Jun. . . . Second edition, with additions.

Worcester: Wood and Son; and Whittaker and Co., London, 1843.

v + 7–34 pp, 7 pls.

24.6 × 15.0 cm

BL

353.3 ‖

A manual of perspective, being a familiar explanation of the science, including the rules necessary for the correct representation of objects, the projection of shadows, reflections in water, &c. Adapted more particularly for the use of amateurs. By J. Wood. Third edition.

Worcester: Wood and Son; Whittaker and Co., London, [1849].

v + 7–34 pp, 7 pls.

Reference: Information supplied by Winterthur Museum Library.

The first and second editions are dated 1841 and 1843, respectively, on the title page. The third edition was dated [1849] by the British Museum, perhaps on the basis of an entry for that year in ECB. The contents of Plates 5 and 7, discussed below, are the same in all editions, but the location of these plates within the volume varies from edition to edition.

To justify publication of yet another treatise on perspective, Wood noted that most of those currently available were too "voluminous" to be affordable (1841, p. iii). A few others, recently published, were full of technicalities and thus unintelligible. The rest were too "fanciful" (1841, p. iii). The present work, therefore, would include the fundamental rudiments of perspective, explained concisely without the use of technical terms, and illustrated by examples (1841, p. iv). As completed, Wood's text includes six principal sections that treat general principles first, then objects set at an angle to the picture plane, objects set at an angle to the horizon, objects angled toward both picture plane and horizon, shadows, and reflections in water.

Wood's illustrations include a variety of geometric diagrams, perspective views of boxes, a bookcase, a bridge, and a distant church steeple, plus four examples of domestic architecture. Plate 3 illustrates the interior of an unfurnished room, with two doorways and three floor-length windows. In Plate 5 there is a row of three houses, each two stories high.[1] Plate 5 also contains a view of a masonry cottage with rudimentary Tudor moldings, partly hidden by a wall and dense foliage. In Plate 7 there is a view of a large Greek Revival mansion. Its facade, symmetrical except for a tetrastyle Ionic portico at one end, is distinguished by a projecting, pilastered, segmental bow at the center.

1. This figure is similar to illustrations in contemporary treatises by John Cart Burgess (1819) and William Rider (1836), *qq.v.*

354.1
WOOD, John George, F.S.A.
Six lectures, on the principles and practice of perspective as applicable to drawing from nature: accompanied with a mechanical apparatus. By John George Wood.

London: Printed by Bye and Law, for the author; and sold by R. Faulder, C. Law, and J. Taylor, 1804.

ix + 77 pp, 1 + 7 pls.

27.0 × 21.6 cm

BL

354.2
————

Lectures on the principles and practice of perspective, as delivered at the Royal Institution, accompanied with a mechanical apparatus, and illustrated by engravings. By John George Wood, F.A.S. The second edition, corrected and enlarged.

London: Printed for T. Cadell and W. Davies, Strand. By J. M'Creery, 1809.

vii + 95 pp, 13 pls (incl. frontisp.).

28.5 × 22.5 cm

PPL

354.3
————

Lectures on the principles and practice of perspective, as delivered at the Royal Institution. Illustrated by engravings. By John George Wood, F.A.S. The third edition. Corrected and enlarged.

London: Printed for T. Cadell and W. Davies, 1844.

vii + 95 pp, 16 pls (frontisp., 5 unnumbered, 1–9, X).

27.2 × 20.8 cm

NIC

The book is organized in a practical and straightforward manner, with no prefatory claim to originality or uniqueness. In the final edition the first chapter or "Lecture" begins with definitions and procedures for preparing pictures. The next five "Lectures" cover the fundamentals of perspective drawing. The last "Lecture" devotes special attention to representing meanders in a river, reflections in water, buildings, natural scenery, and other subjects.

The plates include geometric diagrams, two views of a small church, and landscape scenes, but also include more sophisticated domestic subjects than many perspective treatises of Wood's day. Among the first seven numbered plates, which appear in all editions, there are several examples of row houses and single detached houses. Figure 2 in Plate 2 shows a two-story row house in oblique and end view, and Figure 4 shows a two-story mansion, five windows wide and five windows deep, in oblique view. Plate 3 includes the facade of a two-story house, a bridge, and a row of Gothic vaults. Figure 4 in Plate 6 shows six attached houses, each two stories high and three windows wide, rising stepwise on one side of a street ascending a hill. By the final edition Wood had added several complex and detailed views of urban subjects. The frontispiece is a view of Portland Place, flanked on both sides by three-story terrace houses. Three unnumbered plates show an interior view of a fashionably furnished room, and ascending and descending views of the structures flanking Hay Hill.

355.1

WOODS, Joseph, Jr. (1776–1864)
"An essay on the situations and accompaniments of villas," *Essays of the London Architectural Society* (1808), 97–124, and 4 pls.

NNC

"My object," Woods stated, "is to enquire what situations, and what accompaniments, are to be chosen to make a house appear *beautiful*" (p. 100). He also wanted to analyze certain characteristics of dwellings that accorded in a picturesque manner with landscape scenery.[1]

To these ends Woods examined three different types of dwelling—the cottage, the box, and the villa—but considered the first two only briefly. "The ideas" that a cottage "suggests are those of quiet, seclusion from the world, and domestic comfort." All architectural features must be "simple" and "unassuming" in order to preserve the neat and comfortable "character" of the cottage. Therefore Woods recommended that a cottage should have no pointed windows, nor even any ornament, and that it should be located "in a garden" and "in a sheltered situation" (pp. 101–102). The box, a type of dwelling in between the cottage and villa, offers neither the "seclusion of the cottage" nor "the dignity of the villa," but it does have the potential to unite "neatness and comfort, prospect and some display of wealth" (p. 103).

Woods characterized the villa as "a house in the country, apparently calculated for the residence of a gentleman" (p. 100). He suggested various forms a villa might take, all based on Doric or Ionic temples, some with added porticoes and wings. He indicated that in all cases the design should be symmetrical; indeed he was "astonished that any one should have thought it necessary to build irregular houses, for the sake of variety and picturesque beauty." Symmetrically balanced variations in plan and elevation, he argued, could produce a wide "difference of character and expression" (pp. 114–115). The first three plates include designs for villas based on Greek temple forms and surrounded by picturesque scenery. The fourth plate depicts various types of wings, which Woods discussed at length (pp. 107ff). Following brief remarks on landscape parks and trees (pp. 115–120), the article concludes with an analysis of "castle" and "abbey" styles, which Woods dismissed as unpleasant and impractical to live in (pp. 120ff).

1. Fourteen years earlier Humphry Repton had taken up this problem in *Sketches and Hints on Landscape Gardening* (1794; *q.v.*). Edmund Bartell also touched on the subject in *Hints for Picturesque Improvements* (1804; *q.v.*). In support of his observations, Woods cited the writings of Repton, Richard Payne Knight, Uvedale Price, and Edmund Burke (p. 98). For Knight, see the commentary above on his poem *The Landscape* (1794; *q.v.*). For Price, see *An Essay on the Picturesque* (London, 1794); and for Burke, see *A Philosophical Enquiry into the Origin of Our Ideas of the Sublime and the Beautiful* (London, 1757 and later editions).

356.1
WOOLFE, John (-1793), and James GANDON (1743–1823)

Vitruvius Britannicus, or the British architect; containing plans, elevations, and sections; of the regular buildings both public and private, in Great Britain. Comprised in one hundred folio plates, engrav'd by the best hands; taken from the buildings, or original designs by Woolfe and Gandon Architects. Vol. IV.

Vitruvius Britannicus, ou l'architecte Britannique; contenant les plans, elevations et, sections; des batimens reguliers, tant, particuliers que publics, de la Grande Bretagne compris en cent planches gravées en taille douce par les meilleurs maitres, tirées des batimens, ou copiees des desseins originaux. Par messrs. Woolfe et Gandon Architectes. Tome, IV.

[N. loc.: N. pub.], 1767.

12 pp, 100 pls (including title page, dedication, and nos. 1–98).

Vitruvius Britannicus, or the British architect; containing plans elevations and sections; of the regular buildings both public and private, in Great Britain. Comprised in one hundred folio plates, engrav'd by the best hands; taken from the buildings, or original designs by Woolfe and Gandon architects. Vol. V.

Vitruvius Britannicus, ou l'architecte Britannique; contenant les plans, elevations et, sections; des batimens reguliers, tant, particuliers que publics, de la Grande Bretagne compris en cent planches gravees en taille douce par les meilleurs maitres, tirees des batimens, ou copiees des desseins originaux. Par messrs. Woolfe et Gandon Architectes. Tome, V.

[N. loc.: N. pub.], 1771.

10 pp, 100 pls (including title page, dedication, and nos. 3–100).

44.8 × 28.9 cm

MBAt

In 1715 Colen Campbell suggested that the destiny of modern British architecture was to surpass that of France and Italy.[1] In 1767 James Paine announced that British architecture was rapidly approaching a level not seen since the Roman empire.[2] In the same year Woolfe and Gandon published the "fourth" volume of *Vitruvius Britannicus*,[3] ostensibly a sequel to Campbell's treatise, and they were eager to assert that British architecture had in fact equaled that of the Ancients:

the many elegant and sumptuous buildings already recently erected, and still erecting throughout Great Britain, have furnished us with an opportunity of convincing the world and posterity, that architecture was brought to as great a point of perfection in this kingdom in the eighteenth century, as ever it was known to be among the Greeks and Romans. (p. 1)

Thus they adhered to Campbell's program: "We have throughout this production considered Mr. Campbell as our leader; and have, therefore, no way deviated from his plan" (pp. 1–2).

The first volume consists of an engraved title page and dedication to the king, and Introduction in English and French (pp. 1–2), an explanation of the plates in English and French (pp. 3–10), a list of subscribers (pp. 11–12), and plates. The second volume contains an engraved title page and dedication, a new list of subscribers (pp. 1–2), an explanation of the plates in English and French (pp. 3–10), and plates.

The plates consist almost entirely of plans and elevations of dwellings, with far fewer examples of other architectural types than in Campbell's volumes.[4] The residences illustrated are almost uniformly in the Palladian style. Among the architects represented are Robert Adam, Matthew Brettingham, Lancelot Brown, the Earl of Burlington, John Carr of York, William Chambers, Kenton Couse, George Dance, John Donowell, Henry Flitcroft, James Gandon, William Hiorne, John James, William Kent, Stiff Leadbetter, James Leoni, Roger Morris, James Paine, Joseph Pickford, John Sanderson, Robert Taylor, James Thornhill, John Vardy, Isaac Ware, John Wood, John Woolfe, Stephen Wright, and Thomas Wright. In addition there are two historical designs: Coleshill House, here attributed to Inigo Jones, and Longford Castle (1591), both apparently included because "His lordship, as a great promoter and encourager of this work, made us a present of these plates" (1771, p. 10).

1. Colen Campbell, *Vitruvius Britannicus* (1715; *q.v.*).

2. James Paine, *Plans, Elevations and Sections* (1767; *q.v.*), p. i.

3. In 1739 Badeslade and Rocque published *Vitruvius Brittanicus, Volume the Fourth* (*q.v.*), essentially a collection of topographical views that Woolfe and Gandon clearly chose to ignore.

4. Woolfe and Gandon illustrated the following subjects that are not of a strictly residential nature: in Volume I, a bridge, the York Assembly Rooms, several stables and other offices, and the semi-official Mansion House in London; in Volume II, the Horse Guards, the County Hall in Nottingham, and a bridge.

357.1

WRIGHT, Thomas (1711–1786)

Universal architecture, Book I. Six original designs of arbours. By Thomas Wright, of Durham.

London: Printed for the author, 1755.

3 printed leaves, 12 pls.

Universal architecture, Book II. Six original designs of grottos. By Thomas Wright, of Durham.

London: Printed for the author, 1758.

2 printed leaves, 12 pls.

27.9 × 45.1 cm

CtY-BA

Universal Architecture is an attractive collection of designs for arbors and grottoes, but the title is hardly appropriate. There are two parts, or Books, each with a title page, two or three leaves of letterpress, and twelve plates. Altogether there are designs for six arbors and six grottoes, each shown in plan and elevation.

The title page of Book I is embellished with a view of a rustic arbor with a conical roof supported by tree-trunk columns. The list of subscribers is arranged in two columns flanking a view of a different design. On the recto of the next leaf is an "index" of the designs for arbors, giving a description of each in one or two lines; on the verso brief remarks "To the Reader" caution that the word "Arbour . . . is to be understood in the artificial, not in its natural Sense," but Wright did not expand on this distinction. A third leaf at the end of Book I includes suggestions for appropriate types of scenery—plants, rocks, ground—among which to locate these designs.[1] The twelve plates are elevations and plans of arbors "of the Cave or Cabin Kind," "of the Hut or Hovel-kind," "of the Parasol Kind," "of the Aviary Kind," "of the Hermitage Kind," and "for Entertainments in the open Air." Book II is arranged in a similar manner, but lacks a list of subscribers. The six designs for grottoes are "of the Cell or Cavern Kind," "of the Rustic Kind," "of the Bramage Kind," "of the Moresk Kind," an object to terminate a romantic view, and "of the Antique Ruin Kind."

The scenery that surrounds each structure is the most elaborate and complex found to date in a British architectural treatise. Two years earlier Halfpenny hesitantly had added single trees to the left and right of his designs in *The Country Gentleman's Pocket Companion* (1753; q.v.). Wright now established a complex visual dialogue between the Rococo forms of his architectural designs and their exuberant natural surroundings. Some designs clearly were prepared with an extensive natural context in mind— the grotto intended to terminate a view, for example, or the arbor "of the Parasol Kind suited to a Situation commanding an extensive Prospect." In other cases Wright exploited the variety, form, and texture of natural elements in the immediate vicinity of his designs. For example the "Druid's Cell, or Arbour of the Hermitage Kind, purposely designed for a Study or philosophical Retirement" is shown set into the side of a hill and surrounded overhead and on the sides by dense foliage. Conversely the arbor "of the Tholus Kind, proposed for Entertainments in the open Air" is a light and open structure, set on a raised level in a clearing in the midst of a forest.

•

On Wright's career as an architect and garden designer see the catalogue of his works prepared by Eileen Harris and included with the reprint of *Universal Architecture* (London: Scolar Press, 1979).

1. This concern for suiting buildings to particular types of scenery suggests an awareness of contemporary landscape theory. See John Shebbeare, *Letters on the English Nation* (London, 1755), pp. 270–272.

358.1
WRIGHTE, William

Grotesque architecture, or, rural amusement; consisting of plans, elevations, and sections, for huts, retreats, summer and winter hermitages, terminaries, Chinese, Gothic, and natural grottos, cascades, baths, mosques, Moresque pavillions, grotesque and rustic seats, green houses, &c. Many of which may be executed with flints, irregular stones, rude branches, and roots of trees. The whole containing twenty-eight entire new designs, beautifully engraved on copper plates, with scales to each. To which is added, a full explanation, in letter press, and the true method of executing them. By William Wrighte, Architect.

London: Printed for Henry Webley, 1767.

14 pp, frontisp. + 28 pls.

22.9 × 14.6 cm

MH

358.2
————

Grotesque architecture, or rural amusement; consisting of plans, elevations, and sections, for huts, retreats, summer and winter hermitages, terminaries, Chinese, Gothic, and natural grottos, cascades, baths, mosques, Moresque pavilions, grotesque and rustic seats, green houses, &c. Many of which may be executed with flints, irregular stones, rude branches, and roots of trees. The whole containing twenty-eight new designs, with scales to each. To which is added, an explanation, with the method of executing them. By William Wrighte, Architect. A new edition.

London: Printed for I. and J. Taylor, 1790.

14 pp, frontisp. + 28 pls.

23.5 × 14.0 cm

Soane

358.3

———

Grotosque [*sic*] architecture, or rural amusement consisting of plans, elevations, and sections, for huts, retreats, summer and winter hermitages, terminaries, Chinese, Gothic, and natural grottos, cascades, baths, mosques, Moresque pavillions, grotesque and rustic seats, green houses, &c. Many of which may be executed with flints, irregular stones, rude branches, and roots of trees. The whole containing twenty-eight new designs, with scales to each. To which is added, an explanation, with the method of executing them. By William Wrighte, Architect, a new edition.

London: Printed for I. Taylor, [n.d.].

13 pp, frontisp. + 28 pls.

23.5 × 14.0 cm

MBAt

358.4

———

Grotesque architecture; or, rural amusement: consisting of plans, elevations, and sections, for huts, retreats, summer and winter hermitages, terminaries, Chinese, Gothic, and natural grottos, cascades, baths, mosques, Moresque pavilions, grotesque and rustic seats, green-houses, &c. Many of which may be executed with flints, irregular stones, rude branches, and roots of trees. The whole containing twenty-eight new designs, with scales to each. To which is added, an explanation, with the method of executing them. By William Wrighte, Architect. A new edition.

London: Printed by W. Stratford; for J. Taylor, 1802.

8 pp, frontisp. + 28 pls.

24.8 × 15.2 cm

MB

358.5

———

———

London: Printed by W. Stratford; for J. Taylor, 1815.

8 pp, frontisp. + 28 pls.

24.1 × 15. 2 cm

MB

Grotesque Architecture consists of a frontispiece, title page, plate descriptions (pp. 3–14 in the 1767 and 1790 editions), and 28 plates.

Unlike frontispieces to many other eighteenth- and nineteenth-century architectural books, Wrighte's is not simply a portrait or an illustration of one of his own designs, but is an imaginary scene depicting several of his designs in a natural landscape setting. A glen or dell in the foreground is enclosed by a tree-covered ridge to the sides and rear. Examples of Wrighte's designs appear throughout this setting: there is a mosque, a ruined arch, a hermitage or grotto, and a rude hut made of thatch, mud, and sticks. In the middle ground two men hold plans for another small building, and in the foreground two laborers prepare its foundations. In the distance are three men who appear to be hermits or ascetics, presumably inhabitants of the hermitage. At the bottom of the frontispiece are ten lines of verse on the subject of grottoes, taken from Robert Morris's poem *The Art of Architecture* (1742).[1] The frontispiece was designed to aid the viewer—especially the prospective client—in imagining Wrighte's building designs in a landscape setting. Indeed Wrighte was the first to publish such a scene in a book of architectural designs—showing specific designs set into natural surroundings in a consciously artful way.

The plate descriptions include little more than a discussion of building materials. Occasionally there is a suggestion of some greater aesthetic concern, as in the case of the first plate, a hut, "intended to represent the primitive State of the Dorick Order," or Plate 14, a grotto "built of large rough stones rudely put together, so that the building may as near as possible imitate the beautiful appearance of nature" (1790, pp. 3, 8).

The plates include 25 designs for garden structures: a hut, seven hermitages, five grottoes, four cascades, a seat, a bath, four mosques, a "moresque" temple, and "a greenhouse of the grotesque kind." The plans reveal Wrighte's concern for Palladian principles of proportion and symmetry.[2] Typical examples are composed of squares, circles, and other regular figures: the hut in Plate 1 is square in plan, 10 feet 9 inches on a side, and the plan of the mosque in Plate 22 consists of a circle, 20 feet in diameter, plus four squares, eight feet on a side, attached symmetrically to the perimeter of the circle. The facades of many designs consist of rootwork, shells, thatch, and tree branches that enliven the elevations in a Rococo manner but also contribute a "rustic" quality that dominates other stylistic characteristics. The tree-trunk columns and thatch roof of the "Chinese" hermitage (Plate 4), for example, clearly suggest a rustic character. Likewise in the "Gothic" grotto (Plate 10) the decorative infill "composed of flints and irregular stones, and studded with small pebbles" (p. 6) suggests a grotto-like character more than any other. Most rustic of all is the "grotesque" or rural bath in Plate 20, which appears to be a domed hut made entirely of rootwork and dried mud.

1. The lines appear on pp. 13–14. Morris's book is included below in Appendix C.

2. In some cases Wrighte's debt to the Palladians is obvious. The hut "intended to represent the primitive State of the Dorick Order" (Plate 1), for example, is clearly derived from "The Third sort of Huts which gave birth to the Doric ORDER," illustrated in the first plate of Sir William Chambers's *Treatise* (1759; *q.v.*).

359.1

WYATT, Lewis William (1777–1853)

A collection of architectural designs, rural and ornamental. Executed in a variety of buildings, upon the estates of the Right Hon. Lord Penrhyn, in Carnarvonshire and Cheshire. Accurately delineated by Lewis W. Wyatt. The whole to be illustrated by thirty original designs of cottages, farm=

houses, lodges, inns, villas, &c. &c. to be comprised in ten numbers quarto, one in every two months, with letter-press description, and two perspective views, elegantly engraved by James Basire.

[*First number:*]

London: Published for the editor, by J. Taylor, 1800.

2 printed leaves, 6 pls.

[*Second number:*]

London: Published for the editor, by J. Taylor, 1800.

3 printed leaves, 6 pls.

[*Third number:*]

London: Printed by Nichols and Son; and published for the editor by J. Taylor; R. Faulder; and Vernor and Hood, 1801.

3 printed leaves, 6 pls.

29.8 × 23. 5 cm

RIBA

Of ten numbers and 30 designs promised in the title, only three numbers and eight designs—numbered 4, 7, 11, 13, 19, 20, 25, and 28—are known. The plates depict a back lodge adjoining the farmyard at Penrhyn, a double cottage, a design for a dwelling in "the ornamental style of cottage architecture," a cattle shed, a farmyard with farm house and outbuildings, stables, an inn near Bangor on the road to Holyhead, and Lime Grove House near Bangor. The facade of this house is two stories high in the center, with an upper story three windows wide and a lower story five windows wide. It is ornamented in a fashionably Neoclassical manner.

Work at Penrhyn also is discussed in Robert Beatson's article "On Cottages" (1797), in the report to the Board of Agriculture on North Wales (1810; see above, under "Great Britain. Board of Agriculture"), and in Abraham Rees's *Cyclopaedia* ([1802]–1820), *qq.v.* For more information on improvements by Lord Penrhyn, Samuel Wyatt, and Benjamin Wyatt in Caernarvonshire and Cheshire see John Martin Robinson, *Georgian Model Farms: A Study of Decorative and Model Farm Buildings in the Age of Improvement, 1700–1846* (Oxford: Clarendon Press, 1983), pp. 16, 57, 58, 75, 104, 134, and 145.

YOUNG, Arthur (1741–1820)

See Annals of agriculture, *Entry 479.*

360.1
YOUNG, Arthur (1741–1820)
"Oeconomical dwellings for small proprietors of land," *Communications to the Board of Agriculture; on Subjects Relative to the Husbandry, and Internal Improvement of the Country* VI:1 (1808), 261, and pls. IV–V.

MH

Although several articles in the first volume of *Communications to the Board of Agriculture* include designs for cottages and farm houses, this is the only such article to appear thereafter.

The article consists of a brief text and two plates illustrating a design for a house. Young indicated that it was suitable "for the residence of small proprietors. . . . Such a house as this, will not be burthensome to a gentleman with £800., (clear income), and a prudent man, with from £2000. to £2500. per annum, will not regret the want of a better" (p. 261). The house was designed "on as oeconomical principles as possible; and also as to render few servants necessary" (p. 261). The first plate includes an elevation of the facade and a plan of the chamber story. The second plate shows the ground-floor plan with the attached stable court and offices. The ground floor includes an entrance hall, dining room, drawing room, study, sitting room, butler's pantry, and smaller service rooms. The facade is 68 feet wide, with pairs of thin pilaster strips running its full height, a small Tuscan portico framing the front door, and a Regency fanlight over the door.

ZIEGLER, Henry Bryan (1798–1874)
The royal lodges in Windsor Great Park.

See Entry 457.

Appendixes

Appendix A

Short-Title Checklist of Additional Publications by John Crunden, William and John Halfpenny, Batty and Thomas Langley, Peter and Michael Angelo Nicholson, William Pain, George Richardson, William Salmon, and Abraham Swan

The principal entries above (Nos. 1–360) are limited to books and periodicals containing at least one design for a whole dwelling; the structure must be shown in at least one view, or in one elevation plus one plan. The principal types of publication thus excluded are builder's handbooks, artisan's manuals, and collections of ornaments. These contain designs for the orders, doors, windows, staircases, moldings, and ornaments, instruction in carpentry, and a host of other designs and practical information. The most prolific authors of such publications were John Crunden, William and John Halfpenny, Batty and Thomas Langley, Peter and Michael Angelo Nicholson, William Pain, George Richardson, William Salmon, and Abraham Swan. This appendix is a checklist of books and periodical articles by these 11 authors, apart from publications that appear in the principal entries above.

In compiling this list I have relied on 11 standard sources of bibliographic information. These are described fully in the List of Symbols and Abbreviations at the beginning of the principal entries and are abbreviated here as APSD, Avery (1968), BM (with BLC and BM Supplements to 1975), Colvin (1978), DNB, ECB, ECBB, NUC (and NUC-S), RIBA (1937–1938), Univ. Cat., and WML. In consulting these sources I have tried to select just one copy of each edition for inclusion here; unfortunately it is often difficult to determine whether two similar references actually pertain to the same edition. When in serious doubt as to the equivalence of two similar references, I have included both.

The standards of bibliographic description used here are similar to those explained at the beginning of the principal entries. The following special considerations apply to the entries in Appendix A:

• *Titles* are truncated after the first several words. Up to the point of truncation each title is given exactly as it appears in the source cited. A five-em dash (————) used in place of a title indicates that its wording and punctuation, as truncated, are unchanged from the previous entry.

• Indications of *size* are omitted entirely.

• Descriptions of *pagination and plates* are given as they appear in the source cited, although I have made minor modifications in format to be more consistent with the principal entries above. The abbreviation "p.l.," found on many Library of Congress catalogue cards, stands for "preliminary leaf" or "preliminary leaves." In some books the numeration of the plates does not tally with the actual number of plates; in the bibliographic sources that I consulted such cases often are described by giving both figures, with the correct count in parentheses—for example, "184 (i.e., 187) pls."

• In some cases I have changed conjectural *publication dates*—e.g., "[1758?]"—to "[n.d.]," particularly when the date conjectured is inconsistent with the known active dates of the publisher(s).

• For each entry I have given a *reference* indicating the source of my information. References to the National Union Catalogue (NUC) are followed by an NUC location symbol in square brackets ([ ]), indicating the library originally reporting the information to NUC. The location symbols are explained in the List of Symbols and Abbreviations at the beginning of the principal entries. I have not systematically searched for additional titles and editions beyond the 11 standard sources listed above. Nevertheless I have included a few additional titles and editions that are available in the Bodleian Library, British Library, University of Minnesota Library, and Victoria and Albert Museum; in each case I have stated the library in which the item may be found.

• Some entries are followed by the instruction *"See note. . . ."* All notes are gathered at the end of the appendix.

The following remarks concern material that I have excluded from this appendix:

• I have excluded all publications issued as single sheets. For those by Halfpenny see Colvin (1978), pp. 378–379.

• Several encyclopedia articles by Peter Nicholson are mentioned in the DNB, p. 470. I have not included references to those articles because the DNB omits page numbers and publication dates.

• Pain's *List of Prices of Materials* (1793) is cited by Colvin (1978), p. 606, but is not included here. Instead see Entries 241.3ff above.

• Many of the titles listed below appeared in new and abridged editions well into the twentieth century. As with the principal entries, I have included all new editions and reprints through 1950, but have excluded all abridged editions.

Finally, a list of so many entries arranged in such a condensed manner requires a few practical remarks. First, it is important to note that for any given work there may be frequent and major changes of title. In the arrangement below, works are arranged first according to author and then in alphabetical order according to the title of the first edition. Thus for each author all the first editions (entries ending in ".1") are in alphabetical order. Later editions are entered in chronological order following the appropriate first edition, regardless of any changes in title. For example, all editions of Nicholson's *Carpenter's New Guide* (Entries 410.2ff) follow the first edition, which is titled *The New Carpenter's Guide* (Entry 410.1). Cross-references have been added where appropriate; these titles are alphabetized as if they were first editions (entries ending in ".1"). Nevertheless care is required in locating and recognizing cross-references, since they are not headed by entry numbers, and because authors' names usually are replaced by dashes.

361.1

CRUNDEN, John (ca. 1745–1835), and J. H. MORRIS
The carpenter's companion for Chinese railing and gates.

London: Henry Webley, 1765.

16 pls.

WML

361.2

———

———

London, 1770.

BM

361.3

———

The carpenters companion, for Chinese railing and gates.
New edition.

London: Printed for I. Taylor, [n.d.].

16 pls (including title page).

Avery (1968)

361.4

———

The carpenter's companion: containing thirty-three designs for all sorts of Chinese railings and gates.

London: Printed for I. and J. Taylor, [n.d.].

[17] leaves, 16 pls.

NUC [C]

362.1

CRUNDEN, John (ca. 1745–1835), Thomas MILTON, and Placido COLUMBANI
The chimney-piece-maker's daily assistant.

London: H. Webley, 1766.

1 p.l., frontisp., 54 pls.

NUC [DLC]

363.1
CRUNDEN, John (ca. 1745–1835)
[Engravings of designs for ornamental ceilings.]

[London]: Henry Webley, 1765.

12 pls.

BM

364.1
————
The joyner and cabinet-maker's darling, or pocket director.

London, 1765.

1 l., 25 pls.

NUC-S [RPJCB]

See note 1.

364.2
————

————
London: A. Webley, 1770.

26 pls.

BM

364.3
————
The joyner and cabinet-maker's darling.

London, 1786.

Copy in V&A.

364.4
————
The joiner's and cabinet maker's darling.

London, 1796.

Univ. Cat.

See note 2.

365.1
HALFPENNY, William (–1755)
Andrea Palladio's first book of architecture.

[N.d.; ca. 1750].

Colvin (1978)

365.2

———

Andrea Palladio's first book.

1751.

ECBB

See note 3.

366.1

———

Arithmetick and measurement, improv'd by examples and plain demonstrations.

London: Printed for R. Ware, 1748.

1 p.l., v–vii + [1] + 164 pp.

NUC [MiU]

367.1

HOARE, Michael [pseud. for William HALFPENNY (–1755)]
The builder's pocket-companion.

London: Printed for T. Worrall, 1728.

viii + 44 pp, 6 pls.

NUC [MiU-C]

367.2

———

———

Second edition.

London: Printed for T. Worrall, 1731.

1 p.l., v–viii + 53 pp, 13 folding diagrs.

NUC [CU]

367.3

———

———

Third edition.

London: Printed for R. Ware, 1747.

vi + 53 pp, 13 pls.

NUC [PU-FA]

368.1

HALFPENNY, William (–1755)

Geometry, theoretical and practical.

London: Robert Sayer, 1752.

43 + [1] pp, folding diagrs.

NUC [WU]

368.2

————

[N.d.]

APSD

369.1

————

Magnum in parvo, or the marrow of architecture.

1722.

APSD

369.2

————

Magnum in parvo: or, the marrow of architecture.

London: Printed for J. Wilcox [etc.], 1728.

1 p.l., 19 pp, pls, folding diagrs.

NUC [DLC]

370.1

————

Practical architecture; or, a sure guide to the true working according to the rules of that science.

London, [n.d.].

Univ. Cat.

370.2

————

Practical architecture . . . five orders . . . from Inigo Jones.

[London], 1724.

ECBB

370.3

Practical architecture, or a sure guide to the true working according to the rules of that science.

[London]: Printed for & sold by Tho: Bowles Printseller, by Jer. Batley Bookseller, & by J. Bowles Printseller, [1724?].

3 p.l., 48 numbered leaves (including plates).

NUC [MH]

370.4

Practical architecture; or, a ⟨ . . . as previous edition . . . ⟩.
Fifth edition.

[London]: Printed for & sold by Tho: Bowles, 1730.

[3] + 48 numbered leaves (including plates).

NUC [NNC]

370.5

Practical architecture, or a ⟨ . . . as previous edition . . . ⟩.
Fifth edition.

[London]: Printed for & sold by Tho. Bowles, Printseller, 1736.

48 leaves (including plates).

NUC [FTaSU]

370.6

Practical architecture, or sure guide to the rules of science.

1748.

APSD

370.7

1751.

APSD

371.1
———

"Preface" to John Miller, *Andrea Palladio's elements of architecture*.

London, [ca. 1748].

DNB

See note 4.

371.2
———

———

London: Printed for R. Sayer, Map and Printseller, 1759.

4 + 19 pp, 28 pls.

NUC [MCM]

See note 5.

372.1
———

[Twenty new designs of Chinese lattice, and other works for stair-cases, gates, palings, hatches, &c on six folio copper plates.]

London: Printed for R. Sayer, 1750.

Without title page; 6 double pls.

NUC [NNC]

373.1
[LANGLEY, Batty (1696–1751)]
An accurate description of Newgate.

London: Printed for T. Warner, 1724.

1 p.l., 56+ pp.

NUC [CtY] (entered under title)

LANGLEY, Batty (1696–1751)
Ancient masonry.

See Entry 387.

———

The builder's bench-mate.

See Entry 376.2.

374.1

The builder's chest-book.

London: Printed for J. Wilcox, 1727.

[vi] + vi + 139 pp, tables, 2 pls.

WML

374.2

The builder's vade-mecum.

London; Dublin: S. Fuller, 1729.

138 pp, 7 pls.

WML

374.3

London, printed; and Dublin, reprinted by and for S. Fuller, 1735.

3 p.l., vi + 139 + [9] pp, 7 pls, tables.

NUC [NNC]

374.4

The builder's chest-book
Second edition.

London: Printed for J. Wilcox and J. Hodges, 1739.

vi + vi + 142 pp, 7 pls.

NUC [DLC]

375.1

The builder's compleat assistant.

London: R. Ware, 1738.

2 vols.

NUC [DSI]

375.2

———

The builder's compleat chest-book.

London: Printed by H. Woodfall for the author, 1738.

200 pp, 77 pls.

NUC [NjP]

375.3

———

The builders compleat assistant.
Second edition.

London: Printed for Richard Ware, [1738].

2 p.l., 201 + [3] pp, 77 pls.

Avery (1968)

375.4

———

———

Second edition.

London: Printed for Richard Ware, [ca. 1740].

2 vols. (77 pls).

NUC [MiU-C]

375.5

———

———

Third edition.

London, [1738].

NUC [DLC]

375.6

———

The builder's compleat assistant.
Third edition.

London, [1750].

2 vols.

BM

375.7

The builders complete assistant.
Fourth edition.

London: Printed for C. and R. Ware, 1766.

2 vols.

NUC [PU-FA]

375.8

The builder's complete assistant.
Fourth edition.

London: I. and J. Taylor, [n.d.].

2 p.l., 201 pp.

NUC [CtY]

See note 6.

The builder's compleat chest-book.
See Entry 375.2.

376.1

The builder's director, or bench mate.

1746.

APSD

376.2

The builder's bench-mate.

London: Printed only for Archimedes Langley, 1747.

xxiv pp, 184 pls on 92 leaves.

NUC [CtY]

376.3

The builder's director, or bench-mate.

London: Printed for and sold by Mess. Piers and Wentz, 1747.

xxiv pp, 184 pls on 92 leaves.

Avery (1968)

376.4

———

———

London: Printed for and sold by H. Piers, 1751.

xxiv pp, 184 pls on 92 leaves.

Avery (1968)

376.5

———

———

London: A. Webley, 1761.

xxiv pp, 184 pls on 92 leaves.

NUC [MH-BA]

376.6

———

———

London: A. Webley, 1763.

xxiv pp, 184 pp of illus.

NUC [Vi]

376.7

———

———

London: H. Webley, 1767.

xxiv pp, 184 pls on 92 leaves.

NUC [MH-BA]

376.8

———

———

London: Printed and sold by I. Taylor; and by all booksellers in town and country, [n.d.].

xxiv pp, 184 pls on 92 leaves.

NUC [MiU-C]

See note 7.

376.9

———

———

London: Printed for I. and J. Taylor, [n.d.].

xxiv pp, 184 pls on 92 leaves.

NUC [DLC]

See note 8.

377.1

LANGLEY, Batty (1696-1751), and Thomas LANGLEY (1702-1751)
The builder's jewel.

London: Printed for R. Ware, 1741.

32 pp, frontisp. + 99 pls.

NUC [MB]

377.2

————

————

London: Printed for R. Ware [etc.], 1746.

34 pp, 99 pls.

NUC [GAT]

377.3

————

————

London: R. Ware, 1751.

34 pp, frontisp. + 99 pls.

NUC [NN]

377.4

————

————

London: R. Ware, 1754.

34 pp, 99 pls.

BM

377.5

————

————

London: Printed for R. Ware, 1757.

34 pp, 99 pls.

NUC [NcU]

377.6

———

———

Tenth edition.

London: Printed for C. and R. Ware, 1763.

34 + [2] pp, 100 pls.

Avery (1968)

377.7

———

———

Eleventh edition.

Dublin: Printed for J. Williams,1766.

34 pp, 100 pls.

Avery (1968)

377.8

———

———

Eleventh edition.

London, 1766.

RIBA (1937-1938)

377.9

———

———

Eleventh edition.

London: Printed for C. and R. Ware, 1768.

34 pp, frontisp. + 99 pls.

NUC [IU]

377.10

———

———

Twelfth edition.

Dublin: Printed for J. Williams, 1768.

34 pp, 99 pls.

Copy in MnU Library.

377.11

————

————

Twelfth edition.

Edinburgh: R. Clark, 1768.

34 pp.

NUC [CtY]

377.12

————

————

New edition.

London: Printed for J. F. and C. Rivington [etc.], 1787.

24 pp, 99 pls.

NUC [NBuU]

377.13

————

————

New edition.

London: Printed for T. Longman, B. Law, H. Baldwin, G. G. and J. Robinson, W. Lowndes, and I. and J. Taylor, 1797.

iv + 5–46 pp, frontisp. + 99 pls.

Avery (1968)

377.14

————

————

New edition.

Haddington: G. Miller, 1805.

62 pp, frontisp. + 99 pls.

NUC [DLC]

377.15
_____

Edinburgh, 1808.

Colvin (1978)

377.16
_____

London, 1808.

BM

LANGLEY, Batty (1696–1751)
The builder's treasury.

See Entry 378.4.

_____

The builder's vade-mecum.

See Entry 374.

378.1
_____

The city and country builder's, and workman's treasury of designs.

London: Printed by J. Ilive, for Thomas Langley, 1740.

iv + 24 pp, 184 (i.e., 187) pls.

NUC [ViU]

378.2
[LANGLEY, Batty (1696–1751)]
The city and country builder's and workman's treasury of designs.

London: Printed for and sold by S. Harding, 1741.

1 p.l., 22 pp, 186 + 14 pls.

NUC [CtY]

378.3
_____

London: S. Harding, 1745.

1 p.l., 22 pp, 200 pls.

NUC [CtY]

378.4
LANGLEY, Batty (1696–1751)
The builder's treasury of designs, for piers, gates, etc., pulpits, etc., roofs.

[N.d.; before 1750].

APSD

See note 9.

378.5
[LANGLEY, Batty (1696–1751)]
The city and country builder's and workman's treasury of designs.

London: Printed for and sold by S. Harding, 1750.

22 pp, 200 pls.

NUC [NIC]

378.6

—————

—————

London: Printed for S. Harding, and sold by B. Dod [etc.], 1756.

24 pp, 199 pls.

NUC [DLC]

378.7

—————

—————

London: Printed for John and Francis Rivington, [n.d.].

24 pp, 186 + 14 pls.

Avery (1968)

See note 10.

378.8

—————

The city and country builder's and workman's treasury of designs.

London: John & Francis Rivington, 1770.

24 pp, 186 + 14 pls.

Citation in *British Museum General Catalogue of Printed Books. Five-year Supplement 1966–1970* (London: The Trustees, 1971–1972), XIV, col. 604.

378.9
LANGLEY, Batty (1696–1751)
City . . . country . . . treasury . . . architecture.

1777.

ECBB

379.1
[LANGLEY, Batty (1696–1751)]
"The critical review of the publick buildings, &c. examined," *The Grub=
street Journal* 237 (11 July 1734).

Continued as: "A continuation of the critical review of the publick buildings,
&c. examined by Mr. Hiram," *The Grub-street Journal* 238–245 (18 July
to 5 September 1734).

Continued as: "A new critical review of the public buildings, &c. by Mr.
Hiram," *The Grub-street Journal* 246–249 (12 September to 3 October
1734), 251–256 (17 October to 21 November 1734), 258–259 (5 December
to 12 December 1734), 261 (26 December 1734), 267 (6 February 1735),
271 (6 March 1735).

Copy in MnU Library.

See note 11.

380.1
LANGLEY, Batty (1696–1751)
A design for the bridge at New Palace Yard, Westminster.

London: The author [etc.], 1736.

30 pp, frontisp.

NUC [NN]

[LANGLEY, Batty (1696–1751)]
The landed gentleman's useful companion.

See Entry 390.3.

381.1
LANGLEY, Batty (1696–1751)
London prices of bricklayers' materials and work.

1747.

APSD

381.2

The London prices of bricklayers materials and works.

London: Printed for A. Langley, 1748.

xvii + 389 pp, 32 pls.

NUC [IU]

381.3

London: Printed for R. Adams and J. Wren, 1749.

xvii + 384 pp, 32 pls.

NUC [Vi]

381.4

Second edition.

London: Printed for R. Adams [etc.], 1750.

1 p.l., xvii + [1] + 389 + [1] pp, 32 pls.

NUC [DLC]

381.5

Second edition.

London, 1790.

32 pls.

NUC [MH]

381.6

London prices of bricklayers' materials and work.

1818.

APSD

382.1

———

The measurer's jewel.

London: Printed for J. Wilcox, 1742.

2 p.l., 176 pp, illus., diagrs., tables.

NUC [NNC]

[LANGLEY, Batty (1696–1751)]
"A new critical review of the public buildings."

See Entry 379.

383.1
LANGLEY, Batty (1696–1751)
New principles of gardening.

London: Printed for A. Bettesworth and J. Batley [etc.], 1728.

2 p.l., iii–xvi + [8] + 25–207 + 191 pp, frontisp. + pls.

NUC [DNAL]

384.1
[LANGLEY, Batty (1696–1751)?]
Observations on a pamphlet lately published, entitled, remarks on the different constructions of bridges.

1749.

RIBA (1937–1938)

See note 12.

385.1
LANGLEY, Batty (1696–1751)
The plan of Windsor Castle.

[London], 1743.

5 pls.

BM

386.1

———

Pomona: or, the fruit-garden illustrated.

London: G. Strahan [etc.], 1729.

xviii + 150 pp, 79 pls.

NUC [DLC]

387.1

The principles of ancient masonry.

London: Printed by Mechell & Crichley [etc.], 1733.

434 + xi + [21] pp.

WML

See note 13.

387.2

Ancient masonry.

London: The author [etc.], 1736.

2 p.l., xi + [22] + 3–434 (i.e., 430) pp, 466 (i.e., 490) pls.

NUC [DLC]

See note 13.

388.1

A reply to Mr. John James's review of the several pamphlets and schemes, that have been offer'd to the publick, for the building of a bridge at Westminster.

London: Printed for the author, 1737.

iv + 3–54 pp, frontisp.

NUC [MH-BA]

389.1

A supplement to the builder's jewel.

Edinburgh: Printed for R. Clark, 1769.

40 pp, pls.

NUC [CtY]

390.1

A sure method of improving estates.

London: Printed for F. Clay and D. Browne, 1728.

5 p.l., xx + 274 pp, frontisp.

NUC [DNAL]

390.2
_____

A sure and easy method of improving estates.
Second edition.

London: Printed for F. Noble, 1740.

5 p.l., xx + 274 pp, frontisp.

NUC [MB]

390.3
[LANGLEY, Batty (1696–1751)]
The landed gentleman's useful companion.

London: J. Hodges, 1741.

5 p.l., xxii (i.e., xx) + 274 pp, frontisp.

NUC [MH-BA]

391.1
LANGLEY, Batty (1696–1751)
A survey of Westminster Bridge.

London: M. Cooper, 1748.

viii + 47 pp, pl.

NUC [DLC]

392.1
_____

The workman's golden rule for drawing and working the five orders.

London: R. Ware, 1750.

8 pp, 48 pls.

BM

392.2
_____

[London]: R. Ware, 1756.

[2] + 3–12 + [13–16] pp, 48 pls.

NUC [RPJCB]

393.1
NICHOLSON, Michael Angelo (ca. 1796–1842)
The carpenter & joiner's companion.

London: Caxton Press, H. Fisher, Son, and Co., 1826.

viii + 264 pp, frontisp. + 132 pls.

NUC [CtY]

394.1
————
The carpenters' and joiners' new practical work on hand-railing.

London, 1836.

20 pls.

BM

395.1
————
The five orders.

London, 1826.

RIBA (1937–1938)

395.2
————
————
London, 1834.

BM

396.1
NICHOLSON, Peter (1765–1844)
Analytical and arithmetical essays.

London, 1820.

DNB

396.2
————
————
London: Printed for the author, published by Davis and Dickson, 1821.

1 vol. (various pagings).

NUC [NIC]

397.1
———————

The carpenter and builder's complete measurer.

[London: Jones & Co., 1826].

240 pp, 25 pls.

NUC [DLC]

397.2
———————

———————

London, 1827.

DNB

397.3
———————

A practical treatise on mensuration.

[London: Jones & Co., 1828?].

240 pp.

NUC [DeU]

398.1
———————

The carpenter and joiner's assistant.

London: Printed for I. and J. Taylor, [1792?].

xi + 79 + [1] pp, 79 pls.

NUC [NBuG]

398.2
———————

The carpenter's and joiner's assistant.

London, 1793.

DNB

398.3
———————

The carpenter and joiner's assistant.

London: Printed for I. and J. Taylor, 1797.

xi + 79 pp, 79 pls.

NUC [MdBP]

398.4

The carpenter's and joiner's assistant.

London, 1798.

DNB

398.5

The carpenter and joiner's assistant.
Second edition.

London: Printed for J. Taylor, 1805.

xi + 79 + [1] pp, pls.

NUC [NjR]

398.6

———

Third edition.

London: Printed for J. Taylor, 1810.

x + 82 pp.

NUC [IU]

398.7

———

Fourth edition.

London: Printed for J. Taylor, 1815.

x + 82 + [6] pp, 79 pls.

NUC [PPCC]

398.8

———

Sixth edition.

London, 1826.

RIBA (1937–1938)

399.1
————

Carpenter, joiner, and builder's companion.

London, 1846.

Univ. Cat.

See note 14.

399.2
————

The carpenter, joiner, and builder's companion, in the geometrical construction of working drawings.

London: [188–?]

264 pp, 132 pls.

NUC-S [TxU]

————

The carpenter's new guide.

See Entry 410.

400.1
————

Carpentry; being a comprehensive guide book for carpentry and joinery.

London, 1849.

BM

See note 14.

400.2
[NICHOLSON, Peter (1765–1844)]
————

London: J. Weale, 1852.

2 vols.

NUC [NN]

400.3
————

Carpentry.

1857.

DNB

401.1

NICHOLSON, Peter (1765–1844)
Carpentry, joinery, and building.

[London]: Weale, 1836.

2 vols.

ECB

401.2

———

Carpentry, joining, and building.

London, 1851.

2 vols.

Univ. Cat.

402.1

———

Essay on involution and evolution.

London: Davis and Dickson, 1820.

xxvi + 50 + 16 pp.

NUC [DAU]

402.2

———

Essay on involution & evolution.
New edition.

London: Printed for the author, 1820.

2 p.l., xxvi + 82 + 16 pp.

NUC [NNU]

403.1

———

Essays on the combinatorial analysis.

London: Printed for the author, and published by Longman, Hurst, Rees, Orme, and Brown; and by the author, 1818.

4 p.l., xxxi + [1] + 30 + 30A–30Z + 30*A–30*L + 31–104 pp, 1 leaf, 62 pp.

NUC [MiU]

404.1

———

Guide to railway masonry.

Newcastle, 1839.

DNB

404.2

———

The guide to railway masonry.
Second edition.

London, 1840.

BM

404.3

———

Guide to railway masonry.

Carlisle, 1846.

DNB

404.4

———

The guide to railway masonry.
Third edition.

London: Groombridge & Sons [etc.], 1846.

10 + lxviii + 57 pp, frontisp. + 42 (i.e., 41) pls.

NUC [DLC]

404.5

———

———

Third edition.

London: Spon, 1860.

4 parts in 1 vol.

NUC [NN]

———

An improved and enlarged edition of Nicholson's new carpenter's guide.
See Entry 410.

405.1

An introduction to the method of increments.

London: Davis and Dickson, 1817.

xxxviii + 130 pp.

NUC [GU]

406.1

A key to Nicholson and Rowbotham's practical system of algebra.

London: Baldwin, Cradock & Joy, 1825.

iv + 245 pp.

BM

407.1

A key to Nicholson's popular course of the pure and mixed mathematics.

London: Sir Richard Phillips and Co., 1822.

NUC [MH]

407.2

————

London: G. and W. B. Whittaker, [1823].

1 p.l., 190 pp, diagr.

NUC [DLC]

407.3

————

London: Sherwood, Gilbert, and Piper, [1838?].

1 p.l., 190 (i.e., 198) pp, diagrs.

NUC [MiU]

408.1

————

Key [to rudiments of algebra].

[London]: Longman, 1825.

ECB

409.1

_____

Mechanical exercises.

London, 1811.

DNB

409.2

_____

_____

London: J. Taylor, 1812.

xxvi pp, 1 leaf, 396 pp, 1 leaf, pls.

NUC [DLC]

409.3

_____

_____

London, 1819.

Univ. Cat.

409.4

_____

The mechanic's companion.

London, 1824.

DNB

409.5

_____

_____

Oxford, 1825.

BM

410.1

_____

The new carpenter's guide.

London, 1792.

BM

410.2
———

The carpenter's new guide.

London: Printed for I. and J. Taylor, 1793.

1 p.l., v–xii + 76 pp, 78 pls.

NUC [MiU-C]

410.3
———
———

London, 1797.

DNB

410.4
———
———

Third edition.

London: Printed for J. Taylor, 1801.

x + 76 pp, pl.

NUC [NjR]

410.5
———
———

Fourth edition.

London, 1805.

BM

410.6
———
———

New edition.

London: J. Taylor, 1808.

x + 76 pp, 78 pls.

NUC [Vi]

410.7

—————

Sixth edition.

London: Architectural Library, 1814.

1 vol. (various pagings).

NUC [NcRS]

410.8

—————

Seventh edition.

London: J. Taylor, 1819.

vii + 92 + 8 pp, 84 pls.

WML

410.9

—————

Eighth edition.

London: Printed for J. Taylor, 1823.

vii + 92 pp.

NUC [PKsL]

410.10

—————

An improved and enlarged edition of Nicholson's new carpenter's guide.

London: Printed for Jones & Co., 1825 [–1826].

iv + 83 pp, frontisp. + 80 pls.

NUC [IU]

410.11

—————

London: Printed for Jones & Co., W. Davy, Printer, 1825 [–1826].

iv + xii + 121 pp, 1 leaf, frontisp. + 86 pls.

NUC [ViW]

410.12

———

London: Printed for Jones & Co., 1825 [-1827?].

iv + xii + 62 pp, 1 leaf, 63–121 + 240 pp, frontisp. + 145 pls.

NUC [DLC]

410.13

———

The carpenter's new guide.
Eighth edition, corrected and enlarged.

Oxford: Bartlett & Hinton, 1826.

vi + 94 pp, 84 pls.

Citation in *British Museum General Catalogue of Printed Books. Ten-year Supplement 1956–1965* (London: The Trustees, 1968), XXXIII, col. 309.

410.14

———

———

Eighth edition.

Oxford: Bartlett and Hinton, 1827.

vi + 94 pp, 84 pls.

Avery (1968)

410.15

———

An improved and enlarged edition of Nicholson's new carpenter's guide.

London: Printed for Jones & Co., 1828.

xii + 121 pp.

NUC [DeU]

410.16

———

———

London: Jones and Co., 1831.

xii + 121 pp, pls.

WML

410.17

———

New carpenter's guide.

[London]: Jones, 1831.

iv + iv + 83 pp, 84 pls.

NUC [CU]

410.18

———

An improved and enlarged edition of Nicholson's new carpenter's guide.

[London]: Jones and Co., 1833.

iv + xii + 164 pp, frontisp. + 88 pls.

WML

410.19

———

The carpenter's new guide.

London, 1835.

DNB

410.20

———

———

London and Philadelphia, 1854.

DNB

410.21

———

———

London and Philadelphia, 1856.

DNB

410.22

———

———

New edition.

London, 1857 [1856].

3 parts.

BM

410.23

———

London and New York: George Virtue, [n.d.].

xii + 122 + 240 pp, 147 pls.

NUC [IU]

See note 15.

410.24

———

Nicholson's new carpenter's guide.
An enlarged and improved edition, by John Hay.

London and New York: George Virtue, [n.d.].

122 pp, frontisp. + 89 pls.

WML

See note 15.

410.25

———

Nicholson's carpenter's guide.

London and New York: G. Virtue, [n.d.].

xii + 121 pp, 1 leaf, 81–83 pp, 119 pls.

NUC [NNC]

See note 15.

410.26

———

Nicholson's new carpenter's guide.

London [etc.], G. Virtue, [n.d.].

xii + 122 pp, frontisp. + 121 pls.

NUC [IU]

See note 15.

410.27

――――――

An enlarged and improved edition by John Hay.

London & New York: George Virtue, [ca. 1860].

xii + 122 pp, pls.

Citation in *British Library General Catalogue of Printed Books. Five-year Supplement 1971–1975* (London: British Museum Publications, 1978–1979), IX, col. 1657.

See note 15.

410.28

――――――

New carpenter's guide.

London and New York: J. S. Virtue, [n.d.].

xii + 122 + 8 pp, pls.

NUC [CLSU]

See note 15.

410.29

――――――

Nicholson's new carpenter's guide.

London and New York: James S. Virtue, [n.d.].

xii + 122 pp, 89 + 16 + 16 pls.

NUC [NNC]

See note 15.

411.1

――――――

"New Demonstrations of the Method Invented by Budan, and Improved by Others, of Extracting the Roots of Equations," *The Philosophical Magazine and Journal* LX:293 (September 1822), 173–178.

Copy in MnU Library.

412.1

――――――

A popular and practical treatise on masonry and stone-cutting.

London, 1827.

BM

412.2

———

London: T. Hurst, E. Chance, 1828.

viii + v–vii + 111 pp, pls.

NUC [Vi]

412.3

———

A practical treatise on the art of masonry and stone-cutting. Second edition.

London: J. Taylor, 1832.

111 pp, pls.

NUC [NhD]

412.4

———

———

Third edition.

London: Printed for J. Maynard, 1835.

viii + v–vii + 111 pp, 1 leaf, 43 pls.

NUC [DLC]

412.5

———

A popular and practical treatise on masonry and stone-cutting.

London, 1838.

Univ. Cat.

412.6

———

Practical treatise on the art of masonry and stone-cutting.

London, 1839.

NUC [MdBP]

413.1

———

A popular course of pure and mixed mathematics.

London: Printed for Sir R. Phillips & Co., 1822.

2 p.l., ii + vii–xvi + xxxii + 777 + [96] pp, pls, diagrs.

NUC [CtY]

413.2

————

————

London, 1823.

2 parts.

BM

413.3

————

Popular course of pure and mixed mathematics.

London, 1825.

NUC [MdBP]

413.4

————

A popular course of pure and mixed mathematics.

London: Sherwood, Gilbert, and Piper, 1835.

xvi + xxxii + 800 + 72 pp, pls, maps, diagrs.

NUC [DLC]

414.1
[NICHOLSON, Peter (1765–1844)]
Practical carpentry, joinery, and cabinet-making.

London: T. Kelly, 1826.

iv + 132 + 36 + 133–140 + v–vii pp.

NUC [NN]

See note 16.

414.2

————

————

London: Printed for Thomas Kelley, by J. Rider, 1835.

vii + 140 + 36 + [1] pp, 84 + 6 pls.

NUC [NNC]

414.3
NICHOLSON, Peter (1765–1844)

——————

London: Thomas Kelly, 1837.

viii + 140 + 36 pp, 90 pls.

WML

414.4

——————

——————

London: Thomas Kelly, 1839.

viii + 140 + 36 pp, 90 pls.

WML

414.5

——————

——————

London: Thomas Kelly, 1846.

viii + 140 + 36 pp, 90 pls.

WML

414.6

——————

——————

London: T. Kelly, 1849.

NUC [InU]

414.7

——————

——————

London: Thomas Kelly, 1851.

xxxvi + 140 + 36 + 40 pp, 86 (i.e., 102) + 7 pls, portr.

NUC [NNC]

414.8

——————

——————

London: Thomas Kelly, 1852.

xxxvi + 140 + 36 + 40 pp, 85 + 7 pls.

Citation in *British Museum General Catalogue of Printed Books. Ten-year Supplement 1956–1965* (London: The Trustees, 1968), XXXIII, col. 309.

414.9

———

London: Kelly, 1854.

xxxvi + 40 + 140 + 36 pp, portr., pls.

NUC [MB]

415.1
[NICHOLSON, Peter (1765–1844)]
Practical masonry, bricklaying, and plastering.

London: Printed for Thomas Kelly, 1830.

vii + 232 pp, 45 pls.

Avery (1968)

415.2

———

London: Printed for Thomas Kelly, 1838.

vii + [1] + 232 pp, pls.

NUC [ViU]

415.3

———

London: T. Kelly, 1847.

vii + [1] + 232 pp, 45 (i.e., 60) pls.

NUC [ViU]

415.4

———

1851.

vii + 232 pp, 45 pls.

BM

415.5
NICHOLSON, Peter (1765–1844)
———

London, [n.d.].

NUC [MdBP]

416.1

NICHOLSON, Peter (1765–1844), and John ROWBOTHAM
A practical system of algebra.

London, 1824.

BM

416.2

————

Second edition.

London: Printed for Baldwin and Cradock, 1831.

NUC [MH]

416.3

————

Third edition.

London, 1837.

BM

416.4

————

1844.

DNB

416.5

————

1855.

DNB

416.6

————

1858.

DNB

NICHOLSON, Peter (1765–1844)
A practical treatise on mensuration.

See Entry 397.3.

A practical treatise on the art of masonry and stone-cutting.
See Entry 412.

417.1
———
The principles of architecture.
London: Printed for the proprietors, by J. Barfield, [1795]–1798.
3 vols., 195 pls.
Avery (1968)

417.2
———
———
Second edition.
London: Printed by J. Barfield, 1809.
NUC [CoU]

417.3
———
———
Third edition.
London: Printed by J. Barfield, 1827.
3 vols., 216 (i.e., 218) pls.
NUC [DLC]

417.4
———
———
Fourth edition.
London: Bohn, 1836.
3 vols., pls, diagrs.
NUC [MB]

417.5
———
———
Fifth edition.
London: H. G. Bohn, 1841.
3 vols., 216 (i.e., 218) pls.
NUC [DLC]

417.6

Principles of architecture.
Sixth edition.

London: H. G. Bohn, 1848.

xx + 280 pp, 216 (i.e., 219) pls.

NUC [DLC]

418.1

"Propositions Respecting the Mechanical Power of the Wedge," *The Philosophical Magazine* I:3 (August 1798), 316–319.

Copy in MnU library.

419.1

The rudiments of algebra.

London: Printed by J. Barfield, 1819.

xiv + 261 + [1] pp.

NUC [DLC]

419.2

1824.

DNB

419.3

Rudiments of algebra.

[London]: Longman, 1825.

ECB

419.4

The rudiments of algebra.

1837.

DNB

419.5

———

———

1839.

DNB

420.1

———

The school of architecture and engineering.

London, 1828.

BM

See note 17.

421.1

———

The student's instructor in drawing and working the five orders of architecture.

London: Printed for I. and J. Taylor, 1795.

29 pp.

NUC [CtY]

421.2

———

———

Second edition.

London: J. Taylor, 1804.

iv + 29 pp, 33 pls (including frontisp.).

WML

421.3

———

———

Third edition.

London: J. Taylor, 1810.

viii + 39 pp, 41 pls.

WML

421.4

———

Fourth edition.

London: J. Taylor, 1815.

39 pp, pls.

NUC [CtY]

421.5

———

———

Fifth edition.

London: Printed for J. Taylor, 1823.

viii + 39 pp, 41 pls.

Avery (1968)

421.6

———

———

Sixth edition.

Oxford, 1825.

Copy in Bodleian Library.

421.7

———

The student's instructor.

1837.

DNB

421.8

———

The student's instructor in drawing and working the five orders of architecture.
Seventh edition.

London: M. Taylor, 1839.

1 p.l., v–x + 11–88 pp, 41 pls.

NUC [DLC]

421.9

———————

———————

New edition.

London: M. Taylor, 1845.

88 pp, 41 pls.

WML

421.10

———————

———————

London: M. Taylor, 1854.

BM

421.11

———————

———————

London: M. Taylor, [n.d.].

88 pp, 41 pls.

NUC [MH, NIC]

See note 18.

422.1

———————

A treatise on dialling.

Newcastle: The author, 1833.

vi + 58 pp.

BM

422.2

———————

Treatise on dialling.

[London]: Weale, 1834.

ECB

422.3

———————

———————

Newcastle, 1836.

DNB

423.1
———

A treatise on the construction of staircases and handrails.

London: Printed for J. Taylor, 1820.

vii + 45 pp, diagrs., pls.

NUC [NN]

423.2
———

A treatise on the construction of staircases and hand-rails. Second edition.

London: Printed for M. Taylor, 1835.

vii + 45 pp, 39 pls.

Avery (1968)

423.3
———

A treatise on the construction of stair-cases and hand-rails. New ed.

London: M. Taylor, 1847.

40 pp, 39 pls.

NUC [DLC]

424.1
PAIN, William (1730?–1790?)
The builder's sketch book.

London: Printed for and sold by the author, 1793.

[22] + 1 + 52 pp, 50 pls.

WML

424.2
———
———

Second edition.

London: Printed for and sold by the author, 1794.

[22] pp, 1 p.l., 52 pp, 50 (i.e., 51) pls.

Avery (1968)

425.1

———

The carpenter's and joiner's repository.

London: Printed for the author; and sold by I. Taylor, 1778.

14 leaves, 69 pls including frontisp.

Avery (1968)

425.2

———

———

New edition.

London: Printed for I. and J. Taylor, 1787.

1 vol. (unpaged), 61 pls.

NUC [CtY]

425.3

———

———

London: I. and J. Taylor, 1792.

14 p.l., 4 pp, 69 pls.

NUC [NN]

426.1

———

The carpenter's pocket directory.

London: Printed for I. Taylor, 1781.

[28] pp, 24 pls.

Avery (1968)

426.2

———

———

New edition.

London: Printed for I. and J. Taylor, [n.d.].

2 p.l., [24] pp, 24 pls.

NUC [N]

See note 19.

426.3

———

New edition.

London: J. Taylor, 1803.

2 p.l., 24 pls, with explanations.

NUC [NN]

426.4

———

Carpenter's pocket dictionary.

[London]: Taylor, [ca. 1810].

ECB

———

A list of prices for materials.

See Entries 241.3ff.

426 *bis*.1

———

The practical measurer, or youth's instructor.

London: Printed for the author, 1783.

iii pp, 1 printed leaf, 83 pp, 4 pls (numbered A, B, I, IV).

Copy in BL.

427.1
RICHARDSON, George (1736?–ca. 1813)
Aedes Pembrochianae.

London, 1774.

Univ. Cat.

427.2

———

Tenth edition.

Wilton, 1784.

ECBB

427.3
[RICHARDSON, George (1736?–ca. 1813)]

———————

Eleventh edition.

1788.

xv + 129 pp.

BM

427.4
RICHARDSON, George (1736?–ca. 1813)

———————

Twelfth edition.

Wilton, 1795.

ECBB

427.5
[RICHARDSON, George (1736?–ca. 1813)]

———————

Thirteenth edition.

Salisbury: Printed at the Salisbury Press, and sold by W. Morris and B. C. Collins, 1798.

xvi + 133 pp.

NUC [NIC]

428.1
RICHARDSON, George (1736?–ca. 1813)
A book of ceilings.

London, 1774.

3 p.l., v pp, 48 pls.

NUC [AAP]

428.2

———————

———————

Londres: L'auteur, 1776.

4 p.l., ii + ii + 11 pp, 48 pls.

NUC [DLC]

428.3

A book of ornamented ceilings.

1781.

48 pls.

APSD

428.4

A collection of ceilings.
Second edition.

London: Printed for the author, 1793.

12 pp, 48 pls.

Avery (1968)

429.1

Capitals of columns and frieses measured from the antique.

London: I. & J. Taylor, 1793.

Frontisp. + 17 pls.

WML

A collection of ceilings.
See Entry 428.4.

A collection of ornaments in the antique style.
See Entry 433.3.

430.1

Iconology; or, a collection of emblematical figures.

London: Printed for the editor, 1777 [–1779].

4 books in 2 vols.

NUC [TxU]

430.2

———————

London, 1778–1779.

2 vols.

BM

430.3

———————

1779.

2 vols.

Citation in *British Museum General Catalogue of Printed Books. Five-Year Supplement 1966–1970* (London: The Trustees, 1971–1972), XX, col. 999.

430.4

———————

Iconology, or a collection of emblematical figures.

1779–1780.

2 vols.

Colvin (1978)

431.1

———————

A new collection of chimney pieces.

London: Printed for the author, 1781.

1 p.l., 16 pp, 36 pls.

NUC [CtY]

432.1

———————

New designs of vases and tripods decorated in the antique taste.

London: The author, 1793.

25 pls.

NUC [DLC]

433.1
———

A new drawing book of ornaments in the antique style.

London, 1796.

37 pls.

Avery (1968)

433.2
———

Ornaments in the Grecian, Roman, and Etruscan tastes.

17— .

37 pls.

APSD

433.3
———

A collection of ornaments in the antique style.

London, 1816.

1 p.l., 37 pls.

NUC [DLC]

———

Ornaments in the Grecian, Roman, and Etruscan tastes.
See Entry 433.2.

434.1
———

A treatise on the five orders of architecture.

Londres: L'auteur, 1787.

x + 32 + [2] pp, 22 pls.

NUC [DLC]

435.1
SALMON, William (ca. 1703–1779)
The builder's guide, and gentleman and trader's assistant.

London: Printed for James Hodges, 1736.

xvi + 155 + [5] pp, incl. frontisp.

NUC [MiU-C]

435.2

The builders' guide and gentlemen's and traders' assistant.

[N.d.; 1748?]

APSD

435.3

The builders' guide, and gentleman and trader's assistant.

London: J. Hodges, [1759].

xvi + 155 pp.

BM

436.1

The country builder's estimator.

London: Printed for James Hodges, 1737.

[x] + 96 pp, 4 tables.

WML

436.2

Second edition.

London: J. Hodges, 1737.

6 p.l., 131 pp, tables, diagrs.

NUC [MH-BA]

436.3

Third edition.

London: J. Hodges, 1746.

128 pp.

BM

436.4

———

———

Fourth edition.

London: Printed for J. Hodges, 1752.

[12] + 131 pp, tables.

Avery (1968)

436.5

———

———

Sixth edition.

London: S. Crowder, 1758.

6 p.l., 131 pp, tables, diagrs.

NUC [MH-BA]

436.6

———

———

Seventh edition.

London: Printed for Stanley Crowder and Co., 1759.

6 p.l., 131 + [1] pp, tables.

NUC [MiU-C]

436.7

———

———

Eighth edition.

London, 1770.

BM

436.8

———

———

Ninth edition.

London: For S. Crowder, 1774.

xii + 108 pp, 4 tables in 6.

NUC [RPJCB]

437.1

_____

London and country builder's vade mecum.

London: J. Hodges, 1745.

ii + 187 pp.

BM

437.2

_____

The London and country builder's vade mecum.
Second edition.

London: J. Hodges, 1748.

1 p.l., ii + [8] + 187 pp, frontisp.

NUC [MH-BA]

437.3

_____

_____

Third edition.

London: Printed for J. Hodges, 1755.

1 p.l., ii + 187 + [9] pp, frontisp.

NUC [MiU-C]

437.4

_____

_____

Fourth edition.

London: Printed for S. Crowder, 1760.

[12] + 187 pp, frontisp.

NUC [ICU]

437.5

_____

_____

Fifth edition.

London: S. Crowder, 1773.

184 pp, frontisp.

NUC [Vi]

438.1

Palladio Londinensis: or, the London art of building.

London: Ward and Wicksteed, 1734.

[xii] + 128 + [28] pp, 37 pls.

RIBA (1937–1938)

438.2

Second edition.

London: Printed for A. Ward; J. Clarke; J. Oswald; T. Osborne; and E. Wicksteed, 1738.

6 p.l., 132 + [28] pp, frontisp. + pls, tables, diagrs.

NUC [CtY]

438.3

Palladio Londinensis; or, the London art of building.

London, 1743.

With 52 pls.

Univ. Cat.

438.4

Palladio Londinensis: or, the London art of building.
Third edition.

London: Printed for S. Birt [etc.], 1748.

6 p.l., 132 (i.e., 136) + [27] pp, frontisp. + pls, tables, diagrs.

NUC [DLC]

438.5

Fourth edition.

London: Printed for S. Birt [etc.], 1752.

6 p.l., 132 + [27] pp, 52 pls.

NUC [NBuG]

438.6

———

Palladio Londinensis; or, the London art of building.
Fifth edition.

London: Printed for S. Birt [etc.], 1755.

132 (i.e., 136) + [27] pp, diagrs., plans.

NUC [NIC]

438.7

———

———

Sixth edition.

London: Printed for C. Hitch [etc.], 1762.

2 p.l., 132 (i.e., 136) + [27] pp, 54 pls.

NUC [TxHU]

438.8

———

———

Seventh edition.

London: Printed for J. Rivington [etc.], 1767.

[12] + 132 + [28] pp, pls.

NUC [IEN]

438.9

———

———

Eighth edition.

London: Printed for J. and F. Rivington [etc.], 1773.

[10] + 132 + [27] pp, 54 pls., tables, diagrs.

NUC [DeU]

439.1
SWAN, Abraham
The British architect.

London: Printed for the author, and sold by Thomas Meighan and W. Meadows, 1745.

viii + 20 pp, 60 leaves of plates.

NUC [InU]

439.2

―――――
―――――

Second edition.

London: Printed for the author: and sold by T. Meighan [etc.], 1750.

viii + 20 pp, pls, diagrs.

NUC [DLC]

439.3

―――――
―――――

London, 1758.

viii + 16 pp, 60 pls.

NUC [DLC]

439.4

―――――
―――――

London: Printed for the author: and sold by author [etc.], [n.d.].

viii + 16 pp, pls, diagrs.

WML

439.5

―――――
―――――

London: Printed for and sold by R. Sayer, [n.d.].

viii + 164 [*sic*] pp, pls, diagrs.

NUC [IU]

439.6

―――――
―――――

London: Robert Sayer, [ca. 1760].

viii + 16 + 4 pp, 60 pls.

Citation in *British Museum General Catalogue of Printed Books. Five-year Supplement 1966–1970* (London: The Trustees, 1971–1972), XXIII, col. 941.

―――――

The carpenters complete instructor.

See Entry 440.2.

Designs for chimnies.

See Entry 441.

440.1

Designs in carpentry.

London: The author, 1759.

8 pp, 55 pls.

NUC [DLC]

440.2

The carpenters complete instructor.

London: R. Sayer, 1768.

1 p.l., 55 pls.

NUC [CtY]

441.1

One hundred and fifty new designs for chimney pieces.

1758.

Colvin (1978)

See note 20.

441.2

1763.

Colvin (1978)

See note 20.

441.3

Designs for chimnies.

London: Printed for the author, [1765].

31 pp, 54 [pls].

BM

441.4

Upwards of one hundred and fifty new designs, for chimney pieces.

London: Printed for Robert Sayer, 1768.

31 + [1] pp, 54 pls.

Avery (1968)

441.5

Designs for chimnies.

London: Printed for the author, [n.d.].

31 pp, 54 pls.

NUC [CtY]

Upwards of one hundred and fifty new designs, for chimney pieces.
See Entry 441.4.

Notes

1. This edition, dated 1765, is the earliest. WML erroneously indicates a "1760" edition; in fact the entry in WML should read "1770."

2. The date is likely a misprint for 1786: there is a copy dated 1786 at V&A, and that is the location of the copy cited in Univ. Cat.

3. The 1751 edition also is mentioned in Rudolf Wittkower, *Palladio and Palladianism* (New York: Braziller, 1974), p. 90; and George Smith and Frank Benger, *The Oldest London Bookshop* (London: Ellis, 1928), p. 18. Also cf. Entry 371.

4. Entered in DNB under "Miller, John." I have presumed that Halfpenny contributed a preface to this edition, since a preface by him appears in the 1759 edition, which was published after his death (Entry 371.2). Cf. also Entry 365.

5. Entered in NUC under "Palladio, Andrea." The NUC entry states that the Preface is signed by William Halfpenny.

6. This edition must have appeared between 1787 and 1797, based on the active dates of I. and J. Taylor. See Ian Maxted, *The London Book Trades 1775–1800* (Folkestone: Dawson, 1977), p. 222.

7. The publisher traded as Isaac Taylor only from 1781 to 1787. See Maxted, *London Book Trades*, p. 222.

8. The publishers traded as Isaac and Josiah Taylor from 1787 to 1798. See Maxted, *London Book Trades*, p. 222.

9. The title page of the 1740 edition lists piers, gates, and pulpits among its contents, and so I have presumed that Entry 378.4 is another edition of the same book.

10. The publishers traded as John and Francis Rivington from 1768 to 1777. See Maxted, *London Book Trades*, p. 189.

11. The final installment concludes with the words "to be continued" but no further installments appear. In every case the article begins on the first page of the issue.

12. Attributed to Langley by Colvin (1978).

13. The NUC [MB] entry indicating a 1730 edition is erroneous. The date in the WML entry is likely that of the first fascicle, which appeared in January 1733: see R. M. Wiles, *Serial Publication in England before 1750* (Cambridge: Cambridge University Press, 1957), p. 291. The Introduction is dated January 15, 1732 (i.e., 1733 in "new style"?). The Advertisement to the Reader is dated 10 September 1736. The date in the imprint is 1736.

14. N.B. the titles in Entries 399 and 400 were first published posthumously.

15. George Virtue traded from 1823 to 1857. J. S. Virtue traded from 1855 to 1865. See Philip A. H. Brown, *London Publishers and Printers* (London: British Museum, 1961), p. 98.

16. This book also was issued as the first volume of Nicholson's *New and Improved Practical Builder* (1835 and later; Entry 225).

17. Colvin (1978), p. 593, indicates that Nicholson intended to complete this book in 12 numbers, and that it was "abandoned after the fifth number owing to the bankruptcy of the publishers."

18. The MH and NIC copies may have been issued in 1861: the ECB indicates that a new edition ("n.e.") appeared in that year. I have not listed the ECB reference separately since it is likely the same as the MH and NIC copies.

19. The publishers traded as Isaac and Josiah Taylor from 1787 to 1798. See Maxted, *London Book Trades*, p. 222.

20. Only Colvin (1978) indicates editions in 1758 and 1763.

The following works do not include a full elevation or plan of a dwelling, and so were not included among the principal bibliographical entries above. Yet because these books are unusual in offering schemes for the decoration of entire rooms, illustrated in elevations and views, they are collected here in a brief appendix.

The entries are arranged in manner similar to the principal entries above, but the bibliographic information is not based on direct examination. It is derived from information in ten standard bibliographic sources. These are described fully in the List of Symbols and Abbreviations at the beginning of the principal entries and abbreviated here as APSD, Avery (1968), BM, Colvin (1978), DNB, ECB, NUC, RIBA (1937–1938), Univ. Cat., and WML.

The final line of each entry indicates which of the ten sources list that particular edition. The first source shown is the basis of the information recorded here. All other sources listing the same edition follow in alphabetical order. If the first source shown is NUC, it is followed by an NUC location symbol in square brackets ([ ]) to indicate the library originally reporting that information to NUC.

442.1
ARROWSMITH, Henry William, and A. ARROWSMITH
The house decorator and painter's guide; containing a series of designs for decorating apartments, suited to the various styles of architecture.

London: T. Kelly, 1840.

iv + 120 pp, 61 pls.

Square 4°

NUC [NN]; Avery (1968), Univ. Cat., WML.

443.1
BRIDGENS, Richard H.
Furniture, with candelabra and interior decoration, designed by R. Bridgens.

London: W. Pickering, 1838.

1 printed leaf, 60 pls (including engraved title page).

22 cm

NUC [DLC]; Avery (1968), BM, Colvin (1978), ECB, RIBA (1937–1938), WML. N.B. the date given in RIBA (1937–1938) is 1825.

444.1
BUSBY, Charles Augustus (1788–1834)
A collection of designs for modern embellishments suitable to parlours, dining & drawing rooms, folding doors, chimney pieces, varandas, frizes, &c. on 25 plates, by C. A. Busby, Architect.

London: E. Lumley, [1810]. (Imprint on plates except for title page: London: J. Taylor.)

25 pls (including title page).

22 × 28 cm

Avery (1968); Colvin (1978), ECB, NUC, RIBA (1937–1938), Univ. Cat., WML. N.B. NUC and WML also give the date [1808?], and ECB indicates the book was announced in December 1807.

445.1
COOPER, George
Designs for the decoration of rooms in the various styles of modern embellishment, with pilasters and frizes at large, on 20 folio plates. Designed and etched by G. Cooper, draftsman & decorator.

London: J. Taylor, [1807].

20 pls.

25.5 × 36.5 cm

WML; ECB, Univ. Cat.

446.1
Designs for architects, upholsterers, cabinet-makers, etc., forming a series of plans and sections for various apartments; with plates.

London, 1808.

NUC [PPL]. N.B. the copy at CtY-BA consists of 11 pp, 30 pls.

446.2
Desseins à l'usage des architectes, tapissiers, &c. formant une collection de plans et sections pour des appartemens, tels que salles déjeuné, de diné et de compagnie; chambres a coucher, bain, bibliotheque, boudoir, antichambres, escalier, &c. &c. en trente planches, accompagnées de descriptions. Vol. I.

Londres: R. Ackermann; a Leipzick, Beygang au musée; de l'imprimerie d'A. Dulau et co. et L. Nardini, 1801.

2 printed leaves, 5–11 pp, 30 pls.

36 cm

NUC [NNC].

447.1
FAULKNER, Thomas
Designs for shop fronts doors door-cases roofs &c with the details to each plate and various useful and ornamental designs for internal and external finish of houses also the Grecian orders of architecture.

London: [1831].

24 pls.

26.7 × 21.0 cm

RIBA (1937–1938); Colvin (1978). N.B. additional information supplied from personal examination of RIBA copy.

448.1
HOPE, Thomas (1769–1831)
Household furniture and interior decoration, executed from designs by Thomas Hope.

London: Longman, Hurst, Rees, and Orme, 1807.

2 printed leaves, 53 pp, 60 pls.

48.5 × 30.5 cm

NUC [DLC]; Avery (1968), BM, Colvin (1978), DNB, ECB, RIBA (1937–1938), Univ. Cat., WML.

448.2
_____

Household furniture and interior decoration, executed from the designs by Thomas Hope.

London: J. Tiranti & Co., 1937.

[6] pp, 60 pls (on 30 leaves).

38.0 x 25.5 cm

NUC [CSt]; BM. N.B. this reprint omits the text of the original.

448.3
_____

Household furniture and interior decoration, executed from designs by Thomas Hope.

London: Tiranti, [1946].

[2] pp, 60 pls.

38 cm

NUC [DSI]; Avery (1968), BM, WML. N.B. this reprint omits the text of the original.

449.1
LANDI, Gaetano
Architectural decorations; a periodical work of original designs, invented from the Egyptian, the Greek, the Roman, the Estruscan, the Attic, the Gothic &c. for exterior and interior decoration of galleries, halls, apartments &c. either in painting or relief and whatever relates to furniture, as vases, tripods . . . &c. drawn by and under the direction of G. Landi. . . .

London: Landi, 1810.

30 pls.

54 cm

Avery (1968); Univ. Cat.

The following works are not entered among the principal bibliographic entries above because they fail to meet the criteria for inclusion specified in the Introduction (e.g., the illustrations are entirely topographical, or do not illustrate a complete dwelling). Nevertheless they deserve notice here because of their significance in the history of domestic design. The same standards of bibliographic description used for the principal entries are used again here, but the scope of the commentaries has been reduced.

Over half the titles (Entries 458–467) pertain to Fonthill Abbey, a subject chosen to demonstrate the large number of publications that could be devoted to a single residence and its contents.[1] Neither William Beckford (1760–1844), who envisioned this tall Gothic tower and vast baronial hall as early as 1777,[2] nor his architect James Wyatt (1746–1813) published illustrations or descriptions of their work. In 1812, five years after Beckford took up residence, James Storer completed his early description of the romantic beauties and sublimities of the still uncompleted building. In 1818 Fonthill was essentially finished, but the next year part of it began to collapse. In 1822 the failure of Beckford's business interests forced sale of the Abbey, an event marked by publication of illustrated sale catalogues as well as descriptive guides for tourists, now admitted to the premises more readily than in the past. In 1825 the tower collapsed, and shortly thereafter nearly the whole of the structure was demolished.[3]

1. Only works completely devoted to Fonthill have been included here. More general topographical and historical studies that include individual plates or descriptions of Fonthill have been excluded.

2. John Wilton-Ely, "The Genesis and Evolution of Fonthill Abbey," *Architectural History* 23 (1980), 41.

3. Also on the subject of Fonthill see: Boyd Alexander, *England's Wealthiest Son* (London: Centaur Press, 1962); Alexander, ed., *Life at Fonthill 1807–1822* (London: Hart-Davis, 1957); Alexander, "Fonthill, Wiltshire," *Country Life* CXL (1 and 8 December 1966), 1430–1434, 1572–1576; Lewis Saul Benjamin, *The Life and Letters of William Beckford* (London: Heinemann, 1910); Harold Alfred Nelson Brockman, "Fonthill Abbey," *Architectural Review* XCV:570 (June 1944), 149–156; Brockman, *The Caliph of Fonthill* (London: Laurie, 1956); Guy Chapman, *Beckford* (London: Cape, 1937); Chapman, *A Bibliography of William Beckford* (London: Constable, 1930); Brian Fothergill, *Beckford of Fonthill* (London: Faber and Faber, 1979); James Lees-Milne, *William Beckford* (Tisbury, Wiltshire: Compton Russell, 1976); John Walter Oliver, *The Life of William Beckford* (London: Oxford University Press, 1932); John Wilton-Ely, "A Model for Fonthill Abbey," in H. M. Colvin and John Harris, eds., *The Country Seat* (London: Allen Lane, 1970), pp. 199–204; and Yale University Library, *William Beckford of Fonthill* (New Haven: Yale University Library, 1960).

450.1

BRITTON, John (1771–1857)

The union of architecture, sculpture, and painting; exemplified by a series of illustrations, with descriptive accounts of the house and galleries of John Soane. . . . By John Britton. . . .

London: Printed for the author; sold by Longman and Co.; J. Taylor; and J. and A. Arch, 1827.

v–xvi + 60 pp, 18 + 3 + 2 pls.

27.0 × 21.7 cm

MnU

Sir John Soane's residence in Lincoln's Inn Fields was planned both as a private dwelling and as a museum for displaying architectural fragments, sculpture, and paintings acquired throughout Europe and the Mediterranean region. The aesthetic unity ostensibly created by this display, and announced in Britton's title, is explained in the Dedication by a political analogy: "As in our wisely-framed Constitution, the three degrees of King, Lords, and Commons tend mutually to protect and give energy to each other, so the three Sister Arts, by cordial co-operation, promote the harmony and dominion of the whole. Architecture, like the monarch, is, however, the head, the paramount power" (p. v).

The Preface (pp. vii–xiv) includes comments on the usefulness of museums, on the history and influence of architecture, and on the need to establish an "Architectural Academy" in Britain. Chapter I offers general remarks on domestic design, especially interior decoration. Chapter II includes a discussion of the building history and plan of Soane's house, and conducts the reader on a room-by-room itinerary. Chapter III concerns the furnishings of individual rooms, while Chapter IV describes the museum artifacts under five headings: Egyptian antiquities, Grecian antiquities, Roman architecture and sculpture, pictures and drawings, and books. The text concludes with a discussion of Soane's designs for the National Debt Redemption Office and the Royal Gallery of the House of Lords.

Plate I is a plan of the house, Plates II–IV, VII, VIII, and XII are interior elevations and sections, and the rest, through Plate XVIII, are illustrations of room interiors and individual artifacts. The final five plates are Soane's proposals for the Debt Redemption Office and the Royal Gallery.

451.1

GIBBS, James (1682–1754)

Rules for drawing the several parts of architecture, in a more exact and easy manner than has been heretofore practised, by which all fractions, in dividing the principal members and their parts, are avoided. By James Gibbs.

London: Printed by W. Bowyer for the author, 1732.

3 printed leaves, 42 pp, 64 pls.

46.1 × 29.3 cm

NNC

451.2

———

The second edition.

London: Printed by W. Bowyer for the author, 1736.

3 printed leaves, 42 pp, 64 pls.

43.8 × 28.1 cm

NNC

451.3

———

The second edition.

London: Printed for A. Bettesworth and C. Hitch, W. Innys and R. Manby, and J. and P. Knapton, 1738.

3 printed leaves, ii + 40 pp, 64 pls.

43.8 × 28.0 cm

CtY

451.4

———

The third edition.

London: Printed for W. Innys and J. Richardson, J. and P. Knapton, C. Hitch and L. Hawes, R. Manby and H. S. Cox, 1753.

vi + [2] + 28 pp, 64 pls.

39.8 × 24.7 cm

NNC

451.5

———

The rules for drawing the several parts of architecture by James Gibbs the first edition reduced with an introduction by Christian Barman.

London: Hodder and Stoughton Limited, [1924].

xxiv pp, 4 printed leaves, 111 pp (including 64 pls).

21.7 × 14.3 cm

MnU

In a prefatory essay "To the Reader" Gibbs announced his discovery of a "Method" of mechanical construction that would facilitate drawing the five orders in perfect proportion without the use of fractional numbers (pp. 1–2). The principal text opens with brief remarks on the proportions of columns, on entablatures, and on pedestals. There follow a series of plate descriptions devoted to each of the five orders and their individual parts (Plates I–XXVII). Subsequent plates, also described in the text, illustrate intercolumniations, arches, columns over columns, doors and gates, windows and niches, chimney pieces, moldings, ceilings, quoins, balusters, balconies, and modilions. This remained an authoritative source book for British and American architects throughout the eighteenth century.

452.1
HARDING, James Duffield (1798–1863)
Nine lithographic views of the cottages, composing Blaise Hamlet, (with a ground plan of each, and a general ground plan of the whole), situated in the grounds of Blaise Castle, near Bristol, the seat of I. S. Harford, Esq. and published under his patronage. Drawn on stone by I. D. Harding, and sketched from nature by H. O'Neil; and the ground plans by G. C. Ashmead, Surveyor, Bristol. With an introduction explaining their object, at one guinea per set, and with the ground plans, one pound eleven shillings and sixpence; proofs on India paper, one pound eleven shillings and six pence, and with the ground plans, two guineas.

Bristol: Printed & published by T. Bedford, and sold by Colnaghi and Co. Printsellers, London, and by the principal book and printsellers in town and country, [1826].

9 pls.

55.9 × 38.1 cm

CtY-BA

According to Nigel Temple,[1] this work appeared in at least two versions. The main portion of the title was the same in both, but in only one were the individual cottage plans attributed to G. C. Ashmead. In the copy at the Yale Center for British Art, which includes the attribution to Ashmead, the title page letterpress indicates that the purchaser could choose, for additional cost, to have proofs on India paper and to have additional illustrations of the ground plans.

The Yale copy contains only the lithographed views of the nine dwellings, named Diamond, Dial, Double, Dutch, Rose, Circular, Vine, Oak, and Sweet Briar cottages. J. S. Harford of Blaise Castle, just outside of Bristol, erected this group of cottages in 1810–1811 to house the elderly members of his estate staff. Grouped together around a common green and articulated in a highly picturesque style, the cottages are an early and important monument in the history of romantic village planning.[2]

1. Nigel Temple, *John Nash & the Village Picturesque* (Gloucester: Alan Sutton, 1979), Plate 56.

2. Further on Blaise Hamlet see: Gillian Darley, *Villages of Vision* (London: Architectural Press, 1975), pp. 25–28; Donald Hughes, "Blaise Hamlet," *Country Life* XCIV:2433 (3 September 1943), 429; "National Trust Property Acquired during the War," *Architects Journal* C:2604 (21 December 1944), 472–473; and John Summerson, "Blaise Hamlet," *Country Life* LXXXVI:2230 (14 October 1939), 396–397.

453.1

[MARSHALL, William (1745–1818)]

Planting and ornamental gardening; a practical treatise.

London: Printed for J. Dodsley, 1785.

xi pp, 1 printed leaf, 638 pp.

21.0 × 12.7 cm

MB

453.2

MARSHALL, William (1745–1818)
[*Volume I:*]

Planting and rural ornament. Being a second edition, with large additions, of planting and ornamental gardening, a practical treatise. In two volumes. Volume the first.

London: Printed for G. Nicol; G. G. and J. Robinson; and J. Debrett, 1796.

xxxii + 408 + [viii] pp.

[*Volume II:*]

Planting 〈 . . . as Vol. I . . . 〉 treatise. Volume the second.

London: 〈 . . . as Vol. I . . . 〉, 1796.

xx + 454 + [iv] pp.

20.8 × 12.8 cm

MnU

453.3

On planting and rural ornament. A practical treatise, by Mr. Marshall. The third edition. In two volumes. Vol. I [*or* II].

London: Printed by W. Bulmer and Co.; for G. and W. Nicol; G. and J. Robinson; and T. Cadell and W. Davies, 1803.

[*Volume I:*] xxxii + 408 + [vii] pp.

[*Volume II:*] xx + 454 + [iv] pp.

20.9 × 13.4 cm

NNC

In all editions the principal subject matter is an alphabetical listing of plants.[1] Marshall also included a lengthy essay on the subject of "Rural Ornament" that addressed many of the current issues in gardening theory and practice.[2] This begins with a reprinting of Walpole's essay "On Modern Gardening," first published in 1771. Marshall then identified three fundamental principles of landscape design: nature, which was to be imitated;

taste, which was to be exercised in design; and utility. He implicitly rejected current theories of picturesque garden design by asking that art not be used to shape nature into the form of a picture. He explained that nature is not a "landscape" but rather is a whole unto itself with requirements far different from those of easel painting (1803, II, 270–272). He then discussed several individual elements of garden design, including ground, water, wood, natural accompaniments (e.g., sheep), and factitious accompaniments (e.g., fences and buildings). Among the latter he found "seats" to be useful as places of rest "and as guides to the points of view," but temples were just "useless ornament" (ibid., pp. 263–265).

Marshall identified four different types of architecture for use in landscape gardens: the hunting box, the ornamental cottage, the villa, and the principal residence (ibid., pp. 268–269). The hunting box should be in a "masculine" style but not intrude on nature (ibid., pp. 277–278). As for the ornamented cottage, "Neatness and simplicity ought to mark the style of this rational retreat," so there must be no ostentation or attempts at elegance. Still, the design should "exhibit a cultivated Nature, in the first stage of refinement" (ibid., pp. 278–280). The style of the villa, in contrast, should be "elegant," "rich," or "grand," according to the state of surrounding nature, and the artist should work to connect the design of the house with the country environment (ibid., p. 280). Finally, designing a principal residence offers an opportunity for the full display of the artist's taste and genius: Marshall recommended that views connect the house with distant corners of the whole estate (ibid., p. 283). The essay concludes with descriptions of individual landscape gardens and suggested solutions to specific design problems.

1. In the first edition, pp. 41ff. In the later editions, Vol. II, 1–435.

2. In the first edition, pp. 557–638. In the later editions, Vol. I, 193–408.

454.1
[MORRIS, Robert (ca. 1702–1754)]
The art of architecture, a poem. In imitation of Horace's Art of Poetry. Humbly inscribed to the Rt. Honble the Earl of --------- .

London: Printed for R. Dodsley; and sold by T. Cooper, 1742.

iii + 5–34 pp.

25.0 × 19.5 cm

NNC

Once considered to be the work of John Gwynn (d. 1786), this poem may be attributed more convincingly to Robert Morris.[1] The illustration on the title page is the facade of a two-story house with the outlines of four circles superimposed to reveal the underlying geometric harmony of the composition. This illustration is nearly identical to Plate 8, facing page 209, in Morris's *Lectures* (1734–1736; *q.v.*).

Throughout the poem Morris compared the historical origin of architecture in Greece and Rome with the work of British architects of recent generations. He repeatedly emphasized the need for certain fundamental qualities in architectural design, including order, symmetry, art, convenience, beauty, and strength (e.g., pp. 5, 9, 23). He also addressed the problem of expression, mentioning that the Doric order was originally formulated "for Use," while the Corinthian, a "gayer Dress," was appropriate for "Ease and Luxury" (p. 24). To combine such styles in one structure would be unthinkable, but separately they could express gravity, gaiety, solemnity, grandeur, and so forth (pp. 27–29). An architect's success depended in part on following rules—the laws of art and nature (pp. 31–32)—as well as on having a clear, unified conception of the whole:

He that intends an Architect to be,
Must seriously deliberate, like me;
Must see the Situation, Mode and Form,
Of every Structure, which they would adorn:
All Parts External, and Internal, view;
Before they aim to raise, a something new. (p. 32)

1. Colvin (1978), p. 558. An extended introduction—attributing the work to Gwynn and analyzing various literary and aesthetic problems—accompanies a reprint of the poem, ed. William A. Gibson (Los Angeles: William Andrews Clark Memorial Library, 1970).

455.1 ‖

NORTON, Charles

Proposals, with the plan & specification, for building the crescent, in Birmingham. By C. Norton, Builder.

Birmingham: Printed by Thomas Pearson, 1795.

Reference: Information supplied by Birmingham Central Libraries.

About 1790 architect John Rawstorne completed plans for a large residential crescent to be erected in Birmingham. An engraved view[1] shows a three-story terrace 75 windows across, with low screens on each side connecting to three-story wings. The central portion of the crescent, five windows wide and emphasized by a low attic story, was to be used as a chapel.

Builder Charles Norton undertook to "bring forward and complete" this plan in his *Proposals* of 1795, promising as well "to have a street laid open on the back part of the houses, which will afford an opportunity of having coach houses, stables, and other offices erected, but no shopping or manufactory of any kind." Thus only "coaches, or such like carriages, will be suffered to pass in front of the houses," and the area in front could be fenced off to "prevent all nuisances and encroachments" (p. 1). Following three pages of such introductory remarks, Norton included four pages of financial and legal "proposals" for the sale of subscriptions, an elevation and floor plans of a typical house within the crescent, and seven pages of building specifications. Each house would be three windows wide, but "two houses may be laid into one" to accommodate more "genteel" families (p. 3). The principal floor consisted of a dining room and a sitting room, while the story above comprised three chambers and a dressing room. The top story included a bedroom and several "attick" rooms.

Norton obviously published these proposals in the hope of some financial return. Ultimately only the ends of the crescent were built.[2] But publication of such a set of specifications was unusual, and these offer useful insight into design considerations and financial arrangements for late eighteenth-century terrace housing.

1. There is a copy in the Birmingham Central Library, and another in the British Library (King's Maps.42.82.m).

2. Colvin (1978), p. 672. Also see Nikolaus Pevsner and Alexandra Wedgwood, *Warwickshire* (Harmondsworth: Penguin, 1966), p. 141.

456.1
WEALE, John (1791–1862)
Designs of ornamental gates, lodges, palisading, and iron work of the royal parks; with some other designs equal in utility and taste: intended for those designing, and making parks, terraces, pleasure walks, recreative grounds, &c. &c. Principally taken from the executed works of Decimus Burton, Arch. John Nash, Arch. Sydney Smirke, Arch. Sir John Soane, Arch. Robert Stevenson, C.E. Sir John Vanbrugh, Arch. Christopher Wren, Arch. With fifty engravings, and two woodcuts.

London: Edited and published by John Weale, 1841.

20 pp, 50 pls.

36.2 × 27.3 cm

CU

The first 12 pages contain brief histories of four royal parks in London: St. James's Park, Green Park, Hyde Park, and Regent's Park. Some of these pages are illustrated with vignettes showing picturesque scenes in and near the parks. Following is a seven-page "List of Plates," and then (pp. 19–20) a list of the buildings of London illustrated in the recently issued new edition of Britton and Pugin's *Illustrations of the Public Buildings of London* (ed. W. H. Leeds, 1838).

Weale's illustrations of lodges and other park structures are devoid of scenery. Those depicting lodges are Plates 7 and 10–16, showing respectively the Royal Lodge at Buckingham Gate, a lodge at the Colonnade Entrance into Hyde Park, the Humane Society's Receiving House in Hyde Park, Stanhope Lodge and Grosvenor Lodge in Hyde Park, and Cumberland, Gloucester, and Hanover lodges in Regent's Park. Other major structures illustrated by Weale include the Marble Arch and the Colonnade Entrance into Hyde Park. Plates 3 through 5 show the four parks in plan. Altogether the illustrations depict the work of several major architects, and thus were likely of some influence in the design of lodges and other structures on private estates throughout Britain.

457.1

ZIEGLER, Henry Bryan (1798–1874)

The royal lodges in Windsor Great Park. From drawings by H. B. Ziegler, executed by L. Haghe in lithography, by express command, for Her Gracious Majesty Queen Victoria.

London: Ackermann & Coy. Printsellers, Booksellers, Stationers, &c, 1839.

1 printed leaf, 16 pls.

54.3 × 35.7 cm

NNC

This was not intended to be a didactic treatise, but rather a collection of pictorial and topographical views, composed "by express command" for Queen Victoria. Nevertheless since all the lodges were in a royal park, and since many had patriotic and romantic associations, the illustrations may well have influenced the design of lodges for private estates. The plates include a plan and a view for each of eight structures: the Keeper's Lodges at Bishop's Gate, at Forest Gate, at Blacknest Gate, at the double gates in the Long Walk, on the Windsor Road, and at the Sandpit Gate, the Head Keeper's Lodge on the road from Windsor, and the Royal Lodge Chapel.

458.1–467.1

FONTHILL ABBEY **Monographs, Guides, and Catalogues of Fonthill Abbey, 1812–1836.**

458.1

BRITTON, John (1771–1857)

Graphical and literary illustrations of Fonthill Abbey, Wiltshire; with heraldical and genealogical notices of the Beckford family. By John Britton. . . .

London: Printed for the author. Sold by Longman, Hurst, Rees, Orme, Brown, and Green; Taylor; Clarke; etc., 1823.

viii + 5–68 + [4] pp, additional engraved title page + 10 pls.

30.0 × 24.1 cm

NNC

The text consists of wide-ranging commentary on the armorial bearings of the Beckford family, the family's genealogy, the architectural sources of Fonthill Abbey's design, and the associations engendered by the design in the imagination of the beholder. Britton offered brief remarks on the English mansion as general type, noting that it required not only architectural excellence, but also a substantial collection of art and literature within, and beautiful and picturesque scenery on the exterior (pp. 23–25).

The principal rooms of the abbey are described individually, and several are illustrated in the plates. Most of the plates were engraved after drawings by G. Cattermole, and convey well the striking elevations and vistas that made Fonthill such a prominent monument of the early nineteenth-century

Gothic Revival. The ten plates include a plan, five exterior views, and interior views of the Hall, the Octagon, King Edward's Gallery, and the room in which Beckford so lavishly displayed his supposed ancestral heritage, St. Michael's Gallery.

459.1 †
Magnificent effects at Fonthill Abbey, Wilts. To be sold by auction, by Mr. Christie, on the premises, on Tuesday, September 17, 1822, and eight following days. . . .

[London]: George Sidney, [1822].

iii + 87 pp.

4°

Reference: BLC

459.2 †
Magnificent effects at Fonthill Abbey, Wilts. To be sold by auction, by Mr. Christie on . . . October 1, 1822. . . .
Third edition.
[London]: George Sidney, [1822].

95 pp.

4°

Reference: BLC

These catalogues were prepared for two of the several auctions of personal effects that followed the collapse of Beckford's financial interests.

460.1
NEALE, John Preston (1780–1847)
Graphical illustrations of Fonthill Abbey, the seat of John Farquhar, Esq. By J. P. Neale. With an historical description and notices of works of art formerly preserved there.

London: Published by Sherwood, Jones, and Co.; Longman, Hurst, Rees, Orme, Brown, and Green; and Thomas Moule. And sold by Brodie, Dowding, and Co., Salisbury, 1824.

[i] + 16 pp, frontisp. + 4 pls.

24.6 × 15.4 cm

DLC

In 1823 William Beckford sold Fonthill Abbey and approximately 5,500 acres of land to John Farquhar, and Farquhar soon added another 3,200 acres (pp. 1–2). The text includes a brief history of this transaction, the ancient Manor of Fonthill Gifford, and the building of Fonthill Abbey, plus a description of the house and grounds. At the end (pp. 13–16) there is "A List of the most celebrated Pictures and other splendid effects at Fonthill Abbey." The five plates (one bound as a frontispiece) depict the exterior from the southwest, the western entrance hall, the east oriel of St. Michael's Gallery and the postern towers, the oratory, and a distant view from the lake. A vignette at the top of page 1 depicts the eastern towers.

461.1

A new guide to Fonthill Abbey, Wiltshire, the seat of William Beckford, Esq. comprising a description of the park and buildings; together with brief notices of most of the remarkable productions of nature and art, which are now deposited there, and which are exhibited and offered for sale by the proprietor. Accompanied with an engraved view of the west front of the abbey.

London: Printed for G. and W. B. Whittaker; and P. Youngman, Witham and Maldon, Essex, 1822.

xii + 60 pp, frontisp.

19.9 × 11.5 cm

CtY

The only illustration is a view of the west front, bound as a frontispiece. As indicated on the title page, this is a guidebook prepared for tourists visiting the Abbey at the time of the sale.

462.1

[NICHOLS, John Bowyer (1779–1863)]
Historical notices of Fonthill Abbey, Wiltshire. With eleven plates, and fifteen other embellishments.

London: Nichols and Son; sold also by Brodie and Co. Salisbury, and by all the booksellers in Wiltshire, Dorsetshire, and Somersetshire, 1836.

52 pp, 11 pls.

28.0 × 21.6 cm

NNC

According to the "Advertisement," which follows the title page, the description of the grounds is taken from Britton's *Graphical and Literary Illustrations* (1823; q.v.), and most of the other "descriptions," as well as the "Embellishments," are borrowed from Rutter's *Delineations* (1823; q.v.). The "Advertisement" is signed "J. B. N." and dated January 6, 1836.

The text is divided into nine chapters, treating the history of the Manor and of former mansions, the building of the Abbey, the Abbey as it stood in 1822, the estate sale in 1823, the plates in this book, Beckford's armorial bearings, Fonthill Gifford Church, the approaches and the grounds "without the Barrier," and the "American Plantations" and grounds "within the Barrier."

The plates include a plan, two sections, views of the "Great Western Hall" and of the grand drawing room, details of ceiling ornament, exterior views from various angles, and a view of the remains after the collapse.

463.1
RUTTER, John (1796–1851)
Delineations of Fonthill and its abbey. By John Rutter, Shaftesbury.

Shaftesbury: Published by the author. London: by Charles Knight and Co.; Longman, Hurst, and Co.; Hurst, Robinson, and Co.; John and Arthur Arch, &c. &c., 1823.

1 printed leaf, vii–xxvi + 127 pp, 14 pls.

28.7 × 22.3 cm

MnU

Rutter issued a quarto impression (ca. 29 cm) and also an impression on large paper (ca. 36 cm). The two impressions are identical in imprint, in pagination, and in content of the plates.

Rutter offered this work as a major improvement over his *Description of Fonthill Abbey*, published one year earlier (p. vii). He expanded the text considerably, beginning with a description of the approaches to the estate from London, Bath, and Shaftesbury (pp. 1–6). He devoted 59 pages to detailed description of individual chambers, galleries, and other rooms, followed by a description of the exterior from several viewpoints (pp. 66–81). In the next 19 pages Rutter described the surrounding landscape, focusing on the "Walk within the Barrier," the "Walk without the Barrier," and a "Ride through the Domain." Three appendixes concerned the history of the manor, a history of the Abbey itself, and Beckford's genealogy.

The most impressive feature of the book is the complement of plates, some elegantly colored. Plate 8, serving as a frontispiece, shows an altarpiece with the title of the book displayed in the central panel. Other plates show the exterior in four different views, St. Michael's Gallery, the Hall, the Drawing Room, and King Edward's Gallery. Another plate shows a plan of the Abbey, two show sections, and one shows specimens of various ceiling designs. A large folding plate is a map of "Fonthill Domain." Other subjects are illustrated in headpieces and tailpieces to individual chapters.

464.1
RUTTER, John (1796–1851)
A description of Fonthill Abbey, and demesne, Wilts; the seat of William Beckford, Esq. Including a list of its numerous and valuable paintings, cabinets, and other curiosities. Intended as a guide to the visitor, and to convey information to the more distant enquirer. By John Rutter.

Shaftesbury: Printed and published by J. Rutter; to be had of Longman, Hurst and Co. London; and of all other booksellers in England; also of Hitchcock, at Amsterdam; Nieuwenhuys's, Brussells: and at Galignani's office, Paris, 1822.

2 printed leaves, 66 pp, frontisp.

21.0 × 13.5 cm

CtY

464.2

A description of Fonthill Abbey and demesne, in the county of Wilts; including a list of its paintings, cabinets, and other curiosities. Intended as a guide ⟨ . . . as 1st edition . . . ⟩ Rutter. Second edition, enlarged and corrected.

Shaftesbury: Printed and published by J. Rutter; to be had of Longman, Hurst and Co. London; and of all booksellers, 1822.

4 printed leaves, 74 pp, frontisp.

20.5 × 13.5 cm

CtY

464.3

A description of Fonthill Abbey and demesne, in the county of Wilts; including a list of its paintings, cabinets, &c. By John Rutter. Third edition.

Shaftesbury: Printed and published by J. Rutter; to be had of Longman, Hurst and Co. London; and of all booksellers, 1822.

viii pp, 2 printed leaves, 74 pp, frontisp.

20.6 × 13.0 cm

NN

464.4

A description ⟨ . . . as 3rd edition . . . ⟩ Rutter. Fifth edition.

Shaftesbury: Printed ⟨ . . . as 3rd edition . . . ⟩ booksellers, 1822.

viii pp, 2 printed leaves, 74 pp, frontisp.

19.2 × 12.7 cm

CtY

464.5

A description ⟨ . . . as 3rd edition . . . ⟩ Rutter. Sixth edition.

Shaftesbury: Printed and published by J. Rutter; to be had of Longman, Hurst, and Co. London; and of all booksellers, 1822.

viii pp, 2 printed leaves, 74 pp, frontisp.

20.6 × 13.3 cm

CtY

Similar to the *New Guide to Fonthill* issued in the same year, Rutter's *Description* was prepared for the use of tourists now more freely able to visit the Abbey following the collapse of Beckford's financial interests. The only illustration, the frontispiece, shows a southwest view of the Abbey.

465.1
RUTTER, John (1796–1851)
A new descriptive guide to Fonthill Abbey and demesne, for 1823, including a list of its paintings and curiosities. By John Rutter.

Shaftesbury: Printed and published by J. Rutter; to be had of Longman, Hurst, and Co.; J. and A. Arch; and Charles Knight, London; and of all booksellers; also to be had at the abbey gates, [1823].

viii + 98 pp, frontisp. + additional engraved title page.

13.8 × 21.2 cm

CtY

The text is divided into four sections. The first is a general description of the Abbey and a "survey of its Exterior." The second is a description of the interior and an account of paintings, cabinets, and curiosities in the Abbey. The third is a description of the "inner park," the "Domain," and the "outer park." The final section is an "historical sketch" of Fonthill and its "possessors," and brief remarks on former mansions at Fonthill.

The frontispiece, dated 1823, shows a view of the Abbey from the southwest. The engraved title page includes a view of Fonthill "from the Barrier."

466.1
STORER, James Sargant (1771–1853)
A description of Fonthill Abbey, Wiltshire. Illustrated by views, drawn and engraved by James Storer.

London: Published by W. Clarke; J. Carpenter; W. Miller; C. Chappel; White and Cochrane; Sherwood, Neely, and Jones; Brodie and Co. Salisbury; and J. Storer, Pentonville. Coe, Printer, London, 1812.

24 pp, 8 pls.

34.6 × 24.0 cm

ICN

466.2 ‖

Description of Fonthill Abbey, Wiltshire, with views.

London: William Clarke, 1817.

24 pp, 8 pls.

24 × 16 cm

Reference: Information supplied by The Lilly Library, Indiana University.

466.3

Fonthill Abbey. Storer's description of Fonthill Abbey; with eight interior and exterior views. The description was written and the drawings made by permission of Mr. Beckford, whilst the building and all its internal arrangements were in pristine splendour.

Salisbury: Published by Brodie & Co.; and Sherwood, Jones & Co., London, [1824?].

[*The cover transcribed above is followed by another, with text as follows:* The port-folio: a collection of engravings, from antiquarian, architectural, and topographical subjects; curious works of art, &c. &c. with descriptions. *There is no imprint.*]

16 pp, 9 pls.

22.5 × 14.4 cm

ICN

Storer's book was completed five years after Beckford moved in, at a time when the Abbey was substantially complete, and only a year before its principal architect, James Wyatt, died. Storer offered descriptions and views to assuage the "public curiosity" that "has been much excited for several years" over this "lofty Tower in the conventual style of architecture, among the woody eminences of Fonthill, in the county of Wilts" (p. 1). The first six pages discuss approaches to Fonthill from several directions, and describe distant views of the Abbey. Nearly four pages are devoted to the building's exterior (pp. 6–9), followed by detailed description of individual parlors, galleries, the Octagon, and other rooms. The illustrations show two views of the Abbey from a distance, four views of the exterior from close at hand, a view through the west door toward the Octagon, and a view into the Oratory.

The edition of 1824 differs considerably from the previous two editions. It was intended as the first in a series of publications illustrating "antiquarian, architectural, and topographical subjects." The nine plates, dated 1822–1823, are different from those in the earlier editions. Eight are views of Fonthill, including two that show its appearance in 1566 and in 1755. The ninth plate illustrates the "Handle of Qn. Mary's Coffin." The first 14 pages of text offer a history, description, and tour of Fonthill, much of it taken from Storer's earlier editions. The final two pages of text are a description of the handle of Queen Mary's coffin.

467.1

The valuable library of books, in Fonthill Abbey. A catalogue of the magnificent, rare, and valuable library, (of 20,000 volumes) illustrated, in many instances, with two and three sets of proof and other plates; generally of the most choice editions; selected with great care, and the utmost liberality, during the last forty years; also, of the books of prints, galleries of art, curious missals and manuscripts, the Persian and Chinese drawings, &c. &c. &c. Which will be sold by auction, by Mr. Phillips, at the Abbey, on Tuesday, the 9th of September, 1823, and nine following days, on Friday, the 3d of October, & four following days, and on Thursday, 23d October, 1823, & four following days, (Sundays and Mondays excepted) at half-past twelve each day precisely.

[London, 1823].

5 printed leaves, 113 pp, 1 leaf, 1 printed leaf, 121–175 pp, 1 printed leaf, 291–342 pp, 1 leaf, 4 printed leaves, 231–278 + [i] + 176–222 pp, 1 printed leaf, 343–391 pp, frontisp.

23.6 × 15.0 cm

MnU

Of two copies examined, both were assembled in the following order: Part 1, books; Part [2], furniture and other furnishings; Part [5], books; Part [4], pictures and miniatures; Part [3], furniture and other furnishings; and Part [6], books and prints. This arrangement reflects the sequence in which the individual objects listed were sold. In one copy the colophon "Printed by J. Davy" appears on page 391.

The catalogue consists of six parts describing portions of Beckford's effects that were auctioned off during September and October 1823. The frontispiece to Part 1 shows a view of the central tower framed by the lower towers at the end of the eastern wing.

The following items became available too late for inclusion among the principal entries. These entries are arranged in two separate alphabetical sequences—an arrangement made necessary by greater delays in obtaining information for the final group. The second sequence begins with Entry 479.1. Cross-references to all items here have been entered among the principal entries. The standards of bibliographic description used here are the same as those printed at the beginning of the principal entries. All entries in Appendix D are represented, as appropriate, in Appendixes E and F.

468.1

ATKINSON, James

An account of the state of agriculture & grazing in New South Wales; including observations on the soils and general appearance of the country, and some of its most useful natural productions; with an account of the various methods of clearing and improving lands, breeding and grazing live stock, erecting buildings, the system of employing convicts, and the expense of labour generally; the mode of applying for grants of land; with other information important to those who are about to emigrate to that country: the result of several years' residence and practical experience in those matters in the colony. By James Atkinson, Esq. . . .

London: Printed and published by J. Cross, 1826.

vi pp, 1 printed leaf, 146 pp, 5 pls.

22.0 × 12.5 cm

NN

468.2

————

An account of agriculture and grazing in New South Wales, and of some of its most useful natural productions, with other information, important to those who are about to emigrate to that country, the result of several years' residence and practical experience. By the late James Atkinson, Esq.

Second edition, revised and corrected. To which have been added some useful data and remarks derived from other authentic sources.

London: J. Cross; Simpkin, Marshall, and Co.; and sold by all booksellers, 1844.

x pp, 1 printed leaf, 188 pp [*pages 77–78 and 83–86 are wanting in this copy*].

17.1 × 10.7 cm

CSt

The copy of the second edition at Stanford has no plates. From the text it appears that pages 77–78 and 83–86, which have been torn out, contained two illustrations of silos.

The two editions differ considerably. The commentary below is primarily a discussion of the first edition, followed by a few remarks on the second.

The first three chapters proceed methodically through descriptions of the topography, flora and fauna, and "state of agriculture" in New South Wales. The fourth chapter concerns breeding and management of livestock. The fifth chapter introduces methods of clearing and draining land, paring and burning, fencing and enclosing, and erecting buildings. Atkinson acknowledged that some settlers would find it necessary, due to limited capital, to live in a bark hut for the first several years. Settlers of greater means might construct a "decent dwelling," in which "grandeur and ornament" must nevertheless "be kept out of sight" (p. 95). He included a design for such a house (Plate 3), with a sitting room, three bedrooms, a kitchen, a storeroom, and a veranda on the ground floor, plus a loft above to be used for storage. The veranda extends the full width of the house, and is fronted by seven thin columns supporting a gambrel roof.[1] Atkinson accompanied the design with a few remarks on siting and construction (pp. 95–97). Chapter VI concerns labor and "domestic manufactures." A "Supplementary Chapter" touches on trade, manufacturing, transportation, revenue, climate, police, military forces, churches, schools, government, and "Black Natives."

Other subjects in the plates of the first edition include a view of Port Jackson, "An Exploring Party in New South Wales," a "Party Preparing to Bivouac," a ground plan of a milking yard, a "Party Bivouac'd for the Night," and a map of New South Wales with "Additions to 1826."

The "Editor's Preface" to the second edition (pp. iii–x) notes the progress of settlement in New South Wales since 1826, and the consequent need to omit much of what Atkinson—now deceased—had originally included. The first three chapters concern the history, topography, flora, and fauna of the colony. Chapter IV is a discussion of "Systems of Agriculture." The next three chapters touch on livestock, clearing land, and vineyards. The final chapter treats such topics as trade, manufacturing, banking, travel, climate, the "Advantages of Colonization," and wages and prices.

1. This design and Atkinson's description were reprinted in *Mechanics' Magazine* IX (1828; *q.v.*).

469.1

DICKSON, R. W.

Practical agriculture; or, a complete system of modern husbandry: with the methods of planting, and the management of live stock. By R. W. Dickson, M.D. In two volumes. Vol. I [*or* II].

London: Printed for Richard Phillips; by R. Taylor and Co., 1805.

[*Volume I:*] xix pp, 10 printed leaves, 618 pp, 51 printed leaves, frontisp. + 53 pls.

[*Volume II:*] 4 printed leaves, 583–1234 + 801–817 + 1218–1262 pp, 6 printed leaves, 33 pls (numbered II–XXXIV; pl. I is bound as the frontispiece to Vol. I).

26.6 × 21.4 cm

MnU

469.2 †

──────

Practical agriculture; or, a complete system of modern husbandry: with the best methods of planting, and the improved management of live stock. A new edition.

London: Printed for Richard Phillips, 1807.

2 vols.

Reference: NUC

469.3 ‡

──────

The farmer's companion; being a complete system of modern husbandry: including the latest improvements and discoveries, in theory and practice. Illustrated by numerous engravings. By R. W. Dickson, M.D. . . . .

London: Printed for Richard Phillips; by R. Wilks, 1810.

946 pp, pls.

8°

Reference: Goldsmiths'-Kress Library of Economic Literature (microfilm). Segment 2. Printed Books 1801–1850. Reel 1981, No. 19975.

469.4 †

──────

Farmer's companion.

[London]: Sherwood, 1811.

Royal 8°

Reference: ECB

469.5

The farmer's companion; ⟨ . . . as 1810 . . . ⟩ engravings. By R. W. Dickson, M.D. . . . Second edition. In two volumes. Vol. I [*or* II].

London: Printed for Sherwood, Neely, and Jones; and to be had of all booksellers, 1813.

[*Volume I*:] 1 printed leaf, 336 pp, 83 pls (numbered I–LXII, LXII–LXXXI, LXXXIV).

[*Volume II*:] 337–946 pp, 21 pls (numbered LXXXII–LXXXIII, LXXXV–CIII).

23.0 × 14.4 cm

MnU

469.6 †

Practical agriculture; ⟨ . . . as 1807 . . . ⟩ live stock. Illustrated with numerous engravings. By R. W. Dickson. . . . A new edition. In two volumes. . . .

London: Sherwood, Neely, and Jones, 1814.

2 vols. (including 2 frontisps., 85 pls).

27.0 × 21.5 cm

Reference: NUC

469.7 †

The farmer's companion; ⟨ . . . as 1810 . . . ⟩ Dickson. . . . Second edition.

London: Printed for Sherwood, Gilbert, and Piper, [n.d.].

2 leaves, 948 pp, 103 pls.

24 cm

Reference: NUC

An entry in the ECB indicates that a book by Dickson titled *Complete System of Agriculture* was announced in October 1804. This is no doubt a reference to the edition of *Practical Agriculture* dated 1805.[1]

The edition of *The Farmer's Companion* published by Sherwood, Gilbert, and Piper can be dated 1826 or later, since the publisher did not trade under that name until 1826.[2]

In the Preface to the first edition (I, iii–vi) Dickson noted "numerous alterations and improvements" recently "introduced in the different branches of the art of husbandry," which he now proposed to bring "into better order" and "into a more intimate connexion with the principles on which they depend" (I, iii–iv).[3] The Introduction (I, vii–xix) is a lengthy essay concerning agricultural improvement. The text of the first volume is divided into 11 "Sections," treating farm implements, farm houses and offices, farm cottages, "inclosing" land, road construction, soil, manure, drainage, paring and burning, fallowing, and cultivation of arable land. The last section is continued at the beginning of Volume II, followed by two more sections, concerning cultivation of grassland and livestock. Pages 583–618 at the end of Volume I are "Additions and Corrections to the First Volume." Pages 1226–1234 are likewise "Additions and Corrections to the Second Volume." At the very end is "An Appendix, Containing a Compendious View of the Principal Laws Relating to Agriculture," a text running continuously on pages numbered 801–817 and 1218–1265.

Fifty-seven of the 87 plates are accompanied by single unnumbered leaves containing descriptive letterpress. Among the architectural subjects illustrated is Woburn Park Farm: Plate I depcits its stables, barn, exhibition room, mill house, shops, and bailiff's house in plan. Section II, on farm houses, and Section III, on farm cottages, contain designs for dwellings. In Section II, Plates XXV–XXVII include plans and elevations of six farm houses, together with plans of stables and other offices. The designs are slightly modified reproductions of illustrations accompanying A. Crocker's "Essay on Farm Houses" (1797; q.v.). Dickson's text (I, 69–75) includes excerpts from other agricultural treatises.[4] In Section III, Plate XXVIII includes designs for eight cottages previously published by Crocker, Sir John Sinclair, and Nathaniel Kent.[5] The text is a pastiche of observations by these and other authors.[6] Figures 4 and 5 in Plate XLII (Section VIII) both illustrate techniques of draining land near houses, and each includes a tiny representation of a two-story house, three windows wide.

In 1810 Dickson prepared "an abridged and cheap Edition," to be sold "at a price suited to the literary views of Practical Farmers, and not exceeding what public-spirited Landlords might choose to give for Copies to distribute among their tenantry." Titled *The Farmer's Companion*, this edition retained "every established Principle, Fact, and Improvement" included in the first edition, and also was "carefully revised" to include "all the recent improvements in Agricultural Practice."[7] The first ten chapters of *The Farmer's Companion* closely parallel the first ten "Sections" of the first edition; the remaining three "Sections" of the first edition were divided up to make Chapters XI–XXII in *The Farmer's Companion*. For the abridged edition Dickson only slightly modified his discussion of the "Situation and Arrangement of Farm-Houses and Offices" (pp. 97–102), and in Plate LXI retained three of the six designs for farm houses that appeared in the previous edition. The revised discussion of "Farm-Cottages" (pp. 102–114) closely parallels that in the first edition, but the illustrations are entirely different. On page 107 Dickson added a new "Plan of a Cottage-Farm." The eight cottage designs that appeared in Plate XXVIII in the first edition were replaced by just two designs, titled "Plan 1, Cottage House" and "Plan 3, Cottage House for a Labourer," each shown in one elevation and two floor plans. These designs, which appear on separate plates each marked "Pl. LXII Page 113," were taken from Richard Parkinson's report to the Board of Agriculture on the county of Rutland (1808).[8] The small figures of houses illustrating the discussion of drainage appear on Plate LXXVI in Chapter VIII of the second edition.

1. The 1805 edition includes a dedication dated 19 October 1804, followed by a preface dated 13 October 1804.

2. See Philip A. H. Brown, *London Publishers and Printers* (London: British Museum, 1961), p. 85.

3. In the discussion of *Practical Agriculture* all page references are to the 1805 edition.

4. These include Robert Beatson, "On Farm Buildings in General" (1797; *q.v.*), and Nathaniel Kent, *Hints to Gentlemen* (1775; *q.v.*).

5. Figs. 1–4 are taken from A. Crocker and Son, "On Cottages" (1797; *q.v.*); Figs. 5–9 are from Sir John Sinclair, *Projet d'un plan pour établir des fermes expérimentales* ([1800?]; see Entry 308), Pl. 2; and Figs. 10–21 are from Nathaniel Kent, *Hints to Gentlemen* (1775; *q.v.*).

6. These include Robert Beatson, "On Cottages" (1797; *q.v.*); Arthur Young's report on the agriculture of Lincolnshire (1799; *q.v.* under "Great Britain. Board of Agriculture"); and Thomas Davis, "Address to the Landholders" (1795; *q.v.*).

7. The quotations are from the "Advertisement," dated 17 April 1810, in the 1813 edition.

8. See the commentary on Parkinson's report above, under "Great Britain. Board of Agriculture."

470.1
FIELDING, Theodore Henry Adolphus (1781–1851)
The art of engraving, with the various modes of operation, under the following different divisions: etching. Soft-ground etching. Line engraving. Chalk and stipple. Aquatint. Mezzotint. Lithography. Wood engraving. Medallic engraving. Electrography. And photography. Illustrated with specimens of the different styles of engraving. By T. H. Fielding. . . .

London: Published by Ackermann & Co., 1841.

vii + [i] + 109 + [iii] pp, 10 pls.

25.0 × 14.7 cm

OO

470.2

The art of engraving, ⟨ . . . as 1841 . . . ⟩ with ten specimens ⟨ . . . as 1841 . . . ⟩ .

London: M. A. Nattali, 1844.

vii + [i] + 109 + [iii] pp, 10 pls.

24.0 × 15.4 cm

MiU

In the Preface (pp. iii–iv) Fielding explained that his book was "arranged with a view of serving the professor as well as the amateur." The text begins with a brief essay on the invention of engraving. Individual chapters treat each subject specified on the title page.[1] The final chapter, on photography, discusses three different processes: "First, that it in which the representation is obtained on paper prepared with the nitrate or chloride of silver. Second, that in which it is produced on resins, bitumens, or the residua of essential oils. Third, that in which iodine is the receiving surface" (p. 101). Following the text is a "list of Requisites for engravers" and a two-page list of "Modern Engravings arranged according to the Engravers."

Plate I, bound as a frontispiece, shows engraving tools. Plates II and III, examples of etching and soft-ground etching, depict picturesque country scenes. Plate IV, a line engraving, is a view of the "Giant's Staircase, Doge's Palace, Venice."[2] Plate V depicts eight examples of aquatint grounds, and Plate VI is an aquatint view of a scene along a river or canal. Plate VII shows two mezzotint examples of a landscape with a windmill.[3] Plate VIII is a stipple engraving of a half-length female figure. There are two lithographed views in Plate 9, one showing a small village with several two- and three-story cottages flanking a narrow road, and the other showing a landscape with a castle on a distant hill. Plate 10 is "A Drawing on Zinc" of a lake scene with a castle in the right foreground and a large mansion on a hill in the left distance.

1. The table of contents (pp. v–vi) shows a separate chapter devoted to the subject of "Zincography," but in fact the material (pp. 88–90) is run on as part of the chapter on lithography (pp. 77–90).

2. This caption appears only in the 1844 edition.

3. This plate, marked "VII" in the 1844 edition, is incorrectly marked "V" in the 1841 edition.

471.1 ‡

GREAT BRITAIN. Parliament. House of Commons. Select Committee on Buildings Regulation, and Improvement of Boroughs.

Report from select committee on buildings regulation and improvement of boroughs; together with the minutes of evidence, appendix, index, and plans. Ordered, by the House of Commons, to be printed, 27 June 1842. [*In:* Reports from committees: ten volumes. —(6.)— Courts of Law and Equity; buildings regulation and improvement of boroughs; health of towns (effect of interment of bodies). Session 3 February—12 August 1842. Vol. X. 1842.]

viii + 166 pp, 7 pls.

Reference: Readex microprint edition, New York, N.Y., n.d.

471.2 ‡

Report from the select committee on buildings regulation, and improvement of boroughs; together with the minutes of evidence, appendix, index, and plans. [Communicated by the Commons to the Lords.] Ordered to be printed 4th August 1842.
[*In:* The sessional papers printed by order of the House of Lords, or presented by Royal command, in the Session 1842, (5° & 6° Victoriae,) arranged in volumes. Vol. XVII. Reports from select committees of the House of Commons, and evidence, communicated to the Lords, (two volumes,) the subjects alphabetically arranged. Subjects of this volume: bonded corn; buildings regulation, &c.; health of towns. 1842.]

viii + 166 pp, 7 pls.

Reference: Microfilm edition by Oceana Publications Inc., Dobbs Ferry, N.Y., 1970, Reel 233.

The preliminaries commence with an account of the orders that established this committee and conferred its powers, plus a table of contents (page ii).[1] Next there is a brief "Report" transmitting the minutes of evidence to the House of Commons (p. iii). Pages iv–viii contain an account of the proceedings of the committee and a list of witnesses. The minutes of evidence obtained in proceedings before the committee are printed on pages 1–131, followed by three appendixes (pp. 132–139) and an index (pp. 141–166).

Seven plates bound at the end pertain to testimony presented by George Shorland of Manchester (pp. 94–116). Shorland's remarks principally concern increased costs for first- through fourth-rate houses that would result from passage of an Act establishing new building regulations. Detailed cost estimates printed on pages 100–102 apply to designs numbered 1 through 5, which appear in the first six plates.

All the plates contain plans and elevations for attached row houses. There is little ornament except for cornices, semicircular fanlights over the entrances, and engaged columns *in antis* flanking the entrances to first-rate houses. The first plate depicts designs for first-rate houses, each two stories high and two openings wide, with a parlor, sitting room, kitchen, scullery, yard, privy, and midden on the ground floor. The second-rate houses in the next plate are likewise two stories high and two openings wide, with a parlor, sitting room, kitchen, scullery, yard, and privy on the ground floor. The third-rate houses are two stories high, with a door and window on the ground floor and one window upstairs. The ground plan includes a parlor, kitchen, scullery, yard, and privy. The facades of fourth-rate houses shown in the fourth and fifth plates are similar to the third-rate designs. Shorland provided five different plans for fourth-rate houses, each with a front room, yard, and privy; two of the plans also include a back kitchen. Three additional designs, numbered 5 through 7, are depicted in plan and elevation in the final two plates. No. 5 has a basement and two stories, while No. 6 has a basement and four stories. No. 7 contains just two stories. These designs depict various methods of building attached dwellings back to back.

1. This description refers to the version printed for the House of Commons, which differs only slightly from that printed for the House of Lords.

472.1

GREAT BRITAIN. Poor Law Commissioners.
Report to Her Majesty's Principal Secretary of State for the Home Department, from the Poor Law Commissioners, on an inquiry into the sanitary condition of the labouring population of Great Britain; with appendices. Presented to both Houses of Parliament, by command of Her Majesty, July, 1842.

London: Printed by W. Clowes and Sons, for Her Majesty's Stationery Office, 1842.

xxx + [i] + 457 pp, 20 pls.

21.1 × 13.2 cm

NN

472.2 ‡

[*In:* The sessional papers printed by order of the House of Lords, or presented by Royal command, in the session 1842, (5° & 6° Victoriae,) arranged in volumes. Vol. XXVI. Reports from commissioners, (twelve volumes,) continued; the subjects alphabetically arranged. Subject of this volume: sanitary condition of the labouring population of Great Britain (general report). 1842.]

London: Printed by W. Clowes and Sons, for Her Majesty's Stationery Office, 1842.

xxx + [i] + 457 pp, 20 pls.

Reference: Microfilm edition by Oceana Publications Inc., Dobbs Ferry, N.Y., 1970, Reel 237.

The first chapter of the report concerns the problem of living conditions among the "labouring classes" and the corresponding high incidence of disease. The seven following chapters take up such specific considerations as drainage, sewerage, water supply, "internal economy," ventilation, "domestic habits," life expectancy, economic consequences of neglecting public health, possible measures for preventing disease, "principles of legislation," and living conditions in common lodging houses. The ninth chapter is a "Recapitulation of Conclusions," followed by a lengthy series of appendixes (pp. 373–457).

Apart from three maps of urban areas, one chart, and a double plate illustrating sewer plans, all the plates illustrate model housing for laborers. Following page 266 there are nine plates; they include a view of a "group of Northumbrian cottages," views of four groups of cottages at Harlaxton, one with a "village shop," plans of a "treble cottage" at Harlaxton, plans and elevations of a double cottage and a triple cottage built at Culford, Suffolk, plans and elevations of a quadruple cottage and two double cottages at Holkham, plans and elevations of a double cottage erected at Closeburn, plans and elevations of two cottages built at Egerton, plans of a double cottage erected at Bollington, and an elevation, plan, and section of double cottages on the estates of the Earl of Rosebery. The accompanying text includes remarks by John Claudius Loudon, Sydney Smirke, and others on the subject of cottage design and construction. Facing page 274 is a design by Smirke for a three-story "public lodging house" for needy individuals, shown in elevation and plan. Appendix 8 includes a plate with a view and plan of a cottage "for an Agricultural labourer in the north of England or in Scotland," designed by Loudon and described by him on pages 395–396. Appendix 9 (pp. 396–399), also by Loudon, enumerates 15 "essential requisites" for a comfortable laborer's cottage, and includes text figures illustrating such a cottage in a perspective view and two interior details. Following page 402 are four plates of model residences, perhaps intended to accompany those following page 266: elevations and plans of two more cottages erected at Egerton, an elevation and plans of houses in Great Russell Street, Birmingham, and plans and elevations of "two new courts of houses in Bradford Street, Birmingham."

Appendix 13 concerns the "Arrangement of Public Walks in Towns" and includes text figures on pages 406–407 illustrating the plan of the Derby Arboretum as laid out by Loudon.

•

The annual reports of the Poor Law Commissioners, published in the House of Commons Sessional Papers, sometimes included architectural plans, usually for workhouses or prisons. See particularly the following three reports for workhouse designs:

First Annual Report of the Poor Law Commissioners for England and Wales. Ordered, by the House of Commons, to Be Printed, 10 August 1835. vi + 3–252 pp, 1 printed leaf, 10 pls. Appendix (A.), "Documents Issued by the Central Board," contains ten plates and a printed leaf with captions. Plate 1 depicts a "Plan of a Rural Workhouse, for 500 Persons. By Sir Francis Bond Head." Plates 2–5 illustrate a design by Sampson Kempthorne (1809–1873) for a "Square Plan" workhouse for 300 paupers. Plate 6 is a plan of a workhouse designed by Kempthorne for 200 paupers. Plates 7–10 depict a "Hexagon Plan" workhouse designed by Kempthorne to contain 300 paupers.

Second Annual Report of the Poor Law Commissioners for England and Wales; Together with Appendixes A. B. C. D. Ordered, by the House of Commons, to Be Printed, 19 August 1836. 574 pp, 3 pls. Appendix (A.), "Documents Issued by the Central Board," includes "Plans of an Improved Workhouse for the Less Pauperised Districts" intended to hold 200 paupers. The design, by Kempthorne, is shown in two plans and a perspective view.

Fifth Annual Report of the Poor Law Commissioners: with Appendices. Presented to Parliament in Pursuance of the Act 1 & 2 Vict., Cap. 56. Ordered, by the House of Commons, to Be Printed, 2 May 1839. iv + 149 pp, 4 pls. Appendix (B.), "Documents Issued by the Board under the Irish Poor Relief Act," includes "Papers as to the Providing of Workhouses in Ireland" (pp. 81–90), and "Plans, &c. of Workhouses"—for plates containing perspective views and ground plans of one workhouse for "400 or 800" paupers, and another for 800 paupers.

473.1
GREAT BRITAIN. Poor Law Commissioners.
Sanitary inquiry:—England. Local reports on the sanitary condition of the labouring population of England, in consequence of an inquiry directed to be made by the Poor Law Commissioners. Presented to both Houses of Parliament, by Command of Her Majesty, July, 1842.

London: Printed by W. Clowes and Sons, for Her Majesty's Stationery Office, 1842.

iv + 444 pp, 8 pls.

20.9 × 12.7 cm

MnU

473.2 ‡

[*In:* The sessional papers printed by order of the House of Lords, or presented by Royal command, in the session 1842, (5° & 6° Victoriae,) arranged in volumes. Vol. XXVII. Reports from commissioners, (twelve volumes,) continued; the subjects alphabetically arranged. Subject of this volume: sanitary condition of the labouring population of England (local reports). 1842.]

London: Printed by W. Clowes and Sons, for Her Majesty's Stationery Office, 1842.

iv + 444 pp, 8 pls.

Reference: Microfilm edition by Oceana Publications Inc., Dobbs Ferry, N.Y., 1970, Reel 237.

This volume consists of 26 separate reports on the state of sanitation and housing among the laboring classes in English towns, counties, and other geographic divisions. Report No. 9, concerning dwellings in Norfolk and Suffolk, includes two plates. One depicts plans and elevations of two double cottages and one quadruple cottage erected at Holkham. Edward Twisleton, author of the report, described these cottages as, "perhaps, the most substantial and comfortable which are to be seen in any part of England, and if all the English peasantry could be lodged in similar ones it would be the realization of an Utopia" (p. 136). The other plate shows elevations and plans of a double cottage and a triple cottage built at Culford, in Suffolk, part of "a remarkable village of about fifty cottages, built within the last twenty years by Mr. Benyon de Beuvoir." Compared to the cottages at Holkham, these were "a more attainable standard of excellence" (p. 137).[1]

Report No. 12, on "the State of the Public Health in the Borough of Birmingham," includes six plates. These depict a pair of "three-quarter houses, in Tennant Street," row houses in Great Russell Street, houses in Bromsgrove Street, plans of "two new courts of houses in Bradford Street," elevations of those houses, and plans and elevations of houses in Ann Street and Pershore Street.[2] These plates are not discussed in the text.

•

Also in 1842 the Poor Law Commission completed a volume titled: *Sanitary Inquiry:—Scotland. Reports on the Sanitary Condition of the Labouring Population of Scotland, in Consequence of an Inquiry Directed to Be Made by the Poor Law Commissioners. Presented to Both Houses of Parliament, by Command of Her Majesty, July, 1842.* Organized in the same manner as the volume on England, this volume contains 18 separate reports in iv + 334 pages, with no illustrations.

1. These plates also appear following p. 266 of the Commission's *Report . . . on an Inquiry into the Sanitary Conditions* (1842; *q.v.*).

2. The second, fourth, and fifth of these plates also appear ibid., following p. 402.

474.1

The horticultural register, and general magazine. Vol. I. By Joseph Paxton, . . . and Joseph Harrison.

London: Published by Baldwin and Cradock, [1831–1832].

The horticultural register, and general magazine, of all useful and interesting discoveries connected with natural history and rural subjects. Vol. II. By Joseph Paxton. . . .

London: Printed for Baldwin and Cradock, 1833.

The horticultural register, and general magazine, of all useful & interesting ⟨ . . . as Vol. II . . . ⟩ subjects. Vol. III. By Joseph Paxton. . . .

London: Printed for Baldwin and Cradock, 1834.

The horticultural register. Edited by Joseph Paxton, . . . Joseph Harrison, and James Main. . . . In five volumes. Vol. IV.

London: William Smith, [1835?].

The horticultural register. Edited by Joseph Paxton, . . . Joseph Harrison, and James Main. . . . In five volumes. Vol V.

London: William Smith, [1836?].

[*Volumes I through III:*] MnU

[*Volumes IV and V:*] IU

Although this periodical primarily concerns horticulture, several articles include designs for dwellings and ornamental garden structures:

• **Artus**, "On Labourers' Cottages, Recently Erected at Thurlby, in Lincolnshire," I:2 (1 August 1831), 62–64. The article describes Sir Edward ffrench Bromhead's recent improvements at Thurlby, including six two-story double cottages for laborers. Built of brick and roofed with tile or thatch, these cottages "are plain buildings, and destitute of all those external ornaments, which . . . proclaim the dependence of the possessor. Yet covered as they are with fruit-trees, shrubs and climbers, they are not void of beauty" (p. 63). One example is shown in a perspective view on page 63. This design also was published in *Paxton's Magazine of Botany*, I (1834; *q.v.*).

• **A Bricklayer's Labourer**, "Remarks on the Erection of Labourers' Cottages," I:4 (1 October 1831), 152–155. This author disagreed with "Artus," arguing that "external ornaments of a cottage" in fact " '*proclaim*' the taste of the proprietor" (pp. 152–153). The "Bricklayer's Labourer" also included a design for a picturesque double cottage in the hope of encouraging landowners to improve living conditions for their "dependents" and so unite "utility and comfort with the picturesque" (p. 152). He declared that a "neat cottage and small garden" would "have great effect upon the morals of the labourer"; indeed "there ought to be a national pride implanted in every individual who intends building a cottage"

(p. 153). As shown on page 154, each cottage includes a kitchen, washhouse, closet, privy, and pigsty on the ground floor, with bedrooms upstairs. The elevation is irregular and picturesque, with a thatch roof, ornamented chimneys, hipped gables, and lattice windows. This design also was published in *Paxton's Magazine of Botany*, I (1834; *q.v.*).

• **A Bricklayer's Labourer**, "Remarks on Labourers' Dwellings, with a Design for the Erection of a Double Cottage," I:8 (1 February 1832), 353–357. Although he conceded that "there is a great deal of quackery about the terms, 'landscape gardening,' and 'picturesque village scenery,'" the author had no doubt about the scenic character of the site for which he intended this design. The "ground," he said, should be "greatly elevated above the surrounding surface" so that "the irregular form of the roof may be seen against the sky." He suggested that "broken ascents and rugged pathways; together with something bold and expressive, such as rocks, large trees, &c." would produce a particularly "pleasant effect" (p. 354). As shown on page 353 the plan of this double cottage includes a kitchen, washhouse, and other offices for each dwelling, plus bedrooms upstairs. The elevation is asymmetrical, irregular, and eclectic, with pointed arches, Regency trelliswork, and rustic tree-trunk columns. As in his previous article, the author recommended that landowners adopt his design for the picturesque improvement of their estates as well as for the welfare of their tenants. This design also was published in *Paxton's Magazine of Botany*, I (1834; *q.v.*).

• **A. B. L.**, "Design for an Old English Gate Lodge," II:27 (1 September 1833), 404–405. The author introduced the design by observing that the architectural character of a gate lodge reflects the personal character of the landowner (p. 404). The elevation is highly picturesque, with a thatch roof, one hipped gable and two pointed gables with finials, ornamental chimneys, lattice windows, bargeboards, and trelliswork. The plan includes a parlor, sitting room, back kitchen, and pantry on the ground floor, and three bedrooms upstairs. The design and description also were published in *Paxton's Magazine of Botany*, I (1834; *q.v.*).

• **The Bricklayer's Labourer**, "A Design for Four Labourers' Dwellings United, with a Few Remarks on the State of the British Peasantry," III:38 (1 August 1834), 356–366. The author again urged landowners to recognize "the necessity of their union and sympathy with their tenantry," and as one means of accomplishing this submitted "the present design . . . in the anxious hope that it will be adopted by some benevolent landlord" (p. 356). This quadruple residence is shown in two plans, an elevation, and a perspective view, plus a plan for a garden. The ground floor of each dwelling contains a kitchen, back room, pantry, and other small offices; upstairs there are two closets and one bedroom. The elevation is in an Italianate style, with round arches over the windows and a tile roof. Following brief remarks on materials and construction, the author included an extended essay on "The Condition of the British Peasantry" (pp. 362–366), with suggestions for increasing employment among laborers and for improving their education. This design also was published in *Paxton's Magazine of Botany*, I (1834; *q.v.*).

• **R. Mallet, Esq., of Dublin**, "Garden Architecture. On the Various Forms and Characters of Arbours as Objects of Use or Ornament, Either in Garden or Wild Scenery," IV:XLVII (May 1835), 175–180. Following references to Milton, the Bible, Horace, and Virgil, Mallet classified arbors into three types: purely natural, partly natural and partly artificial, and wholly artificial. Five text figures provide examples of all three types, including lone trees (Figs. 1 and 2), a tree ornamented with climbing plants (Fig. 3), a ring of trees planted to enclose a circular space (Fig. 4), and a large pedimented arch with wings, largely constructed of treillage (Fig. 5). This article also appears in *Paxton's Magazine of Botany*, IV (1838; *q.v.*). An unillustrated continuation of the article appears in *The Horticultural Register*, IV:XLVIII (June 1835), 217–226.

• **A. B.**, "Letter I. from A. B. to a Friend in London," IV:XLIX (July 1835), 251–255. The article is the first in a series of installments giving the author's "impressions and feelings" during a "visit to Fairfax Hall" (p. 252). A vignette at the head of the article depicts the one-story entrance lodge: the facade includes a small entrance porch flanked by single windows on either side, all framed by pilasters and an entablature. The series continued monthly, from "Landscape Gardening. Letter Second" (August 1835) through "Landscape Gardening. Letter Eighteen" (December 1836). There were no further illustrations of dwellings.

475.1
HULLMANDEL, Charles Joseph (1789–1850)
The art of drawing on stone, giving a full explanation of the various styles, of the different methods to be employed to ensure success, and of the modes of correcting, as well as of the several causes of failure, by C. Hullmandel.

London: Published by C Hullmandel. & by R. Ackermann, [1824].

xvi + 92 + vii pp, 19 pls.

22.8 × 18.5 cm

MnU

475.2 †
————

————

London: Longman & Co., 1833.

1 leaf, vii + 92 pp, 19 pls.

26 cm

Reference: NUC

475.3 †

London: Longman & Co., 1835.

xii + 79 pp.

23 cm

Reference: NUC

475.4 †

Art of drawing on stone.

[London]: Longman, 1840.

Royal 8°

Reference: ECB

In 1820 Hullmandel completed *A Manual of Lithography* (London: Rodwell and Martin), a translation of Antoine Raucourt's treatise of 1819.

In the Introduction to the first edition of *The Art of Drawing on Stone* ([1824]) Hullmandel indicated that the book would consist of "a few hints, which my experience has suggested" might be of use to others. Most of the Introduction is a defense of lithography against charges that it is "a *degrading art*, and the means of bringing the works of artists into contempt" through reproduction (p. ii). He countered that due to the invention of lithography "excellent drawing-books and models can now be given to the Public at a cheap rate" (pp. xiv–xv), providing examples for study and instruction. He noted extensive government support for lithographers in France, Bavaria, and Russia, and argued for the same in England.[1]

Following brief preliminary remarks (pp. 1–5) Hullmandel discussed both "Polished" and "Grained" stones, used respectively in the "two principal styles" of lithography, the "Ink" and "Chalk" styles (pp. 5–8). He also gave directions for supporting, cleaning, and preparing stones, tracing drawings, and using certain tools (pp. 8–23). The greatest portion of the text is devoted to "Chalk Drawings" (pp. 24–57), followed by shorter remarks on the "Dabbing Style" (pp. 58–73) and the "Pen and Ink Style" (pp. 73–76). He concluded with instructions for mixing the ink and chalk styles, making transfers and wrappers for books, transferring copperplate impressions to stone, printing with two plates, making corrections, discovering "causes of failure," picking, and packing up stones.

The plates illustrate tools, instruments, and examples of lithographed landscapes, portraits, mechanical diagrams, geometric patterns, hand-writing facsimiles, and maps. The only architectural subject is a rustic cottage that figures prominently in Plate XV, a picturesque landscape scene that also includes a human figure, a stream, and a waterwheel.

1. On the importance of Hullmandel's contribution to English lithography, with detailed remarks concerning his *Art of Drawing on Stone*, see Michael Twyman, *Lithography 1800–1850* (London: Oxford University Press, 1970), pp. 40, 114–131.

476.1

[*Volume I:*]

The imperial magazine; or, compendium of religious, moral, & philosophical knowledge: comprehending religion, literature, moral philosophy, or ethics, natural philosophy, chemistry, review of books, historical narrative, antiquities, domestic economy, trade, miscellaneous articles, poetry.

Liverpool: Printed at the Caxton Press, by Henry Fisher, Printer in Ordinary to His Majesty; published at 87, Bartholomew Close, London, [1819].

[*Volume II:*]

⸻

Liverpool: ⟨ . . . as Vol. I . . . ⟩ London; and sold by all booksellers, [1820].

[*Volume III:*]

The imperial magazine; ⟨ . . . as Vol. I . . . ⟩ moral, and philosophical ⟨ . . . as Vol. I . . . ⟩ poetry.

London: Printed at the Caxton Press, by Henry Fisher, Printer in Ordinary to His Majesty; published at 87, Bartholomew Close; and sold by all booksellers, [1821].

[*Volume IV:*]

⸻

London: ⟨ . . . as Vol. III . . . ⟩; published at 38, Newgate-street; and sold by all booksellers, [1822].

[*Volume V:*]

⸻

⸻ , [1823].

[*Volume VI:*]

⸻

⸻ , [1824].

[*Volume VII:*]

⸻

London: Printed at the Caxton Press, by H. Fisher, Son, and Co. Printers in Ordinary to His Majesty; published at 38, Newgate-street; and sold by all booksellers, [1825].

[*Volume VIII:*]

⸻

⸻ , [1826].

[*Volume IX:*]

———————

London: ⟨ . . . as Vol. VII . . . ⟩ Majesty. Published ⟨ . . . as Vol. VII . . . ⟩, [1827].

[*Volume X:*]

———————

——————— , [1828].

[*Volume XI:*]

The imperial magazine; ⟨ . . . as Vol. I . . . ⟩ moral, and philosphical knowledge; comprehending ⟨ . . . as Vol. I . . . ⟩ poetry.

——————— , [1829].

[*Volume XII:*]

———————

——————— , [1830].

[*Second series, Volume I:*]

The imperial magazine; and, monthly record of religious, philosophical, historical, biographical, topographical, and general knowledge; embracing literature, science, & art. Edited by Samuel Drew, M.A.

London: Fisher, Son, & Jackson, [1831].

[*Second series, Volume II:*]

———————

H. Fisher, R. Fisher, & P. Jackson, [1832].

[*Second series, Volume III:*]

The imperial magazine; ⟨ . . . as 2nd ser. Vol. I . . . ⟩, & art.

——————— , [1833].

[*Second series, Volume IV:*]

———————

——————— , [1834].

[*Volumes I through IV, and second series Volume III:*] MnU
‡ [*All other volumes:*] Early British Periodicals, General Series (microfilm), published by University Microfilms, Ann Arbor, Michigan.

Only one article includes an illustration of domestic architecture:

• "View, and Summary, of Mr. Owen's Plan, for the Permanent Relief of the Working Classes," V:50 (February 1823), 151–158. The view, printed in columns 151–152, shows Owen's proposed community at Motherwell, near New Lanark. Set within a tract of 600 to 1,200 acres, the community forms a large square, with dormitory ranges along the four sides and communal buildings in the center. Designed to accommodate 1,200 people, the buildings "have been accurately designed, working drawings for the builders prepared, and every expense attending their erection has been estimated with great care" (cols. 153–154). The cost of establishing this community, including interest, ground rent, initial farming stock, clothing, and taxes would be £10,750. According to the article the annual labor value of the residents would be £19,916, leaving a surplus after just one year of £9,166. This compared with a surplus of only £6,416 for the same number of families paying rent in conventional housing. The difference was that in this community "Each person, according to his ability, . . . [would] labour for the good of the whole," and the proceeds could be "applied to the payment of rent, interest, taxes, and expenses of the establishment" and provide for its "probable increase" (cols. 153–154). The article concludes with a series of comparisons between the social and economic conditions of "Manufacturing Towns" and those of Owen's "proposed Villages."

477.1
Mechanics' magazine.

[*Ten volumes, 1825–1829:*]

[*Volume I:*] London: Printed for Knight and Lacey. And sold by their agents throughout the United Kingdom, 1825.
[*Volume II:*] London: Published by Knight and Lacey; Dublin, Westley and Tyrrell, 1824.
[*Volume III:*] London: Knight and Lacey; and Westley and Tyrrell, Dublin, 1825.
[*Volume IV:*] ——————— , 1825.
[*Volume V:*] ——————— , 1826.
[*Volume VI:*] ——————— , 1827.
[*Volume VII:*] London: Printed for Knight and Lacey; and sold by Westley and Tyrrell, Dublin, and all other booksellers, 1827.
[*Volume VIII:*] London: Printed for Knight and Lacey; and sold by all booksellers, 1828.
[*Volume IX:*] ——————— , 1828.
[*Volume X:*] London: Printed for John Knight; and sold by all booksellers, 1829.

The mechanics' magazine, museum, register, journal, and gazette.

[*Twenty-seven volumes, 1829–1842:*]

[*Volume XI:*] London: Published by M. Salmon, 1829.
[*Volume XI:*] ——————— , 1830.
[*Volume XIII:*] ——————— , 1830.
[*Volume XIV:*] ——————— , 1831.
[*Volume XV:*] ——————— , 1831.
[*Volume XVI:*] ——————— , [1832].
[*Volume XVII:*] ——————— , 1832.

[*Volume XVIII:*] ———— , 1833.
[*Volume XIX:*] ———— , 1833.
[*Volume XX:*] ———— , 1834.
[*Volume XXI:*] ———— , 1834.
[*Volume XXII:*] London: Published by J. Cunningham, 1835.
[*Volume XXIII:*] ———— , 1835.
[*Volume XXIV:*] ———— , 1836.
[*Volume XXV:*] ———— , 1836.
[*Volume XXVI:*] London: Published for the proprietor, by W. A. Robertson, 1837.
[*Volume XXVII:*] ———— , 1837.
[*Volume XXVIII:*] ———— , 1838.
[*Volume XXIX:*] ———— , 1838.
[*Volume XXX:*] London: Published for the proprietor by W. A. Robertson, 1839.
[*Volume XXXI:*] ———— , 1839.
[*Volume XXXII:*] London: Edited printed and published, by J. C. Robertson, 1840.
[*Volume XXXIII:*] ———— , 1840.
[*Volume XXXIV:*] London: Edited, printed and published, by J. C. Robertson, 1841.
[*Volume XXXV:*] ———— , 1841.
[*Volume XXXVI:*] ———— , 1842.
[*Volume XXXVII:*] ———— , 1842.

CtY, MnU

The first issue appeared 30 August 1823. The title page of Volume I transcribed above is of the "Twenty-First Edition," and dated 1825. Beginning with Volume XVI the title of each volume incorporates the inclusive dates of issues in that volume. For the sake of brevity, this information is not recorded in the listing above. For volumes published after 1842, see the entry for *Iron* in the *Union List of Serials* (3rd ed., III, 2117).

Although not primarily an architectural journal, the *Mechanics' Magazine* frequently included articles on matters of architectural construction, criticism, and design. From the magazine's inception through 1842 eight articles presented designs for domestic structures:

• "Design for a Cottage," III:77 (12 February 1825), 321–322. The design is shown in cellar, ground-floor, and "One Pair Floor" plans, and in front and side elevations. The ground floor consists of a 12-foot-square living room and a smaller kitchen, and there are two bedrooms upstairs. The facade consists of a door and four windows with pointed arches made of rusticated voussoirs. The design was submitted in response to a previous article, "Inquiries. No. 58.—Plan for a Cottage Wanted," II:52 (21 August 1824), 383.

• **A Country Clergyman,** "Plan of a Farming Establishment for Emigrants," IX:249 (24 May 1828), 273–276. Except for some editorial observations, this article is simply a reprint of James Atkinson's illustrations and descriptions of a farm house and milking yard, originally published in *An Account of the State of Agriculture & Grazing in New South Wales* (1826; *q.v*).

• **Henry D.,** "An Itinerant Observatory, or Pleasure House," XV:403 (30 April 1831), 129–130. A telescoping structure with three sections, this observatory could be transported on a wheeled carriage when collapsed. When fully extended, it would rise 25 or 30 feet above the ground, forming "three separate apartments," one above the other. The author thought it would be useful when exploring "the interior of a strange country" or else in "the domains of most of our nobility and gentry" at "favourite spots commanding interesting views of the surrounding country."

• **J. C. Loudon,** "Colleges for Working Men," XVI:443 (4 February 1832), 321–324. Loudon provided an elevation, plan, and brief description of a design he had prepared in 1818 for a nine-story structure intended to house working men. Loudon submitted the design in response to an article that appeared two months earlier: Junius Redivivus [pseud. for William Bridges Adams], "Plan for the Better Housing of the Working Classes," XVI:434 (3 December 1831), 165–171. Adams's article examines the needs of working-class families and includes a proposal for housing them economically in a large building similar to that proposed by Loudon. Further discussion occurs in four subsequent articles: Junius Redivivus, "Colleges for Working Men—Witty's Furnace—Frost's Roofs and Floors," XVI:446 (25 February 1832), 371–372; T., "Improved Dwellings for the Working Classes," XVI:448 (10 March 1832), 410; T. M. B., "Remarks on the Plans for Better Housing the Working Classes," XVI:453 (14 April 1832), 18–20; and J. W. H., "Labourers' Cottages," XVIII:481 (28 October 1832), 55–56.

• "Mile-stone Cottages and Cottage Architecture Generally," XVII:457 (12 May 1832), 81–84. The article includes two views, two plans, two details, and a description of Design XV from John Claudius Loudon's *Encyclopaedia* (1833; *q.v.*). The elevation is two stories high at the center and one story high at either side. The plan of the ground floor consists of a porch, kitchen, pantry, back kitchen, and offices; there is one bedroom upstairs.

• **P. M.,** "A Temporary Cottage for Australia," XVII:458 (19 May 1832), 97–98. The author suggested that his design might be manufactured in parts "ready to pack up for exportation *as is a dressing-case*." As shown in two elevations and one plan, this one-story dwelling consists of a kitchen, back kitchen, bedroom, "eating or bed-room," dairy, larder, cellar, and balcony, all raised above grade on six support columns.

• **Caballais,** "Design for a Milestone Cottage," XVII:460 (2 June 1832), 129–130. In response to a suggestion published three months earlier (T., "Improved Dwellings for the Working Classes," XVI:448 [10 March 1832], 410), Caballais submitted this design for one of a series of cottages that would replace milestones along major roads and house laborers who would be responsible for the roads' upkeep. The plan is square, with four rooms on the ground story plus an octagonal tower rising from the center. On the same subject also see the following unillustrated articles: Kalopino, "Mile-stone Cottages," XVII:462 (16 June 1832), 174–175; Kalopino, "Milestone Cottages," XVII:464 (30 June 1832), 221; T., "Mail-Coach Road Cottages and Gardens," XVIII:482 (3 November 1832), 78–79; "Mile Houses," XVIII:503 (31 March 1833), 448; An Observer, "Mile-Houses," XIX:507 (27 April 1833), 64; and T., "Road-labourers' Cottages and Gardens," XIX:508 (4 May 1833), 77.

• **M. Saul,** "Design of a Toll-gate Cottage, with Machinery for Opening the Gate from Within," XVIII:484 (17 November 1832), 97–99. The article includes diagrams of a mechanism allowing the gate keeper to open the gate without going outside. The house itself is circular in plan, one story high, and surrounded by a veranda.

478.1

SENEFELDER, Alois (1771–1834)

A complete course of lithography: containing clear and explicit instructions in all the different branches and manners of that art: accompanied by illustrative specimens of drawings. To which is prefixed a history of lithography, from its origin to the present time. By Alois Senefelder, inventor of the art of lithography and chemical printing. With a preface by Frederic von Schlichtegroll, Director of the Royal Academy of Sciences at Munich. Translated from the original German, by A. S.

London: Printed for R. Ackermann, 1819.

xxix pp, 1 printed leaf, 85 pp, 1 printed leaf, 91–342 pp, 1 printed leaf, 14 pls (including frontisp. and portr.).

25.5 × 20.9 cm

NNC

This translation of Senefelder's *Vollständiges Lehrbuch der Steindruckerey* (Munich, 1818) was the first treatise on lithography to appear in English.[1] A prefatory "Advertisement" (pp. iii–v) by the book's English publisher, Rudolph Ackermann, touted the benefits that lithography would bring not only to painters, sculptors, and architects, but also to collectors, politicians, merchants, and businessmen—all of whom could benefit from a quick method for creating copies of drawings, documents, accounts, or tables (p. iii). Ackermann regretted that he could not include impressions from Senefelder's original plates, due to prohibitive customs duties, and instead provided a new set of entirely different plates.

In the Preface (pp. ix–xxi) Frederic von Schlichtegroll introduced this book as the outcome of his own persistent efforts to have Senefelder produce an account of his invention of lithography together with "a complete course of Instructions" in its use (p. xii).

The first part of the text (pp. 1–85) is indeed a chronology of Senefelder's invention and perfection of the process, beginning in 1796 and ending in 1817. The second part (pp. 91–342) is divided into two sections. The first treats stones, ink, chalk, etching ground, colors, acids, gum arabic, instruments, utensils, paper, and presses. The second concerns "the different manners of lithography." Senefelder discussed such raised or "Elevated" manners as pen drawing, the "Chalk Manner," the "Transfer and Tracing Manner," the "Wood-cut Manner," "India-Ink Drawing," and the "sprinkled Manner," as well as several intaglio or "Engraved Manners," including "Etching on Stone," the "Aquatinta manner," and the "reversed Chalk, and Soft-ground Manner." He concluded with remarks on the "Mixed Manner," consisting of "Elevated" and "Engraved" methods combined.

Ackermann's plates include a portrait of Senefelder, a line drawing of a woman in the manner of antique Greek vase painting, plus illustrations of printing equipment, a rustic two-story stone cottage drawn by Samuel Prout, other rustic country subjects, vegetal ornaments, handwriting, an ancient piece of papyrus, St. Matthew (executed with and without "Tint-plate"), and a scene of "Etruscan" figures on black ground.

1. For a detailed discussion of this treatise and its importance in the history of English lithography see Michael Twyman, *Lithography 1800–1850* (London: Oxford University Press, 1970), especially pp. 96–108.

479.1

Annals of agriculture, and other useful arts. Collected and published by Arthur Young. . . .

[*Volume I:*] London: Printed by H. Goldney; and sold by all the booksellers in London and Westminster, 1784.

MnU

[*Volumes II–XLV: the imprint varies frequently; only a summary of publication dates is provided here:*]

Volume II: 1784.
Volumes III, IV: 1785.
Volumes V, VI, VII: 1786.
Volume VIII: 1787.
Volumes IX, X: 1788.
Volumes XI, XII: 1789.
Volumes XIII, XIV: 1790.
Volumes XV, XVI: 1791.
Volumes XVII, XVIII: 1792.
Volumes XIX, XX, XXI: 1793.
Volume XXII: 1794.
Volumes XXIII, XXIV: 1795.
Volumes XXV, XXVI, XXVII: 1796.
Volumes XXVIII, XXIX: 1797.
Volumes XXX, XXXI: 1798.
Volumes XXXII, XXXIII: 1799.
Volumes XXXIV, XXXV: 1800.
Volumes XXXVI, XXXVII: 1801.
Volume XXXVIII: 1802.
Volumes XXXIX, XL: 1803.
Volumes XLI, XLII: 1804.
Volume XLIII: 1805.
Volume XLIV: 1806.
Volume XLV: 1808.

MnU

‡ [*Volume XLVI. There is no general title page; the volume includes two numbers:*]

[*Number 270:*] "An enquiry into the progressive value of money in England," 1812.

[*Number 271:*] "An enquiry into the rise of prices in Europe during the last twenty-five years," 1815.

Reference: MH (much of the original copy is intact, but a portion that is wanting has been replaced by a photocopy provided for MH by Yale University Library).

Arthur Young (1741–1820), editor of the *Annals*, was one of the most influential writers on British agriculture. His voluminous output was instrumental in furthering agricultural improvement in the late eighteenth and early nineteenth centuries. In addition to preparing agricultural surveys of six English counties, Young wrote several important agricultural monographs, and is reputed to have written as much as a third of the *Annals* himself (DNB). In the *Annals*, articles by Young and others concern agricultural experiments and techniques, new improvements in husbandry and technology, reports of conditions and practices throughout rural Britain, and many other topics. Articles with illustrations of dwellings are discussed here.

• **William Pitt,** "Buildings of a Farm," IX:52 (1788), 398–409, and 1 pl. Pitt stressed the economic and practical advantages of well-laid-out farms and well-constructed farm buildings. He cited insufficient barn space as a major cause of inconvenience and waste. As remedies he proposed making barns larger, adding new ranges of open barns (barns without walls), and other improvements. For an enclosed farm of 300 acres, he offered a design for a farm house and offices that he estimated would cost £1,415 16s 9d. In elevation the house is three stories high and three openings wide. The ground-floor plan includes a common sitting room (14 1/4 feet by 18 1/4 feet), a parlor (17 1/4 feet by 18 1/4 feet), a pantry (4 1/2 feet by 7 1/2 feet), a kitchen (22 1/2 feet by 18 1/4 feet), a dairy (17 1/4 feet by 18 1/4 feet), a brewhouse, an "accompting-house," and a back court.

• **[Arthur Young],** "A Week in Norfolk," XIX:109–110 (1793), 441–499, and 1 pl. The article is an account of a visit to several Norfolk estates. About the first quarter of the article is devoted to Holkham, where Young made remarks on sheep, tree planting, bricks, drilling, the formation of a lawn near the house, farm buildings, manure, cattle, and other subjects. The plate, which is captioned "New Cottages built at Holkham by Thos. Wm. Coke Esqr.," shows a quadruple cottage in side elevation, front elevation, and plan. Each cottage consists of two rooms on the ground floor (one room is 14 feet by 14 feet, the other is 11 feet by 7 1/2 feet) plus a coal house. Stairs lead down to a cellar and pantry, and up to a bedroom.[1]

• **Sir John Sinclair,** "Proposals for Establishing by Subscription, a Joint Stock Farming Society, for Ascertaining the Principles of Agricultural Improvement," XXXIV:194 (1800), 360–394, and 3 pls. Citing a list of reasons for which the Board of Agriculture had been established,[2] Sinclair addressed the ongoing need for agricultural experiments. Ideally these would be conducted on "a number of experimental farms scattered over the kingdom" (p. 362). He suggested that "public spirited" individuals could found improvement societies, with a common capital of £80,000, to establish such farms. Sinclair promised that these farms would still yield a profit while furthering agricultural research.

Sinclair actually advanced two major "objects" in this proposal: establishing experimental farms, and expanding the area of forest "plantations" in Britain. He indicated that the capital necessary to operate one 400-acre farm would vary from £1,500 to £4,000, depending on the geographic region. He hoped that by locating the farms throughout Britain, sufficiently varied experiments could be conducted to ascertain "the fundamental principles of agriculture" (p. 369). He included a plate illustrating a design for one such farm, divided into 52 separate fields, with indications of appropriate crops for each field. On the subject of forests, he proposed planting a total of 5,000 acres throughout Britain. He recommended larch trees because of their rapid growth.

Sinclair added a short appendix, "On Cottages and Villages." This includes a plate showing designs for four circular cottages, one or two stories high, with two or three rooms per floor, and to be constructed primarily of stone or brick. Detailed estimates showed that a one-story cottage would cost £37 18s 4d, and a two-story cottage would cost £42 0s 5d.[3] In another plate he illustrated an "improved" design for a village, consisting of 20 circular cottages, to be set in a circle in the center of a field of five to 20 acres. Private garden plots radiate outward from the cottages, while the center of the circle is devoted to a lawn for children to play on. At the very center is a square area containing workshops and a kitchen. The article concludes with a second appendix, "On the Profit to be derived from Plantations," and an essay enumerating the advantages of locating an experimental farm near London.

Circa 1800 a French version of this article was published, along with additional commentary, by the Institut National in Paris. The same three plates were included, with inscriptions translated into French. See the commentary to Entry 308.

• **Mr. Birchwold**, "Extract of an Agricultural and Statistick Journey," XXXVII:210 (1801), 175–190, and 4 pls. The article is a mélange of observations on rural conditions and agricultural practices on the Continent. The plates illustrate farm implements, a school, and farm buildings that incorporate peasant housing. One plate depicts a large building with a steeply pitched roof, containing a "lobby and threshing floor," a cow stall, horse stables, a corn chamber, a kitchen, pantries, a baking oven, a bread room, a daily room, one chamber, and several small areas marked "Bed Place."

• **[Arthur Young]**, "The Husbandry of His Grace the Late Duke of Bedford," XXXIX:227 (1803), 385–454, and 4 pls. The article is divided into sections devoted to a wide variety of topics, including chicory, irrigation, rouen (grass) for sheep, disease in sheep, the weight and price of sheep and of wool, a threshing mill, building in pisé, a piggery, a chaff cutter, a cesspool, poultry, cattle, Speedwell Farm, experiments on oxen and on sheep, soiling, drilling, improvement of wasteland, and crops. The plates depict Speedwell Farm, the chaff cutter, the piggery, and the house of the Clerk of the Works on Woburn Park Farm. On the plate illustrating the house, the legend, dated 1798, indicates that the outside walls were built of pisé "in New Constructed Moulds & faced in an Improved Manner by Robert Salmon." The two-story house, three openings wide, is shown in elevation and two floor plans. The ground floor includes a common parlor, best parlor, kitchen, and pantry. Upstairs there are four bedrooms. The text describes an improved method of building with pisé, involving the addition of lime, and gives detailed cost accounts of building pisé walls at Woburn Park.[4]

• **[Arthur Young]**, "Cottages Built by His Grace the Duke of Grafton in Northamptonshire," XLII:245 (1804), 259–262, and 1 pl. The plate contains ground plans of two cottages. The first, estimated to cost £65, includes a kitchen (12 feet by 15 feet), workroom, combination cellar and pantry, and staircase leading to bedrooms upstairs. The second, estimated at £52 10s, has similar features but is smaller. The text includes brief descriptions of the two cottages, plus a lengthy "List of the Cottages built, and others repaired and put in good Plight, . . . on the Estate of His Grace the Duke of Grafton, . . . from June 24, 1801 to August 1803."

• **[Arthur Young]**, "Idea of a Cottage Cheap to Build and Warm to Inhabit," XLII:246 (1804), 284–286, and 1 pl. Young opened with the charge that "Cottages are, perhaps, one of the greatest disgraces to this country that remain to be found in it" (p. 284). He presented a design that incorporated three features intended to increase cottagers' comfort: a vestibule just inside the front door, serving as an air lock to prevent drafts; instead of a fireplace, an iron fire grate in the center of the room, allowing heat to radiate all around; and a small iron tube instead of a brick chimney, helping to conserve heat. As shown in the plate, the cottage is a gable-roofed rectangular box, 14 feet by 21 feet in plan, with a single window. The floor plan shows the vestibule, a "keeping room" with two beds at one end and a fire grate in the center, and a dairy.

1. For additional discussion of improvements at Holkham, examined in the broader context of eighteenth-century agriculture, see John Martin Robinson, *Georgian Model Farms: A Study of Decorative and Model Farm Buildings in the Age of Improvement, 1700–1846* (Oxford: Clarendon Press, 1983).

2. Sinclair was instrumental in establishing the Board. See the entry for "Great Britain. Board of Agriculture."

3. These designs were reproduced later in several articles on cottage design. See *The English Encyclopaedia* (1802); *The Complete Farmer* (1807); and Abraham Rees, *Cyclopaedia* ([1802]–1820), *qq.v.*

4. For additional discussion of pisé building and other improvements at Woburn Abbey, see Robinson, *Georgian Model Farms*.

480.1 ‖

Architectural recreations (being a sequel to the geometrical recreations); illustrating, in an entertaining and familiar manner, the most essential principles of solid geometry and architectural elevations; as also the effect of perspective, light and shadow, by means of cubic sections, figures, and diagrams, capable of endless transformation: accompanied by a case containing the cubic sections.

London: Published by R. Ackermann. Printed by L. Harrison, [n.d.].

iv + 5–39 + [1] pp, 14 pls (numbered A, I–XIII).

14.7 × 10.2 cm

Reference: Information supplied by Winterthur Museum Library.

480.2

Recreaciones arquitectonicas: que forman una secuela de las recreaciones geometricas. Para aprender de un modo familiar y entretenido, los principos mas esenciales de la geometria solida, y del alzado en la arquitectura: como tambien el efecto de la perspectiva, luz y sombra, por medio de las secciones cubicas, figuras, y diagramas, susceptibles de transformaciones interminables. A lo cual va unida una cagita con las secciones cubicas. Traducido del ingles por D. José de Urcullu.

Londres: Lo publica el Sr. R. Ackermann, y en su establecimiento en Megico, 1825.

44 pp, 14 plates (numbered I–XI, XV [instead of XII], XIII, A].

15.0 × 11.0 cm

CtY-BA

480.3 †

Architectural recreations (being a sequel to the geometrical recreations); illustrating . . . the . . . principles of solid geometry and architectural elevations; . . . by means of cubic sections. . . .

London, [1830?].

8°

Reference: BM

An English "second" edition dated 1822 is cited in S. T. Prideaux, *Aquatint Engraving* (London: Duckworth, 1909), pp. 326, 375. I have found no other reference to an 1822 or "second" edition. The undated British Museum copy was destroyed in World War II.

The Introduction to the English edition (pp. iii–iv) describes this book as a sequel to *Geometrical Recreations*, which demonstrated principles of plane geometry. The present volume would treat solid geometry and offer "a variety of useful recreations, to be derived from its study."[1]

The preliminary matter of the Spanish edition includes an "Advertencia" (pp. 3–4) in which the plate titles are translated into Spanish,[2] an "Introduccion" (pp. 5–6), and an "Esplicacion de lo que contiene la cajita" (pp. 7–8), referring to Plate A and concerning a boxed set of 15 wooden pieces in geometric shapes that accompanied this book.

The text is divided into two parts. The first part (1825, pp. 9–19) largely concerns architectural elevations. These are illustrated in Plates I–VII, which show perspective views of the wooden blocks arranged to form rustic houses and cottages, a rustic entrance to a park, simple churches in a small village, an entrance to a fort, a city gate in India, a Chinese pagoda, an entrance to a city, a sepulchral monument, chapels, the entrance to a cemetery, a cenotaph, ancient tombs, and a fortified gate. Plate VIII is a "Key" to Plates I–VII. Plates IX and X show larger elevations that could be made from multiple sets of blocks. The first part concludes with remarks on perspective, light, and shadow.

The second part (1825, pp. 20–24) concerns principles of solid geometry. The remaining two plates in the volume depict plane geometric figures and perspective views of regular solids.[3]

1. Since I have not personally examined the English edition, the remainder of this description concerns the Spanish edition, which I have seen.

2. Although the book's letterpress text is in Spanish, the plates still bear English inscriptions.

3. These plates are numbered XII and XIII in the English edition, but XV and XIII in the Spanish edition.

481.1

BRADLEY, Richard (1688–1732)

A general treatise of husbandry and gardening. Containing such observations and experiments as are new and useful for the improvement of land. With an account of such extraordinary inventions, and natural productions, as may help the ingenious in their studies, and promote universal learning. Vol. I [*or* II, *or* III]. With a variety of curious cutts. By Richard Bradley. . . .

London: Printed for T. Woodward; and J. Peele, 1724.

3 vols. [*Pagination and plates are discussed in the commentary below.*]

19.5 × 12.4 cm

MnU

481.2

A general treatise of husbandry and gardening; containing a new system of vegetation: illustrated with many observations and experiments. In two volumes. Formerly publish'd monthly, and now methodiz'd and digested under proper heads, with additions and great alterations. In four parts.

Part I. Concerning the improvement of land, by fertilizing bad soils. Of stocking of farms with cattle, poultry, fish, bees, grasses, grain, cyder, &c.
Part II. Instructions to a gardener, wherein is demonstrated the circulation of sap, the generation of plants, the nature of soil, air and situation. Of the profits arising from planting and raising timber.
Part III. Of the management of fruit trees, with particular observations relating to grassing, inarching and inoculating.
Part IV. Remarks on the disposition of gardens in general. Of the method of managing exotick plants and flowers, and naturalizing them to our climate; with an account of stoves, and artificial heats.
Adorn'd with cuts. By R. Bradley. . . . Vol. I.

London: Printed for T. Woodward, and J. Peele, 1726.

7 printed leaves, 427 pp, 7 pls.

A general treatise 〈 . . . as Vol. I . . . 〉 a gardiner, wherein 〈 . . . as Vol. I . . . 〉 Vol. II.

London: Printed for T. Woodward, and J. Peele, 1726.

7 printed leaves, 479 pp, 10 pls.

19.8 × 12.4 cm

NNC

481.3

A general treatise of agriculture, both philosophical and practical; displaying the arts of husbandry and gardening: in two parts.
Part I. Of husbandry; treats of the nature of the soil, air, and situation proper for the production of vegetables; the different methods of improving lands; the manner of planting and raising timber; the stocking of farms with cattle, poultry, fish, bees, grass, grain, &c. with estimates of the profits arising thereon, &c.
Part II. Of gardening; treats of the circulation of the sap in vegetables; the generation of plants, and their distribution into genera; the different kinds and particular management of fruit and fruit-trees; the methods of grafting, inarching, and inoculating; the dispositions of gardens in general; the cultivation and improvement of the kitchen and pleasure gardens; the manner of managing exotic plants and flowers, and naturalizing them to our climate; together with an account of stoves, artificial heats, &c.
Originally written by R. Bradley, . . . And now not only corrected and properly methodised, but adapted to the present practice, and improved with the late theories, in many large notes, wherein the several methods of culture, and the different systems of botany and vegetation, according to the most approved writers of the present period upon these subjects,

are delivered. With a compleat index of all the matters contained in the book. Illustrated with twenty copper-plates.

London: Printed for W. Johnston, R. Baldwin, J. Fuller, J. Wren, W. Owen, G. Keith, A. Strahan, T. Field, P. Davey and B. Law, E. Dilly, C. Henderson, A. Linde, and J. Robinson, 1757.

viii + 503 + [xv] pp, frontisp. + 20 pls.

19.9 × 12.2 cm

ICU

Originally this treatise was issued from 1721 to 1723 in 15 parts. The 1724 reissue includes all of these parts, each with its own title page, bound in three volumes which have uniform title pages dated 1724. Since all volumes are paginated irregularly, a separate description of each part is warranted.

In the copy at the University of Minnesota the title page of Volume I is followed by the dedication (one leaf) for the "November" issue. Next appears the title page for the first part: *A general treatise of husbandry and gardening, for the month of April* . . . (London: Printed for J. Peele, [n.d.]). This is followed by xii + 50 pp, and 1 pl. The title page for the second part reads: *A general treatise of husbandry and gardening, for the month of May* . . . (London: Printed for T. Woodward; and J. Peele, 1724); this is the only part-title that is dated. Then appear a dedicatory leaf, 51–110 pp, and 1 pl. Title pages for the next four parts closely resemble that for April, except that "June," "July," "August," and "September" are substituted. Collation of these parts is as follows: dedicatory leaf, 111–170 pp, 1 pl; iv + 173–230 pp, 2 pls; dedicatory leaf, 231–290 pp, 1 pl; dedicatory leaf, 295–358 pp, 1 pl.

The six part-titles for Volume II closely resemble that for April, except that "October," "November," "December," "January," "February," and "March" are substituted. Collation of these parts is as follows: dedicatory leaf, 55 pp, 1 pl; [dedicatory leaf for November bound following title page of Vol. I, as noted above], 59–117 pp, 1 pl; dedicatory leaf, 123–181 pp, 1 pl; dedicatory leaf, 187–246 pp; dedicatory leaf, 251–310 pp; dedicatory leaf, 311–372 pp, 1 pl. The volume concludes with indexes to volumes I and II (7 printed leaves).

Volume III contains three parts. The title page for the first reads: *A general treatise of husbandry and gardening.* . . . *For the months of April and May, the second year* (London: Printed for T. Woodward; and J. Peele, 1724). The title page for the second part closely resembles that for the first part, except that "June" and "July" are substituted. For the final part, the title reads: *A general treatise of husbandry and gardening.* . . . *For the months of August and September, and the remaining part of the second year* (imprint as for the first part). The collation of these parts is as follows: dedication (2 leaves), preface (1 leaf), 94 pp, 1 pl; dedication (2 leaves),

80 pp; dedicatory leaf, 195 pp (pages 193–194 omitted), 4 pls. Page 1 of the first part is headed "The Monthly Register of Experiments and Observations in Husbandry and Gardening. For the Month of April, 1722." Page 57 of the first part has a similar heading, with "May" substituted. Pages 1 and 43 of the second part also have similar headings, with "June" and "July" substituted. At the end of the volume is an index to Volume III (5 leaves).

In the Preface to the first part Bradley announced his intention to advance the "Art of Husbandry" in both the "practical" and the "philosophical" realms (pp. xi, xii). He proposed to do this by publishing his own observations as well as contributions from widespread correspondents. Later, in the Preface to the third volume, Bradley characterized himself more as a "Secretary," and no longer a "Director." Having stimulated a great interest among "Societies" throughout England in corresponding about new agricultural discoveries, he saw his own role more as a collator of information than as a major proponent of change. But the miscellaneous arrangement of information in all three volumes clearly did not suit his successors, and title pages of later editions indicate efforts made to "digest" and "methodise" Bradley's material.

The 16 plates in the first edition reflect the eclectic nature of the contents. Subjects include a microscopic view of a cross section of a vine shoot, a leaf, hothouses, plant frames, a diagram indicating the divergence of sunrise and sunset from true east and west at different times of the year, trees (including some planted in a special manner next to a wall), a water clock, bees, and agricultural implements. Several plates include architectural subjects. The plate facing page 1 in Volume I is meant to demonstrate the relative inefficiency of building structures or raising crops on hillsides; the plate includes minute views of churches, towers, and two-story dwellings. Facing page 115 in the same volume is a design for a garden "House" or "Room" designed to retain cool air in the summer. Cylindrical in form, the structure consists of a thick outer wall and an interior ring of eight Corinthian columns supporting a reservoir of water above. A mechanical apparatus draws water from a nearby stream to feed the reservoir, which then directs the water to six fountains shooting up from the floor and to a cascade spilling down from above. In Volume II a plate facing page 65 depicts techniques for irrigating the grounds of a large estate. In the background at the far right there is a mansion shown in elevation, three stories high and five windows wide. The three stories are separated by string-courses, and there is modest ornament above the door and around the central windows on the upper floors. The plate facing page 338 in Volume II depicts a design for a rabbit warren, including a small Tuscan portio intended to provide the rabbits some shelter from the weather. In Volume III a plate facing page 192 contains a highly architectonic design for a plant stove, ornamented with Ionic pilasters and a balustrade across the top.

482.1 ‡

CLARKE, Henry (1743–1818)

Practical perspective. Being a course of lessons, exhibiting easy and concise rules for drawing justly all sorts of objects. Adapted to the use of schools. By H. Clarke. In two volumes. Vol. I.

London: Printed for the author, and sold by Mr. Nourse, and Mr. Murray, 1776.

xv pp, 2 printed leaves, 17–113 pp, 33 leaves of illustrations (pls. I–LII, figs. 1–4).

Reference: Microfilm supplied by The British Library.

482.2 †

Practical perspective: being a course of lessons, exhibiting easy and concise rules for drawing justly all sorts of objects. . . . By Henry Clarke. . . . New edition, illustrated with fifty-five large copper-plates.

London: Printed for Messrs. Ogilvy and Speare, Mr. Murray, and I. and W. Clarke, 1794.

113 pp, 33 leaves of plates.

Reference: NUC-S

In the Preface (pp. v–xv) Clarke stated clearly that he offered nothing "new in Principle" but that he hoped to present his material in a manner "better adapted to the capacities of Youth" than any other treatise had done so far (p. v). He observed that previous treatises on perspective easily could be divided into just two types: those suited only for mathematicians, and those providing readers with no idea of "the Principles of the Art" that they were trying to learn (pp. v–vi).

The fundamental "principle" of Clarke's method was simple: he posited a plane of glass between an object and the observer; rays of light passing from the object to the observer would intersect the glass and there form a plane representation of the object (p. vi). Working from this notion, Clarke proposed to develop various rules of perspective in a series of 52 "Lessons."

The text begins with definitions and axioms, followed by 30 Lessons devoted to the depiction of lines, planes, and solids parallel to the ground, perpendicular to the ground, and at an angle to the ground. Further Lessons concern "Sciagraphic Perspective" (XXXI–XL), "Catoptric Perspective" (XLI–XLVIII), "Theatrical Perspective" (XLIX), ceiling pictures (L–LI), and a method for making perspective views without the use of any instruments (LII).

Advertising matter at the end of the first edition indicates that a second volume was to be published as soon as the plates were ready; but the second volume never appeared. In the Preface to the first edition Clarke provided an account of what "I have shown" in the second volume (p. viii). This consisted largely of practical applications of rules found in Volume I: making perspective elevations and views of orders, arches, doors, niches, "various Modes of Buildings," squares, streets, and avenues; making maps and charts; making astronomical diagrams; creating aerial perspective; and mixing colors for easel painting.

Most of the illustrations are perspective diagrams or figures and objects shown in perspective. Lesson VII (pp. 34–35) concerns delineation of a ground plan of a house in perspective. The accompanying plate shows a plan with six rooms and a staircase hall, fronted by a facade seven openings wide with a semicircular bow in the center. Lessons XIV and XV (pp. 42–43) treat perspective illustration of an entire house. The accompanying plates show an outline drawing of one house with a gable roof and two chimneys, and a more detailed illustration of a two-story house, three windows wide and two windows deep, with a hip roof. Plate XLVII depicts a chair in perspective. Plate XLIX shows a theatrical drop painted with a street scene, which is lined on both sides by buildings. Plate LI depicts the interior of a room from below, and Plate LII shows a masonry bridge of seven arches.

483.1 ‡
COTTAGE Improvement Society for North Northumberland
Report of the Committee of the Cottage Improvement Society, for North Northumberland, for 1842.

London: Whittaker and Co.; Alnwick: M. Smith. And to be had of all Booksellers, [1842].

55 pp, 7 pls.

Reference: Goldsmiths'-Kress Library of Economic Literature (microfilm). Segment 2. Printed Books 1801–1850. Reel 2995, No. 32946.

The first two pages of the text are minutes of the meeting at which the Cottage Improvement Society was established, on 22 October 1841. The stated goals of the Society included publication of reports from landowners, agents, and residents concerning "any remarkable improvements in cottages and cottage gardens, which they may have effected or promoted, and especially all particulars regarding the plans adopted and the outlay incurred" (p. 1). A committee of the Society was established to collect this information and publish it annually (p. 2). The present volume was the first such annual report. It contains four essays, each illustrated, concerning cottages.

The first essay, "A Few Hints on the Construction of Cottages" (pp. 3–6), includes brief remarks on siting, floors, windows, ceilings, roofs, chimneys, and privies. A plate facing page 4 depicts a floor in section, roof trusses in elevation, and a circular chimney in plan. Two more plates, following page 6, illustrate designs for cottages that are briefly described in the text. The plate labeled "A" shows a group of four attached one-story cottages in plan and elevation. Each cottage, estimated to cost £54 9s, consists of a principal room 15 feet 7 inches wide and a back shed. The plate labeled "B" depicts a single cottage in plan and elevation, with a porch and two rooms on the ground floor and one room above. To the rear are a storeroom, pig house, pig yard, privy, ash pit, and coal pit. The cottage designs in both plates are modestly ornamented with Tudor hood moldings over the doors and windows, plus decorative chimney details.

The next essay, dated June 1842, is titled "Sketches of Cottages, by Robert Dunn, Working Mason" (pp. 7–11). In addition to cost estimates, the text includes remarks on the need for an "upper apartment" over the usual single large room on the ground floor. Dunn argued that cottages with a bedroom upstairs offered a "sacred asylum" for women that would help develop their character and virtues. Dunn also recommended that each cottager be provided with an individual garden plot. He suggested that cultivating one's garden was akin to cultivating one's mind, that it was ennobling to put one's own fruit and vegetables on the table, and that gardening deterred the cottager from idleness and crime. The two plates following page 10 show three pairs of attached cottages. The design on the first plate is shown in plan, end elevation, section, and a choice of two elevations—one exceedingly plain, and the other with Tudor hood moldings, finials on the gable tops, and a slightly ornamented chimney. Each cottage consists of a principal room (16 feet by 18 feet), a stair hall, a bedroom upstairs under the gable roof, a back porch, and a piggery; to the rear are a shared privy and ash pit. Both designs on the next plate are modestly decorated with Tudor hood moldings and other ornaments. A pair of "Small Cottages at Howick" is shown in elevation and plan. Each contains a principal room (16 feet by 18 feet) on the ground floor, another room under the gable roof, and offices to the rear. The other plan and elevation on this plate depict a pair of "Cottages at Howick." The ground floor of each includes a principal room (16 feet by 18 feet), a stair hall, and offices. The upstairs room is provided with a window in the front elevation.

The essay concerning "Hinds' Cottages at Hedgeley, Northumberland" (pp. 13–20) is signed by Ralph Carr, and dated 3 June 1842. The author discussed five cottages that recently had been enlarged by adding an upper story. He noted that putting an entire family in just one large room was detrimental to their "delicacy" (pp. 13–14). He discussed the practical and aesthetic considerations involved in adding another room either on the ground floor or above, noting in particular that adding a room tended to increase ventilation and thus reduce disease (pp. 14–17). The plate facing page 14 illustrates three attached cottages in plan and elevation, showing them with their new upper story.

The final essay, "On Hinds' Cottages," is dated 1 July 1842 and signed "E. F."[1] Following introductory remarks on the nature of housing since prehistoric times (pp. 21–26), the author discussed the positive effect of sound, regular housing on the character of the resident (pp. 26–27) as well as the ill effects of crowding too many people into one room (pp. 29–32). Ensuing remarks on "improved" cottage design (pp. 32–38) are largely paraphrased and quoted from James Cunningham's *Designs for Farm Cottages and Steadings* ([1842?], q.v.). A plate between pages 36 and 37 contains new designs provided by Cunningham. Two attached cottages, estimated to cost £62 apiece, are shown in two plans and one elevation. Each unit is two stories high, with a kitchen, scullery, and privy on the ground floor, plus two bedrooms above. A proposal for improving old cottages, shown in plan, section, and elevation, involves the addition of a "closet" to the large room on the ground floor, plus a new room on the story above. The text examines the economic benefits that would result from providing better living conditions for hinds, and the need to build schools in order to improve the moral and religious character of the people (pp. 39–45). The essay concludes with remarks on siting, constructing, and furnishing cottages, and a review of comments by politicians and others on the need for improving cottage housing.

1. Perhaps Reverend E. Feilde, the "Convenor" of the committee in charge of publishing the *Report*.

484.1
CURWEN, John Christian (1756–1828)
Hints on the economy of feeding stock, and bettering the condition of the poor[.] By J. C. Curwen, Esq. M. P. of Workington-Hall, Cumberland.

London: Printed for B. Crosby and Co.; Jollie and Son, and Hodgson, Carlisle; Bowness, and Mordy, Workington; Hetherington, Wigton; Akenhead, Newcastle; Hazard and Co., Gibbons, Meyler, and Savage, Bath; Richardson, Bristol; Booth, Stevenson and Co., Norwich; Woolstenholme, York; Heaton, Leeds; Brooke, Drury, and Smith, Lincoln; Rooe, and Drakard, Stamford; Ridges, Newark; Sheardown, Doncaster; Wood and Son, Wakefield; Hall, Worcester; Webb, Bedford; Coombe, Leicester, Barratt, Cambridge; Walker, Chester; Watts, Northampton; Dunn, Robinson, and Sutton, Nottingham; Hill, Dumfries, Willan, Liverpool; Clarke and Reddish, Manchester; Constable, and Co., Edinburgh; and Archer, Dublin, 1808.

xvi + 364 + 2 pp, frontisp. + 4 pls + 2 leaves printed with tables.

20.9 cm × 12.9 cm

ICU

484.2

————

Hints on agricultural subjects, and on the best means of improving the condition of the labouring classes. By J. C. Curwen. . . . Second edition, improved and enlarged.

London: Printed for J. Johnson, and B. Crosby and Co., 1809.

xxiv + 385 + [i] + 2 pp, frontisp. + 4 pls + 2 leaves printed with tables.

22.5 × 14.0 cm

MnU

In the preface to the second edition (pp. xi–xxiv) Curwen traced a major decline in British agriculture to changes made in the Corn Laws in 1766. He recounted subsequent efforts by authors and major landowners to reestablish the primacy of agriculture in Britain's economy. He took heart in the fact that by 1807 Britain once again grew enough grain to satisfy its own needs without imports. But he still feared that efforts to expand foreign trade would result in agricultural ruin. He urged that Britain's principal objective be a healthy agricultural economy. Progress in trade and commerce, he said, would follow as a natural consequence. In this manner "probity, industry, and frugality may be generally re-established, and a superiority in happiness as well as liberty" would soon distinguish Britain from the rest of Europe (pp. xxiii–xxiv).

The text is a collection of essays on various subjects:[1] supplying milk for the poor, "soiling" cattle, miscellaneous "hints" on farming, carrots, vegetables, and friendly societies. The frontispiece depicts a southeast view of his model farm in Cumberland, the Schoose Farm.[2] The farm is shown in plan in Plate 2. Major features include a mill and mill pond, a dairy, stables, cow houses, offices, pigsties, a slaughterhouse, several yards, and a dwelling. The interior plan of the house is not shown. Other plates depict the entire Schoose Farm estate, a potato steamer, a plan and elevation of a chaff boiling house, and a plan of a steaming and cutting house.

1. This description is based on examination of the second edition.

2. The frontispiece in the first edition is a different view, captioned "North West View of the Schoose Farm." For more information on Curwen and Schoose Farm see John Martin Robinson, *Georgian Model Farms: A Study of Decorative and Model Farm Buildings in the Age of Improvement, 1700–1846* (Oxford: Clarendon Press, 1983), pp. 9–11, 16, 146.

485.1 ‡

The draughtsman's assistant; or, drawing made easy. Wherein the principles of the art are laid down in a familiar manner, in ten lessons, under the following heads, viz. 1. Of the features and limbs. 2. Of profiles and ovals. 3. Of whole figures. 4. Of drapery. 5. Of light and shade. 6. Of landscapes. 7. Of perspective. 8. Of enlarging and contracting. 9. Of the imitation of life. 10. Of history. Illustrated by a great variety of examples neatly engraved. With an introductory treatise on the utility of the art; and an appendix, containing observations on design as well in regard to theory as practice. By the author of the artist's assistant.

London: Printed for, and sold by, T. Kitchin, Engraver, 1772.

22 pp, 59 pls.

4°

Reference: Microfilm supplied by The British Library.

485.2 †

———

[London: ca. 1775].

16 pp [*this copy is without a title page*].

4°

Reference: BM

485.3

All draughtsmen's assistant; or, drawing made easy: wherein the principles of that art are rendered familiar; in ten instructive lessons, comprised under the following heads: 1. Features and limbs. 2. Profiles and ovals. 3. Whole figures. 4. Drapery. 5. Light and shade. 6. Landscapes. 7. Perspective. 8. Enlarging and contracting. 9. Imitation of life. 10. History.

Explain'd by a great variety of examples from the most approved designs, on copper-plates, neatly engraved: with a suitable introduction on the utility of this noble art; and observations on design, as well in regard to theory as practice. By the author of the artist's assistant.

London: Printed for R. Sayer and J. Bennett, Map and Print-sellers, [n.d.; ca. 1776].

16 pp, 62 pls (most undated; others dated 1763, 1770, 1771, 1775, 1776).

27.3 × 22.5 cm

CtY-BA

485.4

––––––––

London: Printed for R. Sayer and J. Bennett, Map and Print-sellers, [n.d.; ca. 1777].

16 pp, 66 pls (most undated; others dated 1770, 1771, 1775, 1776, 1777).

27.7 × 22.3 cm

NN

485.5
The draughtsmen's assistant; ⟨ . . . as [ca. 1776] . . . ⟩ familiar; in instructive lessons, ⟨ . . . as [ca. 1776] . . . ⟩ Imitation of life. &c. Explained by a great variety of examples from the most approved designs, on seventy-two copper-plates, neatly engraved: with a suitable introduction on the utility of this noble art. And ⟨ . . . as [ca. 1776] . . . ⟩ assistant.

London: Printed by Robert Sayer, Map, Chart, and Printseller, 1786.

16 pp, 72 pls.

27.1 × 22.1 cm

CtY-BA

485.6
The draughtsman's assistant; or, drawing made easy: wherein the principles of that art are rendered familiar, in instructive lessons comprised under the following heads: Features and limbs. Profiles and ovals. Whole figures. Drapery. Light and shade. Landscapes. Perspective. Enlarging and contracting. Imitation of life. &c. &c. Explained by a great variety of examples from the most approved designs, neatly engraved on seventy-two copper plates: with a suitable introduction on the utility of this noble art, and observations on designs, as well in regard to theory as practice. By the author of the artist's assistant.

London: Printed for Robert Sayer and Co., [n.d.; ca. 1787].

16 pp, 72 pls (pls. 41–46 are dated 1787).

29.0 × 23.5 cm

CtY-BA

485.7 ‡

All draughtsmen's assistant; ⟨ . . . as [ca. 1776] . . . ⟩ rendered familiar: in ten instructive lessons. Comprised under the following heads. 1. Features ⟨ . . . as [ca. 1776] . . . ⟩ History. Explained by ⟨ . . . as [ca. 1776] . . . ⟩ approved designs on ⟨ . . . as [ca. 1776] . . . ⟩ noble art. And ⟨ . . . as [ca. 1776] . . . ⟩ assistant.

London: Printed for R. Sayer and J. Bennett, Map and Print-sellers, [n.d.; ca. 1794].

16 pp, 72 pls (pls. 41–46 are dated 1787; pl. 29 is dated 1794).

4°

Reference: Microfilm supplied by The British Library.

485.8

The draughtsman's assistant; ⟨ . . . as [ca. 1787] . . . ⟩.

London: Printed for Robert Sayer and Co., [n.d.; ca. 1794].

16 pp, 72 pls (pls. 41–46 are dated 1787; pl. 29 is dated 1794).

27.5 × 22.0 cm

CtY-BA

485.9

London: Printed for Robert Sayer and Co., [n.d.; ca. 1801].

16 pp, 72 pls (pls. 41–46 are dated 1787; pl. 29 is dated 1794; paper is watermarked 1801).

27.7 × 22.6 cm

CtY-BA

According to the title page, this book was written by the author of *The Artist's Assistant* (Entry 8). Carington Bowles often is presumed to be the author of *The Artist's Assistant*, and so *The Draughtsman's Assistant* frequently is attributed to Bowles as well.

The discussion below is based on examination of the [ca. 1801] edition.

The Introduction (pp. 1–2) indicates that the book was addressed primarily to young people, and extols the pleasures and utility of proficiency in drawing. "General Instructions" (p. 3) include a recommendation that the student work at developing the visual memory. A list of "Materials for Drawing" also appears on page 3. The bulk of the text is devoted to "Instructions, with Examples" for lines, profiles, ovals, human figures, drapery, light and shade, landscape, perspective, "enlarging and contracting," copying, "imitation of life," and history. The text concludes with observations on the history of design.

Subjects illustrated in the plates include perspective diagrams, heads, human figures and groups, animals, ships, and flowers. Several plates contain architectural subjects. In Plate 5, Figure I shows the front wall of a house in elevation and plan. The two-story facade is three openings wide, with a pediment over the door but no other ornament. Figure II is a landscape, depicting a river flanked by houses on both sides. The largest house is four openings wide and two stories high, with dormers in the roof. Figure III is a perspective view of a castle surrounded by a moat. Plates 23 through 28 are paired views (one executed in outline, the other shaded) including houses, cottages, churches, and bridges. Plates 29 through 38 are landscapes that include cottages, towers, and other rustic subjects. Plates 39 and 40 are views of grandiose architectural settings, partly in ruins. Plates 49 and 50 are perspective views of the Queen's Palace, Temple, Summer House, and Dairy in Richmond Gardens.

486.1
HALE, Thomas
A compleat body of husbandry. Containing rules for performing, in the most profitable manner, the whole business of the farmer, and country gentleman, in cultivating, planting, and stocking of land; in judging of the several kinds of seed, and of manures; and in the management of arable and pasture grounds: together with the most approved methods of practice in the several branches of husbandry, from sowing the seed, to getting in the crop; and in breeding and preserving cattle, and curing their diseases. To which is annexed, the whole management of the orchard, the brewhouse, and the dairy. Compiled from the original papers of the late Thomas Hale, Esq; and enlarged by many new and useful commun-ications on practical subjects, from the collections of Col. Stevenson, Mr. Randolph, Mr. Hawkins, Mr. Storey, Mr. Osborne, the Rev. Mr. Turner, and others. A work founded on experience; and calculated for general benefit; consisting chiefly of improvements made by modern practitioners in farming; and containing many valuable and useful discoveries, never before published. Illustrated with a great number of cuts, containing figures of the instruments of husbandry; of useful and poisonous plants, and various other subjects, engraved from original drawings. Published by His Majesty's Royal Licence and authority.

London: Printed for T. Osborne and J. Shipton; J. Hodges; T. Trye; and S. Crowder and H. Woodgate, 1756.

iv pp, 5 printed leaves, 112 pp, 1 printed leaf, 113–719 pp, frontisp. + 12 pls.

44.5 × 27.7 cm

MnU

486.2 ‡
———
A compleat body of husbandry. Containing rules for performing, in the most profitable manner, the whole business of the farmer and country gentleman, in cultivating and planting of land; judging of the several kinds of seeds and manures; and in the management of arable and pasture grounds: together with the most approved methods of practice in the several branches of husbandry, from sowing the seed, to getting in the crop. Compiled from the original papers of the late Thomas Hale, Esq;

and enlarged by many new and useful communications on practical subjects, from the collections of Col. Stevenson, Mr. Randolph, Mr. Hawkins, Mr. Storey, Mr. Osborne, the Rev. Mr. Turner, and others. A work founded on experience, and calculated for general benefit; consisting chiefly of improvements made by modern practitioners in farming; and containing many valuable and useful discoveries, never before published. Illustrated with several cuts of the instruments used in husbandry. Re-printed at the request, and upon the recommendation, of several members of the farmers societies in Ireland. In two volumes. Vol. I.

Dublin: Printed for Peter Wilson, and John Exshaw, 1757.

iv pp, 3 printed leaves, 452 pp, 1 pl.

A compleat body ⟨ . . . as Vol. I . . . ⟩ Ireland. Vol. II.

Dublin: Printed for Peter Wilson, and John Exshaw, 1757.

3 printed leaves, 470 + 473–498 pp, 5 pls.

A compleat body of husbandry. Vol. III. Containing, I. The animals necessary and useful in husbandry and farming. II. Several advantageous articles in husbandry, which are less universal than the others.

Dublin: Printed for P. Wilson and J. Exshaw, 1757.

2 printed leaves, 361 pp, 4 pls.

A compleat body of husbandry. Vol. IV. Containing, I. The natural and artificial products of the farmer's stock. II. The making beer and cyder. III. The accidents to which the cattle and the crops are liable. IV. The diseases of cattle, and their remedies. V. The distemperatures of trees, roots, and herbage, from the injuries done by insects, larger animals, and weeds. VI. The poisonous and hurtful plants, natives of this kingdom. VII. Elevations and plans of small farm houses.

Dublin: Printed for P. Wilson and J. Exshaw, 1757.

3 printed leaves, 380 pp, 7 pls.

Reference: Goldsmiths'-Kress Library of Economic Literature (microfilm). Segment 1. Printed Books through 1800. Reels 698–699, No. 9218.

486.3

A compleat body of husbandry. Containing rules for performing, in the most profitable manner, the whole business of the farmer and country gentleman, in cultivating, planting and stocking of land; in judging of the several kinds of seeds, and of manures; and in the management of arable and pasture grounds: together with the most approved methods of practice in the several branches of husbandry, from sowing the seed, to getting in the crop; and in breeding and preserving cattle, and curing their diseases. To which is annexed, the whole management of the orchard, the brewhouse, and the dairy. Compiled from the original papers of the late Thomas Hale, Esq; and enlarged by many new and useful communications on practical subjects, from the collections of Col. Stevenson, Mr. Randolph, Mr. Hawkins, Mr. Storey, Mr. Osborne, the Reverend Mr. Turner, and others. A work founded on experience; and calculated for general benefit; consisting chiefly of improvements made by modern practitioners in farming; and containing many valuable and useful discoveries, never before published. Illustrated with a great number of cuts, containing figures of the instruments used in husbandry; of useful and poisonous plants, and various other subjects, engraved from original drawings. Published by His Majesty's Royal Licence and authority. Vol. I. The second edition.

London: Printed for Tho. Osborne; Tho. Trye; and S. Crowder and Co., 1758.

x pp, 2 printed leaves, 402 pp, frontisp. + 3 pls.

A compleat body ⟨ . . . as Vol. I . . . ⟩ authority. Vol. II. The second edition.

London: Printed for Tho. Osborne; Tho. Trye; and S. Crowder and Co., 1758.

5 printed leaves, 420 pp, 3 pls.

A compleat body ⟨ . . . as Vol. I . . . ⟩ authority. Vol. III. The second edition.

London: Printed for Tho. Osborne; Tho. Trye; and S. Crowder and Co., 1758.

6 printed leaves, 498 pp, 7 pls.

A compleat body ⟨ . . . as Vol. I . . . ⟩ other subjects engraved ⟨ . . . as Vol. I . . . ⟩ authority. Vol. IV.

London: Printed for Tho. Osborne; Tho. Trye; and S. Crowder, 1759.

viii + 400 pp, 11 printed leaves, 1 pl.

20.2 × 12.5 cm

MnU

The preface to the first edition (pp. iii–iv) includes a description of "The Plan of the Work as published by the Proprietors with the first Numbers." It recounts the purchase of Thomas Hale's papers on husbandry, and the solicitation of additional materials from many other contributors. The intent was to produce a comprehensive treatise on husbandry, both "intelligible to the *Farmer*, and not below the *Gentleman*" (p. iii). The study would adopt a broad historical and geographic perspective, providing a summary of everything already written on husbandry, and then present "all that has been discovered by modern *Practice*" (p. iii). Thus special emphasis would be placed on practical experience: literary assertions would be replaced, where appropriate, by empirical proof. In this manner "the *old* Practice of Husbandry is condemned or established by the *new*" (p. iii). The prospectus promised a methodical arrangement of subjects. In order they would be: soil, manure, fencing, ditching, draining, hedging, coppice wood, timber, methods of stocking the farm, husbandry, the practices of farmers in different counties, seeds, grass, roots, a variety of "less universal" crops, farm products, bad weather, animal diseases, and plant diseases.

The book as published is generally true to this plan. In 1759 a fourth volume was issued to accompany the three volumes of the second edition (1758). This volume includes a short discussion of vineyards and wine, a collection of 134 "Additional Articles in Husbandry," and "The Husbandman's Kalendar," chronologically arranged directions for tending the land and livestock.

Plates in the first edition depict a dung pit, a lime kiln, a sheepfold, coppices, timber, farm animals, plants, farm implements, and an orchard. Several of these plates include views of cottages. The plate facing page 145, for example, shows fields enclosed by means of a "bank fence," a wall fence, coppices, and "timber trees." Adjacent to these fields are two-story cottages, with irregular elevations and thatch roofs; one cottage is half-timbered.[1] The plate facing page 661 contains a design for a two-story "ventilating granary," shown in elevation, section, and three plans.[2]

Pages 378 through 380 in the final volume of the Dublin edition contain descriptions of six designs for small, very plain farm houses, which are shown in plan and elevation in two accompanying plates. Five of these designs were unique to the Dublin edition. A note on page 378 explains that the designs were included here because there was a perceived need for such houses in Ireland. The smallest, just one story high and three openings wide, contains a parlor, kitchen, and bed chamber each 12 feet square, plus another bed chamber, a larder, and a passage, each 12 feet by 6 feet. The largest design, which also appeared in both London editions,[3] is two stories high and two openings wide, with ells to either side. The ground floor includes a parlor (20 feet by 24 feet), kitchen (30 feet by 14 feet), and bed chamber (12 feet by 12 feet).

1. This plate, reduced, appears in Vol. I of the 1758 edition facing p. 256.

2. This plate, reduced, appears in the Dublin edition. It is marked "Vol. 1111 [i.e., IV] Page 247" but in the Goldsmiths' copy it is bound in Vol. III. This plate also appears in the 1758 edition in Vol. III facing p. 398.

3. The design had been redrawn to a larger scale for the Dublin edition. In the London editions, the design appears as part of a plate showing an orchard. In the first edition, this plate appears facing p. 613; in the second edition it faces p. 331 in Vol. III.

487.1
HODSON, Thomas
The cabinet of the arts; being a new and universal drawing book forming a complete system of drawing, painting in all its branches, etching, engraving, perspective, projection, & surveying, with all their various & appendant parts, containing the whole theory and practice of the fine arts in general from the first elements to the most finished principles displaying in the most familiar manner the whole rudiments of imitation, design, disposition, invention & deception, illustrated with upwards of sixty elegant engravings[.] To which is added an appendix, containing several curious and useful miscellaneous articles[.] By T. Hodson author of the accomplished tutor[.]

London: Printed for T. Ostell, 1804.

4 printed leaves, 367 pp, 65 pls.

26.5 × 21.2 cm

DLC

487.2

HODSON, Thomas, and John DOUGALL (1760-1822)

The cabinet ⟨ . . . as 1804 . . . ⟩ miscellaneous articles[.] By T. Hodson & I. Dougall. . . [.]

London: Published by T. Ostell, 1805.

4 printed leaves, 367 pp, 65 pls.

26.0 × 20.5 cm

MnU

487.3

DOUGALL, John (1760-1822), ed.

The cabinet ⟨ . . . as 1804 . . . ⟩ finished principles, displaying ⟨ . . . as 1804 . . . ⟩ invention & surveying, illustrated with one hundred & thirty elegant engravings. Edited by J. Dougall. Second edition with additions. Vol. I.

London: Published by R. Ackermann: and to be had of all booksellers, [1821].

iii + 384 pp, 2 printed leaves, frontisp.

The cabinet of the arts, being a new & universal drawing book, illustrated by 130 engravings, from drawings by various masters. Second edition with additions. Vol. II.

London: Published at R. Ackermann's; & to be had of all other booksellers, [1821?].

frontisp. + 127 plates (numbered 1–101, 97–120, 120, 122).

30.2 × 25.5 cm

DLC

The title pages of all three editions are engraved. The title pages for the 1804 and 1805 editions are in large part identical. There are only three principal differences: in the 1805 edition Dougall's name has been added to the right of Hodson's;[1] the two editions have entirely different vignettes in the space between the title and the imprint; and the imprints differ.

In the 1804 and 1805 editions the Preface is dated 1 October 1805. This suggests that the 1804 title page was issued while the book was being published in parts, and that the 1805 title page was issued as a replacement when the entire book was completed. There are no other major differences between the 1804 and 1805 editions.

The vignette on the title page of the first volume of the 1821 edition is unchanged from the 1805 edition. There are minor changes in the title, and the imprint has been changed to reflect the new publisher.

Two other books, with similar titles but very different contents, should be distinguished from the work under consideration here: *The Cabinet of the Arts. A Series of Engravings; by English Artists* (London, 1799); and Hewson Clarke and John Dougall, *The Cabinet of Arts* (London, 1817; and London, [1825?]).

According to the 1805 Preface this book was conceived as an elementary treatise on drawing and painting for "the education of young artists," to be of modest size and moderately priced. The authors apologized for offering yet another such book in an already saturated market, then obsequiously asked that "what has been thus attempted for the use and advantage of the rising generation, on whom their country has a right to depend for honourable and virtuous pursuits and exertions, . . . be accepted with generosity and indulgence."

The text is divided into six "books," devoted to drawing, etching and engraving, mezzotint and aquatint, painting, perspective, and projection and surveying. A brief Appendix offers remarks on painting transparencies, coloring maps, varnishing, japanning, gilding, and silvering.

The plates are closely related to subjects in the text. They depict details of human anatomy, the human figure alone and in groups, the human skeleton and muscles, the passions, classical statuary, plants, animals, landscape scenes, and perspective exercises, all executed in a variety of intaglio techniques. Several landscape scenes include rustic cottages, two stories high with thatch or slate roofs (Plates [35?], 38, 57, and [58?]). One of the plates devoted to perspective exercises (Plate 58) depicts a two-story house, three openings wide, in front elevation, end elevation, and oblique perspective view. These illustrations were borrowed directly from Plate 2 in James Malton's *Young Painter's Maulstick* (1800; *q.v.*).

Many new plates were added to the 1821 edition, and several incorporate architectural subjects. Plate 67 shows perspective views of a house (two stories high, three openings wide) in a landscape. Plate 68 depicts three-story terrace houses flanking both sides of a street that recedes into the distance. Plates 75, 83–85, 88, 89, and 100 contain views by Samuel Prout of rustic architectural subjects, including cottages, churches, and Dartmouth Castle. Other plates (e.g., 93) incorporate rustic cottages in landscape scenes.

1. From the title page of the 1804 edition it is apparent that Hodson's name originally had been centered, then shifted to the left. (In the space directly to the right of "HODSON" the letters "SO" can be seen, partly obliterated and partially covered by foliage extending out of the vignette below.) In the 1805 edition the space to the right of Hodson's name is occupied by Dougall's name.

488.1

HUMPHREYS, Thomas

The Irish builder's guide, exhibiting the valuation of buildings throughout Ireland; with reference to the rise and fall of materials and workmens' wages, at all times, even in the most remote towns in Ireland. The whole illustrated with plates. Dedicated to Francis Johnston, Esq. Architect to His Majesty's honorable Board of Works. By Thomas Humphreys, Measurer.

Dublin: Printed for the author, by James Charles, 1813.

xii pp, 4 printed leaves, 13–349 pp, frontisp. + 4 pls. [*one of which is wanting in this copy*].

19.1 × 11.0 cm

IU

Humphreys explained in the Preface (pp. v–xii) that in preparing this book he had traveled widely, talking with tradesmen in many cities and towns. Unlike previous authors, he had not inquired simply "what prices they generally charged for such and such work" (p. vi). Rather, he sought to determine the availability of building materials, the price of transportation, workmen's wages, and their degree of productivity. Despite wide variations in costs of materials and in wages, he hoped to establish "a fair and equitable standard price for every city in the kingdom" (p. x). The preliminary matter concludes with a list of subscribers, an index, and a list of errata.

The first several portions of the text concern the quality and price of masonry and brickwork in Dublin, Cork, Waterford, Limerick, and Belfast, in the counties of Antrim, Down, and Armagh, and elsewhere in Ireland. The next section briefly treats stonecutters' work. Carpentry is considered at greater length, with detailed prices given for roofing, joists, flooring, sash frames, sashes, staircases, wainscoting, shop fronts, oak, and mahogany. Two plates depicting four different types of roof trusses accompany the discussion of roof framing. Shorter portions of text are devoted to slating and plastering.

Humphreys next provided separate, very detailed estimates for first-rate houses in Dublin, Cork, Waterford, Limerick, and Belfast. The frontispiece depicts one design for a town house in elevation and plan. An entrance hall on the right side of the ground floor leads back to a staircase; on the left are two rooms, measuring 16 feet by 18 feet, and 16 feet by 20 feet. The elevation is three openings wide. A stringcourse divides the ground story from the three stories above, which in turn are surmounted by a cornice and an attic.

The final portions of the book contain estimates for a stone bridge over the river Liffey in Dublin, and for "a commodious cottage in the vicinity of Dublin" that Humphreys already had executed (p. 349). An accompanying plate shows Richmond Bridge in section. Another plate, wanting in the University of Illinois copy, shows the cottage in plan and elevation.

489.1

LOUDON, John Claudius (1783–1843)

An encyclopaedia of agriculture; comprising the theory and practice of the valuation, transfer, laying out, improvement, and management of landed property; and the cultivation and economy of the animal and vegetable productions of agriculture, including all the latest improvements; a general history of agriculture in all countries; and a statistical view of its present state, with suggestions for its future progress in the British Isles. By J. C. Loudon. . . . Illustrated with upwards of eight hundred engravings on wood by Branston.

London: Printed for Longman, Hurst, Rees, Orme, Brown, and Green, 1825.

xvi + 1226 pp.

22.1 × 14.1 cm

MnU

489.2 †

An encyclopaedia of agriculture; comprising ⟨ . . . as 1825 . . . ⟩ present state; with suggestions for its future progress in the British Isles. Illustrated . . . by Branston.

London: Longman, Hurst, Rees, Orme, Brown and Green, 1826.

1226 pp.

Reference: NUC-S

489.3 †

An encyclopaedia of agriculture: comprising ⟨ . . . as 1825 . . . ⟩. By J. C. Loudon. . . . Second edition. . . .

London: Printed for Longman, Rees, Orme, Brown, and Green, 1831.

xl + 1282 pp.

22 cm

Reference: NUC

489.4

An encyclopaedia of agriculture: comprising ⟨ . . . as 1825 . . . ⟩. By J. C. Loudon. . . . Third edition. Illustrated with upwards of eleven hundred engravings on wood by Branston.

London: Printed for Longman, Rees, Orme, Brown, Green, and Longman, 1835.

xl + 1282 + 1279–1378 pp.

NNC

489.5

An encyclopaedia of agriculture: comprising ⟨ . . . as 1825 . . . ⟩. By J. C. Loudon. . . . Fourth edition. Illustrated with upwards of eleven hundred engravings on wood by Branston.

London: Printed for Longman, Orme, Brown, Green, and Longmans, 1839.

xl + 1282 + 1279–1378 pp.

22.2 × 14.2 cm

NNC

489.6 †

An encyclopaedia of agriculture . . . including . . . supplements bringing down the work to the year 1844. By J. C. Loudon. . . . Fifth edition. Illustrated with upwards of twelve hundred engravings on wood, by Branston.

London: Longman, Brown, Green, and Longmans, 1844.

xl + 1375 + [1] pp.

22.5 cm

Reference: NUC

489.7 †

An encyclopaedia of agriculture. . . . By J. C. Loudon. Fifth edition.

London: Longman, Brown, Green, Longmans & Roberts, 1857.

xl + 1375 pp.

23 cm

Reference: NUC-S

489.8 †

An encyclopaedia of agriculture . . . including . . . supplements bringing down the work to the year 1844. By J. C. Loudon. . . . Sixth edition. Illustrated with upwards of twelve hundred engravings on wood, by Branston.

London: Longman, Brown, Green, and Longmans, 1869.

xl + 1375 + [1] pp.

22.5 cm

Reference: NUC

489.9

An encyclopaedia of agriculture: comprising the theory and practice of the valuation, transfer, laying out, improvement, and management of landed property, and of the cultivation and economy of the animal and vegetable productions of agriculture. With upwards of twelve hundred engravings on wood, by Branston. By J. C. Loudon. . . . Seventh edition.

London: Longmans, Green, and Co., 1871.

xl + 1375 pp.

21.6 × 13.8 cm

NN

489.10

An encyclopaedia of agriculture: comprising ⟨ . . . as 1871 . . . ⟩ Loudon. . . . Eighth edition.

London: Longmans, Green, and Co., 1883.

xl + 1375 pp.

21.8 × 14.0 cm

MnU

Three distinct supplements were issued. The first appeared with the second edition (1831). It consists of six pages (numbered 1277 through 1282); the first page is headed by the single word "Supplement." This also appears in the 1835 and 1839 editions. The next supplement appeared with the 1835 edition, and is titled "First Additional Supplement to Loudon's Encyclopaedia of Agriculture; Being Notices of All the Principal Improvements Which Have Taken Place in Agriculture in Britain, with Historical Notices of Its Progress in Other Countries since the Publication of the Second Edition of the Encyclopaedia of Agriculture, in January, 1831." The pages are numbered 1279 through 1378; prefatory remarks, on page 1279, are dated September 14, 1834. This supplement was advertised separately in 1836, according to ECB, and also appears with the 1839 edition. Later editions have a supplement with a new half-title, "Supplement to Loudon's Encyclopaedia of Agriculture: Bringing Down Improvements in the Art of Field Culture from 1841 to 1843 Inclusive. By J. C. Loudon. . . ." This is page [1277]. The text pages are numbered 1279 through 1375.

In the Preface to the first edition (1825, pp. iii–vi) Loudon described the general division of his book into four parts: (1) a discussion of agriculture "in its most universal sense," treating its origins, progress, and present state in various nations and in different climates; (2) an account of fundamental agricultural principles; (3) an analysis of agricultural practice in Britain; and (4) further comment on the types of people engaged in British agriculture, the different kinds of farms in Britain, different practices in different regions of Britain, agricultural literature, public policy as it relates to agriculture, and the outlook for future progress. In the Preface Loudon also commented on recent agricultural books and indicated the sources from which he obtained some of his information. The front matter also includes a glossary (pp. vii–viii) and a table of contents (pp. ix–xvi).

Part I treats agricultural history as well as farming practices in foreign countries. Loudon illustrated a wide variety of farm and rural dwellings, generally copied from other publications on agriculture, architecture, or travel. Among these are Robert Castell's reconstruction of a Roman villa (p. 19; see also Entry 36), plans and an elevation of a farm house in Tuscany (p. 52), a plan and elevations of a Flemish farmery (pp. 74–75), and views of a Danish farm house (p. 90), houses of Polish "postmasters" and Jews' houses in southern Poland (p. 101), a village and a nobleman's farmery in Russia (p. 105), a Swedish log cottage and conical huts in Lapland (p. 110), a Turkish cottage (p. 122), a Chinese village (p. 158), a Tibetan mansion (p. 166), an Egyptian hut (p. 172) and tent (p. 174), a group of Nubian huts (p. 173), a nomadic settlement in Morocco (p. 176), and tribal settlements in southern Africa (p. 181), plus an elevation of an American log house (p. 188). Closer to home, Loudon depicted plans, views, and an elevation of a Scottish farm house and offices, an elevation of an English double cottage for laborers (pp. 129–130), a view of an Irish cottar's rude cabin (p. 135), and an illustration of an exemplary English house and farmery (p. 186). Taken together, these illustrations are an educated sampling of what was known about rural dwellings around the world in the first quarter of the nineteenth century.

In Part II Loudon undertook a lengthy analysis of the "science of agriculture," in which he paid some attention to the design of farmers' dwellings, cottages for farm servants, and the arrangement of buildings in a farmery. He offered four designs for farmers' residences (pp. 417–419). The plan of the smallest shows an entry, kitchen, dairy and pantry, parlor, light closet, tool house, and water closet on the ground floor, with three bedrooms and a garret above. The largest design has an entry, parlor, kitchen, dairy, pantry, cellar, and cheese room on the ground floor. The facade, two stories high and three openings wide, is ornamented with shallow semicircular relieving arches and pseudo-Venetian lights flanking the window and door openings on the ground floor. Loudon accompanied his brief remarks on servants' cottages (pp. 419–422) with six illustrations. The smallest dwelling is a pair of cottages in Berwickshire, each containing a kitchen, a small parlor (which also serves as a storeroom), offices, and two bedrooms above. More substantial is the "cottage ornamented in the second degree," which has an entrance lobby, kitchen, parlor, back kitchen, cowhouse, water closet, two bedrooms, and two garrets. There is restrained Tudor ornamentation on the facade. Illustrations of six farmeries, each including a dwelling, accompany his discussion of the arrangement of buildings in a farmery (pp. 425–430). The two-story bailiff's house that is part of the "very complete farmery" on page 429 includes a parlor, family room, brewhouse, kitchen, pantry, and milk house, plus bedrooms and attics.

In Part III Loudon turned to the "Practice of Agriculture," a topic that he clearly defined quite broadly, for there are substantial sections that concern landscaping, town planning, and domestic architecture. Book II concerns the "laying out" of estates, and includes a chapter on sites for proprietors' residences. Loudon offered summary remarks on soil, water, exposure, views, gardens, pleasure grounds, and the layout of the "park" (pp. 508–510). Another chapter concerns the founding and development of mills, factories, villages, and markets; as illustrations he included plans of Bridekirk and Torquay (pp. 559–560).[1] The final chapter in Book II returns to the problem of laying out farmeries. There are plans and elevations of seven farmeries with dwellings, intended for farms of 100 to 500 acres (pp. 613–619). Loudon also included seven designs for cottages (pp. 619–620). These range in size from a one-story entrance lodge with kitchen, parlor, pantry, and closet, to a triple cottage providing each tenant with kitchen, parlor, closets, and bedrooms. For cottages "erected as picturesque objects" Loudon recommended grouping several together in one structure, or using elevations in Gothic, Swiss, Italian, or other styles.

Much of Part IV consists of summaries of information pertaining to individual counties. Loudon extracted this information from the county reports to the Board of Agriculture (see Entries 92–123), surveys by William Marshall, and other topographical accounts. Illustrations of typical or exemplary dwellings appear in Loudon's remarks on Essex, Bedfordshire, Berkshire, Shropshire, Staffordshire, Cheshire, North Wales, Berwickshire, Ayrshire, West Lothian, Sutherland, the Hebrides, and King's County (Ireland). Loudon also included a view of the new prison town at Princetown on Dartmoor (p. 1126) and a plan of the town and surrounding lands at Tremadoc (p. 1132).

The first edition closes with a "Kalendarial Index" (an index of topics arranged according to the month of the year for which they are appropriate; pp. 1189–1196) and a "General Index" (pp. 1197–1226).

1. For Bridekirk and Torquay see above, "The Literature of British Domestic Architecture," Chapter III, Section 10.

490.1

LOUDON, John Claudius (1783–1843)
An encyclopaedia of gardening; comprising the theory and practice of horticulture, floriculture, arboriculture, and landscape-gardening, including all the latest improvements; a general history of gardening in all countries; and a statistical view of its present state, with suggestions for its future progress, in the British Isles. By J. C. Loudon. . . . Illustrated with nearly six hundred engravings on wood by Branston.
London: Printed for Longman, Hurst, Rees, Orme, and Brown, 1822.

xviii+ 1469 pp.

22.7 × 14.5 cm

MnU

490.2 †

_____

An encyclopaedia of gardening; comprising ⟨ . . . as 1822 . . . ⟩ present state with suggestions for its future progress in the British Isles. Second edition.

London: Longman, Rees, Orme, Brown and Green, 1824.

1233 pp.

Reference: NUC-S

490.3 †

_____

An encyclopaedia of gardening; comprising ⟨ . . . as 1822 . . . ⟩ Isles. By J. C. Loudon. . . . Third edition.

London: Printed for Longman, Hurst, Rees, Orme, Brown, and Green, 1825.

xii + 1233 + [1] pp.

20.5 cm

Reference: NUC

490.4 †

An encyclopaedia of gardening; comprising ⟨ . . . as 1822 . . . ⟩ present state with suggestions for its future progress in the British Isles. By J. C. Loudon. . . . Illustrated with many hundred engravings on wood by Branston. Fourth edition.

London: Longman, Rees, Orme, Brown and Green, 1826.

xii + 1233 pp.

22 cm

Reference: NUC

490.5 †

An encyclopaedia of gardening; comprising ⟨ . . . as 1822 . . . ⟩ Isles. By J. C. Loudon . . . illustrated with many hundred engravings on wood by Branston. Fifth edition.

London: Printed for Longman, Rees, Orme, Brown, and Green, 1827.

xii + 1233 pp.

22 cm

Reference: NUC

490.6 †

An encyclopaedia of gardening; comprising ⟨ . . . as 1822 . . . ⟩ Isles. By J. C. Loudon. Illustrated with many hundred engravings on wood by Branston. Fifth edition.

London: Prenled [*sic?*] for Longman, Rees, Orme, Brown, and Green, 1828.

xii + 1233 pp.

Reference: NUC

490.7 †

An encyclopaedia of gardening; comprising ⟨ . . . as 1822 . . . ⟩ floriculture, aboriculture, and landscape gardening; including ⟨ . . . as 1822 . . . ⟩ present state; with suggestions for its future progress in the British Isles. By J. C. Loudon. . . . Illustrated with many hundred engravings on wood, by Branston.

London: Longman, Rees, Orme, Brown, and Green, [1830?].

xii + 1233 pp.

Reference: NUC

490.8

An encyclopaedia of gardening; comprising ⟨ . . . as 1822 . . . ⟩ present state; with ⟨ . . . as 1822 . . . ⟩ Isles. By J. C. Loudon. . . . Illustrated with many hundred engravings on wood, by Branston A new edition, considerably improved and enlarged

London: Printed for Longman, Rees, Orme, Brown, Green, and Longman, 1835.

xl + 1270 pp.

21.3 × 13.3 cm

MnU

490.9

An encyclopaedia of gardening; comprising ⟨ . . . as 1822 . . . ⟩ present state; with ⟨ . . . as 1822 . . . ⟩ Isles. By J. C. Loudon. . . . Illustrated with many hundred engravings on wood, by Branston A new edition, considerably improved and enlarged.

London: Printed for Longman, Rees, Orme, Brown, Green, and Longman, [n.d.].

xl + 1270 pp.

21.3 × 13.8 cm

NN

490.10

An encyclopaedia of gardening; comprising ⟨ . . . as 1822 . . . ⟩ and landscape gardening; including ⟨ . . . as 1822 . . . ⟩ present state; with suggestions for its future progress in the British Isles. By J. C. Loudon. . . . Illustrated with many hundred engravings on wood, by Branston. A new edition, corrected and improved, by Mrs. Loudon.

London: Printed for Longman, Brown, Green, and Longmans, 1850.

xl + 1278 pp.

19.5 × 13.0 cm

NN

490.11 †

An encyclopaedia of gardening; comprising ⟨ . . . as 1822 . . . ⟩ and landscape gardening; including ⟨ . . . as 1822 . . . ⟩ present state; with suggestions for its future progress in the British Isles. By J. C. Loudon. . . . .

Illustrated with many hundred engravings on wood, by Branston. A new edition edited by Mrs. Loudon.

London: Longman, Brown, Green, and Longmans, & Roberts, 1859.

xl + 1278 pp.

22.5 cm

Reference: NUC

490.12 †
_____

An encyclopaedia of gardening; comprising the theory and practice of horticulture. . . . . New edition, edited by Mrs. Loudon.

London: Longman, Green, Longman, and Roberts, 1860.

xl + 1278 pp.

Reference: NUC

490.13 †
_____

An encyclopaedia of gardening; comprising the theory and practice of horticulture, floriculture arboriculture, and landscape gardening . . . a general history of gardening in all countries; and a statistical view of its present state; with suggestions for its future progress in the British Isles. By J. C. Loudon. . . . Illustrated with many hundred engravings on wood by Branston. New edition, edited by Mrs. Loudon.

London: Longmans, Green, 1865.

xl + 1278 pp.

23 cm

Reference: NUC

490.14
_____

An encyclopaedia of gardening; comprising ⟨ . . . as 1822 . . . ⟩ and landscape gardening; including ⟨ . . . as 1822 . . . ⟩ present state; with suggestions for its future progress in the British Isles. By J. C. Loudon. . . . Illustrated with many hundred engravings on wood, by Branston New edition edited by Mrs. Loudon.

London: Longmans, Green, and Co., 1869.

xl + 1278 pp.

22.2 × 14.1 cm

MnU

490.15

———
———

London: Longmans, Green, and Co., 1871.

xl + 1278 pp [*this copy is bound in two volumes*].

21.4 × 13.4 cm

NN

490.16 †

———

An encyclopaedia of gardening; comprising ⟨ . . . as 1822 . . . ⟩ and landscape gardening; including ⟨ . . . as 1822 . . . ⟩ present state; with suggestions for its future progress in the British Isles. Illustrated with many hundred engravings on wood, by Branston. New edition edited by Mrs. Loudon.

London: Longmans, Green, 1878.

xl + 1278 pp.

Reference: NUC

NUC shows one undated edition with pagination identical to the third through fifth editions; the preface is dated 1830.

    NUC shows other undated editions, all with pagination similar to the "new" edition of 1835. There are two of these undated editions at the New York Public Library, and each includes a Preface dated 1834 (as does the 1835 "new" edition). In one there is advertising matter, dated 1839, inserted at the front. Otherwise the two copies are indistinguishable.

The Preface to the 1835 edition (pp. iii–vi) touts the advantages of this encyclopedia's systematic (rather than alphabetical) arrangement. Loudon also noted the improvements and additions that he had made to this edition, and indicated that new information would continue to be reported in his *Gardener's Magazine* (Entry 187). The front matter also includes a brief list of contributors (p. vi), a table of contents (pp. vii–xiv), a list of the engravings (pp. xv–xxii), a list of books cited in the text (pp. xxiii–xxxix), and miscellaneous subjects (pp. xxxix–xl).

    Part I treats the "Origin, Progress, and Present State" of gardening among various nations and in different climates. Loudon included plans of ancient Roman villa estates, reconstructed by Robert Castell (pp. 17–19; see also Entry 36), views of castles depicted in Italian landscape paintings, borrowed from G. L. Meason's treatise (pp. 29–30; see Entry 203), a plan and views of the landscape and buildings at Monza (pp. 36–37), a drawing of Petrarch's house at Arqua (p. 37), a view of the Villa Borghese (p. 39), a view of the palace and gardens at Loo (p. 59), and similar subjects of historical interest.

    In Part II Loudon discussed gardening "as a Science, and as an Art." He devoted two chapters to garden architecture, treating such structures as hothouses, mushroom houses, ice houses, apiaries, aviaries, and "decorative buildings." Loudon illustrated a Doric porch and portico (p. 616), trelliswork arbors in French and Italian styles (p. 617), and seats in rustic, "mushroom," and Turkish styles (p. 617).

In Part III Loudon surveyed current gardening practices in Britain. This required further attention to hothouses and aviaries, as well as other decorative garden structures, including a rustic hut, a Greek temple, a log shelter (all on p. 1011), artificial ruins (pp. 1179–1181), and a picturesque gate lodge and cottage (pp. 1180–1181). There is a long section on "Laying Out Private Gardens or Residences" (pp. 1186–1206) in which Loudon divided residences into five types: the mansion and demesne (about which he said little more), the villa, the farm, the temporary residence, and the cottage. He illustrated and discussed at some length "the mode of planting a villa in the modern style," and then made shorter remarks on laying out the grounds of a villa farm, a ferme ornée, and temporary residences (e.g., marine villas or shooting boxes). There follows a lengthy description of the grounds of one small country villa at Wickham, near Fareham, in Hampshire. Loudon also provided views of a parsonage and vicarage whose shrubbery he found praiseworthy. He briefly discussed laying out the grounds of a cottage ornée, a cottage *en verger*, a citizen's villa, a citizen's villa in the Chinese style, a suburban villa, a suburban house, and four other types of house, as well as a common front garden, a farmer's garden, and a laborer's garden. The section concludes with illustrations of a bailiff's cottage, two gardener's houses, and a small lodge, presented as examples of economical and durable dwellings that were suitably picturesque for a large park or estate.

Part IV concerns the different types of people who might engage in gardening, the various kinds of gardens in Britain, the effect of public policy on gardening, and the outlook for future progress in British gardening. This edition concludes with a "Kalendarial Index" (an index of topics arranged according to the month of the year for which they are appropriate; pp. 1243–1260), a "General Index" (pp. 1261–1270), and a leaf of errata and additions.

491.1
MITCHELL, John
"On the dairy husbandry in Holland. By Mr. John Mitchell, Merchant, Leith," *Prize-Essays and Transactions of the Highland and Agricultural Society of Scotland* X (n.s. 4; 1835), 165–185, and pl. IV.

DLC

Mitchell stated that he prepared this essay in hopes of winning the premium offered by the Highland Society of Scotland for the best account of current dairy practices in Holland. His discussion is divided into seven parts, treating pastures, cows, methods of manufacturing dairy products, utensils, milk houses, cheese houses, and general remarks. In the final section he briefly described Dutch farm houses. They were generally of one story, he said, and usually had thatch roofs. Figures 11 and 12 in Plate IV show one of these houses in oblique view and in plan. The hip roof has a very steep pitch, rising approximately three times the height of the single story below. The plan shows a "Large Room," a kitchen, and a bedroom arranged along one side of the building. Most of the area under the roof, however, is for dairy purposes—there are rooms for "dairy operations," drying cheese, "shade," and storing hay and straw, plus a cooler, a byre, and a milk house.

492.1

The new complete dictionary of arts and sciences; or, an universal system of useful knowledge. Containing a full explanation of every art and science, whether liberal or mechanical, in which the difficulties attending a thorough knowledge of them are clearly pointed out, and such directions given as cannot fail of making their acquisition easy and familiar to every capacity. Exhibiting, among the various other branches of literature, a copious elucidation of the following, viz. agriculture, algebra, anatomy, architecture, arithmetick, astronomy, book-keeping, botany, carving, catoptricks, chemistry, chronology, commerce, conicks, cosmography, dialing, dioptricks, ethicks, farriery, fluxions, fortification, gardening, gauging, geography, geometry, grammar, gunnery, handicrafts, heraldry, history, horsemanship, husbandry, hydraulicks, hydrography, hydrostaticks, law, levelling, logick, maritime and military affairs, mathematicks, mechanicks, medicine, merchandize, metaphysicks, meteorology, musick, navigation, opticks, oratory, painting, perspective, pharmacy, philology, philosophy, physick, pneumatics, rhetorick, sculpture, series and staticks, statuary, surgery, surveying, theology, trigonometry, &c. The whole upon an improved plan, the marrow and quintessence of every other dictionary and work of the kind being preserved, and their superfluities and obscurities entirely omitted. Particular attention has been given to every thing valuable in Chambers, the Encyclopedie, printed at Paris; the Encyclopediae [sic] Britannica, and other publications of later date. Including not only all the valuable modern improvements which have been made by several eminent members of the Royal Society, the Royal Academy, and the Society for the Encouragment of Arts, Manufactures and Commerce, but also a great variety of other important discoveries; which have been made and communicated to the authors of this work, by some of the most distinguished characters of this and other nations. Eminent engravers and designers in the several departments have been engaged at a very great expence to unite their abilities in producing the most masterly and superb set of copper-plates, representing upwards of one thousand exact figures, such as machines, instruments, implements, tools, plans, schemes, animals, vegetables, minerals, fossils, and other articles relative to the subjects treated of in a work of the utmost consequence to mankind. The theological, philosophical, critical, and poetical branches, by the Rev. Erasmus Middleton. . . ; the medicinal, chemical, and anatomical, by William Turnbull. . . ; the gardening and botanical, by Thomas Ellis. . . ; the mathematical, &c. by John Davidson. . . ; and the other parts by gentlemen of approved abilities in the respective branches which they have engaged to illustrate. [*Volume I.*]

London: Printed, by authority, for the authors; and sold by Alexr. Hogg; and S. Leacroft; and may be had of all booksellers in town and country, 1778.

The new complete ⟨ . . . as Vol. I . . . ⟩, catoptricks, chronology, chymistry, commerce, ⟨ . . . as Vol. I . . . ⟩ marrow and essence of every other dictionary and work of the kind being preserved, and the superfluities ⟨ . . . as Vol. I . . . ⟩ medicinal, chymical, and anatomical, ⟨ . . . as Vol. I . . . ⟩ illustrate. Vol. II.

London: Printed, by authority, for the authors; and sold by Alexr. Hogg, [1778?].

Art. "Bridge, flying or floating," I, 1 p; pl. XII.
Art. "Camera obscura," I, 1 p; pl. XIV.
Art. "Levelling," II, 2 pp; pl. XLIX.

34.9 × 22.6 cm

MB

The article on "Architecture" (I, 2 pp) begins with a brief discussion of civil architecture, including definitions of solidity, convenience, beauty, order, disposition, proportion, decorum, and economy. There are cursory accounts of historical periods (ancient, Gothic, and modern), of the five orders, and of major writers on architecture. Separate sections of this article are devoted to military, naval, and "counterfeit" (trompe-l'oeil) architecture.

Additional information on civil architecture is found in the following articles: "Composite order" (I, 1 p; pl. XXI), "Corinthian order" (I, 1 p; pl. XXV), "Dorick order" (I, 1 p; pl. XXVIII), "Ionick order" (II, 1 p; pl. XLIII), "Order" (II, 2 pp), and "Tuscan order" (II, 1 p; pl. LXXVII).

The article on bridges includes a short subsection devoted to the "Flying or Floating Bridge," illustrated in Figure 7 on Plate XII. The bridge is depicted in the middle of a river. On the far bank of the river is a village with several one- and two-story cottages, none more than two openings wide.

The illustration for "Camera obscura" (Plate XIV, Fig. 3) shows the image of a two-story house and trees projected through a lens onto an interior wall of a second house. The illustration is an enlarged version of one that first appeared in *A New and Complete Dictionary* (1754–1755; *q.v.*).

The article on levelling includes illustrations (Plate XLIX, Figs. 4 and 5) that appeared previously, but reversed, in *A New Royal and Universal Dictionary* (1770–1771; *q.v.*). Figure 4 includes a porticoed and pedimented two-story dwelling set on a raised embankment or podium. In Figure 5 several cottages, apparently part of a rural village, are visible in the distance.

493.1
PROUT, Samuel (1783–1852)
Rudiments of landscape: in progressive studies. Drawn, and etched in imitation of chalk, by Samuel Prout.

London: Published by R. Ackermann. L. Harrison & J. C. Leigh, Printers, 1813.

iv + 5–26 pp, 64 pls.

34.5 × 47.2 cm

IEN

493.2 ‖
_____

Rudiments of landscape: in progressive studies, in imitation of chalk, Indian ink, and colours. Drawn and etched by Samuel Prout.

London: Published by R. Ackermann. L. Harrison and J. C. Leigh, Printers, 1814.

iv + 5–26 pp, 64 pls.

27 × 37 cm

Reference: Information supplied by Winterthur Museum Library.

The Introduction (pp. iii–iv) to this large and lavish book is addressed to students, admonishing them not to copy "too servilely." Instead, Prout recommended drawing from nature as an appropriate means of learning how to draw with chalk or pencil. He indicated that in his plates he would first present the student with "fragments" having "simplicity of form, and determined light or shadow." Thereafter his illustrations would be arranged in a "progressive" manner to facilitate learning. In the first four numbers (including Plates 1–24) he would introduce the student to "the power of drawing from nature." The subjects of the plates would be "drawn and shadowed with chalk." The next four numbers (Plates 25–48) would have subjects drawn in outline and shaded with sepia or India ink. The final four numbers (projected to be six plates each) would have subjects illustrated in a manner imitating colored drawings, to illustrate principles of light and shade, and the use of cold and warm tints.

The text begins with instructions on the use of paper, pencils, and chalk, and the proper stance for drawing. Prout recommended that the beginner carefully study "such objects as are least formal in their general appearance" (p. 7). New buildings, he said, were the worst subjects to study because of their regular lines and uniform color. He also deplored "mechanical representation" of rock, stone, and other natural objects, encouraging the student instead to be an "original artist" (p. 7). But Prout also recommended that students study the work of established artists such as Morland, Gainsborough, and others. Part 2 of the text begins on page 11, where Prout introduced "shadowing" and the use of sepia and India ink. Later, he discussed the use of the camera obscura and camera lucida. At the beginning of Part 3 he discussed warm and cool colors. He then introduced a variety of mechanical and aesthetic considerations in the rendition of color. He gave instructions for laying washes and mixing tints, for example, discussed the need to harmonize hills and mountains with the sky, and presented methods for achieving effects of relief, contrast, and atmospheric distance.

The plates in Part 1 are executed in soft-ground etching. The first six depict architectural details (doors, windows, gables, and the like) and vernacular cottages, often made to appear picturesque due to broken plaster, thatch roofs, or shutters hanging askew. Plates 7 through 24 show one- and two-story cottages, bridges, churches, gateways, and towers. From plate to plate these subjects progressively become more complex, with the gradual introduction of such features as masonry details, half-timbering, and Gothic ornament.

In Part 2 the illustrations are shaded. There are simple architectural details in Plates 25 and 28, cottages and churches in Plates 26, 27, and 30, and towers in Plate 29. Plates 31 through 48 are more complex, showing more cottages, bridges, churches, ruins of an abbey, an old gate house, and a large half-timbered house.

In Part 3 (Plates 49 through 64) the plates are colored, showing cottages, churches, a tower, bridges, a coastal scene, a farmyard, cattle fording a stream, a canal in a town, a barn, boys fishing in a stream, and similar subjects.

This appendix is a chronological survey of all publications listed in the principal entries (Nos. 1–360) and in Appendix D (Nos. 468–493) that were issued from 1715 through 1842.

As an aid to chronological and quantitative studies the list is divided into two columns. The left column includes all first editions.[1] When two distinct editions appeared in the same year, they are listed together in the left column (as, for example, the 35- and 128-page versions of Castell's *Villas of the Ancients*, both of which appeared in 1728). The right column contains all subsequent issues and editions. Although the principal entries and Appendix D include editions issued after 1842, these editions are not represented here; to have included them, without also including works newly issued after 1842, would have provided a distorted picture of architectural publication after 1842.

All entries here are derived from information in the bibliographic descriptions above; thus uncertainties pertaining to some bibliographic descriptions also apply to the corresponding entries here.[2]

Some books appeared in separate volumes over the course of more than one year; in such cases each volume is entered according to the date of its appearance.[3] A book that was issued first in parts, and later was provided with a title page encompassing all parts, is entered according to the date of the imprint on the title page for the whole.[4] Each set of a multivolume encyclopedia or dictionary is entered only once, according to the date when the first part of the set was issued, or else the imprint date of the earliest volume.

As explained at the beginning of the principal entries, a periodical may be entered according to its title, its editor or "conductor," or the names of authors of articles containing designs for dwellings.[5] Each periodical is entered here in the same manner in which it appears among the bibliographic entries above. Sometimes a series of articles by a single author appeared over the course of more than one year; in such cases there is an entry in the left column for each year. Periodicals that are entered according to editor, "conductor," or title are entered only once, under the year in which the first issue or volume appeared.

I have gathered undated first editions together at the end of the left column. A similar listing in the right column, containing all later undated editions, would be too voluminous to be useful.

Additional features of this survey are explained in the following discussion of symbols and notations:

•   A bullet precedes all entries for encyclopedias and dictionaries.[6]

⟨ ⟩   For encyclopedias and dictionaries, each set is entered only once, according to the date when the first part of the set was issued, or else the imprint date of the earliest volume. The date at which the set was completed, if different from the commencement date, is given within angle brackets.

♦   A diamond precedes all entries for agricultural surveys prepared under the auspices of the Board of Agriculture. These surveys appear in the bibliographic entries above under the corporate author, "Great Britain. Board of Agriculture." The diamond entries are alphabetized correspondingly in this list.

(1:6, 1841)   A set of numerals in parentheses appears at the end of each entry.[7]

The numeral preceding the colon indicates the place of this edition in the overall sequence of editions. The numeral following the colon indicates the total number of editions of this title that are listed in the bibliographic entries above.[8] Thus (1:3) indicates the entry at hand is the first of three editions, while (7:7) indicates the entry is the last of seven editions.

In most entries this pair of numerals is accompanied by a date. For entries in the left column (which are first editions), the date shown is that of the final edition. This allows the reader to see at a glance the span of years over which the book was published.[9] For all entries in the right column (which are later editions), the date shown is that of the first known edition.

(1841)   In the case of periodicals entered according to editor, "conductor," or title, the date given in parentheses is that of the final volume.

1. More precisely, the left column contains the first *known* edition of each title. Stated differently, the left column includes those principal entries, and those entries in Appendix D, whose entry numbers end in ".1". Note for example Entry 27.1, John Cart Burgess's *Easy Introduction to Perspective*, which is described on the title page as the second edition, but for which no first edition is known. As an entry ending in ".1", this edition (1819) appears in the left column. Subsequent editions appear in the right column.

2. See the remarks on "ghost" editions at the beginning of the principal entries.

3. For "date of appearance" I have generally used the date shown in the imprint. For books with undated imprints, but for which a date of publication can be determined, I have used the date shown in square brackets ([ ]) in the bibliographic description above. When there is only an approximate date of publication (e.g., "[ca. 1801]"), the book is considered undated. Treatment of undated ("n.d.") books is discussed below.

4. For example the first volume of the Adams' *Works in Architecture* (1778) originally appeared in five parts from 1773 to 1778, but is entered here according to the date on the title page of the first volume, 1778.

5. A list of all periodicals may be found in notes 23 and 24 of the Introduction.

6. Encyclopedias and dictionaries whose contents are restricted to architectural or agricultural subjects are *not* designated in this manner: these include *The Complete Farmer: or, a General Dictionary of Husbandry* (Entry 42); Loudon's *Encyclopaedia of Agriculture* (Entry 489); Loudon's *Encyclopaedia of Cottage, Farm, and Villa Architecture* (Entry 184); Loudon's *Encyclopaedia of Gardening* (Entry 490); and Nicholson's *Architectural Dictionary* and *Encyclopaedia of Architecture* (Entry 223).

7. The only exceptions are entries for periodicals. No numerals follow entries for single periodical articles, since I have not traced the many editions in which several periodicals appeared. See the preliminary remarks on "Editorial Method" at the beginning of the principal entries. For periodicals entered according to editor, "conductor," or title, see the remark at the end of this list of symbols and notations.

8. This number does not necessarily indicate the true number of "editions" for any title. See the remarks concerning "Entry number" at the beginning of the principal entries. The numeral preceding the colon generally corresponds to the numeral following the point in the entry number.

9. I have omitted this date when the first edition was the only edition, or when all editions appeared in the same year.

First (or First Known) Editions	Second and Later Editions
1715	**1715**
Campbell, *Vitruvius Britannicus* v.1 (1:4, n.d.)	
Switzer, *The nobleman . . . recreation* (1:3, 1742)	
1716	**1716**
1717	**1717**
Campbell, *Vitruvius Britannicus* v.2 (1:3, n.d.)	Campbell, *Vitruvius Britannicus* v.1 (1715, 2:4)
1718	**1718**
	Switzer, *Ichnographia rustica* (1715 as *The nobleman . . . recreation*, 2:3)
1719	**1719**
1720	**1720**
1721	**1721**
1722	**1722**
1723	**1723**
Carwitham, *The . . . architectonick sector* (1:2, 1733)	
1724	**1724**
Bradley, *A general treatise of husbandry* (1:3, 1757)	
1725	**1725**
Campbell, *Vitruvius Britannicus* v.3 (1:4 and 2:4, n.d.)	
Halfpenny, *The art of sound building* ed.1 and ed.2 (1:2 and 2:2)	

First (or First Known) Editions	Second and Later Editions
1726	**1726**
Langley, *Practical geometry* (1:3, 1729)	Bradley, *A general treatise of husbandry* (1724, 2:3)
Langley, *A sure guide* (1:2, 1729)	
Leoni, *Some designs* (1:2, 1758)	
1727	**1727**
Kent (W), *The designs of Inigo Jones* (1:3, 1835)	
1728	**1728**
Castell, *The villas of the ancients* (1:2 and 2:2)	Langley, *Practical geometry* (1726, 2:3)
• Chambers, *Cyclopaedia* (1:17, 1795–1797)	
Gibbs, *A book of architecture* (1:2, 1739)	
Morris, *An Essay in defence* (1:1)	
1729	**1729**
	Langley, *Practical geometry* (1726, 3:3)
	Langley, *A sure guide* (1726, 2:2)
1730	**1730**
Langley, *The young builder's rudiments* (1:3, 1736)	
1731	**1731**
Halfpenny, *Perspective made easy* (1:1)	Campbell, *Vitruvius Britannicus* v.3 (1725, 3:4)
1732	**1732**
Rowland, *A general treatise* (1:1)	
1733	**1733**
	Carwitham, *The . . . architectonick sector* (1723, 2:2)
1734	**1734**
Morris, *Lectures* pt.1 (1:2, 1759)	Langley, *The young builder's rudiments* (1730, 2:3)
1735	**1735**
Hoppus, *Andrea Palladio's architecture* (1:2, 1736)	
Ripley, *The plans . . . of Houghton* (1:2, 1760)	
1736	**1736**
Morris, *Lectures* pt.2 (1:1)	Hoppus, *Andrea Palladio's architecture* (1735, 2:2)
	Langley, *The young builder's rudiments* (1730, 3:3)
1737	**1737**
Hoppus, *The gentleman's . . . repository* (1:4, 1760)	
1738	**1738**
	• Chambers, *Cyclopaedia* (1728, 2:17)
	Hoppus, *The gentleman's . . . repository* (1737, 2:4)

First (or First Known) Editions	Second and Later Editions
1739	**1739**
Badeslade and Rocque, *Vitruvius Brittanicus* (1:1)	• Chambers, *Cyclopaedia* (1728, 3:17)
Rowland, *Mensuration* (1:1)	Gibbs, *A book of architecture* (1728, 2:2)
	Jones (W), *The gentlemens or builders companion* (n.d., 2:2)
1740	**1740**
	• Chambers, *Cyclopaedia* (1728, 4:17)
1741	**1741**
• De Coetlogon, *An universal history* ⟨−1745⟩ (1:1)	• Chambers, *Cyclopaedia* (1728, 5:17)
Shortess, *Harmonic architecture* (1:1)	• Chambers, *Cyclopaedia* ⟨−1743⟩ (1728, 6:17)
Wood, *The origin of building* (1:1)	
1742	**1742**
Langley, *Ancient architecture* (1:3, n.d.)	• Chambers, *Cyclopaedia* (1728, 7:17)
	Switzer, *Ichnographia rustica* (1715 as *The nobleman . . . recreation*, 3:3)
1743	**1743**
	Ware, *Designs of Inigo Jones* (n.d., 2:2)
1744	**1744**
Vardy, *Some designs* (1:1)	
1745	**1745**
1746	**1746**
	• Chambers, *Cyclopaedia* (1728, 8:17)
1747	**1747**
Garret, *Designs, and estimates* (1:4, 1772)	Langley, *Gothic architecture* (1742, 2:3)
1748	**1748**
Muller, *Elements of mathematics* (1:3, 1765)	Hoppus, *The gentleman's . . . repository* (1737, 3:4)
1749	**1749**
Halfpenny, *A new and compleat system* and *Système nouveau* (1:5 and 2:5, 1772)	
Halfpenny, *Twelve beautiful designs* (1:4, 1774)	
1750	**1750**
Halfpenny, *New designs for Chinese temples* (1:4, n.d.)	• Chambers, *Cyclopaedia* (1728, 9:17)
Morris, *Rural architecture* (1:4, 1757)	Halfpenny, *Twelve beautiful designs* (1749, 2:4)
1751	**1751**
Halfpenny, *New designs for Chinese bridges* (1:4, n.d.)	• Chambers, *Cyclopaedia* ⟨-1752⟩ (1728, 10:17)
Halfpenny, *New designs for Chinese doors* (1:4, n.d.)	
Halfpenny, *Six new designs* pt.1 and pt.2 (1:1 and 1:1)	
Halfpenny, *Useful architecture* (1:4, 1760)	
Morris, *The architectural remembrancer* (1:3, 1757)	
Paine, *Plans . . . of the mansion-house* (1:1)	

First (or First Known) Editions	Second and Later Editions
1752	**1752**
Halfpenny, *Chinese and Gothic architecture* (1:1)	Halfpenny, *Rural architecture . . . Chinese taste* (1750–1752 as *New designs*, 2:4)
Halfpenny, *New designs for Chinese gates* (1:4, n.d.)	Halfpenny, *Useful architecture* (1751, 2:4)
Halfpenny, *Rural architecture . . . Gothick taste* (1:1)	
Halfpenny, *Thirteen new designs* pt.3 [see *Six new designs*, 1751] (1:1)	
1753	**1753**
Halfpenny, *The country gentleman's . . . companion* (1:2, 1756)	
1754	**1754**
Aheron, *A general treatise* (1:1)	
Edwards and Darly, *A new book of Chinese designs* (1:1)	
Kirby, *Dr. Brook Taylor's . . . perspective* (1:4, 1768)	
• *A new and complete dictionary* ⟨–1755⟩ (1:2, 1763–1764)	
1755	**1755**
The art of drawing (1:19, 1844)	Halfpenny, *Rural architecture . . . Chinese taste* (1750–1752 as *New designs*, 3:4)
Wright, *Universal architecture* bk.1 (1:1)	Halfpenny, *Useful architecture* (1751, 3:4)
	Kirby, *Dr. Brook Taylor's . . . perspective* (1754, 2:4)
	Morris, *Architecture improved* (1751 as *The architectural remembrancer*, 2:3)
	Morris, *Select architecture* (1750 as *Rural architecture*, 2:4)
1756	**1756**
Bardwell, *The practice of painting* (1:3, 1782)	Halfpenny, *The country gentleman's . . . companion* (1753, 2:2)
Hale, *A compleat body of husbandry* (1:3, 1758–1759)	
Ware, *A complete body of architecture* (1:3, 1768)	
1757	**1757**
Chambers, *Designs of Chinese buildings* and *Desseins des edifices . . . chinois* (1:2 and 2:2)	*The art of drawing* (1755, 2:19)
Gentleman, *Twelve designs* (1:1)	Bradley, *A general treatise of agriculture* (1724 as *A general treatise of husbandry*, 3:3)
Halfpenny, Morris, and Lightoler, *The modern builder's assistant* (1:2, n.d.)	Hale, *A compleat body of husbandry* (1756, 2:3)
Swan, *A collection of designs* (1:3, n.d.)	Morris, *Architecture improved* (1751 as *The architectural remembrancer*, 3:3)
	Morris, *Select architecture* (1750 as *Rural architecture*, 4:4)
	Muller, *Elements of mathematics* (1748, 2:3)

First (or First Known) Editions

1772

The draughtsman's assistant (1:9, n.d.)
Rudiments of architecture (1:5, 1799)

1773

Wallis, *The carpenter's treasure* (1:1)

1774

The builder's magazine (1:10, 1823)
Pain, *The practical builder* (1:8, 1804)

1775

Ferguson, *The art of drawing in perspective* (1:8, 1820)
Kent (N), *Hints to gentlemen* (1:4, 1799)
Malton (T), *A complete treatise on perspective* (1:4, 1779)

1776

Clarke, *Practical perspective* (1:2, 1794)

1777

1778

Adam (R & J), *Works* v.1 (1:4, 1931)
• *The new complete dictionary of arts and sciences* (1:1)
Soane, *Designs in architecture* (1:4, 1797)

Second and Later Editions

1772

The artists assistant in drawing (n.d., 2:16)
Garret, *Designs, and estimates* (1747, 4:4)
Halfpenny, *A new and complete system* (1749, 5:5)

1773

Bardwell, *The practice of painting* (1756, 2:3)
Brettingham, *The plans . . . of Holkham* (1761, 2:2)
• Croker, *The complete dictionary* (1764, 5:5)
• *Encyclopaedia Britannica* (1771, 2:9)
Rudiments of architecture (1772, 2:5)

1774

Halfpenny, *Twelve beautiful designs* (1749, 4:4)
Lightoler, *The gentleman and farmer's architect* (1762, 3:3)
Overton, *The temple builder's . . . companion* (1766, 3:3)

1775

Rudiments of architecture (1772, 3:5)

1776

The builder's magazine (1774, 2:10)
Kent (N), *Hints to gentlemen* (1775, 2:4)
Malton (T), *A compleat treatise on perspective* (1775, 2:4)
Pain, *The practical builder* (1774, 2:8)

1777

The art of drawing Dublin ed. (1755, 6:19) and London ed. (1755, 7:19)
The complete farmer (1766, 4:6)

1778

• Chambers, *Cyclopaedia* ⟨–1786⟩ (1728, 11:17 and 12:17)
• *Encyclopaedia Britannica* ⟨–1783⟩ (1771, 3:9)
Ferguson, *The art of drawing in perspective* Dublin ed. (1775, 2:8) and London ed. (1775, 3:8)
Malton (T), *A compleat treatise on perspective* (1775, 3:4)
Pain, *The practical builder* (1774, 3:8)
Rudiments of architecture (1772, 4:5)

1789

Aldrich, *Elements of civil architecture* (1:3, 1824)

The rudiments of ancient architecture (1:5, 1821)

1789

Miller, *The country gentleman's architect* (1787, 2:7)

Pain, *The practical builder* (1774, 5:8)

Pain, *The practical house carpenter* (1788, 2:11)

Rawlins, *Familiar architecture* (1768, 2:3)

Soane, *Designs in architecture* (1778, 2:4)

1790

1790

• *Encyclopaedia Britannica* ⟨–1797⟩ (1771, 4:9)

Pain, *Pain's British Palladio* (1786, 3:6)

Pain, *The practical house carpenter* (1788, 3:11)

Plaw, *Rural architecture* (1785, 2:6)

Soane, *Designs in architecture* (1778, 3:4)

Wrighte, *Grotesque architecture* (1767, 2:5)

1791

Newton, *The architecture of . . . Vitruvius* v.2 (1:1)

1791

The art of drawing (1755, 10:19)

Chambers, *Treatise* (1759, 3:8)

Crunden, *Convenient and ornamental architecture* (1767, 6:9)

• *Encyclopaedia Britannica* ⟨–1797⟩ (1771, 5:9)

Miller, *The country gentleman's architect* (1787, 3:7)

Newton, *The architecture of . . . Vitruvius* v.1 (1771, 2:2)

1792

Richardson, *New designs in architecture* (1:1)

Wood, *A series of plans* (1:4, 1837)

1792

Pain, *The practical house carpenter* (1788, 4:11)

1793

Middleton, *Picturesque and architectural views* (1:2, 1795)

Sheraton, *The cabinet-maker* (1:5, 1895)

Soane, *Sketches in architecture* (1:2, 1798)

1793

The complete farmer (1766, 5:6)

Kent (N), *Hints to gentlemen* (1775, 3:4)

Miller, *The country gentleman's architect* (1787, 4:7)

Pain, *The builder's pocket-treasure* (1763, 4:4)

Pain, *Pain's British Palladio* (1786, 4:6)

Pain, *The practical builder* (1774, 6:8)

1794

♦ Pearce, *Berkshire* (1:1)

♦ Leatham, *East Riding of Yorkshire* (1:1)

Knight, *The landscape* (1:2, 1795)

Morison, *Designs in perspective for villas* (1:1)

Repton, *Sketches and hints* (1:1)

Richardson, *The first part of a complete system* (1:2, 1795)

1794

Clarke, *Practical perspective* (1776, 2:2)

Pain, *The practical house carpenter* (1788, 5:11)

Plaw, *Rural architecture* (1785, 3:6)

Rudiments of ancient architecture (1789, 2:5)

Sheraton, *The cabinet-maker* (1793, 2:5)

1795

Davis in *Letters . . . of the Bath . . . Society*

• *Encyclopaedia Londinensis* ⟨–1829⟩ (1:1)

♦ Robertson, *Mid-Lothian* (1:1)

Plaw, *Ferme ornée* (1:6, 1823)

1795

• Chambers, *Cyclopaedia* (1728, 16:17) and ⟨–1797⟩ (1728, 17:17)

• Hall, *The new royal encyclopaedia* (1788, 2:3)

Knight, *The landscape* (1794, 2:2)

Middleton, *Picturesque and architectural views* (1793, 2:2)

Rawlins, *Familiar architecture* (1768, 3:3)

Richardson, *A series of original designs* (1794 as *The first part of a complete system*, 2:2)

1796

• *Encyclopaedia Perthensis* ⟨–1806⟩ (1:3, 1816)

♦ Pitt, *Stafford* (1:3, 1813)

1796

Plaw, *Ferme ornée* (1795, 2:6)

Plaw, *Rural architecture* (1785, 4:6)

1797

Beatson in *Communications to the Board of Agriculture*

Beatson in *Communications to the Board of Agriculture*

Crocker in *Communications to the Board of Agriculture*

Crocker and son in *Communications to the Board of Agriculture*

Crutchley in *Communications to the Board of Agriculture*

Holland in *Communications to the Board of Agriculture*

Holland in *Communications to the Board of Agriculture*

Hunt (R) in *Communications to the Board of Agriculture*

Lewis, *Original designs* v.2 (1:1)

Pitt, *An address* (1:1)

Smith (J), *Remarks on rural scenery* (1:1)

1797

The art of drawing (1755, 11:19)

Crunden, *Convenient and ornamental architecture* (1767, 7:9)

• *Encyclopaedia Britannica* (1771, 6:9)

Lewis, *Original designs* v.1 (1780, 2:2)

Pain, *Pain's British Palladio* (1786, 5:6)

Soane, *Designs in architecture* (1778, 4:4)

1798

Malton (J), *An essay on . . . cottage architecture* (1:2, 1804)

1798

The art of drawing (1755, 12:19)

Soane, *Sketches in architecture* (1793, 2:2)

1799

♦ Young, *Lincoln* (1:3, 1813)

Middleton, *The architect and builder's miscellany* (1:4, 1843?)

1799

The art of drawing (1755, 13:19)

The artist's assistant in drawing (n.d., 8:16)

Kent (N), *Hints to gentlemen* (1775, 4:4)

Pain, *The practical builder* (1774, 7:8)

Pain, *The practical house carpenter* (1788, 6:11)

Rudiments of architecture (1772, 5:5)

1800

Bradshaw, *Civil architecture* (1:1)

Elison, *Decorations for parks and gardens* (1:1)

(continued)

1800

The builder's magazine (1774, 5:10)

Malton (T), *An appendix* (1783, 2:2)

Plaw, *Ferme ornée* (1795, 3:6)

(continued)

First (or First Known) Editions	Second and Later Editions

1800 *(continued)*

♦ Thomson, *Fife* (1:1)

♦ Tuke, *North Riding of Yorkshire* (1:1)

Laing, *Hints for dwellings* (1:6, 1841)

Malton (J), *The young painter's maulstick* (1:1)

Plaw, *Sketches* (1:5, 1823)

Robertson (W), *Designs in architecture* and *Desseins d'architecture* (1:2 and 2:2)

Wyatt, *A collection of architectural designs* no.1 and no.2 (1:1 and 1:1)

1801

The artist's assistant; or school (1:4, n.d.)

Mitchell (R), *Plans, and views* (1:1)

Wyatt, *A collection of architectural designs* no. 3 (1:1)

1802

Barber, *Farm buildings* (1:2, 1805)

• *The English encyclopaedia* (1:1)

Malton (J), *A collection of designs* (1:1)

Orme, *William Orme's rudiments* (1:1)

• Rees, *The cyclopaedia* 〈–1820〉 (1:1)

Richardson, *The new Vitruvius Britannicus* v.1 (1:2, 1810)

Sinclair, *Hints regarding . . . property* (1:3 and 2:3, 1818)

Soane, *Plans . . . of Pitzhanger* (1:1)

• Willich, *The domestic encyclopaedia* (1:1)

1803

Edwards, *A practical treatise of perspective* (1:2, 1806)

Elsam, *An essay on rural architecture* (1:2, 1805)

Rennie in *Prize essays and transactions of the Highland Society*

Repton, *Observations* (1:2, 1805)

Sinclair, *A sketch of the improvements* (1:1)

1804

Bartell, *Hints for picturesque improvements* (1:1)

♦ Young, *Norfolk* (1:2, 1813)

Hodson, *The cabinet of the arts* (1:3, 1821)

Wood (JG), *Lectures* (1:3, 1844)

1805

Atkinson, *Views of picturesque cottages* (1:1)

Dickson, *Practical agriculture* (1:7, n.d.)

Gandy, *Designs for cottages* (1:1)

(continued)

1800 *(continued)*

Plaw, *Rural architecture* (1785, 5:6)

1801

The artist's assistant in drawing (n.d., 9:16)

Laing, *Hints for dwellings* (1800, 2:6)

Sheraton, *The cabinet-maker* (1793, 3:5)

1802

Ferguson, *The art of drawing in perspective* (1775, 4:8)

Miller, *The country gentleman's architect* (1787, 5:7)

Plaw, *Rural architecture* (1785, 6:6)

Plaw, *Sketches* (1800, 2:5)

Sheraton, *The cabinet-maker* (1793, 4:5)

Wrighte, *Grotesque architecture* (1767, 4:5)

1803

The art of drawing (1755, 14:19)

The artist's assistant, or school (1801, 2:4)

Ferguson, *The art of drawing in perspective* (1775, 5:8)

Plaw, *Ferme ornée* (1795, 4:6)

Plaw, *Sketches* (1800, 3:5)

1804

Laing, *Hints for dwellings* (1800, 3:6)

Malton (J), *An essay on . . . cottage architecture* (1798, 2:2)

Pain, *Pain's British Palladio* (1786, 6:6)

Pain, *The practical builder* (1774, 8:8)

Rudiments of ancient architecture (1789, 3:5)

1805

Barber, *Farm buildings* (1802, 2:2)

Crunden, *Convenient and ornamental architecture* (1767, 8:9)

(continued)

First (or First Known) Editions	Second and Later Editions
1805 *(continued)*	**1805** *(continued)*

Gandy, *The rural architect* (1:2, 1806)

♦ Duncumb, *Hereford* (1:2, 1813)

Lugar, *Architectural sketches* (1:3, 1823)

Pyne, *Nattes's practical geometry* (1:2, 1819)

Elsam, *An essay on rural architecture* (1803, 2:2)

Hodson and Dougall, *The cabinet of the arts* (1804, 2:3)

Miller, *The country gentleman's architect* (1787, 6:7)

Pain, *The practical house carpenter* (1788, 8:11)

Repton, *Observations* (1803, 2:2)

1806

Dearn, *Sketches . . . for public & private buildings* (1:2, 1814)

• Gregory, *A dictionary* ⟨–1807⟩ (1:2, 1815)

Gyfford, *Designs for elegant cottages* (1:1)

Loudon, *A treatise on . . . country residences* (1:2, 1812)

Randall, *A collection of . . . designs* (1:1)

1806

The artist's assistant in drawing (n.d., 10:16)

Edwards, *Practical treatise of perspective* (1803, 2:2)

Gandy, *The rural architect* (1805, 2:2)

Wood, *A series of plans* (1792, 2:4)

1807

Daniel, *A familiar treatise* (1:3, 1821)

Dearn, *Sketches . . . for cottages and . . . dwellings* (1:2, 1823)

♦ Young, *Essex* (1:2, 1813)

♦ Rudge, *Gloucester* (1:2, 1813)

Gyfford, *Designs for small picturesque cottages* (1:1)

Loudon, *Engravings* (1:1)

Lugar, *The country gentleman's architect* (1:4, 1838)

Pocock, *Architectural designs* (1:3, 1823)

1807

The artist's assistant; or school (1801, 3:4)

The complete farmer (1766, 6:6)

Dickson, *Practical agriculture* (1805, 2:7)

Ferguson, *The art of drawing in perspective* (1775, 6:8)

• *The new encyclopaedia* (1796 as *Encyclopaedia Perthensis*, 2:3)

1808

Aikin, *Designs for villas* (1:3, 1852)

• Brewster, *The Edinburgh encyclopaedia* ⟨–1830⟩ (1:1)

Busby, *A series of designs* (1:2, 1835)

Curwen, *Hints on the economy* (1:2, 1809)

♦ Batchelor, *Bedford* (1:2, 1813)

♦ Mavor, *Berkshire* (1:3, 1813)

♦ Vancouver, *Devon* (1:2, 1813)

♦ Parkinson, *Rutland* (1:1)

Repton, *Designs for . . . Brighton* (1:2, n.d.)

Richardson, *The new Vitruvius Britannicus* v.2 (1:1)

Woods in *Essays of the London Architectural Society*

Young in *Communications to the Board of Agriculture*

1808

♦ Young, *Lincolnshire* (1799, 2:3)

♦ Pitt, *Stafford* (1796, 2:3)

Taylor (C), "On perspective" (1788, 2:3)

Taylor (C), "Principles of architecture" (1788, 2:2)

First (or First Known) Editions

1809

Dearn, *The bricklayer's guide* (1:1)

♦ Kerr, *Berwick* (1:2, 1813)

♦ Pitt and Parkinson, *Leicester and Rutland* (1:2, 1813)

♦ Young, *Oxfordshire* (1:2, 1813)

Hassell, *The speculum* (1:2, 1816)

Jones (R), *Every builder his own surveyor* (1:1)

1810

Gillespie in *Communications to the Board of Agriculture*

♦ Vancouver, *Hampshire* (1:2, 1813)

♦ Robertson, *Kincardineshire* (1:3, 1813)

♦ Davies, *North Wales* (1:2, 1813)

♦ Pitt, *Worcester* (1:2, 1813)

1811

Cresswell, *The elements of . . . perspective* (1:2, 1812)

Dearn, *Designs for lodges* (1:2, 1823)

♦ Keith, *Aberdeenshire* (1:1)

♦ Aiton, *Ayr* (1:1)

♦ Worgan, *Cornwall* (1:2, 1815)

♦ Farey, *Derbyshire* v.1 (1:2, 1815)

♦ Trotter, *West-Lothian* (1:1)

Loudon, *Designs for laying out farms* (1:2, 1812)

Lugar, *Plans and views* (1:3, 1836)

Pocock, *Modern finishings* (1:4, 1837)

1812

♦ Souter, *Banff* (1:1)

♦ Henderson, *Caithness* (1:2, 1815)

♦ Henderson, *Sutherland* (1:2, 1815)

• Johnson, *The imperial encyclopaedia* (1:1)

Matthews, *Useful architecture* (1:1)

Pickett, *Twenty-four plates* (1:1)

Wilkins, *The civil architecture of Vitruvius* (1:1)

Second and Later Editions

1809

The artists' assistant in drawing (n.d., 11:16)

Curwen, *Hints on agricultural subjects* (1808 as *Hints on the economy*, 2:2)

♦ Mavor, *Berkshire* (1808, 2:3)

Wood (JG), *Lectures* (1804, 2:3)

1810

The artist's assistant in drawing (n.d., 12:16)

Daniel, *A familiar treatise* (1807, 2:3)

Dickson, *The farmer's companion* (1805 as *Practical agriculture*, 3:7)

• *Encyclopaedia Britannica* (1771, 7:9)

Ferguson, *The art of drawing in perspective* (1775, 7:8)

Miller, *The country gentleman's architect* (1787, 7:7)

Pain, *The builder's companion* (1758, 5:5)

Richardson, *The new Vitruvius Britannicus* v.1 (1802, 2:2)

Rudiments of ancient architecture (1789, 4:5)

1811

Dickson, *Farmer's companion* (1805 as *Practical agriculture*, 4:7)

1812

Cresswell, *Elements of . . . perspective* (1811, 2:2)

Loudon, *Observations on laying out farms* (1811 as *Designs for laying out farms*, 2:2)

Loudon, *A treatise on . . . country residences* (1806, 2:2)

Middleton, *The architect and builder's miscellany* (1799, 2:4)

Plaw, *Sketches* (1800, 4:5)

First (or First Known) Editions	Second and Later Editions
1813	**1813**
♦ Farey, *Derbyshire* v.2 (1:2, 1815)	*The art of drawing* (1755, 15:19)
Hayter, *An introduction to perspective* (1:7, 1845)	*The artist's assistant* (n.d. as *The artists assistant in drawing*, 13:16)
Humphreys, *The Irish builder's guide* (1:1)	Dickson, *The farmer's companion* (1805 as *Practical agriculture*, 5:7)
• *Pantologia* (1:2, 1819)	♦ Batchelor, *Bedford* (1808, 2:2)
Papworth in *The repository of arts*	♦ Mavor, *Berkshire* (1808, 3:3)
Parker (T), *Plans, specifications, estimates* (1:1)	♦ Kerr, *Berwick* (1809, 2:2)
Prout, *Rudiments of landscape* (1:2, 1814)	♦ Vancouver, *Devon* (1808, 2:2)
Society for . . . Oswestry, *First report* (1:1)	♦ Young, *Essex* (1807, 2:2)
	♦ Rudge, *Gloucester* (1807, 2:2)
	♦ Vancouver, *Hampshire* (1810, 2:2)
	♦ Duncumb, *Hereford* (1805, 2:2)
	♦ Robertson, *Kincardineshire* (1810, 3:3)
	♦ Pitt and Parkinson, *Leicester and Rutland* (1809, 2:2)
	♦ Young, *Lincolnshire* (1799, 3:3)
	♦ Young, *Norfolk* (1804, 2:2)
	♦ Davies, *North Wales* (1810, 2:2)
	♦ Young, *Oxfordshire* (1809, 2:2)
	♦ Pitt, *Stafford* (1796, 3:3)
	♦ Pitt, *Worcester* (1810, 2:2)
	Plaw, *Ferme ornée* (1795, 5:6)
1814	**1814**
♦ Sinclair, *Appendix to . . . Scotland* (1:1)	*The artists assistant in drawing* (n.d., 14:16)
♦ Sinclair, *Scotland* (1:1)	Dearn, *Sketches . . . for public and private buildings* (1806, 2:2)
Pasley, *Course of instruction* v.1 (1:4, 1851)	Dickson, *Practical agriculture* (1805, 6:7)
	Prout, *Rudiments of landscape* (1813, 2:2)
	Wood, *A series of plans* (1792, 3:4)
1815	**1815**
Brown, *The principles of . . . perspective* (1:2, 1835)	Crunden, *Convenient and ornamental architecture* (1767, 9:9)
• *Encyclopedia Mancuniensis* (1:2, 1817)	♦ Henderson, *Caithness* (1812, 2:2)
Nicholson, *Treatise on practical perspective* (1:1)	♦ Worgan, *Cornwall* (1811, 2:2)
Smith (James), *The panorama of science and art* (1:8, 1840?)	♦ Farey, *Derbyshire* v.1 (1811, 2:2)
	♦ Farey, *Derbyshire* v.2 (1813, 2:2)
Stevens, *Domestic architecture* and *Views of cottages* and *Picturesque sketches* (1:4, 2:4, and 3:4, 1860)	♦ Henderson, *Sutherland* (1812, 2:2)
	• Gregory, *A new & complete dictionary* (1806 as *A dictionary*, 2:2)
Varley, *A practical treatise* (1:2, 1820)	Hayter, *An introduction to perspective* (1813, 2:7)
	Lugar, *Architectural sketches* (1805, 2:3)
	Lugar, *The country gentleman's architect* (1807, 2:4)
	Pain, *The practical house carpenter* (1788, 9:11)
	Wrighte, *Grotesque architecture* (1767, 5:5)

First (or First Known) Editions

1816

• Burrowes, *The modern encyclopaedia* ⟨–1820⟩ (1:2, 1822)

Elsam, *Hints for improving . . . the peasantry* (1:1)

Papworth in *The repository of arts* (1:3, 1832)

Prout, *Studies of cottages* (1:1)

Repton, *Fragments* (1:1)

Smith (W), *An outline of architecture* (1:2, 1820)

1817

• *Encyclopaedia metropolitana* ⟨–1845⟩ (1:3, 1848–1849)

♦ Farey, *Derbyshire* v.3 (1:1)

Papworth in *The repository of arts* (1:3, 1832)

Pasley, *Course of military instruction* v.2 and v.3 (1:1)

Prout, *Bits for beginners* and *Progressive fragments* (1:3 and 2:3, n.d.)

1818

Laing, *Plans, elevations, and sections* (1:1)

1819

Burgess, *An easy introduction to perspective* (1:4, 1835)

The imperial magazine (1834)

Merigot, *A treatise on practical perspective* (1:1)

Nicholson, *An architectural dictionary* (1:8, n.d.)

Papworth in *The respository of arts* (1:2, 1823)

Prout, *A series of views . . . west of England* (1:1)

Senefelder, *A . . . course of lithography* (1:1)

Stitt, *The practical architect's . . . assistant* (1:1)

Second and Later Editions

1816

• *Encyclopaedia Perthensis* (1796, 3:3)

Hassell, *The speculum* (1809, 2:2)

Smith (James), *The panorama of science and art* (1815, 2:8)

Taylor (C), *A familiar treatise* (1788 as "Of perspective," 3:3)

1817

The art of drawing (1755, 16:19)

• *Encyclopaedia Britannica* (1771, 8:9)

• *The new school of arts* (1815 as *Encyclopedia Mancuniensis*, 2:2)

1818

Aldrich, *Elements of civil architecture* (1789, 2:3)

The art of drawing (1755, 17:19)

The artist's assistant in drawing (n.d., 15:16)

Laing, *Hints for dwellings* (1800, 4:6)

Papworth, *Rural residences* (1816 and 1817 as "Architectural hints" in *The repository of arts*, 2:3)

Sinclair, "Hints regarding . . . property" (1802, 3:3)

1819

Cook, *The new builder's magazine* (1774, 8:10)

• *Pantologia* (1813, 2:2)

Pocock, *Architectural designs* (1807, 2:3)

Pyne, *Nattes's practical geometry* (1805, 2:2)

First (or First Known) Editions

1820

Hassell, [*Cottage designs*] (1:1)

Loch, *An account of the improvements* (1:1)

Papworth in *The repository of arts* (1:2, 1823)

Pinnock, *A catechism of perspective* (1:2, 1823)

Prout, *A series of easy lessons* (1:1)

1821

Hedgeland, *First part of a series of designs* (1:1)

Merigot, *The amateur's portfolio* (1:1)

Papworth in *The repository of arts* (1:2, 1823)

Prout, *A series of views . . . north of England* (1:1)

1822

Adam (R & J), *Works* v.3 (1:3, 1931)

Gwilt, *Sciography* (1:5, 1866)

Loudon, *Encyclopaedia of gardening* (1:16, 1878)

Nicholson, *The rudiments of . . . perspective* (1:3, 1838)

1823

Bartlett, *An essay on design* (1:1)

Nicholson, *The new practical builder* (1:8, 1861)

Robinson, *Rural architecture* (1:5, 1850)

Second and Later Editions

1820

Cook, *The new builder's magazine* (1774, 9:10)

Ferguson, *The art of drawing in perspective* (1775, 8:8)

Hayter, *An introduction to perspective* (1813, 3:7)

Smith (W), *An outline of architecture* (1816, 2:2)

Varley, *A practical treatise* (1815, 2:2)

1821

Daniel, *A familiar treatise* (1807, 3:3)

Dougall, *The cabinet of the arts* (1804 as Hodson, *The cabinet of the arts*, 3:3)

Rudiments of ancient architecture (1789, 5:5)

1822

Adam (R & J), *Works* v.1 (1778, 2:4)

Adam (R & J), *Works* v.2 (1779, 3:5)

Burgess, *An easy introduction to perspective* (1819, 2:4)

• Burrowes, *The modern encyclopaedia* (1820, 2:2)

Pasley, *A complete course of . . . geometry* (1814 as *Course of instruction*, 2:4)

1823

Cook, *The new builder's magazine* (1774, 10:10)

Dearn, *Designs for lodges* (1811, 2:2)

Dearn, *Sketches . . . for cottages and . . . dwellings* (1807, 2:2)

• *Encyclopaedia Britannica* (1771, 9:9)

Laing, *Hints for dwellings* (1800, 5:6)

Lugar, *Architectural sketches* (1805, 3:3)

Lugar, *The country gentleman's architect* (1807, 3:4)

Lugar, *Plans and views* (1811, 2:3)

Pain, *The practical house carpenter* (1788, 10:11)

Papworth, *Hints on ornamental gardening* (1819, 1820, and 1821 as "Hints on ornamental gardening" in *The repository of arts*, 2:2)

Pinnock, *A catechism of perspective* (1820, 2:2)

Plaw, *Ferme ornée* (1795, 6:6)

Plaw, *Sketches* (1800, 5:5)

Pocock, *Architectural designs* (1807, 3:3)

Pocock, *Modern finishings* (1811, 2:4)

Smith (James), *The panorama of science and art* (1815, 5:8)

First (or First Known) Editions

1824

Hullmandel, *The art of drawing on stone* (1:4, 1840)

Nicholson, *The builder & workman's . . . director* (1:11, 1865)

1825

Carlisle, *Hints on rural residences* (1:1)

Elsam, *The practical . . . price-book* (1:10, 1864)

Hall (J), *Novel designs for cottages* (1:1)

Hunt, *Half a dozen hints* (1:4, 1841)

Loudon, *Encyclopaedia of agriculture* (1:10, 1883)

Mechanics' magazine (1873)

Morris (Richard), *Essays on landscape gardening* (1:1)

Nash, *The royal pavilion at Brighton* (1:2, 1838)

Smith (T), *The art of drawing* (1:3, n.d.)

1826

Allen, *Colonies at home* (1:4, 1832)

Atkinson (J), *An account of . . . New South Wales* (1:2, 1844)

Gwilt, *Rudiments of architecture* (1:4, 1839)

Loudon, *The gardener's magazine* (1843)

• Mitchell, *The portable encyclopaedia* (1:5, 1839)

Nicholson, *The practical cabinet-maker* (1:7 and 2:7, 1846)

1827

Hunt, *Architettura campestre* (1:2, 1844)

Hunt, *Designs for parsonage houses* (1:2, 1841)

Robinson, *Designs for ornamental villas* (1:6, 1853)

Robinson, *Vitruvius Britannicus . . . Woburn* (1:3, 1847)

Soane, *Designs for public improvements* (1:4, 1832)

Thomson, *Retreats* (1:5, 1854)

Waistell, *Designs for agricultural buildings* (1:2, n.d.)

Whittock, *The Oxford drawing book* (1:3, n.d.)

Second and Later Editions

1824

Aldrich, *Elements of civil architecture* (1789, 3:3)

Gwilt, *Sciography* (1822, 2:5)

Loudon, *Encyclopaedia of gardening* (1822, 2:16)

Smith (James), *The panorama of science and art* (1815, 6:8)

1825

The art of drawing (1755, 18:19)

The artist's assistant in drawing (n.d., 16:16)

Chambers, *Treatise* (1759, 4:8)

Hayter, *An introduction to perspective* (1813, 4:7)

Loudon, *Encyclopaedia of gardening* (1822, 3:16)

Nicholson, *The builder and workman's . . . director* (1824, 2:11)

Recreaciones arquitectonicas (n.d. as *Architectural recreations*, 2:3)

Smith (James), *The panorama of science and art* (1815, 7:8)

1826

Chambers, *Treatise* (1759, 5:8)

Elsam, *The practical . . . price-book* (1825, 2:10)

Hunt, *Half a dozen hints* (1825, 2:4)

Loudon, *Encyclopaedia of agriculture* (1825, 2:10)

Loudon, *Encyclopaedia of gardening* (1822, 4:16)

Robinson, *Rural architecture* (1823, 2:5)

1827

Allen, *Colonies at home* (1826, 2:4)

Elsam, *The practical . . . price-book* (1825, 3:10)

Loudon, *Encyclopaedia of gardening* (1822, 5:16)

Nicholson, *The builder and workman's . . . director* (1824, 3:11)

Smith (T), *The art of drawing* (1825, 2:3)

First (or First Known) Editions

1828

Davenport, *The amateur's perspective* (1:1)

Jackson, *Designs for villas* (1:2, 1829)

Lugar, *Villa architecture* (1:2, 1855)

Meason, *On the landscape architecture* (1:1)

• *The Oxford encyclopaedia* (1:1)

Rudge, *An introduction to . . . painting* (1:1)

1829

Billington, *The architectural director* (1:4, 1848)

Davenport, *Supplement* (1:1)

Fielding, *Synopsis of practical perspective* (1:3, 1843)

• *The London encyclopaedia* (1:4, 1844–1845)

1830

Hunt, *Exemplars of Tudor* (1:3, 1841)

Loudon, *Illustrations of landscape-gardening* pt.1 (1:1)

Loudon, *A manual of cottage gardening* (1:1; later eds. in Burke, *British husbandry*)

Robinson, *Designs for farm buildings* (1:3, 1837)

Robinson, *Village architecture* (1:2, 1837)

Soane, *Description of the house* (1:4, 1835)

Thompson, *Practical directions* (1:1)

Whitwell, *Description of an architectural model* (1:1)

1831

Facts and illustrations (1834)

The horticultural register (1836)

Legh, *The music of the eye* (1:1)

Loudon, *Illustrations of landscape-gardening* pt.2 (1:1)

Trendall, *Original designs* (1:1)

1832

Parker, *Villa rustica* bk.1 (1:2, 1848)

Second and Later Editions

1828

Allen, *Colonies at home* (1826, 3:4)

Burgess, *An easy introduction to perspective* (1819, 3:4)

Elsam, *The practical . . . price-book* (1825, 4:10)

Loudon, *Encyclopaedia of gardening* (1822, 6:16)

• Mitchell, *The portable encyclopaedia* (1826, 2:5)

Nicholson, *The practical cabinet maker* (1826, 3:7)

Robinson, *Rural architecture* (1823, 3:5)

Soane, *Designs for public improvements* and *Designs for public and private buildings* (1827, 2:4 and 3:4)

1829

Jackson, *Designs for villas* (1828, 2:2)

Robinson, *Designs for ornamental villas* (1827, 2:6)

Whittock, *The Oxford drawing book* (1825, 2:3)

1830

Architectural recreations (n.d., 3:3)

Loudon, *Encyclopaedia of gardening* (1822, 7:16)

Robinson, *Designs for ornamental villas* (1827, 3:6)

Smith (T), *The young artist's assistant* (1825 as *The art of drawing*, 3:3)

Wetten, *Designs for villas* (n.d., 2:2)

1831

Loudon, *Encyclopaedia of agriculture* (1825, 3:10)

• Mitchell, *The portable encyclopaedia* (1826, 3:5)

1832

Allen, *Colonies at home* (1826, 4:4)

Elsam, *The practical . . . price-book* (1825, 5:10)

Hayter, *An introduction to perspective* (1813, 5:7)

Papworth, *Rural residences* (1816 and 1817 as "Architectural hints" in *The repository of arts*, 3:3)

Soane, *Description of the house* (1830, 2:4)

Soane, *Designs for public and private buildings* (1827 as *Designs for public improvements*, 4:4)

First (or First Known) Editions

1833

Goodwin, *Domestic architecture* v.1 (1:4, 1850)

Jopling, *The practice of isometrical perspective* (1:5, 1861)

Loudon, *Encyclopaedia of . . . architecture* (1:14, n.d.)

Parker, *Villa rustica* bk.2 (1:2, 1848)

• Partington, *The British cyclopaedia* ⟨−1835⟩ (1:4, 1838)

Robertson (J), *Supplement to Loudon's manual* (1:1)

Robinson, *Designs for lodges* (1:2, 1837)

Robinson, *Vitruvius Britannicus . . . Hatfield* (1:2, 1847)

Whittock, *The youth's . . . drawing book* (1:3, 1836)

1834

Burke, *British husbandry* v.1 (1:3, 1847)

Goodwin, *Domestic architecture* v.2 (1:4, 1850)

Loudon, *The architectural magazine* (1839)

Nicholson, *. . . treatise on the five orders* (1:4, 1850)

Paxton's magazine of botany (1849)

Smith (G), *Essay on . . . cottages* (1:3, 1850)

Sopwith, *A treatise on isometrical drawing* (1:2, 1838)

1835

Goodwin, *Cottage architecture* (1:1)

Jones (E), *Athenian; or, Grecian villas* (1:1)

Mitchell in *Prize-essays and transactions of the Highland and Agricultural Society* (1:1)

Robinson, *Vitruvius Britannicus . . . Hardwicke* (1:2, 1847)

Wilds, *Elementary . . . instructions* (1:1)

Wilson, *Helps* (1:2, 1842)

(continued)

Second and Later Editions

1833

Billington, *The architectural director* (1829, 2:4)

Gwilt, *Sciography* (1822, 3:5)

Hullmandel, *The art of drawing on stone* (1824, 2:4)

Hunt, *Half a dozen hints* (1825, 3:4)

Robinson, *Vitruvius Britannicus . . . Woburn* (1827, 2:3)

Thomson, *Retreats* (1827, 2:5)

1834

Billington, *The architectural director* (1829, 3:4)

Gwilt, *Rudiments of architecture* (1826, 2:4)

Loudon, *Encyclopaedia of . . . architecture* (1833, 2:14)

Nicholson, *The builder's and workman's . . . director* (1824, 4:11)

Nicholson, *The practical cabinet-maker* (1826, 4:7)

• Partington, *The British cyclopaedia* ⟨−1836⟩ (1833, 2:4)

Whittock, *The youth's . . . drawing book* (1833, 2:3)

1835

Aikin, *Designs for villas* (1808, 2:3)

Brown, *The principles of . . . perspective* (1815, 2:2)

Burgess, *An easy introduction to perspective* (1819, 4:4)

Busby, *A series of designs* (1808, 2:2)

Goodwin, *Rural architecture* (1833–1834 as *Domestic architecture*, 2:4)

Gwilt, *Rudiments of architecture* (1826, 3:4)

Hullmandel, *The art of drawing on stone* (1824, 3:4)

Kent (W), *The designs of Inigo Jones* (1727, 3:3)

Loudon, *Encyclopaedia of agriculture* (1825, 4:10)

Loudon, *Encyclopaedia of . . . architecture* (1833, 3:14)

Loudon, *Encyclopaedia of gardening* (1822, 8:16)

(continued)

First (or First Known) Editions

1838

Loudon, *The suburban gardener* (1:2, 1850)

Robinson, *A new series of designs* (1:3, 1853)

1839

Brooks, *Designs for cottage . . . architecture* (1:1)

Highland and Agricultural Society of Scotland in *Prize-essays*

1840

Burke, *British husbandry* v.3 (1:2, 1847)

Davy, *Architectural precedents* (1:4, 1841)

Jewitt, *Hand-book of practical perspective* (1:3, n.d.)

Prout, *Elementary drawing book* (1:2, 1858?)

Repton, *The landscape gardening* (1:1)

Ricauti, *Rustic architecture* (1:2, 1842)

Wightwick, *The palace of architecture* (1:1)

1841

Brown, *Domestic architecture* (1:3, 1852)

Cotton, *Short and simple letters* (1:1)

Deacon, *Elements of perspective* (1:2, 1853)

Fielding, *The art of engraving* (1:2, 1844)

Francis, *A series of original designs* (1:1)

Parker, *Villa rustica* bk.3 (1:2, 1848)

Robinson, *Vitruvius Britannicus . . . Castle Ashby* (1:1)

Taylor (A), *Designs for agricultural buildings* (1:1)

Wood (J, Jr), *A manual of perspective* (1:3, 1849)

Second and Later Editions

1838

Lugar, *The country gentleman's architect* (1807, 4:4)

Nash, *Illustrations of . . . Brighton* (1825 as *The royal pavilion at Brighton*, 2:2)

Nicholson, *The new . . . practical builder* (1823, 3:8)

Nicholson, *Rudiments of . . . perspective* (1822, 3:3)

• Partington, *The British cyclopaedia* (1833, 4:4)

Pasley, *Complete course of . . . geometry* (1814 as *Course of instruction*, 3:4)

Sopwith, *A treatise on isometrical drawing* (1834, 2:2)

1839

Gwilt, *Rudiments of architecture* (1826, 4:4)

Jopling, *The practice of isometrical perspective* (1833, 2:5)

• *The London encyclopaedia* (1829, 3:4)

Loudon, *Encyclopaedia of agriculture* (1825, 5:10)

Loudon, *Encyclopaedia of . . . architecture* (1833, 5:14)

• Mitchell, *The portable encyclopaedia* (1826, 5:5)

Nicholson, *. . . treatise on the five orders* (1834, 2:4)

Robinson, *A new series of designs* (1838, 2:3)

1840

Hullmandel, *Art of drawing on stone* (1824, 4:4)

Nicholson, *A treatise on projection* (1837, 2:2)

Parsey, *The science of vision* (1836 as *Perspective rectified*, 2:2)

Smith (James), *The panorama of science and art* (1815, 8:8)

Thomson, *Retreats* (1827, 4:5)

1841

Burke, *British husbandry* v.2 (1837, 2:4)

Davy, *Architectural precedents* [2 separate editions; see also Walker] (1840, 2:4 and 3:4)

Elsam, *The practical . . . price-book* (1825, 6:10)

Hunt, *Designs for parsonage houses* (1827, 2:2)

Hunt, *Exemplars of Tudor* (1830, 3:3)

Hunt, *Half a dozen hints* (1825, 4:4)

Laing, *Hints for dwellings* (1800, 6:6)

Loudon, *Encyclopaedia of . . . architecture* (1833, 6:14)

Walker, *Architectural precedents* (1840 and 1841 by Davy, 4:4)

First (or First Known) Editions

1842

• Brande, *A dictionary of science* (1:8, 1875)

Cottage Improvement Society, *Report* (1:1)

Gt. Brit., *Report . . . on buildings regulation* (1:2 and 2:2)

Gt. Brit., *Report . . . from . . . Poor Law Commissioners* (1:2 and 2:2)

Gt. Brit., *Sanitary inquiry:—England* (1:2 and 2:2)

Loudon, *First additional supplement* (1:1)

Ricauti, *Sketches for rustic work* (1:3, 1848)

n.d.

Undated first and sole editions not included in the above list:

Adam (W), *Vitruvius Scotius* (1:1)

Architectural recreations (1:3, 1830?)

The artists assistant in drawing (1:16, 1825)

Cottingham, *Working drawings for Gothic* (1:1)

Cunningham, *Designs for farm cottages* (1:1)

Domvile, *Eighteen designs* (1:2, n.d.)

Hassell, *Hassell's drawing magazine*

Jones (W), *The gentlemens or builders companion* (1:2, 1739)

Rawlins (TJ), *Elementary perspective* (1:1)

Searles, [*Designs and estimates*] (1:1)

Ware, *Designs of Inigo Jones* (1:2, 1743)

Wetten, *Designs for villas* (1:2, 1830?)

Whittock, *The British drawing-book* (1:1)

Second and Later Editions

1842

Brown, *Domestic architecture* (1841, 2:3)

Elsam, *The practical . . . price-book* (1825, 7:10)

Gwilt, *Sciography* (1822, 4:5)

Jopling, *The practice of isometrical perspective* (1833, 3:5)

Loudon, *Encyclopaedia of . . . architecture* (1833, 7:14)

Ricauti, *Rustic architecture* (1840, 2:2)

Wilson, *Helps* (1835, 2:2)

This appendix contains the names of printers, publishers, and booksellers that appear in the imprints of books included in the principal entries (Nos. 1–360) and in Appendix D (Nos. 468–493). To make this list representative of the architectural book trade, I have not included information from periodicals, general encyclopedias and dictionaries, or agricultural surveys prepared under the auspices of the Board of Agriculture.[1]

In the left column names and initials of printers, publishers, and sellers are given exactly as they appear in the bibliographic entries above. I have not "corrected" variations in spelling, so one name may appear in several versions (e.g., Ackerman, Ackermann, Akermann). In some instances I have added the notation [pr] following a name; this indicates that in the imprint the name appears in conjunction with "printed by," "printed and published by," "printer," or similar words. When the words "the Author" or the actual name of the author appears in the imprint, I have used the term "Author." The result is a convenient list of authors engaged in the printing, publication, and selling of their own books.

"No Imprint" indicates that no imprint appears on the title page. "No Information" indicates that I have no information concerning the imprint. "No Publisher" indicates that the imprint does not contain the name of a publisher, printer, or seller. These designations are gathered at the end of the list.

The entries in the right column represent the individual editions printed, published, or sold by the persons listed in the left column. Each edition is listed by author, short title, and date.

The computer program that I used for sorting these entries permitted certain irregularities in alphabetizing.[2] Since the number of such irregularities is minimal, and they cause little if any confusion, I have not attempted to reorder the entries manually.

A select bibliography of articles and monographs on publishers and printers listed below may be found in Chapter I, Section 1, Note 64, of the essay "The Literature of British Domestic Architecture, 1715–1842" above.

1. For a list of the excluded periodicals, see notes 23 and 24 of the Introduction. All general encyclopedias and dictionaries are marked in the short-title chronological list (Appendix E) by a bullet (•) preceding the entry. All agricultural reports are indicated in the same list by a diamond (♦) preceding the entry.

2. In alphabetizing titles the program did not ignore initial articles ("A," "An," or "The"). Thus in the listing of books published by R. Ackermann, *A Series of Views* by Samuel Prout precedes *Progressive Fragments* by the same author. In addition the program ordered all uppercase characters before lowercase "a" (resulting for example in "Longman, Hurst, Rees . . . " placed before "Longman, Hurst, and Co.").

Ackerman	Burgess, *An easy introduction to perspective*, 1828
Ackerman	Goodwin, *Domestic architecture* v. 1, 1833
Ackerman (R)	Prout, *Progressive fragments*, n.d.
Ackerman (R)	Varley, *A practical treatise*, 1820
Ackerman's Repository	Prout, *Bits for beginners*, 1817
Ackermann	Burgess, *An easy introduction to perspective*, 1819
Ackermann	Burgess, *An easy introduction to perspective*, 1822
Ackermann	Goodwin, *Domestic architecture* v. 2, 1834
Ackermann (R)	Brown, *The principles of . . . perspective*, 1815
Ackermann (R)	Dougall, *The cabinet of the arts*, 1821
Ackermann (R)	Elsam, *Hints for improving . . . the peasantry*, 1816
Ackermann (R)	Hullmandel, *The art of drawing on stone*, 1824
Ackermann (R)	Papworth, *Hints on ornamental gardening*, 1823
Ackermann (R)	Papworth, *Rural residences*, 1818
Ackermann (R)	Papworth, *Rural residences*, 1832
Ackermann (R)	Prout, *A series of easy lessons*, 1820
Ackermann (R)	Prout, *A series of views . . . north of England*, 1821
Ackermann (R)	Prout, *A series of views . . . west of England*, 1819
Ackermann (R)	Prout, *Progressive fragments*, 1817
Ackermann (R)	Prout, *Rudiments of landscape*, 1813
Ackermann (R)	Prout, *Rudiments of landscape*, 1814
Ackermann (R)	Prout, *Studies of cottages*, 1816
Ackermann (R)	Robertson (W), *Designs in architecture*, 1800
Ackermann (R)	Robertson (W), *Desseins d'architecture*, 1800
Ackermann (R)	Senefelder, *A . . . course of lithography*, 1819
Ackermann (R)	Stevens, *Picturesque sketches*, 1815
Ackermann (R)	Stevens, *Views of cottages*, 1815
Ackermann (R)	*Architectural recreations*, n.d.
Ackermann (R)	*Recreaciones arquitectonicas*, 1825
Ackermann & Co.	Fielding, *The art of engraving*, 1841
Ackermann and Co.	Burgess, *An easy introduction to perspective*, 1835
Ainsworth (J)	Billington, *The architectural director*, 1833
Akenhead	Curwen, *Hints on the economy*, 1808
Akermann (R) & Co.	Jones (E), *Athenian; or, Grecian villas*, 1835
Allen (M) [pr]	Cook, *The new builder's magazine*, n.d. [RIBA copy]
Allen (WH) & Co.	Fielding, *Synopsis of practical perspective*, 1836
Appleton and Co.	Nicholson, *An architectural . . . dictionary*, 1835
Arch (J and A)	Allen, *Colonies at home*, 1826
Arch (J and A)	Allen, *Colonies at home*, 1827
Arch (J and A)	Robinson, *Vitruvius Britannicus . . . Hardwicke*, 1835
Arch (J and A)	Robinson, *Vitruvius Britannicus . . . Hatfield*, 1833

Arch (J and A)	Robinson, *Vitruvius Britannicus . . . Woburn*, 1833
Arch (John and Arthur)	Allen, *Colonies at home*, 1828
Arch (John and Arthur)	Allen, *Colonies at home*, 1832
Archer	Curwen, *Hints on the economy*, 1808
Archer (J)	Sheraton, *The cabinet-maker*, 1802
Archer & Ward	Ferguson, *The art of drawing in perspective*, 1803
Aris (S) [pr]	Carwitham, *The . . . architectonick sector*, 1723
Aris (Sam) [pr]	Halfpenny, *The art of sound building* ed.1, 1725
Asperne (J)	Elsam, *An essay on rural architecture*, 1803
Atchley	Rider, *Principles of perspective*, 1849
Auld (William) [pr]	*The rudiments of architecture*, 1773
Author	Adam (R & J), *Works* v.1, 1778
Author	Adam (R & J), *Works* v.2, 1779
Author	Adam (R & J), *Works* v.2, 1786
Author	Aheron, *A general treatise*, 1754
Author	Barber, *Farm buildings*, 1802
Author	Bardwell, *The practice of painting*, 1756
Author	Bartlett, *An essay on design*, 1823
Author	Burgess, *An easy introduction to perspective*, 1819
Author	Burgess, *An easy introduction to perspective*, 1822
Author	Burgess, *An easy introduction to perspective*, 1828
Author	Burgess, *An easy introduction to perspective*, 1835
Author	Campbell, *Vitruvius Britannicus* v.1, 1715
Author	Campbell, *Vitruvius Britannicus* v.1, 1717
Author	Campbell, *Vitruvius Britannicus* v.2, 1717
Author	Campbell, *Vitruvius Britannicus* v.3 (2 different editions), 1725
Author	Castell, *The villas of the ancients* (128-page edition), 1728
Author	Castell, *The villas of the ancients* (35-page edition), 1728
Author	Chambers, *Designs of Chinese buildings*, 1757
Author	Chambers, *Desseins des edifices . . . chinois*, 1757
Author	Chambers, *Plans . . . and . . . views . . . at Kew*, 1763
Author	Chambers, *Treatise*, 1759
Author	Chambers, *Treatise*, 1768
Author	Clarke, *Practical perspective*, 1776
Author	Collis, *The builders' portfolio*, 1837
Author	Crunden, *Convenient and ornamental architecture*, 1767
Author	Crunden, *Convenient and ornamental architecture*, 1770
Author	Davenport, *Supplement*, 1829
Author	Davenport, *The amateur's perspective*, 1828
Author	Dearn, *Sketches . . . for public & private buildings*, 1806
Author	Decker, *Chinese architecture* pt.1, 1759
Author	Decker, *Chinese architecture* pt.2, 1759
Author	Decker, *Gothic architecture* pt.1, 1759
Author	Decker, *Gothic architecture* pt.2, 1759
Author	Edwards and Darly, *A new book of Chinese designs*, 1754
Author	Elsam, *An essay on rural architecture*, 1803
Author	Elsam, *Hints for improving . . . the peasantry*, 1816
Author	Fielding, *Synopsis of practical perspective*, 1829
Author	Fielding, *Synopsis of practical perspective*, 1836
Author	Fielding, *Synopsis of practical perspective*, 1843
Author	Fournier, *A treatise of . . . perspective*, 1761
Author	Fournier, *A treatise of . . . perspective*, 1764

Author	Gentleman, *Twelve designs*, 1757
Author	Goodwin, *Cottage architecture*, 1835
Author	Goodwin, *Domestic architecture* v.1, 1833
Author	Goodwin, *Domestic architecture* v.2, 1834
Author	Goodwin, *Rural architecture*, 1835
Author	Halfpenny, *The art of sound building* ed.1, 1725
Author	Hall (J), *Novel designs for cottages*, 1825
Author	Hassell, *The speculum*, 1809
Author	Hassell, *The speculum*, 1816
Author	Hayter, *An introduction to perspective*, 1813
Author	Hayter, *An introduction to perspective*, 1815
Author	Humphreys, *The Irish builder's guide*, 1813
Author	Jameson, *Thirty three designs*, 1765
Author	Jones (E), *Athenian; or, Grecian villas*, 1835
Author	Jones (R), *Every builder his own surveyor*, 1809
Author	Jones (W), *The gentlemens or builders companion*, 1739
Author	Jopling, *The practice of isometrical perspective*, 1833
Author	Kirby, *Dr. Brook Taylor's . . . perspective*, 1754
Author	Kirby, *Dr. Brook Taylor's . . . perspective*, 1755
Author	Kirby, *Dr. Brook Taylor's . . . perspective*, 1765
Author	Kirby, *Dr. Brook Taylor's . . . perspective*, 1768
Author	Kirby, *The perspective of architecture*, 1761
Author	Lewis, *Original designs* v.1, 1780
Author	Lewis, *Original designs* v.1, 1797
Author	Lewis, *Original designs* v.2, 1797
Author	Loudon, *A manual of cottage gardening*, 1830
Author	Loudon, *The suburban gardener*, 1830
Author	Malton (J), *A collection of designs*, 1802
Author	Malton (J), *An essay on British cottage arcitecture*, 1798
Author	Malton (J), *The young painter's maulstick*, 1800
Author	Malton (T), *A compleat treatise on perspective*, 1776
Author	Malton (T), *A compleat treatise on perspective*, 1778
Author	Malton (T), *A compleat treatise on perspective*, 1779
Author	Malton (T), *A complete treatise on perspective*, 1775
Author	Malton (T), *An appendix*, 1783
Author	Malton (T), *An appendix*, 1800
Author	Martin, *The principles of perspective*, 1770
Author	Middleton, *The architect and builder's miscellany*, 1799
Author	Middleton, *The architect and builder's miscellany*, 1812
Author	Mitchell (R), *Plans, and views*, 1801
Author	Morison, *Designs in perspective for villas*, 1794
Author	Morris, *Lectures* pt.2, 1736
Author	Morris, *Rural architecture*, 1750
Author	Morris, *The architectural remembrancer*, 1751
Author	Muller, *Elements of mathematics*, 1748
Author	Nicholson, *A treatise on practical perspective*, 1815
Author	Orme, *William Orme's rudiments*, 1802
Author	Overton, *Original designs of temples*, 1766
Author	Pain, *A supplement to the builder's golden rule*, 1782
Author	Pain, *Pain's British Palladio*, 1786
Author	Pain, *The builder's companion*, 1758
Author	Pain, *The builder's companion*, 1762

Author	Pain, *The builder's golden rule*, 1781
Author	Pain, *The builder's golden rule*, 1782
Author	Pain, *The builder's golden rule*, 1787
Author	Pain, *The practical house carpenter*, 1788
Author	Pain, *The practical house carpenter*, 1789
Author	Pain, *The practical house carpenter*, 1790
Author	Paine, *Plans . . . of the mansion-house*, 1751
Author	Paine, *Plans . . . of . . . gentlemen's houses* v.1, 1767
Author	Paine, *Plans . . . of . . . gentlemen's houses* v.1, 1783
Author	Paine, *Plans . . . of . . . gentlemen's houses* v.2, 1783
Author	Parker, *Villa rustica* bk.2, 1833
Author	Parker, *Villa rustica* bk.3, 1841
Author	Peacock, Οικιδια, 1785
Author	Plaw, *Rural architecture*, 1785
Author	Plaw, *Rural architecture*, 1790
Author	Rawlins, *Familiar architecture*, 1768
Author	Ricauti, *Rustic architecture*, 1840
Author	Richardson, *A series of original designs*, 1795
Author	Richardson, *New designs in architecture*, 1792
Author	Richardson, *The first part of a complete system*, 1794
Author	Richardson, *The new Vitruvius Britannicus* v.1, 1802
Author	Richardson, *The new Vitruvius Britannicus* v.1, 1810
Author	Richardson, *The new Vitruvius Britannicus* v.2, 1808
Author	Riou, *The Grecian orders*, 1768
Author	Robinson, *Vitruvius Britannicus . . . Hardwicke*, 1835
Author	Robinson, *Vitruvius Britannicus . . . Hatfield*, 1833
Author	Robinson, *Vitruvius Britannicus . . . Woburn*, 1833
Author	Rowland, *A general treatise*, 1732
Author	Rowland, *Mensuration*, 1739
Author	Sheraton, *The cabinet-maker*, 1793
Author	Sheraton, *The cabinet-maker*, 1794
Author	Sopwith, *Practical observations*, 1836
Author	Stitt, *The practical architect's ready assistant*, 1819
Author	Swan, *A collection of designs* v.1, n.d. [ca. 1770–1775?]
Author	Swan, *A collection of designs* v.2, n.d. [ca. 1770–1775?]
Author	Swan, *A collection of designs*, 1757
Author	Taylor (C), *A familiar treatise on perspective*, 1816
Author	Thomas, *Original designs*, 1783
Author	Trendall, *Original designs*, 1831
Author	Vardy, *Some designs*, 1744
Author	Varley, *A practical treatise*, 1815
Author	Ware, *Designs of Inigo Jones*, n.d.
Author	Wood (JG), *Six lectures*, 1804
Author	Wright, *Universal architecture* bk.1, 1755
Author	Wright, *Universal architecture* bk.2, 1758
Author	*The artist's assistant, in . . . mechanical sciences*, n.d.
Author	*The artists assistant in drawing* ed.2, n.d. [ca. 1764–1765]
Author	*The builder's magazine*, 1774
Author	*The builder's magazine*, 1776
Author	*The complete farmer*, 1766
Author	*The complete farmer*, 1767
Author [pr]	Smith (W), *An outline of architecture*, 1816
Author [pr]	Smith (W), *An outline of architecture*, 1820

Bagster	Hayter, *Treatise on perspective drawing*, 1844
Bagster (S)	Hayter, *An introduction to perspective*, 1832
Bagster (Samuel) and Sons	Hayter, *An introduction to perspective*, 1845
Baldwin (R)	Bradley, *A general treatise of agriculture*, 1757
Baldwin (R)	Ware, *A complete body of architecture*, 1756
Baldwin (R)	Ware, *A complete body of architecture*, 1767
Baldwin (R)	Ware, *A complete body of architecture*, 1768
Baldwin (R)	*The complete farmer*, 1769
Baldwin (R)	*The complete farmer*, 1777
Baldwin (R)	*The complete farmer*, 1793
Baldwin (R)	*The complete farmer*, 1807
Baldwin (Robert)	Burke, *British husbandry* v.1, 1847
Baldwin (Robert)	Burke, *British husbandry* v.2, 1848
Baldwin (Robert)	Burke, *British husbandry*, 1847
Baldwin & Co.	Pyne, *Nattes's practical geometry*, 1819
Baldwin and Cradock	Burke, *British husbandry* v.1, 1834
Baldwin and Cradock	Burke, *British husbandry* v.2, 1837
Baldwin and Cradock	Burke, *British husbandry* v.2, 1841
Baldwin and Cradock	Burke, *British husbandry* v.3, 1840
Baldwin, Cradock, and Joy	Smith (W), *An outline of architecture*, 1820
Barfield (J) [pr]	Nicholson, *A treatise on practical perspective*. 1815
Barfield (J) [pr]	Nicholson, *An architectural dictionary*, 1819
Barker (B)	Switzer, *Ichnographia rustica*, 1718
Barker (B)	Switzer, *The nobleman . . . recreation*, 1715
Barker (B and B)	Switzer, *Ichnographia rustica*, 1742
Barratt	Curwen, *Hints on the economy*, 1808
Bass (J) [pr]	Matthews, *Useful architecture*, 1812
Baxter (W) [pr]	Aldrich, *Elements of civil architecture*, 1818
Baxter (W) [pr]	Aldrich, *Elements of civil architecture*, 1824
Baynes	Sheraton, *The cabinet maker*, 1801
Baynes (C) [pr]	Hall (J), *Novel designs for cottages*, 1825
Baynes (W)	Sheraton, *The cabinet-maker*, 1802
Baynes (William)	Dearn, *Sketches . . . for public and private buildings*, 1814
Becket	Malton (T), *A compleat treatise on perspective*, 1776
Becket	Malton (T), *A compleat treatise on perspective*, 1778
Becket	Malton (T), *A compleat treatise on perspective*, 1779
Becket	Malton (T), *A complete treatise on perspective*, 1775
Becket	Malton (T), *An appendix*, 1783
Becket	Paine, *Plans . . . of . . . gentlemen's houses* v.1, 1783
Becket (T)	Adam (R & J), *Works* v.1, 1779 (individual title pages for nos. 1–4 only, 1773–1776)
Becket (T)	Chambers, *Plans . . . and . . . views . . . at Kew*, 1763
Beckett	Paine, *Plans . . . of . . . gentlemen's houses* v.2, 1783
Bell (Andrew)	Campbell, *Vitruvius Britannicus* v.1, 1715
Bell (Andrew)	Campbell, *Vitruvius Britannicus* v.1, 1717
Bell (Andrew)	Campbell, *Vitruvius Britannicus* v.2, 1717
Bell (W)	Langley, *Practical geometry*, 1726
Bennett (John)	Billington, *The architectural director*, 1834
Bensley (T) [pr]	Laing, *Hints for dwellings*, 1804
Bensley (T) [pr]	Lugar, *Architectural sketches*, 1805
Bensley (T) [pr]	Repton, *Designs for . . . Brighton*, 1808

Bensley (T) [pr]	Repton, *Observations*, 1803
Bensley (T) [pr]	Repton, *Observations*, 1805
Bensley (T) [pr]	Richardson, *The new Vitruvius Britannicus* v.1, 1810
Bensley (T) [pr]	Richardson, *The new Vitruvius Britannicus* v.2, 1808
Bensley (T) [pr]	Sheraton, *The cabinet-maker*, 1793
Bensley (T) [pr]	Sheraton, *The cabinet-maker*, 1794
Bensley (T) [pr]	Sheraton, *The cabinet-maker*, 1802
Bensley (T) and Son [pr]	Repton, *Fragments*, 1816
Bensley and Sons [pr]	Laing, *Plans, elevations, and sections*, 1818
Bentham (C)	Allen, *Colonies at home*, 1826
Bentham (C)	Allen, *Colonies at home*, 1827
Bettesworth (A)	Hoppus, *The gentleman's . . . repository*, 1738
Beygand (JG)	Robertson (W), *Desseins d'architecture*, 1800
Beygang (JB)	Robertson (W), *Designs in architecture*, 1800
Bickerton (W)	Morris, *An essay in defence*, 1728
Birt (Sam)	Halfpenny, *The art of sound building* ed.2, 1725
Black	Loudon, *Encyclopaedia of . . . architecture*, 1833
Black	Loudon, *Encyclopaedia of . . . architecture*, 1834
Black	Robertson (J), *Supplement to Loudon's manual*, 1833
Black (A & C)	Repton, *The landscape gardening*, 1840
Black (Adam)	Adam (W), *Vitruvius Scotius*, n.d.
Black (W)	Loudon, *The suburban gardener*, 1830
Black, Kingsbury, Parbury, and Allen	Hayter, *An introduction to perspective*, 1820
Black, Parry, and Co.	Hayter, *An introduction to perspective*, 1815
Blackie	Smith (G), *Essay on . . . cottages*, 1850
Blackie & Son	Smith (G), *Essay on . . . cottages*, 1834
Blackwood (William) & Sons	Cunningham, *Designs for farm cottages*, n.d.
Blythe (F)	*The complete farmer*, 1766
Bohn (H)	Ricauti, *Sketches for rustic work*, 1845
Bohn (H)	Robinson, *A new series of designs*, 1839
Bohn (H)	Robinson, *Designs for ornamental villas*, 1837
Bohn (Henry G)	Billington, *The architectural director*, 1848
Bohn (Henry G)	Goodwin, *Domestic architecture*, 1843
Bohn (Henry G)	Goodwin, *Domestic architecture*, 1850
Bohn (Henry G)	Gwilt, *Sciography*, 1866
Bohn (Henry G)	Hunt, *Architettura campestre*, 1844
Bohn (Henry G)	Hunt, *Designs for parsonage houses*, 1841
Bohn (Henry G)	Hunt, *Exemplars of Tudor*, 1841
Bohn (Henry G)	Hunt, *Half a dozen hints*, 1841
Bohn (Henry G)	Ricauti, *Sketches for rustic work*, 1848
Bohn (Henry G)	Robinson and Britton, *Vitruvius Britannicus*, 1847
Bohn (Henry G)	Robinson, *A new series of designs*, 1838
Bohn (Henry G)	Robinson, *A new series of designs*, 1853
Bohn (Henry G)	Robinson, *Designs for farm buildings* ed.2, 1837
Bohn (Henry G)	Robinson, *Designs for farm buildings* ed.3, 1837
Bohn (Henry G)	Robinson, *Designs for gate cottages, lodges*, 1837
Bohn (Henry G)	Robinson, *Designs for ornamental villas*, 1836
Bohn (Henry G)	Robinson, *Designs for ornamental villas*, 1853
Bohn (Henry G)	Robinson, *Rural architecture*, 1836
Bohn (Henry G)	Robinson, *Rural architecture*, 1850

Bohn (Henry G)	Robinson, *Village architecture*, 1837
Book and print-sellers in the United Kingdom	Prout, *A series of easy lessons*, 1820
Booker (J)	*The complete farmer*, 1807
Bookseller (any)	Ricauti, *Rustic architecture*, 1840
Booksellers	Atkinson (J), *An account of . . . New South Wales*, 1844
Booksellers	Bardwell, *The practice of painting*, 1782
Booksellers	Brooks, *Designs for cottage . . . architecture*, 1839
Booksellers	Burgess, *An easy introduction to perspective*, 1819
Booksellers	Burgess, *An easy introduction to perspective*, 1822
Booksellers	Cottage Improvement Society, *Report*, 1842
Booksellers	Dickson, *The farmer's companion*, 1813
Booksellers	Dougall, *The cabinet of the arts*, 1821
Booksellers	Parsey, *Perspective rectified*, 1836
Booksellers	Pyne, *Nattes's practical geometry*, 1819
Booksellers	Sheraton, *The cabinet-maker*, 1802
Booksellers	Smith (James), *The panorama of science and art*, 1840?
Booksellers	*The artist's assistant; or school*, 1807
Booksellers (principal)	Malton (J), *A collection of designs*, 1802
Booksellers (principal) of London, Edinburgh, and Dublin	Richardson, *A series of original designs*, 1795
Booksellers and instrument-makers	Jopling, *The practice of isometrical perspective*, 1833
Booksellers in Great Britain and Ireland	*The builder's magazine*, 1774
Booksellers in Great Britain and Ireland	*The builder's magazine*, 1776
Booksellers in Great Britain and Ireland	*The builder's magazine*, 1779
Booksellers in Great Britain and Ireland	*The builder's magazine*, 1788
Booksellers in all parts of the British Empire	Elsam, *The practical . . . price-book*, 1825
Booksellers in all parts of the British Empire	Elsam, *The practical . . . price-book*, 1826
Booksellers in all parts of the British Empire	Elsam, *The practical . . . price-book*, 1827
Booksellers in all parts of the British Empire	Elsam, *The practical . . . price-book*, 1828
Booksellers in the United Kingdom	Hassell, *The speculum*, 1809
Booksellers in the United Kingdom	Hassell, *The speculum*, 1816
Booksellers in the United Kingdom	Smith (James), *The panorama of science and art*, 1823
Booksellers in the United Kingdom	Smith (James), *The panorama of science and art*, 1825
Booksellers in the United Kingdom	Smith (James), *The panorama of science and art*, n.d. [ca. 1816–1822]
Booksellers in the United Kingdom	Smith (James), *The panorama of science and art*, n.d. [ca. 1823]
Booksellers in town and country	Adam (R & J), *Works* v.1, 1778
Booksellers in town and country	Adam (R & J), *Works* v.2, 1779
Booksellers in town and country	Adam (R & J), *Works* v.2, 1786

Booksellers of London & Westminster	Hoppus, *Andrea Palladio's architecture*, 1735
Booksellers of London and Westminster, and other parts of Great-Britain	Rowland, *Mensuration*, 1739
Booth, Stevenson and Co.	Curwen, *Hints on the economy*, 1808
Bowles	Halfpenny, *Twelve beautiful designs*, 1750
Bowles (Carington)	*Bowles's artist's assistant in drawing* ed.7, n.d.
Bowles (Carington)	*Bowles's artists assistant in drawing*, 1787
Bowles (Carington)	*Bowles's artists assistant in drawing*, n.d.
Bowles (Carington)	*The artists assistant in drawing* ed.2, n.d. [ca. 1764–1765]
Bowles (J)	*The artists assistant in drawing* ed.2, n.d. [ca. 1764–1765]
Bowles (Tho)	Halfpenny, *The art of sound building* ed. 1, 1725
Bowness	Curwen, *Hints on the economy*, 1808
Boydell	Paine, *Plans . . . of . . . gentlemen's houses* v.1, 1783
Boydell (J and J)	Repton, *Sketches and hints*, 1794
Boydell (John)	Bardwell, *The practice of painting*, 1773
Boydell and Co.	Repton, *Designs for . . . Brighton*, 1808
Boydell and Co.	Repton, *Designs for . . . Brighton*, n.d.
Boydell's	Paine, *Plans . . . of . . . gentlemen's houses* v.2, 1783
Brash & Reid	*The rudiments of architecture*, 1799
Brindley (I)	Halfpenny, *New designs for Chinese temples*, 1750
Brindley (J)	Garret, *Designs, and estimates*, 1747
Brindley (J)	Garret, *Designs, and estimates*, 1758
Brindley (J)	Halfpenny, *New designs for Chinese bridges*, 1751
Brindley (J)	Halfpenny, *Twelve beautiful designs*, 1750
Brindley (J)	Morris, *Lectures* pt.1, 1734
Brindley (J)	Morris, *Lectures* pt.2, 1736
Brindley (J)	Wood, *The origin of building*, 1741
Brindley (John)	Halfpenny, *A new and compleat system*, 1749
British Association for Promoting Co-operative Knowledge	Thompson, *Practical directions*, 1830
Brooke	Curwen, *Hints on the economy*, 1808
Brotherton	Paine, *Plans . . . of . . . gentlemen's houses* v.1, 1767
Brotherton and Sewell	Kirby, *Dr. Brook Taylor's . . . perspective*, 1768
Brown (A)	*The rudiments of architecture*, 1799
Browne (D)	Morris, *An essay in defence*, 1728
Browne (D)	Switzer, *Ichnographia rustica*, 1718
Browne (D)	Switzer, *Ichnographia rustica*, 1742
Buckland (J)	Swan, *A collection of designs* v.1, n.d. [ca. 1770–1775?]
Buckland (James)	Swan, *A collection of designs* v.2, n.d. [ca. 1770–1775?]
Building News	Chambers, *Treatise*, 1860
Bulmer (W) and Co. [pr]	Knight, *The landscape*, 1794
Bulmer (W) and Co. [pr]	Knight, *The landscape*, 1795
Bulmer (W) and Co. [pr]	Repton, *Sketches and hints*, 1794
Bulmer (W) and Co. [pr]	Richardson, *The new Vitruvius Britannicus* v.1, 1802
Bulmer (W) and Co. [pr]	Robertson (W), *Designs in architecture*, 1800
Bulmer (W) and Co. [pr]	Sinclair, *A sketch of the improvements*, 1803
Bulmer (W) and Co. [pr]	Sinclair, *Hints regarding . . . property*, 1802
Burnet (J)	*The rudiments of architecture*, 1799
Butler (John) [pr]	Aheron, *A general treatise*, 1754
Bye and Law [pr]	Wood (JG), *Six lectures*, 1804

Cadell	Chambers, *Treatise*, 1768
Cadell Jun. and Davies	Kent (N), *Hints to Gentlemen*, 1799
Cadell (T)	Bardwell, *The practice of painting*, 1773
Cadell (T)	Chambers, *Treatise*, 1791
Cadell (T)	Ferguson, *The art of drawing in perspective*, 1775
Cadell (T)	*The complete farmer*, 1777
Cadell (T)	*The complete farmer*, 1793
Cadell (T) and Davies (W)	Wood (JG), *Lectures*, 1809
Cadell (T) and Davies (W)	Wood (JG), *Lectures*, 1844
Cadell (T, Jun) and Davies (W)	Sinclair, "Hints regarding . . . property" in *Essays*, 1802
Cadell (T, Jun) and Davies (W)	Sinclair, "Hints regarding . . . property" in *Essays*, 1818
Cadell and Davies	Repton, *Designs for . . . Brighton*, 1808
Cadell and Davies	Repton, *Designs for . . . Brighton*, n.d.
Cadell and Davies	*The complete farmer*, 1807
Calkin and Budd	Goodwin, *Domestic architecture* v.1, 1833
Calkin and Budd	Goodwin, *Domestic architecture* v.2, 1834
Carey and Lea	Loudon, *Encyclopaedia of . . . architecture*, 1833
Carey and Lea	Loudon, *Encyclopaedia of . . . architecture*, 1834
Carey and Lea	Robertson (J), *Supplement to Loudon's manual*, 1833
Carpenter	Robinson, *Designs for ornamental villas*, 1829
Carpenter (J)	Gyfford, *Designs for elegant cottages*, 1806
Carpenter (J)	Gyfford, *Designs for small picturesque cottages*, 1807
Carpenter (J and T)	Malton (J), *A collection of designs*, 1802
Carpenter (J and T)	Mitchell (R), *Plans, and views*, 1801
Carpenter (James)	Jones (R), *Every builder his own surveyor*, 1809
Carpenter (James)	Ricauti, *Rustic architecture*, 1842
Carpenter (James) and Son	Jackson, *Designs for villas*, 1828
Carpenter (James) and Son	Jackson, *Designs for villas*, 1829
Carpenter (James) and Son	Legh, *The music of the eye*, 1831
Carpenter (James) and Son	Parker, *Villa rustica* bk.1, 1832
Carpenter (James) and Son	Robinson, *Designs for farm buildings*, 1830
Carpenter (James) and Son	Robinson, *Designs for ornamental villas*, 1827
Carpenter (James) and Son	Robinson, *Designs. For ornamental villas*, 1830
Carpenter (James) and Son	Robinson, *Rural architecture*, 1826
Carpenter (James) and Son	Robinson, *Rural architecture*, 1828
Carpenter (James) and Son	Robinson, *Village architecture*, 1830
Carpenter (James) and Son	Robinson, *Vitruvius Britannicus . . . Woburn*, 1827
Carpenter (James) and Son	Trendall, *Original designs*, 1831
Carpenter (James) and Son	Wetten, *Designs for villas*, 1830?
Carpenter (James) and Son	Wetten, *Designs for villas*, n.d.

Carpenter & Son	Fielding, *Synopsis of practical perspective*, 1829
Carpenter and Co.	Malton (J), *The young painter's maulstick*, 1800
Carpenter and Co.	Malton (T), *An appendix*, 1800
Carpenter's	Malton (J), *An essay on British cottage architecture*, 1804
Carvill	Loudon, *Encyclopaedia of . . . architecture*, 1833
Carvill	Loudon, *Encyclopaedia of . . . architecture*, 1834
Carvill	Robertson (J), *Supplement to Loudon's manual*, 1833
Cawthorn (John) [pr]	Dearn, *Sketches . . . for public & private buildings*, 1806
Caxton	Nicholson, *The practical cabinet maker*, 1843
Caxton Press	Nicholson, *Encyclopedia of architecture*, 1852
Caxton Press	Nicholson, *The practical cabinet-maker*, 1846
Caxton Press	Smith (James), *The panorama of science and art*, 1816
Caxton Press	Smith (James), *The panorama of science and art*, 1823
Caxton Press	Smith (James), *The panorama of science and art*, 1825
Caxton Press	Smith (James), *The panorama of science and art*, 1840?
Caxton Press	Smith (James), *The panorama of science and art*, n.d. [ca. 1816–1822]
Caxton Press	Smith (James), *The panorama of science and art*, n.d. [ca. 1823]
Chappelle (Henry)	Badeslade and Rocque, *Vitruvius Brittanicus*, 1739
Charles (James) [pr]	Humphreys, *The Irish builder's guide*, 1813
Charles (James) [pr]	Stitt, *The practical architect's ready assistant*, 1819
Charlwood	Loudon, *A manual of cottage gardening*, 1830
Charlwood (G)	Loudon, *Illustrations of landscape-gardening* pt.1, 1830
Charlwood (G)	Loudon, *Illustrations of landscape-gardening* pt.2, 1831
Cheyne (Stewart)	Ferguson, *The art of drawing in perspective*, 1803
Clark (John) [pr]	Newton, *The architecture of . . . Vitruvius*, 1771
Clarke (I and W)	Clarke, *Practical perspective*, 1794
Clarke and Reddish	Curwen, *Hints on the economy*, 1808
Clarke and Sons	*The complete farmer*, 1807
Clay (T)	Pickett, *Twenty-four plates*, 1812
Clements (Henry)	Campbell, *Vitruvius Britannicus* v.1, 1715
Clements (Henry)	Campbell, *Vitruvius Britannicus* v.1, 1717
Clements (Henry)	Campbell, *Vitruvius Britannicus* v.2, 1717
Clowes (W) and Sons [pr]	Gt. Brit., *Report . . . from . . . Poor Law Commissioners*, 1842
Clowes (W) and Sons [pr]	Gt. Brit., *Sanitary inquiry:—England*, 1842
Coke (W)	*The rudiments of architecture*, 1799
Cole (B)	Hoppus, *The gentleman's . . . repository*, 1738
Cole (B)	Hoppus, *The gentleman's . . . repository*, 1748
Cole (B)	Hoppus, *The gentleman's . . . repository*, 1760
Cole (Benj)	Hoppus, *Andrea Palladio's architecture*, 1735
Cole (Benjamin)	Halfpenny, *The art of sound building* ed.1, 1725
Cole (Benjamin)	Hoppus, *The gentleman's . . . repository*, 1737
Cole (Benjn)	Hoppus, *Andrea Palladio's architecture*, 1736
Cole (J)	Rowland, *A general treatise*, 1732
Cole (J)	Rowland, *Mensuration*, 1739
Collins (B)	Ware, *A complete body of architecture*, 1767
Collins (B)	Ware, *A complete body of architecture*, 1768
Colnaghi	Davenport, *Supplement*, 1829
Colnaghi	Davenport, *The amateur's perspective*, 1828
Colnaghi & Co.	Soane, *Designs for public and private buildings*, 1828
Colyer (E) [pr]	Parker, *Villa rustica* bk.3, 1841
Compton (James) [pr]	Nicholson, *The builder & workman's new director*, 1824
Constable and Co.	Curwen, *Hints on the economy*, 1808

Cooke (HT)	Robinson, *Vitruvius Britannicus . . . Castle Ashby*, 1841
Cooke (HT)	Robinson, *Vitruvius Britannicus . . . Warwick Castle*, 1844
Coombe	Curwen, *Hints on the economy*, 1808
Cooper (J)	Hassell, *[Cottage designs]*, 1820
Cooper and Graham [pr]	Lewis, *Original designs* v.1, 1797
Cooper and Graham [pr]	Lewis, *Original designs* v.2, 1797
Coote (J)	*The complete farmer*, 1766
Cornish (James)	Jewitt, *Hand-book of practical perspective*, 1847
Cornish (James) & Sons	Jewitt, *Hand-book of practical perspective*, n.d.
Craighton (W) [pr]	Kirby, *Dr. Brook Taylor's . . . perspective*, 1754
Craighton (W) [pr]	Kirby, *Dr. Brook Taylor's . . . perspective*, 1755
Creech	*The artist's assistant; or school*, 1801
Crosby (B) and Co.	Curwen, *Hints on agricultural subjects*, 1809
Crosby (B) and Co.	Curwen, *Hints on the economy*, 1808
Crosby (B) and Co.	*The complete farmer*, 1807
Cross (J)	Atkinson (J), *An account of . . . New South Wales*, 1844
Cross (J) [pr]	Atkinson (J), *An account of . . . New South Wales*, 1826
Crowder (S)	Bardwell, *The practice of painting*, 1773
Crowder (S)	Hale, *A compleat body of husbandry* v.4, 1759
Crowder (S)	Hoppus, *The gentleman's . . . repository*, 1760
Crowder (S)	*The complete farmer*, 1766
Crowder (S)	*The complete farmer*, 1769
Crowder (S)	*The complete farmer*, 1777
Crowder (S) and Co.	Hale, *A compleat body of husbandry* v.1–3, 1759
Crowder (S) and Woodgate (H)	Hale, *A compleat body of husbandry*, 1756
Cust's	Plaw, *Rural architecture*, 1790
Cuthell (J) and Martin	*The complete farmer*, 1807
Darton and Harvey	Daniel, *A familiar treatise*, 1807
Darton, Harvey, and Darton	Daniel, *A familiar treatise*, 1810
Davey (P) and Law (B)	Bradley, *A general treatise of agriculture*, 1757
Davies	Paine, *Plans . . . of . . . gentlemen's houses* v.1, 1767
Davies	Paine, *Plans . . . of . . . gentlemen's houses* v.1, 1783
Davies (T)	Bardwell, *The practice of painting*, 1773
Davies (T)	Kirby, *Dr. Brook Taylor's . . . perspective*, 1765
Davies (T)	Kirby, *Dr. Brook Taylor's . . . perspective*, 1768
Davies (T)	Kirby, *The perspective of architecture*, 1761
Davies (T)	Noble, *The elements of linear perspective*, 1771
Davis (L)	Bardwell, *The practice of painting*, 1773
Davis (L)	Ware, *A complete body of architecture*, 1756
Davis (L) and Reymers (C)	Ware, *A complete body of architecture*, 1767
Davis (L) and Reymers (C)	Ware, *A complete body of architecture*, 1768
Davis and Dickson	Nicholson, *A treatise on practical perspective*, 1815
Davison (Thomas) [pr]	Wilkins, *The civil architecture of Vitruvius*, 1812
Day (John)	Nicholson, *The builder & workman's new director*, 1824
Dean	Deacon, *Elements of perspective*, 1853
Debrett (J)	Middleton, *The architect and builder's miscellany*, 1799
Deighton (J)	Cresswell, *The elements of linear perspective*, 1811
Denham & Dick	Ferguson, *The art of drawing in perspective*, 1802
Denham & Dick	Ferguson, *The art of drawing in perspective*, 1803

Dickinson	Burgess, *An easy introduction to perspective*, 1819
Dickinson	Burgess, *An easy introduction to perspective*, 1822
Dickinson	Burgess, *An easy introduction to perspective*, 1828
Dickinson	Burgess, *An easy introduction to perspective*, 1835
Dickson (J)	*The rudiments of architecture*, 1799
Dickson (James)	*The rudiments of architecture*, 1778
Diggens (J) [pr]	Papworth, *Hints on ornamental gardening*, 1823
Diggens (J) [pr]	Papworth, *Rural residences*, 1818
Dilly	Malton (T), *A compleat treatise on perspective*, 1778
Dilly	Malton (T), *A compleat treatise on perspective*, 1779
Dilly	Malton (T), *An appendix*, 1783
Dilly (C)	Peacock, Οικιδια, 1785
Dilly (E)	Bradley, *A general treatise of agriculture*, 1757
Dixwell (J) [pr]	Chambers, *Treatise*, 1768
Dixwell (J) [pr]	Riou, *The Grecian orders*, 1768
Dodsley	Chambers, *Designs of Chinese buildings*, 1757
Dodsley	Kirby, *The perspective of architecture*, 1761
Dodsley	Malton (T), *A compleat treatise on perspective*, 1776
Dodsley	Malton (T), *A complete treatise on perspective*, 1775
Dodsley	Paine, *Plans . . . of . . . gentlemen's houses* v.1, 1767
Dodsley (J)	Kent (N), *Hints to gentlemen*, 1775
Dodsley (J)	Kent (N), *Hints to gentlemen*, 1776
Dodsley (J)	Kent (N), *Hints to gentlemen*, 1793
Dodsley (J)	Kirby, *Dr. Brook Taylor's . . . perspective*, 1765
Dodsley (J)	Newton, *The architecture of . . . Vitruvius*, 1771
Dodsley (J and R)	Chambers, *Treatise*, 1759
Dodsley (R)	Chambers, *Treatise*, 1768
Dodsley (R)	Wood, *The origin of building*, 1741
Dodsley (R and J)	Bardwell, *The practice of painting*, 1756
Dodsley (R and J)	Chambers, *Plans . . . and . . . views . . . at Kew*, 1763
Dodsley (R and J)	Kirby, *Dr. Brook Taylor's . . . perspective*, 1755
Donaldson (John)	*The rudiments of architecture*, 1775
Drakard	Curwen, *Hints on the economy*, 1808
Drury	Curwen, *Hints on the economy*, 1808
Drury (TR) [pr]	Jones (E), *Athenian; or, Grecian villas*, 1835
Dulau (A) et Co. [pr]	Robertson (W), *Desseins d'architecture*, 1800
Duncan (J) & Son	*The rudiments of architecture*, 1799
Dunn	Curwen, *Hints on the economy*, 1808
Durham	Chambers, *Treatise*, 1768
Eddowes	Parker (T), *Plans, specifications, estimates*, 1813
Ede (Robert Best)	Robinson, *Vitruvius Britannicus . . . Warwick Castle*, 1844
Edgerton's Military Library	Elsam, *An essay on rural architecture*, 1803
Editor	Loudon, *The villa gardener*, 1850
Editor	Repton, *The landscape gardening*, 1840
Editor	Waistell, *Designs for agricultural buildings*, 1827
Editor	Wyatt, *A collection of architectural designs* no.1, 1800
Editor	Wyatt, *A collection of architectural designs* no.2, 1800
Editor	Wyatt, *A collection of architectural designs* no.3, 1801
Edlin (Thomas)	Leoni, *Some designs*, 1726
Edwards (T)	Society for . . . Oswestry, *First report*, 1813
Edwards (T) [pr]	Parker (T), *Plans, specifications, estimates*, 1813

Egerton	Davenport, *Supplement*, 1829
Egerton	Davenport, *The amateur's perspective*, 1828
Egerton	Hayter, *An introduction to perspective*, 1815
Egerton (J and T)	Aldrich, *Elements of civil architecture*, 1789
Egerton (T)	Pasley, *A complete course of . . . geometry*, 1822
Egerton (T and J)	Middleton, *Picturesque and architectural views*, 1793
Egerton's Military Library	Malton (J), *An essay on British cottage architecture*, 1798
Egerton's Military Library	Malton (J), *An essay on British cottage architecture*, 1804
Elliot (Charles)	*The rudiments of architecture*, 1778
Elliot (William)	Jopling, *The practice of isometrical perspective*, 1833
Elmsly (P)	Aldrich, *Elements of civil architecture*, 1789
Elmsly (P)	Newton, *Commentaires sur Vitruve*, 1780
Elmsly (P)	Newton, *The architecture of . . . Vitruvius* v.1, 1791
Elmsly (P)	Newton, *The architecture of . . . Vitruvius* v.2, 1791
Elmsly (Peter)	Adam (R & J), *Works* v.1, 1778
Elmsly (Peter)	Adam (R & J), *Works* v.2, 1779
Elmsly (Peter)	Adam (R & J), *Works* v.2, 1786
Elmsly and Bremner	Pitt, *An address*, 1797
Evans	Elsam, *An essay on rural architecture*, 1803
Evans (T)	Mitchell (R), *Plans, and views*, 1801
Ewing (G and A)	Gentleman, *Twelve designs*, 1757
Exshaw (John)	Hale, *A compleat body of husbandry*, 1757
Fairbairn (J)	*The rudiments of architecture*, 1799
Farley (S and F) [pr]	Wood, *The origin of building*, 1741
Faulder	Middleton, *The architect and builder's miscellany*, 1799
Faulder (R)	Aldrich, *Elements of civil architecture*, 1789
Faulder (R)	Lewis, *Original designs* v.1, 1797
Faulder (R)	Middleton, *Picturesque and architectural views*, 1793
Faulder (R)	Mitchell (R), *Plans, and views*, 1801
Faulder (R)	Newton, *The architecture of . . . Vitruvius* v.1, 1791
Faulder (R)	Newton, *The architecture of . . . Vitruvius* v.2, 1791
Faulder (R)	Wood (JG), *Six lectures*, 1804
Faulder (R)	Wyatt, *A collection of architectural designs* no.3, 1801
Faulkner	Burgess, *An easy introduction to perspective*, 1819
Faulkner	Burgess, *An easy introduction to perspective*, 1822
Faulkner (T) [pr]	Collis, *The builders' portfolio*, 1837
Fayram (Francis)	Halfpenny, *The art of sound building* ed.1, 1725
Field (T)	Bradley, *A general treatise of agriculture*, 1757
Fisher	Nicholson, *The practical cabinet maker*, 1828
Fisher (H), Son	Nicholson, *The practical cabinet maker*, 1843
Fisher (H), Son, & Co.	Nicholson, *The practical cabinet-maker* (2 different editions), 1826
Fisher (H), Son, & Co.	Nicholson, *The practical cabinet-maker*, 1836
Fisher (H), Son, & Co.	Nicholson, *The practical cabinet-maker*, [1834?]
Fisher (H), Son, & Co.	Smith (James), *The panorama of science and art*, 1840?
Fisher (Henry) [pr]	Smith (James), *The panorama of science and art*, 1823
Fisher (Henry) [pr]	Smith (James), *The panorama of science and art*, 1825
Fisher (Henry) [pr]	Smith (James), *The panorama of science and art*, n.d. [ca. 1816–1822]
Fisher (Henry) [pr]	Smith (James), *The panorama of science and art*, n.d. [ca. 1823]
Fisher, Son, & Co.	Nicholson, *The practical cabinet-maker*, 1846
Flint (W) [pr]	Hassell, *The speculum*, 1809
Forsyth (I)	*The rudiments of architecture*, 1799
Foster (A)	Wilson, *Helps*, 1842

Foster (Arthur) [pr]	Wilson, *Helps*, 1835
Foster (George)	Badeslade and Rocque, *Vitruvius Brittanicus*, 1739
Foster (William)	Nicholson, *The builder & workman's new director*, 1824
Fourdrinier	Ripley, *The plans . . . of Houghton*, 1760
Fox (J and J)	Switzer, *Ichnographia rustica*, 1742
Francklin (R) [pr]	Kirby, *The perspective of architecture*, 1761
Francklin and Bunce [pr]	Kirby, *Dr. Brook Taylor's . . . perspective*, 1765
Fraser (James)	Wightwick, *The palace of architecture*, 1840
Fry (Edmund)	Allen, *Colonies at home*, 1828
Fry (Edmund)	Allen, *Colonies at home*, 1832
Fullarton (A) and Co.	Nicholson, *The builder's and workman's new director*, 1845
Fullarton (A) and Co.	Nicholson, *The builder's and workman's new director*, 1848
Fullarton (A) and Co.	Nicholson, *The builder's and workman's new director*, 1853
Fullarton (A) and Co.	Nicholson, *The builder's and workman's new director*, 1856
Fullarton (A) and Co.	Nicholson, *The builder's and workman's new director*, 1865
Fuller	Burgess, *An easy introduction to perspective*, 1828
Fuller (J)	Bradley, *A general treatise of agriculture*, 1757
Fuller's, Temple of Fancy	Burgess, *An easy introduction to perspective*, 1835
Gale and Curtis	Jones (R), *Every builder his own surveyor*, 1809
Gardiner (T)	Atkinson, *Views of picturesque cottages*, 1805
Gardiner and Son	Nicholson, *A treatise on practical perspective*, 1815
Gibbings and Company	Sheraton, *The cabinet-maker*, 1895
Gibbons	Curwen, *Hints on the economy*, 1808
Gilbert (R & R) [pr]	Taylor (C), *A familiar treatise on perspective*, 1816
Gleed (J)	Kirby, *Dr. Brook Taylor's . . . perspective*, 1755
Goll (Henry)	Nicholson, *The builder & workman's new director*, 1824
Gosling (F)	Switzer, *Ichnographia rustica*, 1742
Gosling (R)	Switzer, *Ichnographia rustica*, 1718
Gosnell (S) [pr]	Laing, *Hints for dwellings*, 1800
Gosnell (S) [pr]	Laing, *Hints for dwellings*, 1801
Gosnell (S) [pr]	Laing, *Hints for dwellings*, 1818
Gosnell (S) [pr]	Plaw, *Sketches*, 1800
Grant and Bolton	Taylor (A), *Designs for agricultural buildings*, 1841
Gray and Bowen	Loudon, *Encyclopaedia of . . . architecture*, 1833
Gray and Bowen	Loudon, *Encyclopaedia of . . . architecture*, 1834
Gray and Bowen	Robertson (J), *Supplement to Loudon's manual*, 1833
Green (J)	Kirby, *Dr. Brook Taylor's . . . perspective*, 1755
Greene (C) [pr]	Allen, *Colonies at home*, 1826
Greene (C) [pr]	Allen, *Colonies at home*, 1827
Greene (Charles) [pr]	Allen, *Colonies at home*, 1828
Greene (Charles) [pr]	Allen, *Colonies at home*, 1832
Gretton (J)	Chambers, *Treatise*, 1759
Gretton (J)	Kirby, *The perspective of architecture*, 1761
Griffin (Richard) and Company	Prout, *Elementary drawing-book*, 1858?
Griffin (William) [pr]	Newton, *The architecture of . . . Vitruvius*, 1771
Griffiths (V) [pr]	Malton (J), *The young painter's maulstick*, 1800
Griffiths (V) [pr]	Malton (T), *An appendix*, 1800
Groombridge (Richard)	Nicholson, *A treatise on projection*, 1840
Gt. Brit. HMSO	Gt. Brit., *Report . . . from . . . Poor Law Commissioners*, 1842
Gt. Brit. HMSO	Gt. Brit., *Sanitary inquiry:—England*, 1842
Gt. Brit. Parliament. House of Commons	Gt. Brit., *Report . . . on buildings regulation*, 1842

Gt. Brit. Parliament. House of Lords	Gt. Brit., *Report . . . from . . . Poor Law Commissioners*, 1842
Gt. Brit. Parliament. House of Lords	Gt. Brit., *Report . . . on buildings regulation*, 1842
Gt. Brit. Parliament. House of Lords	Gt. Brit., *Sanitary inquiry:—England*, 1842
Haberkorn (J) [pr]	Brettingham, *The plans . . . of Holkham*, 1761
Haberkorn (J) [pr]	Chambers, *Desseins des edifices . . . chinois*, 1757
Haberkorn (J) [pr]	Chambers, *Plans . . . and . . . views . . . at Kew*, 1763
Haberkorn (J) [pr]	Chambers, *Treatise*, 1759
Hall	Curwen, *Hints on the economy*, 1808
Hall (B)	Robinson, *Vitruvius Britannicus . . . Castle Ashby*, 1841
Hall (B)	Robinson, *Vitruvius Britannicus . . . Warwick Castle*, 1844
Hannaford (PA)	Ricauti, *Sketches for rustic work*, 1842
Hansard (Luke) [pr]	Edwards, *A practical treatise of perspective*, 1803
Harding (J)	Barber, *Farm buildings*, 1805
Harding (J)	Brown, *The principles of . . . perspective*, 1815
Harding (J)	Gyfford, *Designs for elegant cottages*, 1806
Harding (J)	Gyfford, *Designs for small picturesque cottages*, 1807
Harding (J)	Loudon, *Designs for laying out farms*, 1811
Harding (John)	Gandy, *Designs for cottages*, 1805
Harding (John)	Gandy, *The rural architect*, 1805
Harding (John)	Gandy, *The rural architect*, 1806
Harding (John)	Loudon, *A treatise on . . . country residences*, 1812
Harding (John)	Loudon, *Observations on laying out farms*, 1812
Harjette (T) [pr]	Burgess, *An easy introduction to perspective*, 1822
Harrison (L) [pr]	Prout, *A series of easy lessons*, 1820
Harrison (L) [pr]	Prout, *Progressive fragments*, 1817
Harrison (L) [pr]	*Architectural recreations*, n.d.
Harrison (L) and Leigh (JC) [pr]	Prout, *Rudiments of landscape*, 1813
Harrison (L) and Leigh (JC) [pr]	Prout, *Rudiments of landscape*, 1814
Harrison (L) and Leigh (JC) [pr]	Stevens, *Views of cottages*, 1815
Hartnell (J) [pr]	Cook, *The new builder's magazine*, n.d. [V&A copy]
Harvey and Darton	Allen, *Colonies at home*, 1826
Harvey and Darton	Allen, *Colonies at home*, 1827
Harvey and Darton	Daniel, *A familiar treatise*, 1821
Hatchard	Burgess, *An easy introduction to perspective*, 1819
Hatchard	Burgess, *An easy introduction to perspective*, 1822
Hatchard	Parker (T), *Plans, specifications, estimates*, 1813
Hatchard (J)	Davenport, *Supplement*, 1829
Hatchard (J)	Davenport, *The amateur's perspective*, 1828
Hatchard (J) and Sons	Wilson, *Helps*, 1835
Hatchard and Co.	Allen, *Colonies at home*, 1828
Hatchard and Co.	Allen, *Colonies at home*, 1832
Hatchard and Son	Burgess, *An easy introduction to perspective*, 1828
Hatchard and Son	Francis, *A series of original designs*, 1841
Hatchards	Allen, *Colonies at home*, 1826
Hatchards	Allen, *Colonies at home*, 1827
Hawes, Clarke and Collins	*The complete farmer*, 1769

Hayes (J) [pr]	Pickett, *Twenty-four plates*, 1812
Hazard and Co.	Curwen, *Hints on the economy*, 1808
Heath	Halfpenny, *Twelve beautiful designs*, 1750
Heath (T)	Langley, *A sure quide*, 1729
Heath (Thomas)	Carwitham, *The . . . architectonick sector*, 1723
Heath (Thomas)	Carwitham, *The . . . architectonick sector*, 1733
Heaton	Curwen, *Hints on the economy*, 1808
Henderson (C)	Bradley, *A general treatise of agriculture*, 1757
Hetherington	Curwen, *Hints on the economy*, 1808
Hewett	Robinson, *Vitruvius Britannicus . . . Castle Ashby*, 1841
Hewett	Robinson, *Vitruvius Britannicus . . . Warwick Castle*, 1844
Hill	Curwen, *Hints on the economy*, 1808
Hill (P)	*The rudiments of architecture*, 1799
Hinton (Isaac Taylor)	Whittock, *The Oxford drawing book*, 1829
Hitch (C)	Gibbs, *A book of architecture*, 1739
Hitch (C)	Hoppus, *The gentleman's . . . repository*, 1738
Hitch (C)	Hoppus, *The gentleman's . . . repository*, 1748
Hitch (C)	Wood, *The origin of building*, 1741
Hitch (C) and Hawes (L)	Hoppus, *The gentleman's . . . repository*, 1760
Hitch and Hawes	Swan, *A collection of designs*, 1757
Hodges (J)	Hale, *A compleat body of husbandry*, 1756
Hodges (J)	Hoppus, *The gentleman's . . . repository*, 1738
Hodges (J)	Hoppus, *The gentleman's . . . repository*, 1748
Hodges (J)	Ware, *A complete body of architecture*, 1756
Hodges (James)	Hoppus, *The gentleman's . . . repository*, 1737
Hodgson	Curwen, *Hints on the economy*, 1808
Hodgson (T and J)	Nicholson, *A treatise on projection*, 1837
Hodson (Francis) [pr]	Cresswell, *The elements of linear perspective*, 1811
Hogg (H) & Co.	Cook, *The new builder's magazine*, n.d. [RIBA copy]
Hogg (H) & Co.	Cook, *The new builder's magazine*, n.d. [V&A copy]
Holdsworth	Whittock, *Oxford drawing book*, 1827
Hood (T) and Co. [pr]	Loudon, *Designs for laying out farms*, 1811
Hookham and Carpenter	Elsam, *An essay on rural architecture*, 1803
Hookham and Carpenter	Malton (J), *An essay on British cottage architecture*, 1798
Hooper (S)	Bardwell, *The practice of painting*, 1773
Horsefield (R)	Kirby, *Dr. Brook Taylor's . . . perspective*, 1765
Howe	Loudon, *Encylcopaedia of . . . architecture*, 1833
Howe	Loudon, *Encylcopaedia of . . . architecture*, 1834
Howe	Robertson (J), *Supplement to Loudon's manual*, 1833
Howlett and Brimmer [pr]	Repton, *Designs for . . . Brighton*, n.d.
Hullmandel (C)	Hullmandel, *The art of drawing on stone*, 1824
Hullmandel (C) [pr]	Cottingham, *Working drawings for Gothic*, n.d.
Hullmandel (C) [pr]	Hall (J), *Novel designs for cottages*, 1825
Hullmandel (C) [pr]	Meason, *On the landscape architecture*, 1828
Hurst Chance & Co.	Whitwell, *Description of an architectural model*, 1830
Hurst, Chance, and Co.	Rudge, *An introduction to . . . painting*, 1828
Innys (W)	Wood, *The origin of building*, 1741
Innys (W) and Manby (R)	Gibbs, *A book of architecture*, 1739
Innys (W and J)	Langley, *Practical geometry*, 1726
Jackson (P)	Nicholson, *The practical cabinet maker*, 1843
Jackson (Peter)	Nicholson, *Encyclopedia of architecture*, 1852
Jeffery (E)	Middleton, *The architect and builder's miscellany*, 1799

Jeffery (Edward)	Middleton, *Picturesque and architectural views*, 1793
Johnson (J)	Curwen, *Hints on agricultural subjects*, 1809
Johnson (J)	*The art of drawing*, 1791
Johnson (J)	*The art of drawing*, 1797
Johnson (Robert)	Nicholson, *The builder & workman's new director*, 1824
Johnston (W)	Bradley, *A general treatise of agriculture*, 1757
Jollie and Son	Curwen, *Hints on the economy*, 1808
Jones (M)	Hassell, *The speculum*, 1809
Jones (W and S)	Nicholson, *A treatise on practical perspective*, 1815
Jordan (JS)	Sheraton, *The cabinet-maker*, 1793
Keith (G)	Bradley, *A general treatise of agriculture*, 1757
Keith (G)	*The art of drawing*, London, 1777
Keith (G)	*The art of drawing*, 1755
Keith (G)	*The art of drawing*, 1757
Keith (G)	*The art of drawing*, 1769
Kelly	Nicholson, *The new and improved practical builder*, 1847
Kelly (T)	Elsam, *The practical . . . price-book*, 1832
Kelly (T)	Nicholson, *A . . . treatise on the five orders*, 1850
Kelly (T)	Nicholson, *A . . . treatise on the five orders*, [184–]
Kelly (Thomas)	Brooks, *Designs for cottage . . . architecture*, 1839
Kelly (Thomas)	Cook, *The new builder's magazine*, 1819
Kelly (Thomas)	Cook, *The new builder's magazine*, 1820
Kelly (Thomas)	Cook, *The new builder's magazine*, 1823
Kelly (Thomas)	Elsam, *Kelly's practical builder's price book*, 1864
Kelly (Thomas)	Elsam, *The practical . . . price-book*, 1825
Kelly (Thomas)	Elsam, *The practical . . . price-book*, 1826
Kelly (Thomas)	Elsam, *The practical . . . price-book*, 1827
Kelly (Thomas)	Elsam, *The practical . . . price-book*, 1828
Kelly (Thomas)	Elsam, *The practical . . . price-book*, 1841
Kelly (Thomas)	Elsam, *The practical . . . price-book*, 1842
Kelly (Thomas)	Elsam, *The practical . . . price-book*, 1844
Kelly (Thomas)	Elsam, *The practical . . . price-book*, 1847
Kelly (Thomas)	Nicholson, *A . . . treatise on the five orders*, 1834
Kelly (Thomas)	Nicholson, *A . . . treatise on the five orders*, 1839
Kelly (Thomas)	Nicholson, *The new and improved practical builder*, 1837
Kelly (Thomas)	Nicholson, *The new and improved practical builder*, 1838
Kelly (Thomas)	Nicholson, *The new and improved practical builder*, 1848
Kelly (Thomas)	Nicholson, *The new and improved practical builder*, 1850
Kelly (Thomas)	Nicholson, *The new practical builder*, 1823
Kent (William)	Kent (W), *The designs of Inigo Jones*, 1727
King (C)	Langley, *Practical geometry*, 1726
King (C)	Switzer, *Ichnographia rustica*, 1718
King (C)	Switzer, *The nobleman . . . recreation*, 1715
King (Mark)	Nicholson, *The builder & workman's new director*, 1824
Kingsbury, Parbury, and Allen	Hayter, *An introduction to perspective*, 1825
Kitchin (T)	*The artists assistant in drawing* ed.2, n.d. [ca. 1764–1765]
Kitchin (T)	*The draughtsman's assistant*, 1772
Knapton (J and P)	Gibbs, *A book of architecture*, 1739
Knapton (J and P)	Kirby, *Dr. Brook Taylor's . . . perspective*, 1755
Knapton and Horsefield	Kirby, *The perspective of architecture*, 1761
Knight and Lacey	Nicholson, *The builder and workman's new director*, 1825

Lacey	Fournier, *A treatise of . . . perspective*, 1761
Lacey (Edward)	Whittock, *The Oxford drawing book*, n.d.
Lackington, Allen and Co.	*The complete farmer*, 1807
Lackington, Allen, and Co.	Elsam, *An essay on rural architecture*, 1805
Lackington, Allen, and Co.	Parker (T), *Plans, specifications, estimates*, 1813
Laurie	Pain, *The builder's companion*, 1810
Laurie (RH)	*The art of drawing*, 1825
Laurie (RH)	*The art of drawing*, 1844
Laurie (RH)	*The artist's assistant in drawing*, 1825
Lauire & Whittle	*The artists' assistant in drawing*, 1809
Laurie and Whittle	*The art of drawing*, 1798
Laurie and Whittle	*The artist's assistant in drawing*, 1799
Laurie and Whittle	*The artist's assistant in drawing*, 1801
Laurie and Whittle	*The artist's assistant in drawing*, 1806
Law (B)	*The complete farmer*, 1769
Law (B)	*The complete farmer*, 1777
Law (B)	*The complete farmer*, 1793
Law (C)	Wood (JG), *Six lectures*, 1804
Law and Whittaker	Aldrich, *Elements of civil architecture*, 1818
Lawrence (E)	Elsam, *An essay on rural architecture*, 1803
Leacroft (S)	Bardwell, *The practice of painting*, 1773
Leacroft (S)	Brettingham, *The plans . . . of Holkham*, 1773
Leake (J)	Wood, *The origin of building*, 1741
Leigh	Edwards, *Practical treatise of perspective*, 1806
Leigh (Samuel)	Brown, *The principles of . . . perspective*, 1815
Leigh and Son	Brown, *The principles of . . . perspective*, 1835
Leigh, Sotheby and Son	Edwards, *A practical treatise of perspective*, 1803
Levey, Robson, and Franklyn [pr]	Soane, *Description of the house*, 1835
Levey, Robson, et Franklyn [pr]	Soane, *Description de la maison*, 1835
Lewis	Ripley, *The plans . . . of Houghton*, 1760
Lewis (Lewis A)	Nicholson, *The builder's and workman's new director*, 1836
Lewis (M)	Wood, *The origin of building*, 1741
Library of the Fine Arts	Walker, *Architectural precedents*, 1841
Limbird (John)	Whittock, *The British drawing-book*, n.d.
Linde (A)	Bradley, *A general treatise of agriculture*, 1757
Lindsell	Hayter, *An introduction to perspective*, 1815
Lintot (B)	Langley, *Practical geometry*, 1726
Lockwood and Co.	Chambers, *Treatise*, 1862
London Printing and Publishing Company, Limited	Nicholson, *Nicholson's dictionary*, [ca. 1861–1864]
London Printing and Publishing Company, Limited	Nicholson, *Nicholson's dictionary*, n.d.
Longman	Cresswell, *Elements of linear perspective*, 1812
Longman	Hullmandel, *The art of drawing on stone*, 1840
Longman (T)	Kirby, *Dr. Brook Taylor's . . . perspective*, 1765
Longman (T)	Kirby, *Dr. Brook Taylor's . . . perspective*, 1768
Longman (T)	Kirby, *The perspective of architecture*, 1761
Longman (T)	*The complete farmer*, 1769
Longman (T)	*The complete farmer*, 1777

Longman (T)	*The complete farmer*, 1793
Longman (T and T)	Kirby, *Dr. Brook Taylor's . . . perspective*, 1755
Longman & Co.	Fielding, *Synopsis of practical perspective*, 1829
Longman & Co.	Hullmandel, *The art of drawing on stone*, 1833
Longman & Co.	Hullmandel, *The art of drawing on stone*, 1835
Longman & Co.	Loudon, *Illustrations of landscape-gardening* pt.1, 1830
Longman & Co.	Loudon, *Illustrations of landscape-gardening* pt.2, 1831
Longman & Co.	Parsey, *The science of vision*, 1840
Longman & Co.	Pyne, *Nattes's practical geometry*, 1819
Longman & Co.	Repton, *The landscape gardening*, 1840
Longman and Co.	Allen, *Colonies at home*, 1826
Longman and Co.	Allen, *Colonies at home*, 1827
Longman and Co.	Allen, *Colonies at home*, 1828
Longman and Co.	Allen, *Colonies at home*, 1832
Longman and Co.	Goodwin, *Domestic architecture* v.1, 1833
Longman and Co.	Goodwin, *Domestic architecture* v.2, 1834
Longman and Co.	Jopling, *The practice of isometrical perspective*, 1833
Longman and Co.	Nicholson, *A treatise on practical perspective*, 1815
Longman and Co.	Robinson, *Vitruvius Britannicus . . . Hardwicke*, 1835
Longman and Co.	Robinson, *Vitruvius Britannicus . . . Hatfield*, 1833
Longman and Co.	Robinson, *Vitruvius Britannicus . . . Woburn*, 1833
Longman and Rees	Kent (N), *Hints to gentlemen*, 1799
Longman, Brown, Green, and Longmans	Loudon, *Encyclopaedia of agriculture*, 1844
Longman, Brown, Green, and Longmans	Loudon, *Encyclopaedia of agriculture*, 1869
Longman, Brown, Green, and Longmans	Loudon, *Encyclopaedia of gardening*, 1850
Longman, Brown, Green, and Longmans	Loudon, *Encyclopaedia of . . . architecture*, 1841
Longman, Brown, Green, and Longmans	Loudon, *Encyclopaedia of . . . architecture*, 1842
Longman, Brown, Green, and Longmans	Loudon, *Encyclopaedia of . . . architecture*, 1846
Longman, Brown, Green, and Longmans	Loudon, *Encyclopaedia of . . . architecture*, 1853
Longman, Brown, Green, and Longmans	Ricauti, *Sketches for rustic work*, 1842
Longman, Brown, Green, and Longmans, & Roberts	Loudon, *Encyclopaedia of gardening*, 1859
Longman, Brown, Green, Longmans & Roberts	Loudon, *Encyclopaedia of agriculture*, 1857
Longman, Brown, Green, Longmans, & Roberts	Loudon, *Encyclopaedia of . . . architecture*, 1857
Longman, Green, Longman, and Roberts	Loudon, *Encyclopaedia of gardening*, 1860
Longman, Green, Longman, Roberts, & Green	Loudon, *Encyclopaedia of . . . architecture*, 1863
Longman, Hurst, and Co.	Smith (W), An outline of architecture, 1820
Longman, Hurst, Rees, and Orme	Loudon, *A treatise on . . . country residences*, 1806
Longman, Hurst, Rees, and Orme	Loudon, *Engravings*, 1807
Longman, Hurst, Rees, and Orme	Repton, *Designs for . . . Brighton*, n.d.
Longman, Hurst, Rees, and Orme	Repton, *Designs for . . . Brighton*, 1808

Longman, Hurst, Rees, and Orme	*The complete farmer*, 1807
Longman, Hurst, Rees, Orme, and Brown	Cresswell, *The elements of linear perspective*, 1811
Longman, Hurst, Rees, Orme, and Brown	Loch, *An account of the improvements*, 1820
Longman, Hurst, Rees, Orme, and Brown	Loudon, *Encyclopaedia of gardening*, 1822
Longman, Hurst, Rees, Orme, and Brown	Wilkins, *The civil architecture of Vitruvius*, 1812
Longman, Hurst, Rees, Orme, and Browne	Loudon, *Designs for laying out farms*, 1811
Longman, Hurst, Kees, Orme, Brown and Green	Loudon, *Encyclopaedia of agriculture*, 1826
Longman, Hurst, Rees, Orme, Brown, and Green	Hunt, *Half a dozen hints*, 1825
Longman, Hurst, Rees, Orme, Brown, and Green	Loudon, *Encyclopaedia of agriculture*, 1825
Longman, Hurst, Rees, Orme, Brown, and Green	Loudon, *Encyclopaedia of gardening*, 1825
Longman, Orme, Brown, Green, & Longmans	Loudon, *Encyclopaedia of . . . architecture*, 1839
Longman, Orme, Brown, Green, and Longmans	Loudon, *Encyclopaedia of agriculture*, 1839
Longman, Orme, Brown, Green, and Longmans	Loudon, *The suburban gardener*, 1830
Longman, Rees, Orme, Brown and Green	Loudon, *Encyclopaedia of gardening*, 1824
Longman, Rees, Orme, Brown and Green	Loudon, *Encyclopaedia of gardening*, 1826
Longman, Rees, Orme, Brown, and Green	Hunt, *Architettura campestre*, 1827
Longman, Rees, Orme, Brown, and Green	Hunt, *Designs for parsonage houses*, 1827
Longman, Rees, Orme, Brown, and Green	Hunt, *Exemplars of Tudor*, 1830
Longman, Rees, Orme, Brown, and Green	Hunt, *Half a dozen hints*, 1826
Longman, Rees, Orme, Brown, and Green	Loudon, *Encyclopaedia of agriculture*, 1831
Longman, Rees, Orme, Brown, and Green	Loudon, *Encyclopaedia of gardening*, [1830?]
Longman, Rees, Orme, Brown, and Green	Loudon, *Encyclopaedia of gardening*, 1827
Longman, Rees, Orme, Brown, and Green	Loudon, *Encyclopaedia of gardening*, 1828
Longman, Rees, Orme, Brown, and Green	Waistell, *Designs for agricultural buildings*, 1827
Longman, Rees, Orme, Brown, Green, & Longman	Loudon, *Encyclopaedia of . . . architecture*, 1833
Longman, Rees, Orme, Brown, Green, & Longman	Loudon, *Encyclopaedia of . . . architecture*, 1834
Longman, Rees, Orme, Brown, Green, & Longman	Loudon, *Encyclopaedia of . . . architecture*, 1835
Longman, Rees, Orme, Brown, Green, & Longman	Loudon, *Encyclopaedia of . . . architecture*, 1836

Longman, Rees, Orme, Brown, Green, & Longman	Robertson (J), *Supplement to Loudon's manual*, 1833
Longman, Rees, Orme, Brown, Green, and Longman	Hunt, *Exemplars of Tudor*, 1836
Longman, Rees, Orme, Brown, Green, and Longman	Hunt, *Half a dozen hints*, 1833
Longman, Rees, Orme, Brown, Green, and Longman	Loudon, *Encyclopaedia of agriculture*, 1835
Longman, Rees, Orme, Brown, Green, and Longman	Loudon, *Encyclopaedia of gardening*, n.d.
Longman, Rees, Orme, Brown, Green, and Longman	Loudon, *Encyclopaedia of gardening*, 1835
Longman, Rees, Orme, Brown, Green, and Longman	Parsey, *Perspective rectified*, 1836
Longmans, Green	Loudon, *Encyclopaedia of gardening*, 1865
Longmans, Green	Loudon, *Encyclopaedia of gardening*, 1878
Longmans, Green, and Co.	Loudon, *Encyclopaedia of agriculture*, 1871
Longmans, Green, and Co.	Loudon, *Encyclopaedia of agriculture*, 1883
Longmans, Green, and Co.	Loudon, *Encyclopaedia of gardening*, 1869
Longmans, Green, and Co.	Loudon, *Encyclopaedia of gardening*, 1871
Longmans, Green, and Co.	Loudon, *Encyclopaedia of . . . architecture*, 1867
Lowndes (T)	*The complete farmer*, 1769
Lowndes (T)	*The complete farmer*, 1777
Lowndes (W)	*The complete farmer*, 1793
Lowndes (W)	*The complete farmer*, 1807
Lumley	Nicholson, *Rudiments of practical perspective*, 1838
Lumley (Edward)	Nicholson, *The rudiments of practical perspective*, 1835
M'Creery (J) [pr]	Wood (JG), *Lectures*, 1809
M'Gowan (J) [pr]	Parker, *Villa rustica* bk.2, 1833
M'Millan (B) [pr]	Barber, *Farm buildings*, 1805
Maiden (T) [pr]	*The builder's magazine*, 1800
Malton (J)	Malton (T), *An appendix*, 1800
Malton (Thomas)	Malton (J), *An essay on British cottage architecture*, 1804
Mason (W) [pr]	*The artist's assistant*, 1813
Mathews (J)	Sheraton, *The cabinet-maker*, 1793
Mathews (J)	Sheraton, *The cabinet-maker*, 1794
Meadows	Swan, *A collection of designs*, 1757
Meadows (W)	Kirby, *Dr. Brook Taylor's . . . perspective*, 1755
Mears (W)	Switzer, *Ichnographia rustica*, 1718
Melville	Loudon, *Encyclopaedia of . . . architecture*, 1833
Melville	Loudon, *Encyclopaedia of . . . architecture*, 1834
Melville	Robertson (J), *Supplement to Loudon's manual*, 1833
Mercier (Dorothy)	Chambers, *Plans . . . and . . . views . . . at Kew*, 1763
Meyler	Curwen, *Hints on the economy*, 1808

Millan (J)	Langley, *The young builder's rudiments*, 1730
Millan (J)	Langley, *The young builder's rudiments*, 1734
Millan (J)	Morris, *Lectures* pt.2, 1736
Millan (J)	Muller, *Elements of mathematics*, 1748
Millan (J)	Muller, *Elements of mathematics*, 1765
Millan (J)	Ware, *Designs of Inigo Jones*, 1743
Millan (John)	Langley, *Gothic architecture*, 1747
Millar (A)	Bardwell, *The practice of painting*, 1756
Millar (A)	Chambers, *Designs of Chinese buildings*, 1757
Millar (A)	Chambers, *Desseins des edifices . . . chinois*, 1757
Millar (A)	Chambers, *Plans . . . and . . . views . . . at Kew*, 1763
Millar (A)	Chambers, *Treatise*, 1759
Miller	Repton, *Designs for . . . Brighton*, 1808
Miller	Repton, *Designs for . . . Brighton*, n.d.
Miller (Thomas)	Bardwell, *The practice of painting*, 1773
Miller (W)	Pyne, *Nattes's practical geometry*, 1805
Milln (G)	*The rudiments of architecture*, 1799
Mitchell (John)	Domvile, *Eighteen designs* (2 different editions), n.d.
Molteno and Co.	Robinson, *Vitruvius Britannicus . . . Hardwicke*, 1835
Molteno and Co.	Robinson, *Vitruvius Britannicus . . . Hatfield*, 1833
Molteno and Co.	Robinson, *Vitruvius Britannicus . . . Woburn*, 1833
Moore	*The artist's assistant; or school*, 1801
Mordy	Curwen, *Hints on the economy*, 1808
Moss	Burgess, *An easy introduction to perspective*, 1835
Motte (B)	Halfpenny, *The art of sound building* ed.2, 1725
Moyes (J)	Soane, *Plans . . . of Pitzhanger*, 1802
Moyes (J) [pr]	Lugar, *The country gentleman's architect*, 1815
Moyes (James) [pr]	Soane, *Description of the house*, 1830
Moyes (James) [pr]	Soane, *Description of the house*, 1832
Moyes (James) [pr]	Soane, *Designs for public improvements*, 1827
Moyes (James) [pr]	Soane, *Designs for public improvements*, 1828
Mozley (H) [pr]	*The artist's assistant in drawing*, 1810
Mozley (Henry)	*The artists assistant in drawing*, 1814
Mundel & Son	*The rudiments of architecture*, 1799
Mundell (Robert) [pr]	*The rudiments of architecture*, 1772
Murdoch (J)	*The rudiments of architecture*, 1799
Murray	Burgess, *An easy introduction to perspective*, 1819
Murray	Burgess, *An easy introduction to perspective*, 1822
Murray	Burgess, *An easy introduction to perspective*, 1828
Murray	Clarke, *Practical perspective*, 1776
Murray	Clarke, *Practical perspective*, 1794
Murray (D) and Co. [pr]	Burgess, *An easy introduction to perspective*, 1835
Murray (John)	Pasley, *Course of instruction* v.1, 1814
Murray (John)	Pasley, *Course of military instruction* v.2 and v.3, 1817
Nairn (AH)	Ferguson, *The art of drawing in perspective*, 1803
Nardini (L) [pr]	Robertson (W), *Desseins d'architecture*, 1800
Nattali (MA)	Fielding, *The art of engraving*, 1844
Nattali (MA)	Stevens, *Domestic architecture*, 1815
Nattes	Pyne, *Nattes's practical geometry*, 1805
Newbery (E)	*The builder's magazine*, 1788
Newbery (E)	*The builder's magazine*, 1800
Newbery (F)	*The builder's magazine*, 1774

Newbery (F)	*The builder's magazine*, 1776
Newbery (F)	*The builder's magazine*, 1779
Newman	Burgess, *An easy introduction to perspective*, 1819
Newman	Burgess, *An easy introduction to perspective*, 1822
Newton (James)	Newton, *The architecture of . . . Vitruvius* v.2, 1791
Nichols (JB) & Son	Nash, *Illustrations . . . of Brighton*, 1838
Nichols (JB) and Son	Kent (W), *The designs of Inigo Jones*, 1835
Nichols (JB) and Son	Middleton, *The architect and builder's miscellany*, 1843?
Nichols (JB) and Son [pr]	Robinson, *Vitruvius Britannicus . . . Castle Ashby*, 1841
Nichols (JB) and Son [pr]	Robinson, *Vitruvius Britannicus . . . Warwick Castle*, 1844
Nichols and Son [pr]	Wyatt, *A collection of architectural designs* no.3, 1801
Nicholson (John)	Campbell, *Vitruvius Britannicus* v.1, 1715
Nicholson (John)	Campbell, *Vitruvius Britannicus* v.1, 1717
Nicholson (John)	Campbell, *Vitruvius Britannicus* v.2, 1717
Nicol (G)	Kent (N), *Hints to gentlemen*, 1799
Nicol (G)	Knight, *The landscape*, 1794
Nicol (G)	Knight, *The landscape*, 1795
Nicol (G)	Repton, *Sketches and hints*, 1794
Nicol (George)	Richardson, *The first part of a complete system*, 1794
Nicol (William) [pr]	Carlisle, *Hints on rural residences*, 1825
Noble (F)	Kirby, *Dr. Brook Taylor's . . . perspective*, 1754
Noble (F)	Kirby, *Dr. Brook Taylor's . . . perspective*, 1755
Noble (J)	Kirby, *Dr. Brook Taylor's . . . perspective*, 1754
Noble (J)	Kirby, *Dr. Brook Taylor's . . . perspective*, 1755
Nourse	Chambers, *Treatise*, 1768
Nourse	Clarke, *Practical perspective*, 1776
Nourse	Fournier, *A treatise of . . . perspective*, 1761
Nourse	Fournier, *A treatise of . . . perspective*, 1764
Nourse (J)	Chambers, *Desseins des edifices . . . chinois*, 1757
Nourse (J)	Chambers, *Treatise*, 1759
Nourse (J)	Emerson, *The elements of optics*, 1768
Nuttall, Fisher & Co.	Smith (James), *The panorama of science and art*, 1815
Nuttall, Fisher, and Dixon [pr]	Smith (James), *The panorama of science and art*, 1816
Offor (G and J)	Sinclair, "Hints regarding . . . property" in *Essays*, 1818
Ogilvy and Speare	Clarke, *Practical perspective*, 1794
Ogles, Duncan, & Co.	Pyne, *Nattes's practical geometry*, 1819
Orme	Burgess, *An easy introduction to perspective*, 1819
Orme	Burgess, *An easy introduction to perspective*, 1822
Orr (Wm S) & Co.	Loudon, *The villa gardener*, 1850
Osborn (J) and Longman (T)	Langley, *Practical geometry*, 1726
Osborn (T) and Co.	Kirby, *Dr. Brook Taylor's . . . perspective*, 1755
Osborn and Smith	Shortess, *Harmonic architecture*, 1741
Osborne (T)	Chambers, *Treatise*, 1759
Osborne (T) and Shipton (J)	Hale, *A compleat body of husbandry*, 1756
Osborne (T) and Shipton (J)	Ware, *A complete body of architecture*, 1756
Osborne (Tho)	Hale, *A compleat body of husbandry*, 1758–1759
Ostell	*Art of drawing*, 1803
Ostell (T)	Ferguson, *The art of drawing in perspective*, 1807
Ostell (T)	Hodson and Dougall, *The cabinet of the arts*, 1805

Ostell (T)	Hodson, *The cabinet of the arts*, 1804
Ostell (T)	*The artist's assistant, or school*, 1803
Ostell (Thomas)	*The artist's assistant; or school*, 1807
Oswald (John)	Halfpenny, *Perspective made easy*, 1731
Otridge (W)	*The complete farmer*, 1793
Otridge (W) and Son	*The complete farmer*, 1807
Ottridge (Wm)	Bardwell, *The practice of painting*, 1773
Owen (W)	Bradley, *A general treatise of agriculture*, 1757
Owen (W)	Kirby, *Dr. Brook Taylor's . . . perspective*, 1755
Owen (W)	Morris, *The architectural remembrancer*, 1751
Owen (W)	Pain, *The builder's pocket-treasure*, 1763
Owen (W)	Pain, *The builder's pocket-treasure*, 1766
Owen (W)	Pain, *The builder's pocket-treasure*, 1785
Owen (W)	Ware, *A complete body of architecture*, 1767
Owen (W)	Ware, *A complete body of architecture*, 1768
Paine	Goodwin, *Domestic architecture* v.1, 1833
Paine	Goodwin, *Domestic architecture* v.2, 1834
Palser	Elsam, *An essay on rural architecture*, 1803
Parbury, Allen, & Co.	Fielding, *Synopsis of practical perspective*, 1829
Parker	Cresswell, *The elements of linear perspective*, 1811
Parker (A) [pr]	Rowland, *Mensuration*, 1739
Parker (C)	Bardwell, *The practice of painting*, 1773
Parker (Henry) [pr]	Rowland, *A general treatise*, 1732
Parker (Henry) and Bake-well (Elirabeth)	Decker, *Chinese architecture* pt.1, 1759
Parker (Henry) and Bake-well (Elirabeth)	Decker, *Gothic architecture* pt.1, 1759
Parker (Henry) and Bake-well (Elizabeth)	Decker, *Chinese architecture* pt.2, 1759
Parker (Henry) and Bake-well (Elizabeth)	Decker, *Gothic architecture* pt.2, 1759
Parker (J)	Aldrich, *Elements of civil architecture*, 1818
Parker (J)	Aldrich, *Elements of civil architecture*, 1824
Parker (WH)	Cotton, *Short and simple letters*, 1841
Parker & Son	Pasley, *Course of practical geometry*, 1851
Payne	Repton, *Designs for . . . Brighton*, 1808
Payne	Repton, *Designs for . . . Brighton*, n.d.
Payne (T)	Kirby, *Dr. Brook Taylor's . . . perspective*, 1765
Payne (T)	Kirby, *Dr. Brook Taylor's . . . perspective*, 1768
Payne (T)	Kirby, *The perspective of architecture*, 1761
Payne (T) and Son	Aldrich, *Elements of civil architecture*, 1789
Payne and Foss	Aldrich, *Elements of civil architecture*, 1818
Payne and Mackinlay	Repton, *Designs for . . . Brighton*, 1808
Payne and Mackinlay	Repton, *Designs for . . . Brighton*, n.d.
Peele (J)	Bradley, *A general treatise of husbandry*, 1724
Peele (J)	Bradley, *A general treatise of husbandry*, 1726
Philanthropic Society [pr]	Elsam, *An essay on rural architecture*, 1803
Phillips (Richard)	Dickson, *Practical agriculture*, 1805
Phillips (Richard)	Dickson, *Practical agriculture*, 1807
Phillips (Richard)	Dickson, *The farmer's companion*, 1810
Phillips (W)	Allen, *Colonies at home*, 1826
Phillips (W)	Allen, *Colonies at home*, 1827
Pickering	Robinson, *Vitruvius Britannicus . . . Hardwicke*, 1835

Pickering	Robinson, *Vitruvius Britannicus . . . Hatfield*, 1833
Pickering	Robinson, *Vitruvius Britannicus . . . Woburn*, 1833
Piers (H) and Partner	Decker, *Chinese architecture* pt.1, 1759
Piers (H) and Partner	Decker, *Chinese architecture* pt.2, 1759
Piers (H) and Partner	Decker, *Gothic architecture* pt.1, 1759
Piers (H) and Partner	Decker, *Gothic architecture* pt.2, 1759
Piers (H) and Partner	Swan, *A collection of designs*, 1757
Piers & Webley	Ripley, *The plans . . . of Houghton*, 1760
Piers and Webley	Chambers, *Treatise*, 1759
Piers and Webley	Garret, *Designs, and estimates*, 1759
Pine (J)	Wood, *The origin of building*, 1741
Pinnock & Maunder	Pinnock, *A catechism of perspective*, 1820
Pote (J)	Morris, *An essay in defence*, 1728
Potts (J) [pr]	*The art of drawing*, Dublin, 1777
Potts (J) [pr]	*The art of drawing*, Dublin, 1786
Potts (J) [pr]	*The art of drawing*, 1763
Potts (J) [pr]	*The art of drawing*, 1768
Priestley & Weale	Legh, *The music of the eye*, 1831
Priestley and Co.	Goodwin, *Domestic architecture* v.1, 1833
Priestley and Weale	Adam (R & J), *Works*, 1822
Priestley and Weale	Chambers, *Treatise*, 1825
Priestley and Weale	Cottingham, *Working drawings for Gothic*, n.d.
Priestley and Weale	Gwilt, *Rudiments of architecture*, 1826
Priestley and Weale	Gwilt, *Sciography*, 1824
Priestley and Weale	Gwilt, *Sciography*, 1833
Priestley and Weale	Robinson, *Designs for lodges*, 1833
Priestley and Weale	Robinson, *Vitruvius Britannicus . . . Hardwicke*, 1835
Priestley and Weale	Robinson, *Vitruvius Britannicus . . . Hatfield*, 1833
Priestley and Weale	Robinson, *Vitruvius Britannicus . . . Woburn*, 1833
Priestley and Weale	Soane, *Designs for public and private buildings*, 1828
Priestley and Weale	Trendall, *Original designs*, 1831
Priestly and Weale	Jopling, *The practice of isometrical perspective*, 1833
Prince (D) and Cooke (J)	Aldrich, *Elements of civil architecture*, 1789
Pringle (James)	Nicholson, *The builder & workman's new director*, 1824
Print & booksellers in town & country	Edwards and Darly, *A new book of Chinese designs*, 1754
Proprietor	Leoni, *Some designs*, 1758
Proprietor	Middleton, *Picturesque and architectural views*, 1795
Proprietor	Robinson, *Vitruvius Britannicus . . . Castle Ashby*, 1841
Proprietor	Robinson, *Vitruvius Britannicus . . . Warwick Castle*, 1844
Proprietors	*The artist's assistant; or school*, 1801
Quaritch (Bernard)	Brown, *Domestic architecture*, 1852
Reid (W)	*The rudiments of architecture*, 1799
Richardson	Curwen, *Hints on the economy*, 1808
Richardson (John)	Billington, *The architectural director*, 1829
Richardson (John)	Billington, *The architectural director*, 1833
Richardson (S) [pr]	Bardwell, *The practice of painting*, 1756
Richardson (W J and J)	*The complete farmer*, 1807
Richardson and Urquhart	Malton (T), *A compleat treatise on perspective*, 1776
Richardson and Urquhart	Malton (T), *A complete treatise on perspective*, 1775
Rider (J) [pr]	Elsam, *The practical . . . price-book*, 1825
Rider (J) [pr]	Elsam, *The practical . . . price-book*, 1826
Rider (J) [pr]	Elsam, *The practical . . . price-book*, 1827

Rider (J) [pr]	Elsam, *The practical . . . price-book*, 1828
Rider (J) [pr]	Elsam, *The practical . . . price-book*, 1832
Rider and Weed [pr]	*The art of drawing*, 1813
Rider and Weed [pr]	*The art of drawing*, 1817
Rider and Weed [pr]	*The complete farmer*, 1807
Ridges	Curwen, *Hints on the economy*, 1808
Ridgeway	Soane, *Designs for public and private buildings*, 1828
Rivington (F C and J)	*The complete farmer*, 1807
Rivington (J)	Ware, *A complete body of architecture*, 1767
Rivington (J)	Ware, *A complete body of architecture*, 1768
Rivington (J F and C)	*The complete farmer*, 1777
Rivington (J F and G)	Cotton, *Short and simple letters*, 1841
Rivington (J G and F)	Wilson, *Helps*, 1835
Rivington (J and J)	Bardwell, *The practice of painting*, 1756
Rivington (James) and Fletcher (J)	Halfpenny, Morris, and Lightoler, *The modern builder's assistant*, 1757
Robertson (J & J)	Adam (W), *Vitruvius Scotius*, n.d.
Robinson	Curwen, *Hints on the economy*, 1808
Robinson (G)	*The artist's assistant, in . . . mechanical sciences*, n.d.
Robinson (G)	*The complete farmer*, 1777
Robinson (G G J and J)	*The complete farmer*, 1793
Robinson (G G & J)	*The artist's assistant; or school*, 1801
Robinson (J)	Bradley, *A general treatise of agriculture*, 1757
Robinson (J)	*The art of drawing*, 1755
Robinson (J)	*The art of drawing*, 1757
Robinson (J)	*The art of drawing*, 1769
Robinson (S)	Merigot, *A treatise on practical perspective*, 1819
Robinson (S)	Merigot, *The amateur's portfolio*, 1821
Robinson and Roberts	*The complete farmer*, 1769
Robson	Malton (T), *A compleat treatise on perspective*, 1776
Robson	Malton (T), *A compleat treatise on perspective*, 1778
Robson	Malton (T), *A compleat treatise on perspective*, 1779
Robson	Malton (T), *A complete treatise on perspective*, 1775
Robson	Malton (T), *An appendix*, 1783
Robson	Paine, *Plans . . . of . . . gentlemen's houses* v.1, 1783
Robson	Paine, *Plans . . . of . . . gentlemen's houses* v.2, 1783
Robson (J)	Kirby, *Dr. Brook Taylor's . . . perspective*, 1765
Robson (J) and Clarke (W)	Aldrich, *Elements of civil architecture*, 1789
Robson (R)	Chambers, *Treatise*, 1791
Rodwell	Robinson, *Vitruvius Britannicus . . . Hardwicke*, 1835
Rodwell	Robinson, *Vitruvius Britannicus . . . Hatfield*, 1833
Rodwell	Robinson, *Vitruvius Britannicus . . . Woburn*, 1833
Rodwell	Soane, *Designs for public and private buildings*, 1828
Rodwell and Martin	Robinson, *Rural architecture*, 1823
Rooe	Curwen, *Hints on the economy*, 1808
Salmon (M)	Jopling, *The practice of isometrical perspective*, 1833
Sanders (Edward)	Nicholson, *The builder & workman's new director*, 1824
Savage	Curwen, *Hints on the economy*, 1808
Sayer	Chambers, *Treatise*, 1768
Sayer (R)	Chambers, *Plans . . . and . . . views . . . at Kew*, 1763
Sayer (R)	Chambers, *Treatise*, 1759
Sayer (R)	Chambers, *Treatise*, 1791

Sayer (R)	Garret, *Designs, and estimates,* 1759
Sayer (R)	Garret, *Designs, and estimates,* 1772
Sayer (R)	Halfpenny, *A new and compleat system,* 1759
Sayer (R)	Halfpenny, *A new and complete system,* 1772
Sayer (R)	Halfpenny, *New designs for Chinese bridges,* 1751
Sayer (R)	Halfpenny, *New designs for Chinese temples,* 1750
Sayer (R)	Halfpenny, *Twelve beautiful designs,* 1750
Sayer (R)	Morris, *Lectures* pt.1, 1759
Sayer (R)	*The art of drawing,* London, 1786
Sayer (R)	*The artists assistant in drawing* ed.2, n.d. [ca. 1764–1765]
Sayer (R)	*The artists assistant in drawing,* 1788
Sayer (R) and Bennet (J)	*The artists assistant in drawing,* 1786
Sayer (R) and Bennett (J)	*All draughtsmen's assistant,* n.d. [ca. 1776]
Sayer (R) and Bennett (J)	*All draughtsmen's assistant,* n.d. [ca. 1777]
Sayer (R) and Bennett (J)	*All draughtsmen's assistant,* n.d. [ca. 1794]
Sayer (Robert)	Bardwell, *The practice of painting,* 1773
Sayer (Robert)	Halfpenny, Morris, and Lightoler, *The modern builder's assistant,* 1757
Sayer (Robert)	Halfpenny, Morris, and Lightoler, *The modern builder's assistant,* n.d.
Sayer (Robert)	Halfpenny, *A complete system,* n.d.
Sayer (Robert)	Halfpenny, *Chinese and Gothic architecture,* 1752
Sayer (Robert)	Halfpenny, *New designs for Chinese doors,* 1751
Sayer (Robert)	Halfpenny, *New designs for Chinese gates,* 1752
Sayer (Robert)	Halfpenny, *Rural architecture in the Gothick taste,* 1752
Sayer (Robert)	Halfpenny, *Six new designs* pt.1, 1751
Sayer (Robert)	Halfpenny, *Six new designs* pt.2, 1751
Sayer (Robert)	Halfpenny, *The country gentleman's pocket companion,* 1753
Sayer (Robert)	Halfpenny, *The country gentleman's pocket companion,* 1756
Sayer (Robert)	Halfpenny, *Thirteen new designs,* 1752
Sayer (Robert)	Halfpenny, *Twelve beautiful designs,* 1759
Sayer (Robert)	Halfpenny, *Twelve beautiful designs,* 1774
Sayer (Robert)	Halfpenny, *Useful architecture,* 1752
Sayer (Robert)	Halfpenny, *Useful architecture,* 1755
Sayer (Robert)	Halfpenny, *Useful architecture,* 1760
Sayer (Robert)	Lightoler, *The gentleman and farmer's architect,* 1762
Sayer (Robert)	Lightoler, *The gentleman and farmer's architect,* 1764
Sayer (Robert)	Lightoler, *The gentleman and farmer's architect,* 1774
Sayer (Robert)	Morris, *Architecture improved,* 1755
Sayer (Robert)	Morris, *Architecture improved,* 1757
Sayer (Robert)	Morris, *Select architecture,* 1755
Sayer (Robert)	Morris, *Select architecture,* 1757
Sayer (Robert)	Morris, *Select architecture,* n.d.
Sayer (Robert)	Over, *Ornamental architecture,* 1758
Sayer (Robert)	Over, *Ornamental architecture,* n.d.
Sayer (Robert)	Pain, *The builder's companion,* 1758
Sayer (Robert)	Pain, *The builder's companion,* 1762
Sayer (Robert)	Pain, *The builder's companion,* 1765
Sayer (Robert)	Pain, *The builder's companion,* 1769
Sayer (Robert)	Sayer [?], *Vignola revived,* 1761
Sayer (Robert)	Swan, *A collection of designs,* n.d.
Sayer (Robert)	*The artists assistant in drawing,* 1772
Sayer (Robert)	*The draughtsmen's assistant,* 1786
Sayer (Robert) and Co.	*The draughtsman's assistant,* n.d. [ca. 1787]

Sayer (Robert) and Co.	*The draughtsman's assistant*, n.d. [ca. 1794]
Sayer (Robert) and Co.	*The draughtsman's assistant*, n.d. [ca. 1801]
Sayer (Robt)	Halfpenny, *Rural architecture in the Chinese taste*, 1752
Sayer (Robt)	Halfpenny, *Rural architecture in the Chinese taste*, 1755
Sayer (Robt)	Halfpenny, *Rural architecture in the Chinese taste*, n.d.
Sayer and Bennett	Paine, *Plans . . . of . . . gentlemen's houses* v.2, 1783
Scribner, Welford, and Co.	Loudon, *Encyclopaedia*, 1869
Sedding and Turtle [pr]	Papworth, *Rural residences*, 1832
Seeley (L and G)	Wilson, *Helps*, 1842
Seeley (L and J)	Wilson, *Helps*, 1835
Seeley (RB) and Burnside (W)	Francis, *A series of original designs*, 1841
Senex (John)	Halfpenny, *The art of sound building* ed.1, 1725
Sewell (T)	Newton, *The architecture of . . . Vitruvius* v.1, 1791
Sewell (T)	Newton, *The architecture of . . . Vitruvius* v.2, 1791
Sheardown	Curwen, *Hints on the economy*, 1808
Sherwood	Dickson, *Farmer's companion*, 1811
Sherwood & Co.	Pyne, *Nattes's practical geometry*, 1819
Sherwood and Co.	Burgess, *An easy introduction to perspective*, 1819
Sherwood and Co.	Burgess, *An easy introduction to perspective*, 1822
Sherwood, Gilbert, and Piper	Dickson, *The farmer's companion*, n.d.
Sherwood, Gilbert, and Piper	Smith (T), *The art of drawing*, 1827
Sherwood, Gilbert, and Piper	Smith (T), *The young artist's assistant*, 1830?
Sherwood, Gilbert, and Piper	Varley, *A practical treatise*, 1820
Sherwood, Jones, and Co.	Smith (T), *The art of drawing*, 1825
Sherwood, Neely, and Jones	Dickson, *Practical agriculture*, 1814
Sherwood, Neely, and Jones	Dickson, *The farmer's companion*, 1813
Sherwood, Neely, and Jones	Hassell, *The speculum*, 1816
Simpkin & Marshall	Pyne, *Nattes's practical geometry*, 1819
Simpkin and Marshall	Burgess, *An easy introduction to perspective*, 1835
Simpkin, Marshall, and Co.	Atkinson (J), *An account of . . . New South Wales*, 1844
Simpkin, Marshall, and Co.	Rider, *The principles of perspective*, 1836
Smeeton (Joseph) [pr]	Chambers, *Treatise*, 1791
Smith	Curwen, *Hints on the economy*, 1808
Smith (IT)	Smith (J), *Remarks on rural scenery*, 1797
Smith (J)	*The artists assistant in drawing* ed.2, n.d. [ca. 1764–1765]
Smith (John)	*The artists assistant in drawing*, 1772
Smith (Jos)	Campbell, *Vitruvius Britannicus* v.1, 1715
Smith (Jos)	Campbell, *Vitruvius Britannicus* v.1, 1717
Smith (Jos)	Campbell, *Vitruvius Britannicus* v.2, 1717
Smith (Joseph)	Campbell, *Vitruvius Britannicus* v.3 (2 different editions), 1725
Smith (M)	Cottage Improvement Society, *Report*, 1842
Smith (Nathaniel)	Smith (J), *Remarks on rural scenery*, 1797
Smith & Elder	Fielding, *Synopsis of practical perspective*, 1829

Smith and Co.	Burgess, *An easy introduction to perspective*, 1819
Smith and Co.	Burgess, *An easy introduction to perspective*, 1822
Society for Bettering the Condition of the Poor, in the Hundred of Oswestry	Society for . . . Oswestry, *First report*, 1813
Society for Improving the Condition of the Lower Order	Allen, *Colonies at home*, 1828
Society of Booksellers for Promoting Learning	Shortess, *Harmonic architecture*, 1741
Souter (J)	Burgess, *An easy introduction to perspective*, 1828
Spilsbury (T) [pr]	Brettingham, *The plans . . . of Holkham*, 1773
Spottiswoode (A & R) [pr]	Loudon, *A manual of cottage gardening*, 1830
Stadler (JC)	Repton, *Designs for . . . Brighton*, 1808
Stadler (JC)	Repton, *Designs for . . . Brighton*, n.d.
Steel (HD) [pr]	Pain, *Pain's British Palladio*, 1786
Steel (HD) [pr]	Pain, *The builder's golden rule*, 1781
Steel (HD) [pr]	Pain, *The builder's golden rule*, 1782
Steel (HD) [pr]	Pain, *The builder's golden rule*, 1787
Stockdale (J)	*The complete farmer*, 1807
Storie (J)	Ferguson, *The art of drawing in perspective*, 1803
Strahan (A)	Bradley, *A general treatise of agriculture*, 1757
Strahan (A) [pr]	Sinclair, "Hints regarding . . . property" in *Essays*, 1802
Strahan (A) [pr]	Sinclair, "Hints regarding . . . property" in *Essays*, 1818
Strahan (W)	Ferguson, *The art of drawing in perspective*, 1775
Strahan (W)	Ferguson, *The art of drawing in perspective*, 1778
Strahan (W)	Ware, *A complete body of architecture*, 1767
Strahan (W)	Ware, *A complete body of architecture*, 1768
Strange	Thompson, *Practical directions*, 1830
Stratford (W) [pr]	Crunden, *Convenient and ornamental architecture*, 1805
Stratford (W) [pr]	Crunden, *Convenient and ornamental architecture*, 1815
Stratford (W) [pr]	Lugar, *Architectural sketches*, 1815
Stratford (W) [pr]	Pain, *Pain's British Palladio*, 1804
Stratford (W) [pr]	Pain, *The practical builder*, 1804
Stratford (W) [pr]	Pain, *The practical house carpenter*, 1805
Stratford (W) [pr]	Pain, *The practical house carpenter*, 1815
Stratford (W) [pr]	Plaw, *Ferme ornée*, 1800
Stratford (W) [pr]	Plaw, *Ferme ornée*, 1803
Stratford (W) [pr]	Plaw, *Sketches*, 1803
Stratford (W) [pr]	Wrighte, *Grotesque architecture*, 1802
Stratford (W) [pr]	Wrighte, *Grotesque architecture*, 1815
Sutton	Curwen, *Hints on the economy*, 1808
Swan (J)	Kirby, *Dr. Brook Taylor's . . . perspective*, 1754
Swan (J)	Kirby, *Dr. Brook Taylor's . . . perspective*, 1755
Swinney (M)	*The artist's assistant, in . . . mechanical sciences*, n.d.
Swinney (M) [pr]	*The artist's assistant, or school*, 1803
Swinney & Hawkins [pr]	*The artist's assistant; or school*, 1801
Swinney and Ferrall [pr]	*The artist's assistant; or school*, 1807
Symon (E)	Langley, *Practical geometry*, 1726
Symonds (HD)	Middleton, *Picturesque and architectural views*, 1795
Symonds (HD)	*The builder's magazine*, 1800
Tallis	Nicholson, *Architectural dictionary*, 1854
Taylor	Burgess, *An easy introduction to perspective*, 1819

Taylor	Burgess, *An easy introduction to perspective*, 1822
Taylor	Goodwin, *Domestic architecture* v.1, 1833
Taylor	Goodwin, *Domestic architecture* v.2, 1834
Taylor	Lewis, *Original designs* v.1, 1797
Taylor	Malton (T), *A compleat treatise on perspective*, 1776
Taylor	Malton (T), *A compleat treatise on perspective*, 1778
Taylor	Malton (T), *A compleat treatise on perspective*, 1779
Taylor	Malton (T), *A complete treatise on perspective*, 1775
Taylor	Malton (T), *An appendix*, 1783
Taylor	Malton (T), *An appendix*, 1800
Taylor	Repton, *Designs for . . . Brighton*, 1808
Taylor	Repton, *Designs for . . . Brighton*, n.d.
Taylor	Soane, *Plans . . . of buildings executed*, 1788
Taylor	Wood, *A series of plans*, 1814
Taylor (I)	Crunden, *Convenient and ornamental architecture*, 1785
Taylor (I)	Garret, *Designs, and estimates*, 1772
Taylor (I)	Kirby, *Dr. Brook Taylor's . . . perspective*, 1768
Taylor (I)	Overton, *The temple builder's . . . companion*, 1774
Taylor (I)	Pain, *The practical builder*, 1774
Taylor (I)	Pain, *The practical builder*, 1776
Taylor (I)	Pain, *The practical builder*, 1778
Taylor (I)	Soane, *Designs in architecture*, 1778
Taylor (I)	Wallis, *The carpenter's treasure*, 1773
Taylor (I)	Wrighte, *Grotosque architecture*, n.d.
Taylor (I & J)	Langley, *Gothic architecture*, n.d.
Taylor (I & J)	Soane, *Designs in architecture*, 1789
Taylor (I & J)	Soane, *Designs in architecture*, 1790
Taylor (I & J)	Soane, *Designs in architecture*, 1797
Taylor (I & J)	*The rudiments of ancient architecture*, 1789
Taylor (I and J)	Chambers, *Treatise*, 1791
Taylor (I and J)	Crunden, *Convenient and ornamental architecture*, 1788
Taylor (I and J)	Crunden, *Convenient and ornamental architecture*, 1791
Taylor (I and J)	Crunden, *Convenient and ornamental architecture*, 1797
Taylor (I and J)	Miller, *The country gentleman's architect*, 1787
Taylor (I and J)	Miller, *The country gentleman's architect*, 1789
Taylor (I and J)	Miller, *The country gentleman's architect*, 1791
Taylor (I and J)	Miller, *The country gentleman's architect*, 1793
Taylor (I and J)	Newton, *The architecture of . . . Vitruvius* v.1, 1791
Taylor (I and J)	Newton, *The architecture of . . . Vitruvius* v.2, 1791
Taylor (I and J)	Pain, *Pain's British Palladio*, 1788
Taylor (I and J)	Pain, *Pain's British Palladio*, 1790
Taylor (I and J)	Pain, *Pain's British Palladio*, 1793
Taylor (I and J)	Pain, *Pain's British Palladio*, 1797
Taylor (I and J)	Pain, *The builder's pocket-treasure*, 1793
Taylor (I and J)	Pain, *The practical builder*, 1787
Taylor (I and J)	Pain, *The practical builder*, 1789
Taylor (I and J)	Pain, *The practical builder*, 1793
Taylor (I and J)	Pain, *The practical house carpenter*, 1792
Taylor (I and J)	Pain, *The practical house carpenter*, 1794
Taylor (I and J)	Plaw, *Ferme ornée*, 1795
Taylor (I and J)	Plaw, *Ferme ornée*, 1796
Taylor (I and J)	Plaw, *Rural architecture*, 1796

Taylor (I and J)	Rawlins, *Familiar architecture*, 1789
Taylor (I and J)	Rawlins, *Familiar architecture*, 1795
Taylor (I and J)	Soane, *Sketches in architecture*, 1793
Taylor (I and J)	Wood, *A series of plans*, 1792
Taylor (I and J)	Wrighte, *Grotesque architecture*, 1790
Taylor (I and J)	*Rudiments of ancient architecture*, 1794
Taylor (Isaac)	Paine, *Plans . . . of . . . gentlemen's houses*, v.1, 1783
Taylor (J)	Adam (W), *Vitruvius Scotius*, n.d.
Taylor (J)	Aikin, *Designs for villas*, 1808
Taylor (J)	Bartell, *Hints for picturesque improvements*, 1804
Taylor (J)	Brown, *The principles of . . . perspective*, 1815
Taylor (J)	Busby, *A series of designs*, 1808
Taylor (J)	Chambers, *Treatise*, 1826
Taylor (J)	Crunden, *Convenient and ornamental architecture*, 1805
Taylor (J)	Crunden, *Convenient and ornamental architecture*, 1815
Taylor (J)	Dearn, *Designs for lodges*, 1811
Taylor (J)	Dearn, *Designs for lodges*, 1823
Taylor (J)	Dearn, *Sketches . . . for cottages and . . . dwellings*, 1807
Taylor (J)	Dearn, *Sketches . . . for cottages and . . . dwellings*, 1823
Taylor (J)	Dearn, *The bricklayer's guide*, 1809
Taylor (J)	Elison, *Decorations for parks and gardens*, 1800
Taylor (J)	Gwilt, *Rudiments of architecture*, 1834
Taylor (J)	Gwilt, *Sciography*, 1822
Taylor (J)	Gyfford, *Designs for elegant cottages*, 1806
Taylor (J)	Gyfford, *Designs for small picturesque cottages*, 1807
Taylor (J)	Jones (R), *Every builder his own surveyor*, 1809
Taylor (J)	Laing, *Hints for dwellings*, 1800
Taylor (J)	Laing, *Hints for dwellings*, 1801
Taylor (J)	Laing, *Hints for dwellings*, 1804
Taylor (J)	Laing, *Hints for dwellings*, 1818
Taylor (J)	Laing, *Hints for dwellings*, 1823
Taylor (J)	Laing, *Plans, elevations, and sections*, 1818
Taylor (J)	Lugar, *Architectural sketches*, 1805
Taylor (J)	Lugar, *Architectural sketches*, 1815
Taylor (J)	Lugar, *Architectural sketches*, 1823
Taylor (J)	Lugar, *Plans and views*, 1811
Taylor (J)	Lugar, *Plans and views*, 1823
Taylor (J)	Lugar, *The country gentleman's architect*, 1807
Taylor (J)	Lugar, *The country gentleman's architect*, 1815
Taylor (J)	Lugar, *The country gentleman's architect*, 1823
Taylor (J)	Lugar, *Villa architecture*, 1828
Taylor (J)	Middleton, *The architect and builder's miscellany*, 1799
Taylor (J)	Middleton, *The architect and builder's miscellany*, 1812
Taylor (J)	Middleton, *The architect and builder's miscellany*, n.d.
Taylor (J)	Miller, *The country gentleman's architect*, 1802
Taylor (J)	Miller, *The country gentleman's architect*, 1805
Taylor (J)	Miller, *The country gentleman's architect*, 1810
Taylor (J)	Mitchell (R), *Plans, and views*, 1801
Taylor (J)	Morris (Richard), *Essays on landscape gardening*, 1825
Taylor (J)	Nicholson, *A treatise on practical perspective*, 1815
Taylor (J)	Nicholson, *The builder's and workman's new director*, 1834
Taylor (J)	Nicholson, *The rudiments of practical perspective*, 1822
Taylor (J)	Pain, *Pain's British Palladio*, 1804

Taylor (J)	Pain, *The practical builder*, 1799
Taylor (J)	Pain, *The practical builder*, 1804
Taylor (J)	Pain, *The practical house carpenter*, 1799
Taylor (J)	Pain, *The practical house carpenter*, 1805
Taylor (J)	Pain, *The practical house carpenter*, 1815
Taylor (J)	Pain, *The practical house carpenter*, 1823
Taylor (J)	Plaw, *Ferme ornée*, 1800
Taylor (J)	Plaw, *Ferme ornée*, 1803
Taylor (J)	Plaw, *Ferme ornée*, 1813
Taylor (J)	Plaw, *Ferme ornée*, 1823
Taylor (J)	Plaw, *Rural architecture*, 1802
Taylor (J)	Plaw, *Sketches*, 1800
Taylor (J)	Plaw, *Sketches*, 1802
Taylor (J)	Plaw, *Sketches*, 1803
Taylor (J)	Plaw, *Sketches*, 1812
Taylor (J)	Plaw, *Sketches*, 1823
Taylor (J)	Pocock, *Architectural designs*, 1807
Taylor (J)	Pocock, *Architectural designs*, 1823
Taylor (J)	Pocock, *Modern finishings*, 1811
Taylor (J)	Pocock, *Modern finishings*, 1823
Taylor (J)	Randall, *A collection of architectural designs*, 1806
Taylor (J)	Repton, *Fragments*, 1816
Taylor (J)	Repton, *Observations*, 1803
Taylor (J)	Repton, *Observations*, 1805
Taylor (J)	Richardson, *The new Vitruvius Britannicus* v.1, 1802
Taylor (J)	Richardson, *The new Vitruvius Britannicus* v.1, 1810
Taylor (J)	Richardson, *The new Vitruvius Britannicus* v.2, 1808
Taylor (J)	Soane, *Sketches in architecture*, 1798
Taylor (J)	Thomson, *Retreats*, 1827
Taylor (J)	Thomson, *Retreats*, 1833
Taylor (J)	Wood (JG), *Six lectures*, 1804
Taylor (J)	Wood, *A series of plans*, 1806
Taylor (J)	Wrighte, *Grotesque architecture*, 1802
Taylor (J)	Wrighte, *Grotesque architecture*, 1815
Taylor (J)	Wyatt, *A collection of architectural designs* no.1, 1800
Taylor (J)	Wyatt, *A collection of architectural designs* no.2, 1800
Taylor (J)	Wyatt, *A collection of architectural designs* no.3, 1801
Taylor (J)	*Rudiments of ancient architecture*, 1804
Taylor (J)	*Rudiments of ancient architecture*, 1810
Taylor (J)	*Rudiments of ancient architecture*, 1821
Taylor (Josiah)	Billington, *The architectural director*, 1829
Taylor (Josiah)	Billington, *The architectural director*, 1833
Taylor (M)	Chambers, *Treatise*, 1836
Taylor (M)	Gwilt, *Rudiments of architecture*, 1839
Taylor (M)	Gwilt, *Sciography*, 1842
Taylor (M)	Jopling, *Practice of isometrical perspective*, 1861
Taylor (M)	Jopling, *The practice of isometrical perspective*, 1839
Taylor (M)	Jopling, *The practice of isometrical perspective*, 1842
Taylor (M)	Jopling, *The practice of isometrical perspective*, n.d.
Taylor (M)	Laing, *Hints for dwellings*, 1841
Taylor (M)	Lugar, *Plans and views*, 1836
Taylor (M)	Lugar, *The country gentleman's architect*, 1838
Taylor (M)	Lugar, *Villa architecture*, 1855

Taylor (M)	Pocock, *Modern finishings*, 1835
Taylor (M)	Pocock, *Modern finishings*, 1837
Taylor (M)	Thomson, *Retreats*, 1835
Taylor (M)	Thomson, *Retreats*, 1840
Taylor (M)	Thomson, *Retreats*, 1854
Taylor (M)	Waistell, *Designs for agricultural buildings*, n.d.
Taylor (R) and Co. [pr]	Dickson, *Practical agriculture*, 1805
Taylor (Tho)	Halfpenny, *The art of sound building* ed.1, 1725
Taylor (W)	Campbell, *Vitruvius Britannicus* v.1, 1715
Taylor (W)	Campbell, *Vitruvius Britannicus* v.1, 1717
Taylor (W)	Campbell, *Vitruvius Britannicus* v.2, 1717
Taylor and Walton	Deacon, *Elements of perspective*, 1841
Taylor's Architectural Library	Elsam, *An essay on rural architecture*, 1803
Taylor's Architectural Library	Malton (J), *A collection of designs*, 1802
Taylor's Architectural Library	Malton (J), *An essay on British cottage architecture*, 1798
Taylor's Architectural Library	Malton (J), *An essay on British cottage architecture*, 1804
Taylors (J and J)	Plaw, *Rural architecture*, 1790
Taylors (J and J)	Plaw, *Rural architecture*, 1794
Tegg (T)	Hassell, *The speculum*, 1809
Terry (G)	Sheraton, *The cabinet-maker*, 1793
Thézard (E, fils)	Adam (R & J), *Works* v.1, 1900
Thézard (E, fils)	Adam (R & J), *Works* v.2, 1901
Thézard (E, fils)	Adam (R & J), *Works* v.3, 1902
Thurlbourn (W)	Kirby, *Dr. Brook Taylor's . . . perspective*, 1755
Tilling and Hughes [pr]	Burgess, *An easy introduction to perspective*, 1819
Tilt (Charles)	Prout, *Elementary drawing book*, 1840
Tilt and Bogue	Rawlins (TJ), *Elementary perspective*, n.d.
Tiranti (John) & Co	Adam (R & J), *Works*, 1931
Treuttel & Wurtz	Loudon, *Illustrations of landscape-gardening* pt.1, 1830
Treuttel & Wurtz	Loudon, *Illustrations of landscape-gardening* pt.2, 1831
Treuttel and Co.	Goodwin, *Domestic architecture* v.2, 1834
Treuttel and Würtz	Loudon, *Encyclopaedia of . . . architecture*, 1833
Treuttel and Würtz	Loudon, *Encyclopaedia of . . . architecture*, 1834
Treuttel and Würtz	Robertson (J), *Supplement to Loudon's manual*, 1833
Treuttel, Würtz and Co.	Goodwin, *Domestic architecture* v.1, 1833
Treuttel, Würtz, and Richter	Loudon, *Encyclopaedia of . . . architecture*, 1833
Treuttel, Würtz, and Richter	Loudon, *Encyclopaedia of . . . architecture*, 1834
Treuttel, Würtz, and Richter	Robertson (J), *Supplement to Loudon's manual*, 1833
Trye (T)	Hale, *A compleat body of husbandry*, 1756
Trye (Tho)	Hale, *A compleat body of husbandry*, 1758–1759
Turnham (Charles)	Nicholson, *A treatise on projection*, 1840
Tyas (Robert)	Jewitt, *Hand-book of practical perspective*, 1840
Tyler (John) [pr]	Barber, *Farm buildings*, 1802
Underwood (T)	Adam (W), *Vitruvius Scotius*, n.d.
Underwood (T)	Nicholson, *A treatise on practical perspective*, 1815
Vernor and Hood	Wyatt, *A collection of architectural designs* no.3, 1801
Vernor and Hood	*The builder's magazine*, 1800

Vernor and Hood	*The rudiments of architecture*, 1799
Virtue (G)	Whittock, *The youth's . . . drawing book*, 1833
Virtue (G)	Whittock, *The youth's . . . drawing book*, 1834
Virtue (G)	Whittock, *The youth's . . . drawing book*, 1836
Virtue (George)	Brown, *Domestic architecture*, 1841
Virtue (George)	Brown, *Domestic architecture*, 1842
Walker	Curwen, *Hints on the economy*, 1808
Walker (J)	Kent (N), *Hints to gentlemen*, 1799
Walker (William)	Legh, *The music of the eye*, 1831
Waller	Goodwin, *Domestic architecture* v.1, 1833
Waller	Goodwin, *Domestic architecture* v.2, 1834
Walter (J)	Chambers, *Plans . . . and . . . views . . . at Kew*, 1763
Walter (J)	Chambers, *Treatise*, 1791
Walthoe (J)	Morris, *An essay in defence*, 1728
Walthoe (John)	Halfpenny, *The art of sound building* ed.1, 1725
Ward	Rudge, *An introduction to . . . painting*, 1828
Ward (Aaron)	Langley, *Practical geometry*, 1729
Ward (J)	Ware, *A complete body of architecture*, 1756
Ware	Halfpenny, *Twelve beautiful designs*, 1750
Ware (I)	Ripley, *The plans . . . of Houghton*, 1735
Warne (Frederick) and Co.	Loudon, *Encyclopaedia*, 1869
Warne (Frederick) and Co.	Loudon, *Encyclopaedia*, n.d.
Watts	Curwen, *Hints on the economy*, 1808
Wayland (L)	Sheraton, *The cabinet-maker*, 1793
Weale	Aikin, *Designs for villas*, 1852
Weale	Goodwin, *Domestic architecture* v.2, 1834
Weale (J)	Brown, *The principles of . . . perspective*, 1835
Weale (J)	Collis, *The builders' portfolio*, 1837
Weale (J)	Jones (E), *Athenian; or, Grecian villas*, 1835
Weale (J)	Middleton, *The architect and builder's miscellany*, 1843?
Weale (John)	Aikin, *Designs for villas*, 1835
Weale (John)	Busby, *A series of designs*, 1835
Weale (John)	Domvile, *Eighteen designs* (2 different editions), n.d.
Weale (John)	Francis, *A series of original designs*, 1841
Weale (John)	Goodwin, *Cottage architecture*, 1835
Weale (John)	Goodwin, *Rural architecture*, 1835
Weale (John)	Loudon, *Encyclopaedia of . . . architecture*, 1835
Weale (John)	Loudon, *Encyclopaedia of . . . architecture*, 1836
Weale (John)	Loudon, *Encyclopaedia of . . . architecture*, 1839
Weale (John)	Loudon, *Encyclopaedia of . . . architecture*, 1841
Weale (John)	Loudon, *Encyclopaedia of . . . architecture*, 1842
Weale (John)	Nicholson, *An architectural . . . dictionary*, 1835
Weale (John)	Pain, *Carpentry. . . . The practical house carpenter*, 1860–1861
Weale (John)	Parker, *Villa rustica*, 1848
Weale (John)	Robinson, *Vitruvius Britannicus . . . Castle Ashby*, 1841
Weale (John)	Robinson, *Vitruvius Britannicus . . . Warwick Castle*, 1844
Weale (John)	Sopwith, *A treatise on isometrical drawing*, 1834
Weale (John)	Sopwith, *A treatise on isometrical drawing*, 1838
Weale (John)	Wilds, *Elementary . . . instructions*, 1835
Webb	Curwen, *Hints on the economy*, 1808
Webley	Chambers, *Treatise*, 1768
Webley	Paine, *Plans . . . of . . . gentlemen's houses* v.1, 1767
Webley (A)	Chambers, *Plans . . . and . . . views . . . at Kew*, 1763

Webley (A)	Crunden, *Convenient and ornamental architecture*, 1770
Webley (H)	Swan, *A collection of designs v.1*, n.d. [ca. 1770–1775?]
Webley (Henry)	Crunden, *Convenient and ornamental architecture*, 1767
Webley (Henry)	Overton, *Original designs of temples*, 1766
Webley (Henry)	Overton, *The temple builder's ... companion*, 1766
Webley (Henry)	Swan, *A collection of designs v.2*, n.d. [ca. 1770–1775?]
Webley (Henry)	Wrighte, *Grotesque architecture*, 1767
Weed and Rider [pr]	Cook, *The new builder's magazine*, 1819
Weed and Rider [pr]	Cook, *The new builder's magazine*, 1820
Weed and Rider [pr]	Cook, *The new builder's magazine*, 1823
Whiston (J)	Bardwell, *The practice of painting*, 1773
White	Middleton, *The architect and builder's miscellany*, 1799
White	Paine, *Plans ... of ... gentlemen's houses v.1*, 1783
White	Repton, *Designs for ... Brighton*, 1808
White	Repton, *Designs for ... Brighton*, n.d.
White (B)	Bardwell, *The practice of painting*, 1773
White (B)	Brettingham, *The plans ... of Holkham*, 1773
White (Benjamin)	Kent (W), *The designs of Inigo Jones*, 1770
White (J)	Mitchell (R), *Plans, and views*, 1801
Whitlege (Bowen)	Halfpenny, *The art of sound building* ed.1, 1725
Whittaker (G and WB)	Hedgeland, *First part of a series of designs*, 1821
Whittaker (Geo B)	Aldrich, *Elements of civil architecture*, 1824
Whittaker (Geo B)	Pinnock, *A catechism of perspective*, 1823
Whittaker and Co.	Cottage Improvement Society, *Report*, 1842
Whittaker and Co.	Wood (J, Jr), *A manual of perspective*, 1843
Whittaker and Co.	Wood (J, Jr), *A manual of perspective*, 1849
Whittingham (C) [pr]	Loudon, *A treatise on ... country residences*, 1806
Whittingham (C) [pr]	Loudon, *Engravings*, 1807
Whittle (J) & Laurie (RH)	*The art of drawing*, 1818
Whittle (J) and Laurie (RH)	*The artist's assistant in drawing*, 1818
Whittle (James) and Laurie (Richard Holmes)	*The art of drawing*, 1813
Whittle (James) and Laurie (Richard Holmes)	*The art of drawing*, 1817
Wilcox (J)	Langley, *A sure guide*, 1729
Wilcox (J)	Morris, *Lectures* pt.2, 1736
Wilcox (John)	Badeslade and Rocque, *Vitruvius Brittanicus*, 1739
Wilcox (John)	Hoppus, *Andrea Palladio's architecture*, 1736
Wilkie (J)	Kirby, *Dr. Brook Taylor's ... perspective*, 1768
Wilkinson	Malton (J), *An essay on British cottage architecture*, 1798
Wilks (R) [pr]	Dickson, *The farmer's companion*, 1810
Willan	Curwen, *Hints on the economy*, 1808
Willcock (R)	Chambers, *Designs of Chinese buildings*, 1757
Williams	Francis, *A series of original designs*, 1841
Williams	Goodwin, *Domestic architecture v.1*, 1833
Williams	Goodwin, *Domestic architecture v.2*, 1834
Williams	Robinson, *Vitruvius Britannicus ... Hardwicke*, 1835
Williams	Robinson, *Vitruvius Britannicus ... Hatfield*, 1833
Williams	Robinson, *Vitruvius Britannicus ... Woburn*, 1833
Williams (J)	Collis, *The builders' portfolio*, 1837
Williams (J)	Jones (E), *Athenian; or, Grecian villas*, 1835
Williams (J)	Robinson, *Designs for lodges*, 1833

Williams (J)	Robinson, *Domestic architecture*, 1837
Williams (James) [pr]	Ferguson, *The art of drawing in perspective*, 1778
Williams (John)	Davy, *Architectural precedents* (2 separate editions), 1841
Williams (John)	Davy, *Architectural precedents*, 1840
Wilson	Chambers, *Treatise*, 1768
Wilson (D)	Chambers, *Plans . . . and . . . views . . . at Kew*, 1763
Wilson (E)	Thompson, *Practical directions*, 1830
Wilson (Effingham)	Whitwell, *Description of an architectural model*, 1830
Wilson (J) [pr]	Ferguson, *The art of drawing in perspective*, 1807
Wilson (Peter)	Hale, *A compleat body of husbandry*, 1757
Wilson & Co. [pr]	Mitchell (R), *Plans, and views*, 1801
Wilson and Durham	Chambers, *Designs of Chinese buildings*, 1757
Wilson and Durham	Chambers, *Treatise*, 1759
Wood & Son	Wood (J, Jr), *A manual of perspective*, 1841
Wood and Son	Curwen, *Hints on the economy*, 1808
Wood and Son	Wood (J, Jr), *A manual of perspective*, 1843
Wood and Son	Wood (J, Jr), *A manual of perspective*, 1849
Woodfall (H)	Ware, *A complete body of architecture*, 1767
Woodfall (H)	Ware, *A complete body of architecture*, 1768
Woodman (J) and Lyons (D)	Langley, *Practical geometry*, 1726
Woodward (T)	Bradley, *A general treatise of husbandry*, 1724
Woodward (T)	Bradley, *A general treatise of husbandry*, 1726
Woolstenholme	Curwen, *Hints on the economy*, 1808
Worrall (Tho)	Halfpenny, *The art of sound building* ed.1, 1725
Wren (J)	Bradley, *A general treatise of agriculture*, 1757
Wright (J) [pr]	*The artist's assistant in drawing*, 1801
Wright (John) & Prosser (Thomas)	Nicholson, *The builder & workman's new director*, 1824
Wright (P)	Pyne, *Nattes's practical geometry*, 1819
Wright (Tho)	Halfpenny, *The art of sound building* ed.1, 1725
Wynne (P and W)	*The complete farmer*, 1807
No Imprint	Bradshaw, *Civil architecture*, 1800
No Imprint	Campbell, *Vitruvius Britannicus* v.1 and v.2, n.d.
No Imprint	Campbell, *Vitruvius Britannicus* v.1, v.2, and v.3, n.d.
No Imprint	Jones (W), *The gentlemens or builders companion*, n.d.
No Imprint	Langley, *Ancient architecture*, 1742
No Imprint	Searles, *[Designs and estimates]*, n.d.
No Information	*Architectural recreations*, [1830?]
No Information	*Art of drawing*, 1799
No Information	Butler, *Model farm-houses*, 1837
No Information	Crunden, *Convenient and ornamental architecture*, 1768
No Information	Ferguson, *The art of drawing in perspective*, 1810
No Information	Ferguson, *The art of drawing in perspective*, 1820
No Information	Gwilt, *Rudiments of architecture*, 1835
No Information	Halfpenny, *Système nouveau*, 1749
No Information	Halfpenny, *Twelve beautiful designs*, 1749
No Information	Halfpenny, *Useful architecture*, 1751
No Information	Langley, *A sure guide*, 1726
No Information	Langley, *Practical geometry*, 1728
No Information	Langley, *The young builder's rudiments*, 1736
No Information	Muller, *Elements of mathematics*, 1757

No Information	Nicholson, *Nicholson's dictionary*, 1855
No Information	Nicholson, *Nicholson's dictionary*, 1857–1862
No Information	Nicholson, *The builder and workman's new director*, 1827
No Information	Nicholson, *The builder and workman's new director*, 1843
No Information	Nicholson, *The new and improved practical builder*, 1853
No Information	Nicholson, *The new and improved practical builder*, 1861
No Information	Pain, *The practical house carpenter*, n.d.
No Information	Pasley, *Complete course of . . . geometry*, 1838
No Information	Peacock, Οικιδια, 1786
No Information	Plaw, *Rural architecture*, 1800
No Information	Pocock, *Architectural designs*, 1819
No Information	Smith (James), *The panorama of science and art*, 1824
No Information	*The draughtsman's assistant*, [ca. 1775]
No Information	Wood, *A series of plans*, 1837
No Publisher	Campbell, *Vitruvius Britannicus* v.3, 1731
No Publisher	Gibbs, *A book of architecture*, 1728
No Publisher	Loudon, *First additional supplement*, 1842
No Publisher	Nash, *The royal pavilion of Brighton*, 1825
No Publisher	Soane, *Designs for public and private buildings*, 1832
No Publisher	Stevens, *Picturesque sketches*, 1860
No Publisher	Woolfe and Gandon, *Vitruvius Britannicus* v.4, 1767
No Publisher	Woolfe and Gandon, *Vitruvius Britannicus* v.5, 1771

Index

Only proper names have been indexed. The portions of the book that have been indexed include the Introduction, the essay on "The Literature of British Domestic Architecture, 1715–1842," the Principal Entries, and Appendixes A through D. Appendixes E and F have not been indexed since they are already systematically arranged.

Titles have been excluded, with three exceptions: titles of anonymous books, periodical titles, and (for the Principal Entries and Appendixes A through D) titles of general dictionaries and encyclopedias. Titles of general dictionaries and encyclopedias are included because the name of the editor or compiler, under which most such books are listed in the Principal Entries, may not be known to the user of this index. Unidentifiable pseudonyms, and personal names that consist only of initials, are excluded. All references to books published by 1842 have been indexed (by author), even if they are not included among the Principal Entries, and even if they are mentioned only in a peripheral way.

Page references are given in roman type, while references to individual entries are given in **boldface**. The letter **t** following an entry number (e.g., **40t**) indicates that the citation refers to the title page of the book, as transcribed at the beginning of the entry. Illustrators and editors often are mentioned in this manner. The letter **n** following an entry number (e.g., **40n**) signifies that the citation refers to a note at the end of the commentary for that entry. An author is cited only once for the entry for his or her own book: the entry number is given without **t** or **n**, regardless of whether the author's name appears in the title transcription or in the notes following the commentary. When two entry numbers are combined (e.g., **16–17**) it is a reference to a single commentary that serves both entries.

Aberdeen, George Hamilton-Gordon, Fourth Earl of, 54, **348**
Aberdeen, publishing in, 16, 124 n.75
Aberdeenshire, agricultural improvement and building in, **92**
Abraham, Robert, **187**
Ackermann, Rudolph, 4, 6, 13, 14, 124 n.69, 124 n.71, 129 n.41, **146n, 246, 247, 248, 290, 478, 480**
Adam, James, 11, **38**. *See also* Adam, Robert and James
Adam, John, 11, **2, 38**
Adam, Robert, 91, 129 n.1, **5n, 30, 103, 243, 284, 285, 331, 346n, 356**
Adam, Robert and James, xv, xxi n.3, xxiii n.18, 19, 20, 45, 63, 74, 76, 91, 92, 120 n.24, 128 n.30, 129 n.38, **1, 10, 26, 178, 207, 260, 283n, 284**
Adam, William (1689–1748), 10, 15, 16, **2, 158n**
Adam, William (1751–1839), **2**
Adams, William Bridges, **477**
Addison, Joseph, 46, **153, 327**
Adelphi, London, 76, **25n, 75**
Aheron, John, 14, 4, **3, 339n**
Aikin, Edmund, 29, 37, 145 n.171, **4**
Ainsty of York, **122t, 122**
Aiton, William, 115, 116, **93, 297n**
Akenside, Mark, 132 n.32
Albert, Prince Consort, **203n**
Alberti, Leone Battista, 10, 26, 59, **3t, 5, 5n, 40, 166, 177, 215n, 319, 339n**
Aldrich, Henry, 15, 24, 38, 60, 62, 118, **3, 5, 176**
Alexander, Fulton, **225**
Alison, Archibald, 135 n.65, **22, 191, 191n, 197n**
All Draughtsmen's Assistant, **485**
Allen, Thomas, **342n**
Allen, William, 16, 85, 117, 124 n.78, **6**
Allom, Thomas, **292t, 295t, 297t**
Alton estate, Staffordshire, 147 n.198, **153**
Anderson, James, 144 n.161, **274**
Anglesey, agricultural improvement and building in, **113t**
Annals of Agriculture, 114, **308n, 479**
Arch, John and Arthur, 122 n.64
Archer, Thomas, **32–33, 88**
Archiestown, 114
Architectural Magazine, The, 22, 51, 142 n.147, **182**

Overton, Thomas Collins, 8, 11, 17, 63, 68, 90, 97, 121 n.44, 143 n.156, **234**
Owen, Robert, 84, 85, 86, 117, 142 n.149, **6**, **332n**, **345t**, **345**, **476**
Oxford, publishing in, 15
Oxford Castle, **343n**
Oxford Encyclopaedia, The, **235**
Oxfordshire
   agricultural improvement and building in, **114**, **183t**
   farm house designs for, **138t**

Paddington, suburban development in, **334**
Paestum, temple at, **342**
Pain, James, **38**, **239**
Pain, William, xvii, 19, 21, 74, 75, 78, 119 n.1, 120 n.24, 143 n.156, **236**, **237**, **238**, **239**, **240**, **241**, **242**, **859**, **860**, **424**, **425**, **426**, **426** *bis*
Paine, James, xv, 11, 17, 19, 20, 39, 44, 119 n.1, 128 n.30, **74**, **74n**, **178**, **206**, **207**, **243**, **244**, **260**, **283**, **284**, **285n**, **356**, Figure 6
Paisley, coffee house in, **223**
Palace of Solomon, **351**
Palace of the Odyssey, **348**
Palaestra, Ephesus, **348**
Palazzo Chiericati, Vicenza, **339**
Palazzo Grimani, Venice, **225n**
Palazzo Porto, **75**
Palazzo Valmarana, 130 n.9, **33n**
Palk, Sir Lawrence, **102**
Palladio, Andrea, 15, 23, 25, 26, 27, 34, 37, 38, 44, 56, 57, 60, 61, 87, 127 n.13, 128 n.33, 130 n.15, 130 n.9, 143 n.156, **3t**, **5**, **5t**, **21**, **22**, **32–33**, **33n**, **40**, **64**, **75**, **132**, **150t**, **150**, **158t**, **158**, **166**, **173**, **174t**, **174**, **175t**, **175**, **177**, **215n**, **220**, **234**, **234n**, **236t**, **236**, **238t**, **238**, **239**, **243**, **287t**, **299t**, **319**, **339**, **340**, **341**, **351**, **365t**, **371t**, 919 n.5
Palladius, **36**
Pall Mall, Soane's design for a house in, 76
Palma Vecchio, **203**
Palmer, Charles John, **154n**
Pantheon, Rome, 26, **40**, **41**, **224n**, **329–330**
Pantologia, **78n**, **245**
Papworth, John Buonarotti, xxiii n.18, 14, 22, 29, 54, 55, 65, 70, 83, 98, 99, 100, 103, 107, 108, 110, 136 n.67, 147 n.194, **34n**, **40t**, **40**, **203**, **208n**, **246**, **247**, **248**, **268n**, **333n**, Figure 7
Papworth, Wyatt, 14
Paragon, Blackheath, 75, 170, **230n**
Paragon, Southwark, **230n**
Park Villages, London, **203**, **203n**, **230**, **297n**
   suburban development in, **334**
Parker, Charles, 99, **153**, **203**, **249**, Figure 8
Parker, Mr., 122
Parker, Thomas Netherton, 15, 81, 124 n.78, **250**, **321**
Parkinson, Richard, **109**, **115**, **469**
Parma, Duke of, 10
Parsey, Arthur, **167n**, **251**, **286**
Parthenon, **274**, **313**
Partington, Charles Frederick, **124**, **252**
Pasley, Sir Charles William, 19, **253**
Pastorini, Benedetto, **1t**
Patterdale, Inn at, **297**
Paty, Thomas, 140 n.130

Paty, William, 140 n.130
Paxton, Sir Joseph, **254**, **254n**, **474**
Paxton's Magazine of Botany, xviii, **254**, **474**
Peacock, James, 64, 78, 93, 94, 128 n.30, **34n**, **255**, **260**, **276n**
Peake, Robert, 128 n.33
Pearce, William, **96**, **97**
Pembroke, Earl of, **174**, **174n**, **243**
Penny, Jane, 44
Penrhyn, Lord, **16–17**, **113**, **274**, **359t**
Penrhyn estate, **359**
   Castle, 96
Penrose, V., of Ethy, **100**
Percy, Thomas, 131 n.28, 144 n.158, **40n**
Perrault, Claude, 23, 25, 26, 27, 34, 36, 46, 52, 53, 127 n.18, 131 n.25, 131 n.26, 131 n.27, **3t**, **5**, **32–33**, **40**, **40n**, **174t**, **178n**, **339**
Perronet, Jean Rodolphe, **225t**
Perth, publishing in, 16
Peruzzi, Baldassare, **5**
Peterborough Cathedral, **182**, **245**
Petrarch, **24**
   villa of, **490**
Petre, Lord, **243**
Pettyward, Mr., **69**
Phillips, Mr., auctioneer, **467t**
Philosophical Magazine and Journal, The, **411**, **418**
Phipps, auctioneer, 148 n.207
Phusin, Kata. *See* Ruskin, John
Piazza Navona, Rome, 148 n.204
Pickering, William, 123 n.64
Pickett, W., xxiii n.20, 139 n.112, 147 n.195, **256**, **324n**
Pickett, William, author of *Public Improvement*, 148 n.203
Pickford, Joseph, **356**
Picton, J. A., **182**
Picturesque Sketches of Rustic Scenery Including Cottages & Farm Houses, **324**
Pimlico, Royal Palace, **225n**
Pinnock, William, **257**
Piranesi, Giovanni Battista, **1t**, **222**
Pitt, William, agricultural writer, **479**
Pitt, William (1749–1823), **109**, **118**, **121**
Pitt, William (1759–1806), 363
Pitt, William Morton, 80, **258**
Pitzhanger Manor House, **315**, **318t**, **318**
Plas Newydd, **279**
Plat, Hugh, **42t**
Plaw, John, 12, 21, 29, 31, 50, 103, 107, 109, 113, 120 n.24, 144 n.162, **74**, **141**, **247n**, **259**, **260**, **261**, **275**, **284**, **284n**, **292n**, **297n**, Figure 9
Pliny, Caius Plinius Caecilius Secundus, 57, 59, 61, 66, 130 n.14, 130 n.18, 132 n.28, **36**, **184**, **203**, **223**, **302t**, **302**, **319**, **341**
Pocock, William Fuller, 29, 31, 45, 46, 65, 69, 70, 81, 83, 113, 129 n.1, 136 n.67, 147 n.194, **18n**, **247n**, **262**, **263**
Pococke, Lady, 11
Poirier, architect, **182**
Polygon, Somers Town, London, **230**, **230n**
Polygon, Southampton, **230n**
Pompeii
   house in, **223**
   remains in, **161**
   villas in, **24**, **203**
Pope, Alexander, 47, 56, **153**, **234**, **329–330**
Porden, William, **218**, **285**

DATE DUE			
		RESERVE	

DEMCO 38-297